THE HISTORY OF WITCHCRAFT

THE HISTORY OF WITCHCRAFT AND DEMONOLOGY

MONTAGUE SUMMERS

Initiati sunt Beelphegor: et comederunt sacrificia mortuorum.
Et immolauerunt filios suos, et filias suas daemoniis.
Et effuderunt sanguinem innocentem. Et fornicati sunt in adinuentionibus suis PSALM CV

A CITADEL PRESS BOOK
Published by Carol Publishing Group

To

PATRICK,

in memory of Loreto and Our Lady's Holy House, as also of Our Lady's miraculous Picture at Campocavallo, Our Lady of Pompeii, La Consolata of Turin, Consolatrix Afflictorum in S. Caterina ai Funari at Rome, la Santissima Vergine del Parto of S. Agostino, the Madonna della Strada at the Gesù, La Nicopeja of San Marco at Venice, Notre-Dame-de-Bonne-Nouvelle of Rennes, Notre-Dame de Grande Puissance of Lamballe, and all the Italian and French Madonnas at whose shrines we have worshipped.

First Carol Publishing Group Edition 1993

A Citadel Press Book
Published by Carol Publishing Group
Citadel Press is a registered trademark of Carol Communications, Inc.
Editorial Offices: 600 Madison Avenue, New York, N.Y. 10022
Sales and Distribution Offices: 120 Enterprise Avenue, Secaucus, N.J. 07094
In Canada: Canadian Manda Group, P.O. Box 920, Station U, Toronto, Ontario M8Z 5P9
Queries regarding rights and permissions should be addressed to Carol Publishing Group, 600 Madison Avenue, New York, N.Y. 10022

Carol Publishing Group books are available at special discounts for bulk purchases, for sales promotions, fund raising, or educational purposes. Special editions can be created to specifications. For details, contact Special Sales Department, Carol Publishing Group, 120 Enterprise Avenue, Secaucus, N.J. 07094

ISBN 0-8065-1452-3

Manufactured in the United States of America

10 9 8 7 6 5 4 3 2 1

CONTENTS

INTRODUCTION

Montague Summers is the great classical author on the occult, and his *History of Witchcraft* is a very important contribution to the literature. I read it as a young witch while doing research for my first book on the subject, and it remains a standard, for me, of what a valuable book on witchcraft should be.

I wrote Mr. Summers after I'd finished his book, and he provided me with a list of books that I should read to round out my education on the subject of witchcraft. Most authors find they do not have the time to answer every reader letter, so I was most impressed by Mr. Summers' response, and keep his letter as a fond memory of my early days as a witch.

The History of Witchcraft is broken into sections pertaining, mostly, to the early days of the religion. Mr. Summers takes us back to Medieval and Dark Ages times and quotes, for example, the material available on general witch trials—and he even quotes the trial papers for individual witches. He paints a vivid picture of the Sabbats that the witches held to celebrate the various occasions of their worship of the devil.

In a chapter on the worship of the witch, he tells us about devil marks that the judges looked for on a person to condemn them to death for their witchcraft. The devil marks were tested to verify that that's what they were by having someone insert a pin three inches into the spot. If the pin entered the mark and there was no feeling in it, then the mark was deigned to be a devil's mark and the witch would be put to death.

In the chapter on demons and familiars we learn that goats and not just cats were familiars. And that familiars were demons who took the shape of an animal. The demons were fed by the witch from a third breast that she had on her body. Many people died because they had third breasts, which is not an uncommon phenomenon.

In the chapter on the Sabbat I learned something I'd never known about cocks. It seems that when the cock crows at dawn, it breaks magic spells, so the witches all had to be home (or at least end their Sabbats) when the dawn came and before the cock crowed.

As Mr. Summers was a priest, the chapter on the witch in holy writ is especially interesting for its scholarship. He delves into the Bible for instances of witchcraft in those ancient times and finds much to enlighten us. In the New Testament there is plenty written about people being possessed by devils. And some of the apostles and their followers were not unfamiliar with sorcery.

While Christ was on earth, He made it possible for his apostles to cast out demons. And throughout the Bible there are references to the magic of the times. Part of the interest of this book lies in the fact that Montague Summers was a gifted priest who interpreted what he knew of Church doctrine and how it had always fought witchcraft. Indeed the witches that lived in those days were diabolic, not like the worshippers of Mother Nature and her spirits that we have now who call themselves witches.

That's why it is so important to read this book—for the history of the Satanism that existed then and exists today. The Satanists of yesteryear had human sacrifices on their Sabbats, and it's been documented that in the United States in recent years the practice has been found to be extant. There were, just a few years ago, some warlocks and witches in Mexico who killed children, and grownups too, at their witchcraft orgies. So the practice is not unknown today.

Read Mr. Summers' book with attention and don't be bogged down by the detail and the quotations. There are many of these and they round out the education that a practicing witch should have. Be grateful that Mr. Summers has done all the hard work for you in referencing the classic documents pertaining to witchcraft. If you don't live in New York or Paris or London or Rome, where the great libraries containing witchcraft documents exist, then this book is the next best thing.

Read and enjoy. You feel as if you really know something after completing this book on the arts of witchcraft. As noted, there were some things I'd forgotten or never knew that Montague Summers enlightened me with. So will he for you.

—SARAH LYDDON MORRISON
Author of *The Modern Witch's Spellbook*
and *The Modern Witch's Spellbook, Book II*

FOREWORD

By FELIX MORROW

IN the pages of this book the reader will quite often come across the name of Margaret A. Murray and it will become clear to him that she is Summers' great antagonist. True, he waxes almost warm toward her when he adduces her common stand with him that witchcraft was widespread and really believed in by friend and foe alike, as against the "liberal" historians who think of it as at most a temporary madness. Beyond that, however, Miss Murray's views are obviously anathema. However, Summers never makes precisely clear what these views are.

I share Miss Murray's views, in the main, and I think it important for the reader to understand what they are. She has made them very clear in two splendid books, *The Witch Cult of Western Europe* and *The God of the Witches,* and in very compact form in the article on Witchcraft in the recent editions of the Encyclopaedia Britannica. I should like to believe that the choice of Miss Murray to write the encyclopaedia article means that her views have now prevailed, but unfortunately it is not so. She begins, significantly, with the fact that witch comes from wit, to know. The witch's knowledge has always been especially foretelling: "When this is done in the name of the deity of one of the established religions it is called prophecy; when, however, the divination is in the name of a pagan god it is mere witchcraft." The word *devil* is a diminutive from the root *div* and from it we get the word *divine;* devil merely means "little god." "It is a well known fact that when a new religion is established in any country, the god or gods of the old religion become the devil of the new. When examining the records of the medieval witches, we are dealing with the remains of a pagan religion which survived, in England at least, until the eighteenth century, twelve hundred years after the introduction of Christianity. The practices of this ancient faith can be found in France at the present day; and in Italy *la vecchia religione* (the old religion) still numbers many followers in spite of the efforts of the Christian churches."

The pagan religion of the witches of Europe, when described without prejudice, is quite familiar to any reader of *The Golden Bough* or other anthropological material. Central to it is a god incarnate in a human being or an animal, appearing to his worshipers dressed in black or disguised in various animal forms, the appearances being at assemblies or *sabbaths*. The sexual orgies reveled in by Summers appear quite differently when Miss Murray reminds us how similar they are to the sacred marriage of the Greeks or the Saturnian revels of the Romans. The use of the religion against enemies, by means of incantations and potions, etcetera, no doubt belongs to pre-literate societies but no objective student of comparative religion could seriously affirm that the witches committed more terrible deeds than their Christian successors.

Miss Murray's endlessly fascinating material is available easily enough to interested readers. The point here is that she does establish to our satisfaction that what has come down to us under the name of witchcraft was a religion of the people which was overcome by Christianity and, in defeat, had its terminology and the description of its rites defined for it and posterity by the victors.

The Christian conquerors made central to the defeated religion the idea of the compact with Satan. As Herbert Thurston tells us in the article on Witchcraft in the Catholic Encyclopaedia, "In the traditional belief, not only of the Dark Ages but of post-reformation times, the witches entered into a compact with Satan." The compact with Satan appears to be an invention of Christian times. The Old Testament, while decreeing death for witches, does not know the compact.

Summers avoids dealing with the question why the main struggle against witchcraft came after the middle of the thirteenth century, when the papal inquisition was constituted. In 1484, the bull of Pope Innocent VIII codified and launched the struggle on a grand scale. From the sixteenth until the eighteenth centuries the extirpation of witches went on cruelly and relentlessly. The figures of scholars estimating the number of witches put to death vary enormously, from 30,000 to several million, and it is really impossible to know, given the records of the times, but it is clear that substantial numbers were put to death. Why the end of the struggle is fairly clear: the total victory of Christianity on the one hand and then the rise of a rationalist spirit which denied the magical efficacy of witchcraft. But why the growth and increasing intensity of the struggle against witchcraft beginning in the fifteenth century? Summers evades this question. Miss Murray's answer appears to me decisive: Until then, Christianity in Western Europe was mainly the religion of the upper classes who felt secure and strong enough to launch the struggle against the old religion of the masses only after fifteen centuries of Christianity.

We now come to a very interesting question: Summers was a Roman Catholic priest but the tone and temper of his book, and certain of his views, as we shall see, are scarcely in consonance with certain official or semi-official statements of the Catholic church. At no point is Summers ashamed of the greatest excesses committed in the seventeenth and eighteenth centuries by the church; on the contrary, he vigorously defends everything the Church ever did to extirpate witchcraft and heresy. The idea that many innocents may have suffered with the guilty, at least in periods of hysteria or excitement over witchcraft, is foreign to him. That prior to 1484 there were popes who forbade the killing of witches; that afterward, too, there were archbishops if not popes who were skeptical of the magical efficacy of witchcraft—this is not in Summers' book or in his spirit. There are, indeed, some really hair-raising items in his book which no serious person could lay at the door of the Vatican. For at least two hundred years the Vatican has repudiated the libel against the Jews which accuses them of using the blood of a Christian child in preparing the unleavened bread for Passover; yet (page 195 and especially footnote 37 on page 197) Summers actually complains that the records of such ritual murders are incomplete! Summers lists the famous last case of ritual murder accusation in Czarist Russia, that of Mendel Beiliss, yet fails to note that even in Czarist Russia this trial led to an acquittal. The point is that Summers is an unreconstructed medievalist who simply refuses to accept the modifications introduced in the last century or two by the Vatican.*

But if we put to one side such extremist extravagances, Summers' views are valuable precisely because they provide us in modern English with what is actually the best account of the Roman Catholic version of the history of witchcraft and the church's fight

* Summers describes Albert Pike (page 8) as the grand master of a society practicing Satanism; this reference to the American founder of Scottish rite masonry would have been quite apropos in Catholic circles in 1800 (or in Spain today).

against it. It was his contention, and we are inclined to agree with him, that his account is not only the true story as it appeared to the Catholic church in the seventeenth and eighteenth centuries, but that this remains, in spite of what Catholic apologists may say in encyclopaedias and other public forums, the true position of the Roman Catholic church today. This really unique character of his book becomes apparent when we contrast Summers' views with such an apologetic article on witchcraft as Father Herbert Thurston's in the Catholic Encyclopaedia.

With many a sigh, Father Thurston concludes that both the Old Testament and the New Testament appear to take the position that "the divining spirit (witchcraft) was not a mere imposture." "We are led to the same conclusion from the attitude of the early church." But, he emphasizes, "In the first thirteen hundred years of the Christian era, we find no trace of that fierce denunciation and persecution of supposed sorceresses which characterized the cruel witch hunts of the later age." Father Thurston finds particularly difficult to handle the long series of church statements on sexual congress between human and demon: "The possibility of such carnal intercourse between human beings and demons was unfortunately accepted by some of the great schoolmen, even, for example, by St. Thomas Aquinas. Nevertheless, within the church itself there was always a common sense reaction against the theorizing . . . " And the Protestants were even more cruel: "On the whole, greater activity in hunting down witches was shown in the Protestant districts of Germany than in the Catholic provinces."

Finally Father Thurston must seize the nettle: "The question of the reality of witchcraft is one upon which it is not easy to pass a confident judgment. In the face of Holy Scripture and the teaching of the fathers and theologians, the abstract possibility of a pact with the devil and of a diabolical interference in human affairs can hardly be denied, but no one can read the literature of the subject without realizing the awful cruelties to which this belief led and without being convinced that in 99 cases out of 100 the allegations rest upon nothing better than pure delusion."

It may not be easy for Father Thurston to pass a confident judgment on the reality of witchcraft, but it is quite easy for us to note that the hesitant formulas of Father Thurston are limited to encyclopaedias and other such places where his language is appropriate. Very different is the language of the Roman Catholic

Church in instructing its own priests and in providing them with material for their flocks.

The Roman Ritual (Rituale Romanum) has a substantial section devoted to the liturgy prescribed for driving evil spirits out of possessed persons. Here the interested reader will find, not Father Thurston's talk about "the abstract possibility of a pact with the devil" but a most solemn exposition of ways and means of ridding the faithful of concrete devils. In the Rituale Romanum published by Benziger Bros. in New York in 1947, and endorsed by the coat of arms and introductory letter of Francis Cardinal Spellman, we find the following in Latin:*

"Instruction #3. In the first place lest one be too easily inclined to believe a person to be possessed by the devil the signs should be watched which will distinguish the sufferer from one suffering from black bile or some other disease. Signs of a possessing devil are: the ability to speak many words of an unknown language or to understand them; the ability to reveal distant or hidden things; a manifestation of strength beyond one's age or natural condition . . ."

"Instruction #5. Be cautious of the arts and deceptions that the devils use to disconcert the exorcist (the priest); they usually lie, and make things so difficult that the priest gets tired, or the patient appears not to be possessed at all."

"Instruction #9. Sometimes the devil will leave the patient and permit him to receive the Holy Eucharist. There are innumerable tricks and frauds that the devil will use to deceive. The priest-exorcist must be cautious."

"Instruction #13. Let the priest-exorcist keep the crucifix in his hand or at least in sight. Relics of the saints, if available, should be carefully touched to the head and the breast of the possessed but let him beware lest these sacred objects be abused or in any way damaged by the devil."

"Instruction #19. When exorcising a woman let the priest always have responsible people, preferably relatives, to hold down the woman while the devil is agitating her and let him be careful not to say or do anything that might provoke obscene thoughts either in himself or in others."

---

* I am indebted for this translation to the former Franciscan priest, Emmet McLoughlin, author of *People's Padre*.

"Instruction #20. The priest should ask the devil if he was forced into the body of the possessed person by some trick or magic or an evil spell, or potion, which if the possessed has taken by mouth he should be made to vomit up. The devil must be forced to reveal any such physical evil things (potions, charms, fetishes, etc.) still outside the body, and these must be burned."

After pages of litanies, psalms, scriptural readings and preliminary prayers the exorcism proper continues:

"I exorcise you, most vile spirit, the very incarnation of our adversary, the specter, the enemy, in the name of Jesus Christ to get out and flee from this creature of God. He himself commands you who ordered you thrown from the heights of heaven to the depths of the earth. He commands you, who rules the sea, the winds and the tempests. Hear, therefore, and shudder, O Satan, you enemy of the Faith, enemy of the human race, cause of death, thief of life, destroyer of justice, source of evils, root of vice, seducer of men, betrayer of nations, source of jealousy, origin of avarice, cause of discord, procurer of sorrows—why do you remain and resist when you know that Jesus Christ blocks your plans? Fear him who in Isaac was immolated, who was sold in Joseph, who was killed in the lamb, who was crucified in man and then became the conqueror of hell . . .

"Most vile dragon, in the name of the immaculate lamb, who trod upon the asp and the basilisk, who conquered the lion and the dragon, I command you to get out of this man, to get out of the Church of God. Tremble and flee at that name which Hell fears; that name to which the virtues of heaven, the powers and the dominations are subject, which the cherubim and seraphim praise with untiring voices, chanting, Holy, Holy, Holy, Lord God of Sabaoth."*

Exorcism is of course seldom resorted to but the existence of rites of exorcism in the Rituale Romanum makes clear the indubitable position of the Roman Catholic Church toward witchcraft and demonology.

Few Roman Catholics have ever heard the rites of exorcism but most have heard the baptismal ceremony of a newborn baby. Here, too, is imbedded a rite of exorcism.

In the baptismal ceremony of a newborn baby, before the water is poured, the priest must drive out the devil: "I adjure you,

* Rituale Romanum (Benziger Bros., New York, 1947) pp. 326-347.

unclean spirit, in the name of God the Father, omnipotent, and in the name of Jesus Christ, his Son, our Lord and Judge, and through the power of the Holy Spirit, that you relinquish this creature of God, which our Lord has deigned to choose as his holy temple, that it may become the temple of the living God and that the Holy Spirit may dwell in it."*

It should be evident from the foregoing that Montague Summers does not exaggerate when he claims that he, and not people like Father Thurston, express the true views of the Roman Catholic Church. For its own reasons, that Church seldom speaks in the vernacular nowadays in the forthright terms employed by Summers. The priest's ritual of the baptismal ceremony and the rites of exorcism are of course in Latin. When I say that the Church seldom speaks in the vernacular, I mean of course in forums where the outside public is present. Between the four walls of the church, the doctrine of the baptismal ceremony and of the rites of exorcism is heard often enough.

The rest of us, or at least those of us who are interested students of this fascinating subject, are indebted to Montague Summers for the most forthright presentation of these views that has ever been written in modern English.

When this book first appeared, the *Times* Literary Supplement wrote of it: "The more Mr. Summers gives proof of general ability, of scholarship and of wide reading, the more the suspicion deepens that a mystification is in progress and that he is amusing us at our expense." This is the kind of error rarely made by the *Times*. The author of that review simply could not believe that Summers was serious. He was incredulous because he failed to understand the deeply held point of view from which Summers wrote. This view has perhaps been most succinctly stated by Summers himself, in the biographical material which he supplied to *Twentieth Century Authors*. He spoke of his view as "an absolute and complete belief in the supernatural, and hence in witchcraft." This is the concept of the supernatural in which God is inconceivable without the devil.

Most objective students will, I think, agree with me that the fascinating and sometimes horrifying book which follows was written by a serious and able priest who held firmly and consistently to his conception of the inseparable connection between the supernatural and witchcraft.

---

* Priests New Ritual, P. J. Kennedy, New York, 1947, p. 21.

AUTHOR'S INTRODUCTION

THE history of Witchcraft, a subject as old as the world and as wide as the world,—since I understand for the present purpose by Witchcraft, Sorcery, Black Magic, Necromancy, secret Divination, Satanism, and every kind of malign occult art,—at once confronts the writer with a most difficult problem. He is called upon to exercise a choice, and his dilemma is by no means made the easier owing to the fact he is acutely conscious that whichever way he may decide he is laying himself open to damaging and not impertinent criticism. Since it is essential that his work should be comprised within a reasonable compass he may elect to attempt a bird's-eye view of the whole range from China to Peru, from the half-articulate, rhythmic incantations of primitive man at the dawn of life to the last spiritistic fad and manifestation at yesterday's séance or circle, in which case his pages will most certainly be thin and often superficial: or again he may rather concentrate upon one or two features in the history of Witchcraft, deal with these at some length, stress some few forgotten facts whose importance is now neglected and unrealized, utilize new material the result of laborious research, but all this at the expense of inevitable omissions, of hiatus, of self-denial, the avoidance of fascinating by-ways and valuable inquiry, of silence when he would fain be entering upon discussion and exposition. With a full sense of its drawbacks and danger I have selected the second method, since in dealing with a topic such as Witchcraft where there is no human hope of recording more than a tithe of the facts I believe it is better to give a documented account of certain aspects rather than to essay a somewhat huddled and confused conspectus of the whole, for such, indeed, even at best is itself bound to have no inconsiderable gaps and lacunæ, however carefully we endeavour to make it complete. I am conscious, then, that there is scarcely a paragraph in the present work which might not easily be expanded into a page, scarcely a page which might not to its great advantage become a chapter, and certainly not a chapter that would not be vastly improved were it elaborated to a volume.

Many omissions are, as I have said, a necessary consequence of the plan I have adopted ; or, indeed, I venture to suppose, of any other plan which contemplates the treatment of so universal a subject as Witchcraft. I can but offer my apologies to these students who come to this History to find details of Finnish magic and the sorceries of Lapland, who wish to inform themselves concerning Tohungaism among the Maoris, Hindu devilry and enchantments, the Bersekir of Iceland, Siberian Shamanism, the blind Pan Sus and Mutangs of Korea, the Chinese Wu-po, Serbian lycanthropy, negro Voodoism, the dark lore of old Scandinavia and Islam. I trust my readers will believe that I regret as much as any the absence of these from my work, but after all in any human endeavour there are practical limitations of space.

In a complementary and companion volume I am intending to treat the epidemic of Witchcraft in particular localities, the British Isles, France, Germany, Italy, New England, and other countries. Many famous cases, the Lancashire witch-trials, the activities of Matthew Hopkins, Gilles de Rais, Gaufridi, Urbain Grandier, Cotton Mather and the Salem sorceries, will then be dealt with and discussed in some detail.

It is a surprising fact that amongst English writers Witchcraft in Europe has not of recent years received anything like adequate attention from serious students of history, who strangely fail to recognize the importance of this tragic belief both as a political and a social factor. Magic, the genesis of magical cults and ceremonies, the ritual of primitive peoples, traditional superstitions, and their ancillary lore, have been made the subject of vast and erudite studies, mostly from an anthropological and folk-loristic point of view, but the darker side of the subject, the history of Satanism seems hardly to have been attempted.

Possibly one reason for this neglect and ignorance lies in the fact that the heavy and crass materialism, which was so prominent a feature during the greater part of the eighteenth and nineteenth centuries in England, intellectually disavowed the supernatural, and attempted not without some success to substitute for religion a stolid system of respectable morality. Since Witchcraft was entirely exploded it would, at best, possess merely an antiquarian interest, and even so, the exhumation of a disgusting and contemptible superstition was not to be encouraged. It were more seemly to forget the uglier side of the past. This was the attitude which prevailed for more than a hundred and fifty years, and when Witchcraft came under discussion by such narrowly prejudiced and inefficient writers as Lecky or Charles Mackay they are not even concerned to discuss the possibility of the accounts given by the earlier authorities, who, as they premise, were all mistaken, extravagant, purblind, and misled. The cycle of time has had its revenge, and this rationalistic superstition is dying fast. The extraordinary vogue of and immense adherence to Spiritism would alone prove that, whilst the widespread interest that is taken in mysticism is a yet healthier sign that the world will no longer be content to be fed on dry husks and the chaff of straw. And these are only just two indications, and by no means the most significant, out of many.

It is quite impossible to appreciate and understand the true lives of men and women in Elizabethan and Stuart England, in the France of Louis XIII and his son, in the Italy of the Renaissance and the Catholic Reaction—to name but three countries and a few definite periods—unless we have some realization of the part that Witchcraft played in those ages amid the affairs of these kingdoms. All classes were concerned from Pope to peasant, from Queen to cottage gill.

Accordingly as actors are "the abstracts and brief chronicles of the time" I have given a concluding chapter which deals with Witchcraft as seen upon the stage, mainly concentrating upon the English theatre. This review has not before been attempted, and since Witchcraft was so formidable a social evil and so intermixed with all stations of life it is obvious that we can find few better contemporary illustrations of it than in the drama, for the playwright ever had his finger upon the public pulse. Until the development of the novel it was the theatre alone that mirrored manners and history.

There are many general French studies of Witchcraft of

the greatest value, amongst which we may name such standard works as Antoine-Louis Daugis, *Traité sur la magie, le sortilège, les possessions, obsessions et maléfices,* 1732; Jules Garinet, *Histoire de la Magie en France depuis le commencement de la monarchie jusqu'à nos jours,* 1818; Michelet's famous *La Sorcière;* Alfred Maury, *La Magie et l'Astrologie,* 3rd edition, 1868; L'Abbé Lecanu, *Histoire de Satan;* Jules Baissac, *Les grands Jours de la Sorcellerie,* 1890; Theodore de Cauzons, *La Magie et la Sorcellerie en France,* 4 vols., 1910, etc.

In German we have Eberhard Hauber's *Bibliotheca Magica;* Roskoff's *Geschichte des Teufels,* 1869; Soldan's *Geschichte der Hexenprozesse* (neu bearbeitet von Dr. Heinrich Heppe), 1880; Friedrich Leitschuch's *Beitræge zur Geschichte des Hexenwesens in Franken,* 1883; Johan Dieffenbach's *Der Hexenwahn vor und nach der Glaubensspaltung in Deutschland,* 1886; Schreiber's *Die Hexenprozesse im Breisgau;* Ludwig Rapp's *Die Hexenprozesse und ihre Gegner aus Tirol;* Joseph Hansen's *Quellen und Untersuchungen zur Geschichte des Hexenwahns,* 1901; and very many more admirably documented studies.

In England the best of the older books must be recommended with necessary reservations. Thomas Wright's *Narratives of Sorcery and Magic,* 2 vols., 1851, is to be commended as the work of a learned antiquarian who often referred to original sources, but it is withal sketchy and can hardly satisfy the careful scholar. Some exceptionally good writing and sound, clear, thinking are to be met with in Dr. F. G. Lee's *The Other World,* 2 vols., 1875; *More Glimpses of the World Unseen,* 1878; *Glimpses in the Twilight,* 1885; and *Sight and Shadows,* 1894, all of which deserve to be far more widely known, since they well repay an unhurried and repeated perusal.

Quite recent work is represented by Professor Wallace Notestein's *History of Witchcraft in England from* 1558 *to* 1718, published in 1911. This intimate study of a century and a half concentrates, as its title tells, upon England alone. It is supplied with ample and useful appendixes. In respect of the orderly marshalling of his facts, garnered from the trials and other sources—no small labour—Professor Notestein deserves a generous meed of praise; his interpretation of the facts and his deductions may not unfairly be criticized. Although his incredulity must surely now and again be shaken by the cumulative force of reiterated and corroborative evidence, nevertheless he refuses to admit even the possibility that persons who at any rate affected supernatural powers held clandestine meetings after nightfall in obscure and lonely places for purposes and plots of their own. If human testimony is worth anything at all, unless we are to be more Pyrrhonian than the famous Dr. Marphurius himself who would never say, "Je suis venu; mais; Il me semble que je suis venu," when in 1612 Roger Nowell had swooped down on the Lancashire coven and carried off Elizabeth Demdike with three other beldames to durance vile in Lancaster Castle, Elizabeth Device summoned the whole Pendle gang to her home at Malking Tower, in order that they might discuss the situation and contrive the delivery of the prisoners. As soon as they had forgathered, they all sat down to dinner, and had a good north country spread of beef, bacon, and roast mutton. Surely there is nothing very remarkable in this; and the evidence as given in Thomas Potts' famous narrative, *The Wonderfull Discoverie of Witches in the countie of Lancaster* (London, 1613), bears the very hall-mark and impress of truth: "The persons aforesaid had to their dinners Beefe, Bacon, and roasted Mutton; which Mutton (as this Examinates said brother said) was of a Wether of Christopher Swyers of Barley: which Wether was brought in the night before into this Examinates mothers house by the said Iames Deuice, the Examinates said brother: and in this Examinates sight killed and eaten." But Professor Notestein will none of it. He writes: "The concurring evidence in the Malking Tower story is of no more compelling character than that to be found in a multitude of Continental stories of witch gatherings which have been shown to be the outcome of physical or mental pressure and of leading questions. It seems unnecessary to accept even a substratum of fact" (p. 124). In the face of such sweeping and dogmatic assertion mere evidence is no use at all. For we know that the Continental stories of witch gatherings are with very few exceptions the chronicle of actual fact. It must be confessed that such feeble scepticism, which repeatedly mars his summary of the witch-trials, is a serious blemish in Professor Notestein's work, and in view of his industry much to be regretted.

Miss M. A. Murray does not for a moment countenance any such summary dismissal and uncritical rejection of evidence. Her careful reading of the writers upon Witchcraft has justly convinced her that their statements must be accepted. Keen intelligences and shrewd investigators such as Gregory XV, Bodin, Guazzo, De Lancre, D'Espagnet, La Reynie, Boyle, Sir Matthew Hale, Glanvill, were neither deceivers nor deceived. The evidence must stand, but as Miss Murray finds herself unable to admit the logical consequence of this, she hurriedly starts away with an arbitrary, "the statements do not bear the construction put upon them," and in *The Witch-Cult in Western Europe* (1921) proceeds to develop a most ingenious, but, as I show, a wholly untenable hypothesis. Accordingly we are not surprised to find that many of the details Miss Murray has collected in her painstaking pages are (no doubt unconsciously) made to square with her preconceived theory. However much I may differ from Miss Murray in my outlook, and our disagreement is, I consider, neither slight nor superficial, I am none the less bound to commend her frank and courageous treatment of many essential particulars which are all too often suppressed, and in consequence a false and counterfeit picture has not unseldom been drawn.

So vast a literature surrounds modern Witchcraft, for frankly such is Spiritism in effect, that it were no easy task to mention even a quota of those works which seem to throw some real light upon a complex and difficult subject. Among many which I have found useful are Surbled, *Spiritualisme et spiritisme* and *Spirites et médiums;* Gutberlet, *Der Kampf um die Seele;* Dr. Marcel Viollet, *Le spiritisme dans ses rapports avec la folie;* J. Godfrey Raupert, *Modern Spiritism* and *Dangers of Spiritualism;* the Very Rev. Alexis Lépicier, O.S.M., *The Unseen World;* the Rev. A. V. Miller, *Sermons on Modern Spiritualism;* Lapponi, *Hypnotism and Spiritism;* the late Monsignor Hugh Benson's *Spiritualism* (*The History of Religions*); Elliot O'Donnell's *The Menace of Spiritualism;* and Father Simon Blackmore's *Spiritism: Facts and Frauds*, 1925. My own opinion of this movement has been formed not only from reading studies and monographs which treat of every phase of the question from all points of view, but also by correspondence and discussion with ardent devotees of the cult, and, not least, owing to the admissions and warnings of those who have abandoned these dangerous practices, revelations made in such circumstances, however, as altogether to preclude even a hint as to their definite import and scope.

The History of Witchcraft is full of interest to the theologian, the psychologist, the historian, and cannot be ignored. But it presents a very dark and terrible aspect, the details of which in the few English studies that claim serious attention have almost universally been unrecorded, and, indeed, deliberately burked and shunned. Such treatment is unworthy and unscholarly to a degree, reprehensible and dishonest.

The work of Professor Notestein, for example, is gravely vitiated, owing to the fact that he has completely ignored the immodesty of the witch-cult and thus extenuated its evil. He is, indeed, so uncritical, I would even venture to say so unscholarly, as naïvely to remark (p. 300): "No one who has not read for himself can have any notion of the vile character of the charges and confessions embodied in the witch pamphlets. It is an aspect of the question which has not been discussed in these pages." Such a confession is amazing. One cannot write in dainty phrase of Satanists and the Sabbat. However loathly the disease the doctor must not hesitate to diagnose and to probe. This ostrich-like policy is moral cowardice. None of the Fathers and great writers of the Church were thus culpably prudish. When S. Epiphanius has to discuss the Gnostics, he describes in detail their abominations, and pertinently remarks: "Why should I shrink from speaking of the things you do not fear to do? By speaking thus, I hope to fill you with horror of the turpitudes you commit." And S. Clement of Alexandria says: "I am not ashamed to name the parts of the body wherein the fœtus is formed and nourished; and why, indeed, should I be, since God was not ashamed to create them?"

A few authors have painted the mediæval witch in pretty colours on satin. She has become a somewhat eccentric but kindly old lady, shrewd and perspicacious, with a knowledge of healing herbs and simples, ready to advise and aid her neighbours who are duller-witted than she; not disdaining in return a rustic present of a flitch, meal, a poult or eggs from the farm-yard. And so for no very definite reason she fell an easy prey to fanatic judges and ravening inquisitors, notoriously the most ignorant and stupid of mortals, who caught her, swum her in a river, tried her, tortured her, and finally burned her at the stake. Many modern writers, more sceptical still, frankly relegate the witch to the land of nursery tales and Christmas pantomime; she never had any real existence other than as Cinderella's fairy godmother or the Countess D'Aulnoy's Madame Merluche.

I have even heard it publicly asserted from the lecture platform by a professed student of the Elizabethan period that the Elizabethans did not, of course, as a matter of fact believe in Witchcraft. It were impossible to imagine that men of the intellectual standard of Shakespeare, Ford, Jonson, Fletcher, could have held so idle a chimæra, born of sick fancies and hysteria. And his audience acquiesced with no little complacency, pleased to think that the great names of the past had been cleared from the stigma of so degrading and gross a superstition. A few uneducated peasants here and there may have been morbid and ignorant enough to dream of witches, and the poets used these crones and hags with effect in ballad and play. But as for giving any actual credence to such fantasies, most assuredly our great Elizabethans were more enlightened than that! And, indeed, Witchcraft is a phase of and a factor in the manners of the seventeenth century, which in some quarters there seems a tacit agreement almost to ignore.

All this is very unhistorical and very unscientific. In the following pages I have endeavoured to show the witch as she really was—an evil liver; a social pest and parasite; the devotee of a loathly and obscene creed; an adept at poisoning, blackmail, and other creeping crimes; a member of a powerful secret organization inimical to Church and State; a blasphemer in word and deed; swaying the villagers by terror and superstition; a charlatan and a quack sometimes; a bawd; an abortionist; the dark counsellor of lewd court ladies and adulterous gallants; a minister to vice and inconceivable corruption; battening upon the filth and foulest passions of the age.

My present work is the result of more than thirty years' close attention to the subject of Witchcraft, and during this period I have made a systematic and intensive study of the older demonologists, as I am convinced that their first-hand evidence is of prime importance and value, whilst since their writings are very voluminous and of the last rarity they have universally been neglected, and are allowed to accumulate thick dust undisturbed. They are, moreover, often difficult to read owing to technicalities of phrase and vocabulary. Among the most authoritative I may cite a few names: Sprenger (*Malleus Maleficarum*); Guazzo; Bartolomeo Spina, O.P.; John Nider, O.P.; Grilland; Jerome Mengo; Binsfeld; Gerson; Ulrich Molitor; Basin; Murner; Crespet; Anania; Henri Boguet; Bodin; Martin Delrio, S.J.; Pierre le Loyer; Ludwig Elich; Godelmann; Nicolas Remy; Salerini; Leonard Vair; De Lancre; Alfonso de Castro; Sebastian Michaelis, O.P.; Sinistrari; Perreaud; Dom Calmet; Sylvester Mazzolini, O.P. (Prierias). When we supplement these by the judicial records and the legal codes we have an immense body of material. In all that I have written I have gone to original sources, and it has been my endeavour fairly to weigh and balance the evidence, to judge without heat or prejudice, to give the facts and the comment upon them with candour, sincerity, and truth. At the same time I am very well aware that several great scholars for whom I have the sincerest personal regard and whose attainments I view with a very profound respect will differ from me in many particulars.

I am conscious that the rough list of books which I have drawn up does not deserve to be dignified with the title, Bibliography. It is sadly incomplete, yet should it, however inadequate, prove helpful in the smallest way it will have justified its inclusion. I may add that my Biblical quotations, save where expressly otherwise noted, are from the Vulgate or its translation into English commonly called the Douai Version.

IN FESTO S. TERESIÆ, *V.*
1925.

THE HISTORY OF WITCHCRAFT

THE HISTORY OF WITCHCRAFT

CHAPTER I

The Witch: Heretic and Anarchist

"Sorcier est celuy qui par moyens Diaboliques sciemment s'efforce de paruenir à quel que chose." ("A sorcerer is one who by commerce with the Devil has a full intention of attaining his own ends.") With these words the profoundly erudite jurisconsult Jean Bodin, one of the acutest and most strictly impartial minds of his age, opens his famous *De la Demonomanie des Sorciers*,[1] and it would be, I imagine, hardly possible to discover a more concise, exact, comprehensive, and intelligent definition of a Witch. The whole tremendous subject of Witchcraft, especially as revealed in its multifold and remarkable manifestations throughout every district of Southern and Western Europe from the middle of the thirteenth until the dawn of the eighteenth century,[2] has it would seem in recent times seldom, if ever, been candidly and fairly examined. The only sound sources of information are the contemporary records; the meticulously detailed legal reports of the actual trials; the vast mass of pamphlets which give eye-witnessed accounts of individual witches and reproduce evidence *uerbatim* as told in court; and, above all, the voluminous and highly technical works of the Inquisitors and demonologists, holy and reverend divines, doctors *utriusque iuris*, hard-headed, slow, and sober lawyers,—learned men, scholars of philosophic mind, the most honourable names in the universities of Europe, in the forefront of literature, science, politics, and culture; monks who kept the conscience of kings, pontiffs; whose word would set Europe aflame and bring an emperor to his knees at their gate.

It is true that Witchcraft has formed the subject of a not inconsiderable literature, but it will be found that inquirers have for the most part approached this eternal and terrible chapter in the history of humanity from biassed, although wholly divergent, points of view, and in consequence it is often necessary to sift more or less thoroughly their partial presentation of their theme, to discount their unwarranted commentaries and illogical conclusions, and to get down in time to the hard bed-rock of fact.

In the first place we have those writings and that interest which may be termed merely antiquarian. Witchcraft is treated as a curious by-lane of history, a superstition long since dead, having no existence among, nor bearing upon, the affairs of the present day. It is a field for folk-lore, where one may gather strange flowers and noxious weeds. Again, we often recognize the romantic treatment of Witchcraft. 'Tis the Eve of S. George, a dark wild night, the pale moon can but struggle thinly through the thick massing clouds. The witches are abroad, and hurtle swiftly aloft, a hideous covey, borne headlong on the skirling blast. In delirious tones they are yelling foul mysterious words as they go: "Har! Har! Har! Altri! Altri!" To some peak of the Brocken or lonely Cevennes they haste, to the orgies of the Sabbat, the infernal Sacraments, the dance of Acheron, the sweet and fearful fantasy of evil, "Vers les stupres impurs et les baisers immondes."[3] Hell seems to vomit its foulest dregs upon the shrinking earth; a loathsome shape of obscene horror squats huge and monstrous upon the ebon throne; the stifling air reeks with filth and blasphemy; faster and faster whirls the witches' lewd lavolta; shriller and shriller the cornemuse screams; and then a wan grey light flickers in the Eastern sky; a moment more and there sounds the loud clarion of some village chanticleer; swift as thought the vile phantasmagoria vanishes and is sped, all is quiet and still in the peaceful dawn.

But both the antiquarian and the romanticist reviews of Witchcraft may be deemed negligible and impertinent so far as the present research is concerned, however entertaining and picturesque such treatment proves to many readers, affording not a few pleasant hours, whence they are able to draw highly dramatic and brilliantly coloured pictures of old time sorceries, not to be taken too seriously, for these things never were and never could have been.[4]

The rationalist historian and the sceptic, when inevitably confronted with the subject of Witchcraft, chose a charmingly easy way to deal with these intensely complex and intricate problems, a flat denial of all statements which did not fit, or could not by some means be squared with, their own narrow prejudice. What matter the most irrefragable evidence, which in the instance of any other accusation would unhesitatingly have been regarded as final. What matter the logical and reasoned belief of centuries, of the most cultured peoples, the highest intelligences of Europe? Any appeal to authority is, of course, useless, as the sceptic repudiates all authority—save his own. Such things could not be. We must argue from that axiom, and therefore anything which it is impossible to explain away by hallucination, or hysteria, or auto-suggestion, or any other vague catch-word which may chance to be fashionable at the moment, must be uncompromisingly rejected, and a note of superior pity, to candy the so suave yet crushingly decisive judgement, has proved of great service upon more occasions than one. Why examine the evidence? It is really useless and a waste of time, because we know that the allegations are all idle and ridiculous; the "facts" sworn to by innumerable witnesses, which are repeated in changeless detail century fter century in every country, in every town, simply did not take place. How so absolute and entire falsity of these facts can be demonstrated the sceptic omits to inform us, but we must unquestioningly accept his infallible authority in the face of reason, evidence, and truth.

Yet supposing that with clear and candid minds we proceed carefully to investigate this accumulated evidence, to inquire into the circumstances of a number of typical cases, to compare the trials of the fifteenth century in France with the trials of the seventeenth century in England, shall we not find that amid obvious accretions of fantastic and superfluous detail a certain very solid substratum of a permanent and invaried character is unmistakably to be traced throughout the whole? This cannot in reason be denied, and here we have the core and the enduring reality of Witchcraft and the witch-cult throughout the ages.

There were some gross superstitions; there were some unbridled imaginations; there was deception, there was legerdemain; there was phantasy; there was fraud; Henri Boguet seems, perhaps, a trifle credulous, a little eager to explain obscure practices by an instant appeal to the supernormal; Brother Jetzer, the Jacobin of Berne, can only have been either the tool of his superiors or a cunning impostor; Matthew Hopkins was an unmitigated scoundrel who preyed upon the fears of the Essex franklins whilst he emptied their pockets; Lord Torphichen's son was an idle mischievous boy whose pranks not merely deluded both his father and the Rev. Mr. John Wilkins, but caused considerable mystification and amaze throughout the whole of Calder; Anne Robinson, Mrs. Golding's maid, and the two servant lasses of Baldarroch were prestidigitators of no common sleight and skill; and all these examples of ignorance, gullibility, malice, trickery, and imposture might easily be multiplied twenty times over and twenty times again, yet when every allowance has been made, every possible explanation exhausted, there persists a congeries of solid proven fact which cannot be ignored, save indeed by the purblind prejudice of the rationalist, and cannot be accounted for, save that we recognize there were and are individuals and organizations deliberately, nay, even enthusiastically, devoted to the service of evil, greedy of such emotions and experiences, rewards the thraldom of wickedness may bring.

The sceptic notoriously refuses to believe in Witchcraft, but a sanely critical examination of the evidence at the witch-trials will show that a vast amount of the modern vulgar incredulity is founded upon a complete misconception of the facts, and it may be well worth while quite briefly to review and correct some of the more common objections that are so loosely and so repeatedly maintained. There are many points which are urged as proving the fatuous absurdity and demonstrable impossibility of the whole system, and yet there is not one of these phenomena which is not capable of a satisfactory, and often a simple, elucidation. Perhaps the first thought of a witch that will occur to the man in the street is that of a hag on a broomstick flying up the chimney through the air. This has often been pictorially impressed on his imagination, not merely by woodcuts and illustrations traditionally presented in books, but by the brush of great painters such as Queverdo's *Le Départ au Sabbat, Le Départ pour le Sabbat* of David Teniers, and Goya's midnight fantasies. The famous Australian artist, Norman Lindsay, has a picture *To The Sabbat*[5] where witches are depicted wildly rushing through the air on the backs of grotesque pigs and hideous goats. Shakespeare, too, elaborated the idea, and "Hover through the fog and filthy air" has impressed itself upon the English imagination. But to descend from the airy realms of painting and poetry to the hard ground of actuality. Throughout the whole of the records there are very few instances when a witness definitely asserted that he had seen a witch carried through the air mounted upon a broom or stick of any kind, and on every occasion there is patent and obvious exaggeration to secure an effect. Sometimes the witches themselves boasted of this means of transport to impress their hearers. Boguet records that Claudine Boban, a young girl whose head was turned with pathological vanity, obviously a monomaniac who must at all costs occupy the centre of the stage and be the cynosure of public attention, confessed that she had been to the Sabbat, and this was undoubtedly the case; but to walk or ride on horseback to the Sabbat were far too ordinary methods of locomotion, melodrama and the marvellous must find their place in her account and so she alleged: "that both she and her mother used to mount on a broom, and so making their exit by the chimney in this fashion they flew through the air to the Sabbat."[6] Julian Cox (1664) said that one evening when she was in the fields about a mile away from the house "there came riding towards her three persons upon three Broom-staves, born up about a yard and a half from the ground."[7] There is obvious exaggeration here; she saw two men and one woman bestriding brooms and leaping high in the air. They were, in fact, performing a magic rite, a figure of a dance. So it is recorded of the Arab crones that "In the time of the Munkidh the witches rode about naked on a stick between the graves of the cemetery of Shaizar."[8] Nobody can refuse to believe that the witches bestrode sticks and poles and in their ritual capered to and fro in this manner, a sufficiently grotesque, but by no means an impossible, action. And this bizarre ceremony, evidence of which—with no reference to flying through the air—is frequent, has been exaggerated and transformed into the popular superstition that sorcerers are carried aloft and so transported from place to place, a wonder they were all ready to exploit in proof of their magic powers. And yet it is not impossible that there should have been actual instances of levitation. For, outside the lives of the Saints, spiritistic séances afford us examples of this supernormal phenomenon, which, if human evidence is worth anything at all, are beyond all question proven.

As for the unguents wherewith the sorcerers anointed themselves we have the actual formulæ for this composition, and Professor A. J. Clark, who has examined these,[9] considers that it is possible a strong application of such liniments might produce unwonted excitement and even delirium. But long ago the great demonologists recognized and laid down that of themselves the unguents possessed no such properties as the witches supposed. "The ointment and lotion are just of no use at all to witches to aid their journey to the Sabbat," is the well-considered opinion of Boguet who,[10] speaking with confident precision and finality, on this point is in entire agreement with the most sceptical of later rationalists.

The transformation of witches into animals and the extraordinary appearance at their orgies of "the Devil" under many a hideously unnatural shape, two points which have been repeatedly held up to scorn as self-evident impossibilities and proof conclusive of the untrustworthiness of the evidence and the incredibility of the whole system, can both be easily and fairly interpreted in a way which offers a complete and convincing explanation of these prodigies. The first metamorphosis, indeed, is mentioned and fully explained in the *Liber Pœnitentialis*[11] of S. Theodore, seventh Archbishop of Canterbury (668–690), capitulum xxvii, which code includes under the rubric *De Idolatria et Sacrilegio* "qui in Kalendas Ianuarii in ceruulo et in uitula uadit," and prescribes: "If anyone at the Kalends of January goes about as a stag or a bull; that is, making himself into a wild animal and dressing in the skin of a herd animal, and putting on the heads of beasts; those who in such wise transform themselves into the appearance of a wild animal, penance for three years because this is devilish." These ritual masks, furs, and hides, were, of course, exactly those the witches at certain ceremonies were wont to don for their Sabbats. There is ample proof that "the Devil" of the Sabbat was very frequently a human being, the Grand Master of the district, and since his officers and immediate attendants were also termed "Devils" by the witches some confusion has on occasion ensued. In a few cases where sufficient details are given it is possible actually to identify "the Devil" by name. Thus, among a list of suspected persons in the reign of Elizabeth we have "Ould Birtles, the great devil, Roger Birtles and his wife, and Anne Birtles."[12] The evil William, Lord Soulis, of Hermitage Castle, often known as "Red Cap," was "the Devil" of a coven of sorcerers. Very seldom "the Devil" was a woman. In May, 1569, the Regent of Scotland was present at S. Andrews "quhair a notabill sorceres callit Nicniven was condemnit to the death and burnt." Now Nicniven is the Queen of Elphin, the Mistress of the Sabbat, and this office had evidently been filled by this witch whose real name is not recorded. On 8 November, 1576, Elizabeth or Bessy Dunlop, of Lyne, in the Barony of Dalry, Ayrshire, was tried for sorcery, and she confessed that a certain mysterious Thom Reid had met her and demanded that she should renounce Christianity and her baptism, and apparently worship him. There can be little doubt that he was "the Devil" of a coven, for the original details, which are very full, all point to this. He seems to have played his part with some forethought and skill, since when the accused stated that she often saw him in the churchyard of Dalry, as also in the streets of Edinburgh, where he walked to and fro among other people and handled goods that were exposed on bulks for sale without attracting any special notice, and was thereupon asked why she did not address him, she replied that he had forbidden her to recognize him on any such occasion unless he made a sign or first actually accosted her. She was "convict and burnt."[13] In the case of Alison Peirson, tried 28 May, 1588, "the Devil" was actually her kinsman, William Sympson, and she "wes conuict of the vsing of Sorcerie and Witchcraft, with the Inuocatioun of the spreitis of the Deuill; speciallie in the visioune and forme of ane Mr. William Sympsoune, hir cousing and moder-brotheris-sone, quha sche affermit wes ane grit scoller and doctor of medicin."[14] *Conuicta et combusta* is the terse record of the margin of the court-book.

One of the most interesting identifications of " the Devil " occurs in the course of the notorious trials of Dr. Fian and his associates in 1590–1. As is well known, the whole crew was in league with Francis Stewart, Earl of Bothwell, and even at the time well-founded gossip, and something more than gossip, freely connected his name with the spells, Sabbats, and orgies of the witches. He was vehemently suspected of the black art; he was an undoubted client of warlocks and poisoners; his restless ambition almost overtly aimed at the throne, and the witch covens were one and all frantically attempting the life of King James. There can be no sort of doubt that Bothwell was the moving force who energized and directed the very elaborate and numerous organization of demonolaters, which was almost accidentally brought to light, to be fiercely crushed by the draconian vengeance of a monarch justly frightened for his crown and his life.

In the nineteenth century both Albert Pike of Charleston and his successor Adriano Lemmi have been identified upon abundant authority as being Grand Masters of societies practising Satanism, and as performing the hierarchical functions of " the Devil " at the modern Sabbat.

God, so far as His ordinary presence and action in Nature are concerned, is hidden behind the veil of secondary causes, and when God's ape, the Demon, can work so successfully and obtain not merely devoted adherents but fervent worshippers by human agency, there is plainly no need for him to manifest himself in person either to particular individuals or at the Sabbats, but none the less, that he can do so and has done so is certain, since such is the sense of the Church, and there are many striking cases in the records and trials which are to be explained in no other way.

That, as Burns Begg pointed out, the witches not unseldom " seem to have been undoubtedly the victims of unscrupulous and designing knaves, who personated Satan "[15] is no palliation of their crimes, and therefore they are not one whit the less guilty of sorcery and devil-worship, for this was their hearts' intention and desire. Nor do I think that the man who personated Satan at their assemblies was so much an unscrupulous and designing knave as himself a demonist, believing intensely in the reality of his own dark powers, wholly and horribly dedicated and doomed to the service of evil.

We have seen that the witches were upon occasion wont to array themselves in skins and ritual masks and there is complete evidence that the hierophant at the Sabbat, when a human being played that rôle, generally wore a corresponsive, if somewhat more elaborate, disguise. Nay more, as regards the British Isles at least—and it seems clear that in other countries the habit was very similar—we possess a pictorial representation of "the Devil" as he appeared to the witches. During the famous Fian trials Agnes Sampson confessed: "The deuell wes cled in ane blak goun with ane blak hat vpon his head. . . . His faice was terrible, his noise lyk the bek of ane egle, greet bournyng eyn; his handis and leggis wer herry, with clawes vpon his handis, and feit lyk the griffon."[16] In the pamphlet *Newes from Scotland, Declaring the Damnable life and death of Doctor Fian*[17] we have a rough woodcut, repeated twice, which shows "the Devil" preaching from the North Berwick pulpit to the whole coven of witches, and allowing for the crudity of the draughtsman and a few unimportant differences of detail—the black gown and hat are not portrayed—the demon in the picture is exactly like the description Agnes Sampson gave. It must be remembered, too, that at the Sabbat she was obviously in a state of morbid excitation, in part due to deep cups of heady wine, the time was midnight, the place a haunted old church, the only light a few flickering candles that burned with a ghastly blue flame.

Now "the Devil" as he is shown in the *Newes from Scotland* illustration is precisely the Devil who appears upon the title-page of Middleton and Rowley's Masque, *The World tost at Tennis*, 4to, 1620. This woodcut presents an episode towards the end of the masque, and here the Devil in traditional disguise, a grim black hairy shape with huge beaked nose, monstrous claws, and the cloven hoofs of a griffin, in every particular fits the details so closely observed by Agnes

Sampson. I have no doubt that the drawing for the masque was actually made in the theatre, for although this kind of costly and decorative entertainment was almost always designed for court or some great nobleman's house we know that *The World tost at Tennis* was produced with considerable success on the public stage " By the Prince his Seruants." The dress, then, of " the Devil " at the Sabbats seems frequently to have been an elaborate theatrical costume, such as might have been found in the stock wardrobe of a rich playhouse at London, but which would have had no such associations for provincial folk and even simpler rustics.

From time to time the sceptics have pointed to the many cases upon record of a victim's sickness or death following the witch's curse, and have incredulously inquired if it be possible that a malediction should have such consequences. Whilst candidly remarking that personally I believe there is power for evil and even for destruction in such a bane, that a deadly anathema launched with concentrated hate and all the energy of volition may bring unhappiness and fatality in its train, I would—since they will not allow this—answer their objections upon other lines. When some person who had in any way annoyed the witch was to be harmed or killed, it was obviously convenient, when practicable, to follow up the symbolism of the solemn imprecation, or it might be of the melted wax image riddled with pins, by a dose of subtly administered poison, which would bring about the desired result, whether sickness or death; and from the evidence concerning the witches' victims, who so frequently pined owing to a wasting disease, it seems more than probable that lethal drugs were continually employed, for as Professor A. J. Clark records " the society of witches had a very creditable knowledge of the art of poisoning,"[18] and they are known to have freely used aconite, deadly nightshade (belladonna), and hemlock.

So far then from the confessions of the witches being mere hysteria and hallucination they are proved, even upon the most material interpretation, to be in the main hideous and horrible fact.

In choosing examples to demonstrate this I have as yet referred almost entirely to the witchcraft which raged from the middle of the thirteenth to the beginning of the eighteenth century, inasmuch as that was the period when the diabolic cult reached its height, when it spread as a blight and a scourge throughout Europe and flaunted its most terrific proportions. But it must not for a moment be supposed, as has often been superficially believed, that Witchcraft was a product of the Middle Ages, and that only then did authority adopt measures of repression and legislate against the warlock and the sorceress. If attention has been concentrated upon that period it is because during those and the succeeding centuries Witchcraft blazed forth with unexampled virulence and ferocity, that it threatened the peace, nay in some degree, the salvation of mankind. But even pagan emperors had issued edicts absolutely forbidding goetic theurgy, confiscating grimoires (*fatidici libri*), and visiting necromancers with death. In A.U.C. 721 during the triumvirate of Octavius, Antony, and Lepidus, all astrologers and charmers were banished.[19] Maecenas called upon Augustus to punish sorcerers, and plainly stated that those who devote themselves to magic are despisers of the gods.[20] More than two thousand popular books of spells, both in Greek and Latin, were discovered in Rome and publicly burned.[21] In the reign of Tiberius a decree of the Senate exiled all traffickers in occult arts; Lucius Pituanius, a notorious wizard, they threw from the Tarpeian rock, and another, Publius Martius, was executed *more prisco* outside the Esquiline gate.[22]

Under Claudius the Senate reiterated the sentence of banishment: "De mathematicis Italia pellendis factum Senatus consultum, atrox et irritum," says Tacitus.[23] During the few months he was emperor Vitellius proceeded with implacable severity against all soothsayers and diviners; many of whom, when accused, he ordered for instant execution, not even affording them the tritest formality of a trial.[24] Vespasian, again, his successor, refused to permit scryers and enchanters to set foot in Italy, strictly enforcing the existent statutes.[25] It is clear from all these stringent laws, and the list of examples might be greatly extended, that although under the Cæsars omens were respected, oracles were consulted, the augurs honoured, and haruspices revered, the dark influences and foul criminality of the reverse of that dangerous science were recognized and its professors punished with the full force of repeated legislation.

M. de Cauzons has expressed himself somewhat vigorously when speaking of writers who trace the origins of Witchcraft to the Middle Ages: "C'est une mauvaise plaisanterie," he remarks,[26] "ou une contrevérité flagrante, d'affirmer que la sorcellerie naquit au Moyen-Age, et d'attribuer son existence à l'influence ou aux croyances de l'Eglise." (It is either a silly jest or inept irony to pretend that Witchcraft arose in the Middle Ages, to attribute its existence to the influence or the beliefs of the Catholic Church.)

An even more erroneous assertion is the charge which has been not infrequently but over-emphatically brought forward by partial ill-documented historians to the effect that the European crusade against witches, the stern and searching prosecutions with the ultimate penalty of death at the stake, are entirely due to the Bull *Summis desiderantes affectibus*, 5 December, 1484, of Pope Innocent VIII; or that at any rate this famous document, if it did not actually initiate the campaign, blew to blasts of flame and fury the smouldering and half-cold embers. This is most preposterously affirmed by Mackay, who does not hesitate to write[27]: "There happened at that time to be a pontiff at the head of the Church who had given much of his attention to the subject of Witchcraft, and who, with the intention of rooting out the supposed crime, did more to increase it than any other man that ever lived. John Baptist Cibo, elected to the papacy in 1485,[28] under the designation of Innocent VIII, was sincerely alarmed at the number of witches, and launched forth his terrible manifesto against them. In his celebrated bull of 1488, he called the nations of Europe to the rescue of the Church of Christ upon earth, 'imperilled by the arts of Satan'" which last sentence seems to be a very fair statement of fact. Lecky notes the Bull of Innocent which, he extravagantly declares, "gave a fearful impetus to the persecution."[29] Dr. Davidson, in a brief but slanderous account of this great pontiff, gives angry prominence to his severity "against sorcerers, magicians, and witches."[30] It is useless to cite more of these superficial and crooked judgements; but since even authorities of weight and value have been deluded and fallen into the snare it is worth while labouring the point a little and stressing the fact that the Bull of Innocent VIII was only one of a long series of Papal ordinances dealing with the suppression of a monstrous and almost universal evil.[31]

The first Papal Bull directly launched against the black art and its professors was that of Alexander IV, 13 December, 1258, addressed to the Franciscan inquisitors. And it is worth while here to examine precisely what was the earlier connotation of the terms "inquisitor" and "inquisition," so often misunderstood, as our research, though brief, will throw a flood of light upon the subject of Witchcraft, and, moreover, incidentally will serve to explain how that those writers who assign the beginnings of Witchcraft to the Middle Ages, although most certainly and even demonstrably in error, have at any rate been very subtilely and easily led wrong, since sorcery in the Middle Ages was violently unmasked and the whole horrid craft then first authoritatively exposed in its darkest colours and most abominable manifestations, as had indeed existed from the first, but had been carefully hidden and scrupulously concealed.

By the term Inquisition (*inquirere* = to look into) is now generally understood a special ecclesiastical institution for combating or suppressing heresy, and the Inquisitors are the officials attached to the said institution, more particularly judges who are appointed to investigate the charges of heresy and to try the persons brought before them on those charges. During the first twelve centuries the Church was loath to deal with heretics save by argument and persuasion; obstinate and avowed heretics were, of course, excluded from her communion, a defection which in the ages of faith, naturally involved them in many and great difficulties. S. Augustine,[32] S. John Chrysostom,[33] S. Isidore of Seville[34] in the seventh century, and a number of other Doctors and Fathers held that for no cause whatsoever should the Church shed blood; but, on the other hand, the imperial successors of Constantine justly considered that they were obliged to have a care for the material welfare of the Church here on earth, and that heresy is always inevitably and inextricably entangled with attempts on the social order, always anarchical, always political. Even the pagan persecutor Diocletian recognized this fact, which heretics, until they obtain the upper hand, have throughout the ages consistently denied and endeavoured to disguise. For in 287, less than two years after his accession, he sent to the stake the leaders of the Manichees; the majority of their followers were beheaded, and a few less culpable sent to perpetual forced labour in the government mines. Again in 296 he orders their extermination (*stirpitus amputari*) as a sordid, vile, and impure sect. So the Christian Cæsars, persuaded that the protection of orthodoxy was their sacred duty, began to issue edicts for the suppression of heretics as being traitors and anti-social revolutionaries.[35] But the Church protested, and when Priscillian, Bishop of Avila, being found guilty of heresy and sorcery,[36] was condemned to death by Maximus at Trier in 384, S. Martin of Tours addressed the Emperor in such plain terms that it was solemnly promised the sentence should not be carried into effect. However, the pledge was broken, and S. Martin's indignation was such that for a long while he refused to hold communion with those who had been in any way responsible for the execution, which S. Ambrose roundly stigmatized as a heinous crime.[37] Even more crushing were the words of Pope S. Siricius, before whom Maximus was fain to humble himself in lowliest penitence, and the supreme pontiff actually excommunicated Bishop Felix of Trier for his part in the deed.

From time to time heretics were put to death under the civil law to which they were amenable, as in 556 when a band of Manichees were executed at Ravenna. Pope Pelagius I, who was consecrated that very year, when Paulinus of Fossombrone, rejecting his authority, openly stirred up schism and revolt, merely relegated the recalcitrant bishop to a monastery. Saint Cæsarius of Arles, who died in 547, speaking[38] of the punishment to be meted out to those who obstinately persevere in overt paganism, recommends that they should first be remonstrated with and reprimanded, that they should if possible be thus persuaded of their errors; but if they persist certain corporal chastisement is to be given; and in extreme cases a course of domestic discipline, the cutting of the hair close as a mark of indignity and confinement within doors under restraint, may be adopted. There is no hint of anything more than private measures, no calling in of any ecclesiastical authority, far less an appeal to any punitive tribunal.

In the days of Charlemagne the aged Elipandus, Archbishop of Toledo, taught an offshoot of the Nestorian heresy, Adoptionism, a crafty but deadly error, to which he won the slippery dialectician Felix of Urgel. Felix, as a Frankish prelate, was summoned to Aix-la-Chapelle. A synod condemned his doctrine and he recanted, only to retract his words and to reiterate his blasphemies. He was again condemned, and again he recanted. But he proved shifty and tricksome to the last. For after his death Agobar of Lyons found amongst his papers a scroll asserting that of this heresy he was fully persuaded, in spite of any contradictions to which he might hypocritically subscribe. Yet Felix only suffered a short detention at Rome, whilst no measures seem to have been taken against Elipandus, who died in his errors. It was presumably considered that orthodoxy could be sufficiently served and vindicated by the zeal of such great names as Beatus, Abbot of Libana; Etherius, Bishop of Osma; S. Benedict of Aniane; and the glorious Alcuin.[39]

Some forty years later, about the middle of the ninth century, Gothescalch, a monk of Fulda, caused great scandal by obstinately and impudently maintaining that Christ had not died for all mankind, a foretaste of the Calvinistic heresy. He was condemned at the Synods of Mainz in 848, and of Kiersey-sur-Oise in 849, being sentenced to flogging and imprisonment, punishments then common in monasteries for various infractions of the rule. In this case, as particularly flagrant, it was Hincmar, Archbishop of Rheims, a prelate notorious for his severity, who sentenced the culprit to incarceration. But Gothescalch had by his pernicious doctrines been the cause of serious disturbances; and his inflammatory harangues had excited tumults, sedition, and unrest, bringing odium upon the sacred habit. The sentence of the Kiersey Synod ran: "Frater Goteschale . . . quia et ecclesiastica et ciuilia negotia contra propositum et nomen monachi conturbare iura ecclesiastica præsumpsisti, durissimis uerberibus te cagistari et secundum ecclesiasticas regulas ergastulo retrudi, auctoritate episcopali decernimus." (Brother Gothescalch, . . . because thou hast dared—contrary to thy monastic calling and vows—to concern thyself in worldly as well as spiritual businesses and hast violated all ecclesiastical law and order, by our episcopal authority we condemn thee to be severely scourged and according to the provision of the Church to be closely imprisoned.)

From these instances it will be seen that the Church throughout all those centuries of violence, rapine, invasion, and war, when often primitive savagery reigned supreme and the most hideous cruelty was the general order of the day, dealt very gently with the rebel and the heretic, whom she might have executed wholesale with the greatest ease; no voice would have been raised in protest save that of her own pontiffs, doctors, and Saints; nay, rather, such repression would have been universally applauded as eminently proper and just. But it was the civil power who arraigned the anarch and the misbeliever, who sentenced him to death.

About the year 1000, however, the venom of Manichæism obtained a new footing in the West, where it had died out early in the sixth century. Between 1030–40 an important Manichæan community was discovered at the Castle of Monteforte, near Asti, in Piedmont. Some of the members were arrested by the Bishop of Asti and a number of noblemen in the neighbourhood, and upon their refusal to retract the civil arm burned them. Others, by order of the Archbishop of Milan, Ariberto, were brought to that city since he hoped to convert them. They answered his efforts by attempts to make proselytes; whereupon Lanzano, a prominent noble and leader of the popular party, caused the magistrates to intervene and when they had been taken into the custody of the State they were executed without further respite. For the next two hundred years Manichæism spread its infernal teaching in secret until, towards the year 1200, the plague had infected all Italy and Southern Europe, had reached northwards to Germany, where it was completely organized, and was not unknown in England, since as early as 1159 thirty foreign Manichees had privily settled here. They were discovered in 1166, and handed over to the secular authorities by the Bishops of the Council of Oxford. In high wrath Henry II ordered them to be scourged, branded in the forehead, and cast adrift in the cold of winter, straightly forbidding any to succour such vile criminals, so all perished from cold and exposure. Manichæism furthermore split up into an almost infinite number of sects and systems, prominent amongst which were the Cathari, the Aldonistæ and Speronistæ, the Concorrezenses of Lombardy, the Bagnolenses, the Albigenses, Pauliciani, Patarini, Bogomiles, the Waldenses, Tartarins, Beghards, Pauvres de Lyon.

It must be clearly borne in mind that these heretical bodies with their endless ramifications were not merely exponents of erroneous religious and intellectual beliefs by which they morally corrupted all who came under their influence, but they were the avowed enemies of law and order, red-hot anarchists who would stop at nothing to gain their ends. Terrorism and secret murder were their most frequent weapons. In 1199 the Patarini followers of Ermanno of Parma and Gottardo of Marsi, two firebrands of revolt, foully assassinated S. Peter Parenzo, the governor of Orvieto. On 6 April, 1252, whilst returning from Como to Milan, as he passed through a lonely wood S. Peter of Verona was struck down by the axe of a certain Carino, a Manichæan bravo, who had been hired to the deed.[40] By such acts they sought to intimidate whole districts, and to compel men's allegiance with blood and violence. The Manichæan system was in truth a simultaneous attack upon the Church and the State, a desperate but well-planned organization to destroy the whole fabric of society, to reduce civilization to chaos. In the first instance, as the Popes began to perceive the momentousness of the struggle they engaged the bishops to stem the tide. At the Council of Tours, 1163, Alexander III called upon the bishops of Gascony to take active measures for the suppression of these revolutionaries, but at the Lateran Council of 1179 it was found these disturbers of public order had sown such sedition in Languedoc that an appeal was made to the secular power to check the evil. In 1184 Lucius III issued from Verona his Bull *Ad Abolendam* which expressly mentions many of the heretics by name, Cathari, Patarini, Humiliati, Pauvres de Lyon, Pasagians, Josephins, Aldonistæ. The situation had fast developed and become serious. Heretics were to be sought out and suitably punished, by which, however, capital punishment is not intended. Innocent III, although adding nothing essential to these regulations yet gave them fuller scope and clearer definition. In his Decretals he precisely speaks of accusation, denunciation, and inquisition, and it is obvious that these measures were necessary in the face of a great secret society aiming at nothing less than the destruction of the established order, for all the sectaries were engaged upon the most zealous propaganda, and their adherents had spread like a network over the greater part of Europe. The members bore the title of "brother" and "sister," and had words and signs by which the initiate could recognize one another without betraying themselves to others.[41] Ivan de Narbonne, who was converted from this heresy, in a letter to Giraldus, Archbishop of Bordeaux, as quoted by Matthew of Paris, says that in every city where he travelled he was always able to make himself known by signs.[42]

It was necessary that the diocesan bishops should be assisted in their heavy task of tracking down heretics, and accordingly the Holy See had resource to legates who were furnished with extraordinary powers to cope with so perplexing a situation. In 1177 as legate of Alexander III, Peter, Cardinal of San Crisogono, at the particular request of Count Raymond V, visited the Toulouse district to check the rising tide of Catharist doctrine.[43] In 1181, Henry, Abbot of Clairvaux, who had been in his suite, now Cardinal of Albano, as legate of the same Pope, received the submission of various heretical leaders, and, so extensive were his powers, solemnly deposed the Archbishops of Lyons and Narbonne. In 1203 Peter of Castelnau and Raoul were acting at Toulouse on behalf of Innocent III, seemingly with plenipotentiary authority. The next year Arnauld Amaury, Abbot of Citeaux, was joined to them to form a triple tribunal with absolute power to judge heretics in the provinces of Aix, Arles, Narbonne, and the adjoining dioceses. At the death of Innocent III (1216) there existed an organization to search out heretics; episcopal tribunals at which often sat an assessor (the future inquisitor) to watch the conduct of the case; and above all the legate to whom he might make a report. The legate, from his position, was naturally a prelate occupied with a vast number of urgent affairs—Arnauld Amaury, for example, was absent for a considerable time to take part in the General Chapter at Cluny—and gradually more and more authority was delegated to the assessor, who insensibly developed into the Inquisitor, a special but permanent judge acting in the name of the Pope, by whom he was invested with the right and the duty to deal legally with offences against the Faith. And as just at this time there came into being two new Orders, the Dominicans and Franciscans, whose members by their theological training and the very nature of their vows seemed eminently fitted to perform the inquisitorial task with complete success, absolutely uninfluenced by any worldly motive, it is natural that the new officials should have been selected from these Orders, and, owing to the importance attached by the Dominicans to the study of divinity, especially from their learned ranks.

It is very obvious why the Holy See so sagaciously preferred to assign the prosecution of heretics, a matter of the first importance, to an extraordinary tribunal rather than leave the trials in the hands of the bishops. Without taking into consideration the fact that these new duties would have seriously encroached upon, if not wholly absorbed, the time and activities of a bishop, the prelates who ruled most dioceses were the subject of some monarch with whom they might have come in conflict on many a delicate point which could easily be conceived to arise, and the result of such disagreement would have been fraught with endless political difficulties and internal embarrassments. A court of religious, responsible to the Pope alone, would act more fairly, more freely, without fear or favour. The profligate Philip I of France, for example, during his long, worthless, and dishonoured reign (1060–1108), by his evil courses drew upon himself the censure of the Church, whereupon he banished the Bishop of Beauvais and revoked the decisions of the episcopal courts.[44] In a letter[45] to William, Count of Poitiers, Pope S. Gregory VII energetically declares that if the King does not cease from molesting the bishops and interfering with their judicature a sentence of excommunication will be launched. In another letter the same pontiff complains of the disrespect shown to the ecclesiastical tribunals, and addressing the French bishops he cries: "Your king, who sooth to say should be termed not a king but a cruel tyrant, inspired by Satan, is the head and cause of these evils. For he has notoriously passed all his days in foulest crimes, in seeking to do wickedness and to ensue it."[46] The conflict of the bishops of a realm with an unworthy and evil monarch is a commonplace of history. These troubles could scarcely arise in the case of courts forane.

The words "inquisition" and "inquisitors" began definitely to acquire their accepted signification in the earlier half of the thirteenth century. Thus in 1235 Gregory IX writes to the Archbishop of Sens: "Know then that we have charged the Provincial of the Order of Preachers in this same realm to nominate certain of his brethren, who are best fitted for so weighty a business, as Inquisitors that they may proceed against all notorious evildoers in the aforesaid realm . . . and we also charge thee, dear Brother, that thou shouldest be instant and zealous in this matter of establishing an Inquisition by the appointment of those who seem to be best fitted for such a work, and let thy loins be girded, Brother, to fight boldly the battles of the Lord."[47] In 1246 Innocent IV wrote to the Superiors of the Franciscans giving them leave to recall at will: "those brethren who have been sent abroad to preach the Mystery of the Cross of Christ, or to seek out and take measure against the plague sore of heresy."[48]

All the heresies, and the Secret Societies of heretics, which infested Europe during the Middle Ages were Gnostic, and even more narrowly, Manichæan in character. The Gnostics arose almost with the advent of Christianity as a School or Schools who explained the teachings of Christ by blending them with the doctrines of pagan fantasts, and thus they claimed to have a Higher and a Wider Knowledge, the Γνῶσις, the first exponent of which was unquestionably Simon Magus. "Two problems borrowed from heathen philosophy," says Mansel,[49] "were intruded by Gnosticism on the Christian revelation, the problem of absolute existence, and the problem of the Origin of Evil." The Gnostics denied the existence of Free-will, and therefore Evil was not the result of Man's voluntary transgression, but must in some way have emanated from the Creator Himself. Arguing on these lines the majority asserted that the Creator must have been a malignant power, Lord of the Kingdom of Darkness, opposed to the Supreme and Ineffable God. This doctrine was taught by the Gnostic sects of Persia, which became deeply imbued with the religion of Zoroaster, who assumed the existence of two original and independent Powers of Good and of Evil. Each of these Powers is of equal strength, and supreme in his own dominions, whilst constant war is waged between the two. This doctrine was particularly held by the Syrian Gnostics, the Ophites, the Naasseni, the Peratæ, the Sethians, amongst whom the serpent was the principal symbol. As the Creator of the world was evil, the Tempter, the Serpent, was the benefactor of man. In fact, in some creeds he was identified with the Logos. The Cainites carried out the Ophite doctrines to their fullest logical conclusion. Since the Creator, the God of the Old Testament, is evil all that is commended by the Scripture must be evil, and conversely all that is condemned therein is good. Cain, Korah, the rebels, are to be imitated and admired. The one true Apostle was Judas Iscariot. This cult is very plainly marked in the Middle Ages among the Luciferians; and Cainite ceremonies have their place in the witches' Sabbat.[50]

All this Gnostic teaching was summed up in the gospel of the Persian Mani, who, when but a young man of twenty-six, seems first to have proclaimed in the streets and bazaars of Seleucia-Ctesiphon his supposed message on Sunday, 20 March, 242, the coronation festival of Shapur I. He did not meet with immediate success in his own country, but here and there his ideas took deep root. In 276–277, however, he was seized and crucified by the grandson of Shapur, Bahram I, his disciples being relentlessly pursued. Whenever Manichees were discovered they were brought to swift justice, executed, held up to universal hatred and contempt. They were considered by Moslems as not merely Unbelievers, the followers of a false impostor, but unnatural and unsocial, a menace to the State. It was for no light cause that the Manichee was loathed and abhorred both by faithful Christian and by those who proclaimed Mohammed as the true prophet of Allah. But later Manichæism spread in every direction to an extraordinary degree, which may perhaps be accounted for by the fact that it is in some sense a synthesis of the Gnostic philosophies, the theory of two eternal principles, good and evil, being especially emphasized.

Moreover, the historical Jesus, "the Jewish Messias, whom the Jews crucified," was "a devil, who was justly punished for interfering in the work of the Æon Jesus," who was neither born nor suffered death. As time went on, the elaborate cosmogony of Mani disappeared, but the idea that the Christ must be repudiated remained. And logically, then, worship is due to the enemy of Christ, and a sub-sect, the Messalians or Euchites, taught that divine honours must be paid to Satan, who is further to be propitiated by means of every possible outrage done to Christ. This, of course, is plain and simple Satanism openly avowed. Carpocrates even went so far as to aggravate the teaching of the Cainites, for he made the performance of every species of sin forbidden in the Old Testament a solemn duty, since this was the completest mode of showing defiance to the Evil Creator and Ruler of the World. This doctrine was wholly that of mediæval witches, and is flaunted by modern Satanists. Although the Manichees affected the greatest purity, it is quite certain that not unchastity but the act of generation alone was opposed to their views, secretly they practised the most hideous obscenities.[51] The Messalians in particular, vaunted a treatise *Asceticus*, which was condemned by the Third General Council of Ephesus (431) as "that filthy book of this heresy," and in Armenia, in the fifth century, special edicts were passed to restrain their immoralities, so that their very name became the equivalent for "lewdness." The Messalians survived unto the Middle Ages as Bogomiles.

Attention has already been drawn to the striking fact that even Diocletian legislated with no small vigour against the Manichees, and when we find Valentinian I and his son Gratian, although tolerant of other bodies, passing laws of equal severity in this regard (372), we feel that such interdiction is especially significant. Theodosius I, by a statute of 381, declared Manichees to be without civil rights, and incapable of inheriting; in the following year he condemned them to death, and in 389 he sternly directed the rigorous enforcement to the letter of these penalties.

Valentinian II confiscated their goods, annulled their wills, and sent them into exile. Honorius in 399 renewed the draconian measures of his predecessors; in 405 he heavily fined all governors of provinces or civil magistrates who were slack in carrying out his orders; in 407 he pronounced the sect outlaws and public criminals having no legal status whatsoever, and in 408 he reiterated the former enactments in meticulous detail to afford no loophole of escape. Theodosius II (423), again, repeated this legislation, whilst Valentinian III passed fresh laws in 425 and 445. Anastasius once more decreed the penalty of death, which was even extended by Justin and Justinian to converts from Manichæism who did not at once denounce their former co-religionists to the authorities. This catena of laws which aims at nothing less than extermination is of singular moment.

About 660 arose the Paulicians, a Manichæan sect, who rejected the Old Testament, the Sacraments, and the Priesthood. In 835 it was realized that the government of this body was political and aimed at revolution and red anarchy. In 970 John Zimisces fixed their headquarters in Thrace. In 1115 Alexis Comnenus established himself during the winter at Philippopolis, and avowed his intention of converting them, the only result being that the heretics were driven westward and spread rapidly in France and Italy.

The Bogomiles were also Manichees. They openly worshipped Satan, repudiating Holy Mass and the Passion, rejecting Holy Baptism for some foul ceremony of their own, and possessing a peculiar version of the Gospel of S. John. As Cathari these wretches had their centre for France at Toulouse; for Germany at Cologne; whilst in Italy, Milan, Florence, Orvieto, and Viterbo were their rallying-points. Their meetings were often held in the open air, on mountains, or in the depths of some lone valley; the ritual was very secret, but we know that at night they celebrated their Eucharist or Consolamentum, when all stood in a circle round a table covered with a white cloth and numerous torches were kindled, the service being closed by the reading of the first seventeen verses of their transfigured gospel. Bread was broken, but there is a tradition that the words of consecration were not pronounced according to the Christian formula; in some instances they were altogether omitted.

During the eleventh century, then, there began to spread throughout Europe a number of mysterious organizations whose adherents, in a secrecy that was all but absolute, practised obscure rites embodying their beliefs, the central feature of which was the adoration of the evil principle, the demon. But what is this save Satanism, or in other words Witchcraft? It is true that when these heresies came into sharp conflict with the Catholic Church they developed on lines which lost various non-essential accretions and Eastern subtleties of extravagant thought, but the motive of the Manichæan doctrines and of Witchcraft is one and the same, and the punishment of Manichees and of witches was the same death at the stake. The fact that these heretics were recognized as sorcerers will explain, as nothing else can, the severity of the statutes against them, evidence of no ordinary depravity, and early in the eleventh century Manichee and warlock are recognized as synonymous.

The sorcery of the Middle Ages, says Carl Haas, a learned and impartial authority, was born from the heresies of earlier epochs, and just as Christian authority had dealt with heresy, so did it deal with the spawn witchcraft. Both alike are the result of doubts, of faithlessness, a disordered imagination, pride and presumption, intellectual arrogance; sick phantasy both, they grow and flourish apace in shadow and sin, until right reasoning, and sometimes salutary force, are definitely opposed to them. The authors of the *Malleus Maleficarum* clearly identify heresy and Witchcraft. When the Prince Bishop of Bamberg, John George II Fuchs von Dornheim, (1623–33), built a strong prison especially for sorcerers, the *Drudenhaus*, he set over the great door a figure of Justice, and inscribed above Vergil's words: *Discite iustitiam moniti et non temnere Diuos* (*Æneid*, VI, 620),

(Behold, and learn to practise right,
Nor do the blessed Gods despite).

To the right and the left were engraved upon two panels, the one Latin, the other German, two verses from the Bible, 3 Kings ix. 8, 9; which are Englished as follows: "This house shall be made an example of: every one that shall pass by it shall be astonished, and shall hiss, and say: Why hath the Lord done thus to this land, and to this house? And they shall answer: Because they forsook the Lord their God, who brought their fathers out of the land of Egypt, and followed strange gods, and adored them, and worshipped them: therefore hath the Lord brought upon them all this evil." This is a concise summary of the basic reason for the prosecution of witches, the standpoint of Christian authority, whose professors justly and logically regarded sorcery as being in essence heresy, to be suppressed by the same measures, to be punished with the same penalties.

In connexion with the close correlation between Witchcraft and heresy there is a very remarkable fact, the significance of which has—so far as I am aware—never been noted. The full fury of prosecution burst over England during the first half of the seventeenth century, that is to say, shortly after the era of a great religious upheaval, when the work of rehabilitation and recovery so nobly initiated by Queen Mary I had been wrecked owing to the pride, lust, and baseness of her sister. In Scotland, envenomed to the core with the poison of Calvin and Knox, fire and cord were seldom at rest. It is clear that heresy had brought Witchcraft swiftly in its train. Ireland has ever been singularly free from Witchcraft prosecutions, and with the rarest exceptions —chiefly, if not solely, the famous Dame Alice Kyteler case of 1324—the few trials recorded are of the seventeenth century and engineered by the Protestant party. The reason for this exemption is plain. Until the stranger forced his way into Ireland, heresy had no foothold there. That the Irish firmly believed in witches, we know, but the Devil's claws were finely clipped.

In 1022 a number of Manichees were burned alive by order of Robert I. They had been condemned by a Synod at Orleans and refused to recant their errors.[52] A contemporary document clearly identifies them with witches, worshippers of the Demon, who appeared to them under the form of an animal. Other abominable rites are fully set forth, comparable to the pages of Sprenger, Bodin, Boguet, De Lancre, Guazzo, and the rest. The account runs as follows: "Before we proceed to other details I will at some length inform those who are as yet ignorant of these matters, how that food which they call Food from Heaven is made and provided. On certain nights of the year they all meet together in an appointed house, each one of them carrying a lantern in his hand. They then begin to sing the names of various demons, as though they were chanting a litany, until suddenly they perceive that the Devil has appeared in the midst of them in the shape of some animal or other. As he would seem to be visible to them all in some mysterious way they immediately extinguish the lights, and each one of them as quickly as he can seizes upon the woman, who chances to be nearest at hand. . . . When a child happens to be born . . . on the eighth day they all meet together and light a large fire in their midst, and then the child is passed through the fire, ceremonially, according to the sacrifices of the old heathen, and finally is burnt in the flames. The ashes are collected and reserved, with the same veneration as Christians are wont to reserve the Blessed Sacrament, and they give those who are on the point of death a portion of these ashes as if it were the Viaticum. There appears to be such power infused by the Devil into the said ashes that a man who belongs to these heretics and happens to have tasted even the smallest quantity of these ashes can scarcely ever be persuaded to abandon his heresies and to turn his thoughts towards the true path. It must suffice to give only these details, as a warning to all Christians to take no part in these abominations, and God forbid that curiosity should lead anybody to explore them."[53]

At Forfar, in 1661, Helen Guthrie and four other witches exhumed the body of an unbaptised infant, which was buried in the churchyard near the south-east door of the church, " and took severall peices thereof, as the feet, hands, a pairt of the head, and a pairt of the buttock, and they made a py thereof, that they might eat of it, that by this meanes they might never make a confession (as they thought) of their witchcraftis."[54]

The belief of 1022 and 1661 is the same, because it is the same organization. The very name of the Vaudois, stout heretics, survives in Voodoo worship, which is, in effect, African fetishism or Witchcraft transplanted to America soil.

In 1028 Count Alduin burned a number of Manichees at Angoulême, and the chronicle runs : " Interea iussu Alduini flammis exustæ sunt mulieres maleficæ extra urbem."[55] (About this time certain evil women, heretics, were burned without the city by the command of Alduin.) The Templars, whose Order was suppressed and the members thereof executed on account of their sorceries, were clearly a Society of Gnostic heretics, active propagandists, closely connected with the Bogomiles and the Mandæans or Johannites.[56]

It is true that in his recent study *The Religion of the Manichees*,[57] Dr. F. G. Buskitt, with a wealth of interesting detail and research, has endeavoured to show that the Bogomiles, the Cathari, the Albigenses, and other unclean bodies only derived fragments of their teaching from Manichæan sources, and he definitely states " I think it misleading to call these sects, even the Albigensians, by the name of Manichees." But in spite of his adroit special pleading the historical fact remains; although we may concede that the abominable beliefs of these various Gnostics were perhaps a deduction from, or a development of, the actual teaching of Mani. Yet none the less their evil was contained in his heresy and a logical consequence of it.

In the early years of this century important discoveries of Manichæan MSS. have been made. Three or four scientific expeditions to Chinese Turkestan brought back some thousands of fragments, especially from the neighbourhood of a town called Turfan. Many of these screeds are written in the peculiar script of the Manichees, some of which can be deciphered, although unfortunately the newly found documents are mere scraps, bits of torn books and rolls, and written in languages as yet imperfectly known. Much of the new doctrine is of the wildest and most fantastic theosophy, and the initiate were, as we know, sufficiently cunning not to commit the esoteric and true teachings to writing, but preferred that there should be an oral tradition. One important piece, the *Khuastuanift*, i.e. " Confession," has been recovered almost in its entirety. It is in the old Turkestan Turkish language, and seems full of the most astounding contradictions or paradoxes, a consensus of double meanings and subtleties.

The question is asked whether we ought to consider Manichæism as an independent religion or a Christian heresy? Eznih of Kolb, the Armenian writer of the fifth century, when attacking Zoroastrianism, obviously treats Manichæism as a variety of Persian religion. The orthodox documents, however, from Mark the Deacon onwards treat Manichæism as in the main a Christian heresy and this is assuredly the correct view. There is in existence a polemical fragment, a single ill-preserved pair of leaves, in which the Manichæan writer pours forth horrid blasphemies and vilely attacks those who call Mary's Son (*Bar Maryam*) the Son of Adonay.

It may be worth while here to say just a word correcting a curious old-fashioned misapprehension which once prevailed in certain quarters concerning the Albigenses, an error of which we occasionally yet catch the echoes, as when Mrs. Grenside wrote that the Albigenses were "a sect of the 14th century which, owing to their secret doctrine, endured much ecclesiastical persecution."[58] The impression left, and it is one which was not altogether uncommon some seventy years ago, is that the Albigensian was a stern old Protestant father, Bible and sword in hand, who defended his hearth and home against the lawless brigands spurred on to attack him by priestly machinations. Nothing, of course, could be further from the truth. The Albigensian was a Satanist, a worshipper of the powers of evil, and he would have found short shrift indeed, fire and the stake, in Puritan England under Cromwell, or in Calvinistic Scotland had his practices been even dimly guessed at by the Kirk. As Dr. Arendzen well says[59]: "Albigensianism was not really a heresy against Christianity and the Catholic Church, it was a revolt against nature, a pestilential perversion of human instinct."

Towards the end of the nineteenth century a *Neo-Gnostic Church* was formed by Fabre des Essarts, but that great pontiff Leo XIII promptly condemned it with fitting severity as a recrudescence of the old Albigensian heresy, complicated by the addition of new false and impious doctrines. It is said still to have a number of unhappy adherents. These Neo-Gnostics believe that the world is created by Satan, who is a powerful rival to the omnipotence of God. They also preach a dangerous communism, speciously masqued under some such titles as the "Brotherhood of Man" or the "Brotherhood of Nations."

In 1900, after a letter from Joanny Bricaud,[60] the patriarch of universal Gnosticism at Lyons, where, in 1913, he was residing at 8, rue Bugeaud, the Neo-Gnostics joined with the Valentinians, a union approved by their pseudo-Council of Toulouse in 1903. But some years later Dr. Fugairon of Lyons, who adopted the name of Sophronius, amalgamated all the branches, with the exception of the Valentinians, under the name of the *Gnostic Church of Lyons*. These, however, although excluded, continued to follow their own way of salvation, and in 1906 formally addressed a legal declaration to the Republican Government defending their religious rights of association. Truly might Huysmans tell us that Satanism flourished at Lyons, " où toutes les hérésies survivent," " where every heresy pullulates and is green." These Gnostic assemblies are composed of " perfected ones," male and female. The modern Valentinians, it is said, have a form of spiritual marriage, bestowing the name of Helen upon the mystic bride. The original founder of this sect, Valentinus, was, according to S. Epiphanius (*Hæresis* XXXI) born in Egypt, and educated at Alexandria. His errors led to excommunication and he died in Cyprus, about A.D. 160–161. His heresy is a fantastic medley of Greek and Oriental speculation, tinged with some vague colouring of Christianity. The Christology of Valentinus is especially confused. He seems to have supposed the existence of three redeemers, but Christ, the Son of Mary, did not have a real body and did not suffer. Even his more prominent disciples, Heracleon, Ptolemy, Marcos, and Bardesanes, widely differed from their master, as from one another. Many of the writings of these Gnostics, and a large number of excerpts from Valentinus's own works yet survive.

One or two writers of the nineteenth century remarked that there seemed to be some connexion between certain points of the Sabbat ceremonial and the rites of various pagan deities, which is, of course, a perfectly correct observation. For we have seen that Witchcraft as it existed in Europe from the eleventh century was mainly the spawn of Gnostic heresy, and heresy by its very nature embraced and absorbed much of heathendom. In some sense Witchcraft was a descendant of the old pre-Christian magic, but it soon assumed a slightly different form, or rather at the advent of Christianity it was exposed and shown in its real foul essence as the worship of the Evil Principle, the Enemy of Mankind, Satan.

It may freely be acknowledged that there are certain symbols common to Christianity itself and to ancient religions. It would in truth be very surprising if, when seeking to propagate her doctrines in the midst of Græco-Roman civilization, the Church had adopted for her intercourse with the people a wholly unknown language, and had systematically repudiated everything that until then had served to give expression to religious feeling.

Within the limits imposed by the conventions of race and culture, the method of interpreting the emotions of the heart cannot be indefinitely varied, and it was natural that the new religion should appropriate and incorporate all that was good in a ritual much of which only required to be rightly interpreted and directed to become the language of the Christian soul aspiring to the one True God. Certain attitudes of prayer and reverence, the use of incense and of lamps burning day and night in the sanctuary, the offering of ex-votos as a testimony to benefits received, all these are man's natural expressions of piety and gratitude towards a divine power, and it would be strange indeed if their equivalents were not met with in all religions.

Cicero tells us that at Agrigentum there was a much-venerated statue of Hercules, of which the mouth and chin were worn away by the many worshippers who pressed their lips to it.[61] The bronze foot of the statue of the first Pope, S. Peter, in Rome has not withstood any better the pious kisses of the faithful. Yet he were a very fool who imagined that modern Christians have learned anything from the Sicilian contemporaries of Verres. What is true is that the same thought in analogous circumstances has found natural expression after an interval of centuries in identical actions and attitudes.

Among the Greeks, heroes, reputed to be the mortal sons of some divinity, were specially honoured in the city with which they were connected by birth and through the benefits they had conferred upon it. After death they became the patrons and protectors of these towns. Every country, nay, almost every village, had such local divinities to whom monuments were raised and whom the people invoked in their prayers. The centre of devotion was generally the hero's tomb, which was often erected in the middle of the agora, the nave of public life. In most cases it was sheltered by a building, a sort of chapel known as ἡρῷον. The celebrated temples, too, were not infrequently adorned with a great number of cenotaphs of heroes, just as the shrines of Saints are honoured in Christian churches.[62] More, the translations of the bones or ashes of heroes were common in Greece. Thus in the archonship of Apsephion, 469 B.C., the remains of Theseus were brought from Scyros to Athens, and carried into the city amid sacrifices and every demonstration of triumphal joy.[63] Thebes recovered from Ilion the bones of Hector, and presented to Athens those of Œdipus, to Lebadea those of Arcesilaus, and to Megara those of Aigialeus.[64]

The analogy between these ancient practices and Christianity may be pushed further yet. Just as, in our own churches, objects that have belonged to the Saints are exposed for the veneration of the faithful, so in the old temples visitors were shown divers curiosities whose connexion with a god or a hero would command their respect. At Minihi Tréguier we may reverence a fragment of the Breviary of S. Yves, at Sens the stole of S. Thomas of Canterbury, at Bayeux the chasuble of S. Regnobert, in S. Maria Maggiore the cincture and veil of S. Scholastica; so in various localities of Greece were exhibited the cittara of Paris, the lyre of Orpheus, portions of the ships of Agamemnon and Æneas. Can anything further be needed to prove that the veneration of Holy Relics is merely a pagan survival?

Superficially the theory seems plausible enough, and yet it will not stand a moment before the judgement of history. The cultus of the Saints and their Relics is not an outcome of ancient hero-worship, but of reverence for the Martyrs, and this can be demonstrated without any possibility of question. So here we have two very striking parallels, each of which has an analogous starting-point, two cults which naturally develop upon logical and similar lines, but without any interdependence whatsoever. Needless to say, the unbalanced folklorist, who is in general far too insufficiently equipped for any such inquiry, has rushed in with his theories—to his own utter undoing. And so, with regard to Witchcraft, there appear in the rites of the Sabbat and other hellish superstitions to be ceremonies which are directly derived from heathendom, but this, as a matter of fact, is far from the case. Accordingly we recognize that the thesis of Miss M. A. Murray in her anthropological study *The Witch-*

Cult in Western Europe,[65] although worked out with nice ingenuity and no little documentation, is radically and wholly erroneous. Miss Murray actually postulates that "underlying the Christian religion was a cult practised by many classes of the community" which "can be traced back to pre-Christian times, and appears to be the ancient religion of Western Europe." We are given a full account of the chief festivals of this imaginary cult, of its hierarchy, its organization, and many other details. The feasts and dances —the obscene horrors of the Sabbat—"show that it was a joyous religion"! It is impossible to conceive a more amazing assertion. Miss Murray continues to say that "as such it must have been quite incomprehensible to the gloomy Inquisitors and Reformers who suppressed it." The Reformers, for all their dour severity, perfectly well appreciated with what they were dealing, and the Inquisitors, the sons of S. Dominic who was boundless in his charity and of S. Francis, whose very name breathes Christ-like love to all creation, were men of the profoundest knowledge and deepest sympathies, whose first duty it was to stamp out the infection lest the whole of Society be corrupted and damned. Miss Murray does not seem to suspect that Witchcraft was in truth a foul and noisome heresy, the poison of the Manichees. Her "Dianic cult," which name she gives to this "ancient religion" supposed to have survived until the Middle Ages and even later and to have been a formidable rival to Christianity, is none other than black heresy and the worship of Satan, no primitive belief with pre-agricultural rites, in latter days persecuted, misinterpreted, and misunderstood. It is true that in the Middle Ages Christianity had—not a rival but a foe, the eternal enemy of the Church Militant against whom she yet contends to-day, the dark Lord of that city which is set contrariwise to the City of God, the Terrible Shadow of destruction and despair.

Miss Murray with tireless industry has accumulated a vast number of details by the help of which she seeks to build up and support her imaginative thesis. Even those that show the appropriation by the cult of evil of the more hideous heathen practices, both of lust and cruelty, which prevailed among savage or decadent peoples, afford no evidence whatsoever of any continuity of an earlier religion, whilst by far the greater number of the facts she quotes are deflected, although no doubt unconsciously, and sharply wrested so as to be patent of the signification it is endeavoured to read into them. Miss Murray speaks, for example, of witches "who, like the early Christian martyrs, rushed headlong on their fate, determined to die for their faith and their God."[66] And later, discussing the "Sacrifice of the God," a theme which it is interesting and by no means impertinent to note, folklorists have elaborated in the most fanciful manner, basing upon the scantiest and quite contradictory evidence an abundant sheaf of wildly extravagant theories and fables, she tells us that the burning of witches at the hands of the public executioner was a "sacrifice of the incarnate deity."[67] One might almost suppose that the condemned went cheerfully and voluntarily to the cruellest and most torturing punishment, for the phrase "Self-devotion to death" is used in this connexion. On the contrary, we continually find in the witch-trials that the guilty, as was natural, sought to escape from their doom by any and every means; by flight, as in the case of Gilles de Sillé and Roger de Bricqueville, companions of Gilles de Rais; by long and protracted defences, such as was that of Agnes Fynnie, executed in Edinburgh in 1644; by threats and blackmail of influential patrons owing to which old Bettie Laing of Pittenween escaped scot-free in 1718; by pleading pregnancy at the trial as did Mother Samuel, the Warbois witch, who perished on the gallows 7 April, 1593; by suicide as the notorious warlock John Reid, who hanged himself in prison at Paisley, in 1697.

Of the theoretical "Sacrifice of the incarnate deity" Miss Murray writes: "This explanation accounts for the fact that the bodies of witches, male or female, were always burnt and the ashes scattered; for the strong prejudice which existed, as late as the eighteenth century, against any other mode of disposing of their bodies; and for some of the otherwise inexplicable occurrences in connexion with the deaths of certain of the victims."[68] Three instances are cited to prove these three statements, but it will be seen upon examination that not one of these affords the slightest evidence in support of the triple contention. In the first place we are informed that "in the light of this theory much of the mystery which surrounds the fate of Joan of Arc is explained." How is not divulged, but this is capped by the astounding and indecorous assertion that S. Joan of Arc "belonged to the ancient religion, not to the Christian." It is superfluous to say that there is not a tittle of evidence for such an amazing hypothesis in reference to the Saint.

Gilles de Rais, whose execution is next quoted by Miss Murray in support of her postulate, proves a singularly unfortunate example. We are told that "like Joan he was willing to be tried for his faith," by which is meant the imaginary "Dianic cult." This is a purely gratuitous assertion, not borne out in any way by his behaviour at his trial, nor by the details of any authoritative account or report of the proceedings. Gilles de Rais was hanged on a gibbet above a pyre, but when the heat had burned through the rope the body was quickly taken up from the blazing wood, and afterwards buried in the neighbouring Carmelite church. One may compare the execution of Savonarola and his two fellow friars on 25 May, 1498. They were strangled at the gallows, their bodies committed to the flames, and their ashes carefully gathered and thrown into the Arno. Gilles de Rais was condemned by three distinct courts; by the Holy Inquisition, the presidents being Jean de Malestroit, Bishop of Nantes, and Jean Blouyn, vice-inquisitor, O.P., S.T.M., on charges of heresy and sorcery; by the episcopal court on charges of sacrilege and the violation of ecclesiastical rights; by the civil court of John V, Duke of Brittany, on multiplied charges of murder.

The third case quoted by Miss Murray is that of Major Weir, who "offered himself up and was executed as a witch in Edinburgh." Thomas Weir, who was a hypocritical Puritan, a leader "among the Presbyterian strict sect," and regarded as a Saint throughout Edinburgh, had all the while secretly led a life of hideous debauchery and was stained with the most odious and unnatural crimes. In 1670, which was the seventieth year of his age, he appears to have been stricken with terrible fits of remorse and despair; the pangs of his guilty conscience drove him to the verge of madness and his agony could only be eased by a full, ample, and public confession of his misdeeds. For a few months his party, in order to avoid the scandal and disgrace, contrived to stifle the matter, but a minister "whom they esteemed more forward than wise" revealed the secret to the Lord Provost of the city, and an inquiry was instituted. The wretched old man, insistently declaring that "the terrors of God which were upon his soul urged him to confess and accuse himself," was arrested, together with his crazy sister Jean, who was implicated in his abominations. "All the while he was in prison he lay under violent apprehension of the heavy wrath of God, which put him into that which is properly called despair," and to various ministers who visited him he declared, "I know my sentence of damnation is already sealed in Heaven . . . for I find nothing within me but blackness, darkness, Brimstone, and burning to the bottom of Hell."[69] The whole account gives a complete and perfectly comprehensible psychological study. So sudden a revulsion of feeling, the loathing of foul acts accompanied by the sheer inability to repent of them, is quite understandable in a septuagenarian, worn out in body by years of excess and enfeebled in mind owing to the heavy strain of hourly acting an artificial and difficult rôle. The intense emotionalism of the degenerate has not infrequently been observed eventually to give way to a state of frenzied anguish, for which the alienist Magnan coined the name "Anxiomania," a species of mental derangement that soon drives the patient to hysterical confession and boundless despair. "I am convinced," says one writer with regard to Major Weir, "of the prisoner having been delirious at the time of his trial."[70] His sister frantically accused her brother of Witchcraft, but it is remarkable that in his case this charge was not taken up and examined. I do not say that Weir was not supposed to be a warlock; as a matter of fact he was notoriously reputed such, and strange stories were told of his magic staff and other enchantments, but Witchcraft was not the main accusation brought against him in the official courts. He was found guilty of adultery, fornication, incest, and bestiality, and on these several counts sentenced to be strangled at a stake betwixt Edinburgh and Leith, on Monday, 11 April, 1670, and his body to be burned to ashes. Jean Weir was condemned for incest and Witchcraft and hanged on 12 April in the Grassmarket at Edinburgh. To the last this miserable lunatic placed "a great deal of confidence in her constant adherence to the Covenant, which she called *the cause and interest of Christ.*"[71]

It will be seen that Miss Murray's citation is incorrect and therefore impertinent. Major Weir was not executed "as a witch." Moreover, both he and Gilles de Rais were actually strangled, and such examples must entirely fail to account "for the fact that the bodies of witches, male or female, were always burnt and the ashes scattered," especially since in the latter case, as we have noticed, the body was honourably buried in the church of the Whitefriars. In fine, to endeavour to connect, however ingeniously, the fate of S. Joan of Arc, the execution of Gilles de Rais and Major Weir, with the folklorists' theory of "the sacrifice of the incarnate deity" is merest fantasy.

The gist of the whole matter lies elsewhere. Death at the stake was the punishment reserved for heretics. As we have already noticed, Diocletian ruthlessly burned the Manichees: "We order then that the professors and teachers be punished with the utmost penalties, which is to say they are to be burned with fire together with all their execrable books and writings."[72] The Visigoth code condemned pagans or heretics who had committed sacrilege to the flames, and together with them it grouped all Manichees: "It is known that many Proconsuls have thrown blasphemers to the beasts, nay, have even burned some alive."[73] The Visigoth code of Rekeswinth (652–672) punishes Judaizers with death, "aut lapide puniatur, aut igne cremetur." (Let them be stoned or burned with fire.) But it was actually in the eleventh century that the civil power first generally ordained the penalty of the stake for the heretics, who were, it must always be remembered, mad anarchists endeavouring to destroy all social order, authority, and decency. "In Italy even many adherents of this pestilential belief were found, and these wretches were slain with the sword or burned at the stake,"[74] writes Adhémar de Chabannes, a monk of Angoulême, about the middle of the eleventh century. In a letter of Wazon, Bishop of Liège, there is an allusion to similar punishments which were being inflicted in Flanders.

A striking example of the heretical anarchists who troubled Europe about the beginning of the twelfth century may be seen in Tanchelin[75] and his followers. This fanatic, who was originally a native of Zealand, journeyed throughout Flanders preaching his monstrous doctrines everywhere he could find listeners and especially concentrating upon the city of Antwerp. In 1108 and 1109 he appeared at Arras and Cambrai, persuading many evil and ignorant persons to accept his abominable tenets. The tares were thickly sown, and it is terribly significant that some three centuries later, about 1469, there was a fearful epidemic of sorcery throughout the whole district of the Artois, in reference to which the anonymous author—probably an Inquisitor—of a contemporary work entitled *Erreurs des Gazariens ou de ceux que l'on prouve chevaucher sur un balai ou un bâton* expressly identified such heretics as the Gazariens, who are Cathari, and the Vaudois (Poor Lombards) with warlocks and sorcerers. In 1112 Tanchelin, who had actually visited Rome itself, was upon his return arrested and thrown into prison at Cologne, whence, however, he managed to escape, and accompanied by an apostate priest Everwacher and a Jew Manasses, who had formerly been a blacksmith, at the head of a formidable band of three thousand ruffians, outlaws, cast gamesters, brigands, murderers, beggars and thieves, the parbreak of every slum and stew, he terrorized the whole countryside, the people being afraid, the bishops and secular princes seemingly unable to resist him.

The teaching of Tanchelin was, as might be expected, largely incoherent and illogical, the ravings of a frantic brain, but none the less dangerous and wholly abominable. The Church was, of course, directly attacked and blasphemed. With abuse and foul language, extraordinarily like the language of the so-called Reformers in the sixteenth century, the hierarchy and all ecclesiastical order were repudiated and contemned, priests and religious in particular were to be persecuted and exterminated since the priesthood was a fiction and a snare; the Sacrifice of Holy Mass was a mockery, all Sacraments were void and empty forms, useless for salvation[76]; the churches themselves were to be accounted as brothels and markets of shame. "This very spawn of Satan and black angel of woe declared that the churches, dedicated to God's worship, were bawdy-houses. That, at Holy Mass there was no Sacrifice at the hands of the priest; the Service of the Altar was filth, not a Sacrament."[77]

Tanchelin declared himself to be the Messiah, God, the Son of God, the Perfect Man, the sum of all the divine emanations in one system, upon whom had descended and in whom abode the pleroma of the Holy Spirit. "This miserable wretch advanced from evil to evil and at length proceeded to such an extremity of unheard-of wickedness that he gave himself out to be God, asserting that if Christ be God because the Holy Ghost dwelt in Him, he himself was not less than and of the same nature as God, seeing that he enjoyed the plenitude of the Holy Ghost."[78] Here the Gnostic character of his teaching is very apparent. He even caused a temple to be erected in his honour where he was worshipped with sacrifice and hymns. His followers, indeed, regarded this lunatic wretch with such an excess of veneration that the dirty water from his bath was actually collected in phials and solemnly distributed among them, whereof they partook as of a sacrament.

It must be borne in mind that Tanchelin's programme did not solely comprise a negation of Christian dogma; this we find in most of the innovators at the time of the so-called Reformation, but his ultimate aim was to effect a social revolution, to overturn the existing order of things and produce communistic chaos with himself as overlord and dictator. The way for anarchy could only have been paved by the destruction of the Church, the supreme representative of authority and order throughout the world, and it was accordingly against the Church that this superman launched his fiercest diatribes. To further his ends he encouraged, nay, commanded, the open practice of the foulest vices; incest, adultery, fornication were declared to be works of spiritual efficacy; unmentionable abominations flaunted themselves in the face of day; virtue became an offence; men were driven to vice and crime, and anon they gradually sank in a stupor of infamy and sheer boneless degradation.

The unfortunate town of Antwerp came directly under Tanchelin's influence. Here he reigned as king, surrounded by vile and obsequious satellites who ground the miserable citizens to the dust and filled each street and corner with orgies of lust and blood. There is a strange and striking parallel between the details of his foul career and the Russian tyranny to-day. Little wonder that in 1116 a priest, maddened by the outrages and profanities of this hellish crew, scattered the heretic's brains upon the deck of his royal barge as one afternoon he was sailing in pompous state down the river Schelde: "After a life of infamy, bloodshed, and heresy, whilst he was sailing on the river he was struck on the head by a certain priest and falling down died there."[79] All unfortunately, however, the pernicious errors of Tanchelin did not expire with their author. Antwerp remained plunged in dissipation and riot, and although strenuous efforts were made to restore decency and order, at first these seemed to be entirely nugatory and fruitless. Burchard, the Bishop of Cambrai, at once sent twelve of his most revered and learned canons under the conduct of Hidolphe, a priest of acknowledged sagacity and experience, to endeavour to reform the town by word and example, but it seemed as though their efforts were doomed to failure and ill-success. At length, almost in despair, the good prelate begged S. Norbert,[80] who some three years before had founded his Order at Prémontré, to essay the thankless and wellnigh impossible task. Without demur or hesitation the Saint cheerfully undertook so difficult a mission and accompanied only by S. Evermonde,[81] and Blessed Waltman, together with a few more of his most fervent followers he arrived at Antwerp without delay to begin his work there towards the end of 1123. Success at once crowned his efforts; in an incredibly short space of time the people confessed their errors, abuses were reformed, the leprous town cleansed of its foulness, public safety, order, and decorum once again established, and, what is extremely striking to notice, the old chroniclers draw attention to the fact that a large number both of men and women in deepest penitence brought to S. Norbert quantities of consecrated Hosts which they had purloined from the tabernacles and kept concealed in boxes and other hiding-places to utilize for charms and evil invocations, to profane in devil-worship and at the Sabbat. So marvellous was the change from darkness to light that year by year the Premonstratensian Order upon the Saturday[82] after the Octave of Corpus Christi solemnly observes a fitting memorial thereof in the glad Feast of the Triumph of Holy Father Norbert.

In this incident of the stolen Hosts the connexion between

Gnostic heresy and Satanism is clearly seen. It was in such soil as the antinomianism of Tanchelin that the poisoned weeds of sorcery would thrive apace. The authorities recognized that drastic measures must be employed, and at Bonn a company of impure fanatics who attempted to disseminate his ideas were incontinently sent to the stake.

The other arguments brought forward by Miss Murray to support her thesis of the continuity of a primitive religion are mainly "the persistence of the number thirteen in the Covens, the narrow geographical range of the domestic familiar, the avoidance of certain forms in the animal transformations, the limited number of personal names among the women-witches, and the survival of the names of some of the early gods."[83] Even if these details could be proved up to the hilt and shown to be pertinent the evidence were not convincing; it would at best point to some odd survivals, such as are familiar in an hundred ways to every student of hagiography, history, myths and legends, old religions, geography, iconography, topography, etymology, anthropology, and antiquarian lore in a myriad branches. If we examine the matter broadly we shall find that these circumstances are for the most part local, not general, that in many instances they cannot be clearly substantiated, for the evidence is conflicting and obscure.

"The 'fixed number' among the witches of Great Britain," Miss Murray notes, "seems to have been thirteen,"[84] and certainly in many cases amongst the English trials the coven appears to have consisted of thirteen members, although it may be borne in mind that very probably there were often other associates who were not traced and involved and so escaped justice. Yet Miss Murray does not explain why the number thirteen should form any link with an earlier ritual and worship. On the other hand, the demonologists are never tired of insisting that Satan is the ape of God in all things, and that the worshippers of evil delight to parody every divine ordinance and institution. The explanation is simple. The number thirteen was adopted by the witches for their covens in mockery of Our Lord and His Apostles.

"The narrow geographical range of the domestic familiar" is not at all apparent, and it were futile to base any presumption upon so slender a line of argument. "The avoidance of certain forms in the animal transformation" is upon a general view of Witchcraft found to be nothing other than the non-occurrence of the lamb and the dove, and these two were abhorred by sorcerers, seeing that Christ is the Lamb of God, Agnus Dei, whilst the Dove is the manifestation of the Holy Ghost.[85] There is one instance, the trail of Agnes Wobster at Aberdeen in 1597, when the Devil is said to have appeared to the witch "in the liknes of a lamb, quhom thou callis thy God, and bletit on the, and thaireftir spak to the."[86] But this rare exception must be understood to be a black and deformed lamb, not the snow-white Agnus Dei. In pictures of the Doctors of the Church, particularly perhaps S. Gregory the Great and S. Alphonsus de Liguori, the Dove is seen breathing divine inspiration into the ear of the Saint who writes the heavenly message, thus directly given by God the Holy Ghost. So in a Franco-German miniature of the eleventh century in the *Hortus Deliciarum* we see a black hideous bird breathing into the ear of a magician thoughts evil and dark. This cloudy and sombre spirit, violent in its attitude and lean in body stretches its meagre throat towards the ear of the wicked man, who, seated at a desk, transcribes upon a parchment the malevolent and baleful charms which it dictates. It is in fact the Devil.[87]

With reference to the argument based upon "the limited number of personal names among the women-witches" this simply resolves itself into the fact that in the sixteenth and seventeenth centuries there were in general use (particularly amongst the peasantry) far fewer personal names than have been employed of more recent years. To assert "that the name *Christian* clearly indicates the presence of another religion"[88] is simple nonsense. It may be noticed, too, how many of the names which Miss Murray has catalogued in such conscientious and alas! impertinent detail are those of well-known Saints whose cult was universal throughout Europe: Agnes, Alice, Anne, Barbara, Christopher, Collette, Elizabeth, Giles, Isabel, James, John, Katherine, Lawrence, Margaret, Mary, Michael, Patrick, Thomas, Ursula—and the list might be almost indefinitely prolonged.

"The survival of the names of some of the early gods" is also asserted. In connexion with Witchcraft, however, very few examples of this can be traced even by the most careful research. An old charm or two, a nonsense rhyme, may now and again repeat some forgotten meaningless word or refrain. Thus in a spell used by the witches of the Basses-Pyrénées, cited by De Lancre (1609), we find mention of the old Basque deity Janicot: "In nomine patrica, Aragueaco Petrica, Gastellaco Ianicot, Equidæ ipordian pot." Bodin gives a dance-jingle, "Har, har, diable, diable, saute icy, saute là, ioüe icy, ioüe là," to which the chorus was "sabath sabath." Miss Murray tells us that the Guernsey version "which is currently reported to be used at the present day," runs: "Har, har, Hon, Hon, danse ici."[89] Hon was an old Breton god, and there are still remote districts whose local names recall and may be compounded with that of this ancient deity. It is significant that in one case we have a Basque deity, in the other a Breton; for Basque and Breton are nearly, if obscurely, correlated. Such traces are interesting enough, but by no means unique, hardly singular indeed, since they can be so widely paralleled, and it were idle to base any elaborate argument concerning the continuity of a fully organized cult upon slight and unrelated survivals in dialect place-names and the mere doggerel lilt of a peasant-song.

There is in particular one statement advanced by Miss Murray which goes far to show how in complete unconsciousness she is fitting her material to her theory. She writes: "There is at present nothing to show how much of the Witches' Mass (in which the bread, the wine, and the candles were black) derived from the Christian ritual and how much belonged to the Dianic cult [the name given to this hypothetical but universal ancient religion]; it is, however, possible that the witches' service was the earlier form and influenced the Christian."[90] This last sentence is in truth an amazing assertion. A more flagrant case of hysteron-proteron is hardly imaginable. So self-evident is the absurdity that it refutes itself, and one can only suppose that the words were allowed to remain owing to their having been overlooked in the revision of a long and difficult study, a venial negligence. Every prayer and every gesture of Holy Mass, since the first Mass was celebrated upon the first Maundy Thursday, has been studied in minutest detail by generations of liturgiologists and ceremonialists, whose library is almost infinite in its vastness and extent from the humblest pamphlets to the hugest folios. We can trace each inspired development, when such an early phrase was added, when such a hallowed sign was first made at such words in such an orison. The witches' service is a hideous burlesque of Holy Mass, and, briefly, what Miss Murray suggests is that the parody may have existed before the thing parodied. It is true that some topsy-turvy writers have actually proclaimed that magic preceded religion, but this view is generally discredited by the authorities of all schools. Sir James Frazer, Sir A. L. Lyall, and Mr. F. B. Jevons, for example, recognize "a fundamental distinction and even opposition of principle between magic and religion."[91]

In fine, upon a candid examination of this theory of the continuity of some primitive religion, which existed as an underlying organization manifested in Witchcraft and sorcery, a serious rival feared and hated by the Church, we find that nothing of the sort ever survived, that there was no connexion between sorcery and an imaginary "Dianic cult." To write that "in the fifteenth century open war was declared against the last remains of heathenism in the famous Bull of Innocent VIII"[92] is to ignore history. As has been emphasized above, the Bull *Summis desiderantes affectibus* of 1484 was only one of a long series of Papal ordinances directed against an intolerable evil not heathenism indeed, but heresy. For heresy, sorcery, and anarchy were almost interchangeable words, and the first Bull launched directly against the black art was that of Alexander IV, 1258, two hundred and twenty-six years before.

That here and there lingered various old harmless customs and festivities which had come down from pre-Christian times and which the Church had allowed, nay, had even sanctified by directing them to their right source, the Maypole dances, for example, and the Midsummer fires which now honour S. John Baptist, is a matter of common knowledge. But this is no continuance of a pagan cult.

From the first centuries of the Christian era, throughout the Middle Ages, and continuously to the present day there has invariably been an open avowal of intentional evil-doing on the part of the devotees of the witch-cult, and the more mischief they did the more they pleased their lord and master. Their revels were loathly, lecherous, and abominable, a Sabbat where every circumstance of horror and iniquity found expression. This in itself is an argument against Miss Murray's theory, as none of the earlier religions existed for the express purpose of perpetrating evil for evil's sake. We have but to read the eloquent and exquisite description of the Eleusinian Mysteries by that accomplished Greek scholar Father Cyril Martindale, S.J.,[93] to catch no mean nor mistaken glimpse of the ineffable yearning for beauty, for purity, for holiness, which filled the hearts of the worshippers of the goddess Persephoneia, whose stately and impressive ritual prescribing fasts, bathing in the waters of the sea, self-discipline, self-denial, self-restraint, culminated in the Hall of Initiation, hallowed by the Earth-Mother, Demeter, where the symbolic drama of life, death, and resurrection was shown by the Hierophant to those who had wrestled, and endured, and were adjudged worthy. How fair a shadow was this, albeit always and ever a shadow, of the imperishable and eternal realities to come! How different these Mysteries from the foul orgies of witches, the Sabbat, the black mass, the adoration of hell.

In truth it was not against heathenism that Innocent VIII sounded the note of war, but against heresy. There was a clandestine organization hated by the Church, and this was not sorcery nor any cult of witches renewing and keeping green some ancient rites and pagan creed, but a witch-cult that identified itself with and was continually manifested in closest connexion with Gnosticism in its most degraded and vilest shapes.

There is a curious little piece of symbolism, as it may be, which has passed into the patois of the Pyrenees. Wizards are commonly known as *poudouès* and witches *poudouèros*, both words being derived from *putere*, which signifies to have an evil smell. The demonologists report, and it was commonly believed, that sorcerers could often be detected by their foul and fetid odour. Hagiographers tell that S. Philip Neri could distinguish heretics by their smell, and often he was obliged to turn away his head when meeting them in the street. The same is recorded of many other Saints, and this tradition is interesting as it serves to show the close connexion there was held to be between magic and heresy.[94] Saint Pachomius, the cenobite, could distinguish heretics by their insupportable stench; the abbot Eugendis could tell the virtues and vices of those whom he met by the perfume or the stink. Saint Hilarion, as S. Jerome relates, could even distinguish a man's sins by the smell of a warm garment or cloak. Blessed Dominica of Paradise, passing a soldier in the street, knew by the foul smell that he had abandoned the faith, to which, however, her fervid exhortations and prayers eventually restored him. Saint Bridget of Sweden was wellnigh suffocated by the fetor of a notorious sinner who addressed her. Saint Catherine of Siena experienced the same sensations; whilst Saint Lutgarde, a Cistercian nun, on meeting a vicious reprobate perceived a decaying smell of leprosy and disease.

On the other hand, the Saints themselves have diffused sweetest fragrances, and actually "the odour of sanctity" is more than a mere phrase. One day in 1566, when he had entered the church at Somascha, a secluded hamlet between Milan and Bergamo, S. Charles Borromeo exclaimed: "I know by the heavenly fragrance in this sanctuary that a great Servant of God lies buried here!" The church, in fact, contained the body of S. Jerome Emiliani, who died in 1537. S. Herman Joseph could be traced through the corridors of Steinfeld by the rare perfumes he scattered as he walked. The same was the case with that marvellous mystic S. Joseph of Cupertino. S. Thomas Aquinas smelt of male frankincense. I myself have known a priest of fervent faith who at times diffused the odour of incense. Maria-Vittoria of Genoa, Ida of Louvain, S. Colette, S. Humiliana, were fragrant as sweet flowers. S. Francis of Paul and Venturini of Bergamo scattered heavenly aromas when they offered the Holy Sacrifice. The pus of S. John of the Cross gave forth a strong scent of lilies.

Miss Murray has worked out her thesis with no inconsiderable ingenuity, but when details are considered, historically examined, and set in their due proportions, it must be concluded that the theory of the continuity of an ancient religion is baseless. Her book is called *A Study in Anthropology*, and here we can, I think, at once put our finger upon the fundamental mistake. Anthropology alone offers no explanation of Witchcraft. Only the trained theologian can adequately treat the subject. An amount of interesting material has been collected, but the key to the dark mystery could not be found.

Yet, as our investigations have shown, it was not so far to seek. In the succinct phrase of that profound and prolific scholar Thomas Stapleton[95]: Crescit cum magia hæresis, cum hæresi magia." (The weed heresy grows alongside the weed witchcraft, the weed witchcraft alongside the weed heresy.)

NOTES TO CHAPTER I.

[1] *Paris. Jacques du Puys.* 4to. 1580. The preface, addressed to De Thou, is signed: "De *Laon,* ce xx iour de *Decembre,* M.D.LXXIX." There were nine editions before 1604. The most complete is *Paris,* 4to. 1587. In addition to the text it contains ten extra pages only found here giving the trial of a sorcerer, Abel de la Rue, executed in 1582.

[2] The first Papal bull dealing with sorcery was issued by Alexander IV, 13 December, 1258. The last Papal Constitution concerned with this crime is that of Urban VIII, *Inscrutabilis iudiciorum Dei altitudo,* 1 April, 1631. The last regular English trial seems to have been that of an old woman and her son, acquitted at Leicester in 1717. In 1722 the last execution of a Scottish witch took place at Loth; both English and Scottish statutes were repealed in 1735. The Irish Statute was not repealed until 1821. At Kempten in Bavaria, a mad heretic, a woman, was executed for sorcery in 1775. In the Swiss canton of Glaris, a wench named Anna Goeldi, was hanged as a witch, 17 June, 1782. Two hags were burned in Poland on the same charge as late as 1793.

[3] Roland Brévannes. *Les Messes Noires,* I[ier] tableau, scène VII.

[4] I have actually heard it categorically laid down by a speaker in a Shakespearean debate, a litterateur of professed culture, that the Elizabethans could not, of course, really have believed in witchcraft.

[5] In the Exhibition of this artist's work at the Leicester Galleries, London, in March, 1925.

[6] . . . qu'elle, & sa mère montoient sur vne ramasse, & que sortans le contremont de la cheminée elles alloient par l'air en ceste façon au Sabbat. Boguet, *Discours,* p. 104.

[7] Glanvill, Part II. p. 194.

[8] Julius Wellhausen. *Reste arabischen Heidenthums,* p. 159. Berlin, 1897.

[9] *Apud* Miss Murray's *The Witch-Cult.* (1921). Appendix V. pp. 279–80.

[10] Boguet, *Discours.* XVI. 4.

[11] Benjamin Thorpe, *Monumenta Ecclesiastica,* II. p. 34. London, 1840. The *Liber Poenitentialis* was first published complete by Wasserschleben in 1851; a convenient edition is Migne, *P.L.* XCIX.

[12] *Calendar of State Papers.* Domestic, 1584.

[13] Sir Walter Scott, *Demonology and Witchcraft,* Letter V, gives the narrative of this case, but in the light of later research his version must be slightly corrected.

[14] Pitcairn. I. pt. ii. p. 162.

[15] *Proceedings of the Society of Antiquaries of Scotland,* New Series, vol. X. Edinburgh.

[16] Sir James Melville, *Memoirs.* Bannatyne Club, Edinburgh. pp. 395–6.

[17] London. "for *William Wright.*" N.D. [1591]. The woodcut is on the title-page verso, and signature [c.ij.] verso. The pages are not numbered.

[18] *Flying Ointments. Apud* Miss Murray's *Witch-Cult in Western Europe,* p. 279. It may be noted that the scandals of the Black Mass under Louis XIV were closely concerned with wholesale accusations of poisoning. La Voisin was a notorious vendor of toxic philtres. The possibility of poisoning the King, the Dauphin, Colbert and others was frequently debated.

[19] Dio Cassius. XLIX. 43. p. 756. ed. Sturz.

[20] *Idem*. LII. 36. p. 149.

[21] Suetonius. *Augustus*. 31.

[22] Tacitus. *Annales*. II. 32. *More prisco*. "Ut eum infelici arbori alligatum uirgis cædi, et postremo securi percuti iuberent." Muret.

[23] XII. 32.

[24] Suetonius. *Vitellius*. 14.

[25] Dio Cassius. LXVI. 10.

[26] *La Magie et la Sorcellerie*. Paris. (1912.) I. p. 33.

[27] *Memoirs of Extraordinary Popular Delusions*, II. p. 117.

[28] The dates are as inaccurate as the statements. Giovanni Battista Cibò was elected Pope 29 August, 1484; and the Bull was issued in the December of that year, not in 1488.

[29] *Rise and Influence of Rationalism in Europe*, c. 1.

[30] *Dictionary of Universal Biography*. VIII. (1890).

[31] A more detailed treatment will be found in the present writer's *The Geography of Witchcraft*, where the Bull is given *in extenso*.

[32] *Epist*., c.n. 1.

[33] *Hom*., XLVI. c. 1.

[34] *Sententianum*, III. iv. nn. 4–6.

[35] Theodosius II. *Nouellæ*, tit. III. A.D. 438.

[36] Uanissimus [Priscillianus] et plus iusto inflatior profanarum rerum scientia: quin et magicas artes ab adolescentia cum exercuisse creditum est. Sulpicius Severus. II. 47.

[37] H. C. Lea in his *History of the Inquisition in the Middle Ages*, (1888) I. 215, asserts that Leo I justified the act, and that successive edicts against heresy were due to ecclesiastical influence. This is the exact opposite of historical truth, and the writer has not hesitated to transfer words of the Emperor to the Pope.

[38] In a sermon published in 1896 by Dom Morin *Revue benédictine*, c. xiii. p. 205.

[39] *Epistola Elipandi ad Alcuinum*, Migne. Pat. Lat. CXCVI. p. 872. Alcuin. *Opera Omnia*. Migne Pat. Lat. C–CI., especially *Liber Albini contra hæresim Felicis; Libri VII aduersus Felicem; Aduersus Elipandum Libri IV*. Florez, *España sagrada*. V. p. 562. Menendez y Pelayo, *Historia de los heterodoxos españoles*, Madrid, 1880, I. p. 274.

[40] The martyrdom of S. Peter is a well-known subject in art. Titian's masterpiece in the Dominican church of SS. Giovanni e Paolo at Venice was destroyed by a fire on 16 August, 1867. But there are exquisite paintings of the scene by Lorenzo Lotto and Bellini. S. Peter, whose shrine is in San Eustorgio, Milan, was canonized 25 March, 1253, by Innocent IV. Major Feast, 29 April.

[41] Muratori. *Antiquitates italicæ medii æui*, Milan, 1738–42.

[42] Gabriel Rossetti, *Disquisitions*, vol. I. p. 27.

[43] Gervasius Dorobernensis, *Chronicon*.

[44] *Vita S. Romanæ*. n. 10; Acta SS. die, 3 Oct. p. 138. S. Gregorii VII. Lib. I. Epistola 75, *ad Philippum*.

[45] Labbe. *Sacrosancta concilia*. 18 vols. folio. 1671. Vol. X. col. 84.

[46] Quarum rerum rex uester, qui non rex sed tyrannus dicendus est, suadente diabolo, caput et causa est, qui omnem aetatem suam flagitiis et facinoribus polluit. *Idem*, vol. X. col. 72.

[47] Sane . . . prouinciali ordinis prædicatorum in eodem regno dedimus in mandatis, ut aliquibus fratribus suis aptis ad hoc, inquisitionem contra illos committeret in regno præfato . . . fraternitati tuæ . . . mandamus quatenus . . . per alios qui ad hoc idonei uidebuntur, festines . . . procedere in inquisitionis negotio et ad dominicum certamen accingi. Ripoll et Brémond, *Bullarium ordinis S. Dominici*, I. p. 80. (8 vols. Romæ. 1737, *sqq*.).

[48] Fratres . . . qui ad prædicandum crucem uel inquirendum contra prauitatem hæreticam . . . sunt deputati. Wadding. *Annales Minorum*. ed. secunda. 24 vols. Romæ, 1732, *sqq*. III. 144.

[49] *Gnostic Heresies*.

[50] Jules Bois. *Le Satanisme et la Magie*, c. 6.

[51] It is true that S. Augustine does not bring a charge of depravity against the Manichæans, but they veiled their vices with the greatest caution, and S. Augustine was simply a catechumen, one of the Auditors, who would have known nothing of these esoteric abominations.

[52] Extra ciuitatis educti muros in quodam tuguriolo copioso igne accenso . . . cremati sunt. *Gesta synodi Aurelianensis.* Arnould. *L'Inquisition.* (Paris, 1869). VI. p. 46.

[53] Sed antequam ad conflictum ueniamus, de cibo illo, qui cœlestis ab illis dicebatur, quali arte conficiebatur, nescientibus demonstrare curabo. Congregabantur si quidem certis noctibus in domo denominata, singuli lucernas tenentes in manibus, ad instar letaniæ demonum nomina declamabant, donec subito Dæmonem in similitudine cuiuslibet bestiolæ inter eos uiderent descendere. Qui statim, ut uisibilis ille uidebatur uisio, omnibus extinctis luminaribus, quamprimum quisque poterat, mulierem, quæ ad manum sibi ueniebat, ad abutendum arripiebat, sine peccati respectu, et utrum mater, aut soror, aut monacha haberetur, pro sanctitate et religione eius concubitus ab illis æstimabatur; ex quo spurcissimo concubitu infans generatus, octaua die in medio eorum copioso igne accenso probabatur per ignem more antiquorum Paganorum; et sic in igne cremabatur. Cuius cinis tanta ueneratione colligebatur atque custodiebatur, ut Christiana religiositas Corpus Christi custodire solet, ægris dandum de hoc sæculo exituris ad uiaticum. Inerat enim tanta uis diabolicæ fraudis in ipso cinere ut quicumque de præfata hæresi imbutus fuisset, et de eodem cinere quamuis sumendo parum prælibauisset, uix unquam postea de eadem heresi gressum mentis ad uiam ueritatis dirigere ualeret. De qua re parum dixisse sufficiat, ut Christicolæ caueant se ab hoc nefario opere, non ut studeant sectando imitari. Schmidt. *Histoire et doctrine des Cathares ou Albigeois.* Paris. 1849. I. p. 31.

[54] G. R. Kinloch. *Reliquiæ Antiquæ Scoticæ.* Edinburgh, 1848.

[55] Adhémar de Chabannes. (A monk of Angoulême.) *Chronicon, Recueil des historicus,* vol. X. p. 163.

[56] Fabré Palaprat. *Recherches Historiques sur les Templicrs,* Paris. 1835.

[57] Cambridge University Press, 1925.

[58] *The Philosopher,* July–August, 1924.

[59] *The Philosopher,* January–March, 1925. *The Albigenses,* pp. 20–25. The whole article, which is written with extraordinary restraint, should be read.

[60] He is the author of *Éléments d'Astrologie ; Un disciple de Cl. de Saint-Martin, Dutoit-Membrini ; Premiers Éléments d'Occultisme ; La petite Église anticoncordataire, son histoire, son état actuel ; J. K. Huysmans et le Satanisme ; Huysmans, Occultiste et Magicien.*

[61] *In Uerrem.* IV. 43.

[62] H. Th. Pyl, *Die griechischen Rundbauten,* 1861, pp. 67, *sqq.*

[63] Plutarch, *Theseus* 36 ; *Cimon* 8.

[64] Pausanias is the chief authority on this point. See Rohde *Psyche,* I. p. 161.

[65] Clarendon Press, 1921.

[66] *The Witch-Cult in Western Europe,* p. 16. It is true that the Brethren of the Free Spirit, anarchists, who vaunted the Adamite heresy, in the Thirteenth century, went to the stake with pæans of joy. But they were probably drugged. J. L. Mosheim, *Ecclesiastical History.* London. 1819. III. p. 278. *sqq.* The Adamites were a licentious sect who called their church Paradise and worshipped in a state of stark nudity. They were Gnostics and claimed complete emancipation from the moral law. They lived in shameful communism. Bohemian Adamites existed as late as 1849. In Russia the *telcschi,* a branch of the sect known as the "Divine Men," performed their religious rites in a state of nature, following the example, as they asserted, of Adam and Eve in Paradise. These assemblies were wont to end in promiscuous debauchery.

[67] *Idem.* p. 161.

[68] *Witch-Cult in Western Europe,* p. 161.

[69] *Additional Notices of Major Weir and his Sister ;* Sinclar's *Satan' Invisible World.* (Reprint. 1875).

[70] *Criminal Trials*, 1536–1784; Hugo Arnot, 4to, 1785.

[71] *Ravillac Rediuius*, Dr. George Hickes, 4to, 1678.

[72] Iubemus namque, auctores quidem et principes, una cum abominandis scripturis eorum seueriori pœnæ subiici, ita ut flammeis ignibus exurantur. Baronius, 287, 4.

[73] Scio multos [Proconsu[esl et ad bestias damnasse sacrilegos, nonnullos etiam uiuos exussisse. *Lex Romana Visigothorum nouella*, XLVIII. tit. xiii. c. 6–7.

[74] Plures etiam per Italiam tunc huius pestiferi dogmatis sunt reperti, qui aut gladiis, aut incendiis perierunt.

[75] Tanchelinus, Tandemus, Tanchelmus. The history of this important revolutionary movement has been carefully studied. The following authoritative books are a few from many of great value and learning. *Corpus documentorum Inquisitionis hereticæ prauitatis neerlandicæ*, ed. Dr. Paul Frédéricq, vol. I, p. 15 *et sqq.* Ghent. 1889; *Tanchelijn* by Janssen in the *Annales de l'académie Royale d'archéologie de Belgique*, vol. XXIII, p. 448 *et sqq.* 1867; Foppens, *Historia Episcopatus Antuerpiensis*, p. 8 and p. 146, Brussells, 1717; Dierxsens, *Antuerpia Christo nascens et crescens*, vol. I, p. 88, Antwerp, 1773; Poncelet, *Saint Norbert et Tanchelin* in the *Analecta bollandiniana*, vol. XIII, p. 441, 1893; Schools, *Saint Norbert et Tanchelin à Anvers* in the *Bibliothèque norbertine*, vol. II, p. 97, 1900; De Schapper, *Réponse à la question: Faites connaître l'hérésiarque Tanchelin et les erreurs qu'il répandit au commencement du XIIIe siècle* [an error for *XIIe siècle*] in the *Collationes Brugenses*, vol. XVII, p. 107, 1912. L. Vander Essen, *De Katterij van Tanchelm in de XIIe eeuw* in *Ons Geloof*, vol. II, p. 354, 1912; *Antwerpen en de H. Norbertus* in the *Bode van Onze Lieve Vrouw van het H. Hert van Averbode*, Nos. 18 and 19, pp. 207–211 and 217–220, 1914.

[76] "That most vile and abandoned scoundrel had become so open and utterly depraved an enemy to the Christian faith and all religious observance that he denied any respect was due to Bishops and priests; moreover, he affirmed that the reception of the most holy Body and Blood of Our Lord availed nothing to eternal life and man's salvation." "Erat quidem ille sceleratissimus et christianæ fidei et totius religionis inimicus in tantum ut obsequium episcoporum et sacerdotum nihil esse diceret, et sacrosancti corporiset sanguinis Domini J. C. perceptionem ad salutem perpetuam prodesse denegeret." *Vita Noberti archiepiscopi Magdeburgensis, Vita A. Monument. Germ. Scriptores*, vol. XII. p. 690, ed. G. A. Pertz, Hanover, Berlin.

[77] "Immo uere ipse angelus Sathanæ declamabat eccelsias Dei lupinaria esse reputanda. Nihil esse, quod sacerdotum officio in mensa dominica conficeretur; pollutiones, non sacramenta nominanda." *Lettre des chanoines d'Utrecht au nom de leur diocèse à Frédéric, archevêque de Cologne. Apud* Frédéricq, vol. I. n. 11.

[78] Talibus nequitiæ successibus misero homini tanta sceleris accessit audacia, ut etiam se Deum diceret, asserens, quia, si Christus ideo Deus est, quia Spiritum Sanctum habuisset, se non inferius nec dissimilius Deum, quia plenitudinem Spiritus Sancti accepisset. *Idem.*

[79] Qui tandem post multos errores et cædes, dum nauigaret, a quodam presbytero percussus in cerebro occubuit. *Sigiberti continuatio.* Apud *Monument. Germ. Scriptores*, vol. VI, p. 449. See also, Johannes Trithemius, *Annales Hirsaugienses*, vol. I, p. 387, Saint-Gall, 1690; Du Plessis d'Argentré, *Collectio iudiciorum*, vol. I, p. 11 *sqq.* Paris, 1728; Schmidt, *Histoire et doctrine des Cathares ou Albigeois*, vol. I, p. 49, Paris, 1849.

[80] There is a contemporary *Uita Norberti* of which two recensions have been published: *Uita A.* by R. Wilmans in the *Mon. Germ. Hag.*, SS., vol. XIII, pp. 663–706, Hanover, 1853; *Uita B.* by Surius, *De probatis Sanctorum historiis*, vol. III, pp. 517–547, Cologne, 1572. Other authoritative works are: J. Van der Sterse, *Uita S. Norberti*, Antwerp, 1622; Du Pré, *La Vie du bienhereux saint Norbert*, Paris, 1627; Ch. Hugo, *La Vie de St. Norbert*, Luxembourg, 1704; G. Madelaine, *Histoire de St. Norbert*, Lille, 1886; B. Wazasek, *Der Hl. Norbert*, Vienna, 1914. An excellent brief but

scholarly account is *The Life of S. Norbert*, London, 1886, by my late revered friend Abbot Geudens, C.R.P.

[81] Feast, 17 February.

[82] Formerly kept upon the Sunday.

[83] *Op. cit.*, pp. 16, 17.

[84] *Op. cit.*, p. 191.

[85] For a full and detailed statement see Didron's great work, *Iconographie chrétienne*, Paris, 1843.

[86] *Spalding Club Miscellany*, I, p. 129. Aberdeen, 1841.

[87] At their black mass the witches of the Basses-Pyrénées (1609) when the host was elevated said "Corbeau noir, corbeau noir." De Lancre, *Tableau de l'Inconstance des mauvais Anges*, Paris, 1613.

[88] *Op. cit.*, p. 255.

[89] *Op. cit.*, p. 165. It is not at all evident that "the word *diable* is clearly Bodin's own interpellation for the name of the god," indeed this assumption is purely gratuitous to support the argument, and cannot be admitted.

[90] *Op. cit.*, pp. 14, 15. I would not dwell upon the offensiveness of this suggestion, since it is, I am sure, unintentional.

[91] *Golden Bough*, Part I. vol. I. p. xx. Third Edition. 1911.

[92] *Op. cit.*, p. 19.

[93] *The Goddess of Ghosts*, pp. 137–158.

[94] Cassiodorus, *Hist. Eccl.*, VII, 11. *fin.* speaks of the *fetidissimus fons* of heresy.

[95] 1535–1598. His works were collected in four folio volumes, Páris, 1620, prefaced by Henry Holland's *Uita Thomæ Stapletoni*. An original portrait is preserved at Douai Abbey, Woolhampton.

CHAPTER II

The Worship of the Witch

In order clearly to understand and fully to realize the shuddering horror and heart-sick dismay any sort of commerce between human beings and evil spirits, which is the very core and kernel of Witchcraft, excited throughout the whole of Christendom, to appreciate why tome after tome was written upon the subject by the most learned pens of Europe, why holiest pontiffs and wisest judges, grave philosopher and discreet scholar, king and peasant, careless noble and earnest divine, all alike were of one mind in the prosecution of sorcery; why in Catholic Spain and in Puritan Scotland, in cold Geneva and at genial Rome, unhesitatingly and perseveringly man sought to stamp out the plague with the most terrible of all penalties, the cautery of fire; in order that by the misreading of history we should not superficially and foolishly think monk and magistrate, layman and lawyer were mere tigers, mad fanatics—for as such have they, too, often been presented and traduced,—it will be not wholly impertinent briefly to recapitulate the orthodox doctrine of the Powers of Darkness, facts nowadays too often forgotten or ignored, but which to the acute mediæval mind were ever fearfully and prominently in view.

And here, as in so many other beliefs, we shall find a little dogma; certain things that can hardly be denied without the note of temerity; and much concerning which nothing definite can be known, upon which assuredly no pronouncement will be made.

In the first place, the name Devil is commonly given to the fallen angels, who are also called Demons. The exact technical distinction between the two terms in ecclesiastical usage may be seen in the phrase used in the decree of the Fourth Lateran Council[1]: "Diabolus enim et alii dæmones." (The devil and the other demons), i.e. all are demons, and the chief of the demons is called the Devil. This distinction is preserved in in the Vulgate New Testament, where *diabolus* represents the Greek διάβολος, and in almost every instance refers to Satan himself, whilst his subordinate angels are described, in accordance with the Greek, as *dæmones* or *dæmonia*. But save in some highly specialized context when the most meticulous accuracy is required, we now use the words "devil," "demon" indifferently, and employ the definite article to denote Lucifer (Satan), chief of the devils, The Devil. So in S. Matthew xxv. 41, is written "the devil and his angels." The Greek word διάβολος means a slanderer, an accuser, and in this sense is it applied to him of whom it is said "the accuser [ὁ κατήγορος] of our brethren is cast forth, who accused them before our God day and night" (Apocalypse xii. 10). Thus it answers to the Hebrew name Satan, which signifies an adversary, an accuser.

Mention is made of the Devil in many passages both of the Old and New Testaments, but much is left in obscurity, and the full Scriptural teaching on the legions of evil can best be ascertained by combining the scattered notices and reading them in the light of patristic and theological tradition. The authoritative teaching of the Church is declared in the Decrees of the Fourth Lateran Church (cap. 1. *Firmiter credimus*), wherein, after setting forth that God in the beginning had created two creatures, the spiritual and corporeal; that is to say, the angelic and the earthly, and lastly man, who was made of both earth and body; the Council continues: "For the Devil and the other demons were created by God naturally good; but they themselves of themselves became evil."[2] The dogma is here clearly laid down that the Devil and the other demons are spiritual or angelic creatures created by God in a state of innocence, and that they became evil by their own free act. It is added that man sinned by suggestion of the Devil, and that in the next world the reprobate and impenitent will suffer punishment with him. This then is the actual dogma, the dry bones of the doctrine, so to speak. But later theologians have added a great deal to this,—the authoritative Doctor Eximius, Francisco Suarez, S.J.,[3] *De Angelis*, VII, is especially valuable —and much of what they deduce cannot be disputed without such rejection incurring the grave censure technically known as "Erroneous."[4]

It is remarkable that for an account of the Fall of the angels, which happened before the creation of the world, we must turn to the last book in the Bible, the Apocalypse of S. John. For although the picture of the past be blended with prophecies of what shall be in the future, thus must we undoubtedly regard the vision of Patmos. "And there was a great battle in heaven, Michael and his angels fought with the dragon, and the dragon fought and his angels: and they prevailed not, neither was their place found any more in heaven. And that great dragon was cast out, that old serpent, who is called the Devil, and Satan, who seduceth the whole world; and he was cast down unto the earth, and his angels were thrown down with him" (Apocalypse xii. 7–9). To this may be added the words of S. Jude: "And the angels who kept not their principality, but forsook their own habitation, he hath reserved under darkness in everlasting chains, unto the judgement of the great day." To these references should be added a striking passage from the prophet Isaiah: "How art thou fallen from heaven, O Lucifer, who didst rise in the morning! how art thou fallen to the earth, that didst wound the nations! And thou saidst in thy heart: I will ascend into heaven, I will exalt my throne above the stars of God, I will sit in the mountain of the covenant, in the sides of the north. I will ascend above the heights of the clouds, I will be like the most High. But yet thou shalt be brought down to hell, into the depth of the pit" (Isaiah xiv. 12–15). The words of the prophet may in one sense, perhaps primarily, be directed against Merodach-baladan, King of Babylon, but all the early Fathers and later commentators are agreed in understanding the passage as applying with deeper significance to the fall of the rebel angel. This interpretation is confirmed by the words of Our Lord to His disciples: "I saw Satan like lightning falling from heaven." (Uidebam Satanam sicut fulgur de cœlo cadentem.) S. Luke x. 18.

An obvious question which next arises and which has been amply discussed by the theologians is: What was the nature of the sin of the rebel angels? This point presents some difficulty, for theology has logically formed the highest estimate of the perfection of the angelic nature, the powers and possibilities of the angelic knowledge. Sins of the flesh are certainly impossible to angels, and from many sins which are purely spiritual and intellectual they would seem to be equally debarred. The great offence of Lucifer appears to have been the desire of independence of God and equality with God.

It is theologically certain that Lucifer held a very high rank in the celestial hierarchy, and it is evident that he maintains some kind of sovereignty over those who followed him in his rebellion: "Si autem," says Our Lord, "et Satanas in seipsum diuisus est quomodo stabit regnum eius?" (If Satan also be divided against himself, how shall his kingdom stand?) And S. Paul speaks of "Principem potestatis æris huius, qui nunc operatur in filios diffidentiæ." (The Prince of the power of this air, who now worketh in the sons of disobedience) Ephesians ii. 2. It may seem strange that those rebellious spirits who rose against their Maker should be subordinate to and obey one of their fellows who led them to destruction, but this in itself is a proof that Lucifer is a superior intelligence, and the knowledge of the angels would show them that they can effect more mischief and evil by co-operation and organization, although their unifying principle is the bond of hate, than by anarchy and division. There can be little doubt that among their ranks are many mean and petty spirits[5]—to speak comparatively—but even these can influence and betray foolish and arrogant men. We shall be on safe ground if we follow the opinion of Suarez, who would allow Lucifer to have been the highest of all angels negatively, i.e. that no one was higher, although many (and among these the three great Archangels, S. Michael, S. Gabriel, S. Raphael) may have been his equals.

It has been argued that the highest of the angels, by reason of their greater intellectual illumination, must have entirely realized the utter impossibility of attaining to equality with God. So S. Anselm, *De Casu Diaboli* (IV), says: "Non enim ita obtusæ mentis [diabolus] erat, ut nihil aliud simile Deo cogitari posse nesciret?" (The devil was surely not so dull of understanding as to be ignorant of the inconceivability of any other entity like to God?) And S. Thomas writes, in answer to the question, whether the Devil desired to be "as God," "if by this we mean equality with God, then the Devil would not desire it, since he knew this to be impossible." But as the Venerable Duns Scotus, Doctor subtilis, admirably points out, we must distinguish between efficacious volition and the volition of complaisance, and by the latter act an angel could desire that which is impossible. In the same way he shows that, though a creature cannot directly will its own destruction, it may do this *consequenter*, i.e. it can will something from which this would inevitably follow.

And although man must realize that he cannot be God, yet there have been men who have caused themselves to be saluted as God and even worshipped as God. Such was Herod Agrippa I, who on a festival day at Cæsarea, had himself robed in a garment made wholly of silver, and came into the crowded theatre early in the morning, so that his vesture shone out in the rays of the sun with dazzling light, and the superstitious multitude, taught by his flatterers, cried out that he was a god, and prayed to him as divine, saying: "Be thou merciful unto us, for although we have hitherto reverenced thee only as a man yet henceforth we own thee to be god."[6] Caligula, also, arrogated to himself divinity. "Templum etiam numini suo proprium, et sacerdotes et excogitatissimas hostias instituit."[7] (He also built a temple in honour of his own godhead, and consecrated priests to offer him most splendid sacrifices.) This emperor, moreover, set up his statue in the Temple at Jerusalem, and ordered victims to be sacrificed to him. Domitian, with something more than literary compliment, is addressed by Martial as "Dominus Deusque noster"[8] (Our Lord and our God), and he lived up to his title. Heliogabalus identified himself in some mystic way with the deity of Edessa, and ordered no god save himself to be worshipped at Rome, nay, throughout the wide world: "Taking measures that at Rome no god should be honoured save Heliogabalus alone. . . . Nor did he wish to stamp out only the various Roman cults, but his desire was that all the whole wide world through, only one god, Heliogabalus, should everywhere be worshipped."[9] To cite further examples, and they are numerous, from Roman history were superfluous.[10] Perhaps the most astounding case of all was that of the Persian king, Khosroes (Khusrau) II, who in the seventh century sacked Jerusalem and carried off the True Cross to his capital. Intoxicated with success he announced by solemn proclamation that he was Almighty God. He built an extraordinary palace or tower, in which there were vast halls whose ceilings were painted with luminous suns, moons, and stars to resemble the firmament. Here he sat upon a lofty throne of gold, a tiara upon his head, his cope so sewn with diamonds that the stuff could not be seen, sceptre and orb in his hands, upon one side the Cross, upon the other a jewelled dove, and here he bade his subjects adore him as God the Father, offering incense and praying him " Through the Son." This insane blasphemy was ended when the Persians were vanquished by the Emperor Heraclius, and in the spring of 629 the Cross was restored to Jerusalem.[11]

Montanus, the Phrygian heretic of the second century, who had originally, as S. Jerome tells us, been a priest of Cybele, actually claimed to be the Trinity. " I am the Father, the Word, and the Paraclete,"[12] he said, and again, " I am the Lord God omnipotent who have descended into a man . . . neither an angel, nor an ambassador, but I, the Lord, the Father, am come."[13] Elipandus of Toledo in the eighth century spoke of Christ as " a God among gods," inferring that there were many others who had been divine. One may compare the incarnate gods adored in China and Tibet to-day. A Bohemian woman named Wilhelmina, who died in Milan, 1281, declared herself to be an incarnation of the Third Person of the Blessed Trinity, and was actually worshipped by crowds of fanatics, who caused great scandal and disorder. The Khlysti in Russia have not only prophets but " Christs " and " Redeemers," and they pray to one another. About 1830 there appeared in one of the American states bordering upon Kentucky an impostor who declared himself to be Christ. He threatened the world with immediate judgement, and a number of ill-balanced and hysterical subjects were much affected by his denunciations. One day, when he was addressing a large gathering in his usual strain, a German standing up humbly asked him if he would repeat his warnings in German for the benefit of those present who only knew that tongue. The speaker answered that he had never been able to learn that language, a reply which seemed so ludicrous in one claiming divinity that many of the auditors were convulsed with laughter and so profane a charlatan soon lost all credit. Monsignor Flaget, Bishop of Bardstoun, wrote an account of this extraordinary imposture in a letter dated 4 May, 1833,[14] where he says the scene took place some three years before. About 1880 at Patiala in the Punjaub, a fanatic of filthy appearance named Hakim Singh gave himself out to be Christ, and in a short time had a following of more than four thousand persons, but within a few months they melted away.[15] Many "false Christs" have organized Russian sects. In 1840 a man drained the peasants of Simboisk and Saratov of their money by declaring himself to be the Saviour; about 1880 the founder of the *bojki*, an illiterate fanatic named Sava proclaimed that he was the Father, and his kinsman, Samouil, God the Son. Ivan Grigorieff, founder of the "Russian Mormons," taught that he was divine; and other frenzied creatures, Philipoff, Loupkin, Israil of Selengisk, have all claimed to be the Messiah and God.

It is apparent then, that although rationally it should be inconceivable that any sentient creature could claim divinity, actually the contrary is the case. The sin of Satan would appear to have been an attempt to usurp the sovereignty of God. This is further borne out by the fact that during the Temptation of our Lord the Devil, showing Him "omnia regna mundi, et gloriam eorum" (all the kingdoms of the world and the glory of them), said, "Hæc omnia tibi dabo, si cadens adoraueris me." (All these will I give Thee, if Thou wilt fall down and worship me.) And he is rebuked: "Uade Satana: Scriptum est enim: Dominum Deum tuum adorabis, et illi soli seruies." (Begone, Satan: for it is written: The Lord thy God shalt thou adore, and Him only shalt thou serve.) It should be remarked that Lucifer was telling a lie. The kingdoms of this world are not his to offer, but only its sins and follies, disappointment and death. But here the Devil is demanding that divine honours should be paid him. And this claim is perpetuated throughout the witch trials. The witches believed that their master, Satan, Lucifer, the fiend, the principle of evil, was God, and as such they worshipped him with latria, they adored him, they offered him homage, they addressed prayer to him, they sacrificed. So Lambert Danéau, *Dialogue of Witches* (trans. 1575), asserts: "The Diuell cōmaundeth them that they shall acknowledge him for their god, cal vpō him, pray to him, and trust in him.—Then doe they all repeate the othe which they haue geuen vnto him; in acknowledging him to be their God." Cannaert records that the accusation against Elisabeth Vlamynex of Alost, 1595, was "You were not even ashamed to kneel before Belzebuth, whom you worshipped."[16] De Lancre, in his *Tableau de l'Inconstance des mauvais Anges* (1613), informs us that when the witches presented a young child they fell on their knees before the demon and said: "Grand Seigneur, lequel i'adore." (Great Lord, whom I worship.) The novice joining the witches made profession in this phrase: "I abandon myself wholly to thy power and I put myself in thy hands, acknowledging no other god; and this since there art my god."[17] The words of Silvain Nevillon, tried at Orleans in 1614, are even plainer: "We say to the Devil that we acknowledge him as our master, our god, our creator."[18] In America[19] in 1692, Mary Osgood confessed that "the devil told her he was her God, and that she should serve and worship him."

There are numberless instances of prayer offered to the Devil by his servants. Henri Boguet, in his *Discours des Sorciers* (Lyons, 1608), relates that Antide Colas, 1598, avowed that "Satan bade her pray to him night and morning, before she set about any other business."[20] Elizabeth Sawyer, the notorious witch of Edmonton (1621), was taught certain invocations by her familiar. In her confession to the Rev. Henry Goodcole, who visited her in Newgate, upon his asking "Did the Diuell at any time find you praying when he came unto you, and did not the Diuell forbid you to pray to Iesus Christ, but to him alone? and did he not bid you to pray to him, the Diuell as he taught you?" She replied: "He asked of me to whom I prayed, and I answered him to Iesus Christ, and he charged me then to pray no more to Iesus Christ, but to him the Diuell, and he the Diuell taught me this prayer, *Sanctibecetur nomen tuum, Amen.*"[21] So as Stearne reports in *Confirmation and Discovery of Witchcraft* (1648), of the Suffolk witches: "*Ellen*, the wife of *Nicholas Greenleife* of *Barton* in *Suffolke*, confessed, that when she prayed she prayed to the Devill and not to God."

In imitation of God, moreover, the Devil will have his miracles, although these are θαύματα, mere delusive wonders which neither profit nor convince. Such was the feat of Jannes and Mambres, the Egyptian sorcerers, who in emulation of Moses changed their rods to serpents. To this source we can confidently refer many tricks of Oriental jugglers. "I am satisfied," wrote an English officer of rank and family, "that the performances of the native 'wise-men' are done by the aid of familiar spirits. The visible growth of a mango tree out of an empty vessel into which a little earth is placed, a growth which spectators witness, and the secret of which has never been discovered, may not be unreasonably referred to the same occult powers which enabled the Egyptian magicians of old to imitate the miraculous acts which Moses, by God's command, openly wrought in the face of Pharaoh and his people."[22] In the basket-trick, which is performed without preparation in any place or spot—a greensward, a paved yard, a messroom—a boy is placed under a large wicker basket of conical shape, which may be examined and handled by all, and this is then stabbed through and through by the fakir with a long sword that pierces from side to side. Screams of pain follow each thrust, and the weapon is discerned to be covered with fresh blood. The cries grow fainter and at length cease altogether. Then the juggler uttering cries and incantations dances round the basket, which he suddenly removes, and no sign of the child is to be seen, no rent in the wicker-work, no stain on the steel. But in a few seconds the boy, unharmed and laughing, appears running forward from some distant spot. In this connexion we may well recall the words of Suarez: "[The Devil] can deceive and trick the senses so that a head may appear to be cut off and blood to flow, when in truth no such thing is taking place."[23]

The wizards of Tartary and Tibet, *bokte*, upon certain special days will with great ceremony appear in the temples, which are always thronged on these occasions, and whilst their disciples howl and shriek out invocations, they suddenly throw aside their robes and with a sharp knife seem to rip open their stomachs from top to bottom, whilst blood pours from the gaping wound. The worshippers, lashed to frenzy, fall prostrate before them and grovel frantically upon the floor. The wizard appears to scatter his blood over them, and after some five minutes he passes his hands rapidly over the wound, which instantly disappears, not leaving even the trace of a scar. The operator is noticed to be overcome with intense weariness, but otherwise all is well. Those who have seen this hideous spectacle assure us that it cannot be explained by any hallucination or legerdemain, and the only solution which remains is to attribute it to the glamour cast over the deluded crowd by the power of discarnate evil intelligences.[24]

The portentous growth of Spiritism,[25] which within a generation passed beyond the limits of a popular and mountebank movement and challenged the serious attention and expert inquiry of the whole scientific and philosophical world, furnishes us with examples of many extraordinary phenomena, both physical and psychical, and these, in spite of the most meticulous and accurate investigation, are simply inexplicable by any natural and normal means. Such phenomena have been classified by Sir William Crookes, in his *Researches in the Phenomena of Spiritualism.* They include the movement of heavy bodies without contact, or with contact altogether insufficient to explain the movement; the alteration of weight of bodies; the rising of tables and chairs off the ground without contact with any human person; the levitation of human beings; "apports," objects such as flowers, coins, pieces of stone conveyed into a hermetically closed room without any visible agency to carry them; luminous appearances; more or less distinct phantom faces and forms. In spite of continual and most deliberate trickery, repeated and most humiliating exposure, and this not only in the case of cheap charlatans but also of famous mediums such as William Eglinton, there occur and have always occurred phenomena which are vouched for upon the evidence of names whose authority cannot be gainsaid. Do such manifestations proceed from the spirits of the departed or from intelligences which have never been in human form? Even avowed believers in a beneficent Spiritism, anxious to establish communication with dead friends, are forced to admit the frequent and irresponsible action of non-human intelligences. This conclusion is based upon lengthy and detailed evidence which it is only possible very briefly to summarize. It proves almost impossible satisfactorily to establish spirit identity, to ascertain whether the communicator is actually the individual he or it purports to be; the information imparted is not such as would naturally be expected from those who have passed beyond this life but trivial and idle to a degree; the statements which the spirits make concerning their own condition are most contradictory and confused; the moral tone which pervades these messages, at first vague and unsatisfactory, generally becomes repulsive and even criminally obscene. All these particulars unmistakably point to demoniac intervention and deceit.[26] The Second Plenary Council of Baltimore (1866) whilst making due allowance for fraudulent practice and subtle sleights in Spiritism declares that some at least of the manifestations are to be ascribed to Satanic intervention, for in no other manner can they be explained. (*Decreta*, 33–41.) A decree of the Holy Office, 30 March, 1898, condemns Spiritistic practices, even though intercourse with evil spirits be excluded and intercourse sought only with good angels.

Not only with miracles but also in prophecies does Lucifer seek to emulate that God Whose Throne he covets. This point is dealt with by Bishop Pierre Binsfeld, who in his *De Maleficis* (1589) writes: " Nunc uidendum est an dæmones præscientiam habeant futurorum et secretorum, ita ut ex eorum reuelatione possit homo prognosticare[27] et occulta cognoscere? . . . Prima conclusio: Futura, si in seipsis considerentur, anullo præterquam a solo Deo cognosci possunt." (Next we will inquire whether devils can have any foreknowledge of future events or of hidden things so that a man might from their revelations to him foretell the future and discover the unknown? . . . First conclusion: The future, precisely considered, can be known to none save to God alone.) But it must be borne in mind that the intelligence of angels, though fallen, is of the acutest order, as Simon Maiolo in his *Dies caniculares* explains: " Astutia, sapientia, acumine longe superant homines, et longius progrediuntur ratiocinando." (In shrewdness, knowledge, perspicuity, they far excel mankind, and they can look much further into the future by logical deduction.) And it is in this way that a demon will often rightly divine what is going to happen, although more often the response will either be a lie or wrapped up in meaningless and ambiguous phrase, such as were the pagan oracles. A notable example of false prophets may be found in the Camisards (probably from *camise*, a black blouse worn as a uniform), a sect of evil fanatics who terrorized Dauphiné, Vivarais, and chiefly the Cévennes at the beginning of the eighteenth century. Their origin was largely due to the Albigensian spirit, which had never been wholly stamped out in that district, and which was fanned to flame by the anarchical preaching and disordered pamphlets of the French Calvinists, such as Jurieu's *Accomplissement des prophéties*. Pope Clement XI styles the Camisards "that execrable race of ancient Albigenses." De Serre, a rank old Calvinist of Dieulefit in Dauphiné, became suddenly inspired and a wave of foul hysteria spread far and wide. In 1702 the saintly abbé de Chaila was treacherously murdered by these wretches, who seized arms and formed themselves into offensive bands under such ruffians as Séguier, Laporte, Castanet, Ravenal, and Cavalier. Louis XIV sent troops to subdue them, but the Catholic leaders at first do not seem to have appreciated the seriousness of the position, and a desultory guerilla warfare dragged on for some years. Cavalier escaped to England,[28] whence he returned in 1709, and attempted to kindle a revolt in Vivarais. On 8 March, 1715, by a proclamation and medals, Louis XIV announced that these demoniacs were entirely extinct.

A number of these prophets fled to England, where they created great disturbances, and Voltaire, *Siècle de Louis XIV*, XXXVI, tells us that one of the leading refugees, a notorious rebel, Elie Marion, became so obnoxious on account of his *avertissements prophétiques* and false miracles, that he was expelled the country as a common nuisance.[29]

The existence of evil discarnate intelligences having been orthodoxly established, a realm which owns one chief, and it is reasonable to suppose, many hierarchies, a kingdom that is at continual warfare with all that is good, ever striving to do evil and bring man into bondage; it is obvious that if he be so determined man will be able in some way or another to get into touch with this dark shadow world, and however rare such a connexion may be it is, at least, possible. It is this connexion with its consequences, conditions, and attendant circumstances, that is known as Witchcraft. The erudite Sprenger in the *Malleus Maleficarum* expressly declares that in his opinion a denial of the possibility of Witchcraft is heresy. "After God Himself hath spoken of magicians and sorcerers, what infidel dare doubt that they exist?" writes Pierre de Lancre in his *L'Incredulité et Mescreance du Sortilège* (Paris, 1622)[30]. That eminent lawyer Blackstone, in his *Commentaries* (1765), IV, 4, asserts: "To deny the possibility, nay, actual existence of Witchcraft and Sorcery, is at once flatly to contradict the revealed Word of God in various passages both of the Old and New Testament; and the thing itself is a truth to which every Nation in the World hath in its turn borne testimony, either by examples seemingly well attested, or by prohibitory laws, which at least suppose the possibility of commerce with evil spirits." Even the ultra-cautious—I had almost said sceptical—Father Thurston acknowledges: "In the face of Holy Scripture and the teaching of the Fathers and theologians the abstract possibility of a pact with the Devil and of a diabolical interference in human affairs can hardly be denied." Imposture, trickery, self-deception, hypnotism, a morbid imagination have, no doubt, all played an important part in legends of this kind. It is not enough quite sincerely to claim magical powers to possess them in reality. Plainly, a man who not only firmly believes in a Power of evil but also that this Power can and does meddle with and mar human affections and human destinies, may invoke and devote himself to this Power, may give up his will thereunto, may ask this Power to accomplish his wishes and ends, and so succeed in persuading himself that he has entered into a mysterious contract with evil whose slave and servant he is become.[31] Moreover, as we should expect, the records teem with instances of common charlatanry, of cunning villainies and crime masquerading under the cloak of superstition, of clever fraud, of what was clearly play acting and mumming to impress the ignorant and vulgar, of diseased vanity, sick for notoriety, that craved the name and reputation of witch, of quackery and cozening that proved lucrative and comfortable enough.

But when every allowance has been made, as we examine in detail the long and bloody history of Witchcraft, as we recognize the fearful fanaticism and atrocious extravagances of the witch mania, as we are enabled to account for in the light of ampler knowledge, both psychological and physical, details and accidents which would have inevitably led to the stake without respite or mercy, as we can elucidate case after case—one an hysterical subject, a cataleptic, an epileptic, a sufferer from some obscure nervous disorder even to-day not exactly diagnosed; another, denounced by the malice of private enemies, perhaps on political grounds; a third, some doting beldame the victim of idlest superstition or mere malignity; a fourth, accused for the sake of gain by a disappointed blackmailer or thief; others, silly bodies, eccentrics, and half-crazed cranks; and the even greater number of victims who were incriminated by poor wretches raving in the agonies of the rack and boots;—none the less after having thus frankly discounted every possible circumstance, after having completely realized the world-wide frenzy of persecution that swept through those centuries of terror, we cannot but recognize that there remain innumerable and important cases which are not to be covered by any ordinary explanation, which fall within no normal category. As a most unprejudiced writer has well said: "The underlying and provocative phenomena had really been present in a huge number of cases."[32] And there is no other way of accounting for these save by acknowledging the reality of Witchcraft and diabolic contracts. It must be steadily remembered that the most brilliant minds, the keenest intelligences, the most learned scholars, the noblest names, men who had heard the evidence at first hand, all firmly believed in Witchcraft. Amongst them are such supreme authorities as S. Augustine, "a philosophical and theological genius of the first order, dominating, like a pyramid, antiquity and the succeeding ages"[33]; Blessed Albertus Magnus, the "Universal Doctor" of encyclopædic knowledge; S. Thomas Aquinas, Doctor Angelicus, one of the profoundest intellects the world has ever seen; the Seraphic S. Bonaventura, most loving of mystics; Popes not a few, Alexander IV, the friend of the Franciscans, prudent, kindly, deeply religious, "assiduous in prayer and strict in abstinence"[34]; John XXII,

" a man of serious character, of austere and simple habits, broadly cultivated "[35]; Benedict XII, a pious Cistercian monk, most learned in theology; Innocent VIII, a magnificent prelate, scholar and diplomatist; Gregory XV, an expert in canon and civil law, most just and merciful of pontiffs, brilliantly talented. We have the names of learned men, such as Gerson, Chancellor of Notre-Dame and of the University of Paris, " justly regarded as one of the master intellects of his age "[36]; James Sprenger, O.P., who for all his etymological errors was a scholar of vast attainments; Jean Bodin, " one of the chief founders of political philosophy and political history "[36]; Erasmus; Bishop Jewell, of Salisbury, " one of the ablest and most authoritative expounders of the true genius and teaching of the reformed Church of England "[37]; the gallant Raleigh; Lord Bacon; Sir Edward Coke; Cardinal Mazarin; the illustrious Boyle; Cudworth, " perhaps the most profound of all the great scholars who have adorned the English Church "[36]; Selden; Henry More; Sir Thomas Browne; Joseph Glanvill, who " has been surpassed in genius by few of his successors "[36]; Meric Casaubon, the learned Prebendary of Canterbury; Sir Matthew Hale; Sir George Mackenzie; William Blackstone; and many another divine, lawyer, scholar, of lesser note. It is inconceivable that all these, mistaken as they might be in some details, should have been wholly deluded and beguiled. The learned Sinistrari in his *De Dæmonialitate*,[38] upon the authoritative sentence of Francesco-Maria Guazzo, an Ambrosian, (*Compendium Maleficarum*, Liber I. 7), writes: " Primo, ineunt pactum expressum cum Dæmone aut alio Mago seu Malefico uicem Dæmonis gerente, et testibus præsentibus de seruitio diabolico suscipiendo: Dæmon uero uice uersa honores, diuitias, et carnales delectationes illis pollicetur." (Firstly, the Novices have to conclude with the Demon, or some other Wizard or Magician acting in the Demon's place, an express compact by which, in the presence of witnesses, they enlist in the Demon's service, he giving them in exchange his pledge for honours, riches, and carnal pleasures.)

It is said that the formal pact was sometimes verbal, sometimes a signed document. In every case it was voluntary, and as Görres points out, the usual initiation into these foul mysteries was through some secret society at an asseblym of which the neophyte bound himself with terrific oathsnd a blasphemy to the service of evil. But there are cases which can only be explained by the materialization of a dark intelligence who actually received a bond from the worshipper. These are, of course, extremely rare; but occasionally the judges were able to examine such parchments and deeds. In 1453 Guillaume Edelin, Prior of S. Germain-en-Laye, signed a compact with the Devil, and this was afterwards found upon his person. Pierre de Lancre relates that the witch Stevenote de Audebert, who was burned in January, 1619, showed him "le pacte & conuention qu'elle auoit faict auec le Diable, escrite en sang de menstrues, & si horrible qu'on auoit horreur de la regarder."[39] In the library at Upsala is preserved the contract by which Daniel Salthenius, in later life Professor of Hebrew at Köningsberg, sold himself to Satan.

In the archives of the Sacred Office is preserved a picture of the Crucifixion of which the following account is given: A young man of notoriously wicked life and extreme impiety having squandered his fortune, and being in desperate need, resolved to sell himself body and soul to Lucifer on condition that he should be supplied with money enough to enable him to indulge in all the luxuries and lusts he desired. It is said the demon assumed a visible form, and required him to write down an act of self-donation to hell. This the youth consented to do on one proviso. He asked the demon if he had been present on Calvary, and when he was answered in the affirmative he insisted that Lucifer should trace him an exact representation of the Crucifixion, upon which he would hand over the completed document. The fiend after much hesitation consented, and shortly produced a picture. But at the sight of the racked and bleeding Body stretched on the Cross the youth was seized with such contrition that falling upon his knees he invoked the help of God. His companion disappeared, leaving the fatal contract and picture. The penitent, in order to gain absolution for so heinous guilt, was obliged to have recourse to the Cardinal Penitentiary, and the picture was taken in charge by the Holy Office. Prince Barberini afterwards obtained permission to have any exact copy made of it, and this eventually he presented to the Capuchins at S. Maria della Concezione.

A contract with Satan was said always to be signed in the blood of the executor. " The signature is almost invariably subscribed with the writer's own blood. . . . Thus at Augsburg Joseph Egmund Schultz declared that on the 15 May, 1671, towards midnight, when it was betwixt eleven and twelve of the clock, he threw down, where three cross-roads met, an illuminated parchment, written throughout in his own blood and wrapped up in a fair kerchief, and thus he sealed the compact . . . Widmann also tells us how that unhappy wretch Faust slightly cut his thumb and with the drops of blood which trickled thence devoted himself in writing body and soul to the Devil, utterly repudiating God's part in him."[40] From the earliest times and in many nations we find human blood used inviolably to ratify the pledged word.[41] Rochholz, I, 52, relates that it is a custom of German University freshmen (Burschen) for the parties to write " mutually with their own blood leaves in each other's albums." The parchment is still said to be in existence on which with his own blood Maximilian, the great and devout Bavarian elector, religiously dedicated himself to the Most Holy Mother of God. Blood was the most sacred and irrevocable of seals, as may be seen in the custom of blood-brotherhood when friendship was sworn and alliances concluded. Either the blood itself was drunk or wine mixed with blood. Herodotus (IV, 70) tells us that the Scythians were wont to conclude agreements by pouring wine into an earthen vessel, into which the contracting parties having cut their arms with a knife let their blood flow and mingle. Whereupon both they and the most distinguished of their following drank of it. Pomponius Mela, *De Situ Orbis*, II, 1, records the same custom as still existing among them in his day : " Not even their alliances are made without shedding of blood : the partners in the compact wound themselves, and when the blood gushes out they mingle the stream and taste of it when it is mixed. This they consider to be the most assured pledge of eternal loyalty and trust."[42] Gyraldus, *Topographia Hibernorum*, XXII, p. 743, says : " When the Ireni conclude treaties the one drinks the blood of the other, which is shed voluntarily for this purpose." In July, 1891, a band of brigands which had existed for three years was discovered and broken up in South Italy. It was reported that in the ritual of these outlaws, who were allied to the " Mala Vita " of Bari, " the neophytes drank blood-brotherhood with the captain of the band by sucking out and drinking the blood from a scratch wound, which he had himself made in the region of his heart."

In several grimoires and books of magic, such as *The Book of Black Magic and of Pacts, The Key of Solomon the King, Sanctum Regnum,* may be found goetic rituals as well as invocations, and if these, fortunately for the operators, are occasionally bootless, it can only be said that Divine Power holds in check the evil intelligences. But, as Suarez justly observes, even if no response be obtained from the demon " either because God does not allow it, or for some other reason we may not know,"[43] the guilt of the experimenter in this dark art and his sin are in no wise lightened.[44] Towards the end of the eighteenth century a certain Juan Perez, being reduced to the utmost misery, vowed himself body and soul to Satan if he were revenged upon those whom he suspected of injuring him. He consulted more than one magician and witch, he essayed more than one theurgic ceremonial, but all in vain. Hell was deaf to his appeal. Whereupon he openly proclaimed his disbelief in the supernatural, in the reality of devils, and mocked at Holy Scripture as a fairy tale, a nursery fable. Naturally this conduct brought him before the Tribunal of the Holy Office, to whom at his first interrogation he avowed the whole story, declaring himself ready to submit to any penance they might seem fit to inflict.

Any such pact which may be entered into with the demon is not in the slightest degree binding. Such is the authoritative opinion of S. Alphonsus, who lays down that a necromancer or person who has had intercourse with evil spirits now wishing to give up his sorceries is bound : " 1. Absolutely to abjure and to renounce any formal contract or any sort of commerce whatsoever he may have entered into with demonic intelligences ; 2. To burn all such books, writings, amulets, talismans, and other instruments as appertain to the black art (i.e. crystals, planchettes, ouija-boards, pagan periapts, and the like) ; 3. To burn the written contract if it be in his possession, but if it be believed that it is held by the demon, there is no need to demand its restoration since it is wholly annulled by penitence; 4. To repair any harm he has done and make good any loss."[45] It may be remarked that these rules have been found exceedingly useful and entirely practical in dealing with mediums and others who forsake spiritism, its abominations and fearful dangers.

There are examples in history, even in hagiography, of sorcerers who have been converted. One of the most famous of these is S. Theophilus the Penitent;[46] and even yet more renowned is S. Cyprian of Antioch who, with S. Justina, suffered martyrdom during the persecution of Diocletian at Nicomedia, 26 September, 304.[47] Blessed Gil of Santarem, a Portuguese Dominican, in his youth excelled in philosophy and medicine. Whilst on his way from Coimbra to the University of Paris he fell into company with a courteous stranger who offered to teach him the black art at Toledo. As payment the stranger required that Gil should make over his soul to the Devil and sign the contract with his blood. After complying with the conditions he devoted seven years to magical studies, and then proceeding to Paris easily obtained the degree of doctor of medicine. Gil, however, repented, burned his books of spells, and returned to Portugal, where he took the habit of S. Dominic. After a long life of penitence and prayer he died at Santarem, 14 May, 1205, and here his body is still venerated.[48] His cult was ratified by Benedict XIV, 9 March, 1748. His feast is observed 14 May.

The contract made by the witch was usually for the term of her life, but sometimes it was only for a number of years, at the end of which period the Devil was supposed to kill his votary. Reginald Scot remarks: "Sometimes their homage with their oth and bargaine is receiued for a certeine terme of yeares; sometimes for ever."[49] Magdalena de la Cruz, a Franciscan nun, born at Aquilar in 1487, entered the convent of Santa Isabel at Cordova in 1504. She acquired an extraordinary reputation for sanctity, and was elected abbess in 1533, 1536, and 1539. Scarcely five years later she was a prisoner of the Inquisition, with charges of Witchcraft proven against her. She confessed that in 1499 a spirit who called himself by the grotesque name Balbar, with a companion Pithon, appeared to her at the tender age of twelve, and she made a contract with him for the space of forty-one years. In 1543 she was seized with a serious illness, during which she confessed her impostures and demonic commerce. She was confined for the rest of her life as a penitent in a house of the utmost austerity. Joan Williford, a witch of Faversham, acknowledged "that the Devil promised to be her servant about twenty yeeres, and that the time is now almost expired."[50] In 1646 Elizabeth Weed, a witch of Great Catworth in Huntingdonshire, confessed that "the Devill then offer'd her that hee would doe what mischiefe she should require him; and said she must covenant with him that he must have her soule at the end of one and twenty years which she granted."[51] In 1664, a Somerset sorceress, Elizabeth Style, avowed that the Devil "promised her Mony, and that she should live gallantly, and have the pleasure of the World for Twelve years, if she would with her Blood sign his Paper, which was to give her Soul to him."[52]

Satan promises to give his votaries all they desire; knowledge, wealth, honours, pleasure, vengeance upon their enemies; and all that he can give is disappointment, poverty, misery, hate, the power to hurt and destroy. He is ever holding before their eyes elusive hopes, and so besotted are they that they trust him and confide in him until all is lost. Sometimes in the case of those who are young the pact is for a short while, but he always renews it. So at Lille in 1661 Antoinette Bourignon's pupils confessed: "The Devil gives them a Mark, which Marks they renew as often as those Persons have any desire to quit him. The Devil reproves them the more severely, and obligeth them to new Promises, making them also new Marks for assurance or Pledge, that those Persons should continue faithful to him."[53]

The Devil's Mark to which allusion is here made, or the Witches' Mark, as it is sometimes called, was regarded as perhaps the most important point in the identification of a witch, it was the very sign and seal of Satan upon the actual flesh of his servant, and any person who bore such a mark was considered to have been convicted and proven beyond all manner of doubt of being in league with and devoted to the service of the fiend. This mark was said to be entirely insensible to pain, and when pricked, however deeply, it did not bleed. So Mr. John Bell, minister at Gladsmuir, in his tract *The Trial of Witchcraft; or Witchcraft Arraigned and Condemned*, published early in the eighteenth century, explains: "The witch mark is sometimes like a blew spot, or a little tate, or reid spots, like flea biting; sometimes also the flesh is sunk in, and hollow, and this is put in secret places, as among the hair of the head, or eye-brows, within the lips, under the arm-pits, and in the most secret parts of the body." Robert Hink, minister at Aberfoill, in his *Secret Commonwealth* (1691), writes: "A spot that I have seen, as a small mole, horny, and brown-coloured; throw which mark, when a large pin was thrust (both in buttock, nose, and rooff of the mouth), till it bowed and became crooked, the witches both men and women, nather felt a pain nor did bleed, nor knew the precise time when this was doing to them, (their eyes only being covered)." This mark was sometimes the complete figure of a toad or a bat; or, as Delrio says, the slot of a hare, the foot of a frog, a spider, a deformed whelp, a mouse.[54] The same great authority informs us on what part of the body it was usually impressed: "In men it may often be seen under the eyelids, under the lips, under the armpits, on the shoulders, on the fundament; in women, moreover, on the breast or on the pudenda."[55]

In his profound treatise *De Dæmonialitate* that most erudite Franciscan Ludovico Maria Sinistrari writes: "[Sagæ seu Malefici] sigillantur a Dæmone aliquo charactere, maxime ii, de quorum constantia dubitat. Character uero non est semper eiusdem formæ, aut figuræ: aliquando enim est simile lepori, aliquando pedi bufonis, aliquando araneæ, uel catello, uel gliri; imprimitur autem in locis corporis magis occultis: uiris quidem aliquando sub palpebris, aliquando sub axillis, aut labiis, aut humeris, aut sede ima, aut alibi: mulieribus autem plerumque in mammis, seu locis muliebribus. Porro sigillum, quo talia signa imprimuntur, est unguis Diaboli." (The Demon imprints upon [the Witches or Wizards] some mark, especially on those whose constancy he suspects. That mark, moreover, is not always of the same shape or figure: sometimes it is the image of a hare, sometimes a toad's leg, sometimes a spider, a puppy, a dormouse. It is imprinted on the most hidden parts of the body: with men, under the eye-lids, or the armpits, or the lips, on the shoulder, the fundament, or somewhere else:

with women it is usually on the breasts or the privy parts. Now, the stamp which imprints these marks is none other but the Devil's claw.)

This Mark was made by the Devil, or by the Devil's vicegerent at the Sabbats upon the admission of a new witch. " The Diuell giveth to euerie nouice a marke, either with his teeth or his clawes," says Reginald Scot, *Discoverie of Witchcraft*, 1584. The young witches of Lille in 1661 confessed that " the Devil branded them with an iron awl upon some part of the body."[56] In Scotland, Geillis Duncane, maid-servant to the deputy bailiff of Tranent, one David Seaton, a wench who was concerned in the celebrated trial of Doctor Fian, Agnes Sampson, Euphemia McCalyan, Barbara Napier, and their associates, would not confess even under torture, " whereuppon they suspecting that she had been marked by the devill (as commonly witches are) made diligent search about her, and found the enemies mark to be in her fore crag, or fore part of her throate ; which being found, shee confessed that all her doings was done by the wicked allurements and entisements of the devil, and that she did them by witchcraft."[57] In 1630 Catharine Oswald of Niddrie was found guilty of sorcery, " the advocate for the instruction of the assyze producing the declaration of two witnesses, that being in the tolbuith, saw Mr. John Aird, minister, put a pin in the pannell's shoulder, (where she carries the devill's mark) up to the heid, and no bluid followed theiron, nor she shrinking thereat ; which was againe done in the justice-depute his own presence." In 1643 Janet Barker at Edinburgh confessed to commerce with the demon, and stated that he had marked her between the shoulders. The mark was found " and a pin being thrust therein, it remained for an hour unperceived by the pannell."[58]

On 10 March, 1611, Louis Gaufridi, a priest of Accoules in the diocese of Marseilles, was visited in prison, where he lay under repeated charges of foulest sorcery, by two physicians and two surgeons who were appointed to search for the Devil's mark. Their joint report ran as follows : " We, the undersigned doctors and surgeons, in obedience to the directions given us by Messire Antholne de Thoron, sieur de Thoron, Councillor to the King in his Court of Parliament, have visited Messire L. Gaufridy, upon whose body we observed three little marks, not very different in colour from the natural skin. The first is upon his right thigh, about the middle towards the lower part. When we pierced this with a needle to the depth of two fingers breadth he felt no pain, nor did any blood or other humour exude from the incision.

"The second is in the region of the loins, towards the right, about an inch from the spine and some four fingers breadth above the femoral muscles. Herein we drove the needle for three fingers breath, leaving it fixed in this spot for some time, as we had already done in the first instance, and yet all the while the said Gaufridy felt no pain, nor was there any effluxion of blood or other humour of any kind.

"The third mark is about the region of the heart. At first the needle was introduced without any sensation being felt, as in the previous instances. But when the place was probed with some force, he said he felt pain, but yet no moisture distilled from this laceration. Early the next morning we again visited him, but we found that the parts which had been probed were neither swollen nor red. In our judgement such callous marks which emit no moisture when pierced, cannot be due to any ancient affection of the skin, and in accordance with this opinion we submit our report on this tenth day of March, 1611.

Fontaine, *Grassy*, Doctors;
Mérindol, *Bontemps*, Surgeons."[59]

On 26 April, 1634, during the famous Loudun trials, Urbain Grandier, the accused was examined in order to discover the witch-mark. He was stripped naked, blindfolded, and in the presence of the officials, René Mannoury, one of the leading physicians of the town, conducted the search. Two marks were discovered, one upon the shoulder-blade and the other upon the thigh, both of which proved insensible even when pierced with a sharp silver pin.

Inasmuch as the discovery of the devil-mark was regarded as one of the most convincing indications—if not, indeed, an infallible proof—that the accused was guilty since he bore indelibly branded upon his flesh Satan's own sign-manual, it is easy to see how the searching for, the recognition and the probing of, such marks actually grew to be a profession in which not a few ingenious persons came to be recognized as experts and practical authorities. In Scotland, especially, the "prickers," as they were called, formed a regular gild. They received a good fee for every witch they discovered, and, as might be expected, they did not fail to reap a golden harvest. At the trial of Janet Peaston, in 1646, the magistrates of Dalkeith "caused John Kincaid of Tranent, the common pricker, to exercise his craft upon her. He found two marks of the Devil's making; for she could not feel the pin when it was put into either of the said marks, nor did the marks bleed when the pin was taken out again. When she was asked where she thought the pins were put into her, she pointed to a part of her body distant from the real place. They were pins of three inches in length."[60] Another notorious pricker was John Bain, upon whose unsupported evidence a large number of unfortunate wretches were sentenced to death. About 1634 John Balfour of Corhouse was feared over all the countryside for his exploits; whilst twenty years later one John Dick proved a rival to Kincaid himself. The regular trade of these "common prickers" came to be a serious nuisance, and confessedly opened the door to all sorts of roguery. The following extraordinary incident shows how dangerous and villainous in mountebank hands the examinations could become, which, if conducted at all, ought at least to be safeguarded by every precaution and only entrusted to skilled physicians, who should report the result to grave and learned divines. "There came then to Inverness one Mr. Paterson, who had run over the kingdom for triall off witches, and was ordinarily called the Pricker, because his way of triall was with a long brass pin. Stripping them naked, he alledged that the spell spot was seen and discovered. After rubbing over the whole body with his palms he slips in the pin, and, it seemes, with shame and fear being dasht, they felt it not, but he left it in the flesh, deep to the head, and desired them to find and take it out. It is sure some witches were discovered but many honest men and women were blotted and break by this trick. In Elgin there were two killed; in Forres two; and one Margret Duff, a rank witch, burned in Inverness. This Paterson came up to the Church of Wardlaw, and within the church pricked 14 women and one man brought thither by the Chisholm of

Commer, and 4 brought by Andrew Fraser, chamerlan of Ferrintosh. He first polled all their heads and amassed the heap of haire together, hid in the stone dich, and so proceeded to pricking.[61] Severall of these dyed in prison never brought to confession. This villan gaind a great deale off mony, haveing two servants; at last he was discovered to be a woman disguished in mans cloathes. Such cruelty and rigure was sustained by a vile varlet imposture."[62] No doubt in very many, in the majority of instances, these witch-marks were natural malformations of the skin, thickened tissue, birthmarks—I myself have known a subject who was by prenatal accident stamped upon the upper part of the arm with the complete figure of a rat—moles, callous warts, or spots of some kind. But this explanation will not cover all the cases, and even the sceptical Miss Murray who writes: "Local anæsthesia is vouched for in much of the evidence, which suggests that there is a substratum of truth in the statements," is bound candidly to confess, "but I can at present offer no solution of this problem."[63] Moreover, as before noticed, this mark was not infrequently branded upon the novice at admission, often by the Witch-Master, who presided over the rout, sometimes—it must be admitted—by non-human agency.

The "little Teat or Pap," so often found on the body of the wizard or witch, and said to secrete milk which nourished the familiar, must be carefully distinguished from the insensible devil-mark. This phenomenon, for no explainable reason, seems to occur only in the records of England and New England, where, however, it is of exceedingly frequent occurrence. It is worth remarking that in the last act of Shadwell's play, *The Lancashire Witches* (1681), the witches are searched by a woman, who reports "they have all great Biggs and Teats in many Parts, except Mother *Madge*, and hers are but small ones." Shadwell, who in his voluminous notes has citations from nearly fifty authors, on this point writes: "The having of Biggs and Teats all modern Witch-mongers in *England* affirm."[64] In 1597 at the trial of a beldame, Elizabeth Wright, of Stapenhill, near Burton-on-Trent: "The old woman they stript, and found behind her right sholder a thing much like the vdder of an ewe that giueth sucke with two teates, like vnto two great wartes, the one behinde vnder her armehole, the other a hand off towardes the top of her shoulder. Being demanded how long she had those teates, she answered she was borne so."[65] In the case of the Witch of Edmonton, Elizabeth Sawyer, who was in spite of her resistance searched upon the express order of the Bench, it was found by Margaret Weaver, a widow of an honest reputation, and two other grave matrons, who performed this duty that there was upon her body "a thing like a Teate the bignesse of the little finger, and the length of half a finger, which was branched at the top like a teate, and seemed as though one had suckt it."[66] John Palmer of St. Albans (1649) confessed that "upon his compact with the Divel, hee received a flesh brand, or mark, upon his side, which gave suck to two familiars."[67] The Kentish witch, Mary Read of Lenham (1652), "had a visible Teat, under her Tongue, and did show it to many."[68] At St. Albans about 1660 there was a wizard who "had like a Breast on his side."[69] In the same year at Kidderminster, a widow, her two daughters, and a man were accused; "the man had five teats, the mother three, and the eldest daughter, one."[70] In 1692 Bridget Bishop, one of the Salem witches, was brought to trial: "A Jury of Women found a preternatural Teat upon her Body: But upon a second search, within 3 or 4 hours, there was no such thing to be seen."[71] There is similar evidence adduced in the accounts of Rose Cullender and Amy Duny, two Suffolk witches, executed in 1664; Elizabeth Horner, a Devon witch (1696); Widow Coman, an Essex witch, who died in her bed (1699); and, indeed, innumerable other examples might be quoted affording a whole catena of pertinent illustrations. No doubt many of these are explicable by the cases of polymastia (*mammæ erraticæ*) and polythelia (supernumerary nipples) of which there are continual records in recent medical works. It must be freely admitted that these anatomical divagations are commoner than is generally supposed; frequently they are so slight that they may pass almost unnoticed; doubtless there is exaggeration in many of the inexactly observed seventeenth-century narratives. However, it has to be said, as before, that when every most generous allowance is made, the facts which remain, and the details are very ample, cannot be covered by physical peculiarities and malformations.

There is far more truth in the records of the old theologians and witch finders than many nowadays are disposed to allow.

NOTES TO CHAPTER II.

1 Under Innocent III, 1215.

2 Diabolus enim et alii dæmones a Deo quidem natura creati sunt boni, sed ipsi per se facti sunt mali.

3 Bossuet says that the writings of Suarez contain the whole of Scholastic Philosophy.

4 Since it contradicts a definite (*certa*) theological conclusion or truth clearly consequent upon two premises, of which one is an article of faith (*de fide*), the other naturally certain.

5 Which explains much of the trifling and silliness in Spiritism; the idle answers given through the mediums of the influences at work.

6 Josephus, *Antiquities*, XIX. 8. 2.

7 Suetonius, *Caligula*, XXII. Here ample details of Caligula's worship may be read.

8 *Epigrammatum*, V. 8. 1. See also IX. 4, *et sæpius*.

9 . . . id agens ne quis Romæ deus nisi Heliogabalus coleretur. . . . Nec Romanas tantum extinguere uoluit religiones, sed per orbem terræ unum studens ut Heliogabalus deus unus ubique coleretur. Ælius Lampridius, *Antoninus Heliogabalus*, 3; 6.

10 Even the Christian (Arian) Constantius II suffered himself to be addressed as "Nostra Æternitas."

11 Now commemorated on 14 September, the Feast of the Exaltation of Holy Cross. Shortly after the Restoration of the Cross to Jerusalem, the wood was cut up (perhaps for greater safety) into small fragments which were distributed throughout the Christian world.

12 Didymus, *De Trinitate*, III. xli.

13 Epiphanius, *Hœr.*, xlviii. 11.

14 *Annales de la Propogation de la Foi*, VII (1834), p. 84.

15 D. C. J. Ibbetson, *Outlines of Punjaub Ethnography*, Calcutta. 1883. p. 123.

16 . . . vous n'avez pas eu honte de vous agenouiller devant votre Belzebuth, que vous avez adoré. J. B. Cannaert, *Olim procès des Sorcières en Belgique*, Gand, 1847.

17 Ie me remets de tout poinct en ton pouuoir & entre tes mains, ne recognois autre Dieu: si bien que tu es mon Dieu.

18 On dit au Diable nous vous recognoissons pour nostre maistre, nostre Dieu, nostre Createur.

19 John Hutchinson, *History of the Province of Massachusett's Bay*, 1828, II. p. 31.

20 Satan luy commãda de le prier soir & matin, auant qu'elle s'addonat à faire autre œuure.

21 *Wonderful Discoverie of Elizabeth Sawyer*, London, 1621.

22 Rev. F. G. Lee, *More Glimpses of the World Unseen*, 1878, p. 12.

23 Potest [diabolus] eludere sensus et facere ut appareat caput abcisum, *De Religione*, l. 2, c. 16, n. 13, t. 13, p. 578.

24 Huc. *Voyage dans la Tartarie, le Thibet et la Chine*, I, ix, p. 308. The author remarks: Ces cérémonies horribles se renouvellent assez souvent dans les grandes lamaseries de la Tartarie et du Thibet. Nous ne pensons nullement qu'on puisse mettre toujours sur le compte de la supercherie des faits de ce genre: car d'après tout ce que nous avons vu et entendu parmi les nations idolâtres, nous sommes persuadé que le démon y joue un grand rôle. (These horrible ceremonies frequently occur in the larger lamaseries of Tartary and Tibet. I am very certain that we cannot always ascribe happenings of this sort to mere juggling or trickery; for, after all that I have seen and heard among heathen people, I am confident that the powers of evil are very largely concerned therein.)

[25] I use this term rather than the more popular "Spiritualism." Spiritism obtains in Italy, France and Germany. "Spiritualism" is correctly a technical name for the doctrine which denies that the contents of the universe are limited to matter and the properties and operations of matter.

[26] For fuller, and, indeed, conclusive details see Godfrey Raupert's *Modern Spiritism*, London, 1904; and Monsignor Benson's *Spiritualism, Dublin Review*, October, 1909, and reprinted by the Catholic Truth Society.

[27] *Prognosticare* is a late word. Strictly to prognosticate is to deduce from actual signs, to prophesy is to foretell the future without any such sign or token.

[28] The Camisards were agreeably satirized by D'Urfey in his comedy *The Modern Prophets; or, New Wit for a Husband*, produced at Drury Lane, 5 May, 1709, (*Tatler*, 11), and printed quarto, 1709, (no date). One of the principal characters is "*Marrogn*, A Knavish French Camizar and Priest," created by Bowen. This is a portrait of Elie Marion. In his preface D'Urfey speaks of "the abominable Impostures of those craz'd Enthusiasts" whom he lashes. The play had been composed in 1708, but production was postponed owing to the death of the Prince Consort, 28 October of that year. Swift, *Predictions for the Year 1708*, has: "*June*. This month will be distinguished at home, by the utter dispersing of those ridiculous deluded enthusiasts, commonly called the *prophets*; occasioned chiefly by seeing the time come, when many of their prophecies should be fulfilled, and then finding themselves deceived by contrary events."

[29] See also Fléchier's *Récit fidèle* in *Lettres choisies*, Lyons, 1715; and Brueys' *Histoire du fanatisme de notre temps*, Montpellier, 1713.

[30] Après que Dieu a parlé de sa propre bouche des magiciens et sorciers, qui est l'incredule qui on peut justement douter?

[31] In the fourteenth century bas-reliefs on cathedrals frequently represent men kneeling down before the Devil, worshipping him, and devoting themselves to him as his servants. Martonne, *Piété au Moyen Âge*, p. 137.

[32] George Ives, *A History of Penal Methods*, p. 75. His admirable and documented chapter II, "The Witch Trials," should be carefully read.

[33] Philip Schaff, *History of the Christian Church*.

[34] Matthew Paris, *Chronica Maiora*.

[35] J. P. Kirsch.

[36] All these quotations are from W. H. Lecky, *History of Rationalism in Europe*. c. 1.

[37] Rev. Peter Lorimer, D.D.

[38] First published by Isidore Liseux, 1875. p. 21. XIII. Ludovico Maria Sinistrari, Minorite, was born at Ameno (Novara) 26 February, 1622. He was Consultor to the Supreme Tribunal of the Holy Office; Vicar-general of the Archbishop of Avignon, and Theologian Advisory to the Archbishop of Milan. He is described as "omnium scientiarum uir." He died 6 March, 1701.

[39] *L'Incredulité et Mescreance du Sortilege*, Paris, 1622, p. 38.

[40] Subscriptio autem sæpissime peragitur proprio sanguine. . . . Sic Augustæ referebat Joseph Egmund Schultz, se anno 1671. d. 15. Maji sanguine proprio tinctum manuscriptum, in membrana, nomine picto, obuolutoque muccinio, in media nocte, cum hora undecima & duodecima agebatur, in compitum iecisse, atque pactum sic corroborasse . . . Sic de infausto illo Fausto *Widmannus* refert, proprio sanguine ex leuiter uulnerato pollice emisso illum se totum diabolo adscripsisse, Deoque repudium misisse. *De Sagis*, Christian Stridtheckh, Lipsiæ, 1691. (XXII).

[41] See Götz, *De subscriptionibus sanguine humano firmatis*, Lübeck, 1724. Also Scheible, *Die Sage vom Faust*. Stuttgart, 1847. So far as I am aware this point has been neglected by writers on Witchcraft.

[42] Ne fœdora quidem incruenta sunt: sauciant se, qui paciscuntur, exemtumque sanguinem, ubi permiscuere, degustant. Id putant mansuræ fidei pignus certissimum.

[43] . . . uel quia Deus non permittit, uel propter alias rationes nobis occultas. *De Superstitione*, VIII. i. 13.

[44] Tunc autem propria culpa diuinationis iam commissa est ab homine,

etiamsi effectus desideratus non fuerit subsecutus. (For the sin of divination is actually committed by the sinner and that willingly, although he obtain not the desired effect of his action.) *Idem.*

[45] *Theologia moralis*, l. iii. n. 28. Monendi sunt se teneri 1. Pactum expressum, si quod habent cum dæmone, aut commercium abiurare et dissoluere; 2. Libros suos, schedas, ligaturas, aliaque instrumenta artis comburere; 3. Comburere chirographum, si habeat: si iuro solus dæmon id habeat, non necessario cogendus est ut reddat, quia pactum sufficienter soluitur per pœnitentiam; 4. Damna illata resarcire.

[46] Bollandists, 4 February.

[47] *Breuiarium Romanum*, Paris Autumnalis, 26 September, lectio iii. of Matins. Upon this history Calderon has founded his great drama *El Magico Prodigioso.*

[48] Bollandists, 14 May. *Breuiarium iuxta S. Ordinis Prœdicatorum.* 14 May. In Nocturno, Lectiones ii, iij. Touron *Histoire des hommes illustres de l'ordre de Saint Dominique.* (Paris, 1743.)

[49] *Discoverie of Witchcraft*, Book III.

[50] *Examination of Joane Williford*, London, 1643.

[51] John Davenport, *Witches of Huntingdon*, London, 1646.

[52] Glanvill, *Sadducismus Triumphatus.*

[53] Antoinette Bourignon, *La Vie exterieure*, Amsterdam, 1683.

[54] Delrio. *Disquisitiones magicœ*, l. v. sect. 4. t. 2. Non eadem est forma signi; aliquando est simile leporis uestigio, aliquando bufonis pedi, aliquando araneæ, uel catello, uel gliri.

[55] *Idem.* In uirorum enim corpore sæpe uisitur sub palpebris, sub labiis, sub axillis, in humeris, in sede ima: feminis etiam, in mammis uel muliebribus locis.

[56] . . . le Diable leur fait quelque marque comme avec une aleine de fer en quelque partie du corps.

[57] *Newes from Scotland*, London. (1592.) Roxburgh Club reprint, 1816.

[58] *Abbreviate of the Justiciary Record.*

[59] Nous, medecins et chirurgiens soussignés, suivant le commandement à nous fait par messire Anthoine de Thoron, sieur de Thoron, conseiller du roy en sa cour de parlement, avons visité messire L. Gaufridy au corps duquel avons remarqué trois petites marques peu differentes en couleur du reste du cuir. L'une en sa cuisse sénestre sur le milieu et en la partie inferieure, en laquelle ayant enforcé une aiguille environ deux travers de doigts n'a senti aucune douleur, ni de la place n'est sorti point de sang ni autre humidité.

La seconde est en la region des lombes en la partie droite, un poulce près de l'épine du dos et quatre doigts au-dessus les muscles de la fesse, en laquelle nous avons enfoncé l'aiguille trois travers de doigts, la laissons comme avions fait à la première plantée en cette partie quelque espace de temps, sans toutefois que le dit Gaufridy ait senti aucune douleur et que sang ni humeur quelconque en soit sorti.

La troisième est vers la région du cœur. Laquelle, au commencement qu'on mit l'aiguille parut comme les autres sans sentiment; mais à mesure que l'on enfonçait fort avant, il dit sentir quelque douleur; ne sortant toutefois aucune humidité, et l'ayant visité le lendemain au matin, n'avons reconnu aux parties piquées ni tumeur, ni rougeur. A cause de quoi nous disons telles marques insensibles en rendant point d'humidité étant piquées, ne pouvoir arriver par aucune maladie du cuir précédante, et tel faisons notre rapport ce 10 mars, 1611. *Fontaine, Grassy*, médecins; *Mérindol, Bontemps*, chirurgiens.

So great was the importance attached to the discovery of a witch-mark upon the body of the accused that when the above medico-legal report was read in court, Father Sebastian Michaelis, a learned Dominican, who was acting as consultor in the case, horror-struck, involuntarily exclaimed: "Good sooth, were we at Avignon this man would be executed to-morrow!" Gaufridi confessed: "J'advoue que les dites marques sont faites pour protestation qu'on sera toujours bon et fidèle serviteur du diable toute la vie." (I confess that these marks were made as a sign that I shall be a good and faithful servant to the Devil all my life long.)

[60] Pitcairn, *Records of Justiciary*. In 1663 Kincaid was thrown into jail, where he lay nine weeks for "pricking" without a magistrate's warrant. He was only released owing to his great age and on condition that he would "prick" no more.

[61] This shaving of the head and body was the usual procedure before the search for the devil-mark. We find it recorded in nearly every case. Generally a barber was called in to perform the operation: e.g. the trials of Gaufridi and Grandier, where the details are very ample.

[62] *The Wardlaw Manuscript*, p. 446. Scottish History Society publication, Edinburgh.

[63] *The Witch-Cult in Western Europe*, p. 86.

[64] Angelica in *Love for Love* (1695), II, mocking her superstitious old uncle, Foresight, and the Nurse, cries: "Look to it, Nurse; I can bring Witness that you have a great unnatural Teat under your Left Arm, and he another; and that you Suckle a young Devil in the shape of a Tabby-Cat by turns, I can."

[65] *The most wonderfull . . . storie of a . . . Witch named Alse Gooderidge*. London. 1597.

[66] Goodcole's *Wonderfull Discoverie of Elizabeth Sawyer*, London, 1621. There is an allusion in Ford and Dekker's drama, IV:

> *Sawyer*. My dear *Tom-boy*, welcome . . .
> Comfort me: thou shalt haue the teat anon.
> *Dog*. Bow, wow! . I'll haue it now.

[67] W. B. Gerish. *The Devil's Delusions*, Bishops Stortford, 1914.

[68] *Prodigious and Tragicall Histories*, London, 1652.

[69] W. B. Gerish, *Relation of Mary Hall of Gadsden*, 1912

[70] T. B. Howell, *State Trials*, London, 1816.

[71] Cotton Mather, *Wonders of the Invisible World*.

CHAPTER III

Demons and Familiars

One of the most authoritative of the older writers upon Witchcraft, Francesco-Maria Guazzo, a member of the Congregation of S. Ambrose ad Nemus,[1] in his encyclopædic *Compendium Maleficarum*, first published at Milan, 1608, has drawn up under eleven heads those articles in which a solemn and complete profession of Witchcraft was then held to consist:

First: The candidates have to conclude with the Devil, or some other Wizard or Magician acting in the Devil's stead, an express compact by which, in the presence of witnesses they devote themselves to the service of evil, he giving them in exchange his pledge for riches, luxury, and such things as they desire.

Secondly: They abjure the Catholic Faith, explicitly withdraw from their obedience to God, renounce Christ and in a particular manner the Patronage and Protection of Our Lady, curse all Saints, and forswear the Sacraments. In Guernsey, in 1617, Isabel Becquet went to Rocquaine Castle, "the usual place where the Devil kept his Sabbath: no sooner had she arrived there than the Devil came to her in the form of a dog, with two great horns sticking up: and with one of his paws (which seemed to her like hands) took her by the hand: and calling her by her name told her that she was welcome: then immediately the Devil made her kneel down: while he himself stood up on his hind legs; he then made her express detestation of the Eternal in these words: *I renounce God the Father, God the Son, and God the Holy Ghost;* and then caused her to worship and invoke himself."[2] De Lancre tells us that Jeannette d'Abadie, a lass of sixteen, confessed that she was made to "renounce & deny her Creator, the Holy Virgin, the Saints, Baptism, father, mother, relations, Heaven, earth, & all that the world contains."[3]

In a very full confession made by Louis Gaufridi on the second of April, 1611, to two Capuchins, Father Ange and Father Antoine, he revealed the formula of his abjuration of the Catholic faith. It ran thus: "I, Louis Gaufridi, renounce all good, both spiritual as well as temporal, which may be bestowed upon me by God, the Blessed Virgin Mary, all the Saints of Heaven, particularly my Patron S. John-Baptist, as also S. Peter, S. Paul, and S. Francis, and I give myself body and soul to Lucifer, before whom I stand, together with every good that I may ever possess (save always the benefit of the sacraments touching those who receive them). And according to the tenour of these terms have I signed and sealed."[4] Madeleine de la Palud, one of his victims, used a longer and more detailed declaration in which the following hideous blasphemies occurred: "With all my heart and most unfeignedly and with all my will most deliberately do I wholly renounce God, Father, Son, and Holy Ghost; the most Holy Mother of God; all the Angels and especially my Guardian Angel, the Passion of Our Lord Jesus Christ, His Precious Blood and the merits thereof, my lot in Paradise, all the good inspirations which God may give me in the future, all prayers which are made or may be made for me."[5]

Thirdly: They cast away with contempt the most Holy Rosary, delivered by Our Lady to S. Dominic;[6] the Cord of S. Francis; the cincture of S. Augustine; the Carmelite scapular bestowed upon S. Simon Stock; they cast upon the ground and trample under their feet in the mire the Cross, Holy Medals, *Agnus Dei,*[7] should they possess such or carry them upon their persons. S. Francis girded himself with a rough rope in memory of the bonds wherewith Christ was bound during His Passion, and a white girdle with three knots has since formed part of the Franciscan habit. Sixtus IV, by his Bull *Exsupernæ dispositionis,* erected the Archconfraternity of the Cord of S. Francis in the basilica of the Sacro Convento at Assisi, enriching it with many Indulgences, favours which have been confirmed by pontiff after pontiff. Archconfraternities are erected not only in Franciscan but in many other churches and aggregated to the centre at Assisi. The Archconfraternity of Our Lady of Consolation, or of the Black Leathern Belt of S. Monica,

S. Augustine and S. Nicolas of Tolentino, took its rise from a vision of S. Monica, who received a black leathern belt from Our Lady. S. Augustine, S. Ambrose, and S. Simplicianus all wore such a girdle, which forms a distinctive feature of the dress of Augustinian Eremites. After the canonization of S. Nicolas of Tolentino it came into general use as an article of devotion, and Eugenius IV in 1439 erected the above Archconfraternity. A Bull of Gregory XIII *Ad ea* (15 July, 1575) confirmed this and added various privileges and Indulgences. The Archconfraternity is erected in Augustinian sanctuaries, from the General of which Order leave must be obtained for its extension to other churches.

Fourthly: All witches vow obedience and subjection into the hands of the Devil; they pay him homage and vassalage (often by obscene ceremonies), and lay their hands upon a large black book which is presented to them. They bind themselves by blasphemous oaths never to return to the true faith, to observe no divine precept, to do no good work, but to obey the Demon only and to attend without fail the nightly conventicles. They pledge themselves to frequent the midnight assemblies.[8] These conventicles or covens[9] (from *conuentus*) were bands or companies of witches, composed of men and women, apparently under the discipline of an officer, all of whom for convenience'sake belonged to the same district. Those who belonged to a coven were, it seems from the evidence at trials, bound to attend the weekly Esbat. The arrest of one member of a coven generally led to the implication of the rest. Cotton Mather remarks, "The witches are organized like Congregational Churches."

Fifthly: The witches promise to strive with all their power and to use every inducement and endeavour to draw other men and women to their detestable practices and the worship of Satan.

The witches were imbued with the missionary spirit, which made them doubly damnable in the eyes of the divines and doubly guilty in the eyes of the law. So in the case of Janet Breadheid of Auldearne, we find that her husband "enticed her into that craft."[10] A girl named Bellot, of Madame Bourignon's academy, confessed that her mother had taken her to the Sabbat when she was quite a child. Another girl alleged that all worshippers of the Devil "are constrained to offer him their Children." Elizabeth Francis of Chelmsford, a witch tried in 1566, was only about twelve years old when her grandmother first taught her the art of sorcery.[11] The famous Pendle beldame, Elizabeth Demdike "brought vp her owne Children, instructed her Graund-children, and tooke great care and paines to bring them to be Witches."[12] At Salem, George Burroughs, a minister, was accused by a large number of women as "the person who had Seduc'd and Compell'd them into the snares of Witchcraft."

Sixthly: The Devil administers to witches a kind of sacrilegious baptism, and after abjuring their Godfathers and Godmothers of Christian Baptism and Confirmation they have assigned to them new sponsors—as it were—whose charge it is to instruct them in sorcery: they drop their former name and exchange it for another, generally a scurrilous and grotesque nickname.

In 1609 Jeanette d'Abadie, a witch of the Basses-Pyrénées, confessed "that she often saw children baptized at the Sabbat, and these she informed us were the offspring of sorcerers and not of other persons, but of witches who are accustomed to have their sons and daughters baptized at the Sabbat rather than at the Font."[13] June 20, 1614, at Orleans, Silvain Nevillon amongst other crimes acknowledged that he had frequented assemblies of witches, and "that they baptize babies at the Sabbat with Chrism. . . . Then they anoint the child's head therewith muttering certain Latin phrases."[14] Gentien le Clerc, who was tried at the same time, "said that his mother, as he had been told, presented him at the Sabbat when he was but three years old, to a monstrous goat, whom they called l'Aspic. He said that he was baptized at the Sabbat, at Carrior d'Olivet, with fourteen or fifteen other children. . . ."[15]

Among the confessions made by Louis Gaufridi at Aix in March, 1611, were: "I confess that baptism is administered at the Sabbat, and that every sorcerer, devoting himself to the Devil, binds himself by a particular vow that he will have all his children baptized at the Sabbat, if this may by any possible means be effected. Every child who is thus baptized at the Sabbat receives a name, wholly differing from his own name. I confess that at this baptism water, sulphur, and salt are employed: the sulphur renders the recipient the Devil's slave whilst salt confirms his baptism in the Devil's service. I confess that the form and intention are to baptize in the name of Lucifer, Belzebuth and other demons making the sign of the cross beginning backwards and then tracing from the feet and ending at the head."[16]

A number of Swedish witches (1669) were baptized: "they added, that he caused them to be baptized too by such Priests as he had there, and made them confirm their Baptism with dreadful Oaths and Imprecations."[17]

The giving of a new name seems to have been very general. Thus in May, 1569, at S. Andrews "a notabill sorceres callit Nicniven was condemnit to the death and burnt." Her Christian name is not given merely her witch's name bestowed by the demon. In the famous Fian case it was stated that when at the meeting in North Berwick kirk Robert Grierson was named great confusion ensued for the witches and warlocks "all ran hirdie-girdie, and were angry, for it was promised that he should be called Robert the Comptroller, for the expriming of his name."[18] Euphemia McCalyan of the same coven was called Cane, and Barbara Napier Naip. Isabel Goudie of Auldearne (1662) stated that many witches known to her had been baptized in their own blood by such names as "Able-and-Stout," "Over-the-dike-with-it," "Raise-the-wind," "Pickle-nearest-the-wind," "Batter-them-down-Maggy," "Blow-Kate," and similar japeries.

Seventhly: The witches cut off a piece of their own garments, and as a token of homage tender it to the Devil, who takes it away and keeps it.

Eighthly: The Devil draws on the ground a circle wherein stand the Novices, Wizards, and Witches, and there they confirm by oath all their aforesaid promises. This has a mystical signification. "They take this oath to the Demon standing in a circle described upon the ground, perchance because a circle is the Symbol of Divinity, & the earth God's footstool and thus he assuredly wishes them to believe that he is the lord of Heaven and earth."[19]

Ninthly: The sorcerers request the Devil to strike them out of the book of Christ, and to inscribe them in his own. Then is solemnly brought forward a large black book, the same as that on which they laid their hands when they did their first homage, and they are inscribed in this by the Devil's claw.

These books or rolls were kept with great secrecy by the chief officer of the coven or even the Grand Master of a district. They would have been guarded as something as precious as life itself, seeing that they contained the damning evidence of a full list of the witches of a province or county, and in addition thereto seems to have been added a number of magic formulæ, spells, charms, and probably, from time to time, a record of the doings of the various witches. The signing of such a book is continually referred to in the New England trials. So when Deliverance Hobbs had made a clean breast of her sorceries, " She now testifi'd, that this *Bishop* [Bridget Bishop, condemned and executed as a long-continued witch] tempted her to sign the *Book* again, and to deny what she had confess'd." The enemies of the notorious Matthew Hopkins made great capital out of the story that by some sleight of sorcery he had got hold of one of these Devil's memorandum-books, whence he copied a list of witches, and this it was that enabled him to be so infallible in his scent. The Witch-Finder General was hard put to it to defend himself from the accusation, and becomes quite pitiful in his whining asseverations of innocence. There is a somewhat vague story, no dates being given, that a Devil's book was carried off by Mr. Williamson of Cardrona (Peebles), who filched it from the witches whilst they were dancing on Minchmoor. But the whole coven at once gave chase, and he was glad to abandon it and escape alive.

Sometimes the catalogue of witches was inscribed on a separate parchment, and the book only used to write down charms and spells. Such a volume was the Red Book of Appin known to have actually been in existence a hundred years ago. Tradition said it was stolen from the Devil by a trick. It was in manuscript, and contained a large number of magic runes and incantations for the cure of cattle diseases, the increase of flocks, the fertility of fields. This document, which must be of immense importance and interest, when last heard of was (I believe) in the possession of the now-extinct Stewarts of Invernahyle. This strange volume, so the story ran, conferred dark powers on the owner, who knew what inquiry would be made ere the question was poised;

and the tome was so confected with occult arts that he who read it must wear a circlet of iron around his brow as he turned those mystic pages.

Another volume, of which mention is made—one that is often confused[20] with, but should be distinguished from, these two—is what we may term the Devil's Missal. Probably this had its origin far back in the midst of the centuries among the earliest heretics who passed down their evil traditions to their followers, the Albigenses and the Waldenses or Vaudois. This is referred to by the erudite De Lancre, who in his detailed account of the Black Mass as performed in the region of the Basses-Pyrénées (1609) writes: "Some kind of altar was erected upon the pillars of infernal design, and hereon, without reciting the *Confiteor* or *Alleluya*, turning over the leaves of a certain book which he held, he began to mumble certain phrases of Holy Mass."[21] Silvain Nevillon (Orleans, 1614) confessed that "the Sabbat was held in a house. . . . He saw there a tall dark man opposite to the one who was in a corner of the ingle, and this man was perusing a book, whose leaves seemed black & crimson, & he kept muttering between his teeth although what he said could not be heard, and presently he elevated a black host and then a chalice of some cracked pewter, all foul and filthy."[22] Gentien le Clerc, who was also accused, acknowledged that at these infernal assemblies "Mass was said, and the Devil was celebrant. He was vested in a chasuble upon which was a broken cross. He turned his back to the altar when he was about to elevate the Host and the Chalice, which were both black. He read in a mumbling tone from a book, the cover of which was soft and hairy like a wolf's skin. Some leaves were white and red, others black."[23] Madeleine Bavent, who was the chief figure in the trials at Louviers (1647), acknowledged: "Mass was read from the book of blasphemies, which contained the canon. This same volume was used in processions. It was full of the most hideous curses against the Holy Trinity, the Holy Sacrament of the Altar, the other Sacraments and ceremonies of the Church. It was written in a language completely unknown to me."[24] Possibly this blasphemous volume is the same as that which Satanists to-day use when performing their abominable rites.

Tenthly: The witches promise the Devil sacrifices and

offerings at stated times; once a fortnight, or at least once a month, the murder of some child, or some mortal poisoning, and every week to plague mankind with evils and mischiefs, hailstorms, tempest, fires, cattle-plagues and the like.

The *Liber Pœnitentialis* of S. Theodore, Archbishop of Canterbury 668–690, the earliest ecclesiastical law of England, has clauses condemning those who invoke fiends, and so cause the weather to change "si quis emissor tempestatis fuerit." In the *Capitaluria* of Charlemagne (died at Aachen, 28 January, 814), the punishment of death is declared against those who by evoking the demon, trouble the atmosphere, excite tempests, destroy the fruits of the earth, dry up the milk of cows, and torment their fellow-creatures with diseases or any other misfortune. All persons found guilty of employing such arts were to be executed immediately upon conviction. Innocent VIII in his celebrated Bull, *Summis desiderantes affectibus*, 5 December, 1484, charges sorcerers in detail with precisely the same foul practices. The most celebrated occasion when witches raised a storm was that which played so important a part in the trial of Dr. Fian and his coven, 1590–1, when the witches, in order to drown King James and Queen Anne on their voyage from Denmark, "tooke a Cat and christened it," and after they had bound a dismembered corpse to the animal "in the night following the said Cat was convayed into the middest of the sea by all these witches, sayling in their riddles or cives, . . . this doone, then did arise such a tempest in the sea, as a greater hath not bene seene."[25] The bewitching of cattle is alleged from the earliest time, and at Dornoch in Sutherland as late as 1722, an old hag was burned for having cast spells upon the pigs and sheep of her neighbours, the sentence being pronounced by the sheriff-depute, Captain David Ross of Little Dean. This was the last execution of a witch in Scotland.

With regard to the sacrifice of children there is a catena of ample evidence. Reginald Scot[26] writes in 1584: "This must be an infallible rule, that euerie fortnight, or at the least euerie month, each witch must kill one child at the least for hir part." When it was dangerous or impossible openly to murder an infant the life would be taken by poison, and in 1645 Mary Johnson, a witch of Wyvenhoe, Essex, was tried for poisoning two children, no doubt as an act of sorcery.[27] It is unknown how many children Gilles de Rais devoted to death in his impious orgies. More than two hundred corpses were found in the latrines of Tiffauges, Machecoul, Champtocé. It was in 1666 that Louis XIV was first informed of the abominations which were vermiculating his capital "des sacrilèges, des profanations, des messes impies, des sacrifices de jeunes enfants." Night after night in the rue Beauregard at the house of the mysterious Catherine la Voisin the abbé Guibourg was wont to kill young children for his hideous ritual, either by strangulation or more often by piercing their throats with a sharp dagger and letting the hot blood stream into the chalice as he cried: "Astaroth, Asmodée, je vous conjure d'accepter le sacrifice que je vous présente!" (Astaroth! Asmodeus! Receive, I beseech you, this sacrifice I offer unto you!) A priest named Tournet also said Satanic Masses at which children were immolated; in fact the practice was so common that la Chaufrein, a mistress of Guibourg, would supply a child for a crown[28] piece.

Eleventhly: The Demon imprints upon the Witches some mark. . . . When this has all been performed in accordance with the instructions of those Masters who have initiated the Novice, the latter bind themselves by fearful oaths never to worship the Blessed Sacrament; to heap curses on all Saints and especially to abjure our Lady Immaculate; to trample under foot and spit upon all holy images, the Cross and Relics of Saints; never to use the Sacraments or Sacramentals unless with some magical end in view; never to make a good confession to the priest, but always to keep hidden their commerce with hell. In return the Demon promises that he will at all times afford them prompt assistance; that he will accomplish all their desires in this world and make them eternally happy after their death. This solemn profession having been publicly made each novice has assigned to him a several demon who is called *Magistellus* (a familiar). This familiar can assume either a male or a female shape; sometimes he appears as a full-grown man, sometimes as a satyr; and if it is a woman who has been received as a witch he generally assumes the form of a rank buck-goat.

It is obvious that there is no question here of animal familiars, but rather of evil intelligences who were, it is believed, able to assume a body of flesh. The whole question is, perhaps, one of the most dark and difficult connected with Witchcraft and magic, and the details of these hideous connexions are such—for as the Saints attain to the purity of angels, so, on the other hand, will the bond slaves of Satan defile themselves with every kind of lewdness—that many writers have with an undue diffidence and modesty dismissed the subject far too summarily for the satisfaction of the serious inquirer. In the first place, we may freely allow that many of these lubricities are to be ascribed to hysteria and hallucinations, to nightmare and the imaginings of disease, but when all deductions have been made—when we admit that in many cases the incubus or succubus can but have been a human being, some agent of the Grand Master of the district,—none the less enough remains from the records of the trials to convince an unprejudiced mind that there was a considerable substratum of fact in the confessions of the accused. As Canon Ribet has said in his encyclopædic *La Mystique Divine*, a work warmly approved by the great intellect of Leo XIII: "After what we have learned from records and personal confessions we can scarcely entertain any more doubts, and it is our plain duty to oppose, even if it be but by a simple affirmation on our part, those numerous writers who, either through presumption or rashness, treat these horrors as idle talk or mere hallucination."[29] Bizouard also in his authoritative *Rapports de l'homme avec le démon* writes of the incubus and succubus: "These relations, far from being untrue, bear the strongest marks of authenticity which can be given them by official proceedings regulated and approved with all the caution and judgement brought to bear upon them by enlightened and conscientious magistrates who, throughout all ages, have been in a position to test plain facts."[30]

It seems to me that if unshaken evidence means anything at all, if the authority of the ablest and acutest intellects of all ages in all countries is not to count for merest vapourings and fairy fantasies, the possibility—I do not, thank God, say the frequency—of these demoniacal connexions is not to be denied. Of course the mind already resolved that such things cannot be is inconvincible even by demonstration, and one can only fall back upon the sentence of S. Augustine: "Hanc assidue immunditiam et tentare et efficere, plures talesque asseuerant, ut hoc negare impudentiæ uideatur."[31] In which place the holy doctor explicitly declares: "Seeing it is so general a report, and so many aver it either from their own experience or from others, that are of indubitable honesty and credit, that the sylvans and fawns, commonly called incubi, have often injured women, desiring and acting carnally with them: and that certain devils whom the Gauls call *Duses*, do continually practise this uncleanness, and tempt others to it, which is affirmed by such persons, and with such confidence that it were impudence to deny it."

The learned William of Paris, confessor of Philip le Bel, lays down: "That there exist such beings as are commonly called incubi or succubi and that they indulge their burning lusts, and that children, as it is freely acknowledged, can be born from them, is attested by the unimpeachable and unshaken witness of many men and women who have been filled with foul imaginings by them, and endured their lecherous assaults and lewdness."[32]

S. Thomas[33] and S. Bonaventura,[34] also, speak quite plainly on the subject.

Francisco Suarez, the famous Jesuit theologian, writes with caution but with directness: "This is the teaching on this point of S. Thomas, who is generally followed by all other theologians. . . . The reason for their opinion is this: Such an action considered in its entirety by no means exceeds the natural powers of the demon, whilst the exercise of such powers is wholly in accordance with the malice of the demon, and it may well be permitted by God, owing to the sins of some men. Therefore this teaching cannot be denied without many reservations and exceptions. Wherefore S. Augustine has truly said, that inasmuch as this doctrine of incubi and succubi is established by the opinion of many who are experienced and learned, it were sheer impudence to deny it."[35] The Salmanticenses—that is to say, the authors of the courses of Scholastic philosophy and theology, and of Moral theology, published by the lecturers of the theological college of the Discalced Carmelites at Salamanca—in their weighty *Theologia Moralis*[36] state: "Some deny this, believing it impossible that demons should perform the carnal act with human beings," but they affirm, "None the less the opposite opinion is most certain and must be followed."[37] Charles René Billuart, the celebrated Dominican, in his *Tractatus de Angelis* expressly declares: "The same evil spirit may serve as a succubus to a man, and as an incubus to a woman."[38] One of the most learned—if not the most learned—of the popes, Benedict XIV, in his erudite work *De Seruorum Dei Beatificatione*, treats this whole question at considerable length with amplest detail and solid references, Liber IV, Pars i. c. 3.[39] Commenting upon the passage "The sons of God went unto the daughters of men" (Genesis vi. 4), the pontiff writes: "This passage has reference to those Demons who are known as incubi and succubi. . . . It is true that whilst nearly all authors admit the fact, some writers deny that there can be offspring. . . . On the other hand, several writers assert that connexion of this kind is possible and that children may be born from it, nay, indeed, they tell us that this has taken place, although it were done in some new and mysterious way which is ordinarily unknown to man."[40]

S. Alphonsus Liguori in his *Praxis confessariorum*, VII, n.111, writes: "Some deny that there are evil spirits, incubi and succubi; but writers of authority for the most part assert that such is the case."[41]

In his *Theologia Moralis* he speaks quite precisely when defining the technical nature of the sin witches commit in commerce with incubi.[42] [43] This opinion is also that of Martino Bonacina,[44] and of Vincenzo Filliucci, S.J.[45] "Busembaum has excellently observed that carnal sins with an evil spirit fall under the head of the technical term *bestialitas*."[46] This is also the conclusion of Thomas Tamburini, S.J. (1591–1675); Benjamin Elbel, O.F.M. (1690–1756);[47] Cardinal Cajetan, O.P. (1469–1534) "the lamp of the Church"; Juan Azor, S.J. (1535–1603); "in wisdom, in depth of learning and in gravity of judgement taking deservedly high rank among theologians" (Gury); and many other authorities.[48] What a penitent should say in confession is considered by Monsignor Craisson, sometime Rector of the Grand Seminary of Valence and Vicar-General of the diocese, in his Tractate *De Rebus Uenereis ad usum Confessariorum.*[49] Jean-Baptiste Bouvier (1783–1854) the famous bishop of Le Mans, in his *Dissertatio in Sextum Decalogi Præceptum*[50] (p. 78) writes: "All theologians speak of . . . evil spirits who appear in the shape of a man, a woman, or even some animal. This is either a real and actual presence, or the effect of imagination. They decide that this sin . . . incurs particular guilt which must be specifically confessed, to wit an evil superstition whereof the essence is a compact with the Devil. In this sin, therefore, we have two distinct kinds of malice, one an offence against chastity; the other against our holy faith."[51] Dom Dominic Schram,[52] O.S.B., in his *Institutiones Theologiæ Mysticæ* poses the following: "The inquiry is made whether a demon . . . may thus attack a man or woman, whose obsession would be suffered if the subject were wholly bent upon obtaining perfection and walking the highest paths of contemplation. Here we must distinguish the true and the false. It is certain that—whatever doubters may say—there exist such demons, incubi and succubi: and S. Augustine asserts (*The City of God*, Book XV, chapter 23) that it is most rash to advance the contrary. . . . S. Thomas, and most other theologians maintain this too. Wherefore the men or women who suffer these impudicities are sinners who either invite demons . . . or who freely consent to demons when the evil spirits tempt them to commit such abominations. That these and other abandoned wretches may be violently assaulted by the demon we cannot doubt . . . and I myself have known several persons who although they were greatly troubled on account of their crimes, and utterly loathed this foul intercourse with the demon, were nevertheless compelled sorely against their will to endure these assaults of Satan."[53]

It will be seen that great Saints and scholars and all moral theologians of importance affirm the possibility of commerce with incarnate evil intelligences. The demonologists also range themselves in a solid phalanx of assent. Hermann Thyraus, S.J.,[54] in his *De Spirituum apparitione* says: "It is so rash and inept to deny these (things) that so to adopt this attitude you must needs reject and spurn the most weighty and considered judgements of most holy and authoritative writers, nay, you must wage war upon man's sense and consciousness, whilst at the same time you expose your ignorance of the power of the Devil and the empery evil spirits may obtain over man."[55] Delrio, in his *Dis-*

quisitiones Magicæ, is even more emphatic: "So many sound authors and divines have upheld this belief that to differ from them is mere obstinacy and foolhardiness; for the Fathers, theologians, and all the wisest writers on philosophy agree upon this matter, the truth of which is furthermore proved by the experience of all ages and peoples."[56] The erudite Sprenger in the *Malleus Maleficarum* has much the same.[57] John Nider, O.P. (1380–1438) in his *Formicarius*, which may be described as a treatise on the theological, philosophical, and social problems of his day, with no small acumen remarks: "The reason why evil spirits appear as incubi and succubi would seem to be that . . . they inflict a double hurt on man, both in his soul and body, and it is a supreme joy to devils thus to injure humankind."[58] Paul Grilland in his *De Sortilegio* (Lyons, 1533) writes: "A demon assumes the form of the succubus. . . . This is the explicit teaching of the theologians."[59]

"It has often been known by most certain and actual experience that women in spite of their resistance have been overpowered by demons." Such are the words of the famous Alfonso de Castro, O.F.M.,[60] whose authoritative pronouncements upon Scripture carried such weight at the Council of Trent, and who was Archbishop-elect of Compostella when he died. Pierre Binsfeld, *De confessione maleficarum*, sums up: "This is a most solemn and undoubted fact not only proved by actual experience, but also by the opinion of all the ages, whatever some few doctors and legal writers may suppose."[61]

Gaspar Schott, S.J. (1608–66), physicist, doctor, and divine, "one of the most learned men of his day, his simple life and deep piety making him an object of veneration to the Protestants as well as to the Catholics of Augsburg," where his declining years were spent, lays down: "So many writers of such high authority maintain this opinion, that it were impossible to reject it."[62] Bodin, de Lancre, Boguet, Görres, Bizouard,[63] Gougenot des Mousseaux,[64] insist upon the same sad facts. And above all sounds the solemn thunder of the Bull of Innocent VIII announcing in no ambiguous phrase: "It has indeed come to our knowledge and deeply grieved are we to hear it, that many persons of both sexes, utterly forgetful of their souls' salvation and straying far from the Catholic Faith, have (had commerce) with evil spirits, both incubi and succubi."[65]

I have quoted many and great names, men of science, men of learning, men of authority, men to whom the world yet looks up with admiration, nay, with reverence and love, inasmuch as to-day it is difficult, wellnigh inconceivable in most cases, for the modern mind to credit the possibility of these dark deeds of devilry, these foul lusts of incubi and succubi.[66] They seem to be some sick and loathly fantasy of dim mediæval days shrieked out on the rack by a poor wretch crazed with agony and fear, and written down in long-forgotten tomes by fanatics credulous to childishness and more ignorant than savages. "Even if such horrors ever could have taken place in the dark ages,"—those vague Dark Ages!—men say, "they would never be permitted now." And he who knows, the priest sitting in the grated confessional, in whose ears are poured for shriving the filth and folly of the world, sighs to himself, "Would God that in truth it were so!" But the sceptics are happier in their singleness and their simplicity, happy that they do not, will not, realize the monstrous things that lie only just beneath the surface of our cracking civilization.

It may not impertinently be inquired how demons or evil intelligences, since they are pure spiritual beings, can not only assume human flesh but perform the peculiarly carnal act of coition. Sinistrari, following the opinion of Guazzo, says that either the evil intelligence is able to animate the corpse of some human being, male or female, as the case may be, or that, from the mixture of other materials he shapes for himself a body endowed with motion, by means of which he is united to the human being: "ex mixtione aliarum materiarum effingit sibi corpus, quod mouet, et mediante quo homini unitur."[67] In the first instance, advantage might be taken, no doubt, of a person in a mediumistic trance or hypnotic sleep. But the second explanation seems by far the more probable. Can we not look to the phenomena observed in connexion with ectoplasm as an adequate explanation of this? It must fairly be admitted that this explanation is certainly borne out by the phenomena of the materializing séance where physical forms which may be touched and handled are built up and disintegrated again in a few moments of time. Miss Scatcherd, in a symposium, *Survival*,[68] gives certain of her own experiences that go far to prove the partial re-materialization of the dead by the utilization of the material substance and ectoplasmic emanations of the living. And if disembodied spirits can upon occasion, however rare, thus materialize, why not evil intelligences whose efforts at corporeality are urged and aided by the longing thoughts and concentrated will power of those who eagerly seek them ?

This explanation is further rendered the more probable by the recorded fact that the incubus can assume the shape of some person whose embraces the witch may desire.[69] Brignoli, in his *Alexicacon*, relates that when he was at Bergamo in 1650, a young man, twenty-two years of age, sought him out and made a long and ample confession. This youth avowed that some months before, when he was in bed, the chamber door opened and a maiden, Teresa, whom he loved, stealthily entered the room. To his surprise she informed him that she had been driven from home and had taken refuge with him. Although he more than suspected some delusion, after a short while he consented to her solicitations and passed a night of unbounded indulgence in her arms. Before dawn, however, the visitant revealed the true nature of the deceit, and the young man realized he had lain with a succubus. None the less such was his doting folly that the same debauchery was repeated night after night, until struck with terror and remorse, he sought the priest to confess and be delivered from this abomination. "This monstrous connexion lasted several months; but at last God delivered him by my humble means, and he was truly penitent for his sins."[70]

Not infrequently the Devil or the familiar assigned to the new witch at the Sabbat when she was admitted must obviously have been a man, one of the assembly, who either approached her in some demoniacal disguise or else embraced her without any attempt at concealment of his individuality, some lusty varlet who would afterwards hold himself at her disposition. For we must always bear in mind that throughout these witch-trials there is often much in the evidence which may be explained by the agency of human beings; not that this essentially meliorates their offences, for they were all bond-slaves of Satan, acting under his direction and by the inspiration of hell. When the fiend has ministers devoted to his service there is, perhaps, less need for his interposition *in propria persona.* Howbeit, again and again in these cases we meet with that uncanny quota, by no means insignificant and unimportant, which seemingly admits of no solution save by the materialization of evil intelligences of power. And detailed as is the evidence we possess, it not unseldom becomes a matter of great difficulty, when we are considering a particular case, to decide whether it be an instance of a witch having had actual commerce and communion with the fiend, or whether she was cheated by the devils, who mocked her, and allowing her to deem herself in overt union with them, thus led the wretch on to misery and death, duped as she was by the father of lies, sold for a delusion and by profitless endeavour in evil. There are, of course, also many cases which stand on the border-line, half hallucination, half reality. Sylvine de la Plaine, a witch of twenty-three, who was condemned by the Parliament of Paris, 17 May, 1616, was one of these.[71] Antoinette Brenichon, a married woman, aged thirty, made a confession in almost exactly the same words. Sylvine, her husband Barthélemi Minguet, and Brenichon were hanged and their bodies burned.

Henri Boguet, a Judge of the High Court of Burgundy, in his *Discours des Sorciers*, devotes chapter xii to "The carnal connexion of the Demons with Witches and Sorcerers." He discusses: 1. The Devil knows all the Witches, & why. 2. He takes a female shape to pleasure the Sorcerers, & why. 3. Other reasons why the Devil (has to do) with warlocks and witches.[72] Françoise Secretain, Clauda Ianprost, Iaquema Paget, Antoine Tornier, Antoine Gandillon, Clauda Ianguillaume, Thieuenne Paget, Rolande du Vernois, Ianne Platet, Clauda Paget, and a number of other witches confessed "their dealings with the Devil."[73] Pierre Gandillon and his son George also confessed to commerce with the Demon. Under his third division Boguet lays down explicit statements on the matter.[74] [75]

This unnatural physical coldness of the Demon is commented upon again and again by witches at their trials in every country of Europe throughout the centuries. I have already suggested that in some cases there was a full materialization due to ectoplasmic emanations. Now, ectoplasm is described[76] as being to the touch a cold and viscous mass comparable to contact with a reptile, and this certainly seems to throw a flood of light upon these details. It may be that here indeed we have a solution of the whole mystery. In 1645 the widow Bash, a Suffolk witch, of Barton, said that the Devil who appeared to her as a dark swarthy youth "was colder than man."[77] Isobel Goudie and Janet Breadheid, of the Auldearne coven, 1662, both asserted that the Devil was "a meikle, blak, rock man, werie cold; and I fand his nature als cold, a spring-well-water."[78] Isabel, who had been rebaptized at a Sabbat held one midnight in Auldearne parish church, and to whom was assigned a familiar named the Red Riever, albeit he was always clad in black, gave further details of the Devil's person: "He is abler for ws that way than any man can be, onlie he ves heavie lyk a malt-sek; a hudg nature, uerie cold, as yce."[79]

In many of the cases of debauchery at Sabbats so freely and fully confessed by the witches their partners were undoubtedly the males who were present; the Grand Master, Officer, or President of the Assembly, exercising the right to select first for his own pleasures such women as he chose. This is clear from a passage in De Lancre: "The Devil at the Sabbat performs marriages between the warlocks and witches, and joining their hands, he pronounces aloud

Esta es buena parati
Esta parati lo toma."[80]

And in many cases it is obvious that use must have been made of an instrument, an artificial phallus employed.[81]

The artificial penis was a commonplace among the erotica of ancient civilizations; there is abundant evidence of its use in Egypt, Assyria, India, Mexico, all over the world. It has been found in tombs; frequently was it to be seen as an ex-voto; in a slightly modified form it is yet the favourite mascot of Southern Italy.[82] Often enough they do not trouble to disguise the form. Aristophanes mentions the object in his *Lysistrata* (411 B.C.), and one of the most spirited dialogues (VI) of Herodas (*circa* 300–250 B.C.) is that where Koritto and Metro prattle prettily of their *βαύβων*, whilst (in another mime, VII) the ladies visit Kerdon the leather-worker who has fashioned this masterpiece. Truly Herodas is as modern to-day in London or in Paris as he ever was those centuries ago in the isle of Cos. *Fascinum*, explains the *Glossarium Eroticum Linguæ Latinæ*,[83] "Penis fictitius ex corio, aut pannis lineis uel sericis, quibus mulieres uirum mentiebantur. Antiquissima libido, lesbiis et milesiis feminis præsertim usitatissima. *Fascinis* illis abutebantur meretrices in tardos ascensores." As one might expect Petronius has something to say on the subject in a famous passage where that savage old hag[84] Œnothea fairly frightened Encolpius with her *scorteum fascinum*, upon which an erudite Spanish scholar, Don Antonio Gonzalez de Salas, glosses: "Rubrum penem coriaceum ut Suidas exsertim tradit uoce φαλλόι. Confecti & ex uaria materia uarios in usus olim *phalli* ex ligno, *ficu* potissimum qui *ficulnei* sæpius adpellati, ex *ebore*, ex *auro*, ex *serico*, & ex *lineo panno*, quibus Lesbiæ tribades abutebantur."[85] And Tibullus, speaking of the image of Priapus, has:[86]

Placet Priape? qui sub arboris coma
Soles sacrum reuincte pampino caput
Ruber sedere cum rubente fascino.

The Church, of course, condemned with unhesitating voice all such practices, whether they were connected (in however slight a degree) with Witchcraft or not. Arnobius, who regards all such offences as detestable, in his *Aduersus Nationes*, V (*circa* A.D. 296), relates a curiously obscene anecdote which seems to point to the use of the fascinum by the Galli, the priests of Berecynthian Cybele,[87] whose orgies were closely akin to those of Dionysus. And the same story is related by Clement of Alexandria Προτρεπτικὸς πρὸς Ἕλληνας (*circa* A.D. 190); by Julius Firmicus Maternus, *De Errore profanarum Religionum* (A.D. 337–350); by Nicetas (*ob. circa* A.D. 414) in a commentary on S. Gregory of Nanzianzus, oratio XXXIX; and by Theodoret (*ob. circa* A.D. 457) *Sermo octaua de Martyribus*. Obviously some very primitive rite is in question.

Lactantius, in his *De Falsa Religione* (*Diuinarum Institutionum*, I, *circa* A.D. 304), speaks of a phallic superstition, akin to the fascinum, as favoured by the vestals, and implies it was notoriously current in his day. That eminent father, S. Augustine, *De Ciuitate Dei*, VII, 21, gives some account of the fascinum as used in the rites of Bacchus, and when he is detailing the marriage ceremonies (VI, 9), he writes: " Sed quid hoc dicam, cum tibi sit et Priapus nimius masculus, super cuius immanissimum et turpissimum fascinum sedere nona nupta iubeatur, more honestissimo et religiosissimo matronarum." The historian, Evagrius Scholasticus (*ob.* post A.D. 504), in his *Historia Ecclesiastica* (XI, 2), says that the ritual of Priapus was quite open in his day, and the fascinum widely known. Nicephorus Calixtus, a later Byzantine, who died about the middle of the fourteenth century but whose Chronicle closed with the death of Leo Philosophus, A.D. 911, speaks of phallic ceremonies and of the use of ithy-phalli.[88]

Council after council forbade the use of the fascinum, and their very insistence of prohibition show how deeply these abominations had taken root. The Second Council of Châlon-sur-Saône (813) is quite plain and unequivocal; so are the synods of de Mano (1247) and Tours (1396). Burchard of Worms (died 25 Aug., 1025) in his famous *Decretum* has: " Fecisti quod quædam mulieres facere solent, ut facere quoddam molimen aut mechinamentum in modum uirilis membri, ad mensuram tuæ uoluptatis, et illud loco uerendorum tuorum, aut alterius, cum aliquibus ligaturis colligares, et fornicationem faceres cum aliis mulierculis, uel aliæ eodem instrumento, siue alio, tecum? Si fecisti, quinque annos per legitimas ferias pœniteas." And again: " Fecisti quod quædam mulieres facere solent, ut iam supra dicto molimine uel alio aliquo machinamento, tu ipsa in te solam faceres fornicationem? Si fecisti, unum annum per legitimas ferias pœniteas."

Other old Penitentials have: " Mulier qualicumque molimine aut per seipsum aut cum altera fornicans, tres annos pœniteat; unum ex his in pane et aqua."

" Cum sanctimoniali per machinam fornicans annos septem pœniteat; duos ex his in pane et aqua."

"Mulia qualicumque molimine aut seipsam polluens, aut cum altera fornicans, quatuor annos. Sanctimonialis femina cum sanctimoniali per machinamentum polluta, septem annos."

It is demonstrable, then, that artificial methods of coition, common in pagan antiquity, have been unblushingly practised throughout all the ages, as indeed they are at the present day, and that they have been repeatedly banned and reprobated by the voice of the Church. This very fact would recommend them to the favour of the Satanists, and there can be no doubt that amid the dark debaucheries which celebrated the Sabbats such practice was wellnigh universal. Yet when we sift the evidence, detailed and exact, of the trials, we find there foul and hideous mysteries of lust which neither human intercourse nor the employ of a mechanical property can explain. Howbeit, the theologians and the inquisitors are fully aware what unspeakable horror lurks in the blackness beyond.

The animal familiar was quite distinct from the familiar in human shape. In England particularly there is abundance of evidence concerning them, and even to-day who pictures a witch with nut-cracker jaws, steeple hat, red cloak, hobbling along on her crutch, without her big black cat beside her? It is worth remark that in other countries the domestic animal familiar is rare, and Bishop Francis Hutchinson even says: "I meet with little mention of *Imps* in any Country but ours, where the Law makes the feeding, suckling, or rewarding of them to be Felony."[89] Curiously enough this familiar is most frequently met with in Essex, Suffolk, and the Eastern counties. We find that animals of all kinds were regarded as familiars; dogs, cats, ferrets, weasels, toads, rats, mice, birds, hedgehogs, hares, even wasps, moths, bees, and flies. It is piteous to think that in many cases some miserable creature who, shunned and detested by her fellows, has sought friendship in the love of a cat or a dog, whom she has fondled and lovingly fed with the best tit-bits she could give, on the strength of this affection alone was dragged to the gallows or the stake. But very frequently the witch did actually keep some small animal which she nourished on a diet of milk and bread and her own blood in order that she might divine by its means. The details of this particular method of augury are by no means clear. Probably the witch observed the gait of the animals, its action, the tones of its voice easily interpreted to bear some fanciful meaning, and no doubt a dog, or such a bird as a raven, a daw, could be taught tricks to impress the simplicity of inquirers.

The exceeding importance of blood in life has doubtless been evident to man from the earliest times. Man experienced a feeling of weakness after the loss of blood, therefore blood was strength, life itself, and throughout the ages blood has been considered to be of the greatest therapeutic, and the profoundest magical, value. The few drops of blood the witch gave her familiar were not only a reward, a renewal of strength, but also they established a closer connexion between herself and the dog, cat, or bird as the case might be. Blood formed a psychic copula.

At the trial of Elizabeth Francis, Chelmsford, 1556, the accused confessed that her familiar, given to her by her grandmother, a notorious witch, was "in the lykenesse of a whyte spotted Catte," and her grandmother "taughte her to feede the sayde Catte with breade and mylke, and she did so, also she taughte her to cal it by the name of Sattan and to kepe it in a basket. Item that euery tyme that he did any thynge for her, she sayde that he required a drop of bloude, which she gaue him by prycking herselfe, sometime in one place and then in another."[90] It is superfluous to multiply instances; in the witch-trials of Essex, particularly whilst Matthew Hopkins and his satellite John Stearne were hot at work from 1645 to 1647 the animal familiar is mentioned again and again in the records. As late as 1694 at Bury St. Edmunds, when old Mother Munnings of Hartis, in Suffolk, was haled before Lord Chief Justice Holt, it was asserted that she had an imp like a polecat. But the judge pooh-poohed the evidence of a pack of clodpate rustics and directed the jury to bring a verdict of Not Guilty.[91] "Upon particular Enquiry," says Hutchinson, "of several in or near the Town, I find most are satisfied it was a very right Judgement." In 1712 the familiar of Jane Wenham, the witch of Walkerne, in Hertfordshire, was, at her trial, stated to be a cat.

In Ford and Dekker's *The Witch of Edmonton* the familiar appears upon the stage as a dog. This, of course, is directly taken from Henry Goodcole's pamphlet *The Wonderfull Discouerie of Elizabeth Sawyer* (London, 4to, 1621), where in answer to this question the witch confesses that the Devil came to her in the shape of a dog, and of two colours, sometimes of black and sometimes of white. Some children had informed the Court that they had seen her feeding imps, two white ferrets, with white bread and milk, but this she steadfastly denied. In Goethe's *Faust*, Part I, Scene 2, Mephistopheles first appears to Faust outside the city gates as a black poodle and accompanies him back to his study, snarling and yelping when *In Principio* is read. This is part of the old legend. Manlius (1590), in the report of his conversation with Melanchthon, quotes the latter as having said: "He [Faust] had a dog with him, which was the devil." Paolo Jovio relates[92] that the famous Cornelius Agrippa always kept a demon attendant upon him in the shape of a black dog. But John Weye, in his well-known work *De Præstigiis Dæmonum*,[93] informs us that he had lived for years in daily attendance upon Agrippa and that the black dog, *Monsieur*, respecting which such strange stories were spread was a perfectly innocent animal which he had often led about himself in its leash. Agrippa was much attached to his dog, which used to eat off the table with him and of nights lie in his bed. Since he was a profound scholar and a great recluse he never troubled to contradict the idle gossip his neighbours clacked at window and door. It is hardly surprising when one considers the hermetic works which go under Agrippa's name that even in his lifetime this great man should have acquired the reputation of a mighty magician.

Grotesque names were generally given to the familiar: Lizabet; Verd-Joli; Maître Persil (parsley); Verdelet; Martinet; Abrahel (a succubus); and to animal familiars in England, Tissy; Grissell; Greedigut; Blackman; Jezebel (a succubus); Ilemanzar; Jarmara; Pyewackett.

The familiar in human shape often companied with the witch and was visible to clairvoyants. Thus in 1324 one of the accusations brought against Lady Alice Kyteler was that a demon came to her "quandoque in specie cuiusdam æthiopis cum duobus sociis." The society met with at Sabbats is not so easily shaken off as might be wished.

NOTES TO CHAPTER III.

[1] Two local Milanese Orders, the Apostolini of S. Barnabas and the Congregation of S. Ambrose *ad Nemus*, were united by a Brief of Sixtus V, 15 August, 1589. 11 January, 1606, Paul V approved the new Constitutions. The Congregation retaining very few members was dissolved by Innocent X in 1650. The habit was a tunic, broad scapular, and capuche of chestnut brown,

They were calced, and in the streets a wide cloak of the same colour as the habit.

[2] E. Goldsmid, *Confessions of Witches under Torture*, Edinburgh, 1886.

[3] . . . renoncer & renier son Createur, la saincte Vierge, les Saincts, le Baptesme, pere, mere, parens, le ciel, la terre & tout ce qui est au monde. *Tableau de l'Inconstance des mauvais Anges*, Paris, 1613.

[4] Je, Louis Gaufridi, renonce à tous les biens tant spirituels que temporels qui me pouvraient être conferés de la part de Dieu, de la Vierge Marie, de tous les Saints et Saintes du Paradis, particulièrement de mon patron Saint Jean-Baptiste, Saints Pierre, Paul, et François, et me donne corps et âme à vous Lucifer ici présent, avec tous les biens que je posséderai jamais (excepté la valeur des sacrements pour le regard de ceux qui les recurent). Ainsi j'ai signé et attesté. *Confession faicte par messire Loys Gaufridi, prestre en l'église des Accoules de Marseille, prince des magiciens . . à deux pères capucins du couvent d'Aix, la veille de Pasques le onzième avril mil six cent onze.* A Aix, par Jean Tholozan, MVCXI.

[5] Je renonce entièrement de tout mon cœur, de toute ma force, et de toute ma puissance à Dieu le Père, au Fils et au Saint-Esprit, à la très Sainte Mère de Dieu, à tous les anges et spécialement à mon bon ange, à la passion de Notre Seigneur Jésus Christ, à Son Sang, à tous les mérites d'icelle, à ma part de Paradis, à toutes les inspirations que Dieu me pourrait donner à l'avenir, à toutes les prières qu'on a faites et pourrait faire pour moi.

[6] S. Pius V, Bull *Consueuerunt*, 17 September, 1569: Bl. Francisco de Possadas, *Vida di Santo Domingo*, Madrid, 1721.

[7] In England at this date it was felony to possess an *Agnus Dei.*

[8] *Spondent quod . . . ad conuentus nocturnos diligenter accedent.*

[9] Coven, coeven, covine, curving, covey, are among the many spellings of this word.

[10] R. Pitcairn, *Criminal Trials*, Edinburgh, 1833.

[11] *Examination of Certain Witches*, Philobiblion Society, London, 1863–4.

[12] Thomas Potts, *Discoverie of Witches.*

[13] . . . qu'elle a veu souuent baptiser des enfans au sabbat, qu'elle nous expliqua estre des enfans des sorcieres & non autres, lesquelles ont accoutumé faire plustost baptiser leurs enfans au sabbat qu'en l'église. Pierre de Lancre, *Tableau de l'Inconstance des mauvais Anges*, Paris, 1613.

[14] . . . qu'on baptise des enfans au Sabbat auec du Cresme, que des femmes apportent, & frottent la verge de quelque homme, & en font sortir de la semence qu'elles amassent, and la meslent auec le Cresme, puis mettant cela sur la teste de l'enfant en prononçant quelques paroles en Latin. Contemporary tract, *Arrest & procedure faicte par le Lieutenant Criminel d'Orleans contre Siluain Neuillon.*

[15] . . . dit que sa mère le presenta (dit-on) en l'aage de trois ans au Sabbat, à vn bouc, qu'on appelloit l'Aspic. Dit qu'il fut baptisé au Sabbat, au Carrior d'Oliuet, auec quatorze ou quinze autres, & que Jeanne Geraut porta du Chresme qui estoit jaune dans vn pot, & que ledit Neuillon ietta de la sèmence dans ledit pot, & vn nommé Semelle, & brouilloient cela auec vne petite cuilliere de bois, & puis leur en mirent à tous sur la teste.

[16] J'advoue comme on baptise au Sabath et comme chacun sorcier fait vœu particulièrement se donnant au diable et faire baptiser tous ses enfants au Sabath (si faire se peut). Comme aussi l'on impose des noms à chacun de ceux qui sont au Sabath, différents de leur propre nom. J'advoue comme au baptême on se sert de l'eau, du soufre et du sel: le soufre rend esclave le diable et le sel pour confirmer le baptême au service du diable. J'advoue comme la forme et l'intention est de baptiser au nom de Lucifer, de Belzebuth et autres diables faisant le signe de la croix en le commençant par le travers et puis le poursuivant par les pieds et finissant à la tête. Contemporary tract, *Confession faicte par messire Loys Gaufridi, prestre en l'église des Accoules de Marseille, prince des magiciens*, MVCXI.

[17] Anthony Hornech's appendix to Glanvill's *Sadducismus Triumphatus*, London, 1681.

[18] *Newes from Scotland*, London, W. Wright, 1592.

[19] Præstant Dæmoni . . . iuramentum super circulo in terram sculpto fortasse quia cum circulus sit Symbolum Divinitatis, & terra scabellum Dei sic certe uellet eos credere se esse Dominum cœli & terræ. Guazzo, *Compendium*, I. 7, p. 38. I have corrected the text, which runs "uellet eos credere eum esset . . ."

[20] Even by so industrious a searcher as Miss M. A. Murray.

[21] Dressant quelque forme d'autel sur des coloñes infernales, & sur iceluy sans dire le *Confiteor*, ny l'*Alleluya*, tournant les feuillets d'vn certain liure qu'il a en main, il commence à marmoter quelques mots de la Messe. De Lancre, *Tableau*, p. 401.

[22] . . . que le Sabbat se tenoit dans vne maison . . . Vit aussi vn grand homme noir à l'opposite de celuy de la cheminée, qui regardoit dans vn liure, dont les feuillets estoient noirs & bleuds, & marmotait entre ses dents sans entendre ce qu'il disoit, leuoit vne hostie noire, puis vn calice de meschant estain tout crasseux.

[23] On dit la Messe, & que c'est le Diable qui la dit, qu'il a vne Chasuble qui a vne croix : mais qu'elle n'a que trois barres : & tourne le dos à l'Autel quand il veut leuer l'Hostie & le Calice, qui sont noirs, & marmote dans vn liure, duquel le couuerture est toute velue comme d'vne peau de loup, auec des feuillets blancs & rouges, d'autres noirs.

[24] On lisait la messe dans le livre des blasphèmes, qui servait de canon et qu'on employait aussi dans les processions. Il renfermait les plus horribles malédictions contre la sainte Trinité, le Saint Sacrement de l'autel, les autres sacrements et les cérémonies de l'Eglise, et il était écrit dans une langue qui m'était inconnue. Görres, *La Mystique Divine*, trad., Charles Sainte-Foi, V. p. 230. There is a critical recension of *Die christliche Mystik* by Boretius and Krause, Hanover, 1893–7.

[25] *Newes from Scotland*, London, W. Wright (1592).

[26] Book III. p. 42.

[27] T. B. Howell, *State Trials*, London, 1816. IV, 844, 846.

[28] S. Caleb, *Les Messes Noires*, Paris, s.d.

[29] Après ce que nous ont appris les livres et les âmes, il ne nous est pas permis de douter, et notre devoir est de combattre, ne fût-ce que par un simple affirmation, les nombreux auteurs qui, effrontément ou témérairement, traitent ces horreurs de fables ou d'hallucinations. *La Mystique Divine*, nouvelle édition, Paris, 1902. III, pp. 269, 270.

[30] Ces histoires, loin d'être fabuleuses, ont toute l'authenticité que peut leur donner une procédure instruite avec tout le zèle et le talent que pouvaient y apporter des magistrats éclairés et consciencieux, auxquels, à toutes les époques, les faits ne manquaient pas. Libre III. c. 8.

[31] *De Ciuitate Dei*, xv. 23. I quote Healey's translation, 1610.

[32] Esse eorum (qui usualiter incubi uel succubi nominantur) et concupiscentiam eorum libidinosam, necnon et generationem ab eis esse famosam atque credibilem fecerunt testimonia uirorum et mulierem qui illusiones ipsorum, molestiasque et improbitates, necnon et uiolentias libidinis ipsorum, se passos fuisse testificati sunt et adhuc asserunt. *De Universitate*, Secunda Pars, III. 25.

[33] Si tamen ex coitu dæmonum aliqui interdum nascuntur, hoc non est per semen ab eis decisum, aut a corporibus assumptis; sed per semen alicuius hominis ad hoc acceptum, utpote quod idem dæmon qui est succubus ad uirum, fiat incubus ad mulierem. *Summa*, Pars Prima, quæstio 1, a 3. at 6.

[34] Succumbunt uiris in specie mulieris, et ex eis semen pollutionis suscipiunt, et quadam sagacitate ipsum in sua uirtute custodiunt, et postmodum, Deo permittente, fiunt incubi et in uasa mulierum transfundunt. *Sententiarum*, Liber II, d. viii, Pars Prima, a 3. q. 1.

[35] Docet S. Thomas . . . et consentiunt communiter reliqui theologi. . . . Ratio huius sententiæ est quia tota illa actio non excedit potestatem naturalem dæmonis, usus autem talis potestatis est ualde conformis prauæ uoluntati dæmonis, et iuste a Deo permitti potest propter aliquorum hominum peccata. Ergo non potest cum fundamento negari, et ideo non immerito dixit Augustinus, cum de illo usu multis experientiis et testimoniis constet, non sine impudentia negari. *De Angelis*, l. iv. c. 38. nn. 10, 11.

[36] Begun in 1665 by Fra Francisco de Jésus-Maria (*ob.* 1677).

[37] Negant aliqui, credentes impossible esse quod dæmones actum carnalem cum hominibus exercere ualent. Sed tenenda est ut omnino certa contraria sententia. *Theologia moralis*, Tr. xxi. c. 11. p. 10. nn. 180, 181.

[38] Idem dæmon qui est succubus ad uirum potest fieri incubus ad mulierem. In his monumental *Summa S. Thomæ hodiernis Academiarum moribus accommodata*, 19 vols. Liège, 1746–51.

[39] *De Seruonem Dei Beatificatione*, Romæ, MDCCXC, Cura Aloysii Salvioni. Tom. VII. pp. 30–33.

[40] Quæ leguntur de Dæmonibus incubis et succubis. . . . Quamuis enim prædicti concubitus communiter admittantur, sed generatis a nonnullis excludetur . . . alii, tamen, tum concubitum, tum generationem fieri posse, et factam fuisse existimauerunt, modo quodam nouo et inusitate, et hominibus incognito. Sancho de Avila, bishop of Murcia, Jaen, and Siguenza, S. Teresa's confessor (*ob.* December, 1625), in a commentary on Exodus discusses the curious question : *An Angeli de se generare possint ?*

[41] Quidam hos dæmones incubos uel succubos dari negarunt ; sed communiter id affirmant auctores.

[42] Ad bestialitatem autem reuocatur peccatum cum dæmone succubo, uel incubo ; cui peccato superadditur malitia contra religionem ; et præterea etiam sodomiæ, adulterii, uel incestus, si affectu uiri, uel mulieris, sodomitico, adulterino uel incestuoso cum dæmone coeat. Lib. III, Tract iv. c. 2. Dubium 3.

[43] The word *bestialitas* has theologically a far wider signification than the word *bestiality*. In 1222 a deacon, having been tried before Archbishop Langton, was burned at Oxford on a charge of bestiality. He had embraced Judaism in order to marry a Jewess. Professor E. P. Evans remarks : "It seems rather odd that the Christian lawgivers should have adopted the Jewish code against sexual intercourse with beasts, and then enlarged it so as to include the Jews themselves. The question was gravely discussed by jurists whether cohabitation of a Christian with a Jewess, or *vice versa*, constitutes sodomy. Damhouder (*Prax. rer. crim.* c. 96 n. 48) is of the opinion that it does, and Nicolaus Boer (*Decis.*, 136, n. 5) cites the case of a certain Johannes Alardus, or Jean Alard, who kept a Jewess in his house in Paris and had several children by her : he was convicted of sodomy on account of this relation and burned, together with his paramour, 'since coition with a Jewess is precisely the same as if a man should copulate with a dog' (*Dopl. Theat.* ii, p. 157). Damhouder includes Turks and Saracens in the same category." *The Criminal Prosecution and Capital Punishment of Animals*, p. 152. London, 1906.

[44] An oblate of S. Charles, d. 1631.

[45] 1566–1622. His *Synopsis Theologiæ Moralis* is a posthumous work, published 1626.

[46] Bene ait Busembaum quod congressus cum dæmone reducitur ad peccatum bestialitatis. Hermann Busembaum, S.J., 1600–1668.

[47] *Theologia moralis decalogalis et sacramentalis.* Venice, 1731.

[48] Præter autem crimen bestialitatis accedit scelus superstitionis. An autem, qui coit cum dæmone apparente in forma conjugatæ, monialis, aut consanguiniæ, peccet semper affective peccato adulterii, sacrilegii, aut incestus ? Uidetur uniuerse affirmare Busembaum cum aliis ut supra.

[49] Paris, 1883.

[50] A private manual only delivered to priests.

[51] Omnes theologi loquuntur de congressu cum dæmone in forma uiri, mulieris aut alicuius bestiæ apparente, uel ut præsente per imaginationem repræsentato, dicuntque tale peccatum ad genus bestialitatis reuocandum esse, et specialem habere malitiam in confessione declarandam, scilicet superstitionem in pacto cum dæmone consistentem. In hoc igitur scelere duæ necessario reperiuntur malitiæ, una contra castitatem, et altera contra uirtutem religionis. Si quis ad dæmonem sub specie uiri apparentem affectu sodomitico accedat, tertia est species peccati, ut patet. Item si sub specie consanguineæ aut mulieris conjugatæ fingatur apparere, adest species incestus uel adulterii ; si sub specie bestiæ, adest bestialitas.

[52] 1722–1797. He was a monk of Bans, near Bamberg.

[53] Quæri potest utrum dæmon per turpem concubitum possit uiolenter opprimere marem uel feminam cuius obsessio permissa sit ob finem perfectionis et contemplationis acquirendæ. Ut autem uera a falsis separemus, sciendum est quod dæmones (incubi et succubi, quidquid dicant increduli) uere dantur: immo hoc iuxta doctrinam Augustini (lib. 15, *de Ciuit. Dei*, cap. 23) sine aliqua impudentia negari nequit:... Hoc idem asserit D. Thomas, aliique communiter. Hic uero, qui talia patiuntur, sunt peccatores qui uel dæmones ad hos nefandos concubitus inuitant, uel dæmonibus turpia hæc facinora intentantibus ultro assentiuntur. Quod autem hi aliique praui homines possint per uiolentiam a dæmone opprimi non dubitamus: . . . et ego ipse plures inueni qui quamuis de admissis sceleribus dolerent; et hoc nefarium diaboli commercium exsecrarentur, tamen illud pati cogebantur inuiti. D. Schram, *Theologia Mystica*, I. 233, scholium 3, p. 408. Paris, 1848.

[54] 1532–1591. Provincial of the Jesuit province of the Rhine.

[55] Congressus hos dæmonum cum utriusque sexus hominibus negare, ita temerarium est, ut necessarium sit simul conuellas et sanctissimorum et grauissimorum hominum grauissimas sententias, et humanis sensibus bellum indicas, et te ignorare fatearis quanta sit illorum spirituum in hæc corpora uis utque potestas. C. x. n. 3.

[56] Placuit enim affirmatio axiomatis adeo multis, ut uerendum sit ne pertinaciæ et audaciæ sit ab eis discedere; communis namque hæc est sententia Patrum, theologorum et philosophorum doctiorum, et omnium fere sæculorum atque nationum experientia comprobata. Liber II, quæstio 15.

[57] Asserere per incubos et succubos dæmones homines interdum procreari in tantum est catholicum, quod eius oppositum asserere est nedum dictis Sanctorum, sed et traditioni sacræ Scripturæ contrarium. *Pars prima, quæstio* 3.

[58] Causa autem quare dæmones se incubos faciunt uel succubos esse uidetur, ut per luxuriæ uitium hominis utramque naturam lædant, corporis uidelicet et animæ, qua in læsione præcipue delectari uidentur. This divine was a prominent figure at the Council of Bâle. I have used the Douai edition, 5 vols. 1602.

[59] Dæmon in forma succubi se transformat, et habet coitum cum uiro . . .; accedit ad mulierem in forma scilicet uiri. . . . Ita firmant communiter Theologi.

[60] Certissima experientia sæpe cognitum est fœminas etiam inuitas a dæmonibus fuisse compressas. *De justa hæreticorum punitione*, Lib. I. c. xviii. Salamanca, 1547.

[61] Hæc est indubitata ueritas quam non solum experientia certissima comprobat, sed etiam antiquitas confirmat, quidquid quidam medici et iurisperiti opinentur. *Conclusio quinta.*

[62] Affirmatiuam sententiam tam multi et graues tuentur auctores, ut sine pertinaciæ nota ab illa discedi non posse uidatur.

[63] *Rapports de l'homme avec le démon.*

[64] *Les hauts phenomènes de la magic.*

[65] Sane ad nostrum, non sine ingenti molestia, peruenit auditum quod . . . complures utriusque sexus personæ, propriæ salutis immemores et a fide catholica deuiantes, cum dæmonibus incubis et succubis abuti.

[66] The Dean of S. Paul's (*Christian Mysticism*, 1899, p. 265) urbanely dismisses the whole subject with a quotation from Lucretius:

> Hunc igitur terrorem animi, tenebrasque necessest
> Non radii solis, neque lucida tela diei
> Discutiant, sed naturæ species ratioque. (I. 147–49.)
>
> These Fears, that darkness that o'erspreads our Souls,
> Day can't disperse, but those *eternal* rules
> Which from firm Premises true *Reason* draws,
> And a deep insight into *Natures* laws. (*Creech.*)

[67] *De Dæmonialitate*, 24.

[68] *Survival*, by various authors. Edited by Sir James Marchant, K.B.E., LL.D. London and New York.

[69] So in Middleton's *The Witch*, when the young gallant Almachildes visits Hecate's abode, she exclaims :

'Tis Almachildes—the fresh blood stirs in me—
The man that I have lusted to enjoy :
I've had him thrice in incubus already.

And in a previous scene Hecate has said :

What young man can we wish to pleasure us,
But we enjoy him in an incubus ?

[70] Ce commerce monstreux dura plusiers mois ; mais Dieu le délivra enfin par mon entremise et il fit pénitence de ses péchés.

[71] Auoir esté au Sabbat ; ne sçait comme elle y fut transportée . . . qu'au Sabbat le Diable cogneust charnellement toutes les femmes qui y estoient, & elle aussi la marqua en deux endroicts. . . . Que le Diable la cogneu vne autrefois, & qu'il a le membre faict comme un cheual, en entrant est froid comme glace, iette la semence fort froide, & en sortant la brusse comme si c'estoit du feu. Qu'elle receut tout mescontentement que lors qu'il eut habité auec elle au Sabbat, vn autre homme qu'elle ne cognoist fit le semblable en presence de tous, que son mary s'appercut quand le Diable eut affaire auec elle, & que le Diable se vint coucher auprez d'elle fort froid, luy mit la main sur le bas du ventre, dont elle effrayée en ayant aduerty son mary, il luy dict ces mots, Taise-toy folle, taise-toy. Que son mary vit quand le Diable la cogneust au Sabbat, ensemble cet autre qui la cogneust après.

[72] L'accouplement du Demon avec la Sorciere et le Sorcier. . . . 1. Le Demon cognoit toutes les Sorcieres, & pourquoy. 2. Il se met aussi en femme pour les Sorciers, & pourquoy. 3. Autres raisons pour lesquelles le Demon cognoit les Sorciers, & Sorcieres.

[73] . . . qui Satan l'auoit cogneue charnellement. . . . Et pource que les hommes ne cedent guieres aux femmes en lubricité.

[74] Il y a encor deux autres raisons pour lesquelles le Diable s'accouple auec le Sorcier : La premiere, que l'offense est de tant plus grande : Car si Dieu a en si grande haine l'accouplement du fidelle auec l'infidele (Exodus xxxiv., Deuteronomy xxxvii.), à combien plus forte raison detesterait celuy de l'homme auec le Diable. La seconde raison est, que parce moyen la semence naturelle de l'homme se pert, d'où vient que l'amitié qui est entre l'homme & la femme, se conuertit le plus souuent en haine, qui est l'vn des plus grands mal-heurs, qui pourroient arriuer au mariage.

[75] In chapter xiii Boguet decides : l'accouplement de Satan auec le Sorcier est réel & non imaginaire. . . . Les vns donc s'en mocquēt . . . mais les confessions des Sorciers qui j'ay eu en main, me font croire qu'il en est quelque chose ! dautant qu'ils ont tout recogneu, qu'ils auoient esté couplez auec le Diable, & que la semence qu'il iettoit estoit fort froide . . . Iaquema Paget adioustoit, qu'elle auoit empoigné plusiers fois auec la main le mēbre du Demon, qui la cognoissoit, & que le membre estoit froid comme glace, lōg d'vn bon doigt, & moindre en grosseur que celuy d'vn homme : Tieuenne Paget, & Antoine Tornier adioustoient aussi, que le membre de leurs Demons estoit long, & gros comme l'vn de leurs doigts.

[76] Heuze, *Do the Dead Live ?* 1923.

[77] John Stearne's *Confirmation and Discovery of Witchcraft.*

[78] Robert Pitcairn, *Criminal Trials*, Edinburgh, 1833, III. pp. 603, 611, 617.

[79] *Idem.*

[80] Le Diable faict des mariages au Sabbat entre les Sorciers & Sorcieres, & leur joignant les mains, il leur dict hautement

Esta es buena parati
Esta parati lo toma.

Mais auant qu'ils couchent ensemble, il s'accouple auec elles, oste la virginité des filles. Lancre, *Tableau de l'Inconstance*, p. 132.

[81] This has been emphasized by Miss Murray in *The Witch-Cult in Western Europe* (" The Rites "), but she did not realize that the fascinum was well-known to demonologists, and the use thereof severely reprobated *sub mortali* by the Church.

[82] See G. Belluci, *Amuletti Italiani antichi e contemporanei*; also *Amuletti italiani contemporanei*. Perugia, 1898.

[83] Auctore P.P. Parisiis, MDCCCXXVI.

[84] Crudelissima anus. *Petronii Satirae*. 138. p. 105. Tertium edidit Buecheler. Berlin. 1895.

[85] *Titi Petronii Satyricon*, Concinnante Michaele Hadrianide. Amstelodami, 1669. Amongst the figures on the engraved title-page is a witch mounted on her broomstick.

[86] *Priapeia*. LXXXIV.

[87] For whose impudicities see S. Augustine, *De Ciuitate Dei*, VII. 26.

[88] Priapi lignei in honorem Bacchi.

[89] Francis Hutchinson, *Historical Essay*, London, 1718.

[90] *Witches at Chelmsford*, Philobiblion Society, VIII.

[91] Francis Hutchinson, *Historical Essay on Witchcraft*, 1718.

[92] *Elogia Doctorum Uirorum*, c. 101.

[93] Liber II.; c. v.; 11, 12.

CHAPTER IV

The Sabbat

The Assemblies of the witches differed very much from each other in an almost infinite number of ways. On certain ancient anniversaries the meeting was always particularly solemn, with as large an attendance as possible, when all who belonged to the infernal cult would be required to present themselves and punishment was meted out to those who proved slack and slow; at other times these gatherings would be occasional, resorted to by the company who resided within a certain restricted area, it might be by only one coven of thirteen, it might be by a few more, as opportunity served. There were also, as is to be expected, variations proper to each country, and a seemingly endless number of local peculiarities. There does not clearly appear to be any formal and fair order in the ceremonies throughout, nor should we look for this, seeing that the liturgy of darkness is of its essence opposed to the comely worship of God, wherein, as the Apostle bids, all things are to be done "decently and in order."[1] The ceremonial of hell, sufficiently complex, obscure, and obscene, is even more confused in the witches' narratives by a host of adventitious circumstances, often contradictory, nay, even mutually exclusive, and so although we can piece together a very complete picture of their orgies, there are some details which must yet remain unexplained, incomprehensible, and perhaps wholly irrational and absurd. "Le burlesque s'y mêle à l'horrible, et les puérilités aux abominations." (Ribet, *La Mystique Divine*, III. 2. Les Parodies Diaboliques.) (Mere clowning and japery are mixed up with circumstances of extremest horror; childishness and folly with loathly abominations.) In the lesser Assemblies much, no doubt, depended upon the fickle whim and unwholesome caprice of the officer or president at the moment. The conduct of the more important Assemblies was to a certain extent regularized and more or less loosely ran upon traditional lines. The name Sabbat may be held to cover every kind of gathering,[2] although it must continually be borne in mind that a Sabbat ranges from comparative simplicity, the secret rendezvous of some half a dozen wretches devoted to the fiend, to a large and crowded congregation presided over by incarnate evil intelligences, a mob outvying the very demons in malice, blasphemy, and revolt, the true face of pandemonium on earth.

The derivation of the word Sabbat does not seem to be exactly established. It is perhaps superfluous to point out that it has nothing to do with the number seven, and is wholly unconnected with the Jewish festival. Sainte-Croix and Alfred Maury[3] are agreed to derive it from the debased Bacchanalia. Sabazius (Σαβάζιος) was a Phrygian deity, sometimes identified with Zeus, sometimes with Dionysus, but who was generally regarded as the patron of licentiousness and worshipped with frantic debaucheries. He is a patron of the ribald old Syrian eunuch in Apuleius: "omnipotens et omniparens Dea Syria et sanctus Sabadius et Bellona et Mater Idaea (ac) cum suo Adone Venus domina"[4] are the deities whom Philebus invokes to avenge him of the mocking crier. Σαβαζεῖν is found in the Scholiast on Aristophane (*Birds*, 874), and σαβαῖ, a Bacchic yell, occurs in a fragment of the *Baptæ* of Eupolis; the fuller phrase εὐοῖ Σαβοῖ being reported by Strabo the geographer. The modern Greeks still call a madman ζαβός. But Littré entirely rejects any such facile etymology. "Attempts have been made to trace the etymology of the Sabbat, the witches' assembly, from *Sabazies;* but the formation of the word does not allow it; besides, in the Middle Ages, what did they know about *Sabazies*?"[5]

Even the seasons of the principal Assemblies of the year differ in various countries. Throughout the greater part of Western Europe one of the chief of these was the Eve of May Day, 30 April;[6] in Germany[7] famous as Die Walpurgis-Nacht. S. Walburga (Walpurgis; Waltpurde; at Perche Gauburge; in other parts of France Vaubourg or Falbourg) was born in Devonshire *circa* 710. She was the daughter of S. Richard, one of the under-kings of the West Saxons, who married a sister of S. Boniface. In 748 Walburga, who was then a nun of Wimbourne, went over to Germany to found claustral life in that country. After a life of surpassing holiness she died at Heidenheim, 25 February, 777. Her cultus began immediately, and about 870 her relics were translated to Eichstadt, where the Benedictine convent which has charge of the sacred shrine still happily flourishes. S. Walburga was formerly one of the most popular Saints in England, as well as in Germany and the Low Countries. She is patroness of Eichstadt, Oudenarde, Furnes, Groningen, Weilburg, Zutphen, and Antwerp, where until the Roman office was adopted they celebrated her feast four times a year. In the Roman martyrology she is commemorated on 1 May, but in the Monastic Kalendar on 25 February. The first of May was the ancient festival of the Druids, when they offered sacrifices upon their sacred mountains and kindled their May-fires. These magic observances were appropriately continued by the witches of a later date. There was not a hill-top in Finland, so the peasant believed, which at midnight on the last day of April was not thronged by demons and sorcerers.

The second witches' festival was the Eve of S. John Baptist, 23 June. Then were the S. John's fires lit, a custom in certain regions still prevailing.[8] In olden times the Feast was distinguished like Christmas with three Masses; the first at midnight recalled his mission as Precursor, the second at dawn commemorated the baptism he confessed, the third honoured his sanctity.

Other Grand Sabbat days, particularly in Belgium and Germany, were S. Thomas' Day (21 December) and a date, which seems to have been movable, shortly after Christmas. In Britain we also find Candlemas (2 February), Allhallowe'en (31 October), and Lammas (1 August), mentioned in the trials. Wright, *Narratives of Sorcery and Magic* (I. p. 141), further specifies S. Bartholomew's Eve, but although a Sabbat may have been held on this day, it would seem to be an exceptional or purely local use.

During a famous trial held in the winter of 1610 at Logrono, a town of Old Castille, by the Apostolic Inquisitor, Alonso Becerra Holguin, an Alcantarine friar, with his two assessors Juen Valle Alvarado and Alonso de Salasar y Frias, a number of Navarrese witches confessed that the chief Sabbats were usually held at Zugarramurdi and Berroscoberro in the Basque districts, and that the days were fixed, being the vigils of the "nine principal feasts of the year," namely, Easter, Epiphany, Ascension Day, the Purification and Nativity of Our Lady, the Assumption, Corpus Christi, All Saints, and the major festival of S. John Baptist (24 June). It is certainly curious to find no mention of Christmas and Pentecost in this list, but throughout the whole of the process not one of the accused—and we have their evidence in fullest detail—named either of these two solemnities as being chosen for the infernal rendezvous.[9]

Satan is, as Boguet aptly says, " Singe de Dieu en tout,"[10] and it became common to hold a General Sabbat about the time of the high Christian festivals in evil mockery of these holy solemnities, and he precisely asserts that the Sabbat " se tient encor aux festes les plus solemnelles de l'année."[11] (Is still held on the greatest festivals of the year.) So he records the confession of Antide Colas (1598), who " auoit esté au Sabbat à vn chacun bon iour de l'an, comme à Noel, à Pasques, à la feste de Dieu." The Lancashire witches met on Good Friday; and in the second instance (1633) on All Saints' Day; the witches of Kinross (1662) held an assembly on the feast of Scotland's Patron, S. Andrew, 30 November, termed " S. Andrew's Day at Yule," to distinguish it from the secondary Feast of the Translation of S. Andrew, 9 May. The New England witches were wont to celebrate their chief Sabbat at Christmas. In many parts of Europe where the Feast of S. George is solemnized with high honour and holiday the vigil (22 April) is the Great Sabbat of the year. The Huzulo of the Carpathians believe that then every evil thing has power and witches are most dangerous. Not a Bulgarian or Roumanian farmer but closes up each door and fastens close each window at nightfall, putting sharp thorn-bushes and brambles on the lintels, new turf on the sills, so that no demon nor hag may find entry there.

The Grand Sabbats were naturally held in a great variety of places, whilst the lesser Sabbats could be easily assembled in an even larger number of spots, which might be convenient to the coven of that district, a field near a village, a wood, a tor, a valley, an open waste beneath some blasted oak, a cemetery, a ruined building, some solitary chapel or semi-deserted church, sometimes a house belonging to one of the initiates.

It was advisable that the selected locality should be remote and deserted to obviate any chance of espionage or casual interruption, and in many provinces some wild ill-omened gully or lone hill-top was shudderingly marked as the notorious haunt of witches and their fiends. De Lancre says that the Grand Sabbat must be held near a stream, lake, or water of some kind,[12] and Bodin adds: "The places where Sorcerers meet are remarkable and generally distinguished by some trees, or even a cross."[13] These ancient cromlechs and granite dolmens, the stones of the Marais de Dol, the monolith that lies between Seny and Ellemelle (Candroz), even the market-crosses of sleepy old towns and English villages, were among the favourite rendezvous of the pythons and warlocks of a whole countryside. On one occasion, which seems exceptional, a Sabbat was held in the very heart of the city of Bordeaux. Throughout Germany the Blocksburg or the Brocken, the highest peak of the Hartz Mountains, was the great meeting-place of the witches, some of whom, it was said, came from distant Lapland and Norway to forgather there. But local Blocksburgs existed, or rather hills so called, especially in Pomerania, which boasted two or three such crags. The sorcerers of Corrières held their Sabbat at a deserted spot, turning off the highway near Combes; the witches of la Mouille in a tumbledown house, which had once belonged to religious; the Gandillons and their coven, who were brought to justice in June, 1598, met at Fontenelles, a forsaken and haunted spot near the village of Nezar. Dr. Fian and his associates (1591) "upon the night of Allhollen-Even" assembled at "the kirke of North-Berrick in Lowthian." Silvain Nevillon, who was executed at Orleans, 4 February, 1615, confessed "que le Sabbat se tenoit dans vne maison," and the full details he gave shows this to have been a large château, no doubt the home of some wealthy local magnate, where above two hundred persons could assemble. Isobel Young, Christian Grinton, and two or three other witches entertained the Devil in Young's house in 1629. Alexander Hamilton, a "known warlock" executed at Edinburgh in 1630, confessed that "the pannel

took him one night to a den betwixt Niddrie and Edmiston, where the devill had trysted hir." Helen Guthrie, a Forfar witch, and her coven frequented a churchyard, where they met a demon, and on another occasion they "went to Mary Rynd's house, and sat doune together at the table . . . and made them selfes mirrie, and the divell made much of them all" (1661). The Lancashire witches often held their local Sabbat at Malking Tower. From the confession of the Swedish witches (1670) at Mohra and Elfdale they assembled at a spot called *Blockula* "scituated in a delicate large Meadow . . . The place or house they met at, had before it a Gate painted with divers colours; . . . In a huge large Room of this House, they said, there stood a very long Table, at which the Witches did sit down; And that hard by this Room was another Chamber in which there were very lovely and delicate Beds."[14] Obviously a fine Swedish country house, perhaps belonging to a wealthy witch, and in the minds of the poorer members of the gang it presently became imaginatively exaggerated and described.

Christian Stridtheckh *De Sagis* (XL) writes: "They have different rendezvous in different districts; yet their meetings are generally held in wooded spots, or on mountains, or in caves, and any places which are far from the usual haunts of men. Mela, Book III, chapter 44, mentions Mount Atlas; *de Vaulx*, a warlock executed at Etaples in 1603, confessed that the witches of the Low Countries were wont most frequently to meet in some spot in the province of Utrecht. In our own country, the Mountain of the Bructeri, which some call Melibœus, in the duchy of Brunswick, is known and notorious as the haunt of witches. In the common tongue this Mountain is called the *Blocksberg* or *Heweberg*, *Brockersburg* or *Vogelsberg*, as *Ortelius* notes in his *Thesaurus Geographicus*."[15] The day of the week whereon a Sabbat was held differed in the various districts and countries, although Friday seems to have been most generally favoured. There is indeed an accumulation of evidence for every night of the week save Saturday and Sunday. De Lancre records that in the Basses-Pyrénées "their usual rendezvous is the spot known as Lane du Bouc, in the Basque tongue *Aquelarre de verros*, *prado del Cabron*, & there the Sorcerers assemble to worship their master on three particular nights, Monday, Wednesday, Friday."[16] Boguet says that the day of the Sabbat varied, but usually a Thursday night was preferred.[17] In England it was stated that the "Solemn appointments, and meetings . . . are ordinarily on Tuesday or Wednesday night."[18] Saturday was, however, particularly avoided as being the day sacred to the immaculate Mother of God.

It is true that the hysterical and obscene ravings of Maria de Sains, a witness concerned in the trial of Louis Gaufridi and who was examined on 17–19 May, 1614, assert that the Sabbat used to be held on every day of the week. Wednesday and Friday were the Sabbats of blasphemy and the black ass. To the other days the most hideous abominations of which humanity is capable were allotted. The woman was obviously sexually deranged, affected with mania blasphematoria and coprolalia.

Night was almost invariably the time for the Sabbat, although, as Delrio says, there is no actual reason why these evil rites should not be performed at noon, for the Psalmist speaks of "the terror of the night," the "business that walketh about in the dark," and of "the noonday devil."[19] ("Non timebis a timore nocturno . . . a negotio perambulante in tenebris; ab incursu et dæmonio meridiano.") And so Delrio very aptly writes: "Their assemblies generally are held at dead of night when the Powers of Darkness reign; or, sometimes, at high noon, even as the Psalmist saith, when he speaks of 'the noonday devil.' The nights they prefer are Monday and Thursday."[20]

The time at which these Sabbats began was generally upon the stroke of midnight. "Les Sorciers," says Boguet, "vont enuiron la minuict au Sabbat."[21] It may be remembered that in the *Metamorphoseon* of Apuleius, I, xi, the hags attack Socrates at night "circa tertiam ferme uigiliam." Agnes Sampson, "a famous witch"—as Hume of Godscroft in his Account of Archibald, ninth Earl of Angus, calls her—commonly known as the wise wife of Keith, who made a prominent figure[22] in the Fian trials, 1590, confessed that the Devil met her, "being alone, and commanded her to be at North-Berwick Kirk the next night," and accordingly she made her way there as she was bid "and lighted at the Kirk-yard, or a little before she came to it, about eleven hours at even."[23] In this case, however, the Sabbat was preceded by a dance of nearly one hundred persons, and so probably did not commence until midnight. Thomas Leyis, Issobell Coky, Helen Fraser, Bessie Thorn, and the rest of the Aberdeen witches, thirteen of whom were executed in 1597, and seven more banished, generally met " betuixt tuell & ane houris at nycht."[24] Boguet notes that in 1598 the witch Françoise Secretain "adioustoit qu'elle alloit tousiours au Sabbat enuiron la minuit, & beaucoup d'autres sorciers, que i'ay eu en main, ont dit le mesme." In 1600 Anna Mauczin of Tubingen confessed that she had taken part in witch gatherings which she dubbed *Hochzeiten.* They seem to have been held by a well just outside the upper gate of Rotenburg, and her evidence insists upon " midnight dances " and revelling. A Scotch witch, Marie Lamont, "a young woman of the adge of Eighteen Yeares, dwelling in the parish of Innerkip " on 4 March, 1662, confessed most ingenuously " that when shee had been at a mietting sine Zowle last, with other witches, in the night, the devill convoyed her home in the dawing."[25]

The Sabbat lasted till cock-crow, before which time none of the assembly was suffered to withdraw, and the advowal of Louis Gaufridi, executed at Aix, 1610, seems somewhat singular: " I was conveyed to the place where the Sabbat was to be held, and I remained there sometimes one, two, three, or four hours, for the most part just as I felt inclined."[26] That the crowing of a cock dissolves enchantments is a tradition of extremest antiquity. The Jews believed that the clapping of a cock's wings will make the power of demons ineffectual and break magic spells. So Prudentius sang: " They say that the night-wandering demons, who rejoice in dunnest shades, at the crowing of the cock tremble and scatter in sore affright."[27] The rites of Satan ceased because the Holy Office of the Church began. In the time of S. Benedict Matins and Lauds were recited at dawn and were actually often known as *Gallicinium*, Cock-crow. In the exquisite poetry of S. Ambrose, which is chanted at Sunday Lauds, the praises of the cock are beautifully sung:

Light of our darksome journey here,
With days dividing night from night!
Loud crows the dawn's shrill harbinger,
And wakens up the sunbeams bright.

Forthwith at this, the darkness chill
  Retreats before the star of morn;
And from their busy schemes of ill
  The vagrant crews of night return.

Fresh hope, at this, the sailor cheers;
  The waves their stormy strife allay;
The Church's Rock at this, in tears,
  Hastens to wash his guilt away.

Arise ye, then, with one accord!
  No longer wrapt in slumber lie;
The cock rebukes all who their Lord
  By sloth neglect, by sin deny.

At his clear cry joy springs afresh;
  Health courses through the sick man's veins;
The dagger glides into its sheath;
  The fallen soul her faith regains.[28]

A witch named Latoma confessed to Nicolas Remy that cocks were most hateful to all sorcerers. That bird is the herald of dawn, he arouses men to the worship of God; and many an odious sin which darkness shrouds will be revealed in the light of the coming day. At the hour of the Nativity, that most blessed time, the cocks crew all night long. A cock crew lustily at the Resurrection. Hence is the cock placed upon the steeple of churches. Pliny and Ælian tell us that a lion fears the cock; so the Devil "leo rugiens" flees at cock-crow.

"Le coq," says De Lancre, "s'oyt par fois es Sabbats sonnât la retraicte aux Sorciers."[29]

The witch resorted to the Sabbat in various manners. If it were a question of attending a local assembly when, at most, a mile or two had to be traversed, the company would go on foot. Very often the distance was even less, for it should be remembered that in the sixteenth and seventeenth centuries, and indeed, as a matter of fact, up to a quite recent date, when the wayfarer had gone a few steps outside the gates of a town or beyond the last house in the village he was enfolded in darkness, entirely solitary, remote, eloined. If footmen with flambeaux, at least the humbler linkboy, were essential attendants after nightfall in the streets of the world's great cities, London, Rome, Paris,

Madrid,[30] how black with shadows, dangerous, and utterly lonesome was the pathless countryside! Not infrequently the witches of necessity carried lanterns to light them on their journey to the Sabbat. The learned Bartolomeo de Spina, O.P.,[31] in his *Tractatus de Strigibus et Lamiis* (Venice, 1533), writes that a certain peasant, who lived at Clavica Malaguzzi, in the district of Mirandola, having occasion to rise very early one morning and drive to a neighbouring village, found himself at three o'clock, before daybreak, crossing a waste tract of considerable extent which lay between him and his destination. In the distance he suddenly caught sight of what seemed to be numerous fires flitting to and fro, and as he drew nearer he saw that these were none other than large lanthorns held by a bevy of persons who were moving here and there in the mazes of a fantastic dance, whilst others, as at a rustic picnic, were seated partaking of dainties and drinking stoups of wine, what time a harsh music, like the scream of a cornemuse, droned through the air. Curiously no word was spoken, the company whirled and pirouetted, ate and drank, in strange and significant silence. Perceiving that many, unabashed, were giving themselves up to the wildest debauchery and publicly performing the sexual act with every circumstance of indecency, the horrified onlooker realized that he was witnessing the revels of the Sabbat. Crossing himself fervently and uttering a prayer he drove as fast as possible from the accursed spot, not, however, before he had recognized some of the company as notorious evil-doers and persons living in the vicinity who were already under grave suspicion of sorcery. The witches must have remarked his presence, but they seem to have ignored him and not even to have attempted pursuit. In another instance Fra Paolo de Caspan, a Dominican of great reputation for piety and learning, reports that Antonio de Palavisini, the parish priest of Caspan in the Valtellina, a territory infected with warlocks, most solemnly affirmed that when going before daybreak to say an early Mass at a shrine hard by the village he had seen through clearings in the wood an assembly of men and women furnished with lanterns, who were seated in a circle and whose actions left no doubt that they were witches engaged in abominable rites. In both the above cases the lanterns were not required in the ceremonies of the Sabbat, and they must have been carried for the purely practical purpose of affording light.

Very often when going to a local Sabbat the coven of witches used to meet just beyond the village and make their way to the appointed spot in a body for mutual help and security. This is pointed out by Bernard of Como, a famous scholar, who says: "When they are to go to some spot hard by they proceed thither on foot cheerily conversing as they walk."[32] The fact that the dark initiates walked to the Sabbat is frequently mentioned in the trials. Boguet, who is most exact in detail, writes: "Sorcerers, nevertheless, sometimes walk to the Sabbat, and this is generally the case when the spot where they are to assemble does not lie very far from their dwellings."[33] And in the interrogatory, 17 May, 1616, of Barthélemi Minguet of Brécy, a young fellow of twenty-five, accused with seventeen more, we have: "He was then asked in what place the Sabbat was held the last time he was present there.

"He replied that it was in the direction of Billcron, at a cross-road which is on the high-road leading to Aix, in the Parish of Saint Soulange. He was asked how he proceeded thither. He replied that he walked to the place."[34]

When Catharine Oswald of Niddrie (1625) one night took Alexander Hamilton "a known warlock" "to a den betwixt Niddrie and Edmiston, where the devill had trysted hir," it is obvious that the couple walked there together.

On one occasion the truly subtle point was raised whether those who walked to the Sabbat were as guilty as those who were conveyed thither by the Devil. But De Lancre decides: "It is truly as criminal & abominable for a Sorcerer to go to the Sabbat on foot as to be voluntarily conveyed thither by the Devil."[35]

Major Weir and his sister seem to have gone to a meeting with the Devil in a coach and six horses when they thus drove from Edinburgh to Musselburgh and back again on 7 September, 1648. So the woman confessed in prison, and added "that she and her brother had made a compact with the devil."[36]

Agnes Sampson, the famous witch of North Berwick (1590), confessed "that the *Devil* in mans lickness met her going out to the fields from her own house at *Keith*, betwixt five and six at even, being alone and commanded her to be at *North-berwick* Kirk the next night. To which place she came on horse-back, conveyed by her Good-son, called Iohn Couper."[37] The Swedish witches (1669) who carried children off to Blockula "set them upon a *Beast* of the *Devil's* providing, and then they rid away." One boy confessed that "to perform the Journey, he took his own Fathers horse out of the Meadow, where it was feeding."[38] Upon his return one of the coven let the horse graze in her own pasture, and here the boy's father found it the next day.

In the popular imagination the witch is always associated with the broomstick, employed by her to fly in wild career through mid-air. This belief seems almost universal, of all times and climes. The broomstick is, of course, closely connected with the magic wand or staff which was considered equally serviceable for purposes of equitation. The wood whence it was fashioned was often from the hazel-tree, witch-hazel, although in De Lancre's day the sorcerers of Southern France favoured the "Souhandourra"—*Cornus sanguinea*, dog-wood. Mid hurricane and tempest, in the very heart of the dark storm, the convoy of witches, straddling their broomsticks, sped swiftly along to the Sabbat, their yells and hideous laughter sounding louder than the crash of elements and mingling in fearsome discord with the frantic pipe of the gale.

There is a very important reference to these beliefs from the pen of the famous and erudite Benedictine Abbot, Regino of Prüm (A.D. 906), who in his weighty *De ecclesiasticis disciplinis* writes: "This too must by no means be passed over that certain utterly abandoned women, turning aside to follow Satan, being seduced by the illusions and phantasmical shows of demons firmly believe and openly profess that in the dead of night they ride upon certain beasts along with the pagan goddess Diana and a countless horde of women, and that in those silent hours they fly over vast tracts of country and obey her as their mistress, whilst on certain other nights they are summoned to do her homage and pay her service."[39] The witches rode sometimes upon a besom or a stick, sometimes upon an animal, and the excursion through the air was generally preceded by an unction with a magic ointment. Various recipes are given for the ointment, and it is interesting to note that they contain deadly poisons: aconite, belladonna, and hemlock.[40] Although these unguents may in certain circumstances be capable of producing definite physiological results, it is Delrio who best sums up the reasons for their use: "The Demon is able to convey them to the Sabbat without the use of any unguent, and often he does so. But for several reasons he prefers that they should anoint themselves. Sometimes when the witches seem afraid it serves to encourage them. When they are young and tender they will thus be better able to bear the hateful embrace of Satan who has assumed the shape of a man. For by this horrid anointing he dulls their senses and persuades these deluded wretches that there is some great virtue in the viscid lubricant. Sometimes too he does this in hateful mockery of God's holy Sacraments, and that by these mysterious ceremonies he may infuse, as it were, something of a ritual and liturgical nature into his beastly orgies."[41]

Although the witch is universally credited with the power to fly through the air[42] to the Sabbat mounted upon a besom or some kind of stick, it is remarkable in the face of popular belief to find that the confessions avowing this actual mode of aerial transport are extraordinarily few. Paul Grilland, in his tractate *De Sortilegiis* (Lyons, 1533), speaks of a witch at Rome during whose trial, seven years before, it was asserted she flew in the air after she had anointed her limbs with a magic liniment. Perhaps the most exactly detailed accounts of this feat are to be found in Boguet,[43] than whom scarcely any writer more meticulously reports the lengthy and prolix evidence of witches, such evidence as he so laboriously gathered during the notorious prosecutions throughout Franche-Comté in the summer of 1598. He records quite plainly such statements as: "Françoise Secretain disoit, que pour aller au Sabbat, elle mettoit un baston blanc entre ses iambes & puis prononcait certaines paroles & dés lors elle estoit portée par l'air iusques en l'assemblée des Sorciers." (Françoise Secretain avowed that in order to go to the Sabbat she placed a white stick between her legs & then uttered certain words & then she was borne through the air to the sorcerers' assembly). In another place she confessed "qu'elle avoit esté vne infinité de fois au Sabbat . . . & qu'elle y alloit sur vn baston blanc, qu'elle mettoit entre ses iambes." (That she had been a great number of times to the Sabbat . . . and that she went there on a white stick which she placed between her legs.) It will be noticed that in the second instance she does not explicitly claim to have been borne through the air. Again: "Francoise Secretain y estoit portée [au Sabbat] sur vn baston blanc. Satan y trãsporta Thieuenne Paget & Antide Colas estant en forme d'vn homme noir, sortans de leurs maison le plus souuent par la cheminée." "Claudine Boban, ieune fille confessa qu'elle & sa mère montoient sur vne ramasse, & que sortans le contremont de la cheminée elles alloient par l'air en ceste façon au Sabbat." (Françoise Secretain was carried [to the Sabbat] on a white stick. Satan, in the form of a tall dark man conveyed thither Thieuenne Paget & Antide Colas, who most often left their house by way of the chimney. . . . Claudine Boban, a young girl, confessed that both she and her mother mounted on a besom, & that flying out by the chimney they were thus borne through the air to the Sabbat.) A marginal note explains *ramasse* as "autrement balai, & en Lyonnois coiue."

Glanvill writes that Julian Cox, one of the Somerset coven (1665), said "that one evening she walkt out about a Mile from her own House and there came riding towards her three persons upon three Broom-staves, born up about a yard and a half from the ground. Two of them she formerly knew, which was a Witch and a Wizzard." It might easily be that there is some exaggeration here. We know that a figure in one of the witch dances consisted of leaping as high as possible into the air, and probably the three persons seen by Julian Cox were practising this agile step. A quotation from Bodin by Reginald Scot is very pertinent in this connexion. Speaking of the Sabbat revels he has: "And whiles they sing and dance, euerie one hath a broome in his hand, and holdeth it vp aloft. Item he saith, that these night-walking or rather night-dansing witches, brought out of *Italie* into *France*, that danse which is called *La Volta*."[44] Sir John Davies in his *Orchestra or A Poeme on Dauncing* (18mo, 1596) describes the lavolta as "A loftie iumping, or a leaping round." De Lancre observes that after the regular country dance at the Sabbat the witches sprang high into the air. "Après la dance ils se mettent par fois à sauter."[45] At their assembly certain of the Aberdeen witches (1597) "danced a devilish dance, riding on trees, by a long space." In an old representation of Dr. Fian and his company swiftly pacing round North Berwick church withershins the witches are represented as running and leaping in the air, some mounted on broomsticks, some carrying their besoms in their hands.

There was discovered in the closet of Dame Alice Kyteler of Kilkenny, who was arrested in 1324 upon the accusation of nightly meeting a familiar Artisson and multiplied charges of sorcery, a pipe of ointment, wherewith she greased a staff "upon which she ambolled and gallopped thorough thicke and thin, when and what manner she listed."[46] In the trial of Martha Carrier, a notorious witch and "rampant hag" at the Court of Oyer and Terminer, held by adjournment at Salem, 2 August, 1692, the eighth article of the indictment ran: "One *Foster*, who confessed her own share in the Witchcraft for which the Prisoner stood indicted, affirm'd, that she had seen the prisoner at some of their *Witch-meetings*, and that it was this *Carrier*, who perswaded her to be a Witch. She confessed that the Devil carry'd them on a pole, to a Witch-meeting: but the pole broke, and she hanging about *Carriers* neck, they both fell down, and she then received an hurt by the Fall, whereof she was not at this very time recovered."[47]

In many of these instances it is plain that there is no actual flight through the air implied; although there is a riding a-cock-horse of brooms or sticks, in fact, a piece of symbolic ritual.

It is very pertinent, however, to notice in this connexion the actual levitation of human beings, which is, although perhaps an unusual, yet by no means an unknown, phenomenon in the séances of modern spiritism, where both the levitation of persons, with which we are solely concerned, and the rising of tables or chairs off the ground without contact with any individual or by any human agency have occurred again and again under conditions which cannot possibly admit of legerdemain, illusion, or charlatanry. From a mass of irrefutable evidence we may select some striking words by Sir William Crookes, F.R.S., upon levitation. "This has occurred," he writes, "in my presence on four occasions in darkness; but . . . I will only mention cases in which deductions of reason were confirmed by the sense of sight. . . . On one occasion I witnessed a chair, with a lady sitting on it, rise several inches from the ground. . . . On another occasion the lady knelt on the chair in such manner that the four feet were visible to us. It then rose about three inches, remained suspended for about ten seconds, and then slowly descended. . . .

" The most striking case of levitation which I have witnessed has been with Mr. Home. On three separate occasions have I seen him raised completely from the floor of the room. . . . On each occasion I had full opportunity of watching the occurrence as it was taking place. There are at least a hundred recorded instances of Mr. Home's rising from the ground."[48]

Writing in July, 1871, Lord Lindsay said: " I was sitting with Mr. Home and Lord Adare and a cousin of his. During the sitting Mr. Home went into a trance, and in that state was carried out of the window in the room next to where we were, and was brought in at our window. The distance between the windows was about seven feet six inches, and there was not the slightest foothold between them, nor was there more than a twelve-inch projection to each window, which served as a ledge to put flowers on. We heard the window in the next room lifted up, and almost immediately after we saw Home floating in air outside our window."[49]

William Stainton Moses writes of his levitation in August, 1872, in the presence of credible witnesses: " I was carried up . . . when I became stationary I made a mark [with a lead pencil] on the wall opposite to my chest. This mark is as near as may be six feet from the floor. . . . From the position of the mark on the wall it is clear that my head must have been close to the ceiling. . . . I was simply levitated and lowered to my old place."[50]

When we turn to the lives of the Saints we find that these manifestations have been frequently observed, and it will suffice to mention but a few from innumerable examples.

S. Francis of Assisi was often " suspended above the earth, sometimes to a height of three, sometimes to a height of four cubits"; the same phenomenon has been recorded by eye-witnesses in many instances throughout the centuries. Among the large number of those who are known to have been raised from the ground whilst wrapt in prayer are the stigmatized S. Catherine of Siena; S. Colette; Rainiero de Borgo San-Sepolcro; S. Catherine de Ricci; S. Alphonsus Rodriguez, S.J.; S. Mary Magdalen de Pazzi; Raimond Rocco; Bl. Charles de Sezze; S. Veronica Giuliani the Capuchiness; S. Gerard Majella, the Redemptorist thaumaturge; that wondrous mystic Anne Catherine Emmerich; Dominica Barbagli (died in 1858), the ecstatica of Montesanto-Savino (Florence), whose levitations were of daily occurrence. S. Ignatius Loyola whilst deeply contemplative was seen by John Pascal to be raised more than a foot from the pavement; S. Teresa and S. John of the Cross were levitated in concurrent ecstasies in the shady locutorio of the Encarnacion, as was witnessed by Beatriz of Jesus and the whole convent of nuns;[51] S. Alphonsus Liguori whilst preaching in the church of S. John Baptist at Foggia was lifted before the eyes of the whole congregation several feet from the ground;[52] Gemma Galgani of Lucca, who died 11 April, 1903, was observed whilst praying one evening in September, 1901, before a venerated Crucifix, to rise in the air in a celestial trance and to remain several minutes at some distance from the floor.[53] Above all, S. Joseph of Cupertino (1603–63), one of the most extraordinary mystics of the seventeenth century, whose whole life seemed one long series of unbroken raptures and ecstasies, was frequently lifted on high to remain suspended in mid-air. Such notice was attracted by this marvel that his superiors sent him from one lonely house of Capuchins or Conventuals to another, and he died at the little hill town of Osimo, where his remains are yet venerated. For many years he was obliged to say Mass at a private altar so inevitable were the ecstasies that fell upon him during the Sacrifice. There are, I think, few sanctuaries more sweet and more fragrant with holiness than this convent at Osimo. During a most happy visit to the shrine of S. Joseph I was deeply touched by the many memorials of the Saints, and by the kindness of the Fathers, his brethren to-day. S. Philip Neri and S. Francis Xavier were frequently raised from the ground at the Elevation, and of the ascetic S. Paul of the Cross the Blessed Strambi writes: "Le serviteur de Dieu s'éleva en l'air à la hauteur de deux palmes, et cela, à deux reprises, avant et après la consecration."[54] (The servant of God during Holy Mass was twice elevated in the air to a height of two hand-breadths from the ground both before and after the Consecration.) It is well known that in a certain London church a holy religious when he said Mass was not unseldom levitated from the predella, which manifestation I have myself witnessed, although the father was himself unconscious thereof until the day of his death.

But, as Görres most aptly remarks,[55] although many examples may be cited of Saints who have been levitated in ecstasy, and although it is not impossible that this phenomenon may be imitated by evil powers—as, indeed, it undoubtedly is in the cases of spiritistic mediums—yet nowhere do we find in hagiography that a large number of Saints were in one company raised from the earth together or conveyed through the air to meet at some appointed spot. Is it likely, then, that the demons would be allowed seemingly to excel by their power a most extraordinary and exceptional manifestation? It must be remembered, also, that save in very rare and singular instances, such as that of S. Joseph of Cupertino, levitation is only for a height of a foot or some eighteen inches, and even this occurs seldom save at moments of great solemnity and psychic concentration.

A question which is largely discussed by the demonologists then arises: Do the witches actually and in person attend the Sabbat or is their journey thither and assistance thereat mere diabolic illusion? Giovanni Francesco Ponzinibio, in his *De Lamiis*,[56] wholly inclines to the latter view, but this is superficial reasoning, and the celebrated canonist Francisco Peña with justice takes him very severely to task for his temerity. Peña's profound work, *In Bernardi Comensis Dominicani Lucernam inquisitorum notæ et eiusdem tractatum de strigibus*,[57] a valuable collection of most erudite glosses, entirely disposes of Ponzinibio's arguments, and puts the case in words of weighty authority.

Sprenger in the *Malleus Maleficarum*, I, had already considered "How witches are bodily transported from one place to another," and he concludes "It is proven, then, that sorcerers can be bodily transported."[58] Paul Grilland inquires: "Whether magicians & witches or Satanists are bodily & actually conveyed to and fro by the Devil, or whether this be merely imaginary ?" He freely acknowledges the extraordinary difficulty and intricacy of the investigation, beginning his answer with the phrase "Quaestio ista est multum ardua et famosa."[59] (This is a very difficult and oft-discussed question.) But S. Augustine, S. Thomas, S. Bonaventure, and a score of great names are agreed upon the reality of this locomotion, and Grilland, after balancing the evidence to the nicety of a hair wisely concludes : "Myself I hold the opinion that they are actually transported."[60]

In his *Compendium Maleficarum* Francesco Maria Guazzo discusses (Liber I. 13) "Whether Witches are actually and bodily conveyed from place to place to attend their Sabbats"; and lays down : "The opinion which many who follow Luther & Melancthon hold is that Witches only assist at these assemblies in their imagination, & that they are choused by some trick of the devil, in support of which argument the objectors assert that the Witches have very often been seen lying in one spot and not moving thence. Moreover, what is related in the life of S. Germain is not impertinent in this connexion, to wit, when certain women declared that they had been present at a banquet, & yet all the while they slumbered and slept, as several persons attested. That women of this kind are very often deceived in such a way is certain ; but that they are always so deceived is by no means sure. . . . The alternative opinion, which personally I hold most strongly, is that sometimes at any rate Witches are actually conveyed from one place to another by the Devil, who under the bodily form of a goat or some other unclean & monstrous animal himself carries them, & that they are verily and indeed present at their foul midnight Sabbats. This opinion is that generally held by the authoritative Theologians and Master Jurisprudists of Italy and Spain, as also by the Catholic divines and legalists. The majority of writers, indeed, advance this view, for example, Torquemada in his commentary on Grilland, Remy, S. Peter Damian, Silvester of Abula, Tommaso de Vio Gaetani, Alfonso de Castro, Sisto da Siena, O.P., Père Crespet, Bartolomeo Spina in his glosses on Ponzinibio, Lorenzo Anania, and a vast number of others, whose names for brevity's sake I here omit."[61]

This seems admirably to sum up the whole matter. In the encyclopædic treatise *De Strigibus*[62] by an earlier authority, Bernard of Como, the following remarkable passage occurs: "The aforesaid abominable wretches actually & awake & in full enjoyment of their normal senses attend these assemblies or rather orgies, and when they are to go to some spot hard by they proceed thither on foot, cheerily conversing as they walk. If, however, they are to meet in some distant place then are they conveyed by the Devil, yet by whatsoever means they proceed to the said place whether it be on foot or whether they are borne along by the Devil, it is most certain that their journey is real and actual, and not imaginary. Nor are they labouring under any delusion when they deny the Catholic Faith, worship and adore the Devil, tread upon the Cross of Christ, outrage the Most Blessed Sacrament, and give themselves up to filthy and unhallowed copulations, fornicating with the Devil himself who appears to them in a human form, being used by the men as a succubus, & carnally serving the woman as an incubus."[63]

The conclusion then is plain and proven. The witches do actually and individually attend the Sabbat, an orgy of blasphemy and obscenity. Whether they go thither on foot, or horseback, or by some other means is a detail, which in point of fact differs according to the several and infinitely varied circumstances.

It is not denied that in some cases hallucination and self-deception played a large part, but such examples are comparatively speaking few in number, and these, moreover, were carefully investigated and most frequently recognized by the judges and divines. Thus in the *Malleus Maleficarum* Sprenger relates that a woman, who had voluntarily surrendered herself to be examined as being a witch, confessed to the Dominican fathers that she nightly assisted at the Sabbat, and that neither bolts nor bars could prevent her from flying to the infernal revels. Accordingly she was shut fast under lock and key in a chamber whence it was impossible for her to escape, and all the while carefully watched by lynx-eyed officers through a secret soupirail. These reported that immediately the door was closed she threw herself on the bed where in a moment she was stretched out perfectly rigid in all her members. Select members of the tribunal, grave and acute doctors, entered the room. They shook her, gently at first, but presently with considerable roughness. She remained immobile and insensible. She was pinched and pulled sharply. At last a lighted candle was brought and placed near her naked foot until the flesh was actually scorched in the flame. She lay stockish and still, dumb and motionless as a stone. After a while her senses returned to her. She sat up and related in exact detail the happenings at the Sabbat she had attended, the place, the number of the company, the rites, what was spoken, all that was done, and then she complained of a hurt upon her foot. Next day the fathers explained to her all that had passed, how that she had never stirred from the spot, and that the pain arose from the taper which to ensure the experiment had been brought in contact with her flesh. They admonished her straightly but with paternal charity, and upon the humble confession of her error and a promise to guard against any such ill fantasies for the future, a suitable penance was prescribed and the woman dismissed.

In the celebrated cases investigated by Henri Boguet, June, 1598, young George Gandillon confessed to having walked to the Sabbat at a deserted spot called Fontenelles, near the village of Nezar, and also to having ridden to the Sabbat. Moreover, in his indictment the following occurs: "George Gandillon, one Good Friday night, lay in his bed, rigid as a corpse, for the space of three hours, & then on a sudden came to himself. He has since been burned alive here with his father & his sister."[64]

Since Boguet, who is one of our chief authorities, discusses the Sabbat with most copious details in his *Discours des Sorciers* it will not be impertinent to give here the headings and subdivisions of his learned and amply documented chapters.[65]

Chapter XVI. How, & in what way Sorcerers are conveyed to the Sabbat.

1. *They are sometimes conveyed there mounted on a stick, or a broom, sometimes on a sheep or a goat, & sometimes by a tall black man.*
2. *Sometimes they anoint themselves with ointment, & sometimes not.*

3. *There are some people, who although they are not Sorcerers, if they are anointed, are none the less carried off to the Sabbat. The reason for this.*
4. *The unguent, & the ointment are actually of no use to the Sorcerers, and do not in effect carry them to the Sabbat.*
5. *Sorcerers are sometimes conveyed to the Sabbat by a blast of wind & a sudden storm.*

Chapter XVII. Sorcerers may sometimes walk to the Sabbat on foot.

Chapter XVIII. Is the journey of Sorcerers to the Sabbat merely imagination ?

1 & 3. *Reasons for supposing this to be the case, & examples.*
2. *Indications, owing to which it may be supposed, that a certain woman paid a purely imaginary visit to the Sabbat.*
4. *Reasons for supposing that the journey of Sorcerers to the Sabbat, is a real expedition and not imaginary.*
5. *How we are to understand what is related concerning Erichtho, & Apollonius ; the first of whom raised a soldier to life, & the latter a young girl.*
6. *Sorcerers cannot raise the dead to life. Examples.*
7. *Neither can heretics perform miracles. Examples.*
8. *The Author's opinion concerning the subject of this chapter.*
9. *Satan most frequently deceives mankind. Examples.*

Chapter XIX.

1. *Sorcerers go to the Sabbat about midnight.*
2. *The reason why the Sabbat is generally held at night.*
3. *Satan delights in darkness & blackness, which are opposite to the whiteness and light that please Heaven.*
4. *At the Sabbat Sorcerers dance back to back. For the most part they wear masks.*
5 & 8. *When the cock crows the Sabbat immediately comes to an end, and vanishes away. The reason for this.*
6. *The voice of the cock frightens Satan in the same way as it terrifies lions & serpents.*
7. *Several authors relate that demons fear a naked sword.*

Chapter XX. The days on which the Sabbat is held.

1. *The Sabbat may be held on any day of the week, but particularly on a Friday.*
2. *It is also held on the greatest festivals of the year.*

Chapter XXI. The places where the Sabbat is held.

1. *According to many writers the place where the Sabbat is held is distinguished by a clump of trees, or sometimes by a cross. The Author's opinion on this point.*
2. *A remarkable account of a place where the Sabbat was held.*
3. *There must be water near the place where the Sabbat is held. The reason for this.*
4. *If there is no water in the place, the Sorcerers dig a hole in the ground and urinate in this.*

Chapter XXII. The proceedings at the Sabbat.

1. *The Sorcerers worship the Devil who appears under the form of a tall black man, or as a goat. They offer him candles & kiss his posterior.*
2. *They dance. A description of their dances.*
3. *They give themselves up to every kind of filthy abomination. The Devil transforms himself into an Incubus & into a Succubus.*
4. *The hideous orgies & foul copulations practised by the Euchites, & Gnostics.*
5. *The Sorcerers feast at the Sabbat. Their meat & their drink. The way in which they say grace before and after table.*
6. *However, this food never satisfies their appetites, & they always arise from table as hungry as before.*
7. *When they have finished their meal, they give the Devil a full account of all their actions.*
8. *They again renounce God, their baptism, &c. How Satan incites them to do evil.*
9. *They raise dark storms.*
10. *They celebrate their mass. Of their vestments, & holy water.*
11. *Sometimes to conclude the Sabbat Satan seems to be consumed in a flame of fire, & to be completely reduced*

to ashes. All present take a small part of these ashes, which the Sorcerers use for their charms.

12. *Satan is always the Ape of God in everything.*

As the procedure in the various Sabbats differed very greatly according to century, decade, country, district, nay, even in view of the station of life and, it would seem, the very temperaments of the assembly, it is only possible to outline in a general way some of the most remarkable ceremonies which took place on the occasions of these infernal congregations. An intimate and intensive study of the Sabbat would require a large volume, for it is quite possible to reconstruct the rites in every particular, although the precise order of the ritual was not always and everywhere the same.

Dom Calmet, it is true, has very mistakenly said: "To attempt to give a description of the Sabbat, is to attempt a description of what does not exist, & what has never existed save in the fantastic & disordered imagination of warlocks & witches: the pictures which have been drawn of these assemblies are merely the phantasy of those who dreamed that they had actually been borne, body & soul, through the air to the Sabbat."[66] Happy sceptic! But unfortunately the Sabbat did—and does—take place; formerly in deserted wastes, on the hill-side, in secluded spots, now, as often as not, in the privacy of vaults and cellars, and in those lone empty houses innocently placarded "To be Sold."

The President of the Sabbat was in purely local gatherings often the Officer of the district; in the more solemn assemblies convened from a wider area, the Grand Master, whose dignity would be proportionate to the numbers of the company and the extent of his province. In any case the President was officially known as the "Devil," and it would seem that his immediate attendants and satellites were also somewhat loosely termed "devils," which formal nomenclature has given rise to considerable confusion and not a little mystification in the reports of witch trials and the confessions of offenders. But in many instances it is certain—and orthodoxy forbids us to doubt the possibility—that the Principle of Evil, incarnate, was present for the hideous adoration of his besotted worshippers. Such is the sense of the Fathers, such is the conclusion of the theologians who have dealt with these dark abominations. Metaphysically it is possible; historically it is indisputable.

When a human being, a man, occupied the chief position at these meetings and directed the performance of the rites, he would sometimes appear in a hideous and grotesque disguise, sometimes without any attempt at concealment. This masquerade generally took the shape of an animal, and had its origin in heathendom, whence by an easy transition through the ceremonial of heretics, it passed to the sorcerer and the witch. As early as the *Liber Pœnitentialis* of S. Theodore, Archbishop of Canterbury, 668–690, we have a distinct prohibition of this foul mummery. Capitulum xxvii denounces the man who "in Kalendas Ianuarii in ceruulo et in uitula uadit." "If anyone at the kalends of January goes about as a stag or a bull; that is making himself into a wild animal and dressing in the skin of a herd animal, and putting on the head of beasts; those who in such wise transform themselves into the appearance of a wild animal, penance for three years because this is devilish."

Among the many animal forms which the leader of the Sabbat (the "Devil") assumed in masquerade the most common are the bull, the cat, and above all the goat. Thus the Basque term for the Sabbat is "Akhelarre," "goat pasture." Sometimes the leader is simply said to have shown himself in the shape of a beast, which possibly points to the traditional disguise of a black hairy skin, horns, hoofs, claws, and a tail, in fact the same dress as a demon wore upon the stage.[67] In an old German ballad, *Druten Zeitung*, printed at Smalcald in 1627, "to be sung to the tune of *Dorothea*," it is said that the judges, anxious to extort a confession from a witch, sent down into her twilight dungeon the common hangman dressed in a bear's skin with horns, hoofs, and tail complete. The miserable prisoner thinking that Lucifer had indeed visited her at once appealed to him for help:

Man shickt ein Henkersnecht
Zu ihr in Gefängniss n'unter,
   Den man hat kleidet recht,
Mit einer Bärnhaute,
   Als wenns der Teufel wär;
Als ihm die Drut anschaute
   Meints ihr Bühl kam daher.

Here we have a curious and perhaps unique example of the demoniac masquerade subtly used to obtain evidence of guilt by a trick. The Aberdeen witch Jonet Lucas (1597) said that the Devil was at the Sabbat "beand in likenes of ane beist." But Agnes Wobster of the same company declared that "Satan apperit to them in the likenes of a calff," so possibly two masquerades were employed. Gabriel Pellé (1608) confessed that he attended a Sabbat presided over by the Devil, and "le Diable estoit en vache noire."[68] Francoise Secretain, who was tried in August, 1598, saw the Devil "tantost en forme de chat." Rolande de Vernois acknowledged "Le Diable se presenta pour lors au Sabbat en forme d'vn groz chat noir."[69] To the goat there are innumerable allusions. In the Basses-Pyrénées (1609): "Le Diable estoit en forme de bouc ayant vne queue & audessous vn visage d'homme noir." (The Devil appeared in the form of a goat having a tail & his fundament was the face of a black man.) Iohannis d'Aguerre said that the Devil was "en forme de bouc."[70] "Marie d'Aguerre said that there was in the midst of the ring an immense pitcher whence the Devil issued in the form of a goat." Gentien le Clerc, who was tried at Orleans in 1614, "said that, as he was told, his mother when he was three years old presented him at the Sabbat to a goat whom they saluted as l'Aspic."[71] "Sur le trône," writes Görres, "est assis un bouc, ou du moins la forme d'un bouc, car le démon ne peut cacher ce qu'il est."[72]

In 1630 Elizabeth Stevenson, *alias* Toppock, of Niddrie, avowed to her judges that in company with Catharine Oswald, who was tried for being by *habite and repute* a witch, and Alexander Hamilton, "a known warlock," she went "to a den betwixt Niddrie and Edmiston, where the devill had trysted hir, where he appeared first to them like a foall, and then like a man, and appointed a new dyet at Salcott Muire." When one of Catharine Oswald's intimates, Alexander Hunter, *alias* Hamilton, *alias* Hattaraick, a "Warlok Cairle" who "abused the Countrey for a long time,"[73] was apprehended at Dunbar he confessed that the Devil would meet him riding upon a black horse, or in the shape of a *corbie*, a cat, or a dog. He was burned upon Castle Hill, Edinburgh, 1631.

Sometimes those who are present at the Sabbat are

masked. Canon Ribet writes: "Les visiteurs du sabbat se cachent quelquefois sous des formes bestiales, on se couvrent le visage d'un masque pour demeurer inconnus."[74] (Those who attend the Sabbat sometimes disguise themselves as beasts, or cover their faces to conceal their identities.)

At the famous Sabbat of one hundred and forty witches in North Berwick churchyard on All Hallow e'en, 1590, when they danced "endlong the Kirk-yard" "John Fian, missellit [masked] led the ring." The Salamanca doctors mention the appearance at the Sabbats of persons "aut aperta, aut linteo uelata facie,"[75] "with their faces sometimes bare, sometimes shrouded in a linen wimple." And Delrio has in reference to this precaution: "Facie interdum aperta, interdum uelata larua, linteo, uel alio uelamine aut persona."[76] (Sometimes their faces are bare, sometimes hidden, either in a vizard, a linen cloth, or a veil, or a mask.)

In the latter half of the eighteenth century the territory of Limburg was terrorized by a mysterious society known as "The Goats." These wretches met at night in a secret chapel, and after the most hideous orgies, which included the paying of divine honours to Satan and other foul blasphemies of the Sabbat, they donned masks fashioned to imitate goats' heads, cloaked themselves with long disguise mantles, and sallied forth in bands to plunder and destroy. From 1772 to 1774 alone the tribunal of Foquemont condemned four hundred Goats to the gallows. But the organization was not wholly exterminated until about the year 1780 after a regime of the most repressive measures and unrelaxing vigilance.

Among certain tribes inhabiting the regions of the Congo there exists a secret association of Egbo worshippers. Egbo or Ekpé is the evil genius or Satan. His rites are Obeeyahism, the adoration of Obi, or the Devil, and devil-worship is practised by many barbarous races, as, for instance, by the Coroados and the Tupayas, in the impenetrable forests between the rivers Prado and Doce in Brazil, by the Abipones of Paraguay, as well as by the Bachapins, a Caffre race, by the negroes on the Gold Coast and the negroes of the West Indies. In the ju-ju houses of the Egbo sorcerers are obscene wooden statues to which great veneration is paid, since by their means divination is solemnly practised. Certain festivals are held during the year, and at these it is interesting to note that the members wear hideous black masks with huge horns which it is death for the uninitiated to see.

The first ceremony of the Sabbat was the worship of, and the paying homage to the Devil. It would seem that sometimes this was preceded by a roll-call of the evil devotees. Agnes Sampson confessed that at the meeting in North Berwick, when the whole assembly had entered the church, "The *Devil* started up himself in the *Pulpit* like a mickle black man, and calling the Row, every one answered *Here. Mr. Robert Grierson* being named, they all ran *hirdie girdie,* and were angry: for it was promised he should be called *Robert* the *Comptroller, alias Rob* the *Rower,* for expriming of his name. The first thing he demanded was whether they had been good servants, and what they had done since the last time they had convened."

The witches adored Satan, or the Master of the Sabbat who presided in place of Satan, by prostrations, genuflections, gestures, and obeisances. In mockery of solemn bows and seemly courtesies the worshippers of the Demon approach him awkwardly, with grotesque and obscene mops and mows, sometimes straddling sideways, sometimes walking backwards, as Guazzo says: Cum accedunt ad dæmones eos ueneraturi terga obuertunt & cessim eum cancrorum more supplicaturi manus inuersas retro applicant.[77] But their chief act of homage was the reverential kiss, *osculum infame.* This impious and lewd ritual is mentioned in detail by most authorities and is to be found in all lands and centuries. So Delrio writes: "The Sabbat is presided over by a Demon, the Lord of the Sabbat, who appears in some monstrous form, most generally as a goat or some hound of hell, seated upon a haughty throne. The witches who resort to the Sabbat approach the throne with their backs turned, and worship him . . . and then, as a sign of their homage, they kiss his fundament." Guazzo notes: "As a sign of homage witches kiss the Devil's fundament." And Ludwig Elich says: "Then as a token of their homage—with reverence be it spoken—they kiss the fundament of the Devil."[78] "Y al tiempo que le besan debajo de la cola, da una ventosidad de muy horrible olor," adds the Spanish *Relacion,* "fetid, foul, and filthy."

To cite other authorities would be but to quote the same words. Thomas Cooper, indeed, seems to regard this ceremony as a part of the rite of admission, but to confine it to this occasion alone is manifestly incorrect, for there is continual record of its observance at frequent Sabbats by witches of many years standing. "Secondly," he remarks, "when this acknowledgement is made, in testimoniall of this subiection, Satan offers his back-parts to be kissed of his vassall."[79] But in the dittay of the North Berwick witches, all of whom had long been notorious for their malpractices, "*Item*, the said Agnis Sampson confessed that the divell being then at North Barrick Kerke, attending their comming, in the habit or likenesse of a man,[80] and seeing that they tarried over long, hee at their comming enjoyned them all to a pennance, which was, that they should kisse his buttockes, in sign of duety to him, which being put over the pulpit bare, every one did as he had enjoyned them."[81]

One of the principal charges which was repeatedly brought against the Knights Templars during the lengthy ecclesiastical and judicial processes, 1307–1314, was that of the *osculum infame* given by the juniors to their preceptors. Even so prejudiced a writer as Lea cannot but admit the truth of this accusation. In this case, however, it has nothing to do with sorcery but must be connected with the homosexuality which the Order universally practised.

There are some very important details rehearsed in a Bull, 8 June, 1303, of the noble but calumniated Boniface VIII, with reference to the case of Walter Langton, Bishop of Lichfield and Coventry (1296–1322), and treasurer of Edward I, when this prelate was accused of sorcery and homage to Satan: "For some time past it has come to our ears that our Venerable Brother Walter Bishop of Coventry and Lichfield has been commonly defamed, and accused, both in the realm of England and elsewhere, of paying homage to the Devil by kissing his posterior, and that he hath had frequent colloquies with evil spirits."[82] The Bishop cleared himself of these charges with the compurgators. Bodin refers to Guillaume Edeline, who was executed in 1453 as a wizard. He was a doctor of the Sorbonne, and prior of St. Germain en Laye: "The aforesaid sire Guillaume confessed . . . that he had done homage to the aforesaid Satan, who appeared in the shape of a ram, by kissing his buttocks in token of reverence and homage."[83] A very rare tract of the fourteenth century directed against the Waldenses among other charges brings the following: "Item, in aliquibus aliis partibus apparet eis dæmon sub specie et figura cati, quem sub cauda sigillatim osculantur." (The Devil appears to them as a cat, and they kiss him *sub cauda.*)[84]

Barthélemy Minguet of Brécy, a young man of twenty-five, who was tried in 1616, said that at the Sabbat "he often saw [the Devil] in the shape of a man, who held a horse by its bridle, & that they went forward to worship him, each one holding a pitch candle of black wax in their hands."[85] These candles, as Guazzo tells us, were symbolic and required by the ritual of the Sabbat, not merely of use for the purpose of giving light: "Then they made an offering of pitch black candles, and as a sign of homage kissed his fundament."[86] The candles were ordinarily black, and one taper, larger than the rest, was frequently carried by the Devil himself. At the North Berwick meeting when the witches were all to assemble in the church, "*Iohn Fein* blew up the Kirk doors, and blew in the lights, which wer like *Mickl black candles sticking round about the Pulpit.*"[87] Boguet relates that the witches whom he tried confessed that the Sabbat commenced with the adoration of Satan, "who appeared, sometimes in the shape of a tall dark man, sometimes in the shape of a goat, & to express their worship and homage, they made him an offering of candles, which burned with a blue light."[88] John Fian, also, when doing homage to the Devil "thought he saw the light of a candle . . . which appeared blue lowe." This, of course, was on account of the sulphurous material whence these candles were specially compounded. De Lancre expressly states that the candles or flambeaux used at the Sabbat were made of pitch.

An important feature of the greater Sabbats was the ritual dance, for the dance was an act of devotion which has descended to us from the earliest times and is to be found in every age and every country. Dancing is a natural movement, a primitive expression of emotion and ideals. In the ancient world there can have been few things fairer than that rhythmic thanksgiving of supple limbs and sweet voices which Athens loved, and for many a century was preserved the memory of that day when the young Sophocles lead the choir in celebration of the victory of Salamis.[89] The Mystæ in the meadows of Elysium danced their rounds with the silver clash of cymbals and with madly twinkling snow-white feet. At the solemn procession of the Ark from Cariathiarim (Kirjath Jearim) King David " danced with all his might before the Lord, . . . dancing and leaping before the Lord." S. Basil urges his disciples to dance on earth in order to fit themselves for what may be one of the occupations of the angels in heaven. As late as the seventeenth century the ceremonial dance in church was not uncommon. In 1683 it was the duty of the senior canon to lead a dance of choir-boys in the Paris cathedral. Among the Abyssinian Christians dancing forms no inconsiderable part of worship. Year by year on Whit Tuesday hundreds of pilgrims dance through the streets of Echternach (Luxemburg) to the shrine of S. Willibrod in S. Peter's Church. Formerly the devotees danced three times round the great Abbey Courtyard before proceeding to the sanctuary. But beyond all these the dance has its own place in the ritual of Holy Church even yet. Three times a year in Seville Cathedral—on Holy Thursday, upon Corpus Christi and the Immaculate Conception—Los Seises dance before a specially constructed altar, exquisitely adorned with flowers and lights, erected near the outer door of the grand western entrance of the cathedral. The ceremony in all probability dates from the thirteenth century.

The dresses of the boys, who dance before the improvised altar at Benediction on Corpus Christi, are of the period of Philip III, and consist of short trousers and jackets that hang from one shoulder, the doublets being of red satin, with rich embroidery. Plumed white hats with feathers are worn, also shoes with large scintillating buckles. On Holy Thursday the costume is also red and white, whilst it is blue and white for " the day of the Virgin."

The eight boy choristers—with eight others as attendants—dance, with castanets in their hands, to a soft organ obbligato, down the centre of the cathedral to the decorated altar, advancing slowly and gracefully. Here they remain for about a quarter of an hour, singing a hymn, and accompanying it (as the carols of the olden time) with dance and castanets.

They sing a two-part hymn in front of the altar, forming in two eights, facing each other, the clergy kneeling in a semicircle round them.

Assuredly I cannot do better than quote Mr. Arthur Symons' verdict on this dance as he saw it a few years back in Seville : " And, yes, I found it perfectly dignified, perfectly religious, without a suspicion of levity or indecorum. This consecration of the dance, this turning of a possible vice into a means of devotion, this bringing of the people's art, the people's passion, which in Seville is dancing, into the church, finding it a place there, is precisely one of those acts of divine worldly wisdom which the Church has so often practised in her conquest of the world."

Not too fantastically has a writer suggested that High Mass itself in some sense enshrines a survival of the ancient religious dance—that stately, magnificent series of slow movements which surely may express devotion of the most solemn and reverent kind, as well as can the colour of vestment or sanctuary, or the sounds of melody.

Since the dance is so essentially religious it must needs be burlesqued and buffooned by God's ape. For the dance of the witches is degraded, awkward, foul, and unclean. These very movements are withershins, as Guazzo points out: " Then follow the round dances in which, however, they always tread the measure to the left."[90] " The Sorcerers," says Boguet, " dance a country-dance with their backs turned one to the other."[91] This, of course, being the exact reverse of the natural country-dance. " Sometimes, although seldom," he adds, " they dance in couples, & sometimes one partner is there, another here, for always everything is in confusion."[92] De Lancre writes of witches' revels : " They only dance three kinds of brawls. . . . The first is *à la Bohêmienne* . . . the second with quick trippings : these are round dances."[93] In the third Sabbat measure the dancers were placed one behind another in a straight line.

An old Basque legend reported by Estefanella Hirigaray describes how the witches were wont to meet near an old limekiln to dance their rounds, a ceremony regarded throughout that district as an essential feature of the Sabbat. De Lancre notes the brawls *à la Bohêmienne* as especially favoured by sorcerers in Labourd. Sylvester Mazzolini, O.P.

(1460–1523), Master of the Sacred Palace, and the great champion of orthodoxy against the heresiarch Luther, in his erudite *De Strigimagia*[94] relates that in Como and Brescia a number of children between eight and twelve years old, who had frequented the Sabbat, but had been happily converted by the unsparing patience of the Inquisitors, at the request of the Superiors gave exhibitions of these dances when they showed such extraordinary adroitness and skill in executing the most intricate and fantastic figures that it was evident they had been instructed by no mere human tutelage. Marco de Viqueria, the Dominican Prior of the Brussels monastery, closely investigated the matter, and he was a religious of such known acumen and exceptional probity that his testimony soon convinced many prelates at Rome who were inclined to suspect some trickery or cunning practice. In Belgium this Sabbat dance was known as *Pauana*.

In the Fian trial Agnes Sampson confessed that " They danced along the *Kirk-yeard, Geilic Duncan* playing on a *Trump*, and *John Fein* mussiled led the *Ring*. The said *Agnes* and her daughter followed next. Besides these were *Kate Gray, George Noilis* his wife, . . . with the rest of their Cummers above an hundred Persons."[95] She further added " that this Geillis Duncane did goe before them, playing this reill or daunce uppon a small trumpe, called a Jewe's trumpe, untill they entered into the Kerk of North Barrick."[96] " These confessions made the King [James I, then James VI of Scotland] in a wonderfull admiration, and sent for the saide Geillis Duncane, who, upon the like trumpe, did play the saide daunce before the kinges maiestie."

Music generally accompanied the dancers, and there is ample evidence that various instruments were played, violins, flutes, tambourines, citterns, hautboys, and, in Scotland, the pipes. Those of the witches who had any skill were the performers, and very often they obliged the company awhile with favourite airs of a vulgar kind, but the concert ended in the most hideous discords and bestial clamour ; the laws of harmony and of decency were alike rudely violated. In August, 1590, a certain Nicolas Laghernhard, on his way to Assencauria, was passing through the outskirts of a wood when he saw through the trees a number of men and women dancing with filthy and fantastic movements. In amaze he signed himself and uttered the Holy Name, whereupon the company perceiving him took to flight, but not before he had recognized many of these wretches. He was prompt to inform the ecclesiastical tribunals, and several persons being forthwith questioned freely acknowledged their infamies. Amongst these a shepherd named Michael, who enjoyed a considerable reputation for his musical talents and strangely fascinating voice, confessed that he was the piper at the local Sabbat and that his services were in constant requisition. At the lesser Sabbats (*aquelarre*) of Zugarramurdi, a hamlet of Navarre, some six hundred souls, in the Bastan valley, some twelve leagues from Pampluna, one Juan de Goyburu was wont to play upon the flute, and Juan de Sansin the tambourine. These two unhappy wretches, having shown every sign of sincerest contrition, were reconciled to the Church.

Sinclar in his Relation XXXV, "Anent some Prayers, Charms, and Avies, used in the *Highlands*," says: "As the Devil is originally the Author of *Charms*, and *Spells*, so is he the Author of several baudy Songs, which are sung. A reverend Minister told me, that one who was the Devils Piper, a wizzard confest to him, that at a Ball of dancing, the Foul Spirit taught him a Baudy song to sing and play, as it were this night, and ere two days past all the Lads and Lasses of the town were lilting it throw the street. It were abomination to rehearse it." Philip Ludwig Elich precisely sums up the confused scene: "The whole foul mob and stinkard rabble sing the most obscene priapics and abominable songs in honour of the Devil. One witch yells, *Harr, harr;* a second hag, Devil, Devil; jump hither, jump thither; a third, Gambol hither, gambol thither; another, *Sabaoth, Sabaoth*, &c.; and so the wild orgy waxes frantic what time the bedlam rout are screeching, hissing, howling, caterwauling, and whooping lewd wassail."[97] Of all the horrors of the Sabbat the climax was that appalling blasphemy and abominable impiety by which the most Holy Sacrifice of the Altar was mocked and burlesqued in hideous fashion. And since no Christian will receive the Blessed Sacrament save he be duly fasting as the Church so strictly enjoins, the witches in derision of Christ's ordinance satiate their appetites with a wolfish feast and cram themselves to excess with food of all kinds, both meat and drink, before they proceed to the ritual of hell. These orgies were often prolonged amid circumstances of the most beastly gluttony and drunkenness.

Guazzo writes: "Tables are laid and duly furnished, whereupon they set themselves to the board & begin to gobbet piecemeal the meats which the Devil provides, or which each member of the party severally brings with him."[98] De Lancre also says: "Many authors say that sorcerers at the Sabbat eat the food which the Devil lays before them: but very often the table is only dressed with the viands they themselves bring along. Sometimes there are certain tables served with rare dainties, at others with orts and offal." "Their banquets are of various kinds of food according to the district & the quality of those who are to partake."[99] It seems plain that when the local head of the witches, who often presided at these gatherings *absente diabolo*, was a person of wealth or standing, delicacies and choice wines would make their appearance at the feast, but when it was the case of the officer of a coven in some poor and small district, possibly a meeting of peasants, the homeliest fare only might be served. The Lancashire witches of 1613, when they met at Malking Tower, sat down to a goodly spread of "Beefe, Bacon, and roasted Mutton," the sheep having been killed twenty-four hours earlier by James Device; in 1633 Edmund Robinson stated that the Pendle witches offered him "flesh and bread upon a trencher, and drink in a glass," they also had "flesh smoaking, butter in lumps, and milk," truly rustic dainties. Alice Duke, a Somerset witch, tried in 1664, confessed that the Devil "bids them *Welcome* at their *Coming*, and brings them *Wine*, *Beer*, *Cakes*, and *Meal*, or the like."[100] At the trial of Louis Gaufridi at Aix in 1610 the following description of a Sabbat banquet was given: "Then they feasted, three tables being set out according to the three aforesaid degrees. Those who were employed in serving bread had loaves made from wheat privily stolen in various places. They drank malmsey in order to excite them to venery. Those who acted as cup-bearers had filched the wine from cellars where it was stored. Sometimes they ate the tender flesh of little children, who had been slain and roasted at some Synagogue, and sometimes babes were brought there, yet alive, whom the witches had kidnapped from their homes if opportunity offered."[101] In many places the witches were not lucky enough to get bumpers of malmsey, for Boguet notes that at some Sabbats "They not unseldom drink wine but more often water."[102]

There are occasional records of unsavoury and tasteless viands, and there is even mention of putrefying garbage and carrion being placed before his evil worshippers by their Master. Such would appear to have been the case at those darker orgies when there was a manifestation of supernatural intelligences from the pit.

The Salamanca doctors say: "They make a meal from food either furnished by themselves or by the Devil. It is sometimes most delicious and delicate, and sometimes a pie baked from babies they have slain or disinterred corpses. A suitable grace is said before such a table."[103] Guazzo thus describes their wine: "Moreover the wine which is usually poured out for the revellers is like black and clotted blood served in some foul and filthy vessel. Yet there seems to be no lack of cheer at these banquets, save that they furnish neither bread nor salt. Isabella further added that human flesh was served."[104]

Salt never appeared at the witches' table. Bodin gives us the reason that it is an emblem of eternity,[105] and Philip Ludwig Elich emphatically draws attention to the absence of salt at these infernal banquets.[106] "At these meals," remarks Boguet, "salt never appears."[107] Gentien le Clerc, who was tried in Orleans in 1615, confessed: "They sit down to table, but no salt is ever seen."[108] Madeleine de la Palud declared that she had never seen salt, olives, or oil at the Devil's feasts.[109]

When all these wretches are replete they proceed to a solemn parody of Holy Mass.

At the beginning of the eighteenth century Marcelline Pauper of the Congregation of the Sisters of Charity of Nevers was divinely called to offer herself up as a victim of reparation for the outrages done to the Blessed Sacrament, especially by sorcerers in their black masses at the Sabbat. In March, 1702, a frightful sacrilege was committed in the convent chapel. The tabernacle was forced open, the ciborium stolen, and those of the Hosts which had not been carried away by the Satanists were thrown to the pavement and trampled under foot. Marcelline made ceaseless reparation, and at nine o'clock of the evening of 26 April, she received the stigmata in hands, feet, and side, and also the Crown of Thorns. After a few years of expiation she died at Tulle, 25 June, 1708.

The erudite Paul Grilland tells us that the liturgy is burlesqued in every detail: "Those witches who have solemnly devoted themselves to the Devil's service, worship him in a particular manner with ceremonial sacrifices, which they offer to the Devil, imitating in all respects the worship of Almighty God, with vestments, lights, and every other ritual observance, and with a set liturgy in which they are instructed, so that they worship and praise him eternally, just as we worship the true God."[110] This abomination of blasphemy is met with again and again in the confessions of witches, and although particulars may differ here and there, the same quintessence of sacrilege persisted throughout the centuries, even as alas! in hidden corners and secret lairs of infamy it skulks and lurks this very day.

What appears extremely surprising in this connexion is the statement of Cotton Mather that the New England witches "met in Hellish *Randezvous*, wherein the Confessors (i.e. the accused who confessed) do say, they have had their Diabolical Sacraments, imitating the *Baptism* and the *Supper* of our Lord."[111] At the trial of Bridget Bishop, *alias* Oliver, at the Court of Oyer and Terminer, held at Salem, 2 June, 1692, Deliverance Hobbs, a converted witch, affirmed "that this *Bishop* was at a General Meeting of the Witches, in a Field at *Salem*-Village, and there partook of a Diabolical Sacrament in Bread and Wine then administered." In the case of Martha Carrier, tried 2 August, 1692, before the same court, two witnesses swore they had seen her "at a Diabolical Sacrament . . . when they had Bread and Wine Administered unto them." Abigail Williams confessed that on 31 March, 1692, when there was a Public Fast observed in Salem on account of the scourge of sorcery "the Witches had a *Sacrament* that day at an house in the Village, and that they had *Red Bread* and *Red Drink*." This "Red Bread" is certainly puzzling. But the whole thing, sufficiently profane no doubt, necessarily lacks the hideous impiety of the black mass. A minister, the Rev. George Burroughs, is pointed to by accumulated evidence as being the Chief of the Salem witches; "he was Accused by Eight of the Confessing Witches as being an Head Actor at some of their Hellish Randezvouses, and one who had the promise of being a King in Satan's kingdom"; it was certainly he who officiated at their ceremonies, for amongst others Richard Carrier "affirmed to the jury that he saw Mr. George Burroughs at the witch meeting at the village and saw him administer the sacrament," whilst Mary Lacy, senr., and her daughter Mary "affirmed that Mr. George Burroughs was at the witch meetings with witch sacraments."[112]

The abomination of the black mass is performed by some apostate or renegade priest who has delivered himself over to the service of evil and is shamefully prominent amongst the congregation of witches. It should be remarked from this fact that it is plain the witches are as profoundly convinced of the doctrines of Transubstantiation, the Totality, Permanence, and Adorableness of the Eucharistic Christ, and of the power also of the sacrificing priesthood, as is the most orthodox Catholic. Indeed, unless such were the case, their revolt would be empty, void at any rate of its material malice.

One of the gravest charges brought against the Templars and in the trials (1307–1314) established beyond any question or doubt was that of celebrating a blasphemous mass in which the words of consecration were omitted. It has, indeed, been suggested that the liturgy used by the Templars was not the ordinary Western Rite, but that it was an Eastern Eucharist. According to Catholic teaching the Consecration takes place when the words of institution are recited with intention and appropriate gesture, the actual change of the entire substances of bread and wine into the Body and Blood of Christ being effected in virtue of the words *Hoc est enim Corpus meum; Hic est enim Calix sanguinis mei. . . .* This has been defined by a decree of the Council of Florence (1439): "Quod illa uerba diuina Saluatoris omnem uirtutem transsubstantiationis habent." (These divine words of Our Saviour have full power to effect transubstantiation.) But the Orthodox Church holds that an Epiklesis is necessary to valid consecration, the actual words of Our Lord being repeated "as a narrative" [διηγηματικῶς],[113] which would seem logically to imply that Christ's words have no part in the form of the Sacrament. In all Orthodox liturgies the words of Consecration are found together with the Epiklesis, and there are in existence some few liturgies, plainly invalid, which omit the words of Consecration altogether. These are all of them forms which have been employed by heretical sects; and it may be that the Templars used one of these. But it is far more probable that the words were purposely omitted; the Templars were corroded with Gnostic doctrines, they held the heresies of the Mandæans or Johannites who were filled with an insane hatred of Christ in much the same way as witches and demonolaters, they followed the tenets of the Ophites who venerated the Serpent and prayed to him for protection against the Creator, they adored and offered sacrifice before an idol, a Head, which, as Professor Prutz holds, represented the lower god whom Gnostic bodies worshipped, that is Satan. At his trial in Tuscany the knight Bernard of Parma confessed that the Order firmly believed this idol had the power to save and to enrich, in fine, flat diabolism. The secret mass of the Templars may have burlesqued an Eastern liturgy rather than the Western rite, but none the less it was the essential cult of the evil principle.

In 1336 a priest who had been imprisoned by the Comte de Foix, Gaston III Phébus, on a charge of celebrating a Satanic mass, was sent to Avignon and examined by Benedict XII in person. The next year the same pontiff appointed his trusty Guillaume Lombard to preside at the trial of Pierre du Chesne, a priest from the diocese of Tarbes, accused of defiling the Host.

Gilles de Sillé, a priest of the diocese of S. Malo, and the Florentine Antonio Francesco Prelati, formerly of the diocese of Arezzo, were wont to officiate at the black masses of Tiffauges and Machecoul, the castles of Gilles de Rais, who was executed in 1440.

A priest named Benedictus in the sixteenth century caused great scandal by the discovery of his assistance at secret and unhallowed rites. Charles IX employed an apostate monk to celebrate the eucharist of hell before himself and his intimates, and during the reign of his brother the Bishop of

Paris burned in the Place de Grève a friar named Séchelle who had been found guilty of participating in similar profane mysteries. In 1597 the Parliament of Paris sentenced Jean Belon, curé of S. Pierre-des-Lampes in the Bourges diocese, to be hanged and his body burned for desecration of the Sacrament and the repeated celebration of abominable ceremonies.[114] The Parliament of Bordeaux in 1598 condemned to the stake Pierre Aupetit, curé of Pageas, near Chalus Limousin. He confessed that for more than twenty years he had frequented Sabbats, especially those held at Mathegoutte and Puy-de-Dôme, where he worshipped the Devil and performed impious masses in his honour.[115] August 14, 1606, a friar named Denobilibus was put to death at Grenoble upon a similar conviction. In 1609 the Parliament of Bordeaux sent Pierre De Lancre and d'Espagnet to Labourd in the Bayonne district to stamp out the sorcerers who infested that region. No less than seven priests were arrested on charges of celebrating Satan's mass at the Sabbat. Two, Migalena, an old man of seventy, and Pierre Bocal, aged twenty-seven, were executed, but the Bishop of Bayonne interfered, claimed the five for his own tribunal and contrived that they should escape from prison. Three other priests who were under restraint were immediately set free, and wisely quitted the country. A twelvemonth later Aix and the whole countryside rang with the confessions of Madeleine de la Palud who "Dit aussi que ce malheureux Loys magicien . . . a controuvé le premier de dire la messe au sabatt et consacrer Véritablement et présenter le sacrifice à Lucifer."[116] It was, of course, mere ignorance on her part to suppose that " that accursed Magician Lewes did first inuent the saying of Masse at the Sabbaths," although Gaufridi may have told her this to impress her with a sense of his importance and power among the hierarchies of evil. Certainly in her evidence the details of the Sabbat worship are exceptionally detailed and complete.

They are, however, amply paralleled, if not exceeded, by the narrative of Madeleine Bavent, a Franciscan sister of the Third Order, attached to the convent of SS. Louis and Elizabeth at Louviers. Her confessions, which she wrote at length by the direction of her confessor, des Marets, an Oratorian, meticulously describe scenes of the most hideous blasphemy in which were involved three chaplains, David, Maturin Picard, the curé of Mesnil-Jourdain, and Thomas Boullé, sometime his assistant. Amongst other enormities they had revived the heresy of the Adamites, an early Gnostic sect, and celebrated the Mass in a state of stark nudity amid circumstances of the grossest indecency. Upon one Good Friday Picard and Boullé had compelled her to defile the crucifix and to break a consecrated Host, throwing the fragments upon the ground and trampling them. David and Picard were dead, but Boullé was burned at Rouen, 21 August, 1647.[117]

During the reign of Louis XIV a veritable epidemic of sacrilege seemed to rage throughout Paris.[118] The horrors of the black mass were said in many houses, especially in that of La Voisin (Catherine Deshayes) who lived in the rue Beauregard. The leading spirit of this crew was the infamous abbé Guibourg, a bastard son—so gossip said—of Henri de Montmorency. With him were joined Brigallier, almoner of the Grande Mademoiselle; Bouchot, director of the convent of La Saussaye; Dulong, a canon of Notre-Dame; Dulausens, vicar of Saint-Leu; Dubousquet; Seysson; Dussis; Lempérier; Lépreux; Davot, vicar of Notre-Dame de Bonne-Nouvelle; Mariette, vicar of Saint-Séverin, skilled in maledictions; Lemeignan, vicar of Saint-Eustache, who was convicted of having sacrificed numberless children to Satan; Toumet; Le Franc; Cotton, vicar of St. Paul, who had baptized a baby with the chrism of Extreme Unction and then throttled him upon the altar; Guignard and Sébault of the diocese of Bourges, who officiated at the black mass in the cellars of a house at Paris, and confected filthy charms under conditions of the most fearful impiety.

In the eighteenth century the black mass persisted. In 1723 the police arrested the abbé Lecollet and the abbé Bournement for this profanity; and in 1745 the abbé de Rocheblanche fell under the same suspicion. At the hotel of Madame de Charolais the vilest scenes of the Sabbat were continued. A gang of Satanists celebrated their monstrous orgies at Paris on 22 January, 1793, the night after the murder of Louis XVI. The abbé Fiard in two of his works, *Lettres sur le diable*, 1791, and *La France Trompée* . . . Paris, 8vo, 1803, conclusively shows that eucharistic blasphemies were yet being perpetrated but in circumstances of almost impenetrable secrecy. In 1865 a scandal connected with these abominations came to light, and the Bishop of Sens, in whose diocese it occurred, was so horrified that he resigned his office and retired to Fontainebleau, where he died some eighteen months later, practically of shock. Similar practices were unmasked at Paris in 1874 and again in 1878, whilst it is common knowledge that the characters of Joris Karl Huysmans' *Là-Bas* were all persons easy of identification, and the details are scenes exactly reproduced from contemporary life.[119] The hideous cult of evil yet endures. Satanists yet celebrate the black mass in London, Brighton, Paris, Lyons, Bruges, Berlin, Milan, and alas! in Rome itself. Both South America and Canada are thus polluted. In many a town, both great and small, they have their dens of blasphemy and evil where they congregate unsuspected to perform these execrable rites. Often they seem to concentrate their vile energies in the quiet cathedral cities of England, France, Italy, in vain endeavour to disturb the ancient homes of peace with the foul brabble of devil-worship and all ill.

They have even been brought upon the public stage. One episode of *Un Soir de Folie*, the revue (1925–6) at the Folies Bergère, Paris, was "Le Sabbat et la Herse Infernale," where in a Gothic cathedral an actor (Mons. Benglia) appeared as Satan receiving the adoration of his devotees.

At the more frequented Sabbats the ritual of Holy Mass was elaborately burlesqued in almost every detail. An altar was erected with four supports, sometimes under a sheltering tree, at others upon a flat rock, or some naturally convenient place, "auprès d'vn arbre, ou parfois auprès d'vn rocher, dressant quelque forme d'autel sur des colonés infernales," says De Lancre.[120] In more recent times and to-day when the black mass is celebrated in houses such an altar is often permanent and therefore the infernal sanctuary can be builded with a display of the full symbolism of the hideous cult of evil. The altar was covered with the three linen cloths the ritual enjoins, and upon it were six black candles in the midst of which they placed a crucifix inverted, or an image of the Devil. Sometimes the Devil himself occupied this central position, standing erect, or seated on some kind of monstrous throne. In 1598, at a celebrated witch-trial before the Parliament of Bordeaux with the Vicar-general of the Bishop of Limoges and a learned councillor Peyrat as assessors, Antoine Dumons of Saint-Laurent confessed that he had frequently provided a large number of candles for the Sabbat, both wax lights to be distributed among those present and the large black tapers for the altar. These were lit by Pierre Aupetit, who held a sacristan's reed, and apparently officiated as Master of the Ceremonies when he was not actually himself saying the Mass.[121]

In May, 1895, when the legal representatives of the Borghese family visited the Palazzo Borghese, which had been rented for some time in separate floors or suites, they found some difficulty in obtaining admission to certain apartments on the first floor, the occupant of which seemed unaware that the lease was about to expire. By virtue of the terms of the agreement, however, he was obliged to allow them to inspect the premises to see if any structural repairs or alterations were necessary, as Prince Scipione Borghese, who was about to be married, intended immediately to take up his residence in the ancestral home with his bride. One door the tenant obstinately refused to unlock, and when pressed he betrayed the greatest confusion. The agents finally pointed out that they were within their rights to employ actual force, and that if access was longer denied they would not hesitate to do so forthwith. When the keys had been produced, the cause of the reluctance was soon plain. The room within was inscribed with the words *Templum Palladicum*. The walls were hung all round from ceiling to floor with heavy curtains of silk damask, scarlet and black, excluding the light; at the further end there stretched a large tapestry upon which was woven in more than life-size a figure of Lucifer, colossal, triumphant, dominating the whole. Exactly beneath an altar had been built, amply furnished for the liturgy of hell: candles, vessels, rituals, missal, nothing was lacking. Cushioned prie-dieus and luxurious chairs, crimson and gold, were set in order for the assistants; the chamber being lit by electricity, fantastically arrayed so as to glare from an enormous human eye. The visitors soon quitted the accursed spot, the scene of devil-worship and blasphemy, nor had they any desire more the celebrant "wore a chasuble which was embroidered with a Cross; but there were only three bars."[129] Later a contemporary witness points to the use of vestments embroidered with infernal insignia, such as a dark red chasuble, the colour of dried blood, upon which was figured a black buck goat rampant; a chasuble that bore the inverse Cross, and similar robes adorned by some needle with the heraldry of hell.

In bitter mockery of the *Asperges* the celebrant sprinkled the witches with filthy and brackish water, or even with stale. "The Devil at the same time made water into a hole dug in the earth, & used it as holy water, wherewith the celebrant of the mass sprinkled all present, using a black aspergillum."[130] Silvain Nevillon, a sorcerer who was tried at Orleans in 1614–1615, said: "When Tramesabot said Mass, before he commenced he used to sprinkle all present with holy water which was nothing else than urine, saying meanwhile *Asperges Diaboli.*"[131] According to Gentien le Clerc: "The holy water is yellow . . . & after it has been duly sprinkled Mass is said."[132] Madeleine de la Palud declared that the sorcerers were sprinkled with water, and also with consecrated wine from the chalice upon which all present cried aloud: *Sanguis eius super nos et super filios nostros.*[133] (His blood be upon us and upon our children.)

This foul travesty of the holiest mysteries began with an invocation of the Devil, which was followed by a kind of general confession, only each one made mock acknowledgement of any good he might have done, and as a penance he was enjoined to utter some foul blasphemy or to break some precept of the Church. The president absolved the congregation by an inverse sign of the Cross made with the left hand. The rite then proceeded with shameless profanity, but De Lancre remarks that the *Confiteor* was never said, not even in a burlesque form, and *Alleluia* never pronounced. After reciting the Offertory the celebrant drew back a little from the altar and the assembly advancing in file kissed his left hand. When the Queen of the Sabbat—the witch who ranked first after the Grand Master, the oldest and most evil of the witches ("en chasque village," says De Lancre, "trouuer vne Royne du Sabbat")—was present she sat on the left of the altar and received the offerings, loaves, eggs, nearly to examine the appointments of this infernal chapel.[122]

The missal used at the black mass was obviously a manuscript, although it is said that in later times these grimoires of hideous profanity have actually been printed. It is not infrequently mentioned. Thus De Lancre notes that the sorcerers of the Basses-Pyrénées (1609) at their worship saw the officiant " tournant les feuillets d'vn certain liure qu'il a en main."[123] Madeleine Bavent in her confession said: " On lisait la messe dans le livre des blasphèmes, qui servait de canon et qu'on employait aussi dans les processions."[124] The witches' missal was often bound in human skin, generally that of an unbaptized babe.[125] Gentien le Clerc, tried at Orleans, 1614–1615, confessed that " le Diable . . . marmote dans un liure duquel la couuerture est toute veluë comme d'vne peau de loup, auec des feuillets blancs & rouges, d'autres noires."

The vestments worn by the celebrant are variously described. On rare occasions he is described as being arrayed in a bishop's pontificalia, black in hue, torn, squalid, and fusty. Boguet reports that a witch stated: " Celuy, qui est commis à faire l'office, est reuestu d'vne chappe noire sans croix,"[126] but it seems somewhat strange that merely a plain black cope should be used, unless the explanation is to be found in the fact that such a vestment was most easily procurable and no suspicion of its ultimate employment would be excited. The abbé Guibourg sometimes wore a cope of white silk embroidered with fir-cones, which again seems remarkable, as the symbolism is in no way connected with the Satanic rites he performed. But this is the evidence of Marguerite, La Voisin's daughter, who was not likely to be mistaken.[127] It is true that the mass was often, perhaps, partially erotic and not wholly diabolic in the same sense as the Sabbat masses were, but yet Astaroth, Asmodeus, and Lucifer were invoked, and it was a liturgy of evil. On other occasions Guibourg seems to have donned the orthodox eucharistic chasuble, stole, maniple, girdle, alb, and amice. In the thirty-seventh article of his confession Gaufridi acknowledged that the priest who said the Devil's mass at the Sabbat wore a violet chasuble.[128] Gentien le Clerc, tried at Orleans in 1614–1615, was present at a Sabbat mass when any meat or country produce, and money, so long as the coins were not stamped with a cross. In her hand she held a disc or plate " vne paix ou platine," engraved with a figure of the Devil, and this his followers devoutly kissed. In many places to-day, especially Belgium, during Holy Mass the pax-brede (*instrumentum pacis*) is kissed by the congregation at the Offertory, and universally when Mass is said by a priest in the presence of a Prelate the pax-brede is kissed by the officiant and the Prelate after the *Agnus Dei* and the first appropriate ante-communion prayer.

Silvain Nevillon, who was tried at Orleans in 1614–15, avowed : " The Devil preached a sermon at the Sabbat, but nobody could hear what he said, for he spoke in a growl."[134]

At the Sabbat a sermon is not infrequently delivered, a farrago of impiety and evil counsel.

The hosts are then brought to the altar. Boguet describes them as dark and round, stamped with a hideous design ; Madeleine Bavent saw them as ordinary wafers only coloured red ; in other cases they were black and triangular in shape. Often they blasphemed the Host, calling it " Iean le blanc," just as Protestants called it " Jack-in-the-box." The chalice is filled, sometimes with wine, sometimes with a bitter beverage that burned the tongue like fire. At the *Sanctus* a horn sounded harshly thrice, and torches burning with a sulphurous blue flare " qui est fort puante " were kindled. There was an elevation, at which the whole gang, now in a state of hysterical excitement and unnatural exaltation, burst forth with the most appalling screams and maniac blasphemies, rivalling each other in filthy adjurations and crapulous obscenities. The protagonist poured out all the unbridled venom that diabolic foulness could express, a stream of scurrility and pollution ; hell seemed to have vomited its reeking gorge on earth. *Domine adiuua nos, domine adiuua nos,* they cried to the Demon, and again *Domine adiuua nos semper.* Generally all present were compelled to communicate with the sacrament of the pit, to swallow morsels soiled with mud and ordures, to drink the dark brew of damnation. Gaufridi confessed that for *Ite missa est* these infernal orgies concluded with the curse : " Allez-vous-en tous au nom du diable ! " Whilst the abbé Guibourg cried : " *Gloria tibi, Lucifero !* "

The black mass of the Sabbat varied slightly in form according to circumstances, and in the modern liturgy of the Satanists it would appear that a considerable feature is made of the burning of certain heavy and noxious weeds, the Devil's incense. In the sixteenth and seventeenth centuries the use of incense is very rare at the Sabbat, although Silvain Nevillon stated that he had seen at the Sabbat "both holy water and incense. This latter smelled foul, not fragrant as incense burned in church."[135]

The officiant nowadays consecrates a host and the chalice with the actual sacred words of Holy Mass, but then instead of kneeling he turns his back upon the altar,[136] and a few moments later—*sit uenia uerbis!*—he cuts and stabs the Host with a knife, throwing it to the ground, treading upon it, spurning it. A part, at least, of the contents of the chalice is also spilled in fearful profanation, and not infrequently there further has been provided a ciborium of consecrated Hosts, all stolen from churches[137] or conveyed away at Communion in their mouths by wretches unafraid to provoke the sudden judgement of an outraged God. These the black priest, for so the celebrant is called by the Devil worshippers, scatters over the pavement to be struggled and fought for by his congregation in their madness to seize and outrage the Body of Christ.

Closely connected with the black mass of the Satanists and a plain survival from the Middle Ages is that grim superstition of the Gascon peasant, the Mass of S. Sécaire.[138] Few priests know the awful ritual, and of those who are learned in such dark lore fewer yet would dare to perform the monstrous ceremonies and utter the prayer of blasphemy. No confessor, no bishop, not even the Archbishop of Auch, may shrive the celebrant; he can only be absolved at Rome by the Holy Father himself. The mass is said upon a broken and desecrated altar in some ruined or deserted church where owls hoot and mope and bats flit through the crumbling windows, where toads spit their venom upon the sacred stone. The priest must make his way thither late attended only by an acolyte of impure and evil life. At the first stroke of eleven he begins; the liturgy of hell is mumbled backward, the canon said with a mow and a sneer; he ends just as midnight tolls. The host is triangular, with three sharp points and black. No wine is consecrated but foul brackish water drawn from a well wherein has been cast the body of an unbaptized babe. The holy sign of the cross is made with the left foot upon the ground. And the man for whom that mass is said will slowly pine away, nor doctor's skill nor physic will avail him aught, but he will suffer, and dwindle, and surely drop into the grave.[139]

Although there is, no doubt, some picturesque exaggeration here the main details are correct enough. A black, triangular wafer is not infrequently mentioned in the witch-trials as having been the sacramental bread of the Sabbat, whilst Lord Fountainhall[140] in describing the devilish communion of the Loudian witches says: "the drink was sometimes blood, sometimes black moss-water," and many other details may be closely paralleled.

When the blasphemous liturgy of the Sabbat was done all present gave themselves up to the most promiscuous debauchery, only interrupting their lasciviousness to dance or to spur themselves on to new enormities by spiced foods and copious draughts of wine. "You may well suppose," writes Boguet, "that every kind of obscenity is practised there, yea, even those abominations for which Heaven poured down fire and brimstone on Sodom and Gomorrah are quite common in these assemblies."[141] The erudite Dominican, Father Sebastian Michaelis, who on the 19 January, 1611, examined Madeleine de la Palud concerning her participation in Sabbats, writes[142] that she narrated the most unhallowed orgies.[143] The imagination reels before such turpitudes! But Madeleine Bavent (1643) supplied even more execrable details.[144] Gentien le Clerc at Orleans (1614–1615) acknowledged similar debauchery.[145] Bodin relates that a large number of witches whom he tried avowed their presence at the Sabbat.[146] In 1459 "large numbers of men & women were burned at Arras, many of whom had mutually accused one another, & they confessed that at night they had been conveyed to these hellish dances."[147] In 1485 Sprenger executed a large number of sorcerers in the Constance district, and "almost all without exception confessed that the Devil had had connexion with them, after he had made them renounce God and their holy faith."[148] Many converted witches likewise confessed these abominations "and let it be known that whilst they were witches demons had swived them lustily. Henry of Cologne in confirmation of this says that it is very common in Germany."[149] Throughout the centuries all erudite authorities have the same monstrous tale to tell, and it would serve no purpose merely to accumulate evidence from the demonologists. To-day the meetings of Satanists invariably end in unspeakable orgies and hideous debauchery.

Occasionally animals were sacrificed at the Sabbat to the Demon. The second charge against Dame Alice Kyteler, prosecuted in 1324 for sorcery by Richard de Ledrede, Bishop of Ossory, was "that she was wont to offer sacrifices to devils of live animals, which she and her company tore limb from limb and made oblation by scattering them at the cross-ways to a certain demon who was called Robin, son of Artes (Robin Artisson), one of hell's lesser princes."[150]

In 1622 Margaret McWilliam "renounced her baptisme, and he baptised her and she gave him as a gift a hen or cock."[151] In the Voodoo rites of to-day a cock is often the animal which is hacked to pieces before the fetish. Black puppies were sacrificed to Hecate; Æneas offers four jetty bullocks to the infernal powers, a coal-black lamb to Night;[152] at their Sabbat on the Esquiline Canidia and Sagana tear limb from limb a black sheep, the blood streams into a trench.[153] Collin de Plancy states that witches sacrifice black fowls and toads to the Devil.[154] The animal victim to a power worshipped as divine is a relic of remotest antiquity.

The presence of toads at the Sabbat is mentioned in many witch-trials. They seem to have been associated with sorcerers owing to the repugnance they generally excite, and in some districts it is a common superstition that those whom they regard fixedly will be seized with palpitations, spasms, convulsions, and swoons: nay, a certain abbé Rousseau of the eighteenth century, who experimented with toads, avowed that when one of these animals looked upon him for some time he fell in a fainting fit whence, if help had not arrived, he would never have recovered.[155] A number of writers—Ælian, Dioscorides, Nicander, Ætius, Gesner—believe that the breath of the toad is poisonous, infecting the places it may touch. Since such idle stories were credited it is hardly to be surprised at that we find the toad a close companion of the witch. De Lancre says that demons often appeared in that shape. Jeannette d'Abadie, a witch of the Basses-Pyrénées, whom he tried and who confessed at length, declared that she saw brought to the Sabbat a number of toads dressed some in black, some in scarlet velvet, with little bells attached to their coats. In November, 1610, a man walking through the fields near Bazas, noticed that his dog had scratched a large hole in a bank and unearthed two pots, covered with cloth, and closely tied. When opened they were found to be packed with bran, and in the midst of each was a large toad wrapped in green tiffany. These doubtless had been set there by a person who had faith in sympathetic magic, and was essaying a malefic spell. No doubt toads were caught and taken to the Sabbat, nor is the reason far to seek. Owing to their legendary venom they served as a prime ingredient in poisons and potions, and were also used for telling fortunes, since witches often divined by their toad familiars. Juvenal alludes to this when he writes:

> "I neither will, nor can Prognosticate
> To the young gaping Heir, his Father's Fate
> Nor in the Entrails of a Toad have pry'd."[156]

Upon which passage Thomas Farnabie, the celebrated English scholar (1575–1647) glosses thus: "He alludes to the office of the Haruspex who used to inspect entrails & intestines. Pliny says: The entrails of the toad (*Rana rubeta*), that is to say the tongue, tiny bones, gall, heart, have rare virtue for they are used in many medicines and salves. Haply he means the pud-dock or hop-toad, thus demonstrating that these animals are not poisonous, their entrails being completely inefficacious in confecting poisons."[157] In 1610 Juan de Echalar, a sorcerer of Navarre, confessed at his trial before the Alcantarine inquisitor Don Alonso Becerra Holguin that he and his coven collected toads for the Sabbat, and when they presented these animals to the Devil he blessed them with his left hand, after which they were killed and cooked in a stewpot with human bones and pieces of corpses rifled from new-made graves. From this filthy hotch-potch were brewed poisons and unguents that the Devil distributed to all present with directions how to use them. By sprinkling corn with the liquid it was supposed they could blight a standing field, and also destroy flowers and fruit. A few drops let fall upon a person's garments was believed to insure death, and a smear upon the shed or sty effectually diseased cattle. From these crude superstitions the fantastic stories of dancing toads, toads dressed *en cavalier*, and demon toads at the Sabbat were easily evolved.

There is ample and continuous evidence that children, usually tender babes who were as yet unbaptized, were sacrificed at the Sabbat. These were often the witches' own offspring, and since a witch not unseldom was the midwife or wise-woman of a village she had exceptional opportunities of stifling a child at birth as a non-Sabbatial victim to Satan. " There are no persons who can do more cunning harm to the Catholic faith than midwives," says the *Malleus Maleficarum*, Pars I, q. xi: "*Nemo fidei catholicæ amplius nocet quam obstetrices.*" The classic examples of child-sacrifice are those of Gilles de Rais (1440) and the abbé Guibourg (1680). In the process against the former one hundred and forty children are explicitly named: some authorities accept as many as eight hundred victims. Their blood, brains, and bones were used to decoct magic philtres. In the days of Guibourg the sacrifice of a babe at the impious mass was so common that he generally paid not more than a crown-piece for his victim. " Il avait acheté un écu l'enfant qui fut sacrifié à cette messe." (" The child sacrificed at this mass he had bought for a crown.") These abominable ceremonies were frequently performed at the instance of Madame de Montespan in order that Louis XIV should always remain faithful to her, should reject all other mistresses, repudiate his queen, and in fine raise her to the throne.[158] The most general use was to cut the throat of the child, whose blood was drained into the chalice and allowed to fall upon the naked flesh of the inquirer, who lay stretched along the altar. La Voisin asserted that a toll of fifteen hundred infants had been thus murdered. This is not impossible, as a vast number of persons, including a crowd of ecclesiastics, were implicated. Many of the greatest names in France had assisted at these orgies of blasphemy. From first to last no less than two hundred and forty-six men and women of all ranks and grades of society were brought to trial, and whilst thirty-six of humbler station went to the scaffold, one hundred and forty-seven were imprisoned for longer or shorter terms, not a few finding it convenient to leave the country, or, at any rate, to obscure themselves in distant châteaux. But many of the leaves had been torn out of the archives, and Louis himself forbade any mention of his favourite's name in connexion with these prosecutions. However, she was disgraced, and it is not surprising that after the death of Maria Teresa, 31 July, 1683, the king early in the following year married the pious and conventual Madame de Maintenon.

Ludovico Maria Sinistrari writes that witches "promise the Devil sacrifices and offerings at stated times: once a fortnight, or at least each month, the murder of some child, or an homicidal act of sorcery," and again and again in the trials detailed accusation of the kidnapping and murder of children are brought against the prisoners. In the same way as the toad was used for magical drugs so was the fat of the child. The belief that corpses and parts of corpses constitute a most powerful cure and a supreme ingredient in elixirs is universal and of the highest antiquity. The quality of directly curing diseases and of protection has long been attributed to a cadaver. Tumours, eruptions, gout, are dispelled if the afflicted member be stroked with a dead hand.[159] Toothache is charmed away if the face be touched with the finger of a dead child.[160] Birthmarks vanish under the same treatment.[161] Burns, carbuncles, the herpes, and other skin complaints, fearfully prevalent in the Middle Ages, could be cured by contact with some part of a corpse. In Pomerania the "cold corpse hand" is a protection against fire,[162] and Russian peasants believe that a dead hand protects from bullet wounds and steel.[163] It was long thought by the ignorant country folk that the doctors of the hospital of Graz enjoyed the privilege of being allowed every year to exploit one human life for curative purposes. Some young man who repaired thither for toothache or any such slight ailment is seized, hung up by the feet, and tickled to death! Skilled chemists boil the body to a paste and utilize this as well as the fat and the charred bones in their drug store. The people are persuaded that about Easter a youth annually disappears in the hospital for these purposes.[164] This tradition is, perhaps, not unconnected with the Jewish ritual sacrifices of S. William of Norwich (1144); Harold of Gloucester (1168); William of Paris (1177); Robert of Bury S. Edmunds (1181); S. Werner of Oberwesel (1286); S. Rudolph of Berne (1294); S. Andreas of Rinn (1462); S. Simon of Trent, a babe of two and a half years old (1473); Simon Abeles, whose body lies in the Teyn Kirche at Prague, murdered for Christ's sake on 21 February, 1694, by Lazarus and Levi Kurtzhandel; El santo Niño de la Guardia, near Toledo (1490), and many more.[165]

The riots which have so continually during three centuries broken out in China against Europeans, and particularly against Catholic asylums for the sick, foundling hospitals, schools, are almost always fomented by an intellectual party who begin by issuing fiery appeals to the populace: "Down with the missionaries! Kill the foreigners! They steal or buy our children and slaughter them, in order to prepare magic remedies and medicines out of their eyes, hearts, and from other portions of their dead bodies." Baron Hübner in his *Promenade autour du monde*, II (Paris, 1873) tells the story of the massacre at Tientsin, 21 June, 1870, and relates that it was engineered on these very lines. In 1891 similar risings against Europeans resident in China were found to be due to the same cause. Towards the end of 1891 a charge was brought in Madagascar against the French that they devoured human hearts and for this purpose kidnapped and killed native children. Stern legislation was actually found necessary to check the spread of these accusations.[166]

In the Navarrese witch-trials of 1610 Juan de Echelar confessed that a candle had been used made from the arm of an infant strangled before baptism. The ends of the fingers had been lit, and burned with a clear flame, a "Hand of Glory" in fact. At Forfar, in 1661, Helen Guthrie and four other witches exhumed the body of an unbaptized babe and made portions into a pie which they ate. They imagined that by this means no threat nor torture could bring them to confession of their sorceries. This, of course, is clearly sympathetic magic. The tongue of the infant had never spoken articulate words, and so the tongues of the witches would be unable to articulate.

It is a fact seldom realized, but none the less of the deepest significance, that almost every detail of the old witch-trials can be exactly paralleled in Africa to-day. Thus there exists in Bantu a society called the "Witchcraft Company," whose members hold secret meetings at midnight in the depths of the forest to plot sickness and death against their enemies by means of incantations and spells. The owl is their sacred bird, and their signal call an imitation of its hoot. They profess to leave their corporeal bodies asleep in their huts, and it is only their spirit-bodies that attend the magic rendezvous, passing through walls and over the tree-tops with instant rapidity. At the meeting they have visible, audible, and tangible communication with spirits. They hold feasts, at which is eaten the "heart-life" of some human being, who through this loss of his heart falls sick and, unless "the heart" be later restored, eventually dies. Earliest cock-crow is the warning for them to disperse, since they fear the advent of the morning-star, as, should the sun rise upon them before they reach their corporeal bodies, all their plans would not merely fail, but recoil upon themselves, and they would pine and languish miserably. This hideous Society was introduced by black slaves to the West Indies, to Jamaica and Hayti, and also to the Southern States of America as Voodoo worship. Authentic records are easily procurable which witness that midnight meetings were held in Hayti as late as 1888, when human beings, especially kidnapped children, were killed and eaten at the mysterious and evil banquets. European government in Africa has largely suppressed the practice of the black art, but this foul belief still secretly prevails, and Dr. Norris[167] is of opinion that were white influence withdrawn it would soon hold sway as potently as of old.

A candid consideration will show that for every detail of the Sabbat, however fantastically presented and exaggerated in the witch-trials of so many centuries, there is ample warrant and unimpeachable evidence. There is some hallucination no doubt; there is lurid imagination, and vanity which paints the colours thick; but there is a solid stratum of fact, and very terrible fact throughout.

And as the dawn broke the unhallowed crew separated in haste, and hurried each one on his way homewards, pale, weary, and haggard after the night of taut hysteria, frenzied evil, and vilest excess.

"Le coq s'oyt par fois és sabbats sonnãt le retraicte aux Sorciers."[168] (The cock crows; the Sabbat ends; the Sorcerers scatter and flee away.)

NOTES TO CHAPTER IV

[1] Omnia autem honeste et secundum ordinem fiant. 1 Cor. xiv. 40.

[2] Miss Murray, misled no doubt by the multiplicity of material, postulates two separate and distinct kinds of assemblies: The Sabbat, the General Meeting of all members of the religion; the Esbat "only for the special and limited number who carried out the rites and practices of the cult, and [which] was not for the general public." *The Witch-Cult in Western Europe*, p. 97. Görres had already pointed out that the smaller meetings were often known as *Esbats*. The idea of a "general public" at a witches' meeting is singular.

[3] On a voulu trouver l'etymologie du sabbat, réunion des sorciers, dans les *sabazies;* mais la forme ne le permet pas; d'ailleurs comment, au moyen âge aurait on connu les sabazies? Saint-Croix, *Recherches sur les mystères du paganisme;* Maury, *Histoire des religions de la Grèce antique.*

[4] *Metamorphoseon*, VIII. 25.

[5] Miss Murray thinks that Sabbat "is possibly a derivative of *s'esbattre*, 'to frolic,'" and adds "a very suitable description of the joyous gaiety of the meetings"!!

[6] Miss Murray mistakenly says (p. 109) that May Eve (30 April) is called Roodmas or Rood Day. Roodmas or Rood Day is 3 May, the Feast of the Invention of Holy Cross. An early English calendar (702–706) even gives 7 May as Roodmas. The Invention of Holy Cross is found in the Lectionary of Silos and the Bobbio Missal. The date was not slightly altered. The Invention of Holy Cross is among the very early festivals.

[7] Especially in the North and North-East. Bavaria, Wurtemberg, and Baden, knew little of this particular date.

[8] In the *Rituale* we have "Benedictio Rogi, quæ fit a Clero extra Ecclesiam in Uigilia Natiuitatis S. Joannis Baptistæ. (Blessing of a pyre, which the Clergy may give on the Vigil of the Nativity of S. John Baptist, but outside the Church.) This form is especially approved for the Diocese of Tarbes.

[9] *Relacion de las personas que salieron al auto de la fé que los inquisidores apostólicos del reino de Navarra y su distrito, celebraron en la ciudad De Logroño, en* 7 *y* 8 *del mes de noviembre de* 1610 *años*, 1611.

[10] *Discours des Sorciers*, XXII. 12. Tertullian's *Diabolus simia Dei*.

[11] *Idem*, XX. 2.

[12] *Tableau*, p. 65.

[13] Les lieux des assemblées des Sorciers sont notables et signalez de quelques arbres, ou croix. *Fleau*, p. 181.

[14] Anthony Horneck; Appendix to Glanvill's *Sadducismus Triumphatus*. London, 1681.

[15] Locus in diuersis regionibus est diuersus; plerumque autem comitia in syluestribus, montanis, uel subterraneis atque ab hominum conuersatione dissitis locis habentur. *Mela. Lib.* 3. *cap.* 44. montem Atlantem nominat; *de Vaulx* Magus Stabuleti decollatus, fatebatur 1603, in Hollandia congregationem frequentissimam fuisse in Ultraiectinæ ditionis aliquo loco. Nobis ab hoc conuentu notus atq; notatus mons Bructerorum, Meliboeus alias dictus in ducatu Brunsuicensi, uulgo *der Blocksberg oder Heweberg*, Peucero, *der Brockersberg*, & Tilemanno Stellæ, *der Vogelsberg*, perhibente *Ortelio in Thesauro Geographico*. For the Bructeri see Tacitus, *Germania*, 33: Velleius Paterculus, II, 105, i. *Bructera natio*, Tacitus, *Historiæ*, IV, 61.

[16] . . . le lieu où on le trouue ordinairement s'appelle Lanne de bouc, & en Basque *Aquelarre de verros, prado del Cabron*, & là des Sorciers

le vont adorer trois nuicts durant, celle du Lundy, du Mercredy, & du Vendredy. De Lancre, *Tableau*, p. 62.

[17] Boguet, *Discours des Sorciers*, p. 124.

[18] *A Pleasant Treatise of Witches*, London, 1673.

[19] Psalm xc.

[20] Conuentus, ut plurimum ineuntur uel noctis mediæ silentio, quando uiget potestas tenebrarum ; uel interdiu meridie, quo sunt qui referant illud Psalmistæ notum de dæmonio meridiano. Noctes frequentiores, quæ feriam tertiam et sextam præcedunt. Delrio, *Disquisitiones Magicæ*, Lib. II. xvi.

[21] *Discours*, XIX. 1. "The Sorcerers assemble at the Sabbat about midnight."

[22] Her indictment consists of fifty-three points.

[23] Spottiswoode's *Practicks*.

[24] Spalding Club, *Miscellany*, I.

[25] MS. formerly in the possession of Michael Stewart Nicolson, Esq.

[26] . . . je me trouvais transporté au lieu où le Sabatt se tenait, y demeurant quelquefois une, deux, trois, quatre heures pour le plus souvent suivant les affections.

[27] Ferunt uagantes Dæmonas
Lætas tenebras noctium
Gallo canente exterritos
Sparsim timere et credere.

[28] Nocturna lux uiantibus
A nocte noctem segregans,
Præco diei iam sonat,
Iubarque solis euocat.
Hoc nauta uires colligit,
Pontique mitescunt freta :
Hoc, ipsa petra Ecclesiæ,
Canente, culpam diluit.
Surgamus ergo strenue :
Gallus iacentes excitat,
Et somnolentos increpat,
Gallus negantes arguit.
Gallo canente, spes redit,
Ægris salus refunditur,
Mucro latronis conditur,
Lapsis fides reuertitur.

The translation in text is by Caswall, 1848.

[29] *Tableau*, p. 154.

[30] For London, see Dr. Johnson's *London* (1738) :

Prepare for death, if here at night you roam,
And sign your will before you sup from home.

In 1500 Paolo Capello, the Venetian Ambassador, wrote : "Every night they find in Rome four or five murdered men, Prelates and so forth." During the reign of Philip IV (1621–1665) the streets of Madrid, noisome, unpaved, were only lit on the occasion of festal illuminations.

[31] 1475–1546.

[32] Quando uadunt ad loca propinqua uadunt pedestres mutuo se inuicem inuitantes. *De Strigibus*, II.

[33] Les Sorciers neâtmoins vont quelquefois de pied au Sabbat, ce qui leur aduient principalement, lors que le lieu où ils font leur assemblée, n'est pas guieres eslongé de leur habitation. *Discours*, c. xvii.

[34] Enquis en quel lieu se tint le Sabbat le dernier fois qu'il y fut.
Respond que ce fut vers Billeron à un Carroy qui est sur le chemin tendant aux Aix, Parroisse de Saincte Soulange, Iustice de ceans.
Enquis de quelle façon il y va.
Respond qu'il y va de son pied.
De Lancre, *Tableau*, pp. 803–805.

[35] Aussi vilain & abominable est au Sorcier d'y aller de son pied que d'y estre transporté de son consentement par le Diable. *Tableau*, p. 632.

[36] Sinclar, *Satan's Invisible World Discovered* (Reprint 1875), VII.

[37] *Idem*, p. 25.

[38] *Idem*, pp. 175, 178.

[39] Illud etiam non omittendum quod quædam sceleratæ mulieres retro post Satanam conuersæ, dæmonum illusoribus et phantasmatibus seductæ credunt se et profitentur nocturnis horis cum Diana paganorum dea et innumera multitudine mulierum equitare super quasdam bestias et multa terrarum spatia intempestæ noctis silentio pertransire eiusque iussionibus uelut dominæ obedire, et certis noctibus ad eius seruitium euocari. Minge, *Patres Latini*, CXXXII. 352.

[40] See Professor A. J. Clark's note upon "Flying Ointments." *Witch-Cult in Western Europe*, pp. 279–280.

[41] Posset dæmon eas transferre sine unguento, et facit aliquando; sed unguento mauult uti uariis de causis. Aliquando quia timidiores sunt sagæ, ut audeant; uel quia teneriores sunt ad horribilem illum Satanæ contactum in corpore assumpto ferendum; horum enim unctione sensum obstupefacit et miseris persuadet uim unguento inesse maximam. Alias autem id facit ut sacrosancta a Deo instituta sacramenta inimice adumbret, et per has quasi cerimonias suis orgiis reuerentiæ et uenerationis aliquid conciliat. Delrio, *Disquitiones magicæ*, Liber II, q[to] xvi.

[42] In antiquity we have the case of Simon Magus, who was levitated in the presence of Nero and his court.

[43] Henri Boguet, the High Justice of the district of Saint-Claude, died in 1616. The first edition (of the last rarity) of his *Discours des Sorciers* is Lyons, 1602; second edition, Lyons 1608; but there is also a Paris issue, 1603. Pp. 64 and 104.

[44] Scot, *Discoverie of Witchcraft* (1584). Book III. p. 42.

[45] De Lancre, *Tableau*, p. 211.

[46] Thomas Wright, *Proceedings against Dame Alice Kyteler*, Camden Society. 1843.

[47] Cotton Mather, *Wonders of the Invisible World*, 1693. (Reprint, 1862. P. 158.)

[48] *Quarterly Journal of Science*, January, 1874.

[49] J. Godfrey Raupert, *Modern Spiritism*. 1904. Pp. 34, 35. See also Sir W. Barrett, *On the Threshold of the Unseen*, p. 70.

[50] Arthur Lillie, *Modern Mystics and Modern Magic*, 1894, pp. 74, 75.

[51] David Lewis, *Life of S. John of the Cross* (1897), pp. 73–4.

[52] See the Saint's own letter (written in 1777) to the Bishop of Foggia. *Lettere di S. Alfonso Maria de' Liguori* (Roma, 1887), II. 456 f.

[53] Philip Coghlan, O.P. *Gemma Galgani* (1923), p. 62. For fuller details see the larger biography by Padre Germano.

[54] *Vie du B. Paul de la Croix*. (French translation.) I. Book ii. c. 3.

[55] *La Mystique Divine*. Traduit par Sainte-Foi. V. viii. 17. p. 193.

[56] Giovanni Francesco Ponzinibio was a lawyer whose *De Lamiis* was published at Venice, 1523–4. It called forth a reply, *Apologiæ tres aduersum Joannem Franciscum Ponzinibium Iurisperitum*, Venice, 1525. The edition of *De Lamiis* I have used is Venice, 1584, in the *Thesaurus Magnorum iuris consultorum*. This reprint was met by Peña's answer and two treatises by Bartolomeo Spina, O.P.

[57] Rome, 1584.

[58] De modo quo localiter transferentur [sagæ] de loco ad locum. . . . Probatur quod possint malefici corporaliter transferri.

[59] An isti Sortilegi & Strigimagæ siue Lamiæ uere & corporaliter deferantur a dæmone uel solum in spiritu? *De Sortilegiis*, VII.

[60] Sum modo istius secundæ opinionis quod deferantur in corpore.

[61] Doctrina multi eorum qui sequuti sunt Lutherum, & Melanctonem, tenuerent Sagas ad conuentus accedere animi duntaxat cogitatione, & diabolica illusione interesse, allegantes quod eorum corpora inuenta sunt sæpe numero eodem loco iacentia, nec inde mora fuisse, ad hoc illud pertinens quod est in uita D. Germani, de mulierculis conuiuantibus, vt uidebantur, & tamē dormierant dormientes. Huiusmodi mulierculas sæpe numero decipi

certum est, sed semper ita fieri non probatur. . . . Altera, quam uerissimam esse duco, est, nonnunquam uere Sagas transferri a Dæmone de loco ad locum, hirco, uel alteri animali fantastico vt plurimum eas simul asportanti corporaliter, & conuentu nefario interesse, & hæc sententia est multo communior Theologorum, imò & Iurisconsultorum Italiæ, Hispaniæ, & Germaniæ inter Cathoiicos; hoc idem tenent alii quam plurimi. Turrecremata super Grillandum,[1] Remigius,[2] Petrus Damianus,[3] Siluester Abulensis,[4] Caietanus[5] Alphonsus a Castro[6] Sixtus Senensis[7] Crespetus[8] Spineus[9] contra Ponzinibium, Ananias,[10] & alii quam plurimi, quos breuitatis gratia omitto. *Per Fratrem Franciscum Mariam Guaccium Ord. S. Ambrosii ad Nemus Mediolani compilatum.* Mediolani. Ex Collegii Ambrosiani Typographia. 1626.

[62] *De Strigibus*, II. I have used the reprint, 1669, which is given in the valuable collection appended to the *Malleus Maleficarum* of that date, 4 vols 4to.

[63] Ad quam congregationem seu ludum præfatæ pestiferæ personæ uadunt corporaliter & uigilantes ac in propriis earũ sensibus & quando uadunt ad loca propinqua uadunt pedestres mutuo se inuicem inuitantes. Si autẽ habent congregari in aliquo loco distanti tunc deferuntur a diabolo, & quomodocunque uadant ad dictum locum siue pedibus suis siue adferantur a diabolo uerũ est quod realiter et ueraciter & nõ phãtastice, neque illusorii abnegant fidẽ catholicam, adorant diabolum, conculcant crucem, & plura nefandissima opprobria committunt contra sacratissimum Corpus Christi, ac alia plura spurcissima perpetrant cum ipso diabolo eis in specie humana apparenti, & se uiris succubum, mulieribus autem incubum exhibenti.

[64] George Gandillon, la nuict d'vn Ieudy Sainct, demeura dans son lict, comme mort, pour l'espace de trois heures, & puis reuint à soy en sursaut. Il a depuis esté bruslé en ce lieu auec son père & vne sienne sœur.

[65] Chapitre xvi. Comme, & en quelle façon les Sorciers sont portez au Sabbat.

1. *Ils y sont portez tantost sur un baston, ou ballet, tantost sur un mouton ou bouc, & tantost par un homme noir.*
2. *Quelquefois ils se frottẽt de graisse, & à d'autres non.*
3. *Il y en a, lesquels n'estans pas Sorciers, & s'estans frottez, ne delaissent pas d'estre transportez au Sabbat, & la raison.*
4. *L'onguent, & la graisse ne seruent de rien aux Sorciers, pour leur transport au Sabbat.*
5. *Les Sorciers sont quelquefois portez au Sabbat par un vent & tourbillon.*

Chapitre xvii. Les Sorciers vont quelques fois de pied au Sabbat.

Chapitre xviii. Si les Sorciers vont en ame seulement au Sabbat.

1 & 3. *L'affirmatiue, & exemples.*

2. *Indices, par lesquels on peut coniecturer, qu'vne certaine femme estoit au Sabbat en ame seulement.*
4. *La negatiue.*
5. *Comme s'entend ce que l'on dit d'Erichtho, & d'Apollonius lesquels resusciterent l'un un soldat, & l'autre une ieune fille.*
6. *Les Sorciers ne peuuent resusciter un mort, & exemples.*
7. *Non plus que les heretiques & exemples.*
8. *Opinion de l'Autheur sur le suiect de ce chapitre.*
9. *Satan endort le plus souuent les personnes, & exemples.*

[1] *De haereticis et sortilegiis.* Lugduni. 1536.
[2] Nicolas Remy, *De la démonolâtrie.*
[3] Epistolarum, IV. 17.
[4] Silvester of Avila.
[5] Tommaso de Vio Gaetani, O.P. 1469–1534.
[6] Alfonso de Castro, Friar Minor. (1495–1558). Confessor to Charles V and Philip II of Spain.
[7] Sisto da Siéna, O.P. Bibliotheca Sancta . . . (Liber V). Secunda editio. Francofurti. 1575. folio.
[8] Père Crespet, Celestine monk. *Deux livres de la haine de Satan et des malins esprits contre l'homme.* Paris. 1590.
[9] Bartholomeo Spina, O.P. *De lamiis. De strigibus.* Both folio, Venice, 1584. *Apologia tres aduersus Joannem Franciscum Ponzinibium Jurisperitum.* Venice. 1525. Giovanni Francesco Ponzinibio wrote a *Dedamiis* of which I have used a late edition. Venice, 1584.
[10] Giovanni Lorenzo Anania, *De natura dæmonum*: libri iiii. Venetiis. 1581. 8vo.

Chapitre xix.
1. *Les Sorciers vont enuiron la minuict au Sabbat.*
2. *La raison pourquoy le Sabbat si tient ordinairement de nuict.*
3. *Satan se plait aux tenebres, & à la couleur noire, estant au contraire la blancheur agreable à Dieu.*
4. *Les Sorciers dansent doz contre doz au Sabbat, & se masquent pour la plus part.*
5, 8. *Le coq venant à chanter, le Sabbat disparoit aussi tost, & la raison.*
6. *La voix du coq funeste à Satan tout ainsi qu'au lyon, & au serpent.*
7. *Le Demon, selon quelques uns a crainte d'vne espée nue.*

Chapitre xx. Du iour du Sabbat.
1. *Le Sabbat se tient à un chacun iour de la semaine, mais principalement le Ieudy.*
2. *Il se tient encor aux festes les plus solemnelles de l'année.*

Chapitre xxi. Du lieu du Sabbat.
1. *Le lieu du Sabbat est signalé, selon aucuns, de quelques arbres ou bien de quelques croix, & l'opinion de l'autheur sur ce suiect.*
2. *Chose remarquable d'vn lieu pretendu pour le Sabbat.*
3. *Il faut de l'eau au lieu, où se tient le Sabbat, & pourquoy.*
4. *Les Sorciers, à faute d'eau, urinent dans un trou, qu'ils font en terre.*

Chapitre xxii. De ce qui se fait au Sabbat.
1. *Les Sorciers y adorent Satan, estãt en forme d'homme noir, ou de bouc, & luy offrent des chandelles, & le baisent aux parties honteuses de derriere.*
2. *Ils y dansent, & de leurs danses.*
3. *Ils se desbordent en toutes sortes de lubricitez, & comme Satan se fait Incube & Succube.*
4. *Incestes, & paillardises execrebles des Euchites & Gnostiques.*
5. *Les Sorciers banquettent au Sabbat, de leurs viandes, & breuuages, & de la façon qu'ils tiennent à benir la table, & à rendre graces.*
6. *Ils ne prennent cependant point de gout aux Viandes, & sortent ordinairement auec faim du repas.*
7. *Le repas paracheué, ils rendent conte de leurs actions à Satan.*
8. *Ils renoncent de nouueau à Dieu, au Chresme, &c. Et comme Satan les sollicite à mal faire.*
9. *Ils y font la gresle.*
10. *Ils y celebrent messe, & de leurs chappes, & eau benite.*
11. *Satan se consume finalement en feu, & se reduit en cendre, de laquelle les Sorciers prennent tous, & a quel effet.*
12. *Satan Singe de Dieu en tout.*

[66] Vouloir donner une description du Sabbat, c'est vouloir decrire ce qui n'existe point, & n'a jamais subsisté que dans l'imagination creuse & séduite des Sorciers & Sorcieres : les peintures qu'on nous en fait, sont d'après les rêveries de ceux & de celles qui s'imaginent d'être transportés à travers les airs au Sabbat en corps & en ame. *Traité sur les Apparitions des Esprits*, par le R. P. Dom Augustin Calmet, Abbé de Sénones. Paris, 1751, I. p. 138.

[67] See the woodcut upon the title-page of Middleton & Rowley's *The World tost at Tennis*, 4to, 1620.

[68] De Lancre, *L'Incredulité*, p. 769.

[69] Boguet, *Discours des Sorciers.*

[70] De Lancre, *Tableau*, p. 217.

[71] De Lancre, *L'Incredulité*, p. 800.

[72] Görres, *La Mystique Divine*, traduit par Charles Sainte-Foi. V. viii. 19. p. 208.

[73] George Sinclar, *Satan's Invisible World Discovered*, Relation XVII.

[74] *La Mystique Divine*, 1902 (Nouvelle édition). III. p. 381.

[75] *Tractatus*, xxi. c. 11. P. xi. n. 179.

[76] *Disquisitiones Magicæ*, Lib. II. q^{to} x.

[77] *Compendium Maleficarum*, p. 78.

[78] Solent ad conuentum delatæ dæmonem conuentus præsidem in solio considentem forma terrifica, ut plurimum hirci uel canis, obuerso ad illum tergo accedentes, adorare . . . et deinde, homagii quod est indicium, osculari eum in podice."[1] Guazzo notes: "Ad signum homagii dæmonem podice osculantur."[2] And Ludwig Elich says: "Deinde quod homagii est indicium (honor sit auribus) ab iis ingerenda sunt oscula Dæmonis podici."[3]

[79] *Mystery of Witchcraft.*

[80] It may be remembered that, as related elsewhere, there is strong reason to suppose Francis Stewart, Earl of Bothwell, grandson of James V, was "the Devil" on this occasion, as he was certainly the Grand Master of the witches and the convener of the Sabbat.

[81] *Newes from Scotland, declaring the damnable Life of Doctor Fian.* London. W. Wright. [1592].

[82] Dudum ad audientiam nostram peruenit, quod uenerabilis frater noster G. Conuentrensis et Lichefeldensis episcopus erat in regno Angliæ et alibi publice defamatur quod diabolo homagium fecerat et eum fuerat osculatus in tergo eique locutus multotius.

[83] Confessa ledit sire Guillaume . . . avoir fait hommage audit ennemy en l'espèce et semblance d'ung mouton en le baisant par le fondement en signe de révérence et d'hommage. Jean Chartier, *Chronique de Charles VII* (ed. Vallet de Viriville). Paris, 1858. III. p. 45. Shadwell, who has introduced this ceremony into *The Lancashire Witches*, II, (The Scene Sir *Edward's* Cellar), in his notes refers to "Doctor *Edlin* . . . who was burn'd for a Witch."

[84] *Reliquiæ Antiquæ*, vol. I. p. 247.

[85] Il a veu [le diable] quelque fois en forme d'homme, tenant son cheval par le frein, & qu'ils le vont adorer tenans vue chandelle de poix noir en leurs mains, le baisent quelque fois au nombril, quelque fois au cul. De Lancre, *L'Incredulité*, p. 25.

[86] Tum candelis piceis oblatis, vel vmbilico infantili, ad signum homagii eum in podice osculantur, Liber I. xiii.

[87] *Satan's Invisible World Discovered*, Relation III.

[88] . . . qui apparait là, tantost en forme d'vn grand homme noir, tantost en forme de bouc, & pour plus grand hommage, ils luy offrent des chandelles, qui rendent vne flamme de couleur bleüe. *Discours des Sorciers*, p. 131.

εἴθε λύρα καλὴ γενοίμην ἐλεφαντίνη,
καί με καλοὶ παῖδες φέροιεν Διονύσιον ες χορόν.

(Fain would I be a fair lyre of ivory, and fair boys carrying me to Dionysus' choir.)

[90] Sequuntur his choree quas in girum agitant semper tamen ad læuam progrediendo. *Compendium Maleficarum*, I. xiii.

[91] Les Sorciers, dansent & font leurs danses en rond doz contre doz.

[92] Quelquefois, mais rarement, ils dansent deux à deux, & par fois l'vn çà & l'autre là, & tousiours en confusion.

[93] On n'y dançoit que trois sortes de bransles. . . . La premiere c'est à la Bohemienne. . . . La seconde c'est à sauts: ces deux sont en rond. Sir John Davies in his *Orchestra or A Poeme on Dauncing*, London, 18mo, 1596, describes the seven movements of the Cransles (Crawls) as:

Upward and *downeward, forth* and *back againe,*
To this side and *to that*, and *turning round.*

[94] II. 1.

[95] Sinclar, *Satin's Invisible World Discovered*, III.

[96] *Newes from Scotland*, (1592).

[97] Tota turba colluuiesque pessima fescenninos in honorem dæmonum cantat obscenissimos. Hæc cantat *Harr, harr;* illa Diabole, Diabole, salta huc, salta illuc; altera lude hic, lude illic; alia Sabaoth, Sabaoth, &c.;

[1] *Disquisitiones Magicæ*, Lib. II. qto xvi.
Compendium Maleficarum, I. 13.
[3] *Dæmonomagia*, Quæstis x.

immo clamoribus, sibilis, ululatibus, propicinis furit ac debacchatur. *Dæmonomagia*, Quæstio x.

[98] Hi habent mensas appositas & instructas accumbunt & incipiunt conuiuari de cibis quos Dæmon suppeditat uel iis quos singuli attulere, *Compendium Maleficarum*, I. xiii.

[99] Les liures disent que les sorciers mangent au Sabbat de ce que le Diable leur a apresté : mais bien souuēt il ne s'y trouue que des viandes qu'ils ont porté eux mesmes. Parfois il y a plusieurs tables seruies de bons viures & d'autres fois de tres meschans. "Les Sorciers . . . banquettent & se festoient," remarks Boguet, "leur banquets estans composez de plusieurs sortes de viandes, selon les lieux & qualitez des personnes." *Tableau*, p. 197. *Discours des Sorciers*, p. 135.

[100] Sinclar, *Invisible World Discovered*, Relation XXIX.

[101] Ils banquêtent, dressant trois tables selon les trois diversités des gens susnommés. Ceux qui ont la charge du pain, ils portent le pain qu'ils font de blé dérobé aux aires invisiblement en divers lieux. Ils boivent de la malvoisie, pour eschauffer la chair à la luxure, que les deputés portent, la dérobant des caves où elle se trouve. Ils y mangent ordinairement de la chair des petits enfants que les députés cuisent à la Synagogue et parfois les y portent tout vifs, les derobant à leurs maisons quand ils trouvent la commodité. Père Sébastien Michaëlis, O.P. *Histoire admirable de la possession*, 1613.

[102] On y boit aussi du vin, et le plus souvent de l'eau.

[103] Conuiuant de cibis a se uel a dæmone allatis, interdum delicatissimis, et interdum insipidis ex infantibus occisis aut cadaueribus exhumatis, præcedente tamen benedictione mensæ tali coetu digna. *Salamanticenses*, Tr. xxi. c. 11. P. 11. n. 179.

[104] Uinum eorum præterea instar atri atque insinceri sanguinis in sordido aliquo scipho epulonibus solitum propinari. Nullam fere copiam rerum illic deesse afferunt præterquā panis et salis. Addit Dominica Isabella apponi etiam humanas carnes. *Compendium Maleficarum*, I. xiii.

[105] *De la Démonomanie*, III. 5.

[106] *Dæmonomagio*, Quæstio vii.

[107] Il n'y a jamais sel en ces repas. *Discours des Sorciers*.

[108] On se met à table, où il n'a iamais veu de sel.

Shadwell draws attention to this detail: *The Lancashire Witches*, II, the Sabbat scene; where Mother Demdike says:

> See our Provisions ready here,
> To which no Salt must e'er come near!

[109] Père Sébastien Michaëlis, O.P. *Histoire admirable*, 1613.

[110] Isti uero qui expressam professionem fecerunt, reddunt etiam expressum cultum adorationis dæmoni per solemnia sacrificia, quæ ipsi faciunt diabolo, imitantes in omnibus diuinum cultum, cum paramentis, luminaribus, et aliis huiusmodi, ac precibus quibusdam et orationibus quibus instructi sunt, adeo ipsum adorant et collaudant continue, sicut nos uerum Creatorem adoramus. *De Sortilegiis*, Liber II. c. iii. n. 6.

[111] *The Wonders of the Invisible World*. A Hortatory Address. p. 81.

[112] J. Hutchinson, *History of Massachusett's Bay*, II. p. 55. (1828.)

[113] *Euchologion* of the Orthodox Church, ed. Venice, 1898, p. 63.

[114] Baissac, *Les grands jours de la Sorcellerie* (1890), p. 391.

[115] Calmeil, *De la folie*, I. p. 344.

[116] Sébastien Michaëlis, *Histoire admirable*. 1613. Translated as *Admirable Historie*. London, 1613.

[117] Desmarest, *Histoire de Magdelaine Bavent*. Paris. 4to. 1652.

[118] For full details see François Ravaisson, *Archives de la Bastille*, Paris, 1873, where the original depositions are given.

[119] *Là-Bas* appeared in the *Echo de Paris*, 1890–1.

[120] *Tableau*, p. 401. For the full account of these ceremonies I have chiefly relied upon Guazzo; Boguet, *Discours*, XXII, 10; De Lancre, pp. 86, 122, 126, 129; and Görres, *Mystique*, V. pp. 224–227. It hardly seems necessary to give particular citations here for each circumstance.

[121] Do Lancro, *Tableau*, IV. 4.
[122] *Corriere Nazionale di Torino*, Maggio. 1895
[123] De Lancre, *Tableau*, p. 401.
[124] Görres, *Mystique*, V. p. 230.
[125] Roland Brévannes, *L'Orgie Satanique*, IV. Le Sabbat, p. 122.
[126] *Discours*, p. 141.
[127] S. Caleb, *Messes Noires*, p. 153.
[128] *Confession faicte par Messire Loys Gaufridi*, A Aix. MVCXI.
[129] A vne Chasuble qui a vne croix ; mais qu'elle n'a que trois barres.
[130] Le Diable en mesme temps pisse dans vn trou à terre, & fait de l'eau beniste de son vrine, de laquelle celuy, qui dit la messe, arrouse tous les assistants auec vn asperges noir. Boguet, *Discours*, p. 141.
[131] . . . lors que Tramesabot disoit la Messe, & qu'auant la commencer li iettoit de l'eau beniste qui estoit faicte de pissat, & faisoit la reverence de l'espaule, & disoit *Asperges Diaboli*. De Lancre, *L'Incredulité*.
[132] L'eau beniste est iaune comme du pissat d'asne, & qu'apres qu'on la iettée on dit la Messe.
[133] Michaëlis *Histoire admirable*, 1613. Miss Murray, *The Witch-Cult*, p.149, suggests that this sprinkling was " a fertility rite " ! An astounding theory. This blasphemy, of course, alludes to the curse of the Jews. S. Matthew xxvii. 25.
[134] Que le Diable dit le Sermo au Sabbat, mais qu'on n'entend ce qu'il dit, parce qu'il parle com̄e en grōdant. Which suggests the wearing of a mask, or, at least, a voice purposely disguised.
[135] Dit qu'il a veu bailler au Sabbat du pain benist & de l'encens, mais il ne sentoit bon comme celuy de l'Eglise.
[136] So in the Orleans trial Gentil le Clerc confessed that the Devil "tourne le dos à l'Autel quand il veut leuer l'Hostie & le Calice, qui sont noirs."
[137] Silvain Nevillon, (1614–1615). Dit aussi auoir veu des Sorciers & Sorcieres qui apportoient des Hosties au Sabbat, lesquelles elles auoient gardé lors qu'on leur auoit baillé à communier à l'Eglise.
[138] Presumably S. Cæsarius of Arles, 470–543, who incidentally was famous for eradicating the last traces of Pagan superstitions and practices. He imposed the penalty of excommunication upon all those who consulted augurs and wore heathen amulets. The Gnostics were especially notorious for their employment of such periapts, talismans, and charms.
[139] J. F. Bladé, *Quatorze superstitions populaires de la Gascogne*, pp. 16 *sqq.* Agen. 1883.
[140] *Decisions*. Edinburgh, 1759.
[141] Ie laisse à penser si l'on n'exerce pas là toutes les especes de lubricités veu encor que les abominations, qui firent foudre & abismer Sodome & Gomorrhe, y font fort communes. Boguet, *Discours*, c. xxii. p. 137.
[142] *Histoire admirable*, 1613.
[143] Finalement, ils paillardent ensemble : le dimanche avec les diables succubes ou incubes ; le jeudi, commettent la sodomie ; le samedi la bestialité ; les autres jours à la voie naturelle.
[144] The Louviers process lasted four years, 1643–7.
[145] Après la Messe on dance, puis on couche ensemble, hommes auec hommes, & auec des femmes. Puis on se met à table. . . . Dit qu'il a cognu des hommes & s'est accouplé auec eux ; qu'il auoit vne couppe on gondolle par le moyen de laquelle toutes les femmes le suiuoient pour y boire.
[146] Apres la danse finie les diables se coucherẽt auecques elles, & eurẽt leur cōpagnie.
[147] . . . grand nombre d'hommes & femmes furent bruslees en la ville d'Arras, accusees les vns par les autres, & cōfesserent qu'ellés estoient la nuict transportees aux danses, & puis qu'ils se couploient auecques les diables, qu'ils adoroient en figure humaine.
[148] . . . toutes generalement sans exception, confessoient que le diable auoit copulation charnelle auec elles, apres leur auoir fait renoncer Dieu & leur religion.
[149] . . . c'est à sçauoir que les diables, tāt qu'elles auoient esté Sorcieres,

auoiēt eu copulation auec elles. Henry de Cologne confirmant ceste opinion dit, qu'il y a rien plus vulgaire en Alemaigne.

[150] . . . quod sacrificia dabant dæmonibus in animalibus uiuis, quæ diuidebant membratim et offerebant distribuendo in inferne quadruuiis cuidam dæmoni qui se facit appellari Artis Filium ex pauperioribus inferni. *Dame Alice Kyteler*, ed. T. Wright. Camden Society. 1843. pp. 1–2.

[151] *Highland Papers*, III. p. 18.

[152] *Æneid*, VI. 243–251.

[153] Horace, *Sermonum*, I. viii.

[154] *Dictionnaire Infernal*, ed. 1863, p. 590.

[155] Salgues, *Des erreurs et des prejugés*, I. p. 423.

[156] III. 44–45.

[157] Alludit ad Haruspicis officium, qui exta & viscera inspiciebat. Plinius inquit: *Ex ranæ rubetæ uisceribus; id est, lingua, ossiculo, licne, corde, mira fieri posse constat, sunt enin plurimis medicaminibus referta.* Forte intelligit rubetam uel bufonem, indicans se non esse ueneficum, nec rubetarum extis uti ad uenefica. Cf. also Pliny, *Historia Naturalis*, XXXII. 5.

[158] Ravaisson, *Archives de la Bastille*, VI. p. 295 *et alibi*. The interrogatories of these scandals may be found in volumes IV and V of this work.

[159] L. Strackerjan, *Aberglaube und Sagen aus dem Herzogthum Oldenburg* (1867), I. 70.

[160] *Königsberger Hartung'sche Zeitung*, 1866. No. 9.

[161] V. Fossel. *Volksmedicin und medicinischer Aberglaube in Steiermark*, Graz, 1886.

[162] U. Jahn, *Zauber mit Menschenblut und anderen Teilen des menschlichen Körpers*, 1888.

[163] A. Löwenstimm, *Aberglaube und Strafecht*, (*Die Volksmedizin*), 1897.

[164] V. Fossel, *Volksmedicin, ut supra.*

[165] Adrian Kembter, O.R.P., writing in 1745 enumerates 52 instances, and his last is dated 1650. This number might be doubled, and extends until the present century. H. C. Lee, in an article, *El santo nino de la Guardia*, has signally failed to disprove the account. See the series of forty-four articles in the *Osservatore Cattolico* March and April, 1892, Nos. 8438–8473.

[166] *Le Temps*, Paris, 1 Feb. and 23 March, 1892.

[167] *Fetichism in West Africa*, New York, 1904.

[168] De Lancre, *Tableau*, p. 154.

CHAPTER V

The Witch in Holy Writ

In the course of the Holy Scriptures there occur a great number of words and expressions which are employed in connexion with witchcraft, divination, and demonology, and of these more than one authority has made detailed and particular study. Some terms are of general import, one might even venture to say vague and not exactly defined, some are directly specific: of some phrases the signification is plain and accepted; concerning others, scholars are still undecided and differ more or less widely amongst themselves. Yet it is noteworthy that from the very earliest period the attitude of the inspired writers towards magic and related practices is almost wholly condemnatory and uncompromisingly hostile. The vehement and repeated denunciations launched against the professors of occult sciences and the initiate in foreign esoteric mysteries do not, moreover, seem to be based upon any supposition of fraud but rather upon the "abomination" of the magic in itself, which is recognized as potent for evil and able to wreak mischief upon life and limb. It is obvious, for example, that the opponents of Moses, the sorcerers[1] Jannes and Mambres, were masters of no mean learning and power, since when, in the presence of Pharaoh, Aaron's rod became a live serpent, they also and their mob of disciples "fecerunt per incantationes Ægyptiacas et arcana quædam similiter," casting down their rods, which were changed into a mass of writhing snakes. They were able also to bring up frogs upon the land, but it was past their wit to drive them away. We have here, however, a clear acknowledgement of the reality of magic and its dark possibilities, whilst at the same time prominence is given to the fact that when it contests with the miraculous power divinely bestowed upon Moses it fails hopelessly and completely. The serpent, which was Aaron's rod, swallows all the other serpents. The swarms of mosquitoes and gadflies which Aaron caused to rise in myriads from the dust the native warlocks could not produce, nay, they were constrained to cry "Digitus Dei est hic"; whilst a little later they were unable to protect even their own bodies from the pest of blains and swelling sores. None the less a supernatural power was possessed by Jannes and Mambres as truly as by Moses, although not to the same extent, and derived from another, in fact, from an opposite and antagonistic source.

Even more striking is the episode of Balaam, who dwelt at Pethor, a city of Mesopotamia (the Pitru of the cuneiform texts), and who was summoned thence by Balak, King of Moab, to lay a withering curse upon the Israelites, encamped after their victory over the Amorrhites at the very confines of his territory. The royal messengers come to Balaam "with the rewards of divination in their hand," a most illuminating detail, for it shows that already the practice of magical arts is rewarded with gifts of great value.[2] In fact when Balaam refuses, although with reluctance, to accompany the first embassy, princes of the highest rank are then sent to him with injunctions to offer him rank and wealth or whatsoever he may care to ask. "I will promote thee to very great honour, and I will do whatsoever thou sayest unto me; come, therefore, and curse this people," are the king's actual words. After great difficulties, for Balaam is, at first, forbidden to go and only wins his way on condition that he undertakes to do what he is commanded and to speak no more than he is inspired to say, the seer commences his journey and is met by the king at a frontier town, and by him taken up "unto the high places of Baal," to the sacred groves upon the hill-tops, where seven mystic altars are built, and a bullock and a ram offered upon each. Balaam then senses the imminent presence of God, and withdraws swiftly apart to some secret place where "God met" him. He returns to the scene of sacrifice and forthwith blesses the Israelites. Balak in consternation and dismay hurries him to the crest of Pisgah (Phasga), and the same ceremonies are performed. But again Balaam pours forth benisons upon the people. A third attempt is made, and this time was chosen the summit of Peor (Phogor), a peculiarly sacred sanctuary, the centre of the local cult of Baal Peor, whose ancient worship comprised a ritual of most primitive obscenity.[3] Again the sevenfold sacrifice is offered upon seven altars, and this time Balaam deliberately resists the divine control, a vain endeavour, since he passes into trance, and utters words of ineffable benediction gazing down the dim avenues of futurity to the glorious vision of the Madonna, Stella Jacob, and her Son, the Sceptre of Israel. Beating his clenched hands together in an access of ungovernable fury the choused and exasperated king incontinently dismisses his guest.

It must be remarked that throughout the whole of this narrative, the details of which are as interesting as they are significant, there is on the part of the writer a complete recognition of the claims put forth by Balaam and so amply acknowledged and appreciated by Balak. Balaam was a famous sorcerer, and one, moreover, who knew and could launch the mystic Word of Power with deadly effect. Among the early Arabs as among the Israelites the magic spell, the Word of Blessing or the Curse, played a prominent part. In war, the poet, by cursing the enemy in rhythmic runes, rendered services not inferior to the heroism of the warrior himself. So the Jews of Medina used to bring into their synagogues images of their hated enemy Malik b. al-Aglam; and at these effigies they hurled maledictions each time they met. The reality of Balaam's power is clearly the key-note of the Biblical account. Else why should his services be transferred to the cause of Israel? Balak's greeting to the seer is no empty compliment but vitally true: "I wot that he whom thou blessest is blessed, and he whom thou cursest is cursed." Not impertinent is the bitter denunciation in the song of Deborah, Judges v. 23, "Curse ye me Meroz, said the angel of the Lord, curse ye bitterly the inhabitants thereof; because they came not to the help of the Lord against the mighty!" (A.V.) Belief in the potency of the uttered word has existed at all times and in all places, and yet continues to exist everywhere to-day.

Although Balaam prophesied it must be borne in mind that he was not a prophet in the Scriptural sense of the term; he was a soothsayer, a wizard; the Vulgate has *hariolus*,[4] which is derived from the Sanskrit *hira*, entrails, and equivalent to *haruspex*. This term originally denoted an Etruscan diviner who foretold future events by an inspection of the entrails of sacrificial victims. It was from the Etruscans that this practice was introduced to the Romans. It is probable that Balaam employed the seven bullocks and rams in this way, the technical *extispicium*, a method of inquiry and forecasting which seems to have been almost universal, although the exact manner in which the omens were read differed among the several peoples and at various times. It persisted, none the less, until very late, and indeed it is resorted to, so it has been said, by certain occultists even at the present day. It is known to have been practised by Catherine de' Medici, and it is closely connected with the dark Voodoo worship of Jamaica and Hayti. S. Thomas, it is true, has spoken of Balaam as a prophet, but the holy doctor hastens to add " a prophet of the devil." The learned Cornelius à Lapide, glossing upon Numbers xxii and xxiii writes : " It is clear that Balaam was a prophet, not of God, but of the Devil. . . . He was a magician, and he sought for a conference with his demon to take counsel with him."[5] He is of opinion that the seven altars were erected in honour of the Lords of the Seven Planets. Seven is, of course, the perfect number, the mystic number, even as three ; and all must be done by odd numbers. The woman in Vergil who tries to call back her estranged lover Daphnis by potent incantations cries: *numero deus impare gaudet.* (Heaven loves unequal numbers.) Eclogue viii. 75 (*Pharmaceutria*). S. Augustine, S. Ambrose, and Theodoret consider that when Balaam on the first occasion withdrew hastily saying " Peradventure the Lord will come to meet me," he expected to meet a demon, his familiar. But " God met Balaam." The very precipitation and disorder seem to point to the design of the sorcerer, for as in the Divine Liturgy all is done with due dignity, grace, and comeliness, so in the functions of black magic all is hurried, ugly, and terrible.

One of the most striking episodes in the Old Testament is concerned with necromancy, the appearance of Samuel in the cave or hut at Endor. Saul, on the eve of a tremendous battle with the Philistines, is much dismayed and almost gives away to a complete nervous collapse as he sees the overwhelming forces of the ruthless foe. To add to his panic, when he consulted the Divine Oracles, no answer was returned, "neither by dreams, nor by Urim, nor by prophets." And although he had in the earlier years of his reign shown himself a determined represser of Witchcraft, in his dire extremity he catches at any straw, and bids his servants seek out some woman "that hath a familiar spirit," and his servants said to him, "Behold there is a woman that hath a familiar spirit at Endor," which is a miserable hamlet on the northern slope of a hill, lying something south of Mount Tabor.

The phrase here used, rendered by the Vulgate "pytho" (Quærite mihi mulierem habentem pythonem) and by the Authorized Version "familiar spirit," is in the original *'ôbh*,[6] which signifies the departed spirit evoked, and also came to stand for the person controlling such a spirit and divining by its aid. The Witch of Endor is described as the possessor of an *'ôbh*. The LXX. translates this word by ἐγγαστράμυθος, which means ventriloquist, either because the real actors thought that the magician's alleged communication with the spirit was a mere deception to impose upon the inquirer who is tricked by the voice being thrown into the ground and being of strange quality—a view which mightily commends itself to Lenormant[7] and the sceptical Renan[8] but which is quite untenable—or rather because of the belief common in antiquity that ventriloquism was not a natural faculty but due to the temporary obsession of the medium by a spirit. In this connexion the prophet Isaias has a remarkable passage: Quærite a pythonibus, et a diuinis qui strident in incantationibus suis. (Seek unto them that have familiar spirits, and unto wizards that peep and that mutter. *A.V.*) Many Greek and Latin poets attribute a peculiar and distinctive sound to the voices of spirits. Homer (*Iliad*, XXIII, 101; *Odyssey*, XXIV, 5, and 9) uses τρίζειν, which is elsewhere found of the shrill cry or chirping of partridges, young swallows, locusts, mice, bats,[9] and of such other sounds as the creaking of a door, the sharp crackling of a thing burned in a fire. Vergil *Æneid*, III, 39, speaks of the cry of Polydorus from his grave as *gemitus lacrimabilis*, and the clamour of the spirits in Hades is *uox exigua*. Horace also in his description of the midnight Esbat on the Esquiline describes the voice as *triste et acutum ;* (*Sermonum*, I. viii, 40–1) :

> singula quid memorem, quo pacto alterna loquentes
> umbrae cum Sagana resonarent triste et acutum.

Statius, *Thebais*, VII, 770, has " stridunt animæ," upon which Kaspar von Barth, the famous sixteenth-century German scholar, annotates " Homericum hoc est qui corporibus excedentes animas stridere excogitauit." So in Shakespeare's well-known lines, *Hamlet* I, 1 :

> the sheeted dead
> Did squeak and gibber in the Roman streets.

When he had been informed of this witch Saul, accordingly, completely divested himself of the insignia of royalty and in a close disguise accompanied only by two of his most trusted followers similarly muffled in cloaks, he painfully made his way at dead of night to her remote and squalid hovel. He eagerly requested her to exercise her powers, and to raise the spirit of the person whom he should name. At first she refused, since some years before the laws had been stringently enforced and the penalty of death awaited all sorcerers and magicians. Not unreasonably she feared that these mysterious strangers might be laying a trap for her, to imperil her life. But the concealed king persuaded her, and bound himself by a mighty oath that she should come to no harm. Whereupon she consented to evoke the soul of the prophet Samuel, as he desired. The charm commenced, and after the vision of various familiars—the woman said : Deos uidi ascendentes de terra—and S. Gregory of Nyssa explains these as demons, τὰ φαντάσματα,—Samuel appeared amid circumstances of great terror and awe, and in the same moment the identity of her visitant was recognized (we are not informed how) by the sybil.[10] In a paroxysm of rage and fear the haggard crone turned to him and shrieked out : " Why hast thou deceived me ? For thou art Saul." The king, however, tremblingly reassured her for her own safety, and feeling that he was confronted by no earthly figure—he could not see the phantom, although he sensed a presence from beyond the grave—he asked : " What form is he of ? " And when the beldame, to whom alone the prophet was visible, described the spirit : " An old man cometh up, and he is covered with a mantle," Saul at once recognized Samuel, and fell prostrate upon the ground, whilst the apparition spake his swiftly coming doom.

Here we have a detailed scene of necromancy proper There are, it is true, some remarkable, and perhaps unusual, features: the witch alone sees the phantom, but Saul instantly knows who it is from her description; he directly addresses Samuel, and he hears the prediction of the dead prophet. The whole narrative undoubtedly bears the impress of actuality and truth.

There are several interpretations of these incidents. In the first place some writers have denied the reality of the vision, and so it is claimed that the witch deceived Saul by skilful trickery. This hardly seems possible. It is not likely that she would have run so grave a risk as the exercise, or pretended exercise, of magical arts must entail were she a mere charlatan; an accomplice of remarkably quick wit and invention would have been necessary to carry out the details of the plot; it is surely incredible that they should have ventured upon so uncompromising a denunciation of the king and have foretold so evil an end to his house. In fact the whole tenor of the story conflicts with this explanation, which is not allowed by the Fathers. Theodoret, it is true, inclines to suppose that some deception was practised, but he hesitates to maintain an unequivocal opinion in the matter. In his *Quæstiones in I Regum* Cap. xxviii he asks *πῶς τὰ κατὰ τὴν ἐγγαστρίμυθον νοητέον;*[11] and says that some think that the witch actually evoked Samuel, others believe the Devil took the likeness of the prophet. The first opinion he characterizes as impious, the second foolish.

S. Jerome, whose authority would, of course, be entirely conclusive, does not perhaps pronounce definitely; but his comments sufficiently show, I think, that he regarded the apparition as being really Samuel. In his tractate *In Esaiam*, III, vii, he writes: "Most authors think that a clear sign was given Saul from the earth itself and from the very depths of Hades when he saw Samuel evoked by incantations and magic spells."[12] And again, *In Ezechielem*, Lib. IV; xiii, the holy doctor, speaking of witches, has: "they are inspired by an evil spirit. The Hebrews say that they are well versed in baleful crafts, necromancy and soothsayings, such as was the hag who seemed to raise up the soul of Samuel."[13]

Some authors directly attribute this appearance of Samuel to an evil spirit, who took the form of the prophet in order to dishearten Saul and tempt him to despair. Thus S. Gregory of Nyssa in his letter *De pythonissa ad Theodosium*[14] says that the Devil deceived the witch, who thus in her turn deceived the king. S. Basil expressly lays down (*In Esaiam*, VIII. 218): "They were demons who assumed the appearance of Samuel."[15] And he conjectures that, inasmuch as the denunciation of Saul was strictly true in every detail, the demons having heard the sentence delivered by God merely reported it. Among the Latins Tertullian, more than a century before, had written: "And I believe that evil spirits can deceive many by their lies; for a lying spirit was allowed to feign himself to be the shade of Samuel."[16]

The preponderance of opinion, however, is decidedly in favour of a literal and exact understanding of the event, that it was, in effect, Samuel who appeared to the guilty monarch and foretold his end. Origen argues upon these lines, basing his reasons upon the plain statements of Holy Writ: "But it is distinctly stated that Saul knew it was Samuel."[17] And later he adds: "The Scripture cannot lie. And the words of Scripture are: And the woman saw Samuel."[18] Elsewhere when treating of evil spirits he precisely states: "And that souls have their abiding place I have made known to you from the evocation by the witch of Samuel, when Saul requested her to divine."[19] S. Ambrose also says: "Even after his death Samuel, as Holy Scripture informs us, prophesied of what was to come."[20] We have further the overwhelming witness of S. Augustine, who in more than one place discusses the question at some length, and decides that the phantom evoked by the sibyl was really and truly the soul of the prophet Samuel. Thus in that important treatise *De Doctrina Christiana*, commenced in 397 and finally revised for issue in 427, he has: "The shade of Samuel, long since dead, truly foretold what was to come unto King Saul."[21] Whilst a passage in the even more famous and weighty *De Cura pro mortuis gerenda*, written in 421, asserts: "For the prophet Samuel, who was dead, revealed the future to King Saul, who was yet alive."[22]

Josephus believed the apparition to have been summoned by the witch's necromantic powers, for in his *Jewish Antiquities*, VI, xiv, 2, when dealing with the story of Endor, he chronicles: "[Saul] bade her bring up to him the soul of Samuel. She, not knowing who Samuel was, called him out of Hades,"[23] a remarkable testimony.

Throughout the whole of the Old Testament the sin of necromancy is condemned in the strongest terms, but the very reiteration of this ban shows that none the less evocation of the dead was extensively and continuously practised, albeit in the most clandestine and secret manner. The Mosaic law denounces such arts again and again: "Go not aside after wizards, neither ask any thing of soothsayers, to be defiled by them: I am the Lord your God" (Leviticus xix. 31); "The soul that shall go aside after magicians and soothsayers, and shall commit fornication with them, I will set my face against that soul, and destroy it out of the midst of its people" (Leviticus xx. 6). Even more explicit in its details is the following prohibition: "Neither let there be found among you any one . . . that consulteth soothsayers, or observeth dreams and omens, neither let there be any wizard, nor charmer, nor any one that consulteth pythonic spirits, or fortune tellers, or that seeketh the truth from the dead. For the Lord abhorreth all these things" (Deuteronomy xviii. 10–12). Hence it is obvious that the essential malice of the sin lay in the fact that it was *lèse-majesté* against God, such as is also the sin of heresy.[24] This is, moreover, clearly brought out in the fact that the temporal penalty was death. "A man, or woman, in whom there is a pythonical or divining spirit, dying, let them die" (Leviticus xx. 27). And the famous statute, Exodus xxii. 18, expressly says: "Wizards thou shalt not suffer to live." Nevertheless, necromancy persisted, and on occasion, such as during the reign of Manasses, thirteenth king of Juda (692–638 B.C.),[25] it no longer lurked in dark corners and obscene hiding-holes, but flaunted its foul abomination unabashed in the courts of the palace and at noon before the eyes of the superstitious capital. In the days of this monarch divination was openly used, omens observed, pythons publicly appointed, whilst soothsayers multiplied "to do evil before the Lord, and to provoke Him" (4 Kings [2 Kings] xxi. 6). The ghastly rites of human sacrifice were revived, and it was common knowledge that the sovereign himself, upon the slightest and most indifferent pretexts, resorted to *extispicium*, the seeking of omens from the yet palpitating entrails of boys devoted to this horrid purpose. " Manasses shed also very much innocent blood, till he filled Jerusalem up to the mouth " (4 Kings [2 Kings] xxi. 16). We may parallel the foul sorceries of the Jewish king with the detailed confession of Gilles de Rais, who at his trial "related how he had stolen away children, detailed all his foul cajolements, his hellish excitations, his frenzied murders, his ruthless rapes and ravishments: obsessed by the morbid vision of his poor pitiful victims, he described at length their long-drawn agonies or swift torturings; their piteous cries and the death-rattle in their throats; he avowed that he had wallowed in their warm entrails; he confessed that he had torn out their hearts through large gaping wounds, as a man might pluck ripe fruit."[26] The demonolatry of the sixth century before Christ is the same as that of fourteen hundred years after the birth of Our Lord.

As has been previously noticed, Balaam employed bullocks and rams for *extispicium*, and nine centuries later, in the book of Ezechiel (xxi. 21), Esarhaddon is represented as looking at the liver of an animal offered in sacrifice with a view to divination. " For the king of Babylon stood in the highway, at the head of two ways, seeking divination, shuffling arrows: he inquired of the idols, and consulted entrails. On his right hand was the divination of Jerusalem, to set battering rams, to open the mouth in slaughter." The mode of sortilege by arrows, belomancy, to which allusion is here made was extensively practised among the Chaldeans, as also by the Arabs. Upon this passage S. Jerome comments: " He shall stand in the highway, and consult the oracle after the manner of his nation, that he may cast arrows into a quiver, and mix them together, being written upon or marked with the names of each people, that he may see whose arrow will come forth, and which city he ought first to attack."

Among the three hundred and sixty idols which stood round about the Caaba of Mecca, and which were all destroyed by Mohammed when he captured the city in the eighth year of the Hejira, was the statue of a man, made of agate, who held in one hand seven arrows such as the pagan Arabs used in divination. This figure, which, it is said, anciently represented the patriarch Abraham, was regarded with especial awe and veneration.

The arrows employed by the early Arabs for magical practices were more generally only three in number. They were carefully preserved in the temple of some idol, before whose shrine they had been consecrated. Upon one of them was inscribed "My Lord hath commanded me"; upon another "My Lord hath forbidden me"; and the third was blank. If the first was drawn the inquirer looked upon it as a propitious omen promising success in the enterprise; if the second were drawn he augured failure; if the third, all three were mixed again and another trial was made. These divining arrows seem always to have been consulted by the Arabs before they engaged in any important undertaking, as, for example, when a man was about to go upon a particular journey, to marry, to commence some weighty business.

In certain cases and in many countries rods were used instead of arrows. Small sticks were marked with occult signs, thrown into a vessel and drawn out; or, it might be, cast into the air, the direction they took and the position in which they fell being carefully noted. This practice is known as rhabdomancy. The LXX, indeed, Ezechiel xxi. 21, has *ῥαβδομαντεία* not *βελομαντεία*, and rhabdomancy is mentioned by S. Cyril of Alexandria.

In the Koran, chapter V, The Table or The Chapter of Contracts, "divining arrows" are said to be "an abomination of the work of Satan," and the injunction is given "therefore avoid them that ye may prosper."

It is noticeable that in the early Biblical narrative one form of divination is mentioned, if not with approval, at any rate without overt reproach. Upon the occasion of the second journey of Jacob's sons to Egypt to buy corn in the time of famine, Joseph gave orders that their sacks were to be filled with food, that each man's money was to be put in the mouth of his sack, but that in the sack of Benjamin was also to be concealed the "cup, the silver cup." And the next morning when they had set out homewards and were gone a little way out of the city they were overtaken by a band of Joseph's servants under the conduct of his steward who arrested their progress and accused them of the theft of the cup : " Is not this it in which my lord drinketh, and whereby indeed he divineth ? Ye have done evil in so doing " (*A.V.*). The Vulgate has : " Scyphus quem furati estis, ipse est in quo bibit dominus meus et in quo augurari solet : pessimam rem fecistis " (Genesis xliv. 5). And later when they are brought back in custody and led into the presence of Joseph he asks them : " Wot ye not that such a man as I can certainly divine ? " Vulgate : " An ignoratis quod non sit similis mei in augurandi scientia ? "

In the first place it cannot be for a moment supposed that Joseph's claim, which here he so publicly and so emphatically states, to be a diviner of no ordinary powers was a mere device for the occasion. From the prominence given to the cup in the story it is clear that his steward regarded it as a vessel of especial value and import, dight with mysterious properties.

This cup was used for that species of divination known as hydromantia, a practice almost universal in antiquity and sufficiently common at the present day. The seer, or in some cases the inquirer, by gazing fixedly into a pool or basin of still water will see therein reflected as in a mirror a picture of that which it is sought to know. Strabo, XVI, 2, 39, speaking of the Persians, writes : *παρὰδε τοῖς πέρσαις οἱ Μάγοι καὶ νεκυομάντεις καὶ ἔτι οἱ λεγόμενοι λεκανομάντεις καὶ ὑδρομάντεις.* King Numa, according to one very ancient tradition, divined by seeing gods in a clear stream. " For Numa himself, not being instructed by any prophet or Angel of God, was fain to fall to hydromancy : making his gods (or rather his devils) to appear in water, and instruct him in his religious institutions. Which kind of divination, says Varro, came from Persia and was used by Numa and afterwards by Pythagoras, wherein they used blood also and called forth spirits infernal. Necromancy, the Greeks call it, but necromancy or hydromancy, whether you like, there it is that the dead seem to speak " (*S. Augustine De Ciuitate Dei.* VII. 35).[27]

Apuleius in his *De Magia*,[28] quoting from Varro, says : " Trallibus de euentu Mithridatici belli magica percontatione consultantibus puerum in aqua simulacrum Mercuri contemplantem, quæ futura erant, centum sexaginta uersibus cecinisse." In Egypt to-day the Magic Mirror is frequently consulted. A boy is engaged to gaze into a splash of water, or it may be ink or some other dark liquid poured into the palm of the hand, and therein he will assuredly see pictorially revealed the answers to those questions put to him. When a theft has been committed the Magic Mirror is invariably questioned thus. In Scandinavia the country folk, who had lost anything, would go to a diviner on a Thursday night to see in a pail of water who it was had robbed them.[29] All the world over this belief prevails, in Tahiti and among the Hawaiians, in the Malay Peninsula, in New Guinea, among the Eskimos.

Similar forms of divination are those by things dropped into some liquid, a precious stone or rich amulet is cast into a cup, and the rings formed on the surface of the contents were held to predict the future. Again warm wax or molten lead is poured into a vessel of cold water, and significant letters of the alphabet may be spelled out or objects discerned from the shapes this wax or lead assumes; or again, the empty tea-cup is tilted and from the leaves, their size, shape, and the manner in which they lie, prognostications are made. This is common in England, Scotland, Ireland, Sweden, Lithuania, whilst in Macedonia coffee-dregs are employed in the same manner.

But whether the seer be Hebrew patriarch or Roman king and the divination dignified by some occult name, Ceromancy (the melting of wax), Lecanomancy (basins of water), Oinomancy (the lees of wine), or whether it be some old plaid-shawled grandam by her cottage fire peering at the leaves of her afternoon tea, the object is the same throughout the ages, for all systems of divination are merely so many methods of obscuring the outer vision, in order that the inner vision may become open.

As was inevitable hydromantia lent itself to much trickery, and Hippolytus of Rome, presbyter and antipope (*ob. circa* A.D. 236), in his important polemic against heretics, *Philosophumena*,[30] IV, 35, explains in detail how persons were elaborately duped by the pseudo-magicians. A room was prepared, the roof of which was painted blue to resemble the sky, there was set therein a large vessel full of water with a glass bottom, immediately under which lay a secret chamber. The inquirer gazed steadfastly into the water, and the actors walking in the secret chamber below would seem as though they were figures appearing in the water itself.

In view of the severe and general condemnation of magical practices found throughout Holy Writ it is remarkable that the Pentateuchal narrative does not censure Joseph's hydromantic arts. Indeed, except in the book Genesis, it is seldom that any forms of presaging or the use of charms are noted save with stern reprobation. In Isaias iii. 2, however, the Kōsēm, magician or diviner, is mentioned with singular respect. "Ecce enim dominator Dominus exercituum auferet a Jerusalem et a Juda ualidum et fortem omne robur panis et omne robur aquæ, fortem, et uirum bellatorem, iudicem, et prophetam, et *hariolum*, et senem." Here the Authorized Version deliberately mistranslates and obscures the sense: "For, behold, the Lord, the Lord of hosts, doth take away from Jerusalem and from Judah, the stay and the staff, the whole stay of bread and the whole stay of water, the mighty man and the man of war, the judge and the prophet, and *the prudent*, and the ancient." "The Prudent" is by no means a rendering of Kōsēm which "hariolus" perfectly represents.

In the thirteenth chapter of Genesis we have a most detailed and striking narrative of sympathetic magic. Jacob, who is serving Laban, is to receive as a portion of his hire all the speckled and spotted cattle, all the brown among the sheep, and the spotted and speckled among the goats. But the crafty old Syrian prevented his son-in-law by removing to a distance, a journey of three days, all such herds as had been specified, "and Jacob fed the rest of Laban's flocks. Thereupon Jacob took rods of green poplar, hazel, and chestnut, and peeled these rods in alternate stripes of white and bark, and he put them in the gutters in the watering-troughs when the flocks came to drink." The animals duly copulated, and "the flocks conceived before the rods, and brought forth cattle, ringstraked, speckled, and spotted." Moreover, it was only when the stronger cattle conceived that Jacob set the rods before their eyes, so that eventually all the best of the herds fell to his share. The names of the trees are in themselves significant. The poplar in Roman folklore was sacred to Hercules,[31] and as it grew on the banks of the river Acheron in Epirus it was connected with Acheron, the waters of woe in the underworld, a confused tradition which is undoubtedly of very early origin. So Pausanias has: *τὴν λευκην ὁ Ἡρακλῆς πεφυκυῖαν παρὰ τὸν Ἀχέροντα εὕρετο ἐν Θεσπρωτιᾳ ποταμόν·* In seventeenth-century England poplar-leaves were accounted an important ingredient in hell-broths and charms. The hazel has been linked with magic from remotest antiquity, and the very name witch-hazel remains to-day. The chestnut-tree and its nuts seem to have been associated with some primitive sexual rites. The connexion is obscure, but beyond doubt traceable. In that most glorious marriage song, the Epithalamium of Catullus, as the boys sang their Fescennines of traditional obscenity nuts were scattered among the crowd.[32] Petronius (Fragmentum XXXIII, ed. Buecheler, Berolini, 1895) mentions chestnuts as an amatory gift:

> aurea mala mihi, dulcis mea Marcia, mittis
> mittis et hirsutae munera castaneae.

In Genesis again is recorded a most interesting and instructive example of the belief in the magic efficacy of plants. "And Reuben went in the days of wheat harvest and found mandrakes in the field and brought them to his mother Leah" (xxx. 14 A.V.). Reuben brings his mother mandrakes (Love Apples), which Rachel desires to have. Whereupon Leah bargains with Rachel, and the latter for a portion of the fruit consents that Jacob shall that night return to the bed of his elder wife, who indeed conceives and in due time she bare Issachar. Leah ate of the mandrake as a charm to induce pregnancy, and no disapproval of such use is expressed.

A similar theme is treated in Machiavelli's famous masterpiece of satirical comedy *La Mandragola*,[33] written between 1513 and 1520, and performed by request before Leo X in the April of the latter year. It had already been acted in Florence. In this play Callimaco is bent upon securing as his mistress Lucrezia, the wife of a gullable doctor of laws, Messer Nicia, whose one wish in life is to get a son. Callimaco is introduced as a physician to Nicia, to whom he explains that a potion of mandragora administered to the lady will remove her sterility, but that it has fatal consequences to the husband. He must perish unless some other man be first substituted whose action will absorb the poison, and leave Lucrezia free to become the mother of a blooming family. This plot is fully worked out, and by the services of his supple confederates Callimaco is introduced to Lucrezia's bedchamber as the necessary victim, and gains his desire.

Mandrakes and mallows were potent in all forms of enchantment, and about the mandrake in particular has grown up a whole library of legend, which it would require much time and space thoroughly to investigate. Western lore is mainly of somewhat a grim character, but not entirely, and by the Orientals mandrake is regarded as a powerful aphrodisiac. So in Canticles VII, 13, we have: Mandragoræ dederunt odorem. (The mandrakes give a fragrant smell.) In antiquity mandrakes were used as an anæsthetic. Dioscorides alludes to the employment of this herb before patients have to be cut or burned; Pliny refers to its odour as causing sleep during an operation; Lucian speaks of it as used before cautery; and both Galen and Isidorus have passages which mention its dormitive quality. The Shakespearean allusions have rendered this aspect familiar to all.

The Arabs and ancient Germans thought that a powerful spirit inhabited the plant, an idea derived, perhaps, from the fancied resemblance of the root to the human form. Ducagne has under Mandragore: "Pomi genus cuius mentio fit, Gen. xxx. 14. nostris etiam notis sub nomine *Mandragores*, quod pectore asseruatum sibi diuitiis acquirendis idoneum somniabunt." And Littré quotes the following from an old chronicle of the thirteenth century: "Li dui compaignon [un couple d'éléphants] vont contre Orient près du paradis terreste, tant que la femelle trouve une herbe que on apele mandragore, si en manjue, et si atize tant son masle qu'il en manjue avec li, et maintenant eschaufe la volenté de chascun, et s'entrejoignent à envers et engendrent un filz sanz plus." In the *Commentaria ad Historiam Caroli VI et VII* it is related that several mandrakes found in the possession of Frère Richard, a Cordelier, were seized and burned as savouring of witchcraft.

It seems certain that the teraphim, which Rachel stole

from her father (Genesis xxxi, 19, and 31–35), and which when he was in pursuit she concealed by a subtle trick, were used for purposes of divination. From the relation of the incident it is obvious that they were regarded of immense value—he who had conveyed them away was, if found, to die the death —and invested with a mysterious sanctity. Centuries later, during the period of drastic reform, King Josias (639–608 B.C.) would no longer tolerate them: "Moreover the workers with familiar spirits, and the wizards, and the images [teraphim], and the idols, and all abominations that were spied in the land of Judah and in Jerusalem did Josiah put away" (2 Kings xxiii. 24. A.V.). The Vulgate has: "Sed et pythones, et hariolos, et figuras idolorum, et immunditias, et abominationes, quæ fuerant in terra Juda et Jerusalem, abstulit Josias." In Ezechiel xxi. 21, Esarhaddon is said to have divined bŷ teraphim as well as by belomancy; and in Zacharias (x. 2) the teraphim are stated on occasion to have deceived their inquirers, "simulacra locuta sunt inutile," "the idols have spoken vanity." Notwithstanding this it is obvious from Osee (Hosea) iii. 4, that divination by teraphim was sometimes permitted: "Dies multos sedebunt filii Israel sine rege, et sine principe, et sine sacrificio, et sine altari, et sine ephod, et sine teraphim." "The children of Israel shall abide many days without a king, and without a prince, and without a sacrifice, and without an image, and without an ephod, and without teraphim."

The learned Cornelius à Lapide glossing on Genesis xxxi writes: "Idola, *teraphim* quod significat statuæ humanæ siue humaneas formas habentes ut patet, I. Reg. xix." The allusion is to the deception practised by Michal on Saul's messengers, when putting one of the teraphim in bed and covering it with quilts she pretended it was David who lay sick. "Secundo," continues à Lapide, "nomen *theraphim* non appropriatum est in eas statuas, quæ opera dæmonorum deposci debent, ut patet Judicum, xviii, 18," the reference being to the history of Micas. Calvin very absurdly says: "Theraphim sunt imagines quales habent papistæ."

Spencer[34] is of opinion that these teraphim were small images or figures, and the point seems conclusively settled by S. Jerome, who in his twenty-ninth Epistle, *De Ephod et Teraphim*, quotes 1 Kings xix. 15, and uses "figuras siue figurationes" to translate μορφώματα of Aquila of Pontus. This writer was the author of a Greek version of the Old Testament published *circa* A.D. 128. About eight years before he seems to have been expelled from the Christian community, by whom he was regarded as an adept in magic. The work of Aquila, who studied in the school of Rabbi Akiba, the founder of Rabbinical Judaism, is said by S. Jerome to have attained such exactitude that it was a good dictionary to furnish the meaning of the obscurer Hebrew words. The Targum of Jonathan commenting upon Genesis xxxi. 19, puts forward the singular view that the teraphim, concealed by Rachel, consisted of a mummified human head.

In the book Tobias we have a detailed and important account of exorcism, and one, moreover, which throws considerable light upon the demonology of the time. Tobias, the son of Tobias, is sent under the guidance of the unknown Angel, S. Raphael, to Gabelus in Rages of Media, to obtain the ten talents of silver left in bond by his father. Tobias, whilst bathing in the Tigris is attacked by a monstrous fish, of which he is told by his Angel protector to reserve the heart, liver, and gall; the first two of these are to prevent the devil who had slain seven previous husbands of Sara, the beautiful daughter of Raguel, from attacking him. They arrive at the house of Raguel, and Tobias seeks the hand of Sara. She, however, is so beloved by the demon Asmodeus that seven men who had in turn married her were by him put to death the night of the nuptials, before consummation. Tobias, however, by exorcism, by the odour of the burning liver of the fish, and by the help of S. Raphael, routs Asmodeus, "Then the Angel Raphael took the Devil, and bound him in the desert of upper Egypt." The story which must be accepted as fact-narrative was originally written during the Babylonian exile in the early portion of the seventh century, B.C. It plainly shows that demons were considered to be capable of sexual love, such as was the love of the sons of God for the daughters of men recorded in Genesis (vi. 2). One may compare the stories of the Jinns in Arabian lore. Asmodeus is perhaps to be identified with the Persian *Aēshma daēva*, who in the *Avesta* is next to Angromainyus, the chief of the evil spirits. The introduction of Tobias's dog should be remarked. The dog accompanies his master on the journey and when they return home "the dog, which had been with them in the way, ran before, and coming as if he had brought the news, shewed his joy by his fawning and wagging his tail." Among the Persians a certain power over evil spirits was justly assigned to the faithful dog.

The New Testament evidence for the reality of magic and divination is such that cannot be disregarded by any who accept the Christian revelation.

In the Gospels we continually meet with possession by devils; the miracle wrought in the country of the Gerasenes (Gergesenes) (S. Matthew viii. 28–34), the dumb man possessed by a devil (S. Matthew ix. 32–34), the healing of the lunatic boy who was obsessed (S. Matthew xvii. 14–21), the exorcism of the unclean spirit (S. Mark i. 23–27), the casting out of devils whom Christ suffered not to speak (S. Mark i. 32–34), the exorcism in the name of Jesus (S. Mark ix. 38), the demons who fled our Lord's presence crying out "Thou art Christ, the son of God" (S. Luke iv. 41), the healing of those vexed with unclean spirits (S. Luke vi. 18), and many instances more.

Very early in the Apostolic ministry appears one of the most famous figures in the whole history of Witchcraft, Simon, who is as Simon Magus, sorcerer and heresiarch. At the outbreak of that persecution (*circa* A.D. 37) of the Christian community in Jerusalem which began with the martyrdom of S. Stephen, when Philip the Deacon went down to Samaria, Simon, a native of Gitta, was living in that city. By his magic arts and by his mysterious doctrine, in which he announced himself as "the great power of God," he had made a name for himself and gained many adherents. He listened to Philip's sermons, was greatly impressed by them, he saw with wonder the miracles of healing and the exorcisms of unclean spirits, and like many of his countrymen was baptized and united with the community of believers in Christ. But it is obvious that he only took this step in order to gain, as he hoped, greater magical power and thus increase his influence. For when the Apostles S. Peter and S. John came to Samaria to bestow upon those who had been baptized by Philip the outpouring of the Holy Ghost which was accompanied by heavenly manifestations Simon offered them money, saying, " Give me also this power," which he obviously regarded as a charm or occult spell. S. Peter forthwith sharply rebuked the unholy neophyte, who, alarmed at this denunciation, implored the Apostles to pray for him.

Simon is not mentioned again in the New Testament, but the first Christian writers have much to say concerning him. S. Justin Martyr, in his first *Apologia* (A.D. 153–155) and in his dialogue *Contra Tryphonem* (before A.D. 161), describes Simon as a warlock who at the instigation of demons claimed to be a god. During the reign of the Emperor Claudius, Simon came to Rome, and by his sorceries won many followers who paid him divine honours. He was accompanied by a lewd concubine from Tyre, Helena, whom he claimed was Heavenly Intelligence, set free from bondage by himself the " great power."

In the *Pseudo-Clementine Homilies* (probably second century) Simon appears as the chief antagonist of S. Peter, by whom his devilish practices are exposed and his enchantments dissolved. The apocryphal *Acts of S. Peter*, which are of high antiquity,[35] give in detail the well-known legend of the death of Simon Magus. By his spells the warlock had almost won the Emperor Nero to himself, but continually he was being foiled and thwarted owing to the intercession of the Apostle. At last when Cæsar demanded one final proof of the truth of his doctrines, some miracle that might be performed at midday in the face of all Rome, Simon offered to take his flight into the heavens—a diabolical parody of the Ascension—so that men might know his power was full as mighty as that of Him whom the Christians worshipped as God.

A mighty concourse gathered in the Forum: Vestal Virgins, Senators, Equites, their ladies, and a whole rabble of lesser folk. In the forefront of a new Imperial box sat the Lord Nero Claudius Cæsar Augustus Germanicus, on one side his mother, Agrippina, on the other Octavia his wife. Magic staff in hand the magician advanced into the midst of the arena: muttering a spell he bade his staff await his return, and forthwith it stood upright, alone, upon the pavement. Then with a deep obeisance to the ruler of the known world Simon Magus stretched forth his arms, and a moment more with rigid limbs and stern set face he rose from the ground and began to float high in air toward the Capitol. Like some monstrous bird he rose, and hovered fluttering in space awhile. But among the throng stood S. Peter, and just as the sorcerer had reached the topmost pinnacles of the shrine of Juno Moneta, now Santa Maria in Aracœli, where brown Franciscans sing the praises of God, the first Pope of Rome kneeled down, lifted his right hand and deliberately made a mighty Sign of the Cross towards the figure who usurped the privileges of the Incarnate Son of Mary. Who shall say what hosts of hells fled at that moment? The wizard dropped swift as heavy lead; the body whirled and turned in the air; it crashed, broken and breathless, at the foot of the Emperor's seat, which was fouled and bespattered with black gouts of blood. At the same moment with a ringing sound the staff fell prone on the pavement. The flag upon which S. Peter kneeled may be seen even until this day in the Church of Santa Francesca Romana. For, in order to commemorate the defeat of the warlock, Pope S. Paul I (757–767) built a church upon the site of his discomfiture, and in 850 Pope S. Leo IV reconstructed it as Santa Maria Nova, which gave place to the present fane dedicated in 1612.

But the fame of Simon Magus as a wizard has been swallowed up in his ill repute as a heretic; so early do heresy and magic go hand in hand. He was the first Gnostic, whose disciples the Simonians, an Antinomian sect of the second century, indulged the sickest fantasies. Menander, the successor of Simon, proclaimed himself the Messiah and asserted that by his baptism immortality was conferred upon his followers. He also was regarded as a mighty magician, and the sect which was named after him, the Menandrians, seems to have lasted for no inconsiderable time.

In his missionary journeys S. Paul was continually combating Witchcraft. At Paphos he was opposed by the sorcerer Elymas; in Philippi a medium, "a certain damsel possessed with a spirit of divination," "spiritum pythonem," followed him along the streets crying out and naming him as "a servant of the most high God," until he exorcized the spirit; at Ephesus, a hotbed of sorcery and superstition, he converted many diviners and witches, who cleansed their souls by the Sacrament of Penance, and burned their conjuring books, a library of no mean value. It amounted indeed to fifty thousand drachmas (£2000), and one may suppose that in addition to manuscripts there were amulets of silver and gold, richly wrought and jewelled. In Ephesus, also, had foregathered a large number of vagabond Jews, exorcists. The chief characteristic of a Jewish exorcism was the recitation of names believed to be efficacious, principally names of good angels, which were used either alone, or in combination with El (God); and, indeed, a blind reliance upon the sound of mere names had long been a settled practice with these amateur sorcerers, who considered that the essence of their charms lay in the use of particular names declaimed in a particular order, which differed on several occasions. It was this belief, no doubt, that induced the seven sons of Sceva, who had witnessed S. Paul's exorcisms in the name of Jesus, to try upon their own account the formula "I conjure thee by Jesus whom Paul preacheth," an experiment disastrous to their credit. For in one case the patient cried out "Jesus I know, and Paul I know, but who are ye?" and leaped upon them with infernal strength, beating and wounding them, so that they fled for safety from the house, their limbs bruised and their garments torn, to the great scandal of the neighbourhood.

For the fact of demoniac possession the authority of Christ Himself is plainly pledged; whilst Witchcraft is explicitly ranked by S. Paul with murder, sedition, hatred, and heresy (Galatians v. 20–21). S. John, also, twice mentions sorcerers in a hideous catalogue of sinners. There can be no doubt whatsoever that the reality of Witchcraft is definitely maintained by the New Testament writers,[36] and any denial of this implicitly involves a rejection of the truth of the Christian revelation.

Among the Jews of a later period, and probably even to-day, various diseases are said to be induced by demons, who, it is instructive to notice, haunt marshy places, damp and decayed houses, latrines, squalid alleys, foul atmospheres where sickness is bred and ripened.

Josephus (*ob.* A.D. 100) relates that God taught Solomon how demons were to be expelled, a "science useful and sanitative to men." He also gives an account of Eliezar, a celebrated exorcist of the time, whom, in the presence of the Emperor Vespasian, the historian actually saw casting out evil spirits. The operator applied to the nose of the possessed a ring having attached to it a root which Solomon is said to have prescribed—" Baaras," a herb of magical properties, and one dangerous for the uninitiate to handle. As the devils came forth Eliezar caused them to pass into a basin filled with water, which was at once poured away. It may be noticed also that demonology plays an important part in the Book of Enoch (before 170 B.C.). Even in the Mishna there are undoubted traces of magic, and in the Gemara demonology and sorcery loom very largely. Throughout the Middle Ages Jewish legend played no insignificant part in the history of Witchcraft, and, especially in Spain, until the nineteenth century at least, there were prosecutions, not so much for the observance of Hebrew ceremonies as is often suggested and supposed, but for the practice of the dark and hideous traditions of Hebrew magic. Closely connected with these ancient sorceries are those ritual murders, of which a learned Premonstratensian Canon of Wilthin, Adrian Kembter, writing in 1745, was able to enumerate no less than two-and-fifty,[37] the latest of these having taken place in 1650, when at Cadan in Bohemia, Matthias, a lad of four years old, was killed by certain rabbis with seven wounds. In many cases the evidence is quite conclusive that the body, and especially the blood of the victim, was used for magical purposes. Thus with reference to little S. Hugh of Lincoln, after various very striking details, the chronicler has: " Et cum exspirasset puer, deposuerunt corpus de cruce, et nescitur qua ratione, euiscerarunt corpusculum; dicitur autem, quod ad magicas artes exercendas." In 1261 at Forcheim in Bavaria the blood of a murdered boy was used to sprinkle certain thresholds and doors. In 1285 at Munich a witch was convicted of selling Christian children to the Jews, who carefully preserved the blood in curious vessels for secret rites. In 1494 at Tyrnau twelve vampires were executed for having opened the veins of a boy whom they had snared, and having drunk his warm blood thence whilst he was yet alive. A deed of peculiar horror was discovered at Szydlow in 1597 when the victim was put to death in exquisite tortures, the blood and several members of the body being partaken of by the murderers. In almost every case the blood was carefully collected, there can be no doubt for magical purposes, the underlying idea being the precept of the Mosaic law: Anima enim omnis carnis in sanguine est :[38] For the life of all flesh is in the blood thereof

NOTES TO CHAPTER V

[1] *Khartummim.* The same word is used to describe the magicians whom Pharaoh summoned to interpret his dream, *Genesis* xli. 8, where the Vulgate has *coniectores*. *Exodus* viii. 11, the Vulgate reads: "Uocauit autem Pharao sapientes et maleficos."

[2] It is perhaps worth mentioning that even the most modernistic commentators assign the history of Balaam to the oldest document of the Hexateuch, that they call the Jehovistic.

[3] In his commentary on the ninth chapter of the prophet Osee (Hosea), S. Jerome says: "Ingressi [sunt] ad Beel-Phegor, idolum Moabitarum quem nos PRIAPUM possumus appelare." And Rufinus on the same prophet has: "Beel-Phegor figuram Priapi dixerunt tenere." (They entered in unto Beel-Phegor, the idol of the Moabites, whom we may identify with PRIAPUS. . . . Beel-Phegor is said to have had the same shape as Priapus.)

[4] Balaam hariolus a Domino mittitur ut decipiat Balac filium Beor. *In Ezechielem*, IV. xiv. Migne, *Patres Latini*, XXV. p. 118. (Baalam, a soothsayer, is sent by God to deceive Balac, son of Beor.)

[5] Balaam fuisse prophetam non Dei, sed diaboli constat. . . . Fuit ipse magus, et dæmonis alloquium quærebat, eumque consulere.

[6] The word is usually found with *yidde 'onim* (from *yada*, "to know,") and they are generally considered to be identical in meaning. But W. R. Smith, *Journ. Phil.*, XIV. 127, makes the following distinction: Yidde 'oni is a familiar spirit, one known to him who calls it up; the 'ôbh is any spirit who may be invoked by a spell and forced to answer questions.

[7] *Divination, et la science des présages*, Paris, 1875. p. 161 ff.

[8] *History of the People of Israel*, 3 vols., London, 1888–91. I. p. 347.

[9] Cf. Ovid, *Metamorphoseon*, IV, 412–3, of bats:

Conatæque loqui, minimam pro corpore uocem
Emittunt; peraguntque leues stridore querelas.

[10] Josephus says that Samuel told the witch it was Saul.

[11] Migne, *Patres Græci*, LXXX. p. 589.

[12] Plerique putant Saulem signum accepisse de terra et de profundo inferni quando Samuelem per incantationes et artes magicas uisus est suscitasse. Migne, *Patres Latini*, XXIV. p. 106.

[13] . . . inspirantur diabolico spiritu. Has autem dicunt Hebræi maleficis artibus eruditas per necromantias et pythicum spiritum qualis fuit illa quæ uisa est suscitare animam Samuelis. *Idem*, XXV. p. 114.

[14] Migne, *Patres Græci*, XLV. pp. 107–14.

[15] *Δαίμονες γαρ ἦσαν οἱ κατασχηματίζοντες ἑαυτοὺς εἰς τὸ τοῦ Σαμουὴλ πρόσωπον.* *Idem*, XXX. p. 497.

[16] Et credo quia [spiritus immundi] mendacio possunt; nec enim pythonico tunc spiritui minus liciut animam Samuelis effingere. (*De Anima*, LVII.) Migne, *Patres Latini*, II. p. 749.

[17] Ἀλλὰ γέγραπται, ὅτὶ ἔγνω Σαουλ ὅτι Σαμουὴλ ἔστι.

[18] *ἐπεὶ οὐ δύναται ψευδέσθαι ἡ Γραφη. τὰ δε ῥήματα τῆς Γραφῆς ἐστὶν· Καὶ εἶδεν ἡ γυνὴ τὸν Σαμουήλ.* (*In librum Regum.* Homilia II.) Migne, *Patres Græci*, XII. p. 1013.

[19] *καὶ ὅτι μένουσιν αἱ ψυχαί, ἀπέδειξα ὑμῖν ἐκ τôυ καὶ τὴν Σαμουὴλ ψυχὴν κληθῆναι ὑπὸ τῆς ἐγγαστριμμύθου, ὡς ἠξίωσιν ὁ Σαουλ.* (*In I. Regum.* XXVIII.) *Idem*, XII.

[20] Samuel post mortem, secundum Scripturæ Testimonium futura non tacuit. *I. Regum.* XXVIII. 17 *et seq.* (*In Lucam.* I. 33.) Migne, *Patres Latini*. XV. p. 1547.

[21] Imago Samuelis mortui Saul regi uera prænuntiauit. *Idem*, XXXIV. p. 52. And *De Cura*, XL. p. 606.

[22] Nam Samuel propheta defunctus uiuo Sauli etiam regi futura prædixit.

[23] Whiston's translation. Ed. 1825. Vol. I, p. 263.

[24] So 1 *Kings* (*Samuel*) xv. 23 : "Because it is like the sin of witchcraft, to rebel." Heresy and rebellion are fundamentally the same.

[25] Schrader, *Die Keilenscheiften und das alte Testament*, Giessen, 2nd ed., 1883.

[26] . . . raconta ses rapts d'enfants, ses hideuses tactiques, ses stimulations infernales, ses meurtres impétueux, ses implacables viols ; obsédé par la vision des ses victimes, il décrivit leurs agonies ralenties ou hâtées, leurs appels et leurs râles ; il avoua s'être vautré dans les élastiques tiédeurs des intestins ; il confessa qu'il avait arraché des cœurs par des plaies élargies, ouvertes, telles que des fruits mûrs. *Là-Bas*, J. K. Huysmans, c. xviii.

[27] Healey's translation, 1610.

[28] *De Magia*, XLVII.

[29] *The Primitive Inhabitants of Scandinavia*, Sven Nilsson. 3rd edition. 1868. p. 241.

[30] The original title is *κατὰ πασῶν αἱρέσεων ἔλεγχος*. A Refutation of all Heresies. The first book had long been known ; books IV–X, which had been discovered a short time previously, were first published in 1851 (Oxford) by Miller as the work of Origen, but edited by Duncker and Schneidewin as by Hippolitus, eight years later, Göttingen, 1859. The first chapters of the Fourth, and the whole of the Second and Third Books are still missing.

[31] Theocritus, II. 121. Κρατὶ δ' ἔχων λεύκαν Ἡρακλέος ἱερὸν ἔρνος. Vergil. *Eclogue* VIII, 61 : Populus Alcidæ gratissima. *Æneid*, VIII, 276 : Herculea bicolor quem populus umbra . . .

[32] Pliny (*Historia Naturalis*, XV. 86) says walnuts were thrown, and it appears from an inscription that this custom prevailed on birthdays as well as at weddings. But originally, at any rate, chestnuts were also used. In time the meaning became obscured, and as nuts were used in all kinds of games they merely became synonymous with playthings.

[33] The play is referred to in 1520 as *Messer Nicia*, and the first edition printed at Florence *circa* 1524 has the title *The Comedy of Callimaco and Lucrezia*, but the Prologue definitely gives the name *La Mandragola* (*The Mandrake*), and this is used in all later editions. The story has been imitated by La Fontaine ; the play itself (which is still acted in Italy) has been repeatedly translated, at least six times into French and five times into German, but as yet no English version has been published.

[34] *De Legibus Hebrœorum ritualibus earumque rationibus*, 2 vols., Tubingæ, 1732.

[35] Not later than A.D. 200. They were well known to Commodian, who wrote about A.D. 250.

[36] This is, of course, the view of the Fathers, and even later theological writers (e.g. Alfred Edersheim, Delitzsch, Rev. Walter Scott) accept this literal truth.

[37] In his book *Acta pro Ueritate Martyrii corporis, & cultus publici B. Andreœ Rinnensis*, Innsbruck, 1745. Blessed Andrew, a child, was killed at Rinn in the Tyrol, 12 July, 1462. A systematic investigation would, no doubt, wellnigh double the number of instances recorded by Kembter, and there are 15 for the eighteenth, 39 for the nineteenth century. In 1913 Mendil Beiliss was tried upon the charge of ritually murdering a Russian lad, Yushinsky.

[But see Foreword to this present book, page ix, for correction — Editor.]

[38] Leviticus xvii. 14.

[Publisher's note: The intelligent reader need scarcely be told that the publisher abhors the author's views, and publishes them only for the reasons indicated in Felix Morrow's Foreword to this edition.]

CHAPTER VI

Diabolic Possession and Modern Spiritism

The phenomenon of diabolic possession, the mere possibility of which materialists and modernists in recent years have for the most part stoutly denied, has, nevertheless, been believed by all peoples and at all periods of the earth's history. In truth he who accepts the spiritual world is bound to realize all about him the age-long struggle for empery of discarnate evil ceaselessly contending with a thousand cunning sleights and a myriad vizardings against the eternal unconquerable powers of good. Nature herself bears witness to the contest; disease and death, cruelty and pain, ugliness and sin, are all evidences of the mighty warfare, and it would be surprising indeed if some were not wounded in the fray—for we cannot stand apart, each man, S. Ignatius says, must fight under one of the two standards—if some even did not fall.

The ancient Egyptians, whose religion of boundless antiquity is pre-eminent in the old world for its passionate earnestness, its purity, and lofty idealism certainly held that some diseases were due to the action of evil spirits or demons, who in exceptional circumstances had the power of entering human bodies and of vexing them in proportion to the opportunities consciously or unconsciously given to their malign natures and influences. Moreover, the Egyptians were regarded as being supremely gifted in the art of curing the diseases caused by demoniacal possession, and one noteworthy instance of this was inscribed upon a stele and set up in the temple of the god Khonsu at Thebes so that all men might learn his might and his glory.[1] When King Rameses II was in Mesopotamia the various princes made him many offerings of gold and gems, and amongst other came the Prince of Bekhten, who brought his daughter, the fairest maiden of that land. When the king saw he loved her and bestowed upon her the title of "Royal spouse, chief lady,

Rā-neferu" (the beauties of Ra, the Sun-god), and taking her back to Egypt he married her with great pomp and hallowed solemnity. In the fifteenth year of the king's reign there arrived at his court an ambassador from the Prince of Bekhten, bearing rich presents and beseeching him "on behalf of the lady Bent-ent-resht, the younger sister of the royal spouse Rā-neferu, for, behold, an evil disease hath laid hold upon her body, "wherefore," said the envoy, "I beseech thy Majesty to send a physician[2] to see her." Rameses ordered the books of the "double house of life" to be brought and the wise men to choose from their number one who might be sent to Bekhten. They selected the sage Tehuti-em-heb, who in company with the ambassador forthwith departed on their journey, and when they had arrived the Egyptian priest soon found the lady Bent-ent-resht was possessed of a demon or spirit over which he was powerless. Wellnigh in despair the Prince of Bekhten sent again to the king begging him to dispatch even a god to his help.

When the ambassador arrived a second time Rameses was worshipping in the temple of Khonsu Nefer-hetep at Thebes, and he at once besought that deity to allow his counterpart Khonsu to go to Bekhten and to deliver the daughter of the prince of that country from the demon who possessed her. Khonsu Nefer-hetep granted the request, and a fourfold measure of magical power was imparted to the statue of the god which was to go to Bekhten. The god, seated in his boat, and five other boats with figures of gods in them, accompanied by a noble attendance of horses and chariots upon the right and the left, set out for Bekhten, where in due course they were received with great honour. The god Khonsu was brought to the place where the princess was, magical ceremonies were performed, and the demon incontinently departed. Khonsu remained in Bekhten three years, four months, and five days, being worshipped with the utmost veneration. One night, however, the Prince had a dream in which he saw a hawk of gold issue from the sacred shrine and wing its way towards Egypt. In the morning the Egyptian priests interpreted his dream as meaning that the god now wished to return, and accordingly he was escorted back in superb state, and with him were sent grateful gifts and thank offerings innumerable to be laid in the temple of Khonsu Nefer-hetep at Thebes.

The Greeks of the earlier civilization were inclined generally to attribute all sickness to the gods, who again often by this particular means took almost immediate revenge upon those who had insulted their images, profaned their sanctuaries, or derided their worship. Thus Pentheus who resists the introduction of the mysteries of Dionysus into Thebes is driven mad by the affronted deity.[3] The madness of Ajax, and that of the daughters of Proetus,[4] who imagined themselves changed into cows, shows us that this belief went back to heroic times. In later days Demaratus and his brother Alopecos were driven lunatic (*παραφρονήσαν*) after having found the statue of Artemis Orthosia, and this was considered to be the power of the goddess.[5] The frenzy which attacked Quintus Fulvius was regarded as a punishment, a possession by evil spirits on account of his sacrilege in having stolen the marble roof of the temple of Juno Lacinia at Locri.[6]

Pythagoras taught that the ailments both of men and of animals are due to demons who throng the regions of the air, and this doctrine does no more than state clearly what had been more or less vaguely believed from the dawn of human history. Wherefore Homer in the *Odyssey*, speaking of a man who is racked by a sore disease, says that a hateful demon is tormenting him: *στυγερὸς δέ οἱ ἔχραε δαίμων*, V, 396. (But a hateful demon griped him fast.) The word *κακοδαιμονία*, possession by an evil spirit, in Aristophanes signifies "raving madness," and the verb *κακοδαιμονάω*, to be tormented by an evil spirit, is used by Xenophon, Demosthenes, Dinarchus, and Plutarch[7] amongst other authors.

Many philosophers believed that each man has a protecting daimon, who in some sense personifies his individuality. It followed that lunatics and the delirious were afflicted with madness by these spirits who guided them, and accordingly the Greek names for those distraught are highly significant: *ἐνεργούμενοι* (in later Greek, persons possessed of an evil spirit), *δαιμονιόληπτοι* (influenced by devils), *θεόληπτοι*, *θεόβλαβες* (stricken of God), *θεόμανες* (maddened by the gods); and so Euripides has *λύσσα θεομανής*, and again *θεομανης πότμος*.[8] The very name *μανία* given by the Greeks to madness was derived from the root-word *man*, *men*,[9] which occurs in the Latin *Manes*, and indeed the Romans thought that a madman was tormented by the goddess Mania, the mother of the Lares, the hallucinations of lunatics being taken to be spectres who pursued them.[10] And so a madman was *laruarum plenus, laruatus*,[11] one whom phantoms disturbed; as in Plautus, where the doctor says: "What kind of a disease is this? Explain. Unfold, old sire, I say. Art thou crazed (*laruatus*) or lunatic? Tell me now."[12]

The frantic exaltation which thrilled the Galli, and the Corybantes when they celebrated the Dionysia, seems to have been epidemic, and was universally attributed to divine possession. There are many allusions to the connexion between the rites of Cybele and Dionysus. Apollodorus[13] says Dionysus was purified from madness by Rhea at the Phrygian Cybela, and was then initiated into her rites and took her dress; thence he passed into Thrace with a train of Bacchanals and Satyrs. Strabo,[14] on the other hand, thinks the rites were brought from Thrace by colonists from that country into Phrygia; he even quotes a fragment from the *Edoni* of Æschylus[15] as proving the identity of the cultus of Dionysus and Cybele. So also we have in Euripides, *Bacchæ*, 58,

> Up, and wake the sweet old sound,
> The clang that I and mystic Rhea found,
> The Timbrel of the Mountains.[16]

It is interesting to remark that Nicander of Claros,[17] who was a physician, in his *Alexipharmaca* (Ἀλεξιφάρμακα), speaking of a particular form of lunacy, compares the shrieks uttered by patients with those of a priestess of Rhea, when on the ninth day she makes all whom she encounters in the streets tremble at the hideous howl of the Idæan Mother; κερνοφόρος ζάκορος βωμίστρια Ῥείης is the exact phrase.[18] In the *Hippolytus* (141 *sqq.*) the Chorus speaking to Phaedra says:

> Is this some spirit, O child of man?
> Doth Hecat hold thee perchance, or Pan?
> Doth She of the Mountains work her ban,
> Or the Dread Corybantes bind thee?[19]

And in the *Medea* (1171–2) we have: "She seemed, I wot, to be one frenzied, inspired with madness by Pan or some other of the gods."[20]

Here τινὸς θεῶν, says Paley, alludes to Dionysus or Cybele. Madness was sometimes thought to be sent by Pan for any neglect of his worship, so in the *Rhesus* Hector cries (36–7): "Can it be that you are scared by the fear-causing stroke of Pan of old Kronos's line?"[21]

Aretæus, the medical writer, who is especially celebrated for his accuracy of diagnosis, in his *De signis chronicorum morborum*, VI, describes Corybantic frenzy as a mental malady and says that patients may be soothed and even cured by the strains of soft music.[22] We have here then the same remedy as was applied in the case of Saul, whom, we are told, "an evil spirit from the Lord troubled,"[23] and to whose court David, the sweet harper, was summoned. This seems to be the only instance of demoniac possession in the Old Testament and although the Hebrew word *rûah* need not absolutely imply a personal influence, if we may judge from Josephus[24] the Jews certainly gave the word that meaning in this very passage.

It may be well here clearly to explain the difference between possession and obsession, two technical terms sometimes confounded. By obsession is meant that the demon attacks a man's body from without;[25] by possession is meant that he assumes control of it from within. Thus S. Jerome describes the obsessions which beset S. Hilarion: "Many were his temptations; day and night did the demons change and renew their snares. . . . As he lay down how often did not nude women encircle him? When he was an hungered how often a plenteous board was spread before him?"[26] S. Antony the Great, also was similarly attacked: "The devil did not let to attack him, at night assuming the form of some maiden and imitating a woman's gestures to deceive Antony."[27] These painful phenomena are not uncommon in the lives of the Saints. Very many examples might be cited, but one will suffice, that of S. Margaret of Cortona,[28] the Franciscan penitent,[29] who was long and terribly tormented: "Following her to and fro up and down her humble cell as she wept and prayed [the devil] sang the most filthy songs, and lewdly incited Christ's dear handmaid, who with tears was commending herself to the Lord, to join him in trolling forth bawdy catches . . . but her prayers and tears finally routed the foul spirit and drove him far away."[30] The theologians, however, warn us to be very cautious in dealing with so difficult a matter, and the supreme authority of S. Alphonsus Liguori advises us that by far the greater part of these obsessions are distressing hallucinations, neurasthenia, imagination, hysteria, in a word, pathological: "It is advisable always to be very suspicious of such diabolic attacks, for it cannot be gainsaid that for the most part they are fancy, or the effect of imagination, or weakness, especially when women are concerned."[31] Dom Dominic Schram presses home the same point with equal emphasis: "Very often what are supposed to be demoniacal obsessions are nothing else than natural ailments, or morbid imaginings, or even distractions or actual lunacy. Wherefore it is necessary to deal with these cases most carefully, until the peculiar symptoms clearly show that it is actual obsession."[32]

Demoniac possession is frequently presented to us in the New Testament, and we have the authority of Christ Himself as to its reality. The infidel argument is to deny the possibility of possession in any circumstances, either on the hypothesis that there are no evil spirits in existence, or that they are powerless to influence the human body in the manner described. But whatever view Rationalists may adopt—and they are continually shifting their ground—no reader of the Scriptural narrative can deny that Christ by word and deed showed His entire belief in possession by evil spirits. And if Christ were divine how came He to foster and encourage a delusion? Why did He not correct it? Only two answers can be supposed. Either He was ignorant of a religious truth, or He deliberately gave instructions that He knew to be false, frequently acting in a way which was something more than misleading. To a Christian either of these explanations is, of course, unthinkable. The theory of accommodation formulated by Winer[33] may be accepted by Modernists, but will be instantly condemned by all others. Accommodation is understood as the toleration of harmless illusions of the day having little or no connexion with religion. Even if this fine piece of profanity were allowed, which, of course, must not be the case, the argument could not be applied here, indeed it seems wholly repugnant even in regard to a Saint, but entirely impossible in consideration of the divinity of Christ.

The victims of possession were sometimes deprived of speech and sight: "Then was offered to him one possessed of a devil, blind and dumb: and he healed him, so that he spoke and saw" (S. Matthew xii. 22). Sometimes they had lost speech alone: "Behold, they brought him a dumb man, possessed with a devil, and after the devil was cast out the dumb man spoke" (S. Matthew ix. 32, 33); also "And he was casting out a devil, and the same was dumb: and when he had cast out the devil the dumb spoke" (S. Luke xi. 14). In many cases the mere fact of possession is mentioned without further details: "they presented to him such as were possessed by devils, and lunatics . . . and he cured them" (S. Matthew iv. 24); "and when evening was come, they brought to him many that were possessed with devils, and he cast out the spirits with his word" (S. Matthew viii. 16); "And, behold a woman of Canaan, who came out of those coasts, crying out, said to him: Have mercy on me, O Lord, thou son of David: my daughter is grievously troubled by a devil . . . Then Jesus answering, said to her: O woman, great is thy faith: be it done to thee as thou wilt: and her daughter was cured from that hour" (S. Matthew xv. 22–28); "And when it was evening after sunset they brought to him all that were ill and that were possessed with devils"; "And he cast out many devils, and he suffered them not to speak, because they knew him"; "And he was preaching in their synagogues, and in all Galilee, and casting out devils" (S. Mark i. 32, 34, 39); "And the unclean spirits, when they saw him, fell down before him: and they cried, saying: Thou art the Son of God" (S. Mark iii. 11, 12); "And devils went out from many, crying out and saying: Thou art the Son of God" (S. Luke iv. 41); "And they that were troubled with unclean spirits were cured" (S. Luke vi. 18); "And in that same hour, he cured many of their diseases, and hurts, and evil spirits" (S. Luke vii. 21). The exorcism of the man "who had a devil now a very long time," and who dwelt among the tombs in the country of the Gerasens (Gadarenes) is related by S. Luke (viii. 27–39). The possessed is tormented by so many unclean spirits that they proclaim their name as Legion: he is endowed with supernatural strength so that he breaks asunder bonds and fetters: the devils recognize Christ as God, and Our

Lord converses with them, asking how they are called. Immediately the devils have been cast out the man is clothed, peaceable, reasonable, and quiet, "in his right mind."

At the foot of Mount Tabor a young man is brought by his father to be healed. The youth is possessed of a dumb spirit, "who, wheresoever he taketh him dasheth him, and he foameth, and gnasheth with the teeth, and pineth away." When Jesus approached, "immediately the spirit troubled him; and being thrown down upon the ground, he rolled about foaming." The patient had been thus afflicted "from his infancy, and oftentimes hath he cast him into the fire and into waters to destroy him." Our Lord threatened the spirit, and forthwith expelled it. (S. Mark ix. 14–28.) It should be noticed that it is the demons who are addressed on these occasions, not their victims. In the face of this catena of Biblical evidence and the various circumstances attending these exorcisms it is impossible to maintain that the possessed suffered merely from epilepsy, paralysis, acute mania, or any other such disease. In fact the Evangelists carefully separate natural maladies from diabolic possession: "He cast out the spirits with his word: and all that were sick he healed" (S. Matthew viii. 16); "They brought to him all that were ill and that were possessed with devils . . . and he healed many that were troubled with divers diseases and he cast out many devils" (S. Mark i. 32, 34). In the original Greek the distinction is still more clearly and unmistakably shown: *πάντας τοὺς κακῶς ἔχοντας καὶ τοὺς δαιμονιζομένους.* Saint Matthew, again, differentiates: "they presented to him all sick people that were taken with divers diseases [*ποικίλαις νόσοις*] and torments [*βασάνοις*] and such as were possessed by devils [*δαιμονιζομένους*] and lunatics [*σεληνιαζομένους*] and those who had the palsy [*παραλυτικούς*] and he cured them," iv. 24. Moreover, Our Lord expressly distinguishes between possession and natural disease; "Behold I cast out devils and do cures," are the Divine Words; *ἰδοὺ ἐκβάλλω δαιμόνια καὶ ἰάσεις ἀποτελῶ* (S. Luke xiii. 32).

That the demoniacs were often afflicted with other diseases as well is highly probable. The demons may have attacked those who were already sick, whilst the very fact of obsession or possession would of itself produce disease as a natural consequence.

According to S. Matthew x. 1, Our Lord gave special powers to the Apostles to exorcize demons: "And having called his twelve disciples together, he gave them power over unclean spirits to cast them out, and to heal all manner of diseases, and all manner of infirmities." And S. Peter, when describing the mission and miracles of Christ, stresses this very point: "Jesus of Nazareth: how God anointed him with the Holy Ghost, and with power, who went about doing good, and healing all that were possessed by the devil," *τοὺς καταδυναστευομένους ὑπὸ τοῦ διαβόλου* (Acts x. 38). Our Lord Himself directly appeals to His power over evil spirits as a proof of His Messiahship: "If I by the finger of God cast out devils; doubtless the kingdom of God is come upon you"; *εἰ δὲ ἐν δακτύλῳ Θεοῦ ἐκβάλλω τά δαιμόνια, ἄρα ἔφθασεν ἐφ' ὑμᾶς ἡ βασιλεία τοῦ Θεοῦ* (S. Luke xi. 20).

Whilst yet on earth Christ empowered the Apostles to cast out demons in His Name, and in His last solemn charge He promised that the same delegated power should be perpetuated: "These signs shall follow them that believe: in my name they shall cast out devils"; *σημεῖα δὲ τοῖς πιστεύσασι ταῦτα παρακολουθήσει· ἐν τῷ ὀνόματί μου δαιμόνια ἐκβαλοῦσι* (S. Mark xvi. 17.) But the efficacy of exorcism was conditional, not absolute as in the case of Our Lord Himself, for He explained, upon an occasion when the Apostles seemed to fail, that certain spirits could only be expelled by prayer and fasting. Moreover, a perfect belief and complete command are necessary for the exorcizer. *τότε προσέλθοντες οἱ μαθηταὶ τῷ Ἰησοῦ κατ ἰδίαν εἶπον, Διατί ἡμεῖς οὐκ ἠδυνήθημεν ἐκβαλεῖν αὐτό; ὁ δὲ Ἰησοῦς λέγει αὐτοῖς, Διὰ τὴν ὀλιγοπιστίαν ὑμῶν· . . . τοῦτο δὲ τὸ γένος οὐκ ἐκπορεύεται εἰ μὴ ἐν προσευχῇ καὶ νηστείᾳ* (S. Matthew xvii. 19–21). S. Paul, and no doubt the other Apostles and Disciples, regularly made use of this exorcizing power. Thus, at Philippi, where the girl "having a pythonical spirit . . . who brought to her masters much gain by divining" (*παιδίσκην τινὰ ἔχουσαν πεῦνμα πύθωνα . . . ἥτις ἐργασίαν πολλὴν παρεῖχε τοῖς κυρίοις αὐτῆς μαντευομένη*)[34] met S. Paul and S. Luke and proclaimed them as servants of the most high God, S. Paul "being grieved, turned, and said to the spirit: I command thee, in the name of Jesus Christ, to go out from her. And he went out the same hour" (Acts xvi. 16–18). And at Ephesus, a hot-bed of magic and necromancy, "God wrought by the hand of Paul more than common miracles. So that even there were brought from his body to the sick, handkerchiefs and aprons, and the diseases departed from them, and the wicked spirits went out of them" (Acts xix. 11, 12). Those who do not imagine that the powers Our Lord perpetually bestowed upon the Apostles and their followers abruptly ceased with the thirty-first verse of the twenty-eighth chapter of The Acts of the Apostles, realize that the charisma of exorcism has continued through the ages, and in truth the Church has uninterruptedly practised it until the present day.

The Exorcist is ordained by the Bishop for this office, ordination to which is the second of the four minor orders of the Western Church. Pope Cornelius (251–252) mentions in his letter to Fabius that there were then in the Roman Church forty-two acolytes, and fifty-two exorcists, readers, and door-keepers, and the institution of these orders together with the organization of their functions, seems to have been the work of the predecessor of Cornelius, Pope Saint Fabian the Martyr (236–251).

The rite of the Ordination of Exorcists, "De Ordinatione Exorcistarum," is as follows: First, the Book of Exorcisms, or in its place the Pontifical or Missal must be ready at hand; *Pro Exorcistis ordinandis paretur liber exorcismorum, cuius loco dari potest Pontificale uel Missale* (A Book of Exorcisms must be prepared for those who are to be ordained Exorcists. Howbeit in place thereof the Pontifical or the Missal may be handed to them) runs the rubric. When the Lectors have been ordained, the Bishop resuming his mitre takes his place upon his seat or faldstool at the Epistle side of the altar, and the Missal with the bugia being brought by his acolytes he proceeds to read the Gradual, or (if it be within the Octave of Pentecost) the *Alleluia.* Meantime the Gradual is sung by the choir. When it is finished, he rises, takes off his mitre, and turning to the altar intones the third collect. He next sits again, resumes his mitre, and the third Lection is read. Two chaplains assist him with bugia and book whence he reads the Lection. The Archdeacon now summons the ordinandi, who approach, holding lighted tapers in their hands, and kneel before the Bishop, who solemnly admonishes them with the prayer:

"Dearest children who are about to be ordained to the office of Exorcists, ye must duly know what ye are about to undertake. For an Exorcist must cast out devils; and announce to the people that those that may not be present at the sacrifice should retire; and at the altar minister water to the priest. Ye receive also the power of placing your hand upon energumens, and by the imposition of your hands and the grace of the Holy Spirit and the words of exorcism unclean spirits are driven out from the bodies of those who are obsessed. Be careful therefore that as ye drive out devils from the bodies of others, so ye banish all uncleanness and evil from your own bodies lest ye fall beneath the power of those spirits who by your ministry are conquered in others. Learn through your office to govern all imperfections lest the enemy may claim a share in you and some dominion over you. For truly will ye rightly control those devils who attack others, when first ye have overcome their many crafts against yourselves. And this may the Lord vouchsafe to grant you through His Holy Spirit."[35] After which the Bishop hands to each severally the Book of Exorcisms (or Pontifical or Missal), saying: "Receive this and commit it to thy memory and have power to place thy hands upon energumens, whether they be baptized, or whether they be catechumens."[36] All kneel, and the Bishop, wearing his mitre, stands and prays:

"Dearest brethren, let us humbly pray God the Father Almighty that He may vouchsafe to bless these his servants to the office of Exorcists that they may have the power to command spirits, to cast forth from the bodies of those who are obsessed demons with every kind of their wickedness and deceit. Through His only begotten Son Jesus Christ Our Lord who with Him liveth and reigneth in the unity of the Holy Spirit, one God, world without end. *R.* Amen."[37] Then, his mitre having been removed, he turns to the altar with "Oremus" to which is given the reply "Flectamus genua" with "Leuate," and the last prayer is said over the kneeling exorcists: "Holy Lord, Almighty Father, Eternal God vouchsafe to bless these thy servants to the office of Exorcists; that by the imposition of our hands and the words of our mouth they may have power and authority to govern and restrain all unclean spirits: that they may be skilful physicians for Thy Church, that they may heal many and be themselves strengthened with all Heavenly Grace. Through Our Lord Jesus Christ Thy Son who with Thee liveth and reigneth in the unity of the Holy Spirit one God world without end. *R.* Amen." And then, at a sign from the Archdeacon, they return to their places.[38]

It should be remarked that the Exorcist is specifically ordained "to cast out demons," and he receives "power to place his (your) hands upon the possessed, so that by the imposition of his (your) hands,[39] the grace of the Holy Ghost, and the words of exorcism, evil spirits are driven out from the bodies of the possessed." The very striking term *spiritualis imperator* is strictly applied to him, and God the Father is earnestly entreated to grant him the grace "to cast out demons from the bodies of the possessed with all their many sleights of wickedness." Nothing could be plainer, nothing could be more solemn, nothing could be more pregnant with meaning and intention. The Order and delegated power of Exorcists cannot be minimized; at least, so to do is clean contrary to the mind of the Church as emphatically expressed in her most authoritative rites. In actual practice the office of Exorcist has almost wholly been taken over by clerics in major orders, but this, of course, in no way affects the status and authority of the second of the four minor orders.

Every priest, more especially perhaps if he be a parish priest, is liable to be called upon to perform his duty as Exorcist. In doing so he must carefully bear in mind and adhere to the prescriptions of the *Rituale Romanum*, and he will do well to have due regard to the laws of provincial or diocesan synods, which for the most part require that the Bishop should be consulted and his authorization obtained before exorcism be essayed.

The chief points of importance in the detailed instructions under twenty-one heads prefixed to the rite in the *Rituale* may thus be briefly summarized: (1) The priest or exorcist should be of mature age, humble, of blameless life, courageous, of experience, and well-attested prudence. It is fitting he should prepare himself for his task by special acts of devotion and mortification, by fervent prayer and by fasting (S. Matthew xvii. 20). (2) He must be a man of scholarship and learning, a systematic student and well versed in the latest trends and developments of psychological science. (3) Possession is not lightly to be taken for granted. Each case is to be carefully examined and great caution to be used in distinguishing genuine possession from certain forms of disease. (4) He should admonish the possessed in so far as the latter is capable, to dispose himself for the exorcism by prayer, fasting, by confession, and Holy Communion, and while the rite is in progress he must excite in his heart a most lively faith in the goodness of God, and perfect resignation to the divine will. (5) The exorcism should take place in the Church, or some other sacred place, if convenient, but no crowd of gazers must be suffered to assemble out of mere curiosity. There should, however, be a number of witnesses, grave and devout persons of standing, eminent respectability, and acknowledged probity, not prone to idle gossip, but discreet and silent. If on account of sickness or for some legitimate reason the exorcism takes place in a private house it is well that members of the family should be present; especially is this enjoined, as a measure of precaution, if the subject be a woman. (6) If the patient seems to fall asleep, or endeavours to hinder the exorcist in any way during the rite he is to continue, if possible with greater insistence, for such actions are probably a ruse to trick him. (7) The exorcist, although humble and having no reliance upon himself alone, is to speak with command and authority, and should the patient be convulsed or tremble, let him be more fervent and more insistent; the prayers and adjurations are to be recited with great faith, a full and assured consciousness of power. (8) Let the exorcist remember that he uses the words of Holy Scripture and Holy Church, not his own words and phrases. (9) All idle and impertinent questioning of the demon is to be avoided, nor should the evil spirit be allowed to speak at length unchecked and unrebuked. (10) The Blessed Sacrament is not to be brought near the body of the obsessed during exorcism for fear of possible irreverence; Relics of the Saints may be employed, but in this case every care must be most scrupulously observed that all due veneration be paid to them; the Crucifix and Holy Water are to be used. (11) If expulsion of the evil spirit, who will often prove obstinate, is not secured at once, the rite should be repeated as often as need be.

It will be seen that the Church has safeguarded exorcism with extraordinary precautions, and that everything which is humanly possible to prevent superstition, indecorum, or abuse is provided for and recommended. Again and again the warning is repeated that so solemn, and indeed terrible, an office must not lightly be undertaken. The actual form in present use is as follows:[40]

THE FORM OF EXORCISING THE POSSESSED

[TRANSLATED FROM THE "ROMAN RITUAL."]

The Priest, having confessed, or at least hating sin in his heart, and having said Mass, if it possibly and conveniently can be done, and humbly implored the Divine help, vested in surplice and violet stole, the end of which he shall place round the neck of the one possessed, and having the possessed person before him, and bound if there be danger of violence, shall sign himself, the person, and those standing by, with the sign of the Cross, and sprinkle them with holy water, and kneeling down, the others making the responses, shall say the Litany as far as the prayers.

At the end the Antiphon. Remember not, Lord, our offences, nor the offences of our forefathers, neither take Thou vengeance of our sins.

Our Father. *Secretly.*

℣ And lead us not into temptation.

℟ But deliver us from evil.

Psalm liii.

Deus, in Nomine.

The whole shall be said with Glory be to the Father.

℣. Save Thy servant,

℟. O my God, that putteth his trust in Thee.

℣. Be unto him, O Lord, a strong tower,

℟. From the face of his enemy.

℣. Let the enemy have no advantage of him,
℟. Nor the son of wickedness approach to hurt him.

℣. Send him help, O Lord, from the sanctuary,
℟. And strengthen him out of Sion.

℣. Lord, hear my prayer,
℟. And let my cry come unto Thee.

℣. The Lord be with you,
℟. And with thy spirit.

Let us pray.

O God, Whose property is ever to have mercy and to forgive: receive our supplications and prayers, that of Thy mercy and loving-kindness Thou wilt set free this Thy servant (or handmaid) who is fast bound by the chain of his sins.

O holy Lord, Father Almighty, Eternal God, the Father of our Lord Jesus Christ: Who hast assigned that tyrant and apostate to the fires of hell; and hast sent Thine Only Begotten Son into the world, that He might bruise him as he roars after his prey: make haste, tarry not, to deliver this man, created in Thine Own image and likeness, from ruin, and from the noon-day devil Send Thy fear, O Lord, upon the wild beast, which devoureth Thy vine. Grant Thy servants boldness to fight bravely against that wicked dragon, lest he despise them that put their trust in Thee, and say, as once he spake in Pharaoh: I know not the Lord, neither will I let Israel go. Let Thy right hand in power compel him to depart from Thy servant N. (or Thy handmaid N.) ✠, that he dare no longer to hold him captive, whom Thou hast vouchsafed to make in Thine image, and hast redeemed in Thy Son; Who liveth and reigneth with Thee in the Unity of the Holy Spirit, ever One God, world without end. Amen.

Then he shall command the spirit in this manner.

I command thee, whosoever thou art, thou unclean spirit, and all thy companions possessing this servant of God, that by the Mysteries of the Incarnation, Passion, Resurrection and Ascension of our Lord Jesus Christ, by the sending of the Holy Ghost, and by the Coming of the same our Lord to judgment, thou tell me thy name, the day, and the hour of thy going out, by some sign: and, that to me, a minister of God, although unworthy, thou be wholly obedient in all things: nor hurt this creature of God, or those that stand by, or their goods in any way.

Then shall these Gospels, or one or the other, be read over the possessed.

The Lesson of the Holy Gospel according to S. John i. 1. *As he says these words he shall sign himself and the possessed on the forehead, mouth, and breast.* In the beginning was the Word . . . full of grace and truth.

The Lesson of the Holy Gospel according to S. Mark xvi. 15. At that time: Jesus spake unto His disciples: Go ye into all the world . . . shall lay hands on the sick, and they shall recover.

The Lesson of the Holy Gospel according to S. Luke x. 17. At that time: The seventy returned again with joy . . . because your names are written in heaven.

The Lesson of the Holy Gospel according to S. Luke xi. 14. At that time: Jesus was casting out a devil, and it was dumb . . . wherein he trusted, and divideth his spoils.

℣. Lord, hear my prayer,
℟. And let my cry come unto Thee.

℣. The Lord be with you,
℟. And with thy Spirit.

Let us pray.

Almighty Lord, Word of God the Father, Jesus Christ, God and Lord of every creature: Who didst give to Thy Holy Apostles power to tread upon serpents and scorpions: Who amongst other of Thy wonderful commands didst vouchsafe to say—Put the devils to flight: by Whose power Satan fell from heaven like lightning: with supplication I beseech Thy Holy Name in fear and trembling, that to me Thy most unworthy servant, granting me pardon of all my faults, Thou wilt vouchsafe to give constancy of faith and power, that shielded by the might of Thy holy arm, in trust and safety I may approach to attack this cruel devil, through Thee, O Jesus Christ, the Lord our God, Who shalt come to judge the quick and the dead, and the world by fire. Amen.

Then defending himself and the possessed with the sign of the Cross, putting part of his stole round the neck, and his right hand upon the head of the possessed, firmly and with great faith he shall say what follows.

℣. Behold the Cross of the Lord, flee ye of the contrary part,

℟. The Lion of the tribe of Judah, the Root of David, hath prevailed.

℣. Lord, hear my prayer,

℟. And let my cry come unto Thee.

℣. The Lord be with you,

℟. And with thy spirit.

Let us pray.

O God, and Father of our Lord Jesus Christ, I call upon Thy Holy Name, and humbly implore Thy mercy, that Thou wouldest vouchsafe to grant me help against this, and every unclean spirit, that vexes this Thy creature. Through the same Lord Jesus Christ.

The Exorcism.

I exorcise thee, most foul spirit, every coming in of the enemy, every apparition, every legion; in the Name of our Lord Jesus ✠ Christ be rooted out, and be put to flight from this creature of God ✠. He commands thee, Who has bid thee be cast down from the highest heaven into the lower parts of the earth. He commands thee, Who has commanded the sea, the winds, and the storms. Hear therefore, and fear, Satan, thou injurer of the faith, thou enemy of the human race, thou procurer of death, thou destroyer of life, kindler of vices, seducer of men, betrayer of the nations, inciter of envy, origin of avarice, cause of discord, stirrer-up of troubles: why standest thou, and resistest, when thou knowest that Christ the Lord destroyest thy ways? Fear Him, Who was sacrificed in Isaac, Who was sold in Joseph, was slain in the Lamb, was crucified in man, thence was the triumpher over hell. *The following signs of the Cross shall be made upon the forehead of the possessed.* Depart therefore in the Name of the Father ✠, and of the Son ✠, and of the Holy ✠ Ghost: give place to the Holy Ghost, by this sign of the holy ✠ Cross of Jesus Christ our Lord: Who with the Father, and the same Holy Ghost, liveth and reigneth ever one God, world without end. Amen.

℣. Lord, hear my prayer.
℟. And let my cry com : unto Thee.
℣. The Lord be with you.
℟. And with thy spirit.

Let us pray.

O God, the Creator and Protector of the human race, Who hast formed man in Thine own Image: look upon this Thy servant N. (*or* this Thy handmaid N.), who is grievously vexed with the wiles of an unclean spirit, whom the old adversary, the ancient enemy of the earth, encompasses with a horrible dread, and blinds the senses of his human understanding with stupor, confounds him with terror, and harasses him with trembling and fear. Drive away, O Lord, the power of the devil, take away his deceitful snares: let the impious tempter fly far hence: let Thy servant be defended by the sign ✠ (*on his forehead*) of Thy Name, and be safe both in body, and soul. (*The three following crosses shall be made on the breast of the demoniac.*) Do Thou guard his inmost ✠ soul, Thou rule his inward ✠ parts, Thou strengthen his ✠ heart. Let the attempts of the opposing power in his soul vanish away. Grant, O Lord, grace to this invocation of Thy most Holy Name, that he who up to this present was causing terror, may flee away affrighted, and depart conquered; and that this Thy servant, strengthened in heart, and sincere in mind, may render Thee his due service. Through our Lord Jesus Christ. Amen.

The Exorcism.

I adjure thee, thou old serpent, by the Judge of the quick and the dead, by thy Maker, and the Maker of the world: by Him, Who hath power to put thee into hell, that thou depart in haste from this servant of God N., who returns to the bosom of the Church, with thy fear and with the torment of thy terror. I adjure Thee again ✠ (*on his forehead*), not in my infirmity, but by the power of the Holy Ghost, that thou go out of this servant of God N., whom the Almighty

God hath made in His Own Image. Yield, therefore, not to me, but to the minister of Christ. For His power presses upon thee Who subdued thee beneath His Cross. Tremble at His arm, which, after the groanings of hell were subdued, led forth the souls into light. Let the body ✠ (*on his breast*) of man be a terror to thee, let the image of God ✠ (*on his forehead*) be an alarm to thee. Resist not, nor delay to depart from this person, for it has pleased Christ to dwell in man. And think not that I am to be despised, since thou knowest that I too am so great a sinner. God ✠ commands thee. The majesty of Christ ✠ commands thee. God the Father ✠ commands thee. God the Son ✠ commands thee. God the Holy ✠ Ghost commands thee. The Sacrament of the Cross ✠ commands thee. The faith of the holy Apostles Peter and Paul, and of all the other Saints ✠, commands thee. The blood of the Martyrs ✠ commands thee. The stedfastness (*continentia*) of the Confessors ✠ commands thee. The devout intercession of all the Saints ✠ commands thee. The virtue of the Mysteries of the Christian Faith ✠ commands thee. Go out, therefore, thou transgressor. Go out, thou seducer, full of all deceit and wile, thou enemy of virtue, thou persecutor of innocence. Give place, thou most dire one: give place, thou most impious one: give place to Christ in Whom thou hast found nothing of thy works: Who hath overcome thee, Who hath destroyed thy kingdom, Who hath led thee captive and bound thee, and hath spoiled thy goods: Who hath cast thee into outer darkness, where for thee and thy servants everlasting destruction is prepared. But why, O fierce one, dost thou withstand? why, rashly bold, dost thou refuse? thou art the accused of Almighty God, whose laws thou hast broken. Thou art the accused of Jesus Christ our Lord, whom thou hast dared to tempt, and presumed to crucify. Thou art the accused of the human race, to whom by thy persuasion thou hast given to drink thy poison. Therefore, I adjure thee, most wicked dragon, in the Name of the immaculate ✠ Lamb, Who treads upon the lion and adder, Who tramples under foot the young lion and the dragon, that thou depart from this man ✠ (*let the sign be made upon his forehead*), that thou depart from the Church of God ✠ (*let the sign be made over those who are standing by*): tremble, and flee away at the calling upon the Name of that Lord, of Whom hell is afraid; to Whom the Virtues, the Powers, and the Dominions of the heavens are subject; Whom Cherubim and Seraphim with unwearied voices praise, saying: Holy, Holy, Holy, Lord God of Sabaoth. The Word ✠ made Flesh commands thee. He Who was born ✠ of the Virgin commands thee. Jesus ✠ of Nazareth commands thee; Who, although thou didst despise His disciples, bade thee go bruised and overthrown out of the man: and in his presence, having separated thee from him, thou didst not presume to enter into the herd of swine. Therefore, thus now adjured in His Name ✠, depart from the man, whom He has formed. It is hard for thee to wish to resist ✠. It is hard for thee to kick against the pricks ✠. Because the more slowly goest thou out, does the greater punishment increase against thee, for thou despisest not men, but Him, Who is Lord both of the quick and the dead, Who shall come to judge the quick and the dead, and the World by fire. ℟. Amen.

℣. Lord, hear my prayer.
℟. And let my cry come unto thee.

℣. The Lord be with you.
℟. And with thy spirit.

Let us pray.

O God of heaven, God of earth, God of the Angels, God of the Archangels, God of the Prophets, God of the Apostles, God of the Martyrs, God of the Virgins, God, Who hast the power to give life after death, rest after labour; because there is none other God beside Thee, nor could be true, but Thou, the Creator of heaven and earth, Who art the true King, and of Whose kingdom there shall be no end: humbly I beseech Thy glorious majesty, that Thou wouldest vouchsafe to deliver this Thy servant from unclean spirits, through Christ our Lord. Amen.

The Exorcism.

I therefore adjure thee, thou most foul spirit, every appearance, every inroad of Satan, in the Name of Jesus Christ ✠ of Nazareth, Who, after His baptism in Jordan, was led into the wilderness, and overcame thee in thine own stronghold: that thou cease to assault him whom He hath formed from the dust of the earth for His own honour and glory: and that thou in miserable man tremble not at human weakness, but at the image of Almighty God. Yield, therefore, to God ✠ Who by His servant Moses drowned thee and thy malice in Pharaoh and his army in the depths of the sea. Yield to God ✠, Who put thee to flight when driven out of King Saul with spiritual song, by his most faithful servant David. Yield thyself to God ✠, Who condemned thee in the traitor Judas Iscariot. For He touches thee with Divine ✠ stripes, when in His sight, trembling and crying out with thy legions, thou saidst: What have I to do with Thee, Jesus, Son of the Most High God? Art Thou come hither to torment us before the time? He presses upon thee with perpetual flames, Who shall say to the wicked at the end of time—Depart from Me, ye cursed, into everlasting fire, prepared for the devil and his angels. For thee, O impious one, and for thy angels, is the worm that dieth not; for thee and thy angels is the fire unquenchable prepared: for thou art the chief of accursed murder, thou the author of incest, thou the head of sacrileges, thou the master of the worst actions, thou the teacher of heretics, thou the instigator of all uncleanness. Therefore go out ✠, thou wicked one, go out ✠, thou infamous one, go out with all thy deceits; for God hath willed that man shall be His temple. But why dost thou delay longer here? Give honour to God the Father ✠ Almighty, before Whom every knee is bent. Give place to Jesus Christ ✠ the Lord, Who shed for man His most precious Blood. Give place to the Holy ✠ Ghost, Who by His blessed Apostle Peter struck thee to the ground in Simon Magus; Who condemned thy deceit in Ananias and Sapphira; Who smote thee in Herod, because he gave not God the glory; Who by his Apostle Paul smote thee in Elymas the sorcerer with a mist and darkness, and by the same Apostle by his word of command bade thee come out of the damsel possessed with the spirit of divination. Now therefore depart ✠, depart, thou seducer. The wilderness is thy abode. The serpent is the place of thy habitation: be humbled, and be overthrown. There is no time now for delay. For behold the Lord the Ruler approaches closely upon thee, and His fire shall glow before Him, and shall go before Him; and shall burn up His enemies on every side. If thou hast deceived man, at God thou canst not scoff: One expels thee, from Whose Sight nothing is hidden. He casts thee out, to Whose power all things are subject. He shuts thee out, Who hast prepared for thee and for thine angels everlasting hell; out of Whose mouth the sharp sword shall go out, when He shall come to judge the quick and the dead, and the World by fire. Amen.

All the aforesaid things being said and done, so far as there shall be need, they shall be repeated, until the possessed person be entirely set free.

The following which are noted down will be of great assistance, said devoutly over the possessed, and also frequently to repeat the Our Father, Hail Mary, *and* Creed.

The Canticle. Magnificat.

The Canticle. Benedictus.

The Creed of S. Athanasius.

Quicunque uult.

Psalm xc. *Qui habitat.*
Psalm lxvii. *Exurgat Deus.*
Psalm lxix. *Deus in adiutorium.*
Psalm liii. *Deus, In Nomine Tuo.*
Psalm cxvii. *Confitemini Domino.*
Psalm xxxiv. *Iudica, Domine.*
Psalm xxx. *In Te, Domine, speraui.*
Psalm xxi. *Deus, Deus meus.*
Psalm iii. *Domine, quid multiplicasti?*
Psalm x. *In Domino confido.*
Psalm xii. *Usquequo, Domine?*
Each Psalm shall be said with Glory be to the Father, &c.

Prayer after being set free.

We pray Thee, O Almighty God, that the spirit of wickedness may have no more power over this Thy servant N. (*or* Thy handmaid N.), but that he may flee away, and never come back again: at Thy bidding, O Lord, let there come into him (*or* her) the goodness and peace of our Lord Jesus Christ, by Whom we have been redeemed, and let us fear no evil, for the Lord is with us, Who liveth and reigneth with Thee, in the Unity of the Holy Ghost, ever one God, world without end. ℟. Amen.

A shorter form of exorcism, which, being general, differs in aim and use, was published by order of Pope Leo XIII and may be found in the later editions of the *Rituale Romanum*, "Exorcismus in Satanam et Angelos apostalicos."[41] After the customary invocation *In nomine* . . . the rite begins with a prayer to S. Michael, the solemn adjuration of some length follows with versicles and responses, a second prayer is next recited, and the whole concludes by three aspirations from the Litany: "From the deceits and crafts of the Devil; O Lord, deliver us. That it may please Thee to rule Thy Church so it shall alway serve Thee in lasting peace and true liberty; We beseech Thee, hear us. That Thou wouldst vouchsafe to beat down and subdue all the enemies of Thy Holy Church; We beseech Thee, hear us." *And the place is sprinkled with Holy Water*,[42] is the final rubric.

The Baptismal Exorcism and exorcisms such as those of water, salt,[43] and oil, it were perhaps impertinent to treat of here. It may, however, be noticed that in the ceremony of the Blessing of the Waters[44] (approved by the Sacred Congregation of Rites, 6 December, 1890), performed on the Vigil of the Epiphany, there occurs a solemn "Exorcismus contra Satanam et Angelos apostalicos," followed by "Exorcismus salis" and "Exorcismus aquæ."

There are recorded throughout history innumerable examples of obsession and demoniacal possession, as also of potent and successful exorcism. It is, of course, quite possible, and indeed probable, that many of these cases were due to natural causes, epilepsy, acute hysteria, incipient lunacy, and the like. But, none the less, when every allowance has been made for incorrect diagnosis, for ill-informed ascriptions of rare and obscure forms of both physical and mental maladies, for credulity, honest mistakes, and exaggerations of every kind, there will yet remain a very considerable quota which it seems impossible to account for and explain save on the score of possession by some evil and hostile intelligence. But nobody is asked to accept all the instances of diabolic possession recorded in the history of the Church, nor even to form any definite opinion upon the historical evidence in favour of any particular case. That is primarily a matter for historical and medical science. And, perhaps, even at the present day and among civilized races this phenomenon is not so rare as is popularly supposed.

The annals of Bedlam, of many a private madhouse, and many an asylum could tell strange and hideous histories. And if we may judge from the accounts furnished by the pioneers of the Faith in missionary countries the evidences of diabolical agency there are as clearly defined and unmistakable as they were in Galilee in the time of Christ.[45]

Demoniacal possession is frequently described and alluded to by the early fathers and apologists in matter-of-fact terms which leave no shadow of doubt as to their belief in this regard. Indeed the success of Christian exorcism is often brought forward as an argument for the acceptance of the Divinity of the founder of Christianity. It would be an easy, but a very lengthy process, to make a catena of such passages from Greek and Latin authors alike.[46] S. Justin Martyr (*ob. circa* A.D. 165) speaks of demons flying from " the touch and breathing of Christians " (*Apologia*, II, 6), " as from a flame that burns them," adds S. Cyril of Jerusalem (*ob.* 385–6 : *Catechesis*, XX, 3). Origen (*ob.* 253–4) mentions the laying on of hands to cast out devils, whilst S. Ambrose[47] (*ob.* 397), S. Ephrem Syrus[48] (*ob.* 373), and others used this ceremony when exorcizing. The holy sign of the Cross also is extolled by many Fathers for its efficacy against all kinds of diabolic molestation; thus Lactantius writes: " Nunc satis est, huius signi [Crucis] potentiam, quantum ualeat exponere. Quanto terrori sit dæmonibus hoc signum, sciet, qui uiderit, quatenus adiurati per Christum, de corporibus, quæ obsederint, fugiant,"[49] *Diuinarum Institutionum*, IV, xxvii.[50] S. Athanasius (*ob.* 373), *De Incarnatione Uerbi*, XLVII; S. Basil (*ob.* 379), *In Esaiam*, XI, 249; S. Cyril of Jerusalem, *Catechesis*, XIII; S. Gregory of Nazianzus (*ob. circa* 389), *Carmen aduersus Iram*, 415 *sqq.*, all have passages of no little weight to the same effect. S. Cyril, *Procatechesis*, IX; and S. Athanasius, *Ad Marcellum*, XXIII, recommend that the prayers of exorcism and the adjuration should as far as possible repeat the exact words of Holy Scripture.

In the annals of hagiography we find from the earliest days until our own time very many instances of possession, very many cases where a poor afflicted wretch has been released and relieved by the power and prayer of some Saint or holy servant of God.[51]

Thus in the life of S. Benedict, that noble, calm, dignified, prudent, great-souled, and high-minded hero, there are recorded several occasions upon which he was confronted by extraordinary manifestations of evil spirits who resisted the building of his monastery upon the crest of Monte Cassino, where Satanism had been previously practised. It is not said that there were any visible appearances, save to S. Benedict alone,[52] but a succession of untoward accidents, of abnormal occurrences and constant alarms, plainly showed that the Saint was contending against superhuman difficulties. More than once he found it necessary to exorcize certain of his monks,[53] and so marked was his triumph over these malignant and destructive influences that he has always been venerated in the Church as a most potent "effugator dæmonum," and is confidently invoked in the hour of spiritual peril and deadly attack. Great faith also is placed in the Medal of Saint Benedict. This medal, originally a cross, is dedicated to the devotion in honour of the Patriarch. One side bears the figure of the Saint holding a cross in his right hand, and the Holy Rule in his left. Upon the other is a cross together with the following letters arranged on and around it: C.S.P.B., Crux Sancti Patris Benedicti (The Cross of the holy Father Benedict). C.S.S.M.L., Crux Sacra Sit Mihi Lux (May the holy Cross be my Light). N.D.S.M.D., Non Draco Sit Mihi Dux (Let not the Devil be my guide). U.R.S.: N.S.M.U.: S.M.Q.L.: I.U.B.: Uade Retro Satana: Nunquam Suade Mihi Uana: Sunt Mala Quæ Libas: Ipse Uenena Bibas. (Begone, Satan, never suggest things to me, what thou offerest is evil, drink thou thyself thy poison).[54] The "Centenary" form of the medal (struck at Monte Cassino in 1880 to commemorate the 13th centenary of the birth of S. Benedict in 480) has under the figure the words: *Ex S.M. Cassino MDCCCLXXX*. Upon the same side round the edge runs the inscription: Eius in obitu n̄ro præsentia muniamur (May we be protected by his presence at the hour of our death), and the word PAX appears above the cross.

It is doubtful when the Medal of S. Benedict originated, but during a trial for Witchcraft at Natternberg, near the abbey of Metten, in Bavaria, during the year 1647, the accused women testified that they had no power over Metten which was under the particular protection of the cross. Upon investigation a number of painted crosses surrounded by the letters which are now engraved upon Benedictine medals were found on the walls of the abbey, but their signification had been wholly forgotten. At length, in an old manuscript, written in 1415, was discovered a picture representing S. Benedict holding in one hand a staff which ended in a cross, and in the other a scroll. On the staff and scroll were written in full the formulas of which the mysterious letters were the initials. Medals with the figure of S. Benedict, a cross, and these letters began now to be struck and rapidly spread over Europe. The medals were first authoritatively approved by Benedict XIV in his briefs of 23 December, 1741, and 12 March, 1742.

In the case of the possessed boys of Illfurt (Alsace) they exhibited the utmost horror and dread of a Medal of S. Benedict.

These medals are hallowed with a proper rite[55] in which the adjuration commences: "Exorcizo uos, numismata, per Deum Patrem ✠ omnipotentem. . . ." "I exorcize ye, medals, through God the Father ✠ Almighty. . . . May the power of the adversary, all the host of the Devil, all evil attack, every spirit and glamour of Satan, be utterly put to flight and driven far away by the virtue of these medals. . . .[56] The prayer runs: "O Lord Jesus Christ . . . by Thy most Holy Passion I humbly pray and beseech Thee, that Thou wouldest grant that whosoever devoutly invoketh Thy Holy Name in this prayer and petition which Thou Thyself hast taught us, may be delivered from every deceit of the Devil and from all his wiles, and that Thou wouldest vouchsafe to bring Thy servant to the harbour of salvation. Who livest and reignest. . . ."[57]

S. Maurus also, the beloved disciple of S. Benedict, was famous for the cures he wrought in cases of possession.[58] Visiting France in 543 he became founder and superior of the abbey of Glanfeuil, Anjou, later known by his name, St. Maur-sur-Loise.[59] The relics of S. Maurus after various translations were finally enshrined at St. Germain-des-Prez. In the eleventh century an arm of the Saint had been with great devotion transferred to Monte Cassino, where by its touch a demoniac was delivered. This is related by Desiderius,[60] who was abbot at that time, and afterwards became Pope, Blessed Victor III (*ob.* 16 September, 1087). Throughout the Middle Ages the tomb of S. Maur at St. Germain was a celebrated place of pilgrimage, and the possessed were brought here in large numbers to be healed.[61]

The Holy Winding Sheet of Besançon, again, was greatly resorted to for the relief and cure of possession. This venerable relic, being one of the linen cloths used at the burial of Christ, was brought to Besançon in 1206 by Otto de la Roche, and the feast of its arrival (*Susceptio*) was ordered to be kept on 11 July. At present it is a double of the first class in the cathedral, St. Jean, and of the second class throughout the diocese.

Novenas made in the church at Bonnet, near Nantes, were popularly supposed to be of especial efficacy in healing possession.

It is, of course, impossible even briefly to catalogue the most important and striking of the numberless cases of possession recorded throughout the centuries in every country and at every era. Of these a great number are, no doubt, to be attributed to disease; very many to a commixture of hysteria and semi-conscious, or more frequently unconscious, fraud; some few to mere chousing; and, if human evidence is worth anything at all, many actually to diabolic influence.

There were some curious episodes in England during Queen Elizabeth's reign, when a third-rate Puritan minister, John Darrel, made a considerable stir owing to his attempts at exorcism. This idea seems to have been suggested to him by the exorcisms of the famous Jesuit missionary priest, William Weston, who after having been educated at Oxford, Paris, and Douai, entered the Society on 5 November, 1575, at Rome. He then worked and taught in Spain, until he was called to his native mission, actually arriving in England, 20 September, 1584. In the course of his labours, which at that dangerous time were carried on in circumstances of extremest peril, he was required to perform the rite of exorcism upon several distressed persons, who were for the most part brought to him at the houses of two zealous Catholics, Sir George Peckham of Denham, near Uxbridge, and Lord Vaux of Hackney, both of which gentlemen had suffered in many ways for their faith. With regard to the patients we can only say that we lack evidence to enable us to decide whether the cases were genuine, or whether they were merely sick and ailing folk; but we can confidently affirm that there is no suspicion of any fraud or cozenage. Father Weston is acknowledged to have been a man of the most candid sincerity, intensely spiritual, and of no ordinary powers. Although the rites, in which several priests joined, were performed with the utmost secrecy and every precaution was taken to prevent any report being spread abroad, somebody gossiped, and in about a year various exaggerated accounts were being circulated, until the matter came before the Privy Council. A violent recrudescence of persecution at once followed, many of the exorcists were seized and butchered for their priesthood, the rest, including Weston, were flung into jail, August, 1586. A long period of imprisonment ensued, and in 1599 Weston was committed to the Tower, where he suffered such hardships that he wellnigh lost his sight. Eventually in 1603 he was banished, and spent the rest of his days at Seville and Valladolid. He was rector of the latter college at the time of his death, 9 June, 1615.[62]

It was in 1586, just when the exorcisms of the Jesuit fathers had unfortunately attracted so widespread attention and foolish comment, that John Darrel, although a Protestant and lacking both appropriate ordination and training, rashly resolved to emulate their achievements. He was young, not much more than twenty, he was foolhardy and he was ignorant, three qualities which even in our own time often win cheap notoriety. It seems that he was first called in to cure a young girl of seventeen, Katherine Wright, who lived at Mansfield, Nottingham. Darrel forthwith pronounced that she was afflicted by an evil spirit, and he prayed over her from four o'clock in the morning till noon, but entirely without result. He then declared that the wench had been bewitched and that the demon, moreover, was sent by one Margaret Roper, with whom the patient had recently quarrelled. The girl backed his story, and the accused woman was at once taken into custody by the constable. When, however, she appeared before Mr. Fouliamb, a justice of the peace, not only was she incontinently discharged, but Darrel received a smart rebuff and found himself in no small danger of arrest.

This mischance sufficiently scared the would-be exorcist, and for some ten years he disappeared from view, only to come before the public again at Burton-upon-Trent, where he was prominent in the sensation and the scandal that centred round Thomas Darling, a young Derbyshire boy. This imaginative juvenal was subject to fits—real or feigned—during which he had visions of green angels and a green cat. Betimes his conversation became larded with true Puritan cant, and he loved to discourse with godly ministers. A credulous physician suggested that the lad was bewitched, and very soon afterwards it was noticed that the reading aloud of the Bible, especially certain verses in the first chapter of S. John's Gospel, threw him into frantic convulsions. He also began a long prattling tale about "a little old woman" who wore "a broad thrimmed hat," which proved amply sufficient to cause two women, Elizabeth Wright, and her daughter, Alse Gooderidge, long vehemently suspected of sorcery, to be examined before two magistrates, who committed Alse to jail. Next those concerned summoned a cunning man, who used various rough methods to induce the prisoner to confess. After having been harried and even tortured the wretched creature made some rambling and incoherent acknowledgements of guilt, which were twisted into a connected story. By now Darling had been ill for three months, and so far from improving, was getting worse.

At this juncture, exactly the dramatic moment, John Darrel, full of bluff and bounce, appeared upon the scene, and forthwith took charge of affairs. According to his own account his efforts were singularly blessed; that is to say the boy got better and the sly Puritan claimed all the credit. Alse Gooderidge was tried at the assizes, convicted by the jury, and sentenced to death by Lord Chief Justice Anderson; "She should have been executed but that her spirit killed her in prison," says John Denison the pamphleteer! The whole affair greatly increased Darrel's reputation.

Not long after a much-bruited case of alleged possession

in Lancashire gave him further opportunity to pose in the limelight. Ann Starchie, aged nine, and John, her brother, aged ten, were seized with a mysterious disorder; "a certaine fearefull starting and pulling together of her body" affected the girl, whilst the boy was "compelled to shout" on his way to school. Both grew steadily worse until their father, Nicholas Starchie, consulted Edmund Hartley, a notorious conjurer of no very fair repute. Hartley seems to have quieted the children by means of various charms, and the father paid him something like a retaining fee of forty shillings a year. This, however, he insisted should be increased, and when any addition was denied, there were quarrels, and presently the boy and girl again fell ill. The famous Dr. Dee was summoned, but he was obviously nonplussed, and whilst he "sharply reproved and straitly examined" Hartley, in his quandary could do or say little more save advise the help of "godlie preachers." The situation in that accursed house now began to grow more serious. Besides the children three young wards of Mr. Starchie, a servant, and a visitor, were all seized with the strange disease. "All or most of them joined together in a strange and supernatural loud whupping that the house and grounde did sounde therwith again." Hartley fell under suspicion, and was haled before a justice of the peace, who promptly committed him to the assizes. Evidence was given that he was continually kissing the Starchie children, in fact, he kept embracing all the possessed, and it was argued that he had thus communicated an evil spirit to them. He was accused of having drawn magic circles upon the ground, and although he stoutly denied the charge, he was convicted of felony and hanged at Lancaster. John Darrel and his assistant, George More, minister of a church in Derbyshire, undertook to exorcize the afflicted, and in a day or two, after long prayers and great endeavours, they managed to expel the devils. Here we have folly, imposture, and hysteria all blended together to make a horrible tale.

At this time Darrel was officiating as a minister at Nottingham, where there happened to be living a young apprenticed musician, a clever and likely lad, William Somers, who some years before had met Darrel at Ashby-de-la-Zouch, where both had been resident. It appears that the boy had once met a strange woman, whom he offended in some way, and suddenly he " did use such strang and idle kinde of gestures in laughing, dancing, and such like lighte behaviour, that he was suspected to be madd." The famous exorcist was sent for on the 5th of November, 1597, and forthwith recognized the signs of possession. The lad was suffering for the sins of Nottingham. Accordingly sermons were delivered and prayers were read in true ranting fashion, and when Darrel named one after the other fourteen signs of possession the patient, who had been most carefully coached, illustrated each in turn.

It is possible that Darrel had to some extent mesmeric control over Somers, whose performance was of a very remarkable nature at least, for " he tore ; he foamed ; he wallowed ; his face was drawn awry ; his eyes would stare and his tongue hang out " ; together with a thousand other such apish antics which greatly impressed the bystanders. Finally the boy lay as if dead for a quarter of an hour, and then rose up declaring he was well and whole.

However, obsession followed possession. The demon still assailed him, and it was not long before Master Somers accused thirteen women of having contrived his maladies by their sorcery. Darrel, the witch-finder, had by this time attained a position of no small importance in the town, being chosen preacher at S. Mary's, and he was prepared to back his pupil to the uttermost. Yet even his influence for some reason did not serve, and all but two of the women concerned were released from prison. Next certain unbelieving citizens had the bad taste to interfere, and to carry off the chief actor to the house of correction, where he pretty soon confessed his impostures, in which, as he acknowledged, he had been carefully instructed by Darrel. The matter now became a public scandal, and upon the report of the Archdeacon of Derby the Archbishop of York appointed a commission to inquire into the facts. Brought before these ministers, not one of whom could possibly have had any means of forming a correct judgement, Somers retracted his words, asserted that he had been induced to slander Darrel, and thereat fell into such fits, foamings, and contortions that the ignoramuses were convinced of the reality of his demoniac possession.

At the Nottingham assizes, however, things went differently. Summoned to court and encouraged by the Lord Chief Justice, Sir Edmund Anderson,[63] to tell the truth the wretched young man made a clean breast of all his tricks. The case against Alice Freeman, the accused, was dismissed, and Sir Edmund, shocked at the frauds, wrote a weighty letter to Whitgift, the Archbishop of Canterbury. Darrel and More were cited to the Court of High Commission, where Bancroft, Bishop of London, two of the Lord Chief Justices, the Master of Requests, and other high officials heard the case. It is obvious that Bancroft really controlled the examination from first to last, and that he combined the rôles of prosecutor and judge. Somers now told the Court how he had been in constant communication with Darrel, how they had met secretly when Darrel taught him "to doe all those trickes which Katherine Wright did" and later sent him to see and learn of the boy of Burton. In fact Darrel made him go through a whole series of antics again and again in his presence, and it was after all these preliminaries and practice that the lad posed as a possessed person at Nottingham and was prayed over and exhibited. The vulpine Puritan was fairly caught. No doubt the Bishop of London may have been a trifle arbitrary, but after all he was dealing with a rank impostor. Darrel and More were deposed from the ministry, and committed to close prison.

The whole of this case is reported by Samuel Harsnett, chaplain to Bancroft, in a book of three hundred and twenty-four pages, *A Discovery of the Fraudulent Practises of John Darrel, Bacheler of Artes. . . .* London, 1599, and a perfect rain of pamphlets followed. Both Darrel and More answered Harsnett, drawing meantime a number of other persons into the paper fray. We have such works as *An Apologie, or defence of the possession of William Sommers, a young man of the towne of Nottingham. . . . By John Darrell, Minister of Christ Jesus . . .* a black letter brochure which is undated but may be safely assigned to 1599; *The Triall of Maist. Dorrel, or A Collection of Defences against Allegations . . .* 1599;[64] and Darrel's abusive *A Detection of that sinnful, shamful, lying, and ridiculous discours of Samuel Harshnet,* 1600. There are several allusions in contemporary dramatists to the scandal, and Jonson in *The Divell is an Asse*, acted in 1616, V, 3, has:

> It is the easiest thing, Sir, to be done.
> As plaine as fizzling: roule but wi' your eyes,
> And foame at th' mouth. A little castle-soape
> Will do't, to rub your lips: And then a nutshell,
> With toe and touchwood in it to spit fire,
> Did you ner'e read, Sir, little *Darrel's* tricks,
> With the boy o' *Burton*, and the 7 in *Lancashire*,
> Sommers at *Nottingham?* All these do teach it.
> And wee'l give out, Sir, that your wife ha's bewitch'd you.

It is probable that in his books Harsnett is to a large extent the mouthpiece of the ideas of Bancroft,[65] whose opinions must have carried no small weight seeing that in 1604 he became Archbishop of Canterbury. But Harsnett himself was also a man who could well stand alone, a divine marked out for the highest preferments. As Master of Pembroke Hall, Cambridge, Vice-chancellor of that University, Bishop of Chichester, Bishop of Norwich, and finally in 1628 Archbishop of York,[66] he was certainly one of the most prominent men of the day. His views, therefore, are not only of interest, but may be regarded as an expression of recognized Anglican authority. Bancroft, who was a bitter persecutor of Catholics, seems to have turned over a quantity of material he had collected to Harsnett, who in 1603 published a verjuiced attack upon the priesthood in particular and upon the supernatural in general under the title of *A Declaration of Egregious Popish Impostures.*[67] This violent and foolish polemic with its heavy periods of coarse ill-humour and scornful profanity jars upon the reader like the harsh screeching of some cankered scold. True, it has a certain force due to the very vehemence and elaborate gusto of the wrathful ecclesiastic, the force of Billingsgate and deafening vituperation bawled by leathern lungs and raucous tongue. As a sober argument, a reasoned contribution to controversy and debate, the thing is negligible and has been wholly forgotten. Nevertheless, historically Harsnett and Bancroft are important, for it was the latter who drew up, or at least inspired, carried through Convocation, and at once enforced the Canons generally known as those of 1604, of which number 72 lays down: "No minister or ministers shall . . . without the license or direction (*manda-*

tum) of the Bishop . . . attempt upon any pretence whatsoever either of possession or obsession, by fasting or prayer, to cast out any devil or devils, under pain of the imputation of imposture or cozenage, and deposition from the ministry."

This article seems definitely intended to fix the position of the Church of England.[68] The whole question of exorcism had, in common with every other point of Christian doctrine, caused the most acrid disagreement. The Lutherans retained exorcism in the baptismal rite and were both instant and persevering in their exorcisms of the possessed. Martin Luther himself had a most vivid realization of and the firmest belief in the material antagonism of evil. The black stain in the castle of Wartburg still marks the room where he flung his ink-horn at the Devil. The silly body, the blind, the dumb, the idiot, were, as often as not, afflicted by demons; the raving maniac was assuredly possessed. Physicians might explain these evils as natural infirmity, but such physicians were ignorant men; they did not know the craft and power of Satan. Many a poor wretch who was generally supposed to have committed suicide had in truth been seized by the Fiend and strangled by him. The Devil could beget children; had not Luther himself come in contact with one of them?[69] At the close of the sixteenth century, however, an interminable and desperate struggle took place between the believers in exorcism and the Swiss and Silesian sectaries who entirely discarded exorcism,[70] either declaring it to have belonged only to the earliest years of Christianity or else trying to explain away the Biblical instances on purely rationalistic grounds. In England baptismal exorcism was retained in the First Prayer Book of 1549, but by 1552, owing to the authority of Martin Bucer, we find it entirely eliminated. Under Elizabeth the ever-increasing influence of Zurich and Geneva, to which completest deference was paid, thoroughly discredited exorcisms of any kind, and this misbelieving attitude is repeatedly and amply made clear in the sundry "Apologies" and "Defences" of Jewel and his followers.

A letter of Archbishop Parker in 1574[71] with reference to the proven frauds of two idle wenches, Agnes Bridges and Rachel Pinder,[72] shows that he was thoroughly sceptical as to the possibility of possession, and his successor, the stout old Calvinist Whitgift, was certainly of the same mind.

In 1603 five clergymen attempted exorcism in the case of Mary Glover, the daughter of a merchant in Thames Street, who was said to be possessed owing to the sorceries of a certain Elizabeth Jackson. John Swan, "a famous Minister of the Gospel," took the lead in this business, which made considerable noise at the time. The Puritans were not unnaturally anxious to vindicate their powers over the Devil and they seem avidly to have grasped at any such opportunity that offered. Swan did not fail to advertise his supposed triumph in *A True and Breife Report of Mary Glover's Vexation and of her deliverance by the meanes of fastinge and prayer*, 1603; moreover, after her deliverance he took her home to be his servant "least Satan should assault her again." Old Mother Jackson was indicted, committed by Sir John Crook, the Recorder of London, and actually sentenced by Sir Edmund Anderson, the Lord Chief Justice, to be pilloried four times and be kept a year in prison. Unfortunately for the would-be exorcists and their pretensions King James, whose shrewd suspicions were aroused, sent to examine the girl, a physician, Dr. Edward Jorden, who detected her imposture, in which, I doubt not, she had been well coached by the Puritans. Dr. Jorden recounted the circumstance in his pamphlet *A briefe discourse of a disease called the Suffocation of the Mother, Written uppon occasion which hath beene of late taken thereby to suspect possession of an evill spirit* (London, 1603). The ministers were extremely chagrined, and one Stephen Bradwell even took up the cudgels in a tart rejoinder to Jorden, which was singularly futile as his lucubrations remain unpublished.[73] It is not improbable that this performance had its share of influence on Bancroft when he drew up article 72 of the 1604 Canons.

Francis Hutchinson in his *Historical Essay on Witchcraft* (1718)[74] doubts whether any Bishop of the Church of England ever granted a licence for exorcism to any one of his clergy, and indeed the case which is given by Dr. F. G. Lee,[75] who relates how Bishop Seth Ward of Exeter assigned a form under his own signature and seal in January, 1665, to the Rev. John Ruddle, vicar of Altarnon, is probably unique. And even so, this was not strictly speaking an instance of exorcism, at least there was no deliverance of a person possessed. Mr. Ruddle records in his MS. Diary that in a lonely field belonging to the parish of Little Petherick[76] an apparition was seen by a lad aged about sixteen, the son of a certain Mr. Bligh. The ghost, which was that of one Dorothy Durant, who had died eight years before, appeared so frequently to the boy at this same spot which he was obliged to pass daily as he went to and from school, that he fell ill and at last confessed his fears to his family, who treated the matter with ridicule and scolded him roundly when they saw that jest and mockery were of no avail. Eventually Mr. Ruddle was sent for to argue him out of his foolishness. The vicar, however, was not slow to perceive that young Bligh was speaking the truth, and he forthwith accompanied his pupil to the field, where they both unmistakably saw the phantom just as had been described. After a little while Mr. Ruddle visited Exeter to interview his diocesan and obtain the necessary licence for the exorcism. The Bishop, however, asked: "On what authority do you allege that I am entrusted with faculty so to do? Our Church, as is well known, hath abjured certain branches of her ancient power, on grounds of perversion and abuse." Mr. Ruddle quoted the Canons of 1604, and this appears to have satisfied the prelate, who called in his secretary and assigned a form "insomuch that the matter was incontinently done." But the worthy vicar was not permitted to depart without a thoroughly characteristic caution: "Let it be secret, Mr. Ruddle,—weak brethren! weak brethren!" The MS. Diary gives some details of the manner in which the ghost was laid, and it is significant to read that the operator described a circle and a pentacle upon the ground further making use of a rowan "crutch" or wand. He mentions "a parchment scroll," he spoke in Syriac and proceeded to demand as the books advise; he "went through the proper forms of dismissal and fulfilled all, as it was set down and written in my memoranda," and then "with certain fixed rites I did dismiss that troubled ghost." It would be interesting to know what form and ceremonies the Bishop prescribed. It does not sound like the details of a Catholic exorcism, but rather some superstitious and magical ritual. From what is related the form can hardly have been arranged for the nonce.

Although exorcism was not recognized by Protestants

there are instances upon record where an appeal has been made by English country-folk for the ministrations of a Catholic priest. In April, 1815, Father Edward Peach of the Midland District, was implored to visit a young married woman named White, of King's Norton, Worcestershire. She had for two months been afflicted with an extraordinary kind of illness which doctors could neither name nor cure. Her sister declared that a young man of bad repute, whose hand had been rejected, had sworn revenge and had employed the assistance of a reputed wizard at Dudley to work some mischief. However that might be, the unhappy girl seemed to lie at death's door ; she raved of being beset day and night by spirits who mocked and moped at her, threatening to carry her away body and soul, and suggesting self-destruction as the only means to escape them. The clergyman of the parish visited and prayed with her, but no good resulted from all his endeavours. It so happened that a nurse who was called in was a Catholic, and horrified at the hideous ravings of the patient she procured a bottle of holy water, with which she sprinkled the room and bed. A few drops fell upon the sufferer, who uttered the most piercing cries, and screamed out, "You have scalded me! You have scalded me!" The paroxysm, however, passed, and she fell for the first time during many weeks into a sound slumber. After some slight improvement for eight and forty hours she was attacked by violent convulsions, and her relatives, in great alarm, on Tuesday in Rogation Week, 2 May, 1815, sent a special messenger to beg Father Peach to come over immediately.

When the priest appeared the girl was being held down in bed by two women who were forced to put forth all their strength, and as soon as she saw him—he was a complete stranger to her nor could his sacred profession be recognized by his attire—so terrible were her struggles that her husband was bound to lend his aid also to master her writhing limbs. Presently she fell into a state of complete exhaustion, and Father Peach, dismissing the rest of the company, was able to talk to her long and seriously. He seems to have been quite satisfied that it was a genuine case of diabolic possession, and his evidence, carefully expressed and marshalled with great moderation, leave no reasonable doubt that this strange sickness owned no natural origin. In the course of conversation it appeared that she had never been baptized. A simple instruction was given and finding her in excellent dispositions Father Peach at once baptized her. During the administration of this sacrament she trembled like a leaf, and as the water fell upon her she winced pitifully, a spasm of agony distorting her countenance. She afterwards averred that it gave her as much pain as if boiling water had been poured upon her bare flesh. Immediately afterwards there followed a truly remarkable change in her health and spirits; her husband and sister were overjoyed and thought it no less than a miracle. The next day Father Peach visited her again and noticed a rapid improvement. Save for a slight weakness she seemed perfectly restored, and, says the good father, writing a twelvemonth later than the event from notes he had taken at the time, there was no return, nor the least lingering symptom of her terrible and distressing malady.

In its issue of 11 October, 1925, *The Sunday Express*, under the heading "Evil Spirit Haunts A Girl," devoted a prominent column to the record of some extraordinary happenings. The account commences:

"Haunted for twelve months and more by a mischievous spirit—called a Poltergeist—driven almost to a state of distraction, threatened with a lunatic asylum, and then cured by the help of a band of spirit Indians, is the extraordinary experience of the nineteen-year-old Gwynneth Morley, who lives with her widowed mother at Keighley, and who was employed in the spinning mills of Messrs. Hay and Wright."

These phenomena were communicated to Sir Arthur Conan Doyle, who informed Mr. Hewet McKenzie, with the result that the girl was brought to London for psychic treatment, Mr. McKenzie being "honorary principal of the British College of Psychic Science," an institution which is advertised as the "Best equipped Centre for the study of Psychic Science in Britain," and announces "Lectures on Practical Healing," "Public Clairvoyance," "A Small Exhibition of notable water colours . . . representing Soul development, or experience of the Soul in ethereal conditions." "The College" is, I am given to understand, a well-known centre for spiritistic séances.

Gwynneth Morley worked in Mr. McKenzie's family for three months " as a housemaid, under close observation, and receiving psychic treatment.

" Day by day the amazing manifestations of her tormenting spirit were noted down. In between the new and full moon the disturbances were worse. Everything in the room in which Gwynneth happened to be would be thrown about and smashed. Tables were lifted and overturned, chairs smashed to pieces, bookcases upset, and heavy settees thrown over.

" In the kitchen of Holland Park the preparation of meals, when Gwynneth was about, was a disconcerting affair. Bowls of water would be spilt and pats of butter thrown on the floor.

" On another occasion when Gwynneth was in the kitchen the housekeeper, who was preparing some grape fruit for breakfast, found that one half had disappeared and could be found neither in the kitchen nor in the scullery. She got two bananas to take its place, and laid them on the table beside her; immediately the missing grape fruit whizzed past her ear and fell before her and the bananas vanished. Some ten minutes later they were found on the scullery table.

" All this time Gwynneth was being treated by psychic experts. Every week the girl sat with Mr. and Mrs. McKenzie and others. It was found that she was easily hypnotised, and that tables moved towards her in the circle.

" At other times during the cure the Poltergeist seemed to accept challenges. One night after a particularly exciting day, Mrs. Barkel magnetised her head and quietened her, and Mrs. McKenzie suggested that she should go to bed, saying ' Nothing happens when you get into bed.' Going up the stairs a small table and a metal vase crashed over, and a little later a great noise of banging and tearing was heard in Gwynneth's room. When Mrs. McKenzie went into the room it looked as if a tornado had swept over it.

" After an active spell from June 21 to June 25 the spirit behaved itself until July 1, when the girl had a kind of fit. Suddenly she fell off her chair with her hands clenched. They laid her on a bed, and she fell into another fit. She gripped her own throat powerfully.

" Since that evening she has had no further attacks, nor have there been any disturbances."

The main cause of this apparent cure is said to be the mediumship of Mrs. Barkel.

" On many occasions Mrs. Barkel gave Gwynneth excellent clairvoyance, describing deceased relatives, friends, and incidents in her past life which the girl acknowledged and corroborated.

" One near relative, says Mr. McKenzie, whose life had been misspent, and who had been a heavy drinker, was clearly seen. The girl feared and hated this personality, in life and beyond death, and had herself often seen him clairvoyantly before the disturbances began at all. Through Mrs. Barkel's spirit guide, Mr. McKenzie got into touch with him, and he promised to carry out any instructions that might be given for the benefit of the girl.

" The request was made that he should withdraw altogether from any contact with her and not return except by request. ' Professor J.,' a worker on the other side, became interested. Mr. McKenzie asked that a band of Indians, who sometimes profess to be able to help, should take Gwynneth in hand and protect her from the assaults of disturbing influences.

" The following day Mrs. Barkel described an Indian who had come to help, and improvements were noted from about this date. The ' professor ' encouraged the treatment by suggestion, and told Mr. McKenzie that in a few weeks, with the help of the Indian workers, he would place the medium in an entirely new psychic condition. Mr. McKenzie says that the promise was kept."

I have quoted this case at some length owing to the prominence afforded it in a popular and widely read newspaper. That the facts are substantially true I see no reason at all to doubt. It is an ordinary instance of obsession, and will be easily recognized as such by those priests whose duty has required them to study these distressing phenomena. That the interpretation put upon some of the occurrences is utterly false I am very certain. The clairvoyance is merely playing with fire—I might say, with hell-fire—by those who cannot understand what they are about, what forces they are thus blindly evoking. " Professor J." and " the band of Indians," indeed all these " workers on the other side " are nothing else than evil, or at the least gravely suspect intelligences, masquerading as spirits of light and goodness. If, indeed, the girl is relieved from obsession one cannot but suppose some ulterior motive lurks in the background; it is but part of a scheme organized for purposes of their own by dark and secret powers ever alert to trick and trap credulous man. The girl, Gwynneth Morley, should have been exorcized by a trained and accredited exorcist. These amateurs neither know nor even faintly realize the harm they may do, the dangers they encounter. A bold mind, such as that of Guazzo, might specify their attempts—well-meaning as they are, no doubt—in terms I do not care to use.

At Illfurt, five miles south of Mulhausen in Alsace, is a monument consisting of a stone column thirty feet high surmounted with a statue of the Immaculate Conception, and upon the plinth of the pillar may be read the following remarkable inscription: *In memoriam perpetuam liberationis duorum possessorum Theobaldi et Josephi Burner, obtentæ per intercessionem Beatæ Mariæ Uirginis Immaculatæ, Anno Domini* 1869.

Joseph Burner[77] and Anna Maria, his wife, were poor but intelligent persons, who were not merely respected but even looked up to for their probity and industry by their fellow-villagers of Illfurt. The family consisted of five children, the eldest son, Thiébaut, being born on 21 August, 1855, and the second, Joseph, on 29 April, 1857. They were quiet lads of average ability, who, when eight years old, were sent in the usual course to the local elementary school. In the autumn of 1864 both were seized with a mysterious illness which would not yield to the ordinary remedies. Dr. Levy, of Altkirch, who was called in to examine the case acknowledged himself completely baffled, and a number of other doctors who were afterwards consulted declared themselves unable to diagnose such extraordinary symptoms. From 25 September, 1865, the two boys displayed most abnormal phenomena. Whilst lying on their backs they spun suddenly round like whirling tops with the utmost rapidity. Convulsions seized them, twisting and distorting every limb with unparalleled mobility, or again their bodies would for hours together become absolutely rigid and motionless so that no joint could be bent, whilst they lay motionless as stocks or stones. Fearful fits of vomiting often concluded these attacks. Sometimes they were dumb for days and could only gibber and mow with blazing eyes and slabbering lips, sometimes they were deaf so that even a pistol fired close to their ears had not the slightest effect.[78] Often they became fantastically excited, gesticulating wildly and shouting incessantly. Their voices were, however, not their normal tones nor even those of children at all, but the strong, harsh, hoarse articulation of rough and savage men. For hours together they would blaspheme in the foulest terms, cursing and swearing, and bawling out such hideous obscenities that the neighbours took to flight in sheer terror at the horrible scenes, whilst the distracted parents knew not whence to turn for help or comfort. Not only did the sufferers use the filthy vocabulary of the lowest slums, but they likewise spoke with perfect correctness and answered fluently in different languages, in French, Latin, English, and even in most varied dialects of Spanish and Italian, which could by no possible means have been known to them in their normal state. Nor could they at any time have heard conversation in these languages and subconsciously assimilated it. A famous case is on record where a servant girl of mean education fell ill and during a delirium began to mutter and babble in a language which was recognized as Syriac. This was considered to be accounted for when it was discovered that formerly she had been in service in a house where there was lodging a theological student, who upon the eve of his examinations used to walk up and down stairs and pace his room saying aloud to himself Syriac roots and vocables, which she thus often overheard and which in this way registered themselves in her brain. But there could not be any such explanation in the case of Thiébaut and Joseph Burner, since they did not merely reel out disconnected words and phrases in any one or two tongues, but conversed easily and sensibly in a large variety of languages and even in dialects. This has always been considered one of the genuine signs of diabolic possession, as is stated in the third article of *De Exorcizandis Obsessis a Dæmonio:* "3. In primis, ne facile credat, aliquem a dæmonio obsessum esse, sed nota habeat ea signa, quibus obsessus dignoscitur ab iis, qui uel atra bile, uel morbo aliquo laborant. Signa autem obsidentis dæmonis sunt: ignota lingua loqui pluribus uerbis, uel loquentem intelligere; distantia et occulta patefacere; uires super ætatis seu conditionis naturam ostendere; et id genus alia, quæ cum plurima concurrunt, maiora sunt indicia." Moreover, both Thiébaut and Joseph Burner repeatedly and in exactest detail described events which were happening at a distance, and upon investigation their accounts were afterwards found to be precisely true in every particular. Their strength was also abnormal, and often in their paroxysms and convulsions it needed the utmost exertions of three powerful men severally to hold these lads who were but nine and seven years old.

It was noticed at the very beginning of these maladies that the patients were thrown into the most violent fits and every symptom of disease and disorder exacerbated by the presence of any sacramental such as holy water, or medals, rosaries, and other objects which had been blessed according to the ritual. They seemed particularly enraged by the blessed Medal of S. Benedict and pictures of Our Lady of Perpetual Succour. On one occasion Monsieur Ignace Spies, the *Maire* of Selestat, a man of exceptional devotion and piety, held before their eyes a Relic of S. Gerard Majella,[79] the Redemptorist thaumaturge, when their shrieks and yells were truly terrific, finally dying away in inhuman whines and groans of despair. It so happened that a Corpus Christi procession passed the house, opposite which an Altar of Repose had been erected. The children, who were in bed, knew nothing of this and seemed to lie in a deep stupor. However, as the Blessed Sacrament approached their behaviour is said to have been indescribable. They poured forth torrents of filth and profanity, distorting their limbs into a thousand unnatural postures, their eyes almost starting from their heads, a crisis which was succeeded by a sudden horrible composure, whilst they crept away into the furthest corners of the room moaning, panting, and retching as if in mortal agony. Above all, pictures and Medals of Our Lady and the invocation of Her Most Holy Name filled the possessed with terror and rage. At any mention of "the Great Lady," as they termed Her, they would curse and howl in so monstrous a way that all who had heard them shook and sweated with fear.

The abbé Charles Brey, parish priest of Illfurt, quickly

made up his mind as to the diabolic nature of the phenomena. It was an undoubted case of possession, since in no other way could what was taking place be explained. Accordingly he sent to his diocesan, Monsignor Andreas Räss (1842–87) a full account of such extraordinary and fearful events. The Bishop, however, was far from satisfied that these things could not be accounted for naturally. In fact it was only after three or four years' delay that at the instance of the Dean of Altkirch he decided to order a special ecclesiastical investigation. He finally appointed for this task three acute theologians, Monsignor Stumpf,[80] Superior of his Grand Seminary at Strasburg; Monsignor Freyburger, Vicar-General of the diocese; and Monsieur Sester, rector of Mulhausen. These priests, then, presented themselves unexpectedly at the Burner's house on Tuesday morning, 13 April, 1869, at 10 o'clock. It was found that Joseph Burner had already concealed himself, and it was only after a prolonged search he could with difficulty be dragged from under his bed where he had taken refuge. Thiébaut feigned to be unconscious of the presence of strangers. The inquiry lasted for more than two hours, and it was not until past noon that the investigators left the house. Meanwhile they had witnessed the most hideous scenes, and their minds were quite made up as to the reality of the possession. They shortly presented their report to the Bishop, who then, and not until then, allowed himself to be convinced of the facts.

Even so, the prudent prelate ordered fresh precautions to be taken. At the beginning of September, 1869, Thiébaut was conveyed in the company of his unhappy mother, to the orphanage of S. Charles at Schiltigheim, where he was to be lodged whilst the case was investigated *de nouo* by Monsignor Rapp, Monsignor Stumpf, and Father Eicher, S.J., Superior of the Jesuit house at Strasburg. At the same time Father Hausser, the chaplain of S. Charles, and Father Schrantzer, a well-known scholar and psychologist, were to keep the boy systematically but secretly under the closest observation.

It was decided to proceed to exorcism, and a priest of great reverence and experience, Father Souquat, was commissioned by the Bishop to perform the solemn rite. At two o'clock on Sunday, 3 October, Thiébaut was forcibly brought into the chapel of S. Charles, which hitherto he had always sedulously avoided, and when compelled to enter he uttered without intermission such hoarse yells that it was necessary to remove him for fear of scandal and alarming the other inmates. The lad, however, was now held fast by the abbés Schrantzer and Hausser, assisted by Charles André, the gardener of the establishment, a stalwart and muscular Hercules. The sufferer stood upon a carpet spread just before the communion rails, his face turned towards the tabernacle. He struggled and writhed in the grasp of those who were restraining him; his face was scarlet; his eyes closed; whilst from his swollen and champing lips there flowed down a stream of thick yellowish froth which fell in great viscous gouts to the floor. The Litanies began, and at the words "Sancta Maria, ora pro nobis" a hideous yell burst from his throat. The exorcizer unmoved continued the prayers and gospels of the Ritual. Meanwhile the possessed blasphemed and defied their utmost efforts. It was resolved to recommence upon the following day. Thiébaut, accordingly, was confined in a strait jacket and strapped down in a red arm-chair, around which stood the three guards as before. The evil spirit roared and howled in a deep bass voice, raising a terrific din; the boy's limbs strained and contorted but the bonds held tight; his face was livid; his mouth flecked with the foam of slobbering saliva. In a firm voice the priest adjured the demon; he held the crucifix before his eyes, and finally a statue of Our Lady with the words: "Unclean spirit, disappear before the face of the Immaculate Conception! She commands! Thou must obey! Thou must depart!" The assistants upon their knees fervently recited the *Memorare*, when the air was rent by a yell of hideous agony, the boy's limbs were convulsed in one sharp convulsion, and suddenly he lay still wrapped in a deep slumber. At the end of about an hour he awoke gently and gazed about him with wondering eyes. "Where am I?" he asked. "Do you not know me?" questioned the abbé Schrantzer. "No, father, I do not," was the reply. In a few days Thiébaut was able to return home, worn and weak but bright and happy. Of all that happened during those fateful years he had not the smallest recollection. He returned to school, and was in every respect a normal healthy boy.

Joseph, who had grown steadily worse, was meantime secluded from his brother, pending the preparations for his exorcism. On 27 October he was taken very early in the morning to the cemetery chapel near Illfurt. Only the parents, Mons. Ignace Spics, Professor Lachemann, and some half a dozen more witnesses were present, as the affair was conducted in the utmost privacy. At six o'clock the abbé Charles Brey said Mass, after which he exorcized the unhappy victim. During three successive hours they renewed prayers and adjurations, until at last some present began to feel discouraged. But the glowing faith of the priest sustained them, and at length with a loud groan that sounded like a deep roar the boy, who had been struggling and screeching in paroxysms of frantic fury all the while, fell back into a deep swoon and lay motionless. After no long pause he sat up, opened his eyes as awaking from sleep, and was overcome with amazement to find himself in a church with strange people around him.

Neither Thiébaut nor Joseph ever experienced any recurrence of this strange malady. The former died when he was only sixteen years old on 3 April, 1871. The latter, who obtained a situation at Zillisheim, died there in 1882 at the age of twenty-five.

An even more recent case of possession, which has been authoritatively studied in minutest detail and at first hand, presents many of the same features.[81] Hélène-Joséphine Poirier, the daughter of an artisan family—her father was a mason—was born on 5 November, 1834, at Coullons, a small village some ten miles from Gien in the district of the Loire. Whilst still young she was apprenticed to Mlle Justine Beston, a working dressmaker, and soon became skilful with her needle and a remarkable embroideress. Already she had attracted attention by her sincere and modest piety, and was thought highly of by the parish priest, M. Preslier, a man of unusual discernment and the soundest common sense. On the night of 25 March, 1850, she was suddenly awakened by a series of sharp raps, which soon became violent blows, as if struck upon the walls of the small attic where she slept. In terror she rushed into her parents' room next door, and they returned with her to search. Nothing at all could be discovered, and she was persuaded to go back to bed. Although they could actually see no cause for alarm her parents had heard the extraordinary noises. "From this date," says M. Preslier, "the life of Hélène in the midst of such terrible physical and moral suffering that she might well have given utterance to the complaints of holy Job."[82]

These manifestations to Hélène Poirier may not unfittingly be compared with the famous "Rochester knockings," the phenomenon of the rappings at Hydesville in 1848 at the house of the Fox family, which by many writers is considered to be the beginning of that world-wide movement known as Spiritism or Spiritualism in its modern manifestations and recrudescence.[83]

Some months after this event Hélène suddenly fell rigid to the ground as if she had been thrown down by some strong hands. She was able to get up immediately but only to fall again. It was thought she was epileptic or at any rate seized with some unusual attack, some fit or convulsion. But after a careful observation of her case Dr. Azéma, the local practitioner, shrewdly remarked: "Nobody here but the Priest can cure you." From this time disorders of spirit and physical maladies increased with unprecedented rapidity and violence. "Her physical and mental sufferings, which began on 25 March, 1850, continued until her death on 8 January, 1914, that is to say during a period of sixty-four years. But those of diabolic origin ceased towards the end of 1897. So the diabolic attacks actually lasted for some seven-and-forty years, and for six years of this time she was possessed."[84] It was in January, 1863, it first became undeniably evident that her sufferings, her spasms, and painful trances had a supernatural origin. The abbé Bougaud, Archdeacon of Orleans, having interviewed her, advised that she should be brought to the Bishop, Monsignor Dupanloup, and made arrangements for her to stay at a Visitation convent in the suburbs, promising that a commission of theologians and doctors should examine her case. On Thursday, 28 October, 1865, Hélène accordingly commenced a retreat at the convent, where she was kindly received. M. Bougaud saw her for about two minutes, and she was handed an official order which would allow her access to the Bishop without waiting for a summons from his lordship or any other undue delay. But there was some misunderstanding, for on the Friday a doctor of high repute called at the convent, as he had been requested, interrogated and examined her for some three-quarters of an hour and then roundly informed the Mother Superior that she was mad, stark mad, and had better be sent home at once. He seems to have impressed the Bishop with his report, for Monsignor Dupanloup sent a messenger to direct the nuns to dismiss her forthwith, and accordingly she was perforce taken back to Coullons after a fruitless journey of bitter disappointments and discouragement. Many persons now began to regard her with suspicion, but in the following year, 1866, the Bishop, whilst visiting Coullons for an April confirmation, granted her an interview which caused him very considerably to modify his first opinion, and M. Bougaud, who saw her in September, declared himself convinced of the supernatural origin of the symptoms she displayed.

The most terrible obsessions now attacked her, and more than once she was driven to the verge of suicide and despair. "From 25 March, 1850, until March, 1868, Hélène was *only obsessed*. This obsession *lasted* 18 *years*. At the end of this time she was *both obsessed and possessed* for 13 months. From this double agony of obsession and possession she was completely delivered by the exorcisms, which the Bishop had sanctioned, at Orleans, on 19 April, 1869. Four months' peace followed, until with heroic generosity she voluntarily submitted to new inflictions.

"At the end of August, 1869, she accepted from the hands of Our Lord the agony of a new obsession and possession in order to obtain the conversion of the famous general Ducrot. When he was converted, she was delivered from her torments at Lourdes on 3 September, 1875, the cure being effected by the prayers of 15,000 pilgrims who had assembled there. *The obsession and possession in their new form* had lasted five years. During the forty years which passed before her death, she was never again subject to possession, but she was continually obsessed, the attacks now being of short duration, now long and severe. The sufferings of every kind which she endured as well she offered with the intention of the triumph and good estate of God's priests. Why she was originally thus persecuted by the Devil for nineteen years, and with what intention she offered those torments from which she was delivered by the exorcisms directed by the Bishop, must always remain a secret."[85] On Tuesday, 18 August, 1867, a supernormal impulse came over her to write a paper full of the most hideous blasphemies against Our Lord and His Blessed Mother, and, what is indeed significant, to draw blood from her arm and to sign therewith a deed giving herself over body and soul to Satan. This she happily resisted after a terrible struggle. Upon the following 28 August reliable witnesses saw her levitated from the ground on two distinct occasions. With this phenomenon we may compare the levitation of mediums at spiritistic séances. Sir William Crookes in *The Quarterly Journal of Science*, January, 1874, states that "There are at least a hundred recorded instances of Mr. Home's rising from the ground." Of the same medium he writes: "On three separate occasions have seen him raised completely from the floor of the room."

In March, 1868, it became evident that the poor sufferer was actually possessed. Fierce convulsive fits seized her; she suddenly fell with a maniacal fury and a deep hoarse voice uttered the most astounding blasphemies; if the Holy Names of Jesus and Mary were spoken in her presence she gnashed her teeth and literally foamed at the mouth; she was unable to hear the words *Et caro Uerbum factum est* without an access of insane rage which spent itself in wild gestures and an incoherent howling. She was interrogated in Latin, and answered the questions volubly and easily in the same tongue. The case attracted considerable attention, and was reported by the Comte de Maumigny to Padre Picivillo, the editor of the *Civiltá Cattolica*, who gave an account thereof to the Holy Father. The saintly Pius IX[86] showed himself full of sympathy, and even sent through the Comte de Maumigny a message of most salutary advice recommending great caution and the avoidance of all kinds of curiosity or advertisement.

In February, 1869, when interrogated by several priests Hélène gave most extraordinary details concerning bands of Satanists. "In order to gain admission it is necessary to bring one or more consecrated Hosts, and to deliver these to the Devil, who in a materialized form visibly presides over the assembly. The neophyte is obliged to profane the Sacred

Species in a most horrible manner, to worship the Devil with humblest adoration, and to perform with him and the other persons present the most bestial acts of unbridled obscenity, the foulest copulations. Three towns, Paris, Rome, and Tours, are the headquarters of the Satanic bands."[87] She also spoke of a gang of devil-worshippers at Toulouse. It is obvious that a mere peasant woman could have no natural knowledge of these abominations, the details concerning which were unhappily only too true.

In the following April Hélène was taken to Orleans to be examined and solemnly exorcized. The interrogatories were conducted by Monsieur Desbrosses, a consultor in theology for the diocese, Monsieur Bougaud, and Monsieur Mallet, Superior of the Grand Seminary. They witnessed the most terrible crisis; the sufferer was tortured by fierce cramps and spasms; she howled like a wild beast; but they persisted patiently. Mons. Mallet questioned her on difficult and obscure points in theology and philosophy using now Latin, now Greek. She replied fluently in both tongues, answering his queries concisely, clearly, and to the point, incontestable proof that she was influenced by some supernormal power. Two or three days later the Bishop was present at a similar examination, and forthwith commissioned his own director, Monsieur Roy, a professor at the Seminary, to undertake the exorcisms. With him were associated Monsieur Mallet, the parish priest of Coullons, and Monsieur Gaduel, Vicar-General of the diocese. Two nuns and Mlle Preslier held the patient. It was found necessary to repeat the rite five times upon successive days. On the last occasion the cries of the unhappy Hélène were fearful to hear. She writhed and foamed in paroxysms of rage; she blasphemed and cursed God, calling loudly upon the fiends of hell; she broke free from all restraint, hurling chairs and furniture in every direction with the strength of five men; it was with the utmost difficulty she could be seized and restrained before some serious mischief was done; at last with an unearthly yell, twice repeated, her limbs relaxed, and after a short period of insensibility she seemed to awake, calm and composed, as if from a restful slumber. The possession had lasted thirteen months from March, 1868, to April, 1869.

Into the details of her second possession from 23 August,

1869, until 3 September, 1874, it is hardly necessary to enter at any length. Monsieur Preslier noted : " The second crisis of possession was infinitely more terrible than the first; 1st, owing to the length ; the first lasted thirteen months, the second five years. 2nd, the first was relieved was a number of heavenly consolations, but very little solace was obtained during the second. 3rd, there was much bodily suffering in the first, in the second there were far keener mental sufferings and more exquisite pain."[88] She was finally and completely delivered at Lourdes on Thursday, 3 September, 1874. It is not to be supposed that she passed the remaining forty years of her life without occasional manifestations of extraordinary phenomena. After much sickness, cheerfully and smilingly borne, she made a good end in her eightieth year, on 8 January, 1914, and is buried in the little village cemetery of her native place.

We have here the case of a woman who was mediumistic and clairvoyant to an almost unexampled degree, and it is very certain that if these would-be fortune-tellers and mages who so freely advertise their powers in many spiritistic journals to-day truly realized to what terrible dangers and very real psychic perils the use and even the mere possession of such faculties expose them, they would, so far from trafficking in the presumption of abnormal gifts, regard them with caution and indeed shrink from any occult practice at all, lest haply they become the prey of controls and influences so cunning, so potent for evil, as to merge them body and soul in untold miseries and shadows darker even than the bitterness of death.

The modern Spiritistic movement, so strongly supported by recent scientific utterances, is increasingly affecting all classes and conditions of society, and is beginning in every direction to undermine and actually to usurp the religious belief and convictions of thousands of earnest and seriously inclined but not very accurately informed or well-instructed persons. The basis of the movement is the claim that the spirits of the dead are continually seeking to communicate and, indeed, communicating with us through the agency of sensitives, so that it is possible to get into touch and to converse with our dear ones who have passed from this life. It is hardly necessary to emphasize the almost infinite consolation and comfort such a doctrine holds for the bereaved, how eagerly and with what yearning mourners will embrace such teaching, and how perseveringly and with what tender agonies of an hungered love they will devote themselves to the practices they imagine will place them in closest connexion and communion with those whom they have lost awhile, but whose voices they ever long to hear, whose faces they long to see once again. It is a matter of common knowledge that during and since the Great War Spiritism has increased tenfold; many who were wont to laugh at it, who refused to listen to its claims and scorned it as futile nonsense, are now among its most enthusiastic devotees. In truth there must be few of us who cannot appreciate the irresistible influence such beliefs will have upon the mind. Spiritism is seemingly full of joy, and hope, and promise, and happiness. It will wipe all tears of sorrow from poor human eyes; it is balm to the wounded heart; divine solace and sympathy; the barriers of death are broken down; mortality is robbed of its terrors.

Were it true, could we summon to our side the spirits of those whom we have so fondly cherished and converse with them of things holy and eternal, could we learn wisdom from their fuller knowledge, could we be assured in their own sweet accents of their fadeless love, could we now and again be comforted with a sight of their well-known faces, the touch of their hands upon ours, were it God's will that this should be so, then assuredly Spiritism is a most blessed and sacred thing, consolation to the afflicted, succour to the distressed, a shining light upon earth's dark ways, a very ready help to us all. But if on the other hand there is reason and grave reason to suppose that the spirits, with whom it is possible under certain exceptional conditions and by certain remarkable devices to establish a contact, although often claiming to be departed friends or relatives and supporting their contention (we acknowledge) with no little plausibility, are again and again found to be masquerading intelligences, in some cases undoubtedly actors of excellence who play their part for a time with consummate skill, but who have never at any séance whatsoever anywhere been able conclusively to demonstrate their identity, if in fact these manifesting intelligences are deceivers, imposing for purposes of their own a fraudulent impersonation upon those who with breaking hearts are so eagerly longing to communicate with son or husband fallen in battle, it may be, or on some lone shore, if they are proven liars, if their messages are trivial, ambiguous, cryptic, incapable of verification, shifty, ignorant, nay worse, blasphemous and hideously obscene, then are we justified—and we are in point of fact fully and completely justified—in concluding that the spirits are not those of the departed, but evil intelligences who never have been and never will be incarnate, unclean spirits, demons, and then assuredly Spiritism is most foul, most loathly, most dangerous, and most damnable.

The mediums, who of their own will freely open the door to these spirits, who invite them to enter, stand in the most deadly peril. A Spiritist of many years' experience who saw not too late the hazard and abandoned that creed, writes as follows: "Spirit communion soon absorbs all the time, faculties, hopes, fears, and desires of its devotees, and herein lies one of the greatest dangers of spiritualism. Infatuated by communication with the unseen inhabitants of the hidden world, the medium loses his or her interest in the things pertaining to everyday life and interest. A soft and pleasing atmosphere appears to surround them. The realities of flesh and blood are lost in ideal dreaming and there is no incentive to break away from a state of existence so agreeable, no matter how monstrous are the delusions practised by the spirits. Their consciences are so callous as if seared with a hot iron, sin has to them lost its wickedness, and they are willing dupes to unseen beings who delight to control their every faculty. Very seldom has a full-fledged spiritualist been able to comprehend the necessity and blessedness of the religion of Jesus Christ, and to withdraw from the morbid conditions into which he has fallen. . . .

"For about three months I was in the power of spirits, having a dual existence, and greatly tormented by their contradictory and unsatisfactory operations. . . . They tormented me to a very severe extent, and I desired to be freed from them. I lost much of my confidence in them, and their blasphemy and uncleanness shocked me. But they were my constant companions. I could not get rid of them. They tempted me to suicide and murder, and to other sins. I was fearfully beset and bewildered and deluded. There was no human help for me. They led me into some extravagances of action, and to believe, in a measure, a few of their delusions, often combining religion and devilry in a most surprising manner."[89]

In my own experience, I myself, not once, but over and over again, have seen all these symptoms unmistakably marked in those whose sole interest and aim in life seemed to be a constant attendance at séances. I have watched, in spite of every effort unable to check and dissuade, the fearfully rapid development of such characteristics in persons who have begun to dabble with Spiritism, at first no doubt in moods of levity and wanton curiosity, but soon with hectic anxiety and the most morbid absorption. Some fifteen years ago in a well-known English provincial town a circle was formed by a number of friends to experiment with table-turning, psychometry, the planchette, ouija-boards, crystal-gazing, and the like. They were, perhaps, a little tired of the usual round of social engagements, dances, concerts, bridge, the theatre, dinner parties, and all those mildly pleasurable businesses which go to make up life, or at least a great portion of life, for so many. They wanted some new excitement, something a little out of the ordinary. A lady, just returned home from a prolonged visit to London, had (it seems) been taken to some Spiritistic meeting, and she was full of the wonders both witnessed and heard there. The sense of the eerie, the unknown, lent a spice of adventure too. The earlier meetings were informal, first at one house, now at another. They began by being infrequent, almost casual, at fairly long intervals. Next a certain evening each week was fixed for these gatherings, which soon were fully attended by all concerned. No member would willingly miss a single reunion. Before long they met twice, three times, every evening in the week. Professional mediums were engaged who travelled down from London and other great cities, some at no small distance, to give strange exhibitions of their powers. I myself met two of these experts, a man and a woman, both of whose names I have since seen advertised in Spiritistic journals of a very recent date, and I am bound to say that I was most unfavourably impressed in each instance. Not that I for a moment think they were fraudulent, nor do I suspect any vulgar trickery or pose; they were undoubtedly honest, thoroughly convinced and sincere, which makes the matter ten times worse. And so from being mere idle triflers at a new game, incredulous and a little mocking, the whole company became besotted by their practices, fanatics whose thoughts were always and ever centred and concentrated upon their communion with spirits, who talked of nothing else, who seemed only to live for those evenings when they might meet and enter—as it were—another world. Argument, pleading, reproof, authority, official admonishment, all proved useless; one could only stand by and see the terrible thing doing its deadly work. The symptoms were exactly as above described. In two cases, men, the moral fibre was for a while apparently destroyed altogether; in another case, a woman, there was obsession, and persons who either knew nothing of, or had no sort of belief in, Spiritism, whispered of eccentricities, of outbursts of uncontrolled passion and ravings, which pointed to a disordered mind, to an asylum. All sank into a state of apathy; former interests vanished; the amenities of social intercourse were neglected and forgotten; old friendships allowed to drop for no reason whatsoever; a complete change of character for the worse, a terrible deterioration took place; the physical health suffered; their faces became white and drawn, the eyes dull and glazed, save when Spiritism was discussed, and then they lit with hot unholy fires; one heard covert gossip that hinted of crude debauch, of blasphemous speeches, of licence and degradation. Fortunately by a series of providential events the circle was broken up; outside circumstances compelled the principals to fall away, and what was doubtless a more potent factor than any, one or two were suddenly brought to realize the deadly peril and the folly of their proceedings. It proved a hard struggle indeed to rid themselves of the controls to which they had so blindly and so utterly submitted; their wills were weakened, their health impaired; more than once they slid back again into the old danger zone, more than once they were on the verge of giving up the contest in despair. But under direction and availing themselves of those means of grace the Church so bounteously proffers they persevered, and were at length made clean.

There must be many who have had similar experiences, who know intimately, even if they have not actually had to rescue and to guide, those who have been meshed and trapped by Spiritism and are endeavouring to escape. They will appreciate how difficult is the task, they will realize how pernicious, how potent, how evil, such toils may be. Nobody who has had to deal with sensitives, with poor dupes who are eager to abandon their practices, can think lightly of Spiritism.

That Spiritism opens the door to demoniac possession, so often classed as lunacy, is generally acknowledged by all save the prejudiced and superstitious. As far back as 1877 Dr. L. S. Forbes Winslow wrote in *Spiritualistic Madness:* " Ten thousand unfortunate people are at the present time confined in lunatic asylums on account of having tampered with the supernatural." And quoting an American journal he goes on to say : " Not a week passes in which we do not hear that some of these unfortunates destroy themselves by suicide, or are removed to a lunatic asylum. The mediums often manifest signs of an abnormal condition of their mental faculties, and among certain of them are found unequivocal indications of a true demoniacal possession. The evil spreads rapidly, and it will produce in a few years frightful results. . . . Two French authors of spiritualistic works, who wrote *Le Monde Spirituel* and *Sauvons le genre humain*, died insane in an asylum ; these two men were distinguished in their respective professions ; one as a highly scientific man, the other as an advocate well learned in the Law. These individuals placed themselves in communication with spirits by means of tables. I could quote many such instances where men of the highest ability have, so to speak, neglected all and followed the doctrines of Spiritualism only to end their days in the lunatic asylum."

Some half a dozen years ago an inquiry was undertaken and there was circulated an interrogatory or *enquête* which invited opinions upon (1) " the situation as regards the renewed interest in psychic phenomena " ; (2) whether this " psychic renewal " denoted a " passing from a logical and scientific (deductive) to a spiritual and mystic (inductive) conception of life," or " a reconciliation between the two, that is between science and faith " ;[90] (3) " the most powerful argument for, or against, human survival"; (4) "the best means of organizing this (psychic) movement in the highest interest, philosophical, religious and scientific, of the nation, especially as a factor of durable peace." Five-and-fifty of the answers were collected and published under the title *Spiritualism: Its Present-Day Meaning*,[91] a book which certainly makes most interesting and illuminating if extremely varied reading. Being a symposium, all schools of thought are represented, and I would venture to add that among the contributions are some outpourings which evince no thought at all, a fact which is of itself not without considerable significance. We have the unflinching logic and sound common-sense of Father Bernard Vaughan, whose verdict is reiterated by the Rev. James Adderley and the Rev. J. A. V. Magee; the concise, outspoken, pertinent and telling comments of General Booth; the vague hopelessly inadequate flotsam of Dr. Percy Dearmer,[92] vapid stuff which makes a theologian writhe; the sweet sugary sentimentalism of Miss Evelyn Underhill, so anæmic, so obviously popular, and so ingenuously miscalled mysticism; the dull worthless dross of Mr. McCabe's superstitious materialism; the feverish panicky special pleading of the convinced Spiritists. Here, too, we have much that directly bears out our present contention, the medical evidence of such names as Sir Bryan Donkin; Dr. W. H. Stoddart, who treats of "The Danger to Mental Sanity"; with Dr. Bernard Hollander on "The Peril of Spirits"; and Dr. A. T. Schofield on "The Spiritist Epidemic." Thus Dr. Stoddart writes: "In some cases the spiritualistic hallucinations so dominate the whole mental life that the condition amounts to insanity; and I can confirm Sir Bryan Donkin's statement that spiritualistic inquiries tend to induce insanity."[93] Dr. Hollander is even more emphatic: "The practice is a dangerous one. Persons become intoxicated with spirits of that nature as others do with spirits of another kind. And similarly, as not all persons who take alcohol get drunk, so not all spiritualists show the effects of their indulgences. . . . But that is no proof against the harmful nature of these practices, and, as a mental specialist, I confess I have seen victims of both, and that the one addicted to material spirits is the easier to treat."[94] Spiritism, Dr. Schofield points out, "has been known to

Christians for 2000 years. Any benefit derived therefrom is more than neutralized by the very doubtful surroundings and character of the supposed revelation (I say 'supposed' because it has been known so long). If, however, it must be coupled with the dangers, horrors, and frauds that so often in modern Spiritism accompany the knowledge of the unseen, we are almost as well without it, at any rate from such a source. . . . There can be no doubt the epidemic will eventually subside, but before it does, the vast mischief of a spiritual tidal wave of very doubtful origin will be most disastrously done, and thousands of unstable souls will be wrecked in spirit, if not in mind and body as well. . . . To class it as a religion is an insult to the faith of Christ."[95]

Sir William Barrett utters a word of grave import: "All excitable and unbalanced minds need to be warned away from a subject that may cause, and in many cases has caused, serious mental derangement."[96] "Spiritualism," says Father Bernard Vaughan, "only too often means loss of health, loss of morals and loss of faith. Consult not Sir Oliver Lodge or Sir Arthur Conan Doyle or Mr. Vale Owen, but your family medical adviser, and he will tell you to keep away from the séance-room as you would from an opium den. In fact, the drug habit is not more fatal than the practice of Spiritualism in very many cases. Read the warning note sounded by Dr. Charles Mercier, or by Dr. G. H. Robertson or by Colonel R. H. Elliot, and be satisfied that yielding to Spiritualism is qualifying for an asylum. You may not get there but you deserve to be an inmate."[97] The following letter written by Miss Mary G. Cardwell, M.B., Ch.B., from the Oldham Union Infirmary, speaks for itself: "One day recently I admitted a woman of thirty-five years to the hospital of which I have the honour to be resident medical officer. She was sent in as incapable of looking after herself or her family. She told me that she was a medium, having been introduced into Spiritualism by a man, also a medium, who said he could thereby help her over some family worries. As a direct result of this, she has neglected her children, so that the public authorities have removed them from her care, her home is ruined, and she herself is a mental and moral wreck. She had paid the other medium for his services by the sacrifice of her virtue."[98] And this is no isolated, no exceptional, instance. I have myself known precisely similar cases.

Occasionally some particularly shocking incident will find its way into the public Press and we have records such as the following, which was headed " Family of Eleven Mad. Burning Mania after Séance. Child to be Sacrificed.

" The story of an entire family of eleven persons, in the village of Krucktenhofen, Bavaria, going out of their minds after a spiritualistic séance is sent by the Exchange Paris correspondent, quoting the *Berliner Tageblatt.*

" Renouncing the goods of this world, the father, mother, three sons, two elder daughters, and subsequently the remaining four younger members of the family, joined in burning their furniture and bedding.

" Finally, the three-months-old child of one of the daughters was about to be burnt when neighbours interfered. The whole family is now in an asylum." (*Daily Mirror*, 19 May, 1921.)

" Camouflage it as you will, Spiritualism with its kindred superstitions, such as necromancy and occultism, is a recrudescence of the old, old practices cultivated in the days of long ago."[99] In other words this " New Religion " is but the Old Witchcraft. There is, I venture to assert, not a single phenomenon of modern Spiritism which cannot be paralleled in the records of the witch trials and examinations; not a single doctrine which was not believed and propagated by the damnable Gnostic heresies of long ago.

Some of the definitions of Spiritism given by spiritists themselves are sufficiently startling. They frankly tell us that " Spiritualism is the science or art of communion with spirits. . . . It does not follow that because a communication comes from 'the unseen,' it is therefore from God, as a revelation. It may be from the latest dead lounger, as an amusement,"[100] or, I would add, from a demon as a snare. There is something inexpressibly ugly and revolting about this cold-blooded necromancy defined in set categorical terms.

Modern Spiritism is usually considered to have had its origin in America. In the year 1848 there lived at Hydesville, Wayne, New York State, a family of the Methodist persuasion named Fox; a father, mother, and two daughters,

Margaretta and Katie, aged fifteen and twelve respectively. During the month of March all the household began to declare that they were kept awake at night by the most extraordinary noises, loud knockings on the wall, and footsteps. The children amused themselves by trying to imitate the noises; they tapped on the wainscot, and to their great surprise answering taps came back, so that they found they could get into communication with the unknown agency. They would ask a question and invite it to respond with one sharp rap for "no" and three for "yes," and thus it continually replied. They further held actual conversations in this way by repeating the alphabet and establishing a regular code. Mrs. Fox then began to make inquiries concerning the former occupants of the house, and soon discovered that a pedlar named Charles Rayn was said to have been murdered in the very bedroom where her two girls were sleeping, and that his body had been buried in the cellar. Public curiosity was aroused, and it was now generally believed that it was the spirit of the unfortunate victim who haunted the farm-house, endeavouring to convey some message to those whom he had left. Actually no body was found in the cellar, and the alleged murderer whose name was given, appeared at Hydesville and "threw very hot water on the story." Later when the family moved to Rochester—it is said they were practically driven out of Hydesville by the Methodist minister there—the rappings followed them, and the whole town was speedily on the tiptoe of excitement. It was then given out that the noises were communications from the spirits of those recently dead, and that the Fox girls, who apparently attracted them, were gifted with some special faculty which rendered intercourse of this kind possible. People soon began to flock round them asking their assistance in getting messages from their departed relatives and friends; the two girls held regular séances, and netted a fair sum of money. It was not long before other persons discovered that they also possessed this extraordinary faculty of attracting spirit manifestations, and of getting into communication with the other world at will. But the Fox sisters were first in the field, and to them came a continuous stream of persons with well-filled pockets from all parts of America. There was also opposition, which sometimes took a very violent form. As early as November,

1850, an attack was made upon Margaretta Fox, who was staying at West Troy in the house of a Mr. Bouton. A rough mob surrounded the premises, stones were thrown at the windows, and shots fired, whilst both men and women uttered threats and imprecations against the "unholy witch-woman within." At one of the séances Dr. Kane, a famous Arctic explorer was present, and he was so fascinated by the beauty of Margaretta Fox that he never rested until he had taken her away from her sordid and harmful surroundings, had her educated at Philadelphia, and finally, much to the annoyance of his relations, who loathed any connexion with the Fox family, made her his wife.

Dr. Kane died soon after his marriage, but in the book published by his widow there are several references to his abhorrence of Spiritism. "Do avoid spirits," he urges, "I cannot bear to think of you as engaged in a course of wickedness and deception." For ten years Mrs. Kane did indeed abandon it; in fact in August, 1858, she was baptized as a Catholic at New York; but then,[101] owing perhaps to the pinch of poverty, she again took up work as a medium, and was received back with acclamations by the whole Spiritistic community. From that moment dates her steady deterioration, both physical and moral.

Kate Fox, Mrs. Jencken as she had become, the wife of a London barrister, was the mother of a baby whom popular talk credited with mediumistic powers of the most extraordinary kind. The whole Spiritistic following prophesied a brilliant future for the poor child, of whom, however, there is nothing recorded save that he was sadly neglected by his miserable mother, who died of chronic alcoholism in June, 1892. Mrs. Kane survived her sister for nine months, a pitiable and hopeless wreck, craving only for drink. The last few weeks of her life were spent in a derelict tenement house. "This wreck of womanhood has been a guest in palaces and courts. The powers of mind now imbecile were the wonder and the study of scientific men in America, Europe, and Australia. . . . The lips that utter little else now than profanity, once promulgated the doctrine of a new religion."[102] It would, indeed, be difficult to conceive anything more sordid and more miserable than this sad and shocking story of utter degradation. The collapse and moral corruption of the first apostles of modern Spiritism should surely prove a timely warning and a danger signal not to be mistaken.[103]

In the earliest days of Spiritism the subject was investigated by men like Horace Greeley, William Lloyd Garrison, Robert Hare, professor of chemistry in the University of Pennsylvania, and John Worth Edmonds, a judge of the Supreme Court of New York State. Conspicuous among the spiritists we find Andrew Jackson Davis, whose work *The Principles of Nature* (1847), dictated by him in trance, contained theories of the universe closely resembling those of the Swedenborgians. From America the movement filtered through to Europe, and when in 1852 two mediums, Mrs. Haydon and Mrs. Roberts, came to London, not merely popular interest but the careful attention of the leading scientists of the day was attracted. Robert Owen, the Socialist, frankly accepted the Spiritistic explanation of the various phenomena, while Professor De Morgan, the mathematician, in his account of a sitting with Mrs. Haydon declared himself convinced that "somebody or some spirit was reading his thoughts." In the spring of 1855 Daniel Dunglas Home (Hume)—Home was the son of the eleventh Lord Home and a chambermaid at the Queen's Hotel, Southampton, but was brought up in America—who was then a young man of twenty-two, crossed to England from America. In 1856 Home was received into the Church at Rome by Father John Etheridge, S.J., and he then gave a promise to refrain from all exercise of his mediumistic powers, but in less than a year he had broken his pledge and was living as before. This famous medium is almost the only one who, as even Podmore admits, was never clearly convicted of fraud. Sir David Brewster, the scientist, and Dr. J. J. Garth Wilkinson, a scholar of unblemished integrity and one of the leading homœopathic physicians, both avowed that they were incapable of explaining the phenomena they had witnessed by any natural means. It was in 1855 that the first English periodical dealing exclusively with the subject, *The Yorkshire Spiritual Telegraph*, was published at Keighley, in Yorkshire. In 1864 the Davenport brothers visited England, and in 1876 Henry Slade. Amongst English mediums the Rev. William Stainton Moses became prominent in 1872,[104] and about the same year Miss Florence

Cook, so well known for the materializations of "Katie King," which were scrupulously investigated by the late Sir William Crookes. In 1873 and in 1874, however, the trickery of two mediums, Mrs. Bassett and Miss Showers, was definitely exposed.[105] In 1876 and 1877 the sensitive "Dr." Monck was at the height of his reputation, and both Dr. Alfred Russel Wallace, F.R.S., and the late Archdeacon Colley state that in various séances with him they witnessed on several occasions phenomena, including materialization, under rigid test conditions which admitted of no dispute as to their genuineness. It is true that in 1876 Monck had been in trouble and was sentenced to a term of imprisonment under the Vagrant Act. About the same time William Eglinton, who figures in Florence Marryat's work *There is No Death*, appeared on the scenes and for a while loomed largely in the public eye. He became famous for his slate-writing performances as well as his materializations. He was, however, exposed by Archdeacon Colley, who during the discussion which had centred round a medium named Williams, detected in fraudulent practices during séances in Holland, wrote to *The Medium and Daybreak* to say: "It unfortunately fell to me to take muslin and false beard from Eglinton's portmanteau. . . . Some few days before this I had on two several occasions cut pieces from the drapery worn by, and clipped hair from the beard of, the other figure representing Abdullah. I have the pieces so cut off beard and muslin still. But note that when I took these things into my possession I and a medical gentleman (25 years a Spiritualist and well known to the old members of the Movement) found the pieces of muslin cut fit exactly into certain corresponding portions of the drapery thus taken."[106]

The medium Slade, who was famous for slate-writing, was upon one occasion suddenly seized as he was about to put the slate under the table. His hands were held fast, and when the slate was snatched from him it was seen to be already covered with characters. Anna Rothe, who died in 1901, a medium well known for her apports of flowers, suffered a term of imprisonment in Germany on a charge of fraud. When Baily, the Australian sensitive, visited Italy he refused to sit under the strict conditions which were arranged in answer to a challenge of his powers. Charles

Eldred of Clowne, an adept at materialization, employed a chair skilfully made with a double seat, and in this recess were discovered the whole paraphernalia he employed in his performances.

Mrs. Williams, an American medium, who for a long while was a centre of spiritistic attention at Paris, used to materialize a venerable doctor with a flowing beard who was sometimes accompanied by a young girl dressed in white. At one circle Mons. Paul Leymaric gave a prearranged signal. He and a friend each laid hold of one of the apparitions ; a third spectator seized Mrs. Williams' assistant ; and a fourth turned on the lights. Mons. Leymaric was seen to be struggling with the medium, who had donned a grey wig and a long property beard ; the young girl was a mask from which were draped folds of fine white muslin and which she manipulated with her left hand. Miller, a Californian medium, was more than suspected of producing spirits from gauze and nun's veiling.[107] From one of the mediums of Mons. de Rochas, Valentine, there emanated mysterious lights, which moved quickly hither and thither during the séances. Colonel de Rochas, when this manifestation was once at its height, suddenly switched on a powerful electric torch and Valentine was seen to have slipped off his socks and to be waving in the air his feet, which were covered with some preparation of phosphorus.[108] As early as June, 1875, a photographer named Buguet was convicted of selling faked photographs of spirits by which he netted a very pretty sum.[109]

It is notorious that in Spiritistic séances and circles charlatanry and swindling of every kind are rife ; that again and again mediums have been convicted of fraud ; that not infrequently all kinds of properties, stuffed gloves, gauzes, yards of diaphanous muslin, invisible wires, hooks, beards, wigs, have been discovered ; that the use of luminous paint is very effective and far from uncommon ; that a sliding trap or panel may on occasion prove of inestimable service ; that we must allow for self-deception, delusions, suggestion, hypnotism even ; but when all has been said, when we candidly acknowledge the imposture, the adroit legerdemain, the conjurer's clever tricks, the significant *mise en scène*, the verbal wit and quibbling, the deliberate and subtle cozenage contrived by shrewd minds and the full play of dramatic instinct and energy, nevertheless there yet remain numbers of instances when it has been repeatedly proven that acute and trained observers have witnessed phenomena which could not by any possibility whatsoever have been fraudulently produced; that clear-headed, cold-hearted, suspicious, hard men of science with every sense keenly alert at that very moment have conversed with, inspected, nay, actually handled, materialized forms and figures no personation could have devised and manifested.

The proceedings against Monck plainly showed that he had at any rate a firm belief in his own psychic powers, and although Eglinton was detected in a trick upon more than one occasion there is irrefutable evidence to prove that in other instances when he assisted at séances any normal mode of production of the phenomena seen there was quite impossible. A large number of Miller's manifestations also were genuine.[110] The same may be said of very many mediums. This means, in fine, that although the manifestations of almost any medium may in some cases have been artificially contrived, such phenomena are not on any account to be adjudged *always* fraudulent, and even if the charge of imposture could be brought home far more conclusively than has so far been possible as regards the majority of sensitives, yet it were a false inference indeed to deduce therefrom that all phenomena are equally fraudulent and devised. It is only the recklessly illogical mind and the loose thinker who will in the face of absolutely conclusive proof of genuine manifestations continue to maintain that a certain quota of quackery can invalidate the whole. Writers of the temper of Messrs. Edward Clodd, Joseph McCabe, J. M. Robertson must, of course, be expected to condemn Spiritism without knowing the facts or weighing the evidence as an obvious absurdity which calls for no serious refutation. But this, I think, matters little. The superstitious dogmatism of the materialist is gravely discredited nowadays. True, the sort of book he produces is widely circulated and very successful within certain limits. We should expect tenth-rate ideas which could only emanate from a lack of understanding, a total want of imagination, and no training in metaphysics or philosophy, to have a direct appeal to the immature intelligences, the uneducated vulgar and the blatant yet presumptuous ignorance, which alone are eager for this kind of outmoded fare.

In France Spiritism was first proclaimed by a pamphlet of Guillard *Table qui danse et Table qui répond.* The way had been long paved owing to the interest which was generally taken in the doctrines of Emanuel Swedenborg. Balzac had published in 1835 his esoteric hybrid *Séraphita* (*Séraphitus*), a fanciful yet interesting work, in which there are many pages of theosophic philosophy. Perhaps he meant these seriously, but it is impossible to take them as other than flights of romance. In 1848 Cohognet more immediately heralded Guillard by publishing at Paris the first volume of his *Arcanes de la vie future devoilées*, which actually contains what purport to be communications from the dead. In 1853 séances were being held at Bourges, Strasburg, and Paris, and a regular furore ensued. Nothing was talked of but the wonders of Spiritism, which, however, soon met an opponent, Count Agénor de Gasparin, a Swiss Protestant, who carefully investigated table-turning with a circle of his friends and came to the conclusion that the phenomena originated in some physical force of the human body. It must be admitted that his *Des Tables Tournantes* (Paris, 1854) is unconvincing and to some extent superficial, but more perhaps could hardly be expected from a pioneer in so tortuous an investigation. The Baron de Guldenstubbe, on the contrary, declared his firm belief in the reality of these phenomena and spirit intervention in general. His work *La Réalité des Esprits* (Paris, 1857) eloquently argued for his convictions, whilst *Le Livre des Esprits* (Paris, 1853) by M. Rivail or Rival, better known under his pseudonym Allan Kardec, became a world-wide textbook to the whole subject. In these early days the most distinguished men were wont to meet in the rue des Martyrs at Paris for séances. Tiedmen Marthèse, governor of Java; the academician Saint-René-Taillandier; Sardou, with his son; Flammarion; all were constant visitors. The notorious Home was, it is said, expelled from France after a séance at the Tuileries, during which he had touched the arm of the Empress with his naked foot, pretending that it was a caress from the tiny hands of a little child who was about fully to materialize. No one, I think, could be surprised to know that the famous Joris Karl Huysmans, an epicure in the byways of the occult, made many experiments in Spiritism, and séances were frequently held at No. 11 rue de Sèvres where he lived. Extraordinary manifestations took place, and upon one occasion at least the circle effected a materialization of General Boulanger, or an apparition of the General appeared to them.

At the present time Spiritism is as widely spread in France as in England, if indeed not far more widely. Thus *La Science de l'Ame* is a new bi-monthly journal issued under the auspices of *La Revue Spirite*. It has articles on Magnetism and Radio-activity, the analysis of the soul, and vital radiations. In the number of *La Revue Spirite*, which commences the year 1925, Mons. Camille Flammarion prints a signed letter from Heliopolis, which describes a first experience of a séance, where the death of the writer's father was predicted in six months and took place ten days after the allotted time. Elsewhere in the issue are particulars of the International Congress of Spiritism which was to be held at Paris in September, 1925, and would be open to all Federations, Societies, and Groups everywhere. An immense concourse was expected. The President is Mr. George F. Berry, a well-known name in English Spiritistic circles, and the compliment of honorary membership is paid to Léon Denis,[111] Gabriel Delanne, Sir William Barrett, and Ernest Bozzano.

A glance at the pages of any Spiritistic journal in England will show almost endless activities in every direction. In one issue of the weekly *Light* (Saturday, 21 February, 1925) we have amongst other announcements nine " Sunday's Society Meetings " in various districts of London, with addresses on Wednesdays and Thursdays. The following seems sufficiently startling and a close enough imitation : " *St. Luke's Church of the Spiritual Evangel of Jesus the Christ, Queen's-road, Forest Hill, S.E.*—Minister : Rev. J. W. Potter. February 22nd, 6.30, Service, Holy Communion and Address. Healing Service, Wed., Feb. 25th, 7 p.m." In the next column are details of " Rev. G. Vale Owen's Lecture Tour." The " London Spiritualist Alliance, Ltd." has a list of meetings. There are discussion classes and demonstrations of clairvoyance, psychometry, and Mystic Pictures. Among " Books that will Help you " we find *Talks with the Dead, Report on*

Spiritualism, The Aquarian Gospel of Jesus the Christ—(is this used at St. Luke's Church of the Spiritual Evangel ?)—*Spirit Identity, Spiritualism,* and many more of similar import. There is a "British College of Psychic Science" where Mr. Horace Leaf, a medium of some repute, lectures on "The Psychology and Practice of Mediumship," Mrs. Barker demonstrates Trance Mediumship, and Mrs. Travers Smith the Ouija-Board and Automatic Writing. There is a "London Spiritual Mission" and a "Wimbledon Spiritualist Mission." At Brighton "St. John's Brotherhood Church" provides "The Spiritual Evangel of Jesus the Christ," "Minister, Brother John." And all this is scarcely a tithe of the various announcements and advertisements.

However grotesque, and indeed often puerile in its bombast and grandiloquence, such a mass of heterogeneous notices may seem we must remember that these people are in deadly earnest, and I doubt not but their meetings and assemblies are well attended by enthusiastic devotees. In a report of an address by the Rev. G. Vale Owen at the "Spiritualist Community Services in the County Hall" on Sunday evening, 15 February, 1925, I read "all seats were filled long before the advertised hour for starting. The doors were closed and many for a time were denied admission. A little later they were allowed to enter and take up positions along the edges of the dais and other odd places about the hall."[112] This, of course, was possibly some exceptional occasion, but there is no indication that such was the case. Mr. Vale Owen may be a very eloquent speaker and able to hold his audience spell-bound with the magic of his words. It must assuredly be his manner and not his matter, for his so-called revelations of the life beyond the grave, written under control and presumed to be directly derived from spirit agency, which appeared in *The Weekly Dispatch* are vapid, inept, idle, and insipid to the last degree. Such banal ramblings would provoke a smile, were it not for the pity that any person can be so self-deluded, and can apparently induce others to give credit to his silliness.

There have been large numbers of mediums in recent years who owing to one cause or another attracted considerable attention from time to time, and there are many well-known contemporary sensitives widely practising to-day.

Mrs. Verrall and Mrs. Holland, who were believed to have obtained spirit messages from the late F. W. H. Myers, occupied the serious attention of the Society of Psychical Research[113] for a considerable period; Mrs. Piper is an automatic writer of no little repute; Mr. Vout Peters specializes in psychometry and clairvoyance; Mr. Vearncombe and Mrs. Deane have recently enjoyed their full share of notoriety;[114] the Rev. Josie K. Stewart (Mrs. Y.), a lady hailing from the United States, has a gift for the production of "writing and drawings on cards held in her hand"; Mrs. Elizabeth A. Tomson, in spite of being detected of fraud at a Spiritistic "Church" in Brooklyn, still has devoted followers; Franek Kluski, Stella C., and Ada Besinnet, are in the forefront of American mediums; whilst the famous Goligher circle at Belfast was carefully and patiently investigated for no less than three months by Dr. Fournier d'Albe, who has published the result of his experiences.[115] The very cream of these occult manifestations is materialization, the most complex problem of all, which has been described as "the exercise of the power of using of the matter of the medium's and the sitters' bodies in the formation of physical structures on a principle totally unknown to ordinary life, although probably present there."[116] Recently (1922) Erto, the Italian medium, appears to have been the subject of careful experiments at the French Metaphysical Institute during a period of several months, those who assisted being pledged to silence until a decision had been reached. The particular phenomena produced by or in his presence were chiefly characterized by the radiation of an extraordinary light about his person. At the end of 1922 two papers appeared in *La Revue Métapsychique* on the part of Dr. Sanguinetti and Dr. William Mackenzie of Genoa indicating their assurance (1) that every scientific precaution had been taken, and (2) that the phenomena were genuine. However, the experiments seem to have continued and later there appeared in *Le Matin* an enthusiastic contribution by Dr. Stephen Chauvet, which caused Dr. Gustave Geley, Director of the Metaphysical Institute, to come forward in confirmation of the testimony. It is only fair to add that immediately afterwards Dr. Geley to a certain extent retracted his statement, as he suggested that the psychic lights could be produced with *ferro-cerium*, and it was thought that traces of this substance could be found on Erto's clothes. The medium protested his innocence of any deception, and offers himself for further experiments. A writer in *Psychica* is inclined to believe that the phenomena were genuine, but that later some fraud may have been practised owing to waning power. This is possibly the case, for that the radiations were at first supernormal cannot, I think, be gainsaid in view of the high testimony adduced. For this phenomenon Mr. Cecil Hush and Mr. Craddock have sat repeatedly; of the extraordinary manifestations of the late Eusapia Palladino there can be no reasonable doubt at all; the materializations of Mlle "Eva Carrère,"[117] although on several occasions not altogether successful, are at other times supported by the strongest evidence; Nino Pecoraro, who is described as "a remarkably muscular young Neapolitan," is famous for "ectoplasmic effects"; and Stanislava P., Willy S., the Countess Castelvicz, and very many more psychics possess these supernormal powers, although, as we might expect, they have to be used with the utmost caution and often prove very exhausting to the subject. After all, it must be remembered that probably under certain conditions materialization cannot take place, whilst under favourable conditions it can be completely effected. For an exhaustive and authoritative discussion of the whole matter the Baron Von Schrenck-Notzing's *Phenomena of Materialization* (Kegan Paul, 1923), should be consulted. The 225 photographic reproductions are of the utmost importance, whilst the investigations were carried on under conditions of such pitiless severity to eliminate any hypothesis of fraud that the mediums cannot but have been subjected to the intensest physical and moral strain.

Among recent psychic phenomena very general attention has been attracted by what is known as "The Oscar Wilde Script," which was widely discussed in 1923–24. Briefly, this purports to be a number of communications which were delivered by the spirit of the late Oscar Wilde at the rate of 1020 words in an hour by means of automatic writing through the mediumship of Mrs. Travers Smith (Mrs. Hester M. Dowden)[118] and a certain Mr. V. True, there were published in *The Sunday Express* pages which had a superficial resemblance to the more flashy characteristics of Wilde's flamboyant style, but it seemed as if the wit and point had vanished, leaving only a somewhat heavy and imitative prose; one had a sense of damp fireworks, and personally I do not for a moment accept this script as being inspired or dictated by Wilde. I hasten to add that I do not suggest there was any conscious fraud or trickery on the part of those concerned; it is quite probable that these psychic messages were conveyed by some intelligence of no very high standing, and the result in fine is not of any value. It is said that a three act play is being or has been communicated through the ouija-board from what purports to be Wilde. This I have not read, and therefore I am not in a position to pronounce upon it.

Spiritism is upheld by many distinguished names. Sir Oliver Lodge, F.R.S., has battled on its behalf, as also have Sir William Barrett, F.R.S., and Sir William Crookes, F.R.S., Professors Charles Richet, Janet, Bernheim, Lombroso, and Flammarion lend it the weight of their authority, whilst Sir Conan Doyle has poured forth his benedictions upon occultism of every kind.[119] He has even presided over the opening of a most attractive bookshop in Victoria Street, Westminster, where Spiritistic publications are sold.

How then are we to regard this mighty movement at which it were folly to sneer, which it is impossible to ignore? The Catholic Church does neither. But none the less she condemns it utterly and entirely. Not because she disbelieves in it, but because she believes in it so thoroughly, because she knows what is the real nature of the moving forces, however skilfully they may disguise themselves, however quick and subtle their shifts and turns, the intelligences which inform and direct the whole. It is a painful subject since (I reiterate) many good people, no doubt many thoughtful seekers after truth, have been fascinated and swept along by Spiritism. They are as yet conscious of neither physical nor moral harm, and, it may be, they have been playing with the fire for years. Nay more, Spiritism has been a sweet solace to many in most poignant hours of bitter sorrow and loss; wherefore it is hallowed in their eyes by tenderest memories. They are woefully deceived. Hard as it may seem, we must get down to the bed-rock of fact.

Spiritism has been specifically condemned on no less than four occasions by the Holy Office,[120] whose decree, 30 March, 1898, utterly forbids all Spiritistic practices although intercourse with demons be strictly excluded, and communication sought with good spirits only. Modern Spiritism is merely Witchcraft revived. The Second Plenary Council of Baltimore (1866), whilst making ample allowance for prestidigitation and trickery of every kind, warns the faithful against lending any support whatsoever to Spiritism and forbids them to attend séances even out of idle curiosity, for some, at least, of the manifestations must necessarily be ascribed to Satanic intervention since in no other manner can they be understood or explained.

NOTES TO CHAPTER VI

[1] E. de Rougé, *Étude sur une stèle Égyptienne*, Paris, 1858: E. A. W. Budge, *Egyptian Magic*, VII.

[2] *Rekh Khet*, "knower of things."

[3] Euripides, *Bacchæ*: passim; Ovid, *Metamorphoses*. III. 513, *sqq.*; Apollodorus, III. v. 2.; Hyginus, *Fabulæ*, 184; Nonnus, *Dionysiaca* (*Bassarica*), XIV, 46.

[4] Sophocles, *Ajax*; Pindar, *Nemea*, VII, 25; Ovid, *Metamorphoses*, XIII, 1–398.

[5] Pausanias, III, xvi, 6.

[6] Valerius Maximus, I, 11, 5. Lacinium was a promontory on the east coast of Bruttium, a few miles south of Croton, and forming the western boundary of the Tarentine gulf. The remains of the temple of Juno Lacinia are still extant, and have given the modern name to the promontory, *Capo delle Colonne* or *Capo di Nao* (ναός).

[7] Xenophon, *Memorabilia*. II. i. 5; Demosthenes, XCIII, 24; Dinarchus, CI, 41; Plutarch, *Lucullus*, IV.

[8] Euripides, *Orestes*, l. 854, and l. 79.

[9] Cf. μάντις.

[10] Cf. Vergil *Æneid*. IV. 471–3:

> Agamemnonius scænis agitatus Orestes
> armatam facibus matrem et serpentibus atris
> cum fugit, ultricesque sedent in limine Diræ.
>
> (Or as the Atridan matricide
> Runs frenzied o'er the scene,
> What time with snakes and torches plied
> He flees the murdered queen,
> While at the threshold of the gate
> The sister-fiends expectant wait.)

[11] Plautus, *Amphitruo*, II. 2. 145. Nam hæc quidem edepol lauarum plenast.

[12]
> Quid esset illi morbi, dixeras? Narra, senex.
> Num laruatus, aut cerritus? fac sciam.

Menæchmei. V. 1, 2. Apuleuis has *laruans* = a madman: "hunc [pulcherrimam Mercurii imaginem] denique qui laruam putat, ipse est laruans." (*Laruatus* is a poorer reading in this passage.) *Cerritus*. a rare word. is contracted from *cerebritus* (*cerebrum*), and not connected with Ceres, as was formerly suggested. Cf. Horace, *Sermonum*, II, iii. 278.

13 *Bibl.* III, v, 1.

14 471, *sqq.*

15 56, Nauck.

16 τάπιχώρὶ ἐν πόλει φρυγῶν τύμπανα,
Ῥέας τε μητρὸς ἐμά θ' εὑρήματα.

17 *Circa* 185–135 B.C.

18 Professor Leuba, *The Psychology of Religious Mysticism* Kegan Paul, London, 1925, p. 11 *sqq.* has some very important references to the worship of Dionysus.

19 σὺ γὰρ ἔνθεος, ὦ κούρα,
εἴτ' ἐκ Πανὸς εἴθ' Ἑκάτας
ἢ σεμνῶν Κορυβάντων
φοιτᾷς, ἢ ματρὸς ὀρείας.

20 δόξασά που
ἢ Πανὸς ὀργὰς ἢ τινὸς θεῶν μολεῖν.

21 ἀλλ' ἢ Κρονίου Πανὸς τρομερᾷ
μάστιγι φοβεῖ ;

22 Pythagoras prescribes music for mental disorders, Eunapius *Uita philosophorum*, 67 ; and Cælius Aurelianus by his references shows that this was a common remedy in such cases, *De Morbis Chronicis* (*Tardarum Passionum*) VI. Origen, *Aduersus Celsum*, III, x, and Martianus Capella *De Nuptiis Philologiæ et Mercurii* IX, 925, have similar allusions.

23 1 Kings xvi. 14 (A.V. 1 Samuel xvi. 14): "Exagitabat eum [Saul] spiritus nequam a Domino."

24 *Antiquitates Iud.*, VI, viii, 2 ; ii, 2.

25 *La Mystique Divine*, Ribet, II, ix, 4, it is true, speaks of "l'obsession intérieure," but he makes the above distinction, and further says : "L'obsession purement intérieure ne diffère des tentations ordinaires que par la véhémence et la durée."

26 Multæ sunt tentationes eius, et die noctuque uariæ dæmonum insidiæ . . . Quoties illi nudæ mulieres cubanti, quoties esurienti largissimæ apparuere dapes ? *Uita S. Hilarionis.* VII. Migne. vol. XXIII. col. 32.

27 Sustinebat miser diabolus uel mulieris formam noctu induere, feminæque gestus imitari, Antonium ut deciperet. S. Athanasius, *Uita S. Antonii*, V. Migne. vol. XXVI. col. 847.

28 Feast (duplex maius apud Minores), 22 February.

29 It may perhaps not be amiss to point out that S. Margaret before her conversion was by no means the woman of scandalous life so many biographers have painted her.

30 Sectando per cellam orantis et flentis, cantauit [diabolus] turpissimas cantationes, et Christi famulam lacrymantem et se Domino commendantem procaciter inuocabat ad cantum . . . ; tentantem precibus et lacrymis repulit ac eiecit. Bollandists, 22 February. Vol. VI.

31 Ceterum consilium est semper de talibus inuasionibus suspicionem habere, non enim negandum maiorem earum partem esse aut fictiones, aut imaginationes, aut infirmitates, præsertim in mulieribus. *Praxis confessariorum*, n. 120.

32 Sæpissime, quæ putantur dæmonis obsessiones, non sunt nisi morbi naturales, aut Naturales imaginationes, uel etiam inchoata aut perfecta amentia. Quare caute omnino procedendum, usquedum per specialissima signa de obsessione constet. *Theologia mystica*, I. n. 228.

33 *Biblisches Realworterbuch*, Leipsig, 1833.

34 This word is found nowhere else in the New Testament, and wherever it is used in the LXX, it is invariably of the sayings of lying prophets, or those who practised arts forbidden by the Jewish Law. Thus of the witch of Endor (1 Kings (1 Samuel) xxviii. 8) μάντευσαι δή μοι ἐν τῷ ἐγγαστριμύθῳ, and (Ezechiel xiii. 6) βλέποντες ψευδῆ, μαντευόμενοι μάταια.

35 Ordinandi, filii charissimi, in officium Exorcistarum, debitis noscere quid suscipitis. Exorcistam etenim oportet abiicere dæmones ; et dicere populo, ut, qui non communicat, det locum ; et aquam in ministerio fundere. Accipitis itaque potestatem imponendi manum super energumenos, et per

impositionem manuum uestrarum, gratia spiritus sancti, et uerbis exorcismi pelluntur spiritus immundi a corporibus obsessis. Studete igitur, ut, sicut a corporibus aliorum dæmones expellitis, ita a mentibus, et corporibus uestris omnem immunditiam, et nequitiam eiiciatis; ne illis succumbatis, quos ab aliis, uestro ministerio, effugatis. Discite per officium uestrum uitiis imperare; ne in moribus uestris aliquid sui iuris inimicus ualeat uindicare. Tunc etenim recte in aliis dæmonibus imperabitis, cum prius in uobis eorum multimodam nequitiam superatis. Quod nobis Dominus agere concedat per Spiritum suum sanctum.

[36] Accipite, et commendate memoriæ, et habete potestatem imponendi manus super energumenos, siue baptizatos, siue catechumenos.

[37] Deum Patrem omnipotentem, fratres charissimi, supplices deprecamur, ut hos famulos suos bene ✠ dicere dignetur in officium Exorcistarum; ut sint spirituales imperatores, ad abiiciendos dæmones de corporibus obsessis, cum omni nequitia eorum multiformi. Per unigenitum Filium suum Dominum nostrum Iesum Christum, qui cum eo uiuit et regnat in unitate Spiritus sancti Deus, per omnia sæcula sæculorum. *R.* Amen.

[38] Domine sancte, Pater omnipotens, æterne Deus, bene ✠ dicere dignare hos famulos tuos in officium Exorcistarum; ut per impositionem manuum, et oris officium, potestatem, et imperium habeant spiritus immundos coercendi: ut probabiles sint medici Ecclesiæ tuæ, gratia curationum uirtuteque cœlesti confirmati. Per Dominum nostrum Iesum Christum Filium tuum, qui tecum uiuit, et regnat in unitate Spiritus sancti Deus, per omnia sæcula sæculorum. *R.* Amen. *Post hæc, suggerente Archidiacono, redeunt ad loca sua.*

[39] Sulpitius Severus (d. 420–5) in his *Dialogues*, III (II), 6; (Migne, *Patres Latini*, XX, 215) tells us that S. Martin of Tours was wont to cast out demons by prayer alone without the imposition of hands or the use of the formulæ recommended to the clergy. Similar instances occur in the lives of the Saints.

[40] Translated from the *Rituale Romanum*. There are several forms extant, some authorized, but more, perhaps, unauthorized. There is an authorized form in the Greek *Euchologion*. It commences with the Trisagion, and Psalms, *Domine exaudi* (cxlii.), *Dominus regit me* (xxii.), *Dominus illuminatio mea* (xxvi.), *Esurgat Deus* (lxvii.), *Miserere* (lvi.), *Domine ne in furore* (vi.), *Domine exaudi orationem* (ci.). Then follows the Consolatory Canon, with a long Hymn addressed to Our Lord, Our Lady, and All Saints. Next the priest anoints the patient, saying a prayer over him, and so the office closes.

[41] It is also given in the *Horæ Diurnæ O.P.*, Rome, 1903, where an indulgence of 300 days is attached, plenary once a month.

[42] Ab insidiis diaboli, libera nos Domine; Ut Ecclesiam tuam secura tibi facias libertate seruire, te rogamus, audi nos; Ut inimicos sanctæ Ecclesiæ humiliare digneris, te rogamus, audi nos. *Et aspergatur locus aqua benedicta.*

[43] Holy water, the commonest of the sacramentals, is a mixture of exorcised salt and exorcised water.

[44] Of Eastern origin. It should be remembered that the Baptism of Christ in Jordan is commemorated on the Epiphany. In the present Breviary office in Nocturn I the first response for the day, the Octave, and the Sunday within the Octave deal with the Baptism, as does the second response. The antiphon to the Benedictus and the Magnificat antiphon at Second Vespers also make mention of the same mystery. In Rome the Latin rite of the Blessing of the Waters is pontificated by a Cardinal at S. Andrea della Valle on 5 January, about 3.30 p.m., at the church of the Stimmate of S. Francesco at 9.30 a.m. on the Feast itself. On the Vigil the Oriental rite is performed at the Greek church of S. Atanasio, beginning about 3.30 a.m.

[45] See Wilson, *Western Africa;* and the article "Possession diabolique" by Waffelaert in the *Dictionnaire apologétique de la foi catholique*, Paris, 1889. The opinion of the Cistercian Dom Robert de la Trappe (Dr. Pierre-Jean-Corneille Debreyne), who, whilst acknowledging that the demoniac possessions as detailed in the New Testament are *de fide*, supposes that all other cases are to be attributed to fraud or disease, must be severely censured as regrettably rash and even culpable. *Essai sur la théologie morale*, IV. p. 356.

[46] S. Justin Martyr, *Apologia*, VI; *Dialogues*, XXX, LXXXV: Minutius Felix, *Octavius*, XXVII; Origen, *Contra Celsum*, I, 25; VII, 4, 67: Tertullian, *Apologia*, XXII, XXIII.

[47] Paulinus, *Uita Ambrosii*, 28, 43.

[48] S. Gregory of Nyssa, *De Uita Ephraem*

[49] Upon this passage Servatius Galle (1627–1709), a Dutch minister at Haarlem, in his edition of Lactantius, 1660, writes the most absurd note I have ever met with in any commentator.

[50] Published between 304–313. De Labriolle, *Histoire de la Littérature Latine Chrétienne*, p. 272.

[51] A very full and scholarly monograph upon this subject may be recommended: *La Réalité des Apparitions Démoniaques*, by Dom Bernard-Marie Maréchaux, Olivetan, O.S.B., Paris, Téqui, 1899.

[52] It is true that on one occasion S. Maurus, who was with S. Benedict, beheld an apparition, and S. Benedict once enabled a monk to see a similar vision.

[53] One of Sodoma's exquisite frescoes at Monte Oliveto (Siena) depicts an exorcism by S. Benedict.

[54] The letters have been thus translated by Dom Benedict McLaughlin of Ampleforth:

Holy Cross be thou my light,
Put the evil one to flight.
Behind me Satan speedily,
Whisper not vain things to me.
You can give but evil, then
Keep it for yourself. Amen.

[55] All English Benedictine priests hold the special faculty to use this (bestowed 23 February, 1915), and it has also been granted to many others, religious and seculars.

[56] Omnis virtus aduersarii, omnis exercitus diaboli, et omnis incursus, omnis phantasma Satanæ, eradicare et effugare ab his numismatibus . . .

[57] Domine Iesu Christe . . . per hanc tuam sanctissimam passionem humiliter exoro; ut omnes diabolicas insidias et fraudes expellas ab eo, qui nomen sanctum tuum, his litteris ac characteribus a te designatis, deuote inuocauerit, et eum ad salutis portum perducere digneris. Qui uiuis et regnas . . .

[58] The *Rituale Romanum* has "Benedictio Infirmorum cum Ligno SS. Crucis, D.N.J.C. *seu* Signum S. Mauri Abbatis." This is a blessing of the sick with a Relic of the Holy Cross and the invocation of S. Benedict and S. Maurus.

[59] The *Uita S. Mauri* (Mabillon, *Acta S.S. O. S.B.*, I, 274) is ascribed to a companion, the monk Faustus of Monte Cassino. Père Delehaye, in his unfortunate and temerarious work *Légendes Hagiographiques* (translation. London, 1907), indecorously attacks this and treats S. Maurus with scant respect. A worthy defence was made by Adlhoch, *Stud. u. Mittheil.*, 1903, 3; 1906, 185. According to Peter the Deacon he also wrote a *Cantus ad B. Maurum.*

[60] Blessed Victor III. *Dialogues*, I, 2.

[61] Abbé Lebeuf. *Histoire du diocèse de Paris*, V. 129 *sqq.*

[62] Portraits of him are preserved at Rome and Valladolid.

[63] A hearty believer in witchcraft. He had sent at least one witch to the gallows, and another to prison.

[64] Apparently the work of Darrel himself, but in the Huth catalogue (V, 1643) ascribed to James Bamford.

[65] Darrel in his *Detection of that sinnful, shamful, lying, and ridiculous discours of Samuel Harshnet*, 1600, writes: "There is no doubt but that S.H. stand for Samuell Harsnet, chapline to the Bishop of London, but whither he alone, or his lord and hee, have discovered this counterfeyting and cosonage there is the question. Some think the booke to be the Bishop's owne doing: and many thinke it to be the joynt work of them both."

[66] On 10 November, 1629, he was sworn of the Privy Council.

[67] Whence Shakespeare derived the names of various evil spirits whom Edgar mentions in *King Lear.*

[68] I do not conceive that at the present time many, if any, Bishops of the Church of England would license exorcism. Certainly the more scientifically minded and modernistic Lords Spiritual of the Anglican bench have rid themselves of such an idle superstition. How they would explain Our Blessed Lord's words and actions I do not pretend to know, but I suppose that according to their wider knowledge Christ—*sit uenia uerbis*—was mistaken in this as in other particulars.

[69] *Colloquia Mensalia*, passim.

[70] It is difficult to see how the teachings of such a Protestant leader as Gaspar von Schwenckfeld (1489–90—1561) are anything save tantamount to mere personal morality and a vague individual pietism. A critical edition of his numerous works is in course of publication under the editorship of Hartranft, Schlutter, and Johnson: *Corpus Schwenckfeldianorum*, I, Leipzig, 1907.

[71] Parker's *Correspondence*, Parker Society, Cambridge, 1856, pp. 465–6.

[72] By vomiting pins and straws they had made many believe that they were bewitched, but the tricks were soon found out and they were compelled to public penance at S. Paul's. There is a black letter pamphlet *The discloysing of a late counterfeyted possession by the devyl in two maydens within the Citie of London* [1574], which describes this case. See also Holinshed, *Chronicles* (ed. London, 1808), IV, 325, and Stow *Annales*, London, 1631, p. 678. But the fact that there are malingerers does not mean there are none sick.

[73] *Marie Glover's late woefull case. . . . A defence of the truthe against D. J. his scandalous Impugnations*, British Museum, Sloane MSS., 831. Sinclar, *Satan's Invisible World Discovered*, Edinburgh, 1685, Relation XII quotes an account of Mary Glover from Lewis Hughes' *Certaine Grievances* (1641–2); and hence Burton, *The Kingdom of Darkness*, and Hutchinson, *Historical Essay concerning Witchcraft*, both assign a wrong date (1642) to the occurrence.

[74] Enlarged edition, 1720.

[75] *The Other World*, London, 1875, I, pp. 59–69. The incident is narrated by Fortescue Hitchins, *The History of Cornwall*, Helston, 1824, II, pp. 548–51; and also in fuller detail by the Rev. R. S. Hawker, *Footprints of Former Men in Far Cornwall*, London, 1870, who quotes from Ruddle's MS. Diary.

[76] Six miles north of S. Columb and three miles due south from Padstow.

[77] A full and documented account of these strange happenings may be found in *Lucifer, or the True Story of the Famous Diabolic Possession in Alsace*, London, 1922, with the Imprimatur of the Bishop of Brentwood. Compiled from original documents by the abbé Paul Sutter and translated by the Rev. Theophilus Borer.

[78] Jesus . . . comminatus est spiritui immundo, dicens illi: Surde et mute spiritus, Ego præcipio tibi, exi ab eo: et amplius ne introcas in eum. *Euan. sec. Marcum.* IX. 25.

[79] 1726–1755. This great Saint was then Venerable; he was beatified by Leo XIII, 29 January, 1893, and canonized by Pius X, 11 December, 1903. His feast is kept on 16 October.

[80] Peter Paul Stumpf succeeded Andreas Räss as Bishop of Strasburg, 1887–1890.

[81] *Une Possédée Contemporaine* (1834–1914). *Hélène Poirier de Coullons* (*Loiret*). Paris, Téqui, 1924. An ample study, profusely documented, of 517 pages, edited by M. le Chanoine Champault of the diocese of Orleans.

[82] A partir de cette époque, la vie d'Hélène s'écoulera au milieu de souffrances physiques et morales si grandes, que dans sa bouche les plaintes de Job ne seraient point déplacées.

[83] Mr. G. R. S. Mead, however, in this connexion not impertinently recalls the "controlling" of members of the Shaker communities by what purported to be spirits of North American Indians. This was prior to 1848.

[84] Ses souffrances physiques et morales, commencées le 25 mars, 1850, se poursuivirent jusqu'à sa mort, 8 janvier, 1914, soit pendant soixante-quatre ans.

Toutefois les vexations diaboliques cessèrent vers la fin de 1897. Ces vexations durèrent donc près de quarante-sept années, dont six de possession.

[85] Du 25 mars, 1850, au courant de mars, 1868, Hélène *fut seulement obsédée.* Cette *obsession dura donc* 18 *années.* Au bout de ce temps et pendant 13 *mois* elle fut *obsédée et possédée tout ensemble.*

De l'obsession et de la possession elle fut complètement délivrée par les exorcismes officiels, à Orléans, le 19 avril, 1869.

Suivirent quatre mois de tranquillité, jusqu'au recommencement volontaire et généreux de ses peines.

A la fin d'août, 1869, elle accepta de la main de Notre Seigneur les tourments d'une nouvelle obsession et possession afin d'obtenir la conversion du célèbre général Ducrot. La conversion obtenue, elle fut délivrée à Lourdes le 3 septembre, 1875, par les prières des 15,000 pèlerins qui s'y trouvaient réunis. *Obsession et possession renouvelées* avaient duré cinq ans.

Plus jamais, pendant les quarante ans qu'elle avait encore à vivre, elle ne fut possédée ; mais elle continua à être obsédée tantôt plus, tantôt moins. Les souffrances de toutes sortes, qu'elle endura alors, eurent pour but d'obtenir le salut et le triomphe du clergé.

Quant aux raisons et au but des premières persécutions diaboliques qu'elle subit pendant dix-neuf ans et dont elle fut délivrée par les exorcismes officiels, ils sont restés inconnus. *Une Possédée Contemporaine* (1834–1914), pp. 171–2.

[86] A fragment of the soutane of this most holy Pontiff was taken to Hélène and during one of her fits placed upon her forehead. At the contact she cried out : " Le Pape est un saint, oui un grand saint." (The Pope is a Saint, truly a great Saint !)

[87] Pour y être admis, il faut apporter une ou plusiers hosties consacrées, les remettre au démon qui, sous forme corporelle ou visible, préside l'assemblée. Il faut les profaner d'une manière horrible, adorer le démon lui-même et commettre avec lui et les autres sociétaires les actes d'impudicité les plus révoltants. Trois villes : Paris, Rome, et Tours sont les sièges de cette société infernale.

[88] La seconde possession fut plus terrible que la première. 1e : Par la durée ; la première fut de treize mois, la seconde de cinq ans. 2e : La première fut adoucie par de nombreuses consolations surnaturelles ; la seconde très peu. 3e : Les dévices abondèrent dans la première ; dans la seconde les avanies morales l'emportèrent de beaucoup sur les avanies physiques. *Une Possédée Contemporaine* (1834–1914), p. 405.

[89] *Spirit Possession*, Henry M. Hugunin, published in Sycamore, Ill., U.S.A.

[90] One should note the implication that science and faith are opposed. Dr. Wilfred T. Grenfell pointedly comments : " This question seems inept. To me the terms are not in antithesis, i.e. logical *v.* spiritual.

[91] Edited by Huntly Carter. Fisher Unwin, 1920.

[92] Whose contribution, *From Non-Religion to Religion*, opens with the following inepitude : " I think that the renewal of Spiritualism is mainly due to a real increase in our knowledge of psychical facts." This phrase could only have been written by one wholly ignorant of mystical theology, and, it would seem, of historical Christianity.

[93] *Spiritualism, Its Present-Day Meaning*, p. 258.

[94] *Idem*, p. 269.

[95] *Idem*, pp. 270-1.

[96] *Idem*, p. 245.

[97] *Idem*, p. 206.

[98] *Idem*, pp. 206–7.

[99] *Idem*, p. 205. The words are those of Father Bernard Vaughan.

[100] " Seventeen Elementary Facts concerning Spiritualism." *Light*, 21 February, 1925. Here we also have the frank avowal : " Modern Spiritualism is only a revival of phenomena and experiences that were well known in ancient times." It should be remarked that similar phenomena, believed to be a genuine case of haunting, occurred at the house of Mr. Samuel Wesley, at Epworth, Lincolnshire, in 1716, and attracted universal attention. It is

said that the knockings at the house of Parsons, Cock Lane, West Smithfield, in 1760, were proved to be fraud, but I do not know that the case has ever been candidly studied.

101 She took part in a séance on 25 October, 1860, but this seems to have been exceptional.

102 *Washington Daily Star*, 7 March, 1893, quoted in *The Medium and the Daybreak*, 7 April, 1893.

103 In the "educational" primers prepared by certain spiritists for use by children the story of the Fox Sisters is told in glowing colours to a point, but the history of their downfall is suppressed.

104 He died at Bedford, 5 September, 1892. His control was the spirit Imperator, who claimed to be the prophet Malachias. For a very full biography see Arthur Lillie's *Modern Mystics and Modern Magic*. London. 1894.

105 For Mrs. Bassett see *The Medium*, 11 April and 18 April, 1873, pp. 174 and 182; for Miss Showers, *The Medium*, 8 May and 22 May, pp. 294 and 326.

106 *Medium and Daybreak*, 15 November, 1878, p. 730.

107 *L'Eclair*, 6 April, 1909.

108 Dr. Grasset, *L'Occultisme*, pp. 56, *sqq.*; p. 424.

109 *Procès des Spirites*, 8vo. Paris. 1875.

110 *La Revue Spirite* and *L'Echo du Mentalisme*, Nov., 1908.

111 Who apparently believes that Spiritism is authorized by the Scriptures, and that many of the prophets, nay, even Our Divine Lord Himself, were but mediums.

112 *Light*. Saturday, 21 February, 1925, p. 89.

113 Organized in 1882 for the scientific examination of "debatable phenomena."

114 See the Report presented 11 May, 1922, and published by The Magic Circle, Anderton's Hotel, Fleet Street.

115 *The Goligher Circle, May to August*, 1921. Experiences of E. E. Fournier d'Albe, D.SC. London, Watkins, 1922.

116 *The Classification of Psychic Phenomena*, by W. Loftus Hare. *The Occult Review*, July, 1924, p. 38.

117 Her real name appears to be Marthe Béraud. Professor Richet is satisfied that in his experiments with this medium at the Villa Carmen (Algiers) in 1905 genuine materialization was effected.

118 Who, as noted above, specializes in the Ouija-Board and Automatic Writing.

119 He has written such works as *The New Revelation*, and compiled *The Spiritualists' Reader*, "A Collection of Spirit Messages from many sources, specially prepared for Short Readings."

120 In all of whose documents the distinction is clearly drawn between legitimate scientific investigation and superstitious abuses.

CHAPTER VII

The Witch in Dramatic Literature

The English theatre, in common with every other form of the world's drama, had a religious, or even more exactly a liturgical, origin. At the Norman Conquest as the English monasteries began to be filled with cultured French scholars there is evidence that Latin dialogues, the legends of saints and martyrs, something after the fashion of Hrotsvitha's comedies, which we do not imagine to have been a unique phenomenon, found their way here also, and from recitation to the representation of these was an easy and indeed inevitable step. For it is almost impossible to declaim without appropriate action. From the very heart of the liturgy itself arose the Mystery Play.

The method of performing these early English guild plays has been frequently and exactly described, and I would only draw attention to one feature of the movable scaffold which passed from station to station, that is the dark cavern at the side of the last of the three sedes, Hell-mouth. No pains were spared to make this as horrible and realistic as might be. Demons with hideous heads issued from it, whilst ever and anon lurid flames burst forth and dismal cries were heard. Thus the Digby S. Mary Magdalen play has the stage-direction: "a stage, and Helle ondyrneth that stage." At Coventry the Cappers had a "hell-mouth" for the Harrowing of Hell, and the Weavers another for Doomsday. This was provided with fire, a windlass, and a barrel for the earthquake. In the stage-directions to Jordan's Cornish Creation of the World Lucifer descends to hell "apareled fowle wth fyre about hem" and the place is filled with "every degre of devylls of lether and spirytis on cordis." Among the "establies" required for the Rouen play of 1474 was "Enfer fait en maniere d'une grande gueulle se cloant et ouvrant quant besoing en est." The last stage-direction of the

Sponsus, a liturgical play from Limoges,—assigned by M. M. W. Cloetta and G. Paris to the earlier half of the twelfth century—which deals with the Wise and Foolish Virgins runs as follows: "*Modo accipiant eas* [*fatuas uirgines*] *dæmones et præcipitentur in infernum.*"

The Devil himself is one of the most prominent characters in the Mystery, the villain of the piece. So the York cycle commences with *The Creation and the Fall of Lucifer.* Whilst the Angels are singing "Holy, Holy, Holy" before the throne of God, Satan appears exulting in his pride to be cast down speedily into hell whence he howls his complaint beginning "Owte, owte! harrowe!" There is a curious incident in the episode of the Dream of Pilate's wife. Whilst she sleeps Satan whispers in her ear the vision which moves her to try to stay the condemnation of Jesus whereby mankind is to be redeemed. The last play of the York cycle is the *Day of Judgement.*

In like manner the Towneley cycle opens with *The Creation*, and presently we have the stage-direction *hic deus recedit à suo solio & lucifer sedebit in eodem solio.* The scene soon shifts to hell when we hear the demons reproaching Lucifer for his pride. After the creation of Adam and Eve follows Lucifer's lament. In the long episode of *Doomsday* a number of demons appear and are kept inordinately busy.

The Devil was represented as black, with goat's horns, ass's ears, cloven hoofs, and an immense phallus. He is, in fact, the Satyr of the old Dionysiac processions, a nature-spirit, the essence of joyous freedom and unrestrained delight, shameless if you will, for the old Greek knew not shame. He is the figure who danced light-heartedly across the Aristophanaic stage, stark nude in broad midday,[1] animally physical, exuberant, ecstatic, crying aloud the primitive refrain, *Φαλῆς, ἑταῖρε Βακχίου, ξύγκωμε, νυκτεροπλάνητε, μοιχέ, παιδεραστά,* (Phales, boon mate of Bacchus, joyous comrade in the dance, wanton wanderer o' nights, fornicating Phales), in a word he was Paganism incarnate, and Paganism was the Christian's deadliest foe; so they took him, the Bacchic reveller, they smutted him from horn to hoof, and he remained the Christian's deadliest foe, the Devil.[2]

It was long before the phallic demon was banished the stage, for strange as it may seem, positive evidence exists that he was known there as late as Shakespeare's day. In 1620 was published in London by Edward Wright *A Courtly Masque: The Deuice called, The World tost at Tennis.* "As it hath beene diuers times Presented to the Contentment of many Noble and Worthy Spectators: By the Prince his Seruants." It was "Inuented and set downe by Tho: Middleton, Gent. and William Rowley, Gent." The title-page presents a rough engraving of the various characters in this masque, doubtless from a sketch made at the actual performance. Outside the main group stands a hideous black figure "The Diuele," who made his appearance towards the end to take part in the last dance, furnished with horns, hoofs, talons, tail, and a monstrous phallus. It may be remarked that these horns are prominent on the goat-like head (a clear satyr) of the Devil in *Doctor Faustus* as depicted on the title-page of the Marlovian quarto. A phallus, to which reference is made in the text, was also worn by the character dressed up as the monkey (*Bavian*) in the May-dance scene in Shakespeare & Fletcher's *The Two Noble Kinsman*, Act III, 5, 1613. It is worth remembering that troops of phallic demons formed a standing characteristic of the old German carnival comedy. Moreover, several of the grotesque types of the Commedia dell' arte in the second decade of the seventeenth century were traditionally equipped in like manner.[3] That the Devil was so represented in the English theatre is important. It gives us the popular idea of the Prince of Evil, and incidentally throws a side-light upon much of the grotesque and obscene evidence in the contemporary witch-trials.

In Skelton's lost *Nigramansir* one of the stage directions is stated to have been "Enter Balsebub with a beard," no doubt the black vizard with an immense goatish beard familiar to the old religious drama. Presumably the chief use of the Necromancer, who gives his name to this play, was indeed but to speak the Prologue which summons the Devil who buffets and kicks him for his pains. However, we only know the play from Warton, who describes it as having been shown him by William Collins, the poet, at Chichester, about 1759. He says: "It is the Nigramansir, a morall *Enterlude* and a pithie, written by Maister Skelton laureate, and plaid before the King and other estatys at Woodstoke on Palme Sunday. It was printed by Wynkyn de Worde in a thin quarto, in the year 1504. It must have been presented before Henry VII, at the royal manor or palace at Woodstock in Oxfordshire, now destroyed. The characters are a Necromancer or conjurer, the devil, a notary public, Simony, and Philargyria or Avarice. It is partly a satire on some abuses in the Church. . . . The story, or plot, is the trial of Simony and Avarice." Beyond what Warton tells us nothing further is known of the play. Ritson, *Bibliographia Poetica*, 106, declared : " it is utterly incredible that the *Nigramansir* . . . ever existed." It has been shown, too, that Warton as a literary historian is not infrequently suspect, and E. G. Duff, *Hand Lists of English Printers*, can trace no extant copy of this " morall *Enterlude*."

In the English moralities the Devil plays an important part, and, as in their French originals or analogues, he is consistently hampering and opposing the moral purpose or lesson which the action of these compositions is designed to enforce. In the later English plays also which evolved with added regularity from these interludes the Devil is always a popular character. He is generally attended by the Vice, who although in some sort a serving-man or jester in the fiend's employ, devotes his time to twitting, teazing, tormenting, and thwarting his master for the edification, not unmixed with fun, of the audience. In *The Castell of Perseverance* Lucifer appears shouting in good old fashion " Out herowe I rore," just as he was wont to announce himself in the Mysteries, and he is wearing his " devil's array " over the habit of a " prowde galaunt." Wever's *Lusty Juventus* has unmistakable traces of the slime of the evil days of Edward VI, in whose reign it was written, and when the Devil calls Hipocrisy to his aid we are prepared for a flood of empty but bitter abuse which embodies the sour Puritan hatred against the Catholic Church, and towards the end, under the misnomer God's Merciful Promises, we are not surprised to meet a tiresome old gentleman who cantingly expounds the doctrine of Justification by Faith.

In the interlude to which Collier has assigned the name *Mankind* Mischief summons to her aid the fiend Titivillus, who had appeared in the *Judicium* of the Towneley Mysteries. Once the Devil's registrar and tollsman, he is best known as

"Master Lollard." According to a silly old superstition Titivillus was an imp whose business it was to pick up the words any priest might drop and omit whilst saying Mass.

When we pass to the beginnings of the regular drama we find an extremely interesting play that introduces, if not magic, at least fortune-telling, John Lyly's "Pleasant Conceited Comedie" *Mother Bombie*, acted by the children of Paul's and first printed in 1594. Although the plot is of the utmost complexity and artificiality it does not seem to be derived, as are most of Lyly's stories, from any classical or pseudo-classical source, whilst the cunning old woman of Rochester, who supplies the title, has in fact little to say or do, except that her intervention helps to bring about the unravelling of a perfect maze and criss-cross of incidents. When Selena addresses the beldame with "They say, you are a witch," Mother Bombie quickly retorts "They lie, I am a cunning woman," a passage not without significance.

Upon a very different level from Lyly's play stands Marlowe's magnificent drama *The Tragical History of Dr. Faustus*. The legend of a man who sells his soul to the Devil for infinite knowledge and absolute power seems to have crystallized about the sixth century, when the story of *Theophilus* was supposed to have been related in Greek by his pupil Eutychianus. Of course, every warlock had bartered his soul to Satan, and throughout the whole of the Middle Ages judicial records, the courts of the Inquisition, to say nothing of popular knowledge, could have told of a thousand such. But this particular legend seems to have captured the imagination of both Western and Eastern Christendom; it is met with in a variety of forms; it was introduced into the collections of Jacopo à Voragine; it found its way into the minstrel repertory through Rutebeuf, a French *trouvère* of the thirteenth century; it reappeared in early English narrative and in Low-German drama. Icelandic variants of the story have been traced. It was made the subject of a poem by William Forrest, priest and poet, in 1572; and it also formed the material for two seventeenth-century Jesuit "comedies."

That the original Faust was a real personage,[4] a wandering conjurer and medical quack, who was well known in the south-west of the German Empire, as well as in Thuringia,

Saxony, and the adjoining countries somewhere between the years 1510–1540, does not now admit of any serious doubt. Philip Begardi, a physician of Worms, author of an *Index Sanitatis* (1539), mentions this charlatan, many of whose dupes he personally knew. He says that Faust was at one time frequently seen, although of later years nothing had been heard of him. It has indeed been suggested the whole legend originated in the strange history of Pope S. Clement I and his father Faustus, or Faustinianus, as related in the *Recognitions*, which were immensely popular throughout the Middle Ages. But Melanchthon knew a Johannes Faustus born at Knütlingen, in Wurtemberg, not far from his own home, who studied magic at Cracow, and afterwards "roamed about and talked of secret things." There was a doctor Faustus in the early part of the sixteenth century, a friend of Paracelsus and Cornelius Agrippa, a scholar who won an infamous reputation for the practice of necromancy. In 1513 Conrad Mutt, the Humanist, came across a vagabond magician at Erfurt named Georgius Faustus Hermitheus of Heidelberg. Trithemius in 1506, met a Faustus junior whose boast it was that if all the works of Plato and Aristotle were burned he could restore them from memory. It seems probable that it was to the Dr. Faustus, the companion of Paracelsus and Cornelius[5] Agrippa, that the legend became finally and definitely attached. The first literary version of the story was the *Volksbuch*, which was published by Johann Spies in 1587, at Frankfort-on-the-Main, who tells us that he obtained the manuscript " from a good friend at Spier," and it soon afterwards appeared in England as *The History of the Damnable Life and Deserved Death of Dr. John Faustus*, a chap-book to which Marlowe mainly adhered for the incidents in his play. The tragedy was carried across to Germany by the English actors who visited that country in the last years of the sixteenth and the earlier part of the seventeenth century, and thus, while it was itself derived from a German source, it greatly influenced, if it did not actually give rise to, the treatment of the same theme by the German popular drama and puppet-play. These were seldom printed, and usually for the most part extemporized, keeping all the while more or less closely to the theme. Scheible in his *Kloster* (1847), Volume V, gives the excellent Ulm piece, and there are marionette versions edited by W. Hamm (1850; English translation by T. C. H. Hedderwick, 1887), O. Schade (1856), K. Engel (1874), Bielschowsky (1882), and Kralik and Winter (1885).

Lessing projected two presentations of the story, and Klinger worked the subject into a romance, *Fausts Leben, Thaten, und Höllenfahrt* (1791; translated into English by George Barrow in 1826). A bombast tragedy was published by Klingemann in 1815, whilst Lenau issued his epico-dramatic *Faust* in 1836. Heine's ballet *Der Doctor Faust, ein Tanzpoem* appeared in 1851. The libretto for Spohr's opera (1814) was written by Bernard.

Goethe's masterpiece, planned as early as 1774, was given to the world in 1808, but the second part was delayed until 1831.

General evidence points to 1588 as the date of the first production of Marlowe's *Doctor Faustus*, for it seems certain that the ballad of the *Life and Death of Doctor Faustus the great Conjurer*, entered in the Stationers' Register, February, 1589, did not precede but was suggested by the drama. The first extant quarto is 1604, but already it had been subjected to more than one revision. Upon the stage *Doctor Faustus* long remained popular, and in England, at least, however fragmentary Marlowe's tragedy may be it has never been supplemented by any other literary handling of its theme. Old Prynne in his *Histriomastix* (1633) retails an absurd story to the effect that the Devil *in propria persona* " appeared on the stage at the *Belsavage* Playhouse in Queen *Elizabeth's* days " whilst the tragedy was being performed, " the truth of which I have heard from many now alive who well remember it." It was revived after the Restoration, and on Monday, 26 May, 1662, Pepys and his wife witnessed the production at the Red Bull, " but so wretchedly and poorly done that we were sick of it." It was being performed at the Theatre Royal in the autumn of 1675, but no details are recorded. In 1685–6 at Dorset Garden appeared William Mountfort's *The Life and Death of Doctor Faustus, Made into a Farce, with the Humours of Harlequin and Scaramouch*, a queer mixture of Marlowe's scenes with the Italian *commedia dell' arte*. Harlequin was acted by nimble Thomas Jevon, the first English harlequin, and Scaramouch by Antony Leigh, the most whimsical of comedians. At the end of the third act after Faustus has been carried away by Lucifer and Mephistopheles, his body is discovered torn in pieces. Then "Faustus *Limbs come together. A Dance and Song.*" This farce was continually revived with great applause, and during the whole of the eighteenth century Faust was the central figure of pantomime after pantomime. Nearly forty dramatic versions of the Faust legend might be enumerated. Many are wildly romantic and were especially beloved of the minor theatres: such are *Faustus* by G. Soane and D. Terry, produced at Drury Lane 16 May, 1825, with "O" Smith as Mephistopheles; H. P. Grattan's *Faust, or The Demon of the Drachenfels* performed at Sadlers Wells, 5 September, 1842, with Henry Marston, Mephistopheles, T. Lyon, Faust, "the Magician of Wittenberg," Caroline Rankley, Marguerite; T. W. Robertson's *Faust and Marguerite*, played at the Princess's Theatre in April, 1854: some are operatic; the ever-popular *Faust* of Gounod, with libretto by Barbier and Carré, first seen at the Théâtre Lyrique, Paris, in 1859; and Hector Berlioz' *The Damnation of Faust*, which, adapted to the English stage by T. H. Friend, was performed at the Court, Liverpool, 3 February, 1894; many more are burlesques, descendants of the eighteenth-century farces, amongst which may be remembered F. C. Burnard's *Faust and Marguerite*, S. James, 9 July, 1864; C. H. Hazlewood's *Faust: or Marguerite's Mangle*, Britannia Theatre, 25 March, 1867; Byron's *Little Doctor Faust* (1877); *Faust in Three Flashes* (1884); *Faust in Forty Minutes* (1885); and the most famous of all the travesties *Faust Up to Date*, produced at the Gaiety, 30 October, 1888, with E. J. Lonnen as Mephistopheles and Florence St. John as Marguerite. In France the *Faust*—après Goethe—of Theaulou and Gondelier first seen at the Nouveautés, 27 October, 1827, had a great success, and in the following year no less than three pens, Antony Béraud, Charles Nodier, and Merle, combined to produce a *Faust* in three acts, the music of which is by Louis Alexandre Piccini, the grandson of Gluck's famous rival. In 1858 Adolphe Dennery gave the Parisian stage *Faust*, a "drame fantastique" in five acts and sixteen tableaux, a drama of the Grattan school, effective enough in a lurid Sadlers Wells way, which is, at any rate, a vein greater dramatists have exploited with profit and applause.

Of more recent English dramas which have the Faust legend as their theme the most striking is undoubtedly the adaptation by W. G. Wills from the first part of Goethe's tragedy, which was produced at the Lyceum 19 December, 1885, with H. H. Conway as Faust; George Alexander, Valentine; Mrs. Stirling, Martha; Miss Ellen Terry, Margaret; and Henry Irving, Mephistopheles. Not merely in view of the masterpieces of Marlowe and Goethe, but even by the side of theatrical versions of the legend from far lesser men the play itself was naught, a superb pantomime, a thing helped out by a witches' kitchen, by a bacchanalia of demons, by chromo-lithographic effects, by the mechanist and the brushes of Telbin and Hawes Craven, but it was informed throughout and raised to heights of greatness, nay, even to awe and terror, by the genius of Irving as the red-plumed Mephistopheles, that sardonic, weary, restless figure, horribly unreal yet mockingly alert and alive, who dominated the whole.

To attempt a comparison between Marlowe and Goethe were not a little absurd, and it is superfluous to expatiate upon the supreme merits of either masterpiece. In Goethe's mighty and complex work the story is in truth refined away beneath a wealth of immortal philosophy. Marlowe adheres quite simply to the chap-book incidents, and yet in all profane literature I scarcely know words of more shuddering dread and complete agony than Faust's last great speech:

> Ah, Faustus,
> Now hast thou but one bare hour to live.
> And then thou must be damned perpetually!

The scene becomes intolerable. It is almost too painful to be read, too overcharged with hopeless darkness and despair.

As it is in some sense at least akin to the Faust story it may not be impertinent briefly to mention here an early Dutch secular drama, which has been called "one of the gems of Dutch mediæval literature," *A Marvellous History of Mary of Nimmegen, who for more than seven years lived and had ado with the Devil,*[6] printed by William Vorsterman of Antwerp about 1520. It is only necessary to call attention to a few features of the legend. Mary, the niece of the old priest Sir Gysbucht, one night meets the Devil in the shape of *Moonen with the single eye.* He undertakes to teach her all the secrets of necromancy if she will but refrain from crossing herself and change her name to Lena of Gretchen. But Mary, who has had a devotion to our Lady, insists upon retaining at least the M in her new nomenclature, and so becomes Emmekin. "Thus Emma and Moonen lived at Antwerp at the sign of the Golden Tree in the market, where daily of his contrivings were many murders and slayings together with every sort of wickedness." Emma then resolves to visit her uncle, and insists upon Moonen accompanying her to Nimmegen. It is a high holiday and she sees by chance the mystery of *Maskeroon* on a pageant-waggon in a public square. Our Lady is pleading before the throne of God for mankind, and Emma is filled with strange remorse to hear such blessed words. Moonen carries her off, but she falls and is found in a swoon by the old priest, her uncle. No priest of Nimmegen dared shrive her, not even the Bishop of Cologne, and so she journeyed to Rome, where the Holy Father heard her confession and bade her wear in penitence three strong bands of iron fastened upon neck and arms. Thus she returned to Maestricht to the cloister of the Converted Sinners, and there her sorrow was so prevailing and her humility so unfeigned that an Angel in token of Divine forgiveness removed the irons as she slept.

> And go ye to Maestricht, an ye be able
> And in the Converted Sinners shall ye see
> The grave of Emma, and there all three
> The rings be hung above her grave.[7]

Magic and fairy-land loom large in the plays of Robert Greene, whose place in English literature rests at least as much upon his prose-tracts as on his dramas. It seems to me fairly obvious that *The Honourable History of Friar Bacon and Friar Bungay,* which almost certainly dates from 1589, although the first quarto is 1594, was composed owing to the success of Marlowe's *Doctor Faustus.* Greene was not the man to lose an opportunity of exploiting fashion, and with his solid British bent I have no doubt he considered an old English tale of an Oxford magician would be just as effective as imported legends from Frankfort and Wittenberg. To say that the later play is on an entirely different level is not to deny it interest and considerable charm. But in spite of Bacon's avowal

> Thou know'st that I have divèd into hell
> And sought the darkest palaces of fiends;
> That with my magic spells great Belcephon,
> Hath left his lodge and kneeled at my cell,

his sorceries are in lighter vein than those of Faustus; moreover neither his arts nor the magic of Friar Bungay form the essential theme of the play, which also sketches the love of Edward, Prince of Wales (afterwards Edward I) for Margaret, "the fair Maid of Fressingfield." It is true Bacon conjures up spirits enough, and we are shown his study at Brasenose with the episode of the Brazen Head. It may be noted that Miles, Bacon's servant, is exactly the Vice of the Moralities, and at the end he rides off farcically enough on the Devil's back, whilst Bacon announces his intention of spending the remainder of his years in becoming penitence for his necromancy and magic.

In Greene's *Orlando Furioso*, 4to, 1594, which is based on Ariosto, canto XXIII, we meet Melissa, an enchantress: and in *Alphonsus, King of Arragon*, 4to, 1599, which is directly imitative of *Tamburlaine*, a sibyl with the classical name Medea, conjures up Calehas "in a white surplice and cardinal's mitre," and here we also have a Brazen Head through which Mahomet speaks. A far more interesting play is *A Looking Glasse for London and England*, 4to, 1594, an elaborated Mystery upon the history of the prophet Jonah and the repentance of Nineveh. Among the characters are a Good Angel, an Evil Angel, and "one clad in Devil's attire," who is soundly drubbed by Adam the buffoon. In 1598 was published, "As it hath bene sundrie times publikely plaide," *The Scottish Historie of Iames the fourth, slaine at Flodden. Entermixed with a pleasant Comedie, presented by Oboram, King of Fayeries.* But the fairies only appear in a species of prose prologue, and in brief interludes between the acts.

George Peele's charming piece of folk-lore *The Old Wives' Tale* introduces among its quaint commixture of episodes the warlock Sacripant, son of a famous witch Meroe,[8] who has stolen away and keeps under a spell the princess Delia. His power depends upon a light placed in a magic glass which can only be broken under certain conditions. Eventually Sacripant is overcome by the aid of a friendly ghost, Jack, the glass broken, the light extinguished, and the lady restored to her lover and friends.

Other magicians who appear in various dramas of the days of Elizabeth and her immediate successors are Brian Sansfoy in the primitive *Sir Clyomon and Sir Clamydes*, 4to, 1599; the Magician in *The Wars of Cyrus;* Friar Bacon, Friar Bungay, and Jaques Vandermast in Greene's *Friar Bacon and Friar Bungay*, Merlin and Proximus in the pseudo-Shakespearean *The Birth of Merlin*, where the Devil also figures; Ormandini and Argalio in *The Seven Champions of Christendom*, where we likewise have Calib, a witch, her incubus Tarpax, and Suckabus their clownish son; Comus in Milton's masque; Mago the conjurer with his three familiars Eo, Meo, and Areo in Cokain's *Trappolin Creduto Principe*, *Trappolin suppos'd a Prince*, 4to, 1656, excellent light fare, which Nahum Tate turned into *A Duke and No Duke* and produced at Drury Lane in November, 1684, and which in one form or another, sometimes "a comic melodramatic burletta," sometimes a ballad opera, sometimes a farce, was popular until the early decades of the nineteenth century.

Seeing that actors are "the abstracts and brief chronicles of the time," it is not surprising to find that Witchcraft has a very important part in the theatre of Shakespeare. Setting aside such a purely fairy fantasy as *A Midsummer-Night's Dream*, such figures as the "threadbare juggler" Pinch in *The Comedy of Errors*, such scenes as the hobgoblin mask beneath Herne's haunted oak, such references as that to Mother Prat, the old woman of Brainford, who worked "by charms, by spells, by the figure," or the vile abuse by Richard, Duke of Gloucester, of "Edward's wife, that monstrous witch, Consorted with that harlot strumpet Shore," we have one historical drama *King Henry VI*, Part II, in which an incantation scene plays no small part; we have one romantic comedy *The Tempest*, one tragedy *Macbeth*, the very motives and development of which are due to magic and supernatural charms. It must perhaps be remarked that *King Henry VI*, Part I, is defiled by the obscene caricature of S. Joan of Arc, surely the most foul and abominable irreverence that shames English literature. It is too loathsome for words, and I would only point out the enumeration in one scene where various familiars are introduced of the most revolting details of contemporary witch-trials, but to think of such horrors in connexion with S. Joan revolts and sickens the imagination.

In *King Henry VI* (Part II) the Duchess of Gloucester employs John Hume and John Southwell, two priests; Bolingbroke, a conjurer; and Margery Jourdemain, a witch, to raise a spirit who shall reveal the several destinies of the King, and the Dukes of Suffolk and Somerset. The scene is written with extraordinary power and has not a little of awe and terror. Just as the demon is dismissed 'mid thunder and lightning the Duke of York with his guards rush in and arrest the sorcerers. Later the two priests and Bolingbroke are condemned to the gallows, the witch in Smithfield is "burn'd to ashes," whilst the Duchess of Gloucester after three days' public penance is banished for life to the Isle of Man.

The incidents as employed by Shakespeare are fairly correct. It is certain that the Duchess of Gloucester, an ambitious and licentious woman, called to her counsels Margery Jourdemain, commonly known as the Witch of Eye, Roger Bolingbroke an astrologer, Thomas Southwell, Canon of S. Stephen's, a priest named Sir John Hume or Hun, and a certain William Wodham. These persons frequently met in secret, and it was discovered that they had fashioned according to the usual mode a wax image of the King which they melted before a slow fire. Bolingbroke confessed, and Hume also turned informer; and in 1441 Bolingbroke was placed on a high scaffold before Paul's Cross together with a chair curiously carved and painted, found at his lodging, which was supposed to be an instrument of necromancy, and in the presence of Cardinal Beaufort of Winchester, Henry Chicheley, Archbishop of Canterbury, and an imposing array of bishops, he was compelled to make abjuration of his wicked arts. The Duchess of Gloucester, being refused sanctuary at Westminster, was arrested and confined in Leeds Castle, near Maidstone. She was brought to trial with her accomplices in October, when sentence was passed upon her as has been related above. Margery Jourdemain perished at the stake as a witch and relapsed heretic; Thomas Southwell died in prison; and Bolingbroke was hanged at Tyburn, 18 November.

In *The Tempest* Prospero is a philosopher rather than a wizard, and Ariel is a fairy not a familiar. The magic of Prospero is of the intellect, and throughout, Shakespeare is careful to insist upon a certain detachment from human passions and ambitions. His love for Miranda, indeed, is exquisitely portrayed, and once—at the base ingratitude of Caliban—his anger flashes forth, but none the less, albeit superintending the fortunes of those over whom he watches tenderly, and utterly abhorring the thought of revenge, he seems to stand apart like Providence divinely guiding the events to the desired issue of reconciliation and forgiveness. Even so, the situation was delicate to place before an Elizabethan audience, and how nobly and with what art does Shakespeare touch upon Prospero's "rough magic"! In Sycorax we recognize the typical witch, wholly evil, vile, malignant, terrible for mischief, the consort and mistress of devils.

There are few scenes which have so caught the world's fancy as the wild overture to *Macbeth*. In storm and wilderness we are suddenly brought face to face with three mysterious phantasms that ride on the wind and mingle with the mist in thunder, lightning, and in rain. They are not agents of evil, they are evil; nameless, spectral, wholly horrible. And then, after the briefest of intervals, they reappear to relate such exploits as killing swine and begging chestnuts from a sailor's wife, to brag of having secured such talismans as the thumb of a drowned pilot, businesses proper to Mother Demdike or Anne Bishop of Wincanton, Somerset. Can this change have been intentional? I think not, and its very violence and quickness are jarring to a degree. The meeting with Hecate, who is angry, and scolds them "beldames as you are, Saucy and overbold" does not mend matters, and in spite of the horror when the apparitions are evoked, the ingredients of the cauldron, however noisome and hideous, are too material for "A deed without a name." There is a weakness here, and it says much for the genius of the tragedy that this weakness is not obtrusively felt.

Nevertheless it was upon this that the actors seized when for theatrical effect the incantation scenes had to be "written up" by the interpolation of fresh matter. Davenant also in his frankly operatic version of *Macbeth*, produced at Dorset Garden in February, 1672–3 elaborated the witch scenes to an incredible extent, although by ample conveyance from Middleton's *The Witch* together with songs and dances he was merely following theatrical tradition.[9]

There seems no reasonable doubt that *The Witch* is a later play than *Macbeth*, but it is only fair to say that the date of *The Witch* is unknown—it was first printed in 1778 from a manuscript now in the Bodleian—and the date of *Macbeth* (earlier than 1610, probably 1606) is not demonstrably certain. *The Witch* is a good but not a distinguished play. Owing to the incantation scenes and its connexion with *Macbeth* it has acquired an accidental interest, and an enduring reputation. The witches themselves, Hecate and her crew, stand midway between the mystic Norns of the first scene in *Macbeth*, and the miserable hag of Dekker in *The Witch of Edmonton;* they are just a little below the Witches in *Macbeth* as they appear after the opening lines. There is a ghastly fantasy in their revels which is not lessened by the material grossness of Firestone the clown, Hecate's son. They raise "jars, jealousies, strifes, and heart-burning disagreements, like a thick scurf o'er life," and although their figures are often grotesque their power for evil is not to be despised. Much of their jargon, their charms and gaucheries complete, are taken word for word from Reginald Scott's *Discoverie of Witchcraft*, London, 1584.

The village witch, as she appeared to her contemporaries, a filthy old doting crone, hunch-backed, ignorant, malevolent, hateful to God and man, is shown with photographic detail in *The Witch of Edmonton; A known True Story* by Rowley, Dekker, and Ford, produced at the Cockpit in Drury Lane during the autumn or winter of 1621. It seems to have been very popular at the time, and not only was it applauded in the public theatre, but it was presented before King James at Court. It did not, however, find its way into print until as late as 1658.

The trial and execution (19 April, 1621) of Elizabeth Sawyer attracted a considerable amount of attention.

Remarkable numbers of ballads and doggerel songs were made upon the event, detailing her enchantments, how she had blighted standing corn, how a ferret and an owl constantly attended her, and of many demons and familiars who companied with her in the prison. Not only were these ditties trolled out the day of the execution but many were published as broadsides, and sold widely. Accordingly the Newgate Ordinary hastened to pen *The Wonderfull Discoverie of Elizabeth Sawyer, a Witch, Late of Edmonton, Her Conviction, and Condemnation, and Death, Together with the Relation of the Divels Accesse to Her, and Their Conferance Together,* " Written by Henry Goodcole, Minister of the Word of God, and her Continual Visiter in the Gaole of Newgate," Published by Authority, 4to, 1621. This tractate is in the form of a dialogue, question and answer, between Goodcole and the prisoner, who makes ample confession of her crimes.

In some ways *The Witch of Edmonton* is the most interesting and valuable of the witch dramas, because here we have the hag stripped of the least vestige of glamour and romance presented to us in the starkest realism. We see her dwelling apart in a wretched hovel, " shunned and hated like a sickness," miserably poor, buckl'd and bent together, dragging her palsied limbs wearily through the fields, as she clutches her dirty rags round her withered frame. And if she but dare to gather a few dried sticks in a corner she is driven from the spot with hard words and blows. What wonder her mouth is full of cursing and revenge ?

'Tis all one
To be a witch as to be counted one.

Then appears the Black Dog and seals a contract with her blood. She blights the corn and sends a murrain on the cattle of her persecutors; here a horse has the glanders, there a sow casts her farrow; the maid churns butter nine hours and it will not come; above all a farmer's wife, whom she hates, goes mad and dies in frantic agony; mischief and evil run riot through the town. But presently her familiar deserts her, she falls into the hands of human justice, and after due trial is dragged to Tyburn shrieking and crying out in hideous despair. It is a sordid and a terrible, but one cannot doubt, a true picture.

It is obvious that in this drama[10] Frank Thorney, a most

subtle and minute study of weakness and degeneracy, is wholly Ford's. Frank Thorney may be closely paralleled with Giovanni in *'Tis Pity She's a Whore.* Winnifride, too, has all the sentimental charm of Ford's heroines, Annabella and Penthea.

Carter is unmistakably the creation of Dekker. Simon Eyre and Orlando Friscobaldo are the same hearty, bluff, hospitable, essentially honest old fellows. To Dekker also I would assign Mother Sawyer herself.

Rowley's hand is especially discernible in the scenes where Cuddy Banks and the clowns make their appearance.

It may be mentioned that Elizabeth Sawyer figures in Caulfield's *Portraits, Memoirs, and Characters of Remarkable Persons,* 1794; and she is also referred to in Robinson's *History and Antiquities of the Parish of Edmonton* with a woodcut " from a rare print in the collection of W. Beckford, esq."

A second drama which was also actually founded upon a contemporary trial is Heywood and Brome's *The Late Lancashire Witches,* " A Well Received Comedy " produced at the Globe in 1634.[11] In the previous year, 1633, a number of trials for Witchcraft had drawn the attention of all England to Pendle Forest. A boy, by name Edmund Robinson, eleven years of age, who dwelt here with his father, a poor wood-cutter, told a long and detailed story which led to numerous arrests throughout the district. Upon All Saints' Day when gathering " bulloes " in a field he saw two greyhounds, one black, the other brown, each wearing a collar of gold. They fawned upon him, and immediately a hare rose quite near at hand. But the dogs refused to course, whereupon he beat them with a little switch, and the black greyhound started up in the shape of an old woman whom he recognized as Mother Dickenson, a notorious witch, and the other as a little boy whom he did not know. The beldame offered him money, either to buy his silence or as the price of his soul, but he refused. Whereupon taking something like a Bridle " that gingled " from her pocket she threw it over the little boy's head and he became a white horse. Seizing young Robinson in her arms they mounted and were conveyed with the utmost speed to a large house where had assembled some sixty other persons. A bright fire was burning on the hearth with roast meat before it. He was invited to partake of "Flesh and Bread upon a Trencher and Drink in a Glass," which he tasted, but at once rejected. He was next led into an adjoining barn where seven old women were pulling at seven halters that hung from the roof. As they tugged large pieces of meat, butter in lumps, loaves of bread, black puddings, milk, and all manner of rustic dainties fell down into large basins which were placed under the ropes. When the seven hags were tired their places were taken by seven others. But as they were engaged at their extraordinary task their faces seemed so fiendish and their glances were so evil that Robinson took to his heels. He was instantly pursued, and he saw that the foremost of his enemies was a certain Mother Lloynd. But luckily for himself two horsemen, travellers, came up, whereupon the witches vanished. A little later when he was sent in the evening to fetch home two kine, a boy met him in the dusk and fought him, bruising him badly. Looking down he saw that his opponent had a cloven foot, whereupon he ran away, only to meet Mother Lloynd with a lantern in her hand. She drove him back and he was again mauled by the cloven-footed boy.[12]

Such was the story told to the justices and corroborated by Robinson's father. A reign of terror ensued. Mother Dickenson and Mother Lloynd were at once thrown into jail, and in the next few days more than eighteen persons were arrested. The informer and his father netted a good sum by going round from church to church to point out in the congregations persons whom he recognized as having been in the house and barn to which he was led. A little quiet blackmail of the wealthier county families, threats to disclose the presence of various individuals at the witches' feast, brought in several hundreds of pounds.

The trial took place at Lancaster Assizes and seventeen of the accused were incontinently found guilty. But the judge, completely dissatisfied with so fantastic a story, obtained a reprieve. Four of the prisoners were sent up to London, where they were examined by the Court physicians. King Charles himself also questioned one of these poor wretches and, discerning that the whole history was a fraud, forthwith pardoned all who had been involved. Meantime

Dr. John Bridgeman, the Bishop of Chester, had also been holding a special inquiry into the case. Young Robinson was lodged separately, being allowed to hold no communication with his relatives, and when closely interrogated he gave way and confessed that the scare from beginning to end had been manœuvred by his father, who carefully coached him in his lies. In spite of this fiasco the talk did not die down immediately, and there were many who continued to maintain that Mother Dickenson was indeed a witch, however false the evidence on this occasion might be. It must be remembered, moreover, that twenty-two years before, in the very same district, a coven of thirteen witches, of whom the chief was Elizabeth Demdike, had been brought to justice, " at the Assizes and Generall Gaole-Delivery, holden at Lancaster, before Sir Edward Bromley and Sir James Eltham." Old Demdike herself—she was blind and over eighty years of age—died in prison, but ten of the accused were executed, and the trial, which lasted two days, occasioned a tremendous stir.

It seems not at all improbable that Heywood had written a topical play in 1612 dealing with this first sensational prosecution, and that when practically the same events repeated themselves in the same place less than a quarter of a century after he and the ever-ready Brome fashioned anew the old scenes. In the character of the honourable country-gentleman Master Generous, whose wife is discovered to be guilty of Witchcraft, there is something truly noble, and his tender forgiveness of her crime when she repents is touched with the loving pathos that informs *A Woman Kilde with Kindnesse*, whilst his agony at her subsequent relapse is very real, although Heywood has wisely refrained from any attempt to show a broken heart save by a few quite simple but poignant words. The play as a whole is a faithful picture of country life, homely enough, yet not without a certain winsome beauty. The comic episodes are sufficiently broad in their humour ; we have a household turned topsy-turvy by enchantment, a wedding-breakfast bewitched : the kitchen invaded by snakes, bats, frogs, beetles, and hornets, whilst to cap all the unfortunate bridegroom is rendered impotent. In Act II we have the incident of a Boy with a switch (young Edmund Robinson) and the two greyhounds.

Gammer Dickison carries him off against his will "to a brave feast," where we see the witches pulling ropes for food:

Pul for the poultry, foule and fish,
For emptie shall not be a dish.

In Act V the Boy tells Doughty the story of his encounter with the Devil: "He came to thee like a boy, thou sayest, about thine owne bisnesse?" they ask him, and the whole scene meticulously follows the detailed evidence given before the judge at Lancaster. Of the witches, Goody Dickison, Mal Spencer, Mother Hargrave, Granny Johnson, Meg, Mawd, are actual individuals who were accused by Robinson; Mrs. Generous alone is the poet's fiction. When Robin, the blunt serving-man, refuses to saddle the grey gelding she shakes a bridle over his head and using him as a horse makes him carry her to the satanical assembly. There is a mill, which is haunted by spirits in the shape of cats, and here a soldier undertakes to watch. For two nights he is undisturbed, but on the third "*Enter* Mrs. Generous, Mal, *all the* Witches and *their Spirits* (*at severall dores*)." "*The* Spirits *come about him with a dreadfull noise,*" but he beats them thence with his sword, lopping off a tabby's paw in the hurly-burly. In the morning a hand is found, white and shapely, with jewels on the fingers. These Generous recognizes as being his wife's rings, and Mrs. Generous, who is in bed ill, is found to have one hand cut off at the wrist. This seals her fate. All the witches are dragged in and in spite of their charms and bug-words are identified by several witnesses including the boy who "saw them all in the barne together, and many more, at their feast and witchery."

The play was evidently produced just after the Lancaster Assizes, whilst four of the accused were in the Fleet prison, London, for further examination, and the King's pardon had not as yet been pronounced. This is evident from the Epilogue, which commences:

Now while the witches must expect their due,
By lawfull justice, we appeale to you
For favourable censure; what their crime
May bring upon 'em ripens yet of time
Has not reveal'd. Perhaps great mercy may,
After just condemnation, give them day
Of longer life.

It will be convenient to consider in this connexion a drama largely founded upon Heywood and Brome, and produced nearly half a century later at the Duke's House, Dorset Garden, Shadwell's *The Lancashire Witches and Teague o Divelly, the Irish Priest,* which was first seen in the autumn of 1681 (probably in September). The idea of using magic in a play was obviously suggested to Shadwell by his idolized Ben Jonson's *Masque of Queens,* performed at Whitehall, 2 February, 1609. In close imitation of his model Shadwell has further appended copious notes to Acts one, two, three, and five, giving his references for the details of his enchantments. In the Preface (4to, 1682) he naïvely confesses: "For the magical part I had no hopes of equalling *Shakespear* in fancy, who created his witchcraft for the most part out of his own imagination (in which faculty no man ever excell'd him), and therefore I resolved to take mine from authority. And to that end there is not one action in the Play, nay, scarce a word concerning it, but is borrowed from some antient, or modern witchmonger. Which you will find in the notes, wherein I have presented you a great part of the doctrine of witchcraft, believe it who will." And he has indeed copious citations from Vergil, Horace, Ovid, Propertius, Juvenal, Tibullus, Seneca, Tacitus, Lucan, Petronius, Pliny, Apuleius, Aristotle, Theocritus, Lucian, Theophrastus; S. Augustine, S. Thomas Aquinas; Baptista Porta; Ben Jonson (*The Sad Shepherd*); from the *Malleus Maleficarum* of James Sprenger, O.P., and Henry Institor (Heinrich Kramer), written *circa* 1485–89, from Jean Bodin's (1520–96) *La Demonomanie des Sorciers,* 1580; the *Dæmonolatria,* 1595, of Nicolas Remy; *Disquisitionum Magicarum libri six* of Martin Delrio, S.J. (1551–1608); *Historia Rerum Scoticarum,* Paris, 1527, of Hector Boece (1465–1536); *Formicarius,* 5 vols., Douai, 1602, of John Nider, O.P. (1380–1438); *De Præstigiis Dæmonum,* 1563, by the celebrated John Weyer, physician to the Duke of Cleves; *De Gentibus Septentrionalibus,*[13] Rome, 1555, by Olaus Magnus, the famous Archbishop of Upsala; *Discoverie of Witchcraft,* 1584, by Reginald Scot; *Dæmonomagia,* by Philip Ludwig Elich, 1607; *De Strigimagis,* by Sylvester Mazzolini, O.P. (1460–1523), Master of the Sacred Palace and champion of the Holy See against the heresiarch Luther; *Compendium Maleficarum* (Milan,

1608), by Francesco Maria Guazzo of the Congregation of S. Ambrose; *Disputatio de Magis* (Frankfort, 1584), by Johan Georg Godelmann; *Tractatus de Strigiis et Lamiis* of Bartolommeo Spina, O.P.; the *Decretum* (about 1020) of Burchard, Bishop of Worms; the *De Sortilegiis* (Lyons, 1533) of Paolo Grilland; the *De Occulta Philosophia* (Antwerp, 1531) of Cornelius Agrippa; the *Apologie pour tous les Grands Hommes qui ont este faussement supconnez de Magie* (1625) of Gabriel Naudé, librarian to Cardinal Mazarin; *De Subtilitate* (libri XXI, Nuremberg, 1550) of Girolamo Cardano, the famous physician and astrologer; *De magna et occulta Philosophia* of Paracelsus; *IIII Livres des Spectres* (Angers, 1586) by Pierre le Loyer, Sieur de Brosse, of which Shadwell used the English version (1605) *A treatise of Specters . . .* translated by Z. Jones.

It will be seen that no less than forty-one authors, authorities on magic, are quoted by Shadwell in these notes, whilst not infrequently the same author is cited again and again, and extracts of some length, not merely general references, are given.

But for all this parade of learning, perchance because of all this parade of learning, Shadwell's witch scenes are intolerably clumsy, they are gross without being terrible. Shadwell was a clever dramatist, he was able to draw a character, especially a crank, with quite remarkable vigour, and his scenes are a triumph of photographic realism. True, he could not discriminate and select; he threw his world *en masse* higgledy piggledy on to the stage, and as even in the reign of the Merry Monarch there were a few tedious folk about, so now and again—but not very often—one chances upon heavy passages in Shadwell's robust comedies. On the other hand *The Sullen Lovers*, *Epsom Wells*, *The Virtuoso*, *Bury Fair*, *The Squire of Alsatia*, *The Volunteers*, in fact all his native plays, are full of bustle and fun, albeit a trifle riotous and rude as the custom was. Dryden, who very well knew what he was about, for purposes of his own cleverly dubbed Shadwell dull. And dull he has been dubbed ever since by those who have not read him. But Shadwell had not a spark of poetry in his whole fat composition. And so his witches become farcical, yet farcical in a grimy unpleasant way, for we are spared none of the loathsome details of the

Sabbat, and should anyone object, why, there is the authority of Remy or Guazzo, the precise passage from Prierias or Burchard to support the author. Indeed we feel that these witches are very real in spite of their materialism. They present a clear picture of one side of the diabolic cult, however crude and crass.

Even so, these incantation scenes are not, I venture to think, the worst thing in the play. The obscene caricature of the Catholic priest, Teague o Divelly, is frankly disgusting beyond words. He is represented as ignorant, idle, lecherous, a liar, a coward, a buffoon, too simiously cunning to be a fool, too basely mean to be a villain. It is a filthy piece of work, malignant and harmful prepense.[14]

But Shadwell showed scant respect for the Protestants too, since Smerk, Sir Edward Hartfort's chaplain, is described as "foolish, knavish, popish, arrogant, insolent; yet for his interest, slavish."

It is hardly a matter for surprise that after the play had been in the actors' hands about a fortnight complaints from such high quarters were lodged with Charles Killigrew, the Master of the Revels, that he promptly sent for the script, which at first he seems to have passed carelessly enough, and would only allow the rehearsals to proceed on condition that a quantity of scurrilous matter was expunged. Even so the dialogue is sufficiently offensive and profane. There was something like a riot in the theatre at the first performance, and the play was as heartily hissed as it deserved. Yet it managed to make a stand: those were the days of the Third Exclusion Bill and rank disloyalty, but the tide was on the turn, a rebel Parliament had been dissolved on the 28th March, on the 31st of August Stephen College, a perjured fanatic doubly dyed in treason and every conceivable rascality, had met his just reward on the gallows, whilst the atrocious Shaftesbury himself was to be smartly laid by the heels in the November following. That part of the dialogue which was not allowed to be spoken on the stage Shadwell has printed in italic letter,[15] and so we plainly see that the censor was amply justified in his demands. The political satire is of the muddiest; the railing against the Church is lewd and rancorous.

Such success as *The Lancashire Witches* had in the theatre—

and it was not infrequently revived—was wholly due to the mechanist and the scenic effects, the "flyings" of the witches, and the music, this last so prominent a feature that Downes does not hesitate to call it "a kind of Opera."

In Shadwell's Sabbat scenes the Devil himself appears, once in the form of a Buck Goat and once in human shape, whilst his satellites adore him with disgusting ceremonies. The witches are Mother Demdike, Mother Dickenson, Mother Hargrave, Mal Spencer, Madge, and others unnamed.

Elizabeth Demdike and Jennet Hargreaves belonged to the first Lancashire witch-trials, the prosecutions of 1612; Frances Dickenson and Mal Spencer were involved in the Robinson disclosures of 1633; so it is obvious that Shadwell has intermingled the two incidents. In his play we have a coursing scene where the hare suddenly changes to Mother Demdike; the witches raise a storm and carouse in Sir Edward's cellar something after the fashion of Madge Gray, Goody Price, and Goody Jones in *The Ingoldsby Legends;* Mal Spencer bridles Clod, a country yokel, and rides him to a witches' festival, where Madge is admitted to the infernal sisterhood; the witches in the guise of cats beset a number of persons with horrible scratchings and miauling, Tom Shacklehead strikes off a grimalkin's paw and Mother Hargreave's hand is found to be missing: "the cutting off the hand is an old story," says Shadwell in his notes. It will be seen that the later dramatist took many of his incidents from Heywood and Brome, although it is only fair to add that he has also largely drawn from original sources.

Shortly after the Restoration was published a play dealing with one of the most famous of English sibyls, *The Life of Mother Shipton.* "A New Comedy. As it was Acted Nineteen dayes together with great Applause. . . . Written by T[homas] T[homson]." Among the Dramatis Personæ appear Pluto, the King of Hell, with Proserpina, his Queen; Radamon, A chief Spirit; Four other Devils. The scene is "The City of York, or Naseborough Grove in Yorkshire." It is a rough piece of work, largely patched together from Middleton's *A Chaste Maid in Cheapside* and Massinger's *The City Madam,* whilst the episodes in which Mother Shipton is concerned would seem to be founded on one of the many old chap-books that relate her marvellous adventures and prophetic skill. Agatha Shipton (her name is usually given as Ursula) is complaining of her hard lot when she encounters Radamon, a demon who holds high rank in the court of Dis. He arranges to meet her later, and returns to his own place to boast of his success. He reappears to her dressed as a wealthy nobleman; he marries her; and for a while she is seen in great affluence and state. At the commencement of Act III she finds herself in her poor cottage again. As she laments Radamon enters, he informs her who he really is, and bestows upon her magical powers. Her fame spreads far and wide, and as popular story tells, the abbot of Beverley in disguise visits her to make trial of her art. She at once recognizes him, and foretells to his great chagrin the suppression of the monasteries with other events. In the end Mother Shipton outwits and discomforts the devils who attempt to seize her, she is vouchsafed a heavenly vision, and turns to penitence and prayer. The whole thing is a crude enough commixture, of more curiosity than value.

There are some well-written episodes in Nevil Payne's powerful tragedy *The Fatal Jealousie*,[16] produced at Dorset Garden early in August, 1672. Among the characters we have Witch, Aunt of Jasper, the villain of the piece. Jasper, who is servant to Antonio, applies to his aunt to help him in his malignant schemes. At first he believes she is a genuine sorceress, but she disabuses him and frankly acknowledges:

> I can raise no Devils,
> Yet I Confederate with Rogues and Taylors,
> Things that can shape themselves like Elves,
> And Goblins——

Her imps *Ranter* and *Swash*, *Dive*, *Fop*, *Snap*, *Gilt*, and *Picklock*, are slim lads in masquing habits, trained to trickery. None the less they manage an incantation scene to deceive Antonio and persuade him that his wife, Caelia, is false. An "Antick Dance of Devils" which follows is interrupted by the forcible entry of the Watch. The Aunt shows Jasper a secret hiding-place, whereupon he murders her and conceals the body in the hole. He pretends that she was in truth a witch and has vanished by magic. The Captain of the Watch, however, had detected her charlatanry long before, and presently a demon's vizor and a domino are found on the premises.

Later a little boy, who is caught in his devil's attire, confesses the impostures, and trembling adds that in one of their secret chambers they have discovered their mistress's corpse stabbed to death. Finally Jasper is unmasked, and only escapes condign punishment by his dagger. The character of the Witch is not unlike that of Heywood's *Wise Woman of Hogsdon*, although in *The Fatal Jealousie* the events take a tragic and bloody turn. Smith acted Antonio; Mrs. Shadwell, Caelia; Mrs. Norris, the Witch; and Sandford was famous in the rôle of Jasper.

There are incantation scenes in Dryden's tragedies, but these hardly come within our survey, as the magicians are treated romantically, one might even say decoratively, and certainly here no touch of realism is sought or intended. We have the famous episode in *The Indian-Queen* (produced at the Theatre Royal in January, 1663–4), when Zempoalla seeks Ismeron the prophet who raises the God of Dreams to prophesy her destiny;[17] in the fourth act of *Tyrannick Love* (Theatre Royal, June, 1669), the scene is an Indian cave, where at the instigation of Placidius the magician Nigrinus raises a vision of the sleeping S. Catharine, various astral spirits appear only to fly before the descent of Amariel, the Saint's Guardian-Angel; in *Œdipus*, by Dryden and Lee (Dorset Garden, December, 1678), Teresias plays a considerable part, and Act III is mainly concerned with a necromantic spell that raises the ghost of Laius in the depths of a hallowed grove. In *The Duke of Guise*, moreover (Theatre Royal, December, 1682), there is something of real horror in the figures of Malicorne and his familiar Melanax, and the scene[18] when the miserable wizard, whose bond is forfeit, is carried shrieking to endless bale, cannot be read without a shudder even after the last moments of Marlowe's *Faustus*. Act IV of Lee's *Sophonisba* (Theatre Royal, April, 1675) commences with the temple of Bellona, whose priestesses are shown at their dread rites. Cumana is inspired by the divinity, she raves in fury of obsession, there is a dance of spirits, and various visions are evoked.

In Otway's curious rehandling of *Romeo and Juliet* which he Latinized as *The History and Fall of Caius Marius* produced at Dorset Garden in the autumn of 1679, the Syrian witch Martha only appears for a moment to prophesy good fortune to Marius and to introduce a dance of spirits by the waving of her wand.

Charles Davenant's operatic *Circe* (Dorset Garden, March, 1676–7) is an amazing distortion of mythological story. There are songs without number, a dance of magicians, storms, dreams, an apparition of Pluto in a Chariot drawn by Black Horses, but all these are very much of the stage, stagey, born of candle-light and violins, hardly to be endured in cold print. Ragusa, the Sorceress in Tate's *Brutus of Alba : or the Enchanted Lovers* (Dorset Garden, May, 1678) is a far more formidable figure. Tate has managed his magic not without skill, and the conclusion of Act III, an incantation, was deservedly praised by Lamb. Curiously enough the plot of *Brutus of Alba* is the story of Dido and Aeneas, Vergil's names being altered " rather than be guilty of a breach of Modesty," Tate says. But Tate supplied Henry Purcell with the libretto for his opera *Dido and Aeneas*, wherein also witches appear. It must not be forgotten that *Macbeth* was immensely popular throughout the whole of the Restoration period, when, as has been noted above, the witch scenes were elaborated and presented with every resource of scenery, mechanism, dance, song, and meretricious ornament. Revival followed revival, each more decorative than the last, and the theatre was unceasingly thronged. Duffett undertook to burlesque this fashion, which he did in an extraordinary Epilogue to his skit *The Empress of Morocco*, produced at the Theatre Royal in the spring of 1674, but for all his japeries *Macbeth* never waned in public favour.

Spirits in abundance appear in the Earl of Orrery's unpublished tragedy *Zoroastres*,[19] the principal character being described as " King of Persia, the first Magician." He is attended by " several spirits in black with ghastly vizards," and at the end furies and demons arise shaking dark torches at the monarch whom they pull down to hell, the sky raining fire upon them. It was almost certainly never acted, and is the wildest type of transpontine melodrama.

Edward Ravenscroft's " recantation play " *Dame Dobson, or, The Cunning Woman* (produced at Dorset Garden in the early autumn of 1683) is an English version of *La Devineresse ; ou les faux Enchantements* (sometimes known as *Madame Jobin*), a capital comedy by Thomas Corneille and Jean

Donneau de Vise. This French original had been produced in 1679, and both the stage-craft and the adroit way in which the various tricks and conjurations are managed must be allowed to be consummately clever. An English comedy on a similar theme is *The Wise Woman of Hogsdon*, the intricacies of which are a triumph of technique. *La Devineresse* was published in 1680 with a frontispiece picturing a grimalkin, a hand of glory, noxious weeds, two blazing torches and other objects beloved of necromancy. There are, moreover, eight folding plates which embellish the little book, and these have no small interest as they depict scenes in the comedy. But *Dame Dobson* cannot be accounted a play of witchcraft; it is no more than an amusing study of dextrous charlatanry. The protagonist herself[20] is of that immortal sisterhood graced by Heywood's sibyl, of whom it is said "She is a cunning woman, neither hath she her name for nothing, who out of her ignorance can fool so many that think themselves wise."

Mrs. Behn, in her amusing comedy *The Luckey Chance; or, An Alderman's Bargain*, produced at Drury Lane in the late winter of 1686, 4to, 1687, has made some play with pretended magic in the capital scenes where Gayman (Betterton) is secretly brought by the prentice Bredwel (Bowman), disguised as a devil, to the house of Lady Fulbank (Mrs. Barry). Here he is received by Pert, the maid, who is dressed as an old witch, and conducted to his inamorata's embraces. But the whole episode is somewhat farcically treated, and it is, of course, an elaborate masquerade for the sake of an intrigue.[21]

Shadwell in 1681 took Witchcraft seriously, and notwithstanding the half-hearted disclaimer in his address "To the Reader" that prefaces *The Lancashire Witches* I think he was sensible enough to recognize the truth which lies at the core of the matter in spite of the grotesqueness of the formulæ and spells doting hags and warlocks are wont to employ. Witchcraft was still a capital offence when some fifteen years later Congreve lightly laughed it out of court. Foresight (*Love for Love*), "an illiterate old Fellow, peevish and positive, superstitious, and pretending to understand Astrology, Palmistry, Phisiognomy, Omens, Dreams, etc.," is in close confabulation with his young daughter's Nurse, when

Angelica his niece trips in to ask the loan of his coach, her own being out of order. He says no, and presses her to remain at home, muttering to himself some old doggerel which bodes no good to the house if all the womenfolk are gadding abroad. The lady fleers him, twits him with jealousy of his young wife: "Uncle, I'm afraid you are not Lord of the Ascendant, ha! ha! ha!" He is obstinate in his refusal; and she retorts: "I can make Oath of your unlawful Midnight Practices; you and the Old Nurse there. . . . I saw you together, through the Key-hole of the Closet, one Night, like *Saul* and the Witch of *Endor*, turning the Sieve and Sheers, and pricking your Thumbs to write poor innocent Servants' Names in Blood about a little Nutmeg-Grater, which she had forgot in the Caudle-Cup." "Hussy, Cockatrice," storms the old fellow beside himself with rage. Angelica mocks him even more bitterly, accuses him and the Nurse of nourishing a familiar, "a young Devil in the shape of a Tabby-Cat," and with a few last thrusts she departs, trilling with merriment, in a sedan-chair.

To return for a brief space to an earlier generation when it would have hardly been possible, or at least highly inadvisable, to treat Witchcraft in this blithesome mood, of two plays that would almost certainly have been of great interest in this connexion we have only the names, *The Witch of Islington*, acted in 1597, and *The Witch Traveller*, licensed in 1623.

In addition to *The Masque of Queens*, which as has already been noted, served to some extent for a model to Shadwell when inditing his encyclopædic notes on magic, Ben Jonson in that sweet pastoral *The Sad Shepherd* introduces a Scotch witch, Maudlin. The character is drawn with vigorous strokes; realism mingles with romance.

During the quarrel scene which opens *The Alchemist* Face threatens Subtle:

> I'll bring thee, rogue, within
> The statute of sorcerie, *tricesimo tertio*
> Of Harry the Eight.

Dapper the gull asks Subtle for a familiar, as Face explains (I, 2):

> Why, he do's aske one but for cups, and horses,
> A rifling flye: none o' your great familiars.

And later in order to trick him thoroughly Dol Common appears as the "Queene of Faerie." The Queen of Elphin or Elfhame, who is particularly mentioned in the Scotch witch-trials, seems to be identical with the French Reine du Sabbat. In 1670 Jean Weir confessed: "That when she keeped a school at Dalkeith, and teached childering, ane tall woman came to the declarant's hous when the childering were there; and that she had, as appeared to her, ane chyld upon her back, and one or two at her foot; and that the said woman disyred that the declarant should imploy her to spick for her to the Queen of Farie, and strik and battle in her behalf with the said Queen, (which was her own words)."[22]

Beaumont and Fletcher afford us but few instances of witchcraft in the many dramas that conveniently go under their names. We have, it is true, a she-devil, Lucifera, in *The Prophetess*, but the incident is little better than clowning. Delphia herself is a severely classical pythoness far removed from the Sawyers, Demdikes, and Dickensons Sulpitia, in *The Custom of the County* dons a conjurer's robe and at Hippolita's bidding blasts Zenocia almost to death by her spells, but yet she is more bawd than witch. Peter Vecchio in *The Chances*, "a reputed wizard," is as sharp and cozening a practitioner as Forobosco, the mountebank, a petty pilferer, who is exposed and sent to the galleys at the end of *The Fair Maid of the Inn;* or Shirley's Doctor Sharkino[23] whom silly serving-men consult about the loss of silver spoons and napkins; or Tomkis's Albumazar; nay, Jonson's Subtle himself.[24]

In Marston's *Sophonisba* (4to, 1606) appears Erictho, borrowed from Lucan. The Friar in Chapman's *Bassy d'Ambois* (4to, 1607) puts on a magician's habit, and after a sonorous Latin invocation raises the spirits Behemoth and Cartophylax in the presence of Bussy and Tamyra.

A far more interesting drama than these is Shirley's *S. Patrick for Ireland*, acted in Dublin, 1639–40, which has as its theme the conversion of Ireland by S. Patrick and the opposition of the Druids under their leader Archimagus. The character of S. Patrick moves throughout with a quiet spiritual dignity that has true beauty, and the magicians in their baffled potency for evil are only less effective. This drama is a work of stirling merit, to which I would unhesitatingly assign a very high place in Shirley's theatre. We are shown the various attempts upon S. Patrick's life: poison is administered in a cup of wine, the Saint drinks and remains unharmed; Milcho, a great officer, whose servant S. Patrick once was, locks him and his friends in a house and fires it. The Christians pass out unscathed through the flames which devour the incendiary. In the last scene whilst S. Patrick sleeps Archimagus summons a vast number of hideous serpents to devour him, but the Apostle of Ireland wakes, and expels for ever all venomous reptiles from his isle, whereon the earth gapes and swallows the warlock alive. Particularly impressive is the arrival of S. Patrick, when as the King and his two sons, his druids and nobles, are gathered in anxious consultation at the gates of their temple, they see passing in solemn procession through the woods a fair company with gleaming crosses, silken banners, bright tapers and incense, what time the sweet music of a hymn strikes upon the ear:

Post maris sæui fremitus Iernæ
(Nauitas cœlo tremulas beante)
Uidimus gratum iubar enatantes
Littus inaurans.

(Now that we have crossed the fierce waves of ocean to Ireland's coast, and Heaven has blessed its poor fearful wanderers, wending our way along with joy do we see a sunbeam of light gilding these shores.)

As Marlowe's *Dr. Faustus* has already been treated in this connexion it may not be altogether impertinent very briefly to consider some three or four other Elizabethan plays in which the Devil appears among the Dramatis Personæ, even if he act no very prominent part. These for the most part fluctuate between the semi-serious and merest buffoonery. Thus the prologue of *The Merry Devil of Edmonton* (4to, 1608), in which the enchanter Peter Fabell tricks the demon who has come to demand the fulfilment of his contract, is at the opening managed with due decorum, but it soon adopts a lighter, and even trivial, vein. William Rowley's *The Birth of Merlin, or The Childe hath found his Father* (not printed until 1662) is a curious medley of farce and romance, informed with a certain awkward vigour and not wholly destitute of poetry. Dekker's *If it be not good, the Divel is in it* (4to, 1612), which may be traced to the old prose *History of Friar Rush,* depicts the exploits of three lesser fiends who are dispatched to spread their master's kingdom in Naples. It is an unequal play, the satire of which falls very flat, since it is obvious that the poet was not sincere in his extravagant theme.[25]

Ben Jonson's *The Devil is an Ass*, acted in 1616, is wholly comic. Pug, "the less devil," who visits the earth, and engages himself as servant to a Norfolk squire, Fabian Fitzdottrel, is hopelessly outwitted on every occasion by the cunning of mere mortals. Eventually he finds himself lodged in Newgate, and in imminent danger of the gallows were he not rescued by the Vice, Iniquity, by whom he is carried off rejoicing to the nether regions. His fate may be compared with that of Roderigo in Wilson's excellent comedy *Belphegor: or, The Marriage of the Devil* (produced at Dorset Garden in the summer of 1690), who with his two attendant devils flies back to his native hell to escape the woes of earth.

In *The Devil's Charter*, however, by Barnaby Barnes (1607), we have what is undoubtedly a perfectly serious tragedy, which if not exactly modelled upon, at least owes many hints to Marlowe's *Faustus*. It is flamboyant melodrama and wildly unhistorical throughout, a very tophet of infernal horror. The chief character is a loathsome caricature of Pope Alexander VI,[26] and, as we might expect, all the lies and libels of Renaissance satirists and Protestant pamphleteers are heaped together to portray an impossible monster of lust and crime. The filthiest scandals of Burchard, Sanudo, Giustiniani, Filippo Nerli, Guicciardini, Paolo Giovio, Sannazzaro and the Neapolitans, have been employed with one might almost say a scrupulous conscientiousness. The black art, in particular, occupies a very prominent place in these lurid scenes. Alexander has signed a bond with a demon Astaroth, and it is to this contract that all his success is ascribed. In Act IV there is a long incantation when the Pope puts on his magical robes, takes his rod and pentacle, and standing within the circle he has traced conjures in strange terms, commencing a Latin exorcism which tails off into mere gibberish. Various devils appear, and he is shown a vision of Gandia's murder by Cæsar,[27] with other atrocities. At the climax of the piece we have the banquet with Cardinal

Adrian of Corneto, and whilst the guests talk "The Devill commeth and changeth the Popes bottles." The Borgias are poisoned, and in a far too protracted "Scena Ultima" Alexander discourses and disputes frantically with the demons who appear to mock and torment him. There is the old device of an ambiguous contract; presently a "Devil like a Poast" enters winding a horn to summon the unhappy wretch, who raves and shrieks out meaningless ejaculations as he is dragged away amid thunder and lightning. This sort of thing pandered to the most brutalized appetites of the groundlings, and *The Devil's Charter* may be summed up as a disgusting burlesque not without its quota of vile stuff that is so repulsive as to be physically sickening.

Upon a careful consideration of those seventeenth-century plays which have Witchcraft as their main theme, and leaving on one side, for our purpose, the essentially romantic treatment of the subject, however realistic some details of the picture may be, it is, I think, beyond dispute that *The Witch of Edmonton* in the figure of Mother Sawyer offers us the best contemporary illustration of the Elizabethan witch. The drama itself is one of no ordinary merit and power, whilst the understanding and restraint which set the play apart from its fellows also raises it to the level of genuine tragedy. It should be noticed that we see a witch, so to speak, in the process of making. Mother Sawyer is in truth the victim of the prejudices of the village hinds and ignorant yokels. When she first appears it is merely as a poor old crone driven to desperation by her brutal neighbours; the farmers declare she is a witch, and at length persecution makes her one. She is malignant and evil enough once the compact with the demon has been confirmed; she longs from the first to be revenged upon her enemies and mutters to herself "by what art May the thing called Familiar be purchased?" But, in one sense, she is urged and hounded to her destiny, and the authors, although never doubting her compact with the powers of darkness, her vile and poisonous life, show a detached but very real sympathy for her. It is this touch of humanity, the pathos and pity of the poor old hag, repulsive, wicked, and baleful as she may be, which must place *The Witch of Edmonton* in my opinion among the greatest and most moving of all Elizabethan plays.

It is no pleasant task to turn now to the theatre of the eighteenth century in this connexion. The witch became degraded; she was comic, burlesqued, buffooned; a mere property for a Christmas pantomime: *Harlequin Mother Bunch, Mother Goose, Harlequin Dame Trot,* Charles Dibdin's *The Lancashire Witches, or The Distresses of Harlequin*[28] whose tinsel, music, and mummery drew all the macaronis and cyprians in London to the Circus during the winter of 1782–3.

Some subtle premonition of the great success of Harrison Ainsworth's powerful story *The Lancashire Witches*—for this and the macabre *Rookwood* are probably the best of the work of a talented writer now unduly depreciated and decried—seems to have suggested to the prolific Edward Fitzball his "Legendary Drama in Three Acts," *The Lancashire Witches, A Romance of Pendle Forest,* produced at the Adelphi Theatre, 3 January, 1848. It was quick work, for it was only a month before, 3 December, 1847, that Ainsworth, writing to his friend Crossley of Manchester, states that he has accepted the liberal offer of the *Sunday Times*—£1000 and the copyright to revert to the author on the completion of the work—that his new romance *The Lancashire Witches* should make its appearance as a serial in the paper. He had already sketched out the plan, and he must have given Fitzball an idea of this, or at least have allowed the dramatist the use of some few rough notes, for although the play and the novel have little, one might say nothing essential, in common, the chief character in the theatre, Bess of the Woods, "140 years old, formerly Abbess of S. Magdalen's, doomed for her crimes to an unearthly age," is none other than the anchoress Isolde de Heton.[29] The fourth scene of the second act presents the ruins of Whalley Abbey by moonlight. During an incantation the picture gradually changes; the broken arches form themselves into perfect masonry; the ivy disappears from the windows to show the ruby and gold of coloured glass; the decaying altar glitters with piled plate and the gleam of myriad tapers. A choir of nuns rises from the grave to dance with spectral gallants. Among the votaries are Nutter, Demdike, and Chattox "Three Weird Sisters, doomed for their frailties to become Witches." But they utter no word, and have no part save this in the action.

This scene must have proved extraordinarily effective upon the stage. It owes much to the haunted convent in Meyerbeer's *Robert le Diable*, produced at the Académie Royale in November, 1831, and given in a piratical form both at Drury Lane and Covent Garden within a few weeks. Nor is it comparable to its original. In Fitzball's melodrama O. Smith appeared as Gipsy Dallan, a new character; and Miss Faucit (Mrs. Bland) as Bess of the Woods. The play, for what it is, a luridly theatrical and Surrey-side sensation, has merit; but to speak of it in the same breath as Middleton or even as Barnes would be absurd.

Shelley's genius has with wondrous beauty translated for us scenes from Calderon's *El Magico Prodigioso*, one of the loveliest songs of the Spanish nightingale. On another plane, admittedly, but yet, I think, far from lacking a simple comeliness of its own and surely not without most poignant pathos, is Longfellow's New England Tragedy *Giles Corey of the Salem Farms.*[30] The honest sincerity of Cotton Mather, the bluff irascible heartiness of Corey himself, the inopportune scepticism of his wife—which to many would seem sound common sense—the hysteria of Mary Walcot, the villainy of John Gloyd, all these are sketched with extraordinary power, a few quiet telling touches which make each character, individual, alert, alive.

In the French theatre we have an early fourteenth-century *Miracle de Nostre Dame de Robert le Dyable*, and in 1505 was acted *Le mystère du Chevalier qui donna sa femme au Diable*, à dix personnages. As one might well expect during the long classical period of the drama Witchcraft could have found no place in the scenes of the French dramatists. It would have been altogether too wild, too monstrous a fantasy. And so it is not until the 24 floréal, An XIII (11 June, 1805) that a play which interweaves sorcery as its theme is seen at the Théâtre français, when *Les Templiers* of Raynouard was given there. A few years later *Le Vampire*, a thrilling melodrama by Charles Nodier and Carmouche, produced on 13 August, 1820, was to draw all idle Paris to the Porte-Saint-Martin. In 1821 two facile writers quick to gauge the public appetite, Frédéric Dupetit-Méré and Victor Ducagne, found some favour with *La Sorcière, ou l'Orphelin écossais.* Alexandre Dumas, and one of his many ghosts Auguste

Maquet, collaborated (if one may use the term) in a grandiose five-act drama *Urbain Grandier*, 1850. *La Sorcière Canidie*, a one-act play by Aurélien Vivie, produced at Bordeaux in 1888 is of little account. *La Reine de l'Esprit* (1891) of Maurice Pottecher is founded to some extent on the *Comte de Gabalis*, whilst the same author's three-act *Chacun cherche son Trésor*, "histoire des sorciers" (1899) was not a little helped by the music of Lucien Michelet. There are many excuses for passing over with a mere mention *Les Noces de Sathan* (1892), a "drama ésoterique," by Jules Bois, and *Les Basques ou la Sorcière d'Espelette*, a lyric drama in three acts by Loquin and Mégret de Belligny, produced at Bordeaux in 1892, has an interest which is almost purely local. Alphonse Tavan's *Les Mases* (sorciers), a legendary drama of five acts of alternating prose and verse seen in 1897 was helped out by every theatrical resource, a ballet, chorus, mechanical effects, and confident advertisement. Serge Basset's *Vers le Sabbat* "évocation de sorcellerie en un acte" which appeared in the same year need not be seriously considered. Nor does an elaborate episode "Le Sabbat et la Herse Infernale," wherein Mons. Benglia appeared as Satan, that was seen in the Folies Bergère revue, *Un Soir de Folie*, 1925–6, call for more than the briefest passing mention.

In more recent days Victor Sardou's *La Sorcière* is a violent, but effective, melodrama. Produced at the Théâtre Sarah-Bernhardt, 15 December, 1903, with De Max as Cardinal Ximenes and Sarah Bernhardt as the moresque Zoraya, it obtained a not undeserved success. The locale of the tragedy is Toledo, anno domini 1506; Act IV, the Inquisition scene; and Act V, the square before the Cathedral with the grim pyre ready for the torch, were—owing to the genius of a great actress—truly harrowing. Of course it is very flamboyant, very unbalanced, very unhistorical, but in its gaudy theatrical way—all the old tricks are there—*La Sorcière* had an exciting thrill for those who were content to be unsophisticated awhile.

John Masefield's adaptation from the Norwegian of Wiers-Jennsen, *The Witch*,[31] a drama in four acts, is a very different thing. Here we have psychology comparable to that of Dekker and Ford. Nor will the performances of Miss Janet

Achurch as Merete Beyer and Miss Lillah McCarthy as Anne Pedersdotter easily be forgotten. As a picture of the horror of Witchcraft in cold Scandinavia, the gloom and depression of formidable fanaticism engendered by Lutheran dogma and discipline with the shadow of destiny lowering implacably over all, this is probably the finest piece of work dealing in domestic fashion with the warlock and the sorceress that has been seen on the English stage since the reign of wise King James three hundred years ago.

NOTES TO CHAPTER VII

1 The *Floralia*, the most wanton of Roman festivals, commenced on the fourth day before the Kalends of May, and during these celebrations the spectators insisted that the *mimæ* should play naked, " agebantur [*Floralia*] a meretricibus ueste exutis omni cum uerborum licentia, motuumque obscænitate," says the old commentator on Martial I, 1. "Lasciui Floralia laeta theatri" Ausonius names them, *De Feriis Romanis*, 25. Lactantius, *De Institutionibus Diuinis*, I, 20, writes: " Celebrantur ergo illi ludi cum omni lasciuia, conuenientes memoriæ meretricis. Nam praeter uerborum licentiam, quibus obscænitas omnis effunditur; exuuntur etiam uestibus populo flagitante meretrices; quæ tunc mimorum funguntur officio; et in conspectu populi usque ad satietatem impudicorum luminum cum pudendis motibus detinentur." Both S. Augustine and Arnobius reprehend the lewdness of these naked dances. At Sens during the Feast of Fools, when every licence prevailed, men were led in procession *nudi*. Warton (*History of English Poetry*, by T. Warton, edited by W. C. Hazlitt, 4 vols., 1871), II, 223, states that in the Mystery Plays " Adam and Eve are both exhibited on the stage naked, and conversing about their nakedness; this very pertinently introduces the next scene, in which they have coverings of fig-leaves." In a stage-direction of the Chester Plays we find: " Statim nudi sunt. . . . Tunc Adam et Eua cooperiant genitalia sua cum foliis." Chambers, *The Mediæval Stage*, II, 143, doubts whether the players were actually nude, and suggests a suit of white leather. Warton, however, is probably right.

2 Phales was an early deity, very similar to Priapus, and closely associated with the Bacchic mysteries. For the refrain see *The Acharnians*, 263–265.

3 See Callot's series of character-etchings, *I Balli di Sfessanio*.

4 Not to be confused with the printer Fust, as was at one time frequently supposed.

5 In Marlowe's play Faust welcomes " German Valdes and Cornelius." Who Valdes is has not been satisfactorily explained. The suggestion of Dr. Havelock Ellis that Paracelsus seems intended is no doubt correct.

6 Translated from the Middle Dutch by Harry Morgan Ayres, with an Introduction by Adriaan J. Barnouw. *The Dutch Library*, The Hague: Martinus Nijhoff. 1924.

7 The International Theatre Society gave a private subscription performance of *Mary of Nimmegen* at Maskelyne's Theatre on Sunday, 22 February, 1925. But such a play, presenting crowded scenes of burgher life, the streets, the market-place, to be effective demands a large stage and costly production.

8 Meroe is the hag " saga et diuina " in Apuleius, *Metamorphoseon*, I.

9 *Macbeth* was tinkered at almost from the first. Upon the revival of the play immediately after the Restoration the witch scenes were given great theatrical prominence. 7 January, 1667, Pepys declared himself highly delighted with the " divertissement, though it be a deep tragedy."

10 *The Witch of Edmonton* was revived under my direction for two performances at the Lyric Theatre, Hammersmith, 24 and 26 April, 1921.

Sybil Thorndike played the Witch, Russell Thorndike, the Familiar; Ion Swinley, Frank Thorney; Edith Evans, Ann Ratcliffe; and Frank Cochrane, Cuddy Banks.

[11] 4to 1634: *Stationers' Register*, 28 October.

[12] In a famous Scotch trial for witchcraft, 1661, Jonet Watson of Dalkeith confessed "that the Deivill apeired vnto her in the liknes of ane prettie boy, in grein clothes."

[13] Liber III. *De Magis et Maleficis Finnorum.*

[14] Tegue o' Divelly was acted by Antony Leigh, the most famous comedian of his day, and an intimate friend of Shadwell.

[15] Curiously enough Halliwell in *The Poetry of Witchcraft*, a private reprint of Heywood and Shadwell's plays, 80 copies only, 1853, has not reproduced the italic letter but gives all the dialogue in roman to the great detriment of this edition.

[16] Licensed for printing 2 November, 1672, and published quarto with date 1673.

[17] At a later revival Ismeron's recitative "Ye twice ten hundred Deities" was set by Purcell.

[18] Dryden's. He wrote the first scene of the first act, the whole of the fourth act, rather more than one-half of act five, and Lee is responsible for the rest of the tragedy.

[19] For a full analysis and critical examination of *Zoroastres* see my article in the *Modern Language Review*, XII, Jan., 1917.

[20] The title-rôle Dame Dobson was played by Mrs. Corey, a mistress of broad comedy, who was much admired for her humour by Samuel Pepys.

[21] Mrs. Behn owes a hint to Shirley's *The Lady of Pleasure*, licensed by Sir Henry Herbert, 15 October, 1635; 4to. 1637. It must be confessed that she has managed her scenes with more wit and spirit than the older dramatist, whose charming verse is perhaps too seriously poetical for the actual situation.

[22] George Sinclar, *Satan's Invisible World Discovered*, 1685. Reprint, Edinburgh, 1871. Supplement, I, p. xii.

[23] *The Maid's Revenge*, acted 1626, printed 1639.

[24] Compare Mopus in Wilson's *The Cheats* (acted in 1662); Stargaze in *The City Madam*; Rusee, Norbrett, and their accomplices in *Rollo*; Iacchelino in Ariosto's *Il Negromante*; and a score beside.

[25] Sir Adolphus Ward, *English Dramatic Literature*, 1899, II, 465, says that Langbaine wrongly supposed the source of this play to be "Machiavelli's celebrated *Novella* on the marriage of Belphegor." But this is hardly correct. Langbaine wrote: "The beginning of his Play seems to be writ in imitation of *Matchiavel's* Novel of *Belphegor*: where *Pluto* summons the Devils to Councel."

[26] For a fitting account of Alexander VI see *Le Pape Alexandre VI et les Borgia*, Paris, 1870, by Père Ollivier, O.P.; also Leonetti *Papa Alessandro VI secondo documenti e carteggi del tempo*, 3 vols., Bologna, 1880. *Chronicles of the House of Borgia*, by Frederick, Baron Corvo, 1901, may be studied with profit. Monsignor de Roo's *Material for a History of Pope Alexander VI*, 5 vols., Bruges, 1924, is of the greatest value, and completely authoritative.

[27] The murderer of the Duke of Gandia is unknown to history, if not to historians.

[28] The songs only are printed, 8vo, 1783.

[29] Fosbrooke, *British Monachism*, says that in the reign of Henry VI one Isolde de Heton petitioned the King to let her be admitted as an anchoress in the Abbey of Whalley. But afterwards she left the enclosure and broke her vows, whereupon the King dissolved the hermitage.

[30] The incidents are historically correct. See Cotton Mather's *Wonders of the Invisible World*. Corey refusing to plead was pressed to death.

[31] Originally produced 10 October, 1910, at the Royalty, Glasgow: in London, 31 January, 1911, at the Court. Revived at the Court, 29 October, 1913, when it ran for a month, and was afterwards included in the subsequent three weeks' repertory season.

BIBLIOGRAPHY

This Bibliography does not aim at anything beyond presenting a brief and convenient hand-list of some of the more important books upon Witchcraft. It does not even purport to give all those monographs to which reference is made in the body of this study. A large number of books I have thought it superfluous to include. Thus I have omitted general works of reference such as the *Encyclopædia Britannica*, Du Cange's *Glossarium ad scriptores mediæ et infimæ latinitatis*, Dugdale's *Monasticon*; daily companions such as the Missal, the Breviary, the Bible; Homer, Vergil, Horace, Ovid, Petronius, Lucan; Shakespeare, Marlowe, Ford, Dryden, Burton's *Anatomy of Melancholy*, and English classics; those histories which are on every library shelf, Gibbon, Lingard, Ranke; and such histories as the *Cambridge Modern History*.

On the other hand, I have of purpose included various books which may not seem at first sight to have much connexion with Witchcraft, although they are, as a matter of fact, by no means impertinent. In order to appreciate this vast subject in all its bearings, even the desultory or amateur investigator should at least be fairly grounded in theology, philosophy, and psychology. The student must be a capable theologian.

I have devoted some particular attention to the works of the demonologists, now almost universally neglected, but a close study of which is essential to the understanding of occultism and the appreciation of the grave dangers that may lurk there.

I am only too conscious of the plentiful lacunæ in this Bibliography. However, to attempt anything like a complete catalogue—if, indeed, it were possible to essay so illimitable a task—would involve the listing of very many thousands of books, and would itself require no inconsiderable a tale of volumes.

I need hardly point out that side by side with works of the highest importance it has been found necessary to include a few of no great value, which yet have their use to illustrate some one point or special phase.

GENERAL

CAILLET, ALBERT L. *Manuel bibliographique des sciences psychiques ou occultes, science des Mages, hermétique, astrologie, Kabbale, Franc-maçonnerie, médecine ancienne, mesmérisme, sorcellerie, singularités, etc.* 3 vols. Paris, 1913.

GRÆSSE, JOHAN GEORG THEODOR. *Bibliotheca magica et pneumatica.* Leipzig, 1843. (In spite of obvious defects a very valuable bibliography.)

YVE-PLESSIS, R. *Bibliographie française de la sorcellerie.* Paris, 1900. (An immense and exhaustive work on French books.)

AARON THE GREEK [Simon Blocquel]. *La Magie rouge.* Paris, 1821.

ABNER, THEODORE. *Les apparitions du Diable.* Brussels, 1879.

ACONTIUS. *Stratagemata Satanæ.* Libri VIII. Basle, 1565.

Acta Sanctorum. Par les Bollandistes. Antwerp, Tongerloo, Brussels, 1644 *sqq.* Reprinted, Paris, 1863 *sqq.*

ADHÉMAR DE CHABANNES. *Chronicle :* in *Monumenta Germaniæ historica.* Ed. G. A. Pertz, etc. Vol. IV.

AGOBARD, S. *Opera omnia.* Migne, *Patrologia latina.* Vol. CIV.

AGRIPPA, HEINRICH CORNELIUS *La philosophie occulte de Henr. Corn. Agrippa . . . traduite du latin* [par A. Levasseur]. 2 vols. Hague, 1727.

Œuvres magiques . . . mises en français par Pierre d'Aban. Rome, 1744. (Of the last rarity. There are other editions, Liège, 1788 ; Rome, 1800 ; Rome, 1744 (*circa* 1830) ; but all these are extremely scarce.)

ALANUS (Alain de Lille). *Aduersus hæreticos et Waldenses.* Ed. J. Masson. Paris, 1612.

ALANUS, HENRICUS. *Ciceronis de Divinatione et de Fato.* 1839.

ALBERT, LE PETIT. *Alberti Parui Lucii libellus de mirabilibus Naturæ arcanis.* (This treatise which tells how to confect philtres, make talismans, use the hand of glory, discover treasures, etc., has been very frequently translated into French, generally under the running title *Les secrets merveilleux de la magie naturelle et cabalistique. . . .*)

BL. ALBERTUS MAGNUS, O.P. *Opera omnia.* Ed. Father Peter Jammy, O.P. 21 vols. Lyons, 1651, etc.

De alchimia. (This treatise is said to be doubtful.).

De secretis mulierum. (This work is certainly not from the pen of the great Dominican doctor, to whom, however, it was universally ascribed. There are a vast number of editions, and translations, especially into French. *Les secretz des femmes et homes . . . stampato in Torino par Pietro Ranot,* N.D. *circa* 1540. *Les secrets admirables du grand Albert.* Paris, 1895.)

Commentaria. Lib. IV, dist. 34. *An maleficii impedimento aliquis potest impediri a potentia cocundi.* (*Nœud de l'aiguillette.*)

ALEXANDER III, POPE. *Epistolæ* apud *Regesta R. R. Pontificum.* Nos. 10, 584–14, 424. Ed. Jaffé. And Löwenfeld's *Epistolæ Pontif. Rom. ineditæ.* Leipzig, 1885.

ALEXIS. *Secreti del reverendo Donno Alessio Piemontese.* Venice, 1555. (Attributed by Girolamo Muzio to the alchemist Girolamo Ruscelli.)

ALLARD, PAUL. *Histoire des persécutions.* 5 vols. Paris, 1892.

Julien l'Apostat. 3 vols. Paris, 1900.

ALPHONSUS LIGUORI, S. *Theologia Moralis.* 9 vols. Malines, 1828. Also ed. P. Gaudé, C. SS. R. Rome, 1905.

ALVARO, PELAYO. *De Planctu Ecclesiæ.* Venice, 1560.

AMBROISE DA VIGNATE (c. 1408). *Tractatus de Hæreticis.* Rome, 1581.

AMBROSE, S. *Opera omnia.* Ed. Paolo Angelo Ballerini. 6 vols. Folio. Milan, 1875.

ANANIA, GIOVANNI LORENZO. *De Natura Dæmonum.* Apud Vol. II. *Malleus Maleficarum.* 1669.

Anonymi Gesta Francorum et Aliorum Hierosolymitanorum. Oxford.

ANTONELLI, G. PROF. *Lo spiritismo. Fede e Scienza,* II. 11, 12. Rome.

ANTONINUS, O. P. S. *Confessionale.* Florence, 1496.

ANTONIO A SPIRITU SANCTO, O.D.C. *Directorium Mysticum.* Paris, 1904.

AREMI (LE SAGE). *Secrets de vieux Druide.* Lille, 1840.

ARETINI, ANGELO. *Tractatus de maleficiis.* 1521.

ARIES, MARTIN. *De superstitionibus maleficorum.* Rome, 1559.

ARIMINENSIS, AUGUSTINUS. *Additiones in Angeli Aretini Tractatum de maleficiis.* Milan, 1514.

ARNAULD DE VILLENEUVE. *De Maleficiis.* Lyons, 1509.

ARNOULD, ARTHUR. *Histoire de l'Inquisition.* Paris, 1869.

AROUX. *Mystères de la Chevalerie et de l'amour platonique.* 1857–8.

ARPE (PETR. FRID.). *De Prodigiosis Naturæ et Artis Operibus Talismanes et Amuleta.* Hamburg, 1717.

ATHANASIUS, S. *Opera omnia.* Migne, *Pat. Graeci.* Vols. XXIII–XXVIII.

ATWOOD, M. A. *A Suggestive Inquiry into the Hermetic Mystery.*

AUGUSTINE, S. *Opera omnia.* Migne. *Pat. Lat.* Vols. XXXIX–XLVII.

De Ciuitate Dei. Ed. J. E. C. Welldon, D.D., Dean of Durham. 2 vols. 1924. (The introduction and appendices must be used with caution.)

Confessiones. Ed. P. Knöll. *Corpus Scriptorum Eccl. Latinorum* (Vienna.) XXXIII.

D'AUTUN, JACQUES. *L'Incredulité savante.* Lyons, 1674.

D'AVALLON, ANDRÉ, ET CONDIS. *Dictionnaire de droit canonique.*

AZPILCEUTA, MARTIN. *Opera omnia.* 3 vols. Lyons, 1589.

BACO, R. *De secretis operibus magiæ.* Paris, 1542.

BACON, ROGER. *Epistola de secretis operibus.* Hamburg, 1608; 1618. (The same work as *De mirabili potestate artis et naturæ et de nullitate magiæ.* Paris, 1542; Oxford, 1604; London, 1859.

BAISSAC, JULES. *Les grands jours de la sorcellerie.* Paris, 1890.

BALLERINI, ANTONIO, S.J. *Opus theologicum morale.* 7 vols. Prati, 1892.

BANG. *Norske Hexeformularer.* Christiania, 1902.

BARONIUS, CESARE VEN. *Annales ecclesiastici.* 38 vols. Lucca, 1738–59.

BARRETT. *Magus or Celestial Intelligencer; Being a complete system of Occult Philosophy, etc.* 1801.

BASIL, S. *Opera omnia.* Paris, 1839.

BASIN, BERNARDUS. *De artibus magicis.* 1482; and Paris, 1506.

BECANUS, MARTIN, S.J. *Opuscula Theologica sive Controversiæ Fidei inter Catholicos et Hæreticos hujus temporis.* Duaci, 1634.

BEER, M. *Social Struggles in the Middle Ages.* London, 1924.

BEKKER, BALTHASAR. *De Betoverde Wereld.* 4 vols. Amsterdam, 1691–93.

BENEDICT XIII. *Vita del Sommo Pontefice Benedetto XIII.* Venezia, 1737.

BENEDICT XIV, POPE. *De Beatificatione et Canonizatione.* 9 vols. Rome, 1787.

BENOIST, J., O.P. *Histoire des Albigeoises et des Vaudois.* Paris, 1691.

BERNARD, S. *Opera omnia.* Migne, *Pat. Lat.* CLXXXII–CLXXXV.

BERNARD OF COMO, O.P. *Lucerna inquisitorum hæreticæ prauitatis . . . et eiusdem Tractatus de Strigibus. . . .* Milan, 1566; Rome, 1584.

BERNARD OF LUXEMBURG, O.P. *Catalogus hæreticorum omnium.* Erfurt, 1522.

BERTAGNA, J. B. *De casuum reseruatione in Sacramento Pœniten iæ.* Turin, 1868.

BERTHIER, O.P. *L'Étude de la Somme Théologique de S. Thomas d'Aquin.* Paris, 1905. (Appendix III. *Spiritisme et hypnotisme d'après S. Thomas.*)

BESTERMAN, THEODORE. *Crystal-Gazing.*

BIEL, GABRIEL. *Supplementum in 28 distinctiones ultimas 4ti magistri sententiarum.* (1486.) Basle, 1520.
BINSFELD, PETER. *De Confessionibus Maleficorum.* Treves, 1589.
BODIN, JEAN. *De la démonomanie des sorciers.* Paris, 1580.
Le fleav des demons et sorciers. Nyort, 1616.
BOGUET, HENRY. *Discours des Sorciers.* 3rd ed. Lyons, 1590.
BOISSARDUS, JAN. JAC. *De Diuinatione et Magicis Prasetigiis.* Oppenheimii, 1615.
BONAVENTURA, S. *Opera omnia.* 10 vols. Quaracchi, 1882–1902.
BRAND, J. *Observations on Popular Antiquities.* 2 vols. 1813.
BRETT, G. S. *A History of Psychology.* Vol. I, Ancient and Patristic; Vol. II, Mediæval and Early Modern; Vol. III, Modern Psychology.
BROGNOLI, O.F.M. *Alexicacon, hoc est de maleficiis.* Venice, 1714.
BRUNUS, CONRADUS. *De hæreticis et schismaticis.* Rome, 1584.
BUDGE, SIR E. A. WALLIS. *Tutankhamen: Amenism, Atenism, and Egyptian Monotheism, with Hieroglyphic Texts of Hymns to Amen and Aten.*
Egyptian Magic. Third Impression. London, N.D. [1923].
Bullarium Papæ Benedicti XIV. Rome, 1746.
BURCHARD, WORMACIENSIS. *Decretum.* Migne, *Pat. Lat.* Vol. CLX.
BURKITT, F. G. *The Religion of the Manichees.* Cambridge, 1925.
BUTLER, ALBAN. *Lives of the Saints.* 1756–9; 2 vols Dublin, 1833.
BZOVIUS, A. *Historiæ Ecclesiasticæ.* Apud Zilettum, *q.u.*
CÆSALPINUS, ANDREAS. *Dæmonum inuestigatio.* Florence, 1580.
CAIETANUS, THOMAS. *De Maleficiis.* 1500.
CALMET, AUGUSTIN DOM, O.S.B. *Traité sur les Apparitions des Esprits, et sur les Vampires.* 2 vols. Paris, 1751.
CAPPELLO, S.J., FELIX M. *De Censuris.* Rome, 1919.
CARENA. *Tractatus de officio Sanctæ Inquisitionis.* Lyons, 1669.
CASSINIS, SAMUEL DE. *Question de la strie.* 1505.
CAUZ, C. F. DE. *De Cultibus Magicis.* 1771.
CHARLEY, T. *News from the Invisible World.* Wakefield, n.s. (*circa* 1850).
CHRYSOSTOM, S. JOHN. *Opera omnia Græce.* Edidit H. Savile. 8 vols. Etonæ, 1612.
CHURCHWARD, ALBERT. *The Arcana of Freemasonry.*
CIRVELIUS, PETRUS. *De magica superstitione.* 1521.
Clementis Alexandrini Opera. 2 vols. Venice, 1757.
Collectanea Chemica. (Select Treatises on Alchemy and Hermetic Medicine.) 1893.
COLLIN DE PLANCY, J. A. S. *Dictionnaire Infernal.* Editio princeps. 2 vols. Paris, 1818. (I have used the sixth, and last, edition, one vol. Paris, H. Plon. 4to, 1863. The six editions differ widely from one another. This famous work is valuable, but often uncritical and even erroneous.)
COLLIUS, FRANCIS. *De Animabus Paganorum.* Milan, 1622.
CONCONIER. *L'âme humaine.* Paris, 1890.
L'hypnotisme franc. Paris, 1898.
CONDROCHIUS, BAPTISTA. *De morbis ueneficis ac ueneficiis.* Libri IV. Venice, 1595.
COUNCELL, R. W. *Apologia Alchymiæ.*
CRESPET, PÈRE CELESTINE. *La haine de Sathan contre l'homme.* Paris, 1590.
CROWE, CATHERINE. *The Night Side of Nature.* 2 vols. 1848. (A standard work; very frequently reprinted.)
CUTHBERT, O.S.F.C., FATHER. *God and the Supernatural.* London, 1920.
DANEAU, LAMBERT. *Les Sorciers.* 1574. There is an English tr. *A Dialogue of Witches,* 1575. [London ?]
DAYNES, GILVBERT W. *The Untrodden Paths of Masonic Research.*
DE LANCRE, PIERRE. *Tableau de l'inconstance des mavvais anges et démons.* Paris, 1612.
L'incredvlité et mescréance dv sortilège. Paris, 1622.
Du Sortilège. 1627. (This is the rarest of De Lancre's books, and very little known.)
DELASSUS, JULES. *Les Incubes et les Succubes.* Paris, 1897.

DELEHAYE, H., S.J. *Légendes Hagiographiques.* Brussels, 1906. Trans. by Mrs. V. M. Crawford as *The Legends of the Saints.* (*The Westminster Library.*)

DELRIO, MARTIN ANTON, S.J. *Disquisitionum Magicarum Libri Sex.* Louvain, 1599.

Devil, History of the, Ancient and Modern, with a Description of the Devil's Dwellings. Durham, 1822.

DIANA, R. P. D. ANTONINUS. *Resolutiones morales.* Lyons, 1633.

DIDRON, M. *Iconographie chrétienne. Histoire de Dieu.* Paris, 1843. Eng. tr. 2 vols. by E. J. Millington. London, 1851. Bohn's Library.

DOBBINS, F. S. *False Gods, or the Idol Worship of the World.* Boston, *circa* 1870.

DORAT, S.J., JOSEPH. *Psychologia.* Vol. VI of *Summa Philosophiæ Christianæ.* 8 vols. Rome.

DRAGO, LUIGI VINCENZO. *Il materialismo e il dogma. Fede e Scienza.* IV, 40 Rome.

DULAURE, J. A. *Des Cultes qui ont précédé et amené l'idolâtrie.* 1805.
Des Divinités Génératrices. Paris, 1805.

DU PREL, CARL. Tr. C. C. Massey. *The Philosophy of Mysticism.* 2 vols. London, 1889.

ELICH, PHILIP LUDWIG. *Dæmonomagia, siue de dæmonis cacurgia.* Frankfort, 1607.

ENNEMOSER, JOSEPH. *The History of Magic.* 2 vols. London, 1854.

ERASTUS, THOMAS. *De lamiis seu strigibus.* Basle, 1577.

Errores Gazariorum seu illorum qui scobam uel baculum equitare probantur. 1450.

EVENIUS, SIGISMUND. *Dissertatio physica de magia.* 1512.

EWICK, JOHN. *De sagorum quos uulgo ueneficos appellant natura.* Bremen, 1584.

EYMERIC, O.P., NICHOLAS. *Directorium Inquisitorum.* Rome, 1585; Venice, 1607.

FERRERES, S.J., I. B. *Theologia Moralis.* 11th ed. Rome, 1921.

FRANZELIN, S.J., CARDINAL I.B. *De Deo Uno.* Rome.

FRAZER, SIR JAMES. *Folk-Lore in the Old Testament.* London, 1923.

FREDERICQ, DR. PAUL. *Corpus documentorum Inquisitionis hæreticæ prauitatis neerlandicæ.* 5 vols. Ghent, 1889 *sqq.*
Geschiednes der Inquisitie de Neerlanden tot aen hare herinrichting onder Keizer Karel V (1025–1520). Ghent, 1892 *sqq.*

FREUD, SIGISMUND. *Totem and Taboo. Resemblances between the Psychic Lives of Savages and Neurotics.* London, 1919.

GAFFARELLUS, JAC. *Curiositates Inauditæ.* Hamburg, 1706.

GAMS, PIUS BONIFACIUS, O.S.B. *Die Kirchengeschichte von Spanien.* 5 vols. Regensburg, 1862.

GARRIGON-LEGRANGE, O.P., REGINALD. *De Reuelatione.* 2nd ed. 1921.

GAYA, LOUIS DE. *Cérémonies nuptiales de toutes les nations.* Paris, 1680.

GEBHART, EMILE. *L'Italie mystique.* Paris, 1893.

GEILER, JOHANN. *Die Emeis. Dies ist das Buch von der Omeissen.* 1516.

GEMELLI, O.F.M., AGOSTINO. *Psicologia e Biologia.* Rome, 1920.
Non Moechaberis. Milan, 1923.

GERBERT. *Epistolæ.* Migne. *Pat. Lat.* Vol. CXXXIX.

GERUASIUS OF TILBURY. *Otia imperialia.* Written *circa* 1214.

GIESSLER, J. C. L. *Ecclesiastical History.* Eng. tr. 1853.

GILLY, WILLIAM STEPHEN. *Narrative of Researches among the Vaudois.* London, 1824.

GIUSTINIANUS, BERNARDUS. *Historia Generale della Monarchia Spagnuola Antica, e Moderna.* Venezia, 1674.

GODELMANN, JOHAN GEORG. *Disputatio de Magis.* Frankfort, 1584.
Tractatus de Magis. 1591.

GODWIN, WILLIAM. *Lives of the Necromancers.* London, 1834.

GÖRRES, JOHANN JOSEPH. *Die christliche Mystik.* 4 vols. 1836–42. French translation: *La Mystique Divine, Naturelle, et Diabolique. . . .* 5 vols. Paris, 1861.

GOUGENOT DES MOUSSEAU, HENRI ROGER.
Dieu et les Dieux. Paris, 1854.
Mœurs et pratiques des Démons. Paris, 1854.
La magie au dix-neuvième siècle. Paris, 1860.
Les médiateurs et les moyens de la magie. Paris, 1863.
Les hauts phénomènes de la magie. Paris, 1864.
(Vampires ; the Incubus and the Succubus.)
GOUJET, ABBÉ. *Histoire des inquisitions.* 2 vols. Cologne, 1759.
GREGOROVIUS, FERDINAND. *Geschichte der Stadt Rom im Mittlealter.* 7 vols. 5th ed. Stuttgard and Berlin, 1903 *sqq.*
GREGORY VII, POPE S. *Epistolarum libri* apud Mansi *Sacrorum conciliorum nona . . . collectio.* Florence, 1759. Also *S. Gregorii VII epistolæ et diplomata.* Ed. Horoy. Paris, 1877.
GREGORY XV, POPE. *Gesta Pontificum Romanorum.* Venice, 1688. IV, 522–36.
GREGORY THE GREAT, POPE S. *Opera omnia.* Ed. J. B. Gallicoli. 17 vols. Venice, 1765–76. Reprinted by Migne. *Pat. Lat.* LXXV–LXXIX.
GREGORY OF NAZIANZUS, S. *Opera omnia.* Paris, 1609–11. Migne. *Pat. Gr.* 4 vols. XXXV–XXXVIII.
GREGORY OF TOURS, S. *Scriptores Rerum Merouinginarum* apud *monumenta Germaniæ historica.* I, Pt. I, pp. 1–30. 1884–5.
GRILLANDUS, PAULUS. *De sortilegiis.* Lyons, 1533.
GUAITA, STANISLAS DE. *Essais de sciences maudites.* Paris and Brussels, 1886.
GUAZZO, FRANCESCO MARIA, AMBROSIAN. *Compendium Maleficarum.* Milan, 1608. (One of the most valuable of the earlier writers.)
GUI, BERNARD. *Practica Inquisitionis hæreticæ prauitatis.* Ed. Mgr. C. Douais. Paris, 1886.
GURY, S.J., I. P. *Theologia moralis.* 15th ed. Rome, 1907. Cum supplemento, Acta et Decreta nouissima. 2 vols. Rome, 1915.
HALES, ALEXANDER OF. *Summa uniuersæ theologiæ.* Cologne, 1622.
HANSEN, J. *Quellen und Untersuchungen zur Geschichte des Hexenwahns.* Bonn, 1901.
HARTMANN, FRANZ. *The Life of Phillippus Theophrastus Bombast, of Hohenheim, known by the name of Paracelsus, and the Substance of his Teachings.*
Magic, White and Black.
HASKINS, CHARLES HOMER. *Studies in the History of Mediæval Science.* London, 1924.
HAUBER, E. D. *Bibliotheca magica et scripta magica.* 1738–45.
HAURÉAU, B. *Histoire de la Philosophie Scolastique.* Paris, 1880.
HECKETHORN, CHARLES WILLIAM. *Secret Societies of All Ages and Countries.* 2 vols. London, 1897.
HEDELIN, FRANÇOIS. *Des Satyres, Brutes, Monstres et Demons.* Paris, 1627. Reprinted, Liseux, 1888.
HEINER, FREDERICH. *De Processu Criminali Ecclesiastico.* Rome, 1920.
HEISTERBACH, CÆSARIUS. *Dialogus Miraculorum.* *Circa* 1225. Reprints, 1861, 1901.
HERRMANN. *Institutiones Theologiæ Dogmaticæ.* 2 vols. Rome, 1914.
HETZENAUER, O.M.C., MICHAEL. *Commentarius in librum Genesis.* Rome, 1910.
HILDEBERT, S. *Opera omnia.* Paris, 1708.
HINCMAR. *Opera omnia.* Migne, *Pat. Lat.* Vols. CXXV, CXXVI.
HOCHSTRATEN, JACOB VON. *Quam grauiter peccent quærentes auxilium a maleficiis.* 1510.
HOFFMANN, FRIDOLIN. *Geschichte des Inquisition.* 2 vols. Bonn, 1878.
HOLMES, EDMOND. *The Albigensian or Catharist Heresy.* London, 1925. (A truly amazing defence of the Albigensians. The author has completely misunderstood their heresies.)
HOWEY, M. OLDFIELD. *The Horse in Magic and Myth.* London, 1923.
HUEBER. *Menologium S. Francisci.* Munich, 1608.
HUGON, R. P. *De Deo Uno et Trino.* 2 vols. Rome.
Inquisition. Orden que Comunmente se Guarda en el Santo Oficio de la Inquisition. Valencia, 1736. (Contains all the forms and procedure of the Holy Office.)

IVES, GEORGE. *A History of Penal Methods.* 1914. Chapter II: "The Witch Trials." (The whole volume is valuable.)

JACOLLIOT, LOUIS. *Occult Science in India and among the Ancients.*

JACQUERIUS, NICOLAS. *Flagellum Dæmonum Fascinariorum.* 1458.

JADEROSA, FEDERICO. *Theologia Moralis.* Rome, 1922.

JAUER, NICOLAUS VON. *Tractatus de superstitionibus.* 1405.

JENNINGS, HARGRAVE. *The Rosicrucians: their Rites and Mysteries.*

JORDANUS DE BERGAMO. *Quæstio de strigis.* 1476. MS. 3446. Bibliothèque nationale, Paris.

KELLY, EDWARD *The Alchemical Writings of Edward Kelly.* Trans. from the Hamburg Edition of 1676. 1893.

KHUNRATH, H. *Amphitheatrum Sapientiæ Æternæ Solius Veræ, Christiano-Kabalisticum, Diuino-Magicum, nec non Physico-Chymicum, Tertriunum, Catholicon.* Hanover, 1609.

KRAKEWITZ VON, ALBERT JOACHIM. *De theologia dæmonum.* Wittenberg, 1715.

KRONE. *Fra Dolcino und die Patarerer.* Leipzig, 1844.

LAURENT-NAGOUR. *Occultismus und Liebe,* 1903.

LAVATER, LOYS. *De spectris, lemuribus, etc.* Geneva, 1570.

LEA, HENRY CHARLES. *History of the Inquisition of the Middle Ages.* New York, 1887; London, 1888; and 3 vols., 1906.

Superstition and Force. Philadelphia, 1866. 3rd ed., 1878; 4th ed., 1892.

Studies in Church History. Philadelphia, 1869.

History of the Inquisition in Spain. 4 vols. London, 1906–7.

The Inquisition in the Spanish Dependencies. New York, 1908.

(The works of Henry Charles Lea, lengthy and laborious as they are, must be used with the utmost caution and need continually to be corrected. They are insecure, and bitterly biased, since even when facts are not widely distorted a wrong interpretation is inevitably placed upon them. Their value and merit can but be regarded as fundamentally shaken. The following criticism will be found useful: Paul Maria Baumgarten: *Die Werke von Henry Charles Lea und verwandte Bücher,* 1908. Eng. tr.: *H. C. Lea's Historical Writings: A critical inquiry into their method and merit.* 1909.)

LEE, FREDERICK GEORGE, D.D. *The Other World.* 2 vols. London, 1875.

More Glimpses of the World Unseen. 1878.

Glimpses in the Twilight. 1885.

Sights and Shadows. 1894.

(Scholarly and valuable works.)

LEHMANN. *Aberglaube.* 2nd ed. 1908.

LEHMKUHL, S.J., AUG. *Casus conscientiæ.* 2 vols. Rome, 1913.

LE LOYER, PIERRE. *Discours et histoires des spectres.* Paris, 1605.

LÉVI, ELIPHAS (ALPHONSE LOUIS CONSTANT). *The History of Magic.* Trans. by Arthur Edward Waite. 1922.

The Paradoxes of the Highest Science. (Footnotes by a Master of the Wisdom.)

Transcendental Magic. (Translated, annotated, and introduced by Arthur Edward Waite.)

LEYSER, AUGUST. *De crimine magiæ.* Wittenberg, 1737.

LICOSTHENES, CONRAD. *De prodigiis et ostentis.* 1557.

LOCATI, UMBERTO. *Opus iudiciale inquisitorum.* Rome, 1572.

LOMBARD, PETER. *Quatuor Libri Sententiarium.* Printed 1472. Paris, 1892. (Best edition is that found in the Commentary of S. Bonaventura. *Opera S. Bonauenturæ.* Quaracchi, 1885, I–IV.

LOMEIER, J. *Epimenides sive De Ueterum Gentilium Lustrationibus Syntagma.* Zutphen, 1700

LOTTINI, O.P., GIOVANNI. *Compendium Philosophiæ Scholasticæ.* 3 vols. Rome, 1912.

LUANCO, J. RAMÓN DE. *Ramón Lull considerado come Alquimista.* Barcelona, 1870.

LULL, BL. RAMÓN. *Opera omnia.* 10 vols. Mainz, 1721–42.

MACKAY, CHARLES. *Memoirs of Extraordinary Popular Delusions.* 2 vols. London, 1852. (Must be used with caution, very frequently reprinted.)
MADDEN, R. R. *Phantasmata.* 2 vols. 1857.
MAIER, M. *Themis Aurea* (on the Rosicrucians). Frankfurt, 1618.
MAMOR, PIETRO. *Flagellum maleficorum. Circa* 1462.
MANGETUS. *Bibliotheca Chemico Curiosa.* 1702.
MARÉCHAUX, O.S.B., BERNARD-MARIE. *La Réalité des Apparitions Angéliques.* Paris, 1901.
MARCHESE. *Diario Domenicano.* Naples, 1668–81.
MARTINDALE, C. C., S.J. *Antichrist.* C.T.S. (Do. 83).
Theosophy.
MAURITIUS, E. *De denunciatione sagarum.* Tubingen, 1664.
MAYER, J. B. *Ancient Philosophy.* Cambridge, 1895.
MAYO, HERBERT. *On the Truths contained in Popular Superstitions.* Edinburgh, 1851.
MAZZARA. *Leggendario francescano.* Venice, 1721.
MAZZELLA, HOR. *Prælectiones Scholastico-Dogmaticæ.* 4 vols. Rome.
MAZZOLINI (MOZOLINI, PRIERIAS), O.P., SYLVESTER. *De strigimagorum libri III.* Rome, 1521.
MECHLINIA, JOHANNES DE. *Utrum perfecta dei opera possint impediri dæmonis malicia. Circa* 1450.
MEMMINGIUS, NICOLAS. *Admonitio de superstitionibus magicis uitandis. s.l.* 1575.
MENANT, JOACHIM. *Les Yezidiz. Episodes de l'histoire des adorateurs du Diable.* Paris, 1892.
MENGO, GIROLAMO, CAPUCHIN. *Flagellum Dæmonum.* Bologna, 1578.
Euersio dæmonum e corporibus oppressis. Bologna, 1588.
Fustis dæmonum. Bologna, 1589.
Menologium Cisterciense.
MERCER, REV. J. E. *Alchemy : its Science and Romance.*
MERIC, MGR. *L'Autre vie.* 13 ed. Paris, 1919.
L'Imagination et les Prodigues. Paris, 1918.
Revue de Monde Invisible. Edited by Mgr. Meric. 1909—in continuation.
MICHELET, JULES. *La sorcière.* Paris, 1862. (This original edition is of the last rarity. Reprinted 1862.)
MIRANDOLA, G. P. P. DELLA. *Strix siue de ludificatione dæmonum.* 1523.
MOLITOR, ULRICH. *De lamiis et phitonicis mulieribus, teutonice unholden uel hexen.* 1489.
MOREAU, PAUL. *Des Aberrations du Sens Génésique.* 4th ed. 1887.
MOSHEIM, J. J. VON. *Institutes of Ecclesiasticæ History.* Eng. tr. 2nd ed. 1850.
MURNER, O.M., THOMAS. *De phitonico contractu.* 1499.
MURRAY, MARGARET ALICE. *The Witch-Cult in Western Europe.* Oxford, 1921.
NAUDÉ, GABRIEL. *Apologie povr tovs les grands hommes qui ont esté faussement soupconnez de magie.* Paris, 1625.
NEALE, REV. JOHN MASON. *The Unseen World.* 1847.
NEVIUS, REV. JOHN L. *Demon Possession and Allied Themes.* New York, 1893.
NIDER, JOHAN, O.P. *Formicarius.* 5 vols. Douai, 1602.
Occult Review, The. (In continuation.)
PAPUS (pseud. of Gérard Encausse). *Absolute Key to Occult Science : The Tarot of the Bohemians.* Trans. by A. P. Morton. 1896.
PARACELSUS (Aureolus Philippus, i.e. Theophrastus Bombast von Hohenheim). *Philosophy Reformed and Improved.* Made English by H. Pinnell. 2 vols. 1657.
PARAMO, LUDOVICO À. *De origine et progressu officii Sanctæ Inquisitionis.* Madrid, 1598.
PASCH, G. *De operationibus Dæmonum duo problemata curiosa utrum possint generare et utrum homines in bestias transformari.* 1684.
—— PATRICIUS, FR. *Magia Philosophica.* Hamburg, 1593.

PEEBLES, J. M. *The Demonism of the Ages.* Battle Creek, Mich., 1904.
PEÑA, FRANCESCO. *Inquirendorum hæreticorum lucerna.* Rome, 1572.
PERRY, W. J. *The Origin of Magic and Religion.*
PEUCER, CASPAR. *Commentarius De Præcipuis Generibus Diuinationum.* Witenberga, 1560.
PIGNATARO, F. S. J. *De Disciplina Pœnitentiali.*
PONS, VINCENT. *De potentia Dæmonum.* Aquis Sextiis, 1613.
PONZINIBIO, FRANCESCO. *De lamiis.* Apud *Thesaurus iurisconsultorum.* Venice, 1584.
PRUMMER, O.P., DOMINIC. *Manuale Theologiæ Moralis secundum principia S. Thomæ Aquinatis.* 3 vols. Rome, 1915.
PRYCE, F. N. *The Fame and Confession of the Fraternity of R. C., commonly of the Rosie Cross.* London, 1652.
QUÉTIF-ECHARD. *Scriptores Ordinis Prædicatorum.* 2 vols. Paris, 1719.
RAMUS, S.J., LE PÈRE MARIE. *La Dévotion à Sainte Anne.* Lyons, 1888.
REDGROVE, H. STANLEY. *Alchemy, Ancient and Modern.*
REGINO, ABBOT OF PRÜM. *Libri duo de synodalibus causis.* Migne. *Pat. Lat*, Vol. CXXXII.
REMY, NICOLAS (Remigius). *Dæmonolatriæ libri tres.* Lyons, 1595.
Repertorium penitile de prauitate hæreticorum. 1494.
RÉVILLE, A. *The Devil.* London, 1871.
RIBADENEIRA, S.J., PEDRO. *Uita Ignatii.* Naples, 1572.
RIBET, M. J. *La Mystique Divine.* 4 vols. Paris, 1895.
RICARDUS, ANGENTNUS. *De præstigiis et incantationibus dæmonum.* Basle, 1568.
RICHALMUS, B. (Reichhelm). *Liber de Insidiis Dæmonum.* *Circa* 1270.
RÖMER, WILHELM. *Die Hexenbulle des Papster Innocenz VIII.* Schaffhausen, 1889.
ROSKOFF, GUSTAV. *Geschichte des Teufels.* 2 vols. Leipzig, 1859.
ROYAS, À J. *De Hæreticis.* Apud Zilettum, *q.u.*
SABETTI, ALOYSIUS, S.J. *Compendium Theologiæ Moralis.* Ed. Uicesima Quinta. Recog. a Timotheo Barrett, S.J. 1916. (Tractatus VI. 2. *De Uitiis Religioni Oppositis.* 3. *De Diuinatione.* 4. *De Magia et maleficio.*)
SAINT-HEBIN, ALEXANDRE. *Du culte de Satan.* Paris, 1867.
SBARALEA. *Bullarium Franciscanum* 5 vols. Rome, 1759 *sqq.*
SCHELTEMA, JACOBUS. *Geschiedenis der Heksenprocessen, eene bijdrage tot den roem des vaderlands.* Haarlem, 1828.
SCHERARTZ, SIGISMUND. *Libellus de spectris.* Wittenberg, 1620.
SCHMIDT. *Histoire et Doctrine de la secte des Cathares ou Albigeois.* Paris, 1849.
SCHRAM, DOMINIC, O.S.B. *Institutiones Theologiæ Mysticæ.* 2 vols. Ausburg, 1774. (A most valuable work.)
SCHWAB, J. B. *Jean Gerson.* Würzburg, 1858.
SCOTUS, DUNS. *Opera omnia.* 12 vols. Ed. Wadding. Lyons, 1639. Reprint, 26 vols. (Vives) Paris, 1891–95.
SIMANCAS. *De Catholicis Institutionibus.* Apud Zilettum, *q.u.*
SINISTRARI, O.M., LUDOVICO MARIA. *Opera omnia.* Rome. 3 vols. 1753–4. *De Dæmonialitate.* First published by Liseux. Paris, 1875. Eng. tr. *Demonality, or Incubi and Succubi.* Paris, 1879.
SOCINUS, MARIANUS. *De sortilegiis.* *Circa* 1465.
SOLE, JACOBUS. *De Delictis et Pœnis.* Rome, 1920.
SPEE, S.J., FREDERICH. *Cautio criminalis.* 1631. Cologne, 1632.
SPENCE, LEWIS. *An Encyclopedia of Occultism : a Compendium of Information on the Occult Sciences, Occult Personalities, Psychic Sciences, Magic, Demonology, Spiritism, and Mysticism.* London, 1920.
Spicilegium dæmonolatriæ. *Circa* 1330.
SPINA, BARTOLOMEO, O.P. *Tractatus de Strigibus et Lamiis.* Venice, 1523.
SPRENGER, O.P., JAMES and KRAMER (Institor), HEINRICH. (*Editio princeps*) *Malleus Maleficarum.* Nuremburg, 1494 and 1496. Cologne, 1489 and 1494. Frankfort, 1582. Cologne, 1511 and 1520. Lyons, 1595 and (a fuller edition) 1620. (There are several other issues.) Of this authoritative work I have used the Lyons edition.

Sumptibus Claudii Bovrgeat. 4 vols. 1669, which contains the following valuable collections :—
Vol. I.
NIDER, O.P., JOHN. *Formicarius de maleficiis.*
SPRENGER and KRAMER. *Malleus Maleficarum.*
Vol. II.
ANANIA, GIOVANNI LORENZO. *De Natura Dæmonum.*
BASIN, BERNARD. *De Artibus magicis.*
BERNARD OF COMO, O.P. *De Strigibus.* (With the annotations of Francesco Peña.)
CASTRO, O.M., ALFONSO À. *De impia Sortilegarum hæresi.*
DE VIGNATE, AMBROSE. *Quæstio de Lamiis.* (With a commentary by Peña.)
GERSON, JOHN. *De Probatione Spirituum. De erroribus circa artem magicam reprobatis.*
GRILLAND, PAUL. *De Sortilegiis.*
LEONE, GIOVANNI FRANCESCO. *De Sortilegiis.*
MOLITOR, ULRICH. *De Pythonicis mulieribus.*
MURNER, O.M., THOMAS. *De Pythonico Contractu.*
SIMANCAS, IAGO. *De Lamiis.*
SPINA, O.P., BARTOLOMEO. *De Strigibus.*
In Ponzinibium de Lamiis Apolegia.
Vol. III
GORICHEN, HEINRICH DE. *De superstitioris quibusdam casibus.*
MAMOR, PIETRO. *Flagellum maleficorum.*
MENGO, GIROLAMO, CAPUCHIN. *Flagellum Dæmonum.*
Fustis Dæmonum.
STAMPA, PIETRO ANTONIO. *Fuga Satanæ.*
Vol. IV.
Ars exorcistica tribus partibus.
(It is hardly possible to overestimate the value of this collection.)

STEAD, W. T. *Real Ghost Stories* Reprinted from " The Review of Reviews," 1891–2. London, 1897.

STEINER, RUDOLF. *Les Mystères antiques et le Mystère chrétien.* Paris, 1920.

STENGESIUS, G. *De Monstris et Monstrosis.* 1647 (?).

STRIDTHECKH, CHRISTIAN. *De Sagis, siue Fœminis, commercium cum Malo Spiritu habentibus.* Leipzig, 1691.

SUTTER, PAUL ABBÉ. *Lucifer.* Tr. by the Rev. Theophilus Borer. London, 1922.

TAGEREAU, VINCENT. *Discours sur l'impuissance de l'homme et de la femme.* Paris, 1612.

TAILLEPIED, FRÈRE NOEL. *Psichologie, ou traité de l'apparition des Esprits.* Paris, 1588 ; and many other eds.

TARREGA, RAIMUNDUS. *De inuocatione dæmonum. Circa* 1370.

TARTAROTTI, GIROLAMO. *Del Congresso Notturno delle Lammie.* Rovereto, 1749.

TAXIL, JEAN. *Traicté de l'Epilepsie.* Lyons, 1602. C. XVII (pp. 150–162) treats of demoniacs, sorcerers, and possession.

THEATINUS, JOHANN BAPISTA. *Aduersus artem magicam et striges. Circa* 1510.

Theatrum Diabolorum. 1587.

S. THOMAS AQUINAS. *Opera omnia iussu edita Leonis XIII., P.M.* The Leonine edition.

THUMMIUS, THEODORE. *De Sagarum impictate.* Tubingen, 2nd ed., 1666.

TINCTOR, JOHANNES. *Sermo de secta Uaudensium.* 1460.

TOMASETTI. Ed. *Bullarium . . . Romanorum Pontificum.* 22 vols. Turin, 1857, etc. ; and Naples, 1867–85.

TRIEZ, ROBERT DU. *Les ruses, finesses, et impostures des Esprits malins.* Cambrai, 1563.

TRITHEMIUS, JOHANNES. *Liber Octo quæstionum.* 1508.
Antipalus Maleficiorum. 1508.

TUBERVILLE, A. S. *Mediæval Heresy and the Inquisition.* London, 1920.

UGOLINI, ZANCHINO. *De Hæreticis.* Apud Zilettum, *q.u.*

ULRICHS, K. H. *Incubus, Urningsliebe, und Blutgier.* Leipzig, 1869.
ULYSSE, ROBERT. *Les signes d'infamie au Moyen Age.* Paris, 1891.
URSTISIUS. *Germanicæ historiæ scriptores.* Frankfort, 1585.
VAIR, LEONARD. *Trois livres des charmes, sorceleges, ov enchantments. . . . Faits en latin par Leonard Vair et mis en Francois par Iulian Bavdon, Angeuin.* Paris, 1583.
DE VALLE DE MOURA. *De incantationibus.* 1620.
VALOIS, N. *La France et le Grand Schisme d'Orient.* Paris, 1896–1902
VAUGHAN, THOMAS (Eugenius Philalethes). *Magical Writings of Thomas Vaughan.* Edited by Arthur Edward Waite. 1888.
Veritable Dragon Rouge ou il est traite de l'Art de commander les esprits infernaux aeriens et terrestres, faire apparaitre les morts . . . plus La Poule Noire. Sur l'Edition de 1521 [*circa* 1900].
VERPOORTEN, G. P. *De Dæmonum existentia.* 1779.
VICECOMES, GIROLAMO. *Lamiarum siue striarum opusculum.* 1460, printed 1490.
VILLALPANDO, FRANCISCO TORREBLANCA. *Dæmonologia sive de Magia Naturali, Dæmoniaca, licitia, et illicita.* Mainz, 1603.
VINCENTIUS, JOANNES. *Liber aduersus magicas artes et eos qui dicunt eisdem nullam inesse efficaciam. Circa* 1475.
VINETUS, JOANNES. *Tractatus contra dæmonum inuocatores. Circa* 1450. Printed 1480.
VIVET, O.P., JOHN. *Tractatus contra dæmonum inuocatores.* (*Sine l. et d.*) Black letter.
WAITE, ARTHUR EDWARD. *Book of Black Magic, and of Pacts, including the Rites and Mysteries of Goëtic Theurgy, Sorcery, and Infernal Necromancy.* 1898.
Mysteries of Magic. A Digest of the Writings of Eliphas Lévi. 1886.
The Occult Sciences. 1891.
The Real History of the Rosicrucians. 1887
Studies in Mysticism. 1906.
WAKE, C. S. *Serpent Worship.* 1888.
WARD, J. S. M. *Freemasonry and the Ancient Gods.*
WEYER, JOHAN (Wierus). *De præstigiis dæmonum et incantationibus et uenificiis.* Basle, 1563. *De Lamiis* and *Pseudo-monarchia Dæmonum* are appended to the ed. of 1577.
WRIGHT, DUDLEY. *Druidism.* London, 1924.
The Eleusinian Mysteries and Rites.
Masonic Legend and Tradition.
Vampires and Vampirism. 2nd ed. London, 1925.
WRIGHT, THOMAS. *Narratives of Sorcery and Magic.* 2 vols. 1851.
WULF, M. DE. *History of Mediæval Philosophy.* Eng. tr. 1909.
WÜNSCHELBURG, JOHANNES. *Tractatus de superstitionibus. Circa* 1440.
ZANCHERIUS, UGOLINI. *Tractatus de hæreticis.* Mantua, 1567. Rome, 1579.
ZILETTUS. *Tractatus Uniuersi iuris.* Venice, 1633.

SCRIPTURAL AND ORIENTAL

BAUDISSEN, GRAFEN WOLF WILHELM. *Studien zur semitischen Religionsgeschichte.* 2 vols. Leipzig, 1876 and 1878.
BOCHARTUS, SAM. *Hierozoicon.* Ed. Tert. Lugd. et Traj., 1682.
BOUSSET, W. *The Antichrist Legend.* Trans. by A. H. Keane. London, 1896.
BRECHER. *Das transcendentale Magie und magische Heilarten im Talmud.* Wien, 1850.
BRINTON, D. G. *Religions of Primitive Peoples.* London and New York, 1897.
CHARLES, R. H. *The Book of Enoch.* Oxford, 1893.
CONSTANS. *Relation sur une epidemie d'hystero-demonopathie.* Paris, 1863.
CORNILL, CARL HEINRICH. *The Culture of Ancient Israel.*
CROOK, W. *Folklore of Northern India.* 2 vols. 2nd ed. London, 1896.
DAVIES, T. WITTON. *Magic, Divination and Demonology.* London, 1898. (This work should be used with reserve.)

DENNYS, B. N. *The Folklore of China.* London, 1876.
EDERSHEIM, ALFRED. *Life and Times of the Messiah.* London, 1888.
GINSBERG. *The Kabbalah.* London, 1865. Reprinted, 1925.
GRANGER, F. *The Worship of the Romans.* London, 1895.
GRANT, JAMES. *The Mysteries of all Nations.* Leith, 1880.
HILLEBRANDT. *Rituallliteratur. Vedische Opfer und Zauber.* Strasburg, 1897.
HUGHES, T. P. *Dictionary of Islam.* London, 1885.
HUMMELAUR DE, S. J. *Commentarius in libros Samuel.* (*I et II Regum.*) Rome.
KING, J. *Babylonian Magic and Sorcery.* London, 1896.
KOHUT, A. *Jüdische Angel. und Dämonologie.* Leipzig, 1866.
LENORMANT, F. *Chaldean Magic.* London, 1877.
Divination, et la science des presages. Paris, 1875.
LESÊTRE. *Dictionnaire de la Bible.* (Sub uoce *Demoniaques.*)
MARTIGNY. *Dictionnaire des antiquités chrétiennes* (p. 312). Paris, 1877.
MASPERO. *Histoire ancienne des peuples de l'Orient.*
MEINERS, PROF. *Geschichte aller Religionen.* 2 vols. 1806.
MICHAELIS, J. D. *Commentaries on the Laws of Moses.* From the German. 4 vols. London, 1814.
PAUVERT. *La vie de N. S. Jésus-Christ.*
PERRONE, S.J., GIOVANNI. *De Deo creatore.* Pt. I, c. v, prop. 1, 11.
PICK, BERNHARD. *The Cabala.*
SCHENKEL, D. *Bibel-Lexicon.*
SCHRADER. *Die Keilinschriften u. d. alte Testament.* 2nd ed. Geissen, 1883.
SMIT, J. *De Demoniacis in Historia Evangelica Dissertatio Exegetico Apologetica.* Romæ, 1913.
SPENCER. *De Legibus Hebræorum ritualibus earumque rationibus.* Ed. C. M. Pfaff. 2 vols. Tubingae, 1732.
STEHELIN, J. P. *Traditions of the Jews.* 2 vols. London, 1743.
STRAENE, A. W. *A Translation of the Treatise Chagigah, from the Babylonian Talmud.* Cambridge, 1891.
TERTULLIAN. *Apologia.* Migne, *Pat. Lat. I.*
TIELE, C. P. *Geschichte der Religion im Alterthum.* Vol. I. Gotha, 1896.
VIGOUROUX. *Les livres saints et la critique rationaliste.* Paris, 1891.
TORREBLANCA. *De Magia.* Ed. novissima. Lugduni, 1678.
WAFFELAERT. *Dictionnaire apologétique de la foi catholique.* Paris, 1889. (Sub uoce Possession diabolique.)
WEBER, TERD. VON. *Judische Theologie.* 2te verbesserte Auflage. Leipzig, 1897.
WIEDEMANN, ALFRED. *Religion of the Ancient Egyptians.* London, 1897.
ZIMMERN. *Die Beschwörungstafeln Surpu.* Leipzig, 1896.

ENGLAND, SCOTLAND, AND IRELAND

Abbotsford Club Miscellany. Vol. I. Edinburgh, 1837.
ADY, THOMAS. *A Candle in the Dark.* London, 1656.
ARNOT, HUGO. *Criminal Trials.* Edinburgh, 1785.
ASHTON, JOHN. *The Devil in Britain and America.* London, 1896.
BAXTER, RICHARD. *Certainty of the World of Spirits.* London, 1691.
BEAUMONT, JOHN. *Historical Treatise of Spirits.* London, 1705.
BEDE, VEN. *Ecclesiastical History* (ed. Giles). London, 1843.
BERNARD, RICHARD. *Guide to Grand-Iury men.* London, 1627.
BLACK, G. F. *Scottish Antiquary,* Vol. IX. Edinburgh, 1895.
Blackwood's Magazine, Vol. I. Edinburgh, 1817.
BOULTON, R. *Compleat History of Magick, Sorcery and Witchcraft.* 2 vols. London, 1715.
BOVETT, R. *Pandæmonium.* London, 1658.
BRAND, JOHN. *History and Antiquities of . . . Newcastle.* London, 1789.
BROMHALL, THOMAS. *Treatise of Spectres.* London, 1658.
BURNS, BEGG. *Proceedings of Soc. of Antiquaries of Scotland.* New Series. Vol. X. Edinburgh.
BURTON, JOHN HILL. *Criminal Trials.* London, 1852.

BUTLER, SAMUEL. *Hudibras*. (Ed. Zachary Grey.) 2 vols. Cambridge, 1744.
Calendar of State Papers. Domestic. 1584. London, 1865.
Camden Society. Lady Alice Kyteler. London, 1843.
COOPER, THOMAS. *Mystery of Witchcraft.* London, 1617.
Pleasant Treatise of Witches. London, 1673.
COTTA, JOHN. *Infallible, true and assured Witch.* London, 1625.
Trial of Witchcraft. London, 1616.
County Folklore, III. London, 1901.
DALYELL, JOHN GRAHAME. *Darker Superstitions of Scotland.* Edinburgh, 1834.
DAVENPORT, JOHN. *Witches of Huntingdon.* London, 1646.
DAVIES, J. CEREDIG. *Welsh Folklore.* Aberystwith, 1911.
Denham Tracts. London, 1895.
DRAGE, W. *A Physical Nosonomy . . . with Daimonomagia.* 1665.
FAIRFAX, EDWARD. *Demonologia* (ed. W. Grainge). Harrogate, 1882.
FORBES, WILLIAM. *Institutes of the Law of Scotland.* Edinburgh, 1722–30.
FOSTER. *Tryall of Ann Foster.* Northampton, 1881.
FOUNTAINHALL, LORD. *Decisions.* Edinburgh, 1759.
FULLER, THOMAS. *Church History of Britain.* London, 1655. And edition of J. S. Brewer. Oxford, 1845.
GARDINER, RALPH. *England's Grievance Discovered.* London, 1655.
GAULE, JOHN. *Select cases of Conscience.* London, 1646.
GERISH, WILLIAM BLYTH. *Relation of Mary Hall of Gadsden.* 1912.
The Divel's Delusions. Bishops Stortford, 1914.
The Severall Practices of Johane Harrison. 1909.
GIBBONS, A. *Ely Episcopal Records.* Lincoln, 1891.
GIFFARD, GEORGE. *Discourse of the subtill Practices of Devilles.* London, 1587
Dialogue concerning Witches, Percy Society, VIII. London, 1843.
GILBERT, WILLIAM. *Witchcraft in Essex.* London, 1909.
GLANVILL, JOSEPH. *Sadducismus Triumphatus.* London, 1681.
GOLDSMID, E. *Confessions of Witches under Torture.* Edinburgh, 1886.
HALE, JOHN. *A Modest Enquiry* (ed. Burr). New York, 1914.
HALE, SIR MATTHEW. *Collection of Modern Relations.* London, 1693.
HECTOR, WILLIAM. *Judicial Records of Renfrewshire.* Paisley, 1876.
HELE, N. F. *Notes of Jottings about Aldeburgh.* Ipswich, 1890.
HIBBERT, SAMUEL. *Description of the Shetland Isles.* Edinburgh, 1822.
Highland Papers. Vol. III. Witchcraft in Bute. Edinburgh, 1920.
HOLLAND, HENRY. *A treatise against Witchcraft.* Cambridge, 1590.
HOLLINGSWORTH, A. G. *History of Stowmarket.* Ipswich, 1844.
HORNECK, ANTHONY. *Appendix to Glanvill's Sadducismus Triumphatus.* London, 1681.
HORNES, N. *Dæmonologie and Theologie.* London, 1650.
HOWELL, JAMES. *Familiar Letters.* (Ed. Joseph Jacobs.) London, 1890–2
HOWELL, THOMAS BAYLY. *State Trials.* London, 1816.
HUNT, WILLIAM. *History of the English Church.* London, 1901.
HUTCHINSON, BISHOP FRANCIS. *Historical Essay.* London, 1718.
INCH. *Trial of Isabel Inch.* Ardrossan, *circa* 1855.
JAMES, I. *Demonologie.* Edinburgh, 1597.
Journal of Anatomy. Vols. XIII and XXV. London, 1879, 1891.
Justiciary Court of Edinburgh, Records of Proceedings. Edinburgh, 1905.
KINLOCH, GEORGE RITCHIE. *Reliquiæ Antiquæ Scoticæ.* Edinburgh, 1848.
KNAPP AND BALDWIN. *Newgate Calendar.* London, 1825.
LAMONT, JOHN. *Diary, Maitland Club.* Edinburgh, 1830.
LAW, ROBERT. *Memorialls.* (Ed. Sharpe.) Edinburgh, 1818.
Lawes against Witches and Conivration. Published by Authority. London, 1745.
LYNN LINTON, MRS. *Witch Stories.* London, 1861 and 1883. (A diligent but uncritical work.)
MACKENZIE, SIR G. *Laws and Customs of Scotland.* Edinburgh, 1699.
MAITLAND, S. R. *Puritan Thaumaturgy.*
Maitland Club Miscellany. Vol. II. Glasgow, 1840.
MASON, J. *Anatomie of Sorcery.* 1612.

MELVILLE, SIR CHARLES. *Memoirs. Bannatyne Club.* Edinburgh.
Moore Rental. Chetham Society. Vol. XII. Manchester, 1847.
MORE, HENRY. *Antidote against Atheism.* London, 1655.
Narrative of the Sufferings of a young Girle. Edinburgh, 1698.
NICHOLLS, JOHN. *History and Antiquities of the County of Leicester.* London, 1795–1815.
NICOLL, JOHN. *Diary. Bannatyne Club.* Edinburgh, 1836.
NOTESTEIN, WALLACE. *History of Witchcraft in England.* Washington, 1911.
OSBORNE, FRANCIS. *Traditional Memoirs of the Reigns of Q. Elizabeth and King James I.* London, 1658.
Miscellany of Sundry Essays. London, 1659.
OWEN, H. and BLAKEWAY, J. B. *History of Shrewsbury.* London, 1825.
Percy Society, Giffard's Dialogues of Witches. London, 1843.
PERKINS, WILLIAM. *Discourse of the damned Art of Witchcraft.* Cambridge, 1608.
PETERSON. *Tryall of Mrs. Joan Peterson. Thomason Tracts.* London, 1652.
PETTO, SAMUEL. *A faithful Narrative.* London, 1693.
Philobiblion Society. Examination of certain Witches. London, 1863–4.
PIKE, L. O. *History of Crime in England.* London, 1873.
PITCAIRN, ROBERT. *Criminal Trials.* Edinburgh, 1833.
Pittenweem, A true and full Relation of the Witches of. Edinburgh, 1704.
POLLOCK and MAITLAND. *History of English Law.* 2nd ed. Cambridge, 1898.
Prodigious and Tragicall History. London, 1652.
QUIBELL, JAMES EDWARD. *Hierakonpolis.* II. London, 1902.
Register of the Privy Council of Scotland. Edinburgh, 1881.
Registrum Magni Sigilli Regum Scotorum. Edinburgh, 1886.
ROBERTS, ALEXANDER. *Treatise of Witchcraft.* London, 1616.
Sadducismus Debellatus. London, 1698.
SANDYS, GEORGE. *Relation of a Journey.* London, 1632.
SAUNDERS, W. H. B. *Legends and Traditions of Huntingdonshire.* 1888.
SCOT, REGINALD. *Discoverie of Witchcraft.* London, 1584.
SCOTT, SIR WALTER. *Demonology and Witchcraft.*
Scottish History Society. Vol. XXV. Edinburgh, 1896.
SEYMOUR, S. JOHN D. *Irish Witchcraft and Demonology.* Dublin, 1913.
SHARPE, CHARLES K. *Historical Account of Witchcraft in Scotland.* London, 1884.
SHAW. *Elinor Shaw and Mary Phillips.* Northampton, 1866.
SINCLAR, GEORGE. *The Hydrostaticks.* Edinburgh, 1672.
Satan's Invisible World Discovered. Edinburgh, 1871.
SMITH, CHARLOTTE FELL. *John Dee* (1527–1608). London, 1909.
Spalding Club Miscellany. Aberdeen, 1841.
SPOTTISWODE, JOHN. *History of the Church of Scotland.* Edinburgh, 1847–50.
STEPHEN, SIR J. F. *History of the Criminal Law in England.* London, 1883.
STEVENSON, J. *Chronicon de Lanercost. Maitland Club.* Glasgow, 1839.
STEWART, WILLIAM GRANT. *Popular Superstitions of the Highlands.* Edinburgh, 1823.
STRYPE, JOHN. *Annals of the Reformation.* London, 1709–31. Oxford, 1824.
Surtees Society. Vol. XL. Durham, 1861.
TAYLOR, JOHN. *Tracts relating to Northamptonshire.* Northampton, 1866.
THORPE, BENJAMIN. *Monumenta Ecclesiastica.* London, 1840.
VETTER, THEODOR. *Relations between England and Zurich during the Reformation.* London, 1904.
VICKARS, K. H. *Humphrey, Duke of Gloucester.* London, 1907.
WAGSTAFFE, JOHN. *Displaying of Supposed Witchcraft.* London, 1671.
WALSH. *Examination of John Walsh.* London, 1566.
WHITAKER, T. D. *History of Whalley.* London, 1818.
WILKINS, DAVID. *Concilia Magnæ Britanniæ.* London, 1737.
WILSON, ARTHUR. *Life and Reign of James I.* London, 1653.
Witchcraft, Collection of rare and curious tracts on. Edinburgh, 1891.
Witchcraft, Collections of rare and curious Tracts relating to. London, 1838.
Witchcraft Detected. 1826.
ZIMMERMAN, G. *De Mutata Saxonum veterum religione.* 1839.

ENGLAND: THE PAMPHLET LITERATURE

(Arranged in chronological order)

The Examination and confession of certaine Wytches at Chensforde in the Countie of Essex before the Quenes maiesties Judges, the XXVI daye of July Anno 1566.

A Rehearsall both straung and true of hainous and horrible actes committed by Elizabeth Stile, alias Rockingham, Mother Dutten, Mother Devell, Mother Margaret. Fower notorious Witches apprehended at Winsore in the Countie of Barks, and at Abington arraigned, condemned and executed on the 28 daye of Februarie last anno 1579.

A Detection of damnable driftes, practised by three Witches arraigned at Chelmsforde in Essex . . . whiche were executed in Aprill 1579. 1579.

The apprehension and confession of three notorious Witches arraigned and by Justice condemnede in the Countye of Essex the 5 day of Julye last past. 1589.

A True and just Recorde of the Information, Examination and Confessions of all the Witches taken at St. Oses in the countie of Essex: wherefore some were executed, and other some entreated accordingly to the determination of Lawe. . . . Written orderly, as the cases were tryed by evidence, by W. W. 1582.

The most strange and admirable discoverie of the three Witches of Warboys, arraigned, convicted and executed at the last assizes at Huntingdon. London, 1593.

(This was one of the most famous cases of English Witchcraft. A whole literature grew up in connexion therewith. In *Notes and Queries*, Twelfth Series, I, 1916, p. 283 and p. 304, will be found: "The Witches of Warboys: Bibliographical Note," where twenty-eight entries are made.)

The most wonderfull and true storie of a certaine Witch named Alse Gooderidge of Stapenhill, who was arraigned and convicted at Darbie. . . . As also a true Report of the strange Torments of Thomas Darling, a boy of thirteen years of age, that was possessed by the Devill, with his horrible Fittes and terrible apparitions by him uttered at Burton upon Trent, in the county of Stafford, and of his marvellous deliverance. London, 1597. [By John Denison.]

The Arraignment and Execution of 3 detestable Witches, John Newell, Joane his wife, and Hellen Calles; two executed at Barnett, and one at Braynford, 1 *Dec.* 1595.

The severall Facts of Witchcrafte approved on Margaret Haskett of Stanmore, 1585. Black letter.

An Account of Margaret Hacket, a notorious Witch, who consumed a young Man to Death, rotted his Bowells and back bone asunder, who was executed at Tiborn, 19 *Feb.* 1585. London, 1585.

The Examination and Confession of a notorious Witch named Mother Arnold, alias Whitecote, alias Glastonbury, at the Assise of Burntwood in July, 1574*: who was hanged for Witchcraft at Barking.* 1575.

(The four preceding pamphlets although referred to by Lowndes and other bibliographers apparently have not been traced.)

A true report of three Straunge Witches, lately found at Newnham Regis.

(Not traced. Hazlitt, *Handbook*, p. 231.

A short treatise declaringe the detestable wickednesse of magicall sciences, as Necromancie, Coniuration of Spirites, Curiouse Astrologie and such lyke. . . . Made by Francis Coxe. [London, 1561.] Black letter.

The Examination of John Walsh, before Master Thomas Williams, Commissary to the Reverend father in God, William, bishop of Excester, upon certayne Interrogatories touchyng Wytch-crafte and Sorcerye, in the presence of divers gentlemen and others, the XX of August, 1566. 1566. Black letter.

The discloysing of a late counterfeyted possession by the devyl in two maydens within the Citie of London. [1574.] Black letter.

The Wonderfull Worke of God shewed upon a Chylde, whose name is William Withers, being in the Towne of Walsam . . . Suffolk, who, being Eleven Yeeres of age, laye in a Traunce the Space of tenne Days . . . and hath continued the Space of Three Weeks. London, 1581.

A Most Wicked worke of a Wretched Witch (the like whereof none can record these manie yeares in England) wrought on the Person of one Richard Burt, servant to Maister Edling of Woodhall in the Parrish of Pinner in the Countie of Myddlesex, a myle beyond Harrow. Latelie committed in March last, An. 1592 *and newly recognized acording to the truth. By* G. B. *maister of Artes.* [London, 1593.]

A defensative against the poyson of supposed prophecies, not hitherto confuted by the penne of any man; which being eyther uppon the warrant and authority of old paynted bookes, expositions of dreames, oracles, revelations, invocations of damned spirits . . . have been causes of great disorder in the commonwealth and chiefly among the simple and unlearned people. Circa 1581–3.

The scratchinge of the wytches. 1579.

A warnynge to wytches. 1585.

A lamentable songe of Three Wytches of Warbos, and executed at Huntingdon. 1593.

(The three preceding are ballads. See Hazlitt, *Bibliographical Collections and Notes,* 2nd Series. London, 1882.)

A poosye in forme of a visyon, agaynste wytche Crafte, and Sosyrye.

A Breife Narration of the possession, dispossession, and repossession of William Sommers . . . Together with certaine depositions taken at Nottingham. 1598.

An Apologie, or defence of the possession of William Sommers, a yong man of the towne of Nottingham. . . . By John Darrell, Minister of Christ Jesus. [1599 ?] Black letter.

The Triall of Maist. Dorrel, or A Collection of Defences against Allegations. . . 1599.

(Apparently written by Darrel himself; but the Huth catalogue (V. 1643) ascribes it to James Bamford.)

A brief Apologie proving the possession of William Sommers. Written by John Dorrel, a faithful Minister of the Gospell, but published without his knowledge. . . . 1599.

A Discovery of the Fraudulent Practises of John Darrel, Bacheler of Artes. . . . London, 1599. (By Samuel Harsnett.)

A True Narration of the strange and grevous Vexation by the Devil of seven persons in Lancashire. . . . 1600. Written by Darrel.

(Reprinted in 1641, and again in the *Somers Tracts,* III.)

A True Discourse concerning the certaine possession and dispossession of 7 *persons in one familie in Lancashire, which also may serve as part of an Answere to a fayned and false Discoverie. . . . By George More, Minister and Preacher of the Worde of God. . . .* 1600.

A Detection of that sinnful, shamful, lying, and ridiculous discours of Samuel Harshnet. 1600. (By Darrel in answer to Harsnett.)

A Summarie Answere to al the Material Points in any of Master Darel his bookes, More especiallie to that one Booke of his, intituled, the Doctrine of the Possession and Dispossession of Demoniaks out of the word of God. By John Deacon [and] *John Walker, Preachers.* London, 1601.

A Survey of Certaine Dialogical Discourses, written by John Deacon and John Walker. . . . By John Darrell, minister of the gospel. . . . 1602.

The Replie of John Darrell, to the Answer of John Deacon, and John Walker concerning the doctrine of the Possession and Dispossession of Demoniakes. . . . 1602.

A True and Breife Report of Mary Glover's Vexation, and of her deliverance by the meanes of fastinge and prayer. . . . By John Swan, student in Divinitie. . . . 1603.

Elizabeth Jackson was indicted on the charge of having bewitched Mary Glover, but Dr. Edward Jorden, who examined the girl declared her an hysterical impostor in his pamphlet

A briefe discourse of a disease called the Suffocation of the Mother, Written uppon occasion which hath beene of late taken thereby, to suspect possession of an evill spirit. . . . London, 1603.

A history of the case of Catherine Wright.

The strange Newes out of Sommersetshire, Anno 1584, *tearmed, a dreadfull discourse of the dispossessing of one Maggaret Cooper at Ditchet, from a devill in the likenes of a headlesse beare. Discovery of the Fraudulent Practices of John Darrel.* 1584.

The Most Cruell and Bloody Murther committed by an Inn-keepers Wife called Annis Dell, and her Sonne George Dell, Foure Years since. . . . With the severall Witch-crafts and most damnable practices of one Iohane Harrison and her Daughter, upon several persons men and women at Royston, who were all executed at Hartford the 4 *of August last past* 1606. London, 1606.

The Witches of Northamptonshire.

Agnes Browne { *Arthur Bill* } *Witches*
Joane Vaughan { *Hellen Jenkenson* }
Mary Barber

Who were all executed at Northampton the 22 *of July last.* 1612. 1612.

The severall notorious and lewd Cosenages of Iohn West and Alice West, falsely called the King and Queene of Fayries . . . convicted. . . . 1613. London, 1613.

The Wonderfull Discoverie of Witches in the countie of Lancaster. With the Arraignment and Triall of Nineteene notorious Witches, at the Assizes and Gaole deliverie, holden at the Castle of Lancaster, upon Munday, the seventeenth of August last, 1612. *Before Sir James Altham, and Sir Edward Bromley.* London, 1613.

(Reprinted by the Chetham Society, edited James Crossley. 1845. One of the most famous of the witch-trials.)

Witches Apprehended, Examined and Executed, for notable villanies by them committed both by Land and Water. With a strange and most true trial how to know whether a woman be a Witch or not. London, 1613.

A Booke of the Wytches Lately condemned and executed at Bedford, 1612–1613.

A Treatise of Witchcraft. . . . With a true Narration of the Witchcrafts which Mary Smith, wife of Henry Smith, Glover, did practise . . . and lastly, of her death and execution. . . . By Alexander Roberts, B.D. and Preacher of Gods Word at Kings-Linne in Norffolke. London, 1616.

The Wonderful Discoverie of the Witchcrafts of Margaret and Phillip Flower, daughters of Joan Flower neere Bever Castle: executed at Lincolne, March 11, 1618. *Who were specially arraigned and condemned . . . for confessing themselves actors in the destruction of Henry, Lord Rosse, with their damnable practises against others the Children of the Right Honourable Francis Earle of Rutland. Together with the severall Examinations and Confessions of Anne Baker, Joan Willimot, and Ellen Greene, Witches of Leicestershire.* London, 1619.

Strange and wonderfull Witchcrafts, discovering the damnable Practises of seven Witches against the Lives of certain noble Personages and others of this Kingdom; with an approved Triall how to find out either Witch or any Apprentise to Witchcraft. 1621. Another edition in 1635.

The Wonderfull discoverie of Elizabeth Sawyer . . . late of Edmonton, her conviction, condemnation and Death. . . . Written by Henry Goodcole, Minister of the word of God, and her continuall Visiter in the Gaole of Newgate. . . . 1621.

(Reprinted in Vol. I (lxxxi–cvii) of Bullen's recension of the Dyce-Gifford *Ford.* 3 vols. London, 1895.)

The Boy of Bilson: or A True Discovery of the Late Notorious Impostures of Certaine Romish Priests in their pretended Exorcisme, or expulsion of the Divell out of a young Boy, named William Perry. . . . London, 1622.

A Discourse of Witchcraft As it was acted in the Family of Mr. Edward Fairfax of Fuystone in the County of York, in the year 1621. Edited by R. Monckton Milnes (Lord Houghton) for Vol. V of *Miscellanies of the Philobiblon Soc.* London, 1858–1859. (The editor says the original MS. is still in existence.)

A Most certain, strange and true Discovery of a Witch, Being overtaken by some of the Parliament Forces, as she was standing on a small Planck-board and sayling on it over the River of Newbury, Together with the strange and true manner of her death. 1643.

A Confirmation and Discovery of Witch-craft . . . together with the Confessions of many of those executed since May, 1645. . . . *By John Stearne.*

The Examination, Confession, Triall, and Execution of Joane Williford, Joan Cariden and Jane Hott: who were executed at Faversham, in Kent . . . all attested under the hand of Robert Greenstreet, Maior of Faversham.

A true and exact Relation of the severall Informations, Examinations, and Confessions of the late Witches arraigned . . . and condemned at the late Sessions, holden at Chelmsford before the Right Honorable Robert, Earle of Warwicke, and severall of his Majesties Justices of Peace, the 29 *of July,* 1645.

A True Relation of the Arraignment of eighteene Witches at St. Edmundsbury, 27*th August,* 1645. . . . *As Also a List of the names of those that were executed.*

Strange and fearfull newes from Plaisto in the parish of Westham neere Bow foure miles from London. London, 1645.

The Lawes against Witches and Conjuration, and Some brief Notes and Observations for the Discovery of Witches. Being very Usefull for these Times wherein the Devil reignes and prevailes. . . . Also The Confession of Mother Lakeland, who was arraigned and condemned for a Witch at Ipswich in Suffolke. . . . By Authority. London, 1645.

Signes and Wonders from Heaven. . . . Likewise a new discovery of Witches in Stepney Parish. And how 20. *Witches more were executed in Suffolk this last Assize. Also how the Divell came to Sofforn to a Farmer's house in the habit of a Gentlewoman on horse backe.* London [1645].

Relation of a boy who was entertained by the Devil to be Servant to him . . . about Credition in the West, and how the Devil carried him up in the aire, and showed him the torments of Hell, and some of the Cavaliers there, etc., with a coppie of a Letter from Maior Generall Massie, concerning these strange and Wonderfull things, with a certaine box of Reliques and Crucifixes found in Tiverton Church. 1645.

(A ridiculous, but not uninteresting, publication.)

The Witches of Huntingdon, their Examinations and Confessions. . . . London, 1646.

(The Dedication is signed by John Davenport.)

The Discovery of Witches: in answer to severall Queries, lately Delivered to the Judges of Assize for the County of Norfolk. And now published by Matthew Hopkins, Witchfinder. For the Benefit of the Whole Kingdome. . . London, 1647.

(The most famous of the "Hopkins series.")

A strange and true Relation of a Young Woman possest with the Devill. By name Joyce Dovey dwelling at Bewdley neer Worcester. . . . Also a Letter from Cambridge, wherein is related the late conference between the Devil (in the shape of a Mr. of Arts) and one Ashbourner, a Scholler of S. Johns Colledge . . . who was afterwards carried away by him and never heard of since onely his Gown found in the River. London, 1647.

The Full Tryals, Examination and Condemnation of Four Notorious Witches, At the Assizes held in Worcester on Tuseday the 4*th of March. . . . As also Their Confessions and last Dying Speeches at the place of Execution, with other Amazing Particulars. . . .* London, no date.

The Divels Delusions or A faithfull relation of John Palmer and Elizabeth Knot two notorious Witches lately condemned at the Sessions of Oyer and Terminer in St. Albans. 1649.

Wonderfull News from the North, Or a True Relation of the Sad and Grievous Torments Inflicted upon the Bodies of three Children of Mr. George Muschamp, late of the County of Northumberland, by Witchcraft. . . . As also the prosecution of the sayd Witches, as by Oaths, and their own Confessions will appear and by the Indictment found by the Jury against one of them, at the Sessions of the Peace held at Alnwick, the 24 *day of April,* 1650. London, 1650.

The strange Witch at Greenwich haunting a Wench, 1650.

A Strange Witch at Greenwich, 1650.

The Witch of Wapping, or an Exact and Perfect Relation of the Life and Devilish Practises of Joan Peterson, who dwelt in Spruce Island, near Wapping; Who was condemned for practising Witchcraft, and sentenced to be Hanged at Tyburn, on Munday the 11th of April, 1652. London, 1652.

A Declaration in Answer to several lying Pamphlets concerning the Witch of Wapping, . . . shewing the Bloudy Plot and wicked Conspiracy of one Abraham Vandenhemde, Thomas Crompton, Thomas Collet, and others. London, 1652.

The Tryall and Examinations of Mrs. Joan Peterson before the Honourable Bench at the Sessions house in the Old Bayley yesterday. [1652.]

Doctor Lamb's Darling, or Strange and terrible News from Salisbury; Being A true, exact, and perfect Relation of the great and wonderful Contract and Engagement made between the Devil, and Mistris Anne Bodenham; with the manner how she could transform herself into the shape of a Mastive Dog, a black Lyon, a white Bear, a Woolf, a Bull, and a Cat. . . . The Tryal, Examinations, and Confession . . . before the Lord Chief Baron Wild. . . . By James [*Edmond ?*] *Bower, Cleric.* London, 1653.

Doctor Lamb Revived, or, Witchcraft condemn'd in Anne Bodenham . . . who was Arraigned and Executed the Lent Assizes last at Salisbury, before the Right Honourable the Lord Chief Baron Wild, Judge of the Assize. . . . By Edmund Bower, an eye and ear Witness of her Examination and Confession. London, 1653. (Bower's second and more detailed account.)

A Prodigious and Tragicall History of the Arraignment, Tryall, Confession, and Condemnation of six Witches at Maidstone, in Kent, at the Assizes there held in July, Fryday 30, *this present year*, 1652. *Before the Right Honorable, Peter Warburton. . . . Collected from the Observations of E. G. Gent, a learned person, present at their Convictions and Condemnation* London, 1652.

The most true and wonderfull Narration of two women bewitched in Yorkshire: Who comming to the Assizes at York to give Evidence against the Witch after a most horrible noise to the terror and amazement of all the beholders, did vomit forth before the Judges, Pins, wool. . . . Also a most true Relation of a young Maid . . . who . . . did . . . vomit forth wadds of straw, with pins a crosse in them, iron Nails, Needles, . . . as it is attested under the hand of that most famous Phisition Doctor Henry Heers. . . . 1658.

A more Exact Relation of the most lamentable and horrid Contract with Lydia Rogers, living in Pump-Alley in Wapping, made with the Divel. . . Together with the great pains and prayers of many eminent Divines. . . 1658.

The Snare of the Devill Discovered: Or, A True and perfect Relation of the sad and deplorable Condition of Lydia the Wife of John Rogers House Carpenter, living in Greenbank in Pumpe alley in Wappin. . . . Also her Examination by Mr. Johnson the Minister of Wappin, and her Confession. As also in what a sad Condition she continues. . . . London, 1658.

Strange and Terrible Newes from Cambridge, being A true Relation of the Quakers bewitching of Mary Philips . . . into the shape of a Bay Mare, riding her from Dinton towards the University. With the manner how she became visible again . . . in her own Likeness and Shape, with her sides all rent and torn, as if they had been spur-galled, . . . and the Names of the Quakers brought to tryal on Friday last at the Assizes held at Cambridge. . . . London, 1659.

The Power of Witchcraft, Being a most strange but true Relation of the most miraculous and wonderful deliverance of one Mr. William Harrison of Cambden in the County of Gloucester, Steward to the Lady Nowel. . . . London, 1662.

A True and Perfect Account of the Examination, Confession, Tryal, Condemnation and Execution of Joan Perry and her two Sons . . . for the supposed murder of William Harrison, Gent. . . . London, 1676.

A Tryal of Witches at the assizes held at Bury St. Edmonds for the County of Suffolk; on the tenth day of March, 1664. London, 1682; and 1716.

The Lord's Arm Stratched Out in an Answer of Prayer or a True Relation of the Wonderful Deliverance of James Barrow, the Son of John Barrow of Olaves Southwark, London, 1664. (A Baptist tract.)

The wonder of Suffolke, being a true relation of one that reports he made a league with the Devil for three years, to do mischief, and now breaks open houses, robs people daily . . . and can neither be shot nor taken, but leaps over walls fifteen feet high, runs five or six miles in a quarter of an hour, and sometimes vanishes in the midst of multitudes that go to take him. Faithfully written in a letter from a solemn person, dated not long since, to a friend in Ship-Yard near Temple-bar, and ready to be attested by hundreds. . . . London, 1677.

Daimonomageia : a small Treatise of Sicknesses and Diseases from Witchcraft and Supernatural Causes. . . . Being useful to others besides Physicians, in that it confutes Atheistical, Sadducistical, and Sceptical Principles and Imaginations. . . . London, 1665.

Hartford-shire Wonder. Or, Strange News from Ware, Being an Exact and true Relation of one Jane Stretton . . . who hath been visited in a strange kind of manner by extraordinary and unusual fits. . . . London, 1669.

A Magicall Vision, Or a Perfect Discovery of the Fallacies of Witchcraft, As it was lately represented in a pleasant sweet Dream to a Holysweet Sister, a faithful and pretious Assertor of the Family of the Stand-Hups, for preservation of the Saints from being tainted with the heresies of the Congregation of the Doe-Littles. London, 1673. (Hazlitt, *Bibliographical Collections,* fourth series, *s. u.* Witchcraft.)

A Full and True Relation of The Tryal, Condemnation, and Execution of Ann Foster . . . at the place of Execution at Northampton. With the Manner how she by her Malice and Witchcraft set all the Barns and Corn on Fire . . . and bewitched a whole Flock of Sheep. . . . London, 1674.

Strange News from Arpington near Bexby in Kent : Being a True Narrative of a yong Maid who was Possest with several Devils. . . . London, 1679.

Strange and Wonderful News from Yowell in Surry ; Giving a True and Just Account of One Elizabeth Burgess, Who was most strangely Bewitched and Tortured at a sad rate. London, 1681.

An Account of the Tryal and Examination of Joan Buts, for being a Common Witch and Inchantress, before the Right Honourable Sir Francis Pemberton, Lord Chief Justice, at the Assizes. . . . 1682. Single leaf.

The Tryal, Condemnation, and Execution of Three Witches, viz., Temperance Floyd, Mary Floyd, and Susanna Edwards. Who were Arraigned at Exeter on the 18*th of August,* 1682. London, 1682.

A True and Impartial Relation of the Informations against Three Witches, viz., Temperance Lloyd, Mary Trembles, and Susanna Edwards, who were . . . Convicted at the Assizes holden . . . at . . . Exon, Aug. 14, 1682. *With their several Confessions . . . as also Their . . . Behaviour, at the . . . Execution on the Twenty fifth of the said Month.* London, 1682.

Witchraft discovered and punished Or the Tryals and Condemnation of three Notorious Witches, who were Tryed the last Assizes, holden at the Castle of Exeter . . . where they received sentence of Death, for bewitching severall Persons, destroying Ships at Sea, and Cattel by Land. To the Tune of Doctor Faustus ; or Fortune my Foe.
(A ballad. Roxburghe Collection. Broadside.)

The Life and Conversation of Temperance Floyd, Mary Lloyd and Susanna Edwards . . .; Lately Condemned at Exeter Assizes ; together with a full Account of their first Agreement with the Devil : With the manner how they prosecuted their devilish Sorceries. . . . London, 1687.

A Full and True Account of the Proceedings at the Sessions of Oyer and Terminer . . . which began at the Sessions House in the Old Bayley on Thursday, June 1st, and Ended on Fryday, June 2nd, 1682. *Wherein is Contained the Tryall of Jane Kent for Witchcraft.*

Strange and Dreadful News from the Town of Deptford in the County of Kent, Being a Full, True, and Sad Relation of one Anne Arthur. 1684–5. One leaf, folio.

Strange newes from Shadwell, being a . . . relation of the death of Alice Fowler, who had for many years been accounted a witch. London, 1685.

A True Account of a Strange and Wonderful Relation of one John Tonken, of Pensans in Cornwall, said to be Bewitched by some Women : two of which on Suspition are committed to Prison. London, 1686.

News from Panier Alley ; or a True Relation of Some Pranks the Devil hath lately play'd with a Plaster Pot there. London, 1687.

A faithful narrative of the . . . fits which . . . Thomas Spatchet . . . was under by witchcraft. . . . 1693.

The Second Part of the Boy of Bilson, Or a True and Particular Relation of the Imposter Susanna Fowles, wife of John Fowles of Hammersmith in the Co. of Midd., who pretended herself to be possessed. London, 1698.

A Full and True Account Both of the Life : And also the Manner and Method of carrying on the Delusions, Blasphemies, and Notorious Cheats of Susan Fowls, as the same was Contrived, Plotted, Invented, and Managed by wicked Popish Priests and other Papists.

The trial of Susannah Fowles, of Hammersmith, for blaspheming Jesus Christ, and cursing the Lord's Prayer. . . . London, 1698.

The Case of Witchcraft at Coggeshall, Essex, in the year 1699. *Being the Narrative of the Rev. J. Boys, Minister of the Parish.* Printed from his manuscript in the possession of the publisher (A. Russell Smith). London, 1901.

A True and Impartial Account of the Dark and Hellish Power of Witchcraft, Lately Exercised on the Body of the Reverend Mr. Wood, Minister of Bodmyn. In a Letter from a Gentleman there, to his Friend in Exon, in Confirmation thereof. Exeter, 1700.

A Full and True Account of the Apprehending and Taking of Mrs. Sarah Moordike, Who is accused for a Witch, Being taken near Pauls' Wharf . . . for having Bewitched one Richard Hetheway. . . . With her Examination before the Right Worshipful Sir Thomas Lane, Sir Oven Buckingham, and Dr. Hambleton in Bowe-lane. 1701.

A short Account of the Trial held at Surry Assizes, in the Borough of Southwark ; on an Information against Richard Hathway . . . for Riot and Assault. London, 1702.

The Tryall of Richard Hathaway, upon an Information For being a Cheat and Imposter. For endeavouring to take away the Life of Sarah Morduck, For being a Witch at Surry Assizes. . . . London, 1702.

A Full and True Account of the Discovery, Apprehending, and taking of a Notorious Witch, who was carried before Justice Bateman in Well-Close on Sunday, July the 23. *Together with her Examination and Commitment to Bridewel, Clerkenwell.* London, 1704.

An Account of the Tryals, Examination, and Condemnation of Elinor Shaw and Mary Phillips. . . . 1705.

The Northamptonshire Witches. . . . 1705.

The Devil Turned Casuist, or the Cheats of Rome Laid open in the Exorcism of a Despairing Devil at the House of Thomas Bennington in Oriel. . . . By Zachary Taylor, M.A., Chaplain to the Right reverend Father in God, Nicholas, Lord Bishop of Chester, and Rector of Wigan. London, 1696.

The Surey Demoniack, Or an Account of Satan's Strange and Dreadful Actings, In and about the Body of Richard Dugdale of Surey, near Whalley in Lancashire. And How he was Dispossest by Gods blessing on the Fastings and Prayers of divers Ministers and People. London, 1697.

The Surey Imposter, being an answer to a late Fanatical Pamphlet, entituled The Surey Demoniack. By Zachary Taylor. London, 1697.

A Vindication of the Surey Demoniack as no Imposter : Or, A Reply to a certain Pamphlet publish'd by Mr. Zach. Taylor, called The Surey Imposter. . . . By T. J., London, 1698.

Popery, Supersitition, Ignorance and Knavery very unjustly by a letter in the general pretended ; but as far as was charg'd very fully proved upon the Dissenters that were concerned in the Surey Imposture. 1698. Written by Zachary Taylor.

The Lancashire Levite Rebuked, or a Vindication of the Dissenters from Popery, Superstition, Ignorance, and Knavery, unjustly Charged on them by Mr. Zachary Taylor. . . . London, 1698.

The Lancashire Levite Rebuked, or a Farther Vindication. 1698.

Popery, Superstition, Ignorance, and Knavery, Confess'd and fully Proved on the Surey Dissenters, from a Second Letter of an Apostate Friend, to Zach. Taylor. To which is added a Refutation of T. Jollie's Vindication. . . . London, 1699. Written by Zachary Taylor.

A Refutation of Mr. T. Jolly's Vindication of the Devil in Dugdale; Or, The Surey Demoniack. London, 1699.

The Portsmouth Ghost, or A Full and true Account of a Strange, wonderful, and dreadful Appearing of the Ghost of Madam Johnson, a beautiful young Lady of Portsmouth, Shewing, 1. Her falling in Love with Mr. John Hunt, a Captain in one of the Regiments sent to Spain. 2. Of his promising her Marriage, and leaving her big With Child. 3. Of her selling herself to the Devil to be revenged on the Captain. 4. Of her ripping open her own Belly, and the Devil's flying away with her Body, and leaving the Child in the room. . . . 7. Of her Carrying [*the Captain*] *away in the night in a flame of fire.* Printed and sold by Cluer Dicey and Co. in Aldermary Church Yard, Bow Lane. *Circa* 1704.

A Looking Glass for Swearers, Drunkards, Blasphemers, Sabbath Breakers, Rash Wishers, and Murderers. Being a True Relation of one Elizabeth Hale, in Scotch Yard in White Cross Street; who having sold herself to the Devil to be reveng'd on her Neighbours, did on Sunday last, in a wicked manner, put a quantity of Poyson into a Pot where a Piece of Beef was a boyling for several Poor Women and Children, Two of which dropt down dead, and Twelve more are dangerously Ill; the Truth of which will be Attested by several in the Neighbourhood. Her Examination upon the Crowners Inquest and her Commitment to Newgate. Printed by W. Wise and M. Holt in Fleet Street, 1708.

The Witch of the Woodlands; Or, The Cobler's New Translation. Printed and Sold in Aldermary Church Yard, Bow Lane, London. No date, but about 1710. This pamphlet merely relates an old legend, but is interesting as reproducing with appropriate woodcuts intimate details of the mediæval Sabbat.

An Account of the Tryal, Examination, and Condemnation of Jane Wenham, on an Indictment of Witchcraft, for Bewitching of Matthew Gilston and Anne Thorne of Walcorne, in the County of Hertford. . . .

A Full and Impartial Account of the Discovery of Sorcery and Witchcraft, Practis'd by Jane Wenham of Walkerne in Hertfordshire, upon the bodies of Anne Thorn, Anne Street, &c. . . . till she . . . receiv'd Sentence of Death for the same, March 4, 1711–12. London, 1712.

Witchcraft Farther Display'd. Containing (I) An Account of the Witchcraft practis'd by Jane Wenham of Walkerne, in Hertfordshire, since her Condemnation, upon the bodies of Anne Thorne and Anne Street. . . . (II) An Answer to the most general Objections against the Being and Power of Witches: With some Remarks upon the Case of Jane Wenham in particular, and on Mr. Justice Powel's procedure therein. . . . London, 1712.

A Full Confutation of Witchcraft: More particularly of the Depositions against Jane Wenham, Lately Condemned for a Witch; at Hertford. In which the Modern Notions of Witches are overthrown, and the Ill Consequences of such Doctrines are exposed by Arguments; proving that, Witchcraft is Priestcraft. . . . In a Letter from a Physician in Hertfordshire, to his Friend in London. London, 1712.

The Impossibility of Witchcraft, Plainly Proving, From Scripture and Reason, That there never was a Witch; and that it is both Irrational and Impious to believe there ever was. In which the Depositions against Jane Wenham, Lately Try'd and Condemned for a Witch, at Hertford, are Confuted and Expos'd. London, 1712.

The Belief of Witchcraft Vindicated; proving from Scripture, there have been Witches; and from Reason, that there may be Such still. In answer to a late Pamphlet, Intituled, The Impossibility of Witchcraft. . . By G. R., A.M. London, 1712.

The Case of the Hertfordshire Witchcraft Consider'd. Being an Examination of a book entitl'd, A Full and Impartial Account. . . . London, 1712.

A Defense of the Proceedings against Jane Wenham, wherein the Possibility and Reality of Witchcraft are Demonstrated from Scripture. . . . In Answer to Two Pamphlets Entituled : (I) The Impossibility of Witchcraft, etc. (II) A Full Confutation of Witchcraft. By Francis Bragge, A.B., London, 1712.

The Impossibility of Witchcraft Further Demonstrated, Both from Scripture and Reason . . . with some Cursory Remarks on two trifling Pamphlets in Defense of the existence of Witches. 1712.

An Account of The Tryals, Examination and Condemnation of Elinor Shaw and Mary Phillips (Two notorious Witches) on Wednesday the 7th of March, 1705, for Bewitching a Woman, and two children. . . . With an Account of their strange Confessions. This is signed at the end, "Ralph Davis, March 8, 1705." It was followed very shortly by a completer account, written after the execution, and entitled :

The Northamptonshire Witches, Being a true and faithful account of the Births, Educations, Lives, and Conversations of Elinor Shaw and Mary Phillips (The two notorious Witches) That were Executed at Northampton on Saturday, March the 17th, 1705 . . . with their full Confession to the Minister, and last Dying Speeches at the place of Execution, the like never before heard of. . . . Communicated in a Letter last Post, from Mr. Ralph Davis of Northampton, to Mr. William Simons, Merchantt in London. London, 1705.

The Whole Trial and Examination of Mrs. Mary Hicks and her Daughter Elizabeth, But of Nine Years of Age, who were Condemn'd the last Assizes held at Huntingdon for Witchcraft, and there Executed on Saturday, the 28th of July, 1716 . . . the like never heard before ; their Behaviour with several Divines who came to converse with 'em whilst under their sentence of Death ; and last Dying Speeches and Confession at the place of execution. London, 1716. There is a copy in the Bodleian Library.

(These last three pamphlets are almost certainly spurious.)

A Terrible and seasonable Warning to young Men. Being a very particular and True Relation of one Abraham Joiner a young Man about 17 or 18 Years of Age, living in Shakesby's Walks in Shadwell, being a Ballast Man by Profession, who on Saturday Night last pick'd up a leud Woman, and spent what Money he had about him in Treating her, saying afterwards if she wou'd have any more he must go to the Devil for it, and slipping out of her Company, he went to the Cock and Lyon in King Street, the Devil appear'd to him, and gave him a Pistole, . . . appointing to meet him the next Night at the World's End at Stepney ; Also how his Brother perswaded him to throw the Money away, which he did ; but was suddenly Taken in a very strange manner ; so that they were fain to send for the Reverend Mr. Constable and other Ministers to pray with him, he appearing now to be very Penitent. . . . Printed for J. Dulton, near Fleet Street. *Circa* 1718.

A Timely Warning to Rash and Disobedient Children Being a strange and wonderful Relation of a young Gentleman in the Parish of Stepheny in the Suburbs of London, that sold himself to the Devil for 12 years to have the Power of being revenged on his Father and Mother, and how his Time being expired, he lay in a sad and deplorable Condition to the Amazement af all Spectators. Edinburgh : Printed Anno 1721.

The Kentish Miracle, Or, a Seasonable Warning to all Sinners Shewn in The Wonderful Relation of one Mary Moore, whose Husband died some time ago, and left her with two Children, who was reduced to great Want. . . . How the Devil appeared to her, and the many great Offers he made to her to deny Christ, and enter into his Service ; and how she confounded Satan by powerful Arguments . . . with an Account how an Angel appeared to her and relieved her. . . . Edinburgh : Printed in the Year 1741.

(This is probably a reprint. The style of the pamphlet seems some thirty or forty years earlier.)

Trial of Thomas Colley, to which is annexed some Further Particulars of the Affair from the Mouth of John Osborne. 1751. (The trial took place at Hertford Assizes, 30 July, 1751.)

Remarkable Confession and Last Dying Words of Thomas Colley. 1751.

FRANCE

BARTHÉTY, H. *La sorcellerie en Béarn et dans le pays basque.* Pau, 1879.

BERNOU, J. *La chasse aux sorcières dans le Labourd* (1609). Agen, 1897.

BEUGNOT, A. *Histoire de la destruction du Paganisme en occident.* 2 vols Paris, 1835.

BOIS, JULES. *Le Satanisme et la magie. Les Petites Religions de Paris.*

BONNEMÈRE, EUGÈNE. *Histoire des Camisardes des Cévennes.* Paris, 1869.

BOUCHARD, H. E. *Annette Taudet, ou les sorciers du Poitou au XIXme siècle* Paris, 1867.

BOURIGNON, ANTOINETTE. *La Parole de Dieu.* Amsterdam, 1683.

La vie extérieure. Amsterdam, 1683.

BOURNON, JACQUES. *Chroniques de la Lorraine.* Nancy, 1838.

BRÉVANNES, ROLAND. *L'Orgie Satanique.* Paris, 1904.

BRICAUD, JOANNY. *J. K. Huysmans et le Satanisme.* Paris, 1912.

Huysmans, occultiste et magicien. Paris, 1913.

Un disciple de Cl. de Saint-Martin. Paris, 1911.

Eléments d'Astrologie. Paris, 1911.

Premiers Elements d'Occultisme. Paris, 1912.

CANNAERT, J. B. *Olim : procès des sorcières en Belgique sous Philippe II* Ghent, 1847.

CAUFEYNON ET JAF, DRS. *Les Messes Noires.* Paris, 1905. (A valuable work.)

CAUZONS, THEODORE DE. *La Magie et la Sorcellerie en France.* 4 vols. Paris, 1900, etc. (A very important study.)

CHABLOZ, FRITZ. *Les sorcières neuchatéloises.* Neuchatel, 1868.

CHRISTIAN, PAUL (Paul Pitois). *Histoire de la Magie.* Paris, 1870.

CLOSMADEUC, DR. G. DE. *Les sorciers de Lorient.* Vannes, 1885.

DEBAY, DR. A. *Histoire des sciences occultes.* Paris, 1860.

DE LA MARTINIÈRE. *Voyage des Pais Septentrionaux.* Paris, 1682.

Discours sur la mort et condamnation de Charles de Franchillon Baron de Chenevieres, exécuté . . . pour Crime de Sortilège et de Magie. Paris, 1626.

DRAZOR, H. R. *Histoire tragique de trois magiciens qvi ont accvsé à la mort Mazarin en Italie.* Paris, 1649.

ELVEN, HENRY VON. *La Tradition.* Vol. V. Paris, 1891.

FIGUIER, LOUIS. *Histoire du merveilleux dans les temps modernes.* 4 vols. Paris, 1860–1.

FONTENELLE, BERNARD LE BOVIER DE. *Histoire des oracles.* Paris, 1687. (Often reprinted.)

FOURNIER, ALBAN. *Epidémie de Sorcellerie en Lorraine.* Nancy, 1891.

GARINET, JULES. *Histoire de la magie en France.* Paris, 1818.

GARSAULT, F. ALEXANDRE. *Faits des causes célèbres et intéressantes.* Amsterdam and Paris, 1757.

HARON, ALFRED. *La Tradition.* Vol. VI. Paris, 1892.

Histoire prodigieuse et espouvantable de plus de deux cens 50 sorciers et sorcières emmenez pour leur estre fait et parfait leur procès au parlement de Tholoze. Paris, 1649.

Histoire véritable des crimes horribles commis à Boulogne par deux moynes, deux gentils-hommes, et deux damoiselles, sur le S. Sacrement de l'Autel, qu'ils ont fait consumer à une Cheure et à un Oye, et sur trois enfants, qu'ils ont fait distiler sur la lambique. Paris, 1651.

Histoire véritable de l'exécrable Docteur Vanini, autrement nommé Luciolo. Paris, 1619.

JAF, LE DR. *Physonomie du vice.* Paris, *circa* 1903.

L'Amour secret. Paris, *circa* 1904.

Journal d'un bourgeois de Paris. Panthéon Litteraire. Paris, 1838.

LADAME, DR. *Procès criminel de la derni re sorcière brulée à Genève, le 6 avril, 1652.* Paris, 1888.
LAVANCHY, L'ABBÉ J. M. *Sabbats ou synagogues sur les bords du lac d'Annecy.* Annecy, 1885.
LECANU, L'ABBE. *Histoire de Satan.* 1861.
LECOCQ, AD. *Les sorciers de la Beauce.* Chartres, 1861.
LEMOINE, JULES. *La Tradition.* Vol. VI. Paris, 1892.
Les Enfers Lubriques. Paris, *circa* 1900.
LES GOUVELLES, LE VICOMTE HIPPOLYTE. *Apparitions d'une âme du Purgatoire en Bretagne.* 4th ed. Paris, 1919. (An apparition which visited Jeanne Audouis [Sœur Marie des Sept Douleurs]).
Les sorceleries de Henry de Valois, et les oblations qu'il faisoit au Diable dans le bois de Vincennes. 15 pp. Paris, 1589.
(This attack on Henry III has been reprinted several times; as by Cimber and Darignon *Archives curieuses de l'Histoire de France.* Vol. XII, and L'Estoile, *Journal de Henri III.*
LILLIE, ARTHUR. *The Worship of Satan in Modern France.* 1896.
LOUÏSE, TH. *De la sorcellerie et de la justice criminelle à Valenciennes.* Valenciennes, 1861.
Magie. 2 vols. Paris, *circa* 1904.
MATTER, JACQUES. *Histoire critique du gnosticisme.* 3 vols. Paris, 1828.
MAURY, ALFRED. *Histoire des religions de la Grèce antique.* 3 vols. Paris, 1857–9.
La Magie et l'Astrologie. Paris, 1860. (Often reprinted.)
MONNOYER, JULES. *La sorcellerie en Hainault . . . avec analyse de procès pour sortilèges* (1568–1683). Mons, 1886.
MONSEUR, EUGÈNE. *Le folklore Wallon.* Brussels, 1892.
ROUÉ, PAUL. *Causes sales.* Paris, 1902.
SALVERTE, A. J. E. B. DE. *Essai sur la Magie.* Brussels, 1817.
SCHURÉ, EDOUARD. *Les grandes légendes de France.* 19th ed. Paris, 1922.
SIMONET, L'ABBE. *Realité de la Magie.* Paris, 1819.
THUIS, L'ABBÉ JEAN-BAPTISTE. *Traite des superstitions qui regardent les Sacraments.* 3 vols. Paris, 1703. Reprinted 4 vols., 1741; and 4 vols., 1777.
Tradition, La. Vol. V contains Van Elvan's *Les Procès de sorcellerie au moyen âge.* Paris, 1891. Vol. VI contains Harou's *Sorciers et sorcières.* Par Paris, 1892, also Lemoine's *Sorcellerie contemporaine.* Paris, 1892.
UN BADAUD (Paul Marrin). *Coup d'œil sur la Magie as XIXme siècle.* Paris, 1891.
Coup d'œil sur les thaumaturges et les médiums du XIXme siècle. Paris, 1891.
WAITE, ARTHUR EDWARD. *Devil-Worship in France.* London, 1896.

FRANCE: SPECIAL CASES

Madeleine Bavent

YVELIN, DR. *Examen de la possession des religieuses de Louviers.* Paris, 1643.
Responce à l'Examen de la possession des religieuses de Louviers, n.d.
Récit véritable de ce qui s'est fait et passé à Louviers, touchant les religieuses possédées, n.d.
LE GAUFFRE. *Exorcismes de plusieurs religieuses de la ville de Louuiers en présence de Monsieur le Penitencier d'Evreux et de Monsieur Le Gauffre.*
LE BRETON, JEAN. *La défense de la vérité touchant la possession des religieuses de Lovviers.* Evreux, 1643.
DELANGLE. *Procès-verbal de Monsieur le Penitencier d'Evreux.* Paris, 1643.
Trois questions touchant l'accident arrivé aux religieuses de Louviers, n.d.
DESMARETS, PÈRE. *Histoire de Magdelaine Bavent, religieuse du monastère de Saint-Louis de Louviers avec sa confession générale et testamentaire, ou elle déclare les abominations, impietez et sacrilèges qu'elle a pratiqué et veu pratiquer, tant dans ledit monastère qu'au Sabbat.* Paris, 1652.
HUMIER. *Discours théologique sur l'histoire de Magdelaine Bavent.* Nyort, 1659.

Morin, Louis René. *Histoire de Louviers.* Rouen, 1822.
Dibon. *Essai historique sur Louviers.* Rouen, 1836.
Du Bois, L. *Recherches archéologiques . . . sur la Normandie.* Paris, 1843.
Pierart, Z. *La magnétisme, le somnambulisme et le spiritualisme dans l'histoire. Affaire curieuse des possédées de Louviers.* Paris, 1858.

Marie Benoist, La Bucaille

Arrest donné par la chambre ordonée par le Roy au temps des vacations contre Marie Benoist. Rouen, 1699.
Le tableau prétendu de la pénitence ou le caractère de la dévotion de sœur Marie Bucaille, accusé d'être sorcière. Rouen, 1699.
Almanach historique, ecclésiastique et politique du Diocèse de Coutances pour l'année 1774.

La Cadière and Père Girard

Justification de demoiselle Catherine Cadière. 1731.
Factum pour Marie Catherine Cadière contre le Père J-B. Girard, jésuite, où ce religieux est accusé de l'avoir portée par un abominable Quietisme aux plus criminels excès de l'impudicité. Hague, 1731.
Louis, Bishop of Toulon. *Mémoires des faits qui se sont passés sous les yeux de M. l'Evêque de Toulon, lors de l'origine de l'affaire du P. Girard, jésuite, et de la Cadière.* Toulon, 1731.
Chaudon. *Réponse a l'écrit qui a pour titre "Memoires des faits, etc."* Aix, 1731.
Les veritables sentiments de Mademoiselle Cadière . . . écrits de sa propre main. Aix, 1731.
Boyer d'Aiguilles. *Conclusions de M. le procureur général du roi . . . au sujet de procès d'entre le P. Girard. . . .* n.d.
Sentence de monsieur l'official de l'évêché de Toulon, qui renvoie le P. Girard absous des accusations . . . n.d.

Leonora Galigai

La Juste pvnition de Lycaon, Florentin, Marquis d'Ancre. Paris, 1617.
Arrest de la Cour de Parlement contre le marechal d'Ancre et sa femmé, prononce et exécuté à Paris le 8 juillet, 1617.
Harangve de la marquise d'Ancre, estant sur l'echaffaut. 1617.
Bref récit de ce qui s'est passé pour l'exécution . . . de la marquise d'Anchre. Paris, 1617.
Discours sur le mort de Eléonor Galligay, femme de Conchine, marquis d'Ancre. Paris, 1617.
La Médée de la France, dépeinte en personne de la Marguerite d'Ancre. Paris, 1617.

Louis Gaufridi and Madeleine de la Palud

Arrest de la Covr de Parlement de Provence, portant condamnation contre Messire Louis Gaufridi . . . convaincu de Magie et autres crimes abominables. . . . Aix, 1611.
Confession faicte par Messire Lovys Gaufridi, prestre en l'église Accoules de Marseille, prince de magiciens depuis Constantinople jusques à Paris. . . . Aix, 1611.
Fontaine, Jacques. *Discovrs des marqves des sorciers . . . sur le subiect di procez de . . . Louys Gauffridy.* Paris, 1611.
Michaëlis, Père. *Histoire admirable de la possession et conversion d'une pénitente séduite par un magicien. . . .* Paris, 1612.
Dooms. *Actes des exorcismes faits à la Sainte-Baume . . . sur Louis Copeau, Magdeleine de la Palud et Louis Gauffridy.* Douai, 1613.
Rosset, François de. *Les histoires tragiqves de nostre temps.* Paris, 1614.
Lenormant de Chiremont, J. *Histoire veritable, mémorable de ce qvi c'est passé sovs l'exorcisme de trois filles possédées ès pais de Flandre . . . ou il est avssi traité de la police du Sabbat.* Paris, 1623.
Gineste, Raoul. *Louis Gaufridi et Magdeleine de la Palud.* Paris, 1904. (A modern study which must be used with reserve.)

Urbain Grandier

Interrogatoire de maistre Urbain Grandier, prêtre, curé de Saint Pierre-du-Marché de Loudun, avec les confrontations des religieuses possédées contre ledict Grandier. Paris, 1634.

Arrest et condamnation de mort contre Maistre Vrbain Grandier . . . atteint et convaincu du crime de magie. Paris, 1634.

Relation veritable de ce qui s'est passé à la mort du curé de Loudun, bruslé tout vif le vendredi 18 *aoust* 1634.

TRANQUILLE, PÈRE. *Véritable relation des justes procédures observées au faict de la possession des Ursulines de Loudun.* Paris, 1634.

La démonomanie de Lodun, qui montre la véritable possession des religieuses urselines et autres séculières. La Flèche, 1634.

DUNCAN, MARC. *Discours de la possession des religieuses Ursulines de Loudun.* 1634.

Récit véritable de ce qui s'est passé à Loudun contre Maistre Urbain Grandier. Paris, 1634.

LA FOUCAULDIÈRE, M. DE. *Les effets miraculeux de l'église romain sur les estranges et affroyables action des démons.* Paris, 1635.

Relation de la sortie du démon Balam du corps de la mère prieure des ursulines de Loudun. Paris, 1635.

SURIN, PÈRE. *Lettre écrite à Monseigneur l'Evêque de Poictiers par un des Pères Jésuites qui exorcisèrent à Loudun.* Paris, 1635.

La gloire de St. Joseph, victorieux des principaux démons de la possession des Ursulines de Loudun. Le Mans, 1636.

LUCHÉ, PÈRE MATHIEU DE. *Les interrogatoires et exorcismes nouvellement faites à un démon sur le sujet de la possession des filles urcellines de Loudun.* Paris, 1637.

SAINTE-CATHERINE. *Le grand pécheur converty, représenté dans les deux estats de la vie de M. de Queriolet.* Lyons, 1690.

AUBIN. *Histoire des diables de Loudun.* Amsterdam, 1693.

LA MÉNARDAYE, M. DE. *Examen et discussion critique de l'histoire des diables de Loudun.* Paris, 1747

Histoire abrégée de la possession des Ursulines de Loudun. Paris, 1828.

DUMAS, ALEXANDRE. *Crimes célèbres.* 6 vols Paris, 1839–41. (A highly romantic treatment. This survey must be used with caution.)

SAUZÉ, CHARLES. *Etude médico-historique sur les possédées de Loudun.* Paris, 1840.

LERICHE, L'ABBÉ. *Etudes sur les possessions en général et sur celle de Loudun en particulier.* Paris, 1859.

LEGUÉ, DR. G. *Documents pour servir à l'histoire médicale des possédées de Loudun.* Paris, 1874.

Urbain Grandier et les possédées de Loudun. Paris, 1880.

JEAN DE POITIERS. *Les diables de Loudun.* Paris, 1878.

S. Joan of Arc

LENGLET-DUFRESNOY, L'ABBÉ N. *Histoire de Jeanne d'Arc.* Paris, 1753–4.

GUILBERT. *Eloge historique de Jeanne d'Arc.* Rouen, 1803.

BUCHON, J. A. *Chronique et procès de la Pucelle d'Orleans.* Paris, 1817.

LE BRUN DES CHARMETTES. *Histoire de Jeanne d'Arc.* Paris, 1817.

QUATREMÈRE-ROISSY, J. A. *Quelques pièces curieuses sur le mariage prétendu de Jeanne d'Arc.* Paris, 1830.

QUICHERAT, JULES. *Aperçus nouveaux sur l'histoire de Jeanne d'Arc.* Paris, 1841.

Relation inédite sur Jeanne d'Arc. Orleans, 1879.

BEAUREGARD, B. DE. *Histoire de Jeanne d'Arc.* Paris, 1847.

MICHELET, JULES. *Jeanne d'Arc.* Paris, 1853.

BRIERE DE BOISMONT, DR. A. *De l'hallucination historique, ou étude . . . sur les voix et les révélations de Jeanne d'Arc.* Paris, 1861.

VALLET DE VIRIVILLE. *Procès de condamnation de Jeanne d'Arc.* Paris, 1867.

O'REILLY, E. *Les Deux Procès de condamnation . . . de Jeanne d'Arc.* Paris, 1869.

ROBILLARD DE BEAUREPAIRE. *Recherches sur le procès de condamnation de Jeanne d'Arc.* Rouen, 1869.
CHEVALIER, A. *Jeanne d'Arc. Bio-Bibliographie.* Montbeliard, 1878.
LUCE, SIMÉON. *Jeanne d'Arc à Domremy.* Paris, 1886.
LÉO TAXIL, G. J. P. and FESCH, PAUL. *Le Martyr de Jeanne d'Arc.* Paris, 1890.
BEAUREPAIRE, CHARLES DE. *Notes sur les juges et les assesseurs du procès de condamnation de Jeanne d'Arc.* Rouen, 1890.

La Voisin and her Confederates

DUFEY DE L'YONNE. *La Bastille, mémoires pour servir à l'histoire secrète. . . .* Paris, 1833.
CLÈMENT, PIERRE. *La police de Paris sous Louis XIV.* Paris, 1866.
RAVAISSON, FRANÇOIS. *Archives de la Bastille.* 17 vols. Paris, 1866–74.
MONTIFAUD, M. DE. *Racine et la Voisin.* Paris, 1878.
LOISELEUR, JULES. *La Saint-Barthélemy, l'affaire des poisons et Mme de Montespan.* Paris, 1882.
JOURDY, G. *La Citadelle de Besançon . . . ou épilogue de l'Affaire des poisons.* 1888.
LEGUÉ, DR. G. *Medécins et empoisonneurs au XVIIme siècle.* Paris, 1890.
NASS, DR. L. *Les empoisonnements sous Louis XIV.* Paris, 1898.
FUNCK-BRENTANO, F. *Le drame des poisons.* Paris, 1899.

Palladism

BATAILLE (Dr. Hacks). *Le diable au XIXme siècle ou les mystères du Spiritisme.* Paris, 1893.
MARGIOTTA, D. *Le Palladisme. Culte de Satan.* Grenoble, 1895.
VAUGHAN, MISS DIANA. (i.e. LÉO TAXIL.) *Le Palladium régénéré et libre. Lien des groupes lucifériens independants.* Paris, 1895.
Mémoires d'une ex-palladiste. Paris, 1896.
La Restauration du Paganisme. Transition décrétée par le Sanctum Regnum, pour préparer l'etablissement du culte public de Lucifer. Paris, 1896.
SURLABRÈCHE, E. *La confusion de Satan.* Paris, 1896.
PAPUS. *Catholicisme, satanisme et occultisme.* Paris, 1897.

Gilles de Rais

MEURET, F. C. *Annales de Nantes.* Nantes, *circa* 1840.
Petite histoire nantaise . . . du Barbe-Bleue nantais, ou du Maréchal de Retz. Nantes, 1841.
STENDHAL, H. BEYLE. *Mémoires d'un touriste.* Paris, 1854.
GUERAUD, ARMAND. *Notice sur Gilles de Rais.* Rennes, 1855.
MARCHEGAY. *Récit authentique de l'exécution de Gilles de Rays.* Nantes, s.d.
LACROIX, PAUL. *Crimes étranges. Le maréchal de Rays.* Brussels, 1855.
BOSSARD, L'ABBÉ E. *Gilles de Rais . . . dit Barbe-Bleue.* Paris, 1885.
HUYSMANS, J. K. *La Magie en Poitou. Gilles de Rais.* 1899.

The Templars

MESSIE, PIERRE (Pedro Mexia). *Les diverses leçons de Pierre Messie.* Paris, 1556.
DUPUY, PIERRE. *Traité concernant l'histoire de France.* Paris, 1654.
Histoire de l'abolition de l'ordre des Templiers. Paris, 1779.
NICOLAÏ, FREDERIC. *Essai sur les accusations intentées aux Templiers et sur le secret de cet ordre.* Amsterdam, 1783.
GROUVELLE, P. *Mémoires historiques sur les Templiers.* Paris, 1805.
RAYNOUARD, F. J. M. *Monumens historiques relatifs à la condamnation des Chevaliers du Temple.* Paris, 1813.
REY, E. *Etude sur les Templiers.* Arcis-sur-Aube, 1891.
HAMNER, JOSEPH DE. *Mémoires sur deux coffrets gnostiques du Moyen-Age du cabinet de M. le duc de Blacas.* Paris, 1832.
BARGINET, F. A. *Discours sur l'histoire civile et religieuse de l'ordre du Temple.* Paris, 1833.

MAILLARD DE CHAMBURE, C. H. *Régles et statuts secrets des Templiers.* Paris, 1841.
HAVEMANN. *Geschichte des Ausgangs des Tempelherernordens.* Stuttgart, 1846.
MIGNARD, T. J. A. P. *Monographie du coffret de M. le duc de Blacas.* Paris, 1852.
DAUNANT, DE. *Le procès des Templiers.* Nimes, 1863.
LOISELEUR, JULES. *La doctrine secrète des Templiers.* Paris, 1872.
GAIDOZ, H. *Note sur un statuette en bronze représentant un homme assis les jambes croisées.*
PRUTZ, HANS DR. *Geheimlehre und Geheimstatuten des Tempelherren-Ordens.* Berlin, 1879.
Entwicklung und Untergang des Tempelherrenordens. Berlin, 1888.
JACQUOT, F. *Défense des Templiers.* Paris, 1882.
CURZON, HENRI DE. *La Règle du Temple.* Paris, 1886.
SCHOTTMULLER. *Der Untergang des Tempelordens.* 2 vols. Berlin, 1887.
LAVOCAT. *Procès des frères et de l'ordre du Temple.* Paris, 1888.
NAEF, F. *Recherches sur les opinions religieuses des Templiers.* Nimes, 1890.
GMELIN. *Schuld oder Unschuld des Templerordens.* Stuttgart, 1893.

ITALY

Archivio storico italiano. 4 serie. Florence, 1842–85.
BOFFITO. *Gli eretici in Piemonte.* 1897.
BONNI, F. *L' Inquisizione e i Calabro-Valdesi.* Milan, 1864.
BORELLI. *Editti antichi e nuovi.* Turin, 1681.
BORGIA, STEFANO. *Memorie istoriche della pontificia città di Benevento.* Rome, 1769.
CANTÙ, CESARE. *Gli Eretici d' Italia.* 3 vols. Turin, 1865–7.
Storia della Diocesi di Como. 2 vols. Como, 1829–31.
CAPPELLETTI. *Le Chiese d' Italia.* Venice, 1844.
CARUTTI. *Storia della citta di Pinerolo.* Pinerolo, 1893.
CASTRO, G. DE. *Il Mondo Segreto.* 9 vols. Milan, 1864.
Arnaldo da Brescia. Leghorn, 1875.
CATTANI, FRA. *Discorso sopra la Superstizione dell' Arte Magica.* Florence, 1567.
CIGOGNA, STROZZI. *Pelagii de gli incanti.* Vicenza, 1605
CORIO, B. *L' Istoria di Milano.* Padua, 1646.
DANDALO, C. T. *La Signora di Monza.* Milan, 1855.
DE BLASIO, PROF. ABELE. *La Mala Vita a Napoli.* Naples, 1905.
DEJOB. *De l'influence du concile de Trente.* Paris, 1884.
FOLENGO, GIROLAMO. *Opus Macaronicum.* 2 vols. Mantua, 1771.
GALVANI. *Osservazioni sulla Poesia de' Trovatori.* Modena, 1839.
GIANNONE, P. *Istoria civile del Regno di Napoli.* 7 vols. Naples, 1770.
GORI. *Storia di Chiusi.*
GRIMALDO, CONSTANTINI. *Dissertatione in cui si investiga quali sian le operazioni che dependono della magia.* Rome, 1751.
GUICCIARDINI, FRANCESCO. *Delle istorie d' Italia.* 8 vols. Florence, 1818. Also ed. Resini. 5 vols. Turin, 1874.
LAMI. *Lezioni d' antichitá toscane.* 2 vols. Florence, 1766.
LELAND, C. G. *Etruscan Remains.* London, 1892.
Lettera dal Inquisitore da Barzalone allo Inquisitore de Novara, n.d.
MASTRIANI, F. *I Vermi.* 2 vols. Naples, 1877.
Misteri dell' Inquisizione. Paris, 1847. (A catchpenny.)
MONNIER, M. *La Camorra.* Paris, 1863.
MURATORI, L. A. *Rerum italicarum scriptores.* 28 vols. Milan, 1723 *et seq.*
Continuatio opera Jo. Mar. Tartini. 2 vols. Florence, 1748–80.
Antiquitates italicæ medii aevi. 6 vols. Milan, 1738.
Annali d' Italia. 5 vols. Milan, 1838.
MUTINELLI. *Storia Arcana d' Italia.* 4 vols. Venice, 1858.
MUZI. *Memorie ecclesiastiche e civili di Città di Castello.* Rome, 1842–7.

Niceforo, A. e Sighele. *La Mala Vita a Roma.* Rome, 1899.
L' Italia barbara. Rome, 1898.
Novellis. *Biografia Saviglianese.* Turin, 1840.
Ogniben, Andrea. *I Guglielmiti del secolo XIII.* Perugia, 1847.
Pecci, Giovanni Antonio. *Storia del vescovado della cittá di Siena.* Lucca, 1748.
Pellet, M. *Naples contemporaine.* Paris, 1894.
Perini, O. *Storia delle Societá Segrete.* 2 vols. Milan, 1863.
Rossetti, Gabriele. *Disquisitions on the Antipapal Spirit . . . its Secret Influence. . . .* 2 vols. 1834. (Translated by Miss C. Ward.)
Segni, Giovanni Battista. *Del vero cristiano contra l' arte planetaria.* Ferrara, 1592.
Silvagni, D. *La Corte e la Societá Romana nei XVIII e XIX secoli.* 2nd ed. 3 vols. Florence, 1882–5.
Successo di Giustitia fatta nella cittá di Munich di sei scelerati strigoni. Genoa, 1641.
Tocco. *L' Eresia nel medio Evo.* Florence, 1884.
Torricello. *Dialogo di Otto Lupano, nel qual si ragiona delle statute e miracoli de demoni e spiriti.* Milan, 1540.
Turletti. *Storia di Savigliano.*
Ughelli. *Italia sacra.* 10 vols. Venice, 1721.
Vayra, P. *Le Streghe nel Canarese (Curiositá di Storia Subalpina).* 1874.
Vizzini, A. *La Mafia.* Rome, 1880.

NORTH AMERICA

A True though Sad Relation of Six Sea-men (Belonging to the Margaret *of* Boston) *Who Sold Themselves to the* Devil *And were Invisibly Carry'd away.* A pamphlet of 8 pages. N.D. *Circa* 1698.
Bancroft. *History of the United States.*
Burr, George Lincoln. *Narratives of the Witchcraft Cases.* New York, 1914.
The Witchcraft Persecutions. Univ. of Pennsylvania Translations and Reprints. Vol. III. No. 4. Philadelphia, 1903.
Calef, Robert. *The Wonders of the Invisible World.* Boston, 1700.
Drake, Samuel G. *Annals of Witchcraft.* 1869.
Green, Samuel Abbott. *Groton in the Witchcraft Times.* Cambridge, Mass., 1883.
Hutchinson, John. *History of the Province of Massachuset's Bay.*
Kittredge, G. L. *Notes on Witchcraft.* American Antiquarian Soc. Proceedings. N.S. xviii. 1906–7.
Mather, Cotton. *The Wonders of the Invisible World.* Boston, 1693.
Mather, Increase. *Remarkable Providences.* Boston, 1683–4.
Neal, D. *History of New England.* London, 1747.
Nevins, W. S. *Witchcraft in Salem Village.* Boston, 1892.
Poole, W. F. *Salem Witchcraft.* Boston, 1869.
Taylor, John. *The Witchcraft Delusion in Colonial Connecticut.* New York, n.d.
Upham, Clement Wentworth. *History of Salem Witchcraft.* 2 vols.
Upham, Caroline E. *Salem Witchcraft in Outline.* Illustrated. 3rd ed. Salem, Mass., 1891.
(This is mainly a compendium of C. W. Upham's larger work.)
Winsor, J. *The Literature of Witchcraft in New England.* 1896. (Reprinted from Proc. Am. Antiq. Soc., 1895.)

GERMANY

Buchinger. *Julius Echter von Melpresbrunn.*
Dieckhoff. *Die Waldenser im Mittelalter.* Gottingen, 1851.
Dieffenbach, Johann. *Der Hexenwahn vor und nach der Glaubensspaltung in Deutschland.* Mainz. 1886.

DUHR. *Stellung des Jesuiten in der deutschen Hexenprozessen.* Freiburg, 1900.
DURINGSFELD. *Das festliche Jahr.* Leipzig.
FLÜGEL, G. *Mani, seine Lehre und seine Schriften.* Leipzig, 1862.
GAAR, G. S. J. *Christliche Anred nächst dem Scheiterhaufen, worauff der Leichnam Mariæ Renatæ, einer durchs Schwert hingerichtetin Zauberin, den 21ten Jun. An.* 1749, *ausser der Stadt Würzburg, verbrennet worden, an ein Zahlreich versammeltes Volk gethan.* . . . (Contemporary and important.)
GLAUBRECHT, OTTO. *Die Schreckensjahre von Lindheim.* Stuttgart, 1886.
Handbuch der deutschen Mythologie.
HANSEN, JOSEPH. *Quellen und Untersuchungen zur Geschichte des Hexenwahns und der Hexenverfolgung im Mittelalter.* Bonn, 1901. (A valuable and important study.)
HELBING. *Die Tortur, Geschichte der Folter, etc.* 2 vols. Berlin, 1902.
Historia tragica adolescentis prœnobilis Ernesti ab Ernberg. (Written by his confessor, a Jesuit father. Collect. Gropp. Vol. II, pp. 287, *sqq.*)
HORST, GEORG CONRAD. *Dæmonomagie, oder Geschichte des Glaubens an Zauberci und dæmonische Wunder.* Frankfort. 2 vols. 1818.
HORST, VICTOR. *Zauberbibliothek.* 6 vols.
KESSLER. *Mâni Forschungen über die manichäissche Religion.* 2 vols. Berlin, 1889, *sqq.*
Kleiner Beitrag zur Geschichte des Hexenwesens im 16 Jahrhundert. Trier, 1830.
KOPP. *Die Hexenprozesse und ihre Gegner in Tyrol.* Innsbruck, 1874.
KRONE. *Fra Dolcino und die Patarerer.* Leipzig, 1844.
LEHMANN. *Aberglaube und Zauberei.* Stuttgart, 1908.
LEITSCHUH, FRIEDRICH DR. *Beitræge zur Geschichte des Hexenwesens in Franken.* Bamberg, 1883.
Der letzte Hexenprocess in Deutschland. Pirna, 1849.
LOSCHART, OSWALD, C.R.P. *Die wahrhafte und umständliche Nachricht von dem Zufalle, so das jungfräuliche Kloster Unterzell Nächst Würzburg betroffen, verfasset im Jahr* 1749. 1749.
MEYER, LUDWIG. *Die Periode der Hexenprocesse.*
MÜLLER, KARL. *Die Waldenser und ihre einzelnen Gruppen bis zum Anfang des* 14 *Iahrhunderts.* Gotha, 1886.
OCHSENBEIN. *Aus dem Schweizer Volksleben des XV Iahrhunderts.* 1881.
PAULUS. *Hexenwahn und Hexenprozess in 16 Jahrh.* Freiburg, 1910.
RAPP, LUDWIG. *Die Hexenprozesse und ihre Gegner aus Tyrol.*
REINSBURG, O. F. VON. *Bavaria Landes und Volkskunde des Königreichs Bayern.* Munich, 1860–66.
RIETZLER. *Hexenprozesse in Bayern.* Stuttgart, 1896.
SCHERR, J. *Hammerschläge und Historien.* Vol. II. sub *Die letzte Reichshexe.*
SCHINDLER. *Der Aberglaube des Mittelalters.* Breslau, 1858.
SCHREIBER. *Die Hexenprozesse im Breisgau.*
SCHUMACHER, H. A. *Die Stedinger, Beitrag zur Geschichte der Wesenmarschen.* Bremen, 1865.
SILBERSTEIN, AUGUST. *Denksäulen im Gebeite der Cultur und Literatur.* Vienna, 1879.
SOLDAN-HEPPE. *Geschichte der Hexenprozesse.* 2 vols. Stuttgart, 1880. (Soldan's famous work "neu gearbitet von Dr. Heinrich Heppe.")
STECK, RUDOLFF. *Die Akten des Jetzerprozesses nebst dem Defensorium.* Basel, 1904.
STEINER. *Geschichte der Stads Dieburg.* Darmstadt, 1829.
TRUMMER, C. *Vorträge über Tortur, Hexenverfolgungen, Vehmgerichte,* etc., in *Der Hamburgischen Rechtsgeschichte.* Vol. I.
VOLK, FR. *Hexen in der Landvogtei Ortenau und Reichstadt Offenburg.*
WITZSCHEL, AUGUST. *Sitten, Sagen, und Gevräuche aus Thuringen.* Vienna, 1878.
Wunderbarliche Geheimnussen der Zauberey. 4to. 1630.
ZINGERLE, IGNAZ, DR. *Barbara Pachlerin, die Sarnthaler Hexe.* Innsbruck, 1858.

SPIRITISM

" ADEPTE, UN." *Katie King, Histoire de ses Apparitions.* Paris, 1879.
BALLOU, ADIN. *Spirit Manifestations.* Boston, 1852; Liverpool, 1853.
BENSON, VERY REV. MGR. HUGH. *Spiritualism.* C.T.S. No. 36.
BLACKMORE, S.J., SIMON AUGUSTINE. *Spiritism, Facts and Frauds.* London, 1925. (The best concise study of the subject. The work is fairly and authoritatively written, and the conclusions are eminently sane.)
BROWSON. *The Spirit-Rapper.* Boston, 1854. In Vol. IX of Works. Detroit, 1884.
BUTT, G. BASEDEN. *Modern Psychism.* London, 1925.
CAPRON, E. W. *Modern Spiritualism.* New York, 1855.
CARRINGTON, HEREWARD. *Physical Phenomena.* 1920.
The Physical Phenomena of Spiritualism. Boston, 1902.
CARTER, HUNTLY. *Spiritualism, Its Present-Day Meaning. A Symposium.* London, 1920.
COATES, JAMES. *Seeing the Invisible: practical studies in Psychometry,* etc.
CRAWFORD, W. J. *Experiments in Psychical Science.*
The Reality of Psychic Phenomena.
Some practical Hints for those investigating . . . Spiritualism.
DELANNE, G. and G. BOURNIQUET. *Ecoutons les Morts.* Paris, 1923.
DUNRAVEN, EARL OF. *Experiences in Spiritualism with D. D. Home.*
DURVILLE. *Le Fântome des Vivants.* Paris, 1909.
FOURNIER D'ALBE, E. E. *The Goligher Circle, May to August,* 1921. London, 1922.
GASPARIN, COUNT AGENOR DE. *Des tables tournantes.* Paris, 1854.
GURNEY, MYERS, and PODMORE. *Phantasms of the Living.* 2 vols. London, 1886.
GUTHERLET. *Der Kampf und die Seele.* 2nd ed. Mainz, 1903.
JUNG, J. H. *Theorie der Geisterkunde.*
LANSLOTO, O.S.B., D. I. *Spiritism Unveiled.* St. Louis, 1913. (An excellent and most valuable work.)
LEPICIER, O.S.M., ALEXIS. *The Unseen World.* London, 1906.
LILLIE, ARTHUR. *Modern Mystics and Modern Magic.* London, 1894.
LODGE, SIR OLIVER. *Raymond, or Life after Death.* London, 1916
PAILLOUX, C. S. *Le Magnetisme, le Spiritisme, et la possession.*
RAUPERT, J. GODFREY. *Spiritistic Phenomena; their interpretation.*
New Black Magic. 1924.
Modern Spiritism. London, 1907.
SARGENT, EPES. *Planchette or the Despair of Science.* Boston, 1869.
SCHRENCK-NOTZING, BARON VON. *Phenomena of Materialization.* Trans. by E. E. Fournier d'Albe. London, 1923.
SEMENOFF, MARC. *Introduction à la vie secrète.* Paris, 1925.
SPICER, HENRY. *Sights and Sounds; the Mystery of the Day.* London, 1853.
SURBLED. *Spiritualism et spiritisme.* Paris, 1898.
Spirites et mediums. Paris, 1901.
THURSTON, S.J., HERBERT F. *The Problems of Materialization. The Month,* Oct., 1922. (And a number of valuable articles which have been published of recent years in *The Month.*)
TRETHEWY, A. W. *The Controls of Stainton Moses.* London, 1925.
WALLACE, A. R. *Miracles and Modern Spiritualism.* London, 1897.

INDEX

Fodor's

GREECE

8th Edition

Where to Stay and Eat for All Budgets

Must-See Sights and Local Secrets

Ratings You Can Trust

Fodor's Travel Publications New York, Toronto, London, Sydney, Auckland
www.fodors.com

FODOR'S GREECE

Editors: Robert I. C. Fisher, *lead editor*; Carissa Bluestone, Diana Varvara

Editorial Production: Tom Holton

Editorial Contributors: : Alexia Amvrazi, Stephen Brewer, Elizabeth Carson, Jeffrey Carson, Linda Coffman, Angelike Contis, Natasha Giannousi, Joanna Kakissis, Diane Shugart, Adrian Vrettos

Maps & Illustrations: David Lindroth, Mark Stroud, Harry Colomb, *cartographers*; William Wu, Bob Blake and Rebecca Baer, *map editors*

Design: Fabrizio LaRocca, *creative director*; Guido Caroti, Siobhan O'Hare, *art directors*; Tina Malaney, Chie Ushio, Ann McBride, *designers*; Melanie Marin, *senior picture editor;* Moon Sun Kim, *cover designer*

Cover Photo: (Temple of Poseidon, Sounion): Philip Coblentz/Brand X Pictures/age fotostock

Production/Manufacturing: Matthew Struble

COPYRIGHT

8th Edition

ISBN 978-1-4000-1911-3

ISSN 0071-6413

SPECIAL SALES

This book is available at special discounts for bulk purchases for sales promotions or premiums. Special editions, including personalized covers, excerpts of existing books, and corporate imprints, can be created in large quantities for special needs. For more information, write to Special Markets/Premium Sales, 1745 Broadway, MD 6-2, New York, New York 10019, or e-mail specialmarkets@randomhouse.com.

AN IMPORTANT TIP & AN INVITATION

Although all prices, opening times, and other details in this book are based on information supplied to us at press time, changes occur all the time in the travel world, and Fodor's cannot accept responsibility for facts that become outdated or for inadvertent errors or omissions. So **always confirm information when it matters,** especially if you're making a detour to visit a specific place. Your experiences—positive and negative—matter to us. If we have missed or misstated something, **please write to us.** We follow up on all suggestions. Contact the Greece editor at editors@fodors.com or c/o Fodor's at 1745 Broadway, New York, NY 10019.

PRINTED IN THE UNITED STATES OF AMERICA
10 9 8 7 6 5 4 3 2 1

Be a Fodor's Correspondent

Your opinion matters. It matters to us. It matters to your fellow Fodor's travelers, too. And we'd like to hear it. In fact, we need to hear it.

When you share your experiences and opinions, you become an active member of the Fodor's community. That means we'll not only use your feedback to make our books better, but we'll publish your names and comments whenever possible. Throughout our guides, look for "Word of Mouth," excerpts of your unvarnished feedback.

Here's how you can help improve Fodor's for all of us.

Tell us when we're right. We rely on local writers to give you an insider's perspective. But our writers and staff editors—who are the best in the business—depend on you. Your positive feedback is a vote to renew our recommendations for the next edition.

Tell us when we're wrong. We're proud that we update most of our guides every year. But we're not perfect. Things change. Hotels cut services. Museums change hours. Charming cafés lose charm. If our writer didn't quite capture the essence of a place, tell us how you'd do it differently. If any of our descriptions are inaccurate or inadequate, we'll incorporate your changes in the next edition and will correct factual errors at fodors.com immediately.

Tell us what to include. You probably have had fantastic travel experiences that aren't yet in Fodor's. Why not share them with a community of like-minded travelers? Maybe you chanced upon a beach or bistro or B&B that you don't want to keep to yourself. Tell us why we should include it. And share your discoveries and experiences with everyone directly at fodors.com. Your input may lead us to add a new listing or highlight a place we cover with a "Highly Recommended" star or with our highest rating, "Fodor's Choice."

Give us your opinion instantly at our feedback center at www.fodors.com/feedback. You may also e-mail editors@fodors.com with the subject line "Greece Editor." Or send your nominations, comments, and complaints by mail to Greece Editor, Fodor's, 1745 Broadway, New York, NY 10019.

You and travelers like you are the heart of the Fodor's community. Make our community richer by sharing your experiences. Be a Fodor's correspondent.

Kaló taxídi! (Or simply: Happy traveling!)

Tim Jarrell, Publisher

CONTENTS

GREECE IN FOCUS

CONTENTS

ABOUT THIS BOOK

Our Ratings

Sometimes you find terrific travel experiences and sometimes they just find you. But usually the burden is on you to select the right combination of experiences. That's where our ratings come in.

As travelers we've all discovered a place so wonderful that its worthiness is obvious. And sometimes that place is so unique that superlatives don't do it justice: you just have to be there to know. These sights, properties, and experiences get our highest rating, **Fodor's Choice**, indicated by orange stars throughout this book.

Black stars highlight sights and properties we deem **Highly Recommended**, places that our writers, editors, and readers praise again and again for consistency and excellence.

By default, there's another category: any place we include in this book is by definition worth your time, unless we say otherwise. And we will.

Disagree with any of our choices? Care to nominate a place or suggest that we rate one more highly? Visit our feedback center at www.fodors.com/feedback.

Budget Well

Hotel and restaurant price categories from ¢ to $$$$ are defined in the opening pages of each chapter. For attractions, we always give standard adult admission fees; reductions are usually available for children, students, and senior citizens. Want to pay with plastic? **AE, D, DC, MC, V** following restaurant and hotel listings indicate whether American Express, Discover, Diners Club, MasterCard, and Visa are accepted.

Restaurants

Unless we state otherwise, restaurants are open for lunch and dinner daily. We mention dress only when there's a specific requirement and reservations only when they're essential or not accepted—it's always best to book ahead.

Hotels

Hotels have private bath, phone, TV, and air-conditioning and operate on the European Plan (aka EP, meaning without meals), unless we specify that they use the Continental Plan (CP, with a Continental breakfast), Breakfast Plan (BP, with a full breakfast), or Modified American Plan (MAP, with breakfast and dinner) or are all-inclusive (AI, including all meals and most activities). We always list facilities but not whether you'll be charged an extra fee to use them, so when pricing accommodations, find out what's included.

Many Listings

- ★ Fodor's Choice
- ★ Highly recommended
- ✉ Physical address
- ✥ Directions
- 📪 Mailing address
- ☎ Telephone
- 📠 Fax
- 🌐 On the Web
- ✉ E-mail
- 🎫 Admission fee
- ⏲ Open/closed times
- Ⓜ Metro stations
- 💳 Credit cards

Hotels & Restaurants

- 🏨 Hotel
- 🛏 Number of rooms
- 👍 Facilities
- 🍽 Meal plans
- ✕ Restaurant
- ✍ Reservations
- 🚬 Smoking
- 🍷 BYOB
- ✕🏨 Hotel with restaurant that warrants a visit

Outdoors

- 🏌 Golf
- ⛺ Camping

Other

- 👶 Family-friendly
- ⇨ See also
- ✉ Branch address
- ☞ Take note

Experience Greece

Caryatids of the Erechtheion. Acropolis, Athens.

WORD OF MOUTH

"Hello to the Fodorites who patiently helped and answered my questions about Santorini and Mykonos (travelerjan, Heimdall, Brotherlee love). Well, my husband and I got back two weeks ago and we loved Greece! What a great country! The people were friendly, the country was beautiful and clean, and the food delicious. We spent one week on the islands and another week on the mainland. We will most definitely return!!"

—nilady

www.fodors.com/forums

WHAT'S NEW

Arriving in a taxi (sorry, no chariots), today's traveler may be surprised to find Athenians garbed by Armani and driving the latest sports car. Shouldn't they look like truncated marble statues in the Acropolis Museum and have brows habitually crowned with wild olive? Incongruous as it may seem, most natives have two arms attached to the torso in the normal place. And if visitors still arrive nurtured on the truth and beauty of Keats's Grecian Urn, they shouldn't be puzzled by the locals talking about the latest hipsterious nightspot.

After all, only the most scholarly bookworm still believes that Greece is a dusty museum. The country is now alive with vibrant trends and styles, especially after the mammoth 2004 Olympic Games were held in Athens. Everything old—even 25 centuries old—is new again. While still an agelessly beautiful land, the post-Olympic "European" Greece is burgeoning with boutique hotels, hot restaurants, and sophisticated nightlife that challenges the Zorba-era conceptions of the Spartan Aegean. To get you acquainted with the "new" Greece, here's a rundown of the topics the natives are busy discussing in neighborhood tavernas or, as the case may be, the latest nouvelle restaurants.

Burning Issues

Scorched earth throughout Greece is a grim reminder of the summer of 2007, when massive fires killed at least 63 people, destroyed up to 100 villages, and burned as many as 6 million acres. You don't have to venture far into the countryside to see the evidence—most of the forests on the slopes of Mt. Parnitha, visible from the Acropolis, went up in flames, as did the pine groves that surround ancient Olympia. The fires have fueled outrage in Greece about the lack of a government fire-prevention strategy and launched endless speculation about what caused the fires.

Some of the hottest temperatures on record following a winter drought certainly contributed, but many Greeks suspect arson, pointing their fingers at developers who take advantage of legal maneuvering to build on forest land that has been cleared by fire and reclassified as abandoned farmland. Changes to close the loopholes are afoot, but real and lasting reform might be as slow to come to fruition as the new trees that are being planted in the fire-ravaged regions.

Pride & Hubris at the Acropolis

The new Acropolis Museum, opening in stages in mid- to late 2008, has awakened a sense of pride in Greeks, happy to see many of their country's greatest treasures housed in appropriately stunning quarters (designed by cutting-edge Swiss architect Bernard Tschumi). As with many events in Greece, though, the good news is laced with a liberal dose of controversy. One concerns what's *not* on display: the Parthenon Marbles.

The opening of the museum is rekindling interest in demands for return of the marble sculptures that British diplomat Lord Elgin had removed from the Acropolis in 1803 and enjoy pride of place at the British Museum. For the time being, the Acropolis Museum has installed copies of the friezes and strikingly covered them with transparent veils to symbolize the absence of the originals. Many Athenians are also outraged at the museum's plans to destroy two 1930s-era buildings that block the view of the Acropolis from the café and lower-floor galleries—critics see

this as a heedless act of hubris on the part of museum officials, a serious offense in ancient Athens that clearly still rankles the Greek spirit.

What Are They Going to Take Away Next, My Worry Beads?

Greece has imposed some anti-smoking measures, but in general these have been as wan as a menthol light—you'll probably find it hard to believe this nation of smokers has ever made an honest attempt to quit. After all, how do you take prohibitions that ban smoking in most public places (and also on the job for municipal employees) seriously when it's common to see everyone from bus drivers to postal workers with cigarettes dangling out of their mouths?

Overall, Greece has the highest prevalence of smoking in the European Union—an estimated 40% of Greeks puff away regularly, and some estimates put the number as lofty as 60%. Stakes are getting tragically high as smoking takes an increasing and costly toll on national health, and efforts to help Greeks kick the habit are stepping up. One deterrent that's worked well in Ireland, England, and other northern climes—making smokers step outside if they want to light up—will probably not work in Greece, where socializing is an outdoor affair for most of the year anyway.

Can Slow Food Get Any Slower?

It seems that Greek cooking might have already set the gold standard for the Slow Food movement (first founded in Italy back in the 1980s and now a worldwide fashion), part of whose credo is to use local produce, grains, meats, and fish. After all, even the simplest taverna will use only fresh ingredients and the chef is often a grandma who's following her grandma's recipes. Isn't *magirefta,* the Greek way of cooking a casserole in the morning and letting it warm and steep all day, the very essence of "slow"? Yet, perhaps to uproot the albeit rather shallowly planted presence of fastfoudadika, the Slow Food movement has many practitioners in Greece.

The not-for-profit Zante's Feast organization, for instance, lures foodies to the Ionian island of Zakynthos for sessions in healthful cooking. Elsewhere, an increasing number of restaurants are making a big show of using fresh local ingredients in traditional dishes, and others just do so without fanfare, as they have for years—either way, enjoying a "slow" meal full of tasty fresh ingredients is still something you can count on in Greece.

The Shock of the New

A country where the spotlight shines most brightly on ancient art got a sometimes shocking glimpse of what contemporary artists are up to when the First Athens Biennial opened at Technopolis in the Gazi district in the fall of 2007. The show was called "Destroy Athens," but given public reaction to many of the provocatively violent and sexually explicit pieces, "Annoy Athens" or "Confuse Athens" might have been more apt.

No one seems to have been able to determine exactly what the work had to do with the title or with the exhibition's stated mission to "deny the precondition of collectivity and abolish any connection or relationship." Hmmmm. Well, until the Second Biennial brings more work to town in 2009, how about a visit to the new IKEA megastore near the airport? Now, there's a surefire hit.

WHAT'S WHERE

3 Athens. The capital has greeted the new millennium with a sleek subway and other spiffy municipal makeovers. But for five million Athenians, it's still the tried-and-true pleasures that put the spin on urban life here: the endless parade of cafés, the charming Plaka district, and, most of all, the glorious remnants of one of the greatest civilizations the West ever produced, such as the Acropolis.

4 Attica, the Saronic Gulf Islands & Delphi. Some of the most important remains of ancient Greece are only an hour away from Athens. Delphi was center of the universe for the ancients; at Marathon, the Athenians defeated the Persians; and the Temple of Poseidon hovers between sea and sky at Sounion. Southward lie three Saronic Gulf shangri-las: the islands of Aegina, Hydra, and Spetses.

5 The Sporades. The northern Sporades delivers quintessential Greek-island pleasures: villages spilling down hillsides like giant sugar cubes, Byzantine monasteries, and ageless paths, where the tinkle of goat bells may be the only sound for miles. Weekenders savor Skiathos but Skopelos has great beaches and Skyros is washed by some of the clearest waters in Greece.

6 Epirus & Thessaly. Less visited than other parts of Greece and none the worse for it, Epirus is a land of stark mountains and swift rivers, where Ali Pasha ruled an 18th-century renegade kingdom from the handsome lakeside city of Ioannina. The route east to Thessaly leads into the Meteora—the name derives from "to hang in midair," which is what the region's mountaintop Byzantine monasteries spectacularly do.

7 Thessaloniki & Central Macedonia. These northern lands shelter two of Greece's most sacred places, Mount Olympus, the stormy heights where Zeus reigned, and Mount Athos, a male-only sanctuary dedicated, ironically, to the Virgin Mary. The hub of the region is Thessoloniki, Greece's second-largest city—a cosmopolitan crossroads leading to Pella and Vergina, remnants of Alexander the Great's Macedonian empire.

8 Corfu. Temperate, multithued Corfu—of turquoise waters lapping rocky coves, and jacaranda spread over cottages—could have inspired Impressionism. The island has a history equally as colorful, reflecting the commingling of Venetians, French, and British. First stop, of course, is Corfu town—a stage set for a Verdi opera.

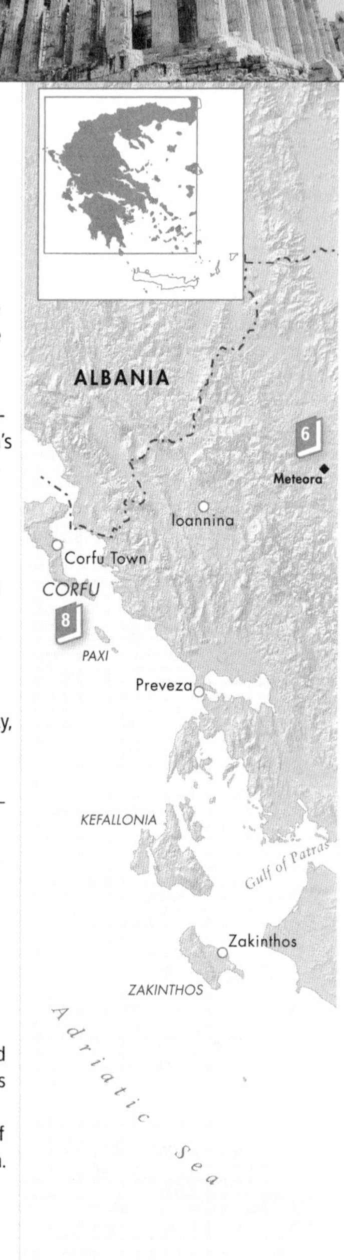

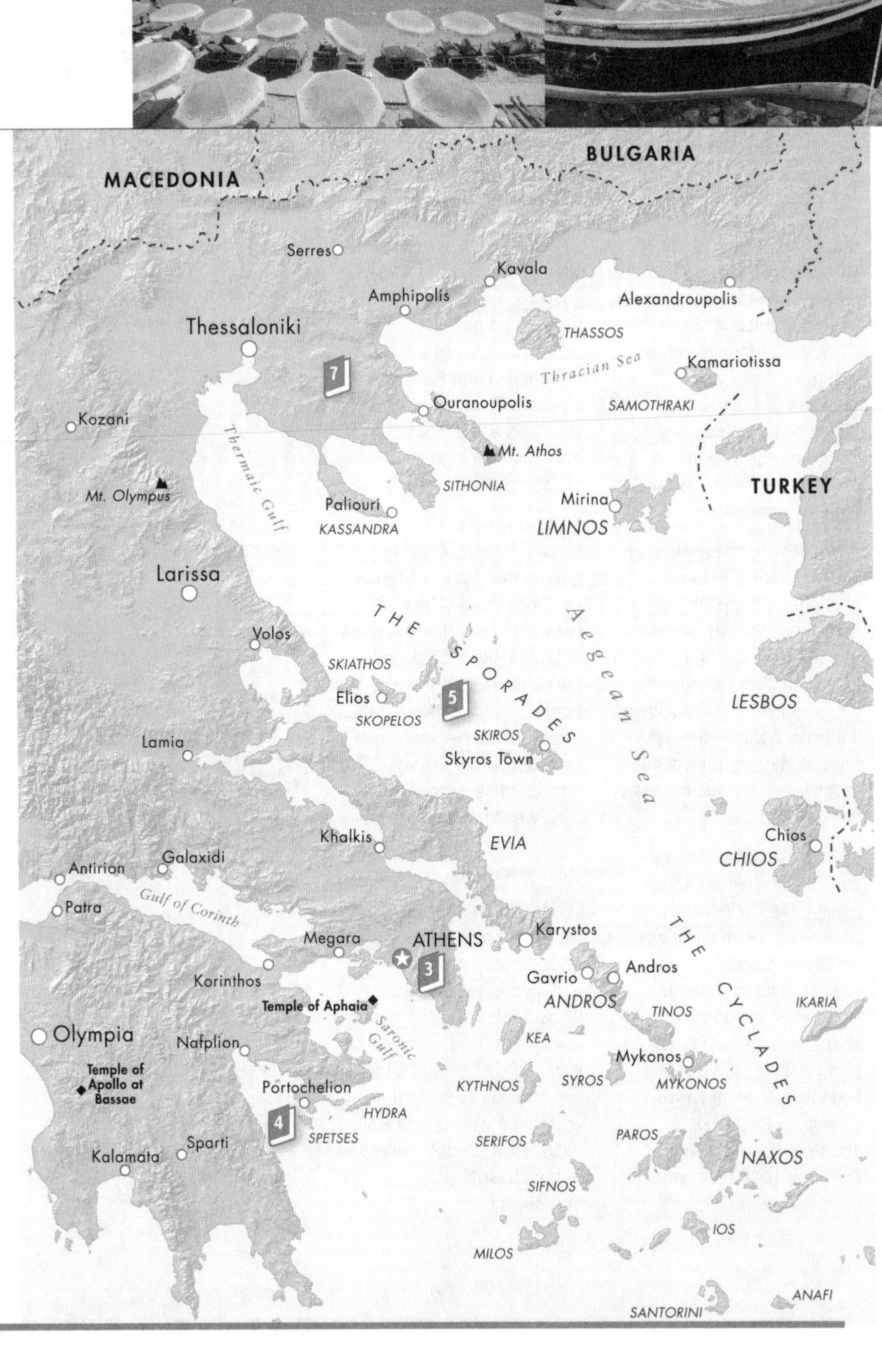
MACEDONIA
BULGARIA
TURKEY
Serres
Kavala
Amphipolis
Alexandroupolis
Thessaloniki
THASSOS
Thracian Sea
Kamariotissa
7
Ouranoupolis
SAMOTHRAKI
Kozani
Thermaic Gulf
Mt. Athos
Mt. Olympus
SITHONIA
Paliouri
KASSANDRA
Mirina
LIMNOS
Larissa
THE SPORADES
Aegean Sea
Volos
SKIATHOS
Elios
5
SKOPELOS
LESBOS
SKIROS
Lamia
Skyros Town
Khalkis
EVIA
Chios
CHIOS
Galaxidi
Antirion
Patra
Gulf of Corinth
Megara
ATHENS
Karystos
3
Korinthos
Gavrio
Andros
ANDROS
THE CYCLADES
Temple of Aphaia
TINOS
IKARIA
Saronic Gulf
KEA
Olympia
Nafplion
Mykonos
Temple of Apollo at Bassae
Portochelion
KYTHNOS
SYROS
MYKONOS
HYDRA
4
SPETSES
SERIFOS
PAROS
Sparti
NAXOS
Kalamata
SIFNOS
IOS
MILOS
ANAFI
SANTORINI

WHAT'S WHERE

9 Northern Peloponnese. The veritable birthplace of Greece, the rugged mountains that loom behind Patras, Greece's third largest city, cradle some of Greece's most important ancient sites—Olympia, Corinth, Mycenae, and more. Nafplion is the work of later empire builders—Byzantines, Venetians, and Turks—and is as mellow as wines from the region's vineyards.

10 Southern Peloponnese. The southern mainland's rugged, often inhospitable mountains were, fittingly, home to the Spartans, whose contempt for ostentation ensured they left little behind. Other powers did leave a mark—the Byzantines at Mystras, the Thebans at Ancient Messene, the Venetians at Methoni.

11 The Cyclades. The ultimate Mediterranean archipelago, the Cyclades easily conjure up the magical words of "Greek islands." Santorini, with its ravishing caldera, is the most picturesque; Mykonos, with its sexy jet-set lifestyle, takes the prize for hedonism. Verdant Naxos, church-studded Tinos, and Brad Pitt–discovered Antiparos have their own distinct charms.

12 Crete. Crete is Greece's southernmost and largest island, and the claims to superlatives don't stop there. Here, too, are some of Greece's tallest mountains, its deepest gorge, many of its best beaches, and a wealth of Venetian and Byzantine wonders. Treasure of treasures is the Palace of Knossos—the high point of Minoan civilization.

13 Rhodes & the Dodecanese. Wrapped enticingly around the shores of Turkey, the Dodecanese ("Twelve Islands") have attracted some notable visitors. St. John the Divine received his Revelations on Patmos, Hippocrates established a healing center on Kos, and the Crusader Knights of St. John lavished their wealth on palaces in Rhodes, still famed for its glitzy resort life.

14 Northern Islands. Flung like puzzle pieces into the Aegean, each of these green and gold islands is distinct: Chios retains an eerie beauty amid its fortified villages and Byzantine monasteries; Lesbos, is a forgetaway favored by artists and writers; and lush, mountainous Samos whispers of the classical wonders of antiquity.

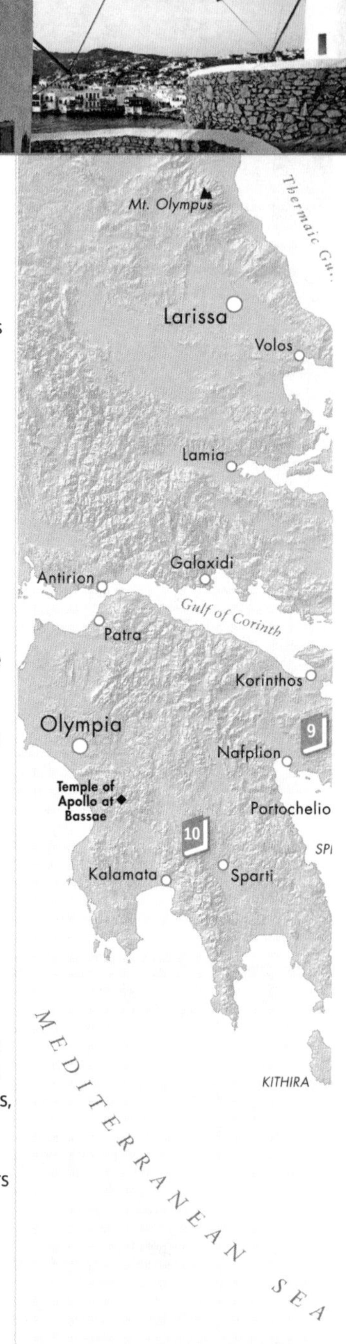

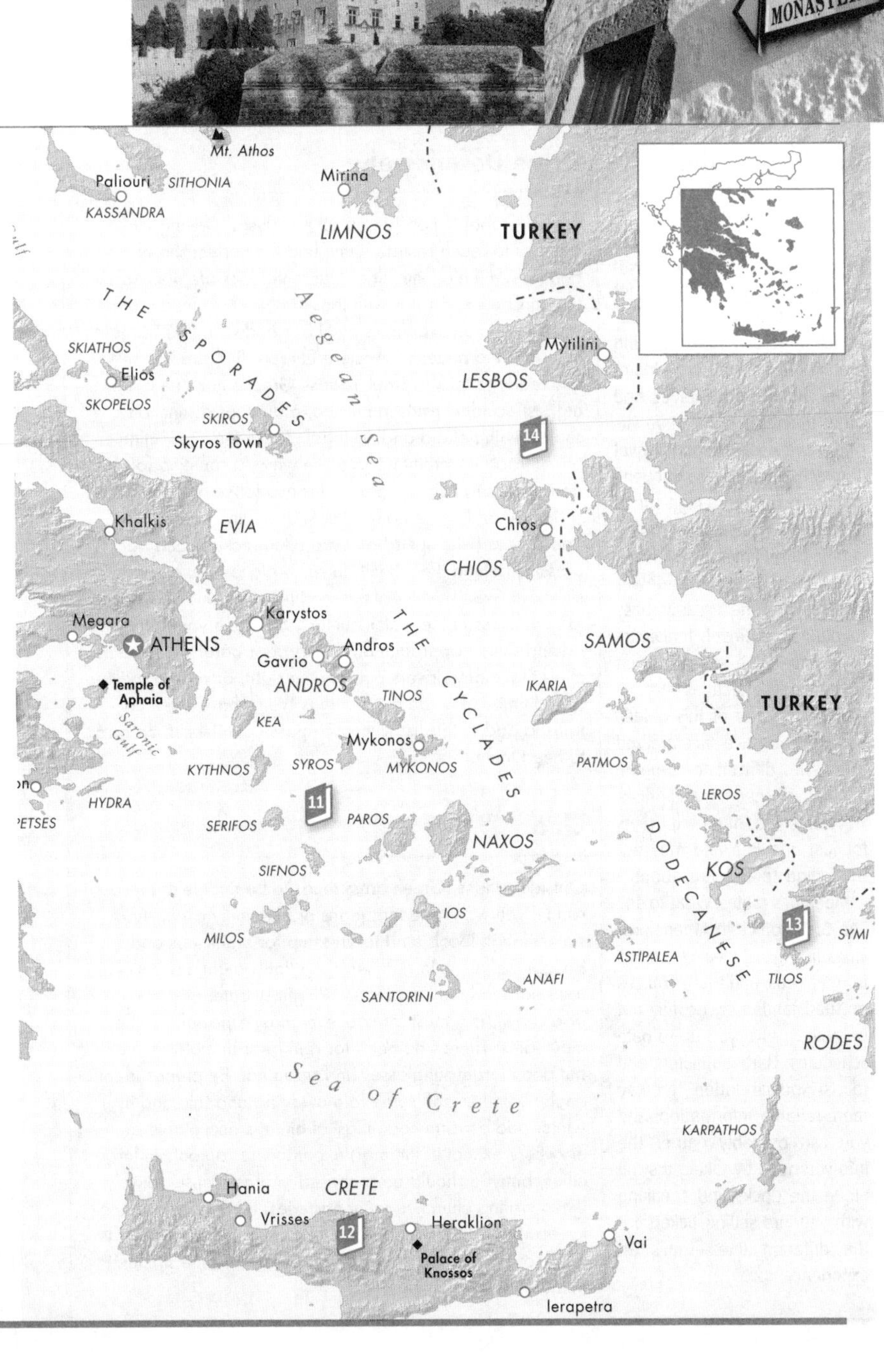
Προς Ι. ΜΟΝΗ
MONASTERY
Mt. Athos
Paliouri
SITHONIA
KASSANDRA
Mirina
LIMNOS
TURKEY
THE SPORADES
Aegean Sea
SKIATHOS
Elios
SKOPELOS
SKIROS
Skyros Town
Mytilini
LESBOS
14
Khalkis
EVIA
Chios
CHIOS
Megara
ATHENS
Karystos
Andros
Gavrio
ANDROS
Temple of Aphaia
Saronic Gulf
THE CYCLADES
SAMOS
IKARIA
TURKEY
TINOS
KEA
Mykonos
KYTHNOS
SYROS
MYKONOS
PATMOS
HYDRA
PETSES
11
SERIFOS
PAROS
NAXOS
LEROS
DODECANESE
SIFNOS
KOS
IOS
MILOS
13
SYMI
ASTIPALEA
ANAFI
TILOS
SANTORINI
RODES
Sea of Crete
KARPATHOS
Hania
CRETE
Vrisses
12
Heraklion
Vai
Palace of Knossos
Ierapetra

GREECE PLANNER

Don't Miss the Boat

Greece's extensive ferry system provides the best way to get from island to island, an experience that can make getting around one of the highlights of a trip. Boats from Piraeus and other mainland ports serve virtually every island; boat travel between islands is also frequent; and more and more high-speed hydrofoils are taking over routes, cutting travel times in half. That's all good news. On the downside, it's not necessarily easy to plan boat travel. Individual lines have Web sites (⇨Boat & Ferry travel sections in each regional chapter of this guide), but in the absence of centralized listings it's difficult to compare alternative schedules and prices. Travel agencies often sell tickets for just one line and may not be willing to tell you about a competitor's routes. What to do? The GNTO office in Athens provides listings of weekly sailings from Piraeus, and tourist offices on the islands may or may not be able to give you up-to-date schedules. Harbor masters and tourist police often provide more-reliable information, and you can probably gather the info you need by taking a stroll along the docks and speaking with vendors selling tickets for the different lines—that's an experience, too.

Drive Defensively

You've probably considered all the pluses. Driving makes it easier to reach remote ruins, find the perfect slip of a beach, see the countryside. Car-rental fees are not exorbitant in Greece, on par with those in North America, and gasoline, while expensive by U.S. standards, is a bargain compared to prices in Western Europe. But, are you really ready to tackle Greek roads? Greece has one of the highest accident rates in Europe, a dubious distinction shared with Ireland and Portugal, and after a few minutes on the road it's pretty easy to see why. Accounting for the perils, not surprisingly, are bad roads (often narrow, poorly surfaced, and full of hairpin turns and blind corners) and bad drivers (who speed and are often reckless and aggressive behind the wheel). In some places you can add stubborn, won't-get-out-of-the-road livestock and slowpoke farm vehicles to the watch-out-fors. So, hone your defensive driving skills—approach any crossroads carefully, keep in mind that many drivers pass on the right, drive at or below speed limits, slow down at curves. You'll have more cautions to add to this list with each passing milepost. Be sure to heed them.

Gear

Outside Athens, Greek dress tends to be middle of the road—you won't see torn jeans or extremely expensive suits, though locals tend to dress up for nightclubs and bouzoukia joints. In summer bring lightweight, casual clothing and good walking shoes. A light sweater or jacket, or a shawl, is a must for cool evenings, especially in the mountains. There's no need for rain gear in high summer, but don't forget sunglasses and a sun hat. Be prepared for cooler weather and some rain in spring and fall, and in winter add a warm coat. Casual attire is acceptable everywhere except in the most expensive restaurants in large cities, but you should be prepared to dress conservatively when visiting churches or monasteries. It's not appropriate to show a lot of bare arm and leg; anyone wearing shorts must cover up, as must women in pants, in some stricter monasteries.

Rooms to Spare

Unless you're visiting Athens or a resort at the height of the tourist season, you'll probably not have a hard time finding a room in Greece. The issue is finding a place you'll enjoy. Chances are you won't want to stay in one of the banal hotels geared to package tourism that have marred many a Greek shoreline, and you will want certain amenities—not necessarily luxuries, mind you, but a terrace, a view of the sea or the mountains, a fridge to keep water and snacks cool. By and large, prices for high-quality accommodations nationwide have reached an almost equal standard—one that doesn't differ that significantly from prices for same-level accommodations in Athens.

When it comes to making reservations, it is probably wise to book at least one month in advance for the months of June, July, and September, and ideally even two to three months in advance for the high season, from late July to the end of August, especially when booking top-end hotels in high-profile destinations like Santorini and Hydra. Sometimes during off-season you can bargain down the official prices (rumor has it to as much as a quarter of the price). The most advisable method is to politely propose a price that's preferable to you, and persevere. The response you get will depend largely on the length of your stay, the hotel's policy, and on the season in question. When booking, it's worth asking whether the hotel provides transportation from the airport/port as part of their services. If you're not certain about directions, ask a travel agent at the port/airport for detailed directions. For low-cost accommodation, consider Greece's ubiquitous "rooms to rent," bed-and-breakfasts without the breakfast. You can count on a clean room, often with such amenities as a terrace and a private bath, at a *very* reasonable price, in the range of €40–€50 for two. Look for signs in any Greek town or village; or, let the proprietors find you—they have a knack for spotting strangers who look like they might need a bed for the night. When renting a room, take a good look first and be sure to check the bathroom before you commit. If there are extra beds in the room, clarify in advance that the amount agreed on is for the entire room—owners occasionally try to put another person in the same room. When approached by one of the touts who meet the island ferries, make sure he or she tells you the location of the rooms being pushed, and look before you commit. Avoid places on main roads or near all-night discos. Rates vary tremendously from month to month; in the off-season, rooms may cost half of what they do in August.

When Less is Not More . . .

Though Greece is becoming more liberal socially, old standards still prevail, especially among the middle-aged and elderly. Some Western habits can cause offense, and the big no-no's include:

Showing public displays of affection. Greeks hug, stroll arm and arm, kiss each cheek in greeting, but an amorous smooch or wandering hand will raise eyebrows.

Baring it all. Nudity is common on Greek beaches, but it's a question of where you decide to drop trou—this is usually appropriate only at the far ends of a strand, away from the areas where Greek families congregate. Topless sunbathing is permissible, but again, discretion is advised.

Showing legs and arms. Appendages, especially female, should be well covered when entering monasteries and churches. An attendant will usually be waiting near the entrance to drape the underclad in cloaks or skirtlike garments. Women might want to bring along a wrap or large scarf for such occasions.

To help you decipher the complexity of Greek culture, read the excellent Exploring the Greek Mosaic, by Benjamin Broome (Intercultural Press, 1996), which thoughtfully analyzes Greece's social landscape and provides insights that are still valuable today.

GREECE TODAY

Being Part of the European Union (E.U.)

It wasn't too long ago that a Greek village was, well, Greek. If there were any outsiders, they were transplants from the other side of the island. But now that E.U. membership has made it easier for residents of other countries to buy property in Greece, properties that have been in Greek families for generations are suddenly vacation getaways for Klaus and Gudrun and Colin and Priscilla. It's common to hear grumblings that the foreigners are snapping up property that's the birthright of Greeks, but no one seems to be complaining about the new influx of cash the newcomers are pouring into local economies. In a case of good things coming to those who wait, Greek women are coming out ahead in many land deals. By tradition, sons inherited flat, farmable land, while daughters received unusable parcels on hillsides—that is, the "view property" that's now going for top euro.

With membership in the E.U., English, the language of tourism, has grown in popularity. That noted, you should still carry a phrase book, because your hosts will appreciate a greeting, thank you, or other occasional kind word in Greek. Also have on hand a list (such as the one at the back of this book) that transliterates the Greek alphabet—this will be helpful in deciphering street names and road signs that are only in Greek (and many signs on country roads still are).

Government & Politics

Greece, it's worth remembering, has only been a bona-fide democracy since the mid-1970s (not forgetting the fact that it invented the concept back in 5th century BC Athens). After years of civil war and military dictatorship, many Greeks aren't so much interested in the politicians who come and go—currently the moderate New Democrats are holding on by their fingernails—as they are in some ages-old issues, most of them having to do with the country's uneasy relationships with its neighbors. Names not to mention unless you have a couple of hours to listen include: Albania, homeland of more than a million immigrants who have flooded into Greece in recent years; Turkey, which for much of the 20th century seemed about to pounce and invade Greece and did indeed persecute Greeks in Turkey on more than one occasion; Cyprus, still uneasily divided between the Greeks and Turks; and the Former Yugoslavian Republic of Macedonia, which Greeks think has no right to use the name of one of their country's most historic regions, birthplace of Alexander the Great.

The Economy

It's a good thing Greeks are optimistic by nature, because the economic news is not particularly sunny. Greece has a huge deficit; unemployment is high; shipping—the mainstay of Greek wealth for centuries—is flat; and that leaves tourism and agriculture, both of which are volatile. The average Greek is likely to gripe about increases in the cost of living, being in debt (credit cards and mortgages were unheard of in Greece until about a decade ago), and how hard it is to find a decent job. At the same time, many Greeks are enjoying cars, second homes, and other bourgeois perks they've never had before.

As a traveler to Greece, you'll find that the country is a lot more expensive than it was even a decade ago, but it's still a bargain compared to other places in Europe. You can, of course, spend a lot of money if you choose to live in the lap of luxury,

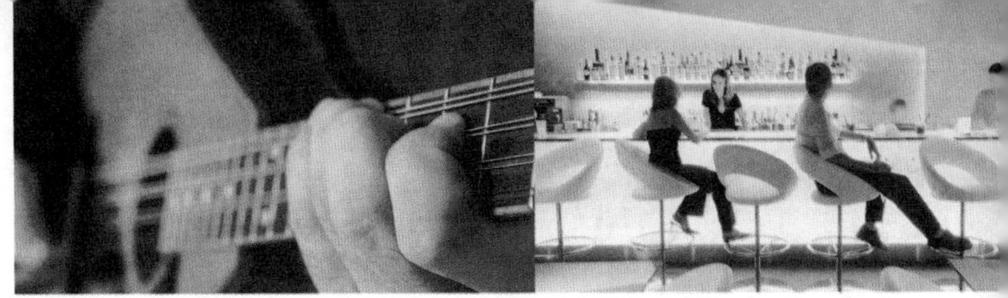

but you can find comfortable lodgings for less than €100 a night for a double and dinner for two needn't clock in at more than €30. The savings will be welcome, because you'll spend a lot of money to get to Greece—as much as $1,500 or $2,000 from New York's J.F.K. airport at the height of the summer season. A lot of travelers take advantage of airline frequent-flyer programs for this trip, but if you want to use miles, make your plans as much as a year in advance—the free seats fly out the door at supersonic speed.

People

You don't have to be a sociologist to note some pretty stellar qualities of the Greek character. For one thing, Greeks are generous, even to the tourists who besiege them—they will often offer a plate of cookies or a bottle of home-brewed *raki* to a traveler, just to create a bond and establish a level of comfort. They are family oriented, to say the least—it's still common for men and women to live with their parents until they marry, and actually, marriage is not necessarily a reason to move out, with extended families living together all their lives. Which brings us to the relationships between men and women, which is, like many aspects of Greek life, somewhat complex. While Greek men might swagger around in what outwardly can seem to be a male-dominated society, women run the home, often take a partnership role in family businesses, and—now that the Greek birthrate is one of the lowest in the E.U., freeing women to pursue careers—are an increasing presence in the white-collar workplace.

Greeks pamper their children, and they'll extend the same affection to yours and probably spoil them rotten. Among other privileges, kids can wander freely around restaurants as you linger over a meal, play safely in many squares and other car-free zones, and stay up late (it's not unusual to see a family enjoying a round of ice cream around midnight on a hot summer evening). Many beaches are family oriented, with shallow waters and concessions that rent floats and other water toys. Young travelers will enjoy wandering around ruins, in limited doses, and will probably be intrigued by stories of gods and goddesses—introducing them to mythology before the trip will enhance their visits to Mt. Olympus, Delphi, and other godly realms.

Culture & Other Pursuits

The father in *My Big Fat Greek Wedding,* who is so quick to point out the Greek roots of any English word, is not really Hollywood hyperbole. Proud of their language and its precision in capturing the complexities of emotion and nuance, Greeks often discuss etymology—as well as the Peloponnesian Wars, Homeric descriptions, and other aspect of their illustrious cultural heritage.

They are eager audiences at the many performances of ancient dramas throughout the country, proud of such recent literary lions as Odysseus Elytis and Nikos Kazantzakis, and put a high value on education—the culture that gave rise to the schools of Socrates and Aristotle offers a free university education these days. At the same time, Greeks are many-times champs in European basketball, and the enthusiasm for football has led to spurts of violence that puts fans firmly in league with other European soccer hooligans.

TOP GREECE ATTRACTIONS

The Acropolis

(C) The great emblem of classical Greece has loomed above Athens (whose harbor of Piraeus is gateway to all the Greek Islands) for 2,500 years. Even from afar, the sight of the Parthenon—the great marble temple that the 5th century BC statesmen Pericles conceived to crown the site—stirs strong feelings about the achievements and failings of Western Civilization.

Corfu

(B) More than a million visitors a year answer the call of the island that inspired the landscapes of Shakespeare's *The Tempest*. Historically, these admirers are in good company—Normans, Venetians, Turks, Napoléon Bonaparte, and the British have all occupied Corfu, leaving fortresses, seaside villas, and an unforgettable patina of cosmopolitan elegance.

Delphi

(E) On Greece's most sacred ground, follow in the footsteps of the ancients and step into the temple of Apollo, where the Pythian oracle may or may not present a garbled answer to your questions. Even if the oracle doesn't send you into a spell, the spectacle of the sanctuary, theater, and treasure-filled museum will.

Knossos

(F) Crete will introduce you to the marvels of the Minoans, the first great European civilization that flourished around 1500 BC. First stop is Knossos, the massive palace complex of King Minos, then it's on to the nearby archaeological museum in Heraklion, where the playful frescoes that once lined the royal chambers show just how urbane these early forbearers were.

Meteora

Getting closer to God, being halfway to Heaven ... however you choose to describe the experience, ascending to these Byzantine monasteries perched atop 1,000-foot-high peaks is a most unearthly experience. With worldly diversions so far below, the religious visions lavishly pictured in frescoes and mosaics are all the more transcendent.

Mykonos

(A) Backbackers and jet-setters alike share the beautiful beaches and the Dionysian nightlife—this island is not called the St-Tropez of the Aegean without reason—but the old ways of life continue undisturbed in fishing ports and along mazelike town streets. Not only are the hotels and cafés picture-perfect, the famous windmills actually seem to be posing for your camera.

Olympia

The games that still hold all the world in their thrall were first staged here in the pine-scented stadium and hippodrome, arranged around a sacred zone of temples, in 776 BC. Natives of Greek city states called a temporary truce and suspended all warfare to compete peacefully in their chariot races, boxing matches, and pentathlons, a tradition we moderns would be wise to follow.

Santorini

(D) One of the world's most picturesque islands cradles the sunken caldera of a volcano that last erupted around 1600 BC. To merely link the phenomenon to the Atlantis myth and the Minoan collapse misses the point—what matters is the ravishing sight of the multicolor cliffs rising 1,100 feet out of sparkling blue waters, a visual treat that makes the heart skip a beat or two.

QUINTESSENTIAL GREECE

The Greek Spirit

"Come back tomorrow night. We're always here at this time," is the gracious invitation that usually terminates the first meeting with your outgoing Greek hosts. The Greeks are open, generous, and above all, full of a frank, probing curiosity about you, the foreigner. They do not have a word for standoffishness, and their approach is direct: American? British? Where are you staying? Are you married or single? How much do you make? Thus, with the subtlety of an atomic icebreaker, the Greeks get to know you, and you, perforce, get to know them.

In many villages there seems to always be at least one English-speaking person for whom it is a matter of national pride and honor to welcome you and, perhaps, insist on lending you his only mule to scale a particular mountain, then offer a tasty dinner meal. This is the typically Greek, deeply moving hospitality which money cannot buy and for which, of course, no money could be offered in payment.

Worry Beads

Chances are that your host—no doubt, luxuriantly moustached—will greet you as he counts the beads of what appears to be amber rosaries. They are *komboloia* or "worry beads," a legacy from the Turks, and Greeks click them on land, on the sea, in the air to ward off that insupportable silence that threatens to reign whenever conversation lags.

Shepherds do it, cops do it, merchants in their shops do it. More aesthetic than thumb-twiddling, less expensive than smoking, this Queeg-like obsession indicates a tactile sensuousness, characteristic of a people who have produced some of the Western world's greatest sculpture.

If you want to get a sense of Greek culture and indulge in some of its pleasures, start by familiarizing yourself with the rituals of daily life. These are a few highlights—things you can take part in with relative ease.

Siestas

When does Greece slow down? In Athens, it seems never. But head out to the countryside villages and you'll find another tradition, the siesta—the only time Greeks stop talking and really sleep it seems. Usually after lunch and until 4 PM, barmen drowse over their bars, waiters fall asleep in chairs, and all good Greeks drift off into slumber wherever they are, like the enchanted courtiers of Sleeping Beauty. Then, with a yawn, a sip of coffee, and a large glass of ice water, Greece goes back to the business of the day.

Folk Music & Dance

It's a rare traveler to Greece who does not at some point in the trip encounter Greek song and folk dancing, sure to be vigorous, colorful, spontaneous, and authentic. The dances are many, often rooted in history or religion, or both: the *zeimbekiko*, a man's solo dance, is performed with a pantherlike grace and an air of mystical awe, the dancer, with eyes riveted to the floor, repeatedly bending down to run his hand piously across the ground. The music, played by bouzoukis, large mandolins, is nostalgic and weighted with melancholy. The most-popular, however, of all Greek dances are the *kalamatianos* and *tsamikos*.

The former is performed in a circle, the male leader waving a handkerchief, swirling, bounding, and lunging acrobatically. The latter, more martial in spirit, represents men going to battle, all to the sound of stamping, springing, and twisting cries of *opa!* Remember that plate-smashing is now verboten in most places. In lieu of flying pottery, however, a more-loving tribute is paid—many places have flower vendors, whose blooms are purchased to be thrown upon the dancers as they perform.

IF YOU LIKE

Ancient Splendors

The sight greets you time and again in Greece—a line of solid, sun-bleached masonry silhouetted against a clear blue sky. If you're lucky, a cypress waves gently to one side. What makes the scene all the more fulfilling is the realization that a kindred spirit looked up and saw the same temple or theater some 2,000 or more years ago. Temples, theaters, statues, a stray Doric column or two, the fragment of a Corinthian capital: these traces of the ancients are thick on the ground in Greece, from the more than 3,000-year-old **Minoan Palace of Knossos** on the island of Crete to such relatively "new" monuments as the **Parthenon.** You can prepare yourself by reading up on mythology, history, and Greek architecture, but get used to the fact that coming upon these magnificent remnants of ancient civilizations is likely to send a chill up your spine every time you see them.

Temple of Poseidon, Sounion, Attica. Set over the sea and showstopper of the Apollo Coast, the extant columns of this great temple are one of the icons of ancient Greece, hallowed by King Aegeus and visited by Lord Byron.

Delphi, west of Attica. Set in a spectacular vale, this was the ancient site of the most venerated and consulted Greek oracle. The site is breathtaking, and the remnant artworks, such as the fabled Charioteer, even more so.

Mycenae, Northern Peloponnese. Haunted by the legendary spirits of Agamennon and Clytemnestra, this royal town of the 13th century BC conjures up the days of Homer, thanks to such staggering relics as the Lion Gate.

Majestic Monasteries

A legacy of the great Byzantine era, and often aligned with great historic churches of the Greek Orthodox church, the monasteries of Greece seems as spiritual and as peaceful as when the land was strode by St. John. A religious mystique hangs over many of these island retreats, infusing them with a sense of calm that you will appreciate even more when escaping from party-central towns like Mykonos or crowded beaches. The natural beauty and calm of these places, many visitors find, heal your body and soul, revitalizing you for the rest of your trip.

Monastery of St. John the Theologian, Patmos. On the hill overlooking Hora is this retreat built to commemorate St. John in the 11th century—not far way is the cave where he wrote the text of *Revelation*, near the Monastery of the Apocalypse.

The Meteora, Thessaly. Set atop soaring rock pinnacles, six heaven-kissing monasteries make up one of Greece's most spectacular sights—everyone from Lord Byron to James Bond has visited.

Osios Loukas, near Delphi, west of Attica. The mosaics here follow to perfection the Byzantine model—set against a gold background they were created by great artists from Thessaloniki and Constantinople.

Profitis Ilias, Sifnos, the Cyclades. This Byzantine extravaganza sits atop the island's highest mountain. After touring the interior with a monk, take in the panoramic views which stop all conversation.

Evangelistria, Skiathos, the Sporades. On Skiathos's highest point, not far from the town of Lalaria, is this late-18th-century jewel, looming above a gorge and set with a magnificent church with three domes.

Natural Wonders

Some countries have serene pastures and unobtrusive lakes, environments beautiful in a subtle way. Not Greece. Its landscapes seem put on Earth to astound outright, and often the intertwined history and spiritual culture are equally powerful. This vibrant modern nation is a land of majestic mountains whose slopes housed the ancient gods long before they nestled Byzantine monasteries or ski resorts. The country's sapphire-rimmed islands served as a cradle of great civilizations before they became playgrounds for sailors and beach lovers. If there are no temples to the ancient gods on many of the mountains on the Greek islands, the looming summits that seem to reach into the heavens, impressive from any perspective, inspired the Greeks to worship natural forces. Many islands have ancient goat and donkey trails that are sublime hikes; prime walking months are April and May, when temperatures are reasonable, wildflowers seem to cover every surface, and birds are on their migratory wing.

Samaria Gorge, Hania, Crete. From Omalos a zigzag path descends steeply 2,500 feet into the tremendous Samaria gorge that splits the cliffs here for 13 km (8 mi) down to Ayia Roumeli on the Libyan Sea. Catch views of the Cretan *kri-kri* goat near the famous "Iron Gates" stone passageway.

The flooded caldera, Santorini, the Cyclades. What may be the most beautiful settlements in the Cyclades straddle the wondrous crescent of cliffs, striated in black and pink, rising 1,100 feet over the haunting, wine-color Aegean Sea.

The Most Beautiful Towns & Villages

Historic, simple, famous, nondescript, or perfectly preserved: almost any Greek village seems to possess that certain balance of charm and mystique that takes your breath away. The sight of miragelike, white clusters of houses appearing alongside blue waters or tumbling down hillsides is one of the top allures of any trip here. Villages are awash in cubical, whitewashed houses—often built atop another along mazelike streets (designed to confound invaders). Add in architectural landmarks—a Byzantine cathedral, a Venetian 16th-century kastro (or fortress), and monasteries that seems sculpted of zabaglione custard—and these villages and towns often look like paintings that belong in anyone's National Gallery.

Rethymnon, Crete. A Venetian *fortessa* rests on a hill above this city, where cobblestone alleyways squirm their way through Turkish and Italianate houses. Bypass the newer parts of town to stroll through the Venetian harbor, packed solid with atmospheric cafés and shops.

Ia, Santorini, the Cyclades. Here is where you will find the cubical white houses you've dreamed of, and a sunset that is unsurpassed.

Pirgi, Chios, Northeast Aegean. Whitewashed buildings stenciled with exuberant traditional patterns create a unique effect here, one of the defensive villages on Chios island founded by the Genoese in the 14th century.

Hydra, the Saronic Gulf Islands. The chicoscenti steal away to this harbor beauty, set with 19th-century merchant's mansions, festive waterside cafés, and some Hollywood pixie dust (Sophia Loren filmed *Boy on a Dolphin* here).

SUNBELIEVABLE: GREECE'S TOP BEACHES

Greeks are very accepting of *xènos* (foreigners) and tend to overlook our strange beach-going habit of seeking out patches of sand as far from the crowds as possible.

For Greeks, the beach is an extension of the *platia* (square) or the *kafenion* (café)—it's another place to gather, gossip, catch up on local news, argue about politics, play a game of tavli, keep an eye on the neighbors, or enjoy a meal in a beachside taverna.

Socializing isn't confined to the sand, either—don't be surprised to hear animated chatter emanating from a sea full of bobbing heads.

The sea is sometimes full of other things, including entire ancient sites—who can forget Roger Moore's and Carole Bouchet's underwater swim through a Greek temple in *For Your Eyes Only*? That should remind you that snorkeling gear is handy on almost any Greek beach and a necessity to see the sunken ancient city of Olous off the shores of Crete's Elounda peninsula.

If you venture to Skantzoura, a tiny islet off Alonissos in the Sporades, you'll want to have a pair of binoculars as well—the ruins of the ancient city of Skandyle lie submerged just offshore, and rare falcons and black-headed Aegean seagulls roost in the pines.

But when night falls, the scuba gear gets put away and the Versace sandals come out.

Dionysus comes on duty when the sun goes down, presiding over Aegean-style nightlife for which a string of Greek islands are justly popular.

Whether the setting is Mykonos, Rhodes, or Corfu, the ingredients are the same—a

Greece is ringed by 15,000 km (9,000 mi) of shoreline, a geographic blessing for sunseekers who pay homage to Helios and Poseidon and bask on seemingly endless expanses of sand. Call it hedonism if you will—after all, that's a Greek term.

view of the sea, an international crowd, and the promise that dawn will bring another flawless day.

Life's a Beach

Choosing the best Greek beach is a task of almost mythic proportions—think of Sisyphus rolling his stone up the hill on his never-to-be-completed task: You will continually come upon a stretch of sand that enchants you, then find an even better spot a little farther down the way.

No one is going to disagree, though, that these get pretty high scores in the idyllic category.

- **Super Paradise, Mykonos, the Cyclades.** Partly gay, partly nude, almost totally "beautiful peopled" by day, and a party scene by night, this golden strand of international fame is aptly named for beachgoers looking for more than sand and surf.
- **Mavra Volia, Chios, Northern Islands.** A "wine-dark sea" washes the black volcanic shores of a cove nestled between sheltering cliffs—little wonder the strangely appealing place is aptly called "Black Pebbles."
- **Plaka, Naxos, the Cyclades.** The most beautiful beach of all on an island of beautiful beaches is backed by sand dunes and bamboo groves, an exotic setting enhanced by a predictably spectacular sunset almost every evening.
- **Vai and Falasarna, Crete.** Here is where you will find the cubical white houses you've dreamed of, and a sunset that is unsurpassed.

LIVING LIKE THE GODS: TOP HOTELS

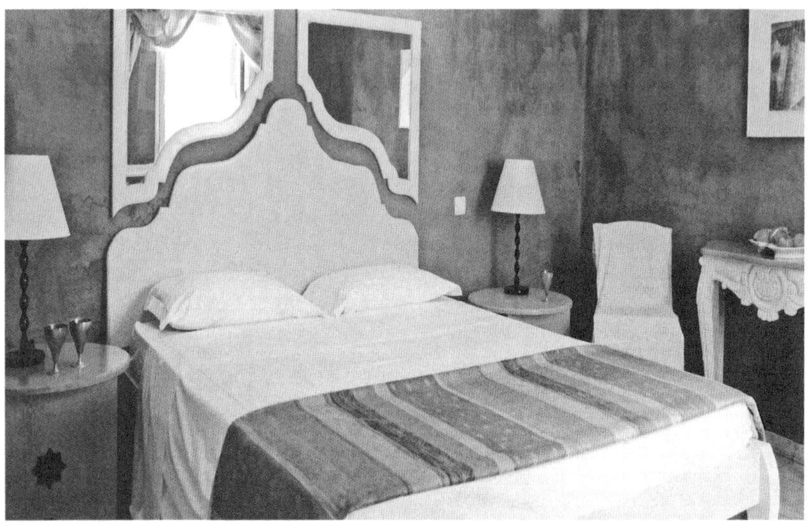

Many Greek getaways may lack worldly amenities but compensate with lots of other luxuries—an abundance of sand and sea, perhaps, or stunning mountain views and other natural enhancements. At these places, the greatest luxury is knowing you don't have to do anything except maybe notice how the water in the pool color-coordinates the sky. But, today, Greece has also a much more stylish side, and not only in Mykonos and Santorini.

Some new Greek resort xanadus would not only please the gods but might even make them blush a bit. Several such temples of hedonism, including the Elounda Mare and the Elounda Beach are nestled on the Elounda peninsula on the coast of Crete. Others, such as the Princess on Skiathos, are set amid a flurry of resort action and nightlife. At their skyward rates, you expect world-class service and accommodation, but the vibe also comes with an easygoing elegance that is distinctly Greek, plus amenities that set the gold standard. Satellite TV, Wi-Fi, gyms, bars, restaurants, lounges—all these are to be taken for granted at top resorts. Some of the other amenities to expect include: your own villa or bungalow, swimming pool, and slip of beach or waterside terrace; a sumptuous marble bathroom with whirlpool, steam room, and/or sauna; a spa with treatment pools and a full range of services; tennis courts and golf courses; a full array of water sports like windsurfing, parasailing, snorkeling, windsurfing, and boating; and a helipad for those harried, overworked CEOs. Although accommodation in Greece can vary from grand hotel to country house, all happily provide the quintessentially Greek quality of *filoxenia*, or welcome—easygoing, heartfelt hospitality.

The new, post-Olympic, European Greece with its boutique hotels, luxury villas, sybaritic spas, and sophisticated nightlife challenges many of the Zorba-era conceptions of "Spartan" Greece.

Greek Chic

- **Aigialos, Santorini, the Cyclades.** No need to venture out to view the jaw-dropping sunset over Santorini's caldera—a cluster of sumptuously restored 18th- to 19th-century village houses near the top of the island in Fira are the perfect perch.
- **Semeli, Mykonos.** Traditional furnishings and elegant surroundings evoke the high Mykoniot style.
- **Palazzino di Corina, Rethymnon, Crete.** The Venetians lived well during their time in Crete, and you will, too, in one of their palaces built around a lovely courtyard now equipped with a swimming pool.
- **Perleas Mansion, Chios, Northern Islands.** More than a thousand citrus trees and shady terraces surround a stone manor house from 1640.
- **Marco Polo Mansion, Rhodes, the Dodecanese.** Live like a pasha in a 15th-century Ottoman mansion fitted out with all the trappings—plush carpets, cushioned divans, and canopied beds.
- **Grande Bretagne, Athens.** The 1842 landmark is still the best of the best in Athens, a haven of grandeur and comfort.
- **Corfu Palace, Corfu, Ionian Islands.** Lush gardens, a sprawling pool, and a sea view from every room complement huge marble baths and elegant furnishings.
- **Miranda, Hyrda, Saronic Gulf Islands.** The 19th-century mansion of a sea captain is decked out with acres of polished wood, Venetian frescoes, and antiques—not just an atmospheric place to stay, but a national monument as well.

GREAT ITINERARIES

THE GLORY THAT WAS GREECE: THE CLASSICAL SITES

Lovers of art, antiquity, and mythology journey to Greece to make a pilgrimage to its great archaeological sites. Here, at Delphi, Olympia, and Epidauros, the gods of Olympus were revered, Euripides' plays were first presented, and some of the greatest temples ever built still evoke the genial atmosphere of Greece's golden age (in spite of 2,500 years of wear and tear). Take this tour and you'll learn that it's not necessary to be a scholar of history to feel the proximity of ancient Greece.

Days 1–2: Athens

Begin at the beginning—the Acropolis plateau—where you can explore the greatest temple of Periclean Greece, the Parthenon, while drinking in heart-stopping views over the modern metropolis. After touring the ancient Agora, the Monument of Lysikrates, and the Odeon of Herod Atticus, finish up at the National Archaeological Museum (check opening hours). *Chapter 1.*

Day 3: Sounion

Sun and sand, art, and antiquity lie southeast of Athens in Sounion. Here, the spectacular Temple of Poseidon sits atop a cliff 195 feet over the Saronic Gulf. Pay your own respects to the god of the sea at the beach directly below or enjoy the coves of the Apollo Coast as you head back west to the seaside resort of Vouliagmeni for an overnight. *Attica in Chapter 2.*

Day 4: Eleusis & Corinth

Heading west of Athens, make a stop at Eleusis, home of the Sanctuary of Demeter and the haunted grotto of Hades, god of the Underworld. Past the Isthmus of Corinth—gateway to the Peloponnese—Ancient Corinth and its sublime Temple of Apollo beckon. Head south to the coast and Nafplion; en route, stop at a roadside stand for some tasty Nemean wine. *Attica in Chapter 2 and Argolid & Corinthiad in Chapter 7.*

Days 5–6: Nafplion, Tiryns, Mycenae, Epidauros

Set up base in Nafplion—a stage set of Venetian fortresses, Greek churches, and neoclassical mansions—then set out to explore the mysteries of forgotten civilizations in nearby Tiryns, Mycenae, and Epidauros. North is Tiryns, where Bronze Age ramparts bear witness to Homer's "well-girt city." Farther north is Agamemnon's blood-soaked realm, the royal citadel of Mycenae, destroyed in 468 BC. Then take a day trip east to the famous ancient Theater at Epidauros, where a summer drama festival still presents the great tragedies of Euripides. *Argolid & Corinthiad in Chapter 7.*

Days 7–8: Olympia & Bassae

After your third overnight in Nafplion, head west via either Argos (with helpful train connections) or Tripoli (by car on the E65) to Olympia—holiest site of the ancient Greek religion, home to the Sanctuary of Zeus, and birthplace of the Olympics. Walk through the olive groves of the sacred precinct; then get acquainted with Praxiteles' *Hermes* in the museum. Overnight here and then make a trip south to the remote Temple of Apollo at Bassae. *Achaea & Elis in Chapter 7 and Arcadia in Chapter 8.*

Day 9: Delphi

Head north through verdant forests of the Elis region to Patras or nearby Rion for the ferry or bridge across the Corinthian Gulf; travel east along the coast and overnight in chic Galaxidi, with its elegant stone seafarers' mansions. The final day, set off to discover Delphi, whose noble dust and ancient ruins are theatrically set amid cliffs. Despite the tour buses, it is still possible to imagine the power of the most famous oracle of antiquity. From here, head back to Athens. *Delphi in Chapter 2.*

BY PUBLIC TRANSPORTATION

KTEL buses leave from the Platia Aigyptou, Liossion, and Odos Kifissou terminals in downtown Athens and connect to most of the major sites: southeast to Sounion along the coast, northwest to Delphi, and west to the Peloponnese.

In some cases you will need to take the bus to the provincial capital (Corinth, Argos, Tripoli), then change to a local bus.

Daily trains connect Athens's Peloponnisou station to Corinth and Argos, with bus connections to Nafplion and Olympia.

Buses travel from Nafplion to Olympia via Argos and Tripoli.

GREAT ITINERARIES

ISLAND-HOPPING: CYCLADES TO CRETE

Cyclades to Crete

There is no bad itinerary for the Greek islands. Whether you choose the Sporades, the Dodecanese, or any of those other getaways floating in the Aegean, the leading isles in Greece differ remarkably, and they are all beautiful. But when the needle may fly off the beauty-measuring gauge when it comes to the Cyclades. It might be possible to "see" any of these famous islands in a day: the "must-see" sights—Byzantine monasteries, ancient temples, Minoan mansions—are often few. Still, it is best to take a slower pace and enjoy a sumptuous, idyllic, 14-day tour. Planning the details of this trip depends on your sense of inclusiveness, your restlessness, your energy, and your ability to accommodate changing boat schedules. Just be warned: the danger of sailing through the Cyclades is that you will never want to leave them. From these suggested landfalls, some of the most justly famous, you can set off to find other idyllic retreats on your own.

Days 1–2: Mykonos

Jewel of the Cyclades, this very discovered island manages to retain its seductive charm. Spend the first day and evening enjoying appealing Mykonos town, where a maze of beautiful streets are lined with shops, bars, restaurants, and discos; spend time on one of the splendid beaches; and, if you want to indulge in some hedonism, partake of the wild nightlife. The next morning take the local boat to nearby Delos for one of the great classical sites in the Aegean. Mykonos is one of the main transport hubs of the Greek islands, with many ferries, boats, and planes connecting to Athens and its port of Piraeus. ⇨ *Mykonos in Chapter 7.*

Days 3–4: Naxos

Sail south to Naxos—easily done in summer, harder in other seasons. Plan on arriving from Mykonos in the late afternoon or evening, and begin with a predinner stroll around Naxos town, visiting the Portara (an ancient landmark), the castle, and other sights in the old quarter. The next morning, visit the Archaeological Museum; then drive through the island's mountainous center for spectacular views. Along the way, visit such sights as the Panayia Drosiani, a church near Moni noted for 7th-century frescoes; the marble-paved village of Apeiranthos; and the Temple of Demeter. If you have time, stop for a swim at one of the beaches facing Paros, say Mikri Vigla. ⇨ *Naxos in Chapter 7.*

Days 5–7: Paros

Go west, young man, to Paros, where the large spaces provide peace and quiet. Paros town has delights profane—buzzing bars—to sacred, such as the legendary Hundred Doors Church. But the highlight will be a meal in the impossibly pretty little fishing harbor of Naousa or, on a morning drive around the island, a visit to the lovely mountain village of Lefkes. Then spend an extra night of magic on the neighboring isle of Antiparos, where off-duty Hollywood celebs hang out and bliss with all the white sands, pink bougainvillea, and blue seas. ⇨ *Paros in Chapter 7.*

Days 8–9: Folegandros

This smaller isle is not only beautiful but, rarer in these parts, authentic. It boasts one of the most stunning Chora towns; deliberately downplayed touristic development; several good beaches; quiet evenings; traditional local food; and respectful visitors. The high point, literally and figuratively, is the siting of the main town—set on a towering cliff over the sea, its perch almost rivals that of Santorini. ⇨ *Folegandros in Chapter 7.*

Days 10–12: Santorini

Take a ferry from Folegandros south to the spectacle of all spectacles. Yes, in summer the crowds will remind you of the running of the bulls in Pamplona but even they won't stop from you gasping at the vistas, the seaside cliffs, and stunning Cycladic cubist architecture. Once you've settled in, have a sunset drink on a terrace overlooking the volcanic caldera but you'll also find many view-providing watering holes in Fira, the capital, or Ia, Greece's most-photographed village. The next day, visit the extensive prehistoric site at Akrotiri and the Museum of Prehistoric Thera; then enjoy a third just swimming one of the black-sand beaches at Kamari or Perissa. ⇨ *Santorini in Chapter 7.*

Days 13–14: Crete

Despite the attractions of sea and mountains, it is still the mystery surrounding Europe's first civilization and empire that draws many travelers to Crete. Like them, you'll discover stunning testimony to the island's mysterious Minoan civilization, particularly at the legendary Palace of Knossos. Along these shores are blissful beaches as well as the enchanting Venetian-Turkish city of Hania. From Heraklion, Crete's main port, there are frequent flights and ferries back to Piraeus, Athens, and reality. ⇨ *Chapter 8.*

WHEN TO GO

The best time to visit Greece is late spring and early fall. In May and June the days are warm, even hot, but dry, and the seawater has been warmed by the sun. For sightseeing or hitting the beach, this is the time. Greece is relatively tourist free in spring, so if the beach and swimming aren't critical, April and early May are good; the local wildflowers are at their loveliest, too. Carnival, usually in February just before Lent, and Greek Easter are seasonal highlights. July and August (most locals vacation in August) are always busy—especially on the islands. If you visit during this peak, plan ahead and be prepared to fight the crowds. September and October are a good alternative to spring and early summer, especially in the cities where bars and cultural institutions reopen. Elsewhere, things begin to shut down in November. Transportation to the islands is limited in winter, and many hotels outside large cities are closed until April.

Climate

Greece has a typical Mediterranean climate: hot, dry summers and cool, wet winters. Chilliness and rain begin in November, the start of Greece's deceptive winters. Any given day may not be very cold—except in the mountains, snow is uncommon in Athens and to the south. But the cold is persistent, and many places are not well heated. Spring and fall are perfect, with warm days and balmy evenings. In the south a hot wind may blow across the Mediterranean from Africa. The average high and low temperatures for Athens and Heraklion and the average temperature for Thessaloniki are presented below.

Forecasts **National Observatory of Athens** www.noa.gr. **Weather Channel Connection** 900/932–8437 95¢ per minute from a touch-tone phone www.weather.com.

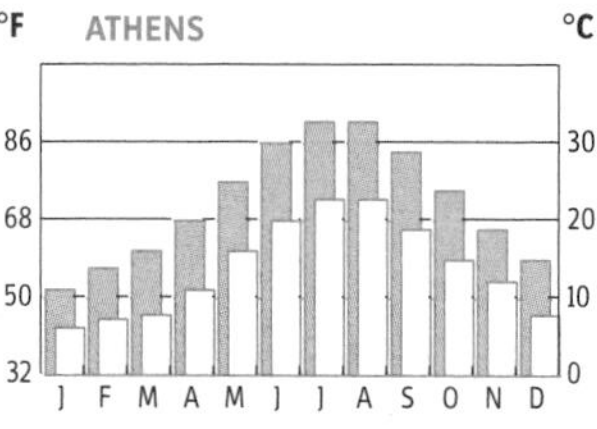

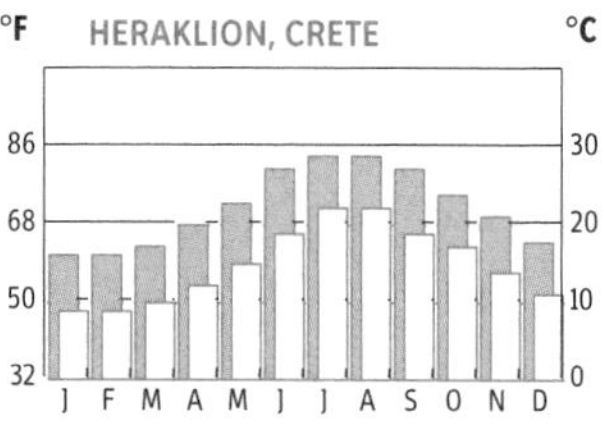

GREEK BY DESIGN

Shopping is now considered an Olympic sport in Greece—get the urge to splurge in the chic shops of Athens's Kolonaki district or head to Rhodes, Mykonos, and Crete, the islands that launched a thousand gifts. For the best in Greek style, here's where to get the goods.

The Greeks had a word for it: *tropos.* Style. You would expect nothing less from the folks who gave us the Venus de Milo, the Doric column, and the lyre-back chair. To say that they have had a long tradition as artisans and craftsmen is, of course, an understatement. Even back in ancient Rome, Greece was the word. The Romans may have engineered the stone vault and perfected the toilet, but when it came to style and culture, they were perfectly content to knock off Grecian dress, sculpture, décor, and architecture, then considered the height of fashion. Fast forward 2,500 years and little has changed. Many works of modern art were conceived as an Aegean paean, including the statues of Brancusi and Le Corbusier's minimalistic skyscrapers—both artists were deeply influenced by ancient Cycladic art. Today, the goddess dress struts the runways of Michael Kors and Valentino while Homer has made the leap to Hollywood in such recent box-office blockbusters as *300* and *Troy*.

Speaking of which, those ancient Trojans may have once tut-tutted about Greeks bearing gifts but would have second thoughts these days. Aunt Ethel has now traded in those plastic souvenir models of the Parthenon for a new Athenian bounty: pieces of Byzantine-style gold jewelry; hand-woven bedspreads from Hydra; strands of amber *komboloi* worry beads; and reproductions of red-figure ceramic vases. These are gifts you cannot resist and will be forever be glad you didn't.

BEARING GIFTS?

Seeing some of the glories of Aegean craftsmanship is probably one of the reasons you've come to Greece. The eggshell-thin pottery Minoans were fashioning more than 3,500 years ago, Byzantine jewelry and icons, colorful rugs that were woven in front of the fire as part of a dowry, not to mention all those bits of ancient masonry—these comprise a magnificent legacy of arts and crafts.

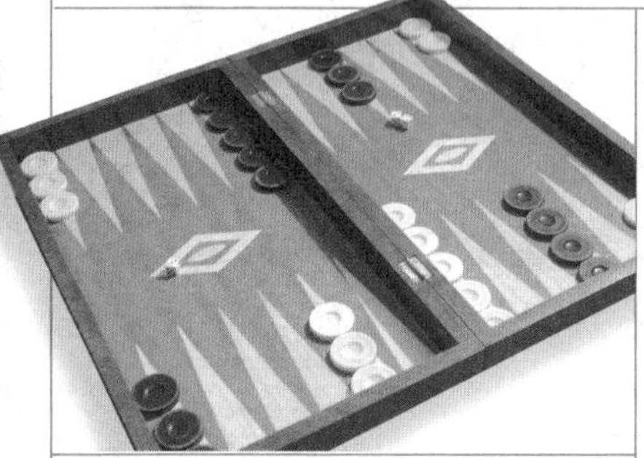

TAVLÍ BOARDS

No matter where you are in Greece, follow the sound of clinking die and you'll probably find yourself in a kafenion. There, enthusiasts will be huddled over Greece's favorite game, a close cousin to backgammon. Tavlí boards are sold everywhere in Greece, but the most magnificent board you'll ever see is not for sale—a marble square inlaid with gold and ivory, crafted sometime before 1500 bc for the amusement of Minoan kings and now on display at the archaeological museum in Heraklion, Crete.

LEATHER SANDALS

Ancient Greek women with means and a sense of style wore sandals with straps that wrapped around the ankles—what today's fashion mags call "strappy sandals," proof that some classics are always in vogue. The most legendary maker is Athens's very own Stavros Melissinos, whose creations were once sported by the Beatles and Sophia Loren. He has been crafting sandals for more than 50 years.

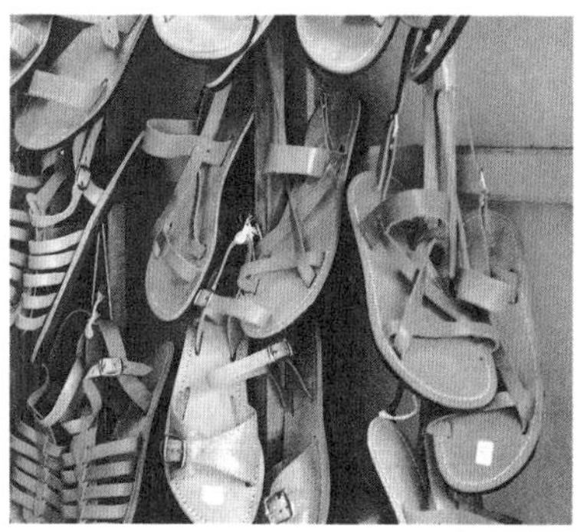

WORRY BEADS

Feeling fidgety? Partake of a Greek custom and fiddle with your worry beads, or komboloi. The amber or coral beads are loosely strung on a long strand and look like prayer beads, yet they have no religious significance. Even so, on a stressful day the relaxing effect can seem like divine intervention. Particularly potent are beads painted with the "evil eye."

ICONS

Icon painting flourished in Greece as the Renaissance took hold of Western Europe, and panels of saints and other heavenly creatures are among the country's greatest artistic treasures. Some, like many of those in the 799 churches on the island of Tinos, are said to possess miraculous healing powers, attracting thousands of cure-seeking believers each year. Icons attract art buyers too, but if you can easily afford one, it's almost certainly a modern reproduction.

JEWELRY

Greece's long gold- and silver-smithing tradition thrives in workshops on Rhodes and Corfu and in such mainland towns and villages as Ioannina and Stemnitsa. Many artisans turn to the past for inspiration—Bronze Age cruciform figures, gold necklaces from the Hellenistic period dangling with pomegranates, Byzantine-style pendants—while others tap out distinctly modern creations using age-old techniques.

WEAVING

Even goddesses spent their idle hours weaving (remember Arachne, so proud of her skills at the loom that Athena turned her into a spider?). From the mountains of Arcadia to such worldly enclaves as Mykonos, mortals sit behind handlooms to clack out folkloric rugs, bedspreads, and tablecloths.

CERAMICS

Ancient Greek pottery was a black-and-red medium: the Spartans and Corinthians painted glossy black figures on a reddish-orange background; later ceramicists switched the effect with stunning results, reddish-hued figures on a black background. Artisans still create both, and potters on Crete and elsewhere in Greece throw huge terracotta storage jars, pithoi, that are appealing, if no longer practical, additions to any household.

BARGAINING FOR BEGINNERS:

In Greece there is often the "first price" and the "last price." Bargaining is still par for the course (except in the fanciest stores). And if you're planning a shopping day, leave those Versace shoes at home—shopkeepers often decide on a price after sizing up the prospective buyer's income bracket.

ATHENS: PASSPORT TO STYLE

If you want to find the best in Greek craftsmanship, head to the shops of Athens. Greece may not have always been a land of great artists, but these top offerings will remind you that it has always been a place for great artistry.

Baba (Ifestou 30, Monastiraki) is Backgammon Central—get a great tavlí board here.

Center of Hellenic Tradition (Mitropoleous 59, Monastiraki) is a mecca for old Greek folk crafts, with regional ceramics, weavings, and antique sheep bells all making for evocative room accents.

Kombologadiko (6 Koumbari, Kolonaki) was praised by *Vogue* a few years ago for its chic take on old traditional komboloi worry beads, having remade this previously for-men-only item into high-fashion necklaces.

Lalaounis (Panepistimiou 6, Syntagma Square), Athens's most famous jeweler, allows jet-setters and collectors to "go for the gold" with necklaces, bracelets, headpieces, and rings inspired by ancient pieces.

Lykeio Ellinidon (Dimokritou 7a, Kolonaki) is famed for its resident weavers who copy folkloric motifs at two on-site looms.

Stavros Melissinos (Ayias Theklas 2, Monastiraki), Athens's most famous sandal-maker, boasts a clientele that has included Jackie Onassis and Gary Cooper.

A. Patnkiadou (58 Pandroussou, Plaka) has fashionistas raving about jewelry that incorporates ancient coins and Byzantine jewels.

Pylarinos (Panepistimious 18, Syntagma Square) is known for its selection of ancient coins and vintage engravings—pick up a 19th-century view of the Acropolis here.

Riza (Voukourestiou 35, Kolonaki) is tops for Greek Island accents like traditional brass candlesticks.

Tanagrea (Voulis 26 and Mitropoleous 15, Syntagma Square) is one of Athens's oldest gift shops and is famed for its hand-painted ceramic pomegranates, symbol of good fortune.

Thiamis (Asklipiou 71, Syntagma Square) gives a new take on an old art form with hand-painted icons.

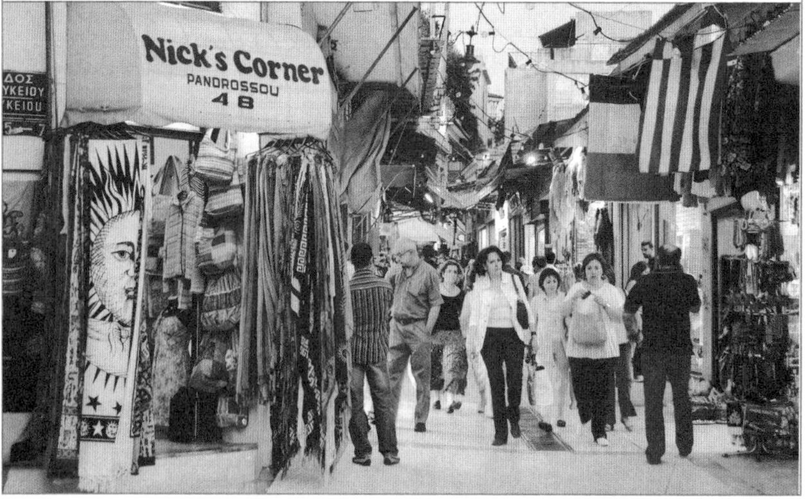

Cruising the Greek Islands

THE BEST SHIPS & ITINERARIES

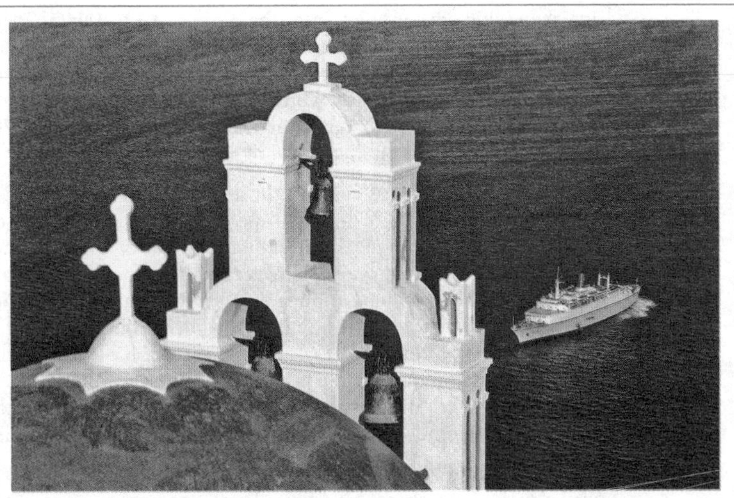

Thira, Santorini

WORD OF MOUTH

"How can anyone pass up a cruise to Greece? Santorini, Mykonos, Crete, and Rhodes: these are the islands that launched a thousand trips! Even Poseidon, god of the waters, would have been jealous of the beautiful cruise ships now sailing the Aegean seas."

—WiseOwl

www.fodors.com/forums

By Linda Coffman

TRAVELERS HAVE BEEN SAILING Greek waters ever since 3,500 B.C.C. (before Chris-Crafts). The good news is that today's visitor will have a much, much easier time of it than Odysseus, the world's first tourist and hero of Homer's *Odyssey.* Back in his day, exploring the Greek islands—1,425 geological jewels thickly scattered over the Aegean Sea like stepping stones between East and West—was a fairly daunting assignment. Zeus would often set the schedule (during the idyllic days in midwinter the master of Mt. Olympus forbade the winds to blow during the mating season of the halcyon or kingfishers); waterlogged wooden craft could be tossed about in summer, when the meltemi, the north wind, would be a regular visitor to these waters; and pine-prow triremes often embarked with a scramble of 170 oarsmen, not all of them pulling in the right direction.

> **SHIP, SHIP, HURRAY!**
>
> Did you know that the Mediterranean cruise ship industry, which is based in Greece, is second only in popularity in number of cruises to the Caribbean region? Nearly 2.2 million passengers a year set sail, with Greece holding the number one spot for the highest embarkation rate of all European Union countries.

Now, in 2008, travelers can sail those same blue highways in effortless fashion. A flotilla of—often—spectacularly outfitted cruise liners helps banish many typical landlubbers' irritations: ferry schedules, hotel reservations, luggage porterage, to name a few. When you add in 21st-century allurements—pulling into Santorini after a deck-side luncheon created by the gastronomic wizard of Nobu; a game of golf in Mykonos via your onboard 18-hole miniature-golf course; a renowned archaeologist illuminating the fascinating history of Rhodes, your next stop—you can see why a vacation aboard one of these gleaming white islands has become one of the most popular travel choices available.

Cruises have always had a magical quality, even without dramatic views of whitewashed Cycladic villages and ancient ruins anchored for eternity above a sheer drop (for a rundown of the ABC's, see the Cruise-Taker's Primer in the second half of this chapter). Sailing into harbor has a grand ceremonial feel lacking in air travel arrivals and Greece, the eastern Mediterranean's showcase, is an ideal cruise destination for travelers with limited time who wish to combine sightseeing with relaxation. This is especially true in the spring and autumn seasons, when milder Aegean and Ionian climates are better suited than the sweltering summer months to, for example, exploring those hilltop ancient ruins.

Although cruises have historically attracted an older group of travelers, more and more young people and family groups are setting sail in Europe. With the peak season conveniently falling during schools' summer hiatus, cruise lines have responded to multigenerational travel with expanded children's programs and discounted shore excursions for youngsters under age 12. Shore excursions have become more varied, too, often incorporating activities that families can enjoy together, such as bicycling and hiking. Cruise lines now offer more programs than ever before for adults as well, including pre- or post-cruise land tours as options, plus extensive onboard entertainment and learning programs. Some lines increasingly hire expert speakers to lead discussions based on local cultures.

Cruise ships may idyllically appear to be floating resorts, but keep in mind that if you should decide you don't like your ship, you can't check out and move somewhere else. Whichever one you choose will be your home for seven days, or more in some cases. The chosen ship will determine the type of accommodations you'll enjoy, the kind of food you'll eat, the entertainment program, and even the destinations you'll visit. That is why the most important endeavor you can undertake when planning a cruise is evaluating the proposed itinerary, the cruise line, and the particular ship.

THE MED FROM STEM TO STERN

Many of today's most popular Greek Island cruises are actually part and parcel of larger itineraries that cover wider swaths of the Mediterranean, extending from Rome to Alexandria, but this has been the Greek way of seafaring for more than 3,000 years. In ancient time, the Aegean and the Mediterranean were propitious for coastal trade, and it was by sea that the Greek way was spread. Greek ships colonized the whole Mediterranean coast to such an extent that for a thousand years the Mediterranean was known as a veritable Greek lake.

CHOOSING YOUR CRUISE

Which cruise is right for you depends on a number of factors, notably the size and style of ship you opt for, the itinerary you choose, and how much you're willing to spend. Prices quoted here are subject to change.

DREAM ITINERARIES

Cruise ships typically follow one of two itinerary types in the eastern Mediterranean: round-trip loops starting and finishing in the same port city; and one-way cruises that pick you up in one port and drop you off at another for the flight home. Itineraries are usually 7 to 10 days, though some lines offer longer sailings covering a larger geographic span. Some cruises concentrate on covering an area that includes the Greek islands, Turkish coast, Cyprus, Israel, and Egypt, while others reach from Gibraltar to the Ionian isles, the western Peloponnese, and Athens.

For an overview of Greece's top sights, choose an itinerary that includes port calls in Piraeus for a shore excursion to the Acropolis and other sights in Athens; Mykonos, a sparkling Cycladic isle with a warren of whitewashed passages, followed by neighboring Delos, with its Pompeii-like ruins; Santorini, a stunning harbor that's actually a partially submerged volcano; Rhodes, where the Knights of St. John built their first walled city before being forced to retreat to Malta; and Heraklion, Crete, where you'll be whisked through a medieval harbor to the reconstructed Bronze Age palace at Knossos. Port calls at Katakolon and Itea mean excursions to Olympia and the Temple of Apollo at Delphi. Some cruises call at Epidauros and Nafplion, offering an opportunity for visits to the ancient theater and the citadel of Mycenae, or at Monemvassia or Patmos, the island where St. John wrote the book of Revelations.

If you'd rather relax by the pool than trek through temples, opt for a cruise with more time at sea and fewer or shorter port calls. If you'd like time to explore each island destination, you'll want to choose a cruise where the ship spends the entire day in port and travels at night. Alternately, if the number of places you visit is more important than the time you spend in each one, book a cruise with a full itinerary and one or two port calls a day.

A cruise spares the planning headaches of solitary island-hopping and the inconvenience of carting luggage from one destination to the next, and, for budget-conscious travelers, cruises offer the advantage of controlled expenses. However, because one disadvantage is that port calls may be long enough only to allow time for a quick visit to one or two main attractions, cruises may be best for an overview, useful for planning a return trip to the more-appealing island stops.

WHEN TO GO

When to go is as important as where to go. In July or August, the islands are crowded with Greek and foreign vacationers, so expect sights, beaches, and shops to be crowded. High temperatures could also limit time spent on deck. May, June, September, and October are the best months—warm enough for sunbathing and swimming, yet not so uncomfortably hot as to make you regret the trek up Lindos. Cruising in the low seasons provides plenty of advantages besides discounted fares. Availability of ships and particular cabins is greater in the low and shoulder seasons, and the ports are almost completely free of tourists.

THE MAIN CRUISE LINES: AZAMARA TO WINDSTAR

Posh or penny-pinching? Two weeks or seven days? EasyCruise burgers or SeaDream Yacht Club's champagne-and-caviar beach barbecues? Large ships or small? There are any number of questions you have to ask yourself when lining up your dream Greek islands cruise but deciding to opt for either a large or small ship may be the most important. Large cruise lines account for the vast majority of passengers sailing in Europe. These typically have both larger cruise ships and megaships in their fleets. Cruise ships have plentiful outdoor deck space, and most have a wraparound outdoor promenade deck that allows you to stroll or jog the ship's perimeter. In the newest vessels, traditional meets trendy, but for all their resort-style innovations, they still feature cruise-

CLOSE UP

10 Questions to Answer Before Visiting a Travel Agent

If you've decided to use a travel agent, ask yourself these 10 simple questions, and you'll be better prepared to help the agent do his or her job:

1. Who will be going on the cruise?
2. What can you afford to spend for the entire trip?
3. Where would you like to go?
4. How much vacation time do you have?
5. When can you get away?
6. What are your interests?
7. Do you prefer a casual or structured vacation?
8. What kind of accommodations do you want?
9. What are your dining preferences?
10. How will you get to the embarkation port?

ship classics—afternoon tea, complimentary room service, and lavish pampering. The smallest cruise ships carry 500 or fewer passengers, while larger vessels accommodate 1,500 passengers and offer a wide variety of diversions. Megaships boast even more amenities and amusements, and carry between 1,500 and 3,000 passengers—enough people to outnumber the residents of many Greek port towns.

Megaships are a good choice if you're looking for nonstop activity and lots of options; they're especially appealing for groups traveling together and families with older kids. Experiences on these ships range from basic, comfortable vacations to white-glove luxury; from traditional cruises with formal nights, afternoon tea, and assigned dining places, to lively ships bustling with activity. All of them allow you the flexibility of seeing a variety of ports while still enjoying such cruise amenities as spas, nightly entertainment, and fine dining. These ships tend to follow conventional itineraries and stop at the best-known, larger ports of call; because of their size they can't venture too close to shore, thus you won't see much scenery from the deck. If you prefer a gentler pace and a chance to get to know your shipmates, consider a smaller ship.

Classic or midsize ships, which are more popular with Europeans than with Americans, offer a range of amenities and comfortable accommodations but are not as flashy as the new megaships. Luxury ships are generally small to midsize and are distinguished by high staff-to-guest ratios, superior cuisine, few onboard charges, and much more space per passenger than you'll find on the mainstream lines' vessels.

SMALL SHIPS

Compact vessels bring you right up to the shoreline where big ships don't fit. Destinations, not casinos or spa treatments, are the focus of these cruises. You'll call into smaller ports, as well as the larger, better-known cities. Port lectures and cultural talks are the norm. But in comparison with those on traditional cruise ships, cabins on these ships can be quite tiny, often with no phone or TV, and some bathrooms are no bigger than cubbyholes. Often, the dining room and the lounge are the only common public areas on these vessels. Some small ships, however, are luxurious yachtlike vessels with cushy cabins, comfy lounges and libraries, and hot tubs on deck. You won't find discos or movie theaters aboard, but what you trade for space and onboard diversions is a unique and detailed glimpse of ports that you're unlikely to forget.

Small-ship cruising can be pricey as costs are spread over a few dozen, rather than hundreds of, passengers. Fares tend to be quite inclusive (except for airfare), with few onboard charges, and, given the size of ship and style of cruise, fewer opportunities to spend money on board. Small ships typically offer the same kinds of early-booking and other discounts as the major cruise lines.

AZAMARA CRUISES

"The adventuresome (yet pampered) soul has met its match" is the catchy new slogan for this fledgling outfit newly launched by parent company Royal Caribbean in 2007. Named partly in honor of the star Acamar—the most-southerly bright star that can be viewed from the latitude of Greece—the firm has two vessels, built for now-defunct Renaissance Cruises, and refitted for the deluxe-cruise crowd. Designed to offer exotic destination-driven itineraries, Azamara offers a more-intimate onboard experience, while allowing access to the less-traveled ports of call experienced travelers want to visit. And the enrichment programs are some of the best on offer.

Itineraries and Ships. *Azamara Quest* (694 passengers) has multiple sailings of its exciting 14-night "Ancient Empires" itinerary, which begins in Rome, then sails to such ports as Sorrento and Greece's Athens, Chios, Heraklion (Crete), with a number of stops in Turkey, including Bodrum and Istanbul, and one in Alexandria, Egypt. Rates begin at $2,499 (note that all itineraries and rates quoted in this chapter are as of fall 2007). *Azamara Journey* (694 passengers) kicks off its "Holyland" 14-day cruise in Athens, then includes such destinations as Greece's Chios, Santorini, Cyprus's Limassol, Israel's Haifa, Egypt's Port Said, Italy's Sorrento and Rome, and Spain's Barcelona. Rates begin at $2,799. The two ships also feature longer "Black Sea" and "Classical Mediterranean" tours.

Your Shipmates. Azamara is designed to appeal to discerning travelers, primarily American couples of any age who appreciate a high level of service in an unstructured atmosphere. The ships are not family oriented and do not have facilities or programs for children.

Food. Expect all the classic dinner favorites but with an upscale twist, such as gulf shrimp with cognac and garlic, or a filet mignon with black truffle sauce. Each ship offers two specialty restaurants: the Mediterranean-influenced Aqualina and the stylish steak-and-seafood restaurant Prime C. Guests in suites receive two nights of complimentary dining in the two restaurants, while guests in staterooms receive one. Daily in-cabin afternoon tea service and delivery of canapés are available to all passengers.

Fitness and Recreation. In addition to a well-equipped gym and an outdoor jogging track, Azamara's fitness program includes yoga at sunset, Pilates, and access to an onboard wellness consultant. Both ships offer a full menu of spa treatments, an outdoor spa relaxation lounge, and an aesthetics suite featuring acupuncture, laser hair removal, and micro-dermabrasion.

HOW TO EARN YOUR SEA MAJOR

A distinguishing aspect of Azamara is a wide range of enrichment programs to accompany the destination-rich itineraries. Programs include guest speakers and experts on a wide variety of topics, including technology, cultural explorations, art, music, and design.

Contact. ✉ *1050 Caribbean Way, Miami, FL33132* ☎ *877/222–2526 or 877/999–9553* 🌐 *www.azamaracruises.com.*

CELEBRITY CRUISES

Founded in 1989, Celebrity has gained a reputation for fine food and professional service. The cruise line has built premium, sophisticated ships and developed signature amenities, including a specialty coffee shop, martini bar, large standard staterooms with generous storage, spas, and butler service for passengers booking the top suites. Although spacious accommodations in every category are a Celebrity standard, the addition of Concierge Class makes certain premium ocean-view and balcony staterooms almost the equivalent of suites in terms of amenities and service.

Itineraries and Ship. *Galaxy* (1,890 passengers) is the European flagship of this popular American line and has some winning cruises. The 10-day "Eastern Mediterranean" kicks off in Rome, then heads to Sicily, Ephesus (Turkey), and winds up back in Naples/Capri but has a sizable chunk in Greece, with stops in Athens, Mykonos, Rhodes, and Santorini; the itinerary, which has multiple sailings from May to November, bumps up to 14 nights and other stops like the Bosphorus Straits in its "Exotic Mediterranean and Black Sea" version. Rates start at $1,029. *Galaxy* is a traditional and quietly elegant ship; the double-height dining room is nothing short of gorgeous with its soaring columns and window walls; there are three pools, with the Oasis pool replete with its own set of palm trees.

Your Shipmates. Celebrity caters to American cruise passengers, primarily couples from their mid-thirties to mid-fifties. Many families enjoy cruising on Celebrity's fleet during summer months and holiday periods. Each vessel has a dedicated playroom and offers a five-tiered program of activities designed for children and teens aged 3 to 17, plus Toddler Time for parents and their children under age 3.

Food. In early 2007, Celebrity announced plans to advance its fleet-wide culinary program to the next level. Every ship in the fleet has a highly experienced team headed by executive chefs and food and beverage managers who now work in concert with the line's new cuisine consultants, Las Vegas–based Blau & Associates, a strategic restaurant planning and development firm.

Fitness and Recreation. Celebrity's fitness centers and AquaSpa by Elemis are some of the most tranquil and nicely equipped at sea. State-of-the-art exercise equipment, a jogging track, and some fitness classes are available at no charge. Spa treatments include a variety of massages, body wraps, and facials. The *Galaxy* has an Acupuncture at Sea program administered by a specialist in Asian medicine. Hair and nail services are offered in the salons.

Contact. ✉ *1050 Caribbean Way, Miami, FL33132* ☎ *305/539–6000 or 800/437–3111* 🌐 *www.celebrity.com.*

COSTA CRUISES

Europe's number one cruise line combines a Continental experience, enticing itineraries, and the classical design and style of Italy with romantic nights at sea. Genoa-based Costa Crociere, parent company of Costa Cruise Lines, had been in the passenger business for almost 50 years when Carnival Corporation completed a buyout of the line in 2000 and began expanding the fleet with larger and more-dynamic ships. "Italian-style" cruising is a mixture of Mediterranean flair and American comfort. Beginning with a *buon viaggio* (bon voyage) celebration, the supercharged social staff works overtime to get everyone in the mood and encourages everyone to be a part of the action.

Itineraries and Ships. *CostaEuropa* (1,488 passengers) was built in 1986, "stretched" in 1990, and in 2002 had her decor brightened up, yet she retains classic touches of elegance such as the teak wraparound promenade deck lined with wooden steamer chairs. As on other ships of her vintage, she has few balconies. Think she looks vaguely familiar? It could be because she starred in *Out to Sea* with Walter Matthau and Jack Lemmon. One sample 11-day cruise leaves from northern Italy's Savona then steams south to Alexandria, Cyprus, and Naples, and stops in Greece at Rhodes, Athens, and Katakolon (Olympia); rates begin at $1,399. *CostaClassica* (1,308 passengers) was designed to bring the Costa fleet up to speed with other cruise lines in the 1990s, and the effort has paid off. Public areas clustered on four upper decks are filled with marble and furnished with sleek, contemporary furnishings and modern Italian artwork. The effect is vibrant, chic, and surprisingly restful. Lounges and bars are sweeping and grand; however, the areas set aside for children are pretty skimpy by today's family-friendly standards. There is no promenade deck, but the Lido areas for sunning and swimming are expansive. One sample 7-day cruise (rates begin at $799) leaves from Trieste in northern Italy, then heads down to Corfu, Athens, Santorini, and Mykonos, and returns to Trieste. *Costa Atlantica* (2,114 passengers) has a Venice vibe, with tons of Murano glass, the Tiziano restaurant as big as an art nouveau football stadium, and an atrium with elevators that soar 12 passenger decks (named after Fellini movies); the knockout is the reproduction of Venice's Caffe Florian. *Costa Romantica* (1,344 passengers) has a 7-day cruise, leaving from Rome, heading to Sicily and Turkey (Izmir), with stops in Greece including Patmos, Santorini, and Mykonos. Every month of the year has cruises scheduled.

SHIP SHAPE

Taking a cue from the ancient Romans, Costa places continuing emphasis on wellness and sybaritic pleasures. Spa treatments include a variety of massages, body wraps, and facials that can be scheduled à la carte or combined in packages to encompass an afternoon or the entire cruise. State-of-the-art exercise equipment in the terraced gym, a jogging track, and basic fitness classes for all levels of ability are available.

Your Shipmates. An international air prevails on board and announcements are often made in a variety of languages. On Mediterranean itineraries approximately 80% of passengers are Europeans, including many from Italy. Youth programs provide daily age-appropriate activities for children ages 3 to 17. Special counselors supervise activities and specific rooms are designed for children and teens, depending on the ship.

Food. Dining features regional Italian cuisines, a variety of pastas, chicken, beef, and seafood dishes, as well as authentic pizza. European chefs and culinary school graduates who are members of Chaîne des Rôtisseurs provide a dining experience that's notable for a delicious, properly prepared pasta course. Vegetarian and healthful diet choices are also offered. Alternative dining is by reservation only in the upscale supper clubs, which serve choice steaks and seafood from a Tuscan Steakhouse menu as well as traditional Italian specialties. Costa chefs celebrate the tradition of lavish nightly midnight buffets.

Contact. *200 S. Park Rd., Suite 200, Hollywood, FL33021-8541 954/266-5600 or 800/462-6782 www.costacruise.com.*

CRYSTAL CRUISES

Winner of accolades and hospitality-industry awards, Crystal Cruises offers the grandeur of the past with all the modern touches discerning passengers demand. Founded in 1990 and owned by Nippon Yusen Kaisha (NYK) in Japan, Crystal ships, unlike other luxury vessels, are large—carrying upward of 900 passengers. Superior service, a variety of dining options, spacious accommodations, and some of the highest ratios of space per passenger of any cruise ships make them distinctive. Beginning with ship designs based on the principles of feng shui, not even the smallest detail is overlooked to provide passengers with the best-imaginable experience. Crystal stands out in their variety of enrichment and educational programs.

Itineraries and Ship. *Crystal Serenity* (1,080 passengers) is stylish, uncrowded, and uncluttered, with clubby drawing rooms done in muted colors and warm woods, creating a refined environment. A West Coast lifestyle laid-back vibe prevails, with sensational restaurants (the alternative choices are yours to enjoy at the cost of a nominal gratuity). Design of smallish standard cabins for this level of luxury ship are disappointing, while public spaces are design-award worthy. Design of even smaller cabins are soigné, while public spaces are design-award worthy. One sample itinerary is the 11-day "Temples of Gods and Pharoahs," which begins in Istanbul, includes Kusadasi and Alexandria/Cairo, and stops in Greece's Rhodes/Lindos, Santorini, and Athens; rates start at $4,345. The 7-day "Greek Gods and Gondolas" kicks off in Athens, then heads to Kusadasi, Santorini, Split (Croatia), and Albania, and ends up in Venice; rates begin at $3,440. Sailings of the many various cruises extend from April to October.

Your Shipmates. Affluent, well-traveled couples, from their late-thirties to retirees, are attracted by Crystal Cruises' destination-rich itineraries, onboard enrichment programs, and the ship's elegant ambience. Children are welcome aboard, but Crystal Cruises reserves the right to restrict the number of children under age three traveling with their parents and is unable to accommodate children younger than six months of age without a signed waiver of parental consent.

Food. The food is a good enough reason to book a cruise on Crystal ships. Dining in the main restaurants is an event starring Continental-inspired cuisine served by trained European waiters. Off-menu item requests are honored when possible. Casual poolside dining from the grills is offered on some evenings in a relaxed, no-reservations-required option. A variety of hot and cold hors d'oeuvres are served in bars and lounges every evening before dinner and again during the wee hours. Where service and the dishes really shine are in the specialty restaurants; the Serenity has Asian-inspired and Italian specialty restaurants.

Fitness and Recreation. Large spas offer innovative pampering therapies, body wraps, and exotic Asian-inspired treatments. Fitness centers feature a range of exercise and weight-training equipment and workout areas for aerobics classes, plus complimentary yoga and Pilates instruction. In addition, golfers enjoy extensive shipboard facilities, including a driving range, practice cage, and putting green.

Contact. ✉ *2049 Century Park E, Suite 1400, Los Angeles, CA90067* ☎ *310/785–9300 or 888/799–4625* 🌐 *www.crystalcruises.com.*

CUNARD LINE

One of the world's most-distinguished names in ocean travel since 1840, Cunard Line's history of transatlantic crossings and worldwide cruising is legendary for its comfortable British style. After a series of owners tried with little success to revive the company's flagging passenger shipping business in the era of jet travel, Carnival Corporation saved the day in 1998 with an infusion of ready cash and the know-how to turn the cruise line around. There is a decidedly British vibe to salons and pubs, while a wide variety of musical styles can be found for dancing and listening in the bars and lounges. Quality enrichment programs are presented by expert guest lecturers in their fields.

SEA & CRUMPETS

Not surprisingly, entertainment and authentic pubs have a decidedly English flavor aboard Cunard, as do some of the grand salons, including the Queen Victoria's double-height Queens Room, a loggia-style venue designed in the manner of the grand ballrooms found in large English country houses, such as Her Majesty's own Osborne House.

Itinerary and Ship. *Queen Victoria* (1,080 passengers) is premiered in 2008 as the third "queen" in Cunard's fleet, with its maiden cruise long sold out. Victoria herself would feel quite at home in the triple-height grand lobby. On board is an extensive Cunardia museum exhibit, a two-deck library connected by a spiral staircase, posh entertainment venues, and shops inspired by London's Burlington and Royal Arcades. More contemporary than traditional, however, is the glass-domed Hemispheres nightclub. Other eye-knocking features include the giant Royal Court Theatre, which touts the first-at-sea private boxes with unobstructed views; the luxe Royal Spa & Fitness Centre; 10,000 square feet of promenade-worthy open deck; wine-tasting classrooms; and staterooms, two-thirds of which boast private balconies to catch the sea winds.

Yours truly, Shipmates. Discerning, well-traveled British and American couples from their late-thirties to retirees are drawn to Cunard's traditional style. The availability of spacious accommodations and complimentary self-service laundry facilities make Cunard liners a good option for families, although there may be fewer children on board than you might expect. Kid-friendly features include a dedicated play area for children ages one to six. Separate programs are reserved for older children ages 7–12 and teens. Toddlers are supervised by English nannies. Children ages one to two sail free (except for government fees).

Food. In the tradition of multiple-class ocean liners, dining room assignments are made according to the accommodation category booked: you get the luxury you pay for. Passengers in junior suites are assigned to single-seating Princess Grill, while the posh Queen's Grill serves passengers booked in the most lavish suites. All other passengers are assigned to one of two seatings in the dramatic Britannia Restaurant. Specialty restaurants require reservations and there is an additional charge.

Fitness and Recreation. Swimming pools, golf driving ranges, table tennis, a paddle tennis court, shuffleboard, and jogging tracks barely scratch the surface of onboard facilities dedicated to recreation. Top-quality fitness centers offer high-tech workout equipment, a separate weight room, and classes ranging from aerobics to healthful living workshops. The spas are top rate with a long menu of treatments and salon services for women and men.

Contact. *24303 Town Center Dr., Valencia, CA91355 661/753–1000 or 800/728–6273 www.cunard.com.*

EASYCRUISE

Introduced with great fanfare in 2005 by Stelios (the guiding force behind budget air carrier easyJet), easyCruise is easily the quirkiest endeavor to hit the cruise industry—and it is one option with a calendar heavily slated for Greek cruises. Aimed at youthful travelers interested in island-hopping and sampling local nightlife, itineraries are scheduled to arrive in port mid-morning, stay until the partying winds down, and then move on to the next destination, somewhat like a cross between a traditional cruise ship and a ferry. Passengers have the flexibility to book as few as three nights, embarking and departing in any port along the way; however, fares are now available in more-traditional 3- to 7-night packages. Rock-bottom prices eliminate all onboard frills and nearly all necessities. Meals aren't included and you'll pay extra for cabin services, including cleaning, fresh towels, and bed linens.

Itineraries and Ships. *EasyCruise 1* (170 passengers) is the more spartan of the two easyCruise ships sailing the Aegean. Although the bright neon-orange hull emblazoned with "easycruise.com" acted in the past as a beacon to late-night revelers returning from shoreside restaurants and clubs, the garish look has undergone a transformation: a new graphite-gray paint job with discreet orange trim gives the ship a more refined appearance but shouldn't hamper the party spirit of its passengers. Even in its new livery, *easyCruise1* is easy to spot late at night—it's likely to be the only ship at the pier. The ship's public spaces have also been redecorated and now have more of the look of a boutique hotel. An ambitious itinerary offered on this ship is the 11-night "Around the Ionian Sea," which kicks off in Piraeus (Athens), then sails to Itea (Delphi), Ithaca, Paxos, Albania, Corfu, Preveza, Kefalonia, Zakynthos, Corinth, Aegina, and back to Athens; rates start at €198. Even though the prices still start as low as €70 per person for a 7-day trip, *easyCruise Life* has ramped up the space (500 passengers) and added amenities like the FusionOn6 bar and restaurant, the Apivita spa, and a range of cabins that even extend to suitelike accommodations. One popular itinerary is the 7-day "Greek Islands and Turkey" cruise, which begins in Piraeus, then goes to Ermoupoli on Syros, then Kalymnos, and on to Turkey's Bodrum, then back to Greece's Kos, Samos, Mykonos, and Paros; rates begin at €140.

Your Shipmates. The plan was to appeal to active adults in their twenties and thirties. In reality, depending on the season and itinerary, passenger ages might lean toward the fortysomething and older set. Most passengers hail from Great Britain or North America, with Brits usually in the majority. There are no provisions made for children's facilities or entertainment. You are unlikely to encounter kids on board.

Food. An upgraded restaurant supplements the diner-quality snacks, sandwiches, and dessert items that have always been available. However, the quality of the food is more like Starbucks or Ruby Tuesday. The best offerings are often found at breakfast. You pay for all food on board; there are no meal plans and individual items are on the pricey side for what you get. You will also pay in euros, which is even more painful for Americans. The best dining is still found ashore when in port.

Fitness and Recreation. A small gym has exercise equipment, but you will be more likely to burn off calories walking in ports and swimming when you head for the beach. There's no pool, but there is a popular hot tub.

Contact. *The Rotunda, 42/43 Gloucester Crescent, London, UKNW1 7DL 30211/211-6211 www.easycruise.com.*

HOLLAND AMERICA LINE

Holland America Line has enjoyed a distinguished record of traditional cruises, world exploration, and transatlantic crossings since 1873—all facets of its history that are reflected in the fleet's multimillion dollar shipboard art and antiques collections. Noted for focusing on passenger comfort, Holland America Line cruises are classic in design and style. Although they may never be considered cutting edge, even with an infusion of younger adults and families on board, they remain refined without being stuffy or stodgy.

Itineraries and Ships. The *Prinsendam* (794 passengers) was launched in 1998 and refurbished with an array of goodies, including a selection of oil paintings of Holland America ships by Captain Stephen Card, an exhilarating Crow's Nest observation lounge, and a tall cylinder of Bolae glass in the atrium area, which is lighted from within by fiber optics so that etched dolphins and sea turtles seem to swim up the center. Unfortunately, a mere 38% of outside cabins and suites have private balconies and some cabins near the bow have portholes instead of large windows—for these reasons, cabin selection must be made carefully. A sample itinerary on the *Prinsendam* is the 14-day "Ancient Mysteries" cruise, which kicks off in Piraeus, and also pulls into Greece's Rhodes, Santorini, and Katakolon (Olympia), with other stops including Alexandria, Jerusalem, Haifa, Kusadasi, Malta, Sicily, and Rome; rates begin at $3,281. The *Noordam* (1,848 passengers) is a more youthful and family-friendly ship, where an exquisite Waterford Crystal sculpture adorns the triple-deck atrium and reflects keep-your-sunglasses-on color schemes throughout; nearly 80% of rooms have a private balcony, although those next to the panoramic elevator are not as "private" as they seem. This ship often sails on extensive 20-day cruises like the "Mediterranean Mosaic," which begins in Rome (Civitavecchia) and stops in Greece's Corfu, Katakolon (Olympia), and Santorini, while ranging from Monte Carlo, Barcelona, Mallorca, Carthage, Palermo, Dubrovnik, Sicily, and Malta; rates begin at $3,768.

Your Shipmates. No longer your grandparents' cruise line, today's Holland America attracts families and discerning couples, mostly from their late thirties on up. Comfortable retirees are often still in the majority, particularly on longer cruises; however, holidays and summer months are peak periods when you'll find more children in the mix. Group activities are planned for children ages 3 to 7 and 8 to

12 in Club HAL, Holland America Line's professionally staffed youth program. Club HAL After Hours offers late-night activities from 10 PM until midnight for an hourly fee. Teens aged 13 to 17 have their own lounge with activities.

Food. You have your choice of two assigned seatings or open seating for evening meals in the formal dining room. In the reservations-required, $20-per-person Pinnacle Grill alternative restaurant, fresh seafood and premium cuts of Sterling Silver beef are used to prepare creative specialty dishes. Delicious onboard traditions are afternoon tea, a Dutch Chocolate Extravaganza, and Holland America Line's signature bread pudding.

Fitness and Recreation. Well-equipped and fully staffed fitness facilities contain state-of-the-art exercise equipment; basic fitness classes are available at no charge. There's a fee for personal training, and specialized classes such as yoga and Pilates. The Greenhouse Spa offers a variety of treatments. Both ships have a jogging track, multiple swimming pools, and sports courts.

Contact. ⊠*300 Elliott Ave. W, Seattle, WA98119* ☎*206/281–3535 or 800/577–1728* 🌐*www.hollandamerica.com.*

MSC CRUISES

Since it began introducing graceful new designs to large-size ships in 2003, MSC (Mediterranean Shipping Cruises) has grown to be a formidable presence in European cruising. The extensive use of marble, brass, and wood in ships' interiors reflect the best of Italian styling and design. Clean lines and bold colors often set the modern sophisticated tone—no glitz, no clutter—elegant simplicity is the standard of MSC's decor.

Itineraries and Ships. Often sailing with a Greece-heavy itinerary, the MSC *Musica* (2,550 passengers) is an extravaganza of curves and seductive colors, crowned by a vast red-and-gold La Scala theater. A highlight is a three-deck waterfall in the central foyer, where a piano is suspended on a transparent floor above a pool of water. Interiors are a blend of art deco and art nouveau themes, with some restaurants saddled with rather cartoony murals. Elsewhere, the elegant Cigar Bar and Giardino restaurant bring things down to earth. A whopping 80% of staterooms have an ocean view and 65% have balconies. Decorated in jewel-tone colors, all are comfortable yet somewhat smaller than the average new-ship cabin. A typical cruise is the 7-night journey that starts in Venice, then calls on Greece's Katakolon (Olympia), Santorini, Mykonos, Piraeus/Athens, and Corfu, plus Dubrovnik. The MSC *Orchestra* (2,550 passengers) is a design beauty, ranging from a three-deck lobby to a Star Trek–like Internet café to a sophisticated Shaker Lounge to a bevy of restaurants that are suave and understated; the main Covent Garden theater is vast, festive, and fun. One of the many cruises sailing to Greece includes an 11-night itinerary that begins in Genoa, and stops at Greece's Katakolon (Olympia), Piraeus/Athens, Rhodes, and Heraklion, with other ports including Alexandria, Cyprus, and Naples. Rates for MSC cruises were not set at press time.

> **THE FACE THAT LAUNCHED A THOUSAND TRIPS**
>
> Garnering plenty of headlines, the MSC *Musica* was launched in 2006 by silver-screen diva Sophia Loren and commentators noted that this curvacious, sexy vessel was one Sophia of a ship.

Your Shipmates. On Mediterranean itineraries you will find a majority of Europeans, including Italians, and announcements are made in a number of languages. Most American passengers are couples in the 35- to 55-year-old range and family groups who prefer the international atmosphere prevalent on board. Children from ages 3 to 17 are welcome to participate in age-appropriate youth programs in groups for ages 3–8 and 9–12. The Teenage Club is for youths 13 years and older.

Food. Dinner on MSC ships is a traditional seven-course event centered around authentic Italian fare. Menus list Mediterranean regional specialties and classic favorites prepared from scratch the old-fashioned way. "Healthy Choice" and vegetarian items are offered as well as tempting sugar-free desserts. A highlight is the bread-of-the-day, freshly baked on board. The nightly midnight buffet is a retro food feature missing from most of today's cruises.

Fitness and Recreation. Up-to-date exercise equipment, a jogging track, and basic fitness classes for all levels are available. Treatments include a variety of massages, body wraps, and facials that can be scheduled à la carte or combined in packages to encompass an afternoon or the entire cruise.

Contact. *6750 N. Andrews Ave., Fort Lauderdale, FL33309 954/662–6262 or 800/666–9333 www.msccruises.com.*

NORWEGIAN CRUISE LINE

A cruise industry innovator since its founding in 1996, Norwegian Cruise Line's "Freestyle" cruising was born when Asian shipping giant Star Cruises acquired the Miami-based line. Confounded that Americans meekly conformed to rigid dining schedules and dress codes, the new owners set out to change the traditional formula by introducing a variety of dining options in a casual, free-flowing atmosphere. Noted for top-quality, high-energy entertainment and emphasis on fitness facilities and programs, NCL combines action, activities, and a resort-casual atmosphere.

Itinerary and Ship. Purpose-built for NCL's revolutionary Freestyle cruising concept (eat when you want and where you want—or almost), the *Norwegian Jewel* (2,224 passengers) has more than a dozen dining options. Decor showstoppers include the theater reminiscent of a European opera house, with lavish production shows and a full proscenium stage. Reflecting perhaps the somewhat gaudy painting of jewels on the exterior of the ship's hull, the Azura main restaurant and a bevy of other public spaces (including the aptly-named Fyzz Lounge & Bar) have some over-the-top jewel-tone carpets; other settings, including Cagney's Steakhouse, the Library, and the Star Bar, are lush, elegant, and elegantly decorated. A popular itinerary is featured on the 12-day "Egypt and Greek Isles" cruise, which sets off from Istanbul, and stops at Greece's Mykonos, Santorini, Heraklion/Crete, Corfu, Katakolon (Olympia), and Piraeus/Athens, and also includes Egypt's Alexandria and Turkey's Ephesus; prices were not available at press time.

Your Shipmates. NCL's mostly American cruise passengers are active couples ranging from their mid-thirties to mid-fifties. Longer cruises and more exotic itineraries attract passengers in the over-55 age group. Many families enjoy cruising on NCL ships during summer months. For children and teens, each NCL vessel offers the "Kid's Crew" program of supervised entertainment for young cruisers ages 2 to 17. Younger children are split into three groups from age 2 to 5, 6 to 9, and 10 to 12. For 13- to 17-year-olds there are clubs where they can hang out in adult-free zones.

Food. Main dining rooms serve what is traditionally deemed Continental fare, although it's about what you would expect at a really good hotel banquet. Where NCL stands above the ordinary is in their specialty restaurants, especially the French-Mediterranean Le Bistro (on all ships), the Pan-Asian restaurants, and steak houses (on the newer ships). In addition, you may find a Spanish tapas bar and an Italian trattoria. Some, but not all, restaurants carry a cover charge or are priced à la carte and require reservations. An NCL staple, the late-night Chocoholic Buffet continues to be a favorite event.

Fitness and Recreation. Mandara Spa offers a long list of unique and exotic spa treatments fleet wide on NCL. State-of-the-art exercise equipment, jogging tracks, and basic fitness classes are available at no charge. There's a nominal fee for personal training, and specialized classes such as yoga and Pilates.

Contact. ✉ *7665 Corporate Center Dr., Miami, FL33126* ☎ *305/436–4000 or 800/327–7030* 🌐 *www.ncl.com.*

OCEANIA CRUISES

This distinctive cruise line was founded by Frank Del Rio and Joe Watters, cruise industry veterans with the know-how to satisfy the wants of inquisitive passengers by offering itineraries to interesting ports of call and upscale touches—all for fares much lower than you would expect. Oceania Cruises set sail in 2003 to carve a unique, almost "boutique" niche in the cruise industry by obtaining midsize "R-class" ships that formerly made up the popular Renaissance Cruises fleet. Intimate and cozy public room spaces reflect the importance of socializing on Oceania ships while varied, destination-rich itineraries are an important characteristic of the line.

Itineraries and Ships. *Nautica* and *Insignia* (684 passengers each) strike some of the most sumptuous, elegant decor notes of any ships sailing—lobbies and public salons are dazzling with old-world gilt-famed paintings, glittery banisters, tapestried rugs, and enough wood paneling to line a hundred libraries—the effect is like a Vanderbilt yacht but magnified to the nth degree. A popular itinerary offered on the *Nautica* is the 12-day "Enchanted Escapade," which embarks in Athens and continues with Greece's Delos, Mykonos, Rhodes, and Santorini, then continues on to such far-flung spots as Malta, Sicily, Capri, Positano, Florence, Monte Carlo, Portofino, and Rome; rates begin at $3,599. A sample itinerary aboard the *Insignia* (684 passengers) is the 10-day "Path of the Phoenicians," which kicks off in Athens, then takes in Greece's Delos, Mykonos, Santorini, and Crete, with other stops in Kusadasi, Albania, Dubrovnik, and Venice; rates begin at $3,699.

Your Shipmates. Oceania Cruises appeal to singles and couples from their late-thirties to well-traveled retirees who have the time for and prefer longer cruises. Most are attracted to the casually sophisticated atmosphere, creative cuisine, and European service. Oceania Cruises are adult oriented and not a good choice for most families, particularly those traveling with infants and toddlers. Teenagers with sophisticated tastes (and who don't mind the absence of a video arcade) would enjoy the emphasis on intriguing ports of call.

Food. Top cruise industry chefs ensure that the artistry of world-renowned master chef Jacques Pépin, who crafted 5-Star menus for Oceania, is carried out. The results are sure to please the most discriminating palate. Oceania simply serves some of the best food at sea, particularly impressive for a cruise line that charges far less than luxury rates. The main open-seating restaurant offers trendy French-Continental cuisine with an always-on-the menu steak, seafood, or poultry choice and vegetarian option. Intimate specialty restaurants require reservations, but there is no additional charge.

Fitness and Recreation. While small, the spa, salon, and well-equipped fitness center are adequate for the number of passengers on board. In addition to individual body-toning machines and complimentary exercise classes, there is a walking/jogging track circling the top of the ship. Spa menus list massages, body wraps, and facials. Forward of the locker rooms you will find a large therapy pool and quiet deck for relaxation and sunning on padded wooden steamer chaises.

Contact. *8300 N.W. 33rd St., Suite 308, Miami, FL33122 ☎305/514–2300 or 800/531–5658 www.oceaniacruises.com.*

OCEAN VILLAGE

This small division of Carnival Corporation is just about as hip as a cruise line can get and still be considered a cruise line. Headquartered and marketed in the United Kingdom, the line's motto promises "the cruise for people who don't do cruises." Quite simply, Ocean Village cruises are flexible and relatively unstructured, although the company follows the typical British holiday scheme of being a total package deal (including airfare to the embarkation port), if that's what you desire.

Although the vessels in the current fleet aren't brand new, they have been extensively refurbished and have many of the amenities typical of much newer ships. They're also family-friendly. Upbeat and trendy, Ocean Village places stress on informal island-hopping and itineraries that include sunny, beach-centric destinations along with major city ports of call.

> **COME AND HEAR THOSE DANCING FEET**
>
> The pool area on the *Ocean Village One* is particularly interesting, with structures devoted to contemporary circus performances. Yes, that's right—the over-the-top "Moonshow" at night is right out of Barnum & Bailey, with acrobats and half-naked dancers tapping up a storm in echt-Riverdance style.

Itineraries and Ship. *Ocean Village One* (1,578 passengers) was redesigned a few years back to appeal to the young, trendy British market, which tends to be a bit unconventional. Interiors are bright and cheerful, with tons of teak and warm woods, and there's no stuffiness in the decor of the public spaces or the cabins. This ship has some of the nicest Greece-based itineraries around. A popular cruise is the 7-night "Olives and Ouzo" Mediterranean cruise that begins in Heraklion, Crete, sets sail for Rhodes, Santorini, and Mykonos, and also puts in at Ephesus, Turkey, and Limassol, Cyprus; rates begin at €1,388. Another typical itinerary is the 7-night "Temples and Tavernas" Mediterranean cruise, which kicks off in Heraklion, Crete, then moves on to Dubrovnik, Corfu, Kefalonia (of Captain Corelli fame), Katakolon (Olympia), and Athens. Rates begin at €1,169.

Your Shipmates. Ocean Village cruises draw mostly active British singles and couples from their thirties to fifties. Many consider themselves unconventional in a don't-tell-us-what-we-want-to-do manner. This relaxed cruising style is ideal for families and particularly for multigenerational family groups. Age-appropriate group programs are offered for children and teens from 2 to 17 years of age.

Food. Dining is buffet style for the most part, and dishes lean heavily toward British favorites with a sprinkling of Mediterranean- and Asian-influenced items for variety. Alternative dining spots with waiter service include menus inspired by British celebrity chef James Martin; these restaurants carry an extra charge. A popular children's tea is served every afternoon.

Fitness and Recreation. The ship has swimming pools, a well-equipped gym, exercise classes—some complimentary, others for a small fee—as well as deck spaces designated for joggers. Spas offer a typical menu of massages, facials, and exotic treatments. There is a fee for the use of saunas and steam rooms. In a unique twist on activities, you can learn to juggle or fly on a trapeze in circus workshops.

Contact. ✉ *Richmond House, Terminus Terr., Southampton, UKSO14 3PN* ☎ *0845/358–5000* 🌐 *www.oceanvillageholidays.co.uk*.

P&O CRUISES

P&O Cruises (originally, Peninsular & Oriental Steam Navigation Company), boasts an illustrious history in passenger shipping since 1837. Although the company's suggestion that they "invented" cruising may not be entirely accurate, P&O is assuredly an industry pioneer. Having set aside such throwbacks as passenger classes, the company remains Britain's leading cruise line, sailing the United Kingdom's largest and most modern fleet. Ships are equipped with every facility you could think of, from swimming pools to stylish restaurants, spas, bars, casinos, theaters, and showrooms. Abundant balcony and outside cabins ensure that a view to the sea is never far away.

Itineraries and Ships. *Artemis* (1,188 passengers) was launched as the *Royal Princess* in 1984 by no less than Diana, Princess of Wales, who added an air of style during her christening that remains undiminished. The ship was a trailblazer—the first mainstream ship to feature only outside cabins. One of the most drastic changes the ship has undergone since joining the P&O fleet is that it is now an adults-only vessel. A popular voyage is the 25-night "Glories of the Mediterranean" cruise, which leaves from Southampton, and takes in Greece's Nafplion, Athens, Heraklion, and Rhodes, while also calling at Ibiza, Cyprus, Cairo, Tripoli, Malta, and Lisbon; rates for the *Artemis* were not available at press time but a good sign is that the October 2007 voyage was "sold out." The *Arcadia* (1,948 passengers) was envisioned adults only, and her sophisticated and fresh elegance is highlighted by an extensive art collection that showcases modern British artists. P&O's first new ship in a decade, it sports a lively British Victorian-style pub; Arcadian Rhodes, the extra-charge specialty restaurant, is the creation of Gary Rhodes, one of Britain's most popular contemporary chefs. A typical cruise is the 17-night "Splendours of the Mediterranean," which sails from Southampton, and puts in at Greece's Corfu and Naxos, along with an extended range visiting Cadiz, Rome, Naples, Dubrovnik, and Malta; rates begin at €1,452.

Your Shipmates. Count on fellow passengers to be predominantly British singles, couples, and families, although you may find Scandinavians, Americans, and Australians aboard for some sailings. *Arcadia* and *Artemis* are adults-only ships; passengers must be 18 or older to sail aboard them.

Food. P&O has jumped on the choice bandwagon in dining and offers a somewhat dizzying number of options, although actual menu offerings vary quite a bit across the fleet. Club Dining, with assigned seating, is available on all ships; Select Dining in specialty restaurants requires reservations and carries a small charge; Freedom Dining is an open-seating dinner offered in certain restaurants on *Arcadia*. Meals are tailored to British tastes, so you will see a lot of curries on the menu. Afternoon tea is served daily.

Fitness and Recreation. Spa and salon facilities for men and women list an extensive range of therapeutic and rejuvenating treatments, from massages to facials, manicures, and body wraps. Each ship has a well-equipped gym and exercise classes. Deck quoits, an informal shipboard form of ring toss (rope rings are thrown alternately by players at round targets on the deck), is popular with passengers, and areas are set aside for the game.

AT SEE LEVEL

Aboard the *Artemis*, a sea view is never far from sight; not only do all cabins have a large window or balcony, there are windows in all public spaces.

Contact. *Richmond House, Terminus Terr., Southampton, UKSO15 2BF 0845/678–0014 www.pocruises.com.*

PRINCESS CRUISES

Princess Cruises may be best known for introducing cruise travel to millions of television viewers when its flagship became the setting for *The Love Boat* TV series in 1977. Since that heady time of small-screen stardom, the Princess fleet has grown both in the number and the size of ships. Although most are large in scale, Princess vessels manage to create the illusion of intimacy in understated, yet lovely public rooms graced by impressive art collections. In today's changing times, Princess has introduced more flexibility; Personal Choice Cruising offers alternatives for open-seating dining and entertainment options as diverse as those found in resorts ashore. Welcome additions to Princess's roster of adult activities are ScholarShip@Sea Enrichment programs featuring guest lecturers, cooking classes, wine-tasting seminars, pottery workshops, and computer and digital photography classes.

Itineraries and Ships. *Star Princess* (2,600 passengers) was built in 2002 and is one of the largest megaships prowling the Mediterranean. These Grand-class Princess ships feature soothing pastel tones with splashy glamour in the sweeping staircases and marble-floor atriums. Four pools, the Skywalker's Disco, and Times Square–style LED screens draw the crowds, while you can escape to your own seaside aerie: 80% of outside staterooms have balconies (although many are stepped, with a resultant loss in total privacy). A typical itinerary is the 12-day "Greek Isles–Venice to Rome" cruise, which embarks in Venice, then calls on Greece's Corfu, Katakolon (Olympia), Mykonos, Athens, Rhodes, and Santorini, along with other ports including Naples and Turkey's Kusadasi; rates are from $1,699; a slightly larger sister ship, *Emerald Princess* (3,100 passengers) offers the same cruise along with the popular 12-day "Greek Isles and Mediterranean," which departs from Rome, stops at Greece's Santorini, Mykonos, Athens, Corfu, and Katakolon (Olympia), with stops in Venice, Naples, Monte Carlo, and Florence; rates start at $2,240. Similar cruises are also offered on sister ship *Grand Princess,* as well as fleetmates *Sea Princess, Pacific Princess,* and *Royal Princess.* Smaller than the larger Grand-class ships, the refined and graceful *Sea Princess* (1,950 passengers) offers the onboard choices attributed to the fleet's larger vessels without sacrificing the smaller-ship atmosphere for which it's noted. A four-story atrium with a circular marble floor, stained-glass dome, and magnificent floating staircase strikes an ideal setting for relaxation, people-watching, and making a grand entrance. *Pacific Princess* (670 passengers) and *Royal Princess* (710 passengers) appear positively tiny beside their megaship fleetmates. In reality, they are medium-size ships that offer real choice to Princess loyalists—a true alternative for passengers who prefer the clubby atmosphere of a smaller "boutique"-style ship, yet one that has big-ship features galore.

CROWD PLEASERS

On Princess ships, personal choices regarding where and what to eat abound, but there's no getting around the fact that most are large and carry a great many passengers. Unless you opt for traditional assigned seating, you could experience a brief wait for a table in one of the open-seating dining rooms. Alternative restaurants are a staple. With a few breaks in service, Lido buffets on all ships are almost always open, and a pizzeria and grill offer casual daytime snack choices.

Your Shipmates. Princess Cruises attract mostly American passengers ranging from their mid-thirties to mid-fifties. Longer cruises appeal to well-traveled retirees and couples who have the time. Families enjoy cruising together on the Princess fleet, particularly during summer months, when many children are on board. For young passengers aged 3 to 17, each Princess vessel has a playroom, teen center, and programs of supervised activities designed for different age groups. To afford parents independent time ashore, youth centers operate as usual during port days.

Food. Menus are varied and extensive in the main dining rooms, and the results are good to excellent considering how much work is going on in the galleys. Vegetarian and healthy lifestyle options are always on the menu, as well as steak, fish, or chicken. A special menu is offered for children. Possible options run from round-the-clock Lido buffets to Ultimate Balcony Dining, where a server is on duty and a photographer stops by to capture the romantic evening.

Fitness and Recreation. Spa and salon rituals include massages, body wraps, facials, and numerous hair and nail services, as well as a menu of special pampering treatments designed specifically for men, teens, and couples. Modern exercise equipment, a jogging track, and basic fitness classes are available at no charge. Grand-class ships have a resistance pool so you can get your "laps" in.

Contact. ✉ *24305 Town Center Dr., Santa Clarita, CA91355-4999* ☎ *661/753–0000 or 800/774–6237* 🌐 *www.princess.com.*

REGENT SEVEN SEAS CRUISES

Regent Seven Seas Cruises (formerly Radisson Seven Seas Cruises) sails an elegant fleet of vessels that offer a nearly all-inclusive cruise experience in sumptuous, contemporary surroundings. The line's tried-and-true formula works; delightful ships feature exquisite service, generous staterooms with abundant amenities, a variety of dining options, and superior enrichment programs. Cruises are destination focused, and most sailings host guest lecturers—historians, anthropologists, naturalists, and diplomats.

Itineraries and Ships. The world's second all-suite, all-balcony ship, the *Seven Seas Voyager* (700 passengers) is a jewel of the fleet, with a high-tech Constellation Theater and four soigné restaurants keeping the beat going. For pure pampering, the Carita Spa—which received the "Best Cruise Line Spa" in *Condé Nast Traveler*'s 2006 Readers Poll—can't be beat. A typical itinerary is featured on the 8-day "Piraeus (Athens) to Venice" voyage, which starts in Piraeus, then sails for Greece's Mykonos, Nafplion, and Corfu, plus Dubrovnik and Venice; rates begin at $5,395. The much smaller *Seven Seas Navigator* (490 passengers) offers a more-intimate experience, and everything is downscaled, with only two restaurants and a large lounge for entertainment. The luxe is upped by some of the highest space and service ratios at sea and all-marble bathrooms. A popular itinerary is the 11-night "Monte Carlo to Piraeus" option, which kicks off in Monte Carlo and then sails to Rome, Sorrento, Sicily, Mytilini (Lesvos) as the first stop in Greece, then on to Istanbul and Kusadasi, then back to Greece for Mykonos, Nafplion, and Piraeus.

Your Shipmates. Regent Seven Seas Cruises are inviting to active, affluent, well-traveled couples ranging from their late thirties to retirees who enjoy the ships' elegance and destination-rich itineraries. Longer cruises attract veteran passengers in the over-60 age group. Regent vessels are adult oriented and do not have dedicated children's facilities. However, a "Club Mariner" youth program for children ages 5 to 9, 10 to 13, and 14 to 17 is offered on selected sailings.

Food. Menus may appear to include the usual cruise ship staples, but in the hands of Regent Seven Seas chefs, the results are some of the most-outstanding meals at sea. Specialty dining varies within the fleet, but the newest ships have the edge with the sophisticated Signatures, which features the cuisine of Le Cordon Bleu of Paris, and Latitudes, offering menus either inspired by regional American favorites or nouveau international cuisine. In addition, Mediterranean-inspired bistro dinners are served in the venues that are the daytime casual Lido buffet restaurants. Wines chosen to complement dinner menus are freely poured each evening.

Fitness and Recreation. Although gyms and exercise areas are well equipped, these are not large ships, so the facilities tend to be on the small side. Each ship has a jogging track, and the larger ones feature a variety of sports courts. Exclusive to Regent Seven Seas, the spa and salon are operated by high-end Carita of Paris.

Contact. ✉ *1000 Corporate Dr., Suite 500, Fort Lauderdale, FL33334* ☎ *954/776–6123 or 877/505–5370* 🌐 *www.rssc.com.*

ROYAL CARIBBEAN INTERNATIONAL

Big, bigger, biggest! More than a decade ago, Royal Caribbean launched the first of the modern megacruise liners for passengers who enjoy traditional cruising with a touch of daring and whimsy tossed in. Expansive multideck atriums and the generous use of floor-to-ceiling glass windows give each RCI vessel a sense of spaciousness and style. A variety of lounges and high-energy stage shows draws passengers of all ages out to mingle and dance the night away. Production extravaganzas showcase singers and dancers in lavish costumes. The action is nonstop in casinos and dance clubs after dark, although daytime hours are filled with games and traditional cruise activities. Port "talks" tend to lean heavily on shopping recommendations and the sale of shore excursions. And then there are those famous rock-climbing walls.

WHAT, NO FERRIS WHEEL?

Royal Caribbean has pioneered such new and unheard-of features as rock-climbing walls, ice-skating rinks, bungee trampolines, and even the first self-leveling pool tables on a cruise ship. Exercise facilities vary by ship class but all Royal Caribbean ships have state-of-the-art exercise equipment and jogging tracks, and passengers can work out independently or participate in a variety of basic exercise classes. Spas are top-notch.

Itineraries and Ships. *Splendour of the Seas* (1,800 passengers) is one of the Royals that are noted for their acres of glass skylights that allow sunlight to flood in and windows that offer wide sea vistas. A double-height dining room with sweeping staircase is a showstopper but has to be, as there are no real specialty restaurants on board. Smaller cabins can be a tight squeeze for more than two people. A popular itinerary, with a good helping of Greece, is the 7-night "Greek Isles" cruise, which sails from Venice, then calls at Mykonos, Piraeus, Katakolon (Olympia), and Corfu, before returning to Venice via Split in Croatia; rates start at $649. *Legend of the Seas* (1,800 passengers) is a sister ship with lots and lots of wide-open space everywhere; the color schemes are both joyous and tranquil in hue, with lots of restful aquas, blues, and whites. A typical itinerary is the 12-night "Greece and the Eastern Mediterranean" tour, which sails from Rome, then mixes up Greece, Turkey, Egypt, and Italy, as it heads to Mykonos, Kusadasi, Rhodes, Cyprus, Alexandria, Piraeus, Naples, and back to Rome; rates start at $1,559.

Your Shipmates. Royal Caribbean cruises have a broad appeal for active couples and singles, mostly in their thirties to fifties. Families are partial to the newer vessels that have larger staterooms, huge facilities for children and teens, and seemingly endless choices of activities and dining options. Supervised age-appropriate activities are designed for children ages 3 through 17. Children are assigned to the Adventure Ocean youth program by age. For infants and toddlers 6 to 36 months of age, interactive playgroup sessions are planned, while a teen center with a disco is an adult-free gathering spot that will satisfy even the pickiest teenagers. Pluses are "family-size" staterooms on most newer ships, but a drawback is the lack of self-service laundry facilities.

Food. Dining is an international experience with nightly changing themes and cuisines from around the world. Passenger preference for casual attire and a resortlike atmosphere has prompted the cruise line to add laid-back alternatives to the formal dining rooms in the Windjammer Café.

Fitness and Recreation. Can a bowling alley be next? Fabled for its range of top-of-the-line recreations, Royal Caribbean also delivers on the basics: most exercise classes, aimed at sweating off those extra calories, are included in the fare (although there's a fee for specialized spinning, yoga, and Pilates classes, as well as the services of a personal trainer). Spas have full spa-style menus and full services for pampering for adults and teens.

Contact. ✉ *1050 Royal Caribbean Way, Miami, FL33132–2096* ☎ *305/539–6000 or 800/327–6700* 🌐 *www.royalcaribbean.com.*

SAGA CRUISES

Saga Holidays, the U.K.-based tour company designed to offer vacation packages to mature travelers, started its cruise program in 1975. After building a 20-year reputation for comfortable cruise travel, Saga purchased its first ship in 1996 and a sister ship was acquired in 2004. Saga Cruises takes care of the details that discerning passengers don't wish to leave to chance—from providing insurance and arranging visas to placing fruit and water in every cabin. Activities and entertainment on board range from dance lessons to presentations of West End–style productions, computer software lessons, and lectures on wide-ranging topics. Both ships have card rooms, but you won't find casinos. With numerous accommodations designed for solo cruisers, Saga Cruises are particularly friendly for senior singles.

Itinerary and Ship. *Saga Ruby* (587 passengers) was originally christened the *Vistafjord* in 1973, but its interiors were fine-tuned in 2005, and the ship is now replete with modern furnishings, a spa, and a top-deck fitness center. She also has a ballroom and cinema, a card room, and a library, where DVDs and computers with Internet access can be found in addition to books. One of her top itineraries is the 16-night "Ancient Mediterranean Treasures" cruise, which sails from Marseilles, then heads to Rome, Katakolon (Olympia) as the first stop in Greece, then onward to Rhodes, Cyprus, Israel's Haifa, Egypt's Alexandria, back to Greece for Piraeus, then on to Malta and Marseilles; rates begin at €2,474.

Your Shipmates. Saga Cruises are exclusively for passengers age 50 and older; the minimum age for traveling companions is 40. The overwhelming majority of passengers are from Great Britain, with a sprinkling of North Americans in the mix. Saga Cruises are adults only—children are strictly not allowed.

Food. In addition to offering a wide selection of dishes to appeal to a variety of discriminating tastes, many British favorites find their way onto menus in the main restaurants. Ingredients are high in quality, well prepared, and served in a single leisurely seating. Traditional English tea is served every afternoon and midnight buffets are set up in the Lido restaurants.

Fitness and Recreation. Gentle exercise classes, tailored to different levels of ability, and fully equipped gyms are available for active seniors, and each ship has two swimming pools, one outdoors and one indoors. Passengers can work on their golf swing at the practice nets, jog on deck, or book a fitness session with a personal trainer. Each ship has a full-service spa tailored especially for mature cruisers.

Contact. *The Saga Bldg., Folkstone, Kent, UKCT20 3SE 1303/771–111 www.sagacruises.com.*

SEABOURN CRUISE LINE

Seabourn was founded on the principle that dedication to personal service in elegant surroundings would appeal to sophisticated, independent-minded passengers whose lifestyles demand the best. Lovingly maintained since their introduction in 1987, the megayachts remain favorites with people who can take care of themselves, but would rather do so aboard a ship that caters to their individual preferences. Recognized as a leader in small-ship, luxury cruising, you can expect complimentary wines and spirits, elegant amenities, and even the pleasure of mini-massages while lounging poolside. Guest appearances by luminaries in the arts and world affairs highlight the enrichment program. Wine tasting, trivia, and other quiet pursuits might be scheduled, but most passengers prefer to simply do what pleases them.

Itinerary and Ship. *Seabourn Spirit* (208 passengers) had its maiden voyage in 1989 but was scheduled to receive a multimillion dollar makeover in January 2008. The ship's intimate scale is a nice plus although decor will never be featured on the cover of *Architectural Digest:* public spaces are beige-on-beige, with little glamour given to white wall treatments (other than paintings). Exotic colors, warm woods, stupendous fabrics, and conversation-piece rooms have been traded in for a restaurant and entertainment lounge that would not upset a staid banker; vast overhead lighting in public areas does not do wonders for a woman's complexion. But if you're looking for tranquillity and oh-so-subtle decor, this ship delivers. It often sails the eastern Mediterranean, and one of its popular itineraries is the 11-day "Glories of Greece" cruise, which kicks off in Alexandria, then sails to Greece's Rhodes, then Turkey's Bodrum, then back to Greece for Santorini, Chania (Crete), Gythion, Pylon, Itea (Delphi), Corinth Canal, Nafplion, and finally Piraeus; rates begin at $6,598. Another typical cruise-tour for Seabourn is the 11-day "Sail and Stay" option of "Greek Isles and Turkey," which allows days to tour Athens and Istanbul with voyages to Mykonos, Patmos, Tethiye and Kusadasi (Turkey), and the Dardanelles; rates start at $5,798.

Your Shipmates. Seabourn's yachtlike vessels appeal to affluent couples of all ages who enjoy destination-rich itineraries, a subdued atmosphere, and exclusive service. Passengers tend to be 50-plus and retired couples who are accustomed to the formality. Seabourn is adult oriented and unable to accommodate children under one year of age.

Food. Exceptional cuisine created by celebrity chef-restaurateur Charlie Palmer is prepared "à la minute" and served in open-seating dining rooms. Creative menu offerings include foie gras, quail, and fresh seafood. Vegetarian dishes and meals low in cholesterol, salt, and fat are prepared with the same care and artful presentation. Wines are chosen to complement each day's luncheon and dinner menus and caviar is always available.

Fitness and Recreation. A full array of exercise equipment, free weights, and basic fitness classes are available in the small gym, while some specialized fitness sessions are offered for a fee. The water-sports marina is popular with active passengers who want to jet ski, windsurf, kayak, or swim in the integrated saltwater "pool" while anchored in calm waters.

Contact. *6100 Blue Lagoon Dr., Suite 400, Miami, FL33126 305/463–3000 or 800/929–9391 www.seabourn.com.*

SEADREAM YACHT CLUB

SeaDream yachts began sailing in 1984 and, after a couple of changes of ownership and total renovation in 2002, they have evolved into the ultimate boutique ships—as they put it, "it's yachting, not cruising." Passengers enjoy an unstructured holiday at sea doing what pleases them, making it easy to imagine the diminutive vessels are really private yachts. The ambience is refined and elegantly casual. Fine dining and socializing with fellow passengers and the ships' captains and officers are preferred pastimes. Other than a tiny piano bar, a small casino, and movies in the main lounge, there is no roster of activities. A well-stocked library has books and movies for those who prefer quiet pursuits in the privacy of their staterooms.

Itineraries and Ships. *SeaDream I* and *SeaDream II* (each 110 passengers) are known for their gorgeously soigné decor, flawless service, and one-of-a-kind delights, such as the Balinese sun beds (so comfortable that passengers sometimes choose to forsake their own quarters to spend the night on them) and beach-barbecue "splashes" replete with champagne and caviar. Although not huge ships, the public areas on board are quite spacious; the chic ambience conjures up a rich man's yacht, with tons of warm woods, brass accents, laid-back rattan chairs, and high-style deck awnings to shade you from the sun. Add in a richly-hued entertainment lounge, an extensive library, and perfect-taste cabins with sleep-inducing mattresses, ultra-deluxe bedding, and a shower big enough for two, and even Onassis would have approved. A popular cruise on *SeaDream I* is a 10-day voyage from Piraeus (Athens) to Venice, with stops in Hydra, Corinth Canal, Itea, Fiskardho, Corfu, and Dubrovnik; rates start at $5,299. A typical itinerary on *SeaDream II* is the 10-day Piraeus (Athens)–to–Dubrovnik cruise, with stops in Mykonos, Santorini, Hydra, Corinth Canal, Zakynthos, Corfu, and Croatia; rates begin at $5,799.

Your Shipmates. SeaDream yachts appeal to energetic, affluent travelers of all ages, as well as groups. Passengers tend to be couples from 45-year-olds and up to retirees who enjoy the unstructured informality, subdued ambience, and exclusive service. No children's facilities or organized activities are available.

> **ROW, ROW, ROW YOUR BOAT**
>
> The SeaDream water-sports marina is well used by active passengers who want to water-ski, kayak, windsurf, or take a Jet Ski for a whirl while anchored in calm waters.

Food. Every meal is prepared to order using the freshest seafood and prime cuts of beef. Menus include vegetarian alternatives and Asian wellness cuisine for the health-conscious. Cheeses, petits fours, and chocolate truffles are offered with after-dinner coffee, and desserts are to die for. All meals are open seating, either in the main restaurant or, weather permitting, alfresco in the canopied Topsider Restaurant daily for breakfast, lunch, and special dinners. Complimentary wines accompany each meal.

Fitness and Recreation. Small gyms on each ship are equipped with treadmills, elliptical machines, recumbent bikes, and free weights. A personal trainer is available. SeaDream's unique Asian Spa facilities are also on the small size, yet offer a full menu of individualized gentle pampering treatments including massages, facials, and body wraps utilizing Eastern techniques. Mountain bikes are available for use ashore.

Contact. *2601 S. Bayshore Dr., Penthouse 1B, Coconut Grove, FL33133 305/856–5622 or 800/707–4911 www.seadreamyachtclub.com.*

SILVERSEA CRUISES

Intimate ships, paired with exclusive amenities and unparalleled hospitality, are the hallmarks of Silversea luxury cruises. Personalization is a Silversea maxim. Their ships offer more activities than other comparably sized luxury vessels, although you can also opt for quiet pursuits. Guest lecturers are featured on nearly every cruise; language, dance, and culinary lessons and excellent wine-appreciation sessions are always on the schedule of events. A multitiered show lounge is the setting for classical concerts, big-screen movies, and folkloric entertainers from ashore.

Itineraries and Ships. *Silver Whisper* (382 passengers) cuts a beautiful picture, large enough for ocean grandeur, small enough for smaller-port charm. Clean, modern decor that defines public areas and lounges verges on stark but it showcases large expanses of glass for sunshine and sea views, and that's a huge plus. Other signature touches include extremely wide passageways roomy enough for display cabinets featuring destination arts and crafts, a Davidoff Humidor, and totally free laundry rooms. A popular itinerary is the 7-day "Rome to Athens" cruise, with ports of call including Sorrento, Dubrovnik, and Greece's Corfu, Kythira, and Mykonos; rates start at $5,180. *Silver Cloud* (296 passengers), a yachtlike gem is all about style, understatement, and personal choice. While simply not large enough for huge public spaces, room on board is more than adequate and functions as well as on her larger fleetmate. A typical itinerary is the "Istanbul to Athens" cruise, with stops at Turkey's Kusadasi, Greece's Patmos, Rhodes, Mykonos, and Santorini; rates begin at $4,548.

Your Shipmates. Silversea Cruises appeals to sophisticated, affluent couples who enjoy the country clublike atmosphere, exquisite cuisine, and polished service. Although Silversea Cruises is adult oriented and unable to accommodate children less than one year of age, occasionally there's a sprinkling of children on board. There are no dedicated children's facilities available.

Food. Dishes from the galleys of Silversea's master chefs are complemented by those of La Collection du Monde, created by Silversea's culinary partner, the world-class chefs of Relais & Châteaux. Special off-menu orders are prepared whenever possible, provided that the ingredients are available. Nightly alternative theme dinners in La Terrazza (by day, the Terrace Café) feature regional specialties from the Mediterranean.

Fitness & Recreation. The rather small gyms are well equipped with cardiovascular and weight-training equipment, and fitness classes are held in the mirror-lined, but somewhat confining, exercise room. South Pacific–inspired Mandara Spa offers numerous treatments including exotic-sounding massages, facials, and body wraps.

Contact. ✉ *110 E. Broward Blvd., Fort Lauderdale, FL33301* ☎ *954/522–4477 or 800/722–9955* 🌐 *www.silversea.com*.

STAR CLIPPERS

Satisfy your inner pirate on Star Clippers' four- and five-masted sailing beauties—the world's largest barkentine and full-rigged sailing ships—which come filled with modern high-tech equipment as well as the amenities of private yachts. They were launched in 1991 as a new, spectacularly lovely tall-ship alternative for sophisticated travelers whose wants included adventure at sea, but not on board a conventional cruise ship. One of their most appealing attractions is that Star Clippers are not cruise ships in the ordinary sense with strict schedules and pages of activities. You are free to do what you please day and night, but many passengers enjoy socializing on deck.

Itineraries and Ship. *Star Clipper* (170 passengers) is a gorgeous four-master with brass fixtures, teak-and-mahogany paneling and rails, and antique prints and paintings of famous sailing vessels—the decor is a homage to the days of grand sailing ships. The library is vaguely Edwardian in style, replete with a belle-epoque fireplace, while the main restaurant has surprisingly vast dimensions but is made cozy by warm red hues, panel detailing, and elegant French Provençal–style chairs. Guest cabins are yachtlike and can be compact, with stepladders to beds. A popular cruise is the 10-night "Mediterranean Sailing," which starts in Venice, then heads to Dubrovnik and two other Croatian ports, before calling on Montenegro and Greece's Corfu, Yithion, Santorini, Mykonos, and ending up in Athens (Piraeus); rates begin at $1,995. A longer version lasts for 12 nights and includes stops at Sorrento and Stromboli. There are also many other idyllic itineraries that chart the northern and southern halves of the eastern Mediterranean.

LOVE FOR SAIL

The Star Clippers ships rely on sail power while at sea unless conditions require the assistance of the engines; you can't help but appreciate the silence and harmony with the sea when the engines are turned off and the ship is under sail.

Your Shipmates. Star Clippers cruises appeal to active, upscale American and European couples from their thirties on up who enjoy sailing, but in a casually sophisticated atmosphere with modern conveniences. Many sailings are about 50-50 from North American and Europe and announcements are made in several languages accordingly. This is not a cruise line for the physically challenged; there are no elevators, ramps, or staterooms/bathrooms with wheelchair accessibility. Star Clippers is adult oriented and there are no dedicated youth facilities.

Food. Not noted for gourmet fare, the international cuisine is what you would expect from a trendy shoreside bistro, albeit an elegant one. Fresh fruits and fish are among the best choices from Star Clippers' galleys. Lunch buffets are quite a spread of seafood, salads, and grilled items.

Fitness and Recreation. Formal exercise sessions take a backseat to water sports, although aerobics classes and swimming are featured on all ships.

Contact. *7200 N.W. 19th St., Suite 206, Miami, FL33126* *305/442–0550 or 800/442–0551* *www.starclippers.com.*

WINDSTAR CRUISES

Are they cruise ships with sails or sailing ships designed for cruises? Since 1986, the Windstar vessels have presented a conundrum. In actuality they are masted sailing yachts, pioneers in the upscale sailing niche. Often found in ports of call inaccessible to large traditional ships, Windstar ships seldom depend on wind alone to sail—their motors are necessary in order to maintain their schedules.

Itineraries and Ships. *Wind Spirit* (148 passengers) is a blue-and-cream-hue essay in Windstar style, with proportionately small public spaces replete with yachtlike touches of polished wood, columns wrapped in rope, and nautical artwork. Lots of time is spent on deck, which can get crowded; you can always escape to your cabin and watch DVDs with room-service popcorn. With its large windows and skylight, the main lounge is flooded with natural light. A popular itinerary is the 7-day "Rome to Athens" sailing, which includes Capri, Sicily, and Greece's Gythion, Nafplion, and Ermoupoli, city capital of the Cyclades; rates begin at $2,399. *Wind Star* (148 passengers) is a sister ship that also offers many voyages through the eastern Mediterranean, including the 7-day "Athens to Venice" cruise, which begins in Athens, then sails to Monemvassia, Katakolon (Olympia), Corfu, Albania, Dubrovnik, and Venice; rates begin at $3,999.

Your Shipmates. Windstar Cruises appeals to upscale professional couples in their late thirties to sixties and on up to retirees who enjoy the unpretentious, yet casually sophisticated atmosphere, creative cuisine, and refined service. The unregimented atmosphere is adult oriented; children, especially toddlers, are not encouraged. No dedicated children's facilities are available.

Food. Since 1994, Windstar menus have featured dishes originated by trendy West Coast chef and restaurateur Joachim Splichal and his Patina Group of bistro-style restaurants. In a nod to healthful dining, low-calorie and low-fat Sail Lite spa cuisine created by chef and cookbook author Jeanne Jones is available. A mid-cruise deck barbecue featuring grilled seafood and other favorites is fine dining in an elegantly casual alfresco setting. With afternoon tea and hot and cold hors d'oeuvres served several times during the afternoon and evening, no one goes hungry.

Fitness and Recreation. Windstar's massage and exercise facilities are quite small on *Wind Star* and *Wind Spirit* as would be expected on ships that carry fewer than 150 passengers. Stern-mounted watersports marinas are popular with active passengers who want to kayak, windsurf, and water-ski.

Contact. *2101 4th Ave., Suite 1150, Seattle, WA98121* ☎ *206/292-9606 or 800/258-7245* *www.windstarcruises.com.*

CRUISE BASICS

BOOKING YOUR CRUISE

According to the Cruise Line International Association (CLIA), cruisers plan their trips anytime from a year to a month in advance, with the majority planning four to six months ahead of time. It follows then that a four- to six-month window should give you the pick of sailing dates, ships, itineraries, cabins, and flights to the port city. You'll need more time if you're planning to sail on a small adventure vessel as some of their more-popular itineraries can be fully booked six to eight months ahead of time. If you're looking for a standard itinerary and aren't choosy about the vessel or dates, you could wait for a last-minute discount, but industry experts warn that these are harder to find than they used to be, now that cruising is so popular in Europe.

If you cruise regularly with the same line, it may be easiest to book directly with them, by phone or Web. Most cruises (90% according to CLIA) are, however, booked through a travel agent. Your best bet is a larger agency that specializes in cruises. They'll be able to sort through the myriad options for you, and often have the buying clout to purchase blocks of cabins at a discount. Cruise Lines International Association *www.cruising.org* lists recognized agents throughout the United States.

A SHORE THING

If a particular shore excursion is important to you, consider booking it when you book your cruise to avoid disappointment later. You can even book your spa services pre-cruise on some cruise lines' Web sites so you can have your pick of popular times, such as sea days or the afternoon before a formal night.

CRUISE COSTS

The average daily price for a cruise varies dramatically depending on when you sail, which ship and grade of cabin you choose, and when you book. At the bargain end, cruising remains one of the best travel deals around: a weeklong cruise on an older ship, for example, with an interior stateroom, in the off-season, can still be had at a basic fare of less than $100 per day (before airfare, taxes, and other costs); or about $150 per day in the high season. At the other end of the scale, a voyage on a luxury line such as Silversea Cruises or a small luxury yacht may cost more than four times as much as a cruise on a mainstream line such as Carnival. Cruises on smaller vessels tend to be pricier than trips on mainstream lines because there are fewer passengers to cover the fixed costs of the cruise.

When you sail will also affect your costs: published brochure rates are highest in July and August; you'll pay less, and have more space on ship and ashore, if you sail in May, June, or September.

Whenever you choose to sail, remember that the brochure price is the highest fare the line can charge for a given cruise. Most lines offer early-booking discounts. Although these vary tremendously, many lines will offer at least some discount if you book several months ahead of time, usually by the end of January for a summer cruise; this may require early payment as well. You may also find a discounted last-minute cruise if a ship hasn't filled all its cabins, but you won't get your pick of cabins or sailing dates, and you may find airfare is sky-high or unavailable. However, since most cruise lines will, if asked, refund the difference in fare if it drops after you've booked and before the final payment date, there's little advantage in last-minute booking. Some other deals to watch for are "kids sail free" specials, where children under 12 sail free in the same cabin as their parents; free upgrades rather than discounts; or discounted fares offered to frequent cruisers from their preferred cruise lines.

SOLO TRAVELERS

Solo travelers should be aware that single cabins are extremely rare or nonexistent on most ships; taking a double cabin for yourself can cost as much as twice the advertised per-person rates (which are based on two people sharing a room). Exceptions are found on some older ships belonging to European-based cruise lines. A few cruise lines will find roommates of the same sex for singles so that each can travel at the regular per-person, double-occupancy rate.

AND ONE LAST TIP

Although most other kinds of travel are booked over the Internet nowadays, for cruises, booking with a travel agent who specializes in cruises is still your best bet. Agents have built strong relationships with the lines, and have a much better chance of getting you the cabin you want, and possibly even a free upgrade.

EXTRAS

Your cruise fare typically includes accommodation, onboard meals and snacks, and most onboard activities. It does not normally include airfare to the port city, shore excursions, tips, soft drinks, alcoholic drinks, or spa treatments. You may also be levied fees for port handling, security and fuel surcharges, as well as sales taxes, which will be added to your cruise fare when you book.

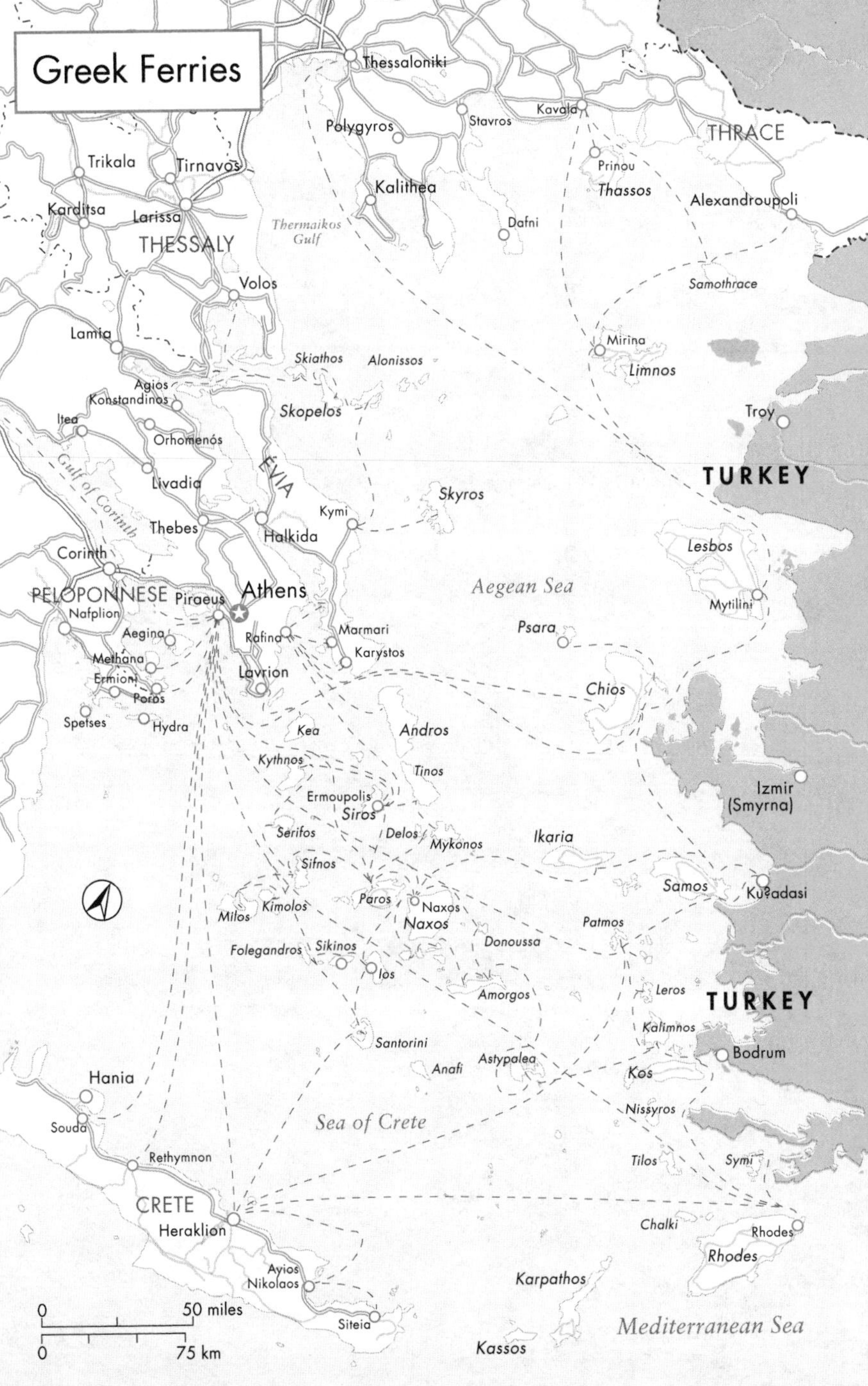
Greek Ferries
Thessaloniki
Polygyros
Stavros
Kavala
THRACE
Prinou
Thassos
Alexandroupoli
Trikala
Tirnavos
Kalithea
Karditsa
Larissa
Thermaikos Gulf
Dafni
THESSALY
Volos
Samothrace
Lamia
Mirina
Limnos
Skiathos
Alonissos
Agios Konstandinos
Skopelos
Troy
Itea
Orhomenós
Gulf of Corinth
ÉVIA
TURKEY
Livadia
Skyros
Kymi
Thebes
Halkida
Lesbos
Corinth
Aegean Sea
PELOPONNESE
Piraeus
Athens
Mytilini
Nafplion
Aegina
Rafina
Marmari
Psara
Methana
Karystos
Ermioni
Lavrion
Chios
Poros
Spetses
Hydra
Kea
Andros
Kythnos
Tinos
Izmir (Smyrna)
Ermoupolis
Siros
Serifos
Delos
Mykonos
Ikaria
Sifnos
Samos
Kuşadasi
Paros
Naxos
Milos
Kimolos
Naxos
Patmos
Folegandros
Sikinos
Donoussa
Ios
Amorgos
Leros
TURKEY
Kalimnos
Santorini
Bodrum
Astypalea
Anafi
Kos
Hania
Nissyros
Sea of Crete
Souda
Rethymnon
Tilos
Symi
CRETE
Heraklion
Chalki
Rhodes
Rhodes
Ayios Nikolaos
Karpathos
0
50 miles
Siteia
Mediterranean Sea
0
75 km
Kassos

Athens

Greek soldiers "evzones", after the flag rise, Sunday morning in Acropolis ancient temple, Athens

WORD OF MOUTH

"As we climb the Parthenon's hill at my very slow pace, stopping for photographs every minute, I feel the weight of all who have climbed before us. It brings tears to my eyes. Even now."

—nikk

"Athenians love their Byzantine churches, so you will find modern buildings over and next to these churches. This is what gives Athens some of its charm."

—TJS

www.fodors.com/forums

WELCOME TO ATHENS

TOP REASONS TO GO

★ **The Acropolis:** An ancient beacon of bygone glory rising above Athens's smog, this iconic citadel represents everything the Athenians were and still aspire to be.

★ **Evzones on Syntagma Square:** Unmistakable in tasseled hats and pompommed shoes, they act out a traditional changing of the guard that falls somewhere between discipline and comedy.

★ **The Ancient Agora & Monastiraki:** Socrates and Plato once discoursed—and scored excellent deals on figs—at the Agora, and today you can do the same at the nearby Monastiraki marketplace.

★ **Opa!:** Whether jamming to post-grunge in Gazi—Athens's Greenwich Village—or dirty dancing on the tables at live bouzouki clubs, the Athenians party like no one else.

★ **Benaki Bounty:** Housed in a neoclassic mansion, the Benaki Museum—Greece's oldest private collection—has everything from ancient sculpture to 19th-century gowns.

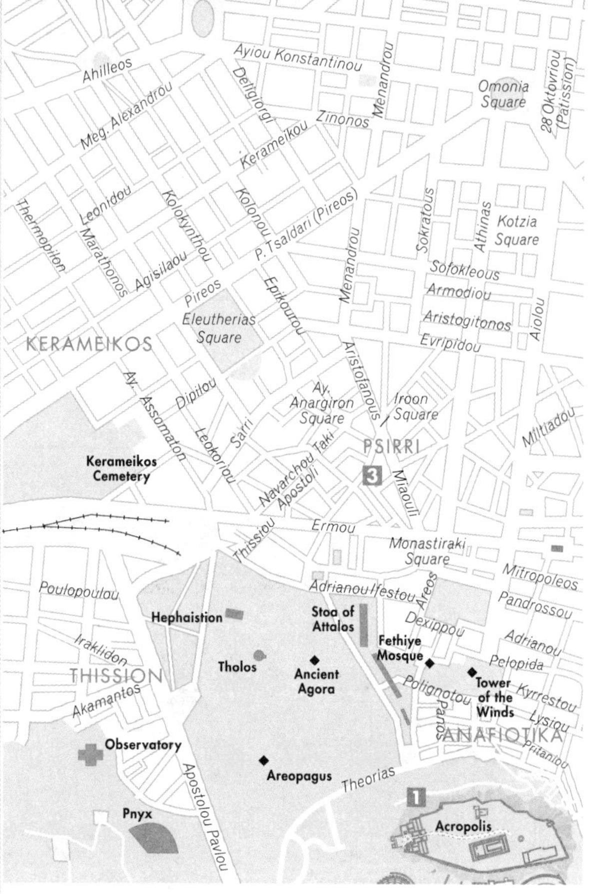

1 Acropolis. A survivor of war, time, and smog, this massive citadel and its magnificent buildings epitomize the glories of classical Greek civilization.

2 Plaka/Anafiotika. This pretty neighborhood remains the last corner of 19th-century Athens, a quiet maze of streets dotted by Byzantine churches. Anafiotika, built on winding lanes climbing up the slope of the Acropolis, looks like a whitewashed Cycladic village.

3 Monastiraki. This area—adjacent to the ancient Agora—once housed the Turkish bazaar and it retains that Near East feel. Go to the flea market here to revel in the bustle of a chaotic, energizing marketplace.

4 Central Athens. Ranging from ancient Athens's majestic Kerameikos cemetery to top people-watching cafés, this is a chaotic mix of 16th-century Byzantine churches and 1970s apartments. Not for the fainthearted is Central Market, where you'll find everything from fresh

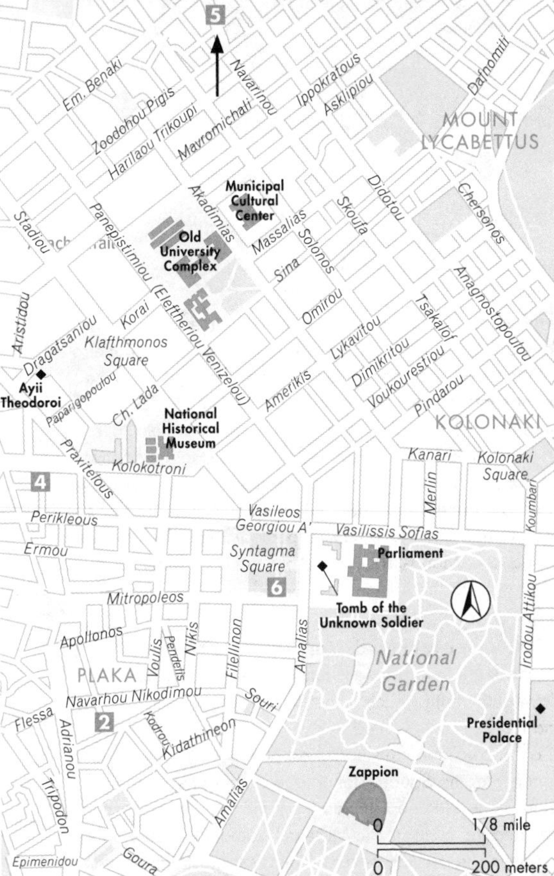

cheeses to suspended carcasses. West lies Psirri, once the decrepit home to knife-wielding "manges" (tough guys) but today a district that beats to the hedonistic pulse of young Athenian clubbers.

5 Exarchia. In the northern reaches of the city, this somewhat run-down neighborhood is Student Central—filled with old-fashioned bars and rembetika clubs—and home to that must-see, the National Archaeological Museum, with its great ancient art.

6 Syntagma Square. The heart of modern Athens, the streets radiating out from Syntagma Square are lined with government agencies, neoclassic mansions, Queen Amalia's National Garden, and the Temple of Olympian Zeus. Here, too, is the museum district, where star attractions include the Goulandris Collection of ancient art and the Benaki Museum. To the east, at the foot of Mt. Lycabettus, lies Kolonaki—a fashionable residential area loaded with see-and-be-seen restaurants.

GETTING ORIENTED

Ancient glory may still define Athens internationally but it also has a modern cachet as a chaotic, exhilarating, spontaneous metropolis. In the midst of a mass of concrete apartment blocks, Athens's Greek, Roman, and Byzantine landmarks are mercifully concentrated around the city center—walk from the Parthenon to many other sites and still find time to sip an icy frappé in a café. The hub stretches from the Acropolis in the southwest to Mt. Lycabettus in the northeast. The main grid consists of three parallel streets—Stadiou, Eleftheriou Venizelou, and Akadimias—that link two main squares, Syntagma and Omonia. But be sure to detour to the Central Market, the shops in Monastiraki and Psirri, and Gazi, the emerging arts district.

ATHENS PLANNER

Those Touristy, Kitschy, Wonderful Guided Bus Tours

Don't be a snob. Leave those three-piece suits at your hotel and enjoy one of the most festive ways to get acquainted with any big city: the basic multi-hour guided bus tour. In Athens, most tours include a visit to the Acropolis and National Archaeological Museum, plus other sites and lunch in a Plaka taverna. There are also "Athens by Night" bus tours. Morning tours begin around 8:45. Reserve through most hotels or travel agencies (many of which are clustered around Filellinon and Nikis streets off Syntagma Square). Tours run daily, year-round, and cost around €50. Book at least a day in advance and ask if you'll be picked up at your hotel or if you have to meet the bus. Two top tour bus companies are CHAT Tours (4 Stadiou, 210/322–3137, *www.chatours.gr*) and Key Tours (4 Kallirois, 210/923–3166, *www.keytours.gr*). Or opt for the "Athens Sightseeing Public Bus Line," or Bus 400, which stops at all the city's main sights. Those buses run every 30 minutes, from 7:30 am to 9 pm and tickets cost €5. The full tour takes 90 minutes, but you can hop on and off as you please. Bus 400 stops are marked by bright-blue waist-high pillars.

Getting Around by Metro

The best magic carpet ride in town is the metro. Cars are not worth the stress and road rage and, happily, the metro is fast, cheap, and convenient; its three lines go to all the major spots in Athens. Line 1, or the Green Line, of the city's metro (subway) system, is often called the *elektrikos*, or the electrical train and runs from Piraeus to the northern suburb of Kifissia, with several downtown stops. Downtown stations on Line 1 most handy to tourists include Victorias Square, near the National Archaeological Museum; Omonia Square; Monastiraki, in the old Turkish bazaar; and Thission, near the ancient Agora and the nightlife districts of Psirri and Thission.

In 2000, the city opened Lines 2 and 3 of the metro, many of whose gleaming stations function as mini-museums, displaying ancient artifacts found on-site. These lines are safe and fast but cover limited territory, mostly downtown. Line 2, or the Red Line, cuts northwest across the city, starting from Syntagma Square station and passing through such useful stops as Panepistimiou (near the Old University complex and the Numismatic Museum); Omonia Square; the Stathmos Larissis stop next to Athens's train stations, and Acropolis, at the foot of the famous site. Line 3, or the Blue Line, runs from the suburb of Aegaleo through Kerameikos (the stop for Gazi) and Monastiraki; some trains on this line go all the way to the airport, but they only pass about every half hour. The stops of most interest for visitors are Evangelismos, near the Byzantine and Christian Museum, Hilton Hotel, and National Gallery of Art, and Megaron Mousikis, next to the U.S. Embassy and concert hall. Work on extending the metro network continues.

The fare is €0.70 if you stay only on Line 1; otherwise, it's €0.80 A daily travel pass, valid for use on all forms of public transportation, is €3; it's good for 24 hours after you validate it. You must validate all tickets at the machines in metro stations before you board. Trains run between 5:30 AM and 11:30 PM. Maps of the metro, including planned extensions, are available in stations. There is no phone number for information about the system, so check the Web site (🌐 *www.ametro.gr*), which has updates on planned extensions.

Getting Around by Bus & Tram

Athens and its suburbs are covered by a good network of buses, with express buses running between central Athens and major neighborhoods, including nearby beaches. During the day, buses tend to run every 15–30 minutes, with reduced service at night and on weekends. Buses run from about 5 AM to midnight. Main bus stations are at Akadimias and Sina and at Kaningos Square. Bus and trolley tickets cost €0.45. No transfers are issued; you validate a new ticket every time you change vehicles.

If you're making several short stops, a 90-minute ticket (€1 for all modes of public transport and €0.70 for bus, trolley, and tram only) may be cheaper. Day passes for €3, weekly passes for €10, and monthly passes for €38 (€35 for metro, trolleys, and buses only and €17.50 for buses only) are sold at special booths at the main terminals. (Passes are not valid for travel to the airport or on the E22 Saronida Express.) Purchase individual tickets at terminal booths or at kiosks.

Maps of bus routes (in Greek) are available at terminal booths or from EOT. KTEL (Greece's regional bus system, made up of local operators) has an English-language Web site. The Web site of the Organization for Urban Public Transportation has an excellent English-language section. You can type in your starting point and destination and get a list of public transportation options for making the journey.

Orange-and-white KTEL buses provide efficient service throughout the Attica basin. Most buses to the east Attica coast, including those for Sounion (€3.70 for inland route and €4.10 on coastal road) and Marathon (€2.40), leave from the KTEL terminal. A tram link between downtown Athens and the coastal suburbs features two main lines.

Line A runs from Syntagma to Glyfada; Line B traces the shoreline from Glyfada to the Peace & Friendship Stadium on the outskirts of Piraeus. Single tickets cost €0.60 or €0.40 for five stops and are sold at machines on the tram platforms.

City trams (🌐 *www.tramsa.gr*). **KTEL Buses** (✉ *Aigyptou Sq. at corner of Mavromateon and Leoforos Alexandras near Pedion Areos park, Pedion Areos* ☎ *210/821–0872, 210/821–3203 for Sounion, 210/821–0872 for Marathon* 🌐 *www.ktel.org*). **Organization for Urban Public Transportation** (✉ *Metsovou 15, Exarchia* 🌐 *www.oasa.gr*).

How's the Weather?

Athens often feels like a furnace in summer, due to the capital's lack of parks and millions of circulating cars. Mornings between 7 AM and 9 AM or evenings after 5 PM are often pleasant but temperatures can still hover in the 90s during heat waves. The capital is far more pleasant in spring and fall. The sunlight is bright but bearable, the air feels crisp and invigorating, and even the famously surly Athenians are friendlier. Winters are mild here, just as they are in all of Greece: it rains but rarely snows, so a light coat is all that is needed.

Multi-Trip Passes

If you are planning to take the bus, trolley, and metro several times in one day during your stay, buy a 24-hour ticket for all the urban network (€3) or a single ticket (€1) valid for all travel completed within 90 minutes. You must use a new ticket (€0.50–€0.70) for each leg of the journey for each method of transportation. A pass also saves you the hassle of validating tickets numerous times. Or opt for a weekly pass or a monthly pass, available at the beginning of the month from terminal kiosks and metro stations (€17.50 for unlimited bus and trolley travel; €35 with metro included). You need a passport-size photograph of yourself for the pass.

Updated by Joanna Kakissis

IT'S NO WONDER THAT ALL roads lead to the fascinating and maddening metropolis of Athens. Lift your eyes 200 feet above the city to the Parthenon, its honey-color marble columns rising from a massive limestone base, and you behold architectural perfection that has not been surpassed in 2,500 years. But, today, this shrine of classical form, this symbol of Western civilization and political thought, dominates a 21st-century boomtown. Athens is now home to 4.4 million souls, many of whom spend the day discussing the city's faults: the murky pollution cloud known as the *nefos,* the overcrowding, the traffic jams with their hellish din, and the characterless cement apartment blocks. Romantic travelers, nurtured on the truth and beauty of Keats's Grecian Urn, are dismayed to find that much of Athens has succumbed to that red tubular glare that owes only its name, neon, to the Greeks.

DISCOUNTS & DEALS

Athens's best deal is the €12 ticket that allows one week's admission to all the sites and corresponding museums along the Unification of Archaeological Sites walkway. You can buy the ticket at any of the sites, which include the Acropolis, ancient Agora, Roman Agora, Temple of Olympian Zeus, Kerameikos, and Theater of Dionysus. Admission to almost all museums and archaeological sites is free on Sunday from mid-November through March. Entrance is usually free every day for European Union students, half off for students from other countries, and about a third off for senior citizens.

To experience Athens—Athìna in Greek—fully is to understand the essence of Greece: ancient monuments surviving in a sea of cement, startling beauty amid the squalor, tradition juxtaposed with modernity—a smartly dressed lawyer chatting on her cell phone as she maneuvers around a priest in flowing robes heading for the ultramodern metro. Locals depend upon humor and flexibility to deal with the chaos; you should do the same. The rewards are immense if you take the time to catch the purple glow of sundown on Mt. Hymettus, light a candle in a Byzantine church beside black-shrouded grandmas while teens outside argue vociferously about soccer, or breathe in the tangy sea air while sipping a Greek coffee after a night at the coastal clubs.

Wander into less-touristy areas and you will often discover pockets of incomparable charm, in refreshing contrast to the dreary repetition of the modern facades. In lovely Athenian neighborhoods you can still delight in the pleasures of strolling. *Peripato,* the Athenians call it, and it's as old as Aristotle, whose students learned as they roamed about in his Peripatetic school. This ancient practice survives in the modern custom of the evening *volta,* or stroll, taken along the pedestrianized Dionyssiou Areopagitou street skirting the base of the Acropolis. Along your way, be sure to stop in a taverna to observe Athenians in their element. They are lively and expressive, their hands fiddling with worry beads or gesturing excitedly. Although often expansively friendly, they are aggressive and stubborn when they feel threatened, and they're also insatiably curious.

Amid the ancient treasures and the 19th-century delights of neighborhoods such as Anafiotika and Plaka, the pickax, pneumatic drill, and cement mixer have given birth to countless office buildings and modern apartments. Hardly a monument of importance attests to the city's history between the completion of the Temple of Olympian Zeus 19 centuries ago and the present day. That is the tragedy of Athens: the long vacuum in its history, the centuries of decay, neglect, and even oblivion. But within the last 150 years the Greeks have created a modern capital out of a village centered on a group of ruined marble columns. And since the late 1990s, inspired by the 2004 Olympics, they have gone far in transforming Athens into a sparkling modern metropolis that the ancients would strain to recognize but would heartily endorse.

COLD RELIEF

The center of modern Athens is small, stretching from the Acropolis in the southwest to Mt. Lycabettus in the northeast, crowned by the small white chapel of Ayios Georgios. The layout is simple: three parallel streets—Stadiou, Eleftheriou Venizelou (familiarly known as Panepistimiou), and Akadimias—link two main squares, Syntagma (Constitution) and Omonia (Concord). Try to detour off this beaten tourist track: seeing the Athenian butchers in the Central Market sleeping on their cold marble slabs during the heat of the afternoon siesta may give you more of a feel for the city than seeing scores of toppled columns.

EXPLORING ATHENS

Although Athens covers a huge area, the major landmarks of the ancient Greek, Roman, and Byzantine periods are close to the modern city center. You can easily walk from the Acropolis to many other key sites, taking time to browse in shops and relax in cafés and tavernas along the way. From many quarters of the city you can glimpse "the glory that was Greece" in the form of the Acropolis looming above the horizon, but only by actually climbing that rocky precipice can you feel the impact of the ancient settlement. The Acropolis and Filopappou, two craggy hills sitting side by side; the ancient Agora (marketplace); and Kerameikos, the first cemetery, form the core of ancient and Roman Athens. Preparations for the 2004 Olympics made these more accessible: along the Unification of Archaeological Sites promenade, you can follow stone-paved, tree-lined walkways from site to site, undisturbed by traffic. Cars have also been banned or reduced in other streets in the historical center. In the National Archaeological Museum, vast numbers of artifacts illustrate the many millennia of Greek civilization; smaller museums such as the Goulandris Cycladic and Greek Ancient Art Museum and the Byzantine and Christian Museum illuminate the history of particular regions or periods.

Athens may seem like one huge city, but it is really a conglomeration of neighborhoods with distinctive characters. The Eastern influences that prevailed during the 400-year rule of the Ottoman Empire are still evident in Monastiraki, the bazaar area near the foot of the Acropolis. On the northern slope of the Acropolis, stroll through Plaka (if possible by moonlight), an area of tranquil streets lined with renovated mansions, to get the flavor of the 19th-century's gracious lifestyle. The narrow lanes of Anafiotika, a section of Plaka, thread past tiny churches and small, color-washed houses with wooden upper stories, recalling a Cycladic island village. In this maze of winding streets, vestiges of the older city are everywhere: crumbling stairways lined with festive tavernas; dank cellars filled with wine vats; occasionally a court or diminutive garden, enclosed within high walls and filled with magnolia trees and the flaming trumpet-shape flowers of hibiscus bushes.

Formerly run-down old quarters, such as Thission and Psirri, popular nightlife areas filled with bars and *mezedopoleia* (similar to tapas bars), are now in the process of gentrification, although they still retain much of their original charm, as does the colorful produce and meat market on Athinas. The area around Syntagma Square, the tourist hub, and Omonia Square, the commercial heart of the city about 1 km (½ mi) northwest, is distinctly European, having been designed by the court architects of King Othos, a Bavarian, in the 19th century. The chic shops and bistros of ritzy Kolonaki nestle at the foot of Mt. Lycabettus, Athens's highest hill (909 feet). Each of Athens's outlying suburbs has a distinctive character: in the north is wealthy, tree-lined Kifissia, once a summer resort for aristocratic Athenians, and in the south and southeast lie Kalamaki, Glyfada, and Vouliagmeni, with their sandy beaches, seaside bars, and lively summer nightlife. Just beyond the city's southern fringes is Piraeus, a bustling port city of waterside fish tavernas and Saronic Gulf views.

THE ACROPOLIS & ENVIRONS ΑΚΡΟΠΟΛΗ & ΠΕΡΙΧΩΡΑ

Although Athens, together with its suburbs and port, sprawls across the plain for more than 150 square miles, most of its ancient monuments cluster around the Acropolis, which rises like a massive sentinel, white and beautiful, out of the center of the city. In mountainous Greece, most ancient towns were backed up by an acropolis, an easily defensible upper town (which is what the word means), but when spelled with a capital "A" it can only refer to antiquity's most splendid group of buildings—the Acropolis of Athens.

Towering over the modern metropolis of 4 million as it once stood over the ancient capital of 50,000, it has remained Athens's most spectacular attraction ever since its first settlement around 5000 BC. It had been a religious center long before Athens became a major city-state in the 6th century BC. It has been associated with Athena ever since the city's mythical founding, but virtually all of the city's other religious cults had temples or shrines here as well. As Athens became the dominant city-state in the 5th century BC, Pericles led the city in making the Acropolis the crowning symbol of Athenian power and successful democracy.

After the Acropolis all will at first seem to be an anticlimax. But there is still much that is well worth seeing on the citadel's periphery, including the neoclassic buildings lining its main street, Dionyssiou Areopagitou; the centuries-old Odeon of Herodes Atticus; the Dionysus theater; and the Ilias Lalaounis Jewelry Museum. Nearby is Filopappou, a pine-clad summit that has the city's best view of the Acropolis; the Pnyx where the Athenian assembly met; and the tiny, rustic church of Ayios Dimitrios Loumbardiaris.

Wear a hat for protection from the sun and low-heel, rubber-sole shoes, as the marble on the Acropolis steps and near the other monuments is quite slippery. Bring plenty of water—you'll need it, and there are usually long lines at the on-site cantinas.

Numbers in the text correspond to numbers in the margin and on the Athens: Acropolis, Plaka, Anafiotika, and Central Athens map.

WHAT TO SEE: THE MAIN ATTRACTIONS

1 **Acropolis.** Towering over a modern city of 12 million much as it stood over the ancient capital of 50,000, the Acropolis (literally "high city") continues to be Athens's most spectacular, photogenic, and visited attraction despite hundreds of years of renovations, bombings, and artistic lootings. The buildings, constructed under the direction of Pericles during the city's Golden Age in the 5th century BC, were designed to be as visually harmonious as they were enormous, and they stand today in a perfect balance of stubborn immortality and elegant fragmentation. For an in-depth look at this emblem of the glories of classical Greek civilization, and the adjacent, headline-making New Acropolis Museum, see our photo-feature, "The Acropolis: Ascent to Glory" in this chapter.

Fodor's Choice ★

2 **Filopappou.** This summit includes **Lofos Mousson** (Hill of the Muses), whose peak offers the city's best view of the Parthenon, which appears almost at eye level. Also there is the **Monument of Filopappus,** depicting a Syrian prince who was such a generous benefactor that the people accepted him as a distinguished Athenian. The marble monument is a tomb decorated by a frieze showing Filopappus driving his chariot. In 294 BC a fort strategic to Athens's defense was built here, overlooking the road to the sea. On the hill of the **Pnyx** (meaning "crowded"), the all-male general assembly (Ecclesia) met during the time of Pericles. Originally, citizens of the Ecclesia faced the Acropolis while listening to speeches, but they tended to lose their concentration as they gazed upon the monuments, so the positions of the speaker and the audience were reversed. The speaker's platform is still visible on the semicircular terrace; from here, Themistocles persuaded Athenians to fortify the city and Pericles argued for the construction of the Parthenon. Farther north is the **Hill of the Nymphs,** with a 19th-century observatory designed by Theophilos Hansen, responsible for many of the capital's grander edifices. He was so satisfied with his work, he had *servare intaminatum* ("to remain intact") inscribed over the entrance. ✉ *Enter from Dionyssiou Areopagitou or Vasileos Pavlou, Acropolis* Ⓜ *Acropolis.*

Continued on page 93

THE ACROPOLIS
ASCENT TO GLORY

One of the wonders of the world, the Acropolis symbolizes Greece's Golden Age. Its stunning centerpiece, the Parthenon, was commissioned in the 5th century BC by the great Athenian leader Pericles as part of an elaborate building program designed to epitomize the apex of an iconic culture. Thousands of years later, the Acropolis pulls the patriotic heartstrings of modern Greeks and lulls millions of annual visitors back to an ancient time.

You don't have to look far in Athens to encounter perfection. Towering above all—both physically and spiritually—is the Acropolis, the ancient city of upper Athens and womb of Western civilization. Raising your eyes to the crest of this *ieros vrachos* (sacred rock), the sight of the Parthenon will stop you in your tracks. The term Akropolis (to use the Greek spelling) means "High City" and today's traveler who climbs this table-like hill is paying tribute to the prime source of civilization as we know it.

A TITANIC TEMPLE

Described by the 19th-century French poet Alphonse de Lamartine as "the most perfect poem in stone," the Acropolis is a true testament to the Golden Age of Greece. While archaeological evidence has shown that the flat-top limestone outcrop, 512 feet high, attracted settlers as early as Neolithic times, most of its most imposing structures were built from 461 to 429 BC, when the intellectual and artistic life of Athens flowered under the influence of the Athenian statesman, Pericles. Even in its bleached and silent state, the Parthenon—the Panathenaic temple that crowns the rise—has the power to stir the heart as few other ancient relics do.

PERICLES TO POLLUTION

Since the Periclean Age, the buildings of the Acropolis have been inflicted with the damages of war, as well as unscrupulous transformations into, at various times, a Florentine palace, an Islamic mosque, a Turkish harem, and a World War II sentry. Since then, a more insidious enemy—pollution—has emerged. The site is presently undergoing conservation measures as part of an ambitious rescue plan. Today, the Erechtheion temple has been completely restored, and work on the Parthenon, Temple of Athena Nike, and the Propylaea is due for completion by the end of 2010. A final phase, involving massive landscaping works, will last through 2020. Despite the ongoing restoration work, a visit to the Acropolis today can evoke the spirit of the ancient heroes and gods who were once worshiped here.

THE PARTHENON

PINNACLE OF THE PERICLEAN AGE

DEDICATED TO ATHENA

At the loftiest point of the Acropolis stands the Parthenon, the architectural masterpiece conceived by Pericles and executed between 447 and 438 BC by the brilliant sculptor Pheidias, who supervised the architects Iktinos and Kallikrates in its construction. It not only raised the bar in terms of sheer size, but also in the perfection of its proportions.

Dedicated to the goddess Athena (the name Parthenon comes from the Athena Parthenos, or the virgin Athena) and inaugurated at the Panathenaic Festival of 438 BC, the Parthenon served primarily as the treasury of the Delian League, an ancient alliance of cities formed to defeat the Persian incursion.In fact, the Parthenon was built as much to honor the city's power as to venerate Athena. Its foundations, laid after the victory at Marathon in 490 BC, were destroyed by the Persian army in 480–79 BC. In turn, the city-state of Athens banded together with Sparta to rout the Persians by 449 BC.

To proclaim its hegemony over all Greece, Athens envisioned a grand new Acropolis. After a 30-year building moratorium, the titanic-scale project of reconstructing the temple was initiated by Pericles around 448 BC.

490 BC
Foundation for Acropolis laid

447-438 BC
The Parthenon is constructed

420 BC
Temple of Athena Nike is completed

TIMELINE

EDIFICE REX: PERICLES

His name means "surrounded by glory." Some scholars consider this extraordinary, enigmatic Athenian general to be the architect of the destiny of Greece at its height, while others consider him a megalomaniac who bankrupted the coffers of an empire, and an elitist who catered to the privileged few at the expense of the masses.

Indeed, Pericles (460–429 BC) plundered the treasury of the Athenian alliance for the Acropolis building program. One academic has even called the Periclean building program the largest embezzlement in human history.

MYTH IN MARBLE

But Pericles' masterstroke becomes more comprehensible when studied against the conundrum that was Athenian democracy. In truth an aristocracy that was the watchdog of private property and public order, this political system financed athletic games and drama festivals; it constructed exquisite buildings. Its motto was not only to live, but to live well. Surrounded by barbarians, the Age of Pericles was the more striking for its high level of civilization, its qualities of proportion, reason, clarity, and harmony, all of which are epitomized nowhere else as beautifully as in the Parthenon. To their credit, the Athenians rallied around Pericles' vision: the respect for the individualistic character of men and women could be revealed through art and architecture.

Even jaded Athenians, when overwhelmed by the city, feel renewed when they lift their eyes to this great monument.

TRICK OF THE TRADE

One of the Parthenon's features, or "refinements," is the way it uses meiosis (tapering of columns) and entasis (a slight swelling so that the column can hold the weight of the entablature), deviations from strict mathematics that breathed movement into the rigid marble. Architects knew that a straight line looks curved, and vice versa, so they cleverly built the temple with all the horizontal lines somewhat curved. The columns, it has been calculated, lean toward the center of the temple; if they were to continue into space, they would eventually converge to create a huge pyramid.

1456
Converted to mosque by occupying Turks

September 26, 1687
The Parthenon, used for gunpowder storage, explodes after being hit by a mortar shell

THE MISSING MARBLES

In Pericles' day, the Parthenon was most famous for two colossal (now vanished) statues fashioned by Pheidias: a tall bronze statue of Athena inside the temple, and one of Athena the Champion (Promachos), which faced anyone approaching the great hill. Neither of these works survive today but a second-century guidebook by the early travel writer Pausanias remembered how a seafarer approaching the harbor Piraeus could see the sun's rays glinting on Athena the Champion's spear and armor.

Today, however the Parthenon is notorious for its "missing" marbles—the legendary statues from the temple frieze and pediments that were shipped to England by Lord Elgin between 1801 and 1805. One of the most evocative sculpted friezes, the Procession of the Panathenaia was 524 feet long, depicting an extraordinary parade of 400 people, including maidens, magistrates, horsemen, and musicians, plus 200 animals. To show ordinary mortals, at a time when almost all sculpture featured mythological or battle scenes, was lively and daring. About 50 of the best-preserved pieces of this panel, called the Parthenon Marbles by Greeks but known as the Elgin Marbles by almost everyone else, are in the British Museum; a few others can be seen in the New Acropolis Museum, while a few—showing scenes of battle: Athenians versus Amazons, and gods and goddesses against giants—remain on the temple itself.

In the first decade of the 19th century, during the time of the Ottoman Empire, Lord Elgin, the British ambassador in Constantinople, was given permission by the Sultan Selim III to remove stones with inscriptions from the Acropolis; he took this as permission to dismantle

Dull is the eye that will not weep to see / Thy walls defaced, thy mouldering shrines removed / By British hands, which it had best behoved / To guard those relics ne'er to be restored.

—From the poem "Childe Harolde's Pilgrimage" by the philhellene Lord Byron, published between 1812–18.

shiploads of sculptures. Some historians say Elgin was neither ethical nor delicate in removing two-thirds of the famous Parthenon friezes and half of the marbles, causing irreparable damage to both the marbles and the Parthenon. On the other side, many argue that the marbles would have been destroyed if left on site. Today, a spirited long-term campaign aims to have them returned to Greece, to be appreciated in their original context. The New Acropolis Museum is being built with a special room for the marbles, in which they would be laid out in their original order; it will be constructed with glass walls, through which the temple the marbles originally adorned will be clearly visible.

(Above): Scenes from the so-called Elgin marbles (c 447- 432 BC) preserved at the British Museum in London; reconstruction of Parthenon interior, showing statue of Athena.

IN THIS CORNER: LORD ELGIN

The British nobleman and future diplomat Thomas Bruce, the seventh Earl of Elgin, became Britain's ambassador to the Ottoman Empire in 1799. His years in Constantinople were not happy: he suffered from what was very likely syphilis (the disease ate away his nose), and his wife soon took off with her personal escort. But Lord Elgin found purpose in "saving" priceless antiquities ignored by the ruling Turks and shipping them to Britain at enormous personal expense. Today, some consider him "a prince among thieves."

IN THIS CORNER: MELINA MERCOURI

She was so beloved as an actress and singer that people called her only by her first name. But behind the smoky eyes and husky voice that lit up the film *Never On Sunday* (1960) lay the heart of a fierce activist. As the country's first female culture minister, Melina led the fight to reclaim the Parthenon Marbles from Britain—"In the world over, the very name of our country is immediately associated with the Parthenon," she proclaimed. After she passed away, in 1994, a bust of her likeness was placed in the Dionysiou Areopagitou pedestrian walkway, in the shadow of the Acropolis.

The Acropolis in Pericles' Time

RAISING A HUE

"Just by color—beige!" So proclaimed Elsie de Wolfe, celebrated decorator to J. Pierpont Morgan, when she first saw the Parthenon. As it turns out, the original Parthenon was anything but beige. Especially ornate, it had been covered with a tile roof, decorated with statuary and marble friezes, adorned with gilded wooden doors and ceilings, and walls and columns so brightly hued that the people protested, "We are adorning our city like a wanton woman" (Plutarch). The finishing touch was provided by the legendary sculptor Pheidias, who created some of the sculpted friezes—these were also brightly hued.

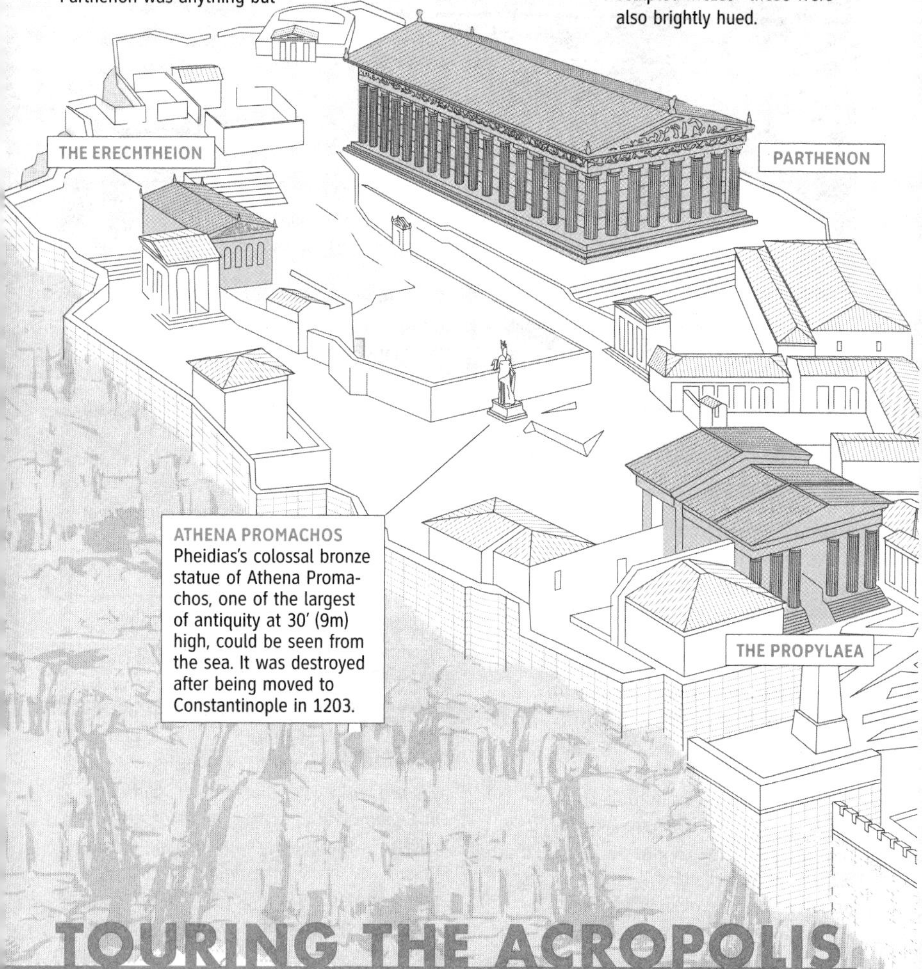

THE ERECHTHEION

PARTHENON

THE PROPYLAEA

ATHENA PROMACHOS

Pheidias's colossal bronze statue of Athena Promachos, one of the largest of antiquity at 30' (9m) high, could be seen from the sea. It was destroyed after being moved to Constantinople in 1203.

TOURING THE ACROPOLIS

Most people take the metro to the Acropolis station, where the New Acropolis Museum is to open in 2008. They then follow the pedestrianized street Dionyssiou Aerogapitou, which traces the foothill of the Acropolis to its entrance at the Beulé Gate. Another entrance is along the rock's northern face via the Peripatos, a paved path from the Plaka district.

THE BEULÉ GATE

You enter the Acropolis complex through this late-Roman structure named for the French archaeologist Ernest Beulé, who discovered the gate in 1852. Made of marble fragments from the destroyed monument of Nikias on the south slope of the Acropolis, it has an inscription above the lintel dated 320 BC, dedicated by "Nikias son of Nikodemos of Xypete." Before Roman times, the entrance to the Acropolis was a steep processional ramp below the Temple of Athena Nike. This Sacred Way was used every fourth year for the Panathenaic procession, a spectacle that honored Athena's remarkable birth (she sprang from the head of her father, Zeus).

THE PROPYLAEA

This imposing structure was designed to instill the proper reverence in worshipers as they crossed from the temporal world into the spiritual world of the sanctuary, for this was the main function of the Acropolis. Conceived by Pericles, the Propylaea was the masterwork of the architect Mnesicles. Conceived to be the same size as the Parthenon, it was to have been the grandest secular building in Greece. Construction was suspended during the Peloponnesian War, and it was never finished. The structure shows the first use of both Doric and Ionic columns together, a style that can be called Attic. Six of the sturdier fluted Doric columns, made from Pendelic marble, correspond with the gateways of the portal. Processions with priests, chariots, and sacrificial animals entered via a marble ramp in the center (now protected by a wooden stairway), while ordinary visitors on foot entered via the side doors. The slender Ionic columns had elegant capitals, some of which have been restored along with a section of the famed paneled ceiling, originally decorated with gold eight-pointed stars on a blue background. Adjacent to the Pinakotheke, or art gallery (with paintings of scenes from Homer's epics and mythological tableaux), the south wing is a decorative portico. The view from the inner porch of the Propylaea is stunning: the Parthenon is suddenly revealed in its full glory, framed by the columns.

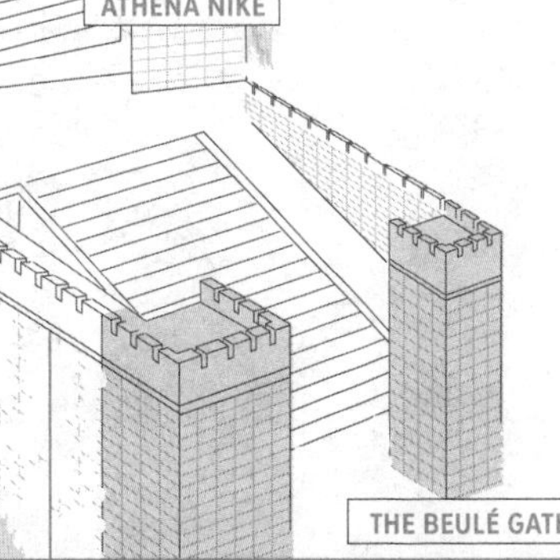

THE TEMPLE OF ATHENA NIKE

The 2nd-century traveler Pausanias referred to this fabled temple as the Temple of Nike Apteros, or Wingless Victory, for "in Athens they believe Victory will stay forever because she has no wings." Designed by Kallikrates, the mini-temple was built in 427–424 BC to celebrate peace with Persia. The bas-reliefs on the surrounding parapet depicting the Victories leading heifers to be sacrificed must have been of exceptional quality, judging from the section called "Nike Unfastening Her Sandal" in the Acropolis Museum. In 1998, Greek archaeologists began dismantling the entire temple for conservation. After laser-cleaning the marble, to remove generations of soot, the team will reconstruct the temple on its original site.

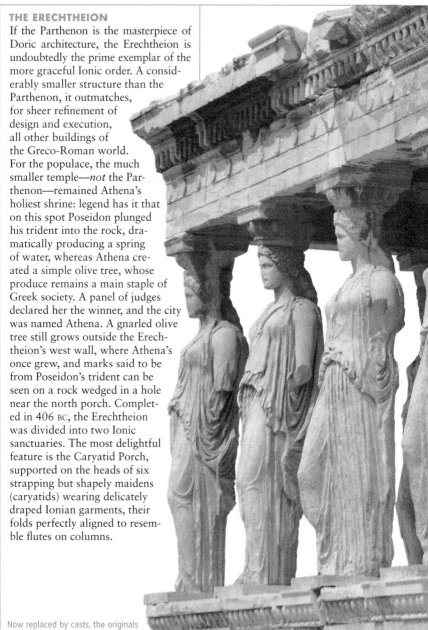

THE ERECHTHEION

If the Parthenon is the masterpiece of Doric architecture, the Erechtheion is undoubtedly the prime exemplar of the more graceful Ionic order. A considerably smaller structure than the Parthenon, it outmatches, for sheer refinement of design and execution, all other buildings of the Greco-Roman world. For the populace, the much smaller temple—*not* the Parthenon—remained Athena's holiest shrine: legend has it that on this spot Poseidon plunged his trident into the rock, dramatically producing a spring of water, whereas Athena created a simple olive tree, whose produce remains a main staple of Greek society. A panel of judges declared her the winner, and the city was named Athena. A gnarled olive tree still grows outside the Erechtheion's west wall, where Athena's once grew, and marks said to be from Poseidon's trident can be seen on a rock wedged in a hole near the north porch. Completed in 406 BC, the Erechtheion was divided into two Ionic sanctuaries. The most delightful feature is the Caryatid Porch, supported on the heads of six strapping but shapely maidens (caryatids) wearing delicately draped Ionian garments, their folds perfectly aligned to resemble flutes on columns.

Now replaced by casts, the originals of the Erechtheion's famous Caryatid maidens are in the New Acropolis Museum.

PLANNING YOUR VISIT

Sooner or later, you will climb the Acropolis hill to witness, close up, its mighty marble monuments whose beauty and grace have not been surpassed in two millennia. When you do, keep these pointers in mind.

What Are the Best Times to Go? Such is the beauty of the Acropolis and the grandeur of the setting that a visit in all seasons and at all hours is rewarding. In general, the earlier you start out the better. In summer, by noon the heat is blistering and the reflection of the light thrown back by the rock and the marble ruins is almost blinding. An alternative, in summer, is to visit after 5 PM, when the light is best for taking photographs. In any season the ideal time might be the two hours before sunset, when occasionally the fabled violet light spreads from the crest of Mt. Hymettus (which the ancients called "violet-crowned") and gradually embraces the Acropolis. After dark the hill is spectacularly floodlighted, creating a scene visible from many parts of the capital. A moonlight visit—sometimes scheduled by the authorities during full moons in summer—is highly evocative. In winter, if there are clouds trailing across the mountains, and shafts of sun lighting up the marble columns, the setting takes on an even more dramatic quality.

How Long Does a Visit Usually Run? Depending on the crowds, the walk takes about four hours, including one spent in the Acropolis Museum.

Are Tour Guides Available? The Union of Official Guides (Apollonos 9A, Syntagma, 210/322-9705, 210/322-0090) offers licensed guides for tours of archaeological sites within Athens. Another option is Amphitrion Holidays (Syngrou 7, Koukaki, 210/900-6000), which offers walking tours of the Acropolis. Guides will also help kids understand the site better.

What's the Handiest Place to Refuel? The Tourist Pavilion (Filoppapou Hill, 210/923-1665), a landscaped, tree-shaded spot soundtracked by chirping birds. It serves drinks, snacks, and a few hot dishes.

Dionysiou Areopagitou, Acropolis

☎ 210/321-4172 or 210/321-0219

www.culture.gr

Joint ticket for all Unification of Archaeological Sites €12. Good for five days—and for free admission—to the Ancient Agora, Theatre of Dionysus, Kerameikos cemetery, Temple of Olympian Zeus, and the Roman Forum.

Apr.–Oct., daily 8–sunset; Nov.–Mar., daily 8–2:30

DON'T FORGET:

- If it's hot, remember to bring water, sunscreen, and a hat to protect yourself from the sun.
- Get a free bilingual pamphlet guide (in English and Greek) at the entrance gate. It is packed with information, but staffers usually don't bother to give it out unless asked.
- An elevator now ascends to the summit of the Acropolis, once inaccessible to people with disabilities.
- All large bags, backpacks, and shopping bags will have to be checked in the site cloakroon.

OPENING 2008: THE NEW ACROPOLIS MUSEUM

Designed by the celebrated New York-based Franco-Swiss architect, Bernard Tschumi, the New Acropolis Museum (🌐 www.newacropolismuseum.gr; admission and hours not set at press time) is finally heralded to open in early 2008. It not only represents the latest in cutting-edge museum design but is seen as the perfect opportunity to showcase the Parthenon Marbles from London's British Museum, which the government of Greece has long been fighting to repatriate to their homeland. Set at the southern foot of the Acropolis hill (in the Makriyanni district), the new museum is a subtle, light-embued blend of high-tech glass and timeless stone.

Long delayed by bureaucracy, the three-story museum will debut in early 2008, when the third floor—devoted to the Parthenon Marbles—will open (it will take a year for all three floors to open). The second floor will contain a restaurant and shop, while the first floor will exhibit ancient art works from the Acropolis and surrounding areas.

CAN YOU DIG IT?

Linking the floors will be a spectacular ramp, presided over by the fabled Caryatid statues from the Erechtheion; its floor will be studded with cutaway glass panels to reveal an ongoing excavation of an ancient Athenian village (discovered as the museum was being constructed). The third floor centerpiece will be a glassed-in rooftop room, built to the exact proportions of the Parthenon, with grand views of the temple itself. There, the Parthenon sculptures that Greece still owns will be arranged in their original order; plaster casts of those still in London will stand in for the originals and will be draped in gauze to dramatically emphasize their absence.

ART'S FOSSILS

Other than the *Caryatid figures* and the *Parthenon Marbles*, the most notable displays of the museum include, in Room IV, the *Rampin Horseman* and the compelling *Hound*, both by the sculptor Phaidimos; the noted pediment sculpted into a calf being devoured by a lioness—a 6th century BC treasure that brings to mind Picasso's *Guernica*; the charismatic *Calf-Bearer*, or Moschophoros, an early Archaic work showing a man carrying on his shoulders a calf intended to be sacrificed; a porous-stone pediment of the Archaic temple of Athena shows *Heracles fighting against Triton*—on its right side, note the rather scholarly looking "three-headed demon," bearing traces of the original color striking pedimental figures from the Old Temple of Athena (525 BC), depicting the battle between Athena and the Giants; and the great *Nike Unfastening Her Sandal*, taken from the parapet of the Temple of Athena Nike.

NEED A BREAK?

The little Tourist Pavilion (✉ *Filopappou hill, Filopappou* ☎ *210/923–1665*) is a blissful hideaway far from the bustle of the archaeological sites and the streets. It is landscaped and shaded by overhanging pines, with chirping birds. Drinks, snacks, and a few hot dishes are served.

THE SCARLET TATTOO

On the hill of the Pnyx (meaning "crowded"), the all-male general assembly (Ecclesia) met during the time of Pericles. Gathering the quorum of 5,000 citizens necessary to take a vote was not always easy, as Aristophanes hilariously points out in his comedy *Ecclesiazusae* (Women of the Assembly). Archers armed with red paint were sent out to dab it on vote dodgers; the offenders were then fined.

3

3 **Odeon of Herodes Atticus.** Hauntingly beautiful, this ancient theater was built in AD 160 by the affluent Herodes Atticus in memory of his wife, Regilla. Known as the Irodion by Athenians, it is nestled Greek-style into the hillside, but with typically Roman arches in its three-story stage building and barrel-vaulted entrances. The circular orchestra has now become a semicircle, and the long-vanished cedar roof probably covered only the stage and dressing rooms, not the 34 rows of seats. The theater, which holds 5,000, was restored and reopened in 1955 for the Elliniko Festival, or Hellenic Festival (formerly known as the Athens Festival). To enter you must hold a ticket to one of the summer performances, which range from the Royal Ballet to ancient tragedies and Attic comedies usually performed in modern Greek. Contact the Elliniko Festival (Hellenic Festival) box office for ticket information. ✉ *Dionyssiou Areopagitou near intersection with Propylaion, Acropolis* ☎ *210/323–2771* ⏲ *Open only during performances* Ⓜ *Acropolis.*

4 **Theater of Dionysus.** It was on this spot in the 6th century BC that the Dionyssia festivals took place; a century later, dramas such as Sophocles's *Oedipus Rex* and Euripides's *Medea* were performed for the entire population of the city. Visible are foundations of a stage dating from about 330 BC, when it was built for 15,000 spectators as well as the assemblies formerly held on Pnyx. In the middle of the orchestra stood the altar to Dionysus. Most of the upper rows of seats have been destroyed, but the lower levels, with labeled chairs for priests and dignitaries, remain. The fantastic throne in the center was reserved for the priest of Dionysus: regal lions' paws adorn it, and the back is carved with reliefs of satyrs and griffins. On the hillside above the theater stand two columns, vestiges of the little temple erected in the 4th century BC by Thrasyllus the Choragus (the ancient counterpart of a modern impresario). ✉ *Dionyssiou Areopagitou across from Mitsaion, Acropolis* ☎ *210/322–4625, 210/323–4482 box office* 🎫 *€2; €12 joint ticket for all Unification of Archaeological Sites* ⏲ *May–Oct., daily 8–7; Nov.–Apr., daily 8:30–2:30* Ⓜ *Acropolis.*

ALSO WORTH SEEING

5 **Ilias Lalaounis Jewelry Museum.** Housing the creations of the internationally renowned artist Ilias Lalaounis, this private foundation also operates as a study center. The 45 collections include 3,000 pieces inspired by subjects as diverse as the Treasure of Priam to the wildflowers of Greece; many of the works are eye-catching, especially the massive necklaces evoking the Minoan and Byzantine periods. Besides the well-made videos that explain jewelry making, craftspeople in the workshop demonstrate ancient and modern techniques, such as chain weaving and hammering. During the academic year the museum can arrange educational programs in English for groups of children. The founder also has several stores in Athens. ✉ *Kallisperi 12, at Karyatidon, Acropolis* ☎ *210/922–1044* 🌐 *www.lalaounis-jewelrymuseum.gr* *€4, free Wed. after 3 and Sat. 9–11* ⏲ *Sept.–mid-Aug., Mon. and Thurs.–Sat. 9–4, Wed. 9–9, Sun. 11–4* Ⓜ *Acropolis.*

PLAKA & ANAFIOTIKA ΠΛΑΚΑ & ΑΝΑΦΙΩΤΙΚΑ

Fanning north from the slopes of the Acropolis, the relentlessly picturesque Plaka is the last corner of 19th-century Athens. Set with Byzantine accents provided by churches, the "Old Town" district extends north to Ermou street and eastward to the Leofóros Amalias. During the 1950s and '60s, the area became garish with neon as nightclubs moved in and residents moved out, but locals, architects, and academicians joined forces in the early 1980s to transform a decaying neighborhood. Noisy discos and tacky pensions were closed, streets were changed into pedestrian zones, and old buildings were well restored. At night merrymakers crowd the old tavernas, which feature traditional music and dancing; many have rooftops facing the Acropolis. If you keep off the main tourist shopping streets of Kidathineon and Adrianou, you will be amazed at how peaceful the area can be, even in summer.

Above Plaka is Anafiotika, built on winding lanes that climb up the slopes of the Acropolis, its upper reaches resembling a tranquil village. In classical times it was abandoned because the Delphic Oracle claimed it as sacred ground. The buildings here were constructed by masons from Anafi island, who came to find work in the rapidly expanding Athens of the 1830s and 1840s. They took over this area, whose rocky terrain was similar to Anafi's, hastily erecting homes overnight and taking advantage of an Ottoman law that decreed that if you could put up a structure between sunset and sunrise, the property was yours. Ethiopians, imported as slaves by the Turks during the Ottoman period, stayed on after independence and lived higher up, in caves, on the northern slopes of the Acropolis.

WHAT TO SEE: THE MAIN ATTRACTIONS

9 **Anafiotika.** Set in the shadow of the Acropolis, this is the closest thing you'll find in Athens to the whitewashed villages of the Cycladic islands
Fodor'sChoice ★ featured on travel posters of Greece. It is populated by many descendants of the Anafi stonemasons who arrived from that small island in

STEP-BY-STEP: A WALK THROUGH PLAKA

Take time to explore the side streets graced by old mansions under renovation by the Ministry of Culture. Begin your stroll at the ancient, jewel-like **Monument of Lysikrates**, one of the few remaining supports (334 BC) for tripods (vessels that served as prizes) awarded to the producer of the best play in the ancient Dionyssia festival. Take Herefondos to Plaka's central square, Filomoussou Eterias (or Kidathineon Square), a great place to people-watch.

Up Kidathineon Square is the small but worthy **Greek Folk Art Museum**, with a rich collection ranging from 1650 to the present, including works by the beloved naive artist Theophilos Hatzimichalis. Across from the museum is the 11th- to 12th-century church of Sotira Tou Kottaki, in a tidy garden with a fountain that was the main source of water for the neighborhood until sometime after Turkish rule. Down the block and around the corner on Hatzimichali Aggelou is the **Center of Folk Art and Tradition**. Continue west to the end of that street, crossing Adrianou to Hill, then right on Epimarchou to the striking Church House (on the corner of Scholeiou), once a Turkish police post and home to Richard Church, who led Greek forces in the War of Independence.

At the top of Epimarchou is Ayios Nikolaos Rangavas, an 11th-century church built with fragments of ancient columns. The church marks the edge of the **Anafiotika** quarter, a village smack dab in the middle of the metropolis: its main street, Stratonos, is lined with cottages, occasional murals painted on the stones, and a few shops. Wind your way through the narrow lanes off Stratonos, visiting the churches Ayios Georgios tou Vrachou, Ayios Simeon, and Metamorphosis Sotiros. Another interesting church is 8th-century Ayioi Anargyroi, at the top of Erechtheos. From the church, make your way to Theorias, which parallels the ancient *peripatos* (public roadway) that ran around the Acropolis. The collection at the **Kanellopoulos Museum** spans Athens's history; nearby on Panos you'll pass the Athens University Museum (Old University), the city's first higher-learning institution. Walk down Panos to the **Roman Agora**, which includes the Tower of the Winds and the Fethiye Mosque. Nearby visit the engaging **Museum of Greek Popular Musical Instruments**, where recordings will take you back to the age of *rembetika* (Greek blues). Also next to the Agora is Athens's only remaining Turkish Bathhouse, providing a glimpse into a daily social ritual of Ottoman times. On your way back to Syntagma Square, cut across Mitropolis Square to the impressive 12th-century church of **Little Mitropolis**.

the 19th century to work in the expanding capital. Anafiotika is an enchanting area of simple stone houses, many nestled right into the bedrock, most little changed over the years, others stunningly restored. Cascades of bougainvillea and pots of geraniums and marigolds enliven the balconies and rooftops, and the prevailing serenity is in blissful contrast to the cacophony of modern Athens. You seldom see the residents—only a line of washing hung out to dry, the lace curtains on the tiny houses, or the curl of smoke from a wood-burning fireplace

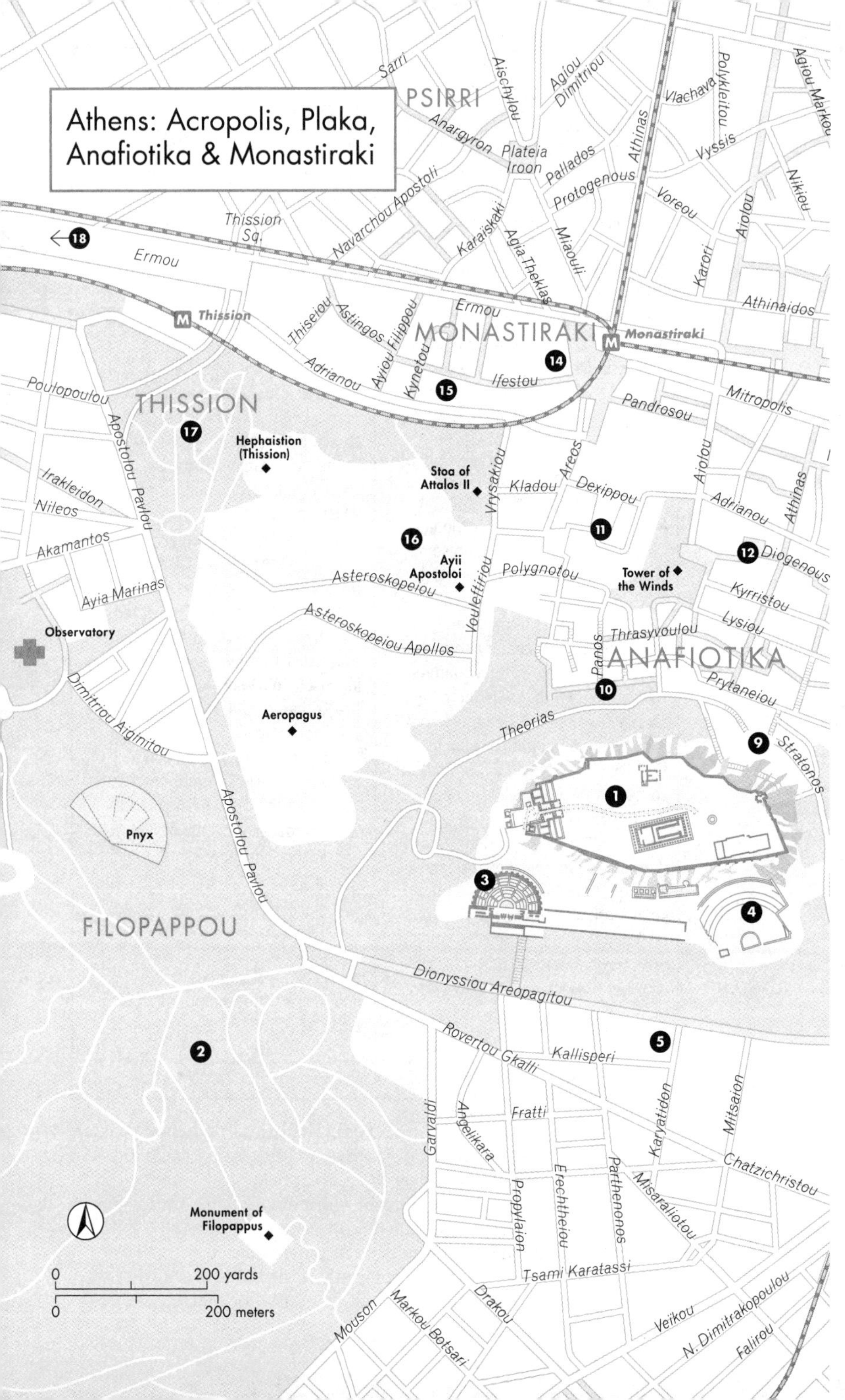
Athens: Acropolis, Plaka, Anafiotika & Monastiraki
PSIRRI
MONASTIRAKI
THISSION
ANAFIOTIKA
FILOPAPPOU
Thission
Monastiraki
Hephaistion (Thission)
Stoa of Attalos II
Ayii Apostoloi
Tower of the Winds
Aeropagus
Observatory
Pnyx
Monument of Filopappus
Sarri
Aischylou
Agiou Dimitriou
Vlachava
Polykleitou
Agiou Markou
Anargyron
Plateia Iroon
Pallados
Athinas
Vyssis
Navarchou Apostoli
Protogenous
Voreou
Nikiou
Thission Sq.
Karaïskaki
Agia Theklas
Miaouli
Aiolou
Karori
Ermou
Athinaidos
Thiseiou
Astingos
Ayiou Filippou
Kynetou
Adrianou
Ifestou
Poulopoulou
Pandrosou
Mitropolis
Apostolou Pavlou
Vrysakiou
Kladou
Areos
Dexippou
Irakleidon
Nileos
Akamantos
Polygnotou
Diogenous
Asteroskopeiou
Vouleftiriou
Kyrristou
Ayia Marinas
Lysiou
Asteroskopeiou Apollos
Thrasyvoulou
Panos
Prytaneiou
Dimitriou Aiginitou
Theorias
Stratonos
Dionyssiou Areopagitou
Rovertou Gkalli
Kallisperi
Garvaldi
Angelikara
Fratti
Karyatidon
Mitsaion
Chatzichristou
Erechtheiou
Parthenonos
Misaraliotou
Propylaion
Tsami Karatassi
Drakou
Mouson
Markou Botsari
Veikou
N. Dimitrakopoulou
Falirou
0
200 yards
0
200 meters
1
2
3
4
5
9
10
11
12
14
15
16
17
18

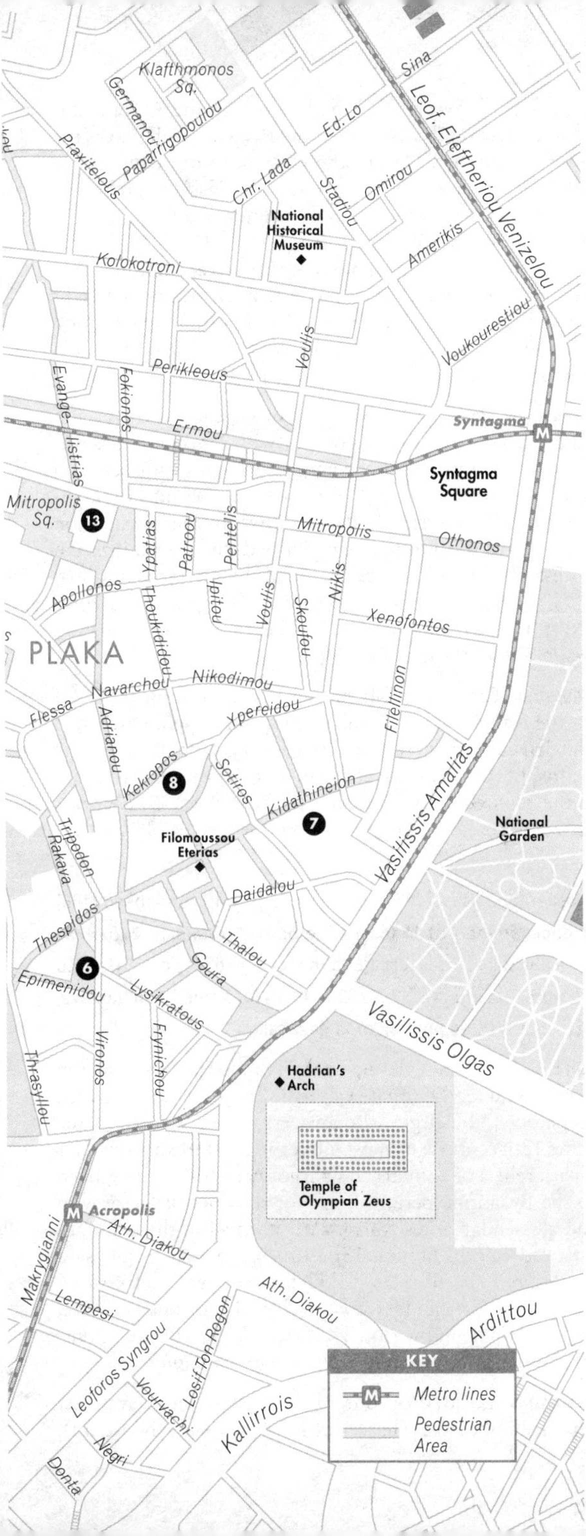

The Acropolis & Environs

- Acropolis 1
- Filopappou 2
- Ilias Lalaounis Jewelry Museum 5
- Odeon of Herodes Atticus 3
- Theater of Dionysus 4

Plaka & Anafiotika

- Anafiotika 9
- Center of Folk Art and Tradition 8
- Greek Folk Art Museum 7
- Kanellopoulos Museum 10
- Little Mitropolis 13
- Monument of Lysikrates 6
- Museum of Greek Popular Musical Instruments 12
- Roman Agora 11

The Ancient Agora, Monastiraki & Thission

- Ancient Agora 16
- Flea Market 15
- Melina Mercouri Cultural Center 18
- Monastiraki Square 14
- Thission 17

Klafthmonos Sq.
Germanou
Paparrigopoulou
Praxitelous
Sina
Ed. Lo
Chr. Lada
Stadiou
Omirou
Leof. Eleftheriou Venizelou
National Historical Museum
Amerikis
Kolokotroni
Voukourestiou
Voulis
Perikleous
Evange-listrias
Fokionos
Ermou
Syntagma
Syntagma Square
Mitropolis Sq.
13
Ypatias
Patroou
Pentelis
Mitropolis
Othonos
Apollonos
Thoukididou
Ipitou
Voulis
Skoufou
Nikis
Xenofontos
PLAKA
Navarchou
Nikodimou
Flessa
Adrianou
Ypereidou
Filellinon
Kekropos
8
Sotiros
Kidathineion
7
Vasilissis Amalias
National Garden
Tripodon
Rakava
Filomoussou Eteriαs
Daidalou
Thespidos
Thalou
6
Goura
Epimenidou
Lysikratous
Vasilissis Olgas
Vironos
Frynichou
Thrasyllou
Hadrian's Arch
Temple of Olympian Zeus
Acropolis
Ath. Diakou
Makrygianni
Lempesi
Ath. Diakou
Arditou
Iosif Ton Rogon
Leoforos Syngrou
Vourvachi
Kallirrois
Negri
Donta

KEY
Metro lines
Pedestrian Area

indicate human presence. Perched on the bedrock of the Acropolis is **Ayios Georgios tou Vrachou** (St. George of the Rock), which marks the southeast edge of the district. One of the most beautiful churches of Athens, it is still in use today. **Ayios Simeon,** a neoclassic church built in 1847 by the settlers, marks the western boundary and contains a copy of a famous miracle-working icon from Anafi, Our Lady of the Reeds. The **Church of the Metamorphosis Sotiros** (Transfiguration), a high-dome 14th-century stone chapel, has a rear grotto carved right into the Acropolis. For those with children, there is a small playground at Stratonos and Vironos. ✉ *On northeast slope of Acropolis rock, Plaka* Ⓜ *Acropolis.*

7 **Greek Folk Art Museum.** Run by the Ministry of Culture, the museum focuses on folk art from 1650 to the present, with especially interesting embroideries, stone and wood carvings, Carnival costumes, and *Karaghiozis* (shadow player figures). Everyday tools—stamps for communion bread, spinning shuttles, raki flasks—attest to the imagination with which Greeks have traditionally embellished the most utilitarian objects. Don't miss the room of uniquely fanciful landscapes and historical portraits by beloved Greek naive painter Theophilos Hatzimichalis, from Mytilini. ✉ *Kidathineon 17, Plaka* ☎ *210/321–3018* 🌐 *www.culture.gr* 🎫 *€3* 🕒 *Tues.–Sun. 10–2.*

10 **Kanellopoulos Museum.** The stately Michaleas Mansion, built in 1884, now showcases the Kanellopoulos family collection. It spans Athens's history from the 3rd century BC to the 19th century, with an emphasis on Byzantine icons, jewelry, and Mycenaean and Geometric vases and bronzes. Note the painted ceiling gracing the first floor. ✉ *Theorias and Panos, Plaka* ☎ *210/321–2313* 🌐 *www.culture.gr* 🎫 *€2* 🕒 *Tues.–Sun. 8:30–3.*

NEED A BREAK?

Stop for an ice-cold frappé (Nescafé frothed with sugar and condensed milk) and a game of backgammon at Ionos (✉ *Geronta 7, Plaka* ☎ *210/322–3139*). If you're craving a good dessert, go to the lovely nearby café Tristrato (✉ *Geronta & Dedalou 34, Plaka* ☎ *210/324–4472*) for some fresh baklava, *galaktoboureko* (custard-filled phyllo), or cheesecake.

13 ★ **Little Mitropolis.** This church snuggles up to the pompous **Mitropolis** (on the northern edge of Plaka), the ornate Cathedral of Athens. Also called Panayia Gorgoepikoos ("the virgin who answers prayers quickly"), the chapel dates to the 12th century; its most interesting features are its outer walls, covered with reliefs of animals and allegorical figures dating from the classical to the Byzantine period. Look for the ancient frieze with zodiac signs and a calendar of festivals in Attica. Most of the paintings inside were destroyed, but the famous 13th- to 14th-century Virgin, said to perform miracles, remains. If you would like to follow Greek custom and light an amber beeswax candle for yourself and someone you love, drop the price of the candle in the slot. ✉ *Mitropolis Sq., Plaka* 🎫 *Free* 🕒 *Hrs depend on services, but usually daily 8–1* Ⓜ *Syntagma.*

6 ★ **Monument of Lysikrates.** Located on one of the ancient city's grandest avenues (which once linked the Theater of Dionysus with the Agora),

this tempietto-like monument is a delightfully elegant jewel of the Corinthian style. It was originally built (335–334 BC) by a *choregos* (theatrical producer) as the support for the tripod (a three-footed vessel used as a prize) he won for sponsoring the best play at the nearby Theater of Dionysus. Six of the earliest Corinthian columns are arranged in a circle on a square base, topped by a marble dome from which rise acanthus leaves. In the 17th century the exceedingly picturesque monument was incorporated into a Capuchin monastery where Byron stayed while writing part of *Childe Harold.* The monument was once known as the Lantern of Demosthenes because it was incorrectly believed to be where the famous orator practiced speaking with pebbles in his mouth in an effort to overcome his stutter. A fresh-looking dirt track at the monument's base is a section of the ancient street of the Tripods (now called Tripodou), where sponsors installed prizes awarded for various athletic or artistic competitions. ✉*Lysikratous and Herefondos, Plaka* Ⓜ*Acropolis.*

3

16 **Museum of Greek Popular Musical Instruments.** An entertaining crash course in the development of Greek music, from regional *dimotika* (folk) to rembetika (blues), this museum has three floors of instruments. Headphones are available so you can appreciate the sounds made by such unusual delights as goatskin bagpipes and discern the differences in tone between the Pontian lyra and Cretan lyra, string instruments often featured on World Music compilations. The museum, which has a pretty shaded courtyard, is home to the Fivos Anoyiannakis Center of Ethnomusicology. ✉*Diogenous 1–3, Plaka* ☎*210/325–0198* 🌐*www.culture.gr* *Free* ⏲*Tues. and Thurs.–Sun. 10–2, Wed. noon–6* Ⓜ*Monastiraki.*

11 ★ **Roman Agora.** The city's commercial center from the 1st century BC to the 4th century AD, the Roman Market was a large rectangular courtyard with a peristyle that provided shade for the arcades of shops. Its most notable feature is the west entrance's Bazaar Gate, or **Gate of Athena Archegetis,** completed around AD 2; the inscription records that it was erected with funds from Julius Caesar and Augustus. Halfway up one solitary square pillar behind the gate's north side, an edict inscribed by Hadrian regulates the sale of oil, a reminder that this was the site of the annual bazaar where wheat, salt, and oil were sold. On the north side of the Roman Agora stands one of the few remains of the Turkish occupation, the **Fethiye (Victory) Mosque.** The eerily beautiful mosque was built in the late 15th century on the site of a Christian church to celebrate the Turkish conquest of Athens and to honor Mehmet II (the Conqueror). During the few months of Venetian rule in the 17th century, the mosque was converted to a Roman Catholic church; now used as a storehouse, it is closed to the public. Three steps in the right-hand corner of the porch lead to the base of the minaret, the rest of which no longer exists.

Fodor'sChoice ★ Surrounded by a cluster of old houses on the western slope of the Acropolis, the world-famous **Tower of the Winds (Aerides)** is the most appealing and well preserved of the Roman monuments of Athens, keeping time since the 1st century BC. It was originally a sundial, water clock, and weather vane topped by a bronze Triton with a metal rod in his hand, which followed the direction of the wind. Its eight sides face the direction of the eight winds into which the compass was divided; expressive reliefs around the tower personify these eight winds, called *I Aerides* (the Windy Ones) by Athenians. Note the north wind, Boreas, blowing on a conch, and the beneficent west wind, Zephyros, scattering blossoms. ✉ *Pelopidas and Aiolou, Plaka* ☎ *210/324–5220* 🌐 *www.culture.gr* 🎫 *€2; €12 joint ticket for all Unification of Archaeological Sites* ⏲ *May–Oct., daily 8–7; Nov.–Apr., daily 8–3* Ⓜ *Monastiraki.*

WATER GAMES

During Ottoman times, every neighborhood in Athens had a *hammam,* or public bathhouse, where men and women met to socialize among the steam rooms and take massages on marble platforms. If you want to see Athens's last remaining example, head to Kyrrestou 8. Sunlight streaming through holes cut on the domed roofs and playing on the colorful tiled floors created a languorous atmosphere here. The pretty 15th-century building now functions as a museum. Admission is free and hours are Wednesday and Sunday 10 to 2.

ALSO WORTH SEEING

8 **Center of Folk Art and Tradition.** Exhibits in the comfortable family mansion of folklorist Angeliki Hatzimichali include detailed costumes, ceramic plates from Skyros, handwoven fabrics and embroideries, and family portraits. ✉ *Hatzimichali Aggelikis 6, Plaka* ☎ *210/324–3987* 🎫 *Free* ⏲ *Sept.–July, Tues.–Fri. 9–1 and 5–9, weekends 9–1.*

NEED A BREAK?

Vyzantino (✉ ***Kidathineon 18, Plaka*** ☎ ***210/322-7368*****) is directly on Plaka's main square—great for people-watching and a good, reasonably priced bite to eat. Try the fish soup, roast potatoes, or baked chicken. Glikis (** ✉ ***Aggelou Geronta 2, Plaka*** ☎ ***210/322-3925*****) and its shady courtyard are perfect for a Greek coffee or ouzo and a** ***mikri pikilia*** **(a small plate of appetizers, including cheese, sausage, olives, and dips).**

THE ANCIENT AGORA, MONASTIRAKI & THISSION
ΑΡΧΑΙΑ ΑΓΟΡΑ, ΜΟΝΑΣΤΗΡΑΚΙ & ΘΗΣΕΙΟ

The Times Square, Piccadilly Circus, and St. Basil's Square of ancient Athens, the Agora was once the focal point of urban life. All the principal urban roads and country highways traversed it; the procession of the great Panthenaea Festival, composed of chariots, magistrates, virgins, priests, and sacrificial animals, crossed it on the way to the Acropolis; the Assembly met here first, before moving to the Pnyx; it was where merchants squabbled over the price of olive oil; the forum where Socrates met with his students; and centuries later, where St. Paul went about his missionary task. Lying just under the citadel of the Acropolis, it was indeed the heart of the ancient city and a general meeting place, where news was exchanged and bargains transacted, alive with all the rumors and gossip of the marketplace. The Agora became important under Solon (6th century BC), founder of Athenian democracy; construction continued for almost a millennium. Today, the site's sprawling confusion of stones, slabs, and foundations is dominated by the best-preserved Doric temple in Greece, the Hephaestion, built during the 5th century BC, and the impressive reconstructed Stoa of Attalos II, which houses the Museum of the Agora Excavations.

You can still experience the sights and sounds of the marketplace in Monastiraki, the former Turkish bazaar area, which retains vestiges of the 400-year period when Greece was subject to the Ottoman Empire. On the opposite side of the Agora is another meeting place of sorts: Thission, a former red-light district. Although it has been one of the most sought-after residential neighborhoods since about 1990, Thission remains a vibrant nightlife district.

TIMING Monastiraki is at its best on Sunday mornings, when the flea market is in full swing; Ermou street, on the other hand, is most interesting Saturday mornings, when it's also most crowded. The ancient Agora has little shade, so in summer it's better to visit the site in early morning or, better, in late afternoon, so you can check out Thission's café scene afterward.

WHAT TO SEE: THE MAIN ATTRACTIONS

16 Fodor's Choice ★ **Ancient Agora.** The commercial hub of ancient Athens, the Agora was once lined with statues and expensive shops, the favorite strolling ground of fashionable Athenians as well as a mecca for merchants and students. The long colonnades offered shade in summer and protection from rain in winter to the throng of people who transacted the day-to-day business of the city, and, under their arches Socrates discussed matters with Plato and Zeno expounded the philosophy of the Stoics (whose name comes from the six *stoa*, or colonnades of the Agora). Besides administrative buildings, it was surrounded by the schools, theaters, workshops, houses, stores, and market stalls of a thriving town. The foundations of some of the main buildings which may be most easily distinguished include the circular Tholos, the principal seat of executive power in the city; the Mitroon, shrine to Rhea, the mother of gods, which included the vast state archives and registry office (*mitroon* is still used today to mean registry); the Bouleterion, where the council met; the Monument of Eponymous Heroes, the Agora's information center, where announcements such as the list of military recruits were hung; and the Sanctuary of the Twelve Gods, a shelter for refugees and the point from which all distances were measured.

The Agora's showpiece was the **Stoa of Attalos II,** where Socrates once lectured and incited the youth of Athens to adopt his progressive ideas on mortality and morality. Today, the Museum of Agora Excavations, this two-story building was first designed as a retail complex and erected in the 2nd century BC by Attalos, a king of Pergamum. The reconstruction in 1953–56 used Pendelic marble and creamy limestone from the original structure. The colonnade, designed for promenades, is protected from the blistering sun and cooled by breezes. The most notable sculptures, of historical and mythological figures from the 3rd and 4th centuries BC, are at ground level outside the museum. In the exhibition hall, chronological displays of pottery and objects from everyday life (note the child's terra-cotta potty) illustrate the settlement of the area from Neolithic times, including fascinating ancient toys and masks.

Take a walk around the site and speculate on the location of Simon the Cobbler's house and shop, which was a meeting place for Socrates and his pupils. The carefully landscaped grounds display a number of plants known in antiquity, such as almond, myrtle, and pomegranate. By standing in the center, you have a glorious view up to the Acropolis. **Ayii Apostoloi** is the only one of the Agora's nine churches to survive, saved because of its location and beauty. Inside, the dome and the altar sit on ancient capitals. Plans displayed in the narthex give an idea of the church's thousand-year-old history.

On the low hill called Kolonos Agoraios in the Agora's northwest corner stands the best-preserved Doric temple in all Greece, the **Hephaestion,** sometimes called the Thission because of its friezes showing the exploits of Theseus. Like the other monuments, it is roped off, but you can walk around it to admire its preservation. A little older than the Parthenon, it is surrounded by 34 columns and is 104 feet in length, and was once filled with sculptures (the only remnant of which is the mutilated frieze, once brightly colored). It never quite makes the impact of the Parthenon, in large part due to the fact that it lacks a noble site and can never be seen from below, its sun-matured columns towering heavenward. The Hephaestion was originally dedicated to Hephaistos, god of metalworkers, and it is interesting to note that metal workshops still exist in this area near Ifestou. Behind the temple, paths cross the northwest slope past archaeological ruins half hidden in deep undergrowth. Here you can sit on a bench and contemplate the same scene that Englishman Edward Dodwell saw in the early 19th century, when he came to sketch antiquities. ✉ *3 entrances: from Monastiraki on Adrianou; from Thission on Apostolou Pavlou; and descending from Acropolis on Ayios Apostoloi, Monastiraki* ☎ *210/321–0185* 🌐 *www.culture.gr* 🎫 *€4; €12 joint ticket for all Unification of Archaeological Sites* ⏲ *May–Oct., daily 8–7; Nov.–Apr., daily 8–5; museum closes ½ hr before site* Ⓜ *Thiseio.*

18 **Melina Mercouri Cultural Center.** Named in honor of the famous *Never on Sunday* Greek actress who became a political figure in the 1980s, this center is installed in the former Poulopoulos hat factory built in 1886. Delightfully, the center gives a rare glimpse of Athens during the 19th century. You can walk through a reconstructed Athens street with facades of neoclassic homes that evoke the civilized elegance of the past, a pharmacy, printing press, dry goods store, *kafeneio* (coffeehouse), and dress shop, all painstakingly fitted out with authentic objects collected by the Greek Literary and Historical Archives. Throughout the year the center showcases temporary exhibitions, usually featuring contemporary Greek art. ✉ *Iraklidon 66a, at Thessalonikis, Thission* ☎ *210/345–2150* 🎫 *Free* ⏲ *Tues.–Sat. 9–1 and 5–9, Sun. 9–1* Ⓜ *Petralona.*

17 **Thission.** This neighborhood, easily accessible by metro and offering a lovely view of the Acropolis, has become one of the liveliest café and restaurant districts in Athens. The area has excellent *rakadika* and *ouzeri*—publike eateries that offer plates of appetizers to go with *raki,* a fiery spirit made from grape must, and the ever-appealing ouzo, as well as barrels of homemade wine. The main strip is the Nileos pedestrian zone across from the ancient Agora entrance, lined with cafés that are cozy in winter and have outdoor tables in summer. The rest of the neighborhood is quiet, an odd mix of mom-and-pop stores and dilapidated houses that are slowly being renovated; take a brief stroll along Akamantos (which becomes Galatias) around the intersections of Dimofontos or Aginoros, or down Iraklidon, to get a feel for the quarter's past. ✉ *West of ancient Agora, Apostolou Pavlou, and Akamantos, Thission* Ⓜ *Thiseio.*

IN & AROUND THE AGORA

After browsing through the market stalls, enter the Ancient Agora at the corner of Kinetou and Adrianou (the latter runs parallel to Ifestou). Be sure to visit the site's Museum of Agora Excavations, which offers a fascinating glimpse of everyday life in the ancient city. Exit at the site's opposite end onto Dionyssiou Areopagitou, crossing the boulevard to the Thission quarter, a lively area with neoclassical homes overlooking trendy cafés and home to the noted Melina Mercouri Cultural Center, where exhibits re-create the streets of Athens during different epochs.

3

NEED A BREAK?

For a fancy coffee (think espresso mixed with sambuca) and sweet crepes (banana and chocolate hazelnut), stop at Athinaion Politeia (✉ *Akamantos 1 and Apostolou Pavlou, Thission* ☎ *210/341–3795*), a restored mansion where you can watch the crowds on Apostolou Pavlou. Thirtysomething hipsters hold court here, telling raucous stories that spill into laughter, making you feel like you're in the middle of the best party in town.

ALSO WORTH SEEING

15 **Flea Market.** Here is where the chaos, spirit, and charm of Athens turn into a feast for the senses. The Sunday morning market has combined sight, sound, and scent into a strangely alluring little world where everything is for sale: 1950s-era scuba masks, old tea sets, antique sewing machines, old tobacco tins, gramophone needles, old matchboxes, and lacquered eggs. Haggle, no matter how low the price. ✉ *Along Ifestou, Kynetou, and Adrianou, Monastiraki* Ⓜ *Monastiraki.*

14 **Monastiraki Square.** The square takes its name from the small **Panagia Pantanassa Church,** commonly called Monastiraki (Little Monastery). It once flourished as an extensive convent, perhaps dating to the 10th century, which stretched from Athinas to Aiolou. The nuns took in poor people, who earned their keep weaving the thick textiles known as *abas.* The buildings were destroyed during excavations and the train (and later metro) line construction that started in 1896. The convent's basic basilica form, now recessed a few steps below street level, was altered through a poor restoration in 1911, when the bell tower was

added. The square's focal point, the 18th-century **Tzistarakis Mosque** (✉*Areos 1, Monastiraki* ☎*210/324–2066* 🎫*€2* ⏲*Wed.–Mon. 9–2:30*), houses a ceramics collection that is beautifully designed, with the exhibits handsomely lighted and labeled. The mosque's creator, a newly appointed Turkish civil governor, knocked down a column from the Temple of Olympian Zeus to make lime for the mosque. Punished by the sultan for his audacity, he was also blamed by Athenians for an ensuing plague; it was believed the toppling of a column released epidemics and disasters from below Earth. ✉*South of Ermou and Athinas junction, Monastiraki.*

NEED A BREAK?

On Mitropoleos off Monastiraki Square are a handful of counter-front places selling souvlaki—grilled meat rolled in a pita with onions, *tzatziki* (yogurt-garlic dip), and tomatoes—the best bargain in Athens. Make sure you specify either a souvlaki sandwich or a "souvlaki plate," an entire meal. Hands down the best kebab in town is Thanassis (✉*Mitropoleos 69, Monastiraki* ☎*210/324–4705*), which is always crowded with Greeks who crave the specially spiced ground meat.

FROM CENTRAL ATHENS TO NATIONAL ARCHAEOLOGICAL MUSEUM ΑΘΗΝΑ (ΚΕΝΤΡΟ) ΤΟ ΕΘΝΙΚΟ ΑΡΧΑΙΟΛΟΓΙΚΟ ΜΟΥΣΕΙΟ

Numbers in the text correspond to numbers in the margin and on the Syntagma Square, Kolonaki, and Exarchia map.

Downtown Athens is an unlikely combination of the squalid and the grand: the cavernous, chaotic Central Market, which replaced the bazaar in Monastiraki when it burned down in 1885, is 10 minutes from the elegant, neoclassic Old University complex. The surrounding area is filled with the remains of the 19th-century mansions that once made Athens world renowned as a charming city. Some of these are crumbling into the streets; others, like the exquisite mansion that has been converted into the Numismatic Museum (once the grand abode of Heinrich Schliemann, discoverer of Troy) have regained their lost loveliness. Such buildings rub shoulders with incense-scented, 12th-century Byzantine churches as well as some of the city's most hideous 1970s apartment blocks, many of which are occupied by Greece's growing migrant population. The mix has become more heady as artists and fashionistas move to the neighborhoods of Psirri and Gazi and transform long-neglected warehouses into galleries, nightclubs, and ultra-chic restaurants.

At the western edge of all this is the wide, green expanse of Kerameikos, the main cemetery in ancient Athens until Sulla destroyed the city in 86 BC. The name is associated with the modern word "ceramic": in the 12th century BC the district was populated by potters who used the abundant clay from the languid Iridanos River to make funerary urns and grave decorations. Kerameikos contains the foundations of two ancient monuments: the Dipylon Gate, where visitors entered the city, and the Sacred Gate, used for both the pilgrimage to the Eleusinian rites and for the Panathenaic procession in which the tunic for the statue of Athena was carted to the Acropolis.

Heading back east, a good 10 blocks directly north of the Old University complex, the glory that was Athens continues at the city's legendary National Archaeological Museum. One of the most exciting collections of Greek antiquities in the world, this is a must-do for any travelers to Athens, nay, Greece. Here are the sensational finds made by Heinrich Schliemann, discoverer of Troy and father of modern archaeology, in the course of his excavations of the royal tombs on the Homeric site of Mycenae in the 1870s. Here, too, are world-famous bronzes such as the *Jockey of Artemision* and a bronze of Poseidon throwing a trident (or is it Zeus hurling a thunderbolt?). An added treat is the neighborhood the museum presides over: Exarchia, a bohemian district that is mentioned in hundreds of Greek folk songs and novels. The area evokes strong feelings in every Athenian for here, in 1973, the students of Athens Polytechnic rose up in protest against Greece's hated military dictatorship. The colonels crushed the uprising and tanks killed many students, but the protests led to the junta's fall the following year. Today, the neighborhood still bubbles with rebellious energy; students, intellectuals, and anarchists often fill its many cafés and tavernas, debating the latest in domestic and global affairs.

WHAT TO SEE: THE MAIN ATTRACTIONS

22 **Central Market.** The market runs along Athinas: on one side are open-air stalls selling fruit and vegetables at the best prices in town, although wily merchants may slip overripe items into your bag. At the corner of Armodiou, shops stock live poultry and rabbits. Across the street, in the huge covered market built in 1870, the surrealistic composition of suspended carcasses and shimmering fish on marble counters emits a pungent odor that is overwhelming on hot days. The shops at the north end of the market, to the right on Sofokleous, sell the best cheese, olives, halvah, bread, and cold cuts, including *pastourma* (spicy cured beef), available in Athens. Small restaurants serving *patsa*, or tripe soup, dot the market; these stay open until almost dawn and are popular stops with weary clubbers trying to ease their hangovers. ✉ *Athinas, Central Market* ⏲ *Weekdays and Sat. morning* Ⓜ *Monastiraki.*

NEED A BREAK?

For a true taste of bygone Athens, don't miss Krinos (✉ *Aiolou 87, Central Market* ☎ *210/321–6852*), an endearingly old-timey café that serves Athens's best *loukoumades*—irresistible, doughnutlike fritters sprinkled with cinnamon and drizzled with a honeyed syrup based on a Smyrna recipe. Krinos has been serving the treat since it opened its doors in the 1920s and also makes excellent *boughatsa* (cream pies), *rizogalo* (rice pudding), and sandwiches; it is closed Sunday. Squeeze into one of the many tables and enjoy your treat with the old gents and ladies who have been regulars for decades.

20 **Kerameikos Cemetery.** From the 7th century BC onward, Kerameikos was the smart cemetery of ancient Athens. During succeeding ages cemeteries were superimposed on the ancient one until the latter was

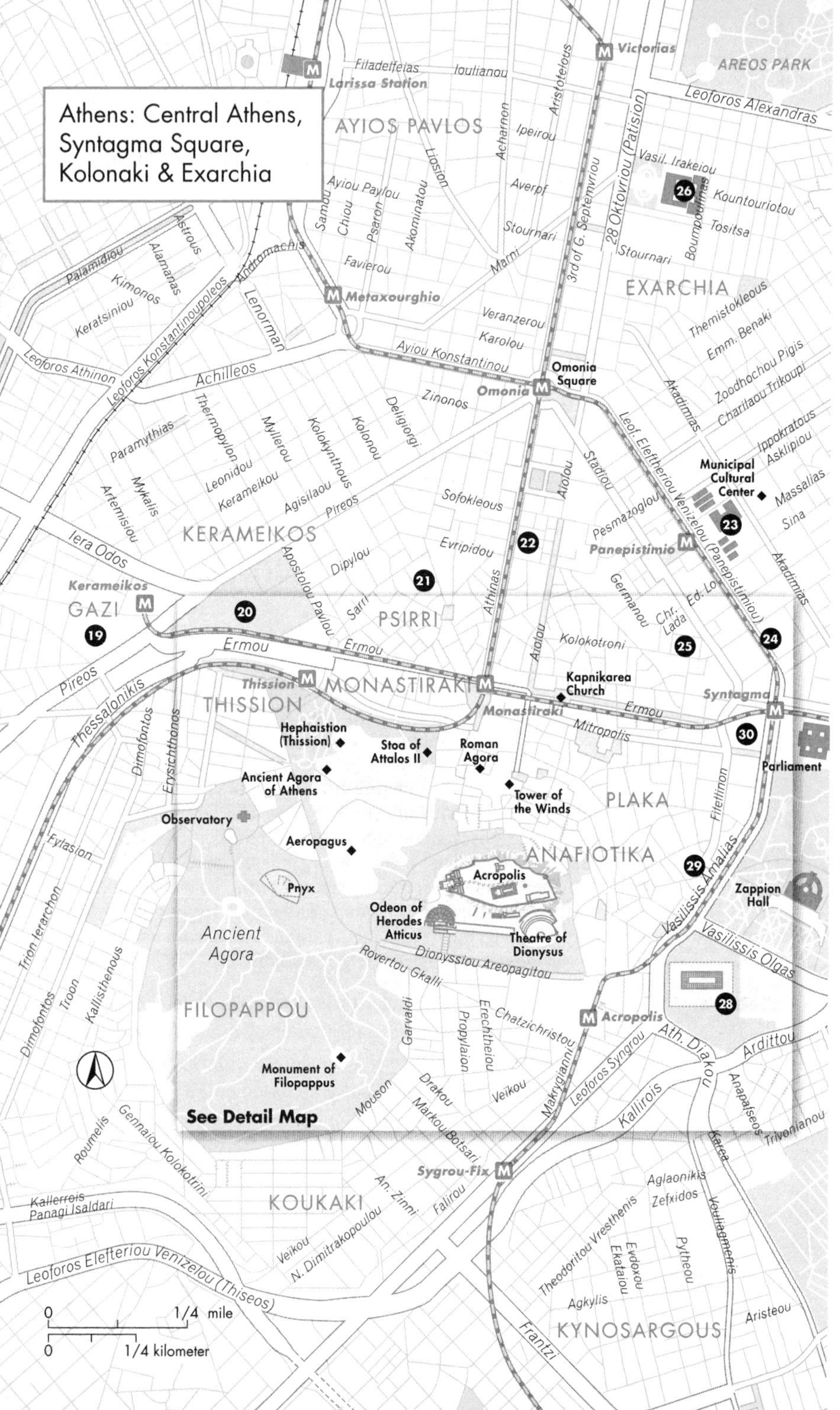

Athens: Central Athens, Syntagma Square, Kolonaki & Exarchia
AYIOS PAVLOS
EXARCHIA
KERAMEIKOS
GAZI
PSIRRI
MONASTIRAKI
THISSION
PLAKA
ANAFIOTIKA
FILOPAPPOU
KOUKAKI
KYNOSARGOUS
AREOS PARK
Victorias
Larissa Station
Metaxourghio
Omonia
Omonia Square
Panepistimio
Kerameikos
Thission
Monastiraki
Syntagma
Acropolis
Sygrou-Fix
Municipal Cultural Center
Kapnikarea Church
Parliament
Hephaistion (Thission)
Stoa of Attalos II
Roman Agora
Ancient Agora of Athens
Tower of the Winds
Observatory
Aeropagus
Pnyx
Acropolis
Odeon of Herodes Atticus
Theatre of Dionysus
Zappion Hall
Ancient Agora
Monument of Filopappus
See Detail Map
0 1/4 mile
0 1/4 kilometer
19
20
21
22
23
24
25
26
28
29
30

From Central Athens to the National Archaeological Museum ▼

Syntagma Square to Kolonaki ▼

discovered in 1861. From the main entrance, you can still see remains of the **Makra Teixoi** (Long Walls of Themistocles), which ran to Piraeus, and the largest gate in the ancient world, the **Dipylon Gate,** where visitors entered Athens. The walls rise to 10 feet, a fraction of their original height (up to 45 feet). Here was also the **Sacred Gate,** used by pilgrims headed to the mysterious rites in Eleusis and by those who participated in the Panathenaic procession, which followed the Sacred Way. Between the two gates are the foundations of the **Pompeion,** the starting point of the Panathenaic procession. It is said the courtyard was large enough to fit the ship used in the procession. On the **Street of Tombs,** which branches off the Sacred Way, plots were reserved for affluent Athenians. A number of the distinctive *stelae* (funerary monuments) remain, including a replica of the marble relief of Dexilios, a knight who died in the war against Corinth (394 BC); he is shown on horseback preparing to spear a fallen foe. To the left of the site's entrance is the **Oberlaender Museum,** also known as the Kerameikos Museum, whose displays include sculpture, terra-cotta figures, and some striking red-and-black-figured pottery. The extensive grounds of Kerameikos are marshy in some spots; in spring, frogs exuberantly croak their mating songs near magnificent stands of lilies. ✉ *Ermou 148, Kerameikos/Gazi* ☎ *210/346–3552* *Site and museum €2; €12 joint ticket for all Unification of Archaeological Sites* ⏲ *May–Oct., daily 7:30–7; Nov.–Apr., daily 8:30–3* Ⓜ *Kerameikos.*

ROUSED TO RALLY

From the terrace near the tombs, Pericles gave his celebrated speech honoring those who died in the early years of the Peloponnesian War, thus persuading many to sign up for a campaign that ultimately wiped out thousands of Athenians.

26 Fodor's Choice ★ **National Archaeological Museum.** The classic culture which was the grandeur of the Greek world no longer exists. It died, for civilizations are mortal, but it left indelible markers in all domains, most particularly in art—and many of its greatest achievements in sculpture and painting are housed here in the most important museum in Greece. Artistic highlights from every period of ancient Greek civilization, from Neolithic to Roman times, make this a treasure trove beyond compare. With a massive renovation scheduled to be completed in 2008, works that have languished in storage for decades are now on view, reorganized displays are accompanied by enriched English-language information, and the panoply of ancient Greek art appears more spectacular than ever.

The museum's most celebrated display is the **Mycenaean Antiquities.** Here are the stunning gold treasures from Heinrich Schliemann's 1876 excavations of Mycenae's royal tombs: the funeral mask of a bearded king, once thought to be the image of Agamemnon but now believed to be much older, from about the 15th century BC; a splendid silver bull's-head libation cup; and the 15th-century BC Vaphio Goblets, masterworks in embossed gold. Mycenaeans were famed for their carving in miniature, and an exquisite example is the ivory statuette of two curvaceous mother goddesses, each with a child nestled on her lap.

Withheld from the public since they were damaged in the 1999 earthquakes, but not to be missed, are the beautifully restored **frescoes from Santorini,** delightful murals depicting daily life in Minoan Santorini. Along with the treasures from Mycenae, these wall paintings are part of the museum's Prehistoric Collection.

SHOELESS IN ATHENS

Some of the museum's most moving displays are those of funerary architecture: the spirited 2nd-century relief of a rearing stallion held by a black groom, which exemplifies the transition from classical to Hellenistic style, the latest period in the museum's holdings. Among the most famous sculptures in this collection is the humorous marble group of a nude *Aphrodite* getting ready to slap an advancing Pan with a sandal, while Eros floats overhead and grasps one of Pan's horns.

Other stars of the museum include the works of Geometric and Archaic art (10th to 6th century BC), and kouroi and funerary stelae (8th to 5th century BC), among them the stelae of the warrior Aristion signed by Aristokles, and the unusual *Running Hoplite* (a hoplite was a Greek infantry soldier). The collection of classical art (5th to 3rd century BC) contains some of the most renowned surviving ancient statues: the bareback *Jockey of Artemision,* a 2nd-century BC Hellenistic bronze salvaged from the sea; from the same excavation, the bronze *Artemision Poseidon* (some say Zeus), poised and ready to fling a trident (or thunderbolt?); and the *Varvakios Athena,* a half-size marble version of the gigantic gold-and-ivory cult statue that Pheidias erected in the Parthenon.

Light refreshments are served in a lower ground-floor café, which opens out to a patio and sculpture garden. ✉*28 Oktovriou (Patission) 44, Exarchia* ☎*210/821–7717* 🌐*www.culture.gr* 🎫*€6* ⏲*Apr. 15–Oct. 15, Mon. 1–7:30, Tues.–Sun. 8–7:30; Oct. 16–Apr. 14, Mon. 1–7:30, Tues.–Fri. 8:30–7:30, weekends 8:30–3. Closed Jan. 1, Mar. 25, May 1, Easter Sun., Dec. 25–26; open reduced hrs other holidays* Ⓜ*Victorias, then 10-min walk.*

25 **National Historical Museum.** After making the rounds of the ancient sites, you might think that Greek history ground to a halt when the Byzantine empire collapsed. A visit to this gem of a museum will fill in the gaps, often vividly, as with Lazaros Koyevina's copy of Eugene Delacroix's *Massacre of Chios.* Paintings, costumes, and assorted artifacts from small arms to flags and ships' figureheads are arranged in a chronological display tracing Greek history from the mid-16th century and the Battle of Lepanto through World War II and the Battle of Crete. A small gift shop near the entrance has unusual souvenirs, like a deck of cards featuring Greece's revolutionary heroes. ✉*Stadiou 13, Syntagma Sq.* ☎*210/323–7617* 🎫*€3, free Sun.* ⏲*Tues.–Sun. 9–2* Ⓜ*Syntagma.*

24 **Numismatic Museum Iliou Melathron.** Even those uninterested in coins might want to visit this museum for a glimpse of the former home of Heinrich Schliemann, who excavated Troy and Mycenae in the 19th century. In this exquisite neoclassical mansion, seemingly haunted by

Fodor's Choice ★

Continued on page 119

CLOSE UP

When Greece Worshipped Beauty

As visitors to the many treasure-filled galleries of the National Archaeological Museum will discover, Greek art did not spring in a blinding flash like Athena fully modeled from the brain of Zeus. The earliest ceramic cup in a Greek museum, said by legend to have been molded after the breast of Helen of Troy, is a libel on that siren's reputation: it is coarse, clumsy, and rough. But fast-forward a millennium or so and you arrive at the Golden Age, when Greek art forevermore set the standard for ideals of beauty, grace, and realism in Western art, when the Parthenon gave proof of an architectural genius unique in history. The time was the 5th century BC, about 2,000 years before the Italian Renaissance. Just as that glorious age flourished, thanks to Italian city-states, so did ancient Greece reach its apogee in its cities. And it was in Athens that Greek citizens realized they could reveal the free blossoming of the human being and respect the individualistic character of men and women through art and architecture. This affirmation was largely the work of one man, Pericles, the famous Athenian general and builder of the Parthenon. During his day, Greek artistic genius fed on a physical ideal—spectacularly represented in the culture with its hero worship of athletes—as it did on religion, and religion itself, far from being an abstraction, was an anthropomorphic reflection of a passion for physical beauty.

The inspiration, however, would not have sufficed to ensure the grandeur of Greek art had it not been served by a perfection of technique. Whoever created any object had to know to perfection every element of his model, whether it was a man or woman or god or goddess. Witness the marvels of the sculpture of the age, such as the *Delphi Charioteer,* the Parthenon frieze figures, or the *Venus de Milo.* Basically the cult of the god was the cult of beauty. The women of Sparta, desirous of having handsome children, adorned their bedchambers with statues of male and female beauties. Beauty contests are not an invention of modern times. The Greeks organized them as early as the 7th century BC, until Christianity came to frown on such practices.

In like form, architecture was also the reflection of the personality of this Greek world. Thus, when we note the buildings of the Acropolis, we note the Doric order is all mathematics; the Ionian, all poetry. The first expresses proud reserve, massive strength, and severe simplicity; the second, suppleness, sensitivity, and elegance. No matter what the order, the column was the binding force—the absolute incarnation of reason in form. Study the columns of the Parthenon and you quickly realize that the Greeks did not propose to represent reality with its clutter of details; their aim was to seize the essence of things and let its light shine forth.

But it would be false to conclude, as certain romantic spirits have done, that the Greeks were mere aesthetes, lost in ecstasy before abstract beauty and subordinating their lives to it. Quite the reverse: it was the art of living which, for the Greeks, was the supreme art. A healthy utilitarian inclination combined with their worship of beauty to such an extent that art within their homes was not an idle ornament, but had a functional quality related to everyday life.

Still from Warner Brother's movie *300*

3

THE MARCH OF GREEK HISTORY

The 21st-century Greeks are one of the oldest peoples on the face of the earth: they have seen *everything*. While Greeks are now subjected to an annual full-scale invasion by an army of camera-toting legions, their ancestors were conquered by numberless encroachers for the past four millennia. During this epic time-span, Greece was forged, torn asunder, and remade into the vital nation it is today.

Paradox is a Greek word and highly applicable to Greek history. Since the rehabilitation of Homer by Hermann Schliemann's excavations, Agamemnon, Great King of Mycenae, and the earliest heroes of ancient Greece have moved from legend into history. Today, the remote 13th century BC sometimes appears more familiar than most Greek events in better documented later periods. Not that subsequent ages were any duller—the one epithet that is utterly unsuitable in Greece—but they lacked the master touch of the great epic poet.

However, while ancient temples still evoke Homer, Sophocles, Plato, and the rest, today's Greeks are not just the watered-down descendants of a noble people living in the ruined halls of their ancestors. From time immemorial the Greeks have been piling the present on top of the past, blithely building, layering, and overlapping their more than 30 centuries of history to create the amazing fabric that is modern Greece.

(top) Gerald Butler as King Leonidas in the 2006 film *300*

Keros-Syros culture of The Cyclades

2000 First palaces built in Crete

2300 BC 2100 BC 1900 BC 1700

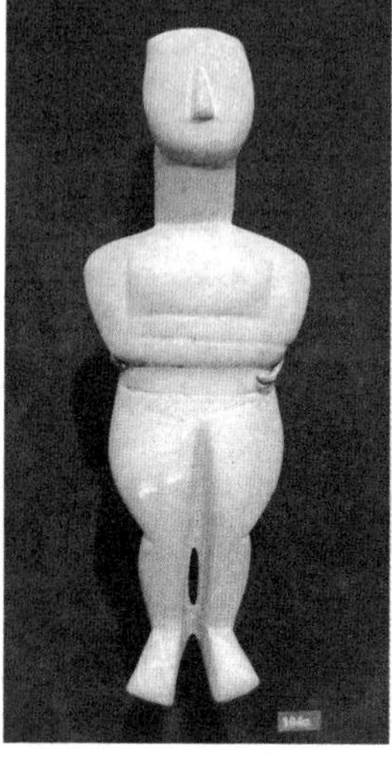

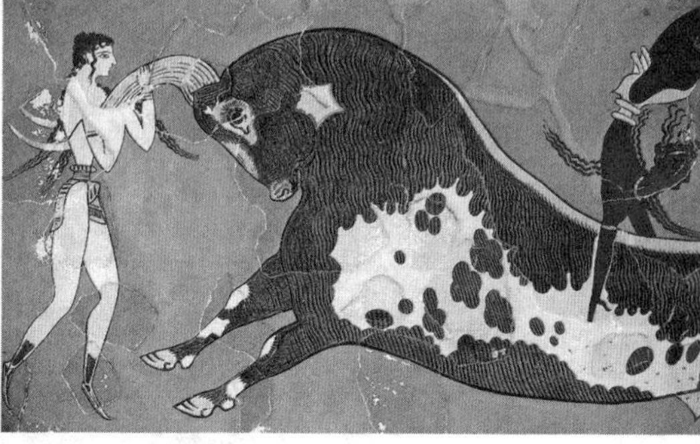

(top left) Cycladic female figure; (top right) Bull fresco from Minoan ruins on Crete; (bottom) Fresco of ladies from Minoan ruins on Crete

3000–1900 BC

CYCLADIC ORIGINS

Greece is far older than the glory days of the Classical age—the 5th-century BC—which gave us the Parthenon. It has been inhabited almost continuously for the past 13,000 years. Tools made on the island of Milos around 11,000 BC have been found in a cave in the Peloponnese, suggesting that even in those long-ago reaches of history Greeks were sailing across the sparkling Aegean between islands and mainland shores. Around 3000 BC, about the time cultures were flourishing in Egypt and Mesopotamia, small cities were springing up throughout the Cycladic islands—the first major Greek settlements, today known as the Keros-Syros culture. These early Cycladic people lived by sea and, as the need for protection from invaders intensified, in fortified towns in the uplands. Objects found in mass graves tell us they made tools, crockery, and jewelry. The most remarkable remnants of Cycladic civilization are flat, two-dimensional female idols, strikingly modern in appearance.

- Museum of Cycladic Art (Goulandris Foundation), Athens

2000–1150 BC

MINOAN BRONZE AGE

By 2000 BC, a great culture—Europe's oldest state (as opposed to mere tribal groupings)—had taken root on the island of Crete. What these inhabitants of Greece's southernmost island actually called themselves is not known; archaeologist Sir Arthur Evans named the civilization Minoan after Minos, the legendary king of the famous labyrinth who probably ruled from the magnificent palace of Knossos. Their warehouses were filled with spices traded throughout the Mediterranean, and royal chambers were decorated with sophisticated art—statuary, delicate rythons, and,

(top) Replica of Trojan Horse; (top, right) Lion Gate at Mycenae; (bottom) Mycenaen gold funeral mask

most evocative of all, alluring frescoes depicting fanciful secular scenes as well as the goddesses who dominated the matriarchal Minoan religion. A system of writing, known as Linear A and Linear B script, appears on seal stones. The cause of the downfall of the Minoans remains a mystery—political unrest, invasions from the mainland, a volcano on nearby Santorini and subsequent earthquakes? Enter the mainland Mycenaeans.

- Palace of Knossos, Crete
- Archaeological Museum, Heraklion

1600–1100 BC

THE MYCENAEANS

By the 14th century BC, the Mycenaeans wielded power throughout main-land Greece and much of the rest of the known world, from Sicily to Asia Minor. Their capital, Mycenae (in the Peloponnese), was one of several great cities they built around palaces filled with art and stories of the new Olympian gods and fortified heavily. As civilized as the Mycenaeans were, they were also warlike. Their exploits inspired the *Iliad* and *Odyssey*, and Agamemnon, legendary hero of the 12th-century Trojan Wars—the starting point in the endless ping-pong match between Europe and Asia—is said to have ruled from Mycenae. For all their might, the Mycenaeans fell into decline sometime around 1100 BC. Soon the Dorians, from northern Greece, moved south, pushing the Mycenaeans into a dark age during which art and writing were lost. But Greeks who sailed across the Aegean to flee the Dorians established Ephesus, Smyrna, and other so-called Ionian cities in Asia Minor, where a rich culture soon flourished.

- Lion Gate, Mycenae, the Argolid
- Cyclopean Walls, Tiryns, the Argolid
- Nestor's Palace, Messinia

First Pan-Hellenic Olympics held

800 BC | 700 BC | 600 BC | 500

(top) Ancient vase depicting Olympic athletes; (left) Bust of Homer; (right) Statue of King Leonidas

1100–800 BC

THE AGE OF HOMER

By the 8th century BC, Greeks were living in hundreds of *poleis*, city-states that usually comprised a walled city that governed the surrounding countryside. Most poleis were built around a raised acropolis and an agora (a marketplace), as well temples and often a gymnasium; limited power lay with a group of elite citizens—the first inklings of democracy. As the need for resources grew, Greeks began to establish colonies in Sicily and Gaul and on the Black Sea, and with this expansion came contact with the written word that laid the foundations of the Greek alphabet. Two essential elements of Greek culture led the new Greek renaissance that forged a nation's identity: Homeric legends began circulating, recounting the deeds of heroes and gods, and athletes showed off their strength and valor at the Olympic Games, first staged in 776 BC.—Participation in these games meant support of Hellenism—the concept of a united Greece.

- Greek colonies set up in Asia Minor, Sicily, and southern Italy
- Persian Invasions
- Marathon Tomb, Marathon, Attica
- Archaeological Museum, Marathon, Attica

499–449 BC

PERSIAN INVASIONS

The most powerful poleis, Athens and Sparta, would soon become two of history's most famous rivals—but for a brief time in the fifth century, they were allies united against a common foe, the Persians, who, in 490 bc, launched an attack against Athens. Though far outnumbered, the Athenians dealt the Persians a crippling blow on the Marathon plain. Ten years later, the Persians attacked again, this time with a massive army and navy commanded by King Xerxes. The Spartan King Leonidas and his "300"—the men of his royal guard (along with an unknown number of

(top) Still from Warner Brothers movie *300;* (top right) Bust of Pericles; (right) Relief sculpture fragment depicting the King of Persia; (bottom) Greek helmet

slaves, or Helots)—sacrificed their lives to hold the Persians off at Thermopylae, allowing the Athenians time to muster ships and sink much of the Persian fleet. Xerxes returned the following year, in the summer of 479 bc, to sack Athens, but an army drawn from city-states throughout Greece and under the command of Pausanias, a Spartan general, defeated the Persians and brought the Persian Wars to an end.

- Marathon Tomb, Marathon, Attica

460–431 BC PERICLES' GOLDEN AGE

Athens thrived for much of the fifth century BC under the leadership of the enlightened statesman Pericles. The city became the center of the Hellenic world—and the cradle of Western civilization—due to a series of revolutionary events. The Parthenon was built; Socrates engaged in the dialogues that, recorded by Plato, became the basis of European thought; Aeschylus, Aristophanes, Euripides, and Sophocles wrote dramas; Praxiteles sculpted his masterpieces; and Herodotus became the "father of history."

- The Parthenon, Athens
- Sanctuary of Apollo, Delphi

431–404 BC PELOPONNESIAN WAR

Athens was leader of the Delian League, a confederation of 140 Greek city-states, and Sparta headed the Peloponnesian League, a formidable alliance of city-states of southern and central Greece. From 431 to 404 bc these two powers engaged in battles that plunged much of Greece into bloodshed. Sparta emerged the victor after Athens suffered two devastating defeats: the destruction of a massive force sent to attack Syracuse, a Spartan ally in Sicily, and the sinking of the Athenian fleet.

- Archaeological Museum, Sparta, Laconia

Greece becomes Roman Achaia

293 Thessaloniki made into a capital of the Roman Empire

0 200 400

(top) Alexander the Great listening to his tutor Aristotle; (top right) Byzantine basilica; (bottom) Alexander the Great on horseback

338 BC–323 AD

ALEXANDER THE GREAT

In the years following the Peloponnesian War, Sparta, Athens, and an emerging power, Thebes, battled for control of Greece. Eventually, the victors came from the north: Macedonians led by Philip II defeated Athens in the Battle of Chaeronea in 338 bc. Philip's son, Alexander the Great, who had been tutored by Aristotle, quickly unified Greece and conquered Persia, most of the rest of the Middle East, and Egypt. In the ensuing 11 years of unparalleled triumphs he spread Greek culture from the Nile to the Indus. Alexander died in Babylon of a mysterious illness in 323 bc and the great empire he amassed soon fell asunder. Roman armies began moving toward Athens, Greece became the Roman province of Achaia in 27 bc, and for the next 300 years of peace Rome readily adapted Greek art, architecture, and thought. This cultural influence during the Pax Romana compensated for the loss of a much abused independence.

- Birthplace, Pella, Central Macedonia
- Royal Tombs, Vergina, Central Macedonia
- Roman Agora, Athens Archaeological Museum, Marathon, Attica

324–1204 AD

BYZANTINE GREECE

With the division of the Roman Empire into East and West, Greece came under the control of the Eastern Empire, administered from the Greek city of Byzantium (later Constantinople) where Emperor Constantine moved the capital, in 324. The Empire had embraced Christianity as its official religion and Byzantium became the seat of the Eastern Orthodox Church, which led to the Great Christian Schism of 1094. Byzantium's Greek culture evolved into a distinct architectural style and religious art forms best represented by mosaics and icon paintings. For centuries Byzantine Greece fended off invasions from Vi-

841 Parthenon transformed into cathedral

Fourth Crusade invades Greece

800 1000 1200 1400

(top) Gold leaf mosaics; (left) Palace of the Grand Masters, Rhodes; (right) Portrait of Mehmet II

sigoths, Vandals, Slavs, Muslims, Bulgars, and Normans. As an ally of the empire, the Republic of Venice developed trading strongholds in Greece in the 11th century. Interested in the control of maritime routes, the Venetians built a network of fortresses and fortified towns along the Ionian coast of Greece. Venice later extended its possessions over several Aegean islands and Crete, which it held until 1669.

- Monastery of Daphni, Attica
- Mt. Athos, Central Macedonia
- Meteora Monasteries, Thessaly

1204–1453 AD

CRUSADERS AND FEUDAL GREECE

The Byzantine Empire, and Greece with it, finally succumbed to Crusaders who pillaged Constantinople in 1204. Frankish knights create vassal feudal states in Thessalonica, the Peloponnese, and Rhodes, while other short-lived kingdoms in Epirus and on the shores of the Black Sea became the refuge of Byzantine Greek populations. Soon, however, a new threat loomed as Ottoman Turks under Sultan Mehmet II began marching into Byzantine lands, occupying most of Asia Minor, Macedonia, and Thessaly.

- Churches of Thessaloniki, Central Macedonia

1453–1821

OTTOMAN AGE

Constantinople fell to the Ottomans in 1453, and by the 16th century Sultan Suleyman the Magnificent had expanded his Empire from Vienna through the Middle East. Greece was the stage of many battles between East and West. In 1687, Athens was besieged and the Parthenon heavily damaged by Venetian bombardments. Only in 1718 all of Greece was conceded to the Ottoman Empire, just in time for a resurgence of Hellenist culture in Europe, Neoclassicism in the arts, and a brand-new interest in Greek archaeology.

- Aslan Mosque, Ioannina, Epirus

(top) 2004 Olympic Greek stadium; (far left) Portrait of Lord Byron; (left) Portrait of Eleftherios Venizelos

1821–1935 AD

A GREEK NATION

Ottoman rulers allowed a degree of autonomy to Greece yet uprisings became increasingly fierce. In 1821, the bloody War of Independence, which started as a successful rebellion in the Peloponnese, spread across the land. Western Europeans, including the Romantic poet Lord Byron, rushed to the Greek cause. After years of setbacks and civil wars, Britain, France, and Russia mediated with the Ottomans to establish Greece as an autonomous region. Otto of Bavaria, only 17, was named sovereign of Greece in 1831, the first of the often-unpopular monarchs who reigned intermittently until 1974. Public favor soon rested with prime ministers like Eleftherios Venizelos, who colonized Crete in 1908. In 1919 Venizelos, a proponent of a "Greater Greece," sought to conquer ethnic Greek regions of the new Turkish nation, but his forces were defeated and hundreds of thousands, on both sides, were massacred. The subsequent peace decreed the massive population exchange of two million people between the two countries, resulting in the complete expulsion of Greeks from Asia Minor, after 3,000 years of history.

- Achilleion Palace, Corfu
- National Garden, Athens

1936–PRESENT

WAR AND THE NEW REPUBLIC

Greece emerged from the savagery of Axis occupation during World War II in the grip of civil war, with the Communist party battling right-wing forces. The right controlled the Greek government until 1963, when Georgios Papandreou became prime minister and proposed democratic reforms that were soon put down by a repressive colonels' junta led by Georgios Papadopoulos. A new republic was proclaimed in 1973, and a new constitution replaced the monarchy with an elective government—democratic ideals born in Greece more than 2,000 years earlier.

- 2004 Olympic Stadium, Athens

the spirit of the great historian, you can see more than 600,000 coins; displays range from the archaeologist's own coin collection to 4th-century BC measures employed against forgers to coins grouped according to what they depict—animals, plants, myths, and famous buildings like the Lighthouse of Alexandria. Instead of trying to absorb everything, concentrate on a few cases—perhaps a pile of coins dug up on a Greek road, believed to be used by Alexander the Great to pay off local mercenaries. There is also a superb 4th-century BC *decadrachm* (a denomination of coin) with a lissome water goddess frolicking among dolphins (the designer signed the deity's headband). A silver *didrachm* (another denomination of coin) issued by the powerful Amphictyonic League after Philip II's death shows Demeter on one side and, on the other, a thoughtful Apollo sitting on the navel of the world. ✉ *Panepistimiou 12, Syntagma Sq.* ☎ *210/361–2190 or 210/364–3774* 🌐 *www.nma.gr* 🎟 *€3* 🕐 *Tues.–Sun., 8:30 AM–3 PM* Ⓜ *Syntagma or Panepistimiou.*

POETRY 101 CLASSROOM

Hermann Schliemann called his magnificent neoclassical house, designed for him by Ernst Ziller, the "Palace of Troy." Note the Pompeiian aesthetic in the ocher, terra-cotta, and blue touches; the mosaic floors inspired by Mycenae; and the dining-room ceiling painted with food scenes, under which Schliemann would recite the *Iliad* to guests.

3

ALSO WORTH SEEING

23 **Old University complex.** In the sea of concrete that is central Athens, this imposing group of marble buildings conjures up an illusion of classical antiquity. The three dramatic buildings belonging to the University of Athens were designed by the Hansen brothers in the period after independence in the 19th century and are built of white Pendelic marble, with tall columns and decorative friezes. In the center is the **Senate House** of the university. To the right is the **Academy,** flanked by two slim columns topped by statues of Athena and Apollo; paid for by the Austro-Greek Baron Sina, it is a copy of the Parliament in Vienna. Frescoes in the reception hall depict the myth of Prometheus. At the left end of the complex is a griffin-flanked staircase leading to the **National Library,** containing more than 2 million Greek and foreign-language volumes and now undergoing the daunting task of modernization. ✉ *Panepistimiou between Ippokratous and Sina, Central Athens* ☎ *210/361–4301 Senate, 210/360–0209 Academy, 210/361–4413 Library* 🕐 *Senate and Academy weekdays 9–2; library Sept.–July, Mon.–Thurs. 9–8, Fri. 9–2* Ⓜ *Panepistimiou.*

NEED A BREAK?

One of the toniest pedestrian malls in Athens is Voukourestiou, where you will find the hippest cafés in the city, Clemente VIII (✉ *Voukourestiou 3, City LinkKolonaki* ☎ *210/321-9340*). With the best espresso and cappuccino (both hot and iced) in town and a fresh daily platter of sandwiches and sweets, this café, which opened in October 2006, can bask in its quality alone. But surrounded by the luxury jewelry stores and the Armani-clad

lunch crowd, it's become the place to see and be seen in the city. This was once the site of one of Athens's most beloved cafés, Brazilian.

21 **Psirri.** Similar to New York City's Tribeca, this district has been targeted by developers who have spurred a wave of renovations and a bevy of new nightspots. At dusk, this quiet quarter becomes a whirl of theaters, clubs, and restaurants, dotted with dramatically lighted churches and lively squares. Defined by Ermou, Kerameikou, Athinas, Evripidou, Epikourou, and Pireos streets, Psirri has many buildings older than those in picturesque Plaka. If you're coming from Omonia Square, walk down Aiolou, a pedestrian zone with cafés and old shops as well as an interesting view of the Acropolis. Peek over the wrought-iron gates of the old houses on the narrow side streets between Ermou and Kerameikou to see the pretty courtyards bordered by long, low buildings, whose many small rooms were rented out to different families. In the Square of the Heroes, revolutionary fighters once met to plot against the Ottoman occupation. Linger on into the evening if you want to dance on tabletops to live Greek music, sing along with a soulful accordion player, hear salsa in a Cuban club, or watch the hoi polloi go by as you snack on updated or traditional *mezedes* (appetizers). ⊠ *Off Ermou, centered on Iroon and Ayion Anargiron Sqs., Psirri* 🌐 *www.psiri.gr* Ⓜ *Monastiraki.*

19 **Technopolis.** Gazi, the neighborhood surrounding this former 19th-century-foundry–turned–arts complex, takes its name from the toxic gas fumes that used to spew from the factory's smokestacks. Today Gazi is synonymous with the hippest restaurants, edgiest galleries, and trendiest nightclubs in town. The smokestacks now glow crimson with colored lights, anchoring a burgeoning stretch that runs from the central neighborhood of Kerameikos to the once-decrepit neighborhood of Rouf. The city of Athens bought the disused foundry in the late 1990s and helped convert it into Technopolis. The transformation preserved all the original architecture and stonework, and includes six exhibition spaces and a large courtyard open to the public. The spaces regularly host shows on a range of topics—war photography, open-air jazz, comic-book art, rock and theater performances, rave nights, and parties. ⊠ *Pireos 100, Gazi* ☎ *210/346–0981* 🎟 *Free* 🕘 *9* AM–*9* PM *during exhibitions* Ⓜ *Thiseio.*

IT'S CALLASTROPHIC!

Hidden within jazzy Technopolis is the small Maria Callas Museum (Andreas Embirikos Hall, Pireos 100, Gazi, open 10 AM–3 PM, Monday through Friday), where you can study the opera diva's personal photo albums, letters, and clothes. To get the real poop on La Divina, however, you'll have to read Nicholas Gage's *Greek Fire*, an in-depth book on her torrid and tragic love affair with Aristotle Onassis. One of the many secrets revealed: Ari was more interested in wooing Jacqueline Kennedy's sister until Lee Radziwill told him that her sister would be a better match. Admission is free to the museum.

SYNTAGMA SQUARE TO KOLONAKI
ΠΛΑΤΕΙΑ ΣΥΝΤΑΓΜΑΤΟΣ & ΚΟΛΩΝΑΚΙ

Dressed in their *foustanelles* (pleated skirts), the Evzone guards standing on duty at the Tomb of the Unknown Soldier; Queen Amalia's National Garden, built as an oasis of green in a desert of marble; a temple to Zeus and an arch built by Emperor Hadrian; and a funicular ride to the top of Mt. Lycabettus, three times the height of the Acropolis. The view from its top—pollution permitting—reveals that this center-city sector is packed with marvels and wonders. Sooner or later, everyone passes through its heart, the spacious Syntagma Square (Constitution Square), which is surrounded by sights that span Athens's history from the days of the Roman emperors to King Othos's reign after the 1821 War of Independence. Some may have likened his palace (now the Parliament) to a barracks but they shouldn't complain: it was paid for by Othos's father, King Ludwig I of Bavaria, who luckily vetoed the plans for a royal residence atop the Acropolis itself, using one end of the Parthenon as the entrance and blowing up the rest. The palace was finished just in time for Othos to grant the constitution of 1843, which gave the name to the square. Neighboring Kolonaki—the chic shopping district and one of the most fashionable residential areas—occupies the lower slopes of Mt. Lycabettus. Besides visiting its several museums, you can spend time window-shopping and people-watching, since cafés are busy from early morning to dawn.

WHAT TO SEE: THE MAIN ATTRACTIONS

31 Fodor'sChoice ★ **Benaki Museum.** Greece's oldest private museum, established in 1926 by an illustrious Athenian family, the Benaki was one of the first to place emphasis on Greece's later heritage at a time when many archaeologists were destroying Byzantine artifacts to access ancient objects. The collection (more than 20,000 items are on display in 36 rooms, and that's only a sample of the holdings) moves chronologically from the ground floor upward, from prehistory to the formation of the modern Greek state. You might see anything from a 5,000-year-old hammered gold bowl to an austere Byzantine icon of the Virgin Mary to Lord Byron's pistols to the Nobel medals awarded to poets George Seferis and Odysseus Elytis. Some exhibits are just plain fun—the re-creation of a Kozani (Macedonian town) living room; a tableau of costumed mannequins; a Karaghiozi shadow puppet piloting a toy plane—all contrasted against the marble and crystal-chandelier grandeur of the Benaki home. The mansion was designed by Anastassios Metaxas, the architect who helped restore the Panathenaic Stadium. The Benaki's gift shop, a destination in itself, tempts with exquisitely reproduced ceramics and jewelry. The second-floor café serves coffee and snacks, with a few daily specials, on a veranda overlooking the National Garden. ✉*Koumbari 1, Kolonaki* ☎*210/367–1000* 🌐*www.benaki.gr* 🎫*€6, free Thurs.* ⏲*Mon., Wed., Fri., and Sat. 9–5; Thurs. 9 AM–midnight; Sun. 9–3* Ⓜ*Syntagma or Evangelismos.*

32 Fodor'sChoice ★ **Museum of Cycladic Art.** Also known as the Nicholas P. Goulandris Foundation, and funded by one of Greece's richest families, this museum has an outstanding collection of 350 Cycladic artifacts dating from the

Bronze Age, including many of the enigmatic marble figurines whose slender shapes fascinated such artists as Picasso, Modigliani, and Brancusi. Other collections focus on Greek art from the Bronze Age through the 6th century AD. A glass corridor connects the main building to the gorgeous adjacent Stathatos Mansion, where temporary exhibits are mounted. There's also a lovely café in a courtyard centered around a Cycladic-inspired fountain. ✉ *Neofitou Douka 4, Kolonaki* ☎ *210/722–8321 through 210/722–8323* 🌐 *www.cycladic.gr* 🎟 *€3.50* ⏲ *Mon. and Wed.–Fri. 10–4, Sat. 10–3* Ⓜ *Evangelismos.*

> **INFORMATION, PLEASE?**
>
> The main office of the Greek National Tourism Organization (GNTO; EOT in Greece) is at Tsochas 7, in the Ambelokipi district, just by the National Gardens, not far from Syntagma Square, the heart of Athens. Their offices generally close around 2 PM. The Web site of the city of Athens (🌐 *www.cityofathens.gr*) has a small but growing section in English.

29 **Hadrian's Arch.** This marble gateway, built in AD 131 with Corinthian details, was intended both to honor the Hellenophile emperor Hadrian and to separate the ancient and imperial sections of Athens. On the side facing the Acropolis an inscription reads THIS IS ATHENS, THE ANCIENT CITY OF THESEUS, but the side facing the Temple of Olympian Zeus proclaims THIS IS THE CITY OF HADRIAN AND NOT OF THESEUS. ✉ *Vasilissis Amalias at Dionyssiou Areopagitou, National Garden* 🌐 *www.culture.gr* 🎟 *Free* ⏲ *Daily* Ⓜ *Acropolis.*

36 ★ **Mt. Lycabettus.** Myth claims that Athens's highest hill came into existence when Athena removed a piece of Mt. Pendeli, intending to boost the height of her temple on the Acropolis. While she was en route, a crone brought her bad tidings, and the flustered goddess dropped the rock in the middle of the city. Kids love the ride up the steeply inclined *teleferique* (funicular) to the summit, crowned by whitewashed **Ayios Georgios** chapel with a bell tower donated by Queen Olga. On a clear day, you can see Aegina island, with or without the aid of coin-operated telescopes. Built into a cave on the side of the hill, near the I Prasini Tenta café, is a small shrine to **Ayios Isidoros.** In 1859 students prayed here for those fighting against the Austrians, French, and Sardinians with whom King Othos had allied. From Mt. Lycabettus you can watch the sun set and then turn about to watch the moon rise over "violet-crowned" Hymettus as the lights of Athens blink on all over the city. ✉ *Base: 15-min walk northeast of Syntagma Sq.; funicular every 10 mins from corner of Ploutarchou and Aristippou (take Minibus 060 from Kanari or Kolonaki Sq., except Sun.), Kolonaki* ☎ *210/722–7065* 🎟 *Funicular €4* ⏲ *Funicular daily 9 AM–3 AM.*

34 **National Gallery of Art.** The permanent collections of Greek painting and sculpture of the 19th and 20th centuries (including the work of naive artist Theophilos) are still on display, but popular traveling exhibitions enliven the gallery. The exhibitions are usually major loan shows from around the world, such as an El Greco retrospective, Dutch 17th-century art, and an exhibit tracing the influence of Greece on works of the Ital-

ian Renaissance. ✉ *Vasileos Konstantinou 50, Ilisia* ☎ *210/723–5857 or 210/723–5937* 🎫 *€6.50* ⏲ *Mon. and Wed. 9–3 and 6–9, Thurs.–Sat. 9–3, Sun. 10–2* Ⓜ *Evangelismos.*

27 **National Garden.** When you can't take the city noise anymore, step into this oasis completed in 1860 as part of King Othos and Queen Amalia's royal holdings. Here old men on the benches argue politics, police officers take their coffee breaks, and animal lovers feed the stray cats that roam among the more than 500 species of trees and plants, many labeled. At the east end is the neoclassic **Zappion hall,** built in 1888 and used for major political and cultural events: it was here that Greece signed its accession to what was then the European Community. Children appreciate the playgrounds, duck pond, and small zoo (✉ *East end of park, National Garden*). Ⓜ *Syntagma.*

NEED A BREAK?

Visit the elegant Aiglí (✉ *National Garden*), an excellent spot for a classic Greek coffee. Nestled among fountains and flowering trees next to the Zappion Exhibition Hall in the National Garden, it's an ideal spot to sample a fresh dessert or some haute cuisine.

30 ★ **Syntagma (Constitution) Square.** At the top of the city's main square stands **Parliament,** formerly King Othos's royal palace, completed in 1838 for the new monarchy. It seems a bit austere and heavy for a southern landscape, but it was proof of progress, the symbol of the new ruling power. The building's saving grace is the stone's magical change of color from off-white to gold to rosy mauve as the day progresses. Here you can watch the **changing of the Evzone guards** at the **Tomb of the Unknown Soldier**—in front of Parliament on a lower level—which takes place at intervals throughout the day. On a wall behind the Tomb of the Unknown Soldier, the bas-relief of a dying soldier is modeled after a sculpture on the Temple of Aphaia in Aegina; the text is from the funeral oration said to have been given by Pericles. Pop into the gleaming **Syntagma metro station** (✉ *Upper end of Syntagma Sq.* ⏲ *Daily 5 AM–midnight*) to examine artfully displayed artifacts uncovered during subway excavations. A floor-to-ceiling cross section of earth behind glass shows finds in chronological layers, ranging from a skeleton in its ancient grave to traces of the 4th-century BC road to Mesogeia to an Ottoman cistern. ✉ *Vasilissis Amalias and Vasilissis Sofias, Syntagma Sq.* Ⓜ *Syntagma.*

NEED A BREAK?

Lovely cafés like Ethnikon (✉ *Syntagma Sq.* ☎ *210/331–0676*) have opened as a result of the city's 2004 Olympics remodeling. This café is shady, atmospheric, and has an excellent selection of desserts, including chocolate cake and homemade spoon sweets, or *glyka koutaliou*.

28 **Temple of Olympian Zeus.** Begun in the 6th century BC, the temple was completed in AD 132 by Hadrian, who also commissioned a huge gold-and-ivory statue of Zeus for the inner chamber and another, only slightly smaller, of himself. Only 15 of the original Corinthian columns remain, but standing next to them may inspire a sense of awe at their bulk, which is softened by the graceful carving on the acanthus-leaf

capitals. The clearly defined segments of a column blown down in 1852 give you an idea of the method used in its construction. The site is floodlighted on summer evenings, creating a majestic scene when you round the bend from Syngrou. On the outskirts of the site to the north are remains of Roman houses, the city walls, and a Roman bath. Hellenic "neopagans" also use the site for ceremonies. ✉ *Vasilissis Olgas 1, National Garden* ☎ *210/922–6330* 🎫 *€2; €12 joint ticket for all Unification of Archaeological Sites* ⏲ *Tues.–Sun. 8:30–3* Ⓜ *Acropolis.*

> **FULL FRONTAL FASHION**
>
> Near the Parliament, you can watch the **changing of the Evzone guards** at the Tomb of the Unknown Soldier—in front of Parliament on a lower level—which takes place at intervals throughout the day. On Sunday the honor guard of tall young men don a dress costume—a short white *foustanella* (kilt) with 400 neat pleats, one for each year of the Ottoman occupation, and red shoes with pompons—and still manage to look brawny rather than silly. A band accompanies them: they all arrive by 11:15 AM in front of Parliament.

ALSO WORTH SEEING

33 ★ **Byzantine and Christian Museum.** One of the few museums in Europe concentrating exclusively on Byzantine art displays an outstanding collection of icons, mosaics, and tapestries. Sculptural fragments provide an excellent introduction to Byzantine architecture. When the museum finishes a massive renovation and extension in late 2008, it will include never-before-seen exhibits such as magnificent illuminated manuscripts. Fans of classical Greece will be happy to know you can explore the on-site archaeological dig of Aristotle's Lyceum. ✉ *Vasilissis Sofias 22, Kolonaki* ☎ *210/721–1027, 210/723–2178, or 210/723–1570* 🌐 *www.culture.gr* 🎫 *€4* ⏲ *Tues.–Sun. 8:30–3; call for periodic closings* Ⓜ *Evangelismos.*

35 **Gennadius Library.** Book lovers who ascend the grand staircase into the hallowed aura of the Reading Room may have difficulty tearing themselves away from this superb collection of material on Greek subjects, from first editions of Greek classics to the papers of Nobel Laureate poets George Seferis and Odysseus Elytis. The heart of the collection consists of thousands of books donated in the 1920s by Greek diplomat John Gennadius, who haunted London's rare-book shops for volumes connected to Greece, thus amassing the most comprehensive collection of Greek books held by one man. He died bankrupt, leaving his wife to pay off his debts, mostly to booksellers. The library's collection includes Lord Byron's memorabilia (including a lock of his hair); Heinrich Schliemann's diaries, notebooks, and letters; and impressionistic watercolors of Greece by Edward Lear. Pride of place is given to the first edition printed in Greek of Homer (The *Iliad* and The *Odyssey*). The Gennadius, which is under the custody of the American School of Classical Studies, is not a lending library. ✉ *Souidias 61, Kolonaki* ☎ *210/721–0536* 🌐 *www.ascsa.edu.gr* ⏲ *Mid-Sept.–mid-Aug., Mon.–Wed. and Fri. 9:30–5, Thurs. 9:30–8, Sat. 9:30–2* Ⓜ *Evangelismos.*

37 **Kolonaki Square.** To see and be seen, Athenians gather not on the square, hub of the chic Kolonaki district, but at the cafés on its periphery and along the Tsakalof and Milioni pedestrian zone. Clothespin-thin models, slick talk show hosts, middle-aged executives, elegant pensioners, and expatriate teen queens all congregate on the square (officially known as Filikis Eterias) for a coffee before work, a lunchtime gossip session, a drink after a hard day of shopping, or for an afternoon of sipping iced cappuccinos while reading a stack of foreign newspapers and magazines purchased from the all-night kiosk. On the lower side of the square is the **British Council Library** (⊠*Kolonaki Sq. 17, Kolonaki* ☏*210/364–5768* ⏲*Mon. and Thurs. 3–8; Tues., Wed., and Fri. 9:30–2:30; closed 3 wks in Aug.*), which has some children's videos and a screening facility. ⊠*Intersection of Patriarchou Ioakeim and Kanari, Kolonaki* Ⓜ*Metro Evangelismos, then 15-min walk.*

RULES OF THE GAME

If you can't understand the menu, just go to the kitchen and point at what looks most appealing, especially in tavernas. In most cases, you don't need to ask—just walk to the kitchen (some places have food displayed in a glass case right at the kitchen's doorway), or point to your eye and then the kitchen; the truly ambitious can ask a question (Bo-*ro* na dtho tee *eh*-he-teh steen koo-*zee*-na?, or "May I see what's in the kitchen?"). When ordering fish, which is priced by the kilo, you often go to the kitchen to pick out your fish, which is then weighed and billed accordingly.

NEED A BREAK?

Enjoy a cappuccino and an Italian sweet standing at Da Capo (⊠*Tsakalof 1, Kolonaki* ☏*210/360–2497*). This place is frequented by young trendsetters, especially on Saturday afternoons; people-watching is part of the pleasure.

WHERE TO EAT

Whether you sample octopus and ouzo near the sea, roasted goat in a 100-year-old taverna, or cutting-edge cuisine in a trendy restaurant, dining in the city is just as relaxing as it is elsewhere in Greece. Athens's dining scene is experiencing a renaissance, with a particular focus on the intense flavors of regional Greek cooking. International options such as classic Italian and French still abound—and a recent Greek fascination with all things Japanese means that sushi is served in every happening bar in town—but today, traditional and nouvelle Greek are the leading contenders for the Athenian palate. The most exciting new, upscale restaurants are contemporary playgrounds for innovative chefs offering a sophisticated mélange of dishes that pay homage to Greek cooking fused with other cuisines. Some of these have also incorporated sleek design, late-night hours, DJs, and adjoining lounges full of beautiful people, forming all-in-one bar-restaurants, renowned for both star Greek chefs and glitterati customers.

Traditional restaurants serve cuisine a little closer to what a Greek grandmother would make, but more formal, and with a wider selection than the neighborhood tavernas. Truly authentic tavernas have wicker chairs that inevitably pinch your bottom, checkered tablecloths covered with butcher paper, wobbly tables that need coins under one leg, and wine drawn from the barrel and served in small metal carafes. The popular hybrid—the modern taverna—serves traditional fare in more-stylish surrounds; most are in the up-and-coming industrial-cum-artsy districts. If a place looks inviting and is filled with Greeks, give it a try. Mezedopoleia serve plates of appetizers—basically Levantine tapas—to feast on while sipping ouzo, though many now serve barrel and bottled wine as well.

In the last three weeks of August, when the city empties out and most residents head for the seaside, many restaurants and tavernas popular among the locals close, though bar-restaurants may reopen in different summer locations by the sea. Hotel restaurants, seafood restaurants in Piraeus, and tavernas in Plaka usually remain open. Most places serve lunch from about noon to 4 (and sometimes as late as 6) and dinner from about 9 to at least midnight.

As in most other cosmopolitan cities, dress varies from casual to fancy, according to the establishment. Although Athens is informal and none of the restaurants listed here requires a jacket or tie, you may feel more comfortable dressing up a bit in the most expensive places. Conservative casual attire (not shorts) is acceptable at most establishments.

WHAT IT COSTS IN EUROS					
	¢	$	$$	$$$	$$$$
AT DINNER	under €8	€8–€16	€16–€22	€22–€30	over €30

Prices are for one main course at dinner, or for two mezedes (small dishes) at restaurants that serve only mezedes.

ACROPOLIS & SOUTH ΑΚΡΟΠΟΛΗ & ΠΡΟΣ ΤΑ ΝΟΤΙΑ

In the shadow of Greece's most famous landmark, arty-chic neighborhoods such as Koukaki and Philopappou offer both historic views and classical-meets-urban ambience.

$$$$ ✕ **Edodi.** Bajazzo—the restaurant that introduced Athenians to haute cuisine—is no more, but when it closed in 1999, several top staffers decided to open an intimate, candlelit dining room (with fewer than 10 tables) in a neoclassic house. Nearly 10 years on, the menu still pays homage to the gastronomic splendor of Bajazzo but in a decidedly new theatrical way: instead of a menu, raw seasonal ingredients are brought to your table, chosen by you, then cooked to order according to your mood and tastes, which the waitstaff are quite skilled at gauging. Offerings are always changing, but the lobster with spicy Parmesan sauce is a perennial favorite. ✉ *Veikou 80, Koukaki* ☎ *210/921–3013* 🌐 *www.edodi.gr* ✍ *Reservations essential* 💳 *AE, DC, MC, V* ⏲ *Closed Sun. and 2 wks in Aug. No lunch.*

$–$$ ✕**Strofi.** Walls lined with autographed photos of actors from the nearby Odeon of Herodes Atticus attest to Strofi's success with the after-theater crowd. Despite the many tourists, the dramatic rooftop garden views of the Acropolis still attract locals who have been coming here for decades. Start with a tangy *taramosalata* (fish roe dip) or velvety tzatziki, which perfectly complements the thinly sliced fried zucchini. Another good appetizer is *fava,* a puree of yellow split peas. For the main coarse, choose roast lamb with *hilopites* (thin egg noodles cut into small squares), rabbit *stifado* (a stew of meat, white wine, garlic, cinnamon, and spices), veal with eggplant, or kid goat prepared with oil and oregano. ✉*Rovertou Galli 25, Makriyianni* ☎*210/921–4130 or 210/922–3787* ▭*DC, MC, V* ⏲*Closed Sun. No lunch.*

PLAKA ΠΛΑΚΑ

Just northeast of the Acropolis, Plaka and Anafiotika delight in their traditional homes, winding alleys, and bustle of cafés and shops.

$$–$$$ ✕**I Palia Taverna tou Psarra.** Founded way back in 1898, this is one of the few remaining Plaka tavernas serving reliably good food as well as having the obligatory mulberry-shaded terrace. The owners claim to have served Brigitte Bardot and Laurence Olivier, but it's the number of Greeks who come here that testifies to Psarra's appeal. Oil-oregano octopus and marinated *gavros* (a small fish) are good appetizers. Simple, tasty entrées include rooster in wine, *arnaki pilino* (lamb baked in clay pots), and pork chops with ouzo. Can't make up your mind? Try the *ouzokatastasi* ("ouzo situation"), a plate of tidbits to nibble while you decide. ✉*Erechtheos 16, at Erotokritou, Plaka* ☎*210/321–8733* ▭*AE, MC, V.*

$–$$ ✕**O Platanos.** Set on a picturesque corner, this is one of the oldest tav-
Fodor'sChoice ★ ernas in Plaka, and it's a welcome sight compared with the many overpriced tourist traps in the area. A district landmark—it is set midway between the Tower of the Winds and the Museum of Greek Popular Musical Instruments—it warms the eye with its pink-hue house, nicely color-coordinated with the bougainvillea-covered courtyard. Although the rooms here are cozily adorned with old paintings and photos, most of the crowd opts to relax under the courtyard's plane trees (which give the place its name). Platanos is packed with locals, who flock here because the food is good Greek home cooking and the waiters fast and polite. Don't miss the oven-baked potatoes, roasted lamb, fresh green beans in savory olive oil, and the exceptionally cheap but delicious barrel retsina. ✉*Diogenous 4, Plaka* ☎*210/322–0666* ▭*No credit cards* ⏲*Closed Sun.*

$–$$ ✕**Taverna Xynos.** Stepping into the courtyard of this Plaka taverna is like entering a time warp back to Athens in the 1950s. In summer, tables move outside and a guitar duo drops by, playing ballads of yesteryear. Loyal customers say little has changed since then—although diners' demands have, making the setup seem somewhat dated. Start with the classic stuffed-grape-leaf appetizer, and then move on to the taverna's strong suit—dishes such as lamb *yiouvetsi* (baked in ceramic dishes with tomato sauce and barley-shape pasta), livers with sweet-

Continued on page 132

EAT LIKE A GREEK

Hailed for its healthfulness, heartiness, and eclectic spicing, Greek cuisine remains one of the country's greatest gifts to visitors. From gyros to galaktoboureko, moussaka to myzthira, and soutzoukakia to snails, food in Greece is rich, exotic, and revelatory.

To really enjoy communal meals of fresh fish, mama's casseroles, flavorful salads, house wine, and great conversation, keep two ground rules in mind.

ORDER LIKE A NATIVE

Go for "*tis oras*" (grilled fish and meat) or "*piato tis imeras*" (or "plate of the day," often stews, casseroles, and pastas). Remember that fish is always expensive but avoid frozen selections and go for the freshest variety by asking the waitstaff what the day's catch is (you can often inspect it in the kitchen). Note that waiters in Greece tend to be impatient—so don't waffle while you're ordering.

DINE LIKE A FAMILY

Greeks share big plates of food, often piling bites of *mezedes*, salads, and main dishes on small dishes. It's okay to stick your fork into communal platters but not in each other's personal dishes (unless you're family or dear friends).

GRECIAN BOUNTY

Greece is a country of serious eaters, which is why there are so many different kinds of eateries. Here is a list of types to seek out.

Estiatorio: You'll often find fine tablecloths, carefully placed silverware, candles, and multipage menus at an *estiatorio*, or restaurant; menus range from traditional to nouvelle.

Oinomageirio: Now enjoying a retro resurgence, these simple eateries were often packed with blue-collar workers filling up on casseroles and listening to *rembetika*, Greece's version of the blues.

Taverna: This is vintage Greece—family-style eateries noted for great spreads of grilled meat "tis oras" (of the hour), thick-cut fried potatoes, dips, salads, and wine—all shared around a big table and with a soundtrack of *bouzouki* music.

Psarotaverna: Every bit like a regular taverna, except the star of the menu is fresh fish. Remember that fish usually comes whole; if you want it filleted, ask "*Mporo na exo fileto?*" Typical fish varieties include *barbounia* (red mullet), *perka* (perch), *sardella* (sardine), *bakaliaros* (cod), *lavraki* (sea bass), and *tsipoura* (sea bream).

Mezedopoleia: In this Greek version of tapas bars, you can graze on a limited menu of dips, salads, and hot and cold mezedes. Wildly popular with the pre-nightclub crowd.

Ouzeri and Rakadiko: *Ouzo* and the Cretan firewater *raki* (also known as *tsikoudia*) are the main attractions here, but there's always a generous plate of hot or cold mezedes to go with the spirits. A mix of old-timers and young scenesters make for great people-watching.

Kafeneio (café): Coffee rules here—but the food menu is usually limited to sandwiches, crepes, *tiropites* (cheese pies), and *spanakopites* (spinach pies).

Zacharoplasteio (patisserie): Most dessert shops are "to go," but some old-style spots have a small klatch of tables to enjoy coffee and that fresh slice of *galaktoboureko* (custard in phyllo dough).

TAKING IT TO THE STREETS

Greeks are increasingly eating on the go, since they're working longer (right through the afternoon siesta that used to be a mainstay). Fortunately, eateries have adapted to this lifestyle change. *Psitopoleia* (grill shops) have the most popular takeaway food: the wrapped-in-pita *souvlaki* (pork, lamb, or chicken chunks), *gyros* (slow-roasted slabs of pork and lamb, or chicken), or *kebabs* (spiced, grilled ground meat). Tzatziki, onions, tomatoes, and fried potatoes are also tucked into the pita. Toasted sandwiches and tasty hot dogs are other yumptious options.

THE GREEK TABLE

Mezedes Μεζέδες (appetizers): Eaten either as a first course or as full meals, they can be hot (pickled octopus, chickpea fritters, dolmades, fried squid) or cold (dips like *tzatziki*; *taramosalata*, puree of salted mullet roe or the spicy whipped feta called *htipiti*). Start with two or three, then keep ordering to your heart's content.

Tzatziki (cucumber in yogurt)

Salata Σαλάτα (salad): No one skips salads here since the vegetables burst with flavor, texture, and aroma. The most popular is the *horiatiki*, or what the rest of the world calls a "Greek salad"—this country-style salad has tomato, onion, cucumber, feta, and Kalamata olives. Other popular combos include *maroulosalata* (lettuce tossed with fresh dill and fennel) and the Cretan *dakos* (bread rusks topped with minced tomato, feta, and onion).

Horiatiki (Greek salad)

Kyrios Piato Κύριο Πιάτο (main course): Main dishes were once served family-style, like mezedes, but the plates are now offered as single servings at many restaurants. Some places serve the dishes as they are ready while more Westernized eateries bring all the plates out together. Order all your food at the same time, but be sure to tell the waiter if you want your main dishes to come after the salads and mezedes. Most grilled meat dishes come with a side of thick-cut fried potatoes, while seafood and casseroles such as *moussaka* are served alone. *Horta*, or boiled greens, drenched in lemon, are the ideal side for grilled or fried fish.

Sardines with rice, potatoes, and salad

Epidorpio Επιδόρπιο (dessert): Most restaurants give diners who have finished their meals a free plate of fresh seasonal fruit or some homemade *halva* (a cinnamony semolina pudding-cake with raisins).

Moussaka

Krassi Κρασί (wine): Greeks almost always have wine with a meal, usually sharing a carafe or two of *hima* (barrel or house wine) with friends. Bitter resinated wine, or *retsina*, has become less common in restaurants. Instead, the choice is often a dry Greek white wine that goes well with seafood or poultry.

Psomi Ψωμί (bread): Bread, often pita-fashion, comes with a meal and usually costs 1 to 2 euros—a *kouver* (cover) charge—regardless of whether you eat it.

Nero Νερό (water): If you ask for water, waitstaff will usually bring you a big bottle of it—and charge you, of course. If you simply want tap water (free and safe to drink) ask for a *kanata*—or a pitcher.

Galaktoboureko (custard filled phyllo pastry)

LIKE MAMA USED TO MAKE

Nearly all Greek restaurants have the same homey dishes that have graced family dinner tables here for years. However, some are hardly ever ordered by locals, who prefer to eat them at home—most Greeks avoid moussaka and pastitsio unless they're made fresh that day. So if you order the following foods at restaurants, make sure to ask if they're fresh ("*tis imeras*").

- Dolmades—grape leaves stuffed with rice and herbs
- Kotopoulo lemonato—whole chicken roasted with thickly sliced potatoes, lemon, and oregano
- Moussaka—a casserole of eggplant and spiced beef topped with béchamel
- Pastitsio—tube-shaped pasta baked with spiced beef, béchamel, and cheese

Best bet: Grape leaves

- Psari plaki—whole fish baked with tomato, onions, garlic and olive oil
- Soupa avgolemono—an egg-lemon soup with a chicken stock base

COFFEE CULTURE

Greeks go out for coffee not because of caffeine addiction but because they like to spend at least two hours mulling the world with their friends. *Kafeneia*, or old-style coffeehouses, are usually full of courtly old men playing backgammon and sipping a tiny but strong cup of *elliniko* (Greek coffee). Modern cafés (*kafeterias*) are more chic, packed with frappé-loving office workers, freddo-swilling college students, and arty hipsters nursing espressos. Order your coffee *sketos* (without sugar), *metrios* (medium sweet), or *glykos* (sweet).

- Frappé—a frothy blend of instant coffee (always Nescafe), cold water, sugar, and evaporated milk.
- Elliniko—the strong traditional coffee made from Brazilian beans ground into a fine powder.
- Freddo—an iced cappuccino or espresso.
- Nes—instant coffee, often served with froth.

Frappé

breads in vinegar and oregano, and piquant *soutzoukakia,* meatballs fried, then simmered in a cinnamon-laced tomato sauce. The entrance is down the walkway next to Glikis Kafenion. ✉*Aggelou Geronda 4, Plaka* ☎*210/322–1065* ▭*No credit cards* ⊗*Closed weekends and July. No lunch.*

¢–$ ✕**Sholarhio.** A favorite with university students, artists, and grizzled workers, this open-hearted tavern offers a tasty daily platter of all the best in home-cooked Greek cuisine. Waiters bring a giant tray of the day's offerings, which include such favorites as taramosalata, tzatziki, cuttlefish stewed with onions, *lahanodolmades* (cabbage rolls), eggplant dip, fried calamari, and *bekri mezedes* (wine-marinated pork cutlets). You can also order a wide range of seafood, pasta, and meat dishes from the menu. Order a carafe of wine and enjoy the feast on the bloom-filled deck. All in all, a great option for lunch or dinner after a day of sightseeing. ✉*Tripodon 14, Plaka* ☎*210/322–0666* ⊕*www.sholarhio.gr* ▭*No credit cards.*

MONASTIRAKI & THISSION ΜΟΝΑΣΤΗΡΑΚΙ & ΘΗΣΕΙΟ

Northwest of Plaka, Monastiraki and Thission retain the gritty charm of an Anatolian bazaar and magnetize the city's hardcore café and bar crowd.

$$$$ Fodor'sChoice ★ ✕**Pil Poul et Jerome Serres.** A century ago, customers arrived on foot or in horse-drawn carriages for fittings at this elegant Jazz Age haberdasher, but today they drive up in SUVs to sample lobster with passion fruit or pan-roasted rooster breast with shallot confit. The prices definitely make this restaurant—which chef Jerome Serres has made one of the best in the city—one for special occasions, but just stepping onto its marble terrace makes it one: the view of the Parthenon is so spectacular you may not fully savor your grouper with lemongrass and winter truffles. White linens and candlelight enhance the romantic aura of this beautifully restored neoclassic building at the edge of the Apostolou Pavlou promenade. If you're just interested in soaking up the atmosphere, stake a spot in the lively ground-floor cocktail lounge. ✉*Apostolou Pavlou 51 and Poulopoulou, Thission* ☎*210/342–3665* ▭*AE, MC, V* ⊗*Closed Mon.*

$$$–$$$$ Fodor'sChoice ★ ✕**Kuzina.** Sleek, dazzlingly decorated, and moodily lighted, this bistro attracts many style-conscious Athenians but Kuzina isn't just a pretty face. The food—especially the inventive seafood and pasta dishes—is among the best in Athens, especially on touristy Adrianou. Happily, the decor is almost as delicious as the Sikomaida fig tart marinated in anise seed and ouzo. Past an outdoor table setting, the main room soars skyward, glittering with birdcage chandeliers and factory ducts, with a vast lemon-yellow bar set below a spotlighted wall lined with hundreds of wine bottles. The menu showcases newfangled Greek as well as old faves; best bets include the grilled and cured octopus with fennel shavings, the soffritto of salted cod, and the beef tenderloin with black truffles. Whether you sit outside on the street, in the spectacular main dining room, or opt for a table on the roof (offering a fantastic view of the Acropolis), finish your meal off with a stroll to the small but

impressive art gallery, Porta, on the second floor. Kuzina's Web site is a winner, too—take a look. ✉*Adrianou 9, Thission* ☎*210/324–0133* 🌐*www.kuzina.gr* ▭*AE, MC, V.*

$$–$$$ ✕**Filistron.** In warm weather it's worth stopping by this place just to have a drink and enjoy the delightful, painterly scene from the roof garden—a sweeping view of the Acropolis and Mt. Lycabettus. In cooler weather, take a seat in the sunny, cheerful dining room off a pedestrian walkway. The long list of mezedes has classics and more unusual dishes: codfish croquettes with herb and garlic sauce; pork with mushrooms in wine sauce; grilled potatoes with smoked cheese and scallions; and an array of regional cheeses, washed down with a flowery white *hima* (barrel wine). The service is top-notch. ✉*Apostolou Pavlou 23, Thission* ☎*210/346–7554 or 210/342–2897* ▭*MC, V* ⊗*Closed 1 wk in Aug. No lunch.*

¢–$ ✕**Bairaktaris.** Run by the same family for more than a century, this is one of the best places to eat in Monastiraki Square. After admiring the painted wine barrels and black-and-white stills of Greek film stars, go to the window case to view the day's *magirefta* (stove-top cooked dish, usually made earlier)—maybe beef *kokkinisto* (stew with red sauce) and *soutzoukakia* (oblong meatballs simmered in tomato sauce) spiked with cloves. Or sit down and order the gyro platter. Appetizers include small cheese pies with sesame seeds, tender mountain greens, and fried zucchini with tzatziki garlic dip. ✉*Monastiraki Sq. 2, Monastiraki* ☎*210/321–3036* ▭*AE, MC, V.*

¢–$ ✕**Steki tou Ilias.** Athenians who love fresh-grilled lamb chops and thick-cut fried potatoes that could have come from *yiayia's* (grandma's) very kitchen flock to this taverna along a quiet pedestrianized street in Thission. It's a place to relax with friends: split a giant plate of *paidakia* (lamb chops), fries, creamy tzatziki, and fava bean spread. ✉*Thessalonikis 7, Thission* ☎*210/342–2407* ▭*No credit cards.*

CENTRAL ATHENS, PSIRRI & OMONIA SQUARE
ΑΘΗΝΑ (ΚΕΝΤΡΟ), ΨΥΡΡΗ & ΠΛΑΤΕΙΑ ΟΜΟΝΟΙΑΣ

Located north of Monastiraki, Omonia, the city's main square, is busy by day and seedy by night, but it bursts with cultural diversity and the kaleidoscopic Central Market. The former warehouse district of Psirri, which is between Omonia and Monastiraki, is party central for Athens.

$$$$ ✕**Hytra.** Don't let the understated bistro ambience fool you: this is one of the city's most fashionable eateries. Applying his French training to his Cretan background, chef Yiannis Baxevanis has created an imaginative menu that has caught the attention of the international press. If you find it hard to choose, sample the range of his culinary combinations—fish soup garnished with sea urchin, the classic lamb in egg-lemon sauce—with a tasting menu of 15 dishes. The wine list features an intriguing selection of vintages to accompany your meal, or you can stick with chilled raki, the traditional tipple of Crete. ✉*Navarhou Apostoli 7, Psirri* ☎*210/331–6767* ✍*Reservations essential* ▭*AE, DC, V* ⊗*Closed Sun. and June–Sept.*

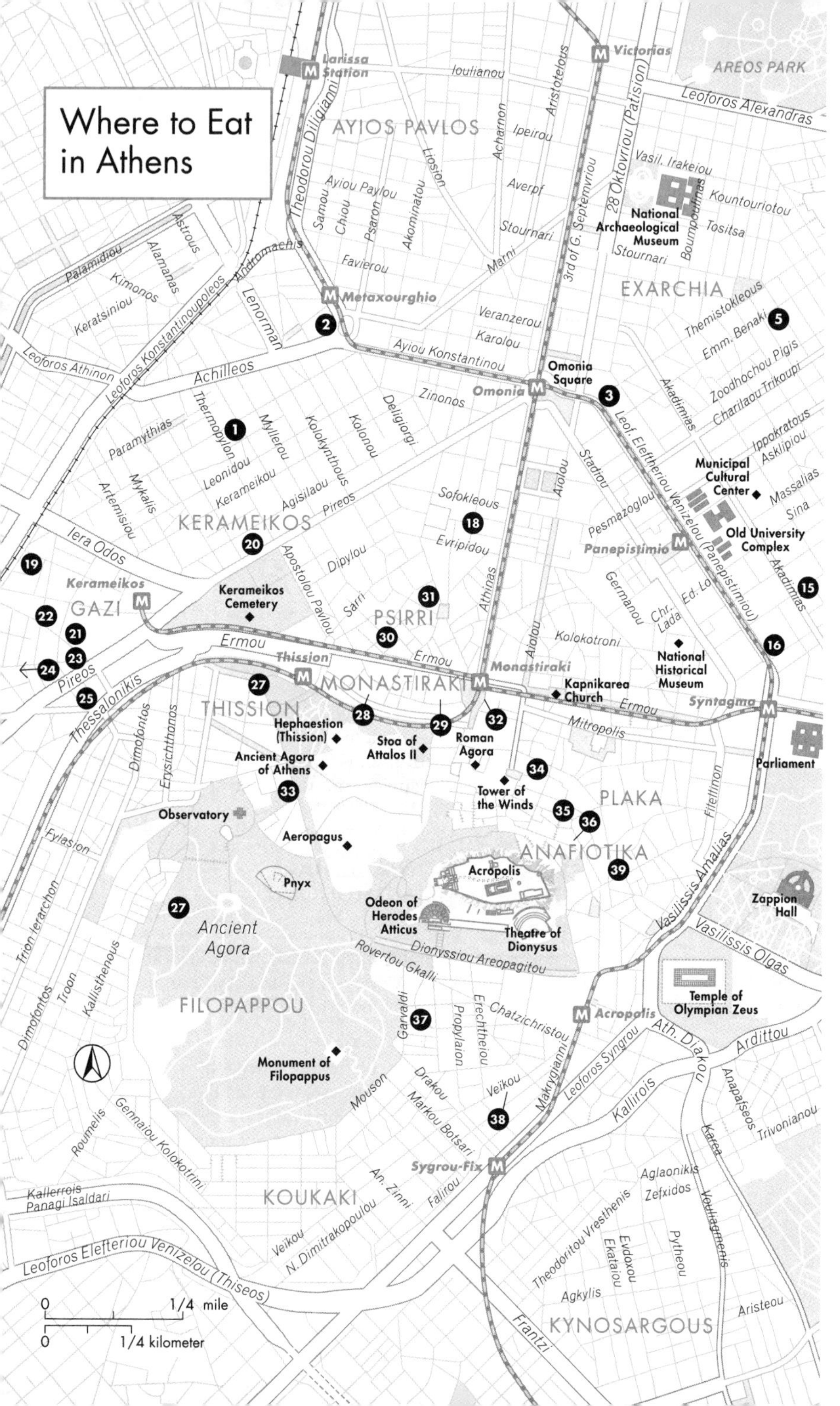
Where to Eat in Athens
Larissa Station
Victorias
AREOS PARK
Leoforos Alexandras
AYIOS PAVLOS
EXARCHIA
KERAMEIKOS
GAZI
PSIRRI
MONASTIRAKI
THISSION
PLAKA
ANAFIOTIKA
FILOPAPPOU
KOUKAKI
KYNOSARGOUS
Metaxourghio
Omonia
Omonia Square
Panepistimio
Keramelkos
Thission
Monastiraki
Syntagma
Acropolis
Sygrou-Fix
National Archaeological Museum
Municipal Cultural Center
Old University Complex
National Historical Museum
Kapnikarea Church
Parliament
Keramelkos Cemetery
Hephaestion (Thission)
Stoa of Attalos II
Roman Agora
Ancient Agora of Athens
Tower of the Winds
Observatory
Aeropagus
Pnyx
Acropolis
Odeon of Herodes Atticus
Theatre of Dionysus
Zappion Hall
Temple of Olympian Zeus
Ancient Agora
Monument of Filopappus
0 1/4 mile
0 1/4 kilometer

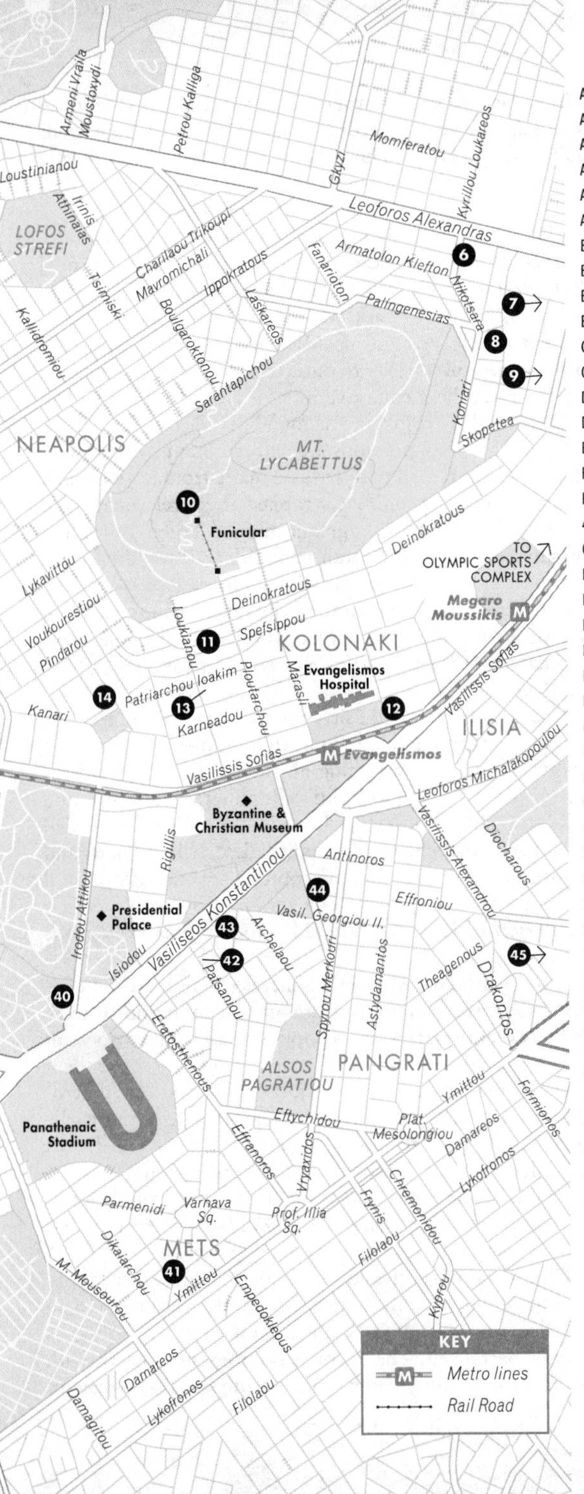

Abyssinia Café 29
Aleria 1
Alexandria 4
Aphrodite 43
Archaion Gefseis 2
Athinaikon 3
Bairaktaris 32
Balthazar 7
Boschetto 12
Butcher Shop 23
Cellier Le Bistrot 16
Cibus 40
Dakos 14
Diporto 18
Edodi 38
Fatsio 44
Filistron 33
48 6
Giantes 5
Hytra 30
I Palia Taverna tou Psarra 35
Kafenio 13
Kainari 9
Kanella 19
Karavitis 42
Kuzina 28
Mamacas 21
Maritsa's 17
O Platanos 34
Orizontes 10
Pil Poul et Jerome Serres 27
Sardelles 21
Sholarhio 36
Skoufia 24
Sophia's Cafe Valaoritou 15
Spondi 41
Steki tou Ilias 26
Strofi 37
Taverna Filipou 11
Taverna Xynos 39
Thalatta 25
To Varoulko 20
To Zeidoron 31
Trata O Stelios 45
Vlassis 8

$$$–$$$$ ✕ **Archaion Gefseis.** The epicurean owners of "Ancient Flavors" combed through texts and archaeological records in an effort to re-create foods eaten in antiquity—not to mention how they were eaten, with spoon and knife only. Dishes like pancetta seasoned with thyme and squid cooked in its ink prove, if anything, the continuity between ancient and modern Greek cuisine. There's an undeniable kitsch factor in the setting: in a torch-lighted garden, waiters in flowing chitons serve diners reclining on couches. ✉ *Kodratou 22, Karaiskaki Sq., Metaxourgeio* ☎ *210/523–9661* *Reservations essential* ▭ *AE, MC, V* ⊗ *Closed Sun.*

$$$–$$$$ Fodor's Choice ★ ✕ **To Varoulko.** Not one to rest on his Michelin star, acclaimed chef Lefteris Lazarou is constantly trying to outdo himself, with magnificent results. Rather than use the menu, give him an idea of what you like and let him create your dish from what he found that day at the market. Among his most fabulous compilations are octopus simmered in sweet red *mavrodafni* wine and served with mousse made from a sourdough pasta called *trahana*, crayfish dolmas wrapped in sorrel leaves, and red snapper with black truffle and eggplant mousse. Some dishes fuse traditional peasant fare like the Cretan *gamopilafo* ("wedding rice" flavored with boiled goat) with unusual flavors like bitter chocolate. The multilevel premises stand next to the Eridanus Hotel; in summer, dinner is served on a rooftop terrace with a wonderful Acropolis view. ✉ *Pireos 80, Gazi* ☎ *210/522–8400* *Reservations essential* ▭ *AE, DC, V* ⊗ *Closed Sun. No lunch.*

$$–$$$ ✕ **To Zeidoron.** This usually crowded Psirri hangout has decent mezedes, but the real draw is its strategic location. Metal tables line the main pedestrian walkway, great for watching all the world go by and for enjoying the sight of the neighborhood's illuminated churches and alleys. Small dishes include hot feta sprinkled with red pepper, grilled green peppers stuffed with cheese, eggplant baked with tomato and pearl onions, shrimp with ouzo, and an impressive array of dips and spreads. The wines are overpriced; opt for ouzo instead. ✉ *Taki 10, at Ayion Anargiron, Psirri* ☎ *210/321–5368* ▭ *No credit cards* ⊗ *Closed Aug.*

$–$$ ✕ **Abyssinia Cafe.** Facing hoary Abyssinia Square, where scores of merchants sell wares such as antique furniture and gleaming bouzoukis, this timeworn but exceptional eatery is popular with locals who want home-cooked traditional food and endless servings of the excellent barrel wine. Try the mussels and rice pilaf, the wine-marinated octopus with pasta, or any of the dips, including the spicy feta-and-garlic spread. Keep this is mind for a great place to relax after a day of shopping at the flea market. Although usually only open 10:30 AM to 2 PM for lunch, it is sometimes open for dinner but call ahead to be sure. ✉ *Plateia Abyssinias, Psirri* ☎ *210/321–7047* ▭ *V* ▭ *No credit cards.*

$–$$ ★ ✕ **Athinaikon.** Choose among classic specialties at this mezedopoleio: grilled octopus, shrimp croquettes, broad beans simmered in thick tomato sauce, and *ameletita* (sautéed lamb testicles). All goes well with the light barrel red. The decor is no-nonsense ouzeri, with marble tables, dark wood, and framed memorabilia. It's a favorite of attorneys and local office workers. ✉*Themistokleous 2, Omonia Sq.* ☎*210/383–8485* ▭*No credit cards* ⊗*Closed Sun. and Aug.*

$–$$ ✕**Maritsa's.** Brokers from the Athens Stock Exchange just a couple of doors down the street have made this mezedopoleio their lunchtime haunt. Choose from classic taverna dishes—pickled octopus, grilled sardines, or deep-fried zucchini—and see if you can catch some insider gossip on the day's trading. ✉*Sofokleous 17–19, Omonia Sq.* ☎*210/325–1421* ▭*MC, V.*

¢–$ ✕**Diporto.** Through the years, everyone in Omonia has come here for lunch—butchers from the Central Market, suit-clad brokers from the nearby stock exchange, artists, migrants, and even bejeweled ladies who lunch; they're often sitting at the same tables when it gets crowded. Owner-chef Barba Mitsos keeps everyone happy with his handful of simple, delicious, and dirt-cheap dishes. There's always an exceptional *horiatiki* (Greek salad), sometimes studded with fiery-hot green pepperoncini; other favorites are his buttery *gigantes* (large, buttery white beans cooked in tomato sauce), *vrasto* (boiled goat, pork, or beef with vegetables), warming chickpea soup, and fried finger-size fish. Wine is drawn directly from the barrels lining the walls. ✉*Theatrou and Sofokleous, Central Market* ☎*No phone* ▭*No credit cards* ⊗*No dinner.*

SYNTAGMA SQUARE & KOLONAKI
ΠΛΑΤΕΙΑ ΣΥΝΤΑΓΜΑΤΟΣ & ΚΟΛΩΝΑΚΙ

Located east of Plaka, Kolonaki is an old-money neighborhood that's a haunt for politicians, expats, and high-maintenance ladies who lunch (and shop). Syntagma, a pretty central square between Parliament and Ermou Street, is also popular with tourists.

$$$$ ★ ✕**Cibus.** The lush Zappion Gardens have always been a tranquil green oasis for stressed-out Athenians, who head here to gaze at the distant views of the Parthenon and Temple of Olympian Zeus, or catch an open-air cinema showing, or chill out at the landmark café. Now, the café is gone and a chic new restaurant is luring both fashionables and families. The food has an Italian touch, thanks to chef Mauro Peressini, and it's expensive but fantastic (reservations are essential for dinner). Try the ravioli with red radicchio and almonds, with a fondue of Montasio cheese and truffles, or one of several outstanding risotto dishes, including one with crayfish and tomatoes. After dinner, have a drink and listen to the latest grooves with the beautiful people at the neighboring Lallabai club. ✉*Zappion Gardens, National Garden* ☎*210/336–9364* ▭*AE, DC, MC, V.*

$$$–$$$$ ★ ✕**Cellier Le Bistrot.** On the same spot occupied by Apotsos, an ouzeri that was a fixture on the Athenian social scene for decades, Cellier Le Bistrot has introduced an upmarket eatery fashioned around wine. The bistro has one of the largest selections of by-the-glass wines in the city, which you can sample with a light dish from the ever-changing menu: maybe fresh pasta, salad, or seafood. The decor is both timeless and contemporary, with leather banquettes and mahogany surfaces. The service is as impeccable as the wine list, which is culled from the

finest vintages from nearby Cellier, one of the city's top wineshops. ✉Panepistimiou 10, in the arcade, Syntagma Sq. ☎210/363–8525 ▭AE, MC, V.

$$$–$$$$ ✕ **Orizontes.** Have a seat on the terrace atop Mt. Lycabettus: the Acropolis glitters below, and, beyond, Athens unfolds like a map out to the Saronic Gulf. It's tough to compete with such a view and, at times, the food and the service (or both) fail to match it. But best bets include the black sea bream with silver beet, mussels, grated tomato, and sea-urchin roe, or the beef paillard with yogurt risotto and glazed tomato. No road goes this high: the restaurant is reached by cable car. ✉*Mt. Lycabettus, Kolonaki* ☎*210/721–0701 or 210/722–7065* ✍*Reservations essential* ▭*AE, DC, MC, V.*

$$ ✕ **Kafenio.** A Kolonaki institution, this ouzeri reminiscent of a French bistro is slightly fancier than the normal mezedopoleio, with cloth napkins, candles on the tables, a handsome dark-wood interior, and society matrons taking a break from retail therapy. The enormous menu offers many unusual creations. For the freshest dishes, ask the waiter for the day's specials, which include traditional fare such as *kolokithokeftedes* (fried zucchini balls), marinated octopus, and pork cooked in wine, as well as more-modern twists such as a mixed greens salad with pomegranates. ✉*Loukianou 26, Kolonaki* ☎*210/722–9056* ▭*No credit cards* ⊙*Closed Sun. and 3 wks in Aug.*

$–$$ ✕ **Dakos.** This sleek new restaurant—named after a scrumptious Cretan salad made of bread rusks, shaved tomato, onions, feta, and olive oil—offers a broad menu of delicacies from Greece's largest island. Some of the best dishes include *hortopitakia* (pies made of wild greens), grilled meats (with excellent sausage), *sfakianopita* (a flat pita stuffed with a ricotta-like cheese and drizzled with honey), and, of course, the *dakos* salad. Wash it all down with a shot of raki, the extremely potent spirit made from grape must. The service is excellent, the waiters informed and very polite, and the decor minimalist and relaxing. ✉*Tsakalof 6, Kolonaki* ☎*210/360–4020* ▭*No credit cards.*

$–$$ ✕ **Sophia's Cafe Valaoritou.** This chic-yet-homey bistro opened recently next to its more-famous sister, the Valaoritou Brasserie, where chef Lefteris Lazarou wins Michelin stars and creates works of art like his cuttlefish risotto with caramelized garlic. Here, the salads are generous and delicious, especially those with the bistro's well-spiced grilled chicken, and there are also a range of pasta dishes and traditional Greek fare like lemon-oregano chicken, lamb, and seafood. But save room for the fabulous desserts, especially the lemon pie and the amazing galaktoboureko made with Camembert cheese instead of the traditional custard. ✉*Valaoritou 15, Kolonaki* ☎*210/364–1530* ▭*MC, V.*

$–$$ ✕ **Taverna Filipou.** This unassuming taverna is hardly the sort of place you'd expect to find in chic Kolonaki, yet its devotees include cabinet ministers, diplomats, actresses, and film directors. The appeal is simple, well-prepared Greek classics, mostly *ladera* (vegetable or meat casseroles cooked in an olive-oil–and–tomato sauce), roast chicken, or fish baked in the oven with tomatoes, onions, and parsley. Everything's home-cooked, so the menu adapts to what's available fresh at the open-air produce market. In summer and on balmy spring or autumn evenings, choose a table on the pavement; in winter, seating is in a cozy dining room a few steps below street level. ✉ *Xenokratous 19, Kolonaki* ☎ *210/721–6390* ▭ *No credit cards* ⊙ *Closed Sat. and mid-Aug.*

PANGRATI & KAISARIANI ΠΑΓΚΡΑΤΙ & ΚΑΙΣΑΡΙΑΝΗ

3

Urbane without being snobby or expensive, Pangrati and Kaisariani are havens for academics, artists, and expats who bask in the homey warmth of these neighborhoods.

$$$$ ✕ **Spondi.** One of Athens's most intensely designed temples to great food, Spondi is a feast for both the eyes and the taste buds. One salon shimmers with arty Swarovski chandeliers, walls of hot pink and cool aubergine, and chic black leather couches; for less glamour opt for the white-linen vaulted room, a beige-on-beige sanctorum; or, in summer, chill in the vast, bougainvillea-draped courtyard. No matter where you sit, however, you'll be able to savor the transcendentally delicious creations of Arnaud Bignon and consultant chef Eric Frechon (of Paris's Hotel Bristol fame). Highlights of their French-inspired Mediterranean menu (which change every summer and winter) include eggplant with tuna, fillet of sea bass in vanilla sauce, black ravioli with honeyed leeks and shrimp, and a feta-and-coriander-flavor ice cream. You may wish to opt for a taxi ride out to Pangrati—but isn't one of the best meals in all of Greece worth it? ✉ *Pirronos 5, Varnava Sq., Pangrati* ☎ *210/752–0658* 📠 *210/756–4021* 🌐 *www.spondi.gr* ✍ *Reservations essential* ▭ *AE, DC, MC, V* ⊙ *No lunch.*

Fodor's Choice ★

$$–$$$ ✕ **Trata O Stelios.** The owner works directly with fishermen, guaranteeing that the freshest catch comes to the table. Just point to your preference and it will soon arrive in the way Greeks insist upon: grilled with exactitude, coated in the thinnest layer of olive oil to seal in juices, and accompanied by lots of lemon. Even those who scrunch up their nose at fish soup will be converted by this version of the dense yet delicate *kakavia*. Stelios is also one of the few remaining places you can get real homemade taramosalata. Avoid the place during Sunday lunch; it's packed with Athenian families. ✉ *Anagenniseos Sq. 7–9, off Ethnikis Antistaseos, Kaisariani* ☎ *210/729–1533* ▭ *No credit cards* ⊙ *Closed 10 days at Orthodox Easter.*

$–$$ ✕ **Aphrodite.** This mezedopoleio's menu changes more often than the faces of its regulars, a mix of locals, politicians, and intellectuals who have elevated this cozy neighborhood square into a city insider's alternative to Kolonaki. Sip the complimentary raki and crunch on bread sticks dipped in olive paste while deciding whether to order the day's special or a round of mezedes: roasted red peppers stuffed with goat cheese, bite-size fried pies with a filling of wild greens, whole grilled squid, marinated anchovies, and a range of salads in season. In warm weather tables go out on the *platia* (square); in winter, seating is in a split-level dining room with a casual island ambience. ✉ *Ptolemeon and Amynta 6, Proskopon Sq., Pangrati* ☎ *210/724–8822* ▭ *MC, V.*

$–$$ ✕ **Fatsio.** Don't be fooled by the Italian name: the food at this old-fashioned restaurant is all home-style Greek. Walk past the kitchen and point at what you want before taking a seat. Favorites include a "souffle"

CLOSE UP

Greek Fast Food

Souvlaki is the original Greek fast food: spit-roasted or grilled meat, tomatoes, onions, and garlicky *tzatziki* wrapped in a pita to go. Greeks on the go have always eaten street food such as the endless variations of cheese pie, *koulouri* (sesame-covered bread rings), roasted chestnuts or ears of corn, and palm-size paper bags of nuts. But modern lifestyles and the arrival of foreign pizza and burger chains have cultivated a taste for fast food—and spawned several local brands definitely worth checking out. **Goody's** serves burgers and spaghetti as well as some salads and sandwiches. Items like baguettes with grilled vegetables or seafood salads are seasonal additions to the menu. At **I Pitta tou Pappou** you can sample several takes on souvlaki: grilled chicken breast or pork-and-lamb patties, each served with a special sauce. **Everest** is tops when it comes to *tost*—oval-shape sandwich buns with any combination of fillings, from omelets and smoked turkey breast to fries, roasted red peppers, and various spreads. It also sells sweet and savory pies, ice cream, and desserts. Its main rival is **Grigoris,** a chain of sandwich and pie shops that also runs the City Espresso Bars. If you want to sit down while you eat your fast food, look for a **Flocafe Espresso Bar.** Along with espresso, frappé, *filtro* (drip), and cappuccino, they also serve a selection of pastries and sandwiches, including brioche with mozzarella and pesto.

that is actually a variation on baked macaroni-and-cheese, with pieces of ham and slices of beef and a topping of eggplant and tomato sauce. Quick service and good value for the money is the reason for Fatsio's enduring popularity among both elder Kolonaki residents and office workers seeking an alternative to fast food. ✉*Effroniou 5–7, off Rizari, Pangrati* ☎*210/721–7421* ▭*No credit cards* ⊙*Closed 1 wk mid-Aug. No dinner.*

$–$$ ★ ✕**Karavitis.** The winter dining room is insulated with huge wine casks; in summer there is garden seating in a courtyard across the street (get there early so you don't end up at the noisy sidewalk tables). The classic Greek cuisine is well prepared, including pungent tzatziki, *bekri mezedes* (lamb chunks in zesty red sauce), lamb ribs (when in season), *stamnaki* (beef baked in a clay pot), and melt-in-the-mouth meatballs. This neighborhood favorite is near the Panathenaic Stadium. ✉*Arktinou 35, at Pausaniou, Pangrati* ☎*210/721–5155* ▭*No credit cards* ⊙*Closed 1 wk mid-Aug. No lunch.*

GAZI, KERAMEIKOS, & ROUF ΓΚΑΖΙ, ΚΕΡΑΜΕΙΚΟΣ, & ΡΟΥΦ

West of Psirri, the greater Gazi district has turned into the city's hottest art, culture, and nightlife zone. The new Kerameikos metro station has also made it ultra-convenient.

$$$–$$$$ ✕**Thalatta.** Walking into this charming renovated house off the factory-lined streets of Gazi feels like stumbling upon a wonderful secret. Owner Yiannis Safos, an islander from Ikaria, has transformed the space into a fresh, modern dining room with a colorful tile-paved

courtyard. He fills the menu with fish pulled daily from the Aegean; ask about the selection, from sea urchins to clams. Perhaps try grilled octopus with pureed pumpkin and sun-dried tomatoes, monkfish carpaccio with wild fennel, or salmon with champagne sauce. Finish with homemade lemon sorbet—bits of zest are left in for added bite. ✉ *Vitonos 5, Gazi* ☎ *210/346–4204* ✍ *Reservations essential* ▭ *MC, V* ⊙ *Closed Sun. No lunch.*

3

$$–$$$ ✕ **Aleria.** Athenian trend-watchers are so enthusiastic about the gritty-cool neighborhood of Metaxourgeio that they say it will soon be like Paris's boho-chic Marais district. Restaurants like Aleria, a gem of neoclassic design and inventive Mediterranean fusion cuisine, are one reason the area's star is rising. Try the canelloni stuffed with shrimp, mussels and carrots in a mango and pineapple sauce, or the pork fillets in ouzo sauce. ✉ *Meg. Alexandrou 57, Metaxourgeio* ☎ *210/522–2633* ✍ *Reservations essential* ▭ *AE, MC, V* ⊙ *Closed Sun. No lunch.*

$$–$$$ ✕ **The Butcher Shop.** A carnivore's paradise, this sleek and simple tavern does its meats superbly. Try the steaks, sausages, and the juicy, gigantic hamburgers. Don't miss the crispy home fries and specialty cheeses from around Greece. For sides, go for a plate of fresh, vinegary beets or the seasonal salads. The menu also offers a selection of cheeses from around Greece as well as an eclectic selection of local wines. ✉ *Persefonis 19, Gazi* ☎ *210/341–3440* ▭ *No credit cards.*

$$ ✕ **Mamacas.** This restaurant started the wave of "modern tavernas," which offer new takes on traditional Greek food amid the chicness of minimalist decor. Mamacas, which means "the mommies" in Greek, was also the first restaurant to spark the rebirth of Gazi, the once-forlorn neighborhood around what was once a gas foundry. Since it opened in 1998, Mamacas has consistently offered fresh, delicious home cooking such as pork with prunes, tomatoes, and peppers stuffed with rice and raisins, and, when they make it, arguably the best walnut cake in town. After hours, the restaurant turns into a bar and draws a flashy crowd of miniskirted young women and open-shirted men who strike poses as if the whole world is looking. Now that the new Kerameikos metro station has opened, it's easier than ever to go to the restaurant that helped turn Gazi into the hottest spot in Athens. ✉ *Persefonis 41, Gazi* ☎ *210/346–4984* ▭ *MC, V* ⊙ *Closed Mon.*

$$ ✕ **Sardelles.** If you love seafood and don't want to pay a fortune for it, don't miss this wonderful and beautifully designed eatery next to Mamacas. The simple lines of Greek island decor are evident in wooden *kafeneion* (coffeehouse) tables and 1950s-style metal-frame garden chairs picked up at auctions and painted dazzling white. Try the cod cutlets, the grilled fish drizzled with mastic-flavored sauce, and the house specialty, the sardines ("sardelles") in rock salt. Also recommended are any of the house salads, especially the mixed greens with goat cheese and pomegranate seeds. Top it off with a shot of *mastiha,* or mastic-flavor liqueur, and a slice of lemon or chocolate tart. ✉ *Persefonis 15, Gazi* ☎ *210/347–8050* ▭ *No credit cards.*

$–$$ ✕ **Kanella.** Housed in a sleek, airy building with modern and traditional touches, this lively restaurant is infused with Gazi's energy. The superb home cooking includes the braised beef in tomato sauce with spaghetti, the simmered pork with mushrooms and mashed potatoes, the Kefalonia-style rooster in red sauce, and an excellent salad with boiled zucchini, sliced avocado, and grated Graviera cheese. Wine comes in beautifully designed glass carafes. Warning: when the place gets busy, it gets almost psychedelically loud. ✉*Konstantinoupoleos 70 and Evmolpidon, Gazi* ☎*210/347–6320* 💳*No credit cards.*

$–$$ ✕**Skoufia.** This pretty, high-quality restaurant has some of the best food in town—and at reasonable prices. Menus are the royal-blue lined notebooks used by Greek schoolchildren; the proprietors have handwritten the Cretan-inspired offerings on the pages. Enjoy Skoufia's signature roasted lamb, which is so tender it just falls off the bone, on one of the tables outside. Other excellent choices include braised beef with eggplant puree, wild-greens pie, and syrupy *ravani* cake with mastic-flavor *kaimaki* ice cream. ✉*Vasileiou Megalou 50, Rouf* ☎*210/341–2252* 💳*No credit cards.*

ATHENS NORTH & EAST ΑΘΗΝΑ, ΒΟΡΕΙΑ & ΑΝΑΤΟΛΙΚΗ

$$$$ ✕**Balthazar.** With its airy neoclassic courtyard—paved with original painted tiles, canopied by huge date palms, and illuminated by colored lanterns—Balthazar truly feels like an oasis in the middle of Athens. The crowd is hip, moneyed, and beautiful, so you might wish to come for dinner, then stay to mingle as the DJ picks up the beat. Talented young chef Yiorgos Tsiktsiras keeps the quality and flavor high on the up-to-the-minute menu, with prices to match. Try any of the creative salads, the East-meets-West fish dishes, and the homemade desserts, especially the grape sorbet. ✉*Tsoha 27, at Soutsou, Ambelokipi* ☎*210/644–1215* *Reservations essential* 💳*AE, MC, V* *Closed Sun. No lunch.*

$$$$ ✕**48.** One of the best and most atmospheric restaurants in Athens, 48
Fodor'sChoice takes the best of traditional Greek fare and transforms it into food so
★ experiential that you will remember it forever. Inspired by the setting—this cavernous space was previously an art gallery—French-trained chef Christophoros Peskiaschas created a menu with definite visual appeal. Rather than fusing Greek recipes with nouvelle ingredients, he has recreated old favorites but given them a twist. Try the sea bass with marinated cucumber and fish roe sauce, the raw and marinated fresh fish platter, or the lamb simmered with artichokes. The desserts are almost orgasmic, especially anything made with chocolate. ✉*Armatolon and Klefton 48, between Leoforos Alexandras and Mt. Lycabettus, Ambelokipi* ☎*210/641–1082* *Reservations essential* 💳*AE, DC, V* *Closed Sun.*

$$$–$$$$ ✕**Boschetto.** The thick greenery of a small urban park, the pampering
★ of an expert maître d', and the flavors of Italian nouvelle cuisine make you forget you're in the center of Athens. The specialty here is fresh pasta, such as the excellent papardelle with rooster ragout and Marsala sauce. Also on the menu is scorpion fish with lobster sauce, as well as more typical (but just as outstanding) fare such as the rack of lamb with polenta and smoked scamorza cheese, and the risotto with lime, mushrooms, and Dry Martini. The desserts, especially the tiramisu and pan-

acotta, are also dreamy, and they go down well with a cup of espresso, the best in Athens. ✉ *Evangelismos Park, near the Hilton, Ilisia, 10676* ☎ *210/721–0893 or 210/722–7324* ✍ *Reservations essential* ▭ *AE, V* ⊙ *Closed Sun. and 2 wks in Aug. No lunch Oct.–Aug.*

$$$ ✕ **Giantes.** The menu here definitely has a modern streak, but meals are served in a lovely flower-filled courtyard. The taverna is co-owned by one of Greece's foremost organic farmers, so almost everything is fresh and delicious, though a little pricier than the norm. The Byzantine pork and chicken with honey, raisins, and coriander are perennial favorites. ✉ *Valtetsiou 44, Exarchia* ☎ *210/330–1369* ▭ *AE, DC, MC, V* ⊙ *Closed Mon. and 1st 2 wks in Aug.*

3

$–$$ Fodor'sChoice ★ ✕ **Vlassis.** Relying on traditional recipes from Thrace, Roumeli, Thessaly, and the islands, cooks whip up what may be the best Greek home-style cooking in Athens. There's no menu: pick from the tray of 20 or so small dishes brought to your table. They're all good, but best bets include *tirokafteri* (a peppery cheese dip), lahanodolmades (cabbage rolls), *pastitsio* (meat pie with macaroni and béchamel sauce), *katsiki ladorigani* (goat with oil and oregano), and the octopus stifado, which is tender and sweet with lots of onions. For dessert, order the halvah or a huge slice of galaktoboureko (custard in phyllo). ✉ *Paster 8, Mavili Sq.* ☎ *210/646–3060* ✍ *Reservations essential* ▭ *No credit cards* ⊙ *Closed Aug.–mid-Sept. No dinner Sun.*

$$ Fodor'sChoice ★ ✕ **Alexandria.** Egyptian spice infuses Greek cuisine with an exotic, eclectic, and dynamic menu at this superb restaurant. The choices include simple but stunning fare such as a tomato salad with thick yogurt and caramelized onions as well as a tender lamb cooked with dried plums and apricots. If you're an adventurous foodie, don't miss Alexandria's signature dish: tender, wine-simmered baby octopus on a creamy bed of fava. The wine list is extensive and well priced, and the service is outstanding. The relaxing, clean-white interior design recalls the cosmopolitan flair of the Egyptian Greeks. ✉ *Metsovou 13 and Rethymnou, behind Park Hotel, near Archaeological Museum, Exarchia* ☎ *210/821–0004* ▭ *No credit cards* ⊙ *Closed Sun. No lunch.*

$–$$ ✕ **Kainari.** Handwoven throws and an odd collection of photographs and mementos adorn the walls of this cozy neighborhood taverna, where you'll rub elbows—literally—with businessmen, doctors, students, and other regulars. But what it lacks in space, it makes up for with an extensive menu combining daily specials (ask the fishmonger sipping ouzo at the next table) and favorites, like spicy grilled pancetta, twisted pites, and hand-cut fries cooked in olive oil. ✉ *Xiromerou 20, behind Archaeological Museum, Erithros Stavros, Ambelokipi* ☎ *210/698–3011* ▭ *No credit cards* ⊙ *Closed Sun. and Aug.*

WHERE TO STAY

As a result of the 2004 Olympics, Athens's hotels have risen both in quality and number of rooms. Nearly every hotel in town underwent a renovation before the games, with luxury hotels paying serious attention to style and design and many adding spas, pools, and gyms. Concept hotels like the Semiramis in Kifissia and Periscope in Kolonaki have not escaped the notice of the international media. Athens's budget hotels—once little better than dorms—now often have air-conditioning and television, along with prettier public spaces. Perhaps best of all is the increase in the number of good-quality, middle-rank family hotels, of which there was long a shortage.

The most convenient hotels for tourists are in the city center. Some of the older hotels in Plaka and near Omonia Square are comfortable and clean, their charm inherent in their age. But along with charm may come leaking plumbing, sagging mattresses, and other lapses in the details—take a good look at the room before you register. The thick stone walls of neoclassic buildings keep them cool in summer, but few of the budget hotels have central heating, and it can be devilishly cold in winter. A buffet breakfast is often served for a few euros extra: cold cuts and cheese, even poached eggs and other meat, but nothing cooked to order.

PRICES

Along with higher quality have come higher hotel prices: room rates in Athens are not much less than in many European cities. Still, there are bargains to be had. Paradoxically, you may get up to a 20% discount if you book the hotel through a local travel agent; it's also a good idea to bargain in person at smaller hotels, especially off-season. When negotiating a rate, bear in mind that the longer the stay, the lower the nightly rate, so it may be less expensive to spend six consecutive nights in Athens rather than staying for two or three nights at either end of your trip through Greece.

WHAT IT COSTS IN EUROS

	¢	$	$$	$$$	$$$$
FOR 2 PEOPLE	under €80	€80–€150	€150–€200	€200–€250	over €250

Hotel prices are for a standard double room in high season, including taxes. Hotels operate on the European Plan (EP, with no meal provided) unless we note that they use the Continental Plan (CP, with Continental breakfast) or Breakfast Plan (BP, with a full breakfast). Hotel rooms have air-conditioning, room phones, and TVs unless otherwise noted.

ACROPOLIS & SOUTH ΑΚΡΟΠΟΛΗ & ΠΡΟΣ ΤΑ ΝΟΤΙΑ

Under Athens's iconic landmark, newly chic neighborhoods such as Koukaki and Philopappou offer both historic vibes and hipsterious ambience.

$$$$ **Ledra Marriott.** The Ledra's main calling cards are its high-performance staff and its style. Guest rooms are gorgeously modern-chic, furnished in warm reds and oranges with feather duvets, with overstuffed armchairs, marble bathrooms, and vast closet space. The fourth-floor executive lodgings are even more spacious and include a private check-in and lounge. The lobby piano bar sits below a spectacular 1,000-crystal chandelier; Kona Kai, the Polynesian restaurant, is excellent; and the Zephyros Café has a bountiful Sunday brunch. While you

can enjoy a gorgeous Acropolis view from the rooftop pool, you'll note you are some distance from the city center. ✉ *Syngrou 115, Neos Kosmos, 11745* ☎ *210/930–0000* 📠 *210/935–8603* 🌐 *www.marriott.com* ⇨ *259 rooms, 11 suites* ♘ *In-room: safe, Ethernet. In-hotel: 3 restaurants, bars, pool* ▭ *AE, DC, MC, V.*

$$$–$$$$ **Herodion Hotel.** A good compromise between the area's budget venues and deluxe digs, this hospitable hotel is down the street from the Odeon of Herodes Atticus, where Hellenic Festival performances are held, and a few minutes from the Acropolis. Service is friendlier and more efficient here than at most other Plaka neighborhood hotels, while the marble in the renovated lobby lends a touch of grandeur. Guest rooms are done in light-wood furnishings and muted olive-color walls. The complimentary buffet breakfast is served in a peaceful, tree-shaded atrium; on the roof, there is a terrace with deck chairs and a Parthenon panorama. Take full advantage of the hotel's location and ask for a room with an Acropolis view. ✉ *Rovertou Galli 4, Acropolis, 11742* ☎ *210/923–6832 through 210/923–6836* 📠 *210/923–5851* 🌐 *www.herodion.gr* ⇨ *86 rooms, 4 suites* ♘ *In-room: refrigerator. In-hotel: restaurant, bar* ▭ *DC, MC, V* 🍽 *BP.*

$$–$$$ **Philippos Hotel.** Just around the corner from its sister hotel, the Herodion, the Philippos shares its good qualities: a quiet location convenient to the Acropolis and friendly, efficient service. Modular dark-veneer beds (in smallish rooms) are offset by pale green carpets and draperies. You can sip a coffee in the light-filled atrium with comfortable couches and patio tables. Prices are kept down by details like the complimentary Continental (rather than full) breakfast, but the overall experience is just as positive. ✉ *Mitseon 3, Makriyianni, 11742* ☎ *210/922–3611* 📠 *210/922–3615* 🌐 *www.philipposhotel.gr* ⇨ *46 rooms, 2 suites* ♘ *In-room: refrigerator. In-hotel: public Internet* ▭ *MC, V* 🍽 *CP.*

$–$$ Fodor's Choice ★ **Acropolis Select.** For only €10 more than many basic budget options, you get to stay in a slick-looking hotel with a lobby full of Philippe Starck–like furniture. Bright, comfortable guest rooms have cheery yellow bedspreads with an abstract red poppy design. Similar in color choice, the dramatic restaurant has daffodil-color walls and contemporary, scroll-back chairs in tomato red. About a dozen rooms look toward the Acropolis: ask for Rooms 401–405 for the best views. There are only 10 no-smoking rooms in the hotel, all on the fifth floor. The residential neighborhood of Koukaki, south of Filopappou Hill, is a 10-minute walk from the Acropolis. ✉ *Falirou 37–39, Koukaki, 11742* ☎ *210/921–1610* 📠 *210/921–1610* 🌐 *www.acropoliselect.gr* ⇨ *72 rooms* ♘ *In-room: refrigerator. In-hotel: restaurant, bar* ▭ *AE, DC, MC, V.*

$–$$ **Art Gallery Pension.** A handsome house on a residential street, this pension is comfortably old-fashioned, with family paintings on the muted white walls, comfortable beds, hardwood floors, and ceiling fans. Many guest rooms have balconies with views of Filopappou or the Acropolis. A congenial crowd of visiting students and single travelers fills the place. In winter, lower rates are available to long-term guests, some of whom stay on for a few months. Rates with and without breakfast are available. Though the residential neighborhood, a

10-minute walk south of the Acropolis, lacks the charm of Plaka, it has many fewer tourists and the metro offers easy access to many of the city's sights. ✉*Erechthiou 5, Koukaki, 11742* ☎*210/923–8376 or 210/923–1933* 📠*210/923–3025* ✎*ecotec@otenet.gr* *21 rooms, 2 suites* *In-room: dial-up. In-hotel: bar* ▭*No credit cards.*

¢ **Marble House.** This popular pension has a steady clientele—even in winter, when it has low monthly and weekly rates. Guest rooms are clean and quiet, with ceiling fans and rustic wooden furniture. Rooms with air-conditioning and private bath cost a few euros extra. The international staff is always willing to help out and the courtyard is a lovely place to relax. It is a little off the tourist circuit, but it's still possible to walk to most ancient sights (it's about 20 minutes from the Acropolis). It's also close to the metro and the Zinni stop on Trolley 1, 5, or 9 from Syntagma. ✉*Andreou Zinni 35, Koukaki, 11741* ☎*210/923–4058 or 210/922–6461* 🌐*www.marblehouse.gr* *16 rooms, 11 with bath* *In-room: no a/c (some), no phone, kitchen (some), refrigerator, no TV* ▭*No credit cards.*

PLAKA ΠΛΑΚΑ

Northeast of the Acropolis, Plaka and Anafiotika are Athens's old-world villages, replete with winding alleys and a bevy of cafés and shops.

$$$–$$$$ ★ **Electra Palace.** If you want simple elegance, excellent service, and a great location in Plaka, this is the hotel for you. Located on an attractive street close to area museums, its guest rooms are comfortable and beautifully decorated, with ample storage space. Rooms from the fifth floor up have a view of the Acropolis–which you can also enjoy from the rooftop garden bar. Before setting out in the morning, fill up with one of the city's best buffet breakfasts—sausage, pancakes, and home fries. In the evening, relax in a steam bath in the hotel spa. ✉*Nikodimou 18–20, Plaka, 10557* ☎*210/337–0000* 📠*210/324–1875* 🌐*www.electrahotels.gr* *131 rooms, 19 suites* *In-room: refrigerator, Wi-Fi. In-hotel: restaurant, pool* ▭*AE, DC, MC, V* *BP.*

$$–$$$ Fodor's Choice ★ **Plaka Hotel.** Tastefully decorated, with deep-blue velvet curtains that match the upholstery on the wood-arm easy chairs, the guest rooms in this charming hotel are a comfortable place to rest while in the heart of old Athens. This hotel, part of the family-owned chain that includes the hotels Hermes and Achilleas, flourishes in its location; some rooms have views of the Acropolis, which you can also enjoy from the roof garden. The staff is helpful, the rooms small but well kept, and breakfast is served in a glassed-in, taverna-style space overlooking the shopping thoroughfare of Ermou, Syntagma, and the Monastiraki metro. ✉*Kapnikareas 7, Plaka, 10556* ☎*210/322–2706 or 210/322–2707* 📠*210/322–2412* 🌐*www.plakahotel.gr* *67 rooms* *In-room: refrigerator* ▭*AE, DC, MC, V* *BP.*

$$ **Hermes Hotel.** Athens's small, modestly priced establishments have generally relied on little more than convenient central locations to draw visitors. Not so at the Hermes: sunny yellow guest rooms with wardrobes and tufted comforters feel warm and welcoming. Breakfast is served in the cheerful dining room, and you can enjoy a sunset cocktail

at the cozy roof-garden bar before setting off to sample the city's nightlife. CHAT tours has an office in the lobby and can help you arrange day trips. Pros: Great staff, happy decor, central location. Con: Small rooms. ✉ *Apollonos 19, Plaka, 10557* ☎ *210/323–5514* 📠 *210/323–2073* 🌐 *www.hermeshotel.gr* *45 rooms* *In-room: no TV (some)* *AE, MC, V* *BP.*

$–$$ **Adrian.** This comfortable pension offers friendly service and an excellent location in the heart of Plaka. Incurable romantics should ask for one of just three rooms looking toward the Acropolis; if you like being in the thick of things, enjoy the Acropolis view from the shaded roof garden and ask instead for one of the rooms with the spacious balconies overlooking the café-lined square. Some room rates include breakfast. ✉ *Adrianou 74, Plaka, 10556* ☎ *210/325–0454* 📠 *210/325–0461* 🌐 *www.douros-hotels.com* *22 rooms* *In-room: refrigerator. In-hotel: bar, public Internet* *MC, V.*

¢–$ ★ **Student and Travellers' Inn.** Not only is it cheap, this place is in the pricey Plaka! Wood floors, regular spruce-ups, and large windows make this spotless hostel cheerful and homey. The renovated house on an attractive and bustling street in Plaka has private rooms and shared dorm bedrooms. You pay extra for a private bathroom, but all rooms have a sink and mirror. There are also public computers with Internet access, and a small garden café. One caveat: the owners forbid food, drinks, or visitors in the rooms. The inn does not accept credit cards for payment, but a credit card number is required to make a reservation. ✉ *Kidathineon 16, Plaka, 10658* ☎ *210/324–4808* 📠 *210/321–0065* 🌐 *www.studenttravellersinn.com* *35 rooms, 14 with bath* *In-room: no a/c, no phone, no TV. In-hotel: public Internet* *No credit cards.*

MONASTIRAKI, PSIRRI & THISSION
ΜΟΝΑΣΤΗΡΑΚΙ, ΨΥΡΡΗ & ΘΗΣΕΙΟ

Northwest of Plaka, Monastiraki and Thission conjure up the gritty charm of an Anatolian bazaar and yet attract the city cognoscenti to hardcore cafés and bars.

$$$–$$$$ Fodor'sChoice ★ **Ochre & Brown.** A beautiful boutique hotel with a soothing, sleek design and an outstanding restaurant-bar, Ochre & Brown opened its doors in early 2006 and has quickly become one of the most talked-about new hotels in town. The guest rooms—from relaxing suites to a dazzling penthouse (with its own terrace)—are all little havens of urban cool; think flat-screen TVs, personal stereo/DVD systems, Pascal Morabito bath products, high-drama color schemes, black minimalistic headboards, and soft white Egyptian cotton sheets. The service is wonderful—you get champagne and fresh fruit when you arrive—and the staff keeps you up to date with all the latest happenings in the area, which are quite a few, since Psirri's legendary nightlife and flea market are right outside your door. ✉ *Leokoriou 7, Psirri, 10554* ☎ *210/331–2950* 📠 *210/331–2942* 🌐 *www.ochreandbrown.com* *9 rooms, 2 suites* *In-room: refrigerator. In-hotel: restaurant, bar* *AE, MC, V* *BP.*

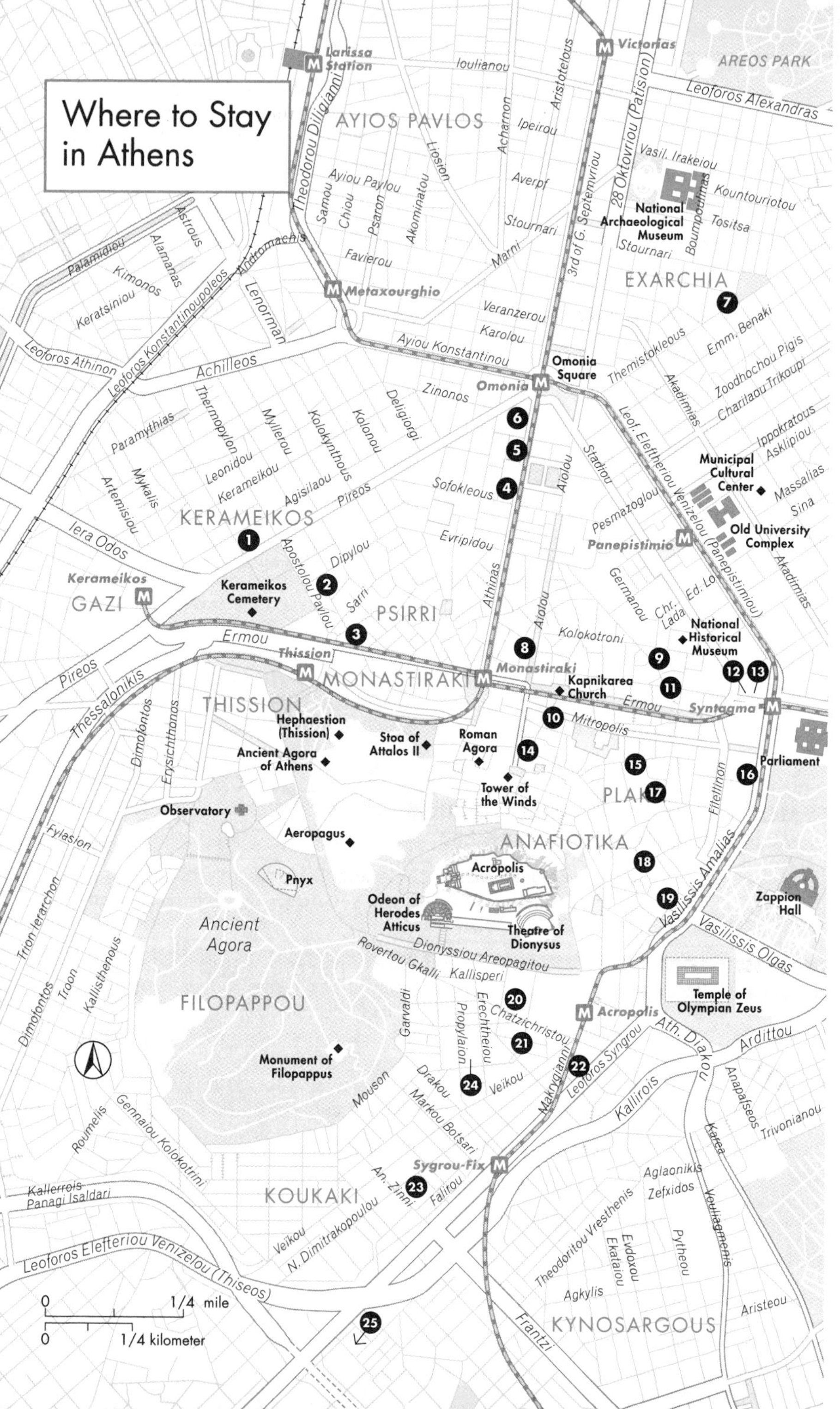
Where to Stay in Athens
Larissa Station
Victorias
AREOS PARK
Leoforos Alexandras
AYIOS PAVLOS
National Archaeological Museum
EXARCHIA
Metaxourghio
Omonia
Omonia Square
Municipal Cultural Center
Old University Complex
Panepistimio
KERAMEIKOS
Kerameikos
GAZI
Kerameikos Cemetery
PSIRRI
National Historical Museum
Thission
MONASTIRAKI
Monastiraki
Kapnikarea Church
Syntagma
THISSION
Hephaestion (Thission)
Stoa of Attalos II
Roman Agora
Ancient Agora of Athens
Tower of the Winds
Parliament
PLAKA
Observatory
Aeropagus
ANAFIOTIKA
Acropolis
Pnyx
Odeon of Herodes Atticus
Theatre of Dionysus
Zappion Hall
Ancient Agora
FILOPAPPOU
Acropolis
Temple of Olympian Zeus
Monument of Filopappus
Sygrou-Fix
KOUKAKI
KYNOSARGOUS
0 1/4 mile
0 1/4 kilometer

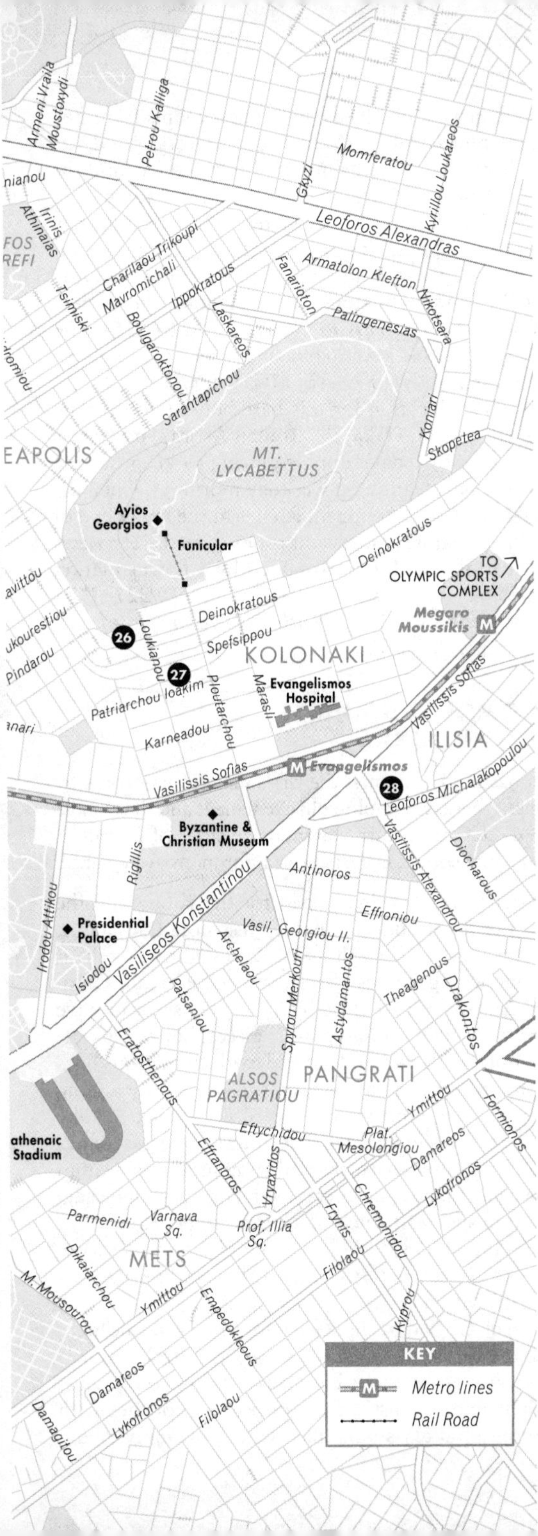

Acropolis Select 22
Adrian 14
Amalia Hotel 16
Art Gallery Pension 24
Athens Cypria Hotel 11
Athens Hilton 28
Baby Grand 5
Classical Athens Acropol 6
Electra Palace 17
Eridanus 1
The Exarcheion 7
Fresh Hotel 4
Grande Bretagne 13
Hermes Hotel 15
Herodion Hotel 20
Hotel Achilleas 9
Hotel Dioskouros 19
Hotel Tempi 8
Jason Inn 2
King George II Palace 12
Ledra Marriott 25
Marble House 23
Ochre & Brown 3
Periscope 27
Philippos Hotel 21
Plaka Hotel 10
St. George Lycabettus 26
Student and Travellers's Inn 18

3

KEY
Metro lines
Rail Road

$-$$ **Jason Inn.** The cool marble lobby leads up to guest rooms furnished in warm peaches and pinks. All have mini-refrigerators, good-size closets, and safes. A buffet breakfast is included in the price, and the rooftop garden restaurant has an intriguing panorama spreading from the Acropolis to the ancient Kerameikos Cemetery to the modern-day warehouse district of Gazi. Though it's on a run-down, seemingly out-of-the-way little corner, the Jason Inn is steps away from the buzzing nightlife districts of Psirri and Thission, not to mention the ancient Agora. ✉*Ayion Assomaton 12, Thission, 10553* ☎*210/325–1106* 📠*210/324–3132* 🌐*www.douros-hotels.com* *57 rooms* *In-room: refrigerator. In-hotel: restaurant, bar* ▭*AE, MC, V* *BP.*

Hotel Tempi. It's all about location for this bare-bones budget hotel just a short, pleasant stroll from Plaka, the Roman Agora, and Psirri's nightlife. Guest room windows have double-glazing to keep out the noise—an especially welcome feature on weekday mornings, when the shops on pedestrians-only Aiolou are open. Rooms at the lower end of the rate scale have shared baths, and several rooms have lovely views to the church of Ayia Irini, which is surrounded by a flower market most mornings. ✉*Aiolou 29, Monastiraki, 10558* ☎*210/321–3175* 📠*210/325–4179* *24 rooms, 12 with bath* *In-room: no phone, kitchen. In-hotel: bar* ▭*AE, MC, V.*

CENTRAL ATHENS, GAZI & OMONIA SQUARE
ΑΘΗΝΑ (ΚΕΝΤΡΟ) & ΠΛΑΤΕΙΑ ΟΜΟΝΟΙΑΣ

Located north of Monastiraki, Omonia, the city's main square roars by day and is seedy by night, but offers multi-culti excitement and that foodie fave, the Central Market. The former warehouse district of Psirri, set between Omonia and Monastiraki, is party central for many Athenians.

$$$–$$$$ Fodor'sChoice ★ **Baby Grand.** Fun yet posh, this dream pad for the young and the young-at-heart is a crazy/cool boutique hotel—just note the vintage convertible parked in the lobby. Though its locale is slightly sketchy if you're not fond of inner-city grit, it is also strategic: City Hall, Omonia, and the Central Market are all close by. Designers seem to have gone a bit overboard with neon art and graffiti pieces, but never fear: guest rooms can be comfortable and understated, with curvaceous lines and art deco modeling. Another array of rooms, however, are among the most dazzling in Europe, with walls covered in psychedelic-like clouds in one or pop art olives in another. The hotel's fantastic restaurant, Meat Me, specializing in juicy steaks and hamburgers, is near an upmarket bar for the champagne and Moët crowd. For true pampering, head to the on-site Carita spa. ✉*Athinas 65 & Lykourgou, Kotzia Sq., 10551* ☎*210/325–0900* 📠*210/325–0900* 🌐*www.classicalhotels.com* *65 rooms, 11 suites* *In-room: refrigerator, Ethernet. In-hotel: restaurant, spa* ▭*AE, DC, MC, V.*

$$$ **Classical Athens Acropol.** Owned by the same family that runs the high-class Grecotel chain, the Classical Athens Acropol has a fresh, assured aesthetic that's style-conscious without being fussy. In the lobby, clusters of cylindrical light fixtures cast a glow on leather couches with beaded fuchsia cushions, and glass pots filled with growing bamboo.

Spacious, quiet rooms are done in olive and cream, with pale patterned coffee tables, art deco–esque armchairs, and other retro details. ✉*Pireos 1, Omonia Sq., 10552* ☎*210/528–2100* 📠*210/523–1361* 🌐*www.grecotel.gr* *164 rooms, 3 suites* *In-room: refrigerator, Ethernet. In-hotel: restaurant* 💳*AE, DC, MC, V.*

$$$ **Eridanus.** Dazzling modern art, a sparkling staircase, luscious beds, top-line bath products—this lovely hotel on the edge of the rising-star neighborhood of Gazi has it all. The building has a neoclassic vibe but the interiors are cool/hot 21st century, thanks to a dramatic, white minimalistic lobby, bedrooms that are designed for the *Wallpaper* crowd, and some high-style marble bathrooms. There are also some stunning antique touches, such as carved wood armoires and a bar lined with vintage Grecian rugs. You can see the Acropolis from seven of the rooms, especially from the gorgeous rooftop suite. The in-house restaurant, Parea, is a great place for meat-lovers (note: the city's best seafood is right next door at the Michelin-starred To Varoulko). Eridanus's staff is professional and well informed and can fill you in on all the hippest happenings in Gazi, a transitioning neighborhood that looks a bit pockmarked in places. ✉*Pireos 78, Kerameikos, 10435* ☎*210/520–5360* 📠*210/520–0550* 🌐*www.eridanus.gr* *27 rooms, 3 suites* *In-room: refrigerator. In-hotel: restaurant* 💳*AE, DC, MC, V.*

Fodor's Choice ★

$–$$ **Fresh Hotel.** Reveling in minimalist glam, this attractive boutique hotel has relaxing and expertly decorated rooms, a plugged-in staff, and a fabulous in-house bar-bistro that features wonderful nouvelle (some might say experimental) Greek cuisine. The nabe is slightly dodgy at night and unattractive by day—the Athens Central Market and Omonia Square are nearby—but this Athenian madness is forgotten quickly as you soak in the hotel's ninth-floor swimming pool or the in-house sauna and steam rooms. ✉*Sofokleous 26, near Kotzia Sq., 10552* ☎*210/524–8511* 📠*210/524–8517* 🌐*www.freshhotel.gr* *133 rooms* *In-room: refrigerator. In-hotel: restaurant, pool, gym, public Wi-Fi* 💳*AE, DC, MC, V.*

SYNTAGMA SQUARE & KOLONAKI
ΠΛΑΤΕΙΑ ΣΥΝΤΑΓΜΑΤΟΣ & ΚΟΛΩΝΑΚΙ

Located east of Plaka, Kolonaki is a posherie favored by politicians, expats, and the ladies who lunch. Syntagma, on the other hand, is a pretty central square, near Parliament, that is a fave with tourists.

$$$$ **Amalia Hotel.** Depending on your needs, the Amalia's best and worst feature is its location: right on one of Athens's biggest, busiest streets, directly across from Parliament. The minute you step outside, you're swept up in the noise and chaos of central Athens—fortunately, double-glazed windows and a view to the pretty National Garden keep things peaceful inside. The newly remodeled rooms are fresh and inviting, and the hotel is close to transport: the airport shuttle is next door, the metro and tram just a few steps away. ✉*Amalias 10, Syntagma Sq., 10557* ☎*210/323–7301* 📠*210/607–2135* 🌐*www.amalia.gr* *98 rooms, 1 suite* *In-room: refrigerator, Internet. In-hotel: restaurant, bar, public Wi-Fi* 💳*AE, DC, MC, V.*

3

$$$$ Fodor'sChoice ★ **Grande Bretagne.** Rest on custom-made silk ottomans in the lobby; drink tea from gold-leafed porcelain in the atrium; call your personal butler 24 hours a day from your room—the landmark Grande Bretagne, built in 1842, remains the most exclusive hotel in Athens. The guest list includes more than a century's worth of royals, rock stars, and heads of state. An all-out-luxury renovation, completed in 2003, recaptured the original grandeur, restoring 19th-century oil paintings, antiques, and hand-carved details as they were a century earlier. There's also a lovely spa where you can pamper yourself with indulgences such as ouzo-oil massages. ✉ *Vasileos Georgiou A' 1, Syntagma Sq., 10564* ☎ *210/333–0000, 210/331–5555 through 210/331–5559 reservations* 📠 *210/322–8034, 210/333–0910 reservations* 🌐 *www.grandebretagne.gr* *290 rooms, 37 suites* *In-room: refrigerator, Ethernet. In-hotel: 3 restaurants, bars, pools, gym, spa* 💳 *AE, DC, MC, V.*

$$$$ ★ **King George II Palace.** A spacious lobby done in marble, mahogany, velvet, leather, and gold trim lures you into a world where antique crystal lamps and frosted glass shower stalls with mother-of-pearl tiles raise standards of luxury to dizzying heights. Each room is individually furnished with one-of-a-kind handcrafted furniture, antique desks, and raw silk upholstery. Heavy brocade curtains are no more than a decorative flourish: the rooms are soundproofed and their lighting calibrated to the natural light. At the Tudor Hall restaurant, savor Mediterranean delicacies and a view of the city skyline stretching from the Panathenaic Stadium to the Parthenon. ✉ *Vasileos Georgiou A' 2, Syntagma Sq., 10564* ☎ *210/322–2210* 📠 *210/325–0564* 🌐 *www.grecotel.gr* *77 rooms, 25 suites* *In-room: refrigerator, Ethernet. In-hotel: restaurant, bars, spa* 💳 *AE, DC, MC, V.*

$$$–$$$$ Fodor'sChoice ★ **St. George Lycabettus.** This small, luxurious hotel on the wooded slopes of Mt. Lycabettus, in upscale Kolonaki, is steps from Athens's museum row and designer shops. Meticulously decorated, most rooms have splendid views (although some have blah ones). Each floor has its own theme, and rooms are designed accordingly, with looks ranging from jewel-tone art nouveau to sleek black-and-white minimalism to soothing neutrals with bamboo. The rooftop pool bar and Le Grand Balcon restaurant have an unbeatable panoramic view. Downstairs the postmodern 1970s-style lounge, Frame, is one of the hottest nightspots in town and also serves a decadent weekend brunch. ✉ *Kleomenous 2, Kolonaki, 10675* ☎ *210/729–0711 through 210/729–0719* 📠 *210/729–0439 or 210/724–7610* 🌐 *www.sglycabettus.gr* *162 rooms, 5 suites* *In-room: dial-up. In-hotel: 2 restaurants, bar, pool, gym, some pets allowed* 💳 *AE, DC, MC, V.*

$$$ **Athens Cypria Hotel.** This modest, friendly oasis in the city center is a good bet for families. It has reasonable prices (considering the location off Syntagma Square) and discounts for children up to 12 years old. Cribs are provided free of charge. There are also several connecting family rooms. Modern, clean, simple blue-and-white rooms overlook a quiet street, but if you'd like a view ask for one of the three rooms looking toward the Acropolis. Breakfast is an American-style buffet (with eggs, not just cold meats). Broadband is being added to some rooms at press time. ✉ *Diomias 5, Syntagma Sq., 10563* ☎ *210/323–8034*

210/324–8792 *diomeia@hol.gr* *71 rooms* *In-room: refrigerator, dial-up (some). In-hotel: bar* *AE, MC, V* *BP.*

$$–$$$ **Periscope.** Like Ochre & Brown, this sleek concept hotel combines minimalist urban-chic design, amenity-filled rooms, and exceptional service for a truly relaxing experience. Business travelers and urbane globe-trotters love the efficient staff, spotless rooms, and the old-money neighborhood of Kolonaki. Guest rooms are a bit small with disappointing views but no one will complain about the flat-screen TVs. Many of the city's best restaurants and cafés are here, and it's only a short walk to the metro. *Haritos 22, Kolonaki, 10675* *210/729–7200* *www.periscope.gr* *17 rooms, 4 junior suites* *In-room: refrigerator. In-hotel: bar, public Internet* *AE, DC, MC, V.*

$$ **Hotel Achilleas.** Like its sisters, the Hermes and Plaka hotels, the Achilleas combines interesting design with the friendly, personal service that comes from being family-run—and a price at the lower end of its category. Black and white diamond tiles alternate down the center of the long, sleek lobby lined by opposing black and white armchairs. The spicy mustard-color guest-room walls contrast nicely with dusky blue bedding and leopard-print curtains. The buffet breakfast is served in a stylish interior courtyard. *Lekka 21, Syntagma Sq., 10562* *210/322–5826* *210/322–2412* *www.achilleashotel.gr* *50 rooms* *In-room: refrigerator, dial-up* *AE, DC, MC, V* *BP.*

¢–$ **Hotel Dioskouros.** The real draws of Dioskouros over similarly cheap, downtown spots are its amicable staff, central but quiet location at Plaka's edge, and its shaded garden, where you can relax with a beer at the end of the day. It's a students' and independent travelers' favorite. Many of the basic rooms have space for the two twin beds and not much more. *Pittakou 6, Syntagma Sq., 10558* *210/324–8165* *210/321–9991* *www.consolas.gr* *18 rooms without bath* *In-room: no TV, no room phones* *AE, DC, MC, V* *CP.*

ATHENS NORTH & EAST ΑΘΗΝΑ, ΒΟΡΕΙΑ & ΑΝΑΤΟΛΙΚΗ

$$$$ **Athens Hilton.** The Hilton reflects the trend sweeping through most of Athens's high-end properties, whose recent revamps have left them with modern, clean-lined, and minimal design. The once-traditional lobby is now a vast expanse of white marble punctuated by sleek, mod benches. Guest rooms are fitted out in light wood, brushed metal, etched glass, and crisp white duvets. Facilities are business-oriented, with a stylish executive check-in lounge and huge conference rooms. Along with a spa, the hotel has the biggest hotel pool in Athens. It also boasts a branch of Estatorio Milos, Manhattan's luxe Greek restaurant. *Vasilissis Sofias 46, Ilisia, 11528* *210/728–1000, 210/728–1100 reservations* *www.athens.hilton.com* *498 rooms, 19 suites* *In-room: refrigerator, Ethernet. In-hotel: 4 restaurants, bars, pool, gym* *AE, DC, MC, V.*

¢ **Exarcheion.** Smack in the center of a lively bohemian bar and café district, this hotel has been a fixture on the international backpacking circuit for years. Guest rooms are plain and slightly worn, but the fact that the National Archaeological Museum is just around the corner makes this a good value. ✉ *Themistokleous 55, Exarchia, 10683* ☎ *210/380–256* ℻ *210/380–3296* *49 rooms* *In-room: refrigerator* *MC, V.*

NIGHTLIFE & THE ARTS

From ancient Greek tragedies in quarried amphitheaters to the chicest disco clubs, Athens rocks at night. Several of the former industrial districts are enjoying a renaissance, and large spaces have filled up with galleries, restaurants, and theaters—providing one-stop shopping for an evening's entertainment. The Greek weekly *Athinorama* covers current performances, gallery openings, and films, as do the English-language newspapers *Athens News,* published Friday, and *Kathimerini,* inserted in the *International Herald Tribune,* available Monday through Saturday. The monthly English-language magazine *Insider* has features and listings on entertainment in Athens, with a focus on the arts. *Odyssey,* a glossy bimonthly magazine, also publishes an annual summer guide in late June, sold at newsstands around Athens with the season's top performances and exhibitions.

NIGHTLIFE

Athens's heady nightlife starts late. Most bars and clubs don't get hopping until midnight and they stay open at the very least until 3 AM. Drinks are rather steep (about €6–€10), but generous. Often there is a cover charge on weekends at the most popular clubs, which also have bouncers. In summer many major downtown bars and clubs close their in-town location and move to the seaside. Ask your hotel for recommendations and summer closings. For a uniquely Greek evening, visit a club featuring rembetika music, a type of blues, or the popular *bouzoukia* (clubs with live bouzouki, a stringed instrument, music). Few clubs take credit cards for drinks.

BARS

★ **Balthazar.** Athenians of all ages come to escape the summer heat at this bar-restaurant in a neoclassic house with a lush garden courtyard and subdued music. ✉ *Tsoha 27, Ambelokipi* ☎ *210/644–1215 or 210/645–2278.*

Baraonda. Beautiful people, breakneck music, and a VIP vibe have made this club a perennial favorite. The food here is also top-line and there's a beautiful garden when you need a breather. ✉ *Tsoha 43, Ambelokipi* ☎ *210/644–4308.*

Mad. Dance in manic fun to '80s pop and all eras of rock at this fun and popular club in the hot Gazi district. ✉ *Persefonis 53, Gazi* ☎ *210/346–2007.*

Memphis. Gregarious is the word for this Athens classic. The music is predominantly 1980s, with some Gothic theme nights and occasional live bands. ✉ *Ventiri 5, behind Hilton, Ilisia* ☎ *210/722–4104.*

Fodor's Choice ★ **Parko.** With low-key music and a romantic setting, Parko is a summer favorite. ✉ *Eleftherias Park, Ilisia* ☎ *210/722–3784.*

Sodade. This gay-friendly bar-club-lounge attracts a standing-room-only crowd every weekend. The draw is the great music, the joyous vibe, and the very fact that it's in Gazi, the hottest place in central Athens. ✉*Triptolemou 10, Gazi* ☎*210/346–8657.*

Soul Garden. Popular Soul Garden is unquestionably hip but also friendly. Relax with a cocktail and snacks in the plant-filled, lantern-lighted courtyard; after 1 AM the dance floor inside picks up pace. ✉*Evripidou 65, Psirri* ☎*210/331–0907.*

Stavlos. All ages feel comfortable at the bar in what used to be the Royal Stables. Sit in the courtyard or in the brick-wall restaurant for a snack like Cretan *kalitsounia* (similar to a calzone), or dance in the long bar. Stavlos often hosts art exhibits, film screenings, miniconcerts, and other happenings, as the Greeks call them, throughout the week. ✉*Iraklidon 10, Thission* ☎*210/345–2502 or 210/346–7206.*

BOUZOUKIA

Many tourists think Greek social life centers on large clubs where live bouzouki music plays while patrons smash up the plates. Plate-smashing is now prohibited, but plates of flowers are sold for scattering over the performer or your companions when they take to the dance floor. Upscale bouzouki clubs line the lower end of Syngrou and stretch out to the south coast, where top entertainers command top prices. Be aware that bouzouki food is overpriced and often second-rate. There is a per-person minimum (€30) or a prix-fixe menu; a bottle of whiskey costs around €200. For those who choose to stand at the bar, a drink runs about €15 to €20 at a good bouzouki place.

Fever. One of Athens's most popular bouzouki clubs showcases the most popular singers of the day, including the ageless Anna Vissi, Greece's own answer to Madonna. It's open Wednesday through Sunday. ✉*Syngrou 259, Neos Kosmos* ☎*210/942–7580 through 210/942–7583.*

Rex. Over-the-top is the way to describe a performance at Rex—it's a laser-light show, multi–costume-change extravaganza, with headlining pop and bouzouki stars. ✉*Panepistimiou 48, Central Athens* ☎*210/381–4591.*

CLUBS

Nightclubs in Greece migrate with the seasons. From October through May, they're in vast, throbbing venues in central Athens and the northern suburbs; from June through September, many relocate to luxurious digs on the south coast. The same spaces are used from year to year, but owners and names tend to bounce around. Before heading out, check local listings or talk to your concierge. Most clubs charge a cover at the door and employ bouncers, aptly called "face-control" by Greeks because they tend to let only the "lookers" in. One way to avoid both of these, since partying doesn't get going until after 1 AM, is to make an earlier dinner reservation at one of the many clubs that have restaurants as well.

Akrotiri Lounge. Luxurious Akrotiri has as much of a reputation for chef Christophe Clessienne's excellent food—think foie-gras bonbons with sautéed pears and spices—as it does for its runway-beautiful clientele, sea views, and a poolside dance floor. ⊠*Vasileos Georgiou 11, Agios Kosmas, Kalamaki* ☎*210/985–9147* ⊕*www.akrotirilounge.gr.*

LEAVE THE DRIVING TO THEM

In summer, the best way to get to Athens's seaside nightclubs is by taxi—driving on the coastal road can be a nightmare. Just tell the taxi the name of the club; drivers quickly learn the location of the major spots once they open each year.

Bios Basement. All the coolest artists, grunge-rockers, revolutionaries, and experimental philosophers hang out in the cavernous basement of this Bauhaus building in the Kerameikos neighborhood, part of the greater Gazi district. Expect to hear the best electronica music in town. ⊠*Piraios 84, Gazi.*

★ **Bo.** A seaside club that actually has a permanent address, Bo is in a huge old beachfront mansion. The beautiful tile floors haven't lost their luster after years of serving as a platform for gyrating club kids. The place is also open during the day for drinks and coffee, served on the terrace. ✣*8 km (5 mi) south of Athens,* ⊠*Konstantinou Karamanli 14, Voula* ☎*210/895–9645.*

Central-Island. From September to May, Athens's hippest people make an appearance at this designer-styled club to groove to ambient music, nibble on sushi, and languidly sip fancy cocktails. From May to September, Central is closed in town; it reopens on the coast as Island, in an atmospheric space in the sunny suburb of Varkiza. ⊠*Kolonak Sq. 14, Kolonaki* ☎*210/724–5938* ⊕*www.island-central.gr Island* ⊠*On Km 27 of Athens-Sounio Ave., Varkiza* ☎*210/892–5000.*

Venti. This successful Psirri club is now open in summer, one of the few in the city center to do so. Its open-air style comes complete with a canopy of olive and palm trees while the crowd dances to a furious beat of Greek pop music. ⊠*Lepeniotou 20, Psirri* ☎*210/325–4504.*

JAZZ & BLUES CLUBS

The jazz scene has built up momentum, and there are several venues from which to choose. Tickets to shows can be purchased at the clubs or major record stores.

Half Note Jazz Club. The original and best venue in town is the place for serious jazz sophisticates. It's a good idea to reserve a table ahead of time, especially for one near the stage; latecomers can always stand at the bar in back. ⊠*Trivonianou 17, Pangrati* ☎*210/921–3310 or 210/923–2460.*

House of Art. This laid-back venue hosts small, mostly blues, groups. ⊠*Santouri 4, at Sarri, Psirri* ☎*210/321–7678.*

Parafono. Leave the big names at other clubs and tap into the homegrown jazz circuit here instead. ⊠*Asklipiou 130A, Exarchia* ☎*210/644–6512* ⊕*www.parafono.gr.*

REMBETIKA

The Greek equivalent of the urban blues, rembetika is rooted in the traditions of Asia Minor and was brought to Greece by refugees from Smyrna in the 1920s. It filtered up from the lowest economic levels to become one of the most enduring genres of Greek popular music, still enthralling clubgoers today. At these thriving clubs, you can catch a glimpse of Greek social life and even join the dances (but remember, it's considered extremely rude to interrupt a solo dance). The two most common dances are the *zeimbekikos,* in which the man improvises in circular movements that become ever more complicated, and the belly-dance-like *tsifteteli.* Most of the clubs are closed in summer; call in advance. Drink prices range from €5 to €8, a bottle of whiskey from €50 to €70, but the food is often expensive and unexceptional; it's wisest to order a fruit platter or a bottle of wine.

Anifori. This friendly, popular club plays both rembetika and *dimotika* (Greek folk music). It's open Friday through Sunday nights. ✉ *Vasileos Georgiou A' 47, Pasalimani, Piraeus* ☎ *210/411–5819.*

Boemissia. Usually crowded and pleasantly raucous, Boemissia attracts many young people, who quickly start gyrating in various forms of the tsifteteli. Doors are shut Monday. ✉ *Solomou 19, Exarchia* ☎ *210/384–3836 or 210/330–0865.*

Mnisikleous. The authentic music of gravel-voiced Bobbis Tsertos, a popular *rembetis* (rembetika singer), draws audience participation Thursday through Sunday. ✉ *Mnisikleous 22, at Lyceiou, Plaka* ☎ *210/322–5558 or 210/322–5337.*

★ **Stoa ton Athanaton.** "Arcade of the Immortals" has been around since 1930, housed in a converted warehouse in the meat-market area. Not much has changed since then. The music is enhanced by an infectious, devil-may-care mood and the enthusiastic participation of the audience, especially during the best-of-rembetika afternoons (3:30–7:30). The small dance floor is always jammed. Food here is delicious and reasonably priced, but liquor is expensive. Make reservations for evening performances, when the orchestra is led by old-time rembetis greats. The club is closed Sunday. ✉ *Sofokleous 19, Central Market* ☎ *210/321–4362 or 210/321–0342.*

Taximi. At one time or other, most of Greece's greatest rembetika musicians have played at this old-time bar; many of their black-and-white pictures are on the smoke-stained walls. ✉ *Isavron 29, at Harilaou Trikoupi, Exarchia* ☎ *210/363–9919.*

TAVERNAS WITH MUSIC

Klimataria. At this century-old taverna, a guitarist (as well as an accordion player in winter) plays sing-along favorites much appreciated by the largely Greek audience. The price of this slice of old-style Greek entertainment is surprisingly reasonable. ✉ *Klepsidras 5, Plaka* ☎ *210/324–1809 or 210/321–1215.*

Stamatopoulou Palia Plakiotiki Taverna. Enjoy good food and an acoustic band with three guitars and bouzouki playing old Athenian songs in an 1822 house. In summer the show moves to the garden. Greeks will often get up and dance, beckoning you to join them, so don't be shy. ✉*Lysiou 26, Plaka* ☎*210/322–8722 or 210/321–8549.*

THE ARTS

Athens's energetic year-round performing arts scene kicks into a higher gear from June through September, when numerous stunning outdoor theaters host everything from classical Greek drama (in both Greek and English), opera, symphony, and ballet, to rock, pop, and hip-hop concerts. In general, dress for summer performances is fairly casual, though the city's glitterati get decked out for events such as a world premiere opera at the Odeon of Herodes Atticus. From October through May, when the arts move indoors, the Megaron Mousikis/Athens Concert Hall is the biggest venue. Athenians consider the Megaron a place to see and be seen, and dress up accordingly. Performances at outdoor summer venues, stadiums, and the Megaron tend to be priced between €20 to €120 for tickets, depending on the location of seats and popularity of performers.

CONCERTS, DANCE & OPERA

Dora Stratou Troupe. The country's leading folk dance company performs Greek folk dances from all regions, as well as from Cyprus, in eye-catching authentic costumes. The programs change every two weeks. Performances are held Tuesday through Sunday from the end of May through September at 9:30 PM and Sunday at 8:15 PM at the Dora Stratou Theater. Tickets cost €13 and can be purchased at the box office before the show. ✉*Arakinthou and Voutie, Filopappou* ☎*210/921–4650 theater, 210/324–4395 troupe's office* 🖷*210/324–6921* 🌐*www.grdance.org.*

Megaron Mousikis/Athens Concert Hall. World-class Greek and international artists take the stage at the Megaron Mousikis to perform in concerts and opera from September through June. Information and tickets are available weekdays 10–6 and Saturday 10–4. Prices range from €18 to €90; there's a substantial discount for students and those 8 to 18 years old. Tickets go on sale a few weeks in advance, and many events sell out within hours. On the first day of sales, tickets can be purchased by cash or credit card only in person at the Athens Concert Hall. From the second day on, remaining tickets may be purchased by phone, in person from the downtown box office (weekdays 10–4), and online. ✉*Vasilissis Sofias and Kokkali, Ilisia* ☎*210/728–2333* 🖷*210/728–2300* 🌐*www.megaron.gr Downtown box office* ✉*Omirou 8, Central Athens* ☎*No phone.*

Philippos Nakas Conservatory. Inexpensive classical music concerts are held November through May at the conservatory. Tickets cost about €11. ✉*Ippokratous 41, Central Athens* ☎*210/363–4000* 🖷*210/360–2827.*

FESTIVALS

★ **Hellenic Festival.** The city's primary artistic event, the Hellenic Festival (formerly known as the Athens Festival), runs from June through September at the Odeon of Herodes Atticus. The festival has showcased performers such as Norah Jones, Dame Kiri Te Kanawa, Luciano Pavarotti, and Diana Ross; such dance troupes as the Royal London Ballet, the Joaquin Cortes Ballet, and Maurice Béjart; symphony orchestras; and local groups performing ancient Greek drama. Usually a major world premiere is staged during the festival. The Odeon theater makes a delightful backdrop, with the floodlighted Acropolis looming behind the audience and the Roman arches behind the performers. The upper-level seats have no cushions, so bring something to sit on, and wear low shoes, since the marble steps are steep. For viewing most performances the Gamma zone is the best seat choice. Tickets go on sale two weeks before performances but sell out quickly for popular shows; they are available from the festival box office. Prices range from €16 to as high as €120 for the big names; student and youth discounts are available. *Odeon of Herodes Atticus* ✉*Dionyssiou Areopagitou, Acropolis* ☎*210/323–2771, 210/323–5582 box office* 🌐*www.greekfestival.gr Festival box office* ✉*Panepistimiou 39, Syntagma Sq.* ☎*210/322–1459.*

MOONLIGHT SERENADES

Every year, on the night of the full moon in August (believed to be the brightest and most beautiful moon of the year), Athens holds an August Moon Festival. The Acropolis, Roman Agora, Odeon of Herodes Atticus, and sometimes other sites are open to the public for free, and performances of opera, Greek dance, and classical music take place amid the ancient columns by moonlight. If you're in Athens in August, this is a must-do. The main venue is the Odeon of Herodes Atticus, at Dionyssiou Areopagitou, phone: 210/323–2771, 210/323–5582 box office.

Lycabettus Theater. A few Elliniko Festival events are held at the Lycabettus Theater, set on a pinnacle of Mt. Lycabettus. The specialty here is popular concerts; past performers have included B. B. King, Bob Dylan, Massive Attack, and Paco de Lucia. Since buses travel only as far as the bottom of the hill, and taxi drivers often won't drive to the top, buy a one-way ticket on the funicular and walk about 10 minutes to the theater. ✉*At top of Mt. Lycabettus, Kolonaki* ☎*210/322–1459, 210/727–2233, 210/722–7209 theater box office.*

Vyronas Festival. Performances by well-known Greek musician Dimitris Mitropanos, international acts such as the Beijing Opera, and ancient Greek theater classics are staged in an old quarry, now the Theatro Vrahon. Shows begin around 9:30 PM. Buy tickets (€10–€15) at the theater before the show, or at any of the chain of Metropolis music stores. ✉*Tatoulon, where Trolley 11 ends, Vyrona* ☎*210/765–5748 or 210/765–3775.*

FILM

Films are shown in original-language versions with Greek subtitles (except for major animated films), a definite boon for foreigners. Downtown theaters have the most advanced technology and most comfortable seats. Tickets run about €7. Check the *Athens News* or *Kathimerini* in the *International Herald Tribune* for programs, schedules, and addresses and phone numbers of theaters, including outdoor theaters. The Hellenic-American Union (www.hau.gr) and the British Council (www.britishcouncil.gr) screen films for free (screenings are usually published in local English-language media).

Unless theaters have air-conditioning, they close from June through September, making way for *therina* (open-air theaters), an enchanting, uniquely Greek entertainment that offers instant escapism under a starry sky. A feature of postwar Mediterranean countries that has survived only in Greece, open-air cinemas saw their popularity decline after the arrival of television. There's been a resurgence in their appeal, and about 75 now operate in the greater Athens area.

Attikon Cinemax Class. With its old-fashioned red-velvet and gold-trim embellishments, huge crystal chandelier, wide screen, enormous seats, and central location, this is the best theater in all of Athens. It screens world premieres and classic rereleases. ✉*Stadiou 19, Syntagma Sq.* ☎*210/322–8821.*

Cine Paris. Kitschy posters of old Greek movies are for sale in the lobby of this rooftop garden theater. It's close to many hotels, on Plaka's main walkway, but the place uses regular stereo instead of Dolby Digital sound. ✉*Kidathineon 22, Plaka* ☎*210/322–2071 or 210/324–8057.*

Elly. Frequent Elly for independent and art films that don't make it to Greece's more-mainstream cinemas. ✉*Akadimias 64, Syntagma Sq.* ☎*210/363–2789.*

Thission. Films at this open-air theater compete with a view of the Acropolis. It's on the Unification of Archaeological Sites walkway. ✉*Apostolou Pavlou 7, Thission* ☎*210/342–0864 or 210/347–0980.*

SHOPPING

For serious retail therapy, most natives head to the shopping streets that branch off central Syntagma and Kolonaki squares. Syntagma is the starting point for popular Ermou, a pedestrian zone where large, international brands like Esprit and Marks & Spencer's have edged out small, independent retailers. You'll find local shops on streets parallel and perpendicular to Ermou: Mitropoleos, Voulis, Nikis, Perikleous, and Praxitelous among them. Poke around here for real bargains, like strings of freshwater pearls, loose semiprecious stones, or made-to-fit hats. Much ritzier is the Kolonaki quarter, with boutiques and designer shops on fashionable streets like Anagnostopoulou, Tsakalof, Skoufa, Solonos, and Kanari. Voukourestiou, the link between Kolonaki and Syntagma, is where you'll find Louis Vuitton, Ralph Lauren, and similar brands. In Monastiraki, coppersmiths have their shops on Ifestou. You can pick up copper wine jugs, candlesticks, cookware, and more for next to nothing. The flea market centered on Pandrossou and Ifestou operates on Sunday mornings and has practically everything, from secondhand guitars to Russian vodka. No matter how low the price, always bargain.

ANTIQUES & ICONS

Antiques are in vogue now, so the prices of these items have soared. Shops on Pandrossou sell small antiques and icons, but keep in mind that many of these are fakes. You must have government permission to export genuine objects from the ancient Greek, Roman, or Byzantine periods.

Alekos Kostas. This *palaiopolio* (junk dealer) is especially popular among collectors of old radio sets and vintage toys, and carries wonderfully quirky items such as mechanized piggy banks. ✉*Abyssinia Sq. 3, Monastiraki* ☎*210/321–1580.*

Kiritisis. Old coins, from Greece and around the world, are for sale at Kiritisis, along with stamps and medals. ✉*Areos 1, at Pandrossou, Monastiraki* ☎*210/324–0544.*

Martinos. Serious antiques collectors should head here to look for items such as exquisite dowry chests, old swords, and Venetian glass. ✉*Pandrossou 5, Monastiraki* ☎*210/321–3110* ✉*Pindarou 24, Kolonaki* ☎*210/360–9449.*

Nasiotis. With a little perseverance, you can make some interesting finds in this huge basement stacked with books, engravings, old magazines, and first editions. ✉*Ifestou 24, Monastiraki* ☎*210/321–2369.*

Pylarinos. Stamp and coin collectors love this packed shop, which also has a good selection of 19th-century engravings. ✉*Panepistimiou 18, Syntagma Sq.* ☎*210/363–0688.*

CLOTHING

Greece is known for its well-made shoes (most shops are clustered around the Ermou pedestrian zone and in Kolonaki), its furs (Mitropoleos near Syntagma), and its durable leather items (Pandrossou in Monastiraki). In Plaka shops you can find fishermen's caps—always a good present—and the natural wool undershirts and hand-knit sweaters worn by fishermen; across the United States these have surfaced at triple the Athens price.

★ **Afternoon.** Prices are lower than what you'll find abroad at this shop with an excellent collection of fashions by Greece's best new designers, including Sophia Kokosalaki, whose work has often graced the pages of *Vogue*. Look for labels from up-and-comers like Deux Hommes, Vasso Consola, and Pavlos Kyriakides. ✉*Deinokratous 1, Kolonaki* ☎*210/722–5380.*

Kaplan Furs. Despite animal rights campaigns, Mitropoleos is lined with fur shops. Kaplan has everything from pieced-together stoles to full-length minks, often from the northern city of Kastoria. ✉*Mitropoleos 22–24, Syntagma Sq.* ☎*210/322–2226.*

Me Me Me. Whether you're shopping around for a new cocktail dress or for funky accessories, this is the place to head for trendsetting creations by emerging Greek designers. ✉*Haritos 19, Kolonaki* ☎*210/722–4890.*

Occhi. Art and the latest clothes and accessories by young Greek designers are displayed side-by-side in this gallery-style shop. ✉*Sarri 35, Psirri* ☎*210/321–3298.*

Stavros Melissinos. A legendary poet and gentle soul, as well as shoemaker, Stavros outfits many tourists with his handmade sandals. The Beatles once visited his shop. ✉*Ayias Theklas 2, Monastiraki* ☎*210/321–9247.*

GIFTS

Athens has great gifts, particularly handmade crafts. Better tourist shops sell copies of traditional Greek jewelry, silver filigree, Skyrian pottery, onyx ashtrays and dishes, woven bags, attractive rugs (including *flokati,* or shaggy goat-wool rugs), and little blue-and-white pendants designed as amulets to ward off the *mati* (evil eye).

Baba. Greeks can spend hours heatedly playing *tavli* (backgammon). To take home a game set of your own, look closely for this hole-in-the-wall, no-name shop, which sells boards and pieces in all sizes and designs. ✉*Ifestou 30, Monastiraki* ☎*210/321–9994.*

Bead Shop. From pinhead-size "evil eyes" to 2-inch-diameter wood beads, you'll find a dizzying selection of beads to string your own *komboloi* (worry beads) or bracelet. ✉*Pal. Venizelou 6, Mitropolis* ☎*210/322–1004.*

Fodor'sChoice ★ **Benaki Museum Gift Shop.** The museum shop has excellent copies of Greek icons, jewelry, and folk art—at fair prices. ✉*Koumbari 1, at Vasilissis Sofias, Kolonaki* ☎*210/362–7367.*

Diplous Pelekys. Wool totes, pillow covers with hand-embroidered folk motifs, and, of course, pins featuring the Cretan double-headed ax (*diplous pelekys*) make excellent, and affordable, gifts. ✉*Voulis 7 and Kolokotroni 3, Syntagma Sq.* ☎*210/322–3783.*

Fresh Line. Among the solid shampoo cakes, body oils, and face packs are a tremendous number of Greek-made soaps that are sliced from big blocks or wheels as though they were cheese; you pay by weight. The strawberries-and-cream soap, Rea, contains real berries; the Orpheus and Eurydice soap for sensitive skin is made with vanilla, milk, and rice, just like Greek *rizogalo* (rice pudding). ✉*Skoufa 10, Kolonaki* ☎*210/364–4015.*

Goutis. One of the more-interesting stores on Pandrossou, Goutis has an eclectic jumble of jewelry, costumes, embroidery, and old, handcrafted silver objects. ✉*Dimokritou 40, Kolonaki* ☎*210/361–3557.*

Ilias Kokkonis. This century-old store stocks any flag you've always wanted, large or small, from most any country. ✉*Stoa Arsakeiou 8, enter from Panepistimiou or Stadiou, Omonia Sq.* ☎*210/322–1189 or 210/322–6355.*

Korres. Natural beauty products blended in traditional recipes using Greek herbs and flowers have graced the bathroom shelves of celebrities like Nicole Kidman. In Athens they are available at most pharmacies for regular-folk prices. For the largest selection of basil-lemon shower gel, coriander body lotion, olive-stone face scrub, and wild-rose eye cream, go to the original Korres pharmacy behind the Panathenaic Stadium. ✉*Eratosthenous and Ivikou, Pangrati* ☎*210/722–2744.*

Mastiha Shop. Medical research lauding the healing properties of gum mastic, a resin from trees only found in an area of Chios, has spawned a range of products, from chewing gum and cookies to cosmetics.

✉Panepistimiou 6, Syntagma Sq. ☎210/363–2750.

Riza. You can pick up wonderful lace, often handmade, in romantic designs at Riza. The shop also carries fabric at fair prices, and decorative items such as handblown glass bowls and brass candlesticks. ✉*Voukourestiou 35, at Skoufa, Kolonaki* ☎*210/361–1157.*

The Shop. A plain or brightly colored olive-oil pourer, traditional kafeneion (coffeehouse) trays, and *fanaria* (birdcagelike contraptions in which to store fresh food) are just some of the items available here that embody Greek village life. Some of the aluminum pieces are handmade. ✉*Lysikratous 3, Plaka* ☎*210/323–0350.*

Tanagrea. Hand-painted ceramic pomegranates, a symbol of fertility and good fortune, are one of the most popular items in one of the city's oldest gift shops. ✉*Voulis 26 and Mitropoleos 15, Syntagma Sq.* ☎*210/322–3366.*

Thiamis. Iconographer Aristides Makos creates beautiful hand-painted, gold-leaf icons on wood and stone. He also paints patron saints to order. ✉*Apollonos 12, Plaka* ☎*210/331–0337.*

ARE YOU GIFTED?

An inexpensive but unusual gift is a string of *komboloi* (worry beads) in plastic, wood, or stone. You can pick them up very cheaply in Monastiraki or look in antiques shops for more expensive versions, with amber, silver, or black onyx beads. Reasonably priced natural sponges from Kalymnos also make good presents. Look for those that are unbleached, since the lighter ones tend to fall apart quickly. They're usually sold in front of the National Bank on Syntagma and in Plaka souvenir shops. The price is set by the government, so don't bother to bargain.

HANDICRAFTS

Amorgos. Wood furniture, hand-carved and hand-painted by the shop's owners, has motifs from regional Greek designs. Needlework, hanging ceiling lamps, shadow puppets, and other decorative accessories are also for sale. ✉*Kodrou 3, Plaka* ☎*210/324–3836.*

★ **Center of Hellenic Tradition.** The Center is an outlet for quality handicrafts—ceramics, weavings, sheep bells, and old paintings. Take a break from shopping in the center's Oraia Ellada café, in clear view of the Parthenon. ✉*Mitropoleos 59 and Pandrossou 36, Monastiraki* ☎*210/321–3023, 210/321–3842 café.*

Lykeio Ellinidon. Resident weavers seated at two looms copy folk motifs from the costumes in the upstairs museum run by the Greek Women's Lyceum. This cozy shop stocks a range of handicrafts, starting at €5, and you can even custom-order a woven tapestry or bedcover. ✉*Dimokritou 7a, basement, Kolonaki* ☎*210/361–1607.*

Oikotechnia. Craftspeople throughout Greece provide folk crafts for sale here by the National Welfare Organization: stunning handwoven carpets, flat-weave kilims, and tapestries from original designs. Hand-embroidered tablecloths and wall decorations make handsome presents; flokati rugs are also for sale. ✉*Filellinon 14, Syntagma Sq.* ☎*210/325–0240.*

JEWELRY

Prices are much lower for gold and silver in Greece than in many Western countries, and the jewelry is of high quality. Many shops in Plaka carry original pieces available at a good price if you bargain hard enough (a prerequisite). For those with more-expensive tastes, the Voukourestiou pedestrian mall off Syntagma Square has a number of the city's leading jewelry shops.

Byzantino. Great values in gold, including certified copies of ancient Greek pieces and many original works designed in the on-site workshop, can be purchased here. ✉ *Adrianou 120, Plaka* ☎ *210/324–6605.*

Elena Votsi. Elena Votsi designed jewelry for Gucci before opening her own boutique, where she sells exquisite creations in coral, amethyst, aquamarine, and turquoise. ✉ *Xanthou 7, Kolonaki* ☎ *210/360–0936.*

Fanourakis. Original gold masterpieces can be had at these shops, where Athenian artists use gold almost like a fabric—creasing, scoring, and fluting it. ✉ *Patriarchou Ioakeim 23, Kolonaki* ☎ *210/721–1762* ✉ *Evangelistrias 2, Mitropolis* ☎ *210/324–6642* ✉ *Panagitsas 6, Kifissia* ☎ *210/623–2334.*

Goulandris Cycladic Museum. Exceptional modern versions of ancient jewelry designs are available here. ✉ *Neofitou Douka 4, Kolonaki* ☎ *210/724–9706.*

Lalaounis. A world-famous Greek jeweler experiments with his designs, taking ideas from nature, biology, and ancient Greek pieces—the last are sometimes so close to the original that they're mistaken for museum artifacts. ✉ *Panepistimiou 6, Syntagma Sq.* ☎ *210/361–1371* ✉ *Athens Tower, Sinopis 2, Ambelokipi* ☎ *210/770–0000.*

Pentheroudakis. Browse among the classic designs; there are even less-expensive trinkets, like silver worry beads that can be personalized with cubed letters in Greek or Latin and with the stone of your choice. ✉ *Voukourestiou 19, Kolonaki* ☎ *210/361–3187.*

★ **Sagianos.** For five generations, the Sagianos family's creations have adorned the fingers, necks, and ears of well-to-do Athenian matrons. The tradition continues, but with more-modern, one-of-a-kind pieces inspired by ordinary objects like bar codes and buttons. ✉ *Makriyianni 3, Makriyianni* ☎ *210/362–5822.*

Xanthopoulos. Shop for traditional gold, silver, and jewels at this store. ✉ *Voukourestiou 4, Kolonaki* ☎ *210/322–6856.*

Zolotas. This jeweler, Lalaounis's main competitor, is noted for its superb museum copies. ✉ *Pandrossou 8, Plaka* ☎ *210/323–2413* ✉ *Stadiou 9, Syntagma Sq.* ☎ *210/322–1212.*

MUSIC

Metropolis. Take your pick of a huge selection of all-Greek music, from rembetika to the latest Greek club hits, all by Greek artists. ✉ *Panepistimiou 54, Omonia Sq.* ☎ *210/380–8549.*

ATHENS ESSENTIALS

TRANSPORTATION

Many major sights, as well as hotels, cafés, and restaurants, are within a fairly small central area of Athens. It's easy to walk everywhere, though sidewalks are sometimes obstructed by parked cars. Most far-flung sights, such as beaches, are reachable by metro, bus, and tram. Check the Organization for Urban Public Transportation (OASA) Web site *(⇨By Bus & Tram Within Athens)* for English-language information on how to use public transport to get to sights around the city. OASA also answers questions about routes (usually only in Greek). The office, open weekdays 7:30–3, distributes maps of bus routes with street names in Greek; these are also distributed at the white ticket kiosks at many bus terminals.

The price of public transportation has risen steeply, but it is still less than that in other western European capitals. Riding during rush hours is definitely not recommended. Upon boarding, validate your ticket in the orange canceling machines at the front and back of buses and trolleys and in metro stations. Keep your tickets until you reach your destination, as inspectors occasionally pop up to check that they have been canceled and validated. They are strict about fining offenders, including tourists. You can buy a day pass covering the metro, buses, trolleys, and trams for €3, a weekly pass for €10, or, at the beginning of each month, a monthly pass for €38.

BY AIR

The opening of Athens's sleek Eleftherios Venizelos International Airport has made air travel around the country much more pleasant and efficient. Greece is so small that few in-country flights take more than an hour or cost more than €200 round-trip. Aegean Airlines and Olympic Airways have regular flights between Athens, Thessaloniki, and most major cities and islands in Greece. *For further information, see Air Travel in the Essentials chapter.*

AIRPORTS & TRANSFERS *For information about Eleftherios Venizelos International Airport near Athens, see Airports in the Essentials chapter.* The best way to get to the airport from downtown Athens is by metro or light-rail. Single tickets cost €6 and include transfers (within 90 minutes of the ticket's initial validation; don't forget to validate the ticket again) to bus, trolley, or tram. Combined tickets for two (€10) and three (€15) passengers are also available; if you're making a stopover in Athens, opt for a round-trip ticket (€10), valid for trips to and from the airport made during a single 48-hour period.

In Athens three reliable express buses connect the airport with the metro (Ethniki Amyna station), Syntagma Square, and Piraeus. These buses are air-conditioned and have space for luggage. Express buses leave the arrivals level of the airport every 10 minutes and operate 24 hours a day. Bus E95 will take you to Syntagma Square (Amalias avenue); E94 goes to the bus terminus at the Ethniki Amyna metro stop (Line 3), which will get you into Syntagma within 10 minutes. Bus E96 takes the Vari–Koropi road inland and links with the coastal road, passing through Voula, Glyfada, and Alimo; it then goes on to Piraeus (opposite Karaiskaki Square).

The Attiki Odos and the expansion of the city's network of bus lanes has made travel times more predictable, and on a good day the E94 can get you to Ethniki Amyna in 40 minutes. Tickets to and from the airport cost €2.90 and are valid on all forms of transportation in Athens for 24 hours from the time of validation. Purchase tickets from the airport terminal, kiosks, metro stations, or even on the express buses. The Greek National Tourism Organization (GNTO, or EOT in Greece) dispenses schedules. You can also obtain brochures at the airport with bus schedules and routes.

Taxis *(⇨Taxis)* are readily available at the arrivals level of the Athens airport; it costs an average of €22 to get into downtown Athens (including tolls). Limousine Service and Royal Prestige Limousine Service provide service to and from Athens; an evening surcharge of up to 50% often applies, and you should call in advance. Prices start at €80 for one-way transfer from the airport to a central hotel.

Limousines Limousine Service (☎ *210/970–6416* ⊕ *www.limousine-service.gr*). **Royal Prestige Limousine Service** (☎ *210/988–3221* 📠 *210/983–0378*).

BY BOAT & FERRY

Boat travel in Greece is common and relatively inexpensive. Every weekend thousands of Athenians set off on one- and two-hour trips to islands like Aegina, Hydra, and Andros, while in summer ferries are weighed down with merrymakers on their way to Mykonos, Rhodes, and Santorini. Cruise ships, ferries, and hydrofoils from the Aegean and most other Greek islands dock and depart every day from Athens's main port, Piraeus, 10 km (6 mi) southwest of Athens. Ships for the Ionian islands sail from ports nearer to them, such as Patras and Igoumenitsa. Connections from Piraeus to the main island groups are good, connections from main islands to smaller ones within a group less so, and services between islands of different groups or areas—such as Rhodes and Crete—are less frequent.

Travel agents *(⇨Travel Agents)* and ship offices in Athens and Piraeus have details. Boat schedules are published in *Kathimerini,* inserted in the *International Herald Tribune*; EOT *(⇨Visitor Information)* distributes boat schedules updated every Wednesday. You can also call a daily Greek recording (listed below) for ferry departure times. Timetables change according to seasonal demand, and boats may be delayed by weather conditions, so your plans should be flexible. Buy your tickets two or three days in advance, especially if you are traveling in summer or taking a car. Reserve your return journey or continuation soon after you arrive. *For further information, see Boat & Ferry Travel in the Essentials chapter.*

To get to and from Piraeus harbor, you can take the green line metro (Line 1) from central Athens directly to the station at the main port.

The trip takes 25–30 minutes. A taxi takes longer because of traffic and costs around €12–€15.

Athens's other main port is Rafina, which serves some of the closer Cyclades and Evia. KTEL buses run every 30 minutes between the port and the Mavromateon terminal in central Athens, from about 5:30 AM until 9:30 PM, and cost €2 (⇨*By Bus & Tram Within Athens*). At Rafina, the buses leave from an area slightly uphill from the port. The trip takes about one hour.

Contacts **Ferry departures** (☎*1440*). **Piraeus** (✉*Port Authority, Akti Miaouli, Piraeus* ☎*210/451–1311 through 210/451–1317*). **Rafina** (☎*22940/22300*).

BY BUS TO & FROM ATHENS

Travel around Greece by bus is inexpensive, usually comfortable, and relatively fast. The journey from Athens to Thessaloniki takes roughly the same time as the regular train, though the InterCity Express train covers the distance 1¼ hours faster. To reach the Peloponnese, buses are speedier than trains. Information and timetables are available at tourist information offices. Make reservations at least one day before your planned trip, earlier for holiday weekends.

Terminal A is the arrival and departure point for bus lines that serve parts of northern Greece, including Thessaloniki, and the Peloponnese destinations of Epidauros, Mycenae, Nafplion, Olympia, and Corinth. Each destination has its own phone number; EOT offices distribute a list. Terminal B serves Evia, most of Thrace, and central Greece, including Delphi. EOT provides a phone list (⇨ *Visitor Information*). Tickets for these buses are sold only at this terminal, so you should call to book seats well in advance in high season or holidays.

To get to the city center from Terminal A, take Bus 051 to Omonia Square; from Terminal B, take Bus 024 downtown. To get to the stations, catch Bus 051 at Zinonos and Menandrou off Omonia Square (for Terminal A) and Bus 024 on Amalias in front of the National Garden (for Terminal B). International buses drop their passengers off on the street, usually in the Omonia or Syntagma Square areas or at Stathmos Peloponnisou (train station).

Information **Terminal A** (✉*Kifissou 100* ☎*210/512–4910 or 210/512–4911*). **Terminal B** (✉*Liossion 260* ☎*210/831–7096 for Delphi, 210/831–7173 for Livadia [Ossios Loukas via Distomo], 210/831–1431 for Trikala [Meteora]*).

BY BUS & TRAM WITHIN ATHENS

See the Athens Planner at front of this chapter.

BY CAR

Greece's main highways to the north and the south link up in Athens; both are called Ethnikis Odos (National Road). Take the Attiki Odos, a beltway around Athens that also accesses Eleftherios Venizelos International Airport, to speed your travel time entering and exiting the city.

At the city limits, signs in English clearly mark the way to both Syntagma Square and Omonia Square in the city center. Leaving Athens, routes to the highways and Attiki Odos are well marked; signs usually name Lamia for points north, and Corinth or Patras for points southwest. From Athens to Thessaloniki, the distance is 515 km (319 mi); to Kalamata, 257 km (159 mi); to Corinth, 84 km (52 mi); to Lamia, 214 km (133 mi); to Patras, 218 km (135 mi); to Igoumenitsa, 472 km (293 mi).

CAR RENTAL If you are coming to Athens from abroad, especially the United States or Canada, and are planning to rent a car from a major international chain, it's almost always cheaper to book from your home country. Agencies are grouped around Syngrou and Syntagma Square in central Athens, and at the arrivals area of the airport. *For further information, see Car Rental in the Essentials chapter.*

DRIVING IN ATHENS Driving in Athens is not recommended unless you have nerves of steel; it can be unpleasant and even unsafe. It's fairly easy to get around the city with a combination of public transportation and taxis; save car rentals for excursions out of town. Red traffic lights are frequently ignored, and motorists often pass other vehicles while driving on hills and while rounding corners. Driving is on the right, and although the vehicle on the right has the right-of-way, don't expect this or any other driving rule to be obeyed. The speed limit is 50 kph (31 mph) in town. Traffic tends toward gridlock or heart-stopping speeding; parking in most parts of the city could qualify as an Olympic sport. Seat belts are compulsory, as are helmets for motorcyclists, though many natives ignore the laws. In downtown Athens do not drive in the bus lanes marked by a yellow divider; if caught, you may be fined.

Downtown parking spaces are hard to find, and the few downtown garages—including ones in vacant lots—are both expensive and perpetually full. You're better off leaving your car in the hotel garage and walking or taking a cab. Gas pumps and service stations are everywhere, and lead-free gas is widely available. Be aware that all-night stations are few and far between.

EMERGENCIES *For information about the Automobile Touring Club of Greece (ELPA), see Car Travel in the Essentials chapter.*

BY METRO

See the Athens Planner at the front of this chapter.

BY TAXI

Most drivers in Athens speak basic English. Although you can find an empty taxi on the street, it's often faster to call out your destination to one carrying passengers; if the taxi is going in that direction, the driver will pick you up. Likewise, don't be alarmed if your driver picks up other passengers (although he should ask your permission first, and he will never pick up another fare if you are a woman traveling alone at night). Each passenger pays full fare for the distance he or she has traveled.

Taxi rates are still affordable compared to fares in other European capitals. Most taxi drivers are honest and hardworking, but a few con artists infiltrate the ranks at the airports and near popular restaurants and clubs frequented by foreigners. Get an idea from your hotel how much the fare should be, and if there's trouble, ask to go to a police station (most disagreements don't ever get this far, however). Make sure the driver turns on the meter and that the rate listed in the lower corner is 1, the normal rate before midnight; after midnight, the rate listed is 2.

Taxi drivers know the major central hotels, but if your hotel is less well known, show the driver the address written in Greek and make note of the phone number and, if possible, a nearby landmark. If all else fails, the driver can call the hotel from his mobile phone or a kiosk. Athens has thousands of short side streets, and few taxi drivers have maps, although newer taxis have GPS installed. Neither tipping nor bargaining is generally practiced; if your driver has gone out of the way for you, a small gratuity (10% or less) is appreciated.

FARES The meter starts at €1, and even if you join other passengers, you must add this amount to your final charge. The minimum fare is €2.65. The basic charge is €0.26 per kilometer (½ mi); this increases to €0.50 between midnight and 5 AM or if you go outside city limits. There are surcharges for holidays (€0.50), trips to and from the airport (€2), and rides to (but not from) the port, train stations, and bus terminals (€0.70). There is also a €0.29 charge for each suitcase over 10 kilograms (22 pounds), but drivers expect €0.29 for each bag they place in the trunk anyway. Waiting time is €7.10 per hour. Radio taxis charge an additional €3 to €5 for the pickup. Athina 1, Ermis, Hellas, and Parthenon are reliable radio taxi services.

Taxi Companies **Athina 1** (☎ *210/921–7942*). **Ermis** (☎ *210/411–5200*). **Hellas** (☎ *210/645–7000 or 210/801–4000*). **Parthenon** (☎ *210/532–3300*).

BY TRAIN

The *proastiakos* ("suburban"), a light-rail network offering travelers a direct link from Athens airport to Corinth for €8, is introducing Athenians to the concept of commuting. The trains now serve the city's northern and eastern suburbs as well as western Attica. The Athens-to-Corinth fare is €6; lower fares apply for points in between. Upgrades are also being made to the segments linking Athens with Halkidha and Thebes. If you plan on taking the train while in Athens, call the Greek Railway Organization (OSE) to find out which station your train leaves from, and how to get there. At this writing, Stathmos Peloponnisou, where the trains from the Peloponnese arrive, has been temporarily closed and operations transferred to the Ayii Anaryiri station. Trains from the north and international trains arrive at, and depart from, Stathmos Larissis, which is connected to the metro. If you want to buy tickets ahead of time, it's easier to visit a downtown railway office. *For further information, see Train Travel in the Essentials chapter.*

Information **Greek Railway Organization (OSE)** (☎ *210/529–7777*) 🌐 *www.ose.gr*. **OSE buses** (☎ *210/513–5768 or 210/513–5769*). **Proastiakos** (☎ *210/529–7777* 🌐 *www.proastiakos.gr*). **Railway Offices** (✉ *Karolou 1, Omonia Sq.* ☎ *210/529–7006 or 210/529–7007* ✉ *Sina 6, Kolonaki* ☎ *210/529–8910* ✉ *Filellinon 17, Syntagma Sq.* ☎ *210/323–6747*). **Stathmos Larissis** (☎ *210/529–8837*). **Stathmos Peloponnisou** (☎ *210/529–8735*).

CONTACTS & RESOURCES

EMERGENCIES

You can call an ambulance in the event of an emergency, but taxis are often faster. For car accidents, call the city police.

Contacts **Ambulance** (☎ *166*). **City Police** (☎ *100*). **Coast Guard** (☎ *108*). **Fire** (☎ *199*). **Tourist Police** (✉ *Dimitrakopoulou 77, Koukaki* ☎ *171*).

> **MARRIED, WITH CHILDREN**
>
> The concept of babysitting agencies hasn't really taken hold in Athens, in part because Greeks are used to taking their children almost everywhere, including restaurants and late-night cafés and cinemas. High-end hotel chains can arrange for staff to babysit children in your hotel for between €10 and €15 per hour.

DOCTORS & DENTISTS Most hotels will call a doctor or dentist for you; you can also contact your embassy for referrals to either. For a doctor on call 2 PM–7 AM on Sunday and holidays, dial 105 (in Greek).

HOSPITALS Dial 106 (in Greek), check the *Athens News* or the English-language *Kathimerini,* inserted in the *International Herald Tribune,* or ask your hotel to check the Greek papers to find out which emergency hospitals are open; not all hospitals are open nightly. Hygeia Hospital is considered one of the best in Greece, as is its sister maternity hospital, Mitera; both have some English-speaking staff. Children go to Aglaia Kyriakou Hospital or Ayia Sofia Hospital. Note that children's hospitals answer the phone with "Pedon" and not the specific name of the institution.

Contacts **Aglaia Kyriakou Hospital** (✉ *Levadias 3 and Thivon, Goudi* ☎ *210/777-5611 through 210/777-5619*). **Asklepion Hospital** (✉ *Vasileos Pavlou 1, Voula* ☎ *210/895-8301 through 210/895-8306*). **Ayia Sofia Hospital** (✉ *Mikras Asias and Thivon, Goudi* ☎ *210/777-1811 through 210/777-1816*). **Hygeia Hospital** (✉ *Erythrou Stavrou 4, at Kifissias, Maroussi* ☎ *210/686-7000* 🌐 *www.hygeia.gr*). **KAT Hospital** (✉ *Nikis 2, Syntagma Sq.* ☎ *210/801-4411, 166 for accidents*). **Mitera** (✉ *Erythrou Stavrou 6, at Kifissias, Maroussi* ☎ *210/686-9000*). **Ygeia** (✉ *Erythrou Stavrou 4, at Kifissias, Maroussi* ☎ *210/682-7940 through 210/682-7949*).

Contacts **Late-night pharmacy hotline (in Greek)** (☎ *107*). **Thomas** (✉ *Papadiamantopoulou 6, near Hilton and Holiday Inn, Ilisia* ☎ *210/721-6101*).

ENGLISH-LANGUAGE MEDIA

English-language books, newspapers, and magazines are readily available in central Athens; international bookstores and kiosks in Kolonaki and Syntagma stock everything from the *Wall Street Journal* to *Wallpaper.* Local English-language publications include the weekly *Athens News,* which offers a mix of politics, features, travel, and style articles written by both Greek and international journalists; the English-language translation of the respected Greek broadsheet *Kathimerini,* sold as an insert with the *International Herald Tribune*; *Odyssey* magazine, a glossy bimonthly on politics, sports, travel, and events in Greece and among Greeks abroad; and *Insider,* a monthly magazine on lifestyle and entertainment in Athens, with a focus on shopping, art exhibits, restaurants, and nightlife.

INTERNET CAFÉS

Though Greeks use the Internet far less than their European Union counterparts, there are still plenty of places to check your e-mails in Athens. Many hotels offer Internet access, but it's usually expensive. If your laptop has a wireless adapter, you can use the Athens Wireless Metropolitan Network for free. A good stop for free Web surfing is the quiet café on the top floor of the Eleftheroudakis bookstore on Panepistimiou Street. If you don't have a laptop, go to the following cafés. Expect to pay between one and two euros an hour.

3

Internet & Mail Information **Arcade** (✉ *Stadiou 5Center* ☎ *210/321–0701*). **Bits & Bytes Net** (✉ *Akadimias 78Center* ☎ *210/330–6590*). **Quick Net Café** (✉ *Gladstonos 4Omonia* ☎ *210/380–3771*).

MAIL & SHIPPING

There are post offices all over Athens; ask your hotel how to get to the closest one. The city's two central post offices are in Syntagma Square and off Omonia Square; both are infamous for long lines and slow service. Avoid all post offices during the first week of the month, when Greeks line up to pay their utility bills. Post offices are open weekdays 8–2; some also open Saturday morning. If you want to mail a letter, you can do it from the yellow mailboxes outside post offices; there are separate boxes for international and domestic mail.

Post Offices **Omonia Square** (✉ *Tritis Septemvriou 28, Omonia Sq.* ☎ *210/522–4949* ⏲ *Weekdays 7:30 AM–8 PM*). **Syntagma Square** (✉ *Corner of Mitropoleos and Filellinon, Suite 134, Syntagma Sq.* ☎ *210/323–7573* ⏲ *Weekdays 7:30 AM–8 PM, Sat. 7:30–2, Sun. 9–1:30*).

SIGHTSEEING TOURS

BUS TOURS For Athens guided bus tours, see the Athens Planner at the front of this chapter.

EXCURSION TOURS Most agencies *(⇨ Travel Agents)* offer excursions at about the same prices, but CHAT is reputed to have the best service and guides. Common excursion tours include a half-day trip to the Temple of Poseidon at Sounion (€29); a half-day tour to the Isthmus and ancient Corinth (€48); a full-day tour to Delphi (€76, €66 without lunch); a two-day trip to Delphi (€116 including half-board—meaning breakfast and dinner—in first-class hotels); a three-day tour taking in Delphi and the monasteries of Meteora with half-board in first-class hotels (€273); a one-day tour to Nafplion, Mycenae, and Epidauros (€76, €66 without lunch); a two-day tour to Mycenae, Nafplion, and Epidauros (€116 including half-board in first-class hotels); a four-day tour covering Nafplion, Mycenae, Epidauros, Olympia, and Delphi (€378 with half-board in first-class hotels); and a five-day "classical" tour covering all major sights in the Peloponnese, as well as Delphi and Meteora (€492 with half-board in first-class hotels). Most tours run two to three times a week, with reduced service in winter. It's best to reserve a few days in advance.

PERSONAL GUIDES Major travel agencies *(⇨ Travel Agents)* can provide English-speaking guides to take you around Athens's major sights. The Union of Official

Guides provides licensed guides for individual or group tours, starting at about €120, including taxes, for a four-hour tour of the Acropolis and its museum. Hire only guides licensed by the EOT—they have successfully completed a two-year state program.

Contact **Union of Official Guides** (✉ *Apollonos 9A, Plaka* ☎ *210/322–9705 or 210/322–0090* 📠 *210/923–6884*).

TRAVEL AGENTS

Several travel agents and tour services in Athens are listed below. Closer to Omonia, try Condor Travel, CHAT tours, or Pharos Travel and Tourism.

Contacts **American Express** (✉ *Ermou 2, Syntagma Sq.* ☎ *210/324–4975* 📠 *210/322–7893*). **Amphitrion Travel LTD** (✉ *Syngrou 7, Central Athens* ☎ *210/924–9701* 📠 *210/924–9671* ✉ *Deuteras Merachias 3, Pasalimani, Piraeus* ☎ *210/411–2045 through 210/411–2049* 📠 *210/417–0742* 🌐 *www.amphitrion.gr*). **CHAT** (✉ *Stadiou 4, Syntagma Sq.* ☎ *210/322–2886* 📠 *210/323–5270*). **Condor Travel** (✉ *Stadiou 43, Central Athens* ☎ *210/321–2453 or 210/321–6986* 📠 *210/321–4296*). **Dolphin Hellas** (✉ *Syngrou 16, Makriyianni* ☎ *210/922–7772* 📠 *210/923–2101* 🌐 *www.dolphin-hellas.gr*). **Key Tours** (✉ *Kallirois 4, Central Athens* ☎ *210/923–3166* 📠 *210/923–2008* 🌐 *www.keytours.gr*). **Magic Travel Service (Magic Bus)** (✉ *Filellinon 20, Syntagma Sq.* ☎ *210/323–7471* 📠 *210/322–0219* 🌐 *www.magic.gr*). **Pharos Travel and Tourism** (✉ *Triti Septemvriou 18, Patissia* ☎ *210/523–3403 or 210/523–6142* 📠 *210/523–3726*). **Travel Plan** (✉ *Christou Lada 9, Syntagma Sq.* ☎ *210/323–8801 through 210/323–8804* 📠 *210/322–2152* 🌐 *www.travelplan.gr*).

VISITOR INFORMATION

Greek National Tourism Organization (GNTO; EOT in Greece) offices generally close around 2 PM. The English-speaking tourist police can answer questions about transportation, steer you to an open pharmacy or doctor, and locate phone numbers of hotels and restaurants. The Web site of the city of Athens has a small but growing section in English.

Contacts **City of Athens Web site** (🌐 *www.cityofathens.gr*). **Greek National Tourism Organization (EOT)** (✉ *Tsochas 7, Ambelokipi, near National Garden and Syntagma Square* ☎ *210/870–7000* ✉ *Eleftherios Venizelos International Airport, arrivals area* ☎ *210/354–5101* ✉ *EOT Bldg., 1st fl., Zea Marina, Pasalimani, Piraeus* ☎ *210/452–2591 or 210/452–2586* 🌐 *www.gnto.gr*). **Tourist Police** (✉ *Veikou 43, 4th fl., Koukaki* ☎ *171*).

Attica, The Saronic Gulf & Delphi

4

Hydra Island

WORD OF MOUTH

"Choosing between Delphi or Sounion? Delphi has the temple ruins, the Roman amphitheater, the stunning views over the valley, the excellent museum. As for Sounion, it has the famed Temple of Poseidon with its famous view. That's it."

—indytravel

"The first glimpse of the church of Osios Loukas is a dazzling sight. Filled with mosaics and light, it stunned both me and my husband."

—smalti2

www.fodors.com/forums

WELCOME TO ATTICA, THE SARONIC GULF & DELPHI

TOP REASONS TO GO

★ **Delphi, "Navel of the World":** Delphi's Sanctuary of Apollo invites you to imagine a time of oracles, enimagic prophecies, and mystical emanations.

★ **Sunset at Sounion:** Perched over the water, the spectacular Temple of Poseidon still summons strong emotions in this land of seafarers.

★ **Mighty Marathon:** Dare you retrace Pheidippides's first marathon when he ran 26 hilly miles from this town to Athens in 490 BC?

★ **Car-Free Isles:** Serene and tasteful Hydra and Spetses are home to carless streets, 19th-century merchant mansions, and welcoming harbors.

★ **Pistachio Perfection:** Those sweet-yet-salty nuts from the isle of Aegina are reputedly the world's best.

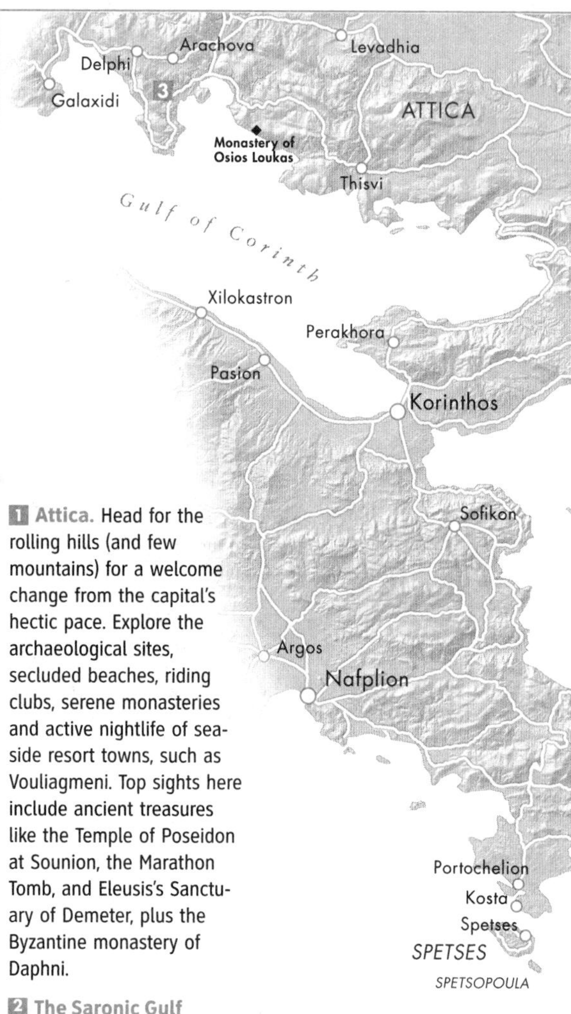

1 Attica. Head for the rolling hills (and few mountains) for a welcome change from the capital's hectic pace. Explore the archaeological sites, secluded beaches, riding clubs, serene monasteries and active nightlife of seaside resort towns, such as Vouliagmeni. Top sights here include ancient treasures like the Temple of Poseidon at Sounion, the Marathon Tomb, and Eleusis's Sanctuary of Demeter, plus the Byzantine monastery of Daphni.

2 The Saronic Gulf Islands. The beauty of Aegina, Hydra, and Spetses remains blissfully unspoiled by mass tourism, though they are popular retreats for Athenians. On Aegina and Spetes, kick back to enjoy a laid-back lifestyle, while sophisticates will love Hydra for its picturesque merchant mansions and bevy of art events.

Left, the beautiful harbor of Hydra. Right, the temple of Poseidon, Cape Sounion.

GETTING ORIENTED

Attica, the southeastern tip of Central Greece, is much more than the home of Athens—it is also a fertile land, with sandy beaches to the south, serene mountains like Parnassus to the north, and beautiful Byzantine monasteries in between. Archaeology abounds, from the sanctuary of Brauron, near Attica's east coast, to the sacred precinct of Delphi, in the westward Boeotia prefecture. South lies three fantasy islands: Aegina, Hydra, and Spetses, jewels of the Saronic Gulf.

3 Delphi & Environs. Closer to Athens, despite modern Eleusis's heavy industry, Delphi's ancient rocks signal a time of ancient worship and secret ritual. Steeped in history, this region is today popular not only with tourists who flock to the sublime Sanctuary of Apollo, its renovated museum, and the nearby monastery of Osios Loukas, but also with skiers, who have turned Arachova into the most cosmopolitan ski resort in the country.

Tholos temple, Delphi.

ATTICA, THE SARONIC GULF & DELPHI PLANNER

When to Go?

June and September offer the benefits of the summer without the July and August crowds.

Athens's nightlife shifts to the southern coast July through August.

Après-ski town Arachova is the place to be in the winter (if expensive), but it's only a stepping stone to Delphi in the summer.

The Saronic islands and Attica's northeastern coast are beautiful anytime, though in the winter, things can feel dead.

Be it the islands or Delphi, be prepared to go head-to-head with the crowds and the heat in summer.

The beaches, of course, are most enjoyable in full summer, but even chic Astir Beach gets engulfed by a rising tide of tourists.

A much better time to visit is April to June, when wildflowers carpet the arid hillsides of Attica and the Marathon plain.

September and October are another beautiful stretch. For nice year-round retreats, head to inland sites, from Eleusis to Marathon.

A Trip to Bountiful

Athenians often forsake traditional Greek tavernas downtown in lieu of the most obscure little taverns in the market towns and villages of Attica, as well as along the backstreets of the Saronic Gulf islands. Not only are the idyllic surrounds a draw but the food is a triumph of local ingredients. Since much of Attica's vegetation is used to support herds of grazing sheep and the omnivorous goat, the meat of both animals is a staple in many country tavernas. Rural tavernas serve big tapsia (pans) of pastitsio (layers of pasta, meat, and chees) or papoutsakia (sliced eggplant with minced meat or with tomatoes and onion)—all tasty, inexpensive meals. That noted, vegetarians will be able to put together an unforgettable meal of wild greens, pies, homemade noodles cooked in fresh tomato sauce, fasolia (baked broad beans), and thick dips.

On the Saronic Gulf islands and in the coastal town of Galaxidi, fresh fish and seafood courses dominate. Because fresh fish is expensive, and billed by weight, a meal for two may cost more than €50. Ask the price and weight of seafood before ordering (and order an exact amount, as the price is usually more than €60 per kilo), or stick to less-expensive choices like calamari, sardines (excellent grilled), or the finger-size atherina (silver smelts).

Dining & Lodging Prices in Euros

	¢	$	$$	$$$	$$$$
Restaurants	Under €8	€8–€15	€15–€20	€20–€25	Over €25
Hotels	Under €80	€80–€120	€120–€160	€160–€200	Over €200

Restaurant prices are for one main course at dinner, or for two mezedes (small dishes). Hotel prices are for a standard double room in high season, including taxes. Hotels operate on the European Plan (EP, with no meal provided) unless we note that they use the Continental Plan (CP, with Continental breakfast); Breakfast Plan (BP, with a full breakfast); Modified American Plan (MAP, with breakfast and dinner); or the Full American Plan (FAP, with all meals). Inquire when booking if these meal plans (which can entail higher rates) are mandatory. Guest rooms have air-conditioning, room phones, and TVs unless otherwise noted.

Making the Most of Your Time

Two weeks is ideal to really see the region, but a week allows for plenty of exploring, letting you hit the major archeological sites of Delphi and Sounion as well as traverse Marathon at less than breakneck speed. The Saronic isles make fabulous day trips, though an overnight stay—or hop to a second isle—will give you a better feel for the locale. Short on time? In two to three days, you can explore Attica's coasts and visit a few key sites. The ancient Greeks believed Delphi was the center of the world, so you could do worse than making it the focus of a trip. With stunning mountain scenery, a world-famous archaeological site, and an excellent museum, touring it can easily take up two days. (Note: While it's possible to drive from Athens to Delphi and back in a day, we don't recommend it: a night in the crisp mountain air is a pleasant alternative to falling asleep behind the wheel.) If you do need to see Delphi in a day, however, be sure to leave Athens early (it's a three- to four-hour trip), especially in summer, when the heat and crowds can be overbearing. A second or third day could be spent hiking around the mountain village of Arachova. Or, head to the sea and the pretty port town of Galaxidi.

Finding a Place to Stay

Many hotels in Attica take a back-seat to the sights. Often built of reinforced concrete slabs, with spindly metal balconies, they have modern "Greek island" decor of simple pine furnishings. Be forewarned: a few of the large resort hotels require you to take half-board in high season. The southeastern coast, from Glyfada to Sounion, underwent a major pre-Olympic 2004 overhaul and a number of new hotels were built (prices rose, too). Delphi and Arachova have some appealing small lodging establishments but elsewhere these picturesque pensions are rare. Note also that many hotels in this region close in late fall and reopen usually around Easter Week, except in Delphi and Arachova, where high season (with top prices) is during ski season. Many hotels (and restaurants) are closed during summer in Arachova.

Accommodations on the Saronic Gulf islands range from elegant 19th-century mansions, usually labeled as traditional settlements, and boutique-style hotels to spare rental rooms. Ask at small hotels if solar water heaters are used in summer; if so, find out when it's best to bathe. Apart from Arachova and Delphi during ski season or on the islands and coast during the summer, it's a buyer's market.

Getting There & Around

Athens and Attica system buses (and trams) run from Athens's center to the southern and northeastern coast, and points from Marathon to Eleusis.

Taking a bus to Arachova, Delphi, and Galaxidi may help you avoid road fatigue.

Seacraft travel from Piraeus's port to the isles near Athens.

Attica's public bus service is extensive, though buses can be infrequent so, for ambitious exploring in the area, a car is invaluable.

The roads to Arachova, Mt. Parnassus, and Galaxidi are decent, but include hairpin turns and can get icy in winter.

The islands are a different story: Cars are prohibited on Hydra and Spetses.

On Hydra you can travel by mule and on Spetses by buggy and boat—but it's best to confirm prices first, so you don't get taken for a different kind of ride.

Cars and buses zip through Aegina, and scooters are also an option.

Updated by Angelike Contis and Natasha Giannousi

BOUNDED ON THREE SIDES BY SEA, Atikí (Attica) has an indented coastline fringed with innumerable sandy beaches and rocky inlets. Waterfront towns become the summer playgrounds for Athenians; nightclubs move seaward for the season and beach clubs have as many amenities as people. The coves and natural harbors are ideal for seafaring. Much of Attica is mountainous: on the stony foothills only a few shrubs grow in the poor soil; higher up, the feathery Aleppo pine of Attica (from which the resin is tapped to make retsina wine) is supplanted by dramatically tall fir trees. Several fertile plains here are well watered with rivers and seasonal streams. Separated from central Greece by mountains—Pateras, Kithairon, Pastra, and Parnitha—and bordered by the sea, Attica was easily defensible. Over all hangs the famed light, the purest of rays sharply delineating the exquisite configuration of mountains, sea, and plain that is Attica.

For true escape, you may need to head to the sun-gilt sea and the Saronic Gulf islands, which straddle the gulf between Athens and the Peloponnese. Aegina, Hydra, and Spetses are especially popular with Athenians, owing to their proximity and, especially in the case of the latter two, their beauty. Yet they all retain their distinct cultural traditions, best appreciated out of high season, when the isles are not inundated with mainlanders and tourists. Aegina, the closest Saronic island to the port of Piraeus, in ancient times was renowned for its bronze work; it eventually succumbed to the power of Athens and two millennia later played a pivotal role in the War of Independence. Extant proof of Hydra's and Spetses's prosperity in the 18th and 19th centuries are the stately, forbidding mansions built by the fleet-owning shipping magnates; they are now the playground of carefree European vacationers.

Delphi is a region immensely rich in mythological and historical allusions. The heart of ancient Greece, united under Athens in the 5th century BC, was the sacred precinct of Delphi. For the ancient Greeks, this site was the center of the universe, home to Apollo and the most sacred oracle, and today it remains a principal pilgrimage site. Nearby Mt. Parnassus is the destination for skiers, who stay in the mountain village of Arachova. Those who prefer the sea choose Galaxidi, a town of 19th-century stone mansions.

EXPLORING ATTICA, THE SARONIC GULF ISLANDS & DELPHI

Athens lies in a basin defined by three mountain masses: Mt. Hymettos to the east, Mt. Aigaleo and Mt. Parnitha to the west, and Mt. Pendeli to the north. The bulk of Attica, which stretches southeast into the Aegean, lies east and north of the Athens basin. A tram line from Glyfada to downtown Athens, opened in 2004, allows travelers to enjoy the expansive sea views offered by a hotel on the coast while enjoying easy access to the city center. The Saronic Gulf islands, whose ancient city-states rivaled Athens, are now virtually a part of the capital. Aegina is just 30 minutes from Piraeus by hydrofoil, and Spetses, the farthest, is just 90 minutes away. Cradled in the mountains, the Del-

phi region has terraced vineyards, steep cliffs, rocky mountain passes, and deep river gorges around Mt. Parnassus and Arachova. Past the modern town of Delphi, the landscape smooths as it sweeps down into a wide valley full of olive trees, ending at the waters of the Bay of Itea and the harbor-front town of Galaxidi.

ATTICA ΑΤΤΙΚΗ

Want to escape from the cacophony of Athens? Head for the interior of Attica, with its rustic inns, local wineries, small towns, and rolling hills. It is believed that recorded history began near here, in the towns of the Boeotian plain, although where legend leaves off and fact begins is often a matter of conjecture (witness Thebes, home of the luckless Oedipus). Historians can be sure that since the 1st millennium BC, the story of Attica has been almost inextricably bound to that of Athens, the most powerful of the villages that lay scattered over the peninsula. By force and persuasion Athens brought these towns together, creating a unit that by the 5th century BC had become the center of an empire.

Northeast of Mt. Pendeli, between the slopes and the sea, lies the fabled plain of Marathon, its flat expanse now dotted with small agricultural communities and seaside resorts, where many Athenians have summer homes. Attica includes such sites as the Temple of Poseidon, spectacularly perched on Cape Sounion, and, up the coast and around the northern flank of Mt. Pendeli, the enchanting, rural archaeological site at the Amphiareion. It takes in the Fortress of Phyle, on the slopes of Mt. Parnitha; the Sanctuary of Demeter at Eleusis; and the Monastery of Daphni.

It is in the small towns of the interior of Attica that the soul of Attica lies. This once quiet and undulating landscape has changed significantly since the construction of the Eleftherios Venizelos (Athens International Airport) in Spata. The many olive groves and vineyards once gracing this region made way for increased development, as new highways give these once-remote towns almost immediate access to Athens.

GLYFADA ΓΛΥΦΑΔΑ

17 km (10½ mi) southeast of Athens.

A palm-fringed coastal promenade, parks, beautiful villas, golf courses, shopping, and seaside dining have always made Glyfada a popular destination for both young and old. Since the relocation of the former international airport from here to Spata, it's much quieter and less touristy. Athenians come to swim, stroll, and spend quiet moments gazing at the sea. A tram link to downtown Athens and Piraeus (change at Neo Faliro) has eased traffic. On summer weekends trams operate through the night to serve clubbers who come to enjoy the nightlife that has moved here from Athens to escape the heat. Glyfada has several fine hotels and, with Athens city center just a tram ride away, makes a good base for travelers who like being near the beach.

Glyfada hosts a **summer concert festival** with theater and musical performances at the carved-marble open-air theater Aixoni in September. Call the local cultural center for program and ticket information. ✉*Aixoni, Hydras 11* ☎*210/961–4094.*

BEACHES

Attica's southwestern coast is mainly rock, with some short, sandy stretches in Glyfada and Voula that have been made into public pay beaches. Along with snack bars, changing rooms, beach umbrellas, and rental water-sport equipment for windsurfing and waterskiing, there are gardens, parking, and playgrounds. These beaches have received Blue Flags for cleanliness from the European Union despite their proximity to Athens. Most are open from 8 AM to 8 PM in summer, and entry fees are generally from €4 to €15. At some beaches, fees go up on weekends, and at others you may have to pay extra for a lounge chair or parking. In July and August, when temperatures climb past 100°F (38°C), public beaches often stay open until midnight. Farther south or east along the coast, accessible by tram, there are open or free beaches from Flisvos up to Glyfada's Asteria.

The town of **Alimos** (✣*10 km [6 mi] south of Athens, 5 km [3 mi] north of Glyfada* ☎*210/981–3315*) has the nearest developed beach to Athens. It has umbrellas and lounge chairs and is packed in summer.

Asteria Seaside (✉ *15 km [9 mi] south of Athens* ☎ *210/894–1620*) in Glyfada really stands out. The sprawling, upmarket complex, built around a fine sand beach and landscaped grounds shaded by elegant pergolas. Facilities include lounge chairs, umbrellas, pools, lockers, changing rooms, showers, trampolines, a playground, a self-service restaurant, three bars, and water sports. Keep going all day and night at the youthful Balux poolside café-club where you can cool off on abundant pillows with a chilled coffee in hand or sip a cocktail long after sundown.

WHERE TO STAY & EAT

$$$$ ✕ **La Peche.** Chef Jean-Yves Carattoni focuses on seafood with a twist at this seaside—and now poolside—haunt of Athens's beautiful people. Asian ingredients are sprinkled into his Mediterranean recipes. Try risotto with lemongrass or shrimp with wasabi and mango with a perfectly chilled white wine from the extensive list. Linger over dinner before hitting the dance floor at the airy Babae beach club next door. ✉ *Vas. Georgiou II 58, next to Asteria Seaside beach* ☎ *210/894–1620* *Reservations essential* *AE, DC, MC, V* *Closed Oct.–Apr. No lunch.*

$$$$ ✕ **Smaragdi.** Established in 1908, this once-humble fish taverna was the favorite place of Athenian couples, in real life and in Greek movies. In recent years, it has spruced up its image—and raised prices, accordingly—but truth is you can't dine any closer to the water without getting your toes wet. Go around sunset and nibble on fried *atherina* (silver smelts), washed down with ouzo. ✉ *Leoforos Karamanli 10 (an extension of Poseidonos), Voula* ☎ *210/965–7404* *Reservations essential* *AE, DC, MC, V.*

$$–$$$ ✕ **George's Steak House.** When all you really want is a burger, head to George's. The menu's limited to steaks (George learned how to carve a T-bone from a visiting American), fries, salads, and *biftekia* (thick, grilled, hamburger-like patties of ground beef and pork). The service is fast, so don't be disappointed if all the tables are taken when you arrive; there's a continuous stream of diners coming and going. ✉ *Konstantinoupoleos 4–6* ☎ *210/894–6020* *No credit cards.*

$–$$ ✕ **Theodoros & Eleni.** Share a platter of steamed mussels covered in a thin feta sauce, very light deep-fried battered shrimp rolled in sesame seeds, or *saganaki* (any dish fried in a small pan with cheese) cubes while you wait for your fish—perfectly grilled and served with the classic Greek olive-oil-and-lemon dressing on the side. Attentive service is part of the homeyness of this understated restaurant housed in a small, suburban villa with outdoor seating in the shaded garden. ✉ *Kondili 8* ☎ *210/898–3140* *Reservations essential* *DC, MC, V* *No dinner Sun.*

$$$ **Blazer Suites.** The late availability of breakfast service suggests this sparkling-clean all-suites hotel doesn't just cater to executives. The service is friendly and personal—adding to the hotel's clublike panache. Here you can relax with home comforts and conveniences like a well-equipped kitchenette, separate living and sleeping quarters, a second TV, and stereo. Blazer Suites' location, a short walk from Glyfada's shopping and restaurants (and near to a tram line), makes it easy for you to combine sightseeing with languid days by the pool or nearby beach. ✉*Leoforos Karamanli 1, 16673 Voula* ☎*210/965–8801* 🌐*www.blazersuites.gr* *28 suites* *In-room: kitchen. In-hotel: restaurant, bar, pool, public Internet, parking (no fee)* 💳*AE, DC, MC, V* *BP.*

$$ **Emmantina.** Carpeted rooms are simply furnished with beds, bedside tables, and built-in vanities with chairs, in a blue-and-yellow color scheme. Double-glazed windows and balcony doors eliminate any noise from the main road. A covered bar provides a shady place for refreshment next to a small, sky-hugging rooftop pool. A bonus: the hotel provides free transport from the airport. A public wireless Internet system is available for a fee. ✉*Leoforos Poseidonos 33, 16675* ☎*210/898–0683* *210/894–8110* 🌐*www.emmantina.com* *80 rooms* *In-room: ethernet. In-hotel: restaurant, bars, pool, parking (no fee)* 💳*AE, DC, MC, V* *BP.*

NIGHTLIFE

Glyfada is renowned as a summer party spot, since some of Athens's most popular clubs close up shop downtown and move here in summer. Places seem to change their name and style each season to keep up with trends; ask at your hotel for the latest information. Most clubs have a cover charge that includes a drink (€10–€25); if you're a large party, take a tip from the Greeks and share a bottle (whiskey, vodka) to save on the cost of ordering single drinks.

Easygoing music gives way to lively post-midnight clubbing at seaside **Akrotiri Lounge** (✉*Vas. Georgiou II 5, Agios Kosmas* ☎*210/985–9147*). At the hot nightspot, which also contains a ritzy restaurant, five bar benches are scattered around a huge swimming pool under the palm trees. **Babae** (✉*Vas. Georgiou II 58* ☎*210/894–1062*) is on the golden sands at Asteria Seaside beach and is one of the hottest clubs—a favorite of Greek celebrities. Have a drink by the sea at **Bo** (✉*Karamanlis 14, Voula* ☎*210/895–9645*), which draws crowds of all ages for its beachside position, chic geometric decor, big round outside bar, and a short menu of pasta and seafood (including an oyster bar). A huge and impressive club, **Envy Mediterraneo** (✉ *Paralia Agiou Kosma, Hellenikon* ☎*210/985–2994*) offers R&B and Greek nights as well. From Psyrri, its base in winter, **Mao Summer** (✉*Waterfront, Diadochou Pavlou* ☎*210/894–4048*) moves to a man-made beachfront "peninsula" for summer where hip clubbers sip drinks and dance around a lagoon.

SPORTS & THE OUTDOORS

Yachts can be rented year-round, but May, June, September, and October are less expensive than summer, and, even better, the *meltemi* (brisk northern winds) are not blowing then. Many yacht brokers charter boats and organize scuba tours and flotilla cruises in small, rented sailboats around the islands.

In a seaside suburb between Glyfada and Athens, **Vernicos Yachts** (✉*Leoforos Poseidonos 11, Alimos* ☎*210/989–6000* *210/985–0130* 🌐*www.vernicos.com*) hosts weeklong cruises and charters boats.

VOULIAGMENI ΒΟΥΛΙΑΓΜΕΝΗ

8 km (5 mi) southwest of Glyfada, 25 km (16 mi) south of Athens.

A classy seaside residential suburb, Vouliagmeni is the most prestigious address for an Athenian's summer home or business. It's coveted for the large yacht harbor and the scenic promontory, Laimos Vouliagmenis, which is covered with umbrella pines and includes an area called Kavouri, with several seaside fish tavernas. Much like Glyfada, Vouliagmeni can serve as a convenient base from which to explore Attica, but it is far less crowded.

BEACHES

Here, beaches are quieter, and even cleaner, than the beaches farther north toward Athens.

The upscale beach on the Laimos Vouliagmenis promontory, **Asteras beach** (✉*Apollonos 40* ☎*210/890–2000*) is on the premises of the Arion Resort & Spa but is open to the public from 8:30 AM to 8 PM. Its more-exclusive location has always commanded a hefty fee (€11 on weekdays, €17 on weekends), which means the green lawns and sandy stretch are usually not so crowded.

With a reasonable fee, **Akti Vouliagmenis** (✉*2 km [1 mi] west of Vouliagmeni* ☎*210/985–2993*) has elegant wooden lounge chairs, umbrellas, and shiny cabanas. The free beach **Kavouri** (✉*Western shore of Vouliagmeni headland*) extends south from Voula to Vouliagmeni.

The part-salt, part spring-fed waters of the **lake at Vouliagmeni** (✉*2 km [1 mi] southeast of town* ☎*210/896–2237* *€7*) are reputed to have curative powers, and thus are popular with older Greeks. The lake is open 7 AM to 7:30 PM; facilities include umbrellas and showers, and there's a pleasant snack bar. Most of the lake has a gradual slope and sandy bottom (although caution is recommended, as it deepens suddenly in parts).

With a range of fees, **Yabanaki** (✉*5 km [3 mi] east of Vouliagmeni, Varkiza* ☎*210/897–2414* 🌐*www.yabanaki.gr*) has beach-club amenities—water sports, bars, restaurants, a children's water park, and cabins where you can take a nap—spread across 25 acres. Varkiza's sandy beach park is open 8 AM to 8 PM. Varkiza is popular with windsurfers.

EN ROUTE

South of Vouliagmeni the road threads along a rocky and heavily developed coastline dotted with inlets where intrepid bathers swim off the rocks, after leaving their cars in the roadside parking areas and scrambling down to the inviting *limanakia* (coves) below. (If you're not driving, you can take the urban E22 Saronida Express from the Akadimias terminal in central Athens to Saronida or a KTEL bus from various points in Athens.) If you are a good swimmer and want to join them, take along your snorkel, fins, and mask so you can enjoy the underwater scenery, but avoid the stinging sea urchins (you won't have to be reminded a second time) clustered on rocks.

Stop at **Georgiadis Bakery** (✉*5 km [3 mi] southeast of Vouliagmeni, Varkiza* ☎*No phone*) to pick up a snack. Athenians flock here for the *piroshki,* a Russian turnover filled with spicy ground meat, but leave carrying bags filled with all types of baked goods, from baguettes and hearty peasant loaves to honey-drenched cakes.

WHERE TO STAY & EAT

$$$$ ✕ **Island.** Claim a place at the bar and observe the fashionable exchange air kisses while casting an eye around to see who's watching. People come in waves: some early for drinks, some late for dancing, and some flowing from the bar to the restaurant to the disco in this complex. Palm trees, bamboo, flowering shrubs, and staggered terraces create an elegant and slightly exotic backdrop for one of the city's hottest summer hangouts. The restaurant's imaginative Mediterranean cuisine, using ingredients such as saffron and feta, comes at a price, but you can sample some of these flavors at the bar for less. ✉*27 km (17 mi) mark on Athens–Sounion coastal road, 3 km (2 mi) southeast of Vouliagmeni, 16672 Varkiza* ☎*210/892–5000* *Reservations essential* *DC, MC, V.*

Fodor's Choice ★

$$$–$$$$ ✕ **Garbi.** Athenians flock year-round to share a seafood platter and bottle of white wine or feast on a fisherman's version of bouillabaisse made up of *kakavia* fish (when available). There's meat on the menu, but most opt for the fresh grilled fish that is brought daily from Paros and Leros isles, and a selection of appetizers with subtle influences from the cuisine of Istanbul Greeks. But it's not just the food that attracts locals to this family-run restaurant: there are also elegant wood-beam ceilings and a superb view of the coast, all just 30 minutes from downtown Athens. Reservations are essential weekends. ✉*3 km (2 mi) west of Vouliagmeni, Liou 21, Kavouri* ☎*210/896–3480* *AE, DC, MC, V.*

$$–$$$ ✕ **Penelope Kai Oi Mnistires Tis.** The flowery name of "Penelope and her Suitors" conjures up Odysseus's legendary wife, but her backstory doesn't figure at this airy, multilevel restaurant. Western and Eastern touches accent traditional Greek offerings: saganaki with feta cheese and ouzo or the crayfish in cream and soya sauce are two winning starters, while rump steak or chicken with mushrooms are best-bet main courses. Top off the epic dining experience with some Cyclopes Apple Pie. The restaurant doubles as a pool bar–café that's especially animated in summer. Reservations are handy in summer. ✉*On coastal road to Sounion, 17 km (10½ mi) south of Vouliagmeni, at 41-km (25½-mi) mark, Lagonissi* ☎*22910/70990* *AE, DC, V* *Closed Mon.–Thurs. Nov.–Mar.*

$–$$ ✕ **I Remvi.** The last of the fish tavernas lining the coastal road in Palaia Fokaia, this is the smallest, the cheapest, and the most romantic. *Remvi* means "daydreaming," easy to do as you sit at little tables with checkered tablecloths sipping potent barreled wine and gazing out to sea. The family-run place keeps expanding its delicious menu—the fish soup *sinagrida,* made with the freshest bream, sweet onions, carrots, and potatoes, is worth the wait. Seafood appetizers like crab salad and fried calamari are a good lead-in to the superbly fresh fish, served by the kilo. ✉*52 km (32 mi) point on Athens–Sounion coastal road, 34 km (21 mi) south of Vouliagmeni, Palaia Fokaia* ☎*22910/36236* *DC, MC, V.*

$$$$ Fodor'sChoice ★ **Arion Resort & Spa.** U.S. hotel giant Starwood Hotels & Resorts has recently taken over the management of Vouliagmeni's 80-acre prestigious Astir Palace complex, the gem of a peninsula owned by the National Bank of Greece. They have swiftly started updating the three-hotel complex, while continuing to draw the high-profile customers—from European dignitaries to rock stars—it has attracted since the 1960s. At the Arion Resort & Spa (formerly just Arion), each room has light-color wood furniture, sparkling white linens, a soothing decor, and jaw-dropping perks—like some glass bathroom walls that overlook the sea. Public spaces are regal. There is also a sweetly scented spacious spa with a therapy pool that gazes out to the sea. Luxury suites reach €6,000. Starwood has also transformed the Astir complex's former Nafsika hotel into the 162-room Westin Athens, with more-minimalist room decor and facilities like a water-sports center, a kid's club, and a swimming area that is half-pool, half-sea. The former cliff-top Aphrodite will become a trendy "W" chain hotel by fall 2008. ✉ *Apollonos 40, 16671* ☎ *210/890–2000* 🖷 *210/896–2582* 🌐 *www.luxurycollection.com/arion* *153 rooms, 76 bungalows, 9 suites* *In-room: refrigerator, Wi-Fi. In-hotel: 3 restaurants, bar, tennis courts, pools, gym, spa, beachfront, boating* 💳 *AE, DC, MC, V* *BP.*

$$$–$$$$ ★ **The Margi.** A sculptural stone fireplace in the lobby, a rich brown leather headboard in one guest room, an antique dressing table in another: no detail escapes notice at Margi, an upscale boutique hotel. Individually furnished rooms exude elegance, with marble baths and sweeping views of Vouliagmeni bay. Soothing creams, scented candles, and soft earth tones make your room a private haven in which to relax or work. Even though you are so near the beach, the intimate, greenery-filled pool courtyard might entice you: have a drink at the Malabar lounge-restaurant, sample sushi from an upholstered wicker chaise, or read by lamplight in the covered outdoor living room. The Malabar's pool and its outdoor "beds" are popular with young beachgoers by day and night. ✉ *Litous 11* ☎ *210/892–9000* 🖷 *210/892–9143* 🌐 *www.themargi.gr* *90 rooms, 7 suites* *In-room: safe, DVD, ethernet (some), refrigerator, Internet, Wi-Fi (some). In-hotel: 2 restaurants, bars, pool, public Internet* 💳 *AE, DC, MC, V* *BP.*

$ **Stefanakis Hotel and Apartments.** Sacrifice style for value: here you get a good location, balconies, friendly service, and a generous breakfast buffet (at an extra cost with the apartments). Guest rooms have twin or double beds and mini refrigerators, and the apartments—in a separate building—have two bedrooms and a kitchenette. There's a pool, too, but Varkiza's wonderful sand beach and café-lined waterfront are just a short walk away. Regular bus service runs from Varkiza to downtown Athens and sights like Sounion. ✉ *3 km (2 mi) east of Vouliagmeni, Aphroditis 17, 16672 Varkiza* ☎ *210/897–0528 to 210/897–0530* 🖷 *210/897–0249* 🌐 *www.stefanakishotel.gr* *40 rooms, 12 apartments* *In-room: kitchen (some), refrigerator. In-hotel: bar, pool* 💳 *MC, V* ⊗ *Closed Nov.–Mar.* *BP.*

SOUNION ΣΟΥΝΙΟ

50 km (31 mi) southeast of Vouliagmeni, 70 km (44 mi) southeast of Athens.

Poised at the edge of a rugged 195-foot cliff, the Temple of Poseidon hovers between sea and sky, its "marble steep, where nothing save the waves and I may hear mutual murmurs sweep" unchanged in the centuries since Lord Byron penned these lines. Today the archaeological site at Sounion is one of the most photographed in Greece. The coast's raw, natural beauty has attracted affluent Athenians, whose splendid summer villas dot the shoreline around the temple. There are a tourist café-restaurant by the temple, and a few minimarts on the road, but no village proper. Arrange your visit so that you enjoy the panorama of sea and islands from this airy platform either early in the morning, before the summer haze clouds visibility and the tour groups arrive, or at dusk, when the promontory has one of the most spectacular sunset vantage points in Attica. Be prepared, however, to be shuttled out quickly by guards.

In antiquity, the view from the cliff was matched emotion for emotion by the sight of the cape (called the "sacred headland" by Homer) and its mighty temple when viewed from the sea—a sight that brought joy to sailors, knowing upon spotting the massive temple that they were close to home. Aegeus, the legendary king of Athens, threw himself off the cliff when he saw his son's ship approaching flying a black flag. The king's death was just a Greek tragedy born of misunderstanding: Theseus had forgotten to change his ship's sails from black to white—the signal that his mission had succeeded. So the king thought his son had been killed by the Minotaur. To honor Aegeus, the Greeks named their sea, the Aegean, after him.

Fodor's Choice ★ Although the columns at the **Temple of Poseidon** appear to be gleaming white from a distance in the full sun, when you get closer you can see that they are made of gray-veined marble, quarried from the Agrileza valley 2 km (1 mi) north of the cape, and have 16 flutings rather than the usual 20. Climb the rocky path that roughly follows the ancient route, and beyond the scanty remains of an ancient *propylon* (gateway), you enter the temple compound. On your left is the *temenos* (precinct) of Poseidon, on your right, a *stoa* (arcade) and rooms. The temple itself (now roped off) was commissioned by Pericles, the famous leader of Greece's golden age. It was probably designed by Ictinus, the same architect who helped design the Temple of Hephaistos in the ancient Agora of Athens, and was built between 444 and 440 BC. The people here were considered Athenian citizens, the sanctuary was Athenian, and Poseidon occupied a position second only to Athena herself. The badly preserved frieze on the temple's east side is thought to have depicted the fight between the two gods to become patron of Athens.

The temple was built on the site of an earlier cult to Poseidon; two colossal statues of youths, carved more than a century before the temple's construction (perhaps votives to the god), were discovered in early excavations. Both now reside at the National Archaeological Museum in Athens. The 15 Doric columns that remain stand sentinel over the Aegean, visible from miles away. Lord Byron had a penchant for carving his name on ancient monuments, and you can see it and other graffiti on the right corner pillar of the portico. The view from the summit is breathtaking. In the slanting light of the late-afternoon sun, the landmasses to the west stand out in sharp profile: the bulk of Aegina backed by the mountains of the Peloponnese. To the east, on a clear day, one can spot the Cycladic islands of Kea, Kythnos, and Serifos. On the land side, the slopes of the acropolis retain traces of the fortification walls. ✉ *Cape of Sounion* ☎ *22920/39363* 🌐 *www.culture.gr* 🎫 *€4* 🕐 *Daily 9.30* AM*–dusk.*

BEACHES

If you spend the morning and have lunch on the beach below **Sounion,** you may also want to take a swim. The sandy strip becomes uncomfortably crowded in summer.

On your approach to the Temple of Poseidon, there is a decent beach at **Legrena** (✉ *4 km [2½ mi] north of Sounion, before the turnoff for Haraka*). A few kilometers before you approach Legrena from Athens, look for a "ferry" sign, in order to catch a small boat for a short ride across to the uninhabited isle of Patroklou; the service operates daily and leaves approximately every 10 minutes. The broad sand beach at **Anavyssos** (✉ *13 km [8 mi] northwest of Sounion*) is at this writing free and very popular with windsurfers. It's slated for development into an organized, paying beach with more amenities.

WHERE TO STAY & EAT

$$$–$$$$ ✕ **Theodoros-Eleni.** More than two-thirds of the diners here are returning customers, which says a lot about this taverna run by a Greek-British husband-and-wife team. Like their taverna in Glyfada, the menu is built around fresh fish and seafood, with marvelous additions like a twisted spanakopita, spinach pie made with homemade phyllo (winter/early spring only), and boiled or fresh salads in season. ✉ *Off Athens–Sounion coastal road, 3 km (2 mi) south of Sounion, Legrena* ☎ *22920/5193* 💳 *MC, V* 🕐 *Closed Mon.–Thurs. Nov.–Mar.*

$–$$ ✕ **O Ilias.** All of the tables have a view of the Temple of Poseidon, perching above its cliff, in this restaurant started by owner Vasili Kampiti's uncle, Ilias. The fish tavern's menu remains centered around fish, from "small frys" like marida, atherina, and anchovy to large ones by the kilo. Try the homemade french fries or fried peppers to start with, or either boiled greens or fresh salad. Top off a meal with fresh, seasonal fruit, or—if there's a piece left in the large pan it was baked in—some *ravani* (a traditional Greek honey-covered cake). ✉ *On beach below Temple of Poseidon* ☎ *22920/39114* 💳 *MC, V* 🕐 *No dinner weekdays Nov.–Mar.*

$$$$ 🏨 **Grecotel Cape Sounio.** One of the most luxurious hotels in Greece, this showpiece—looking a bit like a Greek temple left over from a spectacular Cecil B. DeMille movie set—perches amid the verdant pine forest of Sounion National Park: the stunning bay view includes a picture-perfect castle-fort. Accommodations here range from bungalows to villas and all are built as in amphitheater seating, to embrace the coast and maxi-

Fodor'sChoice ★

mize sea vistas. Floor-to-ceiling sliding glass doors open onto walk-on terraces, many facing southeast toward the Temple of Poseidon; some have private pools. If you don't want to leave the comfort of your bungalow or villa, just order from the 24-hour room service menu, but few can resist the restaurant's front-row terrace over the bay. The octagonal glass-wall spa and fitness center overlook the sea, and on the two bays below the hotel is a private beach, with water-sports rentals available. And for those who have everything: Jean-Michel Cousteau has designed a program of fun outdoor environmentally minded activities for children (ages 4–11). ✉ *Athens–Sounion coastal road at 67-km (42-mi) mark, 19500 Sounion* ☎ *22920/69700* 📠 *22920/69770* 🌐 *www.grecotel.gr* *154 bungalows (villas)* *In-hotel: 3 restaurants, bars, tennis courts, pool, gym, spa* 💳 *AE, DC, MC, V* *BP.*

$$$ **Aegeon Beach Hotel.** Nothing can beat this hotel's location—much objected to by environmentalists and archaeologists—*on* the beach below the Temple of Poseidon, at the very harbor where ancient ships once navigated. All rooms have balconies, most have sea views, and a few gaze up at the temple. The hotel was renovated for the 2004 games, opting for a wood-and-marble minimalism. The restaurant, from where you can enjoy the sunset, serves Continental and Greek cuisine and fresh fish. Be warned: the beach gets crowded in high season. It's a 15-minute walk to the ancient temple. ✉ *68-km (42-mi) mark on Athens–Sounion road, Sounion beach, 19500* ☎ *22920/39200* 📠 *22920/39234* 🌐 *www.aegeon-hotel.com* *39 rooms, 6 suites* *In room: safe. In-hotel: restaurant, bar, beachfront, gym* 💳 *MC, V* *BP.*

BRAURON ΒΡΑΥΡΩΝΑ

45 km (28 mi) north of Sounion, 40 km (25 mi) southeast of Athens.

The **Sanctuary of Artemis** rises on the site of an earlier shrine at Brauron, in a waterlogged depression at the foot of a small hill. Found here are a 5th-century BC temple and a horseshoe-shaped stoa. Today it's off the beaten track, but the sanctuary was well known in antiquity: Aristophanes mentions the dance in *Lysistrata,* and in Euripides's drama *Iphigenia in Tauris,* Iphigenia arrives at Brauron with an image of the goddess stolen from Tauris. Here the virgin huntress was worshipped as the protector of childbirth. Every four years the Athenians celebrated the Brauronia, an event in which girls between ages 5 and 10 took part in arcane ceremonies, including a dance in which they were dressed as bears. The museum next to the site contains statues of these little girls, as well as many votive offerings. Those without cars could take the metro from downtown Athens to Ethniki Amyna (Line 3) and then switch to Bus 304 or 316 and ride to the end; the site is a 1-km (½-mi) walk from there. ✉ *Off Markopoulo highway at foot of hill near fork in road to northern Loutsa* ☎ *22990/27020* *€3* *Site Tues.–Sun. 8:30 AM–2:45 PM; museum closed for renovation until Jan. 2009.*

BEACHES

Kakia Thalassa (✉ *14 km [9 mi] south of Brauron, Keratea*), with its public playground, ball courts, and open-air cinema, lends itself to being a relaxed, family outing. This sheltered cove with a sand beach is at the end of a country road that winds through pines past the imposing Keratea Monastery. Reserve one of the tables on the rocks overlooking the water at the beachfront tavernas, Kapetan Christos and fish tavern Yiorgakis (☎22990/28444). They are the perfect perches from which to watch both the sunset and the children playing on the sand. On the way from Brauron, you could pick up a tin of honey sold roadside by local producers whose hives dot the surrounding hills.

The coast road north from Brauron, which skirts an extensively (and poorly) developed coastline, leads to a pleasant beach at **Loutsa** (✉ *8 km [5 mi] north of Brauron*) framed by a backdrop of umbrella pines. With safe shallow waters perfect for small children, it gets extremely congested and noisy in July and August. The port of **Rafina** (✉ *15 km [9 mi] north of Brauron*) has become more developed as the ferry and hydrofoil routes to the Cyclades that depart from here have become more popular. If you have some time to kill before catching your ferry, Rafina has a number of good tavernas on and near the harbor worth the visit. The beach here is a little less crowded in summer than Loutsa.

4

WHERE TO STAY & EAT

$$$–$$$$ ✕ **O Xipolitos.** No longer a closely guarded secret of Athenians with summer homes in Loutsa and nearby Rafina, this simple fish taverna has cast its net wider. Its fresh fish and seaside location have established it as a broader family favorite for the past 50 years. Munch on homemade *tirokafteri,* a spicy dip made with soft white cheese, and marinated anchovies while waiting for the main course. Reservations are often needed in summer. ✉ *8 km (5 mi) north of Brauron, G. Papandreou 1, at 25 Martiou, Paralia Loutsas, Ayios Nikolaos* ☎ *22940/28342* ▭ *No credit cards.*

$–$$ ✕ **Kali Kardia tou Egre.** For more than 35 years, Egre's taverna—as it's known locally—has been a family favorite. The menu is fairly simple, yet there's something about the juicy biftekia and potato-chip-shaped fries that brings folks back. The move from a side street near the harbor to a residence with a pretty garden behind the town hall hasn't changed this homey taverna's prices, service, or food. ✉ *Argonauton 16, Karamanli Park (after the small bridge), Rafina* ☎ *22940/2664* ▭ *No credit cards* ⊙ *Closed weekdays Oct.–Apr.*

$$$–$$$$ 🏨 **Club Thalasso Mare Nostrum.** This sprawling resort and thalassotherapy center has the amenities and "holiday village" spirit of the Club Med brand. Rejuvenate at the spa—the subtle lighting on the ceiling of the indoor saltwater pool has a starlike effect. Treatments include sauna, *hamam* (Turkish steam bath), seaweed and mud wraps, and massage—Swedish, reflexology, and shiatsu. Superior rooms, on the third level of the main building, have carpeting instead of terra-cotta tile. Regular rates don't include spa services, but you can select a package that does. ✉ *Above Brauron (Vravrona) bay, 19003* ☎ *22940/71000, 801/118–0200 toll-free* 📠 *22940/47790* 🌐 *www.mare-nostrum.gr*

300 rooms, 125 bungalows, 3 suites In-room: refrigerator. In-hotel: 2 restaurants, bar, tennis courts, pool, gym, spa AE, DC, MC, V FAP.

$-$$ **Hotel Avra Airport.** Strategically located at the Rafina port, this is a perfect hotel for a stay over when you have an early ferry to catch or arrive late from the islands, although for the same reason it's not recommended for a longer stay—at least not at the height of summer when the harbor is congested and Rafina is packed with Athenians who have holiday homes there. Request a room with a sea view since about a third face towards the town. *Arafinidon Alon 3, Rafina port, 19009 Rafina 22940/22780 22940/23320 www.hotelavra.gr 84 rooms, 16 suites In-hotel: restaurant, bar MC, V BP.*

MARATHON ΜΑΡΑΘΩΝΑΣ

87 km (54 mi) north of Brauron, 42 km (26 mi) northeast of Athens.

Today Athenians enter the fabled plain of Marathon to enjoy a break from the capital, visiting the freshwater lake created by the dam, or sunning at the area's beaches. When the Athenian *hoplites* (foot soldiers), assisted by the Plataians, entered the plain in 490 BC, it was to crush a numerically superior Persian force. Some 6,400 invaders were killed fleeing to their ships, while the Athenians lost 192 warriors. This, their proudest victory, became the stuff of Athenian legends; the hero Theseus was said to have appeared himself in aid of the Greeks, along with the god Pan. The Athenian commander Miltiades sent a messenger, Pheidippides, to Athens with glad tidings of the victory; it's said he ran the 42 km (26 mi) hardly taking a breath, shouted *Nenikikamen!* ("We won!"), then dropped dead of fatigue (more probably of a heart attack)—the inspiration for the marathon race in today's Olympics. To the west of the Marathon plain are the quarries of Mt. Pendeli, the inexhaustible source for a special marble that weathers to a warm golden tint.

The 30-foot-high **Marathon Tomb** is built over the graves of the 192 Athenians who died in the 490 BC battle against Persian forces. At the base, the original gravestone depicts the Soldier of Marathon, a hoplite, which has been reproduced here (the original is in the National Archaeological Museum in Athens). This collective tomb, which contains the cremated remains of the national heroes, was built to honor them. The battle is plotted on illustrated panels, supplemented by a three-dimensional map of local landmarks. *5 km (3 mi) south of Marathon 22940/55462 Combined ticket with Archaeological Museum, the tomb of Plataies (to the northwest), and the 2 ancient cemeteries on the road to the museum €3 Tues.–Sun. 8:30–3.*

About 1½ km (1 mi) north of the Marathon Tomb is the smaller burial mound of the Plataians killed in the same battle, as well as the **Archaeological Museum.** Five rooms contain objects from excavations in the area, ranging from Neolithic pottery from the cave of Pan to Hellenistic and Roman inscriptions and statues (labeled in English and Greek). Eight larger-than-life sculptures came from the gates of a nearby sanctuary of the Egyptian gods and goddesses. In the center of one of the rooms stands part of the Marathon victory trophy—an Ionic column that the Athenians erected in the valley of Marathon after defeating the Persians. ✉ *Plataion 114, approximately 6 km (4 mi) south of Marathon* ☎ *22940/55155* 🎫 *Combined ticket with Marathon Tomb €3* ⏲ *Tues.–Sun. 8:30–3.*

The archaeological site at **Rhamnous,** an isolated, romantic spot on a small promontory, overlooks the sea between continental Greece and the island of Euboia. From at least the Archaic period, Rhamnous was known for the worship of Nemesis, the great leveler, who brought down the proud and punished the arrogant. The site, excavated during many years, preserves traces of temples from the 6th and 5th centuries BC. The smaller temple from the 6th century BC was dedicated to Themis, goddess of Justice. The later temple housed the cult statue of Nemesis, envisioned as a woman, the only cult statue remains left from the high classical period. Many fragments have turned up, including the head, now in the British Museum. The acropolis stood on the headland, where ruins of a fortress (5th and 4th centuries BC) are visible. As you wander over this usually serene, and always evocative, site you discover at its edge little coves where you can enjoy a swim. For those going by public transportation, take a KTEL bus from Athens toward the Ayia Marina port, get off at the Ayia Marina and Rhamnous crossroads, and follow the signs on the flat road, about 3 km (2 mi). Or take a taxi from Marathon village. ✉ *15 km (9 mi) northeast of Marathon* ☎ *22940/63477* 🎫 *€2* ⏲ *Apr.–Nov., daily 8–6.*

4

★ **Lake Marathon** is a huge man-made reservoir formed by the **Marathon Dam** (built by an American company in 1925–31). It claims to be the only dam faced with marble. You may be astonished by the sight of all that landlocked water in Greece and want to contemplate it over a drink or snack at the café-restaurant **Fragma** (☎ *210/814–3615*) on the east side. At the downstream side is a marble replica of the Athenian Treasury of Delphi. This is a main source of water for Athens, supplemented with water from Parnitha and Boeotia. ✉ *8 km (5 mi) west of Marathon, down side road from village of Ayios Stefanos.*

Youngsters tired of trekking through museums may appreciate the distraction of the **Attica Zoological Park.** Spread across 32 acres, the zoo is home to more than 1,600 animals, 50 mammal species, 27 types of reptiles, and 304 birds, from a jaguar and wallaby to a brown bear and snowy owl. Take the Spata exit if you're coming from the airport or the Rafina exit if you're coming from the direction of Eleusis. ✉ *Yalou region, Spata* ☎ *210/663–4724* 🌐 *www.atticapark.gr* 🎫 *€12* ⏲ *Daily 9–dusk.*

BEACHES

The best beach is the long, sandy, pine-backed stretch called **Schinias** (✉ *10 km [6 mi] southeast of Marathon*). It's crowded with Athenians on the weekend, and is frequently struck by strong winds that windsurfers love in summer.

Paralia Varnava (✉ *10 km [6 mi] northeast of Marathon*), less crowded than Schinias, is reached from Varnavas village. The coves at **Rhamnous** (✉ *8 km [5 mi] northeast of Marathon*), about 2,000 feet from the approach, are cozy and remote. These are favorite swimming spots of nudists and free campers, although this is forbidden. Beware of spiny sea urchins when swimming off the rocks.

WHERE TO STAY & EAT

$$$–$$$$ ✕ **Argentina.** While living in South America, owner Nikos Milonas learned how to carve beef, how high to fire up the grill, and exactly how to time a perfect medium-rare steak (size XXL!). The meat-loving population of Greece has been benefiting from his expertise ever since. Salad and home fries round out the menu. On a clear day you get a peek at the sea from the large veranda. It is advised to order meat in advance as grilling takes at least an hour. ✉ *Vitakou 3, Kalentzi, about 1½ km (1 mi) after dam crossing* ☎ *22940/66476 or 22940/67827* *Reservations essential* ▭ *AE, V* ⏲ *Closed Mon. and 3 wks in Aug. No lunch weekdays. No dinner Sun.*

$$–$$$ ✕ **O Hontros.** On the busy main harbor road of the resort community of Nea Makri, O Hontros ("the fat one") is a good choice if you're seeking more variety than the standard meat or seafood tavernas. Try the grilled green peppers filled with feta cheese, the sardines wrapped in vine leaves, and the grilled chicken with parsley. ✉ *5 km [3 mi] south of Marathon, Leoforos Poseidonos and Masaioi, Nea Makri* ☎ *22940/50430* ▭ *No credit cards.*

$–$$ ✕ **Ta Patitiria tou Mpairaktari.** This traditional taverna is located on the major throughway Marathonos avenue, but the renovated former wine-press ("patitiri") building is surrounded in its own greenery, maintaining coolness and serenity. Owner Stefanos Mpairaktaris, a skilled craftsman as well as deputy mayor of Marathon, took a hands-on approach to shifting the decades-old (since 1948) family focus on wine to food. In the taverna with white embroidered curtains, he's worked on details including the vine motif painted onto wood chairs and branch candleholders. Try the stuffed potato *tis Yiayias* (Granny's), the spicy pork with peppers, and ewe cooked in a clay pot. ✉ *3 km [2 mi] south of Marathon, 285 Marathonos* ☎ *22940/55261* ▭ *MC, V.*

¢–$ ✕ **Tehlikidis (Pefkakia).** Introduced to Greece by repatriated Greeks from the Black Sea region, the *peinirli* is the local version of the calzone. The boat-shaped pieces of thick, hand-tossed dough are topped with ham, cheese, bacon, egg, onions, sausage, or ground beef, then drizzled with butter and baked in a wood-burning oven. The classic *peinirli,* originally a workman's snack, is topped in this taverna with *kasseri,* a sharp local cheese. ✉ *19 km (12 mi) west of Marathon, Argonauton and Komninon 4, Drosia* ☎ *210/622–9002* ▭ *DC, MC, V.*

$–$$ **Cabo Verde.** Spacious rooms with sea views that include Evia island's profile across the strait are this hotel's (inaugurated in 2003) main assets. It's small enough to provide personal service, but large enough to have a pool, sauna, and Italian restaurant on the premises. The marina, the beach, and the handful of tavernas that comprise the seaside village of Mati are just steps away. A children's playground is close by as well. ✉ *7 km (4½ mi) south of Marathon, Poseidonos 41, 19009 Mati*

☎*22940/33111, 2810/220088 reservations* 📠*2810/220785* 🌐*www.caboverde.gr* *34 rooms, 4 suites* *In-hotel: restaurant, bar, pool* *MC, V* *CP.*

$ ★ **Aquamarina.** Set 26 km (16 mi) from Athens and 4 km (2½ mi) from the port of Rafina, this hotel offers an ideal combination of city living and seaside relaxation. Its two large buildings have a touch of Cycladic architecture, but also state-of-the-art amenities like a wellness center, business facilities, and plasma televisions. All rooms have a balcony with a full or partial sea view. ✉*Poseidonos 55–57, 19005 Mati* ☎*22940/77555, 210/362–0662 Athens office* 📠*22940/77233* 🌐*www.aquamarina.gr* *130 rooms* *In-hotel: restaurant, bar, pool,* *AE, DC, MC, V* *BP.*

SPORTS

Every year in early November, the **Athens Classic Marathon** is run over roughly the same course taken in 490 BC by the courier Pheidippides, when he carried to Athens the news of victory over the Persians. The 42-km (26-mi) race—organized by Athens-based Hellenic Association of Amateur Athletics and Segas (🌐www.segas.com)—open to men and women of all ages, starts in Marathon and finishes at the Panathenaic Stadium in Athens. You can apply and pay your entry fee either online or by mail. Even if you don't have the stamina for the race, cheer on the runners at the end of the route in Athens—they represent many ages, nationalities, and physiques. Those who finish the course sprint triumphantly into the stadium, where the first modern Olympics were held in 1896. A permanent free "Olympic Marathon" exhibit is housed at the Center for the Promotion of the Marathon Race. ✉*Marathon and 25th March, Marathon* ☎*22940/67632.*

This part of Attica is ideal for all kinds of water sports. If you want to get a taste of windsurfing, drive to nearby Schinias for your first lesson with the accredited instructors of **Moraitis Sports Center.** ✉*Marathon bay, Schinias* ☎*22940/55965* 📠*22940/64473* 🌐*www.moraitis-sports.gr.*

MT. PARNITHA ΠΑΡΝΗΘΑ

62 km (38 mi) west of Marathon, 33 km (20½ mi) northwest of Athens.

The summit of Mt. Parnitha, Attica's highest mountain, has a splendid view of the plain of Athens cradled by Mt. Pendeli and Mt. Hymettos. Tragically, large swathes of the mountain's protected national park, particularly its western side, were destroyed in a 2007 fire. However, lovely nature walks thread through the Mt. Parnitha massif are still possible. Visitors are discouraged from passing through the charred area until the forest regenerates. In April and May the forest blooms with wildflowers, red poppies, white crocuses, purple irises, and numerous species of orchid. Many Athenians come year-round, especially on Sunday, to enjoy the clean air, but some are equally attracted by the gaming tables at the **Regency Casino Mont Parnes** (☎*21024/21234* 🌐*www.regency.gr*).

OUTDOORS

There are 12 marked hiking trails, with varying degrees of difficulty, on Mt. Parnitha—the Alpine Club reports that though the view is beautiful at the cave, en route you pass through the devastating fire area. So it's not recommended for 2008 travelers. The area between Bafi and Flambouri remains unchanged. One of the milder, and most pleasant, hikes follows a marked trail from Ayia Triada through the national park to **Ayios Petros** at Mola. The path leads past the Skipiza spring, providing along the way spectacular views of western Attica and the town of Thebes. The 6-km (4-mi) walk takes about two hours, and you might even spot deer darting among the trees. A 3-km (2-mi) ascent from Ayia Triada (approximately 40 minutes) leads to the **Bafi Refuge** (⊠*Ermou 64, 5th fl., Monastiraki, 10563 Athens* ☎*210/246–9050 refuge, 210/321–2429 club* 📠*210/324–4789 club*), run by the Alpine Club of Athens, where basic board and lodging are available. The refuge has a fireplace and kitchen; water is piped in from a nearby spring. From Bafi, one trail turns south, tracing the fir and pine woods along the Houni ravine, skirting the craggy Flambouri peak—a favorite nesting place of the park's raptors. This trail intersects with another path leading to the **Flambouri Refuge** (⊠*Filadelfias 126, 13671 Aharnes* ☎*210/246–1528* 📠*210/246–9777*), a basic hikers' hut run by the Aharnes Alpine Club.

PHYLE ΦΥΛΗ

16 km (10 mi) south of Mt. Parnitha, 31 km (19 mi) northwest of Athens.

Evidence of the livestock-based economy in the area of Phyle (Fili) is everywhere: in the dozens of whole lambs, pigs, and goats strung up in front of butcher shops; in the numerous tavernas lining the main street; in the many window displays of fresh sheep yogurt. Beyond the nearby village of Khasia, the road climbs Mt. Parnitha.

The Athenians built several fortresses on the ancient road between Mt. Parnitha and Thebes, including the untended 4th-century BC **Fortress of Phyle** (⊠*On a high bluff west of the road to Thebes, 10 km [6 mi] north of Phyle*), now in ruins. The road looping back and around the flank of Mt. Parnitha climbs slowly through rugged, deserted country along the ancient road northwest to Thebes. Here the fortress watched over the passes between Attica and Boeotia, offering a dramatically beautiful vista, with the fortress's rugged rectangular masonry scattered about the site. Fragments of the wall still stand; it was made of blocks, each up to 9 feet high, and was reinforced with five towers (two are still visible). When it snows on Mt. Parnitha, the road up to the fortress may be closed, so check with your hotel about weather conditions on the mountain.

MONASTERY OF DAPHNI ΜΟΝΗ ΔΑΦΝΙΟΥ

35 km (22 mi) southwest of Phyle, 11 km (7 mi) west of Athens.

Sacked by Crusaders, inhabited by Cistercian monks, and desecrated by Turks, the Monastery of Daphni remains one of the most splendid Byzantine monuments in Greece—unfortunately, it is currently closed for long-term restoration work. Dating from the 11th century, the golden age of Byzantine art, the church contains a series of miraculously preserved mosaics without parallel in the legacy of Byzantium: powerful portraits of figures from the Old and New Testaments, images of Christ and the Virgin Mary in the *Presentation of the Virgin*, and, in the golden dome, a stern *Pantokrator* ("ruler of all") surrounded by 16 Old Testament prophets who predicted his coming. The mosaics, made of chips of four different types of marble, are set against gold.

Daphni means "laurel tree," which was sacred to Apollo, whose sanctuary once occupied this site. It was destroyed in AD 395 after the antipagan edicts of the emperor Theodosius, and the Orthodox monastery was probably established in the 6th century, incorporating materials of Apollo's sanctuary in the church and walls. Reoccupied by Orthodox monks only in the 16th century, the Daphni area has since been host to a barracks and mental institution. At this writing, the monastery is closed for restoration; officials hope it will be reopened by late 2008. Based on some of the mosaic work that has been shown privately, it will be well worth the wait. ✉*End of Iera Odos, Haidari* ☎*210/581–1558* 🌐*www.culture.gr.*

ELEUSIS ΕΛΕΥΣΙΝΑ

11 km (7 mi) west of the Monastery of Daphni, 22 km (14 mi) west of Athens.

The growing city of Athens co-opted the land around Eleusis, placing shipyards in the pristine gulf and steel mills and petrochemical plants along its shores. It is hard to imagine that there once stretched in every direction fields of corn and barley sacred to the goddess Demeter, whose realm was symbolized by the sheaf and sickle.

The **Sanctuary of Demeter** lies on an east slope, at the foot of the acropolis, hardly visible amid modern buildings. The legend of Demeter and her daughter Persephone explained for the ancients the cause of the seasons and the origins of agriculture. It was to Eleusis that Demeter traveled in search of Persephone after the girl had been kidnapped by Hades, god of the underworld. Zeus himself interceded to restore her to the distraught Demeter but succeeded only partially, giving mother and daughter just half a year together. Nevertheless, in gratitude to King Keleos of Eleusis, who had given her refuge in her time of need, Demeter presented his son Triptolemos with wheat seeds, the knowledge of agriculture, and a winged chariot so he could spread them to mankind. Keleos built a *megaron* (large hall) in Demeter's honor, the first Eleusinian sanctuary.

The worship of Demeter took the form of mysterious rites, part purification and part drama, and both the Lesser and the Greater Eleusinian rituals closely linked Athens with the sanctuary. The procession for the Greater Eleusinia began and ended there, following the route of the Sacred Way. Much of what you see now in the sanctuary is of Roman construction or repair, although physical remains on the site date back to the Mycenaean period. Follow the old Sacred Way to the great *propylaea* (gates) and continue on to the Precinct of Demeter, which was strictly off-limits on pain of death to any but the initiated. The *Telesterion* (Temple of Demeter), now a vast open space surrounded by battered tiers of seats, dates to 600 BC, when it was the hall of initiation. It had a roof supported by six rows of seven columns, presumably so the mysteries would be obscured, and it could accommodate 3,000 people. The museum, just beyond, contains pottery and sculpture, particularly of the Roman period. Although the site is closed at night, you can see the sacred court and propylae from a distance thanks to special lighting by Pierre Bideau, the French expert who also designed the new lighting for the Acropolis in Athens. ✉ *Eleusis* ☎ *210/554–6019* 🎫 *€4* ⏲ *Tues.–Sun. 8:30–3.*

THE SARONIC GULF ISLANDS
ΝΗΣΙΑ ΣΑΡΩΝΙΚΟΥ ΚΟΛΠΟΥ

Straddling the gulf between Athens and the Peloponnese are the Saronic Gulf islands, the aristocracy of the Greek isles. They're enveloped in a patrician aura that is the combined result of history and their more-recent cachet as the playgrounds of wealthy Athenians. Aegina's pretty country villas have drawn shipping executives, who commute from the island to their offices in Piraeus. Here pine forests mix with groves of pistachio trees, a product for which Aegina is justly famous. Hydra and Spetses are farther south and both ban automobiles. Hydra's stately mansions, restaurants, and boutiques cater to the sophisticated traveler. Spetses has both broad forests and regal, neoclassic buildings. Rather than being spoiled by tourism, all four islands have managed to preserve their laid-back attitude, well suited to the hedonistic lifestyle of weekend pleasure-seekers arriving by yacht and hydrofoil.

AEGINA ΑΙΓΙΝΑ

30 km (19 mi) south to Aegina town from the port of Piraeus.

Although it may seem hard to imagine, by the Archaic period (7th to 6th century BC) Aegina was a mighty maritime power. It introduced the first silver coinage (marked with a tortoise) and established colonies in the Mediterranean. By the 6th century BC, Aegina had become a major art center, known in particular for its bronze foundries—worked by such sculptors as Kallon, Onatas, and Anaxagoras—and its ceramics, which were exported throughout the Mediterranean. This powerful island, lying so close off the coast of Attica, could not fail to come into conflict with Athens. As Athens's imperial ambitions grew, Aegina became a thorn in its side. In 458 BC Athens laid siege to the city, eventually conquering the island. In 455 BC the islanders were forced to migrate from the island, and Aegina never again regained its former power.

From the 13th to the 19th century, Aegina ping-ponged between nations. A personal fiefdom of Venice and Spain after 1204, it was fully claimed by Venice in 1451. Less than a century later, in 1537, it was devastated and captured by the pirate Barbarossa and repopulated with Albanians. Morosini recaptured Aegina for Venice in 1654, but Italian dominance was short-lived: the island was ceded to Turkey in 1718. Its Greek roots were brushed off in the early 19th century, when it experienced a rebirth as an important base in the 1821 War of Independence, briefly holding the fledgling Greek nation's government (1826–28). The first modern Greek coins were minted here. At this time many people from the Peloponnese, plus refugees from Chios and Psara, emigrated to Aegina, and many of the present-day inhabitants are descended from them.

The eastern side of Aegina is rugged and sparsely inhabited today, except for Ayia Marina, a former fishing hamlet now studded with hotels. The western side of the island, where Aegina town lies, is more fertile and less mountainous than the east; fields are blessed with grapes, olives, figs, almonds, and, above all, the treasured pistachio trees. Idyllic seascapes, and a number of beautiful courtyard gardens, make Aegina town attractive. A large population of fishermen adds character to the many waterfront café-taverna hybrids serving ouzo and beer with pieces of grilled octopus, home-cured olives, and other *mezedes* (appetizers). Much of the ancient city lies under the modern. Although some unattractive contemporary buildings mar the harborscape, a number of well-preserved neoclassic buildings and village houses are found on the backstreets. It takes between 60 and 90 minutes for ferries from Piraeus to dock at Souvala, a sleepy fishing village on the island's northern coast, or at the main port in Aegina town. Hydrofoils reach Aegina town in 35 minutes.

As you approach from the sea, your first view of Aegina town takes in the sweep of the harbor, punctuated by the tiny white chapel of **Ayios Nikolaos.** ⊠*Harbor front, Aegina town.*

During the negotiations for Greece during the War of Independence, Ioannis Kapodistrias, the first president of the country, conducted meetings in the medieval **Markelon Tower.** Today the tower houses the town's cultural center and the Spyros Alexiou Center for Social Issues. ⊠*Town center, Aegina town.*

The **Archaeological Museum** is small, but it was the first to be established in Greece (1829). Finds from the Temple of Aphaia and excavations throughout the island, including early– and middle–Bronze Age pottery, are on display. Among the Archaic and classical pottery is the distinctive Ram Jug, depicting Odysseus and his crew fleeing the Cyclops, and a 5th-century BC sphinx. Also notable is a Hercules sculpture from the Temple of Apollo. Just above the Archaeological Museum is the ancient site of the acropolis of Aegina, the island's religious and politi-

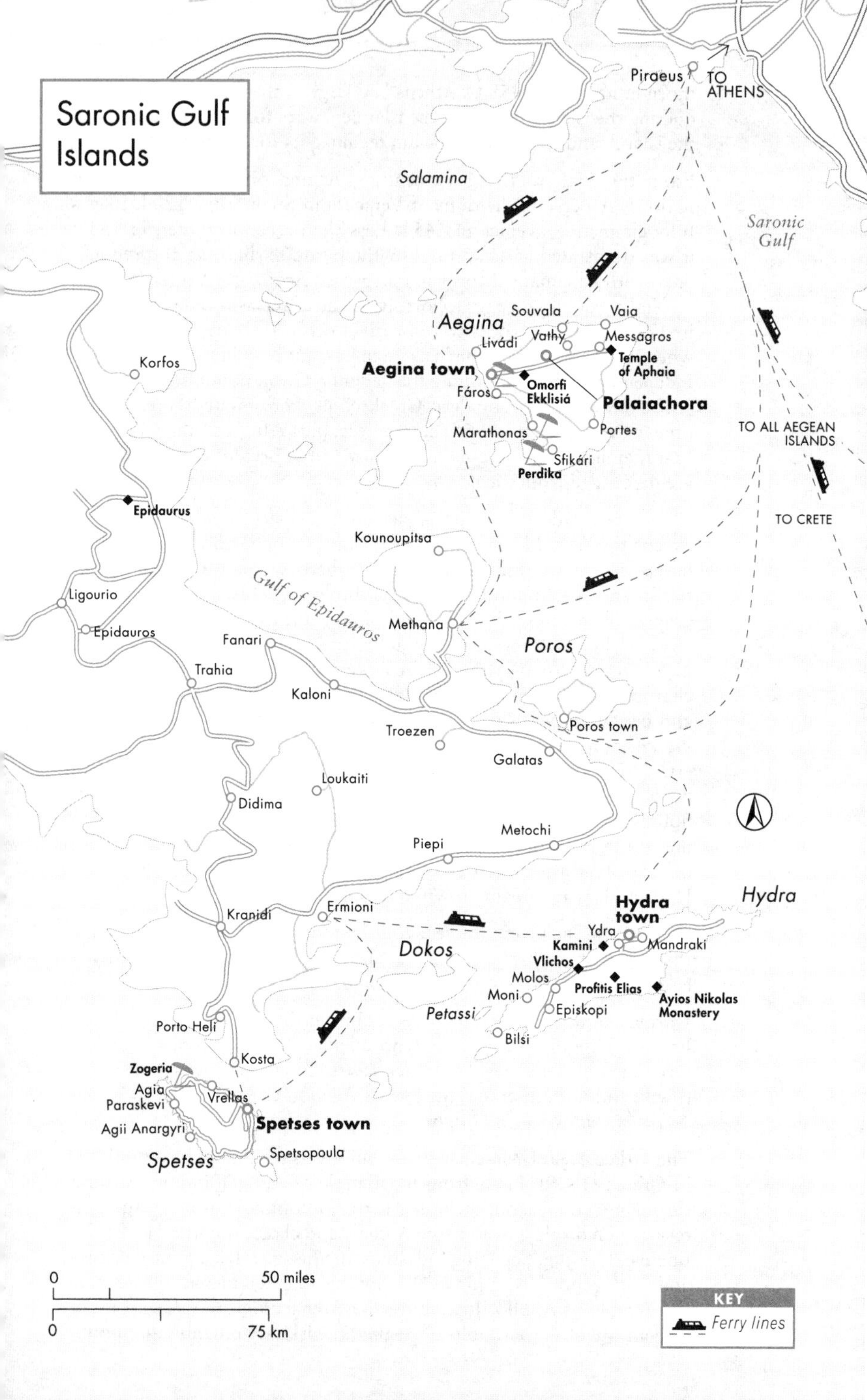

Saronic Gulf Islands
Piraeus
TO ATHENS
Salamina
Saronic Gulf
Aegina
Souvala
Vaia
Livádi
Vathy
Messagros
Temple of Aphaia
Aegina town
Omorfi Ekklisiá
Fáros
Palaiachora
Marathonas
Portes
Sfikári
Perdika
TO ALL AEGEAN ISLANDS
TO CRETE
Korfos
Epidaurus
Kounoupitsa
Gulf of Epidauros
Ligourio
Epidauros
Methana
Fanari
Poros
Trahia
Kaloni
Poros town
Troezen
Galatas
Loukaiti
Didima
Metochi
Piepi
Hydra
Hydra town
Ermioni
Kranidi
Ydra
Kamini
Mandraki
Dokos
Vlichos
Molos
Profitis Elias
Moni
Ayios Nikolas Monastery
Episkopi
Petassi
Bilsi
Porto Heli
Kosta
Zogeria
Agia Paraskevi
Vrellas
Spetses town
Agii Anargyri
Spetsopoula
Spetses
0
50 miles
0
75 km
KEY
Ferry lines

cal center. The settlement was first established in the Copper Age, and was renamed **Kolona,** or "column," in modern times, after the only remaining pillar of the Temple of Apollo that once stood there. You can examine ruins and walls dating back to 1600–1300 BC, as well as Byzantine-era buildings. ✉ *Harbor front, 350 feet from ferry dock, Aegina town* ☎ *22970/22248* 🎫 *€3* ⏲ *Tues.–Sun. 8:30–3:30.*

NEED A BREAK?

Having a bite to eat at the *psaragora* (fish market) is a must in Aegina town. A small dish of grilled octopus at the World War II–era taverna agora (*market* ✉ *Within market on Panayi Irioti, Aegina town* ☎ *22970/27308*) is perfect with an ouzo—if you aren't averse to the smell of raw fish wafting over. Inside, fishermen gather mid-afternoon and early evening, worrying their beads while seated beside glistening octopus hung up to dry—as close to a scene from the film *Zorba the Greek* as you are likely to see in modern Greece.

4

The haunting remains of the medieval **Palaiachora** *(Old Town)* , built in the 9th century by islanders whose seaside town was the constant prey of pirates, are set on the rocky, barren hill above the monastery. Capital of the island until 1826, Palaiachora has the romantic aura of a mysterious ghost town, a miniature Mistras that still has more than 20 churches. They are mostly from the 13th century, and a number of them have been restored and are still in use. They sit amid the ruins of the community's houses abandoned by the inhabitants in the early 19th century. Pick up a booklet from the Aegina Tourist Police that provides a history of the settlement and directs you to several of the most interesting churches. Episkopi (often closed), Ayios Giorgios, and Metamorphosi have lovely but faded (by dampness) frescoes. The frescoes of the church of Ayioi Anargyroi are especially fascinating because they are of pagan subjects, such as the mother goddess Gaia on horseback and Alexander the Great. The massive Ayios Nektarios Monastery, 1 km (½ mi) west of Palaiachora, is one of the largest in the Balkans. ✉ *7 km (4½ mi) south of Aegina town center.*

The small, somewhat-overrun port of **Ayia Marina** has many hotels, cafés, restaurants, and a family-friendly beach. ✉ *13 km (8 mi) east of Aegina town, via small paved road below Temple of Aphaia.*

From the **Temple of Aphaia,** perched on a promontory, you have superb views of Athens and Piraeus across the water—with binoculars you can see both the Parthenon and the Temple of Poseidon at Sounion. This site has been occupied by many sanctuaries to Aphaia; the ruins visible today are those of the temple built in the early 5th century BC. Aphaia was apparently a pre-Hellenic deity, whose worship eventually converged with that of Athena. The temple, one of the finest extant examples of Archaic architecture, was adorned with an exquisite group of pedimental sculptures that are now in the Munich Glyptothek. Twenty-five of the original 32 Doric columns were either left standing or have been reconstructed. You can visit the museum for no extra fee. The exhibit has many fragments from the once brilliantly colored temple interior and inscriptions of an older temple from the

6th and 5th centuries BC, as well as drawings that show a reconstruction of the original building. From Aegina town, catch the bus for Ayia Marina on Ethniyersias Square, the main Aegina town bus station; ask the driver to let you off at the temple. A gift and snack bar is a comfortable place to have a drink and wait for the return bus to Aegina town or for the bus bound for Ayia Marina. ✉ *15 km (9 mi) east of Aegina town, Ayia Marina* ☎ *22970/32398* 🌐 *www.culture.gr* *€4* *Temple Apr.–Nov., daily 8–7:15; Dec.–Mar., daily 8:15–5; museum Tues.–Sun. 8–2:15.*

NO-SWEAT TIP

In July and August visit archaeological sites like the Temple of Aphaia as early in the day as possible. There is little shade at such sites, and the midday heat can be withering. Plus, an early start may help you avoid crowds.

Follow the lead of the locals and visiting Athenians, and for an excursion, take a bus (a 20-minute ride from Ethniyersias Square) to the pretty village of **Perdika** to unwind and eat lunch at a seaside taverna. Places to eat in Perdika have multiplied over the years but are still low key and have a strong island flavor, transporting you light-years away from the bustle of much of modern Greece. Try O Nontas, the first fish taverna after the bus station, for a meal on the canopied terrace overlooking the little bay and the islet of Moni. Antonis, the famous fish tavern, draws big-name Athenians year-round. Other interesting year-round cafés include the inviting Liotrivi, with its corner view on the port, beachside tables, and the antique olive press it's named after on display inside; the Kioski, in a little stone building; and mainstream bar Cafe Aigokeros. There's also a small sand cove with shallow water safe for young children to swim in. ✉ *9 km (5½ mi) south of Aegina town.*

OFF THE BEATEN PATH

Moni. In summer, caïques make frequent trips of 10 minutes from Perdika harbor to this little islet, inhabited only by birds and relocated *kri-kri* (Cretan goats). Trails are good for hiking, after which a swim off a little sand beach in the marvelously clear water is most welcome. If you want to stay for a few hours, it is best to make an appointment for your boatman to return for you (pay him when he does). A small snack bar operates in summer, although you would be better off bringing a picnic lunch.

BEACHES

There are no broad coasts, and most beaches on Aegina are slivers of sand edging the coastal roads. Aegina town's beaches, and notably the pine-surrounded **Kolona** beach (✉ *Near Kolona monument*), are pleasant enough, though crowded. There's a good swimming spot at the sandy **Marathonas** beach (✉ *6 km [4 mi] south of Aegina town*). After Marathonas, **Aiginitissa** (✉ *7 km [4½ mi] south of Aegina town*) is a small, sandy bay that has its own café-restaurant and is lined with umbrellas and lounge chairs. **Klima** (✉ *10 km [6 mi] south of Aegina town*), a semi-secluded sandy beach, has a finely pebbled bay of crystal-clear waters. To reach it, turn left at the intersection before entering Perdika.

Ayia Marina's beach (✉ *15 km [9 mi] east of Aegina town*) is popular with the parenting set, as the shallow water is ideal for playing children.

BEACH BUMMED?

If Aegina's beaches don't wow you, climb aboard one of the many daily boats from Aegina's harbor to the smaller, nearby isle of **Angistri.** Without cars, but with food, drink, and small coves to swim in, Angistri has a relaxed, out-of-the-way feel, and more than its share of lovely beaches, which range from sandy stretches to pine-surrounded pebble beaches, all lapped by crystal waters.

WHERE TO STAY & EAT

$$$–$$$$ ✕**Antonis.** Seafood is the word at this famed taverna run by Antonis and his sons. The octopus grilled in front of the establishment lures bathers and other visitors who tuck into options ranging from teeny fried smelt to enormous lobsters. People-watching is as much of a draw as the food, since the tables afford a view of all the comings and goings of the harbor's small boats as well as some sleek yachts. Bouillabaisse is a good starter. ✉ *Waterfront, Perdika* ☎ *22970/61443* ▭ *MC, V.*

$$$–$$$$ ✕**Taverna O Kyriakos.** Though it doesn't have the cachet of Antonis, this taverna serves some of the freshest seafood on the island; the sea view isn't bad either. Order the red mullet or white sea bream—both expertly grilled for a reasonable price. *Magirefta* (oven-baked dishes) such as oven-roasted lamb and beef *kokkinisto* (slow-cooked in tomato sauce) are cheaper options. Excellent appetizers include eggplant salad, zucchini pie, and bourekakia. ✉ *Marathonas beach, Marathonas* ☎ *22970/24025* ▭ *No credit cards* ⊗ *Closed Dec. and Jan., and weekdays Oct., Nov., Feb., and Mar.*

$$–$$$ ✕**Taverna O Kostas.** Hollowed-out wine barrels used for displaying wines and serving food are more kitsch than antique, but they match the lightheartedness of this country tavern. Cooks showily prepare saganaki over live flames by the table as waiters pull wine from the barrels lining the walls. The menu is solid Greek fare, slightly tweaked for non-Greek palates in search of a "genuine" taverna experience. Yes, it's touristy, but it's also fun. ✉ *Aegina–Alones road, Ayia Marina* ☎ *22970/32424* ▭ *No credit cards.*

$$–$$$ ✕**Vatsoulia.** Ask a local to name the best restaurant in Aegina, and the response is invariably Vatsoulia. In summer the garden is a pleasant oasis, scented with jasmine and honeysuckle; in winter, nestle inside the cozy dining room. Eggplant in garlic sauce and zucchini croquettes are can't-go-wrong starters. Continue with taverna classics such as veal in red sauce; thick, juicy grilled pork chops; or moussaka enlivened with cinnamon and a wonderfully fluffy béchamel. In winter try the hare stew. A 10-minute walk from Aegina town center gets you to this rustic taverna. ✉ *Aphaias 75, Aegina town* ☎ *22970/22711* ⚠ *Reservations essential* ▭ *AE, MC, V* ⊗ *Closed Mon., Tues., Thurs., and Fri.*

$–$$ ✕**Ela Mesa.** It may have relocated to the elegant hotel of the same name, but Ela Mesa hasn't changed its inventive approach to food. Crisp, deep-fried zucchini puffs give va-va-voom to the typically sliced and fried squash starter. And entrées like golden shrimp *bourekia* (wrapped

4

in phyllo, deep-fried, and served in a cream base) and *midopilafo* (mussel risotto) will sate your inner foodie while sparing your wallet. ✉ *Souvala* ☎ *22970/53158* 🌐 *www.elamesa.gr* ▭ *AE, MC, V.*

¢–$ ✕ **Tsias.** For a light bite, try this harborside *meze-ouzeri* (bar serving mezedes) restaurant that's a hangout for locals as well as tourists passing through. Except for the 30 varieties of ouzo, everything is homemade in this small establishment whose warm yellow walls are decorated with stencils. Vouta Vouta *(Dip Dip)*, a shrimp-and-pink-spicy-sauce concoction, is a palate pleaser, but the real don't-miss dishes are baked apple in cognac and the custom omelets for breakfast. Reservations are recommended at night. ✉ *Harbor road (Dimokratias), Aegina town* ☎ *22970/23529* ▭ *MC, V.*

$ **Hotel Apollo.** Take advantage of the beachside location by relaxing on the restaurant terrace or renting a boat to water-ski. Steps lead down from the sundeck to the sand. Spartan guest rooms at this white, block-shaped hotel all have balconies and sea views. The town center of overdeveloped Ayia Marina is a 10-minute walk from the hotel; a bus stop is 750 feet from the hotel. ✉ *Ayia Marina beach, 18010 Ayia Marina* ☎ *22970/32271 through 22970/32274, 210/323–4292 winter in Athens* 🌐 *www.apollohotel.gr* *107 rooms* *In-room: refrigerator. In-hotel: restaurant, pool* ▭ *AE, DC, MC, V* *Closed Nov.–Mar.* *BP.*

$ ★ **Pension Rena.** Come home to the handmade lace curtains and the wood and marble furnishings lovingly tended by friendly proprietor Rena Kappou. The breakfast of homemade cakes, jams, and fresh juice is served family-style in the dining room or courtyard. With an advance request, Rena will cook dinner for you. Her specialties: *yiouvetsaki* (meat baked in ceramic dishes with tomato sauce and barley-shape pasta) and *kasseropita* (a pie made from kasseri cheese). Bonus: all rooms have a balcony. Pension Rena is a 10-minute walk from the town harbor. ✉ *Parodos Ayias Irinis, Faros, 18010 Aegina town* ☎ *22970/24760 or 22970/22086* 📠 *22970/24244* *8 rooms* *In-room: refrigerator* ▭ *AE, MC, V* *BP.*

$ Fodor's Choice ★ **Rastoni.** Quiet and secluded, this hotel's peaceful quality is heightened by the landscaped Mediterranean garden, which has pistachio trees, wood pergolas and benches, and rattan armchairs where you can curl up with a book or just spend the day staring out at sea. A sense of space and reliance on Asian wood trims and furniture adds to the Zen appeal. Rooms have a sleek, minimalist feel, in addition to private verandas with panoramic views. Rastoni overlooks the beach and the Kolona promontory, a short walk (about 900 feet) north of the town center. ✉ *Dimitriou Petriti 31, 18010 Aegina town* ☎ *22970/27039* 🌐 *www.rastoni.gr* *11 studios* *In-room: refrigerator. In hotel: no elevator* ▭ *AE, MC, V* *BP.*

¢–$ **To Petrino Spiti.** A compound of buildings constructed in the traditional village style, "The Stone House" combines modern convenience with Greek character (and among the notable characters we include owner Elpida Thanopoulou, who keeps an eagle eye on the place). Customary pine furniture and folk crafts give old-school flair to rooms with fully equipped kitchens and spare beds. The studio apartments on the second floor have excellent views of the sea and nearby Angistri, although ground-floor rooms open onto the pistachio tree–filled garden. This quiet area of Aegina town is set a little back from the harbor and Ayios Nikolaos church. ✉*Stratigou Petriti 5, 18910 Aegina town* ☎*22970/23837, 22970/23838, 210/867–9787 in Athens* *12 apartments* *In-room: no a/c (some), kitchen. In hotel: no elevator* *No credit cards.*

FESTIVALS

Two of the most important festivals held at **Ayios Nektarios Monastery** (✉*7 km [4½ mi] southeast of Aegina town* ☎*22970/53806*) are Whitmonday, or the day after Pentecost (the seventh Sunday after Easter), and the November 9 saint's day, when the remains of Ayios Nektarios are brought down from the monastery and carried in a procession through the streets of town, which are covered in carpets and strewn with flowers.

4

On the Assumption of the Virgin Mary, August 15—the biggest holiday of summer—a celebration is held at **Panayia Chrysoleontissa** (✉*6 km [4 mi] east of Aegina town*), a mountain monastery.

On September 6 and 7, the feast of the martyr Sozon is observed with a two-day *paniyiri* (saint's day festival), celebrated at **Ayios Sostis** (✉*9 km [5½ mi] south of Aegina town, Perdika*).

NIGHTLIFE

Greek bars and clubs frequently change names, so it's sometimes hard to keep up with the trends. The ever-popular **Avli** (✉*Panayi Irioti 17, Aegina town* ☎*22970/26438*) serves delicious appetizers in a small courtyard that goes from café-bistro by day to bar (playing Latin rhythms) by night. On the outskirts of Aegina town, multilayered **Inn on the Beach** (✉*1 km [½ mi] north of center, Aegina town* ☎*22970/25116*) draws an early crowd with its sunset cocktails and chill-out music, before notching up the music to a beach-party tempo. An Aegina mainstay since 1996, beach bar **Aqua Loca** (✉*1½ km [1 mi] north of Aegina town, on road toward Perdika, Agios Vasilios* ☎*69426/96709*) promises great cocktails (ask for the house special) with some of the best sunsets of your life. Consider nibbling on a *poikilia mezedon* (an hors d'oeuvre assortment) or the shrimp and sea urchin salad.

THE OUTDOORS

Aegina is one of the best islands for hiking, since the interior is gently undulating, older dirt trails are often still marked by white paint markings, and the terrain has many landscapes. Those who are ambitious might want to hike from Aegina town to the Temple of Aphaia or on the unspoiled eastern coast from Perdika to Ayia Marina, two routes described in detail in Gerald Thompson's *A Walking Guide to Aegina,* available at local gift and bookshops.

SHOPPING

Aegina's famous pistachios, much coveted by Greeks, can be bought from stands along the town harbor. They make welcome snacks and gifts. A treat found at some of the Aegean town bakeries behind the harbor is *amigdalota,* rich almond cookies sprinkled with orange flower water and powdered sugar. If you want to have a picnic lunch on the island or on the ferryboat while en route to another Saronic island, check out the luscious fruit displayed on several boats in the center of the harbor.

Cheap secondhand items from lamps to undergarments can be found at the **Animal Respect** (✉*Panayi Irioti 73, behind town hall, Aegina harbor* ☎*22970/27049*) charity shop. Run by the nonprofit organization that cares for stray animals on the island, the shop also sells fashionable pet accessories.

Flip-flops, shoes, and bikinis; jewelry; papier-mâché figures; dangling Turkish charms; and kitchenware form a rainbow of items available at **Fistiki** (✉*Panayi Irioti 15, Aegina town* ☎*22970/28327*). The shop's small entrance opens into a maze of boxy rooms filled with everything you could ever need to stay stylish on your trip.

HYDRA 'ΥΔΡΑ

140 km (87 mi) south of Aegina town port.

As the full length of Hydra stretches before you when you round the easternmost finger of the northern Peloponnese, your first reaction might not, in fact, be a joyful one. Gray, mountainous, and barren, the island has the gaunt look of a saintly figure in a Byzantine icon. But as the island's curved harbor—one of the most picturesque in all of Greece—comes into view, delight will no doubt take over. Because of the nearly round harbor, the town is only visible from a perpendicular angle, a quirk in the island's geography that often saved the island from attack, since passing ships completely missed the port.

Although there are traces of an ancient settlement, the island was sparsely inhabited until the Ottoman period. Hydra took part in the Greek War of Independence, begun in 1821, and by the early 19th century the island had developed an impressive merchant fleet, creating a surge in wealth and exposing traders to foreign cultures. Their trade routes stretched from the mainland to Asia Minor and even America.

In the middle of the 20th century the island became a haven for artists and writers like Canadian singer-songwriter Leonard Cohen and the Norwegian novelist Axel Jensen. In the early 1960s, an Italian starlet named Sophia Loren emerged from Hydra's harbor waters in the Hollywood flick *A Boy and a Dolphin.* The site of an annex of Athens's Fine Arts School, today Hydra remains a favorite haunt of new and established artists. In summer there are continual small art exhibits. And even though the harbor is flush with bars and boutiques, Hydra seems as fresh and innocent as when it was "discovered." The two- and three-story gray and white houses with red tile roofs, many built from

1770 to 1821, climb the steep slopes around Hydra town harbor. The noble port and houses have been rescued and placed on the Council of Europe's list of protected monuments, with strict ordinances regulating construction and renovation.

Although Hydra has a landmass twice the size of Spetses, only a fraction is habitable, and after a day or so on the island, faces begin to look familiar. All motor traffic is banned from the island (except for several rather noisy garbage trucks). When you arrive by boat, mule tenders in the port will rent you one of their fleet to carry your baggage—or better yet, you—to your hotel, for around €10. ■ TIP→ **Make sure to agree on a price before you leave.** Mule transport is the time-honored and most practical mode of transport up to the crest; you may see mules patiently hauling anything from armchairs and building materials to cases of beer.

Impressed by the architecture they saw abroad, shipowners incorporated many of the foreign influences into their *archontika,* old, graystone mansions facing the harbor. The forbidding, fortresslike exteriors are deliberately austere, the combined result of the steeply angled terrain and the need for buildings to blend into the gray landscape. One of the finest examples of this Hydriot architecture is the **Lazaros Koundouriotis Mansion,** built in 1780 and beautifully restored in the 1990s as a museum. The interior is lavish, with hand-painted ceiling borders, gilt moldings, marquetry, and floors of black-and-white marble tiles. Some rooms have pieces that belonged to the Koundouriotis family, who played an important role in the War of Independence; other rooms have exhibits of costumes, jewelry, wood carvings, and pottery from the National Museum of Folk History. The basement level has three rooms full of paintings by Periklis Vyzantinos and his son. ✉ *On a graded slope over port, on west headland, Hydra town* ☎ *22980/52421* 🎫 *€3* ⏲ *Mar.–Oct., Tues.–Sun. 10–4:30.*

Hydra Historical Archives and Museum has a collection of historical artifacts and paintings dating back to the 18th century. A small first-floor room contains figureheads from ships that fought in the 1821 War of Independence. There are old pistols and navigation aids, as well as portraits of the island's heroes and a section devoted to local costume, including the dark *karamani,* pantaloons worn by Hydriot men. There are also temporary Greek-art exhibits. ✉ *On east end of harbor, Hydra town* ☎ *22980/52355* 🎫 *€4* ⏲ *Daily 9–4:30 and 7–9.*

Founded in 1643 as a monastery, the **Church of the Dormition** has since been dissolved and the monks' cells are now used to house municipal offices and a small **ecclesiastical museum.** The church's most noticeable feature is an ornate, triple-tier bell tower made of Tinos marble, likely carved in the early 19th century by traveling artisans. There's also an exquisite marble iconostasis. ✉ *Along central section of harbor front, Hydra town* ☎ *22980/54071 museum* 🎫 *Church: donations accepted; museum: €2* ⏲ *Church daily 10–3 and 6–8; museum Mar.–Nov., daily 10–3.*

Kamini, a small fishing hamlet built around a shallow inlet, has much of Hydra town's charm but none of its bustle—except on Orthodox Good Friday, when the entire island gathers here to follow the funerary procession of Christ. On a clear day, the Peloponnese coast is plainly visible across the water, and spectacular at sunset. Take the 15-minute stroll from Hydra town west; a paved coastal track gives way to a staggered, white path lined with fish tavernas. ✉ *1 km (½ mi) west of Hydra town.*

From Kamini, the coastal track continues to **Vlichos,** another pretty village with tavernas, a historic bridge, and a rocky beach on a bay. It's a 5-minute water-taxi ride from the Hydra town port or a 40-minute walk (25 minutes past Kamini). ✉ *6 km (4 mi) west of Hydra town.*

OFF THE BEATEN PATH

Hydra's monasteries. If you're staying for more than a day, you have time to explore Hydra's monasteries. Hire a mule (■ TIP→ **again, check prices first, as they can soar to more than €70**) for the ascent up Mt. Klimaki, where you can visit the **Profitis Ilias Monastery** (about two hours on foot from Hydra town) and view the embroidery work of an inhabitant of the nearby nunnery of **Ayia Efpraxia.** Experienced hikers might be tempted to set off for the **Zourvas Monastery** at Hydra's tip. It's a long and difficult hike, but compensation comes in the form of spectacular views and a secluded cove for a refreshing dip. An alternative: hire a water taxi to Zourvas.

The convent of **Ayios Nikolaos Monastery** is to the southeast of Hydra town, after you pass between the monasteries of Agios Triadas and Agias Matronis (the latter can be visited). Stop here for a drink and a sweet (a donation is appropriate), and to see the beautiful 16th-century icons and frescoes in the sanctuary. When hiking, wear sturdy walking shoes, and in summer start out early in the morning—even when traveling by mule—to minimized exposure to the midday sun. Your reward: stunning vistas over the island (resplendent with wildflowers and herbs in spring), the western and eastern coasts, and nearby islets on the way to area monasteries.

BEACHES

Beaches are not the island's main attraction; the only sandy stretch is an activity-centered beach by the Mira Mare hotel (☎ *22980/52300*), near Mandraki. There are small, shallow coves at Kaminia and Vlichos, west of the harbor. At **Hydronetta** (✉ *Western edge of harbor, Hydra town*) the gray crags have been blasted and laid with cement to form sundecks. Sunbathing and socializing at the beach bars take priority over swimming, but diving off the rocks into the deep water is exhilarating. Boats ferry bathers from Hydra town harbor near the Mitropolis church to pebble beaches on the island's **southern coast,** including **Bisti** and **Ayios Nikolaos,** where there are sun beds and umbrellas. Large boats have set fees posted for particular beaches; water taxis, whose rates you should negotiate in advance, start at €10.

WHERE TO STAY & EAT

$$$–$$$$ ✕ **Enalion.** A charming young trio of owners—Fanis, Kostas, and Alexandros—imbues the place with energy and attentive service. Their light, imaginative approach to Mediterranean cuisine includes dishes like *skordopitakia* (garlic bread with tomato and shrimp) and mussels flavored with saffron, as well as a good selection of vegetarian options, including spinach and broccoli tarts. All go perfectly with a glass of house wine and the accompanying Mediterranean tunes. ✉ *2½ km (1½ mi) west of Hydra town, 100 feet from beach, Vlichos* ☎ *22980/29680* ▭ *AE, MC, V* ⊙ *Closed Dec.–Mar.*

$$$–$$$$ ★ ✕ **Kondylenia's.** In a whitewashed fisherman's cottage on a promontory overlooking the little harbor of Kaminia, the restaurant is irresistibly charming (if a little pricey). Peek into the kitchen below the terrace to see what's cooking: a whole fish may be char-grilling. When available, order *kritamos* (rock samphire), vegetation which grows on the island's rocky coast, or share an order of fresh-caught grilled squid. ✉ *1 km (½ mi) west of Hydra town, on headland above harbor, Kaminia* ☎ *22980/53520* ▭ *No credit cards* ⊙ *Closed Nov.–Mar.*

$$$–$$$$ ✕ **Omilos.** The spot where Aristotle Onassis and Maria Callas once danced is now a vision in white, reopened in 2007 by one of Enalion's owners. Tables nestle in the small, high-ceiling Hydra Nautical Club and wind around the deck outside, which affords an exquisite sea view. An extensive salad menu joins tempting starters such as Greek caviar with fava bean mash and caramelized onions. Try the risotto entrée with sea urchins or select from six different sauces for grilled meats. By day bathers sip coffee on the deck; by night the feel is more formal, before all reserve melts away in the wee hours of summer mornings, when the restaurant turns club. ✉ *Hydra port, on the way to Hydronetta* ☎ *22980/53800* ✍ *Reservations essential* ▭ *MC, V* ⊙ *Closed Mon.–Thurs. Oct.–Apr.*

$$$–$$$$ ★ ✕ **To Geitoniko.** Christina and her husband, Manolis, cook home-style Greek dishes in a cozy old Hydriot house with stone floors and wooden ceilings. Try the octopus *stifado* (stew) with pearl onions; beef with quince; or eggplant stuffed with ground meat. Grilled meats and fresh fish, including the island's own calamari, are also available. Scrumptious desserts include baklava and two types of halvah. It's a good idea to arrive before 9 PM for dinner; there are only 20 tables under the open-air vine-covered pergola upstairs, and they fill up. ✉ *Spiliou Harami, opposite Pension Antonis, Hydra town* ☎ *22980/53615* ▭ *No credit cards* ⊙ *Closed Dec.–Feb.*

$–$$ ✕ **Kyria Sofia.** This home-based eatery is so popular you have to call to make an appointment. The oldest restaurant in Hydra, it sports bright green, original woodwork inside and, outside, a terrace with half a dozen tables that are quickly snapped up by those in the know. Owner Leonidas lived in New York for many years, and he's more than happy to share his culinary stories as he serves your meal. For tasty appetizers try the small cheese pies with cinnamon, and fresh salads. ✉ *Miaouli 60, past Miranda hotel, Hydra town* ☎ *22980/53097* ✍ *Reservations essential* ▭ *No credit cards* ⊙ *Closed mid-Jan.–mid-Mar. No lunch (except big parties).*

4

$–$$ **Lulus.** It's easy to laze away for hours under the canopied shade of this central taverna, whose tables spill down a little side street, almost to the harbor. The emphasis is on seafood, including lightly fried *gavros* (anchovies) and local *barbounia* (red mullet). Price-conscious menus include salad, moussaka, and fresh fish for €14. A plate of fresh watermelon yields a refreshing end. ✉*Hydra town* ☎*22980/52018* ▭*MC, V* ⊗*Closed Dec.–Feb.*

> **WORD OF MOUTH**
>
> "It is not necessary to take a donkey ride to get to your hotel if you are staying at the Bratsera. We are still laughing about being taken by that tourist trap. However, our friends love the pictures and the story."
>
> —AKNIC

$$$–$$$$ ★ **Bratsera.** An 1860 sponge factory was transformed into this posh hotel, with doors made out of old packing crates still bearing the "Piraeus" stamp. Hints of the building's rustic past are visible in the Hydriot gray stonework, exposed-timber ceilings, and wide-plank floors. Some guest rooms have four-poster ironwork beds, others have cozy lofts, and all are decorated with portraits and engravings. The restaurant operates in the oleander- and bougainvillea-graced courtyard, and its kitchen, which specializes in European cuisine, is considered one of the island's best. Bar-restaurant tables spill out poolside, and quiet Greek music plays on weekends. ✉*On left leaving port, near Hydra Tours office, 18040 Hydra town* ☎*22980/53971 through 22980/53975, 22980/52794 restaurant, 210/721–8102 winter in Athens* ⊕*www.bratserahotel.com* *25 rooms, 3 suites* *In-room: refrigerator. In-hotel: restaurant, bar, pool, public Wi-Fi, no elevator* ▭*AE, DC, MC, V* ⊗*Closed Nov.–Mar.* *BP.*

$$$ **Angelica Hotel.** It's composed of two island villas with Hydra stone, garden areas, and red barrel-tile roofs. The 13-room main villa is currently undergoing extensive reconstruction to bring it up to the high standards of its fully renovated sister, now called the V.I.P. There, streamlined wood furniture and soft neutral colors predominate in eight spacious rooms with names like Sappho and Amazon, each with unique decor. Perks include hot tubs, plasma TVs, and Korres beauty products. It's a three-minute walk from the port. ✉*Miaouli 42, 18040 Hydra town* ☎*22980/53202 or 22980/53264* ⊕*www.angelica.gr* *21 rooms* *In-room: refrigerator. In hotel: no elevator* ▭*AE, DC, MC, V* *BP.*

$$$ **Orloff.** Commissioned in 1796 by Catherine the Great for her lover Count Orloff, who came to Greece with a Russian fleet to try to dislodge the Turks, this archontiko retains its splendor. The thick white walls and white linens are offset by cornflower blue on the deep window wells and matching blue guest-room carpets. Antiques in the public (and some private) rooms have been carefully chosen—curvaceous walnut sofas, chairs, dining sets, and highboys; old paintings and lithographs; and gilt mirrors. Superior rooms are suites with a couch; all rooms have views of the town or the courtyard shaded by a mulberry tree. ✉*Rafalia 9, 350 ft from port, 18040 Hydra town* ☎*22980/52564, 22980/52495, 210/522–6152 winter in Athens* ⊕*www.orloff.gr* *5*

rooms, 4 suites ♿*In room: refrigerator. In-hotel: no elevator* 💳*AE, MC, V* ⊗*Closed Nov.–late Mar.* 🍽*BP.*

$$ ★ **Miranda.** Art collectors might feel right at home among the interesting 18th- and 19th-century furniture and art (Oriental rugs, wooden chests, nautical engravings) at the sparkling clean Miranda. This traditional Hydriot home was built in 1821 by a Captain Danavasis and is now classified by the Ministry of Culture as a national monument. The two suites on the top floor have huge balconies, sea views, and graceful ceiling frescoes done by Venetian painters. There are also paintings by esteemed Greek painters Panagiotis Tetsis and Christos Karras. The large breakfast is served in the interior courtyard, full of fragrant lemon blossoms, jasmine, and bougainvillea. ✉*Miaouli, 2 blocks inland from port center, 18040 Hydra town* ☎*22980/52230, 22980/53953, 210/804–3689 winter in Athens* 🌐*www.mirandahotel.gr* *12 rooms, 2 suites* ♿*In-room: refrigerator. In hotel: no elevator* 💳*MC, V* ⊗*Closed Nov.–Feb.* 🍽*BP.*

WORD OF MOUTH

"I stayed at Angelica hotel . . . and loved it. Very clean, comfortable, and reasonably priced. The hotel itself also looked very nice. It's in a great location—close enough to the main drag to be convenient, but far enough up the hill to give you a glimpse of island life. It's around the corner from two grocery stores and the pharmacy (which is also the Internet café), so that was very convenient."

—DenverDice

FESTIVALS

On **Megali Paraskevi** *(Good Friday)* of Orthodox Easter, a mournful procession of parishioners holding candles follows the *epitaphios* (funeral bier) as it winds its way from Kamini town to its harbor, where the bier is set afloat, illuminated by several fishing boats. Youth dive in to retrieve it. There are also several *epitaphia* in Hydra town. Greek Orthodox Holy Week ends at midnight on the eve of Easter with **Anastasi** *(Resurrection mass)* liturgies. There's joyful singing of hymns, exploding fireworks, and churches competing to see who can raise the Resurrection cross highest.

Status as a weekend destination has made Hydra a popular venue for all sorts of events, from international puppet festivals to open-air performances by British theater troupes. Exhibits, concerts, and performances are usually held June–August; details are available from the **municipality** (✉*Main street, Hydra town* ☎*22980/52210*).

The island celebrates its crucial role in the War of Independence with the **Miaoulia,** which takes place the third week of June. Festivities include dancing, and culminate in a reenactment of the night Admiral Miaoulis loaded a vessel with explosives and sent it upwind to the Turkish fleet. Naturally, the model enemy's ship goes down in flames.

NIGHTLIFE

Bars often change names, ownership, and music—if not location—so check with your hotel for what's in vogue. On the ground floor of an early-19th-century mansion, **Amalour** (✉ *Tombazi, behind port, Hydra town* ☎ *22980/53125*) attracts a thirtysomething crowd who sip expertly made cocktails and listen to ethnic, jazz, soul, and funk music. The trendy **Nautilus Bar** (✉ *West of harbor, Hydra town* ☎ *22980/52687*) hosts Greek music jam sessions.

Café-bar **Pirate** (✉ *South end of harbor, Hydra town* ☎ *22980/52711*) has been a fixture of the island's nightlife since the late 1970s. It got a face-lift, added some mainstream dance hits to its rock music–only playlist, and remains popular and raucous. Drinks include the fruity Tropical Sin. The **Saronicos** (✉ *Harbor front, Hydra town* ☎ *22980/52589*), which plays primarily Greek music, goes wild after midnight and is ideal for die-hard partygoers. The club's easy to spot: there's a fishing boat "sofa" out front.

The minuscule **Hydronetta** (✉ *West of Hydra town, on the way to Kamini, past Kanoni* ☎ *22980/54160*) has an enchanting view from its perch above the harbor. It's jammed during the day and it is *the* place to enjoy an ouzo or fruity long drink at sunset. **Spilia** (☎ *22980/54166*), tucked into the seaside rocks just below the Hydronetta bar, provides a nice escape from the midday sun and is a popular nocturnal haunt, too. It offers both coffee and drinks.

SHOPPING

A number of elegant shops (some of them offshoots of Athens stores) sell fashionable and amusing clothing and jewelry, though you won't save much by shopping here. Worth a visit is the stylish store of local jewelry designer **Elena Votsi** (✉ *Ikonomou 3, Hydra town* ☎ *22980/52637*). Exquisite handmade pieces are more work of art than accessory. Her designs sell well in Europe and New York.

SPETSES ΣΠΕΤΣΕΣ

24 km (15 mi) southwest of Hydra town port.

In the years leading up to the revolution, Hydra's great rival and ally was the island of Spetses. Lying at the entrance to the Argolic Gulf, off the mainland, Spetses was known even in antiquity for its hospitable soil and verdant pine-tree-covered slopes. The pines on the island today, however, were planted by a Spetsiot philanthropist dedicated to restoring the beauty stripped by the shipbuilding industry in the 18th and 19th centuries. There are far fewer trees than there were in antiquity, but the island is still well watered, and the many prosperous Athenians who have made Spetses their second home compete to have the prettiest gardens and terraces. The island shows evidence of continuous habitation through all of antiquity. From the 16th century, settlers came over from the mainland and, as on Hydra, they soon began to look to the sea, building their own boats. They became master sailors, successful merchants, and, later, in the Napoleonic Wars, skilled blockade runners, earning fortunes that they poured into building larger boats and grander houses. With the outbreak of the War of Independence in 1821, the Spetsiots dedicated their best ships and brave men (and women) to the cause.

By most visitors' standards, Spetses town is small—no larger than most city neighborhoods—yet it's divided into districts. Kastelli, the oldest quarter, extends towards Profitis Ilias and is marked by the 18th-century Ayia Triada church, the town's highest point. The area along the coast to the north is known as Kounoupitsa, a residential district of pretty cottages and gardens with pebble mosaics in mostly nautical motifs. A water-taxi ride here from Kosta, across the channel on the mainland, takes about 15 minutes.

Ships dock at the modern harbor, **Dapia,** in Spetses town. This is where the island's seafaring chieftains met in the 1820s to plot their revolt against the Ottoman Turks. A protective jetty is still fortified with cannons dating from the War of Independence. Today, the town's waterfront strip is packed with cafés; and the navy-blue-and-white color scheme adopted by Dapia's merchants hints of former maritime glory. The harbormaster's offices, to the right as you face the sea, occupy a building designed in the simple two-story, center-hall architecture typical of the period and this place.

The waterfront's 1914 **Hotel Poseidonion** was the scene of glamorous Athenian society parties and balls in the era between the two world wars, and was once the largest resort in the Balkans and southeastern Europe. It is currently closed for renovation. ✉ *West side of Dapia, Spetses town.*

In front of a small park is **Bouboulina's House,** where you can take a 45-minute guided tour (available in English) and learn about this interesting heroine's life. Laskarina Bouboulina was the bravest of all Spetsiot revolutionaries, the daughter of a Hydriot sea captain, and the wife—then widow—of two more sea captains. Left with a considerable inheritance and nine children, she dedicated herself to increasing her already substantial fleet and fortune. On her flagship, the *Agamemnon,* the largest in the Greek fleet, she sailed into war against the Ottomans at the head of the Spetsiot ships. Her fiery temper led to her death in a family feud many years later. It's worth visiting the mansion just for the architectural details, like the carved-wood Florentine ceiling in the main salon. Hours are unpredictable but are posted along with tour times on the door. ✉ *Behind Dapia, Spetses town* ☎ *22980/72416* 🎫 *€5* ⏲ *Late Mar.–Oct., daily 9:45–2:30 and 3:45–9* 🌐 *www.bouboulinamuseum-spetses.gr.*

A fine late-18th-century archontiko, built in a style that might be termed Turko-Venetian, contains Spetses's **museum.** It holds articles from the period of Spetses's greatness during the War of Independence, including Bouboulina's bones and a revolutionary flag. A small collection of ancient artifacts is mostly ceramics and coins. As this book went to press, the museum was closing indefinitely for renovation.

⊠ *Archontiko Hatziyianni-Mexi, 600 ft south of harbor, Spetses town* ☎ *22980/72994.*

Spetses actually has two harbors; the **Paleo Limani** *(Old Harbor),* also known as Baltiza, slumbers in obscurity. As you stroll the waterfront, you might imagine it as it was in its 18th- and 19th-century heyday: the walls of the mansions resounding with the noise of shipbuilding and the streets humming with discreet whisperings of revolution and piracy. Today, the wood keels in the few remaining boatyards are the backdrop for trendy bars, cafés, and restaurants. ⊠ *Waterfront, 1½ km (1 mi) southeast of Dapia, Spetses town.*

THE AUTO "BAN" EXPLAINED

Unlike on Hydra, cars are not banned outright on Spetses; residents are permitted to ferry their autos to the island. In some rare cases, for medical or professional reasons, it's possible for nonresidents to get a car permit from the port authority (☎ 22980/72245), but it must be obtained at least two days prior to arrival.

The promontory is the site of the little 19th-century church, **Ayios Mamas.** ⊠ *Above harbor, Spetses town.*

On the headland sits **Ayios Nikolaos,** the current cathedral of Spetses, and a former abbey. Its lacy white-marble bell tower recalls that of Hydra's port monastery. It was here that the islanders first raised their flag of independence. ⊠ *On road southeast of waterfront, Spetses town.*

Anargyios and Korgialenios School is known as the inspiration for the school in John Fowles's *The Magus.* It was established in 1927 as an English-style boarding school for the children of Greece's Anglophilic upper class. Today, tourism management students study amid the elegant amphitheaters, black-and-white-tile floors, and huge windows. Visitors can take a peek (free) inside the school throughout the year. ⊠ *½ km (¼ mi) west of Dapia, Spetses town* ☎ *22980/74306.*

Walk along the coast to **Analipsi,** the old fisherman's village. At Easter, instead of setting off fireworks at midnight to celebrate the resurrection, local tradition dictates that a boat is set afire and put out to sea. Excavations here unearthed pottery shards and coins from the 7th century. ⊠ *1 km (½ mi) south of Spetses town.*

BEACHES

Water taxis at Dapia make scheduled runs to the most-popular outlying beaches but can also be hired for trips to more-remote coves. **Scholes Kaiki** (⊠ *1 km [½ mi] southeast of Spetses town center, in front of Anargyios and Korgialenios School*) is a triangular patch of sand beach that draws a young crowd with its beach volleyball courts, water sports, and bars. The beach at **Ayia Marina** (⊠ *2 km [1 mi] southeast of Spetses town*) is the home of the elegant Paradise Bar. You can hire a horse-drawn buggy from town to arrive in style.

Spetses's best beaches are on the west side of the island, and most easily reached by water taxi or the daily boats from Spetses town. **Ayioi**

Anargyroi (✉6 *km [4 mi] west of Spetses town*) is clean and cosmopolitan, with umbrellas and lounge chairs. The gently sloped seabed has deep waters suitable for snorkeling, waterskiing, and other water sports (rentals available). **Zogeria** (✉7½ *km [4¾ mi] west of Spetses town*), a pine-edged cove with deep sapphire waters, has a gorgeous natural setting that more than makes up for the lack of amenities—there's just a tiny church and a modest taverna. On a clear day you can see all the way to Nafplio. Pine trees, tavernas, and umbrellas line **Ayia Paraskevi** (✉8 *km [5 mi] west of Spetses town*), a sheltered beach with a mostly sandy shore.

WHERE TO STAY & EAT

$$$–$$$$ ✕ **Exedra.** Called Sioras or Giorgos by locals (all three names are on the sign), this waterside taverna lets you ogle mooring yachts while digging into a well-prepared, and thoroughly Greek meal. Mussels saganaki and a dish called Argo, shrimp and lobster baked with feta, are among the specialties, and if you've been stalking the elusive *gouronopoulo kokkinisto* (suckling pig slow-cooked in tomato sauce), your hunt can end here. Fresh fish is always available, and you can also order meats such as souvlaki and even schnitzel. ✉*At edge of Old Harbor, Spetses town* ☎*22980/73497* ▭*MC, V* ⏲*Closed Nov.–Feb.*

$$$–$$$$ ★ ✕ **Patralis.** Sit on a seaside veranda and savor seafood mezedes and fresh fish—fried, grilled, or baked. The house specialties are the fish soup, *astakomakaronada* (lobster with spaghetti), and a kind of paella with mussels, shrimp, and crayfish. *Magirefta* (oven-baked dishes) include stuffed peppers and tomatoes; oven-baked lamb; and *papoutsakia* (literally, "little shoes"), sliced eggplant with minced meat or with tomatoes and onion. The chef makes a mean baked apple for dessert, and the service is especially friendly. ✉*Kounoupitsa, near Spetses Hotel, Spetses town* ☎*22980/72134* ▭*AE, MC, V* ⏲*Closed Nov. and Dec.*

$–$$ ✕ **Lazaros.** A boisterous local crowd fills the small tables—which spill onto the street in summer—and old family photos and barrels of retsina line the walls. A small selection of well-prepared dishes includes some daily specials, such as goat in lemon sauce, chicken kokkinisto, grilled meats, and, occasionally, fresh fish at good prices. Tasty appetizers include homemade *tzatziki* (cucumber-yogurt dip), *taramosalata* (fish roe dip), *mavromatika* (black-eyed pea salad), and tender beets with *skordalia* (potato dip). Order the barrel retsina, priced by the kilo. ✉*Kastelli, 900 ft up hill from harbor, Spetses town* ☎*22980/72600* ▭*No credit cards* ⏲*Closed mid-Nov.–mid-Mar. No lunch.*

$$$$ ★ 🏨 **Nissia Traditional Residences.** The plain, rather austere facade of this restored 1920s industrial complex conceals a village of self-contained villas arranged around a swimming pool. Each apartment is named after an island; cheery white rooms, with wood and built-in furniture, have splashes of a primary color on the pillows and upholstery—lemon yellow, bright blue check, or red-and-white stripe. Even the studios (which overlook the garden) seem roomy, and sea-view apartments have spacious sitting areas with fireplaces. Aristocratic walnut dining sets, love seats, and beds furnish the huge, splurge-worthy, two-story Presidential Residences. ✉*Kounoupitsa, 1,500 feet west of Dapia, 18050 Spetses town* ☎*22980/75000 through 22980/75010, 210/346–*

2879 or 210/342–1279 in Athens ⊕www.nissia.gr 14 studios, 5 maisonettes, 12 suites In-room: kitchen. In-hotel: restaurant, pool, no elevator (except in 2 suites), public Wi-Fi AE, DC, MC, V.

$$$–$$$$ **Archondiko Economou.** Captain Mihail Economou's heirs have converted his 1851 stone mansion into a beautiful seaside spot. The main building's airy rooms feature iron beds and a sprinkling of antiques: the old ship safe, for instance, houses board games. The pebbled gardens contain a small, pretty swimming pool and a handful of live tortoises. The building's additions are less glamorous but feature pluses—in one case, a generous balcony with a cannon facing the sea. Note: no children under 16 are permitted. ⊠*Harbor road, near town hall, Spetses town, 18050* ☎*22980/73400* ⊕*www.spetsestravel.gr 2 suites, 2 studios, 4 apartments In-room: kitchen (some), refrigerator. In-hotel: no elevator, public Wi-Fi AE, MC, V BP.*

$$–$$$ **Spetses Hotel.** Enjoy both privacy—surrounded by greenery, beach, and water—and a short walk's distance to town. Here waiters bring drinks to your lounge chair in the sand, and breakfast can be taken in bed, on your balcony, or in the terrace restaurant. Blue-carpeted rooms have wood-veneer beds covered in plaid spreads, and balconies with either a sea or a town view. The staff can help you arrange excursions to mainland sights. ⊠*Beachfront, 1 km (½ mi) west of Dapia, 18050 Spetses town* ☎*22980/72602 through 22980/72604, 210/821–3126 winter in Athens* ⊕*www.spetses-hotel.gr 77 rooms In-room: refrigerator, dial-up. In-hotel: restaurant, bar, public Wi-Fi MC, V Closed Nov.–Mar. BP.*

$ ★ **Niriides Apartments.** With cheerful exteriors surrounded by myriad flowers, these four-bed apartments a short walk from the main harbor are a good value, especially in the off-season. Old-fashion wood shutters and beds with wrought-iron frames are just the right accents to set off the cool white, minimalist interiors. ⊠*Near square with clock tower, Dapia, 18050 Spetses town* ☎*22980/73392, 210/984–1851 winter in Athens* ⊕*www.niriides-spetses.gr 7 apartments In-room: kitchen, Wi-Fi. In hotel: no elevator MC, V CP.*

FESTIVAL

Spetses puts on an enormous harbor-front reenactment of a **War of Independence naval battle** for one week in early September, complete with costumed fighters and burning ships. Book your hotel well in advance if you wish to see this popular event. There are also concerts and exhibitions the week leading up to it.

NIGHTLIFE

For the newest "in" bars, ask your hotel or just stroll down to the Old Harbor, which has the highest concentration of clubs.

Surviving many years and with ever bigger dimensions, including a seaside patio, is **Baltiza** (⊠*Old Harbor, Spetses town* ☎*No phone*). International rhythms play earlier in the evening; late at night, it's packed with writhing bodies, and when the music switches to Greek at midnight, as the Greeks say, *ginete hamos*—chaos reigns. **Bratsera** (⊠*Waterfront, Spetses town* ☎*No phone*) is a popular mainstream bar in the middle of Dapia.

SPORTS

The lack of cars and the predominantly level roads make Spetses ideal for bicycling. One good trip is along the coastal road that circles the island, going from the main town to Ayia Paraskevi beach.

Ilias Rent-A-Bike (✉ *Ayia Marina road, by Analipsis Sq., Spetses town* ☏ *69738/86407*) rents well-maintained bikes, motorbikes, and equipment.

DELPHI & ENVIRONS ΔΕΛΦΟΙ

4

The region of Delphi is steeped in history: it was in Thebes, according to legend, and so described by Sophocles in *Oedipus Rex,* that the infant Oedipus was left by his father, Laios, on a mountainside to die after an oracle predicted he would murder his father and marry his mother. Some shepherds, ignorant of the curse, rescued him, and he was raised by the king of Corinth. The saga unfolded when, as a young man, Oedipus was walking from Delphi and met his father, Laius, King of Thebes, near the Triple Way. The latter, having struck Oedipus with his whip in order to make room for his chariot to pass, was in turn attacked and accidentally killed by the young man, who did not recognize his father, not having seen his parents since his birth. Journeying to Thebes, he solved the riddle of the terrible Sphinx and, as a reward, was offered the throne and the hand of Jocasta (who was, unbeknownst to him, his mother). When they discovered what had happened, Oedipus blinded himself and Jocasta hanged herself.

The preferred route from Athens follows the National Road to the Thebes turnoff, at 74 km (46 mi). Take the secondary road south past Thebes and continue west through the fertile plain—now planted with cotton, potatoes, and tobacco—to busy Levadia, capital of the province of Boeotia. If you detour in Levadia by following the signs for the *piges* (hot springs), you come to the banks of the ancient springs of Lethe and Mnemosyne, or Oblivion and Remembrance (these springs are about a 10-minute walk from the main square); in antiquity the Erkinas (Hercyne) gorge was believed to be the entrance to the underworld. Today, the plane- and maple-tree-shaded river is spanned by an old stone arch bridge built in Ottoman times. Almost halfway between Levadia and Delphi, the Triple Way (where the roads from Delphi, Daulis, and Levadia meet) is where Oedipus fatefully met his father.

If you turn south toward Dhistomo at the junction, you can visit the monastic complex at Osios Loukas and its Byzantine architecture. The National Road continues to Mt. Parnassus, where the formerly quiet mountain village of Arachova is now a successful confluence of traditional Greek mountain village and Athenian-style cafés, thanks to the proximity of ski lifts. The sublime ruins at Delphi are captivating whether you have little knowledge of ancient Greece or have long awaited a chance to see where the Pythian priestesses uttered their cryptic prophecies. After the Acropolis of Athens, Delphi is the most powerful ancient site in Greece. Its history reaches back at least as far

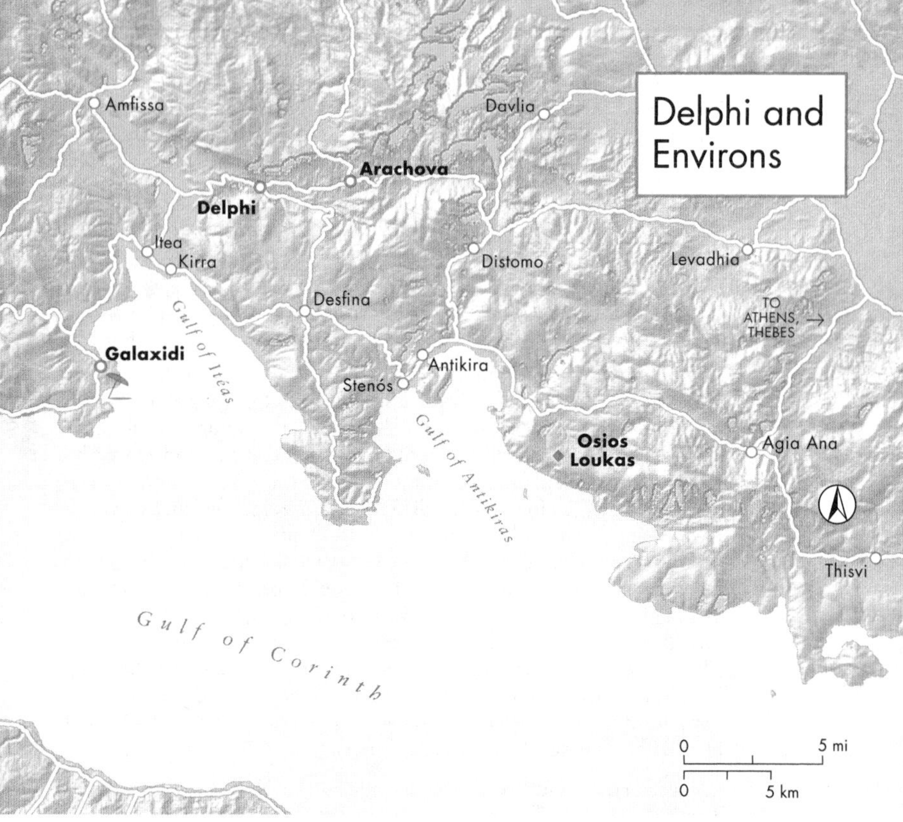

as the Mycenaean period; in Homer's *Iliad* it is referred to as Pytho. Southwest of the Delphi ruins on the coast, picturesque Galaxidi now caters to wealthy Athenians who have restored many of the mansions once owned by shipbuilders.

OSIOS LOUKAS ΌΣΙΟΣ ΛΟΥΚΑΣ

★ *150 km (93 mi) northwest of Athens.*

The monastic complex at Osios Loukas, still inhabited by a few monks, is notable for both its exquisite mosaics and its dramatic stance, looming on a prominent rise with a sweeping view of the Elekonas peaks and the sparsely inhabited but fertile valley. The outside of the buildings is typically Byzantine, with rough stonework interspersed with an arched brick pattern. It is especially beautiful in February when the almond branches explode with a profusion of delicate oval pinkish-white blooms.

Luke (Loukas) the Hermit, not the evangelist who wrote a book of the New Testament, was a medieval oracle who founded a church at this site and lived here until his death in AD 953. He was probably born in Delphi, after his family fled from Aegina during a raid of Saracen pirates. This important monastery was founded by the emperor Romanos II in AD 961, in recognition of the accuracy of Loukas's prophecy that Crete would be liberated by an emperor named Romanos. The katholikon, a masterpiece of Byzantine architecture, was built in the 11th century over the tomb of Luke. It follows to perfection the Byzantine cross-in-a-square plan under a central dome and was inspired by Ayia Sophia in Constantinople; in turn, it was used as a model for both the Monastery of Daphni and Mystra churches. Impressive mosaics in the narthex and in portions of the domed nave are set against a rich gold background and done in the somber but expressive 11th-century hieratic style by artists from Thessaloniki and Constantinople. Particularly interesting are the reactions evident on the faces of the apostles, which range from passivity to surprise as Christ washes their feet in the mosaic of *Niptir,* to the far left of the narthex.

4

In the second niche of the entrance is a mosaic showing Loukas sporting a helmet and beard, with his arms raised. The engaging *Nativity, Presentation in the Temple,* and the *Baptism of Christ* mosaics are on the curved arches that support the dome. Two priceless icons from the late 16th century, *Daniel in the Lion's Den* and *Shadrach, Meshach, and Abednego in the Flames of the Furnace,* by Damaskinos, a teacher of El Greco, were stolen a few years back from the white marble iconostasis in the little apse and have been replaced with copies. The tomb of Osios Loukas is in the crypt of the katholikon; his relics, formerly in the Vatican, were moved here in 1987, making the monastery an official shrine. A highlight of the complex is the Theotokos (Mother of God), a small communal church dedicated to the Virgin Mary, on the left as you enter. On the periphery is the monks' cells and a refectory. To visit you must wear either long pants or a skirt. Bring a small flashlight to help see some of the frescoes. ✉ *On rise above valley* ☎ *22670/22797* 🎟 *€3* ⏲ *May–mid-Sept., daily 8 AM–6 PM; mid-Sept.–Apr., daily 8–5.*

ARACHOVA ΑΡΑΧΩΒΑ

24 km (16 mi) northwest of Osios Loukas, 157 km (97 mi) northwest of Athens.

Arachova's gray-stone houses with red-tile roofs cling to the steep slopes of Mt. Parnassus, the highest mountain in Greece after Mt. Olympus. The last decade brought a boom to this once-quiet region, which in winter is transformed into a busy ski resort. Weekends attract sophisticated Athenians heading for the slopes: hotel prices soar and rooms are snapped up; cobblestone streets fill with jeeps carrying skis aloft; and village taverns get crowded after dark as people warm their weary bones before the fires. Unlike other Greek destinations, in summer there are hardly any Greek tourists in Arachova and not everything may be open.

If you're lucky enough to be in Arachova for the festival on **St. George's Day**—April 23 (or the Monday after Easter if April 23 falls during Lent)—you're in for the time of your life. St. George, the dragon slayer, is the patron saint of Arachova, and the largest church on the top of the highest hill in town is dedicated to him. So, naturally, the festival here lasts three days and nights, starting with a procession behind the generations-old silver icon from the church, in which the villagers don the local costumes, most of them ornately embroidered silken and brocaded heirlooms that testify to the rich cultural heritage of the town. The festival is kicked off in fine form with the race of the *yeroi,* the old men of the town, who are astonishingly agile as they clamber up the hill above the church without so much as a gasp for air. The following days are filled with athletic contests, cooking competitions, and, at night, passionate dancing in the tavernas until long after the goats go home.

WHERE TO STAY & EAT

$$–$$$ ✕ **Taverna To Agnandio.** Warm yourself at your choice of several fireplaces in this old house, and look out at the excellent views of the mountains. *Tirokafteri,* a piquant cheese spread, is the perfect accompaniment to the stone-ground country bread to start. Follow with a sampling of the large purplish Amphissa olives, *fava* (mashed yellow split peas, lemon, and raw onions), or the potent skordalia. Meat dominates the entrées: rooster in tomato sauce, and stuffed lamb shank, for example. ⊠ *Delfon, next to town hall* ☎ *22670/32114* ▭ *No credit cards* ⊗ *Closed June–Aug.*

$–$$ ✕ **Dasargiris.** Arachova's oldest taverna still draws gargantuan crowds—causing occasional staff surliness—simply because of the amazing food. Lamb with oregano and beef in a red sauce are both served with *hilopites,* the thin egg noodles cut into thousands of tiny squares, for which the area is known. Sample the fried *formaella* (a mild local sheep's-milk cheese); the *hortopites* (pastries filled with mountain greens); grilled beef patties stuffed with formaella or Gouda cheese; or the *kokoretsi* (a tasty mix of various lamb organs), which Greek customers swear by. At Easter the cook makes an unforgettable roast lamb and egg-lemon soup. ⊠ *Delfon 56* ☎ *22670/31291* ▭ *No credit cards* ⊗ *Closed Aug.*

$–$$ ✕ **Panayota.** It is well worth climbing the 270 steps leading from the main road up to the church of Ayios Georgios. Behind the churchyard, the lovely smells from this hilltop restaurant's kitchen will prepare you for a tasty meal. The restaurant dates back to the 1930s and has served many a Greek politician and poet. Start with local specialty *opsimotyri* (tart yogurt dip) and the house salad of shredded red cabbage, carrot, and grilled mushrooms. Then, dig into a plump *bifteki* (ground meat) flavored with parsley or *dolmades* (stuffed vine leaves) with a creamy lemon sauce. ⊠ *Ayios Giorgios, Ano Arachova* ☎ *22670/32735* ✍ *Reservations essential in winter* ▭ *MC, V* ⊗ *Closed Mon.–Wed. June–Aug.*

$$ Fodor's Choice ★ **Guesthouse Generali.** You may feel like Goldilocks when you enter this enchanting century-old building that contains many more spaces than it seems it could at first. Colorful little trinkets and toy knickknack decorations are everywhere, and no one can miss the fireplace screens painted by owner Stamatis. Detailed effort has also gone into the romantic decor of the ten varying-size rooms (all motifs like "Love" or "Flowers"); yours may have a hand-sewn linen half canopy draped over the bed, for example. The wintertime small indoor pool steambath (shaped like a little house) and spa are rare treasures. In summer, prices fall significantly. To get here from the center, walk down

the steps next to the old stone schoolhouse and past the church. A breakfast-brunch buffet (service from 8 AM to 1 PM) is available for €15 per person. ✉*Behind local school and church of Panayia, 32004* ☎*22670/31529* 🖷*22670/32287* 🌐*www.generalis.gr* *8 rooms, 1 suite, 1 apartment* *In-room: refrigerator. In-hotel: pool, some pets allowed, public Wi-Fi, no elevator* 💳*AE, DC, MC, V* *Closed for 2–3 wks late Aug.–Sept.*

$ **Guesthouse Maria.** Simple and affordable, this rustic inn is housed in a restored 1800 building on a quiet lane off the main road. The rooms' decor is as spare as the austere stone exterior, but perfectly captures local flavor thanks to well-placed accents like hand-loom wool throws, wooden spindles hung on the wall, and woven curtains embroidered with folk motifs. The three studios have mini refrigerators and a hot plate. ✉*Off Delfon, near village center, 32004* ☎*22670/31803* 🌐*www.mariarooms.com* *4 rooms, 3 studios* *In-room: refrigerator, no a/c. In-hotel: no elevator* 💳*No credit cards* *CP.*

4

NIGHTLIFE

On winter weekends Arachova streets are jammed with Athenians who come almost as much for the nightlife as for the skiing. Clubs change frequently, but favorites remain. Greek music—sometimes live—sets the tone at warm **Aquarella** (☎*22670/32660* ✉*Lakkas Sq.*): drop by for a drink or tuck into a large menu of meaty offerings Friday and Saturday nights. Catch a coffee by day or drink by night at **Café Bonjour** (☎*22670/32330*) in tree-covered Lakkas square. **Emboriko** (✉*Delfon* ☎*22670/32467*) is where an older crowd of politicians, journalists, and artists mingle anonymously. The bar is action-packed; two quieter, rear sections serve light food. Located off of the Ayios Yiorgos steps, **Flox** (☎*6932/288318*) is a restaurant-bar, open October through March and in late December, that is transformed into a club after 1:30 AM. Red wine flows on chilly nights within the carefully lighted rock-wall interior. The rowdy **Snow Me** (✉*Lakka Sq.* ☎*22670/31197*) is a split-level club with young things dancing on the bar and a doorman to keep out the unhip.

SPORTS & THE OUTDOORS

HIKING Arachova and its environs are made for exploring on foot, either by simply walking a country lane to see where it leads or picking up one of the hiking trails like the E4 through Parnassus National Park or the ancient footpath down the mountain. The 8,061-foot summit of **Mt. Parnassus** (✉*28 km [17 mi] north of Arachova*) is now easily accessible, thanks to roads opened up for the ski areas. The less hardy can drive almost up to the summit. You can motor up to the **Sarandari refuge** (☎*22370/25130* 🌐*www.greekmountains.gr*), run by ski shop company Klaoudatos, at 6,201-foot high to spend the night and then walk to the summit in time to catch the sunrise—the best time to be on Mt. Parnassus.

SKIING Rental equipment is available at local shops in Arachova and at the **Parnassos Ski Center** (✉*25 km [17 mi] north of Arachova* ☎*22340/22700* 🌐*www.parnassos-ski.gr*), just 40 minutes from Arachova. The Fterolakka area has a good restaurant and several more-challenging runs.

Stoa of the Athenians 2
Temple of Apollo 3
Theater 4
Treasury of the Athenians 1

Delphi

The Kelaria area is good for beginners. A daily ski pass costs about €27 on weekends, €12 weekdays.

SHOPPING

Arachova was known even in pre-ski days as a place to shop for wool, and stores selling rugs and weavings line the main street. The modern mass-produced bedspreads, *flokates* (woolen rugs, sometimes dyed vivid colors), and kilim-style carpets sold today are reasonably priced. If you poke into dark corners in the stores, you still might turn up something made of local wool; anything that claims to be antique bears a higher price. Also look for local foodstuffs like the delicious Parnassus honey, the local cheese formaella (often served warm), and the fiery *rakomelo,* a combination of anise liqueur and honey, which is served in most of the bars and cafés.

DELPHI ΔΕΛΦΟΙ

10 km (6 mi) west of Arachova, 189 km (118 mi) northwest of Athens.

Nestled in the mountain cliffs, modern Delphi is perched dramatically on the edge of a grove leading to the sea, west of an extraordinary ancient site. A stay in town can prove most memorable—especially if you come at *Pascha* (Easter). The hospitable people of modern Delphi take great pride in their town. They maintain a tradition of comfortable, small hotels and a main street thick with restaurants and souvenir shops. Ancient Delphi, the home of famous oracle in antiquity, can be seen from the town's hotels or terraced village houses. It's easily reached from almost any point in the central town, at most a 5- to 10-minute walk. When the archaeological site is first seen from the road, it would appear that there is hardly anything left to attest to the existence of the ancient religious city. Only the Treasury of the Athenians and a few other columns are left standing, but once you are within the precincts, the plan becomes clearer and the layout is revealed in such detail that it is not impossible to conjure up a vision of what the scene must have once been when Delphi was the holiest place in all Greece.

At first the settlement probably was sacred to Gaia, the mother goddess; toward the end of the Greek Dark Ages (circa 1100–800 BC), the site incorporated the cult of Apollo. According to Plutarch, who was a priest of Apollo at Delphi, the oracle was discovered by chance, when a shepherd noticed that his flock went into a frenzy when it came near a certain chasm in the rock. When he approached, he also came under a spell and began to utter prophecies, as did his fellow villagers. Eventually a *Pythia,* an anointed woman over 50 who lived in seclusion, was the one who sat on the three-footed stool and interpreted the prophecy.

On oracle day, the seventh of the month, the Pythia prepared herself by washing in the Castalian Fountain and undergoing a purification involving barley smoke and laurel leaves. If the male priests of Apollo determined the day was propitious for prophesying, she entered the Temple of Apollo, where she drank the Castalian water, chewed laurel leaves, and presumably sank into a trance. Questions presented to her received strange and garbled answers, which were then translated into verse by the priests. A number of the lead tablets on which questions were inscribed have been uncovered, but the official answers were inscribed only in the memories of questioners and priests. Those that have survived, from various sources, suggest the equivocal nature of these sibylline emanations: perhaps the most famous is the answer given to King Croesus of Lydia, who asked if he should attack the Persians. "Croesus, having crossed the Halys River, will destroy a great realm," said the Pythia. Thus encouraged, he crossed it, only to find his *own* empire destroyed.

During the 8th and 7th centuries BC, the oracle's advice played a significant role in the colonization of southern Italy and Sicily (Magna Graecia) by Greece's Amphictyonic League. By 582 BC the Pythian Games had become a quadrennial festival similar to those held at Olympia. Increasingly an international center, Delphi attracted supplicants from beyond the Greek mainland, including such valued clients as King Midas and King Croesus, both hailing from wealthy kingdoms in Asia Minor. During this period of prosperity many cities built treasure houses at Delphi. The sanctuary was threatened during the Persian War but never attacked, and it continued to prosper, in spite of the fact that Athens and Sparta, two of its most powerful patrons, were locked in war.

Delphi came under the influence first of Macedonia and then of the Aetolian League (290–190 BC) before yielding to the Romans in 189 BC. Although the Roman general Sulla plundered Delphi in 86 BC, there were at least 500 bronze statues left to be collected by Nero in AD 66, and the site was still full of fine works of art when Pausanias visited and described it a century later. The emperor Hadrian restored many sanctuaries in Greece, including Delphi's, but within a century or two the oracle was silent. In AD 385 Theodosius abolished the oracle. Only in the late 19th century did French excavators begin to uncover the site of Apollo.

Start your tour of the old Delphi in the same way the ancients did, with a visit to the **Sanctuary of Athena.** Pilgrims who arrived on the shores of the Bay of Itea proceeded up to the sanctuary, where they paused before going on to the Ancient Delphi site. The most notable among the numerous remains on this terrace is the **Tholos** (Round Building), a graceful 4th-century BC ruin of Pendelic marble, the purpose and dedication of which are unknown, although round temple-like buildings were almost always dedicated to a goddess. By the 2nd millennium BC, the site was already a place of worship of the earth goddess Gaia and her daughter Themis, one of the Titans. The gods expressed themselves through the murmuring of water flooding from the fault, from the rustle of leaves, and from the booming of earth tremors. The Tholos remains one of the purest and most exquisite monuments of antiquity. Theodoros, its architect, wrote a treatise on his work: an indication in itself of the exceptional architectural quality of the monument. Beneath the Phaedriades, in the cleft between the rocks, a path leads to the **Castalian Fountain,** a spring where pilgrims bathed to purify themselves before continuing. (Access to the font is prohibited because of the danger of falling rocks.) On the main road, beyond the Castalian Fountain, is the modern entrance to the sanctuary. ☒ *Below road to Arachova, before Phaedriades* 🎫 *€6 for all Delphi sites, €9 for Delphi sites and Delphi museum* ⏲ *Apr.–Oct., daily 7:30–7; Nov.–Mar., daily 8:30–2:45.*

Fodor's Choice ★

After a square surrounded by late-Roman porticoes, pass through the main gate to **Ancient Delphi** and continue on to the **Sacred Way,** the approach to the Altar of Apollo. Walk between building foundations and bases for votive dedications, stripped now of ornament and statue, mere scraps of what was one of the richest collections of art and treasures in antiquity. Thanks to the 2nd-century AD writings of Pausanias, archaeologists have identified treasuries built by the Thebans, the Corinthians, the Syracusans, and others—a roster of 6th- and 5th-century BC powers. The **Treasury of the Athenians,** on your left as you turn right, was built with money from the victory over the Persians at Marathon. The **Stoa of the Athenians,** northeast of the treasury, housed, among other objects, an immense cable with which the Persian king Xerxes roped together a pontoon bridge for his army to cross the Hellespont from Asia to Europe.

The **Temple of Apollo** visible today (there were three successive temples built on the site) is from the 4th century BC. Although ancient sources speak of a chasm within, there is no trace of that opening in the earth from which emanated trance-inducing vapors. Above the temple is the well-preserved **theater,** which seated 5,000. It was built in the 4th century BC, restored in about 160 BC, and later was restored again by the Romans. From a sun-warmed seat on the last tier, you see a panoramic bird's-eye view of the sanctuary and the convulsed landscape that encloses it. Also worth the climb is the view from the **stadium** still farther up the mountain, at the highest point of the ancient town. Built and restored in various periods and cut partially from the living rock, the stadium underwent a final transformation under Herodes Atticus, the Athenian benefactor of the 2nd century AD. It lies cradled in a grove of pine trees, a quiet refuge removed from the sanctuary below and backed by the sheer, majestic rise of the mountain. Markers for the starting line inspire many to race the length of the stadium. ✉*Road to Arachova, immediately east of modern Delphi* ☎*22650/82312* 🌐*www.culture.gr* 🎫*€6* ⏲*Apr.–Oct., daily 7:30–7; Nov.–Mar., daily 8:30–2:45.*

★ The **Delphi Museum** contains a wonderful collection of art and architectural sculpture, principally from the Sanctuaries of Apollo and Athena Pronoia. Visiting the museum is essential to understanding the site and sanctuary's importance to the ancient Greek world, which considered Delphi its center. (Look for the copy of the *omphalos,* or Earth's navel, a sacred stone from the adytum of Apollo's temple.) Curators have used an additional 15,000 square feet of museum space, opened in 2004, to create contextual, cohesive exhibits. You can now view all the pediments from Apollo's temple together and new exhibits include a fascinating collection of 5th-century BC votives.

One of the greatest surviving ancient bronzes on display commands a prime position in a spacious hall, set off to advantage by special lighting: the *Charioteer* is a sculpture so delicate in size (but said to be scaled to life) it is surprising when you see it in person for the first time. Created in about 470 BC, the human figure is believed to have stood on a terrace wall above the Temple of Apollo, near which it was found in 1896. It was part of a larger piece, which included a four-horse chariot. Scholars do not agree on who executed the work, although Pythagoras of Samos is sometimes mentioned as a possibility. The donor is supposed to have been a well-known patron of chariot racing, Polyzalos, the Tyrant of Gela in Sicily. Historians now believe that a sculpted likeness of Polyzalos was originally standing next to the charioteer figure. The statue commemorates a victory in the Pythian Games at the beginning of the 5th century BC. Note the eyes, inlaid with a white substance resembling enamel, the pupils consisting of two concentric onyx rings of different colors. The sculpture of the feet and of the hair clinging to the nape of the neck is perfect in detail.

Two life-size Ionian *chryselephantine* (ivory heads with gold headdresses) from the Archaic period are probably from statues of Apollo and his sister Artemis (she has a sly smirk on her face). Both gods also figure prominently in a frieze depicting the Gigantomachy, the gods' battle with the giants. These exquisitely detailed marble scenes, dated to the 6th century BC, are from the Treasury of the Siphnians. The *caryatids* (supporting columns in a female form) from the treasury's entrance have been repositioned to offer a more accurate picture of the building's size and depth. The museum's expansion also allowed curators to give more space to the *metopes,* marble sculptures depicting the feats of Greece's two greatest heroes, Heracles and Theseus, from the Treasury of the Athenians. The museum also has a pleasant café. ✉*East of Ancient Delphi* ☎*22650/82312* 🌐*www.culture.gr* 🎫*€6; Ancient Delphi and museum €9* ⏲*Apr.–Nov., Tues.–Sun. 7:30 AM–7:30 PM, Mon. noon–6:30 PM; Dec.–Mar., daily 8:30–3 PM.*

WHERE TO STAY & EAT

$–$$ ✕ **Iniochos.** Local specialties and small dishes, such as zucchini croquettes, roast feta, and the *bekri* ("drunk's") meze—a meat appetizer meant to be consumed slowly with wine—are served at this hotel restaurant also known as "Syndeiraion 1900." Residents stop by late at night to have a nightcap or a snack—fried formaella cheese, *sfongato* (country vegetable omelet), or a sweet baklava—and to sing along to pianist Yiannis's amazing repertoire of old Greek songs. In winter, warm yourself at the fireplace in the dining room; in summer eat on the enormous veranda overlooking the valley of Delphi. Set menus cost as little as €10. ✉*Karamanlis (formerly Friderikis) 19, at Vas. Pavlou* ☎*22650/82710* ✍*Reservations essential* 💳*AE, DC, MC, V.*

$–$$ ✕ **Lekaria.** Escape the noise and the crowds of the main street, and climb up a side lane to dine on typical Greek taverna food in a covered veranda and adjoining courtyard. You can have your rich Lekaria salad, with a variety of veggies, chicken, walnuts, and pineapple. Or you might choose *briam,* thinly sliced eggplant, carrots, potatoes, and fresh chopped tomatoes drizzled with olive oil and cooked in a slow oven. For dessert, follow the Greeks' lead and enjoy a bowl of yogurt with quince. ✉*Apollonos 33* ☎*22650/82864* 📠*22650/82355* 💳*AE, MC, V.*

$–$$ ★ ✕ **Taverna Vakchos.** Owner Andreas Theorodakis, his wife, and their two sons keep a watchful eye on the kitchen and on the happiness of their customers. Choose to eat in the spacious dining room or out on the large sheltered veranda with vines growing across the balcony rail, a Bacchus-themed wall painting, and a stunning valley view. The menu is heavy on meat dishes, either grilled, boiled, or simmered in the oven, but vegetarians can put together a small feast from boiled greens and other homemade meatless Greek classics, like sweet peas in tomato sauce. Seasonal dishes in the winter season include game such as hare and, if you're really lucky, venison. Service is especially efficient. ✉*Apollonos 31* ☎*22650/83186* 💳*MC, V.*

¢–$ ★ ✕ **Epikouros.** Nothing in the uncluttered restaurant design detracts from the view of alpine slopes from the large, open veranda. Even in the colder months, a glass canopy protects the seating area and allows diners to look out year-round. Start with rooster soup. The house specialty is a must: the wild boar stifado is cooked with plenty of baby onions and fresh tomato sauce, fragrantly seasoned with bay leaves and cinnamon. Chicken in tomato sauce with eggplant and feta is an interesting alternative for timid palates. ✉ *Karamanlis (formerly Friderikis) 33, at Vas. Pavlou* ☎ *22650/83250* ▭ *AE, DC, MC, V.*

$$$ **Amalia.** Clean-cut retro chic predominates at this 1965 landmark built by architect Nikos Valsamakis. Thirty-five acres of gardens spread down the mountainside, helping the low-lying Amalia blend seamlessly with the olive groves and pines of surrounding Delphi. Breathtaking views of Itea port seen from various public verandas, the rooms, and the poolside bar add to the hotel's appeal. An open, central hearth in the lobby sitting area is complemented by modern furnishings and a multihue blue-gray slate floor blocked off in large, varied squares. Comfortable, renovated contemporary rooms have light-color wood furniture, olive green cupboards, and balconies. ✉ *Apollonos 1, 33054* ☎ *22650/82101, 210/607–2000 in Athens* 🖷 *22650/82290, 210/607–2135 in Athens* 🌐 *www.amalia.gr* *184 rooms* *In-hotel: restaurant, bar, pool* ▭ *AE, DC, MC, V* 🍽 *BP.*

Fodor'sChoice ★

4

$ **Acropole.** Feel completely secluded, though you're in the heart of the action as you look out over a sea of olive trees from your balcony. Wood furniture and traditional linens and paintings decorate the simple, attractive public and private rooms. Guest rooms on the upper floor have a sloping cathedral ceiling in pine as well. You may want to ask for one of the rooms with a fireplace for cold evenings. The light breakfast includes fresh yogurt drizzled with local honey. The owners offer a 10% discount for Fodor's readers. ✉ *Filellinon 13, 33054* ☎ *22650/82675 through 22650/82677* 🖷 *22650/83171* 🌐 *www.delphi.com.gr* *42 rooms* *In-room: refrigerator. In-hotel: bar, public Wi-Fi* ▭ *AE, DC, MC, V* 🍽 *BP.*

$ ★ **Fedriades.** This hotel in the center of Delphi was purchased by the family that runs Epikouros and Acropole. Their renovation work (to be completed in late 2008) has created a simple, functional look accented by warm colors and a touch of Greek mountain style, while avoiding the "ancient kitsch" of other nearby hotels. The basic amenities and cleanliness offered for a reasonable price make it a good choice. The owners offer a 10% discount for Fodor's readers. ✉ *Karamanlis (formerly Friderikis) 46, at Vas. Pavlou* ☎ *22650/82370* 🖷 *22650/83088* 🌐 *www.fedriades.com* *23 rooms* ▭ *AE, DC, MC, V* 🍽 *BP.*

$ **Hotel Vouzas.** Before the big archaeological digs of the 1890s, the great-great-great-grandfather of the owner of this large hotel used to run Delphi's inn. Ask for a room with a view of the gorge that the hotel sits above; the intimate public living room, with a fireplace, also has a great view. A fantastic large veranda, where breakfast is served half the year, overlooks the olive groves, and the Pleistos River. Despite the unexceptional rooms, the hotel fills up on winter weekends with Athenians who come to challenge the Mt. Parnassus ski slopes 30 minutes away. They leave fortified by the large buffet breakfast; half-board is also available. This is the closest hotel (about 1,600 feet) to the archaeological site of Ancient Delphi. ✉ *Karamanlis (formerly Friderikis) 1, at Vas. Pavlou, 33054* ☎ *22650/82232 through 22650/82234, 210/984–6861 in Athens* 🖷 *22650/82033, 210/982–3772 in Athens*

CLOSE UP

Easter Week in Delphi

Orthodox Easter Week is the most important holiday in Greece, and Delphians celebrate it with true passion. The solemn Good Friday service in Ayios Nikolaos church and the candlelight procession following it, accompanied by the singing of haunting hymns, are one of the most moving rituals in all of Greece. By Saturday evening, the mood is one of eager anticipation as the townspeople are decked out in their nicest finery and the earnest children are carrying *lambades,* beautifully decorated white Easter candles. At midnight the lights of the cathedral are extinguished, and the priest rushes into the sanctuary shouting *Christos anesti!* (Christ is risen). He lights one of the parishioner's candles with his own and the flame is passed on, one to the other, until the entire church is illuminated with candlelight, which is reflected in the radiant faces of the congregation. Firecrackers are set off by the village schoolboys outside to punctuate the exuberance of the moment. After the liturgy is finished, each person tries to get his or her candle home while still lighted, a sign of good luck for the following year, whereupon the sign of the cross is burned over the door. Then the Easter fast is broken, usually with *mayiritsa* (Easter soup made with lamb) and brilliantly red-dyed hard-boiled eggs. On Easter Sunday, the entire village works together to roast dozens of whole lambs on the spit. It is a joyous day, devoted to feasting with family and friends, but you are welcome and may be offered slices of roast lamb and glasses of the potent dark red local wine. In the early evening, a folk-dance performance is held in front of the town-hall square, followed by communal dancing and free food and drink.

58 rooms, 1 suite In-room: refrigerator. In-hotel: restaurant, bar, public Internet MC, V BP.

¢ **Artemis.** A pleasant peach and stone facade reveals a budget-priced lodging option whose fresh appearance makes it stand out from other hotels on this busy main street. The generous lobby floor is covered with large rectangles and small geometric-shaped rocks, while the halls benefit from natural green wood slab details. Guest rooms are comfortable, many with their own interior courtyard or street balconies. *Vas. Pavlou B & Karamanlis (formerly Friderikis) 61, 33054 22650/82294 www.panartemis.gr 20 rooms AE, DC, MC, V CP.*

FESTIVALS

Sit in the ancient stadium of Delphi under the stars and watch everything from the National Beijing Opera Theater's the *Bacchae* to the tragedies of Aeschylus and Euripides, and even folk and traditional music improvisations at the **Summer Arts Festival** (*Stadium, Ancient Delphi 210/331–2781 through 210/331–2785*), organized by the European Cultural Centre of Delphi in July. The festival is in conjunction with an annual symposium. All performances, which begin around 8:30 PM, are open to the public and charge a small fee.

GALAXIDI ΓΑΛΑΞΕΙΔΙ

35 km (22 mi) southwest of Delphi.

Sea captains' homes with classic masonry, and an idyllic seaside location reminiscent of an island, have steadily attracted outsiders recognizing Galaxidi's potential. The heyday of the harbor town was in the 19th century—thanks to shipbuilding and a thriving mercantile economy—but after the invention of steamships it slipped into decline. Today the old town is classified a historical monument and undergoes continual renovation and restoration. If you are a shore person rather than a mountain person, Galaxidi is a good alternative to Delphi as a base for the region. Stroll Galaxidi's narrow streets with their elegant stone mansions and squares with geraniums and palm trees, and then take a late-afternoon swim in one of the pebbly coves around the headland to the north, dine along the waterfront, and enjoy the stunning mountain backdrop over the sea. If you walk to the far side of the sheltered harbor, Galaxidi appears, reflected in the still waters.

If you happen to be in Galaxidi at the start of Greek Orthodox Lent, **Kathara Deftera** *(Clean Monday)*, duck. Locals observe the holiday with flour fights in the town's streets. The common baking flour is tinted with food dye and by the end of the day everyone and everything in sight—buildings, cars, shrubs—is dusted with a rainbow of colors that match spring's bright palette. The custom has pagan roots: every year the dead were thought to be allowed to leave Hades for a day and return to Earth; if they had a good time, a good crop was assured.

Peek into **Ayios Nikolaos** (✉ *Old town*). The cathedral, named after the patron saint of sailors (Nicholas), possesses a beautiful carved 19th-century altar screen.

The little **Nautical Museum** has a collection of local artifacts from ships and the old sea captains' houses. ✉ *Mousiou 4* ☎ *22650/41795* 🎫 *€5* ⏲ *May–Sept., daily 10–1:30 and 5:30–8:30; Oct.–Apr., daily 10–4.*

WHERE TO STAY & EAT

$$$–$$$$ ✕ **To Barko tis Maritsas.** Inside an 1850 captains' *kafeneio* (coffeehouse), this waterfront restaurant is decorated with a nautical theme. Not to be missed are the pies—zucchini with dill, and chicken—as well as the eggplant dip flavored with grated walnut. Fresh fish is always plentiful, but mussels are what Galaxidi is known for—here they're served in a saganaki, steamed, and in a pilaf. There's also seafood risotto and lobster pasta. Homemade sweets include *galaktoboureko* (a sweet custard dough concoction) made with fresh butter. ✉ *Akti Ianthis 34, on waterfront* ☎ *22650/41059* ✍ *Reservations essential* 💳 *AE, DC, MC, V.*

$$–$$$ ✕ **Omilos.** Relax on the shiplike deck as the Bay of Itea stretches before you, the peaks of Mt. Parnassus tower in the distance, and the little gray-stone houses of Delphi topped with rose-slate roofs cluster on inland slopes. If you want really fresh fish, watch as one of the staff casts a line and hauls in your *sargos* or *tsipoura* (respectively, bream or panfish). Have it grilled to a golden brown and lightly embellished with oil, lemon, and oregano. Sunset is a particularly attractive time here, but the place is open early morning to late at night. After your meal, swim off the pebble beach. ✉*Old Yacht Club, main harbor entrance* ☎*22650/42111* ▭*MC, V* ⊙*Closed Nov.–Apr.*

$$–$$$ ✕**O Tassos.** Locals and tourists pack O Tassos's waterfront terrace, the first you see as you approach from the center; they're drawn in year-round by the quality of the seafood. Farm-raised crawfish, *karavidhes,* are simply boiled and sprinkled with lemon—a true delicacy. Crispy fried calamari and whole fish, such as char-grilled snapper, are fresh as can be. Complete the feast with boiled greens and garlic-potato sauce, a large village salad, and a carafe of local wine. ✉*Akti Ianthis 69, at far end of harbor on waterfront* ☎*22650/41291* ▭*V.*

$–$$ ✕**O Bebelis.** The wine barrel by the front door is the first hint that this cozy ouzeri, tucked into a side street off the harbor, is a place for the *meraklis,* people who savor life's every moment. Sit back, order the house wine, and pick at little treats laid before you, like home-cured olives, stuffed onions, steamed mussels, and other seasonal small dishes prepared and served by the genial owner's mother. ✉*Nikolaou Mama, near start of harbor* ☎*22650/41677* ▭*No credit cards.*

¢–$ ★ **Archodiko.** Yianni Schiza, who established the hotel with his wife Argyroula, has a knack for collecting odd items. This hobby paid off tastefully at their nearly decade-old establishment. Each guest room is different, with bathroom fixtures from ships, a sewing machine as a table in one room and a bed-in-a-boat in another. In summer, guests take their pre-packed breakfast (ready in the refrigerator) out on the balcony. ✉*Eleftherias 80, 33052* ☎*22650/42292* ⊕*www.gto.gr/archodiko* *8 rooms* *In room: refrigerator. In hotel: parking, no elevator* ▭*No credit cards* *CP.*

¢–$ ★ ✕**O Dervenis.** Look inland, to O Dervenis, for some of the best small mezedes in town. The friendly young couple that now runs their family's taverna is conscious of providing old-style quality and hospitality—using real feta and virgin olive oil and always offering a complimentary dessert (sometimes it's heavenly panna cotta) or fruit. It will be tough choosing an appetizer from among the homemade tzatziki, the spinach pie made with feta and *kefalograviera* (a soft cheese), the marinated octopus, and the *gavros* (resembles a large anchovy). Other options include minced meat wrapped in fresh vine leaves (tender enough to use only the first few weeks of summer), and a local specialty, *avgopita* (egg pie). They also make rice-filled dolmades, using onion skin instead of vine leaves and *kelemia,* the local version of rice-stuffed tomatoes and other vegetables. Contemplate your selection in the covered garden courtyard. ✉*N. Gourgouris 6* ☎*22650/41177* ▭*DC, V.*

¢–$ ★ **Villa Ianthia.** Superb hospitality is the main reason you won't want to leave Villa Ianthia after you're welcomed into the hotel over an Italianate *tapeto marmo* (marble carpet). The reception room, graced by a stained-glass window, is the perfect setting for enjoying cocktails and popular piano melodies on weekends. Rooms vary in size and are furnished with romantic touches like bed canopies and wall paintings. Look to the sea or Mt. Parnassus over the wrought-iron railing of your small balcony. The breakfast buffet—served until noon—is laden with breads, homemade marmalades, and various baked treats prepared fresh daily. ✉*Anexartisias, opposite town hall, 33052* ☎*22650/42433* 📠*22650/42434* 🌐*www.fokidanet.com/villaianthia* *10 rooms, 2 suites* *In room: refrigerator* *MC, V* *CP.*

¢ ★ **Hotel Ganimede.** Elegant spaces take full advantage of the 19th-century sea captain's house in a lush garden. Outside there are beautiful pebble walkways, and indoors, unpretentious antiques are interspersed with Arachova weavings, small sculptures, and paintings, giving each room personality. There's one single available (€37). In winter a blazing fire beckons from the sitting room. Have the optional breakfast (€9) there, or in the courtyard in summer: the homemade marmalades (apricot, fig, and tangerine), breads, cakes, and bacon/cheese scones are delicious. ✉*N. Gourgouris 20, 33052* ☎*22650/41328* 📠*22650/41664* 🌐*www.ganimede.gr* *5 rooms, 1 studio, 1 suite* *In-room: kitchen (some). In hotel: public Wi-Fi* *MC, V.*

SHOPPING

After a lovely seaside dinner, satisfy your sugar craving at the sweet shop **Mina** (✉*Nikolaou Mama 13, off waterfront* ☎*22650/41117*). Preserves and traditional honey-and-nut sweets are on sale, but don't pass through Galaxidi without trying local specialties: crushed almond, and sugar paste *amagdalopasta* or a *ravani me rizi*, a sweet rice cake flavored with mastic.

Clearly, artists are behind the dazzling selection of gift items at **Ostria** (✉*Akti Ianthis 101, waterfront* ☎*22650/41206* *Daily 11 AM–2 PM and 6 PM–11:30 PM; reduced hrs Nov. and Dec.*). Beautifully displayed items include nautical items like brass compasses and model ships, but also an array of toys, clocks, icons, and jewelry. There's also a huge selection of ceramics, some by owner Petros Skourtis. He and co-owner Katie Kapi, who is a painter, also invite customers to visit their nearby workshop.

ATTICA, SARONIC GULF & DELPHI ESSENTIALS

TRANSPORTATION

BY BIKE & MOPED

On the islands of Aegina and Spetses, many people rent scooters, mopeds, and bicycles from shops along the harbor, but extreme caution is advised: the equipment may not be in good condition, roads can be narrow and treacherous, and many drivers scorn your safety. Wear a helmet, and drive defensively.

BY BOAT & FERRY

The island of Spetses is so close to the Peloponnese mainland that you can drive there, park, and ferry across the channel in any of a number of caïques (price negotiable) at the ports, but to get to them from Athens or to visit the other Saronic Gulf islands, you must take to the sea in a ferry.

Saronikos Ferries carries you and your car from the main port in Piraeus (Gate E8, which is about 1,312 feet from the train station, beyond Karaiskaki Square) to Aegina (1 hour) or you alone—no cars allowed—to Hydra (3 hours, 15 minutes) and Spetses (4 hours, 25 minutes). You can get a weekly boat schedule from the Greek National Tourism Organization (GNTO or EOT). There are approximately a half dozen departures per day, and fares range from about €5 per person for Aegina to about €11 for Spetses. Car rates are usually three to four times the passenger rate. Hydra and Spetses are also serviced by Euroseas catamarans. Ferries are the leisurely and least-expensive way to travel; however, most people prefer the speedier Hellenic Seaways hydrofoils (faster than the catamarans; no cars allowed) that also depart from Piraeus, at Gate E8 or E9. You can get to Aegina in 40 minutes (€12), to Hydra in 90 minutes (€21.50), and to Spetses (€29.50) in just under two hours. There are about a half dozen departures daily to each island), but make reservations ahead of time—boats fill quickly. You can also reserve through a travel agent.

From a small port, Rafina has grown into a bustling harbor with connections to the Cyclades and the northeastern Aegean island of Limnos. The additional travel time to reach Rafina pays off in shorter sea journeys, via Blue Star Ferries, especially to Andros, Tinos, Mykonos, and Syros.

Contacts **Blue Star Ferries** (*☎ 210/891-9800 🌐 www.bluestarferries.com*). **Euroseas** (*☎ 210/413-2188 🌐 www.euroseas.com*). **Hellenic Seaways** (*☎ 210/419-9000 for flying dolphin tickets, 210/411-7341 for ferry tickets 🌐 www.hellenicseaways.gr*). **Saronikos Ferries** (*☎ 210/417-1190 or 210/411-7341*).

BY BUS

Places close to Athens can be reached with the blue city bus lines (€0.50): Bus A16 from Koumoundourou Square for Daphni and Eleusina; Bus 224 from Vassilisis Sofias or Akadimias, coupled with a 25-minute walk, for Kaisariani; Bus A2, A3, or B3 from Syntagma Square for Glyfada; Bus A2 to Voula; Bus A2 to Glyfada, then connect with Bus 114, or 116 to Vouliagmeni; Bus A2 or A3 to Glyfada, then connect with Bus 116, or 149 for Varkiza. For the rest of the destinations, if you can't rent a car, the next most efficient mode of travel is the regional KTEL bus system in combination with taxis. The extensive network serves all points in Attica from Athens, and local buses connect the smaller towns and villages at least daily.

Buses in Aegina leave from the main port for spots around the island, including Agia Marina and Perdika. There are no public buses on Hydra or Spetses. Bus service on the islands becomes more infrequent, and the last bus tends to run earlier, from late October to early May.

FARES & SCHEDULES

KTEL buses for eastern Attica leave hourly from their main station in downtown Athens (Aigyptou Square at the corner of Mavromateon and Leoforos Alexandras). You can also catch this bus from Klathmonos Square or on Filellinon. KTEL buses depart regularly for Marathon (€3.20), Rhamnous (€4.50), and Amphiareion (€3.60). The Greek

National Tourism Organization (EOT) distributes a list of bus schedules, as does the Athens Main terminal in Aigyptou Square.

KTEL buses servicing western Attica depart from Terminal B in Athens. To Delphi (via Arachova), there are six departures, beginning at 7:30 AM. The journey takes about three hours and costs €13. Four buses daily make the four-hour trip to Galaxidi, starting at 7:30 AM; the fare is €16. Buses depart hourly from 5:50 AM to 8:30 PM for Dhistomo near Osios Loukas; the journey takes 2½ hours and costs €12.80. Note that the prices above are one-way fares. To get to Terminal B from downtown Athens, catch Bus 24 on Amalias in front of the National Garden. Tickets for these buses are sold only at this terminal, so you should call to book seats well in advance during high season or holidays.

Information **Aegina bus station** (✉ *Harbor road, across from ferries, Aegina town, Aegina* ☎ *22970/22787*). **Athens Main** (*Terminal A* ✉ *Aigyptou Sq., Athens* ☎ *210/512–4910*). **Athens Terminal B** (✉ *Liossion 260, Athens* ☎ *210/831–7179*). **KTEL Amphiareion** (☎ *210/823–0179*). **KTEL Delphi & Arachova** (☎ *210/831–7096 or 210/831–7173*). **KTEL Marathon** (☎ *210/823–0179*). **KTEL Osios Loukas** (☎ *210/831–7173*). **KTEL Rhamnous** (☎ *210/823–0179*). **KTEL Sounion** (☎ *210/880–8080*).

BY CAR

Points in Attica can be reached from the main Thessaloniki–Athens and Athens–Patras highways, with the National Road (Ethnikos Odos) the most popular route, especially since it has been extended and linked to the new Attica Highway (Attiki Odos). From the Peloponnese, you can drive east via Corinth to Athens, or from Patras, cross the Corinthian Gulf via the Rio–Antirrio bridge, the longest cable suspension bridge in Europe, to visit Delphi first. Most of the roads when you get off the new highway are two-lane secondary arteries; a few of them (notably from Athens to Delphi and Itea, and Athens to Sounion) have been upgraded so are good quality, not to mention spectacularly scenic. Expect heavy traffic to Delphi in the ski season and to and from Athens on summer weekends.

On Aegina, there is a good network of mostly narrow rural roads (two lanes at best). Drivers should be prepared for occasional abrupt turns; major towns and sites are well marked. Karagiannis Klimis Travel, on Aegina, rents both cars and motorcycles. Cars are not allowed on Hydra and Spetses.

CAR RENTALS

Local and international agencies have offices in downtown Athens—most are on Syngrou avenue—as well as at the arrival level at Eleftherios Venizelos–Athens International Airport, in Spata.

CONTACTS & RESOURCES

EMERGENCIES

Keep in mind that hailing a cab may be faster than calling and waiting for an ambulance. The Automobile Touring Club of Greece (ELPA) assists tourists with breakdowns free of charge if they belong to AAA or to ELPA; otherwise, there is a charge. Patients are admitted to regional hospitals according to a rotating system; call the duty hospital number, or in an emergency, an ambulance.

Information **Ambulance** (☎ *166*). **Duty Hospitals and Clinics** (☎ *1434*). **ELPA** (✉ *Mesogeion 395, Ayia Paraskevi* ☎ *104 in emergency, 210/606–8800* 🌐 *www.elpa.gr*). **Fire** (☎ *199*). **Forest Fires** (☎ *191*). **Police** (☎ *100*). **Tourist Police** (☎ *22970/27777 in Aegina, 171 in Attica, 22650/82222 in Delphi, 22980/52205 on Hydra, 22980/73100 on Spetses*).

INTERNET, MAIL & SHIPPING

Internet cafés are scattered throughout the main port towns; they range in services offered. In Hydra, Rafaleas Pharmacy, a fascinating mix of old and new, has speedy Internet connection in an 1890 landmark building—worth skipping the coffee for. Post offices are open weekdays from 7:30 AM–2 PM; Hellenic Post's Web site has more information. Speedex, on Aegina, is one of the few couriers in the Saronic islands. You can arrange with the Athens branches of other couriers for special deliveries to and from the islands.

Information **Aegina Post Office** (✉ *Ethnegersias Sq., Aegina town* ☎ *22970/22398*). **E-global Internet café** (✉ *Phaneromenis 7, across from municipal stadium, Aegina town* ☎ *22970/27819*). **1800 Bar & Internet Café** (✉ *Harbor road, Kounoupitsa, Spetses town* ☎ *22980/29497*). **Hellenic Post** (🌐 *www.elta.gr*). **Hydra Post Office** (✉ *Off main port, Hydra town* ☎ *22980/52262*). **Rafaleas Pharmacy** (✉ *Harbor, behind clock tower, near Angelica Hotel, Hydra town*). **Speedex** (✉ *Neoptolemou 2, Aegina town* ☎ *22970/26430, 210/340–7000 in Athens* 🌐 *www.speedex.gr*). **Spetses Post Office** (✉ *On side street off Dapia harbor road, Dapia, Spetses town* ☎ *22980/72228*).

MEDIA

The English-language weekly newspaper *Athens News* carries entertainment listings for the towns around Athens (and for the Athens clubs that moved to the southern Attica seashore for summer). The daily English language–edition of the Greek newspaper *Kathimerini* is inserted in the *International Herald Tribune*. The bimonthly lifestyle magazine, *The Insider*, is also filled with information on Greek culture and events.

SPORTS & THE OUTDOORS

The Alpine Club of Athens organizes skiing classes for children on Mt. Parnassus. Contact the Hellenic Skiing Federation for more information about skiing Mt. Parnassus. For a booklet on Greece's hiking refuges and information on hiking paths, including the E4 and E6 trails, and on local hiking groups, contact the Greek Federation of Mountaineering Associations. Hiking expeditions are run by Trekking Hellas and the Alpine Club of Athens. The Alpin Club travel agency (not to be confused with the Alpine Club) also arranges all kinds of sports—adventure travel, including hiking, rafting, mountain climbing and biking, and canyoneering.

Hiking **Alpin Club** (*Ioanni Agelopoulou 9, Neo Psihiko, Athens 210/675–3514 or 210/675–3515 210/675–3516 www.alpinclub.gr*). **Alpine Club of Athens** (*Ermou 64, 5th fl., Monastiraki, Athens 210/321–2355 or 210/321–2429 210/324–789 www.eosathinon.gr*). **Greek Federation of Mountaineering Associations** (*Milioni 5, Kolonaki, Athens 210/364–5904 or 210/363–6617 210/364–4687 www.eooa.gr*). **Trekking Hellas** (*Filellinon 7, 3rd fl., Syntagma, Athens 210/331–0323 through 210/331–0326 210/323–4548 www.trekking.gr*).

Skiing **Alpine Club of Athens** (*Ermou 64, 5th fl., Monastiraki, Athens 210/321–2355 or 210/321–2429 210/324–4789*). **Hellenic Skiing Federation** (*Karageorgi Servias 7, 8th fl., Syntagma, Athens 210/323–0182 or 210/323–4412 210/323–0142 www.eox.gr*).

4

TOUR OPTIONS

Most agencies run tour excursions at about the same prices, but CHAT and Key Tours have the best service and guides, plus comfortable air-conditioned buses. Taking a half-day trip to the breathtaking Temple of Poseidon at Sounion (€36) avoids the hassle of dealing with the crowded public buses or paying a great deal more for a taxi. A one-day tour to Delphi with lunch costs €93, but the two-day tour (€135) gives you more time to explore this wonder. A full-day cruise from Piraeus, with either CHAT or Key Tours, visits three nearby islands—Aegina, Poros, and Hydra—and costs around €93 (including buffet lunch on the ship).

The Winemakers' Association of Attica Vineyards has a comprehensive Internet site with plenty of information about the history of wine making in the Attica region and potential wine tour routes encompassing its active members.

Contacts **CHAT** (*Xenofontos 9, Syntagma, Athens 210/322–2886 or 210/323–0827 210/323–1200 www.chatours.gr*). **Key Tours** (*Kallirois 4, Syntagma, Athens 210/923–3166 or 210/923–3266 210/923–2008 www.keytours.gr*). **Winemakers' Association of Attica Vineyards** (*210/603–8019 www.enoaa.gr*).

TRAVEL AGENCIES

Full-service agencies, like those listed below, handle hotel reservations, transportation tickets, and tours.

Contacts **Dolphin Hellas** (*For Attica Leoforos Syngrou 16, Syngrou, Athens 210/922–7772 www.dolphin-hellas.gr*).

Karagiannis Klimi Travel (*Kanaris 2, Aegina town 22970/25664 22970/28779 www.aegina-travel.com*).

VISITOR INFORMATION

The Greek National Tourism Organization offices in Athens may have information on excursions outside the city. For more-detailed information, consult with municipal tourist offices and tourist police offices. Arachova's office is open from December to March only, and the town's tourism development office maintains a site (*www.arahova.gr*).

Information **Aegina Municipality** (*Town hall, Aegina 22970/22220 or 22970/22391*). **Aegina Tourist Police** (*Leonardou Lada 11, Aegina town 22970/27777*). **Arachova Tourist Office** (*Arachova–Delfon road, Arachova 22670/31692*). **Attica Tourist Police** (*Veikou 43–45, Koukaki 171*). **Delphi Tourist Office** (*Karamanlis [formerly Friderikis] 12 and Apollonos, Delphi 22650/82900*). **Delphi Tourist Police** (*Angelou Sikelianou 3, Delphi 22650/82220*). **Hydra Tourist Police** (*Port, Hydra town 22980/52205*). **Spetses Police** (*Hatziyianni-Mexi, near museum, Spetses town 22980/73744 or 22980/73100*).

The Sporades

SKIATHOS, SKOPELOS & SKYROS

Skyros

WORD OF MOUTH

"Skiathos—out of season—is still the quaint, lovely, quiet, and very green island people have fond memories of. The town is still cobbled and whitewashed, old caïques line the harbor quay, fishermen still mend their nets in the mornings and head out to sea to ply their trade. In summer, the nightlife grinds on through the night, and it's a very European, younger crowd, though nothing like Ios or Mykonos. And never are there crowds like there are on Santorini."

—djuna

www.fodors.com/forums

WELCOME TO THE SPORADES

The hub of Skopelos island is Skopelos town

TOP REASONS TO GO

★ **Sun-and-fun Skiathos:** Thousands of international sunseekers head here to enjoy famous beaches and then work on their neon tans in the buzzing nightclubs.

★ **Skyros's Style:** Set against a dramatic rock, the main town of Skyros is a showstopper of Cycladic houses colorfully set with folk wood carvings and embroideries.

★ **Sylvan Skopelos:** Not far from the verdant forests lie 40 picturesque monasteries and Skopelos town, looking like a Sporades Positano.

★ **Beachy Keen:** The beaches are best on Skiathos, the star location being Koukounaries, whose golden sands are famous throughout Greece.

★ **"Forever England":** The grave of Edwardian poet Rupert Brooke draws pilgrims to Vouno on Skyros.

1 Skiathos. The 3,900 residents are eclipsed by the 50,000 visitors who come here each year for clear blue waters and scores of beaches, including the world-famous Koukounaries. Close to the mainland, this island has some of the aura of the Pelion peninsula, with red-roof villages and picturesque hills. Beauty spots include the monastery of Evangelistria and Lalaria beach. Skiathos draws a lot of artists for its scenic villages and spiritual energy.

2 Skopelos. Second largest of the Sporades, this island is lushly forested and more prized by ecologists than funseekers. The steep streets of Skopelos town needs mountain-goat negotiating skills, but the charming alleys are irresistible, as are the island's monasteries, the famous cheese pies, and the traditional *kalivia* farmhouses around Panormos bay.

Celebrants of Clean Monday, Skyros

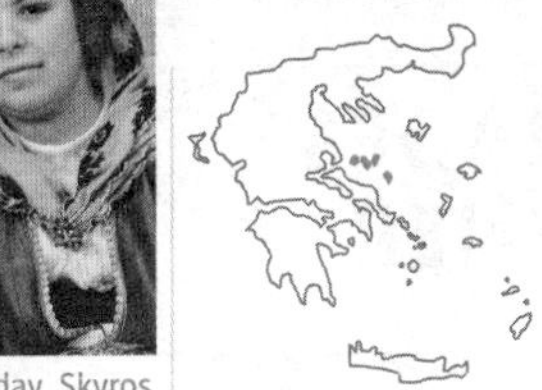

GETTING ORIENTED

This small cluster of islands off the coast of central Greece is just a short hop from the mainland and, consequently, often overrun in high season. Obviously, the Cyclades aren't the only Greek islands that serve up a cup of culture and a gallon of hedonism to travelers looking for that perfect tan. Each of the Sporades is very individual in character. Due east of tourism-oriented Skiathos are eco-blessed Skopelos and folk-craft-famous Skyros.

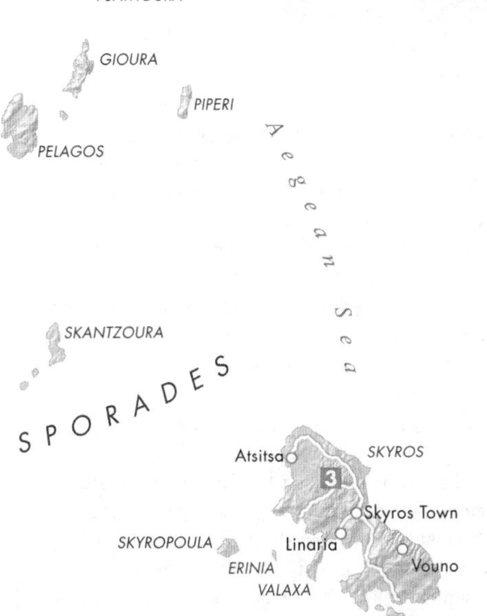

3 Skyros. Located at the virtual center of the Aegean sea, this Sporades Shangri-la is the southernmost of the island group. The top half is covered with pine forests and is home to Skyros town, a Cycladic cubic masterpiece, which climbs a spectacular rock peak and is a tangle of lanes, whitewashed houses, and Byzantine churches. The arid southern half has the site of the grave of the noted Edwardian poet Rupert Brooke at Vouno.

A view of spectacular Skyros town

SPORADES PLANNER

How to Choose?

If you're the can't-sit-still type and think crowds add to the fun, Skiathos is your island. By day you can take in the beautiful, thronged beaches and Evangelistria Monastery or the fortress-turned-cultural-center, and at night stroll the port to find the most hopping nightclub. Day people with a historical bent should explore Skopelos's many monasteries and churches and its 19th-century Folk Art Museum. Skyros should be at the top of your list if you're a handicraft collector, as the island's furniture and pottery is known throughout the country.

Festival Fun

The Carnival (Feb.) traditions of Skopelos, although not as exotic as those of Skyros, parody the expulsion of the once-terrifying Barbary pirates. August 15 is the Panayia (Festival of the Virgin), celebrated on Skyros at Magazia beach and on Skopelos in Skopelos town; its cultural events continue to late August. Skiathos hosts cultural events in summer, including a dance festival in July. Feast days? Skiathos: July 26, for St. Paraskevi; Skopelos: February 25, for St. Reginos.

Finding a Place to Stay

Accommodations reflect the pace of tourism on each particular island: Skopelos has a fair number of hotels, Skiathos a huge number, but there are far fewer on Skyros. Most hotels close from October or November to April or May. Reservations are a good idea, though you may learn about rooms in pensions and private homes when you arrive at the airport or ferry landing. The best bet, especially for those on a budget, is to rent a converted room in a private house—look for the Greek National Tourism Organization (EOT or GNTO) license displayed in windows. Owners meet incoming ferries to tout their location, offer rooms, and negotiate the price.

In Skyros most people take lodgings in town or along the beach at Magazia and Molos: you must choose between being near the sea or the town's bars and eateries. Accommodations are basic, and not generally equipped with television sets. In Skiathos tourists are increasingly renting private apartments, villas, and minivillas through local island travel agents. Rates fluctuate from season to season; the August high-season prices may drop by more than half between October and May. Always negotiate off-season.

Dining & Lodging Prices in Euros

	¢	$	$$	$$$	$$$$
Restaurants	under €8	€8–€11	€11–€15	€15–€20	over €20
Hotels	under €60	€60–€90	€90–€120	€120–€160	over €160

Restaurant prices are for one main course at dinner, or for two mezedes (small dishes). Hotel prices are for a standard double room in high season, including taxes. Hotels operate on the European Plan (EP, with no meal provided) unless we note that they use the Continental Plan (CP, with Continental breakfast); Breakfast Plan (BP, with a full breakfast); Modified American Plan (MAP, with breakfast and dinner); or the Full American Plan (FAP, with all meals). Inquire when booking if these meal plans (which can entail higher rates) are mandatory. Guest rooms have air-conditioning, room phones, and TVs unless otherwise noted.

Getting Around

The road networks on Skiathos, Skopelos, and Skyros are so rudimentary that cars are not really needed.

Still, it's not a bad idea to rent one for a day to get a feel for the island, then use public transport or a scooter thereafter. Car rentals cost €28–€33 per day, while scooters cost about €15–€20 (with full insurance).

If you rent a scooter, however, be extra cautious: many of those for hire are in poor condition. The locals are not used to the heavy summer traffic on their narrow roads, and accidents provide the island clinics with 80% of their summer business.

Bus service is available throughout the Sporades, although some islands' buses run more frequently than others.

Caïques leave from the main ports for the most popular beaches, and interisland excursions are made between Skiathos and Skopelos. You can also hire a caïque (haggle over the price) to tour around the islands; they are generally the preferred way to get around by day.

For popular routes, captains have signs posted showing their destinations and departure times. On Skyros, check with Skyros Travel (See ⇨ Tour Options in Essentials) for caïque tours.

Making the Most of Your Time

Inveterate island-hoppers might spend one night on each island, although your trip might be more comfortable if you plant yourself on one. There are regular cruises that travel around the Sporades in three to four days, but as each of the four islands are so very varied, it's worth spending at least two days on each. That noted, you can get around Skiathos and Skopelos in a total of two days, since there are daily ferry connections between them and they are relatively near each other. Traveling between these islands and Skyros, however, requires advance planning, since ferries and flights to Skyros are much less frequent. Also, make sure that you are arriving and leaving from the correct harbor; some islands, such as Skopelos, have more than one from which to depart. Five days can be just enough for touching each island in summer; off-season you need more days to accommodate the ferry schedule.

When to Go

Winter is least desirable, as the weather turns cold and rainy; most hotels, rooms, and restaurants are closed, and ferry service is minimal. If you do go from November through April, book in advance and leave nothing to chance. The same advice applies to July and August peak season, when everything is open but overcrowded, except on Skyros. The meltemi, the brisk northerly summer wind of the Aegean, keeps things cooler than on the mainland even on the hottest days. Late spring and early summer are ideal, as most hotels are open, crowds have not arrived, the air is warm, and the roadsides and fields of flowers are incredible; September is also mild.

Eating Well

Eating and drinking out in the Sporades is as much about savoring the ambiance as consuming the fresh island food; if in doubt, eat where the locals do; few hangouts geared specifically to tourists are as good. Ask your waiter for suggestions about local specialties—you won't go wrong with the catch of the day. Octopus and juicy prawns, grilled with oil and lemon or baked with cheese and fresh tomatoes, are traditional dishes. Skyros is especially noted for spiny lobster, which is almost as sweet as the North Atlantic variety.

Updated by Adrian Vrettos and Alexia Amvrazi

LIKE EMERALD BEADS SCATTERED ON SAPPHIRE SATIN, the verdant Sporades islands of Skiathos and Skopelos, and a nearby host of tiny, uninhabited islets are resplendent with pines, fruit trees, and olive trees. The lush countryside, marked with sloping slate roofs and wooden balconies, strongly resembles that of the neighboring Pelion peninsula, to which the islands were once attached. Only on Skyros, farther out in the Aegean, will you see a windswept, treeless landscape, or the cubist architecture of the Cyclades. Sitting by itself east of Evia, Skyros is neither geographically nor historically related to the other Sporades.

The Sporades have changed hands constantly throughout history, and wars, plunder, and earthquakes have eliminated all but the strongest ancient walls. A few castles and monasteries remain, but these islands are now geared more for having fun than for sightseeing. Skiathos is the most touristy, to the point of overkill, while less-developed Skopelos has fewer beaches and much less nightlife, but has a main town that is said to be the most beautiful in the Sporades. Late to attract tourists, Skyros is the least traveled of the Sporades. It's also the most remote and quirky, with well-preserved traditions.

The Sporades are (with the exception of Skyros) quite easily reached from the mainland; even so, many parts remain idyllic. They may be close to each other, yet they remain different in character, representing a spectrum of Greek culture, from towns with screaming nightlife to hillsides where the tinkle of goat bells may be the only sound for miles. Quintessential Greek-island delights beckon: sun, sand, and surf, along with starlit dinners. Almost all restaurants have outside seating, often under leafy trees, where you can watch the passing Greek dramas of daily life: lovers arm-in-arm, stealing a kiss; animated conversations between restaurateur and patron that may last for the entire meal; fishermen cleaning their bright yellow nets and debating and laughing as they work. Relax and immerse yourself in the blue-and-green watercolor of it all.

EXPLORING THE SPORADES

Little mentioned in mythology or history, the Sporades confidently rely on their great natural beauty to attract visitors. Some locals poetically claim them to be the handful of colored pebbles the gods were left with after creating the world, and as an afterthought, they flung them over the northwestern Aegean. Bustling with tourists, Skiathos sits closest to the mainland; it has a pretty harbor area and the liveliest nightlife, international restaurants and pubs, and resort hotels. Due east is Skopelos, covered with dense, fragrant pines, where you can visit scenic villages, hundreds of churches, and lovely beaches. The least progressive of the islands, it is the most naturally beautiful and has a fascinating old hill town.

Some visitors return year after year to mythical Skyros, southeast of the other islands, for its quiet fishing villages, expansive beaches, and stunning cubist rabbit warren of a town that seems to spill down a

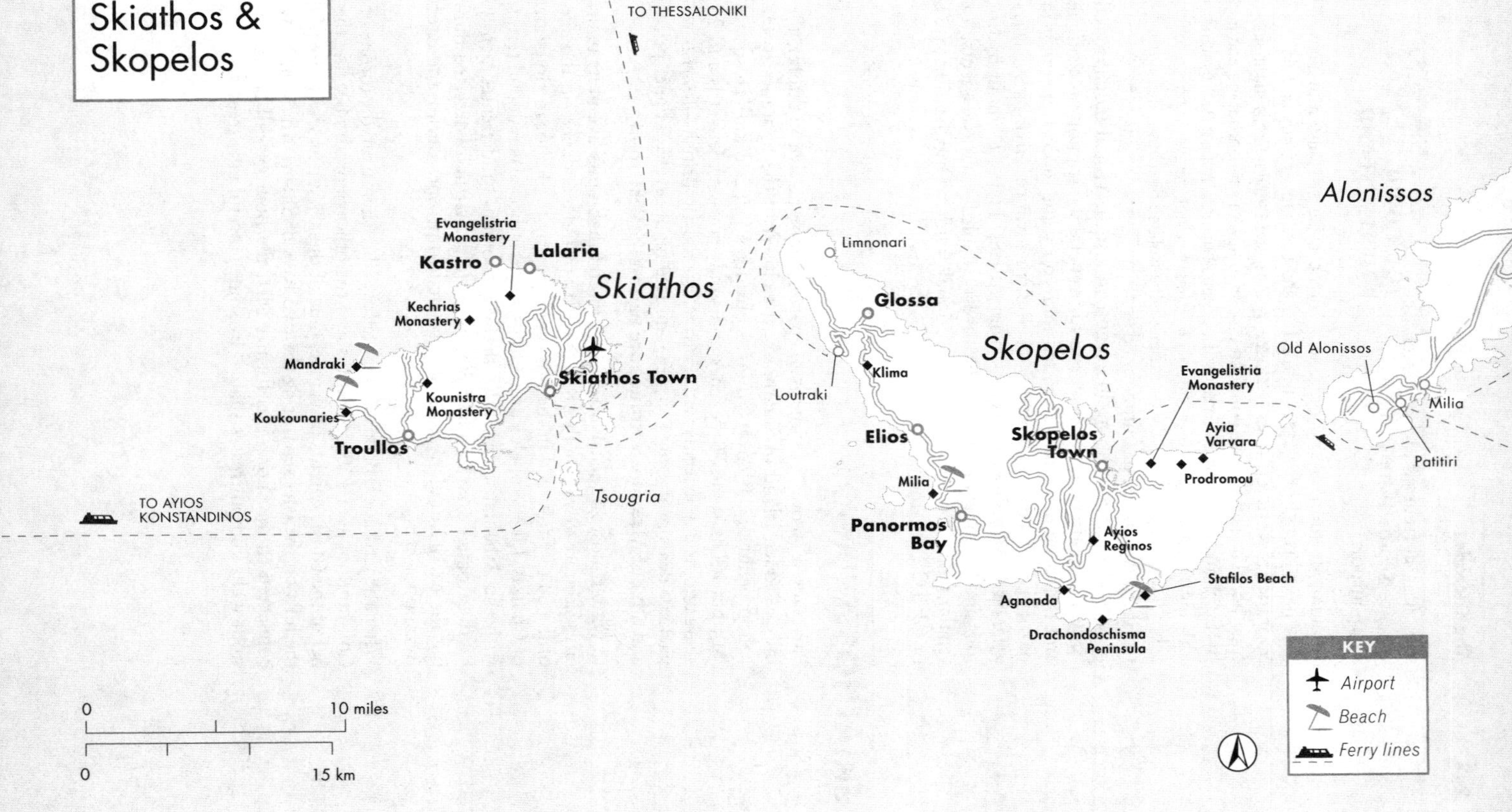
Skiathos &
Skopelos
TO THESSALONIKI
Alonissos
Evangelistria Monastery
Kastro
Lalaria
Skiathos
Kechrias Monastery
Mandraki
Skiathos Town
Kounistra Monastery
Koukounaries
Troullos
TO AYIOS KONSTANDINOS
Tsougria
Limnonari
Glossa
Skopelos
Klima
Loutraki
Elios
Milia
Panormos Bay
Skopelos Town
Evangelistria Monastery
Ayia Varvara
Prodromou
Ayios Reginos
Stafilos Beach
Agnonda
Drachondoschisma Peninsula
Old Alonissos
Milia
Patitiri
0
10 miles
0
15 km
KEY
Airport
Beach
Ferry lines

hill. As a current citadel of Greek defense Skyros also has the bonus of an airport.

> **YOUR OWN PRIVATE ISLAND**
>
> Nine idyllic islets lush with pines and olive groves surround Skiathos, and two lie across the main harbor, with safe anchorage and a small marina. You can sail over, or hire a caïque, to swim and sun on the isolated beaches.

Regular air shuttles and boat service have brought the aptly named Sporades ("scattered ones") closer together. The islands are connected by ferry and sometimes hydrofoil, although some are infrequently scheduled, especially November to April. A number of uninhabited islands in the Sporades archipelago can also be visited by chartered boat. If you are taking it easy, you can generally just jump on a caïque and island-hop. If time is limited and you want to do something in particular, it's best to plan your schedule in advance. Olympic Airways offers a weekly flight to Skyros from Athens. Flying Dolphin hydrofoils and Olympic flight timetables are available from travel agents; for regular ferries, consult the Greek National Tourism Organization (EOT or GNTO), in Athens.

SKIATHOS ΣΚΙΑΘΟΣ

Part sacred (scores of churches), part profane (active nightlife), the hilly, wooded island of Skiathos is the closest of the Sporades to the Pelion peninsula. It covers an area of only 42 square km (16 square mi), but it has some 70 beaches and sandy coves. A jet-set island 25 years ago, today it teems with European—mostly British—tourists on package deals promising sun, sea, and late-night revelry. Higher prices and a bit of Mykonos's attitude are part of the deal, too.

In winter most of the island's 5,000 or so inhabitants live in its main city, Skiathos town, built after the War of Independence on the site of the colony founded in the 8th century BC by the Euboean city-state of Chalkis. Like Skopelos and Alonissos, Skiathos was on good terms with the Athenians, prized by the Macedonians, and treated gently by the Romans. Saracen and Slav raids left it virtually deserted during the early Middle Ages, but it started to prosper during the later Byzantine years.

When the Crusaders deposed their fellow Christians from the throne of Constantinople in 1204, Skiathos and the other Sporades became the fief of the Ghisi, knights of Venice. One of their first acts was to fortify the hills on the islet separating the two bays of Skiathos harbor. Now connected to the shore, this former islet, the Bourtzi, still has a few stout walls and buttresses shaded by some graceful pine trees.

SKIATHOS TOWN ΣΚΙΑΘΟΣ (ΠΟΛΗ)

2½ hrs from Agios Konstantinos.

Though the harbor is picturesque from a distance—especially from a ferry docking at sunset, when a purple light casts a soft glow and the lights on the hills behind the quay start twinkling like faint stars—Skiathos town close-up has few buildings of any distinction. Many traditional houses were burned by the Germans in 1944, and postwar development has pushed up cement apartments between the pleasant, squat, red-roof older houses. Magenta bougainvillea, sweet jasmine, and the casual charm of brightly painted balconies and shutters camouflage most of the eyesores as you wander through the narrow lanes and climb up the steep steps that serve as streets. Activity centers on the waterfront or on Papadiamantis, the main drag, with banks, travel agents, telephones, post offices, police and tourist police stations, plus myriad cafés, fast-food joints, postcard stands, tacky souvenir shops, tasteful jewelry stores, and car- and bike-rental establishments. Shops, bars, and restaurants line the cobbled side streets, where you can also spot the occasional modest hotel and rooms-to-rent signs. The east side of the port (more commonly known as the new port), where the larger boats and Flying Dolphin hydrofoils dock, is not as interesting. The little church and clock tower of Ayios Nikolaos watch over it from a hill reached by steps so steep they're almost perpendicular to the earth.

5

Papadiamantis Museum is devoted to one of Greece's finest writers, Alexandros Papadiamantis (1851–1911), who wrote passionately about traditional island life and the hardships of his day. Skiathos plays a part in his short stories; his most famous novel, *The Murderess,* has been translated to English. Three humble rooms with his bed, the low and narrow divan where he died, some photos, and a few personal belongings are all that is exhibited. ✉*Right of Papadiamantis at fork* ☎*24270/23843* 📠*24270/23841* 🎫*€1* ⏲*July and Aug., daily 9:30–1:30 and 5–8:30; Sept.–June, Tues.–Sun. 9:30–1:30 and 5–8:30.*

The **Bourtzi** (✉*End of causeway extending from port*) is a piney islet that was once a fortress. It divides the harbor and now is a cultural center with periodic events and activities. In July and August, art and antiquities exhibitions and open-air performances are held here. West of the waterfront is the fishing port and the dock where caïques depart for round-the-island trips and the beaches. The sidewalk is filled with cafés and *ouzeri* (casual bars) catering more to people-watchers than to serious culinary aficionados. At the far end of the port, beginning at the square around the 1846 church of Trion Hierarchon, fancier restaurants spread out under awnings, overlooking the sea. A few good restaurants and bars are hidden on backstreets in this neighborhood, many of them serving foreign foods.

BEACHES

Skiathos is known for its beaches, but as has happened so many times before, popularity has a way of spoiling special places. Since the arrival of English expatriates in the early 1960s, the beautiful, piney 14-km (9-mi) stretch of coast running south of town to famed, gold-sand Koukounaries has become one almost continuous ribbon of villas, hotels, and tavernas. One beach succeeds another, and in summer the asphalted coast road carries a constant stream of cars, buses, motorbikes, and pedestrians buzzing beach to beach, like frenzied bees sampling pollen-laden flowers. To access most beaches, you must take little, usually unpaved, lanes down to the sea. Along this coast, the beaches, **Megali Ammos, Vassilias, Achladia, Tzaneria, Vromolimnos,** and **Platania,** all offer water sports, umbrellas, lounge chairs, and plenty of company.

WHERE TO STAY & EAT

$$–$$$ ★ ✕ **The Windmill.** Sit outdoors at this well-preserved 1880 mill–turned–unpretentiously elegant restaurant and a nighttime trek to the hill above Ayios Nikolaos is rewarded with spectacular views of the dimly lighted harbor. White terraces have dark, rough-hewn wood rails, and small balconies poke out from the mill building. The Windmill's friendly and clued-in staff, under the direction of Scottish co-owners Pamela Dance and Karen McCann, serves creative dinners like Thai fish cakes with sweet chili sauce and duck with a honey-and-orange sauce, along with exotic cocktails and a variety of fine Greek and foreign wines. Follow signs to the top of the short but steep staircase. ✉ *Above clock tower* ☎ *24270/24550* ✍ *Reservations essential* ▭ *MC, V* ⊗ *Closed mid-Oct.–mid-May. No lunch.*

$–$$ ✕ **Amphiliki.** Sprawled on a balcony overlooking Siferi bay, this restaurant, open for three meals a day, pairs an inviting breeze with one of the best views in town. The menu's pairings are less reliable: a Mediterranean-fusion approach works for some dishes, like mouthwatering prawns and mushrooms dressed in a zingy lemon sauce. But for others (like mussels drowned in cheese) it detracts from the purity of the fresh ingredients. Service is attentive and the white house wine crisp and cool. Leave space for the feather-light *ekmek* (custard cake) with mastic ice cream if you arrive for lunch or dinner. ✉ *Opposite health center* ☎ *24270/22839* ▭ *MC, V* ⊗ *Oct.–May.*

$–$$ ✕ **Don Quijote Tapas Bar Restaurant.** Mediterranean ingredients inspire at one of the few tapas bars in Greece. Its impressive selection of hot and cold tapas include baked feta in foil, spicy prawns, paella, *jamon* (Spanish crude ham), and tortillas. Between nibbles, sip a traditional Spanish wine, or a refreshing margarita, mojito, or caipirinha. Catalan cream (the Spanish version of crème brûlée) and chocolate soufflé make for a sweet end. Have a question about a dish? The cheerful, friendly waitstaff is happy to answer. Sitting on the cozy, vibrantly colored rooftop terrace allows you to view the harbor's bustle with the sound turned down. ✉ *East harbor* ☎ *24270/21600* ▭ *MC, V* ⊗ *Closed Nov.–Apr.*

$–$$ ★ ✕ **Ta Psarädika.** You can't get any closer to the fish market than this old port taverna, and the fresh seafood dishes (served grilled or fried) prove it. Fish is caught daily by local fishermen expressly for the restaurant, which is family-owned and run. Sit at an outside table facing the sea and sip an icy ouzo while sampling the *mezedes* (appetizers) and finny creatures. ✉ *Far end of old port* ☎ *24270/23412* ▭ *AE, MC, V* ⊗ *Closed Dec. and Jan.*

$–$$ **Fresh.** The warm, inviting owners, Astergios and Spyros, can be counted on to entertain while imparting their in-depth knowledge of Skiathos. Many of the simple studios with modern furnishings have great views of the harbor. For Greek food—*pastitsio* (pasta with aromatic meat sauce and béchamel), moussaka—reasonable prices, and great service, don't pass up the casual boardwalk café (¢), also fun for people-watching. *Portside, 37002 24270/21998 10 studios In-room: kitchen. In-hotel: restaurant, no elevator AE, DC, MC, V Closed Nov.–Apr. CP.*

¢ ★ **Mouria Hotel and Taverna.** A wonderful choice for budget travelers, Mouria first opened in 1830 as a market and taverna and is today an inn and restaurant run by the great-grandchildren of the original owners. Guest rooms, some of which can accommodate up to six people, have air-conditioning as well as access to kitchen and laundry facilities. Ask for a room with a balcony overlooking the courtyard, where Papadiamantis once came to write stories. The reasonably priced taverna ($–$$) serves traditional Greek food and fish brought in from the hotel's own boat. *Areti Ioannou, behind National Bank, 37002 24270/23069 24270/23859 12 rooms In-room: no phone. In-hotel: restaurant, laundry facilities MC, V.*

$$ **Alkyon.** Don't be disappointed by the boxy exterior and the lack of architectural embellishments—this is a discreet, light-filled hotel with many rooms offering lovely views of the new harbor. It's just enough away from the motion and commotion of Skiathos's main artery to provide some tranquillity, but it's also within easy walking distance of terrific nightlife. The rooms are comfortable and sunny (all come with private balconies), and the lounge areas are spacious and inviting. *New port, 37002 24270/22981 through 24270/22985 24270/21643 89 rooms In-room: kitchen, no TV. In-hotel: bar, pool AE, MC, V Closed Nov.–Mar. CP.*

NIGHTLIFE

Skiathos is filled with night owls, and for good reason. Bars for all tastes line main and side streets, from pubs run by Brits to quintessential Greek bouzouki joints in beach tavernas. Most of the nightlife in Skiathos town is centered along the waterfront and on Papadiamantis, Politechniou, and Evangelistrias streets. The most active season, as you might expect, is June through August, when nightclubs catering to all tastes open along the new port.

MUSIC & NIGHTCLUBS

For late-night action along a row of hopping clubs, head to **Kahlua** (*Tasos Antonaros [new port] 24270/23205 Closed Oct.–Apr.*), which has indoor and outdoor dancing and is open in summer until at least 3 AM. The popular **Kentavros Bar** (*Papadiamantis Sq. 24270/22980 Closed Oct.–Apr.*) entertains a young professional crowd with rhythm and blues, funk, soul, and rock starting at 9:30 PM.

Rock 'n' Roll (*Old port 24270/22944 Closed Oct.–Apr.*) is a trendy bar that serves more than 100 cocktails and has a DJ after 9:30 PM. At the funky, white-hot **Slip Inn** (*Old port 24270/21006*) you can indulge in an amazing fresh passion-fruit margarita as you lounge, Dionysian style on multicolor floor cushions.

SPORTS & THE OUTDOORS

SAILING For multiday charters with or without crew, contact *Active Yachts* (✉*Portside* ☎*69722/45391* ✉*activeyachts@ath.forthnet.gr* ⊙*Closed Oct.–Apr.*), which also rents out motorboats by the day.

SCUBA DIVING Popular beaches often have diving-equipment rental and instructors on hand. Skiathos is the only Sporades island with scuba-diving schools. The first in operation, **Dolphin Diving Center** (✉*Porto Nostos beach [off bus stop 12]* ☎*24270/21599* 📠*24270/22525* 🌐*www.ddiving.gr* ⊙*Closed Nov.–Apr.*) offers single or multiple dives, as well as full-certification programs.

SHOPPING

ANTIQUES & CRAFTS The **Archipelago** (✉*Near Papadiamantis Museum* ☎*24270/22163*) is the most impressive shop on the island. Browse here among the antiques, pottery, jewelry made from fossils, and embroideries. **Galerie Varsakis** (✉*Trion Hierarchon* ☎*24270/22255*) has kilims, embroideries, jewelry, icons, and hundreds of antiques, set off by the proprietor's surrealistic paintings. **Loupos and His Dolphins** (✉*Papadiamantis Sq.* ☎*24270/23777*) is two adjacent shops that sell museum copies of Byzantine jewelry, ceramics made in Volos, furniture, and antiques. **Skia** (✉*Off Papadiamantis, behind National Bank* ☎*24270/21728*) sells original paintings, sculptures, and ceramics handcrafted by the owners, Milena and Vladislav.

JEWELRY **Odysseus Jewelry** (✉*Papadiamantis* ☎*24270/24218*) sells gold and silver pieces. **Seraïna** (✉*Near Papadiamantis Museum* ☎*24270/22039*) sells jewelry, ceramic plates, and lamp shades. **Simos** (✉*Papadiamantis* ☎*24270/22916*) has unique silver and gold designs.

KALAMAKI PENINSULA ΚΑΛΑΜΑΚΙ (ΧΕΡΣΟΝΗΣΟΣ)

6 km (4 mi) south of Skiathos town.

The less-developed area on the south coast of Skiathos is the Kalamaki peninsula, where the British built their first villas. Some are available for rent in summer, many above tiny, unfrequented coves. Access here is by boat only, so you can usually find your own private beach to get away from the crowds. Motor launches run at regular intervals to the most popular beaches from Skiathos town, and you can always hire a boat for a private journey.

WHERE TO STAY

$$$$ **Skiathos Princess.** Flanking virtually the whole of Platania bay below Ayia Paraskevi, Skiathos Princess has all the expected amenities of a luxury resort and friendly, professional service to match. The lobby is minimal, airy, and polished. Rooms that look lifted from a magazine have tile floors, elegant marble bathrooms, and patios or balconies—most with garden views, some facing the sea. A poolside bar serves light snacks. Open only for lunch, the property's chic seaside taverna is worth a visit; the unimaginative buffet dinner at the main restaurant is less enticing. ✉*8 km (5 mi) from Skiathos town, 37002Ayia Paraskevi* ☎*24270/49731* 📠*24270/49740* 🌐*www.skiathosprincess.com*

131 rooms, 25 suites, 2 apartments In-room: safe, refrigerator. In-hotel: 2 restaurants, bars, pool, spa, no elevator, parking (no fee) AE, MC, V Closed Nov.–Apr. BP.

TROULLOS ΤΡΟΥΛΛΟΣ

4 km (2½ mi) west of Kalamaki peninsula, 8 km (5 mi) west of Skiathos town.

On the coast road west of Kalamaki peninsula lies Troullos bay, a resort area. Continue west and you come to Koukounaries beach—famous, beautiful, and overcrowded.

The dirt road north of Troullos leads to beaches and to the small, and now deserted, **Kounistra Monastery** (*4 km [2½ mi] north of Troullos*). It was built in the late 17th century on the spot where an icon of the Virgin miraculously appeared, swinging from a pine tree. The icon spends most of the year in the church of Trion Hierarchon, in town, but on November 20 the townspeople parade it to its former home for the celebration of the Presentation of the Virgin the following day. You can enter the deserted monastery church any time, though its interior has been blackened by fire and its 18th-century frescoes are hard to see.

5

BEACHES

Though **Koukounaries** (*4 km [2½ mi] northwest of Troullos, 12 km [8 mi] west of Skiathos town*) has been much touted as Greece's best beach, photos displaying it must either have been taken a long time ago or on a brilliant, deserted winter's day. All summer it is so packed with umbrellas, beach chairs, and blistering tourists that you can hardly see the sand. The multitudes can be part of the fun, however: think of this as an international Greek island beach party. Water activities abound, with waterskiing, sailing (laser boats), paddleboats, and banana-boat rides all available. The beach can only be reached from its ends, as a lagoon separates it from the hinterland.

Around the island's western tip are **Ayia Eleni** and **Krasa** (*1 km [½ mi] west of Koukounaries beach, 13 km [8 mi] west of Skiathos town*), facing the Pelion peninsula, which looms close by. These beaches are also known as Big and Little Banana, perhaps because sun worshippers—mainly gay men on Little Banana—often peel their clothes off. Rocky coves provide some privacy.

Mandraki (*5 km [3 mi] northwest of Troullos bay, 12 km [7½ mi] west of Skiathos town*) has privacy because the beach is a 25-minute walk from the road. Sometimes called Xerxes's harbor, this is where the Persian king stopped on his way to ultimate defeat at the battles of Artemisium and Salamis. The reefs opposite are the site of a monument Xerxes supposedly erected as a warning to ships, the first such marker known in history.

Megalos Aselinos and Mikros Aselinos (*7 km [4½ mi] north of Troullos, 8 km [5 mi] west of Skiathos town*), north of Mandraki beach, can be reached by car or bike.

WHERE TO STAY

$$$$ ★ **Aegean Suites.** In a league of its own on Skiathos, this luxurious boutique hotel pampers eclectic and demanding guests ages 18 and up in what resembles a Mediterranean grand villa. Suites are separated by stairs weaving through a lush garden, and each accommodation has a separate living room and bedroom and its own audacious, original Greek artwork. Balconies peer over the Aegean Sea near Troullos. The beach lies close by, and the outdoor candlelit restaurant, Pelagos, shares the rooms' blue-green sea views. Expect outstanding service and such perks as a champagne bar, Jacuzzi dinners, yacht cruises, helicopter transfers, and occasional wine tastings or barbecue nights. ✉*Megali Ammos beach* *Winter address: Santikmos Hotels & Resorts, 40 Ag. Konstantinou, Aethrio Centre, Office A40, 15124 Maroussi, Athens* ☎*24270/24069* *24270/24070* *www.aegeansuites.com* *20 suites* *In-room: safe, refrigerator, Wi-Fi. In-hotel: 3 restaurants, bar, pool, no elevator, parking (no fee)* *AE, D, MC, V* *Closed Nov.–Apr.* *BP.*

$ **Troullos Bay.** Quiet and peaceful, this homey beachfront hotel invites reading, chatting, and relaxing in bamboo chairs around the lobby's fireplace. Bedrooms have wood furniture, striped duvets, tile floors, and colorful prints. Most rooms have balconies and views of the pretty beach. The restaurant, decorated with bamboo and chintz, serves a combination of good Greek and international food and opens onto the lawn near the sand's edge. ✉*Troullos, 37002Troullos Bay* ☎*24270/49390 or 24270/49391* *24270/49218* *43 rooms* *In-room: refrigerator. In-hotel: restaurant, bar* *MC, V* *Closed Nov.–Apr.*

KASTRO ΚΑΣΤΡΟ

13 km (8 mi) northeast of Troullos, 9 km (5½ mi) northeast of Skiathos town.

Also known as the old town, Kastro perches on a forbidding promontory high above the water, accessible only by steps. Skiathians founded this former capital in the 16th century when they fled from the pirates and the turmoil on the coast to the security of this remote cliff—staying until 1829. Its landward side was additionally protected by a moat and drawbridge, and inside the stout walls they erected 300 houses and 22 churches, of which only 2 remain. The little Church of the Nativity has some icons and must have heard many prayers for deliverance from the sieges that left the Skiathians close to starvation.

You can drive or take a taxi or bus to within 325 feet of the old town, or wear comfortable shoes for a walk that's mostly uphill. Better, take the downhill walk back to Skiathos town; the trek takes about three hours and goes through orchards, fields, and forests on the well-marked paths of the interior.

Four kilometers (2½ mi) southwest of Kastro is the deserted **Kechrias monastery,** an 18th-century church covered in frescoes and surrounded by olive and pine trees. Be warned: the road to Kechrias from Skiathos town and to the beach below is tough going; stick to a four-wheel-drive vehicle.

LALARIA ΛΑΛΑΡΙΑ

Fodor'sChoice ★ *2 km (1 mi) east of Kastro, 7 km (4½ mi) north of Skiathos town.*

The much-photographed, lovely Lalaria beach, on the north coast, is flanked by a majestic, arched limestone promontory. The polished limestone and marble add extra sparkle to the already shimmering Aegean. There's no lodging here, and you can only reach Lalaria by taking a boat from the old port in Skiathos town, where taxi and tourist boats are readily available. In the same area lie **Skoteini (Dark) cave, Galazia (Azure) cave,** and **Halkini (Copper) cave.** If taking a tour boat, you can stop for an hour or two here to swim and frolic. Bring along a flashlight to turn the water inside these grottoes an incandescent blue.

★ The island's best-known and most beautiful monastery, **Evangelistria,** sits on Skiathos's highest point and was dedicated in the late 18th century to the Annunciation of the Virgin by monks from Mt. Athos. It encouraged education and gave a base to revolutionaries, who pledged an oath to freedom and first hoisted the blue-and-white flag of Greece here in 1807. Looming above a gorge, and surrounded by pines and cypresses, the monastery has a high wall that once kept pirates out; today it encloses a ruined refectory kitchen, the cells, a small museum library, and a magnificent church with three domes. A gift shop sells the monastery's own Alypiakos wine, olive oil, preserves, and icons. It's close to Lalaria, and about a 10-minute drive, or an hour's walk, from Skiathos town. ✉*2 km (1 mi) south of Lalaria, 5 km (3 mi) north of Skiathos town* ☎*No phone* 🎫*Donations accepted* ⏲*Daily 9–7.*

NEED A BREAK?

A couple of miles south of Evangelistria Monastery, the dirt road veers off toward the north and northwest of the island. Follow this track for a quick repast; about 2 km (1 mi) on, an enterprising soul has set up a café and snack bar, Platanos (✉***Off main road south of Evangelistria Monastery*** ☎***No phone*** ⏲***Closed Oct.–Apr.*****), where you can stare at the astounding view of the harbor for as long as you like.**

SKOPELOS ΣΚΟΠΕΛΟΣ

This triangular island's name means "a sharp rock" or "a reef"—a fitting description for the terrain on its northern shore. It's an hour away from Skiathos by hydrofoil and is the second largest of the Sporades. Most of its 122 square km (47 square mi), up to its highest peak on Mt. Delphi, are covered with dense pine forests, olive groves, and orchards. On the south coast, villages overlook the shores, and pines line the pebbly beaches, casting jade shadows on turquoise water. Although this is the most populated island of the Sporades, with two major towns, Skopelos remains peaceful and absorbs tourists into its life rather than

5

giving itself up to their sun-and-fun desires. It's not surprising that ecologists claim it's the greenest island in the region.

Legend has it that Skopelos was settled by Peparethos and Staphylos, colonists from Minoan Crete, said to be the sons of Dionysus and Ariadne, King Minos's daughter. They brought with them the lore of the grape and the olive. The island was called Peparethos until Hellenistic times, and its most popular beach still bears the name Stafilos. In the 1930s a tomb believed to be Staphylos's was unearthed, filled with weapons and golden treasures (now in the Volos museum on the Pelion peninsula).

The Byzantines were exiled here, and the Venetians ruled for 300 years, until 1204. In times past, Skopelos was known for its wine, but today its plums and almonds are eaten rather than drunk, and incorporated into the simple cuisine. Many artists and photographers have settled on the island and throughout summer are part of an extensive cultural program. Little by little, Skopelos is cementing an image as a green and artsy island, still unspoiled by success.

SKOPELOS TOWN ΣΚΟΠΕΛΟΣ (ΠΟΛΗ)

3 hrs from Agios Konstantinos, ½ hr from Skiathos town.

Pretty Skopelos town, the administrative center of the Sporades, overlooks a bay on the north coast. On a steep hill below, scant vestiges of the ancient acropolis and medieval castle remain. The town works hard to stay charming—building permits are difficult to obtain, signs must be in native style, pebbles are embedded into the walkways. Three- and four-story houses rise virtually straight up the hillside, reached by flagstone steps, where women sit chatting and knitting by their doorways. The whitewashed houses look prosperous and cared for, their facades enlivened by brightly painted or brown timber balconies, doors, and shutters. Flamboyant vines and potted plants complete the picture. Interspersed among the red-tile roofs are several with traditional gray fish-scale slate—too heavy and expensive to be used much nowadays.

Off the waterfront, prepare for a breath-snatching climb up the almost perpendicular steps in Skopelos town, starting at the seawall. You will encounter many churches as you go—the island has over 300. The uppermost, located near the castle and said to be situated on the ruins of the ancient temple of Minerva, is the 11th-century Ayios Athanasios with a typically whitewashed exterior and an interior that includes 17th-century Byzantine murals. At the stairs' summit you're standing within the walls of the 13th-century castle erected by the Venetian Ghisi lords who held all the Sporades as their fief. It in turn rests upon polygonal masonry of the 5th century BC, as this was the site of one of the island's three ancient acropoli. Once you've admired the view and the stamina of the old women negotiating the steps like mountain goats, wind your way back down the seawall steps by any route you choose. Wherever you turn, you may spy a church; Skopelos claims some 360, of which 123 are in the town proper. Curiously, most of them seem to be locked, but the exteriors are striking—some incorporating ancient artifacts, Byzantine plates or early Christian elements, and slate-capped domes.

★ For a glimpse of the interior of a Skopelan house, visit the **Folk Art Museum,** a 19th-century mansion with period furniture and traditional tools. Check out the example of an elaborate women's festive costume: a silk shirt embroidered with tiny flowers, a velvet coat with wide embroidered sleeves, and a silk head scarf. Even today, women in the villages dress this way for special occasions. ✉ *Hatzistamatis* ☎ *24240/23494* 🎫 *€3* ⏲ *May–Sept., daily 10–10.*

PILGRIMAGE WITH A VIEW

A few of Skopelos's 40 monasteries—dazzling white and topped with terra-cotta roofs—are perched on the nearby mountainside, circling in tiers to the shore. Most offer spectacular views of the town; some are deserted, but others are in operation and welcome you to visit (dress appropriately: no bare legs or arms, and women must wear skirts). You can drive or go by bike, but even by foot, with a good walking guide, you can visit them all in a few hours.

Evangelistria Monastery was founded in 1676 and completely rebuilt in 1712. It contains no frescoes but has an intricately carved iconostasis and an 11th-century icon of the Virgin with Child, said to be miraculous. ✉ *On mountainside opposite Skopelos town, 1½ km (1 mi) to the northeast* ☎ *24240/23230* 🎫 *Free* ⏲ *Daily 9–1 and 3–5.*

★ The **Prodromou** *(Forerunner)*, dedicated to St. John the Baptist, now operates as a convent. Besides being of an unusual design, its church contains some outstanding 14th-century triptychs, an enamel tile floor, and an iconostasis spanning four centuries (half carved in the 14th century, half in the 18th century). The nuns sell elaborate woven and embroidered handiwork. Opening days and hours vary. ✉ *2½ km (1½ mi) east of Skopelos town.*

The tiny port of **Agnonda** has many tavernas along its pebbled beach. It is named after a local boy, Agnonas, who returned here from Olympia in 546 BC wearing the victor's wreath. ✉ *5 km (3 mi) south of Skopelos town.*

The road from the beach at Stafilos runs southwest through the rounded **Drachondoschisma peninsula,** where, legend has it, St. Reginos dispatched a dragon that was picking off the islanders. ✉ *5 km (3 mi) south of Skopelos town.*

BEACHES

Most beaches lie on the sheltered coast, south and west of the main town, and are reached from the road by footpath. The water in this area is calm, and pines grow down to the waterfront. Scattered farms and tavernas, houses with rooms for rent, and one or two pleasant hotels line the road to the beach at **Stafilos** (✉ *8 km [5 mi] southeast of Skopelos town*), the closest to town and the most crowded. Prehistoric

5

walls, a watchtower, and an unplundered grave suggest that this was the site of an important prehistoric settlement. **Velania** (✉ *1 km [½ mi] east of Stafilos*), reachable by footpath, takes its name from the *valanium* (Roman bath) that once stood here, which has since disintegrated under the waves. It's a nude beach today.

WHERE TO STAY & EAT

$–$$ ✕ **Alexander Garden Restaurant.** If you've had enough of the waterfront, follow the signs up to this little garden restaurant in the hills for a made-to-order meal. Especially recommended are *orektika* (appetizers) such as fried eggplant or zucchini, served with *tzatziki* (garlic and yogurt dip) or *tirosalata* (cheese dip). A 200-year-old well in the center of the elegant, leafy terrace produces its own natural spring water, which you can enjoy while dining here. ✉ *Odhos Manolaki; turn inland after corner shop Armoloi* ☎ *24240/22324* ▭ *MC, V* ⊙ *No lunch.*

$–$$ ✕ **Perivoli.** An elegant, imaginative meal awaits at this local favorite with a candlelit garden. The varied menu is chock-full of delicious options; standouts include rolled pork with mushrooms in wine sauce, seafood risotto, and any of the beef fillets. Make sure to leave room for dessert, as the *amigdalopita* (almond cake with chocolate and fresh cream) is a winner. The secret is out, though—this place is usually crowded. Follow the signs up from Platanos Square (aka Souvlaki Square). ✉ *Off Platanos Sq.* ☎ *24240/23758* ▭ *MC, V* ⊙ *Closed Oct.–May. No lunch.*

$ ✕ **Molos.** The best of the cluster of tavernas near the ferry dock, Molos serves excellent grilled meat, stuffed grape leaves, meatballs, and *magirefta* (dishes cooked ahead in the oven, and often served at room temperature). It's one of the few places in town open for lunch, especially delightful at an outdoor table. ✉ *Waterfront* ☎ *24240/22551* ▭ *No credit cards* ⊙ *Closed Nov.–Mar.*

¢–$ ✕ **Mihalis.** Come here for the delicious *Skopelitiki tiropita* (Skopelos cheese pie), or splurge on *rizogalo* (rice pudding). Bougainvillea lines the walls of the courtyard, where you hear the warble of canaries. Opposite stands a barbershop that embodies the charm of another era. ✉ *East side of port, 3 blocks inland from bank* ☎ *24240/22014* ▭ *No credit cards.*

$$$–$$$$ 🏨 **Skopelos Village.** If sprawling is your style, try one of these spacious bungalows. Each sleeps from two to six people and has a balcony or patio, kitchen, large bedroom(s), and living room. The design is traditional northern Greece, with white stucco exterior and interior walls, orange barrel-tile roofs, and rustic pine beds. A sparkling pool is the focus of the central courtyard, and lounge chairs sit poolside. The hotel is steps away from the beach and about a 15-minute walk from the town center. ✉ *1 km (½ mi) west of center, 37003* ☎ *24240/23011 or 24240/22517* 📠 *24240/22958* 🌐 *www.skopelosvillage.gr* ⇨ *36 suites* ♨ *In-room: safe, kitchen. In-hotel: restaurant, bar, pool, no elevator* ▭ *MC, V* ⊙ *Closed Nov.–Apr.*
★

$$ 🏨 **Alkistis.** Geared toward families or couples with cars, this complex of four buildings amid a grove of olive trees makes an agreeable alternative to a beach or town hotel. The cheerful apartments' exteriors are pastel-contemporary; lounges and dining terraces are more traditional,

though airy and bright. Housekeeping is included, and the large pool has a swim-up bar. Room TVs are provided upon request. ✉ *2 km (1 mi) southeast of town on road to Stafilos, 37003* ☎ *24240/23006 through 24240/22517* 🖷 *24240/22116* *25 apartments* *In-room: kitchen. In-hotel: restaurant, bar, pool, no elevator* ▭ *No credit cards* ⏲ *Closed Oct.–May.*

¢ **Pension Sotos.** This cozy, restored old Skopelete house on the waterfront is inexpensive and extremely casual. Tiny rooms look onto one of the hotel's two courtyard terraces. Breakfast is not offered, although you are welcome to bring your own food and use the communal kitchen. ✉ *Waterfront, 37003* ☎ *24240/22549* 🖷 *24240/23668* *12 rooms* *In-room: no a/c (some), no phone, refrigerator (some), no TV (some). In hotel: no elevator* ▭ *No credit cards.*

5

THE OUTDOORS

A big caïque captained by a knowledgeable local guide makes day cruises from Skopelos to Alonissos and the National Marine Park. The tour includes a visit to Patitiri, the port of Alonissos, and to the island of Kyra Panayia, where you can walk, swim, snorkel, and visit a post-Byzantine monastery. You can make reservations at Madro Travel (⇨ *Tour Options in Sporades Essentials).*

NIGHTLIFE

Nightlife on Skopelos is more sedate than it is on Skiathos. There's a smattering of cozy bars playing music of all kinds, and each summer at least one nightclub operates (look for advertisements). The *kefi* (good mood) is to be found at the western end of the waterfront, where a string of bar-nightclubs come to life after midnight. Take an evening *volta* (stroll); most bars have tables outside, so you really can't miss them.

At **Anatoli** (✉ *Old kastro* ☎ *24240/22851*), tap into a truly Greek vein with proprietor Giorgo Xithari, who strums up a storm on his bouzouki and sings *rembetika,* traditional Greek acoustic blues (without the benefit of a microphone). Sometimes other musicians join in, sometimes his sons, and with enough ouzo, you might, too.

Venture into the back alleys and have a drink at **Ionos Blue Bar** (✉ *Skopelos town* ☎ *24240/23731*), which offers cool jazz and blues. **Mercurius** (✉ *Skopelos town* ☎ *24240/24593*), along the waterfront, is an artsy jazz bar with a candlelit terrace and unbeatable sea view. **Platanos Jazz Club** (✉ *Next to ferry dock, Skopelos town* ☎ *24240/23661*), on the eastern part of the harbor, is atmospheric and quietly popular.

SHOPPING

The town's tiny shops are tucked into a few streets behind the central part of the waterfront. Handicrafts include loom-woven textiles made by nuns.

CLOTHING **Mythos** (✉ *Behind port, next to post office* ☎ *24240/23943*) sells fashionable Greek and international styles for women. Try **Pragmata** (✉ *Behind port, above Verdo Bldg.* ☎ *24240/22866*) for clothes, shoes, and other accessories.

LOCAL CRAFTS **Archipelago** (✉ *Waterfront* ☎ *24240/23127*), the sister shop of Archipelago on Skiathos, has modern ceramics and crafts, great jewelry, handbags, and a wonderful selection of pricey antiques. **Armoloi** (✉ *Waterfront* ☎ *24240/22707*), one of the neatest shops, displays ceramics made by local potters, tapestries, embroideries, and bags crafted from fragments of old Asian rugs and kilims. Kilims, bags, hand-painted T-shirts, and jewelry are among the wares at **Ploumisti** (✉ *Waterfront* ☎ *24240/22059*). **Yiousouri** (✉ *Waterfront* ☎ *24240/23983*) sells decorative ceramics.

PANORMOS BAY ΌΡΜΟΣ ΠΑΝΟΡΜΟΥ

6 km (4 mi) west of Skopelos town, 4 km (2½ mi) northwest of Agnonda.

Due northwest of Agnonda is Panormos bay, the smallest of the ancient towns of Peparethos, founded in the 8th century BC by colonists from Chalkis. A few well-concealed walls are visible among the pine woods on the acropolis above the bay. With its long beach and its sheltered inner cove ideal for yachts, this is fast becoming a holiday village, although so far it retains its quiet charm. Inland, the interior of Skopelos is green and lush, and not far from Panormos bay traditional farmhouses called *kalivia* stand in plum orchards. Some are occupied; others have been turned into overnight stops or are used only for feast-day celebrations. Look for the outdoor ovens, which baked the fresh plums when Skopelos was turning out prunes galore. This rural area is charming, but the lack of signposts makes it easy to get lost, so pay attention.

BEACHES

Pebbly **Milia** (✉ *2 km [1 mi] north of Panormos bay*) Skopelos's longest beach, is considered by many to be its best. Though still secluded, Milia bay is up and coming—parasols and recliners are lined across the beach ready and waiting for the summer crowd. There's an enormous taverna, thankfully ensconced by pine trees; the food is only decent, but cold drinks and ice cream are a luxury in the noonday sun. No matter what, Milia is breathtaking, and if you want to minimize the distance between you and the deep blue sea, locate the owner of one of the villas for rent right on the beach. They're well tended and a few short strides from the water's edge. Next to Milia, accessible through the Adrina Beach hotel, **Adrina beach** has gorgeous turquoise water and a feeling of seclusion. Dassia, the verdant islet across the bay, was named after a pirate who drowned there—a woman.

WHERE TO STAY

$$$$ ★ **Adrina Beach.** Atop a picture-book cove, this terraced hotel has uninterrupted views of Panormos bay from every level. Outside there is multihued bougainvillea; indoors, the blue-and-white scheme is carried throughout, complemented by terra-cotta floors. Plates adorn the walls, amphorae (large clay vessels that usually held wine) the corners. The only fly on the baklava might be the many stairs between the private beach, pool, restaurant (which serves scrumptious home-style

food made from local products), and your room, and the steep walk back from the little town. ✉*1 km (½ mi) northwest of Panormos bay, 37003Adrina* ☎*24240/23371 or 24240/23373* 📠*24240/23372* 🌐*www.adrina.gr* *42 rooms, 10 suites* *In-room: refrigerator. In-hotel: restaurant, bar, pool, spa, no elevator, parking (no fee)* 💳*AE, DC, MC, V* ⏲*Closed Nov.–Apr.* 🍽*BP.*

$ **Panormos Beach.** The owner's attention to detail shows in the beautifully tended flower garden, the immaculate rooms with pine furniture and handwoven linens, the country dining room, and the entrance case displaying his grandmother's elaborate costume. The lobby even looks like a little museum decorated with antiques and traditional clothes. This exceptionally peaceful hotel is a five-minute walk from the beach. ✉*Beachfront, 37003* ☎*24240/22711* 📠*24240/23366* *34 rooms* *In-room: refrigerator. In-hotel: no elevator* 💳*No credit cards* ⏲*Closed Nov.–Apr.*

5

ELIOS ΈΛΙΟΣ

10 km (6 mi) north of Panormos bay, 25 km (16 mi) west of Skopelos town.

Residents of Klima who were dislodged in 1965 by the same earthquake that devastated Alonissos now live here. The origin of its name is more intriguing than the village: legend has it that when St. Reginos arrived in the 4th century to save the island from a dragon that fed on humans, he demanded, "Well, where in *elios* (God's mercy) is the beast?"

Klima (✉*3 km [2 mi] north of Elios*) means "ladder," and in this village Kato (Lower) Klima leads to Ano (Upper) Klima, clinging to the mountainside. Some houses destroyed in the 1965 earthquake have not been restored and are still for sale. If you crave an island retreat, this could be your chance.

WHERE TO STAY

$ **Zanétta.** These simple, peaceful apartments are surrounded by pine trees and are close to the sea. Two-bedroom apartments host four people and the three-bedrooms can accommodate six. The white hotel with yellow trim and red barrel-tile roof is about a five-minute walk from the water. ✉*Hovolo beach, 37005* ☎*24240/33140* 📠*24240/33717* *16 apartments* *In-room: no a/c (some), kitchen. In-hotel: tennis court, pool, no elevator* 💳*MC, V* ⏲*Closed Nov.–Apr.*

EN ROUTE

Loutraki is the tiny port village where the ferries and hydrofoils stop to and from Skiathos, and it is not very charming.

Three hundred yards from the port are the remains of the acropolis of Selinous, the island's third ancient city. Unfortunately, everything lies buried except the walls.

GLOSSA ΓΛΩΣΣΑ

38 km (23 mi) northwest of Skopelos town, 14 km (8 mi) northwest of Elios, 3 km (1½ mi) northwest of Klima.

Delightful Glossa is the island's second-largest settlement, where whitewashed, red-roof houses are clustered on the steep hillside above the harbor of Loutraki. Venetian towers and traces of Turkish influence remain; the center is closed to traffic. This is a place to relax, dine, and enjoy the quieter beaches. Just to the east, have a look at Ayios Ioannis monastery, dramatically perched above a pretty beach. There's no need to tackle the series of extremely steep steps to the monastery, as it is not open to visitors.

WHERE TO EAT

$ ★ ✕**Restaurant Agnanti.** With breathtaking views of the sea below, creative dishes, and reasonable prices, this restaurant, opened in a restored home in 1953, has stayed true to the spirit that gave it its renown. Fresh produce and local wines underscore the high quality. Begin with a sun-dried tomato and smoked cheese salad, and move on to the lemon chicken, pork with plums, or goat in a tomato sauce. ⊠*Above bus stop, on left side of Agiou Riginou* ☎*24240/33076* ▭*MC, V* ⊙*Closed Nov.–Apr.*

SKYROS ΣΚΥΡΟΣ

Even among these unique isles, Skyros stands out. Its rugged terrain looks like a Dodecanese island, and its main town, occupied on and off for the last 3,300 years and filled with mythical ghosts, looks Cycladic. It has military bases, and an airport with periodic connections to Athens, yet it remains the most difficult ferry connection in the Sporades. With nothing between it and Lesbos, off the coast of Turkey, its nearest neighbor is the town of Kimi, on the east coast of Evia.

Surprisingly beguiling, this southernmost of the Sporades is the largest (209 square km [81 square mi]). A narrow, flat isthmus connects Skyros's two almost-equal parts, whose names reflect their characters—*Meri* or *Imero* ("tame") for the north, and *Vouno* (literally, "mountain," meaning tough or stony) for the south. The heavily populated north is virtually all farmland and forests. The southern half of the island is forbidding, barren, and mountainous, with Mt. Kochilas its highest peak (2,598 feet). Its western coast is outlined with coves and deep bays dotted with a series of islets.

Until Greece won independence in 1831, the population of Skyros squeezed sardine-fashion into the area under the castle on the inland face of the rock. Not a single house was visible from the sea. Though the islanders could survey any movement in the Aegean for miles, they kept a low profile, living in dread of the pirates based at Treis Boukes bay on Vouno.

Strangely enough, although the island is adrift in the Aegean, the Skyrians have not had a seafaring tradition, and they have looked to the

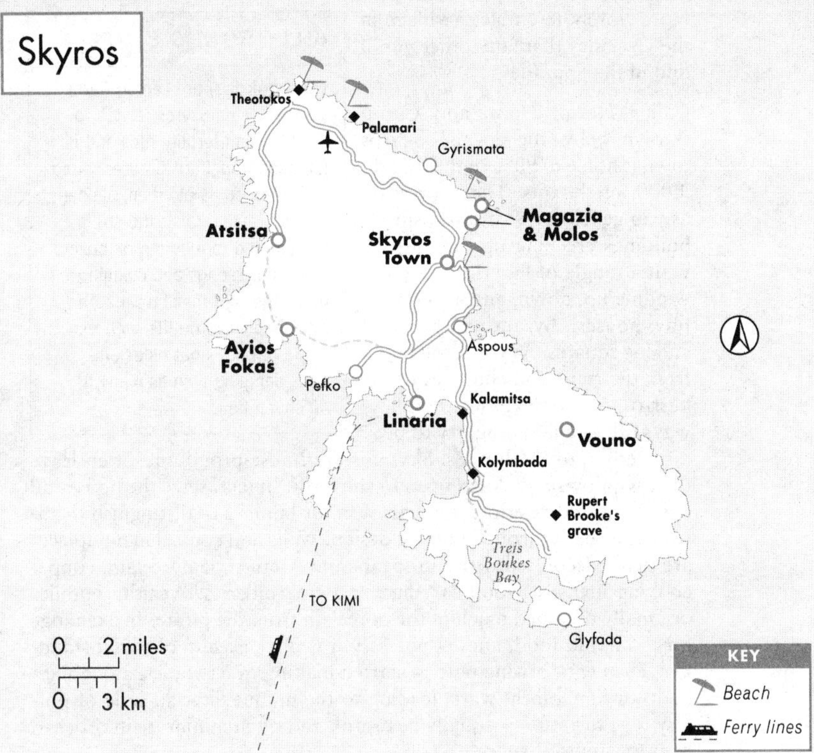

land for their living. Their isolation has brought about notable cultural differences from the other Greek islands, such as pre-Christian Carnival rituals. Today there are more than 300 churches on the island, many of them private and owned by local families. An almost-extinct breed of pony resides on Skyros, and exceptional crafts—carpentry, pottery, embroidery—are practiced by dedicated artisans whose creations include unique furniture and decorative linens. There are no luxury accommodations or swank restaurants: this idiosyncratic island makes no provisions for mass tourism, but if you've a taste for the offbeat, you may feel right at home.

SKYROS TOWN ΣΚΥΡΟΣ (ΧΩΡΙΟ)

Fodor's Choice ★

1 hr 40 mins from Kimi to Linaria by boat, 30 mins from Linaria by car

As you drive south from the airport, past brown, desolate outcroppings with only an occasional goat as a sign of life, Skyros town suddenly looms around a bend. It resembles a breathtaking imaginary painting by Monet, Cézanne, or El Greco: blazing white, cubist, dense, and otherworldly, clinging, precariously it seems, to the precipitous rock beneath it and topped gloriously by a fortress-monastery. This town more closely resembles a village in the Cyclades than any other you'll find in the Sporades.

> **BILLY GOAT'S BLUFF**
>
> The **Apokries,** pre-Lenten Carnival revelry, on Skyros relates to pre-Christian fertility rites and is famous throughout Greece. Young men dressed as old men, maidens, or "Europeans" roam the streets teasing and tormenting onlookers with ribald songs and clanging bells. The "old men" wear elaborate shepherd's outfits, with masks made of baby-goat hides and belts dangling with as many as 40 sheep bells.

Called *Horio, Hora,* and *Chora* ("town") by the locals, Skyros town is home to 90% of the island's 3,000 inhabitants. The impression as you get closer is of stark, simple buildings creeping up the hillside, with a tangle of labyrinthine lanes winding up, down, and around the tiny houses, Byzantine churches, and big squares. As you stroll down from the ruins and churches of the kastro area, or explore the alleyways off the main drag, try to peek discreetly into the houses. Skyrians are house-proud and often leave their windows and doors open to show off. In fact, since the houses all have the same exteriors, the only way for families to distinguish themselves has been through interior design. Walls and conical mantelpieces are richly decorated with European- and Asian-style porcelain, copper cooking utensils, wood carvings, and embroideries. Wealthy families originally obtained much of the porcelain from the pirates in exchange for grain and food, and its possession was a measure of social standing. Then enterprising potters started making exact copies, along with the traditional local ware, leading to the unique Skyrian style of pottery. The furniture is equally beautiful, and often miniature in order to conserve interior space.

Farther up the hill, the summit is crowned with three tiny cubelike churches with blue and pink interiors, and the ruined Venetian cistern, once used as a dungeon. From there you have a spectacular view of the town and surrounding hills. The roofs are flat, the older ones covered with a dark gray shale that has splendid insulating properties. The house walls and roofs are interconnected, forming a pattern that from above looks like a magnified form of cuneiform writing. Here and there the shieldlike roof of a church stands out from the cubist composition of white houses that fills the hillside—with not an inch to spare.

Most commercial activity takes place in or near the agora (the market street), familiarly known as Sisifos, as in the myth, because of its frustrating steepness. Found here are the town's pharmacies, travel agencies, shops with wonderful Skyrian pottery, and an extraordinary number of tiny bars and tavernas but few boutiques and even less kitsch. In the summer heat, all shops and restaurants close from 2 PM to 6 PM, but the town comes alive at night.

★ The best way to get an idea of the town and its history is to follow the sinuous cobbled lanes past the mansions of the old town to the *kastro,* the highest point, and the 10th-century fortified **Monastery of St. George,** which stands on the site of the ancient acropolis and Bronze Age settlement. Little remains of the legendary fortress of King Lykomedes, portrayed in Skyros's two most colorful myths, though lower down on the north and southwest face of the rock are the so-called Pelagian bastions of immense rectangular fitted blocks, dated to the classical period or later.

MYTHIC SKYROS

In the legends of The *Iliad*, before the Trojan War, Theseus, the deposed hero-king of Athens, sought refuge in his ancestral estate on Skyros. King Lykomedes, afraid of the power and prestige of Theseus, took him up to the acropolis one evening, pretending to show him the island, and pushed him over the cliff—an ignominious end. In ancient times, Timon of Athens unearthed what he said were Theseus's bones and sword, and placed them in the Theseion—more commonly called the Temple of Hephaistion—in Athens, in what must be one of the earliest recorded archaeological investigations.

A white marble lion, which may be left over from the Venetian occupation, is in the wall above the entrance to the monastery. This classical symbol is a reminder of when Skyros was under Athenian dominion and heavily populated with Athenian settlers to keep it that way. This part of the castle was built on ancient foundations (look right) during the early Byzantine era and reinforced in the 14th century by the Venetians. The monastery itself was founded in 962 and radically rebuilt in 1600. Today it is inhabited by a sole monk.

5

Unfortunately, the once splendid frescoes of the Monastery of St. George are now mostly covered by layers of whitewash, but look for the charming St. George and startled dragon outside to the left of the church door. Within, the ornate iconostasis is considered a masterpiece. The icon of St. George on the right is said to have been brought by settlers from Constantinople, who came in waves during the iconoclast controversy of the 9th century. The icon has a black face and is familiarly known as Ayios Georgis o Arapis ("the Negro"); the Skyrians view him as the patron saint not only of their island but of lovers as well. ✉*1 km (½ mi) above waterfront.*

Take the vaulted passageway from St. George's Monastery courtyard to the ruined church of **Episkopi,** the former seat of the bishop of Skyros, built in 895 on the ruins of a temple of Athena. This was the center of Skyros's religious life from 1453 to 1837. You can continue up to the summit from here. ✉*Above St. George's Monastery.*

The tiny **archaeological museum** (on the way to Magazia beach as you begin to descend from the town) contains finds, mostly from graves dating from Neolithic to Roman times. Weapons, pottery, and jewelry are represented. ✉*Rupert Brooke Sq. (at far end of Sisifos)* ☎*22220/91327* 🎫*€2* ⏲*Tues.–Sun. 8:30–3.*

★ The **Faltaits Historical and Folklore Museum** has an outstanding collection of Skyrian decorative arts. Built after independence by a wealthy family who still owns it, the house is far larger than the usual Skyros dwelling, and it's almost overflowing with rare books, costumes, photographs, paintings, ceramics, local embroideries, Greek statues, and other heirlooms. The embroideries are noted for their flamboyant colors and vivacious renderings of mermaids, hoopoes (the Skyrians' favorite bird), and human figures whose clothes and limbs sprout flowers. A handwritten copy of the Proclamation of the Greek Revolution against the Ottoman Empire is among the museum's historical documents. The informative guided tour is well worth the extra euros. ✉*Rupert Brooke Sq.* ☎*22220* *€2; tour €5* ⏲*Daily 10–2 and 6–9.*

It'd be hard to miss the classical bronze statue, *To Brooke,* dedicated to the English poet Rupert Brooke. Every street seems to lead either to it or to the kastro, and the statue stands alone with a 180-degree view of the sea behind it. In 1915, Brooke was 28, on his way to the Dardanelles to fight in World War I when he died of septicemia on a French hospital ship off Skyros. Brooke was a socialist, but he became something of a paragon for war leaders such as Churchill. ✉*Rupert Brooke Sq.*

BEACH

Around the northern end of the island is a dirt road to **Theotokos** (✉*15 km [9 mi] northwest of Skyros town*). The large Greek air base near the northern tip of the beach is off-limits.

WHERE TO STAY & EAT

$–$$ ✕ **Margetis Taverna.** A vest-pocket taverna wedged in among shops on the main drag, Margetis is known locally as the best place for fish on the island. It's popular, so get here early (8–8:30). Though fish and lobster are always pricey, they are worth it here, as is the roast pork loin, lamb, or goat chops. Try the flavorful barrel wine, sit outside under the big tree, and watch the folks walk by. ✉*Agora* ☎*22220/91311* 💳*No credit cards* ⏲*No lunch.*

¢–$ ★ ✕ **Papous Ki'Ego.** "My Grandfather and I," as the name translates in English, serves terrific Greek cuisine in an eclectic dining room decorated with hanging spoons, bottles of wine and ouzo, and whole heads of garlic. The proud grandson suggests that diners order a selection of mezedes and share with others at the table. The best include fried pumpkins with yogurt, tzatziki, zucchini croquettes, and meatballs doused with ouzo and served flambé. If you want a single dish, the baby goat served as a casserole tastes delicious. ✉*Agora* ☎*22220/93200* 💳*MC, V* ⏲*Closed Nov. and Dec. No lunch.*

$$–$$$ Fodor'sChoice ★ ✕🏨 **Nefeli.** This superb little hotel is decorated in Cycladic white and soft green trim, with a dazzling pool and elegant bar terrace. The three buildings reflect unique styles, including modern, traditional, and antique, and the guest rooms have handsome furniture and sophisticated amenities. The suites come with hydro-massage baths. Nefeli's restaurant ($–$$) serves organic food from its own local farm, with outstanding service; breakfast is served à la carte. The hotel is about a five-minute walk from the town center and the beach. ✉*Plageiá, 34007* ☎*22220/91964, 22220/92060, or 22220/91481* 📠*22220/92061* 🌐*www.skyros-nefeli.gr* 🛏*4 apartments, 7 studios, 8 rooms, 2 suites* *In-room: kitchen (some), refrigerator. In-hotel: restaurant, bar, pool, no elevator* 💳*AE, DC, MC, V.*

NIGHTLIFE

Skyros town's bars are seasonal affairs, offering loud music in summer. **Apokalypsis** (✉*Next to post office*) plays hits from the '60s and '70s. Jazz and blues are the standards at **Calypso** (✉*Agora*), the oldest bar-club.

At **Rodon** (✉*Agora*), the owner, Takis, is also the DJ spinning the best tunes in town. **Stone** (✉*South of Skyros town*) is popular with the disco crowd.

SHOPPING

Want to buy something really unusual for a shoe lover? Check out the multi-thong *trohadia,* worn with pantaloons by Skyrian men as part of their traditional costume. Just as unique, Skyrian pottery and Skyrian furniture are famous around the country. The pottery is both utilitarian and decorative, and the distinctive wooden furniture is easily recognizable by its traditional carved style. Although you will see it all over town, the best places to shop are all on the agora. Skyrian furniture can be shipped anywhere. Don't try to shop between 2 and 6 PM, as all stores close for siesta.

5

CLOTHING You can find the conversation-stopping trohadia at the **Argo Shop** (✉*Off Rupert Brooke Sq.* ☎*No phone*).

FURNITURE The workshop of **Lefteris Avgoklouris** (✉*About 100 yds from Rupert Brooke Sq. on right side of road heading down hill* ☎*22220/91106*), a carpenter with flair, is open to visitors. Ask around to find other master carpenters and craftspersons who make original furniture and other artistic handicrafts.

POTTERY The best store selling Skyrian handmade ceramics and imports is **Ergastiri** (✉*Agora* ☎*22220/91559*).

MAGAZIA & MOLOS ΜΑΓΑΖΙΑ & ΜΩΛΟΣ

1 km (½ mi) northeast of Skyros town.

Coastal expansions of the main town, these two resort areas are the places to stay if you love to swim. Magazia, where the residents of Horio used to have their storehouses and wine presses, and Molos, a bit farther north, where the small fishing fleet anchors, are both growing fast. You can sunbathe, explore the isolated coastline, and stop at sea caves for a swim. Nearby are rooms to rent and tavernas serving the day's catch and local wine. From here, Skyros town is only 15 minutes away, along the steps that lead past the archaeological museum to Rupert Brooke Square.

At the August 15 **Panagia** *(Festival of the Virgin)* on the beach at Magazia, children race on the island's domesticated small ponies, similar to Shetland ponies.

BEACHES

From **Molos** to **Magazia** is a long, sandy beach. A short walk south of Magazia, **Pourias** offers good snorkeling, and nearby on the cape is a small treasure: a sea cave turned into a chapel. North of Molos, past low hills, fertile fields, and the odd farmhouse, a dirt road leads to the beach at **Palamari.**

WHERE TO STAY

$–$$ **Perigiali.** Unlike other options in this area, Perigiali has many of the comforts of home and a few that home may be lacking—like private terraces and a pretty, verdant garden with plenty of shade, where you can relax over breakfast or drinks in summer. Located near Magazia beach, the accommodations are simple, and simply decorated with traditional touches. Breakfast isn't included, but fridges and cookers in rooms mean you can prep your own with a trip to the nearby minimarket. ✉ *On the beachfront at the foot of Skyros town 34007Magazia* ☎ *22220/91889 or 22220/92075* 🖷 *22220/92770* 🌐 *www.perigiali.com* *12 rooms* *In-room: refrigerator. In-hotel: restaurant, pool, no elevator* 💳 *AE, MC, V.*

$–$$ **Skiros Palace.** With a big freshwater pool and a gorgeous, isolated beach, this is a water lover's dream. Separate white, low-rise cubist buildings have arched windows and flat roofs. Rooms decorated with traditional Aegean furnishings offer simple wood beds, chairs, desks, and verandas; upstairs rooms also have air-conditioning. ✉ *North of Molos, 34007Girismata, Kambos* ☎ *22220/91994 or 22220/92212* 🖷 *22220/92070* 🌐 *www.skiros-palace.gr* *80 rooms* *In-room: no a/c (some), refrigerator, no TV. In-hotel: restaurant, pool, no elevator* 💳 *AE, MC, V* ⏲ *Closed Oct.–June* *CP.*

NIGHTLIFE

For late-night dancing, the best club is **Skiropoulo** (✉ *On beach before Magazia* ☎ *No phone* ⏲ *Closed Oct.–Apr.*). Music is Western at first and later on, Greek. A laser lighting system illuminates the rocks of the acropolis after the sun has gone down. The club can be reached from Rupert Brooke Square by descending the steps past the archaeological museum.

ATSITSA ΑΤΣΙΤΣΑ

14 km (9 mi) west of Molos.

On the northwest coast, pine forests grow down the rocky shore at Atsitsa. The beaches north of town—Kalogriá and Kyra Panagia—are sheltered from the strong northern winds called the *meltemi.*

The road south from Atsitsa deteriorates into a rutted track, nerve-wracking even for experienced motorbike riders. If you're feeling fit and the weather's good, however, consider the challenging 6-km (4-mi) trek around the headland to **Ayios Fokas** (✉ *5 km [3 mi] south of Atsitsa*). There are three lovely white-pebbled beaches and a small taverna where Kyria Kali serves her husband's just-caught fish with her own vegetables, homemade cheese, and bread. She also rents out a couple of very basic rooms without electricity or plumbing.

On July 27, the chapel of **Ayios Panteleimon** (⊠*On dirt road south of Atsitsa*) holds a festival in honor of its patron saint.

Skyros Centre, founded in 1978, was the first and remains the foremost center in Europe for holistic vacations. Participants come for a two-week session, staying in straw huts or in the main building, all surrounded by pines and facing the sea, and can take part in activities as diverse as windsurfing, creative writing with well-known authors, art, tai chi, yoga, massage, dance, drama, and psychotherapy. Courses also take place in Skyros town, where participants live in villagers' traditional houses. Skyros Centre's courses are highly reputed. Contact the London office well in advance of leaving for Greece. ⊠*Atsitsa coast* *Prince of Wales road 92, LondonNW5 3NE, U.K.* ☎*207/267–4424 or 207/284–3065* *207/284–3063* *www.skyros.co.uk*.

THE WAY THE WIND BLOWS

As of this writing, government and conservationists are locked in battle over putting a 100-turbine wind farm in the island's barren southeast. While the government sees it as a means to increase the country's sustainable energy sources, conservationists say it could be the death knell for the rare Skyrian horses and bird species that live there.

5

EN ROUTE

All boats and hydrofoils to Skyros dock at the tiny port of **Linaria** (⊠*18 km [11 mi] southeast of Atsitsa, 10 km [6 mi] south of Skyros town*) because the northeast coast is either straight, sandy beach, or steep cliffs. A bus to Skyros town meets arrivals. To get to the otherwise inaccessible sea caves of Pentekáli and Diatryptí, you can take a caïque from here. This dusty area offers scenes of fishermen tending their bright-yellow nets and not much more.

VOUNO ΒΟΥΝΟ

Via Loutro, 5 km (3 mi) northwest of Linaria; access to southern territory starts at Ahilli, 4 km (2½ mi) south of Skyros town and 25 km (15 ½ mi) from Atsitsa.

In the mountainous southern half of Skyros, a passable dirt road heads south at the eastern end of the isthmus, from Aspous to Ahilli. The little bay of Ahilli (from where legendary Achilles set sail with Odysseus) is a yacht marina. Some beautiful, practically untouched beaches and sea caves are well worth the trip for hard-core explorers.

Thorny bushes warped into weird shapes, oleander, and rivulets running between sharp rocks make up the landscape; only goats and Skyrian ponies can survive this desolate environment. Many scholars consider the beautifully proportioned, diminutive horses to be the same breed as the horses sculpted on the Parthenon frieze. They are, alas, an endangered species, and only about 100 survive.

Pilgrims to **Rupert Brooke's grave** should follow the wide dirt road through the Vouno wilderness down toward the shore. As you reach the valley, you can catch sight of the grave in an olive grove on your left. He was buried the same night he died on Skyros, and his marble grave was immortalized with his prescient words, "If I should die think only this of me:/ That there's some corner of a foreign field/ That is forever England." Restored by the British Royal Navy in 1961, the grave site is surrounded by a stout wrought-iron and cement railing. You also can arrange for a visit by taxi or caïque in Skyros town.

BEACHES

The beach of **Kalamitsa** is 4 km (2½ mi) along the road south from Ahilli. Three tavernas are at this old harbor. The inviting, deserted **Kolymbada** beach is 5 km (3 mi) south of Kalamitsa.

SPORADES ESSENTIALS

TRANSPORTATION

BY AIR

CARRIERS Olympic Airways flies daily in summer to Skiathos from Athens International Airport. The trip takes 50 minutes; the fare is €65 one way. In summer there are also weekly Olympic Airways flights from Athens to Skyros Airport. The flight takes 35 minutes; the fare is €40 one way. Skopelos has no air service.

Contact **Olympic Airways** (*☎80111/44444 within Greece, 210/966-6666 in Athens ⊕www.olympicairlines.gr*).

AIRPORTS Skiathos Airport handles direct charter flights from many European cities.

Contacts **Athens International Airport** (*✉Spata ☎210/353-0000*). **Skiathos Airport** (*✉1 km [½ mi] northeast of Skiathos town ☎24270/22049 or 24270/23300*). **Skyros Airport** (*✉11 km [7 mi] northwest of Skyros town ☎22220/91600*).

BY BOAT & FERRY

Ferry travel to Skiathos and Skopelos requires that you drive or take a bus to Agios Konstantinos, located a couple of hours north of Athens, near Volos. Altogether, there are at least two or three ferries per day (regular, or the fast Flying Dolphin hydrofoils) in summer from Agios Konstantinos to Skiathos and Skopelos; fewer in winter. There are also some ferries from Volos and Thessaloniki. For all ferries, it's best to call a travel agency (Alonissos Travel for Thessaloniki and Agios Konstantinos, Vlaikos Travel for Volos and Agios Konstantinos) ahead of time to check schedules and prices, which change seasonally. Tickets are available from several travel agents on the dock. The fast ferry from Agios Konstantinos costs €23 to Skiathos and takes one hour; the fare is higher to continue on to Skopelos (€27). The regular ferry takes twice as long and costs half as much.

Getting to Skyros is equally tricky. You must drive or take a bus to Kimi—on the large Sporades island of Evia—and then catch one of the two daily ferries, or the weekly hydrofoil, to Skyros. You can buy ferry tickets at the Kimi dock when you get off the bus; the trip to Skyros takes two hours and costs €8.30. Should you choose to book your return when you get to Skyros, note that Skyros Travel *(⇨ Tour Options)* has a virtual monopoly on hydrofoil tickets.

BETWEEN THE ISLANDS Regular ferries connect Skiathos and Skopelos; between Skyros and the other Sporades there is no regular boat service. The once-per-week Flying Dolphin hydrofoil that travels from Kimi, on the large nearby island of Evia, to all the Sporades is by far the quicker, more reliable way to travel between the islands. Because schedules change frequently, check the times listed outside travel agencies in each of the port towns; the agents sell tickets. Connecting through Kimi is the easiest way to get between Skyros and the other islands (the alternative is to fly through Athens).

ON THE ISLANDS On all islands, caïques leave from the main port for the most popular beaches, and interisland excursions are made between Skiathos and Skopelos. You can also hire a caïque (haggle over the price) to tour around the islands; they are generally the preferred way to get around by day. For popular routes, captains have signs posted showing their destinations and departure times. On Skyros, check with Skyros Travel for caïque tours.

Contacts **Flying Dolphin** (☎ *21041/99000* 🌐 *www.hellenicseaways.gr*). **Port Authority** (☎ *22350/31759 in Agios Konstantinos, 22220/22606 in Kimi, 24270/22017 in Skiathos town, 24240/22180 in Skopelos town, 22220/91475 in Skyros town*).

Vlaikos Travel (☎ *24240/65220*).

BY BUS

From central Athens, buses to Agios Konstantinos, the main port for the Sporades (except Skyros), cost €11.50 and take about 2½ hours. Buses from Athens to Kimi, on Evia island (the only port where boats depart for Skyros), cost €11 and take 2½ hours. For those connecting to Agios Konstantinos from Halkidha, on Evia island, the bus costs €8 and takes 1½ hours. Check the **KTEL** (🌐 *www.ktel.org*) site for schedules.

Buses on Skiathos leave Skiathos town to make the beach run as far as Koukounaries every 30 minutes from early morning until 11:30 PM. Buses on Skopelos run six times a day from Skopelos town to Glossa and Loutraki, stopping at the beaches. Skyros buses carry ferry passengers between Linaria and Horio, stopping in Molos in summer.

Information **Athens to Agios Konstantinos** (☎ *210/831–7147 in Athens*). **Athens to Skyros** (☎ *210/831–7163 in Athens*). **Ceres Lines bus** (☎ *210/428–0001 in Piraeus*). **KTEL bus station** (☎ *22210/22026 in Halkidha*).

CLOSE UP

Paradise Found: The Pelion Peninsula

An incredibly charming landscape of stone churches, elegant houses adorned with rose arbors, and storybook town squares lies across the water from Skiathos on the mainland, about 320 km (200 mi) northeast of Athens.

The Pelion peninsula—three hours by ferry or 1½ hrs by hydrofoil traveling east of Skiathos town—looms large in myth and legend. Jason and the Argonauts are said to have embarked from the port of ancient Iolkos, once set opposite modern Volos, on the northwestern tip of the peninsula, to make good a vague claim to the Golden Fleece.

Mt. Pelion, still thickly wooded with pine, cypress, and fruit trees, was the home of the legendary Centaurs, those half-man–half-horse beings notorious for lasciviousness and drunkenness. Here, too, on a cypress-clad hill overlooking Volos, was the site of the wedding banquet of the nymph Peleus and the mortal Thetis. Uninvited, the goddess of discord, Eris, flung a golden apple between Athena and Aphrodite, asking Prince Paris of Troy to decide who was the fairest (and thereby giving Homer one heck of a plot).

Today the peninsula is much more peaceful, dotted with no fewer than 24 lovely villages. As you leave Volos (having explored its waterfront esplanade and splendid archaeological museum), you ascend along serpentine roads into the cooler mountains, enjoying great views over Volos Bay.

Some roads wind down to beautiful white-sand or round-stone beaches, such as Horefto and Milopotamos. Nestled among the forests are villages such as Tsangarades, Milies (with the beautifully frescoed Ag Taxiarchis church), and Vyzitsa, while high above Volos is exquisite Portaria, whose kokkineli (fresh red wine) has to be consumed on the spot, as it does not stand up well to transport.

Neither visitors nor locals complain of this. Separated from Portaria by a deep ravine is Makrynitsa, incredibly rich in local color. The village square is straight out of fairyland: the large, paved terrace overhangs the town and gulf below, yet feels intimate thanks to a backdrop of huge plane trees that shade a small Byzantine church and a lulling fountain.

Most of the Pelion villages have archetypal Greek houses—replete with bay windows, stained glass, and ornamentation—whose elegance cannot be bettered.

To get to Pelion from Skiathos by car, take the three-hour ferry down to Volos; you can also board the hydrofoil and rent a car in Pelion. There is daily train service to Volos from Athens's Stathmos Larissa station (this ride takes six hours).

For information on the Pelion peninsula and accommodations in the lovely government-renovated village inns, contact the **EOT** (✉ *Riga Fereous, Volos* ☎ *24210/23500* ⏲ *open weekdays 7–2:30*).

BY CAR

To get to Skiathos and Skopelos by car you must drive to the port of Agios Konstantinos (Agios) and from there take the ferry. The drive to Agios from Athens takes about two hours. For high-season travel you might have to reserve a place on the car ferry a day ahead.

For Skyros you must leave from the port of Kimi on the big Sporades island of Evia. From Athens, take the Athens–Lamia National Road to Skala Oropou and make the 30-minute ferry crossing to Eretria on Evia (every half hour in the daytime). No reservations are needed. Because it is so close to the mainland, you can skip the ferry system and drive directly to Evia over a short land bridge connecting Agios Minas on the mainland with Halkidha. From Athens, about 80 km (50 mi) away, take the National Road 1 to the Schimatari exit, and then follow the signs to Halkidha. Beware that weekend crowds can slow traffic across the bridge.

ROAD CONDITIONS The road networks on all three islands are so rudimentary that cars are not really needed, but it's not a bad idea to rent one for a day to get a feel for the island, then use the bus or a scooter thereafter. Car rentals usually cost €30–€50 per day, while scooters cost about €15–€25. Four-wheel drives, cars, scooters, and motorbikes can be rented everywhere. If you rent a scooter, however, be extra cautious: many of those for hire are in poor condition. The locals are not used to the heavy summer traffic on their narrow roads, and accidents provide the island clinics with 80% of their summer business. Check with the travel agencies for rental information.

BY TAXI

Taxis wait at the ferry landings on all the islands. They are unmetered, so negotiate your fare in advance.

CONTACTS & RESOURCES

EMERGENCIES

The most efficient way to get to a medical center is to ask a taxi driver to take you to the nearest facility. Emergency services are listed by island.

Skiathos **Tourist Police** (☎ *24270/23172 in Skiathos town*). **Medical Center** (☎ *24270/22040 in Skiathos town*).

Skopelos **Police** (☎ *24240/33333 in Glossa, 24240/22235 in Skopelos town*). **Medical Center** (☎ *24240/22222 in Skopelos town*).

Skyros **Police** (☎ *22220/91274 in Skyros town*). **Medical Center** (☎ *22220/92222 in Skyros town*).

INTERNET, MAIL & SHIPPING

Contacts **Skiathos Sixth Element Internet Café** (✉ *15 G. Panora St., across from National Bank of Greece, Skiathos town* ☎ *24270/29040* ⏲ *9 AM–2 AM*). **Skopelos Net Café** (✉ *In town, Skopelos town* ☎ *24240/23093*). **Internet Café** (✉ *In Patitiri on road going up from port toward Milia and Old Town, Alonissos town*). **Hellenic Postal Services** (✉ *3 Papadiamadi St., Skiathos town* ☎ *24270/22011*). **Hellenic**

Postal Services (✉ *Skopelos Town Center, Skopelos town* ☎ *24240/22203*). **Hellenic Postal Services** (✉ *Skyros highstreet, Skyros town* ☎ *22240/91208*). **DHL Services** (☎ *210/9890-000 in Athens, 24270/29058 in Skiathos, 22210/20004 in Evia Prefecture [Chalkida]*).

BOATING On Skiathos, small motorboats can be rented at the Marine Center. Boats can also be rented at the Marine Center in Alonissos.

Contacts **Marine Center–Skiathos** (✉ *Near airport runway* ☎ *24270/22888* 🖷 *24270/23262*).

TOUR OPTIONS

Thalpos Holidays has a number of boat excursions that start from the island of Skopelos.

Contacts **Creator Tours** (✉ *New port, Skiathos* ☎ *24270/22385 or 24270/21384* 🖷 *24270/21136*). **Madro Travel** (✉ *Waterfront, Skopelos town* ☎ *24240/22145* 🌐 *www.madrotravel.com*). **Skyros Travel** (✉ *Agora, Skyros town* ☎ *22220/91123 or 22220/91600* 🖷 *22220/92123* 🌐 *www.skyrostravel.com*). **Thalpos Holidays** (✉ *Paralia Skopelou, Skopelos town* ☎ *24240/22947* 🖷 *24240/23057* 🌐 *www.holidayislands.com*).

VISITOR INFORMATION

The Greek National Tourism Organization is the authority on the Sporades. Contact the tourist police in Skiathos town for information on the island. In Skopelos, try the Skopelos Municipality.

Contacts **Greek National Tourism Organization (GNTO or EOT)** (✉ *Tsoha 7, Athens* ☎ *210/870-7000* 🌐 *www.gnto.gr*). **Skiathos Municipality** (✉ *Odos Papadiamndiou, Skiathos town* ☎ *24270/22200* 🌐 *www.n-skiathos.gr*). **Skopelos Municipality** (✉ *Waterfront, Skopelos town* ☎ *24240/22205* 🌐 *www.skopelosweb.gr*). **Skyros official Web site** (🌐 *www.skyros.gr*).

Epirus & Thessaly

IOANNINA, METSOVO & THE METEORA MONASTERIES

Fetiche Mosque (Fetihe Tzani) in Ioannina. Epirus, Greece

WORD OF MOUTH

"Our hotel room faced the medieval monoliths of Meteora and we awoke to a fabulous mist-covered view. I kept going out on the balcony to see the changes as the fog would drift in and out, giving you glimpses of the previously hidden monasteries. Don't miss it!"

—newcomer

www.fodors.com/forums

WELCOME TO EPIRUS & THESSALY

TOP REASONS TO GO

★ **Rock Stars:** Even more wondrous than the Meteora's soaring rock pinnacles are the medieval monasteries perched atop them—walk, climb, or drive to these still-inhabited spots where eagles once nested.

★ **Connect with the Gods:** Visiting the ancient site of Dodona in Epirus is a must: many a mystical ceremonies took place in this ancient sanctuary of Zeus.

★ **Experience Metsovo's Traditions:** This mountain village has held on hard to its traditional character—discover its stone houses, customary foods, and winding alleyways (each with its own story).

★ **Haunts of Ali Pasha:** Even Lord Byron was drawn to Ioannina to trace the haunted spirit of the legendary pasha who once made Epirus his own personal potentate.

1 Ioannina. Strongly infused by the influences of Greeks, Jews, and Turks, Ioannina rests on the banks of Lake Pamvotis. Picturesquely medieval and founded by the Emperor Justinian in 527, the town is shadowed by two historic mosques, which reflect the area's marked Asiatic character. While it has an extensive, multicultural history, Ioannina also has a vibrant modern scene.

2 Metsovo. Studded with traditional houses filled with Epirote arts and crafts, this mountain township in famously inhabited by Vlachous who speak their distinct dialect. After visiting the noted Tositsa Museum, head to the hills for an idyllic skiing vacation, nature walks, or wine tours.

Above, Folkloric Museum, Ambelakia. Left, Roussanou Monastery, Meteora.

GETTING ORIENTED

Travelers in search of wild and romantic country will be more than delighted with these two regions of northern Greece. In the markedly Balkan region of Epirus, the route east from Ioannina leads to the thriving traditional village of Metsovo and over the Katara Pass on one of the most dramatic roads in Greece. Westward lies the fertile province of Thessaly, where spectacular rock-pinnacle monasteries are shadowed by the Pindus, Plion, and Olympus mountain ranges.

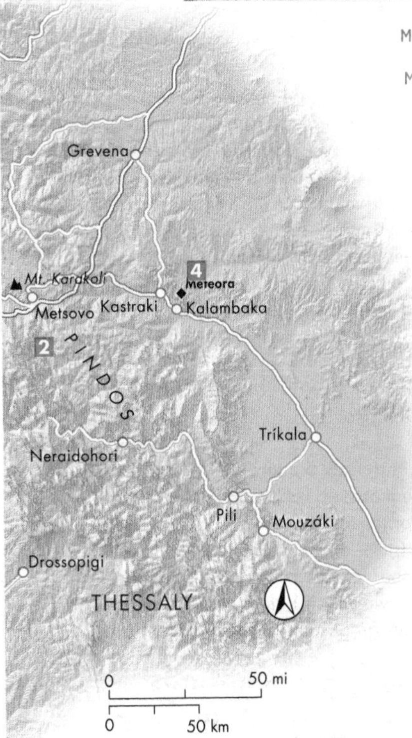

3 Dodona. Mentioned by Homer in the tenth book of the *Iliad*, the Dodona Oracle once presided here, only eclipsed by Delphi in classical times. View the remains of the sanctuary of Zeus and the majestic ancient theater, which once held 17,000 spectators, and still the venue of Greek drama presentations.

4 Meteora. Looming out of the edge of Thessaly's main plain, the sky-kissing medieval monasteries of Meteora seem to float in midair, built atop bizarrely shaped pinnacles that tower over the town of Kalambaka. You can enjoy relaxed, fun nights in this "town near Meteora" on its central Dimoula Square, with the Meteora rocks as a dramatic backdrop.

The Epirus coast.

EPIRUS & THESSALY PLANNER

When to Go

Ioannina is easy to visit year-round, but excursions to the countryside are best May through October, when most places are open.

Winter is great for skiing and curling up by the fire, although spring, when the abundant and broadly variable natural surroundings blossom, is captivating.

Metsovo can be blissfully cool even in high summer (especially at night).

This helps make the town panagyri (saint's day festival) for Ayia Paraskevi, held July 26, quite pleasant, but the heat is oppressive elsewhere in this region at this time.

The Meteora monasteries attract considerably fewer people in winter, but keep in mind the Thessalian plain can bake during summer in the vast oven formed by the surrounding high mountains.

Maximum enjoyment will be obtained in the spring, especially at the Meteora monasteries.

At this point, the mountains are still snow covered and blend harmoniously with the green fields, the red poppies, and the white and pink fruit trees.

Get Stuffed!

With their dramatic winters, these regions are known for some of the heartiest, rib-stickingest meals around. Metsovites are particularly known for their meat specialties, such as kontosouvli (lamb or pork kebab) and boiled goat, their trahanas soup (made from cracked wheat boiled in milk and dried), and their sausages or meatballs stuffed with leeks, as well as their costly but delectable smoked Metsovone cheese. Pites (pies, or pita) are pastry envelopes filled with local and seasonal produce, from savory meats and vegetables to sweet dairy creams and honey. Head to the lakesides, most famously those in Ioannina, to feast on aquatic delights: frogs' legs, trout, eel, and crayfish. Wherever you head, Epirot restaurants generally offer an interesting blend of Greek, Turkish, and Jewish flavors usually prepared with fresh local produce. Some of their tried-and-true recipes are moschato kokkinisto (a tomato-base veal stew with carrots, onions, and peas), lamb in lemon sauce, and lathera (stove-top vegetable stew made with artichoke hearts, beans, okra, and tomatoes). And the best wine to wash it all down with is Katogi red wine pressed from French Bordeaux grapes grown locally in Metsovo.

Dining & Lodging Prices in Euros

	¢	$	$$	$$$	$$$$
Restaurants	Under €8	€8–€15	€15–€20	€20–€25	Over €25
Hotels	Under €80	€80–€120	€120–€160	€160–€200	Over €200

Restaurant prices are for one main course at dinner, or for two mezedes (small dishes). Hotel prices are for a standard double room in high season, including taxes. Hotels operate on the European Plan (EP, with no meal provided) unless we note that they use the Continental Plan (CP, with Continental breakfast); Breakfast Plan (BP, with a full breakfast); Modified American Plan (MAP, with breakfast and dinner); or the Full American Plan (FAP, with all meals). Inquire when booking if these meal plans (which can entail higher rates) are mandatory. Guest rooms have air-conditioning, room phones, and TVs unless otherwise noted.

Finding a Place to Stay

Rooms are usually easy to find in Ioannina and, except at the best hotels, are simply decorated. Reservations might be necessary for Kalambaka, which is packed with tour groups to the Meteora monasteries in late spring and summer, and in Metsovo during ski season or the town's July 26 festival. In these two towns, private rooms are likely to be far cheaper than comparable hotel rooms—look for advertisements as you arrive. Off-season, prices drop drastically from those listed here, and you should always try to negotiate. In some cases, prices will skyrocket for Greek Easter and Christmas. In Epirus, most small hotels are built in the charming and traditional style—usually recognizable by the heavy use of wood and stone, most suited to the cold winter months, when these accommodations make the perfect base for skiing, hiking, and other activities.

Fancy Footwork

In Epirus, local tourist offices and most hotels will provide information about festivals, including the famous Ioannina International Folk Festival (at the Theatro tis Eterias Ipirotcon Meleton) showcasing the region's music and dancing, which takes place in July. For those seeking the haunting traditional klarino (clarinet) music and graceful circle dances of Epirus such as the pogonisios and beratis, this is a fascinating event. Local groups also perform eerie polyphonic singing, another unique folk tradition rooted in the region.

Getting There

Ioannina is a 70-minute flight from Athens and a 50-minute flight from Thessaloniki. From June through August, Olympic Airlines usually has two or three flights daily from Athens to Ioannina. About nine buses a day make the seven-hour trip from Athens's Terminal A (Kifissou) to Ioannina's main Zosimadon station. From Athens's miserable Terminal B (Liossion), seven buses leave daily for the five-hour journey to Kalambaka (Meteora). Most routes require you to hop on a different bus for the final leg from Trikala, but one morning bus goes direct. Around three KTEL buses leave Ioannina daily for Metsovo (about one hour) and two buses for Kalambaka (two hours); frequencies are the same in the opposite direction.

Getting Around

Local buses within the regions are usually on time, clean, air-conditioned, and cheap to travel in.

Since most of the distances between towns are quite considerable, taxis are on the expensive side.

A rented car is by far the best way to explore the region, and one is essential to go beyond the main sights.

Driving to Kalambaka or Ioannina from Athens takes the greater part of a day.

The road from Ioannina to Metsovo to Kalambaka is one of the most scenic in northern Greece.

However, it traverses the famous Katara Pass, which is curvy and possibly hazardous.

This is especially the case December through March (snow chains are necessary).

To reach Ioannina by car take the National Road west past Corinth in the Peloponnese, crossing the magnificent Rion–Antirion bridge.

For Kalambaka, take the National Road north past Thebes; north of Lamia there's a turnoff for Trikala and Kalambaka.

Updated by
Adrian Vrettos

STARK MOUNTAINS, LUSH FORESTS, SWIFT RIVERS, and remote villages marked with unique customs, language, and architecture distinguish the province of Epirus, which is bordered by Albania and the Ionian Sea. Epirus means "the mainland," standing in contrast to the neighboring islands of Corfu, Paxi, and Lefkada, strung along the coast. The land changes abruptly from the delicately shaded green of the idyllic olive and orange groves near the shore to the tremendous solidity of the bare mountains inland. This was the splendid massive landscape that came to cast its spell over Lord Byron, who traveled here to meet tyrant Sinan Ali Pasha (1741–1822). The Epirote capital of Ioannina still bears many vestiges of this larger-than-life figure, who seems to have stepped from the pages of *The Arabian Nights*.

Going back in time, and taking an easy trip southwest of Ioannina, you can visit Dodona, the site of the oldest oracle in Greece. North of Ioannina, in the mountainous region known as Zagorohoria, or the Zagori, dozens of tiny, unspoiled villages contain remnants of the Ottoman period, and outdoor activities such as hiking are abundant. The route east from Ioannina leads to the thriving traditional village of Metsovo in the Pindos mountains and over the Katara pass on one of the most dramatic roads in Greece. It ends in the fertile province of Thessaly, where, on the edge of the plain, the Byzantine-era monasteries of Meteora seem to float in midair, built atop bizarrely shaped pinnacles that tower over the town of Kalambaka. At this spiritual center of Orthodox Greece, the quiet contemplation of generations of monks is preserved in wondrously frescoed buildings. Nearby, spectacular mountain passes reveal shepherd villages with richly costumed women speaking the Vlach vernacular.

All in all, northwestern Greece, which stretches from the northern shore of the Gulf of Corinth to the Albanian frontier west of the Pindos range, was aroused from its centuries-old slumber several decades ago with the advent of the ferryboats from Italy. The nautical crossing from Corfu to Igoumenitsa, the westward gateway town to mainland Greece, is enchanting, with the lush green of the island slowly receding and the stark outlines of the mainland dramatically ahead. The bay is at its best in the early morning, but sunset will do, when the gray rocks likewise flame with deep pinks and violets in an unforgettable welcome. Igoumenitsa is generally unappealing as a port of entry, which means everyone quickly pushes on into the interior and discovers the often-overlooked wonders of Epirus and Thessaly.

EXPLORING EPIRUS & THESSALY

The region consists of two areas: the mountainous province of Epirus, with appealing traditional villages such as Metsovo and its lakeside capital, Ioannina, to the west; and the Thessalian plain, an agricultural heartland with the Meteora at its edge. The mountainous Zagorohoria region, north of Ioannina in Epirus, is becoming very popular for its access to outdoor activities and for its stone-built towns, which have fine examples of Ottoman architecture. In Thessaly, what was once a

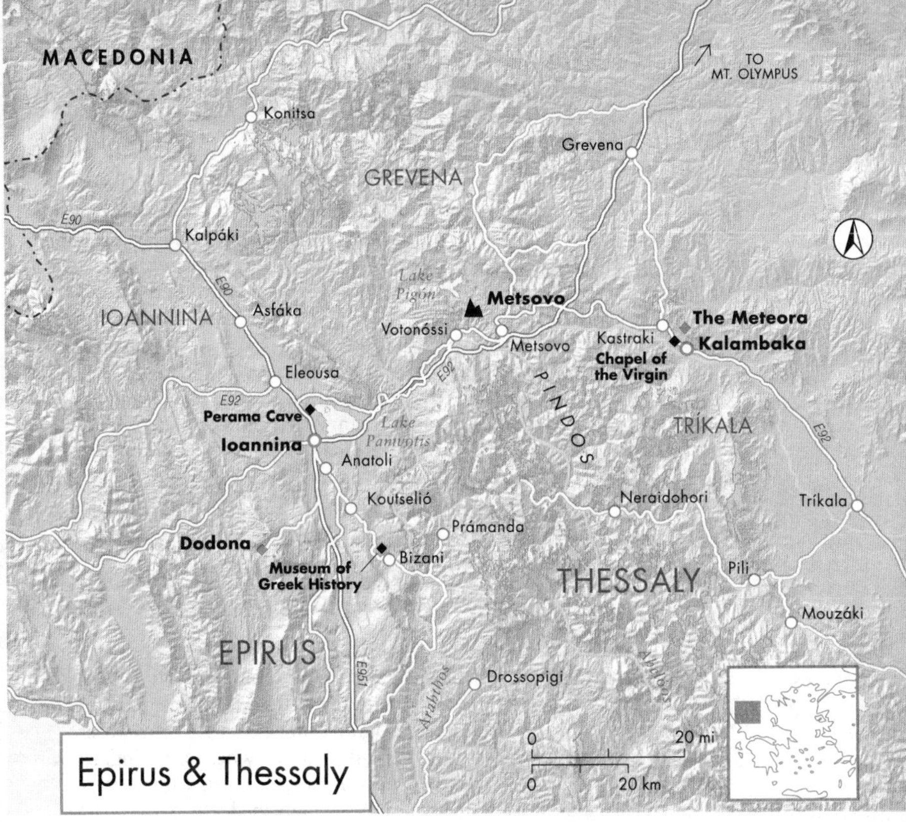

Epirus & Thessaly

lake is now a large, open, fertile plain with cotton, apples, and cherries among other produce cultivated in abundance. In contrast to most of the Thessalian landscape, the area around Kalambaka and the monasteries of the Meteora is rugged and steep.

EPIRUS ΗΠΕΙΡΟΣ

Ipiros (Epirus) fully justifies its name, continent, by an overwhelming concentration of mountains, contrasting with the islands—Corfu, Paxi, Lefkada—strung along its littoral. The abrupt changes from the delicately shaded green of the idyllic olive groves on the coast to the tremendous solidity of the bare mountains have been faithfully depicted by that versatile Victorian, Edward Lear (of limerick fame). But few travelers would nowadays put up with the discomfort, hardship, and very real danger from bandits that Lear seems to have enjoyed. The scenery has kept its grandeur, but has become easily accessible by a good road network, provided with plenty of hotels.

Ancient Epirus was once a huge country that stretched from modern-day Albania (an area the Greeks still call northern Epirus and one in which Greek is still spoken by large communities) to the Gulf of Arta and modern Preveza. The region is bordered by the Ionian Sea to the west, the islands of Lefkada to the south, and Corfu to the north. Inland it is defined by a tangle of mountain peaks and upland plains, and the climate is markedly Balkan.

Although invaded by Normans in 1080, Epirus gained in importance after the influx of refugees from Constantinople and the Morea beginning in 1205 and was made a despotate, a principality ruled by a despot. Ioannina was subsequently made the capital of Epirus and fortified by Michalis Angelos, the first despot. After an invasion by Serbs, Ioannina surrendered to the Ottomans in 1431 and Epirus remained a part of its empire until it became part of Greece in 1913. Besides this great Turkish influence, Metsovo and the surrounding area contain the largest concentration of the non-Greek population known as the Vlachs, nomadic shepherds said to be descendants of legionnaires from garrisons on the Via Egnatia, one of the Roman Empire's main east–west routes. The Vlachs speak a Romance language related to Italian and Romanian.

IOANNINA ΙΩΑΝΝΙΝΑ

305 km (189 mi) northwest of Athens, 204 km (126 mi) west-southwest of Thessaloniki.

On the rocky promontory of Lake Pamvotis lies Ioannina, its fortress punctuated by mosques and minarets whose reflections, along with those of the snowy peaks of the Pindos range, appear in the calm water. The lake contains tiny Nissi, or "small island," where nightingales still sing and fishermen mend their nets. Although on first impression parts of the city may seem noisy and undistinguished, the old quarter preserves a rich heritage. Outstanding examples of folk architecture remain within the castle walls, and in the neighborhoods surrounding them; Ioannina's historic mansions, folk houses, seraglios, and bazaars are a reminder of the city's illustrious past. Set at a crossroads of trading, the city is sculpted by Balkan, Ottoman, and Byzantine influences. Thanks to a resident branch of the Greek national university, today the lively provincial capital city (population 100,000) has a thriving contemporary cultural scene (and a proliferation of good restaurants and lively bars). Things get particularly lively the first two weeks of July, when the city's International Folk Festival takes place.

The name Ioannina was first documented in 1020 and may have been taken from an older monastery of St. John. Founded by Emperor Justinian in AD 527, Ioannina suffered under many rulers: it was invaded by the Normans in 1082, made a dependency of the Serbian kingdom in 1345, and conquered by the Turks in 1431. Above all, this was Ali Pasha's city, where, during its zenith, from 1788 to 1821, the despot carved a fiefdom from much of western Greece. His territory extended from the Ionian Sea to the Pindos range and from Vaona in the north to Arta in the south. The Turks ended his rule in 1821 by using deception to capture him; Ali Pasha was then shot and decapitated.

One of Ioannina's main attractions is the **Kastro** *(Castle)*, with massive, fairly intact stone walls that once dropped into the lake on three sides; Ali Pasha completely rebuilt them in 1815. The city's once-large Romaniote Jewish population, said to date from the time of Alexander the Great, lived within the walls, alongside Turks and Christians. The Jews were deported by the Nazis during World War II, to meet their deaths at extermination camps; of the 4,000-odd inhabitants around the turn of the 20th century, fewer than 100 remain today. The area inside the walls is now a quiet residential area. Outside the citadel walls, near the lake, a **monument** at Karamanli and Soutsou streets commemorates the slaughter of the Jewish community. ✉ *Lakeside end of Odhos Averoff.*

The collections in the remarkably well-preserved **Aslan Mosque,** now the **Municipal Museum,** recall the three communities (Greek, Turkish, Jewish) that lived together inside the fortress from 1400 to 1611. The vestibule has recesses for shoes, and inscribed over the doorway is the name of Aslan Pasha and THERE IS ONLY ONE GOD, ALLAH, AND MUHAMMED IS HIS PROPHET. The mosque retains its original decoration and *mihrab,* a niche that faces Mecca. Exhibited around the room are a walnut-and-mother-of-pearl table from Ali Pasha's period, ornate inlaid *hamam* (Turkish bath) shoes on tall wooden platforms, clothes chests, and a water pipe. There is also a collection of 18th- and 19th-century guns. ✉ *North end of citadel* ☎ *26510/26356* 🎫 *€4.50* ⏲ *Nov.–Apr., daily 8–3; May–Oct., daily 8–7:30.*

6

Within the larger citadel is the **fortress,** called *Its Kale* by the Turks, where Ali Pasha built his palace; these days the former palace serves the city as the **Byzantine Museum.** The museum's small collection of artworks, actually almost all post-Byzantine, includes intricate silver manuscript Bible covers, wall murals from mansions, and carved wooden benediction crosses covered in lacy silver, gathered from all over the countryside of Epirus. It's carefully arranged in the front half of the museum with good English translations. The second half of the museum houses an important collection of icons and remarkable iconostases, painted by local masters and salvaged from 16th- and 17th-century monasteries. The most interesting section is devoted to silver works from Ali Pasha's treasury from the seraglio. Nearby is the **Fethiye (Victory) Mosque,** which purports to contain Ali Pasha's tomb. ✉ *Eastern corner of citadel* ☎ *26510/39580* 🎫 *€3.50* ⏲ *Nov.–Apr., Tues.–Sun. 8–5; May–Oct., Tues.–Sun. 8–7:30.*

Vestiges of 19th-century Ioannina remain in the **old bazaar.** On Anexartisias are some Turkish-era structures, such as the Liabei arcade across from the bustling municipal produce market and, on Filiti, a smattering of the copper-, tin-, and silversmiths who fueled the city's economy for centuries. Some workshops still have wares for sale. ✉ *Around citadel's gates at Ethnikis Antistasios and Averoff.*

NEED A BREAK?

Filistrou (✉ ***Andronikou Paleologou 20*** ☎ ***26510/72429*****), an intimate café on a main street near the citadel area, occupies a 200-year-old residence with a colorful folk interior with decorated ceilings. Pamper yourself with**

some of the most unique drinks in Greece. Try *salepi* and other Arab herbal drinks with a splash of alcohol, or stop by in the late evening for Metaxa brandy and a *visino* (a spoon sweet made up of black cherries preserved in syrup, eaten by the spoonful or added to a beverage). For breakfast, try the thick strained yogurt topped with chestnut-color honey and chopped walnuts. The café is open September to June, daily 11–11.

The **Archaeological Museum** is the best in the area but is, at this writing, closed for refurbishment, possibly until late 2008. Some works in the museum have been lent to museums in the area, and others are in storage. When the museum reopens, it will have multimedia technology and contemporary exhibition space. ✉*25 Martiou Sq., 45221* ☎*26510/33357, 26510/35498, 26510/25490 for updates on renovation* 🌐*www.culture.gr.*

The small **Kostas Frontzos Museum of Epirote Folk Art,** in a restored Ottoman house, has a collection of richly embroidered local costumes, rare woven textiles made by the nomadic tent-dwelling Sarakatsanis, ceramics, and cooking and farm implements. ✉*Michail Angelou 42* ☎*26510/20515 or 26510/23566* 🎫*€3* ⏲*Mon. and Wed. 9–2 and 5:30–8; Tues., Thurs., and Fri. 9–2; weekends 10–3:30.*

The waterfront **Mavili Square** is lined with smart cafés that fill with travelers having breakfast or waiting for the next boat to the nearby island. In the evening the *molos* (seawall) is *the* place to hang out—the youth of Ioannina while away the hours here over frappés or long drinks. The *volta* (ritual evening promenade) is still a favorite way of passing the time and keeping up to date with all the action and gossip, but these days people carry an added accessory—the modern *kinito* (cellular telephone). At night the area is especially gregarious, with vendors selling corn, halvah, and cassettes of Epirote clarinet music.

Lake Pamvotis remains picturesque despite the fact that the water level is so low (the streams that feed it are drying up) it's become too polluted for swimming. Still, it has the longest rowing course in Greece, and teams from all over the Balkans use it for training. The Valkaniadia rowing championships are periodically hosted here.

Look back at the outline of the citadel and its mosques in a wash of green as you take the 10-minute ride from the shore toward small **Nissi island.** The whitewashed lakeside island village was founded in the late 16th century by refugees from the Mani (in the Peloponnese). No outside recreational vehicles are allowed, and without the din of motorcycles and cars, the village seems centuries away from Ioannina. Ali Pasha once kept deer here for hunting. With its neat houses and flower-trimmed courtyards, pine-edged paths, runaway chickens, and reed-filled backwater, it's the perfect place to relax, have lunch, visit some of the monasteries (dress appropriately and carry a small flashlight to make it easier to see the magnificent frescoes), and have a pleasant dinner. Frogs' legs, eel, and carp take center stage, although traditional taverna food can also be found. ✉*Ferry below citadel, near Mavili Sq.* 🎫*Ferry €1.70* ⏲*May–Sept., ferry daily on the ½ hr 6:30*

AM–*midnight; Oct.–Apr., daily on the hr 6:30* AM–*11* PM.

THE PRETTIEST WALK

Set at the lakeside end of Odhos Averoff, tree-lined Dionyssiou Skylosofou, which circles the citadel along the lake, is ideal for a late-afternoon stroll. The street was named for a defrocked Trikala bishop who led an ill-fated uprising against the Turks in 1611 (and was flayed alive as a result). A moat, now filled, ran around the southwest landward side, and today the walls divide the old town—with its rose-laden pastel-color houses, overhanging balconies, cobblestone streets, and birdsong—from the new.

The main attraction on Nissi is the 16th-century Pandelimonos Monastery, now the **Ali Pasha Museum.** Ali Pasha was killed here in the monks' cells on January 17, 1822, after holding out for almost two years. In the final battle, Ali ran into an upstairs cell, but the soldiers shot him through its floorboards from below. (The several bullet holes in the floor were newly drilled because the floor had to be replaced.) A wax version of the assassination can be seen at the Pavlos Vrellis Museum of Greek History in Bizani, south of Ioannina. A happier Ali Pasha, asleep on the lap of his wife, Vasiliki, can be seen in the museum's famous portrait. Here also is the crypt where Vasiliki hid, some evocative etchings and paintings of that era, an edict signed by Ali Pasha with his ring seal (he couldn't write), and his magnificent narghile, a water pipe, standing on the fireplace. The community-run museum is generally open as long as boats are running; if the doors are shut, ask around to be let in. The local ticket taker will give a brief tour of the museum in Greek and broken English (supplemented by an English-language printed guide). A tour is free, but do leave a tip. ✉ *On Nissi, take left from boat landing and follow signs* ☎ *26510/81791* 🎫 *€0.80* ⏲ *Daily 8–1.*

6

Agios Nikolaos ton Filanthropinon has the best frescoes of Nissi's several monasteries. The monastery was built in the 13th century by an important Byzantine family, the Filanthropinos, and a fresco in the northern exonarthex (the outer narthex) depicts five of them kneeling before St. Nikolaos (1542). Many of the frescoes are by the Kontaris brothers, who later decorated the mighty Varlaam in Meteora. Note the similarities in the bold coloring, expressiveness, realism, and Italian influence—especially in the bloody scenes of martyrdom. Folk tradition says the corner crypts in the south chapel were the meeting places of the secret school of Hellenic culture during the Ottoman occupation. A most unusual fresco here of seven sages of antiquity, including Solon, Aristotle, and Plutarch, gives credence to this story. It is not really feasible, however, that the school would have been kept a secret from the Ottoman governors for long; more likely, the reigning Turkish pasha was one who allowed religious and cultural freedom (as long as the taxes were paid). ✉ *On island, follow signs* ☎ *No phone* 🎫 *€1* ⏲ *Daily 8–8.*

★ The **Pavlos Vrellis Museum of Greek History** displays a collection of historical Epirote figures from the past 2,500 years in more than 30 settings (streets, mountains, caves, churches, and more); look for the

CLOSE UP

The Reign of Ali Pasha

Born in the 1740s in Tepeline, Albania, Ali Pasha rose to power by unscrupulous means. The most notorious ruler of Epirus employed assassins to carry out his plots of murder and brigandage. He was made pasha of Trikala in 1787 and a year later seized Ioannina, then the largest town in Greece. For the next 33 years, Ali pursued his ambition: to break from the Ottoman Empire and create his own kingdom. He paid only token tribute to the sultan and allied himself according to his needs with the French, the British, and the Turks. In 1797 he collaborated with Napoléon; the next year he seized Preveza from the French; and by 1817 he was wooing the British and Admiral Nelson, who gave him Parga.

Historical accounts focus on the fact that he had an insatiable libido and combed the countryside looking for concubines, accumulating a harem numbering in the hundreds. He attacked the Turkish Porte ("Sublime Porte" [or gate] of the sultan's palace, where justice was administered; by extension, the Ottoman government), and he brutalized his Greek subjects. Ali's most infamous crime was perhaps the drowning of Kyra Frosini, his son's mistress, and 16 other women, by tying them in stone-laden bags and dumping them in Lake Pamvotis. Apparently, Ali was in love with Frosini, who rejected him, and, spurred on by his son's wife, he had Frosini killed on charges of infidelity. He regretted his deed and ordered that 250 pounds of sugar be thrown into the lake to sweeten the water Frosini would drink. A superstition persists that Frosini's ghost hovers over the lake on moonlit nights.

tableau of Ali Pasha's murder. All the figures were sculpted in wax by artist Pavlos Vrellis, a local legend who embarked on this endeavour at the ripe age of 60. His studio is on the premises. ✉ *11 km (7 mi) south of Ioannina, Ethnikos Odos Ioanninon–Athinon road, Bizani* ☎ *26510/92128* 🌐 *www.vrellis.org* 🎟 *€6* ⏲ *May–Oct., daily 9:30–5; Nov.–Apr., daily 10–4.*

OFF THE BEATEN PATH

Perama Cave. The cave's passageways, discovered in the early 1940s by locals hiding from the Nazis, extend for more than 1 km (½ mi) under the hills. You learn about the high caverns and multihued limestone stalagmites during the 45-minute guided tour; one begins about every 15 minutes. Printed English-language information is available. Be prepared for the many steps you must walk up on the way out. You can catch Bus 8 from Ioannina's clock tower to get here. ✉ *E92, 4 km (2½ mi) north of Ioannina* ☎ *26510/81521* 🎟 *€7* ⏲ *May–Oct., daily 9–7; Nov.–Apr., daily 9–5.*

WHERE TO STAY & EAT

$$–$$$ Fodor's Choice ★ ✕ **Es Aei.** The name means "forever," a telling indication of the dedication of owners Manos Chronakis and Haris Stavrou to showcase the generally "forgotten" regional dishes of Greece and, just as impressively, the authentic ways they were once prepared. Beguilingly, Es Aei is set in a 200-year-old Ottoman residence furnished with the owner's growing collection of traditional Greek antiques. The unique

set menu includes more than 60 meze dishes, such as *Palatiani* (meatballs), made with numerous kinds of meat and nuts. Inventive salads—such as the fresh orange salad with potatoes (Mani)—homemade pies, meat dishes, and an abundance of vegetarian options are made with ingredients from their organic farm in Tzoumerka, so it comes as no surprise that the menu changes seasonally, and month by month the cultured owners celebrate the cuisine of a different Greek region. ✉ *Koundouriotou 50, Ioannina* ☎ *26510/34571* 🌐 *www.esaei.gr* 💳 *MC, V* ⊗ *Closed July and Aug.*

$$–$$$ Fodor's Choice ★ ✕**Gastra.** Mr. Vassilis has run this friendly traditional taverna for more than 30 years. Here you can discover how Greek grandmothers cooked before the comforts of electricity were introduced to Epirus. The *gastra* is basically a large container with hot coals placed on the iron lid over the pot. Your meal (of lamb, chicken, or goat) roasts very slowly in its own juices, resulting in tender, juicy meat with a crispy outer skin. ✉ *Leoforos Kostaki 16a, 7 km (4½ mi) north of Ioannina on the way to the airport, Eleousa* ☎ *26510/61530* ✍ *Reservations essential* 💳 *No credit cards* ⊗ *Closed Mon.*

$$–$$$ ✕**Ithaki.** Among the many restaurants on the trendy lakeside street, Ithaki stands out. You can eat traditional Ioanniotika fare, such as vegetable pies, frogs' legs, and fried Metsovitiko cheese, while enjoying the view of Pamvotis lake with the mosque of Kaplan Pasha reflecting in its waters. The speciality of the house is the spit-roasted *kontosouvli* (tender pork), and the tasty homemade baklava. ✉ *Stratigou Papagou 20a* ☎ *26510/74730* 💳 *MC, V.*

6

¢–$ ✕**Ivi.** Old fashioned and no nonsense, this Ioannina landmark serves excellent *magirefta* (dishes precooked in an oven or on the stove). Open from 5 AM, it's the place to head to after a long night out on the town. Tripe soup and *mageiritsa* (sheep's liver and intestine) are some unusual dishes. There's usually a fish entrée such as grilled *kolios* (mackerel), *bakaliaros* (fried cod), or *galeos* (shark) with *skordalia* (garlic-potato sauce). ✉ *Neomartiros Georgiou Sq. 4* ☎ *26510/73155* 💳 *No credit cards* ⊗ *Closed every other Sun.*

$$$ ★ ✕🏨**Epirus Palace.** Indulging oneself in the city of Ali Pasha seems entirely fitting, and you can do so in style at this stunning, lavish hotel, opened in 1999 by the innovative brothers Natsis. Some of the exquisite furniture, highlighted with gold and silver, was handmade for the hotel. Rooms are spacious, and the marble bathrooms are luxurious. For a more international taste of Greece, dine at the sophisticated à la carte hotel restaurant, which prides itself on its *loukoulia gevmata* (sumptuous feast). ✉ *7 km (4½ mi) south of Ioannina, Ethnikos Odos Ioanninon–Athinon road, 45221* ☎ *26510/93555* 📠 *26510/92595* 🌐 *www.epiruspalace.gr* 🛏 *51 rooms, 2 suites* ♨ *In-room: dial-up, refrigerator, safe. In-hotel: 3 restaurants, bars, pool, no-smoking rooms* 💳 *AE, D, MC, V* 🍽 *BP.*

$$ ★ 🏨**Kentrikon Hotel** Opened in 2005, the architecturally traditional Kentrikon is located in Ioannina's city center (indeed, that's what its name means) and offers all modern amenities. The renovated mansion's wood-and-stone look, the simple but quaintly classic and traditional decor, the friendly service, and the light-filled rooms all make

this a comfortable and cozy place to stay, especially when clients and visitors alike can enjoy mezedes and *tsipouro* (a liquor made from grapes) in the pretty garden in summer. ✉*Koletti 5A, 45444* ☎*26510/71771* 🖷*26510/71945* *12 rooms, 2 suites* *In room: refrigerator, dial-up. In-hotel: bar* 💳*MC, V.*

$ ★ **Kastro Hotel.** A restored neoclassic mansion is the more popular of only two accommodation options within the walls of the citadel, so make reservations well in advance. Wooden beams, painted wooden ceilings, two fireplaces (in the sitting and breakfast rooms), and cast-iron beds are thoroughly delightful. Thick stone walls keep things cool in summer. The owners and staff are very helpful, and breakfast (additional, upon request) is homemade jams, ham, cheese, fruit, and local honey. ✉*Andronikou Paleologou 57, 45444* ☎*26510/22866* 🖷*26510/22780* 🌐*www.epirus.com/hotel-kastro* *7 rooms* *In-hotel: some pets allowed, no elevator* 💳*MC, V.*

¢ **Pension Dellas.** Evangelos Dellas inherited this island lakeshore establishment from his parents; its welcoming hospitality is a delightful change from hotels in town. The pension is immaculate, sunny, and quiet, with two balconies overlooking the lake and sunset. Make the boat ride to the island village from Mavili Square yourself or call to be picked up in the family boat. ✉*Nissi, 45444* ☎*26510/81494 or 26510/89894* *4 rooms* *In-room: no phone, refrigerator. In-hotel: restaurant, bar, some pets allowed, no elevator* 💳*No credit cards.*

FEELING FESTIVE?

Ioannina's local tourist office (✉ Dodonis 39, eotioan@otenet.gr) can provide information about festivals, including a noted bazaar in September. The International Folk Festival, showcasing the region's music and dancing, takes place in July. For those seeking the haunting *klarino* (clarinet) music and graceful circle dances of Epirus such as the *pogonisios* and *beratis*, this is a must. Local groups also perform eerie polyphonic singing, another folk tradition rooted in Epirus.

NIGHTLIFE & THE ARTS

BARS & CAFÉS Even in a relatively small city like Ioannina, the *magazia* (club-cafés) are always changing names and owners; they may close for winter and open elsewhere for summer, usually under the stars. Karamanli, adjacent to the citadel, is lined with trendy *mezedopoleia* (Greek-style tapas bars) and smart pubs. **Club Preview** (✉*Giosif Eligia and Aetorrahis* ☎*26510/64522*), by the Kastro, is a popular club open late—but closed June through August—with lots of loud foreign music. **Iperokeanios** (✉*Mavili Sq. 10* ☎*06510/33781*), by the citadel near Giosif Eligia and Aetorrahis, is one of the hippest coffee shops along the seawall; it serves ice cream and sweets. If it's full, try the adjacent Ploton. The waterfront music taverna **Kyknos** (✉*Stratigou Papagou* ☎*26510/75557*), very popular with students, is a good place to hang out for the night or to charge your batteries before clubbing.

The **Web** (✉*Pirsinella 21* ☎*26510/74115 or 26510/26813*) is the place to check your e-mail as you socialize with other tourists and locals and sip coffee or a strong drink until late at night.

SHOPPING

Ioannina has long been known throughout Greece for its silver craftsmanship and for its jewelry, copper utensils, and woven items. You can find delicate jewelry items on the island of Nissi, but there are also many silver shops on Odhos Averoff (the better place for larger items, like trays, glasses, and vases), near Neomartiros Georgiou Square. Avoid the shinier and brighter items in stores near the entrance to the citadel.

Doublis (✉*Neomartiros Georgiou Sq.* ☎*26510/79287*) is one of the better arts-and-crafts shops in this area; a careful eye can discern some prizes amid the typical tourist paraphernalia.

Antique collectors consider **Papazotos Zikos** (✉*Andronikou Paleologou 2, inside citadel* ☎*26510/83103*), one of the must-go-to shops; it has a large collection of Ali Pasha's original belongings.

DODONA ΔΩΔΩΝΗ

★ *22 km (14 mi) southwest of Ioannina.*

Said to be the oldest in Greece, the **Dodona Oracle** flourished from at least the 8th century BC until the 4th century AD, when Christianity succeeded the cult of Zeus. Homer, in the *Iliad,* mentions "wintry Dodona," where Zeus's pronouncements, made known through the wind-rustled leaves of a sacred oak, were interpreted by priests "whose feet are unwashed and who sleep on the ground." The oak tree was central to the cult, and its image appears on the region's ancient coins. Here Odysseus sought forgiveness for slaughtering his wife's suitors, and from this oak the Argonauts took the sacred branch to mount on their ship's prow. According to one story, Apollo ordered the oracle moved here from Thessaly; Herodotus writes that it was locally believed a dove from Thebes in Egypt landed in the oak and announced, in a human voice, that the oracle of Zeus should be built.

As you enter the archaeological site of Dodona, you pass the **stadium** on your right, built for the Naïa games and completely overshadowed by the **theater** on your left. One of the largest and best preserved on the Greek mainland, the theater once seated 17,000; it is used for summer presentations of ancient Greek drama. Its building in the early 3rd century BC was overseen by King Pyrrhus of Epirus. The theater was destroyed, rebuilt under Philip V of Macedon in the late 3rd century, and then converted by the Romans into an arena for gladiatorial games. Its retaining wall, reinforced by bastions, is still standing. East of the theater are the foundations of the **bouleuterion** (headquarters and council house) of the Epirote League, built by Pyrrhus, and a small rectangular temple dedicated to Aphrodite. The remains of the **acropolis** behind the theater include house foundations and a cistern that supplied water in times of siege.

> **NOT SO CRYSTAL CLEAR**
>
> The Dodona oracle had its ups and downs. Consulted in the heroic age by Heracles, Achilles, and all the best people, it went later into a gentle decline, because of its failure to equal the masterly ambiguity of Delphi.

The remains of the **sanctuary of Zeus Naios** include temples to Zeus, Dione (goddess of abundance), and Heracles; until the 4th century BC there was no temple. The Sacred Oak was here, surrounded by abutting cauldrons on bronze tripods. When struck, they reverberated for a long time, and the sound was interpreted by soothsayers. Fragments of oracular questions and answers from as early as the 8th century have been recovered. In the 4th century BC, a small temple was built near the oak, and a century later the temple and oak were enclosed by a stone wall. By King Pyrrhus's time, the wall had acquired Ionic colonnades. After a 219 BC Aeolian attack, a larger Ionic temple was built, and the surrounding wall was enhanced by a monumental entrance. The oak tree currently on the site was planted by archaeologists; the original was probably cut down by Christians in the 4th century AD.

Two buses leave daily (except Thursday) from Ioannina's Bizaniou station, one at 7 AM and the other at 4 PM. The most efficient way to get here from Ioannina is with a rented car or a taxi; the driver will wait an hour at the site. Negotiate with one of the drivers near Ioannina's clock tower or ask your hotel to call a radio taxi service. Hours may be reduced from October to May. ✉*Signposted off E951, near Dodona* ☎*26510/82287* 🌐*www.culture.gr* 🎫*€3* ⏲*Daily 8–5.*

The Ioannina tourist office has information about summer presentations of **Ancient Greek drama** (*Tourist office* ✉*Dodonis 39, Ioannina* ☎*26510/41868 or 26510/46662*) at Dodona.

METSOVO ΜΕΤΣΟΒΟ

58 km (36 mi) east of Ioannina, 293 km (182 mi) northwest of Athens.

The traditional village of Metsovo cascades down a mountain at about 3,300 feet above sea level, below the 6,069-foot Katara pass, which is the highest in Greece and marks the border between Epirus and Thessaly. Even in summer, the temperatures may be in the low 20°sC (70°sF), and February's average highs are just above freezing. Early evening is a wonderful time to arrive. As you descend through the mist, dazzling lights twinkle in the ravine. Stone houses with gray slate roofs and sharply projecting wooden balconies line steep, serpentine alleys. In the square, especially after the Sunday service, old men—dressed in black flat caps, dark baggy pants, and wooden shoes with pompoms—sit on a bench, like crows on a tree branch. Should you arrive on a religious feast day, many villagers will be decked out in traditional costume. Older women often wear dark blue or black dresses with embroidered trim every day, augmenting these with brightly colored aprons, jackets, and scarves with floral embroidery on holidays.

Although most such villages are fading away, Metsovo, designated a traditional settlement by the Greek National Tourism Organization (GNTO or EOT), has become a prosperous community with a growing population. In winter it draws skiers headed for Mt. Karakoli, and in summer it is—for better or worse—a favorite destination for tourist groups. For the most part Metsovo has preserved its character despite the souvenir shops selling "traditional handicrafts" that may be imports and the slate roofs that have been replaced with easy-to-maintain tile.

The natives are descendants of nomadic Vlach shepherds, once believed to have migrated from Romania but now thought to be Greeks trained by Romans to guard the Egnatia Highway connecting Constantinople and the Adriatic. Metsovo became an important center of finance, commerce, handicrafts, and sheepherding, and the Vlachs began trading farther afield—in Constantinople, Vienna, and Venice. Ali Pasha abolished the privileges in 1795, and in 1854 the town was invaded by Ottoman troops led by Abdi Pasha. In 1912 Metsovo was freed from the Turks by the Greek army. Many important families lived here, including the Averoffs and Tositsas, who made their fortunes in Egyptian cotton. They contributed to the new Greek state's development and bequeathed large sums to restore Metsovo and finance small industries. For example, Foundation Baron Michalis Tositsa, begun in 1948 when a member of the prominent area family endowed it (although he was living in Switzerland), helped the local weaving industry get a start.

6

For generations the Tositsa family had been one of the most prominent in Metsovo, and to get a sense of how Metsovites lived (and endured the arduous winters in style), visit their home, a restored late-Ottoman-period stone-and-timber building that is now the **Tositsa Museum** of popular art and local Epirote crafts. Built in 1661 and renovated in 1954, this typical Metsovo mansion has carved woodwork, sumptuous textiles in rich colors on a black background, and handcrafted Vlach furniture. In the stable are the gold-embroidered saddle used for special holidays and, unique to this area, a fanlight in the fireplace, ensuring that the hearth would always be illuminated. The goatskin bag on the wall was used to store cheese. Wait for the guard to open the door prior to the tour. Guides usually speak some English. ✉ *Up stone stairs to right off Tositsa (main road) as you descend to main town square* ☎ *26560/41084* 🌐 *www.epcon.gr/metsovo* 🎫 *€3* ⏲ *By guided tour, every ½ hr May–Oct., Fri.–Wed. 9–1:30 and 4–6; Nov.–Apr., Fri.–Wed. 9–1:30 and 3–5.*

The freely accessible 18th-century church of **Agia Paraskevi** has a flamboyantly decorated altar screen that's worth a peek. Note that July 26 is its saint's day, entailing a big celebration in which the church's silver icon is carried around the town in a morning procession, followed by feasting and dancing. ✉ *Main square.*

The **Averoff Gallery** displays the outstanding personal art collection of politician and intellectual Evangelos Averoff (1910–90). The 19th- and 20th-century paintings depict historical scenes, local landscapes, and daily activities. Most major Greek artists, such as Nikos Ghikas and Alekos Fassianos, are represented. One painting known to all Greeks is Nikiforos Litras's *Burning of the Turkish Flagship by Kanaris,* a scene from a decisive battle in Chios. Look on the second floor for Pericles Pantazis's *Street Urchin Eating Watermelon,* a captivating portrait of a young boy. Paris Prekas's *The Mosque of Aslan Pasha in Ioannina* depicts what Ioannina looked like in the Turkish period. ✉ *Main square* ☎ *26560/41210* 🌐 *www.epcon.gr/metsovo* 🎫 *€3* ⏲ *Mid-July–mid-Sept., Wed.–Mon. 10–7; mid-Sept.–mid-July, Wed.–Mon. 10–4:30.*

THE WHITE WIDOWS

In winter, while Metsovo lies buried in snow, the area's famed Vlach shepherds move their flocks from the mountains to the lowlands around Trikala; their wives, nicknamed the "white widows," tend to their hearths in isolation. The shepherds' numbers are dwindling, however (they herd about 15,000 sheep today), as many have turned to tourism for their livelihoods.

Call in advance to visit the **winery.** Don't leave without a few bottles of the exquisite, full-bodied, musky red Katogi-Averoff wine. It's about a 45-minute walk, however. ✉ *Eastern edge of village, in Upper Aoos valley* ☎ *26560/41010* 🎫 *Free* ⏲ *Weekdays 8:30–3:30.*

OFF THE BEATEN PATH

Ayios Nikolaos Monastery. Visit a restored 14th-century monastery, about a 30-minute walk into the valley (with the trip back up about an hour). The *katholikon* (main church) is topped by a barrel vault, and what may have once been the narthex was converted to a *ginaikonitis* (women's gallery). Two images of the *Pantocrator* (Godhead), one in each dome—perhaps duplicated to give the segregated women their own view—stare down on the congregation. You can also see the monks' cells, with insulating walls of mud and straw; the abbot's quarters; and the school where Greek children were taught during the Turkish occupation. The keepers will give you a closely guided tour in English and explanation of the unusual 18th-century frescoes created in Epirote style. ✉ *Down into valley via footpath (follow signs near National Bank of Greece; turn left where paving ends)* 🎫 *€1* ⏲ *May–Oct., daily 9–7; Nov.–Apr., daily 9–1.*

WHERE TO STAY & EAT

$–$$ ✕ **Taverna Metsovitiko Saloni.** A large fireplace, Metsovo costumes on the walls, old photos, and carved wooden furniture enliven the dining room. Try the vegetable pies, especially the *kolokithopita* (zucchini pie) made from *bobota* (corn flour), an unusual crust in Greece but an Epirote favorite; in addition, the *saganaki* (fried cheese) made with four Metsovo cheeses is a winner. Savor the large wine selection (good local choices are Katogi and Zitsa) and tender lamb *yiouvetsi* (baked in tomato-wine sauce). ✉ *Tositsa 10, above post office* ☎ *26560/42142* 💳 *No credit cards.*

¢–$ ★ ✕ **To Paradosiako.** The name means "traditional," and that's what this comfortable spot decorated with colorful weavings and folk crafts is. Vasilis Bissas, the chef-owner, has revived many of the more esoteric regional specialties. Try the *fileta tou dasous* (fillet of the forest)—a choice beef fillet stuffed with cheese, ham, tomato, mushrooms, and "woodcutters' potatoes" (potato slices baked with bacon and four kinds of cheese). "Grandmothers' bread" is toasted and stuffed with cheese, bacon, tomato, peppers, and onions, then baked in the oven. Accompany your meal with the house wine, guaranteed to be a well-searched-out regional speciality, or choose the heady local red Katogi. ✉*Tositsa 44* ☎*26560/42773* ▭*No credit cards* ⊙*No lunch.*

$–$$ **Galaxias.** A great place to rest your mountain-weary feet, this small hotel has guest rooms designed in typical Metsovo style: simple, with the splash of color on a *kourelou,* or traditional rug. Some bathrooms have tubs, others showers; still others have their own fireplaces. Happily, a garden restaurant is right next door—enjoy local specialties such as leek pie with a corn pastry, veal with noodles from Metsovo, or boiled goat. Start with half a kilo of house barrel wine, *miso kilo hima.* ✉*Above main square, 44200* ☎*26560/41202 or 26560/41123* 📠*26560/41124* 🌐*hotel-galaxias-metsovo.focusgreece.gr* *10 rooms* *In-room: no a/c. In-hotel: restaurant, some pets allowed* ▭*AE, MC, V.*

$ **Apollon Hotel.** Family-run and refurbished in 1996, the Apollon is centrally located in Metsovo and looks out on the Pindos mountain range. Topped by picturesque coves and built in traditional style, it offers comfortable, modern amenities along with old-world accents. For a true rustic feel plus great views, opt for one of the 10 charming and spacious attic rooms with Jacuzzis. At the hotel's restaurant try delicious local specialties such as the Metsovo pie and succulent baked mountain goat. Conveniently, Apollon organizes mini-bus tours to Aoos lake and river springs, the Valia Calda valley, and Anilio village. ✉*Metsovo central square, 44200* ☎*26560/41844* 📠*26560/42110* 🌐*www.metsovohotels.com* *40 rooms* *In room: refrigerator, Wi-Fi. In-hotel: restaurant, bar* ▭*MC, V* *CP.*

¢–$ ★ **Bitouni.** Local craftsmen created the elegantly carved wooden ceilings in this traditional-style Metsovo mansion. A large fireplace in the main reception room warms the cozy hotel. Six suites have panoramic views of the surrounding mountains. Soothe your weary travelers muscles in the on-site sauna. Two brothers, fluent in English, run this friendly establishment and three times a week mother Bitouni makes a mean vegetable pie. ✉*On main street leading up from the central square, 44200* ☎*26560/41217* 📠*26560/41545* 🌐*www.hotelbitouni.com* *18 rooms, 6 suites* *In-room: no a/c. In-hotel: bar* ▭*AE, MC, V* *CP.*

SHOPPING

Metsovo is famous throughout Greece for its expensive smoked cheeses. You can try them at one of the *tiropolio* (cheese shops) in the main square. You may even be able to get a taste before you buy. Metsovo is also known for its fabrics, folk crafts, and silver. Although many of the "traditional" arts and crafts here are imported, low-quality imitations, with a little prowling and patience you can still make some finds, especially if you like textiles and weavings. Some of them are genuine antiques that cost a good deal more than the newer versions, but they are far superior in quality. Everything's available on the main square. **Aris Talaris** (✉*Hotel Egnatia, Arvantinou 20* ☎*26560/41901*) has two shops: one sells quality silver jewelry made in Talaris's own workshop, and the other displays gold pieces. The Metsovo silver-work trade is one of the oldest trades in the region; members of the Talaris family have been silversmiths for many generations. Near the Hotel Egnatia, the shop of **Vangelis Balabekos** (✉*Arvantinou* ☎*26560/41623*) sells traditional clothing from Epirus and other areas of Greece.

THESSALY ΘΕΣΣΑΛΙΑ

Though Thessaly, with part of Mt. Olympus within its boundaries, is the home of the immortal gods, a Byzantine site holds pride of place: Meteora, the amazing medieval monasteries on top of inaccessible needles of rock. The monasteries' extraordinary geological setting stands in vivid contrast to the rest of Thessaly, a huge plain in central Greece, almost entirely surrounded by mountains: Pindos to the west, Pelion to the east, Othrys to the south, and the Kamvounian range to the north. It is one of the country's most fertile areas and has sizable population centers in Lamia, Larissa, Trikala, and Volos. Thessaly was not ceded to Greece until 1878, after almost five centuries of Ottoman rule; today vestiges of this period remain. Kalambaka and Meteora are in the northwest corner of the plain, before the Pindos mountains. The best time to come here is spring, especially to the Meteora monasteries, when the mountains are still snow covered and blend harmoniously with the green fields, the red poppies, and the white and pink flowering fruit trees.

KALAMBAKA ΚΑΛΑΜΠΑΚΑ

71 km (44 mi) east of Metsovo, 154 km (95 mi) southwest of Thessaloniki.

Kalambaka may be dismissed as one more drab modern town, useful only as a base to explore the fabled Meteora complex north of town. Yet an overnight stay here, complete with a taverna dinner and a stroll in the main squares, provides a taste of everyday life in a provincial Thessalian town. This will prove quite a contrast to an afternoon spent at nearby Meteora, where you can get acquainted with the glorious history and architecture of the Greek Orthodox Church. Invariably, you return to modern Kalambaka and wind up at a poolside bar to sip ouzo and contemplate the asceticism of the Meteora monks. If you'd rather stay in a more attractive place slightly closer to the monasteries, head to Kastraki, a hamlet with some attractive folk-style houses about 2½ km (1 mi) north of Kalambaka.

Burned by the Germans during World War II, Kalambaka has only one building of interest, the centuries-old cathedral church of the **Dormition of the Virgin.** Patriarchal documents in the outer narthex indicate that it was built in the first half of the 12th century by Emperor Manuel Comnenos, but some believe it was founded as early as the 7th century, on the site of a temple of Apollo (classical drums and other fragments are incorporated into the walls, and mosaics can be glimpsed under the present floor). The latter theory explains the church's paleo-Christian features, including its center-aisle *ambo* (great marble pulpit), which is usually to the right of the sanctuary; its rare *synthronon* (four semicircular steps where the priest sat when not officiating) east of the altar; and its Roman-basilica style, originally adapted to Christian use and unusual for the 12th century. The church has vivid 16th-century frescoes, work of the Cretan monk Neophytos, son of the famous hagiographer Theophanes. The marble baldachin in the sanctuary, decorated with crosses and stylized grapes, probably predates the 11th century. The courtyard outside the church provides welcome respite under the cool shade of a eucalyptus tree. Behind the church you can stroll through a small necropolis: boxes upon boxes of bones that have been disinterred and washed in accordance with Orthodox tradition. ⊠*North end of town, follow signs from Riga Fereou Sq.* ☎*24320/24297* 🌐*www.culture.gr* €2 ⏲*Daily 8–1 and 4–8.*

WHERE TO STAY & EAT

$–$$ ★ ✕ **Estiatorio Meteora.** At this spot on the main square, a local favorite since 1925, the Gertzos family serves food prepared by the matriarch, Ketty. Meteora is known for hearty main courses—try Ketty's special wine-and-pepper chicken, veal or pork *stifado* (stew)—and some specialties from Asia Minor, including *tzoutzoukakia Smyrneika,* aromatic meatballs in a red sauce laced with cumin. All customers are ushered through the kitchen to place their order. Do try the local wine with your meal. Call ahead if you want lunch; it's served only several, varying days a week. ⊠*Ekonomou 4, on Dimarchiou Sq.* ☎*24320/22316* ▭*No credit cards* ⏲*Closed Feb.*

$–$$ ✕ **O Kipos Tou Ilia.** This simple taverna with a traditional Greek menu and a waterfall in the garden attracts everyone from visiting royalty to Olympic-medal winners. Kids get their own *paithika piata* (kids' plates). Unusual appetizers include spicy fried feta with peppers and grilled mushrooms. Among the main dishes are beef *stamna* (baked in a covered clay pot with herbs, potatoes, and cheese), rabbit with onions, and vegetable croquettes. ⊠*Trikalon, at terminus of Ayia Triada, before entrance to Kalambaka* ☎*24320/23218* ▭*V.*

$ ✕ **Paradissos.** When a Greek woman cooks with *meraki* (good taste and mood), the world does indeed feel like *paradissos* (paradise). Owner Kyriakoula Fassoula serves up meat dishes cooked *tis oras* (to order), such as grilled pork and lamb chops. Vegetarians can choose from delectable eggplant *papoutsakia* ("little shoes"), fried zucchini with garlic sauce, and various boiled greens. Complimentary fruit is served for the finale, but it would be a shame to pass up the flaky baklava. ⊠*On main road to Meteora across from Spania Rooms, Kastraki* ☎*24320/22723* ▭*No credit cards.*

$$$$ **Amalia.** A low-lying, clay-color complex outside Kalambaka (on the road to Trikala), this hotel has spacious, handsome public rooms that somehow avoided the generic stamp. Relax in the sitting room, with striking antiques, floral murals, and fireplace—you can also enjoy fireplaces in the bar and restaurant—or chill out at the poolside bar, with glistening blue tiles and rustic rafters. Grounds are beautifully landscaped and blissfully quiet. Rooms are done in soothing colors and have

large beds and prints; some also have balconies. ✉*14 km [9 mi] along Ethnikos Odos Trikalon–Ioanninon road, 42200* ☎*24320/72116 or 24320/72117* 📠*24320/72457* 🌐*www.amalia.gr* *170 rooms, 2 suites* ▭*AE, DC, MC, V* *CP.*

$$$ **Hotel Divani.** A few minutes from the center of town, this hotel has optimal views of the Meteora rocks from the rooms' balconies. Its large open spaces, quiet corners, and private garden encourage relaxation. The exterior is plain, as are the rooms, but they're shielded from outside noise. The professional reception staff will arrange and negotiate a price for a leisurely taxi ride to the monasteries. ✉*Ethnikos Odos Trikalon 1, 42200* ☎*24320/23330* 📠*24320/23638* 🌐*www.divanis.gr* *163 rooms, 1 suite* *In-room: refrigerator. In-hotel: restaurant, bars, pool* ▭*AE, DC, MC, V* *BP.*

$ **Hotel Edelweiss.** Every room is spotless, with bare white walls (OK, so you may feel a little like you're in a hospital), but many of them have balcony views. Do request one looking out over the pool and the towering Meteora rocks beyond. The bar attracts a lively local crowd, and the hotel runs a Western-and-Greek popular music club next door. ✉*Eleftherios Venizelou 3, 42200* ☎*24320/23966 or 24320/23884* 📠*24320/24733* *edelweis@hol.gr* *60 rooms* *In-hotel: restaurant, bars, pool* ▭*MC, V* *CP.*

¢–$ ★ **Doupiani House.** Reside in a traditional stone-and-wood hotel set amid vineyards in the upper reaches of the idyllic village of Kastraki. Each room—with a luxurious carved double bed, oak floors, and cupboards—has a balcony with panoramic views of both Meteora and Kastraki. Vivacious owner Toula Naki serves breakfast (extra charge, but the produce is local) around the pergola in the large garden, which is perfumed with the scent of roses, jasmine, and honeysuckle. If you have enough stamina, you can walk to the monasteries from here; Thanassis Naki will happily provide you with his excellent homemade area hiking maps. ✉*Kastrakiou, left off main road to Meteora, near Cave Camping, 42200 Kastraki* ☎📠*24320/77555 or 24320/75326* *doupiani-house@kmp.forthnet.gr* *11 rooms* ▭*MC, V.*

¢ **Arsenis.** This guesthouse is located in an olive grove east of Meteora, and is a cozy, remarkably friendly, and accommodating option. The clean, well-attended rooms in Arsenis overlook spectacular views of the Meteora cliffs, Thessalian valleys, and the Pindos mountains. The family-run guesthouse's restaurant is lauded for its hearty, flavorsome meals, sometimes cooked on the open fire, and people rave as well about its homemade wine. ✉*East road of Meteora, 42200* ☎*24320/23500 or 24320/24150* 🌐*www.arsenis-meteora.gr/home_en.html* *16 rooms* *In-hotel: restaurant, no elevator* ▭*V.*

NIGHTLIFE

Kalambaka isn't the most cosmopolitan city, but you may find some fun places for ice cream or coffee along the main drag, Trikalon. Dimoula Square is all abuzz on weekends as locals descend from the surrounding villages.

Arena (✉*Dimoula Sq.* ☎*24320/77999*) is an Internet bar and café open from around 10 AM until late night.

THE METEORA ΜΕΤΕΩΡΑ

Fodor's Choice ★ *3 km (2 mi) north of Kalambaka, 178 km (110 mi) southwest of Thessaloniki.*

> **WORD OF MOUTH**
>
> "With regards to mass tourism at Meteora, most tourist buses leave in the afternoon. The monasteries are practically empty after 3 PM and you can then really enjoy their serene beauty." —Carlos

As you drive through the mighty Pindos range, strange rock formations rise ever higher from the plain. Just beyond the dramatic sheer cliff that shelters the town of Kalambaka, the legendary monasteries of the Meteora—one of the wonders of the later Middle Ages—begin to appear along a circular road as it winds 6 km (4 mi) through an unearthly forest of gigantic rock pillars. The ancients believed these formations to be meteors hurled by an angry god. Ascending to 1,820 feet above sea level, these towers, in fact, owe their fantastic shapes to river erosion. But they owe their worldwide fame (and Hollywood moment of glory—remember the James Bond *For Your Eyes Only* climax?) to what perches atop six of them: the impregnable monasteries built here by pious hermits in the turbulent 14th century. For a complete overview of these fascinating retreats, see our special photo-feature, "Nearer to Heaven: The Meteora Monasteries" on the next page.

6

EPIRUS & THESSALY ESSENTIALS

TRANSPORTATION

BY AIR

Ioannina is a 70-minute flight from Athens and a 50-minute flight from Thessaloniki. From June through August, Olympic Airlines usually has two or three flights daily from Athens to Ioannina and about five flights per week from Thessaloniki to Ioannina. In other months, two flights daily leave Athens for Ioannina and about four flights per week depart Thessaloniki for Ioannina. Aegean Airlines has one flight per day to Ioannina from Athens. AirSea Lines flies regularly to Corfu from Ioannina in their seaplanes.

Carriers **Aegean Airlines** (✉ *Othonos 10, Athens* ☎ *210/331–5502, 210/331–5503, 801/112–0000 for local charge countrywide, 210/353–4294 Ioannina airport* 🌐 *www.aegeanair.com* ✉ *Pirsinella 11, Ioannina* ☎ *26510/64444, 26510/65200, 26510/65201 Ioannina airport*). **AirSea Lines** (✉ *Spyrou Lambrou 36, Ioannina* ☎ *26510/49800* 🌐 *www.airsealines.com*). **Olympic Airlines** (✉ *Spirou Katsadima 6, Ioannina* ☎ *26510/23120, 801/114–4444 for local charge countrywide* 🌐 *www.olympicairlines.com* ✉ *Ioannina airport, Ioannina* ☎ *26510/22355*).

AIRPORT The Ioannina airport is 8 km (5 mi) north of town.

Contact **Ioannina airport** (✉ *8-km- [5-mi-] mark on Ethnikos Odos Ioanninon–Trikalon road* ☎ *26510/83310 or 26510/83320*).

Continued on page 299

NEARER TO HEAVEN: THE METEORA MONASTERIES

Here in the most remote corner of Greece, landscape and legend conspire to twist reality into fantasy. Soaring skyward out of dense orchards looms a different kind of forest: gigantic rock pinnacles, the loftiest of which rises up 984 feet. But even more extraordinary than these stone pillars are the monasteries that perch atop nature's skyscrapers. Funded by Byzantine emperors, run by ascetic monks, and once scaled by James Bond, these saintly castles-in-air are almost literally "out of this world."

The name Meteora comes from the Greek word *meteorizome* ("to hang in midair"). These world-famous monasteries seem to do just that. The origin of these rocks, which loom up between the Pindos range and the Thessalian plain, is an enigma. Some geologists say a lake that covered the area 30 million years ago swept away the soil and softer stone as it forced its way to the sea. Others believe the inexorable flow of the Peneus River slowly carved out the towering pillars, now greatly eroded by wind and rain. Legend created, as it often does, a more colorful story: the rock needles are meteors hurled to earth by an angry god.

Man first staked claim to the Meteora peaks when the inaccessible pinnacles served as refuge to pious hermits in the turbulent 14th century. As soon as the Turkish rulers of Trikkala began warring with the Byzantine emperors of Constantinople for rights to the fertile valley, these anchorite monks were forced to retreat to the heights of the impregnable rocks. In 1336 they were joined by St. Athanasios, who hailed from fabled Mt. Athos. Notwithstanding the legend that says the saint flew up to the rocks on the back of an eagle, Athanasios began the backbreaking task of building the Megalo Meteoro (1356–72)—the biggest of the Meteora monasteries—using pulleys and ropes to haul construction materials. By the 16th century, 13 monasteries had been established here as bastions of Christianity, supported by revenues from estates in Thessaly and Eastern Europe. During the late-Byzantine period, they are said to have helped "save" Western civilization from the inroads of Turkish domination. In the end, however, the Meteora monasteries came to poignantly epitomize both the glory and the decline of Eastern monasticism. Once the former abodes of emperors and kings, they are now largely supported by tourism.

For centuries, jointed ladders and descending nets were the only way to ascend the rocky peaks. Tourists who may yearn for the days when travelers made the ascent squeezed into an outsize string-bag are cured of their nostalgia after one look at the rusty windlass, especially if accompanied by the gruesome story that the rope was only ever changed "when it broke." Today, stone bridges, rock-hewn stairs, and *monopati* (old paths) guide visitors up hundreds of steps to the monasteries, where they are rewarded with gasp-inducing vistas that fill the soul as much as the eye.

THE MAIN MONASTERIES

Set atop the Meteora's "heavenly columns" are six sky-kissing monasteries. While their dizzying perch seems attributable only to divine intervention, their architecture can be dated from the 14th to 17th centuries. Restricted by space, the buildings rise from different levels. Some are whitewashed; others display the pretty Byzantine pattern of stone and brick, the multiple domes of the many churches dominating the wooden balconies that hang precariously over the frightening abyss.

THE ROAD LESS TRAVELED

Even though **Ayios Nikolaos Anapafsas** (Holy Monastery of St. Nicholas Anapausas) is the first monastic complex you see and is accessed by a relatively unchallenging path, many travelers hurry on to the large Megalo Meteoro, leaving this one relatively uncrowded. Its *katholikon* (church), built 1388, faces north rather than the usual east because of the rock's peculiar shape. The small area precluded the construction of a cloister, so the monks studied in the larger-than-usual narthex. While the monastery dates from the end of the 15th century, its superb frescoes are from the 16th century and the work of Theophanis Strelitzas. Though conservative, his frescoes are lively and expressive: mountains are stylized, and plants and animals are portrayed geometrically. Especially striking are the treatments of the Temptation and the scourging of Christ.

Ayios Nikolaos Anapafsas, ☎ 24320/22375; €2; Apr.–Oct., Sat.–Thurs. 9–5; Nov.–Mar., Sat.–Thurs. 9–1

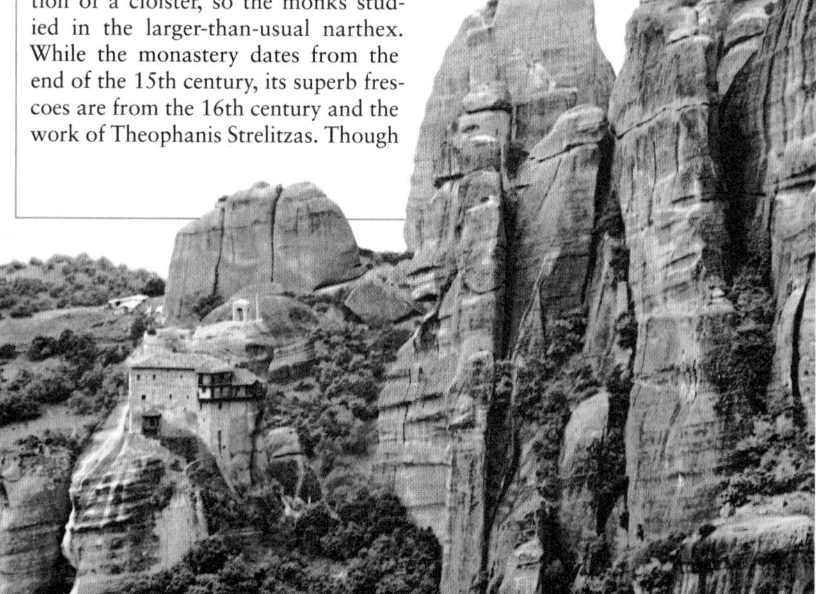

FABLED FRESCOES

The monastery closest to the Megalo Meteoro is the **Varlaam**, which sits atop a ravine and is reached by a bridge and a climb of 195 steps. Originally here were the Church of Three Hierarchs (14th century) and the cells of a hermitage started by St. Varlaam, who arrived shortly after St. Athanasios. Two brothers from the wealthy Aparas family of Ioannina rebuilt the church in 1518, incorporating it into a larger katholikon called Agii Pandes (All Saints). A church document relates how it was completed in 20 days, after the materials had been accumulated atop the rock over a period of 22 years. The church's main attraction, the 16th-century frescoes—including a disturbing Apocalypse with a yawning hell's mouth—completely covers the walls, beams, and pillars. The frescoes' realism, the sharp contrasts of light and dark, and the many-figured scenes show an Italian influence, though in the portrayal of single saints they follow the Orthodox tradition. Note the Pantocrator peering down from the dome. These are the work of Frangos Katellanos of Thebes, one of the most important 16th-century hagiographers. Set around a pretty garden, other buildings include a chapel to Sts. Cosmas and Damien. By the large storerooms is an ascent tower with a net and a winch.

Varlaam, ☎ 24320/22277; 🎫 €2
🕒 May–Oct., Fri.–Wed. 9–4; Nov.–Apr., Sat.–Wed. 9–3

TAKE THEE TO A NUNNERY

On the lowest rock—thought an appropriate tribute to male superiority by the early monks (who first refused to have women in the Meteora)—the compact monastery of **Ayia Barbara** (Holy Monastery of Rousanou) was the only nunnery in the complex centuries ago. With its colorful gardens in and around red- and gray-stone walls, it is a favorite for picture taking. Set on a large mesa-like rock, the squat building was abandoned in the early 1900s and stood empty until a new order of nuns moved in some years ago and restored it. The monastery was thought to have been founded in 1288 by the monks Nicodemus and Benedict. The main church has well-preserved frescoes dating from the mid-16th century. Most depict gory scenes of martyrdom, but one shows lions licking Daniel's feet during his imprisonment. The nunnery is accessible via steps and a new bridge.

Ayia Barbara, ☎ 24320/2269
🎫 €2; 🕒 Apr–Oct., daily 9–6; Nov–Mar., daily 9–2

HIGHEST & GRANDEST

Superlatives can be trotted out to describe the **Megalo Meteoro** (Church of the Metamorphosis [Transfiguration])—the loftiest, richest, biggest, and most popular of the monasteries. Founded by St. Athanasios, the monk from Athos, it was built of massive stones 1,361 feet above the valley floor and is reached by a stiff climb of more than 400 steps. As you walk toward the entrance, you see the chapel containing the cell where St. Athanasios once lived. This monastery, known as the Grand Meteoron, gained imperial prestige because it counted among Athanasius's disciples the Hermit-King Ioasaph of Serbia and John Cantacuzene, expelled by his joint emperor from the Byzantine throne. Dating from 1387–1388, the sanctuary of the present church was the chapel first built by St. Athanasios, later added to by St. Ioasaph. The rest of the church was erected in 1552 with an unusual transept built on a cross-in-square plan with lateral apses topped by lofty domes, as in the Mt. Athos monasteries. To the right of the narthex are the tombs of Ioasaph and Athanasios; a fresco shows the austere saints holding a monastery in their hands. Also of interest are the gilded iconostasis, with plant and animal motifs of exceptional workmanship; the bishop's throne (1617), inlaid with mother-of-pearl and ivory; and the beautiful 15th-century icons in the sanctuary. In the narthex are frescoes of the Martyrdom of the Saints, gruesome scenes of persecution under the Romans. Note the kitchen, blackened by centuries of cooking, and the wine cellar, filled with massive wine barrels. The gift shop is noted for its icons and incense. From November to March the monastery may close early.

Megalo Meteoro, ☎; 24320/22278; 🎟 €2; 🕐 Wed.–Mon. 9–6

FOR YOUR EYES ONLY?

The most spectacularly sited of all the Meteora monasteries, **Ayia Triada** (Monastery of the Holy Trinity) is shouldered high on a rock pinnacle isolated from surrounding cliffs; it is reached via rock tunnels and 130 stone-hewn steps. Primitive and remote, the monastery will also be strangely familiar: James Bond fans will recognize it from its starring role in the the 1981 movie *For Your Eyes Only* (the famous winch is still in place, and you may be shown it in a tour by the one monk who lives here). According to local legend, the monk Dometius was the first to arrive in 1438; the main church, dedicated to the Holy Trinity, was built in 1476, and the narthex and frescoes were added more than 200 years later. Look for the fresco with St. Sisois gazing upon the skeleton of Alexander the Great, meant to remind the viewer that power is fleeting. The apse's pseudo-trefoil window and the sawtooth decoration around it and beneath other windows lend a measure of grace to the structure. Ayia Triada is fabled for its vistas, with Ayios Stephanos and Kalambaka in the south and Varlaam and Megalo Meteoro to the west. Conveniently, a well-traveled footpath near the entrance (red arrows) descends to Kalambaka, about 3 km (2 mi) away.

Ayia Triada, ☎ 24320/22220 ₤ €2; ⏲ Fri.–Wed. 9–12:30 and 3–5

GROWING OLD GRACEFULLY

At the far end of the eastern sector of the Meteora is **Ayios Stephanos**, the oldest monastery—a permanent bridge has replaced the movable one that once connected the monastery with the hill opposite, making this perhaps the most easily accessible, with a car road passing not far below the entrance. According to an inscription that was once on the lintel, the rock was inhabited before 1200 and was the hermitage of Jeremiah. After the Byzantine emperor Andronicus Paleologos stayed here in 1333 on his way to conquer Thessaly, he made generous gifts to the monks, which funded the building of a church in 1350. Today Ayios Stephanos is an airy convent, where the nuns spend their time painting Byzantine icons, writing, or studying music; some are involved in the community as doctors and professors. The katholikon has no murals but contains a carved wooden baldachin and an iconostasis depicting the Last Supper. You can also visit the 15th-century frescoed church of Ayios Stephanos as well as a small icon museum.

Ayios Stephanos, ☎ 24320/22279; ₤ €2; ⏲ Apr.–Oct., Tues–Sun. 9–1:30 and 3:30–5.30; Nov.–Mar., Tues.–Sun. 9:30–2 and 3–5

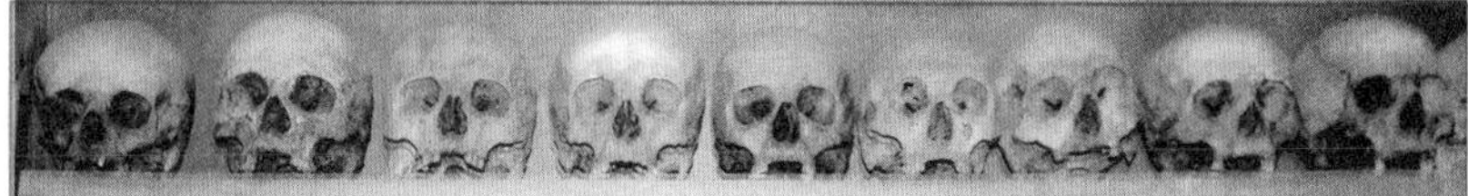

METEORA FAQS

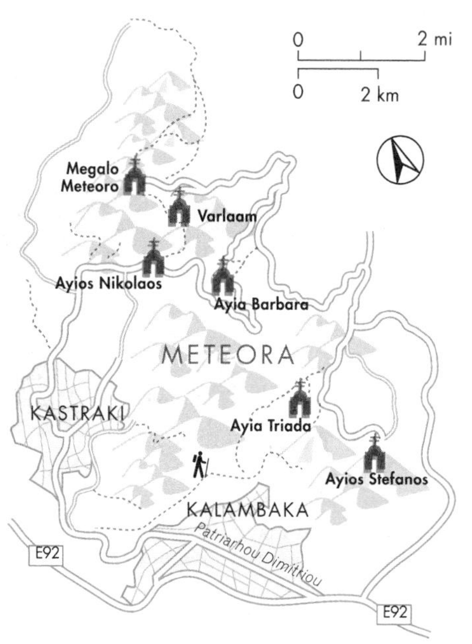

How many monasteries can I see in a day? All monasteries can be visited in a single journey from Kalambaka—a 21-km (13-mi) round-trip by car—but most visitors prefer to do only two or three, especially if they are hiking along the old *monopati* (old paths) that connect the monasteries. Most of the stairs upwards are in fine shape but some of the paths are crumbling in places and require the skill of an inordinately sure-footed goat (no heels, please!). Megalo Meteoro and Varlaam are the two most rewarding monasteries to visit if time is tight. Whatever your mode of transport, buy a map of the monasteries in Kalambaka.

What is the general geographic layout? Heading out from Kalambaka, the comfortable Patriarhou Dimitriou road serpentines past the village of Kastraki and then winds its way ingeniously through the sandstone Meteora labyrinth. The first monastery is Ayios Nikolaos Anapafsas. Beyond it lies the mammoth Megalo Meteoro and, vis-à-vis, Varlaam. Southward is Ayia Barbara and, after a major curving detour, Ayia Triada and Ayios Stephanos. Along the main road, arrowed signposts indicate the turn-offs for the various monasteries. Note, however, that you have to journey along side roads that run for at least one mile (sometimes as much as two) to get to the feet of the monasteries, at which point you then have to get ready for the vertical ascent.

Is there anyplace to eat? Once on the monastery circuit, there are just a few overpriced concession stands; if you plan to make a day of it, stock up on picnic goods in town.

Can I get to the monasteries by bus? A bus leaves Kalambaka for Megalo Meteoro five times daily (once daily in winter); the bus returns to town in late afternoon.

Is there a dress code? When visiting you are expected to dress decorously: men must tuck up long hair and wear long pants, women's skirts (no pants allowed) should fall to the knee, and both sexes should be sure to cover their shoulders. Some monasteries provide appropriate coverings at their entrances.

How changeable are the opening hours? We list official opening hours, but as these can vary depending on the season (winter hours are usually more limited), confirm the information with your hotel receptionist in Kalambaka. And leave plenty of time before setting off up the hundreds of steps: if you don't, you may find the monastery door closed at the top once you get there!

BY BUS

About nine buses a day make the seven-hour trip from Athens's Terminal A (Kifissou) to Ioannina's main Zosimadon station. Some buses take the longer route east through Kalambaka and Trikala rather than the usual southern route to the Rion–Antirion ferry over the suspension bridge which is the largest in Europe. From Athens's dismal Terminal B (Liossion), seven buses leave daily for the five-hour journey to Kalambaka. Most routes require you to hop on a different bus for the final leg from Trikala, but one morning bus goes direct. From Thessaloniki the bus takes you via Konitsa to Ioannina in a little over seven hours.

Around three KTEL buses leave Ioannina daily for Metsovo (about one hour) and two buses for Kalambaka (two hours); frequencies are the same in the opposite direction. Buses for Dodona leave from Ioannina's smaller, Bizaniou station. The several-times-weekly bus heading for Melingi village passes the ancient site. Other bus options drop you off 1 km (½ mi) or ½ km (¼ mi) from the site; ask for information based on the day you want to go. On Sunday, service is reduced for all towns. Regular bus service runs from Ioannina's main terminal to the towns in the Zagorohoria.

Information **Zosimadon station** (*Main terminal ✉ Between Sina and Zosimadou, Ioannina ☎ 26510/27442 for Metsovo and Kalambaka, 26510/25014 for Dodona*). **Bizaniou station** (*Smaller station ✉ Bizaniou 21, Ioannina ☎ 26510/25014 for Dodona*). **KTEL information** (*🌐 www.ktel.org*). **Terminal A** (*✉ Kifissou 100, Athens ☎ 210/512–4910, 210/512–9363 for Ioannina*). **Terminal B** (*✉ Liossion 260, Athens ☎ 210/831–1434 for Trikala Kalambaka and Meteora*).

BY CAR

A rented car is by far the best way to explore the region, and one is essential to go beyond the main sights. Driving to Kalambaka or Ioannina from Athens takes the greater part of a day. To reach Ioannina take the National Road west past Corinth in the Peloponnese, crossing the magnificent Rion–Antirion bridge. The total trip is 445 km (276 mi). For Kalambaka, take the National Road north past Thebes; north of Lamia there's a turnoff for Trikala and Kalambaka (a total of 330 km [204 mi]). The drive from Thessaloniki takes around five hours and winds you over the mountains and river valleys of Kozani and Grevena on the National Road.

The road from Ioannina to Metsovo to Kalambaka is one of the most scenic in northern Greece, but it traverses the famous Katara pass, which is curvy and possibly hazardous, especially December through March (snow chains are necessary). If you have a few people, it might be more relaxing and almost as economical to hire a taxi to drive you around, at least for a day.

Rental Agencies **Avis** (*✉ Dodonis 96, Ioannina ☎ 26510/46333 for city and Ioannina airport 🌐 www.avis.com*). **Budget** (*✉ Dodonis 109, Ioannina ☎ 26510/43901 or 6932/641943 🌐 www.budget.com*). **Hertz** (*✉ Pirsinella 11, Ioannina ☎ 26510/38911 🌐 www.hertz.com ✉ Airport, Ioannina ☎ 26510/27400*). **Tomaso** (*✉ Dodonis 42, Ioannina ☎ 26510/66900 🌐 www.tomaso.gr*).

BY TAXI

In Ioannina your hotel reception desk should be able to help you negotiate with a taxi driver, especially if you want a tour. You can find taxis at the local bus station and in the central square and at other spots around town. If you see a cab along the street, step into the road and shout your destination. The driver will stop if he or she is going in your direction. You can also phone for a taxi. In smaller towns also you can ask the hotel reception desk for help; taxi ranks are normally in the main square.

Radio Taxis **Ioannina** (☎ *26510/46777, 26510/46778, 26510/46779, or 26510/46780*). **Kalambaka** (☎ *24320/22310 or 24320/22822*).

BY TRAIN

Locals normally prefer to travel by bus, because trains generally take longer. However, train travel makes sense on the Athens Larissis station–Kalambaka route if you take the express Intercity (five hours). It costs around the same as a bus—about €19.10 for the train and €18.10 for the bus. Investing in a first-class seat (*proti thesi*) for €26 means more room and comfort. The nonexpress train is agonizingly slow (at least eight hours) and requires a change at Palaiofarsalo.

Information **OSE Railway** (✉ *Larissis station, Theodorou Deliyanni 31, Athens* ☎ *210/513–1601* 🌐 *www.ose.gr* ✉ *Pindou and Kondyli, Kalambaka* ☎ *24320/22451*).

CONTACTS & RESOURCES

EMERGENCIES

Ioannina **Emergencies** (☎ *100, 171 for tourist police*). **Panepistimiako General Hospital** (✉ *Panepistimiou* ☎ *26510/99111*). **Police** (✉ *28th October 11* ☎ *26510/25673, 0651/26431 tourist police*).

Kalambaka **Health Center** (✉ *Ioanninon, 546 yards from Kalambaka on road to Ioannina* ☎ *24320/22222*). **Police** (✉ *Pindou and Ioanninon* ☎ *24320/76500*). **Tourist Police** (✉ *Hatzipetrou 10* ☎ *24320/22813 or 24320/22109*).

Metsovo **Health Center/First Aid** (✉ *Metsovo main road* ☎ *26560/41111, 26560/41112, or 26560/41071*). **Police** (✉ *Metsovo main road* ☎ *26560/41233*).

SPORTS & THE OUTDOORS

HIKING & WALKING In Ioannina, contact the Greek Alpine Club for walking-tour information. It can organize treks to the Pindos mountains. Aris Talaris can arrange excursions, in his eight-seater minibus, around the Metsovo area and Kalambaka, as well as hiking trips to the Vikos gorge, mainly during summer season. Metsovo Alpine Club has information on hiking trails and the nearby ski center.

Robinson Expeditions in Ioannina specializes in outdoor tours and can make arrangements for single travelers or groups to hike the Vikos gorge; other programs are hang gliding, rafting, kayaking, and studying nature. The company also schedules rock-climbing excursions around the Meteora. For alternative adventures and extreme sports, contact

Trekking Hellas and No Limits (both for the Zagorohoria) and Ecoexperience (for Metsovo).

Contacts **Aris Talaris** (✉ *Hotel Egnatia, Arvantinou 20, Ioannina* ☎ *26560/41263 or 26560/41900* 📠 *26510/75060*). **Ecoexperience** (✉ *Metsovo* ☎ *26560/41770 or 26560/41719* 🌐 *www.ecoexperience.gr*). **Greek Alpine Club** (✉ *Despotatou Ipirou 2, Ioannina* ☎ *26510/22138*). **Metsovo Alpine Club** (✉ *2, Nik. Gotsou, 44200 Metsovo* ☎ *26560/41249*). **No Limits** (✉ *Central square, Konitsa* ☎ *26550/23777* 🌐 *www.nolimits.com.gr*). **Robinson Expeditions** (✉ *Mitropoleos 23, Ioannina* ☎ *26510/74989 or 26510/29402* 📠 *26510/25071* 🌐 *www.robinson.gr*). **Trekking Hellas** (✉ *Nap. Zerva 7, Ioannina* ☎ *26510/71703* 🌐 *www.trekking.gr*).

TOURS

CHAT and Key Tours have similar guided trips to Meteora and northern Greece from Athens. A two-day, one-night tour to Delphi and Meteora with lodging and half-board costs €138. In Metsovo, Kassaros Travel has summer tours (€15 includes picnic) that explore the rugged countryside in an off-road vehicle; in winter, try the snowmobile tour for about €100.

Contacts **CHAT** (✉ *Stadiou 4, Athens* ☎ *210/322–2886* 🌐 *www.chatours.gr*). **Kassaros Travel** (✉ *Kassaros Hotel, Triantafyllou Tsoumaka 3, Metsovo* ☎ *26560/41800, 26560/41346, 26560/41662, or 6944/383131* 📠 *26560/41262*). **Key Tours** (✉ *Kallirois 4, Athens* ☎ *210/923–3166* 🌐 *www.keytours.com*).

VISITOR INFORMATION

The Greek National Tourism Organization (GNTO or EOT) in Ioannina is open weekdays 7:30–2:30 and 5:30–8, Saturday 9–1 in July and August; hours vary other months. Mornings are always best. In summer a tourist information booth is usually erected in the main square of Kalambaka, but it's best to visit the town hall for information.

Contacts **Greek National Tourism Organization** (✉ *Dodonis 39, 45332 Ioannina* ☎ *26510/41868 or 26510/46662* 📠 *26510/49139* 🌐 *www.eot.gr*). **Kalambaka Municipality** (✉ *Vlahava and Trikalon, Kalambaka* ☎ *24320/22339 or 24320/22346*).

Thessaloniki & Central Macedonia

Megisti Lavra Monastery, Mount Athos

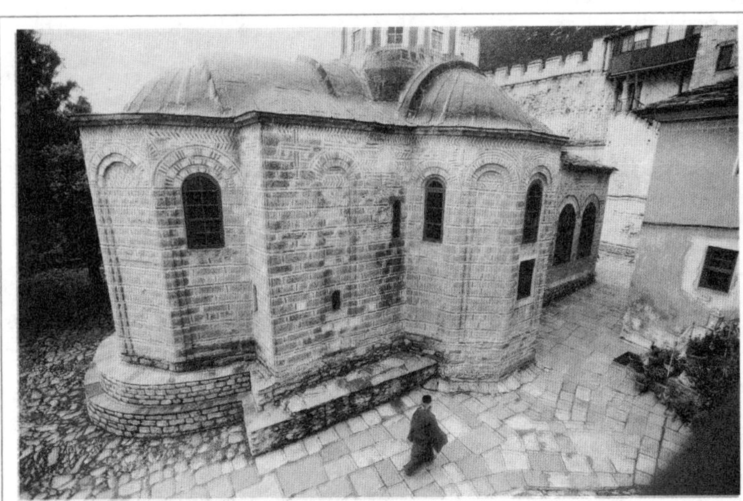

WORD OF MOUTH

"Don't underestimate Thessaloniki itself. [There's an] astonishing range of things to see, from its extraordinary Macedonian gold jewelery, through its late Roman and early Christian remains, through its Jewish history to the relatively untouristy bustling place it's become."

—flanneruk

WELCOME TO THESSALONIKI & CENTRAL MACEDONIA

TOP REASONS TO GO

★ **Mount Olympus:** Bask in a god's-eye view from the top of Greece's highest peak, often covered in clouds and lighting as if to prove Zeus still holds sway—ascend skyward thanks to numerous enchanting trails.

★ **Thrilling Thessaloniki:** In this great commercial hub, the Armani suits and five-euro coffees provide a startling contrast to the ruins of the ancient city walls, Byzantine monuments, and the spirited bartering of the city's bazaar.

★ **Between Heaven and Earth:** Mt. Athos, pinpointed with monasteries, is Greece's most solemn precinct; off-limits to women, it is an exclusive bastion as well.

★ **Alexander the Great Sites:** The fabled ancient ruler made this region the crossroads of the ancient world—walk in his footsteps in Pella, his birthplace and Vergina, home to the royal tomb of his father, Phillip II.

1 Thessaloniki. Named after Alexander the Great's stepsister, this bustling, commercial center is Greece's second city, and has always played a supporting role—to Pella in ancient times, Constantinople during the Byzantine Empire, Istanbul after the Ottoman Empire, and Athens in modern times. Rather than wallow in this eternal bridesmaid status, Thessaloniki has excelled as a cultural and business center, with some of Greece's best food and nightlife (it is known as the country's Liverpool for the jazz and rock groups founded here). Concentrated around its architecturally rich city center, where lovely pedestrian squares give the city a distinctively European urbanity, are such sights as the White Tower, Aristotelous Square, and the Aghia Sophia church; to the north is the picturesque district of Ano Polis.

A fruit-stall in the Thessaloniki market.

GETTING ORIENTED

At the crossroads of East and West, Macedonia bears the traces of many civilizations: Macedonian, Hellenic, Roman, Byzantine, and Ottoman. Bounded as it is by the vast mountain ranges of Olympus and Pindus, it gives an illusion of being cut off from the rest of the country—of having more in common with the adjoining Balkans than with peninsular Greece. From here Alexander the Great once set out to conquer the world but, today, the world heads to Thessaloniki, Macedonia's gateway port and Greece's second city.

2 Central Macedonia. Just southwest of Thessaloniki, central Macedonia dazzles with natural beauty and archaeological wonders, especially at Dion and Vergina. Don't miss an excursion to Mount Olympus, Greece's highest and most storied peak (Zeus had his throne there, after all), and the Royal Tombs of Vergina, where Philip II of Macedonia, father of Alexander the Great, was buried.

3 On the Road to Mt. Athos. Monks got to northern Greece long before tour groups, and the sites they chose for their monasteries are truly beautiful. In this region of extraordinary Byzantine architecture, one of the most impressive monastic complexes in the world is near the Ayion Oros (Holy Mountain) of Mt. Athos, a male-only community for Greek Orthodox monks. Women can cool their heels in nearby Ouranopoulis—known as "Heaven's City," this village lies near Proviakas Bay.

Fresco at the Xeropotamou monastery, Mount Athos.

THESSALONIKI & CENTRAL MACEDONIA PLANNER

When to Go

Travel throughout Northern Greece is best from May through October.

The fall is beautiful; the air is cool and clear and the forests are dressed in burnished hues of orange, red, and copper.

Spring is also lovely, especially in Dion, with its blooming fields of wildflowers scenting the breeze.

Winters are mild, though there's usually enough snow on Olympus to keep ski resorts in business.

July and August are most crowded but best for sunning, swimming, and chatting with northern Europeans and Greek families on holiday.

In the summer, Thessaloniki gets hot and humid but rarely reaches the scorching temperatures that sizzle southern Greece.

But as a whole, northern Greece is rainier and cooler than the rest of Greece, especially in mountainous areas.

Autumn and winter rains, besides turning some roads to mud, do not enhance the appearance of Thessaloniki, a city designed for the sun.

Loosen Those Belts!

The cosmopolitan, multiracial character of Thessaloniki—building on its historic Byzantine and Ottoman influences—has created a multifaceted cuisine of sometimes subtle sophistication; many Greeks feel Thessaloniki has the best food in the country. It is distinguished by its liberal use of fragrant Levantine spices, including hot red peppers from Florina called florines and sweet peppers known as boukova. Traditional Thracian and Macedonian cooks adapt to the seasons: in winter, rich game such as boar and venison is served, and in summer, there are mussels and other seafood from the Aegean, and fruits and vegetables from the fertile plains. The relatively cooler climate here is reflected in rich chicken soups, roast chicken, stuffed vegetables, and stewed lamb and pork.

Thessaloniki is especially known for its mezedes, or small portions of food; every little ouzeri (casual bar serving ouzo and mezedes) or taverna has at least one prized house recipe. Leisurely lunches consisting of a multitude of little plates are the focal point of a typical Thessaloniki day. Specialties include medhia (mussels), which come from farms outside the bay and are served in different styles including saganaki (fried in a pan with tomatoes, peppers, and feta) and achnista (steamed in broth with herbs). Also look for soutzoukakia (Anatolian-style meatballs in tomato sauce, seasoned with cumin). Peinerli (an open-faced boat of bread filled with cheese and ham) is a Black Sea specialty brought here by the Pontii, Greeks who emigrated from that area.

Meals are complemented by generous amounts of wine, ouzo, and tsipouro, the local version of grappa. Try the excellent barrel or bottled local wines, especially reds under labels such as Naoussa or Porto Carras or a little bottle of Mavromatina retsina, considered the best bottled version in Greece. Throughout the city, little shops and cellars specialize in a Macedonian treat called a submarine (or ipovrihio), a spoonful of sweets such as visino (black) cherries in syrup, dipped in a glass of ice water. As for dinnertime, you can arrive around 8, earlier than most Greeks like to eat dinner (many places do not open before then)—but it's much more fun to come at 9 or 10 and mix with the locals.

Making the Most of Your Time

Thessaloniki makes a great base for a trip to northern Greece. Most of the city's sights are concentrated within the easily walkable center, and the city is also the main hub for regional buses and rental cars. There are wonderful museums, a great counterculture vibe, and you could spend days exploring Greece's second-largest city, especially if you're an ecclesiastical buff (the five-aisled basilica Ayios Dimitrios is Greece's largest church) or a foodie (Thessaloniki has outstanding food). From Thessaloniki, go west to Pella, the birthplace of Alexander the Great. Then go south to the town of Vergina, home of the magnificent Royal Tombs, and the ancient city of Dion, tucked into the lush foothills of Mount Olympus. You'll need at least two days to hike the great summit of the gods, including an overnight stay in Litochoro, a pretty village full of enticing tavernas and openhearted locals.

Where to Stay

Thessaloniki's hotels are geared mostly to the practical needs of transient businesspeople, with little emphasis on capturing the spirit of the place—in fact, "high season" here is September, during the major trade fair. City accommodation is fairly pricey compared to regional towns, and if you're driving, parking is a major consideration. The selection of hotels elsewhere varies from exclusive seaside resorts in Chalkidiki to spartan affairs, with charm that comes mainly from their surroundings.

Dining & Lodging Prices in Euros

	¢	$	$$	$$$	$$$$
Restaurants	Under €8	€8–€15	€15–€20	€20–€25	Over €25
Hotels	Under €80	€80–€120	€120–€160	€160–€200	Over €200

Restaurant prices are for one main course at dinner, or for two mezedes (small dishes). Hotel prices are for a standard double room in high season, including taxes. Hotels operate on the European Plan (EP, with no meal provided) unless we note that they use the Continental Plan (CP, with Continental breakfast); Breakfast Plan (BP, with a full breakfast); Modified American Plan (MAP, with breakfast and dinner); or the Full American Plan (FAP, with all meals). Inquire when booking if these meal plans (which can entail higher rates) are mandatory. Guest rooms have air-conditioning, room phones, and TVs unless otherwise noted.

Getting Around

Thessaloniki doesn't have good public transportation, though a new metro is in the works.

However, getting around the city on foot is fairly easy, since most of the sights are fairly close together.

Taxis are also an option, if you don't mind drivers who tend to grouse over the slightest inconvenience.

If you choose to drive, know that the traffic here can be as bad as the gridlock in Athens. That changes once you get out of Thessaloniki.

The national highway is easy to navigate and the smaller roads in central Macedonia are well-paved.

If you wish to rent a car, there are several reliable car rental agencies in Thessaloniki.

There are also buses daily that go to major sites in central Macedonia, many belonging to the giant KTEL company.

English-Language Media

In Thessaloniki, newspapers and magazines are sold at the international press kiosks on Egnatia Odos and Ayias Sofias, Aristotelous Square and Tsimiski, Ionos Dragoumi and Leoforos Nikis by the entrance to the port, and the newsstand at Ayias Sofias 37.

Updated by Joanna Kakissis

A LAND SHAPED BY GODS, warriors, and ghosts, Northern Greece sparkles with the sights, sounds, scents, and colors of its melting-pot history and epic geography. The area called Northern Greece in this guide borders Albania, the Former Yugoslav Republic of Macedonia (FYROM), Bulgaria, and Turkey. Here you will find remnants of the powerful civilizations that battled each other: temples and fortifications built by Athens and Sparta, Macedonian tombs, the arches and rotundas of imperial Rome, the domes of Byzantium, and the minarets and *hamams* (baths) of the Ottomans. "Even today, house-owners sometimes dream that beneath their cellars lie Turkish janissaries and Byzantine necropolises," wrote historian Mark Mazower in his 2004 book *Salonica: City of Ghosts*. "One reads stories of hidden Roman catacombs, doomed love-affairs, and the unquiet souls who haunt the decaying villas near the sea."

Around 316 BC, the Macedonian leader Cassander founded what is now the area's centerpiece, Thessaloniki. The city grew into a culturally rich and politically strategic metropolis where Christians, Muslims, and Jews lived together for hundreds of years. Today it remains the second-largest city in Greece, is a major anchor for arts and culture in the Balkans, and also brims with antiquities, old-style street markets, and old-world European flavor. Beyond Thessaloniki lies central Macedonia, where you can explore ancient monasteries, admire the frescoed tomb of Philip II of Macedon, hike the bloom-filled trails leading to Mt. Olympus, commune with farmers over grilled wild mushrooms, and enjoy some of Greece's finest beaches and seaside resorts.

The region was established as the state of Macedonia in the 8th century BC, and an illustrious monarchy was ensconced by about the 7th century BC. Philip II (382–336 BC) and his son Alexander the Great conquered all of Greece except Sparta and all of Persia as well. After Alexander's death, his brother-in-law, Cassander, established Thessaloniki as the capital (316 BC), naming it for his new bride, Thessalonica, Alexander's half sister and daughter of the much-married Philip. (Philip had named her after his famous *nike* (victory) in Thessaly, where her mother had been one of the prizes.) The Romans took Macedonia as Alexander's successors squabbled, and by 146 BC, the rest of Greece had fallen under Roman rule. After the assassination of Julius Caesar, Marc Anthony defeated Brutus and Cassius at the battles of Philippi in Macedonia in 42 BC. Under Pax Romana, St. Paul twice traveled through on his way to Corinth.

Greek and Macedonian culture bloomed again during the Byzantine Empire (circa AD 312–1453), when the center of Greek civilization shifted from Athens to Constantinople (today Istanbul). Thessaloniki became the second most important city in the empire and it remained so during the Ottoman domination that lasted from the fall of Constantinople until the 1912–13 Balkan Wars. That's when Macedonia became part of Greece, and the 1923 Treaty of Lausanne established the present borders with Thrace. But the fighting did not stop in Northern Greece. In 1941 Mussolini's troops invaded Northern Greece but were pushed back into Albania, prompting the German army to fight its way through the country. (The Nazis also deported 96% of Thessaloniki Jews to their death in concentration camps, almost wiping out the community). And at the end of World War II, Epirus and Macedonia were the principal arenas for the Greek Civil War (1946–49) between the Communists and the Royalists. The political tensions of the time prompted the murders of a prominent leftist Greek politician, Grigoris Lambrakis, and a rising CBS radio journalist, George Polk, who was reporting on the war.

The collapse of Yugoslavia in the 1990s rekindled ethnic and religious animosities. Today's northern Greeks are fiercely nationalist, and they strongly oppose the Former Yugoslav Republic of Macedonia's (FYROM) insistence on calling itself "Macedonia" and using ancient Macedonian symbols such as the star of Vergina on its flag. Tempers flared again in December 2006, when FYROM announced plans to name its international airport in Skopje after Alexander the Great.

Name-game squabbling aside, Northern Greece is flourishing. It's a hub for southeast European commerce and culture, and is home to Aristotle University, Greece's largest. The area is also expected to benefit massively from the Egnatia Odos, a 669-km (416-mi) road project connecting the Greek–Turkish border with the western port of Igoumenitsa. An influx of immigrants, many of them from Eastern Europe and the Middle East, is once again returning a multicultural flavor to Thessaloniki. The beautiful beaches of Halkidiki continue to draw more tourists every year, giving hope to the Greek government's wish to turn the coast into the "Olympian Riviera."

EXPLORING NORTHERN GREECE

A delightful geographic mix awaits you: in the mountains, from snow-covered Mt. Olympus in the west to the mineral-rich eastern ranges, forests of pine, spruce, juniper, oak, and chestnut abound, and ski resorts and centers for climbing beckon. Cosmopolitan Thessaloniki lies in the strategic center of Macedonia, nestled gracefully in the wide but protective arms of the Thermaic gulf and buttressed on its inland side by a low-lying mountain range around which the Axios River flows south to the Aegean. This is a vast, fertile plain of grain, vegetables, and fruit. In the lowlands of Halkidiki the turquoise sea laps at miles of white-sand beach along coastal inlets. You don't have to travel far from Thessaloniki to find these pleasures: the famed three-fingered peninsulas, with their vistas of mountain and sea, and tipped by famed Mt. Athos monasteries, are only a few hours away by car on good highways.

THESSALONIKI ΘΕΣΣΑΛΟΝΙΚΗ

At the crossroads of East and West, where North blends into South, Thessaloniki (accent on the "ni") has seen the rise and fall of many civilizations: Macedonian, Hellenic, Roman, Byzantine, Ottoman, and that of the Jews and the modern Greeks. Each of its successive con-

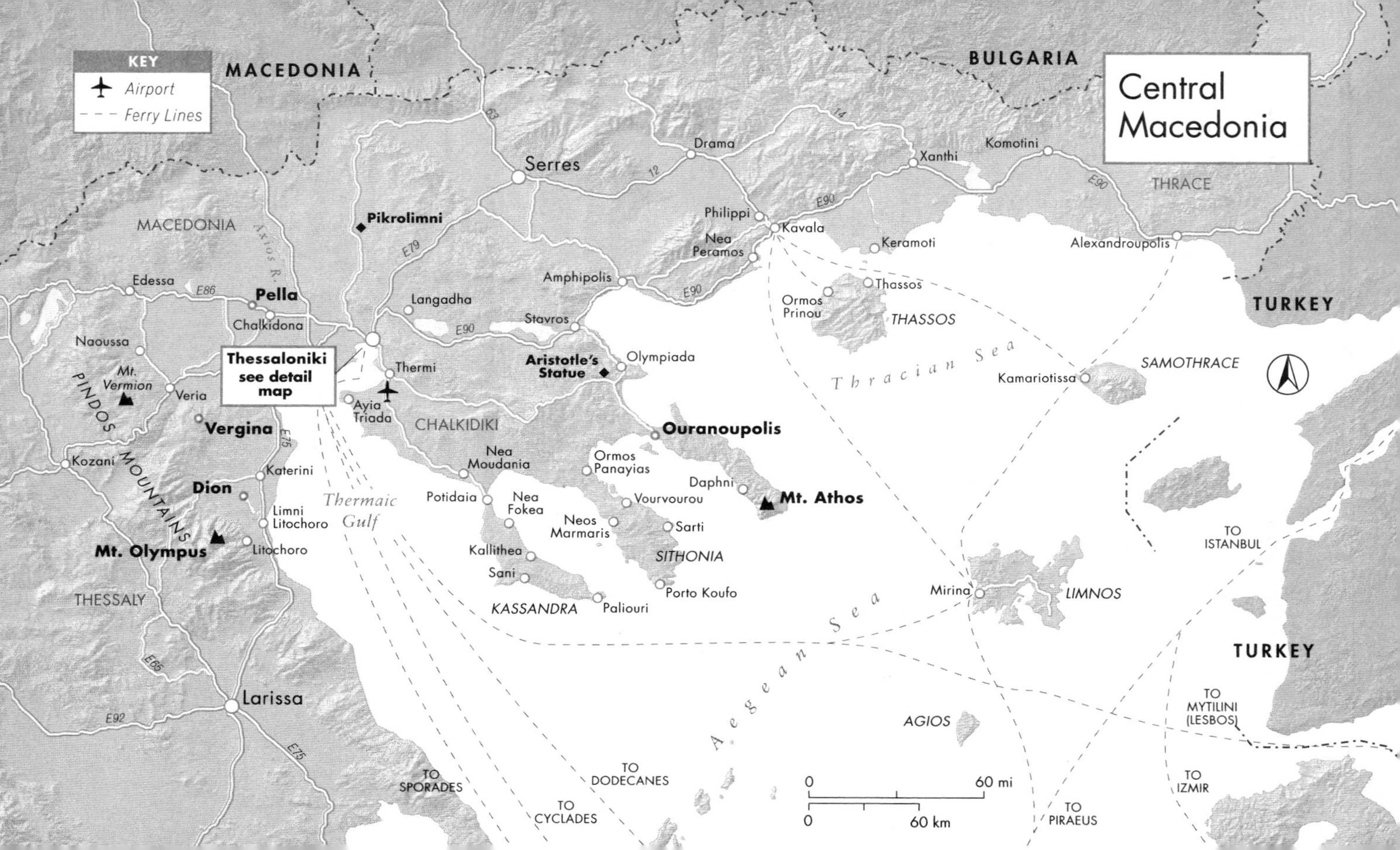
Central Macedonia
KEY
Airport
Ferry Lines
MACEDONIA
BULGARIA
TURKEY
TURKEY
THRACE
MACEDONIA
CHALKIDIKI
THESSALY
PINDOS MOUNTAINS
Serres
Drama
Xanthi
Komotini
Alexandroupolis
Philippi
Kavala
Keramoti
Nea Peramos
Amphipolis
Thassos
Ormos Prinou
THASSOS
SAMOTHRACE
Kamariotissa
Thracian Sea
Aegean Sea
Pikrolimni
Langadha
Stavros
Olympiada
Aristotle's Statue
Edessa
Pella
Chalkidona
Axios R.
Naoussa
Mt. Vermion
Veria
Vergina
Thessaloniki see detail map
Thermi
Ayia Triada
Ouranoupolis
Mt. Athos
Daphni
Ormos Panayias
Vourvourou
Sarti
Neos Marmaris
SITHONIA
Porto Koufo
Nea Moudania
Potidaia
Nea Fokea
Kallithea
Sani
KASSANDRA
Paliouri
Kozani
Katerini
Dion
Limni Litochoro
Litochoro
Mt. Olympus
Thermaic Gulf
Larissa
Mirina
LIMNOS
AGIOS
TO ISTANBUL
TO MYTILINI (LESBOS)
TO IZMIR
TO PIRAEUS
TO SPORADES
TO DODECANES
TO CYCLADES
E90
E86
E79
E75
E65
E92
63
12
14
0
60 mi
0
60 km

querors has plundered, razed, and buried much of what went before. In 1917 a great fire destroyed much of what was left, but the colorful past can still be seen and sensed. The vibrant city with close to 1.5 million inhabitants today—also known as Thessalonike, Saloniki, Salonika or Salonica—has a spacious, orderly layout that is partly a result of French architect Ernest Hébrard, who rebuilt the city after the fire.

Though Thessaloniki has suburbanized in the last two decades, sprawling to the east and west, the old part of the city is fairly centralized and easy to get used to. Whether you're in Ano Polis (Upper City) or along the bay, short walks here are well rewarded; you may come across parks, squares, old neighborhoods with narrow alleyways and gardens, courtyards draped with laundry, neoclassic mansions, and some of the more than 50 churches and 40 monasteries. Thessaloniki's early Christian and Byzantine monuments, with their distinctive architecture and magnificent mosaics, are UNESCO World Heritage Sites. The ever-changing nature of the city continues and neighborhoods like Ladadika, a former warehouse district (which got its name from the olives and olive oil or *ladi* stored here), have been recycled into pedestrian zones of restaurants and clubs. The neighborhood is filled with young and old, strolling by fountains, snapping fingers to the music in the air, and savoring *mezedes* (appetizers) and microbrewery beers at tables spilling onto the stone squares.

The appeal of Thessaloniki lies in part in its warmth, accessibility, and languid pace. The afternoon *mesimeri*, or siesta, is still sacrosanct (don't call people between 3 and 5 PM). Take your time exploring in-town archaeological sites and Byzantine treasures, making sure to stop for café-style people-watching. The two walks suggest routes for exploring highlights. The best, however, is simply to wander through the streets responding to whatever you encounter. It is hard to get lost, since the entire city slopes downhill to the bay, where you can always align yourself with the White Tower and the city skyline.

KENTRO & LADADIKA ΚΕΝΤΡΟ & ΛΑΔΑΔΙΚΑ

Exploring the area from the White Tower west along the seaside to Aristotelous Square reveals icons of the city's history: grand monuments of Emperor Galerius, artifacts from the Neolithic period through the Roman occupation housed in the Archaeological Museum, and prominent churches, as well as the city's most important landmark, the tower itself. The lively shopping streets, bustling markets, and cafés of the Kentro (City Center) and adjacent areas reward you with the unexpected encounters and sensual treats of a great city.

If you're out to catch the sights, why not begin at the **White Tower**, taking in the city's expanse from the rooftop? Walk east on the seaside promenade, Leoforos Nikis, until you see the dramatic bronze statue of Alexander the Great and his horse, Bucephalus. Meander through the lovely park to the north, with its cafés and children's playground, to get to the renowned **Archaeological Museum**, with finds dating from prehistoric Greece to Alexander's Macedonia. The **Byzantine Museum**

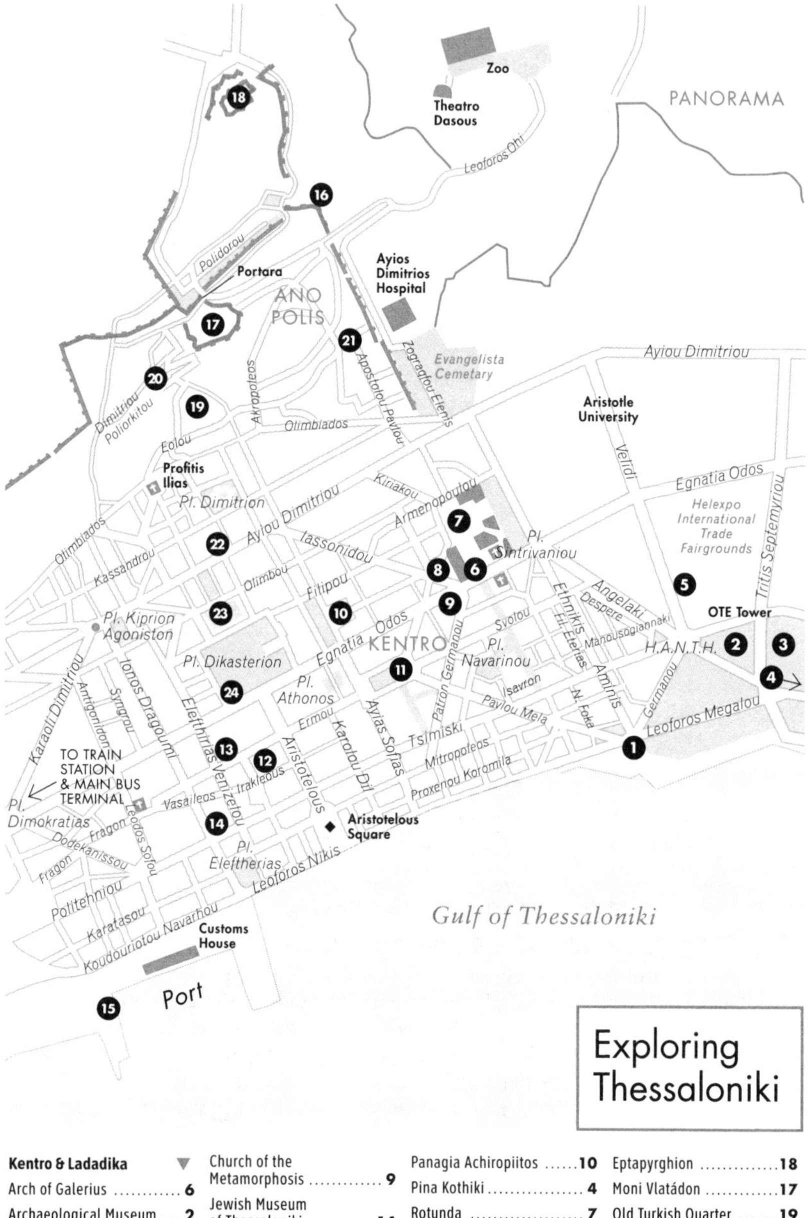

Exploring Thessaloniki

is across Tritis Septemyriou to the east of the museum. Art buffs will head to the new **Pinakothiki** ten or so blocks eastward, then backtrack west to the Macedonia Museum of Contemporary Art. Then head across the enormous square called H.A.N.T.H. toward the city center to the beginning of the city's fanciest shopping street, Tsimiski. Stay on the north side until you reach the beautiful pedestrian Dimitriou Gounari, a street lined with delightful shops and cafés. It crosses Tsimiski and leads you north directly to the **Arch of Galerius**. Even if the **Rotunda** is closed, try to explore the narrow streets surrounding the area, rich with cluttered junk and antiques shops; on Wednesday you can see the eclectic street market. Pass by delightful **Ayios Panteleimon** before crossing Egnatia Odos to the south side of the street and continue west to the lovely 14th-century **Church of the Metamorphosis**. Continuing west on Egnatia Odos, turn right and walk a half block up Ayias Sofias to the oldest Byzantine church in the city, the 5th-century **Panagia Achiropiitos**. Next, head south again on Ayias Sofias for a short downhill walk to reach the 8th-century church of **Ayia Sofia**. From here, it's about an eight-block walk southwest to get to Aristotelous Square, the bustling *platia* (square) by the sea.

GETTING AROUND

Buses traveling throughout Thessaloniki are frequent and the routes practical. Bus 1 plies the route from the train station to the main KTEL Main Terminal; Bus 78 goes from the KTEL Main Terminal to the train station and the airport; Bus 39 from Dikasterion Square (at Aristotelous and Egnatia, in the city center) goes to the KTEL Halkidiki Terminal (for Ouranoupolis, etc). Tickets cost €0.45 and are purchased at bus company booths, and at some kiosks (*periptera*) or corner stores; not on the bus. For complete into, contact O.A.S.T.H., the public transport company of the city.

7

WHAT TO SEE

6 **Arch of Galerius.** The imposing *kamára* (arch) is one of a number of monuments built by Galerius around AD 305, during his reign as co-emperor of Diocletian's divided Roman Empire. It commemorated the Roman victory over Persia in AD 297, and you can still see scenes of those battles on the badly eroded bas-reliefs. Originally, the arch had four pediments and a dome and was intended to span not only the Via Egnatia, the ancient Roman road, but also a passageway leading north to the Rotunda. Only the large arches remain. ✉ *Egnatia Odos, Sintrivaniou Sq., Kentro.*

2 **Archaeological Museum.** The unpretentious, single-story white structure gives no hint from the outside of the treasures within. A superb collection of artifacts from Neolithic times, sculptures from the Archaic, classical, and Roman eras, and remains from the Archaic temple at Thermi, all reside under this roof. Objects discovered during construction of the Egnatia and Thessaloniki–Skopje highways were added in 2005 to the collection displayed in eight galleries. "Thessaloniki, the Metropolis of Macedonia" traces the city's history through artifacts and a multimedia collection. "Towards the Birth of Cities" offers remains from

Fodor's Choice ★

settlements from Kastoria to Mt. Athos that date to as early as the Iron Age. ✉ *Manoli Andronikou 6, H.A.N.T.H., Kentro* ☎ *2310/830538 or 2310/861306* 🌐 *www.amth.gr* 🎫 *€6; combined ticket with Byzantine Museum €8* ⏲ *Apr.–Oct., Mon. 1–7:30, Tues.–Sun. 8–7:30; Nov.–Mar., Mon. 10:30–5, Tues.–Sun. 8–5.*

11 ★ **Ayia Sofia.** The founding date of this church, a UNESCO World Heritage Site and the focal point of the city's Easter and Christmas celebrations, has been the subject of disagreements over the centuries. Ecclesiastics think it was built after the first Council of Nicea (AD 325), when Jesus was declared a manifestation of Divine Wisdom; other church historians say it was contemporaneous with the magnificent church of Ayia Sofia in Constantinople, completed in AD 537, on which it was modeled. From its architecture the church is believed to date to the late 8th century, a time of transition from the domed basilica to the cruciform plan. The rather drab interior contains two superb mosaics: one of the Ascension and the other of the Virgin Mary holding Jesus in her arms. This latter mosaic is an interesting example of the conflict in the Orthodox Church (AD 726–843) between the iconoclasts (icon smashers, which they often literally were) and the iconodules (icon venerators). At one point in this doctrinal struggle, the Virgin Mary in the mosaic was replaced by a large cross (still partly visible), and only later, after the victory of the iconodules, was it again replaced with an image of the Virgin Mary holding baby Jesus. The front gate is a popular meeting spot. ✉ *Ermou and Ayias Sofias, Kentro* ☎ *2310/270253* ⏲ *May–Oct., Mon.–Sun. 7 AM–1 and 6–8; Nov.–Apr., Mon.–Sun. 7 AM–1 and 5–7.*

8 ★ **Ayios Panteleimon.** A prime example of 14th-century Macedonian religious architecture, Ayios Panteleimon is an eye-catching church that draws you in to take a closer look. Restored in 1993 after an earthquake in 1978, the facade reveals the ornamental interplay of brick and stonework, and a dome displays typically strong upward motion. ✉ *Iasonidou and Arrianou, near Egnatia Odos, Kentro* ⏲ *Mon.–Thurs. 9–noon and 4:30–6:30, Fri. 8 PM–10:30 PM, Sat. 9–noon, Sun. 7–10 AM.*

3 ★ **Byzantine Museum.** Awarded the Council of Europe's 2005 Museum Prize, much of the country's finest Byzantine art—priceless icons, frescoes, sculpted reliefs, jewelry, glasswork, manuscripts, pottery, and coins—is on exhibit here. Ten rooms contain striking treasures, notably an exquisite enamel-and-gold "woven" bracelet (Room 4), and an enormous altar with piratical skull-and-crossbones. A mezzanine (Room 7) shows how early pottery was made. Check the Web site for the museum's changeable winter hours. ✉ *Leoforos Stratou 2, Kentro* ☎ *2310/868570* 🌐 *www.mbp.gr* 🎫 *€4; combined ticket with Archaeological Museum €8* ⏲ *June–Sept., Mon. 1–7:30, Tues.–Sun. 8–7:30; Oct.–May closes earlier.*

15 **Center of Contemporary Art.** This moody box of experimental art opened in a remodeled warehouse on Thessaloniki's port in 2005 and now features a wide range of new-media art and video installations. Despite a shoestring budget, it manages to showcase some of the

most exciting young Greek artists around. ✉ *Warehouse B1, Kentro* ☎ *2310/546683* 🌐 *www.cact.gr* 🎫 *€3* ⏲ *Hrs. vary with exhibitions, so call ahead.*

ALL ROADS ALSO LED TO THESSALONIKI

It was during the Byzantine period that Thessaloniki came into its own as a commercial crossroads, because the Via Egnatia, which already connected the city to Rome (with the help of a short boat trip across the Adriatic), was extended east to Constantinople. Today, the avenue called Egnatia Odos virtually follows the same path; it is Thessaloniki's main commercial thoroughfare, although not as upscale as the parallel Tsimiski, two blocks to the south.

9 **Church of the Metamorphosis.** This sunken church, part of which is below ground level, is an example of 14th-century Macedonian church architecture, with a decorative mix of brick and stonework and a dome thrusting upward. ✉ *Egnatia Odos, Kentro.*

14 **Jewish Museum of Thessaloniki.** Among the displays in this museum dedicated to the history of the local Jewish community are tombstones from the city's ancient necropolis, which was on the grounds now inhabited by the Aristotle University. Also on exhibit are objects rescued from the 32 synagogues that existed around the city, some of which were destroyed by the Nazis. The neoclassic building is one of the few Jewish structures that were spared in the great fire of 1917. ✉ *Ayiou Mina 13, Kentro* ☎ *2310/250406 or 2310/250407* 🌐 *www.jmth.gr* 🎫 *Free* ⏲ *Aug. 16–July 14, Tues., Fri., and Sun. 11–2, Wed. and Thurs. 11–2 and 5–8; July 15–Aug. 15, Mon., Tues., and Fri. 11–2, Wed. and Thurs. 11–2 and 5–8.*

5 **Macedonian Museum of Contemporary Art.** A large and expanding permanent collection of Greek and foreign works, as well as an eclectic selection of temporary shows, are on exhibit. After the show, unwind at the museum shop and the quirky art café. ✉ *Egnatia 154, Helexpo, Kentro* ☎ *2310/240002 or 2310/281212* 🌐 *www.mmca.org.gr* 🎫 *€3* ⏲ *Tues.–Sat. 9:30–2 and 6:30–9, Sun. 11–3.*

13 **Memorial to Grigoris Lambrakis.** If you've read the 1966 novel *Z* by Vassilis Vassilikos (or seen the 1969 Costas-Gavras film about the murder of Lambrakis, a leftist member of Parliament, by rightists in 1963), this monument is especially moving. The murder precipitated the events leading to the 1967–74 dictatorship of the colonels. A dramatic bronze head and arm, above which flutters a sculpted dove, marks the spot. ✉ *Corner of Ermou and Eleftheriou Venizelou, Kentro.*

12 **Modiano Market.** Overhauled in 1922 by Jewish architect Eli Modiano, this old landmark is basically a rectangular building with a glass roof and pediment facade. Inside, the rich aromas of food—fish, meats, vegetables, fruits, breads, and spices—compete with music and the noisy, colorful market characters, from the market owners to the bargain hunters. In the little tavernas nearby, ouzo and mezedes are sold at all hours. It is worth a visit—as is the generally cheaper **open-air market** (on the north side of Ermou)—even if you have no intention of buy-

7

ing anything. ✉ *Block bounded by Aristotelous, Ermou, Irakliou, and Komninon, Kentro* ⏲ *Mon., Wed., and Sat. 8:30–2:30; Tues., Thurs., and Fri. 8:30–1:30 and 5:30–8:30.*

10 **Panagia Achiropiitos.** The name *Achiropiitos* means "made without hands" and refers to the icon representing the Virgin that miraculously appeared in this 5th-century Byzantine church during the 12th century. An early example of the basilica form, the church has marvelous arcades, monolithic columns topped by elaborate capitals, and exquisite period mosaics of birds and flowers. It is the second-oldest church in Thessaloniki and probably the oldest in continuous use in the eastern Mediterranean. An inscription in Arabic on a column states that "Sultan Murat captured Thessaloniki in the year 1430," which was the year the church was converted temporarily into a mosque. ✉ *Ayias Sofias 56, Kentro.*

4 **Pinakothiki** *(Municipal Art Gallery).* Nestled amid lush gardens, the art gallery has a distinctive icon collection from the Byzantine and post-Byzantine periods, engravings that highlight the development of the craft of icon making in Greece, and a representative collection of modern Greek art. One section shows the work of three generations of Thessalonian artists, documenting modern art in the city from the turn of the 20th century to 1967. The museum building, the 1905 Villa Mordoh, draws from neoclassic, Renaissance, and art nouveau styles. ✉ *Vasilissis Olgas 162, at 25 Martiou, east of Kentro, Depot* ☎ *2310/425531* 🌐 *www.thessalonikicity.gr* 🎟 *Free* ⏲ *Tues.–Fri. 9–1 and 5–9, Sat. 5–9, Sun. 9–1.*

7 ★ **Rotunda.** Also known as Ayios Giorgios, this brickwork edifice has become a layered monument to the city's rich history. Built in AD 306, it was probably intended as Roman emperor Galerius's mausoleum. However, when he died in Bulgaria, his successor refused to have the body brought back. Under Theodosius the Great, the Byzantines converted the Rotunda into a church dedicated to St. George, adding the impressive 4th-century AD mosaics of early saints. The Ottomans made it a mosque (the minaret still stands). It was restored after damage suffered in a 1978 earthquake, and is undergoing restoration at this writing. Once a month and on major holidays a liturgy is held here, as are occasional art exhibits and concerts. ✉ *Dimitriou Gounari off Sintrivaniou Sq., Kentro* ☎ *2310/968860* ⏲ *May–Oct., Tues.–Sun. 8–7:30; Nov.–Apr., Tues.–Sun. 8–3.*

1 ★ **White Tower.** Formidable seawalls and intermittent towers encircling the medieval city were erected in the 15th century on the site of earlier walls. In 1866, with the threat of piracy diminishing and European commerce increasingly imperative, the Ottoman Turks began demolishing them. The city's most famous landmark, and a symbol of Macedonia, the White Tower is the only medieval defensive tower left standing along the seafront (the other remaining tower, the Trigoniou, is in the Upper City). During the 19th century this was an infamous prison and execution site that became known as the Bloody Tower. In the future, the tower is expected to hold permanent exhibits as the Thes-

saloniki City Museum. ✉*Leoforos Nikis and Pavlou Melas, Kentro* ☎*2310/267832* 🎫€2 ⏲*Tues.–Sun. 8:30–3.*

ANO POLIS TO ARISTOTELOUS SQUARE
ΆΝΩ ΠΟΛΗ ΩΣ ΤΗΝ ΠΛΑΤΕΙΑ ΑΡΙΣΤΟΤΕΛΟΥΣ

Ano Polis, where many fortified towers once bristled along the city's upper walls, is what remains of 19th-century Thessaloniki. It's filled with timber-frame houses with their upper stories overhanging the steep streets. The views of the modern city below and the Thermaic gulf are stunning, but other than Byzantine churches, there are few specific places of historical interest. This elevated northern area of the city gained its other name, Ta Kastra (The Castles), because of the castle of Eptapyrghion and the fortified towers that once dominated the walls. The area within and just outside the remains of the walls is like a village unto itself, a pleasing jumble of the rich, the poor, and the renovated. Rustic one-story peasant houses, many still occupied by the families that built them, sit side by side with houses newly built or restored by the wealthier class. As the area continues to be upgraded, tavernas, café-bars, and restaurants spring up to serve visitors, both Greek and foreign, who flock there for a cool evening out. It's an experience in itself to navigate the steps, past gossipy women, grandfathers playing backgammon in smoky cafés, and giggling children playing tag in tiny courtyards filled with sweet-smelling flowers, stray cats, and flapping laundry.

7

Getting here can be a chore, as taxi drivers often try to avoid the cramped, congested streets and fear missing a fare back down. Have your hotel find a willing driver, or take a local bus. Bus 23 leaves from the terminal at Eleftherias Square (two blocks west of Aristotelous Square, on the waterfront side) every 10 to 15 minutes and follows an interesting route through the narrow streets of Ano Polis. Or you can stroll the 30 minutes north from the White Tower, along Ethnikis Aminis, to get to Ano Polis.

Sightseers should start their Ano Polis excursion with the superb aerial city view from the **Tower of Trigoniou**; then walk west along the inside of the seaward wall (the wall should be to your right). Walk a few yards past the second *portara* (large open gateway), and to your left is the entrance to the grounds of **Moni Vlatádon** and its tiny chapel dedicated to Sts. Peter and Paul. The **Eptapyrghion** is north along Eptapyrghiou. Backtrack to the Tower of Trigoniou and continue west along Eptapyrghiou to the first wide street on your left, Dimitriou Poliorkitou, and take the broad flight of stairs to the beginning of the **Old Turkish Quarter** toward the sea. Follow Dimitriou Poliorkitou west, bearing left, and take the winding descent to the left and then to the right until you come to the doors of the 5th-century **Osios David**. Turn right and continue down the narrow cobblestone street to the first intersection. Below a strange tin "palace" of the self-proclaimed King of the Greeks, follow Akropoleos to the small Romfei Square; walk east along Kryspou, Aiolou, Malea, and Kodrou to Irodotou, in order to see the beautiful frescoes in the exceptional 14th-century **Ayios Nikolaos Orfanos**. Walk downhill toward the modern city on Apostolou Pavlou, the legendary path Apostle Paul took to the Upper City to address the Thessalonians, and cross busy Kassandrou; passing by modern Turkey's founder Ataturk's House.

ATATURK'S HOUSE

The soldier and statesman who established the Turkish republic and became its president, Ataturk (Mustafa Kemal) was born here in 1881. He participated in the city's Young Turk movement, which eventually led to the collapse of the sultanate and the formation of the modern Turkish state. Set about eight blocks east of the Ayios Dimitrios church, the modest pink house is decorated in Ottoman style. For a free tour, apply at the Turkish Consulate (Ayiou Dimitriou 151, ☎2310/248452) down the block and show your passport. ✉*Apostolou Pavlou 17, at Ayiou Dimitriou, Kentro* ⌚*Daily 10–5.*

WHAT TO SEE

Athonos Square. A warren of side streets around a tiny square with a fountain is filled with tavernas and crafts stores. The area is frequently referred to but rarely appears on street maps, as everyone knows where it is. *East of Aristotelous, between Gennadiou and Karolou Dil, between Egnatia and Ermou.*

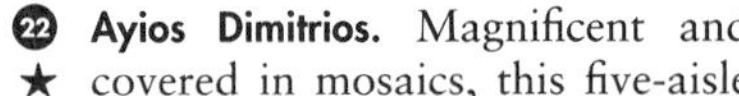

22 ★ **Ayios Dimitrios.** Magnificent and covered in mosaics, this five-aisle basilica is Greece's largest church and a powerful tribute to the patron saint of Thessaloniki. It was rebuilt and restored from 1926 to 1949 with attention to preserving the details of the original; the marks left by a fire can still be seen throughout. In the 4th century, during the reign of Emperor Galerius, the young, scholarly Dimitrios was preaching Christianity in the coppersmith district, in contravention of an edict. He was arrested and jailed in a room in the old Roman baths, on the site of the present church. While he was incarcerated in AD 303, Dimitrios gave a Christian blessing to a gladiator friend named Nestor, who was about to fight Galerius's champion, Lyaios. When Nestor fought and killed Lyaios, after having made Dimitrios's blessing public, the enraged Galerius had Nestor executed on the spot and had Dimitrios speared to death in his cell. His Christian brethren were said to have buried him there. A church was built on the ruins of this bath in the 5th century but was destroyed by an earthquake in the 7th century. The church was rebuilt, and gradually the story of Dimitrios and Nestor grew to be considered apocryphal until the great 1917 fire burned down most of the 7th-century church and brought to light its true past. The process of rebuilding uncovered rooms beneath the apse that appear to be baths; the discovery of a reliquary containing a vial of bloodstained earth helped confirm that this is where St. Dimitrios was martyred. You enter through a small doorway to the right of the altar. The church's interior was plastered over when the Turks turned it into a mosque, but eight original mosaics remain on either side of the altar. Work your way through the crypt, containing sculpture from the 3rd to 5th century AD and Byzantine artifacts, or peruse the parish women's crafts cooperative. ✉*Ayiou Dimitriou 97, Kentro* ☎*2310/270591* *Free* ⌚*Mon. 12:30–7, Tues.–Sat. 8–8, Sun. 11–8.*

21 **Ayios Nikolaos Orfanos.** Noted frescoes here include the unusual *Ayion Mandilion* in the apse, which shows Jesus superimposed on a veil sent to an Anatolian king, and the *Niptir,* also in the apse, in which Jesus is washing the disciples' feet. The artist is said to have depicted himself in the right-hand corner wearing a turban and riding a horse. The 14th-century church, which became a dependency of the Vlatádon Monastery in the 17th century, has an intriguing mix of Byzantine architectural styles and perhaps the most beautiful midnight Easter service in the city. ✉*Irodotou (entrance), Kallithea Sq. and Apostolou Pavlou, Ano Polis* ⏲*Tues.–Sun. 8:30–3.*

18 **Eptapyrghion.** In modern times, this Byzantine fortress—its name means "the seven towers"—was an abysmal prison, closed only in 1988. There's not much to see here except wall ruins and a small museum that documents the building's history. The area is an untended green space, not an unpleasant place to sit and survey Thessaloniki below. The surrounding tavernas accommodate throngs of locals in the evening. ✉*Eptapyrghiou, Ano Polis.*

NEED A BREAK?

Rest your feet and step back in time at the Café Bazaar (✉*Papamarkou 34, Kentro* ☎*2310/241817*), an art deco café and restaurant on a street parallel to Ermou, on Athonos Square. This area was the Jewish quarter prior to the 1917 fire. After that, a French architect built numerous shops known as the bazaar.

17 **Moni Vlatádon.** The Vlatades Monastery, shaded with pine and cypress, is a cruciform structure that displays a mixture of architectural additions from Byzantine times to the present. It's known for its Ecumenical Foundation for Patriarchal Studies, the only one in the world. The small central church to the right of the apse has a tiny **chapel dedicated to Sts. Peter and Paul,** which is seldom open. It is believed to have been built on the spot where Paul first preached to the Thessalonians, in AD 49. Go through the gate entrance to get a panoramic view of the city of Thessaloniki. ✉*Eptapyrghiou 64, Ano Polis.*

19 ★ **Old Turkish Quarter.** During the Ottoman occupation, this area, probably the most picturesque in the city, was considered the best place to live. In addition to the superb city views, in summer it catches whatever breeze there is. Once the home of some of the poorest families in Thessaloniki, the area is rapidly gentrifying, thanks to European Union development funds (which repaired the cobblestones), strict zoning and building codes, and the zeal of young couples with the money to restore the narrow old houses. The most notable houses are on Papadopolou, Kleious, and Dimitriou Poliorkitou streets. ✉*South of Dimitriou Poliorkitou, Ano Polis.*

NEED A BREAK?

A tree shades the terrace and blue, multipaned storefront of the Tsinari Ouzeri (✉*Papadopoulou 72, at Kleious, Ano Polis* ☎*2310/284028*), the last remaining Turkish-style coffeehouse (opened in 1850) and the only one to have survived the fire of 1917. During the 1920s it became the social hub for the refugees from Asia Minor who lived here. Now a café and *ouzeri* (a bar

where appetizers are sold), it is especially popular before siesta time (3:30–4). Try the thick, black coffee, or have an ouzo and share delicious appetizers such as eggplant puree or charcoal-grilled sardines.

20 **Osios David** *(Blessed David).* This entrancing little church with a commanding view of the city was supposedly built about AD 500 in honor of Galerius's daughter, who was secretly baptized while her father was away fighting. It was later converted into a mosque, and at some time its west wall—the traditional place of entrance (in order to look east when facing the altar)—was bricked up, so you enter Osios David from the south. No matter; this entirely suits the church's rather battered magic. You can still see the radiantly beautiful mosaic in the dome of the apse, which shows a rare beardless, somewhat orphic Jesus, as he seems to have been described in the vision of Ezekiel: Jesus is seen with a halo and is surrounded by the four symbols of the Evangelists—clockwise, from top left, are the angel, the eagle, the lion, and the calf. To the right is the prophet Ezekiel and, to the left, Habakuk. To save it from destruction, the mosaic was hidden under a layer of calfskin during the iconoclastic ravages of the 8th and 9th centuries. Plastered over while a mosque, it seems to have been forgotten until 1921, when an Orthodox monk in Egypt had a vision telling him to go to the church. On the day he arrived, March 25 (the day marking Greek independence from the Ottomans), an earthquake shattered the plaster revealing the mosaic to the monk—who promptly died. ✉ *Timotheou 7, near intersection of Dimitriou Poliorkitou and Ayias Sofias, Ano Polis* ☎ *2310/221506* ⏲ *Mon.–Sat. 9–noon and 6–8.*

Fodor's Choice ★

24 **Panagia Chalkeon.** The name *Chalkeon* comes from the word for copper, and the beautiful "Virgin of the Copper Workers" stands in what is still the traditional copper-working area of Thessaloniki. Completed in 1028, this is one of the oldest churches in the city displaying the domed cruciform style and is filled with ceramic ornaments and glowing mosaics. Artisans and workers frequently drop by during the day to light a candle to this patron of physical laborers. The area around Panagia Chalkeon has many shops selling traditional copper crafts at low prices. ✉ *Chalkeon 2, southwest corner of Dikasterion Sq., Kentro.*

★

23 **Roman Forum.** The forum in the ancient agora, or market, dates back to the end of the 2nd century AD. The small amphitheater here, which hosted public celebrations and athletic and musical contests in ancient times, is now often the site of romantic concerts on balmy summer evenings. ✉ *Between Olimbou and Filipou, behind Dikasterion Sq., Kentro* ☎ *2310/221266* 🎫 *Free* ⏲ *May–Oct., Mon.–Sun. 8–7; Nov.–Apr., Mon.–Sun. 8–5.*

16 **Tower of Trigoniou.** From this survivor of the city walls, you can see the city spread out below you in a graceful curve around the bay, from the suburbs in the east to the modern harbor in the west and, on a clear day, even Mt. Olympus, rising near the coastline at the southwest reaches of the bay. There is, however, little of historic interest to see within the walls. ✉ *Eptapyrghiou, Ano Polis.*

WHERE TO EAT

$$–$$$ ★ ✕ **Ouzeri Agora.** Low-key but extremely popular, this ouzeri in the art-grungy Bezesteni neighborhood has excellent food, great service, and a friendly atmosphere where you can vibe with Thessalonians relaxing over lunch or dinner. The fish soup is highly recommended as is the spicy-hot whipped feta, the braised monkfish, and any of the hearty salads. Wash it all down with the distilled spirit made from grapes called *tsipouro.* ✉*Kapodistriou 5, Kentro* ☎*2310/532428* ▭*MC, V* ⊗*Closed Aug.*

$$ ★ ✕ **Ouzeri Aristotelous.** Behind a wrought-iron gate opening to a stoa, artists, scholars, and businesspeople pack marble-topped tables. This convivial place epitomizes the quality and spirit of Thessaloniki dining, down to the traditional spoon desserts. Once you sample the calamari *gemista* (stuffed with cheese), fried eggplant with garlic, or crispy fried smelts, you'll understand why no one is in a hurry to leave. The entrance is on the east side of Aristotelous, between Irakliou and Tsimiski. Be warned: address numbers repeat at the square of the same name down the street. ✉*Aristotelous 8, Kentro* ☎*2310/230762* ▭*AE, MC, V.*

$$ ★ ✕ **Ouzeri Melathron.** "Ouzo's Mansion" was established as Greece's first ouzeri franchise (1993). The chefs here are trained in a style that is essentially Mediterranean, with some French and Turkish influences. Pick from insolently named items, such as "transvestite lamb" (it's chicken) or "Maria's breasts" (cones of fried phyllo filled with ground meat) on the exhaustive menu. Don't forget to order a kilo of house wine. There are also outlets in other cities, such as Lamia, Larissa, Karditsa, Komotini, and Varkiza. ✉*Eleftheriou Venizelou 23, at Ermou, in Stoa Ermeion, Kentro* ☎*2310/220043* ▭*MC, V.*

7

$–$$ ★ ✕ **O Loutros.** Diners at this side-street Thessaloniki institution rub shoulders with lawyers, students, out-of-towners, and workers from the Bezesteni market. The trendy-yet-traditional digs are opposite an old Turkish bath (*loutra* means "baths"). Try grilled *koutsomoura* (baby red mullets), grilled eggplant, mussels in rice pilaf, or smelt or shrimp sautéed in a casserole with cheese and peppers. Do sample the owner's own retsina, which comes straight from the barrel, and check if they have the exquisite *kazan dipi,* a marvelous flan with a slightly burned top, sweetened with a hint of rose water. Live bouzouki music caps an evocative, sultry evening. ✉*M. Kountoura 5, Kentro* ☎*2310/228895* ▭*AE, MC, V.*

$–$$ ✕ **Omorfi Thessaloniki.** The friendly staff at "Beautiful Thessaloniki" and a menu that incorporates around 120 reasonably priced dishes from all over Greece make this a popular choice. Start with the tsipouro (a potent spirit made from grapes) and a few mezedes—oven-cooked octopus with olive oil, for example—and keep adding as your mood strikes; that's how the Greeks do it. ✉*Navarinou Sq. 6, Kentro* ☎*2310/270714* ▭*No credit cards* ⊗*Closed Mon. and 1–2 wks in Aug. No dinner Sun.*

$–$$ ✕ **Ta Nissia.** You're in the city here, even though the furnishings may make you feel as if you've been transported to some Cycladic isle. More than 70 wines and 150 menu items give you plenty of options, such as stuffed squid with cheese and herbs, turkey with ouzo sauce, and veal with smoked eggplant. Reservations are accepted from November through April. ✉*Proxenou Koromila 13, Kentro* ☎*2310/285991* ▭*MC, V* ⊙*Closed Sun. and July and Aug.*

$–$$ ✕**Tsambouro.** One of the favorites in Athonos Square this spot is particularly lively at lunchtime, when the pedestrian walkways are clustered with tables of gregarious (and ravenous) groups attracted by the terrific food and reasonable prices. Good picks are the grilled octopus, as tender and flavorful as lobster; fried *marides* (smelt); and retsina and barrel wine. ✉*Vagdamali 4, Kentro* ☎*2310/281435* ▭*No credit cards.*

$–$$ ★ ✕**Vrotos.** Some of the most delicious and innovative appetizers in Thessaloniki are served at this little ouzeri run by the Vrotos family. You can sit in the noisy interior, decorated with old movie posters, or at the tables out front, all jammed with the cognoscenti. A strong Anatolian influence is evident in the terrific mezedes: try the cheese spread made with Roquefort, eggplant, and walnuts; the *bougiourdi* (feta and other cheeses, tomatoes, and peppers baked in a clay pot); and *prassopita* (leek pie). ✉*Mitropolitou Gennadiou 6, Athonos Sq., Kentro* ☎*2310/223958* ▭*No credit cards* ⊙*Closed 3 wks in Aug., Sun. June–Aug. No dinner Sun.*

$ ★ ✕**Myrovolos Tis Smyrnis.** Go to this beloved hangout—also called Tou Thanassi, after its owner, Thanassis—on a Saturday afternoon when an eclectic mix of Thessalonians fills the Modiano Market. Roaming Gypsy musicians serenade visitors with languid accordion lullabies or swooning violin ballads. The food here is equally diverting, from grilled octopus (sliced off specimens hanging nearby) and stuffed squid to *midhia saganaki* (mussels with cheese-and-tomato sauce). If you do plan to come on Saturday, make a reservation; it's the only day they are accepted. ✉*Komninon 32, Modiano Market, Kentro* ☎*2310/274170* ▭*No credit cards.*

$ ★ ✕**Ta Louloudadika.** Location is everything here: on a lively cul-de-sac across from the *louloudadika* (flower market), this fish restaurant and ouzeri has outdoor seating amid the lunchtime street action. The gold interior with folk accents is mellow, perfect for an ouzo and mezedes. But the food is not an afterthought—crisp calamari rings, sweet morsels of rosy *karavides* (crayfish), and tender stuffed *soupies* (cuttlefish) are some of the delicacies that draw faithful diners. There's live Greek music Wednesday through Saturday night. ✉*Komninon 20, Kentro* ☎*2310/225624* ▭*MC, V* ⊙*No dinner Sun.*

$ ★ ✕**Tiffany's.** Paneled walls, lighting sconces, long tables, and sidewalk dining: this local downtown favorite has some elements of a Parisian bistro. Its grilled meats and stews are the essence of Northern Greece: simple, tasty, and traditional. ✉*Iktinou 3, south of Ayia Sofia church, Kentro* ☎*2310/274022* ▭*AE, MC, V.*

$ ✕**Zythos Dore.** Crowded and lots of fun, Zythos Dore café has a great view of the White Tower as well as a good buzz. Columns tower above tile floors and there are plenty of choices: Greek and international food, bottled or barrel beers, and wine from around the world. Have a drink or a big-deal meal. Zythos, in hip Ladadika, follows the same concept and is one of the best places to hang out in the former warehouse district. ✉ *Tsiroyiannis 7, Kentro* ☎ *2310/279010* 💳 *DC, MC, V Zythos* ✉ *Katouni 5, Ladadika* ☎ *2310/540284* 💳 *V.*

¢–$ ✕ **To Meteoro Vima Tis Garidas.** This casual, friendly place in the midst of busy Modiano Market is known for great *garides* (prawns), served in many different ways, and its humor: the name translates as "the meteoric step of the prawn." Other traditional fare is on the menu, too. Order your ouzo and a selection of mezedes and take in the bustle of market life. ✉ *Irakliou 31, Modiano Market, Kentro* ☎ *2310/279867* 💳 *No credit cards* ⊗ *Closed mid-July–mid-Aug.*

WHERE TO STAY

$$$$ Fodor'sChoice ★ **Capsis Bristol.** An elegant retreat with a touch of history, this exquisite boutique hotel occupies one of the few buildings that survived the great fire of 1917 untouched. During Ottoman rule the structure served as the city's post office. A mixture of handmade furniture, handpicked antiques, and works of art makes this place special. The rooms are named after important Macedonian personalities such as Alexander the Great, Perseus, and Aristotle. Ask about half-price summer discounts. The Capsis Bristol straddles the Ladadika and Kentro neighborhoods, near the waterfront. ✉ *Oplopiou 2, at Katouni, Ladadika, 54625* ☎ *2310/506500* 🖷 *0310/515777* 🌐 *www.capsishotel.gr* *16 rooms, 4 suites* *In-room: dial-up, refrigerator. In-hotel: restaurant, bar* 💳 *AE, DC, MC, V* 🍽 *CP.*

$$$–$$$$ **Makedonia Palace.** You might see a rock star or the president of Albania here; it's that kind of place. Inside you get a real sense of being in Greece, with its mosaics, murals, and artifacts. The luxury Grecotel chain has installed a slew of amenities (mini-stereos, dual-voltage outlets, multimedia convention center) behind a '70s-era facade. The decor is retro-cool, though it's starting to look a little worn and the rooms can sometimes get stuffy in summer. However, this hotel has an excellent location on the waterfront, southeast of the White Tower, with stunning sunset and Mt. Olympus views. There are playgrounds on either side of the building. The rooftop bar and restaurant serve excellent international food. ✉ *Alexandrou 2, at Megalou, Faliro, 54640* ☎ *2310/897197* 🖷 *2310/897211* 🌐 *www.grecotel.gr* *260 rooms, 24 suites* *In-room: refrigerator, DVD, VCR, ethernet, dial-up. In-hotel: 2 restaurants, bars, pools, gym, parking (no fee)* 💳 *AE, DC, MC, V.*

$$$ **Le Palace.** Although it's on one of the city's main thoroughfares, this updated art deco–style hotel is popular with savvy business travelers and Greek tourists. The lounge and restaurant attract neighborhood people as well. Rooms in its five stories have high ceilings, wooden floors, and smartly designed bathrooms, though the decor is a bit weathered. Happily, the breakfast buffet is one of the richest and most eclectic around. Unhappily, rooms can get hot in summer. ✉ *Tsimiski 12, at Eleftheriou Venizelou, Kentro, 54624* ☎ *2310/257400* 🖷 *2310/256589* 🌐 *www.lepalace.gr* *53 rooms, 4 suites* *In-room: dial-up. In-hotel: restaurant, bar* 💳 *AE, DC, MC, V* 🍽 *CP.*

7

$$$ ★ **Mediterranean Palace.** From the abundance of amenities at this six-story hotel near the port and Ladadika, it's easy to see that the Mediterranean Palace caters to business travelers. Besides a phone in the bathroom and soundproof windows, rooms have wireless Internet service and, on request and for a fee, an in-room PC and fax. The chandeliers, black marble-top tables, and richly upholstered furniture are meant to evoke aristocratic 1930s Thessaloniki. Everything is bright and shining, and the polish extends to exemplary service. ☒*Salaminos 3, at Karatasou, Ladadika, 54626* ☎*2310/552554* 🖷*2310/552622* 🌐*www.mediterranean-palace.gr* *118 rooms, 7 suites* *In-room: ethernet, dial-up, Wi-Fi. In-hotel: restaurant, bar, parking (fee)* ▭*AE, DC, MC, V.*

$$$ **Olympia.** Location counts at this hotel on a corner close to the flea market, copper market, Roman Forum, and Ayios Dimitrios. Clean, well kept, and modern, the hotel offers service that is as excellent as the breakfasts. The bar, which has cable TV, is open 24 hours. On this site back in 1931, the Olympia public baths were opened; the hotel wing was added in 1964. Web site under construction at press time. ☒*Olimbou 65, at Papageorgiou, Kentro, 54631* ☎*2310/235421* 🖷*2310/276133* *111 rooms* *In-room: dial-up. In-hotel: restaurant, room service, bar, parking (no fee)* ▭*AE, DC, MC, V* *CP.*

$–$$ **Aegeon.** Don't despair over the garish neon sign outside the Aegeon—it's one of the warmest and best-priced hotels along busy Egnatia street. It's close to the train station, port, city center, and Ladadika districts. Basic but comfy, with folk art decorating the walls, this hotel has small but clean rooms and a staff that is well trained and friendly. Another plus: soundproof rooms. Traffic makes Egnatia noisy but you won't hear the commotion. ☒*Egnatia 19, Kentro, 54630* ☎*2310/522921* 🖷*2310/522922* 🌐*www.aegeon-hotel.gr* *59 rooms* *In-room: refrigerator (some), dial-up. In-hotel: parking (fee)* ▭*AE, DC, MC, V* *CP.*

$ **Mandrino Hotel.** This budget option comes with unexpected amenities, such as an Internet station and no-smoking rooms. The Mandrino Hotel is quite central, along busy Egnatia, near Ayios Dimitrios, Ladadika, and Aristotelous Square. Rooms are nondescript, small, and a little tattered but entirely adequate; go for those in the rear of the building, which are quieter. In a building quirk, the hot water is on the right. Booking through the hotel's Web site may get you a 25% discount on the going rate. ☒*Antigonidon 2, at Egnatia, Kentro, 54630* ☎*2310/526321 through 2310/526325* 🖷*2310/526321* 🌐*www.mandrino.gr* *72 rooms* *In-room: refrigerator, dial-up. In-hotel: bar, public Internet, parking (fee)* ▭*AE, MC, V* *CP.*

$ ★ **Tourist.** A high-ceilinged, turn-of-the-20th-century building houses a modest family-run, three-story hotel that's quite popular with regular foreign visitors—from business-trippers to families. Rooms have high ceilings, and wainscotting figures prominently among the old-fashioned elegance. Three of the 10 single rooms have private bathrooms that are outside the room. Book in advance; the location, just west of Aristotelous Square, is prime. ☒*Mitropoleos 21, at Komninon, Kentro, 54624* ☎*2310/270501* 🖷*2310/226865* 🌐*www.touristhotel.gr* *37* *rooms* ♿*In-room: refrigerator, ethernet, dial-up* 💳*AE, DC, MC, V* 🍽*CP.*

¢–$ **Orestias Kastorias.** Blink and you may miss this circa-1920 hotel on a quiet, narrow street leading from the Roman Forum to Ayios Dimitrios church. The rooms are tiny and the bathrooms even tinier, but front rooms have balconies and views of the ancient ruins. Decor is bland (think Formica and woodlike vinyl flooring) and there's also no elevator in the three-story building, but the price is unbeatable and so is the location. ✉*Agnostou Stratiotou 14, Kentro, 54631* ☎*2310/276517* 📠*2310/276572* 🌐*www.okhotel.gr* *37 rooms* ♿*In-room: no a/c (some), dial-up* 💳*MC, V.*

NIGHTLIFE & THE ARTS

NIGHTLIFE

The Thessaloniki bar and club scene is eclectic, dynamic, and energized. Students, academics, and artists haunt the bars on Zefxidos street near Ayia Sofia church while music lovers crowd the stages at Mylos, a former flour mill that is now Northern Greece's most coveted arts and entertainment complex. In summer, most clubs close, as their clients flock to the beaches of Halkidiki, which functions as an outer suburb of the city. The discos on the road to the airport go in and out of fashion and change names (and concept) from one season to the next, so ask at your hotel for the newest and best.

7

BARS & CLUBS When you hear locals talking about Paralia, they are referring to the road that lines the city center's waterfront, Leoforos Nikis. The cafés and bars here buzz at all hours of the day and night. Walk east along Proxenou Koromila, one block up from the waterfront, to find more intimate, cool bars. Pedestrian Katouni street in Ladadika is lined with cafés and bars; this neighborhood is Thessaloniki's answer to Athens's Psirri and Thission nightlife areas. The club district Sfageia is a short hike or cheap taxi ride southwest of the train station, along 26th Oktovriou street. Restaurants may have live *rembetika* (Greek blues) and other Greek music.

Fodor'sChoice ★ **Mylos** (✉*Andreadou Georgiou 25, Sfageia* ☎*2310/525968*), in a former mill on the southwest edge of the city, has become perhaps the best venue in Greece for jazz, folk, and pop acts, both Greek and foreign. This fabulous complex of clubs, bars, and ouzeri-tavernas, as well as art galleries and a concert stage, exemplifies how a respectful architectural conversion can become a huge success. Don't miss the Xylourgeio stage, which has some of the best alternative acts around. The lively place buzzes with the young and hip as early as 11 PM. **Odos Oneiron** (✉*Vaiou 3, Ladadika* ☎*2310/555036*) is a taverna with live rembetika. It moves to Halkidiki each summer.

Pastaflora Darling! (✉*Zefxidos 6, Kentro* ☎*2310/261518*) is a whimsically decorated hangout for students and artists philosophizing about the latest global trend. Drinks are excellent and inexpensive.

Urban (✉*Zefxidos 7, Kentro* ☎*2310/272821*) is a former art gallery–turned–glam bar for counterculture scenesters, young academics, and lifelong artists. The music is fantastic (Scissor Sisters anyone?) as is the people-watching.

CASINO Next to the airport, the large and elaborate **Regency Casino Thessaloniki** (✉*12th km mark Ethnikos Odos, Thessaloniki–Airport road, Aerodromio* ☎*2310/491234* 🌐*www.thessaloniki.regencycasino.hyatt.com*) is open 24 hours. You must be 23 and have valid identification, such as a passport, to enter (€6 after 8 PM).

THE ARTS

Thessaloniki is an outstanding town for all things cultural: large orchestras and string trios, drama and comedy, and performances by international and local favorites are all part of the scene. For current happenings or information about festivals in the city or area, check with your hotel or the Greek National Tourism Organization (GNTO or EOT).

CONCERTS The **Megaron Moussikis Thessaloniki** (*Thessaloniki Concert Hall* ✉*25th Martiou and Paralia, Kalamaria* ☎*2310/895800, 2310/895938, 2310/895939 box office* 🌐*www.tch.gr*) is a large venue that hosts international and local orchestras (including the Municipal Orchestra of Thessaloniki) and classical, folk, and jazz nights, as well as seminars and lectures.

The live music club **Ydrogeios** (✉*26th Oktovriou 33, Sfageia* ☎*2310/516515*) presents concerts in different genres from September to May, and the venue's jazz café hosts various local and international acts Thursday to Saturday.

FESTIVALS *Apokriés,* or Carnival celebrations, mark the period preceding Lent and ending the night before Clean Monday, the beginning of Lent. These costume-and-parade affairs are particularly colorful (and often bawdy) in Northern Greece. You are welcome to join in the fun in Thessaloniki and other towns. Sohos, 32 km (20 mi) northeast of Thessaloniki, hosts a festive event in which people cavort in animal hides with sheep bells around their waists and phallic headdresses. In Naoussa, 112 km (70 mi) to the west of Thessaloniki, some participants wear *foustanellas* (short, pleated white kilts), special masks, and chains of gold coins across their chests, which they shake to "awaken the Earth." The whole town dons costumes and takes to the streets behind the brass marching bands that have a tradition of playing New Orleans–style jazz.

St. Dimitrios's feast day is celebrated on October 26, but its secular adjunct, the **Dimitria Festival,** has developed into a major series of cultural events that include theater, dance, art exhibits, and musical performances that take place from September to December at venues around Thessaloniki.

More than 1,000 participants from Greece and some 30 countries descend on the **Helexpo International Trade Fair** (✉*Egnatia 154, north of the Archaeological Museum, Kentro* ☎*2310/291115* 🌐*www.helexpo.gr*) to promote their wares—from gadgets to tourism products. An important event in Greek politics, the prime minister traditionally makes the annual state-of-the-economy speech from the fair, which is held in mid-September at the Helexpo fairgrounds.

FILM A must-do in summer, especially for film-lovers, is to see a movie at an open-air cinema. There are usually two showtimes (around 8 and 11 PM, the later one usually at lower volume, depending on the neighborhood). Call ahead to see what's playing—some screen oldies and foreign films (subtitled in Greek), others run the latest Hollywood movies subtitled or dubbed). **Alex** (☒*Ayias Sofias and Olympou, Kentro* ☎*2310/269403*) is the most central.

In November the best films by new directors from around the world are screened and awards given at the **International Film Festival,** southeast Europe's most noted cinematic festival (☒*Olympion Bldg., Aristotelous Sq. 10, Kentro* ☎*2310/378431, 210/870–6000 in Athens* 🌐*www.filmfestival.gr*). Films are usually subtitled; screening tickets are hard to come by. In spring, there's also an international documentary film festival.

PLAYING WITH FIRE

Anastanarides (fire dancers) are a famous part of Northern Greece. On May 21, the feast day of Sts. Constantine and Eleni, religious devotees in the villages of Langadha (25 km [15 mi] north of Thessaloniki) and Ayia Eleni (80 km [50 mi] northeast of Thessaloniki) take part in a three-day rite called the *pirovassia* (literally, "fire dancing"), in which, unharmed, they dance barefoot over a bed of hot coals while holding the saints' icons. The rite is derived from the eastern Thracian village of Kosti. Around 1250 the villagers are famously said to have rescued the original icons from a burning church.

THEATER Performances are in Greek, although there are occasional visits by English-speaking groups. The **Kratiko Theatro** (*State Theater* ☒*Opposite the White Tower, Kentro* ☎*2310/223404*) presents plays, ballets, and special performances of visiting artists year-round. **Theatro Dasous** (*Forest Theater* ☒*In Seich-Sou forest, Ayios Pavlos* ☎*2310/218092 or 2310/245307*) stages theatrical performances in foreign languages in summer, as well as other events, such as concerts.

Children's stages put on well-known plays for kids, usually on Sunday mornings from September to May. They are likely in Greek, but depending on the play and the age of your tot, it might not matter. **Sofouli** (☒*Trapezoundos 5, at Sofouli, Kalamaria* ☎*2310/423925* ✉*info@theatrosofouli.gr*) has three performances on Sunday.

SHOPPING

Among the best buys in Thessaloniki are folk arts and crafts, leather, and jewelry. If it's traditional handmade objects, antiques, and souvenirs you're after, Athonos Square is the place to go. You might want to take home a long-handled, demitasse coffeepot or nautical bric-a-brac. Handmade copper items can be picked up near the Panayia Chalkeon church or at the Bezesteni market, off Egnatia at Eleftherios Venizelou. Is your heart set on handmade jewelry? Head to Aristotelous Square. Don't forget to sample the city's legendary sweets and pastries where- and whenever possible.

SHOPPERS' SIESTA

The government has made efforts to harmonize Thessaloniki's shop opening hours, but the afternoon siesta is still observed by many small establishments. Hours are generally from about 9 to 1:30 or 2; stores reopen in the evenings on Tuesday, Thursday, and Friday. Many shops close for a few weeks in July or August.

ANTIQUES

Antiques shops on Mitropoleos between Ayias Sofias and the White Tower are perfect for leisurely browsing; look also on the streets around Athonos Square.

One block west of the Roman Forum, **Tositsa** is the best junk, antiques, and roaming-peddler street in the city, with good finds from brass beds to antique jewelry. The *paliatzidiko* (flea market) here has a marvelous jumble of fascinating, musty old shops, with the wares of itinerant junk collectors spread out on the sidewalks, intermingled with small, upscale antiques shops.

On Wednesday the narrow streets surrounding the Rotunda are taken over by a **bazaar** with knickknacks and the occasional interesting heirloom, antique, or folk art piece for sale.

BOOKS

The following bookstores are rich with beautifully illustrated children's books on ancient Greek heroes and myths. **Ianos** (✉*Aristotelous 7, Kentro* ☎*2310/277164*) draws travelers because of its stock of foreign-language books. **Malliaris** (✉*Dimitriou Gounari 39, Kentro* ☎*2310/277113* ✉*Aristotelous 10, Kentro* ☎*2310/262485*) carries a large stock of books in English and other foreign languages. **Molho** (✉*Tsimiski 10, west of Eleftheriou Venizelou, Kentro* ☎*2310/275271*), the city's oldest bookshop, sells a wide selection of newspapers and magazines in myriad languages and specializes in English and French books.

CLOTHING

Thessalonians are noted for being tastefully and stylishly dressed. Clothing here is high quality (but notice that sizes are a lot smaller than their American counterparts). The best shopping streets are Tsimiski, with its brand-name boutiques, Mitropoleos, Proxenou Koromila, Mitropolitou Iosif, Karolou Dil, and P. P. Germanou. Cheaper children's clothing (normally extortionate) can be found on Syngrou, south of Egnatia.

GREEK SOUVENIRS

Athonos Square has shops with traditional, handmade items; craftspeople themselves own many of the stores on the narrow streets between Aristotelous and Ayias Sofias. The streets around Panayia Chalkeon have shops selling copper items. Try at the Archaeological Museum for Macedonian-focused souvenirs.

★ **Ergastirio Kouklis** (*Doll Workshop* ✉*Mitropolitou Gennadiou 2, Kentro* ☎*2310/236890*) displays dolls artistically designed by Artemis Papa-

CLOSE UP

Music in Thessaloniki

Thessaloniki was known as the City of Refugees because it was one of the major destinations for the thousands of displaced Asia Minor refugees during the population exchange starting in 1923. Greeks became a majority in Thessaloniki (surpassing the Turks and Jews) and brought along their music, a form of *rembetika* similar to the blues in lyrical content but set to plaintive minor chord music highlighted by the bouzouki. You can still hear it at tavernas and ouzeri, often on weekends. *Pontic*, an ethnic music style rarely heard elsewhere in Greece, was brought along with another group of refugees, from the Black Sea coast. Traditional instruments such as *kemence* (a form of lyra, a string instrument), bagpipe, and *diaouli* (large drum) accompany a staccato rhythm. The music is usually quite loud, as it is now accompanied by heavily amped keyboards and guitars.

Many songs have been written about Thessaloniki, mostly nostalgic tunes of longing. You may want to purchase some of this music, so that you, too, can reminisce. Greece's premier composer (and bouzouki player), Vassilis Tsitanis, wrote "*Omorfi Thessaloniki*" ("Beautiful Thessaloniki"); grab a version of the song interpreted by Glykeria. Dimitris Mitropanos has composed two of the most gut-wrenching tunes; ask for "*S'anazito sti Saloniki*" ("I'm Looking for You in Salonica") and "*Ladadika*," written about the old district. For something more contemporary, try "*Genithika sti Saloniki*" ("I Was Born in Salonica") by Dionysius Savvopoulos, the Greek Bob Dylan. Kristi Stassinopoulou, on the musical edge, performs what she calls a "Balkan ethno-trance" or "Greek techno folk psychedelia." Don't leave a music store without buying something by the amazing Balkan jazz-folk fusion group Mode Plagal (who got their start in Thessaloniki) or by the Athens-based folksinger Savina Yannatou, whose interpretations of Thessaloniki's Ladino (Judeo-Spanish) folk songs are spine-chillingly sublime.

7

dopoulou. **Mastihashop** (✉*Karolou Dil 15, Kentro* ☎*2310/250205* 🌐*www.mastihashop.com*) carries products containing mastic—a tree resin produced on the Aegean island of Chios. Everything from face cream to preserves and sweets come in extremely attractive, easy-to-pack tins.

SWEETS

Thessaloniki is well known for its food, including a vast array of Balkan and Eastern-oriented pastries and desserts. Sit down, sample, and decide which you think is best.

With eight outlets in Thessaloniki, **Agapitos** (✉*Tsimiski 53, between Ayias Sofias and Karolou Dil, Kentro* ☎*2310/235935* 🌐*www.agapitos.gr*) aptly translates as "loved one." The oldest son of a venerable Thessaloniki family owns this chain. **Averof** (✉*Vasilissis Georgiou 11, Kentro* ☎*2310/814284* 🌐*www.averof.gr*) is the only patisserie in Thessaloniki that creates kosher pastries.

★ Sample Thessaloniki's fabled Anatolian sweets at central **Hatzi** (✉*Eleftheriou Venizelou 50, Kentro* ☎*2310/279058*). Specialties include the buffalo milk cream-based *kazan dipi,* a kind of flan; *trigono,* a cream-filled triangle of phyllo; and *kataïfi* (logs of crushed and sugared walnuts wrapped in honey-drenched shredded phyllo) served with *kaïmaki* (mastic-flavored ice cream). Choose a beverage—like iced coffee, granita, or *boza* (a thick, sweet, millet-and-corn drink)—and people-watch from the pedestrian side street that faces the gardens of Panagia Chalkeon church.

Terklenis (✉ *Tsimiski 30, Kentro*) serves an unforgettable *tsoureki* (sweet bread flavored with *mahlepi,* a spice made from the ground-up pits of a Persian cherry) and then filled and dipped in chocolate. This delicacy is so delicious that it disappears within hours from this extremely popular patisserie's shelves.

CENTRAL MACEDONIA ΚΕΝΤΡΙΚΗ ΜΑΚΕΔΟΝΙΑ

Ancient ruins, mountains, beachfront resorts, and sacred sanctuaries lie within easy reach of Thessaloniki in Central Macedonia. Pella, Vergina, and Dion are three major archaeological sites associated with Alexander the Great and his father, Philip II, heroes of the ages. A lovely village, Litochoro, sits beneath the peaks of Mt. Olympus. The region of Halkidiki is best known as Thessaloniki's summer playground with its beaches and resorts, including Ouranoupolis and its offshore islands. Holy Mt. Athos is a males-only monastic peninsula of natural and spiritual beauty.

In the 7th century BC the Dorian Makednoi (Macedonian) tribe moved out of the Pindos mountains (between Epirus and Macedonia), settled in the fertile plains below, and established a religious center at the sacred springs of Dion at the foot of Mt. Olympus. Perdikkas, the first king of the Macedonians, held court at a place called Aigai, now known to have been at Vergina; and in the 5th century BC, the king of that time, Archelaos (413–399), moved his capital from Aigai to Pella, which was then on a rise above a lagoon leading to the Thermaic gulf.

In 359 BC, after a succession of kings and near anarchy exacerbated by the raids of barbarian tribes from the north, the 23-year-old Philip II was elected regent. Philip II pulled the kingdom together through diplomacy and marital alliances and then began expanding his lands, taking the gold mines of the Pangeon mountains and founding Philippi there. In 356 BC, on the day that Alexander the Great was born, Philip II was said to have simultaneously taken the strategic port of Potidea in Halkidiki, received news of his horse's triumph in the Olympic Games, and learned of a general's victory against the Illyrians. That was also the day the temple of Artemis at Ephesus was destroyed by fire, which later prompted people to say that the goddess was away on that day, tending to Alexander's birth. In 336 BC, Philip II was assassinated in Vergina at a wedding party for one of his daughters. (His tomb there was discovered in 1977 by the Greek archaeologist Manolis Andronikos.) Alexander, then 20, assumed power, and within two years he had gathered an army to be blessed at Dion, before setting off to conquer the Persians and most of the known world.

PELLA ΠΕΛΛΑ

★ *40 km (25 mi) west of Thessaloniki.*

Pella was Alexander's birthplace and the capital of the Macedonian state in the 4th century. The modern-day village is not the most alluring, nor is there anywhere to stay. The ancient village ruins and its museum—both best known for their intricate, artful, beautifully preserved floor mosaics, mainly of mythological scenes—are on either side of the main road toward Edessa (where waterfalls invite a possible further trip). It's best to first get an overview at the **Archaeological Museum,** which contains a model of the 4th-century BC dwelling that stood across the road, as well as fascinating artifacts of Neolithic, Bronze, and Iron Age settlers, some as old as the 7th century BC. Note also the unique statuette of a horned Athena (apparently influenced by Minoan Crete), the statue of Alexander sprouting the horns of Pan, and the adorable sleeping Eros (Cupid), reproductions of which can be bought at the gift shop. Descriptions are sparse, but the attendants, pointedly not experts, are happy to share what they know.

In 1914, two years after the Turks' departure, the people who lived on the land were moved to a village north of here, and excavations of the **archaeological site** began. These include portions of the walls; the sanctuaries of Aphrodite, Demeter, and Cybele; the marketplace; cemetery; and several houses. In 1987, on a small rise to the north, the remains of the **palace** came to light; at present they are still excavating. If coming by train, get off at Edessa and take the KTEL bus to the site. If coming by bus, get off the Thessaloniki–Edessa KTEL bus at the site. ✉ *Off E86, Thessaloniki–Edessa road* 🎫 *€6* ⏲ *Tues.–Sun. 8–7:30, Mon. noon–7:30.*

7

VERGINA ΒΕΡΓΙΝΑ

Fodor'sChoice ★ *40 km (25 mi) south of Pella, 135 km (84 mi) southwest of Thessaloniki.*

Some of antiquity's greatest treasures await you at the Royal Tombs of Vergina, opened to the public in 1993, 16 years after their discovery. Today the complex, including a museum, is a fitting shrine to the original capital of the kingdom of Macedonia, then known as Aigai. The entrance is appropriately stunning: you walk down a white sandstone ramp into the partially underground structure, roofed over by a large earth-covered dome approximately the size of the original tumulus. Here on display are some of the legendary artifacts from the age of Philip II of Macedonia.

For years both archaeologists and grave robbers had suspected that the large mound that stood on this site might contain something of value, but try as they might, neither of these groups was successful in penetrating its secret. Locals still remember playing ball on the mound as children. Professor Manolis Andronikos, who discovered the tombs, theorized in his book *The Royal Tombs of Vergina* that one of Alexander's successors, wanting to protect Philip's tomb from robbers, had it covered with broken debris and tombstones to make it appear that the grave had already been plundered, and then built the tumulus so that Philip's tomb would be near the edge rather than the center. When Andronikos discovered it, on the final day of excavation, in 1977, he had been trying one of the last approaches, with little hope of finding anything—certainly not the tomb of Philip II, in as pristine condition as the day it was closed.

This was the first intact Macedonian tomb ever found—imposing and exquisite, with a huge frieze of a hunting scene, a masterpiece similar to those of the Italian Renaissance but 1,800 years older, along with a massive yet delicate fresco depicting the abduction of Persephone (a copy of which is displayed along one wall of the museum). Two of the few original works of great painting survive from antiquity. On the left are two tombs and one altar that had been looted and destroyed in varying degrees by the time Andronikos discovered them. Macedonian Tomb III, on the right, found intact in 1978, is believed to be that of the young Prince Alexander IV, Alexander the Great's son, who was at first kept alive by his "protectors" after Alexander's death and then poisoned (along with his mother) when he was 14. To the left of Tomb III is that of Philip II. He was assassinated in the nearby theater, a short drive away; his body was burned, his bones washed in wine, wrapped in royal purple, and put into the magnificent, solid gold casket with the 16-point sun, which is displayed in the museum. His wife, Cleopatra (not the Egyptian queen) was later buried with him.

The tombs alone would be worth a special trip, but the golden objects and unusual artifacts that were buried within them are equally impressive. Among these finds, in excellent condition and displayed in dramatic dimmed light, are delicate ivory reliefs, elegantly wrought gold laurel wreaths, and Philip's crown, armor, and shield. Especially interesting are those items that seem most certainly Philip's: a pair of greaves (shin guards), one shorter than the other—Philip was known to have a limp. To the right of the tombs there's a gift shop that sells books and postcards; the official gift shop is outside the entrance gate (across from Philippion restaurant), on the same side of the road. Macedonian souvenirs available here are scarce elsewhere.

The winding road to the **site of Philip's assassination** goes through rolling countryside west of modern Vergina, much of it part of the vast royal burial grounds of ancient Aigai. On the way you pass three more **Macedonian tombs** of little interest, being rough-hewn stone structures in typical Macedonian style; the admission to the Royal Tombs includes these. The **palace** itself is nothing more than a line of foundation stones that shows the outline of its walls. It was discovered by French archaeologists in 1861 but not thought to have any particular significance; ancient Aigai was then thought to be somewhere near Edessa. In the field below are the remnants of the **theater,** discovered by Andronikos in 1982. It was on Philip's way here, to attend the wedding games that were to follow the marriage of his daughter to the king of Epirus, that he was murdered and where his son, Alexander the Great, was crowned.

To get to Vergina by bus, go from Thessaloniki KTEL main terminal to Veria, and take a bus to the site from there. If going by train, get off at Veria station. A local "blue" bus takes passengers from the outlying station into town, where you can take the KTEL bus. Be attentive if coming by car: the route is not well marked from Pella. ✉ *Off E90, near Veria* ☎ *23310/92347* *€8* *June–Oct., Mon. noon–7, Tues.–Sun. 8–7; Nov.–May, Tues.–Sun. 8:30–3.*

THE ROAD TO VERGINA

To get to Vergina by bus, go from Thessaloniki KTEL main terminal to Veria, and take a bus to the site from there. If going by train, get off at Veria station. A local "blue" bus takes passengers from the outlying station into town, where you can take the KTEL bus. Be attentive if coming by car: the route is not well marked from Pella. ✉ *Off E90, near Veria* ☎ *23310/92347* *€8* *June–Oct., Mon. noon–7, Tues.–Sun. 8–7; Nov.–May, Tues.–Sun. 8:30–3.*

WHERE TO STAY & EAT

$ Fodor's Choice ★ **Philippion.** Choose from traditional foods such as moussaka or try the highly recommended fresh pasta. The regional vegetables are especially delicious, and fresh frozen yogurt is made from local fruits. Self-serve cafeteria-style lunch is available, but this is also a taverna-restaurant. Reservations are not necessary, but be warned tour buses do stop here. ✉ *Outside archaeological site* ☎ *23310/92892* *AE, MC, V.*

$$$ **Dimitra.** On a quiet street a five-minute walk from the ancient archaeological site at Vergina is the village's luxury lodging. This beautiful two-story hotel was built in 2003. Each of the eight spacious studio suites has its own classic style and features as a fireplace or piano. The owners may offer to give you a private viewing of an oil painting of the hotel's namesake. Consider making this a base for area excursions; discounts are available for extended stays. A hearty breakfast is included in the price. ✉ *Athinas 5, 59031* ☎ *23310/92900* *23310/92901* *zisseka@yahoo.com* *8 suites* *In-room: kitchen, refrigerator. In-hotel: bar, parking* *No credit cards* *BP.*

¢ **Vergina Pension.** Between the modern and ancient village sits a two-story, pine-furniture-and-crisp-sheets accommodation like those found all over the country. It's got all the basics covered and has wraparound balconies and plants in the unusually wide corridors. The café-bar is enormous, and you can relax with a glass of wine, a coffee, or a sweet. Breakfast is generous and fresh. Small pets are allowed, but only have free-run on balconies. ✉ *Aristotelous 55, 59031* ☎ *23310/92510* *23310/92511* *10 rooms* *In-room: no phone, refrigerator (some). In-hotel: bar* *No credit cards.*

7

DION ΔΙΟΝ

Fodor's Choice ★ *90 km (56 mi) south of Vergina, 87 km (54 mi) southwest of Thessaloniki.*

At the foothills of Mt. Olympus lies ancient Dion. Even before Zeus and the Olympian gods, the mountain was home to the Muses and Orpheus, who entranced the men of the area with his mystical music. The story says that the life-giving force of Dion came from the waters in which the murderers of Orpheus (the women of Mt. Olympus, jealous for attention from their men) washed their hands on the slopes of the sacred mountain to remove the stain of their own sin. The waters entered the earth and rose, cleansed, in the holy city of Dion. (Zeus is *Dias* in Greek, it's he for whom the city was named.)

Ancient Dion was inhabited from as early as the classical period (5th century BC) and last referred to as Dion in the 10th century AD according to the archaeological findings. Start at the **museum** to see the videotape (in English) prepared by the site's renowned archaeologist, Dimitris Pandermalis, which describes the excavations, the finds, and their significance. (His efforts to keep the artifacts in the place where they were found have established a trend for decentralization of archaeological finds throughout Greece.) The second floor contains a topographical relief of the area and the oldest surviving pipe organ precursor—the 1st-century BC hydraulis. The basement learning area has an Alexander mosaic, model of the city, and ancient carriage shock absorbers. Labels are very basic. ✉ *Adjacent to archaeological site* ☎ *23510/53206* 🎫 *€3* ⏲ *Tues.–Sun. 8–7:30.*

Unearthed ruins of various buildings include the villa of Dionysos, public baths, a stadium (the Macedonian Games were held here), shops, and workshops. The road from the museum divides the diggings at the archaeological site into two areas. On the left is the **ancient city** of Dion itself, with the juxtaposition of public toilets and several superb floor mosaics. On the right side are the **ancient theaters** and the **Sanctuaries of Olympian Zeus, Demeter, and Isis.** In the latter, which is a vividly beautiful approximation of how it once looked, copies of the original statues, now in the museum, have been put in place.

Dion is about a 1½-hour journey from Thessaloniki; buses leave every half hour or so for Katerini, where you can take the local "blue" bus to the Dion site (€1). From Katerini, you could also hop on the connecting route to Litochoro at the base of Mt. Olympus (€6.50), which has good dining and lodging options, and take a taxi (around €7) to the site. If coming by train get off at Katerini, 17 km (27 mi) south of the site, then take a bus or a taxi to the site or to Litochoro (the isolated Litochoro railway station is outside town). Winter hours are unpredictable. ✣ *7 km (4½ mi) north of Litochoro off E75/1A, Thessaloniki–Athens road* ☎ *23510/53484* 🎫 *€4* ⏲ *May–Oct., daily 8–5; Nov.–Apr. reduced hrs.*

WHERE TO STAY & EAT

$$–$$$ ★ ✕ **Dionysos.** Excellent food and true Greek *filoxenia* (hospitality) await at the combination tourist shop, café, and three-meal-a-day restaurant. Recommended are the *loukanika* (sausages); rolled, spiced, and spit-roasted meat; and the excellent *yemista* (stuffed tomatoes and peppers) and *papoutsakia* (eggplant halves baked with cheese, spiced ground beef, and garlicky tomato sauce). If you want to try the specialty of the area, *katsikaki sti souvla* (roasted goat on a spit), order at least a day ahead. The house barrel wine, *krasi hima,* is locally produced, and the owners serve homemade tsipouro liquor. ✉ *Village center, directly opposite museum* ☎ *23510/53276* ▭ *No credit cards.*

$–$$ Fodor'sChoice ★ **Safeti.** The mauve-color Safeti, opened in 2005, is a most welcome addition to Dion, and Greece in general. Four gorgeous, modern suites—one of which has a hot tub, another, a fireplace—upstairs make good use of chrome, light wood, ceramic tiles, and leather furniture. Downstairs, crafts and products all enterprisingly made by the Safeti family (most right on-site) are for sale: organic preserves, liqueurs, and pasta; loom-made rugs; dolls and bags; mosaics; and copper pots. Full breakfast, made with ingredients from the garden, is available. Two of the suites have a stunning view of Mt. Olympus. ✉ *Opposite ancient Dion museum, on main road, 60100* ☎ *23510/46272, 694/7720343 cell* ℻ *23510/46273* 🌐 *www.safetis.gr* ✉ *info@safetis.gr* *4 suites* *In-room: kitchen* ▭ *MC, V.*

7

MT. OLYMPUS ΌΡ. ΌΛΥΜΠΟΣ

★ *17 km (10 mi) southwest of Dion, 100 km (62 mi) southwest of Thessaloniki.*

To understand how the mountain must have impressed the ancient Greeks and caused them to shift their allegiance from the earth-rooted deities of the Mycenaeans to those of the airy heights of Olympus, you need to see the mountain clearly from several different perspectives. On its northern side, the Olympus range catches clouds in a turbulent, stormy bundle, letting fly about 12 times as many (surely Zeus-inspired) thunder-and-lightning storms as anywhere else in Greece. From the south, if there is still snow on the range, it appears as a massive, flat-topped acropolis, much like the one in Athens; its vast, snowy crest hovering in the air, seemingly capable of supporting as many gods and temples as the ancients could have imagined. As you drive from the sea to Mt. Olympus, this site appears as a conglomeration of thickly bunched summits rather than as a single peak. The truly awe-inspiring height is 9,570 feet.

A PEACEABLE KINGDOM

Today a feeling of tranquility prevails at Dion, at the foot of the mountain of the gods. Few people visit this vast, underrated city site. The silence is punctuated now and then by goats, their bells tinkling so melodically you expect to spy Pan in the woods at any moment. Springs bubble up where excavators dig, and scarlet poppies bloom among the cracks—this is the essence of Greece.

CLOSE UP

Hiking Zeus's Mountain

Mt. Olympus has some of the most beautiful nature trails in Europe. Hundreds of species of wildflowers and herbs bloom in spring, more than 85 of which are found only on this mountain. There are basically three routes to Zeus's mountain top, all beginning in Litochoro. The most-traveled road is via Prionia; the others are by Diastavrosi (literally, "crossroads") and along the Enipeos. You can climb all the way on foot or take a car or negotiate a taxi ride to the end of the road at Prionia (there's a taverna) and trek the rest of the way (six hours or so) up to snow-clad Mytikas summit—Greece's highest peak at 9,570 feet. The climb to Prionia takes about four hours; the ride, on a bumpy gravel road with no guardrails between you and breathtakingly precipitous drops, takes little less than an hour, depending on your nerves. If you can manage to take your eyes off the road, the scenery is magnificent. The trail is snow-free from about mid-May until late October. During your Mt. Olympus hike, you could take a lunch break or stay overnight at **Spilios Agapitos.** The refuge is run by the daughter of Kostas Zolotas, the venerable English-speaking guru of climbers. To bunk down for the night costs €10 per person; there are blankets but no sheets. Bring your own flashlight, towel, and soap. The restaurant is open 6 AM–9 PM. It's 6 km (4 mi), about 2½–3 hours, from Prionia to Refuge A. From here it's 5 km (3 mi), about 2½–3 hours, to the Throne of Zeus and the summit. The trail is easygoing to Skala summit (most of the way), but the last bit is scrambling and a bit hair-raising. Some people turn back. If you plan to hike up Mt. Olympus, be sure to take a map; the best are produced by Anavasi. ✉ *Refuge A* ☎ *23520/81800* ✉ *zolotam@hol.gr* ⏲ *Mid-May–Oct.; overnight guests must arrive by 8 PM.*

Litochoro is the lively town (population 7,000, plus a nearby army base) nestled at the foot of the mountain and is the modern address for Olympus these days. Souvenir shops, restaurants, local-specialty bakeries (stock up before a hike), and hotels vie for customers. Litochoro is 1½ hours by KTEL bus from Thessaloniki (almost every half hour from Thessaloniki and hourly from nearby Katerini). The isolated Litochoro train station is hard to access, about 5 km (3 mi) from the town near the seaside. Better to take the train to Katerini and then a bus from there.

WHERE TO STAY & EAT

$–$$ Fodor'sChoice ★ ✕ **Gastrodromio En Olympo.** A perfect place for the village gourmet, this is just the spot for tantalizing grilled wild mushrooms, wild boar with plums, fresh and fragrant salads, and great house wine. Family-run, friendly, and elegant, it's a fetching place to enjoy outstanding food while taking in the area's rugged beauty. ✉ *Central square of Litochoro, Litochoro 60200* ☎ *23520/21300* 🌐 *www.gastrodromio.gr* 💳 *No credit cards.*

$ ★ ✕ **To Pazari.** This homey restaurant is known for its outstanding seafood—it's always fresh, artfully prepared, and surprisingly cheap. The grilled meats are also good, as are the fresh bread and the dips (especially the *tzatziki* [cucumber-yogurt dip] and *melitzanosalata*, lovingly made from roasted eggplant and garlic). The fish soup in winter is also a specialty. Follow the signs 100 yards past the main square and up to the left around the corner. ✉ *25th Martiou, Litochoro* ☎ *23520/82540 or 23520/84185* ▭ *MC, V.*

$$$$ ★ **Dion Palace Beauty & Spa Resort.** Enjoy excellent views of the sea or the peaks at the Dion Palace. Proximity to the beach, Mt. Olympus, and the archaeological site at Dion is the big draw here. There's also a luxury spa, as well as many activities for kids. Water sports are available through a private operator. KTEL buses on the Thessaloniki-bound Katerini–Litochoro route (Camping Mitikas stop; go through the campground) run every hour in summer, from about 6 AM to 9:30 PM. ✉ *Limni Litochoro, 6 km (4 mi) northeast of Litochoro, 60200 Gritsa* ☎ *23520/61431 through 23520/61434* 🖷 *23520/61435* 🌐 *www.dionpalace.com* *187 rooms, 9 suites* *In-room: refrigerator, dial-up. In-hotel: 3 restaurants, bars, tennis courts, pool, gym, spa* ▭ *AE, DC, MC, V* *BP.*

$$–$$$ ★ **Olympus Mediterranean.** Pretty and friendly, this spa hotel—built in 2004—offers a surprisingly vibe of luxury and comfort for the money. Rooms on each of its four floors are done in different styles, such as traditional or modern, and the third-floor suite has a great view of the area. Some rooms have a fireplace and/or hot tub; all have balconies. There are beauty treatment rooms and an indoor pool in the basement. Follow signs up and left from the main square (not far); it's hidden beside To Pazari taverna. ✉ *Dionyssou 5, 60200 Litochoro* ☎ *23520/81831* 🖷 *23520/83333* *olympus-med@acn.gr* *20 rooms, 3 suites* *In-room: refrigerator. In-hotel: bar, pool, spa* ▭ *DC, MC, V* *BP.*

¢–$ ★ **Villa Pantheon.** You know you're somewhere special when you see this family-run establishment at the trailhead for Mt. Olympus; views stretch to the sea and the mountains. All the suites (with three or four beds) have fireplaces. Prices are cheap, amenities like TV and air-conditioning are available, so that means reservations are a must, especially on weekends and holidays. From the square it's a 10-minute walk up Enipeos past the Aphrodite Hotel. Continue slightly left after the juncture, turn up Ayiou Dimitriou, and keep going over the bridge; the hotel's on the right. ✉ *Ayiou Dimitriou terma (end), 60200Litochoro* ☎ *23520/83931* 🖷 *23520/83932* *4 rooms, 8 suites* *In-room: kitchen, refrigerator. In-hotel: restaurant, bar* ▭ *MC, V.*

SPORTS & THE OUTDOORS

Trekking Hellas runs hiking, rafting, mountain biking, and other outdoor excursions in the region, including some great trips up the mythical Mt. Olympus by foot (or bike) from Litochoro. Hellenic Alpine Club can help with information on hiking Mt. Olympus. Oreivatein is a good online resource for area mountains and hiking.

Hellenic Alpine Club (✉ *Thessaloniki* ☎ *2310/278288*). **Oreivatein** (🌐 *www.oreivatein.com*). **Trekking Hellas** (✉ *3rd fl., Alexandros Bldg., Giannitson 31, West Thessaloniki, Thessaloniki* ☎ *2310/523522* 🌐 *www.trekking.gr*).

OURANOUPOLIS ΟΥΡΑΝΟΥΠΟΛΗ

110 km (68 mi) east of Thessaloniki, 224 km (189 mi) north and east of Mt. Olympus.

Meaning "heaven's city" in Greek, Ouranoupolis (also spelled Ouranopolis) is an appealing cul-de-sac on the final point of land that separates the secular world from the sacred sanctuaries of Mt. Athos. The village, noted for its rug and tapestry weaving, is particularly entrancing because of the bay's aquamarine waters, and the town is full of families on holiday in summer. The narrow village beaches can become overcrowded. There are many pensions and rooms-to-let around town, but the hotels on an islet or slightly outside the main town are quietest.

PAYING YOUR RESPECTS

If you make your own way to Ouranoupolis via Route 16, do stop at Aristotle's Statue in Stagira (west of the modern village, watch for the blink-and-miss road sign), the region of this remarkable man's birthplace. Aristotle's theories and inventions are re-created in engaging hands-on exhibits (small fee) around a grassy knoll with a surveying view.

Ouranoupolis was settled by refugees from Asia Minor in 1922–23, when the Greek state expropriated the land from Vatopedi Monastery on Mt. Athos. The settlement, known as Prosforion, was until then occupied by farming monks, some of whom lived in the Byzantine **Tower of Prosforion,** its origins dating from the 12th century. The tower subsequently became the abode of Joice and Sydney Loch, a couple who worked with Thessaloniki's noted American Farm School to help the refugees develop their rug-weaving industry. The tower was burned, altered, and restored through the centuries. It is rather a breezy and open place to take in the view on a sweltering day. ✉ *Main square, waterfront* ☎ *23770/71389 or 23770/71651* 🎫 *€2* ⏲ *June–Oct., Mon.–Sun. 9–5.*

OFF THE BEATEN PATH

Small Islands. Floating on the Proviakas Bay's turquoise waters are tiny emerald islands which are reachable from Tripiti via a 15-minute caïque or ferry ride that runs every half hour or so in summer—and by small outboard motorboats, which you can rent by the day. All the islets have glorious white-sand beaches, and two—**Gaidoronisi** (part of the Drenia group) and the fishing hamlet of **Amouliani town**—have places to eat. ✉ *Tripiti, 6 km (4 mi) north of Ouranoupolis.*

WHERE TO STAY & EAT

$–$$ Fodor's Choice ★ ✕ **Kritikos.** The owner is a local fisherman, and everything served is catch-of-the-day. Don't confuse this modern, cream-hue restaurant with the eponymous snack bar up the road. Here the family cooks traditional village recipes—the seafood pasta is sublime—and Macedonian specialties, such as *melitzana horiatiki* (an eggplant, tomato, feta, garlic, and olive oil salad). The *kolokithokeftedes* (zucchini-and-potato croquettes) are enormous. The owner's efforts received a citation in the country's top-10 "best of" *Alpha Guide,* yet the place remains unpretentious and very well priced for what you get. They even produce their own wine and tsipouro. ✉ *Main road, away from the tower* ☎ *23770/71222* ✎ *info@okritikos.gr* ▭ *DC, MC, V.*

$$$–$$$$ ★ **Agionissi Resort.** A private boat transports you from Ouranoupolis to the secluded islet of Amouliani, which still has a village of 500 fishing families. Rooms in bungalows are modern and uncluttered, with white walls, dark wooden furniture, and area rugs. The restaurant has marvelous seafood and an impressive selection of wines from Halkidiki and Mt. Athos. The pool bar has a view of Mt. Athos from its terrace. The resort's three beaches have been awarded the European eco-label Blue Flag for water cleanliness. Half-board is available. ✉ *5-min boat ride from Ouranoupolis, 1½ km (1 mi) outside village, 63075 Amouliani Island* ☎ *23770/51102* 📠 *23770/51180* 🌐 *www.papcorp.gr* *68 rooms* *In-room: refrigerator. In-hotel: restaurant, bars, tennis court, pool, spa, beachfront* ▭ *AE, MC, V* ⏲ *Closed Nov.–Apr.* *BP.*

$$$ Fodor'sChoice ★ **Skités.** Find peace and privacy on a bluff off a gravel road south of town. Each of the small, pleasant rooms in this charming complex of garden bungalows has its own entrance. The staff works to make you feel comfortable and the restaurant's home-style meals change daily, with a focus on vegetarian dishes. Sea views from the terrace are lovely. Stays can include three meals a day, with half-board another option. In the evening there are often cultural events to enjoy, such as classical music concerts, poetry readings, and theatrical presentations. ✉ *1 km (½ mi) south of town, c/o Pola Bohn, 63075* ☎ *23770/71140 or 23770/71141* 📠 *23770/71322* 🌐 *www.skites.gr* *21 rooms, 4 apartments* *In-room: refrigerator, kitchen (some), no TV. In-hotel: restaurant, bars, pool, beachfront, public Internet, some pets allowed* ▭ *MC, V* ⏲ *Closed Nov.–Apr.* *BP.*

¢ **Acrogiali.** Built in 1935, this is the town's first hotel, and the only one across the street from the beach. The three-story building is nothing special to look at, but it has been modernized (2002), and the sea view rooms are just fine for basic beach holidays. The same family also runs an off-beach hotel around the corner. ✉ *Beach road, 63075* ☎ *23770/71201* *15 rooms* *In-room: refrigerator. In-hotel: laundry service, some pets allowed* ▭ *No credit cards.*

MT. ATHOS ΌΡ. ΆΘΩΣ

★ *50 km (31 mi) southeast of Ouranoupolis, 120 km (74 mi) southeast of Thessaloniki.*

The third peninsula of Halkidiki, Mt. Athos is called *Ayion Oros* (Holy Mountain) in Greek, although it does not become a mountain until its southernmost point (6,667 feet). The peninsula is prized for its pristine natural beauty, seclusion (no women allowed), and spirituality; its monasteries contain priceless illuminated books and other treasures.

The Virgin Mary, it is said, was brought to Athos by accident from Ephesus, having been blown off course by a storm, and she decreed that it be venerated as her own special place. This story has since become the rationale for keeping it off-limits to all women but the Virgin herself. Hermits began settling here and formed the first monastery in the 10th century. By the 14th century, monasteries on the 650-square-km (250-square-mi) peninsula numbered in the hundreds. In 1924 the Greek state limited the number of monasteries, including Russian, Bulgarian, and Serbian Orthodox, to 20, but a number of hermitages and separate dependencies called *skités* also exist. The semiautonomous community falls under the religious authority of the Istanbul-based Orthodox Ecumenical Patriarch.

Men who want to visit Mt. Athos should contact the **Holy Executive of the Holy Mt. Athos Pilgrims' Bureau** at least six months in advance of arrival. You must obtain a written permit (free) from this office, which issues 10 permits a day for non-Orthodox visitors, and 100 permits a day for Orthodox visitors (Greek or foreign). You will need to pick it up in person, presenting your passport. Enquire about making reservations for a specific monastery, which must be done in advance, noting however, that some might be closed for renovations. The permits are valid for a four-day visit on specific dates, which may be extended by authorities in Karyes. When you arrive at Ouranoupolis, you also need to pick up a *diamonitirio,* or residence permit (€35); ask at the Thessaloniki bureau of the Greek National Tourism Organization (ETO) for more information. The boat departs Ouranoupolis for Daphni on the peninsula at 9:45 AM; it's a two-hour sail. Local transport takes you the last 13 km (8 mi) to Karyes and to monasteries beyond from there. Mt. Athos is a place of religious pilgrimage: proper attire is long pants and shirts with sleeves at least to mid-arm; wearing hats inside the monasteries is forbidden. Video cameras and tape recorders are banned from the mountain, but taking photographs is allowed. ✉ *Egnatia 109, Kentro, Thessaloniki* ☎ *2310/252578* 📠 *2310/222424* ⏲ *Weekdays 9–2, Sat. 10–noon.*

Both men and women can take one of the three-hour boat tours around the edge of Athos peninsula; the **Ouranoupolis Port Authority** (☎ *23770/71248 or 23770/71249*) can help you find a boat.

Athos Sea Cruises (✉ *Near tower on main road, Ouranoupolis* ☎ *23770/71370 or 23770/71606*) sails for the Mt. Athos area from May to October at 10 AM (€16), with an additional afternoon departure in July and August.

THESSALONIKI & CENTRAL MACEDONIA ESSENTIALS

TRANSPORTATION

BY AIR

There are direct flights to Thessaloniki from London, Brussels, Frankfurt, Stuttgart, Munich, Zurich, and Vienna, with good connections from the United States. Olympic Airlines and other international carriers fly from Athens to Thessaloniki. There are usually at least five daily flights to and from Athens; flying time is 40–45 minutes. Domestic carriers including Aegean Air connect Thessaloniki with a number of other cities as well as Mykonos, Santorini, Crete, Rhodes, Corfu, Limnos, Chios, and Lesbos.

Carriers **Aegean Air** (✉ *Leoforos Nikis 1, Port, Thessaloniki* ☎ *2310/239225, reservations, 2310/476470 airport* 🌐 *www.aegeanair.com*). **Olympic Airlines** (✉ *Kountouriotou 3, Kentro, Thessaloniki* ☎ *2310/368311 or 2310/368666* 🌐 *www.olympicairlines.com*).

AIRPORT

Thessaloniki Macedonia International Airport (SKG) is at Mikras, 13 km (8 mi) southeast of the city center on the coast; it's about a 20-minute drive. Bus 78 to and from the airport originates at the KTEL bus terminal, stops at the train station, and makes a stop at Aristotle Square (along Egnatia).

Airport Information **Thessaloniki Macedonia International Airport** (✉ *16th km [10th mi] mark on the Ethnikos Odos, Thessaloniki–Perea road, Mikras* ☎ *2310/473212*).

BY BOAT

Hellenic Seaways, Nel, Minoan, and other sea lines connect Thessaloniki to Chios, Lesbos, Limnos, Samos, Heraklion (Crete), Kos, Rhodes, Skiathos, Skopelos, Alonnisos, Naxos, Mykonos, Paros, Santorini, and Tinos. Buy tickets at the Karacharisis Travel and Shipping Agency, Zorpidis Travel Services (Sporades and Cyclades islands only), or Polaris Travel Agency. Connections from Thessaloniki to Rhodes, Kos, and Samos should be confirmed at Karacharisis Travel and Shipping Agency. You can connect to Piraeus from Kavala, 136 km (85 mi) east of Thessaloniki. In summer you should reserve a month in advance. City port authorities, GNTO/EOT offices, and the Greek Travel Pages online have ferry schedules.

Information **Greek Travel Pages** (🌐 *www.gtp.gr*). **Karacharisis Travel and Shipping Agency** (✉ *Kountouriotou 8, Port, Thessaloniki* ☎ *2310/513005* 📠 *2310/532289*). **Kavala Port Authority** (☎ *2510/224967 or 2510/223716*). **Polaris Travel Agency** (✉ *Egnatia 81, Kentro, Thessaloniki* ☎ *2310/276051, 2310/278613, or 2310/232078* 📠 *2310/265728* ✉ *polarisk@otenet.gr* ✉ *Kountouriotou 19, Port, Thessaloniki* ☎ *2310/548655 or 2310/548290*). **Thessaloniki Port Authority** (☎ *2310/531504 through 2310/531507*). **Zorpidis Travel Services** (✉ *Salaminos 4, at Kountouriotou, Port, Thessaloniki* ☎ *2310/555995* 🌐 *www.zorpidis.gr*).

BY BUS

The trip to Thessaloniki from Athens takes about seven hours, with one rest stop (and no access to onboard toilets). Buy tickets at least one day in advance at Athens's Terminal A or at the Thessaloniki ticket office, which sells departure tickets to Athens; one-way fare is about €30.

Intercity KTEL buses connect Thessaloniki with locations throughout Greece. There are small ticket-office terminals (*praktorio*) for each line and separate ticket offices and telephone numbers for each destination. You can browse the KTEL Web site to get an idea of timetables, or call KTEL Thessaloniki Main Terminal, but it's often best to make ticket inquiries in person. The KTEL main terminal is on Thessaloniki's southwestern outskirts, off the National Road (Ethnikos Odos). It has left-luggage storage.

Information **KTEL Main Terminal** (*✉ Giannitson 194, Menemeni, Thessaloniki ☎ 2310/595408, 2310/510834 lost and found 🌐 www.ktel.org*). **KTEL Halkidiki Terminal** (*For Halkidiki-bound buses ✉ Kifissias 33, at Egeou, Kalamaria, Thessaloniki ☎ 2310/316555*).

KTEL Katerini "blue bus" station (*For Dion site ✉ Katerini ☎ 23510/37600*). **KTEL Katerini station** (*✉ Katerini ☎ 23510/46720 or 23510/23313*). **KTEL Litochoro depot** (*✉ Litochoro ☎ 23520/81271*). **KTEL Monastiriou ticket office** (*✉ Monastiriou 69, West Thessaloniki, Thessaloniki ☎ 2310/555777*). **KTEL reservations** (*☎ 2310/595411, 2310/595435 Athens, 2310/595428 Litochoro, 2310/595432 Veria*). **KTEL Veria station** (*✉ Veria ☎ 23310/22342 or 23310/23334*).

BY CAR

Driving to Greece from Europe through the Former Yugoslav Republic of Macedonia is possible but often time-consuming owing to many border problems. The Athens–Thessaloniki part of the Ethnikos Odos (National Road), the best in Greece, is 500 km (310 mi) and takes five to seven hours. The roads in general are well maintained and constantly being improved and widened throughout the region. A good four-lane highway that begins in Athens goes to the border with Turkey; watch for closures as the new Egnatia Highway (linking Igoumenitsa and Europe in the west to Turkey and points east) is under phased construction. You can get information from the Greek Automobile Touring Club (ELPA). Posted speed limits are up to 120 kph (75 mph), and vehicles regularly use the shoulder as an extra lane.

Driving in Thessaloniki is not recommended because of the congestion, frequent traffic jams, and scarcity of parking. Walking and taking a local bus or taxi are much easier on the nerves. But having a car to get out of town and explore the smaller villages is helpful.

Contact **Greek Automobile Touring Club** (*ELPA ✉ Vasilissis Olgas 228–230, Kalamaria, Thessaloniki ☎ 2310/426319, 2310/426320, 10400 road assistance 🌐 www.elpa.gr*).

Rental Agencies **Akon car rental** (*✉ Main road, Ouranoupolis ☎ 23770/71644 📠 23770/71645*). **Avis** (*✉ Thessaloniki Macedonia International Airport ☎ 2310/473858 🌐 www.avis.com*). **Budget** (*✉ Aggelaki 15, H.A.N.T.H., Kentro, Thessaloniki ☎ 2310/254031 🌐 www.budget.com*). **Hertz** (*✉ Thessaloniki Macedonia International Airport ☎ 2310/473952 🌐 www.hertz.com ✉ Eleftheriou Venizelou 1, Kentro, Thessaloniki ☎ 2310/224906*).

BY TAXI

Lefkos Pyrgos, Makedonia, and Euro are some taxi companies in Thessaloniki. If you try to hail one off the street, you may be expected to call out your destination—the drivers are excellent lip-readers. Enquire about tailored trips: sites such as Vergina, Pella, and Dion can be covered within a few hours, cost should be €50–€100. Lefko has a special-needs taxi (van) service for those with disabilities, as well as regular taxi service. You can take the Litochoro Taxi to Dion, get picked up from Litochoro train station, Katerini bus station, and so on. It is a private taxi, not a company, as are the others in Litochoro.

Contacts **Euro** (☎ *2310/866866 or 2310/551525*). **Lefko** (☎ *2310/861050*). **Lefkos Pyrgos** (*White Tower* ☎ *2310/214900*). **Litochoro Taxi** (☎ *6977/320853 cell*). **Makedonia** (☎ *2310/550500*).

BY TRAIN

Out of some 10 Athens–Thessaloniki trains per day, three are express (4½ hours). Make reservations in advance at Athens Larissis Station (Stathmos Larissis) south office (far-left facing, not the main entrance ticket booths, which are for same-day tickets only), or in Thessaloniki. The fastest Intercity will set you back €50; other express options begin at €33. The standard train fare begins at around €14. A €40 ticket can be purchased that is good for 10 days' (nonexpress) travel in the center and north of the country (i.e., from Larissis Station). Thessaloniki station has a left-luggage office.

Information **OSE Larissis Station** (✉ *Theodorou Deliyanni, Athens* ☎ *1110, 1440 departures recording* 🌐 *www.ose.gr*). **OSE Thessaloniki Train Station** (✉ *Monastiriou 28, West Thessaloniki, Thessaloniki* ☎ *1110, 2310/599068 lost and found* 🌐 *www.ose.gr* ✉ *Aristotelous 18, Kentro, Thessaloniki* ☎ *2310/598120*).

CONTACTS & RESOURCES

EMERGENCIES

Lists of late-night pharmacies and hospitals on emergency duty are published in newspapers and posted in the windows of all pharmacies. In Thessaloniki, you can also contact your consulate for information on hospitals, doctors, and dentists. The European Union emergency hotline has English-speakers.

Emergency Services **Ambulance** (☎ *166*). **European Union Hotline** (☎ *112*). **Police** (☎ *100*). **Thessaloniki Tourist Police** (✉ *4th fl., Dodekanissou 4, Dimokratias Sq., Thessaloniki* ☎ *2310/554871*).

Hospitals **Ahepa Hospital** (✉ *Kyriakidi 1, Kentro, Thessaloniki* ☎ *2310/993111*). **Ippokration Hospital** (✉ *Konstantinoupoleos 49, Kentro, Thessaloniki* ☎ *2310/892000*).

INTERNET CAFÉS

Internet cafés are found near most key spots in Thessaloniki. Meganet, open 24 hours, has about 70 machines and a youthful, tourist-wise staff, along with good music, coffee, and croissants. E-Global has Internet outlets around town.

Information **e-Global** (✉ *Vasilissis Olgas 60, Faliro, Thessaloniki* ☎ *2310/887711*). **Meganet** (✉ *Navarinou Sq. 5, Kentro, Thessaloniki* ☎ *2310/269591 or 2310/250331*).

TOURS

Dolphin Hellas leads organized tours of Northern Greece that begin in Athens and take in the ancient archaeological sites. Like other agencies, the company also arranges tailored tours and books hotels and car rental. Going through an agency often nets a cheaper rate than those quoted to individual walk-ins. Major tour operator Zorpidis runs half-day tours to Vergina–Pella from Thessaloniki, and even arranges honeymoon trips. Velas Tours can also set you up at a thalassotherapy spa near Thessaloniki. To hire a sightseeing guide, contact the Thessaloniki Tourist Guide Association.

Contacts **Dolphin Hellas** (*Main office, Athanassiou Diakou 16, at Syngrou, Acropolis, Athens 210/922–7772 through 210/922–7775 www.dolphin-hellas.gr*). **Thessaloniki Tourist Guide Association** (*2310/546037 guideskg@otenet.gr*). **Velas Tours** (*Egnatia 6, Kentro, Thessaloniki 2310/512032 or 2310/518015 www.velastours.gr*). **Zorpidis Travel** (*Main location 1st fl., Egnatia 76, Kentro, Thessaloniki 2310/244400 www.zorpidis.gr For flights and tours Aristotelous 27, Kentro, Thessaloniki 2310/282600 For ferries Salaminos 4, at Kountouriotou, West Thessaloniki, Thessaloniki 2310/555995*).

VISITOR INFORMATION

In Thessaloniki, the Greek National Tourism Organization (GNTO or EOT) central regional office on Tsimiski is open May–September 15, weekdays 9:30–9:30 and weekends 9–3; September 16–April, weekdays 9–3—but unscheduled breaks and closures are common. There's also a branch at the airport. OTE Directory Assistance is useful for finding oft-changing addresses and phone numbers; most operators speak English.

Contacts **Greek National Tourism Organization** (*GNTO/EOT Tsimiski 136, at Dagli, Kentro, Thessaloniki 2310/221100 or 2310/252170 www.mintour.gr*). **OTE Directory Assistance** (*11888*).

Corfu

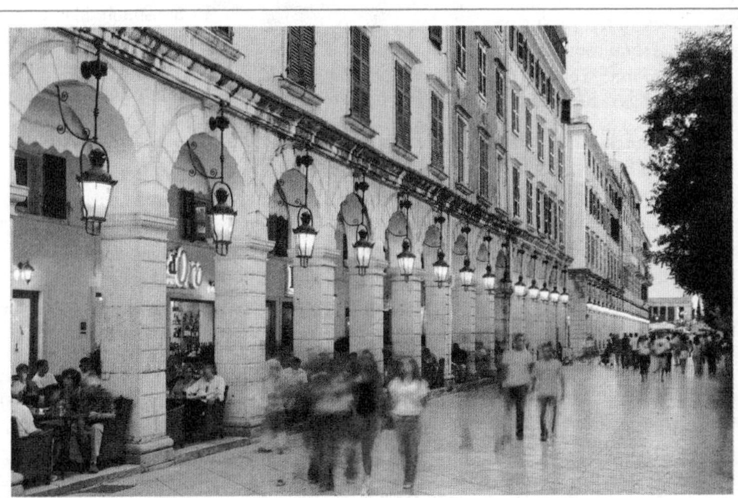

Spianada Promenade, The Liston, Corfu Town

WORD OF MOUTH

"I loved Corfu . . . it's quite different from the dry islands with the white houses that you see in photos. It is lush with greenery and olive trees, for one thing, and also it has such a varied history (various empires owned it at one time or another) that you can go into Corfu town, sit under a Venetian-style arcade, eat Greek food, and hear a discussion about a game of cricket."

—elaine

www.fodors.com/forums

WELCOME TO CORFU

TOP REASONS TO GO

★ **Corfu Town:** No matter how clogged the streets or how sophisticated the resorts, this little beauty of a city glows with a profusion of picturesque remnants of its Venetian, French, and British colonies.

★ **Some Enchanted Islet:** Hero of a 1,001 travel posters, Pontikonisi is crowned by a white-washed chapel—could tiny "Mouse Island" really be Odysseus's ship turned to stone by Poseidon?

★ **The Achilleion:** A neoclassic white elephant, this Corfu villa built for Empress Elizabeth of Austria is more than redeemed by its enchanting seaside gardens.

★ **Homer's City of the Phaeacians:** Once hallowed by Odysseus, Paleokastritsa is still a spectacle of grottoes, cliffs, and turquoise waters.

★ **Hiking Heaven:** The fully marked Corfu Trail runs 220 km (137 mi) from Lake Korisia to Mt. Pantokrator.

Enchanting Corfu town

1 Corfu Town. Along the east coast mid-island, Corfu town occupies the central prong of a three-pronged peninsula; on the southern prong is Paleopolis (Old Town) and on the northern is the Old Fortress. Between the two is the gorgeous and elegant Esplanade, from which extend stage-set streets lined with Venetian and English Georgian houses and Corfiot cafés.

2 South Corfu. Just south of Corfu town is a region that crowned heads—and heads that were once crowned—once made their own. Mon Repos was the summer residence of the British lord high commissioners (and birthplace of Queen Elizabeth II's husband). Another 16 km (10 mi) south is Gastouri, site of the Achilleion, a 19th-century extravaganza studded with a bewildering number of neoclassic statues. To remind yourself you're really in Greece, take in the famed vista of the chapel-covered Mouse Island.

3 West-Central & North Corfu. Corfu town is great for a day or three of sightseeing but you really need to head into the island interiors to find your personal niche. Many head to Paleokastritsa, where you'll discover one of Greece's best beaches; rent a boat to visit the nearby caves. Head inland to Ano Korakiana—"Little Venice"—before chilling out at the picturesque harbor town of Agni.

Hellenic temple on Corfu island

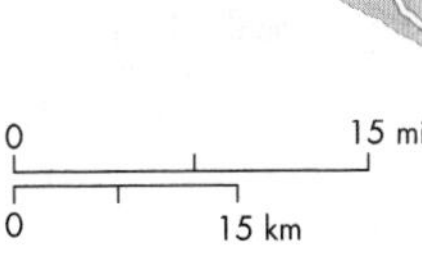

West-Central Corfu is famous for its beaches

GETTING ORIENTED

Scattered along the western coast of Greece the Ionian islands derive their name from the Ionian Greeks, their first colonizers. The proximity of these isles to Italy and their sheltered position on the East–West trade routes tempted many an occupier to the main island jewel, Corfu. Never subjected to Turkish rule, the Corfiots were greatly influenced by the graciousness of Venetian settlers as well as the civilized formality of its 19th-century British Protectorate. With its fairy-tale setting, Corfu (Kerkyra in Greek) is connected by numerous ferries with Italy's Brindisi and is the gateway to Greece for many European travelers.

CORFU PLANNER

Where to Start?

Whether arriving by ferry from the mainland or another island or directly by plane, the best place to start your exploration of the island is Corfu town.

Catch your breath by first relaxing in the shaded Liston arcade over coffee and a Ionian spoon sweet—the island's specialty is kumquat—then stroll the narrow lanes of the pedestrians-only medieval quarter.

For an overview of the immediate area, and a quick tour of the Mon Repos palace, hop on the little tourist train.

Corfu town has a different feel at night, so book a table at one of its famed tavernas near the Town Hall to savor Corfu's unique cuisine.

Getting Around

You need a car to get to some of Corfu's loveliest and most inaccessible places, and the island's gentle climate and rolling hills make Corfu ideal motorbike country.

Your can rent cars and motorbikes in Corfu town. If you only plan to visit a few of the major sights and towns, the inexpensive local bus system will do.

Taxis can be hired for day trips from Corfu town.

Making the Most of Your Time

Corfu is often explored in a day—most people pass through quickly as part of a cruise of the Greek islands. Two days allows enough time to visit Corfu town and its nearby and most famous sites. With four days you can spend time exploring the island's other historic sites and natural attractions along both coasts. Six days allows you time to get a closer look at the museums, churches, and forts and perhaps even take a day trip to Albania. Because Corfu is small, you could make day trips to outlying villages and return to accommodations in Corfu town if you wish. Alternatively, you could spend a night at the hilltop Pelekas or farther north at the seaside Paleokastritsa. Don't forget to see the ruins of Angelokastro in the mountains at Lakones. Take the coast road northeast around the bay to the most mountainous part of the island and historic Kassiopi. Spend the night there so you can explore the northern beaches of Roda and Sidari, or head into the mountains to stay near Ano Korakiana.

Dining & Lodging Prices in Euros

	¢	$	$$	$$$	$$$$
Restaurants	under €8	€8–€15	€15–€20	€20–€25	over €25
Hotels	under €80	€80–€120	€120–€160	€160–€200	over €200

Restaurant prices are for one main course at dinner, or for two mezedes (small dishes). Hotel prices are for a standard double room in high season, including taxes. Hotels operate on the European Plan (EP, with no meal provided) unless we note that they use the Continental Plan (CP, with Continental breakfast); Breakfast Plan (BP, with a full breakfast); Modified American Plan (MAP, with breakfast and dinner); or the Full American Plan (FAP, with all meals). Inquire when booking if these meal plans (which can entail higher rates) are mandatory. Guest rooms have air-conditioning, room phones, and TVs unless otherwise noted.

Finding a Place to Stay

Corfu has both bed-and-breakfasts in renovated Venetian town houses and sleek resorts with children's camps and spas.

The explosion of tourism in recent years has led to prepaid, low-price package tours, and the largest hotels often cater to groups.

These masses can get rowdy and overwhelm otherwise pleasant surroundings, mainly in towns along the southeast coast.

Budget accommodation is scarce, though it can be found with effort; the Greek National Tourism Organization (GNTO or EOT) can often help.

Corfu is popular year-round so reservations are strongly recommended, especially as many hotels are closed from the end of October through March.

At Easter, the island is crammed with Greek tourists, and the availability of charter flights directly from the United Kingdom and other European cities means there's a steady flow of tourists from early spring through fall.

How's the Weather?

Corfu enjoys a temperate climate, with a relatively long rainy season that lasts from late fall through early spring.

Winter showers bring spring flowers, and the countryside is positively abloom starting in April, when the air is perfumed with the fragrances of orange blossoms, jasmine, and wildflowers.

The weather begins warming in May, although nights can be cool—be sure to pack a thick sweater—but even this early in the season the sun can be quite warm, especially when trekking through sights during the day.

By late May swimming is possible, and by June the waters have warmed considerably. July and August are the hottest months and can also be a little humid.

September is gloriously warm and dry, with warm evenings and the occasional cool breeze.

Swimming is often possible through mid-October, although after that the water can be quite cool. Late September through late October are good for hiking and exploring the countryside.

Great Flavors

Corfiot food specialties, which tend to reflect the island's Venetian heritage, are served at most restaurants and tavernas.

Those worth a try are *soffritto* (veal cooked in a sauce of vinegar, parsley, and plenty of garlic) served with rice or potatoes; *pastitsada* (a derivation of the Italian dish *spezzatino*—layers of beef and pasta, called *macaronia* in Greek, cooked in a rich and spicy tomato sauce and topped off with béchamel sauce).

Other tantalizing treats include *bourdetto* (firm-flesh fish stewed in tomato sauce with lots of hot red pepper) and *bianco* (whole fish stewed with potatoes, herbs, black pepper, and lemon juice).

Corfu doesn't have many vineyards, but if you find a restaurant that has its own barrel wine, try it—you'll rarely be disappointed.

Two drinks that are legacies of the British are *tsitsibira* (ginger-beer), often drunk while watching cricket, and the bright-orange liqueur made from kumquats, which the colonists first planted on the island.

Note: locals say the liqueur, available at any tourist shop, is an aphrodisiac.

Bottled water can and should be bought everywhere—Corfu's tap water is *not* one of its pleasures.

Updated by Diane Shugart

THE IONIAN ISLANDS ARE ALL LUSH AND LOVELY, but Kerkyra (Corfu) is the greenest and, quite possibly, the prettiest of all Greek islands—emerald mountains, ocher and pink buildings, shimmering silver olive leaves. The turquoise waters lap rocky, pine-rimmed coves, and plants like bougainvillea, scarlet roses, and wisteria spread over cottages. Homer's "well-watered gardens" and "beautiful and rich land" were Odysseus's last stop on his journey home. Corfu is also said to be the inspiration for Prospero's island in Shakespeare's *The Tempest*. This northernmost of the major Ionian islands has, through the centuries, inspired other artists, as well as conquerors, royalty, and, of course, tourists.

Today more than a million—mainly British—tourists visit every year, and in summer crowd the evocative capital city of Corfu town (population 100,000). As a result, the town has a number of stylish restaurants and hotels, and coastal areas are crammed with package-tour resorts, which blight areas of its beauty. Still, the interior remains largely unspoiled, and the entire island has gracefully absorbed its many layers of history, creating an alluring mix of neoclassic villas and extensive resorts, horse-drawn carriages and Mercedes, simplicity and sophistication.

Corfu's proximity to Europe, 72 km (45 mi) from Italy and 2 km (1 mi) or so from Albania, and its position on an ancient trade route, assured a lively history of conquest and counter-conquest. In classical times, Corinth colonized the northern Ionian islands, but Corfu, growing powerful, revolted and allied itself with Athens, a fateful move that triggered the Peloponnesian War. Subjection followed: to the tyrants of Syracuse, the kings of Epirus and of Macedonia, in the 2nd century BC to Rome, and from the 11th to the 14th century to Norman and Angevin kings. Then came the Venetians, who protected Corfu from Turkish occupation and provided a 411-year period of development. Napoléon Bonaparte took the islands after the fall of Venice. "The greatest misfortune which could befall me is the loss of Corfu," he wrote to Talleyrand, his foreign minister. Within two years he'd lost it to a Russo-Turkish fleet.

For a short time the French regained and fortified Corfu from the Russians, and their occupation influenced the island's educational system, architecture, and cuisine. Theirs was a Greek-run republic—the first for modern Greece—which whetted local appetites for the independence that arrived later in the 19th century. In 1814 the islands came under British protection; roads, schools, and hospitals were constructed, and commercialism developed. Corfu was ruled by a series of eccentric lord high commissioners. Nationalism finally prevailed, and the islands were ceded to Greece in 1864.

Indeed, when you look at Corfu in total, it's hard to believe an island of its size could generate such a large history. The classical remains have suffered from the island's tempestuous history and also from earthquakes; architecture from the centuries of Venetian, French, and British rule is most evident, leaving Corfu with a pleasant combination of contrasting design elements. And although it was bombed during the Italian and Nazi occupation in World War II, the town of Corfu remains one of the loveliest in all of Greece: every nook and cranny tells a story, every street meanders to a myth. The island's northeast section has become geared to tourism, but there are inland farming villages that seem undisturbed by the civilizations that have come and gone. Corfu today is a vivid tapestry of cultures—a sophisticated weave, where charm, history, and natural beauty blend.

CORFU TOWN ΠΟΛΗ ΤΗΣ ΚΕΡΚΥΡΑΣ

34 km (21 mi) west of Igoumenitsa, 41 km (26 mi) north of Lefkimmi.

This lovely capital and cultural, historical, and recreational center is off the middle of the island's east coast. All ships and planes lead to Corfu town, on a narrow strip of land hugged by the Ionian Sea. Though beguilingly Greek, much of Corfu's old town displays the architectural styles of many of its conquerors—molto of Italy's Venice, a soupçon of France, and more than a tad of England. A multi-sight ticket (€8), available at any of the sights, includes admission to the Archaeological Museum, the Museum of Asiatic Art, the Byzantine Museum, and the Old Fortress.

WHAT TO SEE

14 **Archaeological Museum.** Examine finds from ongoing island excavations; most come from Kanoni, the site of Corfu's ancient capital. The star attraction is a giant relief of snake-coiffed Medusa, depicted as her head was cut off by the hero Perseus—at which moment her two sons, Pegasus and Chrysaor, emerged from her body. The 56-foot-long sculpture once adorned the pediment of the 6th-century BC Temple of Artemis at Kanoni and is one of the largest and best-preserved pieces of Archaic sculpture in Greece. ✉ *Vraila 1, off Leoforos Dimokratias, past Corfu Palace hotel* ☎ *26610/30680* 🎫 *€3* ⏲ *Tues.–Sun. 8:30–3.*

British Cemetery. Flowers—rare orchids and lilies, cultivated cyclamens, snowdrops, tulips, and hundreds of wildflowers—bloom in this overgrown cemetery established in 1814, as do fascinating stories told by the stone angels, Celtic crosses, and quirky inscriptions atop the nearly 600 memorials. Along the cypress-lined paths (Greeks believe the pointed trees help guide souls to heaven) are tombs of the British colonizers, soldiers who died during the Crimean and two world wars, and more recently, Brits who so fell so in love with Corfu that they were buried here years after they'd returned home. ✉ *Kolokotroni 22* 🎫 *Free* ⏲ *Daily 9–dusk.*

8 **Byzantine Museum.** Panagia Antivouniotissa, an ornate church dating from the late 15th century, houses an outstanding collection of Byzantine religious art. More than 85 icons from the 13th to the 17th century hang on the walls as the ethereal sounds of Byzantine chants are piped in overhead. Look for works by the celebrated icon painters Tzanes and Damaskinos; they are perhaps the best-known artists of the Cretan style of icon painting, with unusually muscular, active (and sometimes

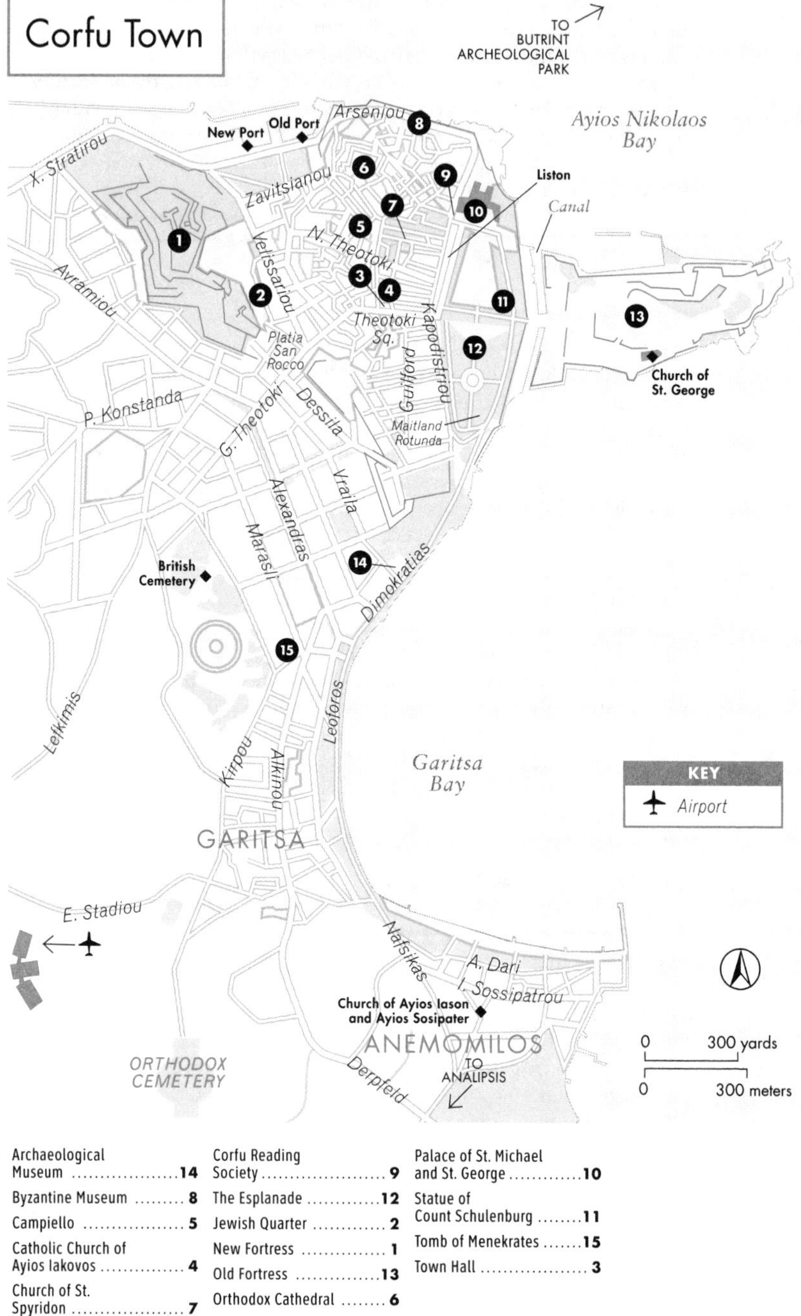

Archaeological Museum 14
Byzantine Museum 8
Campiello 5
Catholic Church of Ayios Iakovos 4
Church of St. Spyridon 7
Corfu Reading Society 9
The Esplanade 12
Jewish Quarter 2
New Fortress 1
Old Fortress 13
Orthodox Cathedral 6
Palace of St. Michael and St. George 10
Statue of Count Schulenburg 11
Tomb of Menekrates 15
Town Hall 3

CORFU TOWN: STEP-BY-STEP

Arriving from mainland Greece by ferry, you dock at the new port, adjacent to the **New Fortress**, with its British citadel. East of the fortress is the area of Velissariou, one of Corfu town's main streets, and the western edge of the historical center. Here is the former **Jewish Quarter**, with its old synagogue. From Velissariou, go southeast toward Voulgareos, turn left on G. Theotoki, and follow the street for about 10 minutes until you reach Theotoki Square. Ahead is the ornate, marble, 17th-century **Town Hall**. Note the elaborate Venetian design, popular throughout the town. Adjacent is the neoclassic **Catholic Church of Ayios Iakovos**, more commonly known as the Cathedral of San Giacomo. Go north on Theotoki to Filarmonikis, four blocks through the medieval area of **Campiello**—narrow winding streets filled with artisans' shops and restaurants—to the **Orthodox Cathedral**. From the cathedral, look up to see the nearby red bell tower of the **Church of St. Spyridon**, dedicated to the island's patron saint. Head north to the waterfront to explore the fascinating **Byzantine Museum**; then backtrack to the cathedral area.

Southeast from the museum, in Kapodistriou, is the historic **Corfu Reading Society**, with its grand outside staircase. From here go south two blocks to Ayios Ekaterinis. East are the colonnade of the **Palace of St. Michael and St. George** and the arcades of the Liston area. Along the central path is the **Statue of Count Schulenburg**, hero of the siege of 1716. The southern half of the **Esplanade** has a Victorian bandstand, Ionic rotunda, and a statue of Ioannis Kapodistrias, a Corfu resident and the first president of modern Greece. Relax a while, and then cross over the bridge to the **Old Fortress** on the northeastern tip of Corfu town. In the southern section of the fort is the Church of St. George, with views of Albania.

8

viscerally gruesome) depictions of saints. Their paintings more closely resemble Renaissance art—another Venetian legacy—than traditional, flat orthodox icons. ✉ *Arseniou Mourayio* ☎ *26610/38313* 🎫 €2 ⏲ *Tues.–Sun. 8:30–3.*

5 **Campiello.** Narrow, winding streets and steep stairways make up the Campiello, the large, traffic-free medieval area of the town. Laundry lines connect balconied Venetian buildings bearing marble porticoes engraved with the original occupant's coat of arms to multistory, neoclassic 19th-century ones built by the British. Small cobbled squares anchored by central wells and surrounded by high-belfry churches and alleyways that lead nowhere and back add to the utterly lovely urban space. ✉ *West of the Esplanade, northeast of New Fortress.*

4 **Catholic Church of Ayios Iakovos.** Built in 1588 and consecrated 50 years later, this elegant cathedral was erected to provide a grand place of worship for Corfu town's Catholic occupiers. If you use the Italian name, San Giacomo, locals will know it. When it was bombed by the Nazis in 1943, the cathedral's original neoclassic facade of pediments, friezes, and columns was practically destroyed; only the bell tower remained intact. ✉ *Dimarcheiou Sq. next to Town Hall* ☎ *No phone.*

Church of Ayios Iason and Ayios Sosipater. The suburb of Anemomilos is crowned by the ruins of the Paleopolis church and by the 11th-century Church of Ayios Iason and Ayios Sosipater. It was named after two of St. Paul's disciples, St. Jason and St. Sosipater, who brought Christianity to the island in the 1st century. The frescoes are faded, but the icons are beautiful, and the exterior is dramatic among the unspoiled greenery. This is one of only two Byzantine churches on the island; the other is in the northern coastal village of Ayios Markos. ⊠*Anemomilos at south end of Garitsa Bay* ☎*No phone.*

7 **Church of St. Spyridon.** Built in 1596, this church is the tallest on the
Fodor's Choice ★ island, thanks to its distinctive red-domed bell tower, and is filled with silver treasures. The patron saint's internal remains—smuggled here after the fall of Constantinople—are contained in a silver reliquary and carried in procession four times a year, along with his mummified body, which can be seen through a glass panel. His slippered feet are actually exposed during the procession so that the faithful can venerate them. The saint was not a Corfiot but a shepherd from Cyprus, who became a bishop before his death in AD 350. His miracles are said to have saved the island four times: once from famine, twice from the plague, and once from the hated Turks. During World War II, a bomb fell on this holiest place on the island but didn't explode. Maybe these events explain why it seems every other man on Corfu is named Spiros. If you keep the tower in sight you can wander as you wish without getting lost around this fascinating section of town. ⊠*Agiou Spyridon* ☎*No phone.*

9 **Corfu Reading Society.** The oldest cultural institution in modern Greece, the Corfu Reading Society was founded in 1836. The building, filled with the archives of the Ionian islands, stands opposite the High Commissioner's Palace and has an impressive exterior staircase leading up to a loggia. ⊠*Kapodistriou* ☎*26610/39528* *Free* ⊙*Weekdays 9:15–1:45 and 5:30–8, Sat. 9:15–1:45.*

12 **The Esplanade.** Central to the life of the town, this huge, open parade ground on the land side of the canal is, many say, the most beautiful *spianada* (esplanade) in Greece. It is bordered on the west by a street lined with seven- and eight-story Venetian and English Georgian houses, and arcades, called the **Liston.** The name refers to a list that the Venetians kept of lucky upper-class townspeople who were allowed to walk and linger here. Today, happily, its beauty can be enjoyed by all. Cafés spill out onto the passing scene, and Corfiot celebrations, games, and trysts occur in the sun and shadows. Sunday cricket matches, a holdover from British rule, are sometimes played on the northern half of the Esplanade, which was once a Venetian firing range. On the southern half is an ornate **Victorian bandstand** and a **statue of Ioannis Kapodistrias,** a Corfu resident and the first president of modern Greece. He was also, unfortunately, the first Greek president to be assassinated, in 1831. The restored **Ionic rotunda** was built in honor of Sir Thomas Maitland, the not-much-loved first British lord high commissioner who was appointed in 1814 when the island became a protectorate of Britain. ⊠*Between Old Fortress and old town.*

2 **Jewish Quarter.** This twist of streets was home to the area's Jewish population from the 1600s until 1940, when the community was decimated, most sent to Auschwitz by the occupying Nazis. Fewer than 100 of 5,000 Jews survived. At the southern edge of the ghetto, a 300-year-old synagogue with an interior in Sephardic style still proudly stands. ✉ *Parados 4, off Velissariou, 2 blocks from New Fortress.*

1 **New Fortress.** Built in 1577–78 by the Venetians, the New Fortress was constructed to strengthen town defenses—only three decades after the construction of the "old" fortress. The French and the British subsequently expanded the complex to protect Corfu town from a possible Turkish invasion. You can wander through the maze of tunnels, moats, and fortifications, and the moat (dry now) is the site of the town's marketplace. A classic British citadel stands at its heart. At the top, there is an exhibition center as well as the trendy Morrison Café, which has stunning views by day and international DJs spinning cool, ambient tunes at night. The best time to tour is early morning or late afternoon. ✉ *Solomou on promontory northwest of Old Fortress* ☎ *26610/27370* *€2* *June–Oct., daily 9 AM–9:30 PM.*

13 **Old Fortress.** Corfu's entire population once lived within the walls of the ★ Old Fortress, or Citadel, built by the Venetians in 1546 on the site of a Byzantine castle. Separated from the rest of the town by a moat, the fort is on a promontory mentioned by Thucydides. Its two heights, or *korypha* ("bosom"), gave the island its Western name. Standing on the peaks, you have a gorgeous view west over the town and east to the mountainous coast of Albania. Inside the fortress, many Venetian fortifications were destroyed by the British, who replaced them with their own structures. The most notable of these is the quirky **Church of St. George,** built like an ancient Doric temple on the outside and set up like a Greek Orthodox church on the inside. In summer there are folk-dancing performances in the fortress, and in August sound-and-light shows tell the fortress's history. ✉ *On northeastern point of Corfu town peninsula* ☎ *26610/48310* *€4* *Weekdays 8–7, weekends 8:30–3.*

6 **Orthodox Cathedral.** This small, icon-rich cathedral was built in 1577. It is dedicated to St. Theodora, the island's second saint. Her headless body lies in a silver coffin by the altar; it was brought to Corfu at the same time as St. Spyridon's remains. Steps lead down to the harbor from here. ✉ *Southwest corner of Campiello, east of St. Spyridon* ☎ *26610/39409.*

10 **Palace of St. Michael and St. George.** Admire Ming pottery in an ornate Fodor's Choice ★ colonial palace as Homer's Ionian Sea shimmers outside the windows. This elegant, colonnaded, 19th-century Regency structure houses the **Museum of Asiatic Art,** a notable collection of Asian porcelains and Sino-Japanese art, as well as the **Municipal Art Gallery,** which displays work by Corfiot artists and depictions of the island's history and famous figures. The building was constructed as a residence for the lord high commissioner and headquarters for the order of St. Michael and St. George; it was abandoned after the British left in 1864 and precisely renovated about a hundred years later by the British ambassador

8

to Greece. Before entering the galleries, stop at the Art Café in the shady courtyard, where you may have trouble tearing yourself away from the fairy-tale view of the lush islet of Vido and the mountainous coast of Albania. ⊠ *North end of the Esplanade* ☎ *26610/30443 Museum of Asiatic Art, 26610/48690 Municipal Art Gallery* 🎫 *€3* ⏲ *Tues.–Sun. 8:30–3.*

11 **Statue of Count Schulenburg.** The hero of the siege of 1716, an Austrian mercenary, is immortalized in this statue. The siege was the Turks' last (and failed) attempt to conquer Corfu. ⊠ *Along central path of Esplanade.*

15 **Tomb of Menekrates.** Part of an ancient necropolis, this site held funerary items that are now exhibited in the Archaeological Museum. ⊠ *South around Garitsa Bay, to right of obelisk dedicated to Sir Howard Douglas.*

3 **Town Hall.** The rich marble, 17th-century Town Hall was built as a Venetian loggia and converted in 1720 into Greece's first modern theater—a far cry from the classic amphitheater pioneered in Epidaurus. A second story was added by the British before it became a grand town hall early in the 20th century. Note the sculpted portraits of Venetian dignitaries over the entrance—one is actually a lion, the symbol of Venice. ⊠ *Theotoki Sq.* ☎ *26610/40401* 🎫 *Free* ⏲ *Weekdays 9–1.*

WHERE TO EAT

$$$–$$$$ ★ ✕ **To Dimarcheio.** Menu items like marinated salmon with fennel and veal carpaccio reflect the chef's classic French training. But ask the waiter what else is in the kitchen, and he may reel off a list of hearty village favorites that includes a rich *soffritto* (veal cooked in a sauce of vinegar, parsley, and plenty of garlic), *pastitsada* (a derivation of the Italian dish *spezzatino*—layers of beef and pasta, called *macaronia* in Greek, cooked in a rich and spicy tomato sauce and topped off with béchamel sauce), and pork stewed with celery, leeks, and wine. You won't go wrong choosing from among them. In June you can sit beneath a jacaranda tree's electric-blue flowers; year-round the outdoor tables of the Town Hall restaurant overlook the comings and goings at that elegant building. Reservations are recommended on weekends. ⊠ *Dimarcheiou Sq.* ☎ *26610/39031* 💳 *AE, DC, MC, V.*

$$$–$$$$ ✕ **Venetian Well.** Tables organized around a 17th-century well, a staff that tiptoes past lingering lovers—the scene is as delicious as the food. In a Venetian building, on the most charming little square in the old town, operatic and traditional music accompanies the Greek and international specialties. Creative entrées include crepes with spinach and green-tea sauce, and wild boar. ⊠ *Kremasti Sq. across from Church of the Panagia* ☎ *26610/44761* ✍ *Reservations essential* 💳 *MC, V* ⏲ *No lunch Sun.*

$$–$$$$ ✕ **Bellisimio.** Contrary to its Italian-sounding name, this is a traditional, family-run Greek taverna where owner Stavros invites you into the kitchen to look at the available food. Here you can relax, away from the bustling crowds, on a quiet square and eat traditional favorites such as *briam* (a mixture of eggplant, zucchini, and potatoes in olive oil and

tomato sauce). Only Corfiot wine is sold, in order to keep prices affordable. ✉*Lemonia Sq. off N. Theotoki* ☎*26610/41112* ▭*No credit cards* ⏲*Closed Nov.–Apr. No lunch Sun.*

$$–$$$ ✕**Aegli.** More than 100 different dishes, both local and international, are on the menu. Start with a plate of baked artichokes, then move on to perfectly executed Corfiot classics such as spicy swordfish *bourdetto* (firm-flesh fish stewed in tomato sauce with lots of hot red pepper), or the more-unusual *arnaki kleftiko* (lamb cooked as the *kleftes,* War of Independence fighters, liked it), with onions, olives, mustard, and feta cheese. Tables in front, with comfortable armchairs and spotless tablecloths, overlook the nonstop parade on the Esplanade at Liston. Aegli keeps late hours, serving drinks and sweets midnight until 2 AM. ✉*Kapodistriou 23, Liston* ☎*26610/31949* ▭*AE, MC, V.*

$$–$$$ ✕**Gerekos.** One of the island's most famous seafood tavernas, Gerekos's raw materials are supplied daily by the family's own fishing boats. The menu varies according to the catch and the season, but the friendly staff will guide your choice. For a light meze, opt for a table on the terrace and try the whitefish *me ladi* (cooked in olive oil, garlic, and pepper) with a salad and some crisp white wine while deciding. ✉*Kondokali Bay, 6 km (4 mi) north of Corfu town* ☎*26610/91281* *Reservations essential* ▭*AE, V.*

$$–$$$ ★ ✕**Rex.** A friendly Corfiot restaurant in a 19th-century town house, Rex has been a favorite for nearly 100 years, and with good reason. Classic local specialties such as a hearty and meaty pastitsada, *stifado* (meat stewed with sweet onions, white wine, garlic, cinnamon, and spices), and *stamna* (lamb baked with potatoes, rice, beans, and cheese) are reliably delicious. Dishes such as rabbit stewed with fresh figs and chicken with kumquats are successful twists on the regional fare. Outside tables are perfect for people-watching on the Liston. ✉*Kapodistriou 66, west of Liston* ☎*26610/39649* ▭*AE, V.*

WHERE TO STAY

$$$$ ★ **Corfu Palace.** Get away from the town center, and gaze out over the bay from spacious rooms decorated with Louis XIV–style furniture. Every room has a sea-view balcony and a huge marble bathroom. The two restaurants both have seating in the lush gardens adjacent to the sprawling pool, and once a week there's a barbecue. You can book a tennis court at the nearby Corfu Tennis Club and hire facilities at the Corfu Yacht Club. Three days a week a shuttle runs to the beach at Glyfada on the west coast. ✉*Leoforos Dimokratias 2, 49100* ☎*26610/39485* 📠*26610/31749* 🌐*www.corfupalace.com* *101 rooms, 11 suites* *In-room: refrigerator. In-hotel: 2 restaurants, bars, pool, spa* ▭*AE, DC, MC, V.*

$$$–$$$$ **Corfu Imperial.** A deluxe resort complex—run by top Greek chain Grecotel—juts into Komeno Bay atop a 14-acre peninsula. Luxury rooms, bungalows, and villas (several with private pools), provide comfortable elegance—and balconies with sea views. The eight suites, all different, have large living rooms and bathrooms with whirlpool tubs, and the Presidential Suite also has a dining room and a dramatic view across the Ionian Sea to the shores of Albania. Though extensive, the prop-

8

erty blends harmoniously with the lush landscape of olive, palm, and cypress trees and colorful gardens. ✉*Komeno Bay, 10 km (6 mi) north of Corfu town, 49100* ☎*26610/88400* 📠*26610/91481* 🌐*www.grecotel.gr* *184 rooms, 119 bungalows, 8 suites, 21 villas* *In-hotel: 2 restaurants, bars, pool* 💳*AE, DC, MC, V* *Closed Nov.–Apr.*

$$$–$$$$ **Daphnila Bay.** Yet another dazzling member of the Grecotel chain, the Daphnila Bay has as its star attraction the impressive Elixir Thalasso Spa, which specializes in thalassotherapy and aromatherapy. Family-oriented guest rooms are large and brightly decorated with spacious balconies; the public lounges are an elegant mix of sophisticated, high-tech design with traditional folk elements. The property is in an olive grove and surrounded by verdant pines, which sweep down to the edge of a beach. The hotel operates on an all-inclusive-rate basis only. ✉*11 km (7 mi) north of Corfu town, 49100Dassia* ☎*26610/91520* 📠*26610/91026* 🌐*www.grecotel.gr* *126 rooms, 134 bungalows, 2 suites* *In-room: refrigerator. In-hotel: 3 restaurants, bar, pools, spa* 💳*AE, D, MC, V* *Closed Nov.–Mar.*

$$–$$$ **Kontokali Bay.**When you tire of exploring the streets and museums in town, this hotel is a fine place to relax away from it all. The pastel guest rooms, with modern wood appointments, are cheerful and sunlit, with balconies facing the sea, the mountains, or the lake. Umbrellas and chaise lounges wait for you on the two beaches. A buffet and a grill restaurant serve Greek and Italian cuisine, or you can order a snack from the beach bar. ✉ *Kondokali Bay, 6 km (4 mi) north of Corfu town, 49100* ☎*26610/90500 through 26610/90509, 26610/99000 through 26610/99002* 📠*26610/91901* 🌐*www.kontokalibay.com* *158 rooms, 83 bungalows* *In-room: safe. In-hotel: 3 restaurants, bars, pool, public Internet* 💳*AE, DC, MC, V* *Closed Nov.–Mar.*

$–$$ **Cavalieri Hotel.** Ask for a room on the fourth or fifth floor, with a number ending in 2, 3, or 4, for a breathtaking view of the Old Fortress near the Liston. The building is swank yet graceful and chock-full of history—it was built in the 18th century and is a landmark of old Corfu. Rooms have polished wood furniture and old brass fixtures, though the bathrooms are a little cramped. The highlight is the roof garden, where, over a drink at sunset, you have the most glorious view in town. Be warned though, the service is not always top-notch. ✉*Kapodistriou 4, 49100* ☎*26610/39041* 📠*26610/39283* 🌐*www.cavalieri-hotel.com* *50 rooms* *In-hotel: restaurant, bar* 💳*AE, DC, MC, V.*

$–$$ **Hotel Bella Venezia.** This colorful two-story Venetian town house in the center of town was operated as a hotel as early as the 1800s. The large lobby has a marble floor; a rich, polished wood ceiling; and chandeliers. The high-ceiling rooms are small but have elegant furniture, and some have canopy beds. Enjoy the buffet breakfast in the huge garden. There are no views, but that's what keeps it affordable. ✉*Zambelli 4, behind Cavalieri Hotel, 49100* ☎*26610/20707 or 26610/44290* 📠*26610/20708* *30 rooms, 1 suite* *In-room: refrigerator. In-hotel: bar* 💳*AE, DC, MC, V* *BP.*

¢ **Hotel Hermes.** The bare-bones Hermes is popular with backpackers because it has clean rooms, comfortable beds (a double, two twins, or a single), and cheap rates (as little as €28 for a double). It's not bad for a short stay, but not the best choice for a summer holiday if you value creature comforts, views, and being near the beach (the hotel is in town). The nearby daily produce market is convenient for stocking up for picnics, but it makes the hotel a bit noisy in the morning. ✉*G. Markora 14, 49100* ☎*26610/39268* *25 rooms* *In-room: no a/c, no TV* *MC, V* *BP.*

A MUSICAL TRADITION

Corfu has a rich musical tradition, partly the result of the Italian, French, and British influences evident throughout the island. The town's numerous marching bands take part in all official ceremonies, even religious observances. Throughout the summer on Sunday you can catch the local philharmonic in concert on the Esplanade in Corfu town.

NIGHTLIFE & THE ARTS

Past the commercial center, 3 km (2 mi) west of town is a string of discos that really don't start swinging until after midnight. They have names like Privelege, Hippodrome, and Apocalypsis, and they throb with the latest Euro-pop and dance hits. Incredibly loud sound systems and futuristic designs are just what the young, flesh-baring crowd wants for dancing into the wee hours. Most of the clubs have a cover charge, which includes the first drink. Greek clubs come and go by the minute, so be sure to ask the concierge and locals for the current hot spots.

BARS & CLUBS For sunsets with your ouzo and *mezedes* (appetizers), try the **Aktaion Bar** (✉*South of Old Fortress* ☎*No phone*) on the water. The rooftop bar at the **Cavalieri Hotel** (✉*Kapodistriou 4* ☎*26610/39041*) is hard to beat for views. Hotel guests happily mingle with locals as the scene slowly enlivens from a mellow, early-evening cocktail crowd to a more energetic partylike atmosphere.

8

Hip but relaxed **Cofineta** (✉*Liston, north end* ☎*26610/25642*) has cane chairs out on the cobblestones and a good view not of nature, but of decked-out promenade strollers. At **Ekati** (✉*Alykes Potamou* ☎*No phone*) crowds are sophisticated and older, but the volume of the live music is nevertheless high at this chichi club, where excessive baubles and Paris designer labels are in evidence. Ekati is at the end of the disco strip west of the commercial center.

Have a drink from the bar at **Internet Cafe Netoikos** (✉*Kalokeretou 12–14* ☎*26610/47479*) while you do business online from 10 AM to midnight every day except Sunday, when the place opens at 6 PM. At the top of the New Fortress, **Morrison Café** (✉*Solomou, on northwest town promontory* ☎*No phone*) overlooks the water and has Corfu's best DJs, who favor cool acid jazz. It stays open long after the rest of the fortress is closed to the public.

FILM Corfu town's **Foinikas** (✉*Akadimias* ☎*No phone*) is said to be the oldest outdoor cinema in Greece. It shows undubbed international movies in a pretty courtyard from June to September. In summer, shows generally start at 9 PM and 11 PM; selections change every two to three weeks.

SHOPPING

Corfu town has myriad tiny shops. Increasingly, designer boutiques, shoe shops, and accessory stores are opening up in every nook and cranny of the town. For traditional goods, head for the narrow streets of the Campiello, where olive wood, lace, jewelry, and wineshops abound. For perishable products such as liqueurs and candies, you may do better checking out the supermarkets than buying in the old town. Most of the shops listed below are in the Campiello and are open May to October, from 8 AM until late (whenever the last tourist leaves); they're generally closed September to April. Stores in outlying shopping areas tend to close Monday, Wednesday, and Saturday afternoons at 2:30 PM, and all day Sunday.

Alexis Traditional Products. For locally made wines and spirits, including kumquat liqueur and marmalade, go to Alexis Traditional Products. Traditional sweets, local olive oil, olives, and olive oil soap—as well as honey, herbs, and spices—are also sold. ✉*Solomou 10–12, Spilia* ☎*26610/21831.*

Katafigio. You can take a replica of your favorite museum artifact home with you from this shop. There's also a display of chess sets, some of which have pieces depicting ancient Greek heroes. ✉*N. Theotoki 113* ☎*26610/43137.*

Mironis Olive Wood. Bowls, sculptures, wooden jewelry, and much more are crammed into two tiny family-run shops. Smaller items are made as you watch. ✉*Filarmonikis 27* ☎*26610/40621* ✉*Agiou Spyridon 65* ☎*26610/40364.*

Nikos Sculpture and Jewellery. Nikos makes original gold and silver jewelry designs, and sculptures in cast bronze; they're expensive, but worth it. ✉*Paleologou 50* ☎*26610/31107* ✉*N. Theotoki 54* ☎*26610/32009* 🌐*www.nikosjewellery.gr.*

Rolandos. Visit the talented artist Rolando and watch him at work on his paintings and handmade pottery. ✉*N. Theotoki 99* ☎*26610/45004.*

SOUTH CORFU ΝΟΤΙΑ ΚΕΡΚΥΡΑ

Outside Corfu town, near the suburb of Kanoni, are several of Corfu's most unforgettable sights, including the lovely view of the island of Pontikonisi. The nearby palace and grounds of Mon Repos were once owned by Greece's royal family and are open to the public as a museum. A few villages south of Benitses, and some on the island's southern tip, are usually overrun with raucous package-tour groups. If you seek a hard-drinking, late-night crowd, and beaches chockablock with activities and tanning bodies, head there. If you're looking for more-solitary nature in the south, take a trip to Korisia.

KANONI KANONI

5 km (3 mi) south of Corfu town.

At Kanoni, the site of the ancient capital, you may behold Corfu's most famous view, which looks out over two beautiful islets. Keep in mind that though the view *of* the islets has sold a thousand postcards, the view *from* the islets is that of a hilly landscape built up with resort hotels and summer homes and of the adjacent airport, where planes take off directly over the churches.

The suburb of Kanoni was once one of the world's great beauty spots, made deservedly famous by countless pictures. The name derives from a French cannon that once stood here, no doubt utterly incongruous in this once sublimely peaceful landscape. The open sea is separated by a long, narrow causeway from the lagoon of Halikiopoulou, with the intensely green slopes of Mount Agia Deka as a backdrop. A shorter breakwater leads to the white convent of Moni Vlahernes on a tiny islet. Beyond, tall cypresses guard **Pontikonisi,** or Mouse Island, a rock rising dramatically from the clear water and topped by a 13th-century chapel—one of the most picturesque setpieces in all Greece. Legend has it that the island is really Odysseus's ship, which an enraged Poseidon turned to stone: the reason why Homer's much-traveled hero was shipwrecked on Phaeacia (Corfu) in The *Odyssey.* June to August a little motorboat runs out to Pontikonisi every 20 minutes.

Fodor'sChoice ★

The island's only casino is in the sleek and curving hotel, **Corfu Holiday Palace.** The nearly 5,500 square feet of gaming space is open daily noon–3 AM. ✉ *Kanoni* ☎ *26610/46941.*

8

★ The royal palace of **Mon Repos** is surrounded by gardens and ancient ruins. It was built in 1831 by Sir Frederic Adam for his wife, and it was later the summer residence of the British lord high commissioners. Prince Philip, the duke of Edinburgh, was born here. After Greece won independence, it was used as a summer palace for the royal family of Greece, but it was closed when the former king Constantine fled the country in 1967, after which the Greek government expropriated it. Throughout the '90s, the estate was tangled in an international legal battle after Constantine petitioned to have the property returned; the Greek government finally paid him a settlement and opened the fully restored palace as a museum on the island's rich history. After touring the palace, wander around the extensive grounds, which include ruins of temples from the 7th and 6th centuries BC as well as the small but lovely beach that was once used exclusively by the Greek royal family and is now open to the public. Ask museum officials for maps and information; the pamphlets are free and useful but aren't handed out unless requested. Opposite Mon Repos are ruins of Ayia Kerkyra, the 5th-century church of the Old City. ✥ *1 km (½ mi) north of Kanoni, near Mon Repos beach* ☎ *26610/41369* 🎫 €3 ⏲ *Tues.–Sun. 8:30–7.*

GASTOURI ΓΑΣΤΟΥΡΙ

19 km (12 mi) southwest of Corfu town.

★ The village of Gastouri, still lovely despite the summer onrush of day-trippers, is the site of the **Achilleion.** Although in remarkably bad taste (Lawrence Durrell called it "a monstrous building"), the palace is redeemed by lovely gardens stretching to the sea. Built in the late 19th century by the Italian architect Rafael Carita for Empress Elizabeth of Austria, this was a retreat for her to nurse her health and her heartbreak over husband Franz Josef's numerous affairs. Elizabeth named the palace after her favorite hero, Achilles, whom she identified with her son. After she was assassinated, Kaiser Wilhelm II bought it and lived here until the outbreak of World War I, during which he still used it as a summer residence. After the armistice, the Greek government received it as a spoil of war.

The interior contains a pseudo-Byzantine chapel, a pseudo-Pompeian room, and a pseudo-Renaissance dining hall, culminating in a vulgar fresco called *Achilles in His Chariot.* One of the more-interesting furnishings is Kaiser Wilhelm II's saddle seat, used at his desk. On the terrace, which commands a superb view over Kanoni and the town, is an Ionic peristyle with a number of statues in various degrees of undress. The best is *The Dying Achilles.* In 1962 the palace was restored, leased as a gambling casino, and later was the set for the casino scene in the James Bond film *For Your Eyes Only.* The casino has since moved to the Corfu Holiday Palace. The exhibits on the ground floor contain mementos and portraits. ✉*Main street* ☎*26610/56210* €6 ⏲*June–Aug., daily 8–7; Sept.–May, daily 9–4.*

WHERE TO STAY & EAT

$$$$ ✕ **Taverna Tripas.** Taken in the right spirit, this most famous (and most touristed) of Corfu's tavernas can be fun. The festivity kicks in when the live music and local dancers fill the courtyard (patrons join in, too), and it's not uncommon to see Greek politicians and their retinues dining here. The fixed menu has a choice of tasty *mezedakia* (small appetizers); the pastitsada and beef *kokkinisto* (roasted in a clay pot with garlic and tomatoes) are especially good. ✉*2 km (1 mi) northwest of Gastouri, Kinopiastes* ☎*26610/56333* 🌐*www.tripas.gr* *Reservations essential* ▭*No credit cards* ⏲*No lunch.*

$$$–$$$$ **Marbella Hotel.** In an olive grove near the emerald waters of Agios Ioannis south lies the deluxe Marbella Hotel complex and bungalows. The spacious, sophisticated Mediterranean-style accommodation has amazing views of the sea or the garden from balconies that adjoin the rooms. Single rooms are available, and prices drop almost by half off-season. The Marbella is on the coast road between Benitses and Moraitika. ✉*10 km (6 mi) south of Gastouri, 49084Agios Ioannis Peristeron* ☎*26610/71183* *26610/71189* 🌐*www.marbella.gr* *375 rooms, 21 suites* *In-room: refrigerator. In-hotel: 5 restaurants, pool, public Internet, parking (no fee)* ▭*AE, D, MC, V* ⏲*Closed Nov.–Apr.* *MAP.*

$$ **San Stefano.** Close to Achilleion palace and 900 feet from the beach, this modern hotel commands a hill overlooking the water in 35 acres of garden. Rooms have standard hotel furniture and are rather uninspiring, but most have balconies from which to savor the coastline vistas. Bungalows have kitchenettes with refrigerators. It's hard to get bored here: there are many activities and water sports available through the hotel, and the beach lies just below. ✉ *1 km (½ mi) south of Gastouri, 49084Benitses* ☎ *26610/71123* 📠 *26610/71124 or 26610/72272* 🌐 *www.ellada.net/sanstef* *216 rooms, 4 suites, 39 bungalows* *In-hotel: 2 restaurants, bars, pool, some pets allowed* 💳 *AE, DC, MC, V* ⊗ *Closed Nov.–Mar.*

WEST-CENTRAL CORFU
ΔΥΤΙΚΗ-ΚΕΝΤΡΙΚΗ ΚΕΡΚΥΡΑ

The agricultural Ropa Valley divides the sandy beaches and freshwater lagoon of the lower west coast past Ermones from the dramatic mountains of the northwest. Hairpin bends take you through orange and olive groves, over the mountainous spine of the island to the rugged bays and promontories of the coast. The road descends to the sea, where two headlands near Paleokastritsa, 130 feet high and covered with trees and boulders, form a pair of natural harbors.

PELEKAS ΠΕΛΕΚΑΣ

11 km (7 mi) northwest of Gastouri, 13 km (8 mi) west of Corfu town.

8

Inland from the coast at Glyfada is Pelekas, a hilltop village that overflows with tourists because of its much-touted lookout point, called **Kaiser's Throne.** German kaiser Wilhelm II enjoyed the sunset here when not relaxing at Achilleion Palace. The rocky hilltop does deliver spectacular views of almost the entire island and sea beyond.

North across the fertile Ropa Valley is the resort town of **Ermones** (✉ *8 km [5 mi] north of Pelekas*), with pebbly sand beaches, heavily wooded cliffs, water with plentiful fish, large hotels, and a backdrop of green mountains. The Ropa River flows into the Ionian Sea here.

BEACHES

The beach at **Pelekas** has soft, golden sand and clear water but is developed and tends to be crowded. There's a huge resort hotel next to it. Free minibuses regularly transport people to the beach from the village, which is a long and steep walk otherwise. The large, golden beaches at **Glyfada** (✉ *2 km [1 mi] south of Pelekas*) are the most famous on the island. Though the sands are inevitably packed with sunbathers—some hotels in Corfu town run daily beach shuttles to Glyfada—many still come. Sun beds, umbrellas, and water-sports equipment is available for rent and there are several tourist resorts.

The isolated **Myrtiotissa** (✉ *3 km [2 mi] north of Pelekas*) beach, between sheer cliffs, is known for its good snorkeling—and its nude sunbathing. Backed by olive and cypress trees, this sandy stretch was called by Lawrence Durrell in *Prospero's Cell* (with debatable overenthusiasm) "perhaps the loveliest beach in the world." Alas, summer crowds are the norm.

WHERE TO STAY & EAT

$$$$ ✕ **Spiros and Vassilis.** Escape the in-town tourist hordes and venture to a timeless restaurant on farmland belonging to the Polimeri family. Steak is a big winner on the classic French menu, as are frogs' legs and escargots. An extensive wine list and truly efficient, discreet service add to the pleasure. ✉ *9 km (6 mi) west of Corfu town on road to Pelekas, Agios Ioannis* ☎ *26610/52552 or 26610/52438* ▭ *AE, D, MC, V* ⊗ *No lunch.*

$$–$$$$ ✕ **Jimmy's.** Only fresh ingredients and pure local olive oil are used at this family-run restaurant serving traditional Greek food. Try *tsigareli*, a combination of green vegetables and spices, or some of Jimmy's own Corfiot meat dishes. There's a nice choice of vegetarian dishes and of sweets. The place opens early in the morning for breakfast and stays open all day. ✉ *Pelekas* ☎ *26610/94284* ▭ *MC, V* ⊗ *Closed Nov.–Apr.*

$$$ ★ **Pelekas Country Club.** The old family mansion of Nikos Velianitis, amid 200 acres of olive and cypress trees, forms the core of this idyllic retreat. Seven impeccably furnished bungalows and four suites are decorated with antiques and family heirlooms from England and Russia; all have large verandas overlooking the gardens. Olive Press House and the François Mitterrand Suite are recommended. Breakfast treats include fresh-squeezed fruit juices and homemade jams served in the mansion dining room. ✉ *Kerkyra–Pelekas road, 49100* ☎ *26610/52239 or 26610/52917* 🖷 *26610/52919* 🌐 *www.country-club.gr* *7 studios, 4 suites* *In-room: no a/c (some), kitchen (some). In-hotel: bar, pool* ▭ *No credit cards* *BP.*

$ **Levant Hotel.** Guest rooms have small balconies to enjoy the breathtaking views (and sunsets) over the Adriatic Sea and across silver-green olive groves. The neoclassic Levant retains a touch of romance in the traditional Corfiot style: canopies hang over the beds in comfortable rooms. Start off your day with a soul-warming breakfast served on the main terrace. This hotel is under Kaiser Wilhelm II's favorite lookout point. ✉ *Near Kaiser's Throne, 49100* ☎ *26610/94230 or 26610/94335* 🖷 *26610/94115* 🌐 *www.levanthotel.com* *24 rooms, 1 suite* *In-hotel: restaurant, bar, pool* ▭ *MC, V* *BP.*

PALEOKASTRITSA ΠΑΛΑΙΟΚΑΣΤΡΙΤΣΑ

21 km (13 mi) north of Pelekas, 25 km (16 mi) northwest of Corfu town.

Identified by archaeologists as the site of Homer's city of the Phaeacians, this spectacular territory of grottoes, cliffs, and turquoise waters has a big rock named Kolovri, which resembles the mythological ship that brought Ulysses home. The natural beauty and water sports of Paleo, as Corfiots call it, have brought hotels, tavernas, bars, and shops to the hillsides above the bays, and the beaches swarm with hordes of people on day trips from Corfu town. You can explore the quiet coves in peace with a pedal boat or small motorboat rented at the crowded main beach. There are also boat operators that go around to the prettiest surrounding beaches; ask the skipper to let you off at a beach that appeals to you and to pick you up on a subsequent trip.

Paleokastritsa Monastery, a 17th-century structure, is built on the site of an earlier monastery, among terraced gardens overlooking the Adriatic Sea. Its treasure is a 12th-century icon of the Virgin Mary, and there's a small museum with some other early icons. Note the Tree of Life motif on the ceiling. Be sure to visit the inner courtyard (go through the church), built on the edge of the cliff, dappled white, green, and black by the sunlight on the stonework, vine leaves, and habits of the hospitable monks. Under a roof of shading vines you look precipitously down to the placid green cove and the torn coastline stretching south. ✉ *On northern headland* ☎ *No phone* *Donations accepted* ⏲ *Daily 7–1 and 3–8.*

The village of **Lakones** is on the steep mountain behind the Paleokastritsa Monastery. Most of the current town was constructed in modern times, but the ruins of the 13th-century **Angelokastro** also loom over the landscape. The fortress was built on an inaccessible pinnacle by a despot of Epirus during his brief rule over Corfu. The village sheltered Corfiots in 1571 from attack by Turkish wannabe conquerors. Look for the chapel and caves, which served as sanctuaries for hermits. The road to this spot was reputedly built by British troops in part to reach Lady Adam's favorite picnic place, the Bella Vista terrace (there's a café here now). Kaiser Wilhelm also came here to enjoy the magnificent view of Paleokastritsa's coves. ✉ *5 km (3 mi) northeast of Paleokastritsa.*

8

WHERE TO STAY & EAT

$$$–$$$$ ✕ **Vrahos** *(The Rock).* Overlooking the rock of the bay in Paleokastritsa, where Homer's wine-dark sea touches forest-green mountains, the view here is one of those Greek keys that explain all. As for the food, the lobster and spaghetti is delicious, and the house salad is a tasty mix of rocket lettuce, spinach, and cabbage with mushrooms and croutons. The prices are reasonable considering the fantastic views. ✉ *North end of beach* ☎ *26630/41233* ▭ *AE, MC, V* ⏲ *Closed Nov.–May.*

¢ **Casa Lucia.** The stone buildings of an olive press have been converted into individually decorated guest cottages, each overlooking a tranquil garden filled with hibiscus, olive trees, and bougainvillea. Cottages have two to five beds with colorful striped linens and a few antiques, and most have their own small kitchens and courtyard. Tai chi and yoga sessions are held out in the garden by the pool. ✉ *Corfu–Paleokastritsa road, 13 km (8 mi) northwest of Corfu town, 49083Sgombou* ☎ *26610/91419* 🌐 *www.casa-lucia-corfu.com* *9 cottages* *In-room: no a/c, no phone, no TV. In-hotel: pool* ▭ *AE, D, MC, V.*

NORTH CORFU
ΒΟΡΕΙΑ ΚΕΡΚΥΡΑ

The main roads along the northeast coast above Corfu town are crowded with hotels, gas stations, touristy cafés, and shops. But head inland a bit and there are more-peaceful settings—dusty villages where olives, herbs, and home-brewed wine are the main products, and where goats roam the squares and chickens peck at the roadsides. Steep Mt. Pantokrator ("ruler of all")—at 2,970 feet the highest peak on Corfu—forms the northeast lobe of the island. The northern coastal area is replete with pretty coves, and it has the longest sand beach in Corfu, curving around Roda to Archaravi.

HIKING CORFU

Corfu's verdant, varied interior is excellent hiking terrain. There are trails to the summit of Mt. Pantokrator from the villages of Strinylas, Spartylas, and Old Perithia. The fully marked Corfu Trail runs 220 km (137 mi), winding through Corfu's most beautiful scenery, from the lake at Korisia to Mt. Pantokrator. It takes about 10 days to hike the entire trail (there are hotels and tavernas along the way), but it's possible to explore small chunks of it in a day or two. For info, read *The Companion Guide to the Corfu Trail* and *The Second Book of Corfu Walks* written by Hilary Whitton Paipeti.

ANO KORAKIANA ΆΝΩ ΚΟΡΑΚΙΑΝΑ

★ *6 km (4 mi) northeast of Paleokastritsa, 19 km (12 mi) north of Corfu town.*

Corfiots call this beautiful village Little Venice, for its narrow lanes winding through old Venetian houses painted in fading peach and ocher. Instead of watery canals, they're set against the silvery-green olive-tree-covered slopes of Mt. Pantokrator, and filled with gardens of pomegranate and lemon trees and brilliantly colored flowers. Life is quiet but happy here: old men bring their chairs out to the square, where they can drink coffee and gossip while looking out to the sea; heavenly aromas drift out from the bakeries, said to make the island's best bread; and some afternoons the town marching band strikes up a tune in the square.

WHERE TO EAT

$$$ Fodor's Choice ★ ✕**Etrusco.** Hidden in the old mansion of a tree-filled village is one of the best restaurants in Greece; it's mentioned regularly on the prestigious Golden Chef's Cap Awards list. Etrusco is run by the Italian-Corfiot Botrini family, whose passion for both cuisines, combined with flawless technique and creativity, results in truly memorable dinners. Chef Ettore Botrini delights with dishes like homemade *pappardelle* (flat pasta with rippled edges) with duck and truffles, and medallions of fish cooked in Triple Sec and sesame seeds. For starters try the extraordinary home-cured meats and marinated fish—particularly delicious is the salmon in aromatic oil and poppy seeds. Ettore's wife, Monica, prepares the desserts; her terrine of peaches and white chocolate is sublime. ✉*1 km (½ mi) east of Ano Korakiana, Kato Korakiana* ☎*26610/93342* *Reservations essential* *MC, V* *No lunch.*

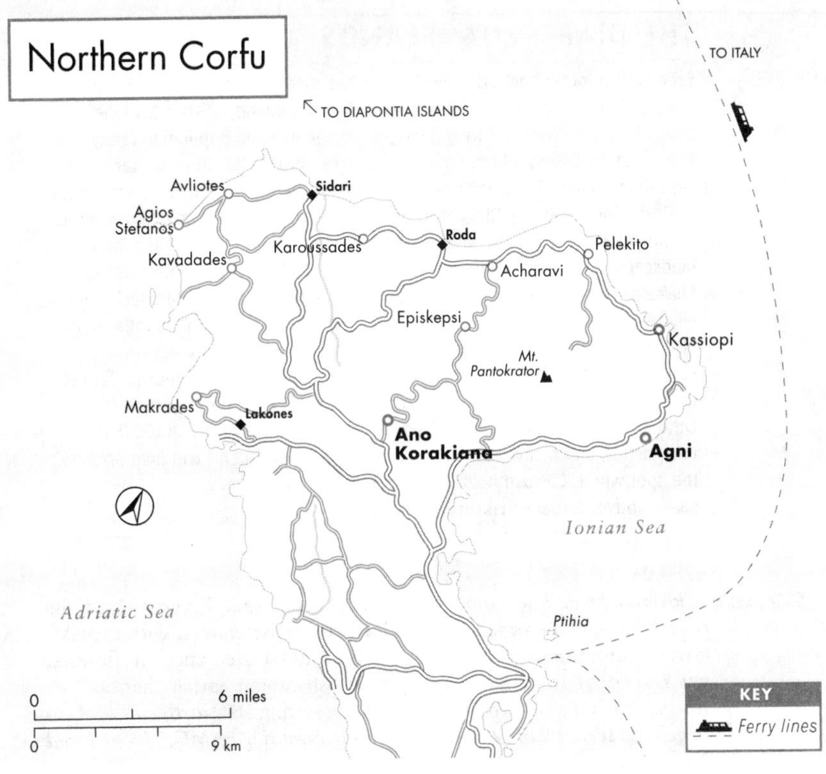

AGNI ΑΓΝΗ

7 km (4½ mi) north of Ano Korakiana, 28 km (17 mi) north of Corfu town.

Tiny, clear-water Agni is little more than a scenic fishing cove. Like the rest of Corfu's coast, it has good swimming, and you can rent small boats to go exploring on your own. What makes it a don't-miss destination is its three outstanding restaurants, all lining the pretty harbor. If you're doing a drive around Corfu's north coast, try to stop at Agni for lunch or dinner—or both.

The harbor town at **Kouloura,** 3 km (2 mi) south of Agni, is on a U-shape bay enclosed by cypress, eucalyptus, and palm trees and has a small shingle beach with close views of the Albanian coastline. This coastline is part of the Corfu immortalized by the Durrell brothers—much of Lawrence Durrell's writing of *Prospero's Cell* was done in what is now a taverna called the White House, south in Kalami. Donkeys still plod the roads, cafés serve local wine, and life here on the lower slopes of Mt. Pantokrator holds its sweet charm, even when besieged by tourists in July and August.

THE DIAPONTIA ISLANDS

Even with a four-wheel drive and a map of dirt roads, it can still be tough to find a stretch of truly pristine coast on cosmopolitan Corfu. Less than 7 km (4.5 mi) northwest of Corfu, the three tiny Diapontia islands look more like the untouched landscape evoked by Homer and Shakespeare. All three have beaches where you won't see anything at all beyond water, white sand, and hilltops where wild herbs and flowers wave in the breeze. The island of Othonoi also has a few ruined Venetian castles, and a cave said to be the spot where Calypso held Odysseus captive. Verdant Erikoussa has excellent fishing and a thickly wooded inland. Mathraki, where the year-round population rarely exceeds 100, has long, solitary, stunningly beautiful beaches. Each makes a memorable day trip. If you want to stay longer, each also has a handful of small hotels; there are tavernas at the harbors where boats dock from Corfu. Boats for the Diapontia islands leave three times a week from Agios Stefanos. San Stefano Travel (18 km [11 mi] northwest of Kassiopi, Agios Stefanos, 26630/51910, steftrav@otenet.gr) can help arrange trips to the islands.

WHERE TO EAT

$$$–$$$$ ✕**Taverna Agni.** The quintessential island taverna, Taverna Agni sits on a white-pebble beach near shallow turquoise waters, with cypress-covered mountains as backdrop. The food—stuffed zucchini flowers, chicken cooked in champagne, grilled fish caught earlier that day—is just as much a reason to stop here as the setting. ✉*North end of Agni beach* ☎*26630/91142* ✍*Reservations essential* ▭*MC, V* ⊗*Closed Nov.–Apr.*

$$$–$$$$ ✕**Toula's.** Of the Agni restaurants, Toula's gets the most creative with the abundant fresh seafood and seasonal produce. Many declare the fragrant shrimp pilaf to be the best they've ever tasted—cooked with lots of garlic, parsley, and chili, and a secret spice Toula's refuses to reveal. The pasta with lobster or prawns is also excellent, as are simpler dishes, like fresh grilled bream and mussels cooked in broth. ✉*Waterfront* ☎*26630/91350* ▭*MC, V* ⊗*Closed Nov.–Apr.*

$$–$$$ ✕**Taverna Nicholas.** Which Corfiot village dishes are available at Taverna Nicholas depends on what produce has been brought down from the mountains, and what fish out of the sea, that day. Likely as not, there will be an exemplary soffritto, cod with garlic sauce, and chicken in white wine with freshly picked herbs. The simple, whitewashed beachfront terrace restaurant has been serving food for several generations. ✉*South end of Agni cove* ☎*26630/91243* ▭*AE, MC, V* ⊗*Closed Nov.–mid-Apr.*

CORFU ESSENTIALS

TRANSPORTATION

BY AIR

Olympic Airlines and Aegean Airlines both have two or three flights a day from Athens to Corfu town. Fares change, but the hour-long flight starts at about €180 round-trip. AirSea Lines has connections to the islands of Paxos, Ithaki, and Lefkas, and to Ioannina and Patras on the mainland; it also connects the region with the Italian port of Brindisi. Between April and October many charter flights arrive in Corfu directly from the United Kingdom and northern Europe.

Carriers **Aegean Airlines** (☎ *210/998–8350, 210/998–8300 in Athens* 🌐 *www.aegeanairlines.gr*). **AirSea Lines** (☎ *26610/99316* 🌐 *www.airsealines.com*). **Olympic Airlines** (☎ *26610/38694, 26610/38695, 26610/49484, or 26610/49485* 🌐 *www.olympicairlines.com*).

AIRPORTS Corfu Airport is northwest of Kanoni, 3 km (2 mi) south of Corfu town. A taxi from the airport to the town center costs around €8; there is no airport bus. Taxi rates are on display in the arrivals hall.

Information **Corfu Airport** (☎ *26610/89600*).

BY BOAT & FERRY

There are no ferries from Piraeus to Corfu town; you need to drive to Patras or to the northwestern city of Igoumenitsa, to catch one of the daily ferries for Corfu. You can buy tickets at the ports, or book in advance through the ferry lines or travel agents. For the most up-to-date information on boat schedules, call the port authority in the city of departure or check the Greek ferry information Web site.

Ferries from Patras to Corfu town (six to seven hours) generally leave around 11 PM or midnight. The ferries are run by Minoan, ANEK, and Blue Star lines and tickets cost about €25 per person, €70 per car, and €40 per person for a cabin. Kerkyra Lines and Cruises runs ferries between Igoumenitsa and Corfu town (two hours); tickets are €8 per person and €32 per car. Petrakis Lines and Cruises hydrofoils go from Igoumenitsa to Corfu town (45 minutes) on Sunday and Corfu town to Igoumenitsa on Tuesday (€12). International ferries between Greece and Italy stop in Corfu town at least several times a week; check with Minoan Lines.

Boat & Ferry Lines **ANEK Lines** (✉ *Akti Kondili 22, Piraeus* ☎ *210/419–7438* 🌐 *www.anek.gr*). **Argostoli Port Authority** (☎ *26710/22224*). **Blue Star Ferries** (✉ *Amalias 30, Athens* ☎ *210/891–9800* 🌐 *www.bluestarferries.com*). **Corfu Port Authority** (☎ *26610/32655*). **Greek ferry info** (🌐 *www.greekferries.gr*). **Igoumenitsa Port Authority** (☎ *26650/22235*). **Kerkyra Lines and Cruises** (✉ *Eleftheriou Venizelou 32, Corfu town* ☎ *26610/23874*). **Minoan Lines** (✉ *25th August 17, Iraklio* ☎ *2810/399800* 🌐 *www.minoan.gr*). **Patras Port Authority** (☎ *2610/341002*). **Petrakis Lines and Cruises** (✉ *Venizelou 9, new port, Corfu town* ☎ *26610/31649*).

BY BUS

KTEL buses leave Athens Terminal A for Corfu town (10 hours, €35 one way), via Patras and the ferry, three or four times a day. The inexpensive local bus network covers Corfu island, with reduced service Sunday, holidays, and off-season. Green KTEL buses leave for long-distance destinations from the Corfu town terminal near the new port. Blue local buses (with destinations including Kanoni and Gastouri) leave from San Rocco Square. You can get timetables and information at both bus depots and in the English-language news magazine *The Corfiot*.

Contacts **Corfu local buses** (*San Rocco Sq., Corfu town 26610/31595*). **KTEL Corfu buses** (*Avramiou, Corfu town 26610/39862 or 26610/30627 Terminal A, Kifissou 100, Athens 210/512–4190 or 210/512–9443*).

BY CAR & MOTORBIKE

The best route from Athens is the National Road via Corinth to Igoumenitsa (472 km [274 mi]), where you take the ferry to Corfu. In winter, during severe weather conditions, the ferries from Igoumenitsa may stop running.

There is little or no system to Greek driving, and "Depend on the other guy's brakes" best expounds the basic philosophy of many drivers. The road surfaces deteriorate as the tourist season progresses, and potholes abound.

As on all Greek islands, exercise caution with regard to steep, winding roads, and fellow drivers equally unfamiliar with the terrain.

RENTALS Corfu town has several car-rental agencies, most clustered around the ports. There's a gamut of options, ranging from international chains offering luxury four-wheel drives to local agencies offering cheap deals on basic wheels. Prices can range from €35 a day for a Fiat 127 (100 km [62 mi] minimum) to €120 a day for a four-wheel-drive jeep with extras. Expect additional charges of around €20 for insurance, delivery, and so forth. It's definitely worth it to shop around: chains have a bigger selection, but the locals will usually give a cheaper price. Don't be afraid to bargain, especially if you want to rent a car for several days. In Corfu town, Ocean Car Hire has good bargains, and Reliable Rent-a-Car has dozens of options. Other agencies include Top Cars and Olympus Rent-a-Car.

A 50cc motorbike can be rented for about €25 a day and €110 a week, or a 125cc motorbike for about €30 a day and €160 a week, but you can bargain, especially if you want it for longer. Helmets are rarely provided, and then only on request. Check the lights, brakes, and other mechanics before you accept a machine. In Corfu town, try Easy Rider; rentals are available in even the most-remote villages.

Contacts **Budget Zakynthos** (*26950/51337*). **Easy Rider** (*Eleftheriou Venizelou 50, Corfu town 26610/43026*). **Kefalonia Rent-A-Car** (*26710/27313*). **Ocean Car Hire** (*New port, Corfu town 26610/44017 www.oceancar.gr*). **Olympus Rent-a-Car** (*National Stadium 29, Corfu town 26610/36147*). **Reliable Rent-a-Car** (*Donzelot 5, Corfu town 26610/35740*). **Top Cars** (*Donzelot, Corfu town 26610/35237 www.topcars.gr*).

BY TAXI

Taxis are available 24 hours a day, and rates, which are set by the government, are reasonable—when adhered to. Many drivers speak English and know the island well. If you want to hire a cab and driver on an hourly or daily basis, negotiate the price before you travel. In Corfu town, taxis wait at Sarokou Square, Theotoki Square, the Esplanade, and the ports.

Contact **Corfu Taxis** (☎ *26610/33811, 26610/30383, or 26610/39911*).

CONTACTS & RESOURCES

EMERGENCIES

In Corfu town there's always one pharmacy open 24 hours; call the 24-hour information line to find out which one.

Information **Corfu Tourist Police** (✉ *Kapodistriou 1, Corfu town* ☎ *26610/30265*). **Hospital** (✉ *Andreadi, Corfu town* ☎ *26610/45811*). **Police** (✉ *Alexandras 19, Corfu town* ☎ *100*). **24-Hour Pharmacy Information** (☎ *107*).

MEDIA

The monthly English news magazine *The Corfiot,* written mostly by and for ex-pats, has information on events; restaurant reviews; and bus, boat, and plane schedules. It's available at newsstands and at English-language bookshops, the largest of which is Lykoudis, which also has memoirs and novels related to the island. Lykoudis also runs a kiosk that sells English-language periodicals, from *Financial Times* to *Seventeen.*

English-Language Bookstores **Lykoudis** (✉ *Polimnias Skaramgka Sq., Corfu town* ☎ *26610/39845 Kiosk* ✉ *Kapodistriou 11, Corfu town* ☎ *No phone*).

TOUR OPTIONS

Many travel agencies run half-day tours of Corfu's old town, and tour buses go daily to all the sights on the island; All-Ways Travel is reliable. Charitos Travel has more than 50 tours of the island and can create custom tours for groups of five or more. International Tours arranges hiking, mountain biking, horseback riding, jeep trips, and other such excursions around the island. Cosmic Travel has east-coast boat trips as well as sunset and moonlight cruises from Kassiopi.

Contacts **All-Ways Travel** (✉ *G. Theotoki 34, Corfu town* ☎ *26610/33955* 🌐 *www.allwaystravel.com*). **Charitos Travel** (✉ *Arseniou 35, Corfu town* ☎ *26610/44611* 🌐 *www.charitostravel.gr*). **Cosmic Travel** (✉ *Kassiopi* ☎ *26630/81624* 🌐 *www.cosmic-kassiopi.com*). **International Tours** (✉ *Eleftheriou Venizelou 32, Corfu town* ☎ *26610/39007 or 26610/38107*). **Petrakis Lines and Cruises** (✉ *Ethnikis Antisaseos 4, Corfu town* ☎ *26610/31649*).

VISITOR INFORMATION

Information **Greek National Tourism Organization (GNTO or EOT)** (✉ *San Rocco Sq., Corfu town* ☎ *26610/20733* 🌐 *www.gnto.com*).

Northern Peloponnese

The Lion gate at Mycenae

9

WORD OF MOUTH

"You're going to adore Nafplion! It feels like Italy.... Don't miss climbing up the steps to the top of the fortress (but do it in the morning). Because all the sites are so close, it's easy to include Mycenae and Ancient Corinth in your agenda. You might also have dinner one night in Tolo—it's 9 km from Nafplion and is pretty happening at night."

–DenverDice

www.fodors.com/forums

WELCOME TO NORTHERN PELOPONNESE

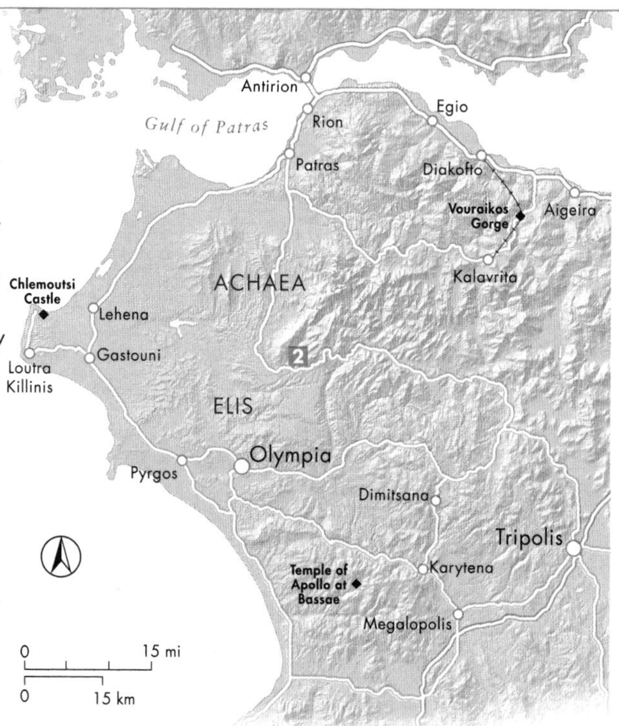

TOP REASONS TO GO

★ **Ancient Ruins A to Z:** Some of Greece's greatest classical ruins, including Ancient Corinth, Mycenae, and Ancient Olympia, are all packed into this region.

★ **Nafplion Grace:** The favorite Greek city of many seasoned travelers has a magnificent setting on the Gulf of Argos, imposing remains, an animated waterfront, and street after street of old houses, churches, and mosques.

★ **Beach Basking:** The beaches along the western coast are some of the best in Greece and are generally less crowded than those in other areas.

★ **High Drama:** The theater at Epidauros, the setting for a highly acclaimed drama festival, still claims acoustics so perfect that every word can be heard—even from the very last of its 55 tiers.

★ **A Thrill-a-Minute Train Ride:** The narrow-gauge Kalavrita Express, delivers an exhilarating journey between seaside Diakofto and alpine Kalavrita.

1 Argolid and Corinthiad. Forgotten civilizations left their mysteries here on the eastern side of the Northern Peloponnese. The ruined city of Mycenae, with giant tombs to the heroes of Homer's *Iliad*, stands sentinel over the Argolid plain. Nearby Nafplion, with its ancient edifices jutting into the Bay of Argos, is perhaps the most beautiful city in Greece—and surrounded by other ancient sites: Tiryns, Epidauros, Ancient Nemea, and Corinth are all within easy reach.

The theater at Epidauros.

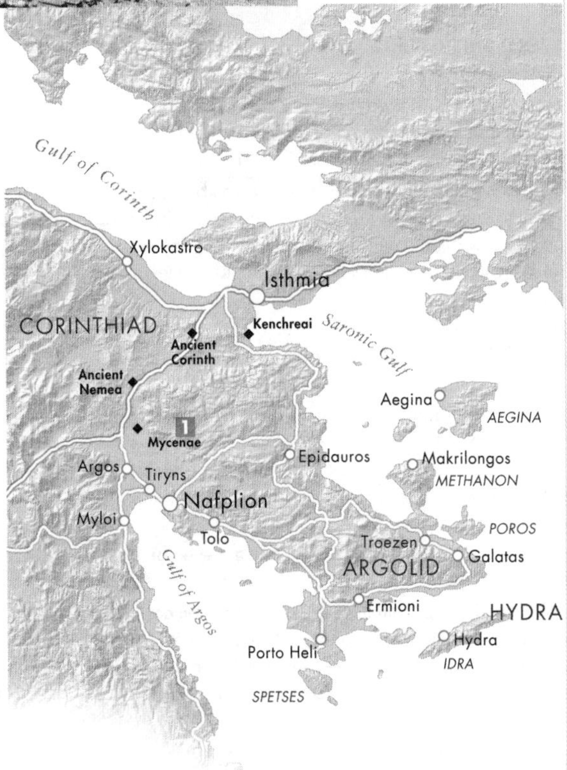

GETTING ORIENTED

The Northern Peloponnese comprises the Argive peninsula, jutting into the Aegean, and runs westward past the isthmus and along the Gulf of Corinth to Patras and the Adriatic coast. The oldest region is the fertile Argive plain (Argolid), the heart of Greece in the late Bronze Age and the home of the heroes of Homer's *Iliad*. Most of the Peloponnese is mountainous and rural, with farms and olive groves on the hillsides and in the valleys. However, Patras, in the far northwestern corner of the Peloponnese, is the third-largest city in Greece and its major port with Europe. Nafplion has maintained its traditional architectural heritage, which is largely inspired by Venetian, Ottoman, and German neoclassic trends.

Nafplion with Fort Bourdzi in background, Argolid.

2 Achaea and Elis. Achaea's wooded mountains rise behind the port of Patras, Greece's gateway to Western Europe. To the south the mountain valleys of Elis shelter small villages and the sleepy town that happens to house one of the most famous sites of the ancient world: Olympia, home to the games that still bring the world together.

NORTHERN PELOPONNESE PLANNER

Making the Most of Your Time

The remains of the ancient world are what draw many visitors to the Northern Peloponnese—Mycenae, Epidauros, and Olympia certainly top of the list of "must-see" sights of anyone with an interest in archaeology. However, the region has a lot more to offer. Nafplion, a delightful city, with Byzantine, Venetian, and Turkish roots, makes an ideal base from which to explore the well-preserved ruins of ancient Greece.

The eastern and western portions of the Northern Peloponnese are easily divided into two separate three-day itineraries; a thorough exploration requires about nine days. Visitors with less time should consider investigating either the eastern or western half only; for travelers entering Greece from Italy, Olympia and environs are logical options, and for those entering Greece through Athens, Nafplion and the Argolid are only a short hop away.

Olympia beckons the Peloponnesian traveler sooner or later, but don't rush. There's plenty to see en route from the Argolid, including the alluring beauty of the Vouraikos Gorge, which you can enjoy on an overnight stop in Diakofto or Kalavrita.

Great Flavors

One of the simplest pleasures of traveling in the Northern Peloponnese is a late dinner of traditional food with good Greek wine, preferably *varelisio* (from the barrel).

From late April until as late as early November, you can expect to enjoy this experience outdoors. With the exception of a few hotel dining rooms in Nafplion, any restaurant that pretends to offer more than this should be viewed with suspicion.

You can usually enjoy a meal of such staples as lamb or moussaka for about €10 a person, even in Nafplion or Patras.

Dress is casual and reservations unnecessary, although you might be asked to wait for a table, if you're dining with the majority at 9 PM or later. Expect to pay quite a bit for most fresh fish and seafood; a single portion is usually about €15.

Never settle for frozen fish, which may not even be from Greek waters.

Look for red wines from the region around Nemea, between Corinth and Argos, and try Patras's sweet *mavrodaphne,* a heavy dessert wine. Another favorite in Patras is *dendoura,* a clove liqueur served after dinner as a digestive.

How's the Weather?

As in much of Greece, late April and May provide optimum conditions for exploration—hotels, restaurants, and sites have begun to extend their hours but the hordes of travelers have not yet arrived.

September and October are also excellent times because the weather is warm but not oppressive, the sea is at its balmiest, and the throngs of people have gone home.

In summer, morning and early-evening activity will avoid the worst of the heat, which can be a formidable obstacle.

Getting Around

Nafplion is the major city in the east of the region, on the Gulf of Argos, about 150 km (90 mi) south of Athens. Patras is in the west, near the Rion Bridge for easy connections to central Greece and ferries to Italy.

The easiest way to get around the Northern Peloponnese is by car, on the region's well-maintained and well-marked roads.

Corinth, Nemea, Tiryns, Argos, and Epidauros are within easy reach of Nafplion, and when it comes time to venture farther, it's easy to get to other parts of the Peloponnese via the E65, a north–south highway that cuts through the region and is four lanes for much of its length.

You can take a bus to Patras or Nafplion and rent a car there, or rent a car at the airport in Athens and head south.

The association of regional bus companies (KTEL) provides frequent service at reasonable prices from Athens to Patras, Pyrgos (for Olympia), Corinth, Argos, Epidauros, Nafplion (for Mycenae), and Xylokastro.

In addition to serving major centers such as Nafplion, Argos, Corinth, and Patras, KTEL buses travel to virtually every village in the Northern Peloponnese.

From Nafplion, an excellent base for exploring the region, you can reach Epidauros, Tiryns, Mycenae, Argos, and many other towns and sites by frequent and dependable bus service.

Traveling by train from Athens to some places in the Northern Peloponnese is sometimes convenient and is relatively inexpensive.

Dining & Lodging Prices in Euros

	¢	$	$$	$$$	$$$$
Restaurants	Under €8	€8–€15	€15–€20	€20–€25	Over €25
Hotels	Under €80	€80–€120	€120–€160	€160–€200	Over €200

Restaurant prices are for one main course at dinner, or for two mezedes (small dishes). Hotel prices are for a standard double room in high season, including taxes. Hotels operate on the European Plan (EP, with no meal provided) unless we note that they use the Continental Plan (CP, with Continental breakfast); Breakfast Plan (BP, with a full breakfast); Modified American Plan (MAP, with breakfast and dinner); or the Full American Plan (FAP, with all meals). Inquire when booking if these meal plans (which can entail higher rates) are mandatory. Guest rooms have air-conditioning, room phones, and TVs unless otherwise noted.

Finding a Place to Stay

Hotels in Nafplion, Patras, and other large towns and cities tend to be open year-round. In beach resorts and in Olympia, many hotels close in late October and reopen in late March or early April. A few resort-type hotels in beach towns cater to an international clientele, and there are business-style hotels in Patras. In Nafplion, many old houses have been converted to pleasant small hotels and do a brisk weekend business as a getaway for Athenians.

In Patras and Nafplion you are likely to find the region's more luxurious and expensive lodgings. Overall, though, lodging is a good value, and even in high season you can usually manage to find a clean and pleasant room for two, with breakfast, for €70 or even less.

The Gifted

Olympia has big-ticket gold jewelry, as do the stores around Constitution Square in Nafplion, but the gifts beyond price in this region are really the folk crafts, usually found in the smaller villages. With a bit of poking around, you can find outstanding examples of strikingly colored old weavings, especially tagaria (shepherd's shoulder bags), which command a higher price than the newer versions. They make wonderful wall hangings.

Updated by Stephen Brewer

THE SOUTHERN SECTION OF THE GREEK MAINLAND, hanging like a leaf from the Corinthian isthmus, the Peloponnese is graced by astounding and imposing ruins that litter a landscape of massive mountains covered with low evergreen oak and pine trees, fertile coastal valleys, and rocky shores and sandy beaches. Over the millennia this rugged terrain nourished kingdoms and empires and witnessed the birth of modern Greece. The region is named for Pelops, son of the mythical Tantalos, whose tragic descendants, including Atreus and Agamemnon, dominate the half-legendary Mycenaean centuries. Traces of these lost realms—ruined Bronze Age citadels, Greek and Roman temples and theaters, and the fortresses and settlements of the Byzantines, Franks, Venetians, and Turks—attest to the richness of the land.

A walk through the Lion Gate into Mycenae, the citadel of Agamemnon, brings the Homeric epic to life, and the massive walls of nearby Tiryns glorify the age of might. The thriving market town of Argos, the successor to Mycenae and Tiryns, engaged in a long rivalry with Sparta. Corinth, the economic superpower of the 7th and 6th centuries BC, dominated trade and established colonies abroad. Although eclipsed by Athens, Corinth earned a reputation for ostentatious wealth and loose living. Today modern Corinth is a bustling, if unremarkable, regional center. Not far from Corinth is Epidauros, the sanctuary of Asklepios, god of healing, where in summer Greek dramas are re-created in the ancient theater, one of the finest and most complete to survive. Olympia, the sanctuary of Zeus and site of the ancient Olympic Games, lies on the western side of the Peloponnese.

By the 13th century, the armies of the Fourth Crusade (in part egged on by Venice) had conquered the Peloponnese after capturing Constantinople in 1204. But the dominion of the Franks was brief, and Byzantine authority was restored under the Palaiologos dynasty. Soon after Constantinople fell in 1453, the Turks, taking advantage of an internal rivalry, crushed the Palaiologoi and helped themselves to the Peloponnese. In the following centuries the struggle between the Venetians and the Ottoman Turks was played out in Greece. The two states alternately dominated the Northern Peloponnese until the Ottomans ultimately prevailed as Venetian power declined in the early 1700s. The Turkish mosques and fountains and the Venetian fortifications of Nafplion recall this epic struggle. Rebellion against Turkish rule ignited in the Peloponnese, and after the Turks withdrew in 1828 in the wake of the Greek War of Independence, Nafplion was the capital of Greece from 1829 until the move to Athens in 1834.

A large portion of Greece's emigrants to the United States in the 20th century (12%–25% of the male population) have roots in the Peloponnese (their family names are often identified with an ending in *poulos,* meaning "son of"); almost all dreamed of returning to their Greek villages when they had raised their families and had accumulated a sufficient *ekonomies* (nest egg). Quite a number of them have done just that, so if you find yourself unable to convey what you need through phrase-book Greek and body language in one of the remote villages here, an elderly *Helleno-Americanos* (Greek-American) may be called upon to assist. Time seems to have stood still in the smaller towns here, and even in the cities you'll encounter a lifestyle that remains more traditionally Greek than that of some of the more developed islands. The joy of exploring this region comes as much from watching life transpire in an animated square as it does from seeing the impressive ruins.

You probably won't need much encouragement to forgo clamoring over ruins to lie on a beach. Excellent stretches of sand near Kastro, under Chlemoutsi Castle, include Katakolo and Spiantza, and Kalogria, closer to Patras, is a 6-km (4-mi) beach bordered by pine forests. Even in urbane Nafplion, the sea is a main attraction, appreciated from long promenades and pleasant nearby town beaches. But knowing travelers venture to this region for far more than suntans. After all, the "cyclopean" walls at Tiryns, the Lion Gate and beehive tombs at Mycenae, the theater in Epidauros, and the world-famous sculptures at Olympia are some of the once-in-a-lifetime wonders to be seen and relished here.

ARGOLID & CORINTHIAD
ΑΡΓΟΛΙΔΑ & ΚΟΡΙΝΘΙΑ

Ancient Tiryns and Mycenae gaze over the plain of Argos, and nearby Epidauros hosts audiences from around the world who come to see performances in its classical theater. The city of Argos lies in the center of the plain, near the beautiful Turkish-Venetian city of Nafplion. Behind the mountains that surround the plain is the Corinthiad, a hilly region overlooked by Ancient Corinth.

ISTHMUS ΙΣΘΜΟΣ

75 km (47 mi) southwest of Athens, 7 km (4½ mi) southeast of Corinth.

More of a pit stop than a town, the isthmus is where the Peloponnese begins. Were it not for this narrow neck of land less than 7 km (4½ mi) across, the waters of the Gulf of Corinth and the Saronic Gulf would meet and would make the Peloponnese an island; hence the name, which means "Pelops's island." The tragic myths and legends surrounding Pelops and his family—Atreus, Agamemnon, Orestes, and Electra, among others—provided the grist for poets and playwrights from Homer to Aeschylus and enshroud many of the region's sites to this day.

For the ancient Greeks the isthmus was strategically important for both trade and defense; Corinth, with harbors on either side of the isthmus, grew wealthy on the lucrative east–west trade. Ships en route from Italy and the Adriatic to the Aegean had to sail around the Peloponnese, so in the 7th century BC a paved roadway called the Diolkos was constructed across the isthmus, over which ships were hauled using rollers. You can still see remnants near the bridge at the western end of the modern canal.

Isthmia, an ancient sanctuary dedicated to Poseidon, 1 km (½ mi) west of the canal, isn't much to look at today, but in antiquity it was an important place. From 580 BC, this was the site of the Isthmian Games, biennial athletic and musical competitions on a par with those at Nemea, Delphi, and Olympia. Little remains of the ancient city, since its buildings were dismantled for stone to repair the Isthmian wall and to build a large fortress. Better preserved are the remains of the fortress, called the **Hexamilion,** and of the **wall** (east of the sanctuary is a stretch that rises more than 20 feet). The remains of a **Roman bath** include some good mosaics. A museum near the site entrance contains objects uncovered in excavations over the years. ✉*Off Hwy. 94* ☎*0741/37244* 🌐*www.culture.gr* 🎫*€2* ⏲*May–Oct., daily 8–7; Nov.–Apr., daily 8–3.*

THE ISTHMUS CANAL

Nero was the first to begin cutting a canal, supposedly striking the first blow, with a golden pickax, in AD 67, a task he then turned over to 6,000 Jewish prisoners. But the canal project died with Nero the following year, and the roadway was used until the 13th century. The modern canal, built 1882–93, was cut through 285 feet of rock to sea level. The impressive sight is a fleeting one if you are speeding by on the highway, so keep a sharp lookout. A well-marked turnoff leads to the tourist area, which has many restaurants (best avoided) and souvenir shops, as well as an overlook above the canal.

EPIDAUROS ΕΠΙΔΑΥΡΟΣ

62 km (38 mi) south of the isthmus, 25 km (15 mi) east of Nafplion.

Fodor'sChoice ★ The Sanctuary of Asklepios, once the most famous healing center in the ancient world, is today best known for the **Theater at Epidauros,** remarkably well preserved because it was buried at some time in antiquity and remained untouched until it was uncovered in the late 19th century. Built in the 4th century BC with 14,000 seats, the theater was never remodeled in antiquity, and because it was rather remote, the stones were never quarried for secondary building use. The extraordinary qualities of the theater were recognized even in the 2nd century AD. Pausanias of Lydia, the 2nd-century AD traveler and geographer, wrote, "The Epidaurians have a theater in their sanctuary that seems to me particularly worth a visit. The Roman theaters have gone far beyond all the others in the world ... but who can begin to rival Polykleitos for the beauty and composition of his architecture?" In addition, the acoustics of his theater are so perfect that even from the last of the 55 tiers every word can be heard. The theater is the setting for a highly acclaimed **summer drama festival,** with outstanding productions.

The **Sanctuary of Asklepios** is dedicated to the god of healing, the son of Apollo who was allegedly born here. The most important healing center in the ancient world, it drew visitors in search of a cure from throughout Greece and the colonies. The sanctuary is in the midst of

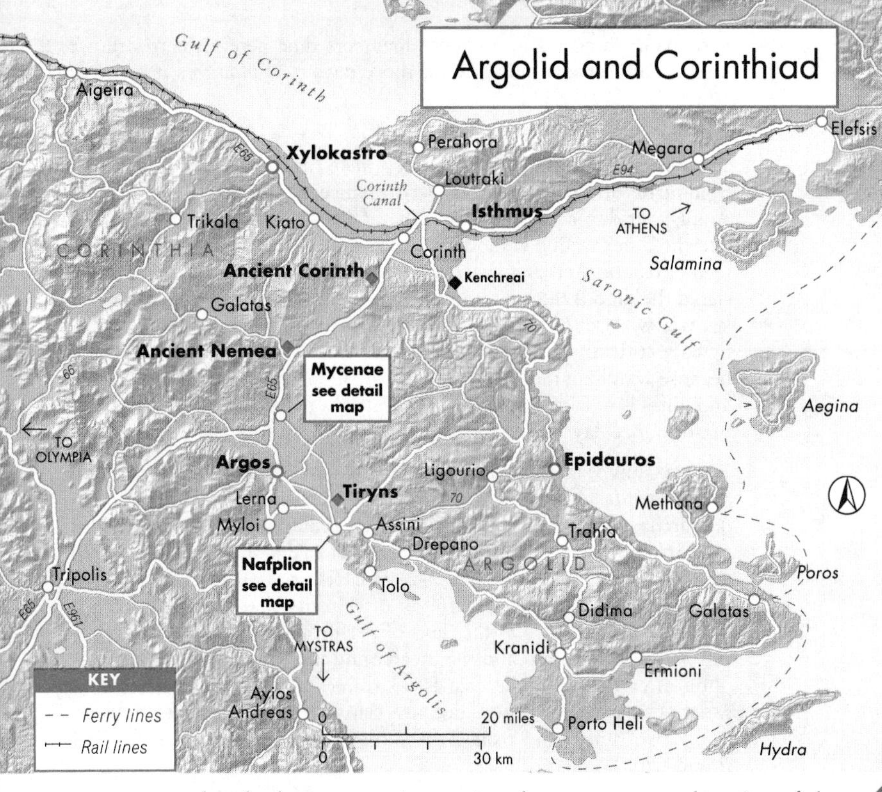

a decades-long restoration project, but you can see the ruins of the Sleeping Hall, where clients slept in order to be visited by the gods in their dreams and told which cure to follow, as well as the enormous Guest House, with 160 rooms. Some copies of sculptures found among the ruins are in the **site museum,** but the originals are in the National Archaeological Museum in Athens. An exhibit of ancient medical implements is of interest, as are detailed models of the sanctuary and blueprints. Heading south from the isthmus on Highway 70, don't take the turnoffs for Nea Epidauros or Palaio Epidauros; follow the signs that say "Ancient Theatre of Epidauros." ✉ *Off Hwy. 70 near Ligourio* ☎ *27530/23009* 🌐 *www.culture.gr* 🎫 *€6* ⏲ *May–Oct., daily 8–7:30; Nov.–Apr., daily 8–5.*

9

WHERE TO EAT

¢–$$ ★ ✕ **Leonidas.** Seating in a rear garden in summer and in front of a fire in winter adds to the pleasure of dining at this friendly taverna, the best dining choice in and around Epidauros. The grilled pork chops are excellent, as are the moussaka and the stuffed vine leaves in egg-lemon sauce. Dessert choices are brandy-and-cinnamon-laced *revani* (semolina cake) or luscious *kataifi* (shredded dough filled with chopped pistachio nuts) topped with *kaimaki* (clotted cream). The owner may walk you around to show off his photos of celebs who have dined here. Many actors and audience members dine here on performance nights, so reserve in advance on those days. ✉*Epidauros main road* ☎*27530/22115* ▭*V*.

THE ARTS

The **Hellenic Festival** (✉*Off Hwy. 70 near Ligourio*) in the theater at Epidauros offers memorable performances from late June through August, Friday and Saturday only, at 9 PM. All productions are of ancient Greek drama in modern Greek, many presented by the national theater troupe. Actors are so expressive (or often wear ancient masks to signal the mood) that you can enjoy the performance even if you don't know a word of Greek. Get to the site early (and bring a picnic lunch or have a drink or a light meal at the excellent Xenia Café on-site), because watching the sun set behind the mountains and fields of olives and pines is unforgettable. The festival sells tickets a short time before performance days at the theater.

You can buy tickets through the **Festival Box Office** (✉*Panepistimiou 39, in arcade, Athens* ☎*210/928–2900* ⏲*Weekdays 8:30 AM–4 PM*) or purchase tickets online at 🌐www.greekfestival.gr. Tickets are also available at the box office of the **Theatre of Epidaurus** (☎*27530/22026* ⏲*Weekdays 8:30–4 and Sat. 9–2*). Tickets are €10–€50. Many tour operators in Athens and Nafplion offer tours that include a performance at Epidauros. On the days of performances, four or five buses run between Nafplion and the theater and there's service back to Nafplion after the play; the cost is €4 round-trip. Look for those that say THEATER or EPIDAUROS, not NEA EPIDAUROS or ARCHEA EPIDAUROS. Buses also run to and from Athens on days of performances for €14 round-trip.

NAFPLION ΝΑΥΠΛΙΟ

Fodor's Choice ★ *65 km (40½ mi) south of Corinth, 27 km (17 mi) west of Epidauros.*

Oraia (beautiful) is the word Greeks use to describe Nafplion. The town's old section, on a peninsula jutting into the Gulf of Argos, mixes Greek, Venetian, and Turkish architecture; narrow streets, often just broad flights of stone stairs, climb the slopes beneath the walls of Acronafplia. Statues honoring heroes preside over tree-shaded plazas surrounded by neoclassic buildings. The Palamidi fortress—an elegant display of Venetian might from the early 1700s—guards the town. Nafplion deserves at least a leisurely day of your undivided attention, and you may want to spend several days or a week here and use the city as the base from which to explore the many surrounding ancient sights.

Little is known about ancient Nafplion, although Paleolithic remains and Neolithic pottery have been found in the vicinity. The town grew in importance in Byzantine times, and it was fought over by the Byzantines and the Frankish crusaders. It has been held by the duke of Athens, the Venetians, and the Turks. In the War of Independence, the Greeks liberated the town, and it briefly became the national capital. During World War II, German troops occupied Nafplion from April

1941 until September 1944. Today Nafplion is once again just a provincial city, busy only in the tourist season and on weekends when Athenians arrive to get away from city pressures.

A full exploration of this lovely town takes an entire day; a quick tour, with some omissions, could be done in three hours. Although a step-by-step itinerary can lead you to all the main sights, you can get a good sample of Nafplion just by following your nose through its winding streets and charming squares. But if you want a mapped-out plan of action, start by making a beeline for the center of the old town: Syntagma (Constitution) Square. In clockwise fashion around it are some top sights, including the Peloponnesian Folklore Foundation Museum, St. Spyridon Chruch, and the Archaeological Museum. The most picturesque avenue around here is Vasileos Konstantinou; the more commercial Amalias is lined with shops. Westward you'll find the Church of the Virgin Mary's Birth, an elaborate post-Byzantine structure. Continuing north, you come to quayside and Philhellenes Square and the St. Nicholas Church.

From St. Nicholas westward along the quayside (called Akti Miaouli) is an unbroken chain of restaurants, most just average, and, farther along, better patisseries. It is pleasant in the afternoon for postcard writing, an iced coffee or ouzo, and conversation. From the quay, you can embark on a boat trip out to the miniature fortress of the Bourtzi in the harbor. Or you can continue walking along the waterfront promenade to the Five Brothers bastion, and then follow the winding Kostouros street up to Psaromachalas, the picturesque fishermen's quarter. Return to the Five Brothers to continue on the promenade that follows the sea along the south side of the Nafplion peninsula, or, instead, go through the tunnel that looks like a James Bond movie set from the parking lot off Kostouros street and take the elevator to the Nafplia Palace hotel and the top of the Acronafplia fortress. The hotel bar is an excellent place to enjoy a sunset. Above all looms the town's Venetian-era Palamidi fortress, the pick of the peak and another top sunset spot (when weekday hours permit).

WHAT TO SEE

15 **Acronafplia.** Potamianou street, actually a flight of stone steps, ascends from St. Spyridon Square toward this imposing hilltop of ruined fortifications, which the Turks once called Its Kalé (Three Castles). Until the Venetian occupation, it had two castles: a Frankish one on the eastern end and a Byzantine one on the west. The Venetians added the massive Castello del Torrione (or Toro for short) at the eastern end around 1480. During the second Venetian occupation, the gates were strengthened and the huge Grimani bastion was added (1706) below the Toro. The Acronafplia is accessible from the elevator on the west side or by the road from the east side, near the Nafplia Palace hotel, which sits on the ruins of the Frankish fort. Most of the remains of fortifications can be explored free of charge on overgrown paths that provide stupendous views over Nafplion and the sea.

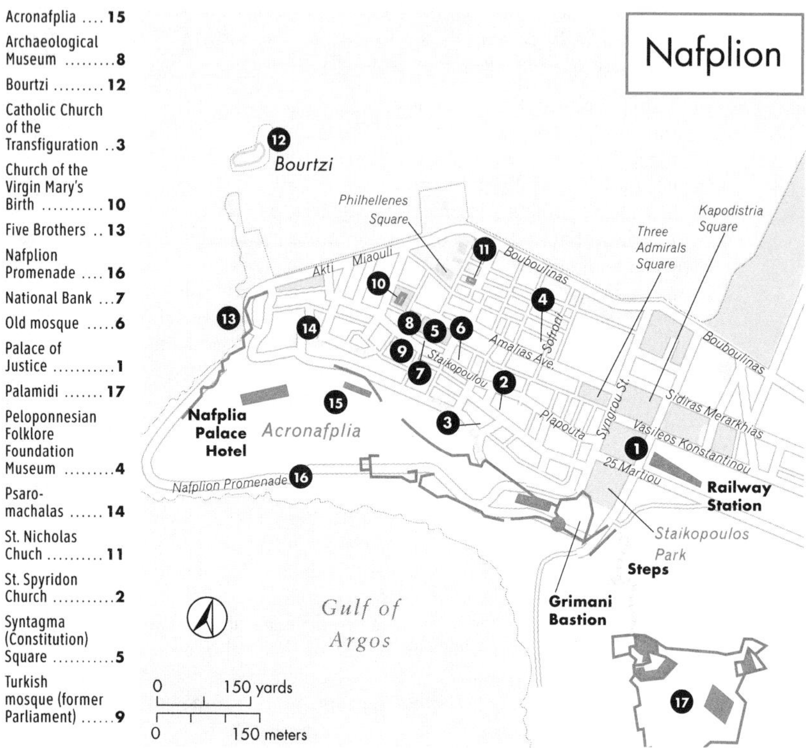

8 **Archaeological Museum.** To say that this red-stone building, built in 1713 to serve as the storehouse for the Venetian fleet, is "well constructed" is an understatement; its arches and windows are remarkably well proportioned, and the thick walls ensure the coolest interior in town. The museum, recently renovated, houses artifacts from such nearby sites as Mycenae, Tiryns, Asine, and Dendra; the loot from Mycenaean tombs is especially rich and includes wonderful masks and a suit of armor. ✉ *West side of Syntagma Sq.* ☎ *27520/27502* 🌐 *www.culture.gr* 🎫 *€2* ⏲ *Tues.–Sun. 8:30–3.*

OFF THE BEATEN PATH

Ayia Moni. Before or after exploring Nafplion, drive out the Epidauros road and turn right after 1 km (½ mi) to visit the Byzantine convent and church of Ayia Moni, a place of Christian devotion with a pagan twist. It was built in 1149 by Leo, the bishop of Argos and Nafplion, and an inscription on the west gate expresses the possibility that the Virgin will reward him by absolving him of his sins. In the monastery garden is a fountain said to be the spring Kanathos, where Hera annually renewed her virginity. Admission to the convent is free, but it is generally closed; ring the bell, and the nuns may admit you. They also sell beautiful embroidery.

12 **Bourtzi.** The sight of the Bourtzi, Nafplion's pocket-size fortress in the middle of the harbor, is captivating. Built in 1471, the Bourtzi (or Castelli) was at first a single tower, on a speck of land generously called St. Theodore's Island. Francesco Morosini is said to have massacred the Turkish garrison when he recaptured it for Venice in 1686. A tower and bastion were then added, giving the building the shiplike appearance it has today. In 1822, after the Bourtzi was captured in the War of Independence, it was used to bombard the Turks defending the town. In the unsettled times following the revolution, the government retreated to the Bourtzi for a while; after 1865, it was the residence of the town executioners; and from 1930 until 1970 it was run as a hotel. During the day the Bourtzi is no longer menacing; a tree blooms bright red in its courtyard in spring. Extending from the extreme end of the quay is a large breakwater, the west mole, built by the Turks as the anchor point for a large chain that could be drawn up between it and the Bourtzi, blocking the harbor completely. Boats leave on no fixed schedule from the eastern end of Akti Miaouli; the trip, including a chance to disembark at the Bourtzi, costs about €5. ✉*In harbor.*

9 **Catholic Church of the Transfiguration.** In the 19th century King Otho returned this Venetian-built church to Nafplion's Catholics. It is best known for the wooden arch erected inside the doorway in 1841, with the names carved on it of philhellenes who died during the War of Independence (Lord Byron is number 10). Note also the evidence of its use as a mosque by the Turks: the mihrab (Muslim prayer recess) behind the altar and the amputated stub of a minaret. The church has a small museum and an underground crypt in which can be found sculptural work commemorating the defeat of the Turks at the hands of the Greeks and philhellenes. ✉*Zigomala, 2 blocks south of St. Spyridon.*

10 **Church of the Virgin Mary's Birth.** The church rises next to an **ancient olive tree,** where, according to tradition, St. Anastasios, a Nafpliote painter, was killed in 1655 by the Turks. Anastasios was supposedly engaged to a local girl, but he abandoned her because she was immoral. Becoming despondent as a result of spells cast over him by her relatives, he converted to Islam. When the spell wore off, he cried out, "I was a Christian, I am a Christian, and I shall die a Christian." A Turkish judge ordered that he be beheaded, but a mob stabbed Anastasios to death. A local tradition holds that he was hanged on this olive tree and that it never again bore fruit. The church, a post-Byzantine three-aisle basilica, was the main Orthodox church during the Venetian occupation. It has an elaborate wooden reredos carved in 1870. ✉*West of Syntagma Sq.*

13 **Five Brothers.** Above the harbor at the western edge of town are the ruins of a fortification known as the Five Brothers, the only remaining part of the wall built around Nafplion in 1502. The name comes from the five guns placed here by the Venetians; there are five here today, all from around 1690 and all bearing the winged lion of St. Mark. ✉*Near promontory of peninsula.*

NEED A BREAK?

Beyond the Five Brothers, near the promontory of the peninsula, a few pleasant cafés and bars line the seaside promenade that follows the southern edge of the peninsula. These are good places to sit with an ouzo and watch

the sun set behind the mountains across the gulf; some establishments have created little swimming areas alongside the tables, so it's not unusual to see patrons bobbing around in the water.

Kolokotronis Park. The centerpiece of this park is a bronze equestrian statue surrounded by four small Venetian cannons, which commemorates the revolutionary hero Theodore Kolokotronis (1770–1843). ⊠*Syngrou and Sidiras Merarkhias.*

Miniature triangular park. This contains, inevitably, a monument to **Admiral Konstantinos Kanaris,** a revolutionary hero; across from its far end is the **bust of Laskarina Bouboulina.** Twice widowed by wealthy shipowners, she built her own frigate, the *Agamemnon.* Commanding it herself, along with three small ships captained by her sons, Bouboulina blockaded the beleaguered Turks by sea, cutting off their supplies. **Bouboulina's pedestal** sits on the corner. ⊠*Syngrou, north of Three Admiral Sq.*

16 **Nafplion Promenade.** This promenade around the Nafplion peninsula is paved with reddish flagstones and graced with an occasional ornate lamppost. Here and there a flight of steps goes down to the rocky shore below. (Be careful if you go swimming here, because the rocks are covered with sea urchins, which look like purple-and-black porcupines and whose quills can inflict a painful wound.) Before you reach the very tip of the peninsula, marked by a ship's beacon, there is a little shrine at the foot of a path leading up toward the Acronafplia walls above. Little Virgin Mary, or **Ayia Panagitsa** (⊠*End of promenade*), hugs the cliff on a small terrace and is decorated with icons. During the Turkish occupation it hid one of Greece's secret schools. Other terraces, like garden sanctuaries, have a few rosebushes and the shade of olive and cedar trees. Along the south side of the peninsula, the promenade runs midway along the cliff—it's 100 feet up to Acronafplia, 50 feet down to the sea. All along there are magnificent views of the cliff on which the Palamidi sits and the slope below, known as the Arvanitia.

7 **National Bank.** This structure displays an amusing union of Mycenaean and modern Greek architectural elements with concrete. (The Mycenaeans covered their tholos tombs [circular vaults] with mounds of dirt; the bank's ungainly appearance may explain why.) Take a look at the **sculptures** (⊠*Square next to National Bank*) of a winged lion of St. Mark (which graced the main gate in the city's landward wall, long since demolished) and of Kalliope Papalexopoulou (a leader of the revolt against King Otho), whose house once stood in the vicinity. ⊠*South of Syntagma Sq.*

6 **Old Mosque.** Immediately to the left as you enter Syntagma Square from Vasileos Konstantinou is this venerable mosque. It was formerly used for various purposes: as a school, a courthouse, municipal offices, and a movie theater. (The writer Henry Miller, who did not care for Nafplion, felt that the use of the building as a movie theater was an example of the city's crassness.) ⊠*Syntagma Sq.*

1 **Palace of Justice.** The gracelessness of this building is magnified by its large size. This monumentality makes it useful as a landmark, however. Nearby, across Syngrou street from the KTEL bus station, is a **square** with a statue honoring Nikitaras the Turk-Killer, who directed the siege of Nafplion during the War of Independence. ⊠*Syngrou, 2 blocks down from Kapodistria Sq.*

17 ★ **Palamidi.** Seen from the old part of Nafplion, this fortress, set on its 700-foot peak, is elegant, with the red-stone bastions and flights of steps that zigzag down the cliff face. A modern road lets you drive up the less-precipitous eastern slope, but if you are in reasonable shape and it isn't too hot, try climbing the stairs. Most guidebooks will tell you there are 999 of them, but 892 is closer to the mark. From the top you can see the entire Argive plain and look across the gulf to Argos or down its length to the Aegean.

Built in 1711–14, the Palamidi comprises three forts and a series of freestanding and connecting defensive walls. The name is taken from the son of Poseidon, Palamedes, who, legend has it, invented dice, arithmetic, and some of the Greek alphabet. Sculpted in gray stone, the lion of St. Mark looks outward from the gates. The Palamidi fell to the Turks in 1715 after only eight days. After the war, the fortress was used as a prison, its inmates including the revolutionary war hero Theodore Kolokotronis; a sign indicates his cell. On summer nights the Palamidi is illuminated with floodlights, a beautiful sight from below. ⊠*Above town* ☎*27520/28036* 🎫*€4* ⏲*Apr.–Oct., daily 8–7:30, weekends 8:30–2:30; Nov.–Mar., daily 8–3.*

NEED A BREAK?

For a respite, head to the pleasant series of tree-shaded Staikopoulou squares (⊠*At foot of Palamidi*). A tranquil café welcomes the weary, benches give your less-than-bionic feet a break, and children will appreciate the playground and duck pond. At the west end of the area, the Nafpliotes have reconstructed the Venetian Gateway, which originally guarded the entrance to the Palamidi; it commemorates the Venetian recapture of the city in 1487. Standing amid Byzantine and classical ruins, the gateway invites contemplation of the passage of time.

4 **Peloponnesian Folklore Foundation Museum.** This exemplary small museum focuses on textiles and displays outstanding costumes, handicrafts, and household furnishings. Many of the exhibits are precious heirlooms that have been donated by Peloponnesian families. The gift shop has some fascinating books and a good selection of high-quality jewelry and handicrafts, such as weavings, kilims, and collector folk items such as *roka* (spindles) and wooden *koboloi* (worry beads). ⊠*Vasileos Alexandrou 1, on block immediately north of Amalias, going up Sofroni* ☎*27520/28947* 🌐*www.pli.gr* 🎫*€4* ⏲*Museum Mon. and Wed.–Sat. 9–3 and 6–9, Tues. 6 PM–9 PM, Sun. 9–3; shop Mon.–Sat. 9–3 and 6–9.*

14 **Psaromachalas.** The fishermen's quarter is a small district of narrow, alleylike streets running between cramped little houses that huddle

beneath the walls of Acronafplia. The old houses, painted in brownish yellow, green, and salmon red, are embellished with additions and overhangs in eclectic styles. The walk is enjoyable, but this is a nontouristed area, so try to keep a low profile to respect the privacy of the locals. The pretty, miniature whitewashed chapel of **Ayios Apostoli** (⊠*Off parking lot of Psaromachalas*) has six small springs that trickle out of the side of Acronafplia. ⊠*Along Kostouros.*

11 **St. Nicholas Church.** Built in 1713 for the use of sailors by Augustine Sagredo, the prefect of the Venetian fleet, this church near the waterfront has a facade and belfry that are recent additions. Inside, the church is furnished with a Venetian reredos and pulpit, and a chandelier from Odessa. ⊠*Off Philhellenes Sq.*

2 **St. Spyridon Church.** This one-aisle basilica with a dome (1702), west of Ayios Georgios, has a special place in Greek history, for it was at its doorway that the statesman Ioannis Kapodistrias, the first president of an independent Greece, was assassinated in 1831 by the Mavromichalis brothers from the Mani, the outcome of a long-running vendetta. The mark of the bullet can be seen next to the Venetian portal. On the south side of the square, opposite St. Spyridon, are two of the four Turkish fountains preserved in Nafplion. A third is a short distance east (away from St. Spyridon) on Kapodistria street, at the steps that constitute the upper reaches of Tertsetou street. ⊠*Terzaki, St. Spirdonas Sq., Papanikolaou.*

5 **Syntagma (Constitution) Square.** The center of the old town is one of Greece's prettiest *platias* (squares), distinguished by glistening, multicolor marble paving bordered by neoclassic and Ottoman-style buildings. In summer the restaurants and patisseries on the square—a focal point of Nafpliote life—are boisterous with the shouts and laughter of children and filled with diners well into the evening. ⊠*Along Amalias and Vasileos Konstantinou.*

9 **Turkish mosque.** Now known as the Vouleftiko (Parliament), this mosque was where the Greek National Assembly held its first meetings. The mosque is well built of carefully dressed gray stones. Legend has it that the lintel stone from the Treasury of Atreus was used in the construction of its large, square-domed prayer hall. ⊠*Staikopoulou next to Archaeological Museum and behind National Bank.*

BEACHES

The closest sandy beach to Nafplion is **Karathona,** about 3 km (2 mi) south of town by road; the pine-backed sands are favored by Greek families with picnic baskets and serviced by buses. This is an ideal spot for kids, since the waters remain shallow far out into the bay. The resort town of Tolo is a short bus ride (€0.90) from the main station; service every hour) or a reasonably priced taxi ride (about €15); beware, though, that the beach at Tolo is packed solid with sunburned northern Europeans in the warm months.

In Nafplion, **Arvanitia Beach** (⊠*South side of town, nestled between Acronafplia and the Palomides*) is not really a beach but a seaside perch made of smooth rocks and backed by fragrant pines. This is a good place for a quick plunge after a day of sightseeing. Changing cabins, shaded cabanas, a snack bar, and an ouzeri are on the premises. You can walk to Arvanitia by following the seaside promenades south of town, and, if you're up for a hike, from there follow a dirt track that hugs the coastline past several coves that are nice for swimming all the way to Karathona.

WHERE TO STAY & EAT

It's a Nafplion tradition to have dessert at one of the cafés on Syntagma Square or the *zacharoplasteia* (patisseries) on the harbor. Lingering over an elaborate ice-cream concoction or after-dinner drink is a memorable way to wrap up an evening. Tempting, too, is the traditional Italian gelato (ice cream) at the **Antica Gelateria di Roma** (✉ *Farmakopoulou 3* ☎ *27520/23520*).

$–$$ ✕ **Arapakos.** Nafplion locals are demanding when it comes to seafood, so it's a credit to this attractive, nautical-theme taverna that locals pack in to enjoy expert preparations of fresh catches. The kitchen sends out such traditional accompaniments as *tzatziki* (yogurt garlic dip) and oven-roasted vegetables of the season, as well as grilled lamb chops and chicken fillets. ✉ *Bouboulinas 79* ☎ *27520/2767* ▭ *No credit cards.*

$–$$ ✕ **Taverna Byzantio.** Charcoal-grilled meats are the specialty at this pleasant little taverna tucked away in the backstreets off the harbor, and the cuisine also strays from Greece into the neighboring Balkans, with some wonderful schnitzels, cheese-filled pork roast, and other dishes that provide a nice change. ✉ *Alexandrou 15* ☎ *27520/21631.*

¢–$$ ★ ✕ **Paleo Archontiko.** Seating here is in the ground floor of an old stone mansion or on the narrow street in front. Tassos Koliopoulos and his wife, Anya, oversee the ever-changing menu, which highlights such specialties as beef *stifado* (stew slow-cooked with tomatoes and small onions) and *krassato* (rooster in wine sauce). It's not unusual for a musician to wander by and serenade the diners, another reason the place is wildly popular with locals (it's best to reserve on weekends and in high season). ✉ *Siokou and Ipsilantou, behind Commercial Bank, 1 block from Epidauros hotel* ☎ *27520/22449* ▭ *No credit cards.*

¢–$ ✕ **Ta Fanaria.** Staikopoulou street is one long outdoor dining room, with dozens of tourist-oriented tavernas serving night and day, and this popular place is leagues ahead of its neighbors. The kitchen concentrates on excellent preparations of such staples as *ladera* (vegetables cooked in olive oil), charcoal-grilled lamb ribs, and *imam bayilda* (eggplant stuffed with onions), and serves them beneath a grape arbor in a quiet lane next to the restaurant. ✉ *Staikopoulou 13* ☎ *27520/27141* ▭ *V.*

$$$$ Fodor's Choice ★ **Amphitryon Hotel.** Sea views fill every window in the airy, stylish, and contemporary guest rooms here, all of which open to teakwood decks. Though the old city is just a few steps away, you may feel like you're mid-sea on a ship, a pretty swanky one: mattresses are remote controlled to conform to the shape of your body, drapes open at the push of a button, bathrooms are equipped with Jacuzzis, and some showers double as steam rooms. Guests may use the pool at the sister hotel, the

Nafplia Palace. ✉*Spiliadou, 21100* ☎*27520/70700* 📠*27520/28783* 🌐*www.amphitryon.gr* 🛏*42 rooms, 3 suites* 👍*In-room: ethernet. In-hotel: restaurant, bar* 💳*AE, MC, V* 🍴*BP.*

$$$$ **Nafplia Palace.** An elevator whisks you from the old town up to the extensive grounds of this dramatic hotel built on the ruins of the Frankish fortification atop Acronafplia. Public spaces tend to be cavernous and austere, but the delightful pine-scented terraces and swimming pools seem to hang in midair, high above the city and bay. Spacious rooms in the main building have exposed stonework, terraces, marble bathrooms, and separate dressing areas, and are, at this writing, undergoing some much-needed renovations. Rooms and suites in the "villas" wing are equipped with sumptuous bathrooms and chic modern furnishings; some have private pools. ✉*Acronafplia, 21100* ☎*27520/28981 through 27520/28985* 📠*27520/28783* 🌐*www.nafplionhotels.gr* 🛏*80 rooms, 4 suites* 👍*In-room: Ethernet (some). In-hotel: 2 restaurants, bar, pools, spa* 💳*AE, MC, V* 🍴*BP.*

$$ **King Othon II.** The family that owns the King Othon I also operates this "branch" in a neighboring mansion. Rooms at this second lodging are larger and have the same high ceilings and ornate, neoclassic detailing. Many are set up like suites, with separate sitting areas; a number have sea views. Breakfast is served on a rear terrace. ✉*Spiliadou 5, 21100* ☎*27520/97790* 🌐*www.kingothon.gr* 🛏*10 rooms* 💳*AE, MC, V* 🍴*BP.*

$ **Byron.** A great deal of charm prevails here, from the simply but tastefully decorated rooms, with Turkish carpets and the odd sloping ceiling, to the outdoor patio set atop an old Turkish *hamam* (bath). The staff is quite welcoming, and the location at the top of the old town, up the street from the church of Ayiou Spiridona, is delightful (though you might want to call ahead and ask for directions on the easiest way to reach the hotel with your baggage). Breakfast is an additional €6. ✉*Platonos 16, Kapodistriou Sq., 21100* ☎*27520/22351* 📠*27520/26338* 🌐*www.byronhotel.gr* 🛏*14 rooms, 4 studios* 👍*In-room: refrigerator* 💳*AE, MC, V.*

$ **Hotel Athina.** One of the best-valued lodgings in Nafplion commands a prime spot on Syntagma Square, and the scene can be enjoyed from the narrow balconies or from the quiet comfort of the simply furnished rooms. A generous buffet breakfast is served in the ground-floor lounge, which does double duty as a café the rest of the day. ✉*Syntagma Sq., 21100* ☎*27250/26647* 🌐*www.athina-hotel.gr* 🛏*12 rooms, 2 suites* 👍*In-room: refrigerator, ethernet* 🍴*BP.*

$ ★ **Hotel Latini.** This handsomely restored old house, just off the waterfront in the center of town, feels like a well-appointed private home. The top-floor suite is especially commodious, with sloping ceilings and two balconies, but all guest rooms are graciously appointed and have sparkling bathrooms, and all have views of the bay or a palm-filled square. An elaborate breakfast is served in a pleasant bar-café that opens onto a narrow lane of the old town; drinks and cheese and other light refreshments are served here throughout the evening. ✉*Othonos 47, 21100* ☎*27520/96470* 📠*27520/96471* 🌐*www.latinihotel.*

gr *9 rooms, 1 suite* *In-hotel: restaurant, no elevator* *AE, MC, V* *BP.*

$ **King Othon I.** This gracious neoclassic mansion has decorative rosette ceilings and a curving wooden staircase leading to the upper floor. The high-ceilinged rooms are pleasantly decorated in a turn-of-the-20th-century style; those on the ground floor are a bit small, as are bathrooms throughout. Breakfast is served in the lovely garden at the side of the house. *Farmakopoulou 4, 21100* *27520/27585* *27520/27595* *www.kingothon.gr* *11 rooms* *In-room: refrigerator. In-hotel: no elevator* *AE, MC, V* *BP.*

¢ **Epidauros.** The owner of this simple hotel brims with pride over his establishment, one of the first hotels in Nafplion, which occupies a former merchant prince's home and an adjoining building. Rooms are spartan, but breezy balconies provide a nice perch above the pedestrian lanes of the old town, and Syntagma Square is a block away. *Kokinou 2, 21100* *27520/27541* *35 rooms, 25 with bath* *In-room: no phone* *No credit cards.*

NIGHTLIFE

Paleo Lichnari (*Bouboulinas 39*), a restaurant-club along the eastern end of the waterfront, presents live Greek *rembetika* (urban blues) and popular music every weekend and some weeknights in summer; it's frequented by vacationing Greeks who usually arrive after midnight.

SPORTS & THE OUTDOORS

It's easy to find **Captain Aris** (*Nafplion harbor* *69443/53200* *www.captainaris.com*), who when not at sea with an excursion is on his deck overlooking the comings and goings on Nafplion's seaside promenade. The captain offers daily excursions and sailing instruction in the Gulf of Argos, with a meal and several stops for swimming included. A trip aboard his sleek sailboat is about €80 per person.

9

SHOPPING

Many stores in Nafplion sell tacky reproductions of bronzes, frescoes, and vase paintings, which your family, friends, and coworkers will probably stash away and soon forget. But a number of tasteful shops sell fine-quality merchandise, including jewelry and smart sportswear. For antiques and woven goods, such as colorful *tagaria* (shepherds' shoulder bags), head toward the end of Vassilos Konstantinou street near the bus station; several shops here also sell dried herbs and natural honey.

★ **Agynthes** (*Siokou 10* *27520/21704 or 27520/22380*) showcases handwoven and naturally dyed woolens, cotton, and silks, some of which have been fashioned into chic scarves and other apparel. **Helios** (*Siokou 4* *27520/22329*) carries a distinctive line of stylish bric-a-brac for the home, along the lines of brass lanterns and candlesticks. **Karonis** (*Amalias 5* *27520/24446*) is a family-run shop that has dispensed fine wines, ouzo, and other spirits since 1869 and offers tastings and a great deal of knowledge about local vineyards. The **Komboloi Museum** (*Staikopoulou 25* *27520/21618* €2) in an old Nafpliote home, has a shop on the ground floor that sells antique and new worry beads and attractive beaded key chains. The museum's exhibits of historic worry beads are fascinating.

★ **Odyssey** (✉*Syntagma Sq.* ☎*27520/23430*) is the best place in Nafplion for newspapers and books in English; the owners are very helpful if you need advice or directions. The **Peloponnesian Folklore Foundation Museum Shop** (✉*Vasileos Alexandrou 1, on block immediately north of Amalias, going up Sofroni* ☎*27520/28947*) stocks an appealing array of merchandise that includes jewelry, candlesticks, and other gift items. **To Kobologaki T'Anaplioy** (✉*Palpouta 19* ☎*27520/23990*) carries a large selection of amber beads, strung into stunning necklaces and bracelets.

TIRYNS ΤΙΡΥΝΘΑ

★ *5 km (3 mi) north of Nafplion.*

Partly obscured by citrus trees are the well-preserved ruins of the Mycenaean acropolis of Tiryns, more than 3,000 years old. Some people skip the site, but if you see this citadel before touring Mycenae, you can understand those rambling ruins more easily. Homer describes Tiryns as "the wall-girt city," and Pausanias, writing in the 2nd century AD, gave the cyclopean walls his highest praise: "Now the Hellenes have a mania for admiring that which is foreign much more than that which is in their own land ... whilst they bestow not a word on the treasure-house of Minyas or the walls of Tiryns, which nevertheless are fully as deserving of admiration." The modern writer Henry Miller was repelled by the place, as he records in *The Colossus of Maroussi:* "Tiryns is prehistoric in character.... Tiryns represents a relapse.... Tiryns smells of cruelty, barbarism, suspicion, isolation." Today the site seems harmless, home to a few lizards who timidly sun themselves on the Bronze Age stones. Archaeological exploration of the site, which still continues, shows that the area of the acropolis was occupied in Neolithic times, about 7,000 years ago.

The citadel makes use of a long, low outcrop, on which was set the circuit wall of gigantic limestone blocks of the type called "cyclopean" because the ancients thought they could have been handled only by the giant cyclopes—the largest block is estimated at more than 15 tons. Via the **cyclopean ramp** the citadel was entered on the east side, through a gate leading to a narrow passage between the outer and inner walls. You could then turn right, toward the residential section in the **lower citadel,** or to the left toward the **upper citadel** and **palace.** The heavy **main gate** and **second gate** blocked the passage to the palace and trapped attackers caught between the walls. After the second gate, the passage opens onto a rectangular **courtyard,** whose massive left-hand wall is pierced by a **gallery of small vaulted chambers,** or casemates, opening off a **long, narrow corridor** roofed by a **corbeled arch.** (The chambers were possibly once used to stable horses, and the walls have been worn smooth by the countless generations of sheep and goats who have sheltered there.) This is one of the famous galleries of Tiryns;

another such gallery at the southernmost end of the acropolis also connects a series of five casemates with sloping roofs.

An elaborate entranceway leads west from the court to the upper citadel and palace, at the highest point of the acropolis. The complex included a colonnaded **court**; the great *megaron* (main hall) opened onto it and held the royal throne. Surviving fragments suggest that the floors and the walls were decorated, the walls with frescoes (now in the National Archaeological Museum in Athens) depicting a boar hunt and women riding in chariots. Beyond the megaron, a large **court** overlooks the houses in the lower citadel; from here, a long **stairway** descends to a small **postern gate** in the west wall. At the excavated part of the lower acropolis a significant discovery was made: two parallel **tunnels,** roofed in the same way as the galleries on the east and south sides, start within the acropolis and extend under the walls, leading to **subterranean cisterns** that ensured a continuous water supply.

From the palace you can see how Tiryns dominated the flat, fertile land at the head of the Gulf of Argos. Pioneering German archaeologist Heinrich Schliemann (1822–90), in his memoirs, waxed rhapsodic when recalling this scene: "The panorama which stretches on all sides from the top of the citadel of Tiryns is peculiarly splendid. As I gaze northward, southward, eastward, or westward, I ask myself involuntarily whether I have elsewhere seen aught so beautiful ..." The view would have been different in the Late Bronze Age: the ancient shoreline was nearer to the citadel, and outside the walls there was an extensive settlement. Profitis Ilias, the prominent hill to the east, was the site of the Tiryns cemetery. ✉ *Off road to Argos, on low hill past suburbs of Nafplion* ☎ *27520/22657* 🌐 *www.culture.gr* 🎫 *€3* ⏲ *Daily 8:30–3.*

9

ARGOS ΆΡΓΟΣ

12 km (7½ mi) northwest of Nafplion, 7 km (4½ mi) northwest of Tiryns.

The city of Argos (population 21,000), set amid citrus groves on the western edge of the Argive plain, is the economic hub of the region, a workaday town with a long past. The fall of Mycenae and Tiryns at the close of the Late Bronze Age proved favorable for Argos, and under King Pheidon in the 7th century BC, it became the chief city in the Peloponnese. In the mid-5th century BC, the city consolidated its hold on the Argive plain by eradicating Mycenae and Tiryns. But like Corinth, Argos was never powerful enough to set its own course, following in later years the leadership of Sparta, Athens, and the Macedonian kings.

Remains of the classical city are scattered throughout the modern one, and you can see in a small area the extensive **ruins** of the Roman bath, *odeon* (a roofed theater), and agora, or market. The theater is especially striking, and its well-preserved seats climb a hillside. ✉ *Tripoleos* 🎫 *Free* ⏲ *Tues.–Sun. 8:30–3.*

The **Archaeological Museum** houses a small but interesting collection of finds from the classical city. ✉ *Off main square, Ayios Petros* ☎ *27510/68819* 🌐 *www.culture.gr* 🎫 *€2* 🕓 *Tues.–Sun. 8:30–3.*

The **Kastro,** a Byzantine and Frankish structure, incorporates remnants of classical walls and was later expanded by the Turks and Venetians. It's quite a hike to get to, but your reward will be an unsurpassed view of the Argolid plain. Nestle yourself into a ruined castle wall to guard against the fierce wind and ponder the mysteries of the long-lost Mycenaean civilization. ✉ *On top of hill above town* 🎫 *Free* 🕓 *Daily 8–6.*

SHOPPING

On Saturday morning the main square is transformed into a huge household-merchandise and produce market (dwarfing that at Nafplion). You can often find unusual household items, such as wooden stamps used to impress designs on bread loaves, at prices that haven't been inflated. Argos is also well known throughout Greece for its ouzo.

MYCENAE ΜΥΚΗΝΕΣ

9 km (5½ mi) north of Argos, 21 km (13 mi) north of Nafplion.

The ancient citadel of Mycenae, which Homer described as "rich in gold," stands on a low hill, wedged between sheer, lofty peaks but separated from them by two deep ravines. The gloomy, gray ruins are hardly distinguishable from the rock beneath; it's hard to believe that this kingdom was once so powerful that it ruled a large portion of the Mediterranean world, from 1500 BC to 1100 BC. The major archaeological artifacts from the dig are in the National Archaeological Museum in Athens, so seeing these first will add to your appreciation. The most famous object from the treasure found here is the so-called Death Mask of Agamemnon, a golden mask that 19th-century archaeologist Heinrich Schliemann found in the last grave he excavated. He was ecstatic, convinced this was the mask of the king of Homeric legend who launched the Trojan War with his brother, Menelaus—but it is now known that this is impossible, since the mask dates from an earlier period. The Archaeological Museum in Nafplion also houses artifacts from this once-great city.

THE HEROINES OF ARGOS

Twice in its history, women are said to have defended Argos: once in 494 BC when Telesilla the poetess (who may be mere legend) armed old men, boys, and women to hold the walls against the Spartans; and again in 272 BC when Pyrrhus, king of Epirus, who was taking the city street by street, was felled from above by an old woman armed with a tile.

In 1841, soon after the establishment of the Greek state, the Archaeological Society began excavations of the **ancient citadel,** and in 1874 Heinrich Schliemann began to work at the site. Today the citadel is
❶ entered from the northwest through the famous **Lion Gate.** The triangle

Cult Center **6**
Granary **2**
Great Courtyard **8**
House of the Columns **10**
House of the Warrior Vase **4**
House of Tsountas **7**
Lion Gate **1**
Ramp House **5**
Stone slabs **3**
Throne room **9**
Treasury of Atreus **11**

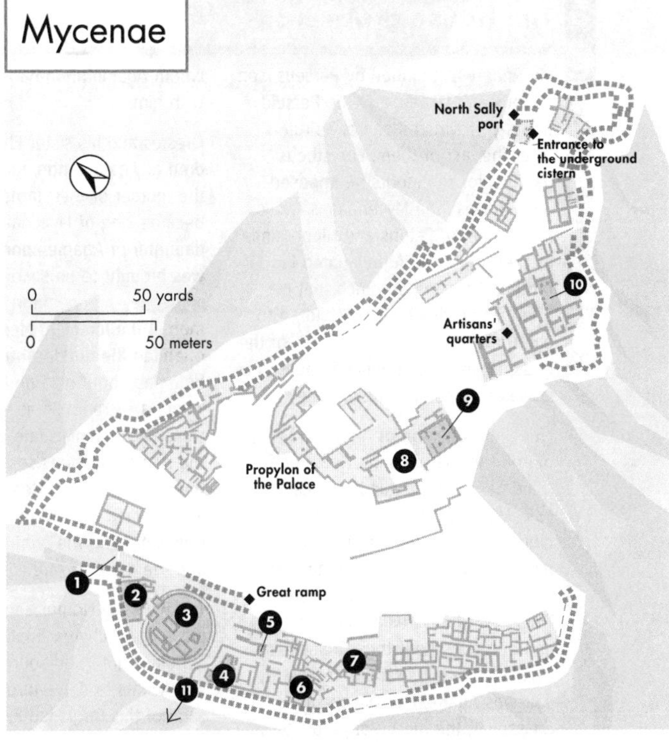

above the lintel depicts in relief two lions, whose heads, probably of
steatite, are now missing. They stand facing each other, their forepaws 9
resting on a high pedestal representing an altar, above which stands a
pillar ending in a uniquely shaped capital and abacus. Above the abacus are four sculptured discs, interpreted as representing the ends of
beams that supported a roof. The gate was closed by a double wooden
door sheathed in bronze. The two halves were secured by a wooden
bar, which rested in cuttings in the jambs, still visible. The holes for the
pivots on which it swung can still be seen in both sill and lintel. Inside
2 on the right stands the **Granary,** so named for the many *pithoi* (clay
storage vessels) that were found inside the building and held carbonized
wheat grains. Between it and the Lion Gate a flight of steps used to lead
to the top of the wall. Today you see a broad ramp leading steeply up
to the palace; the staircase is modern. Beyond the granary is the grave
3 circle, made up of six **stone slabs,** encircled by a row of upright stone
slabs interrupted on the northern side by the entrance. Above each
grave stood a vertical stone stele. The "grave goods" buried with the
dead were personal belongings including gold face masks, gold cups
and jewelry, bronze swords with ivory hilts, and daggers with gold
inlay, now in the National Archaeological Museum of Athens. South of
4 the stone slabs lie the remains of the **House of the Warrior Vase,** the **Ramp**
6 **House,** the **Cult Center,** and others; farther south is the **House of Tsountas** of

CLOSE UP

The House of Atreus

Mycenae was founded by Perseus, son of Zeus and Danae, and the Perseid dynasty provided many of its rulers. After the last of them, Eurystheus (famous for the labors he imposed on Hercules), the Mycenaeans chose Atreus, son of Pelops and Hippodamia, as their ruler. But Atreus hated his brother, Thyestes, so much that he offered Thyestes his own children to eat, thereby incurring the wrath of the gods. Thyestes pronounced a fearful curse on Atreus and his progeny.

Menelaus, one son of Atreus, was married to the beautiful Helen and ruled her lands. It was this Helen who was abducted by Paris, beginning the Trojan War. Atreus's heir, the renowned and energetic Agamemnon, was murdered on his return from the Trojan War by his wife, Clytemnestra, and her lover, Aegisthus (Thyestes's surviving son). Also murdered by the pair was Agamemnon's concubine, Cassandra, the mournful prophetess whom Agamemnon had brought back with him.

Orestes and his sister Electra, the children of Agamemnon, took revenge for the murder of their father, and Orestes became king of Mycenae. Another daughter of Agamemnon, Iphigenia, was brought to be sacrificed because someone—Agamemnon or one of the men in the forces of Menelaus—had offended the goddess Artemis by bragging about his hunting skills or killing a sacred animal. Various versions of Iphigenia's fate exist. During the rule of Orestes's son, Tisamenus, the descendants of Hercules returned and claimed their birthright by force, thus satisfying the wrath of the gods and the curse of Atreus.

The works of Homer and the classical plays of Aeschylus, Sophocles, and Euripides are good sources for anyone who wants to delve further into the saga of this tragic family.

Mycenae. The palace complex covers the summit of the hill and occupies a series of terraces; people entered through a monumental gateway
in the northwest side and, proceeding to the right, beyond it, came to
8 the **Great Courtyard** of the palace. The ground was originally covered
by a plaster coating above which was a layer of painted and decorated
9 stucco. East of the Great Courtyard is the **throne room,** which had four
columns supporting the roof (the bases are still visible) and a circular
hearth in the center. Remains of an **Archaic temple** and a **Hellenistic**
temple can be seen north of the palace, and to the east on the right, on
a lower level, are the **workshops** of the artists and craftsmen employed
by the king. On the same level, adjoining the workshops to the east, is
★ 10 the **House of the Columns,** with a row of columns surrounding its central
court. The remaining section of the east wall consists of an addition
made in around 1250 BC to ensure free communication from the citadel
with the subterranean reservoir cut at the same time. *9 km (5½ mi) north of Argos ☎27510/76585 www.culture.gr Combined ticket with Treasury of Atreus €6 Daily 8:30–7.*

11 On the hill of Panagitsa, on the left along the road that runs to the
citadel, lies another Mycenaean settlement, with, close by, the most-
imposing example of Mycenaean architecture, the **Treasury of Atreus.** Its

construction is placed around 1250 BC, contemporary with that of the Lion Gate. Like the other tholos tombs, it consists of a passageway built of huge squared stones, which leads into a domed chamber. The facade of the entrance had applied decoration, but only small fragments have been preserved. Traces of bronze nails suggest that similar decoration once existed inside. The tomb was found empty, already robbed in antiquity, but it must at one time have contained rich and valuable grave goods. Pausanias wrote that the ancients considered it the Tomb of Agamemnon, its other name. ⊠*Across from citadel of Mycenae* *Combined ticket with Mycenae €6* *Daily 8:30–7.*

BE PREPARED

When you visit Mycenae, make sure that you are adequately protected from the sun by wearing long sleeves and a hat (there is no shade). Carry a bottle of water, and wear sturdy walking shoes. The ground is uneven and often confusing to navigate; every week paramedics carry out people who fell because they were not adequately prepared for the climb. If you have physical limitations, it's best to go only as far as the plateau by the Lion Gate and view the rest from there.

WHERE TO EAT

¢–$ **To Mykinaiko.** At this pleasant, family-run restaurant in the modern village, where summer seating is on the front terrace, always ask what has been cooked up as specials that day. You might try *lachanodolmades* (cabbage rolls) in a tart egg-lemon sauce, *papoutsakia* (eggplant "shoes" filled with tomatoes and garlicky ground beef, topped with béchamel), or spaghetti embellished only with tomato-meat sauce and topped with local *kefalograviera* cheese. Sample the barrel wine from nearby Nemea, especially the potent dark red, known as the Blood of Hercules to the locals. ⊠*Main road* ☎*27510/76724* *AE, MC, V.*

ANCIENT NEMEA ΑΡΧΑΙΑ ΝΕΜΕΑ

18 km (11 mi) north of Mycenae.

The ancient storytellers proclaimed that it was here Hercules performed the first of the Twelve Labors set by the king of Argos in penance for killing his own children—he slew the ferocious Nemean lion living in a nearby cave. Historians are interested in Ancient Nemea as the site of a sanctuary of Zeus and the home of the biennial Nemean games, a Panhellenic competition like those at Isthmia, Delphi, and Olympia (today there is a society dedicated to reviving the games).

The main monuments at the site are the **temple of Zeus** (built about 330 BC to replace a 6th-century BC structure), the **stadium,** and an **early Christian basilica** of the 5th to 6th century AD. Several columns of the temple still stand. An extraordinary feature of the stadium, which dates to the last quarter of the 4th century BC, is its vaulted tunnel and entranceway. The evidence indicates that the use of the arch in building may have been brought back from India with Alexander, though arches were previously believed to be a Roman invention. A spacious **museum** displays finds from the site, including pieces of athletic gear and coins of various city-states and rulers. Around Nemea, keep an eye out for roadside stands where local growers sell the famous red Nemean wine of this region. ✉*North of E65 near modern village of Nemea* ☎*27460/22739* 🌐*www.nemea.org* 🎫*Site €3, site and museum €4* ⏲*May–Oct., Tues.–Sun. 8–7; Nov.–Apr., Tues.–Sun. 8:30–3.*

EN ROUTE

As the road (E65) emerges from the hills onto the flatter terrain around Corinth, the massive rock of **Acrocorinth** peaks on the left. The ancient city sat at the foot of this imposing peak, its long walls reaching north to the harbor of Lechaion on the Gulf of Corinth.

ANCIENT CORINTH ΑΡΧΑΙΑ ΚΟΡΙΝΘΟΣ

★ *35 km (22 mi) northeast of Ancient Nemea, 81 km (50 mi) southwest of Athens.*

West of the isthmus, the countryside opens up into a low-lying coastal plain around the head of the Gulf of Corinth. Modern Corinth, near the coast about 8 km (5 mi) north of the turnoff for the ancient town, is a regional center of some 23,000 inhabitants. Concrete pier-and-slab is the preferred architectural style, and the city seems to be under a seismic curse: periodic earthquakes knock the buildings down before they have time to develop any character. Corinth was founded in 1858 after one of these quakes leveled the old village at the ancient site; another flattened the new town in 1928; and a third in 1981 destroyed many buildings. Most tourists avoid the town altogether, visiting the ruins of Ancient Corinth and moving on.

Anyone interested in folklore will certainly want to stop at the notable **Folk Museum** to views exhibits including rare examples of 300 years of bridal and daily wear, old engravings, and dioramas. ✉*Town wharf, Corinth* ☎*27410/25352* 🌐*www.culture.gr* 🎫*€2* ⏲*Tues.–Sun. 8:30–1:30.*

Ancient Corinth, at the base of the massive Acrocorinth peak (1,863 feet), was huge. Excavations, which have gone on since 1896, have exposed ruins on the slopes of Acrocorinth and northward toward the coast. Most of the buildings that have been excavated are from the Roman era; only a few from before the sack of Corinth in 146 BC were rehabilitated when the city was refounded.

The **Glauke Fountain** is past the parking lot on the left. According to Pausanias, "Jason's second wife, Glauke (also known as Creusa), threw herself into the water to obtain relief from a poisoned dress sent to her by Medea." Beyond the fountain is the **museum,** which displays examples of the pottery decorated with friezes of panthers, sphinxes, bulls, and such, for which Corinth was famous; some mosaics from the Roman period; and marble and terra-cotta sculptures. The remains of a temple (Temple E) adjoin the museum, and steps lead from there left toward the **Temple of Apollo.**

Seven of the original 38 columns of the Temple of Apollo are still standing, and the structure is by far the most striking of Corinth's ancient buildings, as well as being one of the oldest stone temples in Greece (mid-6th century BC). Beyond the temple are the remains of the **North Market,** a colonnaded square once surrounded by many small shops. South of the Temple of Apollo is the main forum of Ancient Corinth. A row of shops bounds the forum at the far western end. East of the market is a series of small temples, and beyond is the forum's main plaza. A long line of shops runs lengthwise through the forum, dividing it into an **upper (southern)** and **lower (northern) terrace,** in the center of which is the bema (large podium), perhaps the very one where the Roman proconsul Gallio refused to act on accusations against St. Paul.

The southern boundary of the forum was the **South Stoa,** a 4th-century building, perhaps erected by Philip II to house delegates to his Hellenic confederacy. There were originally 33 shops across the front, and the back was altered in Roman times to accommodate such civic offices as the council hall, or *bouleuterion,* in the center. The road to Kenchreai began next to the bouleuterion and headed south. Farther along the South Stoa were the entrance to the **South Basilica** and, at the far end, the **Southeast Building,** which probably was the city archive.

In the lower forum, below the Southeast Building, was the **Julian Basilica,** a former law court; under the steps leading into it were found two starting lines (an earlier and a later one) for the course of a footrace from the Greek city. Continuing to the northeast corner of the forum, you approach the facade of the **Fountain of Peirene.** Water from a spring was gathered into four reservoirs before flowing out through the arcadelike facade into a drawing basin in front. Frescoes of swimming fish from a 2nd-century refurbishment can still be seen. The Lechaion road heads out of the forum to the north. A colonnaded courtyard, called the **Peribolos of Apollo,** is directly to the east of the Lechaion road, and beyond it lies a **public latrine,** with toilets in place, and the remains of a **Roman-era bath,** probably the Baths of Eurykles described by Pausanias as Corinth's best known.

Along the west side of the Lechaion road is a large basilica entered from the forum through the **Captives' Facade,** named for its sculptures of captive barbarians. West of the Captives' Facade the row of **northwest shops** completes the circuit.

Northwest of the parking lot is the **odeon,** cut into a natural slope, which was built during the AD 1st century, but it burned down around 175. Around 225 it was renovated and used as an arena for combats between gladiators and wild beasts. North of the odeon is the **theater** (5th century BC), one of the few Greek buildings reused by the Romans, who filled in the original seats and set in new ones at a steeper angle. By the 3rd century they had adapted it for gladiatorial contests and finally for mock naval battles.

North of the theater, inside the city wall, are the **Fountain of Lerna** and the **Asklepieion,** the sanctuary of the god of healing with a small temple (4th century BC) set in a colonnaded courtyard and a series of dining rooms in a second courtyard. Terra-cotta votive offerings representing afflicted body parts (hands, legs, breasts, genitals, and so on) were found in the excavation of the Asklepieion, and many of them are displayed at the museum. A stone box for offerings, complete with copper coins, was found at the entrance to the sanctuary. Off the lower courtyard are the drawing basins of the Fountain of Lerna.

Looming over Ancient Corinth, the limestone **Acrocorinth** was one of the best naturally fortified citadels in Europe, where citizens retreated in times of invasions and earthquakes. The climb up to Acrocorinth is worth the effort for both the medieval fortifications and the views to the Saronic Gulf and the Gulf of Corinth, and over the Isthmus. The entrance is on the west, guarded by a moat and outer gate, middle gate, and inner gate. Most of the fortifications are Byzantine, Frankish, Venetian, and Turkish—but the right-hand tower of the innermost of the three gates is apparently a 4th-century BC original. Corinth's famous Temple of Aphrodite, which had 1,000 prostitutes in attendance, stood here at the summit, too. On the slope of the mountain is the Sanctuary of Demeter, which you can view but not enter. Take the road next to the ticket office in Ancient Corinth, where taxis often wait for visitors (about €5 round-trip); from the tourist pavilion and café, it's a 10-minute walk to Acrocorinth gate. ✉*Off E94, 7 km (4½ mi) west of Corinth* ☎*27410/31207* 🌐*www.culture.gr* 🎫*€6* 🕒*Apr.–Oct., daily 8–7:30; Nov.–Mar., daily 8–5.*

XYLOKASTRO ΞΥΛΟΚΑΣΤΡΟ

34 *34 km (21 mi) west of Ancient Corinth.*

Xylokastro, a pleasant little town, is perfect if you want to soak your feet after trudging around Ancient Corinth. The road west of town that climbs up Sithas valley also climbs up to Ano Trikala, an alpine landscape where the peak (second highest in the Peloponnese) stays covered with snow into June.

BEACH

A wide, paved promenade along the shore, with a beautiful view of the mountains across the gulf, leads to a good if somewhat pebbly **beach** (✉*Beyond east end of town*).

ACHAEA & ELIS ΑΧΑΙΑ & ΗΛΕΙΑ

Achaea's wooded mountains guard the mountains of Arcadia to the south and mirror the forbidding mountains of central Greece on the other side of the Corinthian gulf. Those who venture into Achaea may find their way to Patras, a teeming port city. Elis, farther to the south, is bucolic and peaceful. This is a land of hills green with forests and vegetation, and it is not surprising that the Greeks chose this region as the place in which to hold the Olympic Games.

VOURAIKOS GORGE
ΦΑΡΑΓΓΙ ΤΟΥ ΒΟΥΡΑΙΚΟΥ

★ *Diakofto, the coastal access point: 47 km (29 mi) west of Xylokastro; Kalavrita: 25 km (15 mi) south of Diakofto.*

The Vouraikos Gorge is a fantastic landscape of towering pinnacles and precipitous rock walls that you can view on an exciting train ride. In addition, a road goes directly from Diakofto to Kalavrita; the spectacular 25-km (15-mi) drive negotiates the east side of the gorge.

Diakofto is a peaceful seaside settlement nestled on a fertile plain with dramatic mountains as a background; the village straggles through citrus and olive groves to the sea. If you're taking a morning train up the gorge, plan on spending the night in Diakofto, maybe enjoying a swim off one of the pebbly beaches and a meal in one of several tavernas. After dinner, take a stroll on Diakofto's main street to look at the antique train car in front of the train station, then take a seat at an outdoor table at one of the cafés surrounding the station square and enjoy a *gliko* (sweet). This is unembellished Greek small-town life.

ROAD WARRIORS

Route E65, the highway that skirts the Gulf of Corinth between Corinth and Patras, is one of the most dangerous roads in Greece if not in all of Europe. Magnify the perils of driving on any road in Greece—which has one of the highest accident rates in the Western world—by 10 when driving on this hair-raising stretch. Trucks and cars racing to and from the Patras ferries travel at breakneck speeds, and use the shoulders as extra lanes. Keeping a slow pace on the shoulder is one way to remain relatively safe, but you will probably find yourself crawling behind a tractor or belching truck.

The *Kalavrita Express*, an exhilarating narrow-gauge train ride, makes a dramatic 25-km (15-mi) journey between Diakofto and Kalavrita. Italians built the railway between 1889 and 1896 to bring ore down from Kalavrita, and these days a diminutive train, a cabless diesel engine sandwiched between two small passenger cars, crawls upward, clinging to the rails in the steeper sections with a rack and pinion, through and over 14 tunnels and bridges, rushing up and down wild mountainside terrain. Beyond the tiny hamlet of Zakhlorou, the gorge widens into a steep-sided green alpine valley that stretches the last 11 km (7 mi) to Kalavrita, a lively town of about 2,000 nestled below snowcapped Mt. Helmos. The *Kalavrita Express* makes the round-trip from Diakofto four times daily. The trip takes about an hour, and the first train leaves at 7 AM. Comings and goings are well timed so you can do some exploring; in a day's outing, for example, you can alight at Zakhlorou, make the trek to Mega Spileo, continue on to Kalavrita, explore that town, and return to Diakofto by the last train of the day. Call ahead for schedule, or since little English is spoken, check with the EOT in Athens to make sure the train is operating—repairs can close the line for months at a time; the Chris-Paul hotel *(⇨ below)*

9

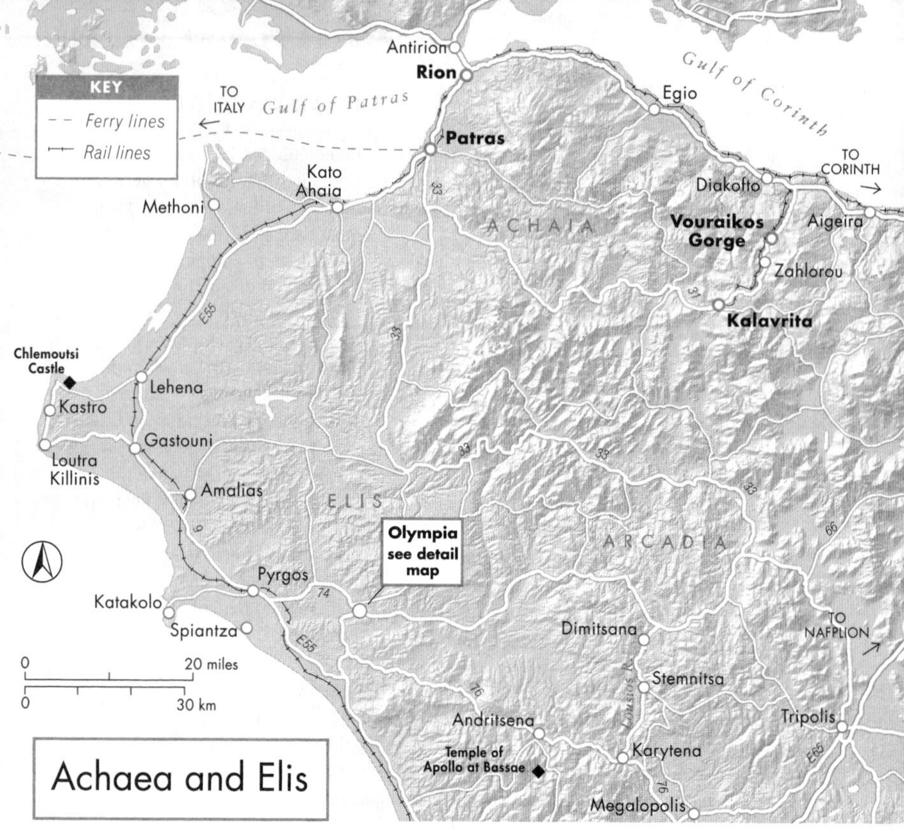

is another good source of information. ✉*Diakofto* ☎*210/323–6747* 🎟*€8 round-trip.*

Forty-five minutes into its trip, the *Kalavrita Express* pauses at the stream-laced mountain village of Zakhlorou, from where you can hike up a steep path through evergreen oak, cypress, and fir to the monastery of **Mega Spileo** (altitude 3,117 feet). This hour-long trek (one-way) along a rough donkey track gives you superb views of the Vouraikos valley and distant villages on the opposite side. The occasional sound of bells, from flocks of goats grazing on the steep slopes above, is carried on the wind. It's also possible to take a cab from the village, though they are not always at hand; if you're driving, the monastery is just off the road between Diakofto and Kalavrita and is well marked. The monastery, founded in the 4th century and said to be the oldest in Greece, has been burned down many times, most recently in 1934. It once had 450 monks and owned vast tracts of land in the Peloponnese, Constantinople (now Istanbul), and Macedonia, making it one of the richest in Greece. Mega Spileo sits at the base of a huge (360-foot-high) curving cliff face and incorporates a large cavern (the monastery's name means "large cave"). You can tour the monastery to see a charred black-wax-and-mastic icon of the Virgin, supposedly painted by St. Luke, found in the cave after a vision of the shepherdess Euphrosyne led some monks there in AD 362. Also on display are ornate vellum manuscripts of early gospels and the preserved heads of the founding monks. Modest dress is required; wraps are available at the entrance. ✉ *Zakhlorou* 🎫 *€2* ⏲ *Daily 8–6.*

WHERE TO STAY & EAT

¢ ✕ **Kostas.** This *psitaria* (grill house) is run by a hospitable Greek-Australian family. Grilled chicken is the main attraction, but *horta* (boiled wild greens), huge *horiatiki* (village) salads with a nut-flavor feta cheese, and stuffed zucchini are other reasons to enjoy a meal on the large terrace in warm months or the cozy dining room in winter. ✉ *Main road coming into town opposite National Bank, Diakofto* ☎ *26910/43228* ▭ *No credit cards.*

¢ **Chris-Paul Hotel.** Rooms in this appealing hotel, just around the corner from the train station, are attractive and well maintained. Each has a balcony overlooking the surrounding orchards. There's a pool in the garden, and the congenial bar and terrace are perfect for a cocktail before dinner. Breakfast is €5 extra, but you'll do better walking over to one of the cafés near the station. ✉ *Clearly signposted, in orchard close to train station, 25100 Diakofto* ☎ *26910/41715* 📠 *26910/42128* 🌐 *www.chrispaul-hotel.gr* *24 rooms* *In-hotel: bar, pool* ▭ *DC, MC, V.*

¢ **Romantzo Hotel.** If you want to spend the night in a romantic setting, the mountain village of Zakhlorou is your place. This aptly named inn is really just a basic refuge. The small, extremely modest rooms have baths and balconies from which you can enjoy the views over the wooded valley. The hotel's restaurant across the way prepares hearty country fare and serves an à la carte breakfast—handy if you're using the hotel as a base for an early-morning hike to the monastery of Mega Spileo. ✉ *Next to railroad station platform, 25001 Zakhlorou* ☎📠 *26920/22758* *9 rooms* *In-room: no a/c, no phone, no TV. In-hotel: no elevator* ▭ *No credit cards.*

EN ROUTE

If you're driving from Diakofto to Kalavrita, make a stop at **Tetramythos vineyards** (✉ *5 km [3 mi] south of Diakofto, Ano Diakofto* ☎ *26910/97224*). The winery attributes the high quality and refined flavor of its reds and whites to the location of its vineyards on the northern slopes of Mt. Helmos, which protects the grapes from hot winds. The winery operates tours and gives tastings year-round, weekdays 9–4, and weekends 9–7.

9

KALAVRITA ΚΑΛΑΒΡΥΤΑ

25 km (15 mi) south of Diakofto.

The mountain air here is refreshing, breezy, and cool at night, even in the middle of summer, making the town a favorite retreat for people from Patras and Diakofto. The ruins of a **Frankish castle, the Church of the Dormition,** and a **small museum** are worth seeing, but Greeks remember Kalavrita primarily as the site of the Nazis' most heinous war crime on Greek soil. On December 13, 1943, the occupying forces rounded up and executed the town's entire male population over the age of 15 (1,436 people) and then locked women and children into the school and set it on fire. They escaped, but the Nazis later returned and burned the town to the ground. The clock on the church tower is stopped at 2:34 PM, marking the time of the execution.

Signs point the way to the **Martyr's Monument** (⊠*Off Vasileos Konstantinou*), a white cross on a cypress-covered hill that stands as a poignant commemoration of the 1943 Nazi massacre.

WHERE TO STAY

$$ **Filoxenia.** Built in traditional style, this modern hotel caters largely to skiers who enjoy the slopes on nearby Mt. Helmos (accordingly, winter rates are approximately double summer rates). All the rooms have balconies that look either to the gorge or the mountains, and are quite welcoming, with wood floors, contemporary wooden furnishings, and sparkling, well-equipped bathrooms. The friendliness of the staff and the public rooms with their fireplaces add an extra touch of charm as well. ⊠*Ethnikis Antistasios 10, 25001* ☎*26920/22290* *26920/23009* *www.hotelfiloxenia.gr* *28 rooms* *In-hotel: bar* *AE, DC, MC, V* *BP.*

SPORTS & THE OUTDOORS

The European path E4 skirts the slopes of Mt. Helmos, and the village of Diaselo Avgou on the mountain has the **B. Leondopoulos Mountain Refuge** for hikers, with a capacity of 12 to 16. Contact the **Kalavrita Alpine Club** (⊠*Top end of Martiou 25 Sq., Kalavrita* ☎*26920/22661*), usually open weekdays 7–3. The leading ski facility in the area, the **Kalavrita Ski Center** (⊠*Near Kalavrita* ☎*26920/22661* *www.kalavrita-ski.gr*), is 14 km (9 mi) from town and has 12 ski runs and seven lifts, as well as a restaurant; facilities are open December–April, daily 9–4. **Trekking Hellas** (⊠*Fillelinon 7, 10557 Athens* ☎*210/331–0323* *www.trekking.gr*) runs a six-day "Mountains and Monasteries" hiking tour on Mt. Ziria and Mt. Helmos.

RION ΡΙΟ

37 *49 km (30 mi) west of Diakofto, 5 km (3 mi) east of Patras.*

Rion was long known as the point from which ferries connected the Peloponnese with Antirion in central Greece; these days, traffic zooms across the Rion–Antirion suspension bridge, providing a much faster route between Rion and the rest of the Peloponnese and other parts of mainland Greece.

Rion is distinguished by the **Castle of the Morea,** built by Sultan Bayazid II in 1499. It sits forlorn amid roadways and a field of oil storage tanks. Here the Turks made their last stand in 1828, holding out for three weeks against the Anglo-French forces. Along with the Castle of Roumeli on Antirion's shore opposite, it guarded the narrows leading into the Gulf of Corinth. ⊠*Waterfront, Rion* ☎*2610/990691* *Free* *Tues.–Sun. 8:30–7.*

BEACH

Ayios Vassilios (✉ *Off E65, near Rion*) has received one of the highest cleanliness ratings from Perpa, Greece's ministry of the environment. Even so, crowds from Patras (this is the closest sandy beach to the city), freighter traffic, and the looming presence of the Rion bridge make for a less than idyllic experience.

PATRAS ΠΑΤΡΑ

5 km (3 mi) west of Rion, 135 km (84 mi) west of Corinth.

Patras, the third-largest city in Greece and a major harbor, begins almost before Rion is passed. Unless you come to town to catch a ferry to Italy or Corfu, you might want to zoom right by. The municipality has launched an extensive improvement plan, paving the harbor roads and creating pedestrian zones on inner-city shopping streets. Even so, earthquakes and mindless development have laid waste to most of the elegant European-style buildings that earned Patras the nickname "Little Paris of Greece" in the 19th and early 20th centuries.

Like all respectable Greek cities, Patras has an ancient history. Off the harbor in 429 BC, Corinthian and Athenian ships fought inconclusively, and in 279 BC the city helped defeat an invasion of Celtic Galatians. Its acropolis was fortified under Justinian in the 6th century, and Patras withstood an attack by Slavs and Saracens in 805. Silk production, begun in the 7th century, brought renewed prosperity, but control passed successively to the Franks, the Venetians, and the Turks, until the War of Independence. Thomas Palaiologos, the last Byzantine to leave Patras before the Turks took over in 1458, carried an unusual prize with him—the skull of the apostle St. Andrew, which he gave to Pius II in exchange for an annuity. St. Andrew had been crucified in Patras and had been made the city's patron saint. In 1964 Pope Paul VI returned the head to Patras, and it now graces St. Andrew's Cathedral, seat of the Bishop of Patras.

Patras is Greece's major western port and the city has the international, outward-looking feel common to port cities. The waterfront is pleasant enough. You'll find lots of mediocre restaurants, some decent hotels, the bus and train stations, and numerous travel agents (caveat emptor for those near the docks). Back from the waterfront, the town gradually rises along arcaded streets, which provide welcome shade and rain protection. Of the series of large platias, tree-shaded Queen Olga Square is the nicest. Patras is built on a grid system, and it is easy to find your way around. For a pleasant stroll, take Ayios Nikolaos street upward through the city until it comes to the long flight of steps leading to the Kastro, the medieval Venetian castle overlooking the harbor. The narrow lanes on the side of Ayios Nikolaos are whitewashed and lined with village-style houses, many of which are being restored.

The **Archaeological Museum's** small rooms are laden with Mycenaean- through Roman-period finds, including sculptures, cups, and jewelry. Many items are from the ancient Roman odeon in town, still in use for a summer festival. It's a pleasant surprise to find these antiquities in a city not known for them. ✉*Mezonos 42* ☎*2610/275070* 🌐*www.culture.gr* 🎫*Free* ⏲*Tues.–Sun. 8:30–2:30.*

Olga Square (✉*2 blocks uptown from Othonos Amalias, off Kolokotronis*) is the most appealing of Patras's many popular squares—locals sip their ouzo and observe their fellow townspeople as they eat, drink, shop, and play in this quintessentially Greek meeting place. Other popular squares include **Martiou 25 Square** and **Ypsila Alonia Square.**

In the evening the **Kastro** (✉*End of Ayios Nikolaos, on hill uptown, southeast of train station*), a Frankish and Venetian citadel overlooking Patras, draws many Greek couples seeking a spectacular view. The sight of the shimmering ships negotiating the harbor stirs even the most travel-weary.

A **Roman odeon** (✉*Off Martiou 25 Sq.*) remains in use in Patras, almost 2,000 years after it was first built. Today the productions of summer arts festivals are staged in the well-preserved theater, which was discovered in 1889 and heavily restored in 1960.

St. Andrew's Cathedral (✉*At end of Trion Navarhon at western edge of city center*) dates from the early 20th century but is built next to a spring that's been used for thousands of years. In antiquity, the waters were thought to have prophetic powers. The church is one of the largest in Greece and an important pilgrimage sight for the faithful—the cavernous interior houses the head of St. Andrew, who spread Christianity throughout Greece and was crucified in Patras in AD 60. The church is open daily 8–8.

Achaia Clauss (✉*8 km [5 mi] west of Patras, Exit 3, Achaia* ☎*2610/325051*) winery operates tours and provides tastings. The oldest in Greece, the winery was founded by the Bavarian Gustav Clauss in 1854, and continues to produce a distinctive line of wines. Mavrodaphne, a rich dessert wine, is the house speciality, and oak barrels still store vintages from Gustav's day. The winery, set on a hilltop amid fragrant pines, is open for visits May–October, daily 9–7:30, and November–April, daily 9–5.

BEACHES

The nicest beach near Patras is **Kalogria** (✉*Off E55, about 32 km [20 mi] west of Patras*), a long, sandy stretch backed by a pine forest and a grassy plain where cattle graze. Much favored by Greeks, Kalogria is crowded on weekends and in August, and it is often buffeted by bracing winds that can whip up a wild surf. The nearest town is Metohi. A river behind the beach forms estuaries that are great for bird-watching. People swim in them as well, but you may feel like Hercules if you are joined by nonvenomous, yard-long snakes.

WHERE TO STAY & EAT

Avoid most of the indistinct restaurants along Patras's waterfront. For lighter fare or after-dinner ice cream, coffee, and pastries, choose one of the cafés along upper Gerokostopoulou street, which is closed to traffic, in Olga Square, or in Ypsila Alonia Square—a favorite watering hole of locals near the Kastro, which, as a bonus, has a panoramic view of the harbor. The streets, including Papadiamatopoulou, leading through the old town up to the south end of the Kastro, have many small *mezedopoleia,* which serve mezedes, Greek-style tapas.

¢–$$ ✕**To Konaki.** Nouli and Andonis Andrikopoulou take pride in offering local specialties at this homey inn near the train station. *Hortopites* (pies filled with wild greens and feta) and *midhia saganaki* (mussels in a tomato, cheese, and pepper casserole) are among the favorites. On Saturday night a group occasionally plays traditional Greek music. In summer this place closes and the family moves down the coast to a seaside restaurant, set under an arbor on the beach in the idyllic village of Kato Ararchovitika, past Rion, 15 km (9 mi) from Patras. ✉*Aratou and Karaiskai 44* ☎*2610/275096* ▭*No credit cards* ⊙*Closed May–Aug.*

¢ ✕**Krini.** The sloping streets heading up to the Kastro are the setting for this *oinopoleia,* or wineshop, which sells wine from barrels to a loyal clientele and serves simple but excellent fare. The rustic taverna room and rear garden are the places to sample delicacies like the spicy sausage meatballs known as soutzoukakia or rabbit braised with white wine and rosemary. ✉*Pandokratoros 57* ☎*No phone* ▭*No credit cards* ⊙*Closed last 2 wks of Aug. No lunch.*

$$$–$$$$ ★ **Primarolia.** Step through the doors of the most distinctive hotel in town (located in a former distillery), and workday Patras seems far away. Modernist furniture by Greek artists fills the soothing public rooms. Dramatic fabrics and wallpapers add flair to the handsome, well-equipped guest rooms, where the emphasis is on comfort as well as design. Some rooms have balconies with harbor views. ✉*Othonos Amalias 33, 26221* ☎*2610/624900* 🖷*2610/623559* ⊕*www.arthotel.gr* *11 rooms, 3 suites* *In-room: Wi-Fi. In-hotel: restaurant, bar* ▭*AE, DC, MC, V* *BP.*

$ **Acropole.** Well kept, comfortable, and even a bit stylish, the tidy rooms here are filled with light and wonderful views. Sitting on your balcony and watching the sunset over the harbor might be the highlight of an evening. The port, train and bus stations, and the center of town are all within an easy walk, making this a satisfactory choice if you're stuck in Patras between connections. ✉*Agiou Andreou 32, 26221* ☎*2610/279809* 🖷*2610/221533* *27 rooms* *In-hotel: bar* ▭*MC, V* *BP.*

¢ **Rannia.** Just off the harbor and near the train and bus stations, this budget option faces a quiet street and is a nice retreat from the hubbub of Patras. Rooms are simply furnished but spotless and appealing, and all have balconies. ✉*Riga Fereou 53, 26500* ☎*2610/220114* 🖷*2610/220537* *30 rooms* ▭*MC, V* *BP.*

NIGHTLIFE & THE ARTS

BARS & CAFÉS For nightlife, in general it's best to ask around when you arrive, as the scene changes. On the northern side of Martiou 25 Square are the steps at the head of Gerokostopoulou street, below the odeon. Closed to traffic along its upper reaches, this street has myriad cafés and music bars, making it a good choice for a relaxing evening. It is the place to be for the young and hip of Patras.

FESTIVALS Patras holds a lively **summer arts festival** (✉ *Office: Ayios Georgios 104* ☎ *2610/278730*) with concerts and dance performances at the Roman odeon. It usually runs from mid-June to early October.

If you're in Patras in late January to February, you're in for a treat: the **Carnival** (✉ *Office: Ayios Georgios 104* ☎ *2610/226063*), which lasts for several weeks before the start of Lent, is celebrated with masquerade balls, fireworks, and the Sunday Grand Parade competition for the best costume. Room rates can double or even triple during this time; tickets for seats (€10) at the Grand Parade, held in front of the Municipal Theater at Georgiou Square, are sold at the Carnival office.

NIGHTCLUBS Worth a spin on the dance floor is the music club **Privé** (✉ *Germanou 55* ☎ *2610/274912*). Especially in summer, though, the nighttime action centers on the waterfront in Rion.

SHOPPING

Patras is a major city, and you'll find fashionable clothing, jewelry, and other products here. The best shops are on Riga Fereou, Maizonas, and Korinthou streets, near Olga Square. An outlet of the venerable London department store **Marks and Spencer** (✉ *Mezonos 68* ☎ *2610/623247*) is a good stop if you realize you're missing a vacation essential. Patras also has shops that sell handmade and machine-made Greek icons, which make beautiful decorations. At night in the narrow streets surrounding the Kastro, Greek craftspeople burn the midnight oil in their workshops and stores painting images of saints on wood and stone.

OLYMPIA ΟΛΥΜΠΙΑ

★ *112 km (69 mi) south of Patras.*

Ancient Olympia, with the Sanctuary of Zeus, was the site of the ancient Olympic Games. Located at the foot of the tree-covered Kronion hill, and set in a valley near two rivers, today it is one of the most popular sites in Greece. Although the fires of 2007 burned many of the pine forests around Olympia, including those on the Kronion hill, a major replanting effort is restoring the greenery. Modern Olympia, an attractive mountain town surrounded by pleasant hilly countryside, has hotels and tavernas, convenient for visitors to the ancient site. For the complete scoop on the ancient sight—one of the must-sees of any trip to Greece—see our special photo-feature, "Ancient Olympia: Let the Games Begin!"

WHERE TO STAY & EAT

¢–$ ✕ **Aegean.** Don't let the garish signs depicting the menu put you off: the far-ranging offerings are excellent. You can eat lightly—a gyro or pizza—but do venture into some of the more serious fare, especially such local dishes as fish, oven-baked with onion, garlic, green peppers, and parsley. The house's barrel wine is a nice accompaniment to any meal. ✉*Douma, near Hotel New Olympia* ☎*262* ▭*MC, V.*

¢–$ ✕**Bacchus.** The best restaurants in Greece are often in villages, and Dimitris Zapantis's family-run taverna in the village of Miraka (3 km [2 mi] outside Olympia, along road to Lambia) is one such establishment. Locals start to trickle in around 10:30 PM. Try the delectable chicken with oregano and enjoy an evening in a small village. ✉*Miraka* ☎*0624/22498* ▭*No credit cards* ⏲*Closed Dec.–Feb.*

¢–$ ✕**Taverna Melathron.** A nice break from the tourist traps that dominate the Olympia dining scene, Melathron offers down-to-earth fare in a simple, traditional taverna. Moussaka and other casseroles, cabbage rolls stuffed with ground beef, and grilled meats dominate the straightforward menu. ✉*Douma 3* ☎*26240/22916* ▭*MC, V* ⏲*Closed mid-Nov.–Mar.*

$–$$ ✕**Europa Best Western.** White stucco, pine, and red tiles offset the somewhat generic package-tour feel of this hilltop hotel, just above the ancient site. Rooms are large, with queen-size beds in many, and marble bathrooms and small terraces; most have sunken sitting areas and face the attractive pool, which is set in an olive-shaded garden. The summertime-only outdoor taverna (¢–$$) serves excellent grilled meats and vegetables. It's the best choice in town for an alfresco meal on a warm night. The Greek fare in the handsome, year-round indoor restaurant is commendable, too. ✉*Oikismou Drouba, off road to Ancient Olympia, 27065* ☎*26240/22650 or 26240/22700* 🖷*26240/23166* 🌐*www.hoteleuropa.gr* *78 rooms, 2 suites* *In-room: refrigerator. In-hotel: 2 restaurants, bars, pool* ▭*AE, DC, MC, V* *BP.*

$$ **Olympia Palace.** There's a slick, big-city air at the best hotel in town, with its spacious public rooms, garden café, sleek bar, and shopping mall. The rooms, too, are more sophisticated than those in most other Greek towns: each has three telephones and most have print bedspreads and wooden furniture. The room rate is often negotiable when the hotel is not full; always ask for the best available price. ✉*Praxitelous Kondili 2, 27065* ☎*26240/23101* 🖷*26240/22525* 🌐*www.olympiapalace.gr* *58 rooms, 6 suites* *In-room: dial-up. In-hotel: 2 restaurants, bar* ▭*AE, DC, MC, V* *BP.*

$ ★ **Hotel Pelops.** Suzanna and Theo Spiliopoulou set the gold standard for a small hotel. The stylish and comfortable wood-floor rooms overlook the nearby mountains and have small terraces, and there is a welcoming breakfast room with a large fireplace. Their hospitality extends to dispensing information about Ancient Olympia and other locations in the Peloponnese. Suzanna, a well-known chef, teaches cooking lessons and serves a Peloponnesian feast for the evening meal (€15), which is a treat not to be missed. Guests can use the Europa Best Western's pool. ✉*Varela 2, 27065* ☎*26240/22543* 🖷*26240/22213* 🌐*www.hotelpelops.gr* *26 rooms* *In-hotel: restaurant, bar* ▭*MC, V* *BP.*

SHOPPING

★ The shop of the **Archaeological Museum** (✉*Off Ethnikos Odos 74, north of Ancient Olympia site* ☎*26240/22742*) carries an appealing line of figurines, bronzes, votives, and other replicas of objects found in the

Continued on page 417

ANCIENT OLYMPIA

LET THE GAMES BEGIN!

Just as athletes from city-states throughout ancient Greece made the journey to compete in the ancient Olympics—in which victory bestowed a laurel wreath and the highest honors in the land—visitors from all over the world today make their way to the small Arcadian town known as the birthplace of the Olympic Games. Home to a sacred sanctuary dedicated to Zeus, Olympia appears to have been a legendary place as long ago as the 10th century BC, and the Olympic Games, first staged around the 8th century BC, were played here in the stadium, hippodrome, and other venues for some 1,100 years.

Olympia's tranquil pine-forested valley, set with weathered stones of peaceful dignity, belies the sweaty drama of the first sporting festivals. Stadium footraces run in the nude; pankration wrestling so violent today's Ultimate Fighting matches look tame; weeklong bacchanals—serviced by an army of pornoi and prostitutes—held in the Olympic Village: Little wonder this ancient event is now called the "Woodstock of its day" by modern scholars (wrestlers, boxers, and discus-throwers being the rock stars of ancient Greece). Using mind over medal, today's traveler to Olympia can get an eye-opening glimpse into the ancient world.

FELLOWSHIP OF THE RINGS

RULES OF THE GAMES

For almost eleven centuries, free-born Greeks from the various city-states gathered to participate in the Olympic Games, held every four years in August or September at this town set at the foot of the tree-covered Kronion hill. These games became so much a part of the culture that the four-year interval between the games became a standard unit of time, an Olympiad. An Olympic truce—the Ekecheiria—allowed safe passage for athletes from the different city-states traveling to the games, and participation in them meant allegiance to a "pan-Hellenic" ideal of a united Greece.

The exact date of the first games is not known, but the first recorded event is a footrace, a stade, run in 776 BC. A longer race, a *diaulos*, was added in 724 BC, and wrestling and a pentathlon—consisting of the long jump, the javelin throw, the discus throw, a footrace, and wrestling—in 708 BC. Boxing and chariot racing were 7th-century BC additions, as was the *pankration*, a no-holds-barred match (broken limbs were frequent and strangulation sometimes the end)—Plato, the great philosopher, was a big wrestling fan.

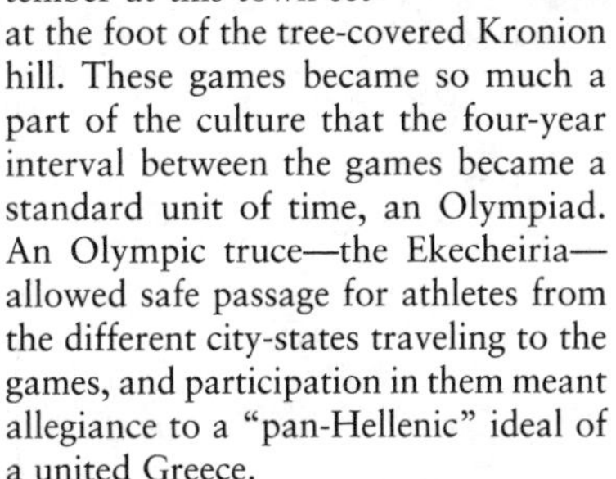

Most of the participants were professional athletes, for whom winning a laurel wreath at Olympia ensured wealth and glory from the city-states that sponsored them. Bruce Jenner and Michael Jordan had nothing on these guys.

Large-scale building at Olympia began around the 6th century BC, with construction of a temple to Hera and Zeus. The 5th and 4th centuries BC, the Golden Age of the ancient games, saw a virtual building boom—the monumental Temple of Zeus, the Prytaneion, and the Metroon went up at this time.

THE HERCULES CONNECTION

Legend claims that Heracles, son of Zeus and the epitome of masculinity and sexual prowess, founded Olympia and the games after he slew his wife and children, and in atonement for the crime, undertook twelve labors. One of these was cleaning the stables of King Augeas, a task he completed by rerouting the river Alpheios, which runs past the site.

Ancient tales tell that he mapped out the outline of the vast stadium with his foot—the starting and finishing lines are still in place, 600 Olympic feet (about 630 feet) apart. The world-famous pediment sculptures of Olympia's Temple of Zeus were also devoted to Heracules's exploits.

Discobolos (Discus Thrower), marble, circa 450 BC

IT'S A JUMBLE OUT THERE: WHAT'S WHERE

Panorama of ancient Olympia as one would have seen it from the viewpoint ✻ below.

There are few extant buildings at ancient Olympia so, to make sense of the scattered stones, a handy map is needed.

↑ To MUSEUM (700 ft)
City Wall
Kronion Hill
ENTRANCE
ALTIS
Stoa of Echo

1 Altis: The sacred quarter was also known as the Sacred Grove of Zeus.

2 Bouleuterion: Here in the seat of the organizers of the games, the Elean senate, athletes swore an oath of fair play.

3 Gymnasion: Athletes practiced for track and field events in an open field surrounded by porticoes.

4 Hippodrome: Horse and chariot races were run on this racecourse.

5 House of Nero: The lavish villa was built for the emperor's visit to the games of AD 67, in which he competed.

6 Leonidaion: This luxurious hostel for distinguished visitors to the games later housed Roman governors.

7 Metroon: A small Doric temple was dedicated to Rhea (also known as Cybele), Mother of the Gods.

8 Nymphaion: A semicircular reservoir stored water from a spring to the east, distributed throughout the site by a network of pipes.

9 Palaestra: This section of the gymnasium complex was used for athletic training; athletes bathed and socialized in rooms around the square field.

10 Pelopeion: This shrine to Pelops, legendary king of the region now known as the Peloponnese, housed an altar in a sacred grove.

11 Pheidias's Workshop: The sculptor crafted the enormous statue of Zeus in this workshop, of the same

15

13

17

9

size and orientation as the nearby Temple of Zeus.

12 **Prytaneion:** Magistrates in charge of the games feted the winners here in a banquet room and a perpetual flame burned in the hearth.

13 **Roman Baths:** The earliest baths at Olympia date to the 5th century BC, though the Romans later replaced them with a more sophisticated complex.

14 **South Hall:** A vast hall surrounded by 34 Doric columns was one of the main entrances to the sanctuary.

15 **Stadium:** As many as 50,000 spectators could crowd onto earthen embankments to watch running events. The starting and finishing lines are still in place.

16 **Temple of Hera:** One of the earliest monumental Greek temples was built in the 7th century BC.

17 **Temple of Zeus:** A great temple and fine example of Doric architecture, this housed an enormous statue of Zeus that was one of the seven wonders of the ancient world.

18 **Treasuries:** These templelike buildings housed valuables and equipment of twelve of the most powerful of the city-states competing in the games.

VISITING ANCIENT OLYMPIA

You'll need at least two hours to see the ruins and the outstanding museum, and three or four hours would be better. Ancient Olympia is located off Ethnikos Odos 74, ½ km (¼ mi) outside modern Olympia. ☎ 26240/22517; 🌐 www.culture.gr; 🎫 €6, combined ticket with Archaeological Museum €9; ⏲ Open May–Oct., daily 8–7; Nov.–Apr., daily 8:30–5. Modern Olympia, an attractive mountain town surrounded by pleasant hilly countryside, has hotels and tavernas, convenient for visitors to the ancient site.

PRAISE BE TO THE GODS

As famous as the Olympic Games were—and still are—Olympia was first and foremost a sacred place, a sanctuary honoring Zeus, king of the gods, and Hera, his wife and older sister.

To honor the cult of Zeus established at Olympia as early as the 10th century BC, altars were first constructed outdoors, among the pine forests that still encroach upon the site. But around the turn of the 6th century BC, the earliest building at Olympia was constructed, the Temple of Hera, which originally honored Zeus and Hera jointly, until the Temple of Zeus was constructed around 470 BC. The Temple of Zeus was one of the finest temples in all of Greece. Thirteen columns flanked the sides and its interior housed the most famous work of ancient Greece—a gold and ivory statue of Zeus. Earthquakes in 551 and 552 finished off the temple. Two of the greatest sculptors of ancient Greece, Pheidias and Praxiteles, executed some of their best-known work for temples here.

Pheidias, who worked between 490 and 430 BC, was renowned for the enormous statue of Athena he completed for the Parthenon in 438 BC. He topped his fame at Olympia thanks to his 42-foot-high statue of Zeus for the Temple of Zeus: one of the Seven Wonders of the Ancient World, the work depicted the god sitting on a throne, holding a winged victory in one hand and a scepter in the other.

While the statue is long gone, one of the most evocative remains at Olympia are those of Pheidias's workshop—despite the ruinous state, the place looks like the sculptor might have stood stepped out and will soon return.

As for Praxiteles—who worked from around 370–330 BC and is credited with infusing Greek sculpture with unequalled grace and sensuality—the only surviving example of his work is today in the Olympia Museum, *Hermes Carrying the Infant Dionysus*, an elegant and delicate piece that once adorned the Temple of Hera.

SCANDALOUS OLYMPIA

Olympia's dreaded pankration made today's Ultimate Fighting matches look mild. Painted red-figure vases (left) depict this sport, which mixed boxing and wrestling techniques—including choke holds and joint locks—to sometimes lethal effect. Sometimes the only form of submission was unconsciousness or death.

LEAVE THOSE FIG LEAVES AT HOME

While these venerated statues of gods conjure up noble scenes of raised Olympic torches and brotherhood pledges, modern scholars—most notably Tony Perrottet (in *The Naked Olympics*, Random House, 2004)—have discovered that the original Olympic Games were far from today's genteel televised spectacles.

In the hottest days of August, 50,000 spectators would have descended on Olympia—only to find no bathing facilities, no seats (many passed out from sunstroke), open-air latrines, hordes of flies, and a sea of touts, thieves, Homer-reciters, fire-breathers, prostitutes, and sports heroes.

Long before the era of Spandex, these athletes competed in the nude, and trainers were asked to leave their clothing at the door, too—a fact that has long titillated scholars.

One theory holds that the nudity rule was imposed when a woman violated the ban on female participation at the events and disguised herself as a trainer to watch her sons compete; she revealed her gender with her screams of delight at the victory of one of her offspring and was summarily executed.

A more likely explanation is that the ancient Greeks, who found nothing shameful about nudity, simply enjoyed the display of athletic bodies. The only "outfit" was a covering of olive oil (applied by specially trained youths).

Victory processions often descended into full-scale orgies, perhaps fueled by a favored love potion for sale—a mixture of horse sweat and minced lizard.

Back on the field, bribery seems to have been the most common offense (steroids not being available).

Olympia also provides the earliest case of the sports-parent syndrome: in the 192nd Olympiad, Damonikos of Elis, whose son Polyktor was to wrestle Sosander of Smyrna, bribed the latter's father in an attempt to buy the victory for his son.

OLYMPIC GLORY: THE ARCHAEOLOGICAL MUSEUM

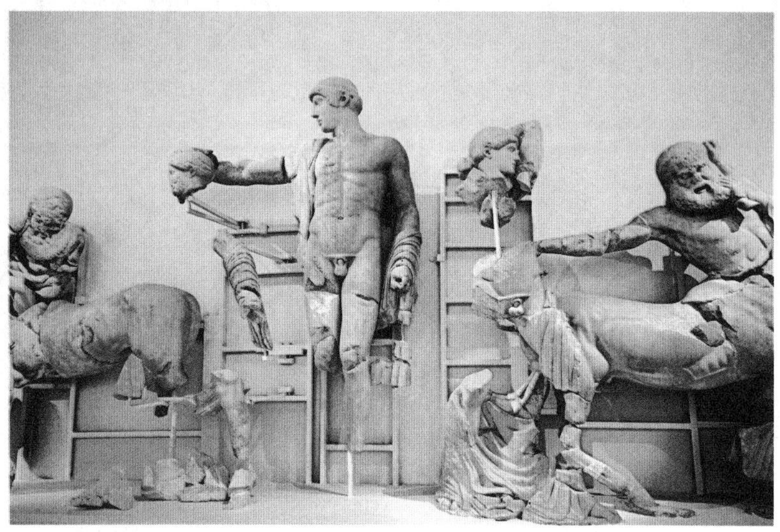

Battle of Lapiths and Centaurs

Of all the sights in ancient Olympia, some say the fabled sculptures in the archaeological museum get the gold. The Archaeological Museum, located in a handsome glass-and-marble pavilion at the edge of the ancient site, has in its magnificent collections the sculptures from the Temple of Zeus and the *Hermes Carrying the Infant Dionysus*, sculpted by the great Praxiteles, discovered in the Temple of Hera in the place noted by the ancient travel writer Pausanias. The Hermes was buried under the fallen clay of the temple's upper walls and is one of the best-preserved classical statues. The central gallery of the museum holds one of the greatest sculptural achievements of classical antiquity: the pedimental sculptures and metopes from the Temple of Zeus, depicting *Hercules's Twelve Labors*. Also on display is the famous *Nike of Paionios*. Other treasures include notable terra-cottas of Zeus and Ganymede; the head of the cult statue of Hera; sculptures of the family and imperial patrons of Herodes Atticus; and bronzes found at the site, including votive figurines, cauldrons, and armor. Of great historic interest are a helmet dedicated by Miltiades, the Athenian general who defeated the Persians at Marathon, and a cup owned by the sculptor Pheidias, which was found in his workshop on the Olympia grounds.

✉ Off Ethnikos Odos 74, north of Ancient Olympia site

☎ 26240/22742

🌐 www.culture.gr

🎫 €6, combined ticket with Ancient Olympia €9

🕒 May–Oct., Mon. 11–7, Tues.–Sun. 8–7; Nov.–Apr., Mon. 10:30–5, Tues.–Sun. 8:30–3

★ ruins. At **Atelier Exekias** (✉ *Kondoli* ☎ *6936/314054*) Sakis Doylas sells exquisite handmade and hand-painted ceramic bowls and urns, fashioned after finds in Ancient Olympia; the glazes and colors are beautiful. **Olympia Alternative Action** (✉ *Kondoli* ☎ *26240/22532*), despite the political-sounding name, is a small shop selling honey, olive oil, herbs, and other locally grown products; the outfit also arranges rafting, cycling, and river-trekking excursions around Olympia.

NORTHERN PELOPONNESE ESSENTIALS

TRANSPORTATION

BY AIR

There is no commercial plane service to the Northern Peloponnese (the small airport at Patras handles private aviation and limited charters). The closest airports are in Athens and in Kalamata (in the Southern Peloponnese).

BY BOAT & FERRY

The Nafplion Port Authority and Patras Port Authority can advise you about entry and exit in their ports for yachts. Patras's tourist office (⇨ *Visitor Information*) is at the port.

HYDROFOILS Hellenic Seaways' high-speed car ferries sail four times daily in summer from Piraeus to Porto Heli (two hours; about €23); you can purchase tickets online. In winter the schedule is much reduced.

Contacts **Hellenic Seaways** (✉ *August 25, Heraklion, Crete* ☎ *2810/346185* 🌐 *www.hellenicseaways.gr*). **Nafplion Port Authority** (☎ *27520/27022*). **Patras Port Authority** (☎ *2610/341002*). **Piraeus Port Authority** (☎ *210/422–6000*).

BY BUS

Buses leave from Terminal A on the outskirts of Athens at Kifissou 100 (take Bus 51 at corner of Zinonos and Menandrou streets, near Omonia Square; from the airport, take Bus E93). Pick up a bus schedule from the Athens EOT (⇨ *Visitor Information*) or call the number listed below for departure times or seat reservations.

Bargain prices and an extensive network make bus travel a viable alternative to renting a car. Service from Athens to Corinth and Patras, for instance, operates as frequently as every half hour from 6 AM to the late evening, takes only three hours, and spares you a hair-raising drive; the cost is €12.25.

Within the Peloponnese, bus schedules are posted at local KTEL stations, usually on the main square or main street.

Information **Nafplion Bus Terminal** (✉ *Sigrou 8, Nafplion* ☎ *27520/27323*). **Terminal A** (✉ *Kifissou 100, Athens* ☎ *210/513–4588* 🌐 *www.ktel.org*).

9

BY CAR

The roads are fairly good in the Northern Peloponnese, and driving can be the most enjoyable way to see the region, giving you the freedom to visit the sights at leisure. The toll highway, known simply as Ethnikos Odos, or National Road, runs from Athens to the Isthmus of Corinth (84 km [52 mi], 1¼ hours), and from there continues (toll only in parts) to Nafplion, Patras, and Olympia; the system is well maintained. Have change ready, as a toll of about €2 is collected intermittently. The highway between Corinth and Patras is two lanes for some of its length and can be dangerous, with impatient drivers using the two lanes as four lanes. Slow-moving traffic is forced onto the shoulder. No speed limit is enforced, and the asphalt becomes very slippery when wet. The accident rate is high.

An alternative route from Athens to Patras is via Delphi and the Rion–Antirion bridge. Many people also enter the region on the car ferry between Italy (Ancona, Bari, or Brindisi) and Patras.

TRAIN TRAVEL

Trains from Athens depart from the Peloponnissos station; take Bus 057, which leaves every 10 minutes from Panepistimiou, or take Line 2 of the metro to the Larissa station, which is adjacent to the Peloponnissos station.

Trains run from Athens to Corinth, and then the route splits; you can go south to Argos and Nafplion or west along the coast to Patras and then south to Pyrgos and Kalamata. Alternatively, you can go directly through the Peloponnese to Kalamata via Tripoli. On the western route the train stops at Kiato, Xylokastro, Diakofto (where a narrow-gauge branch line heads inland to Kalavrita), and Aigion, before arriving in Patras. In summer the trains between Patras and Athens can be crowded with young people arriving from or leaving for Italy on ferries from Patras. Branch lines leave the main line at Kavasila for Loutra Killinis and at Pyrgos for Olympia. If you know you are returning by train, buy a round-trip ticket (good for a month); there is a substantial discount.

There are five departures daily from Athens to Nemea–Mykines–Argos–Nafplion; the trip to Nafplion takes three to five hours. A new commuter service serves Corinth, with trains to and from central Athens and the airport every hour between 8 and 8. The trip takes one hour and costs €6 to and from Athens, €8 to and from the airport. Eight trains leave Athens daily for Patras, a trip of 3½ to 4½ hours; the InterCity express is 4 hours. A line running along the west coast connects Kalamata with Patras (six hours). Going to Olympia by train from Athens isn't worth the trouble; the trip takes almost eight hours, with a change at Pyrgos.

As of this writing, extensive track work is being done on the Peloponnesian line, with a goal of significantly improving service between Athens and Patras. Check for service interruptions and station changes by contacting one of the offices listed below.

Information **Greek National Railway (OSE) offices** (✉ *Fillelinon 17, Athens*

☎ 210/323-6747 ✉ Sina 6, Athens ☎ 210/362-4402). **Patras railway station** (*✉ Patras ☎ 2610/221311, 2610/277441, or 2610/273694*). **Peloponnissos station** (*✉ Leoforos Theodorou Deligianni, Athens ☎ 210/522-4302*).

CONTACTS & RESOURCES

EMERGENCIES

Tourist police, who often speak English, can be useful in emergencies; they can also help you find accommodations, restaurants, and sights. Pharmacies, clearly identified by red-cross signs, take turns staying open late. A listing is published in the local newspaper; it is best to check at your hotel to find out not only which pharmacy is open but how to get there.

Tourist Police **Corinth** (*✉ Ermou 51 ☎ 27410/23282*). **Nafplion** (*✉ Martiou 25 Sq. ☎ 27520/98728*). **Olympia** (*✉ Douma 13 ☎ 26240/22550*). **Patras** (*✉ Patreos 53 ☎ 2610/451833 or 2610/451893*).

TOUR OPTIONS

CHAT Tours is among the many operators who organize whirlwind one-day tours from Athens to Corinth, Mycenae, Epidauros, and Nafplion; cost is about €85. These no-frills tours, aimed at those who don't expect a lot of hand-holding, can be booked at travel agencies and at larger hotels. CHAT and other operators also offer a more-leisurely two-day tour of Corinth, Mycenae, and Epidauros, with an overnight stay in Nafplion; cost is about €140.

If you are in Nafplion or Patras, many local travel agencies can arrange day tours of the classical sites.

Contacts **CHAT Tours** (*✉ Xenofontos 9, Athens ☎ 210/323-0827 🌐 www.chatours.gr*).

VISITOR INFORMATION

The Peloponnese are woefully underserved by tourist offices. The Greek National Tourism Organization (GNTO or EOT) has an office in Patras, and this is a good place to stock up on info for travel throughout the region. Olympia has a locally run tourist office and Nafplion has a municipal tourist office across from the OTE (telephone-company) building, but these are lackluster at best; most towns in the region do not have tourist offices of any sort. For tourist information and general help in places without tourist offices, it's best to contact the local tourist police, who often speak English and can be extremely helpful.

Contacts **Greek National Tourism Organization** (*✉ Tsochas 7, Athens ☎ 210/870-7000 ✉ Airport arrivals hall, Athens ☎ 210/353-0445 ✉ EOT Bldg., 1st fl., Zea Marina, Piraeus ☎ 210/452-2591 or 210/452-2586 🌐 www.gnto.gr*). **Nafplion** (*✉ Martiou 25 Sq. ☎ 27520/24444*). **Olympia** (*✉ Praxitelous Kondili 75 ☎ 26240/23100*). **Patras** (*✉ Filopimenos 26 ☎ 2610/620353*).

Southern Peloponnese

King Leonidas, Sparta

10

WORD OF MOUTH

"Monemvassia is called the Gibraltar of Greece. . . . The main street is about 4 feet wide; all materials coming into town must be carried by pack mule. The streets are a maze of twisting alleyways down to the fortress wall. I felt tempted to turn my watch back about five centuries."

–stanbr

www.fodors.com/forums

WELCOME TO SOUTHERN PELOPONNESE

TOP REASONS TO GO

★ **Breathe in Mountain Air:** Rugged mountains rise across the Southern Peloponnese; you can enjoy the scenery from Stemnitsa, Dimitsana, and other stone mountain villages.

★ **Byzantine Glory:** Two remarkable strongholds, Mystras and Monemvassia, display the region's Byzantine legacy.

★ **Breathtaking Bassae:** Splendidly isolated, this gigantic temple to Apollo was designed by the Parthenon's architect.

★ **Beach Life:** White sand and warm, turquoise waters beckon at Methoni and Elafonisi.

★ **Follow the Trails of the Ancients:** The pleasures of the Southern Peloponnese weren't lost on the ancients, who left vestiges of their rich culture at Nestor's Palace and Ancient Messene.

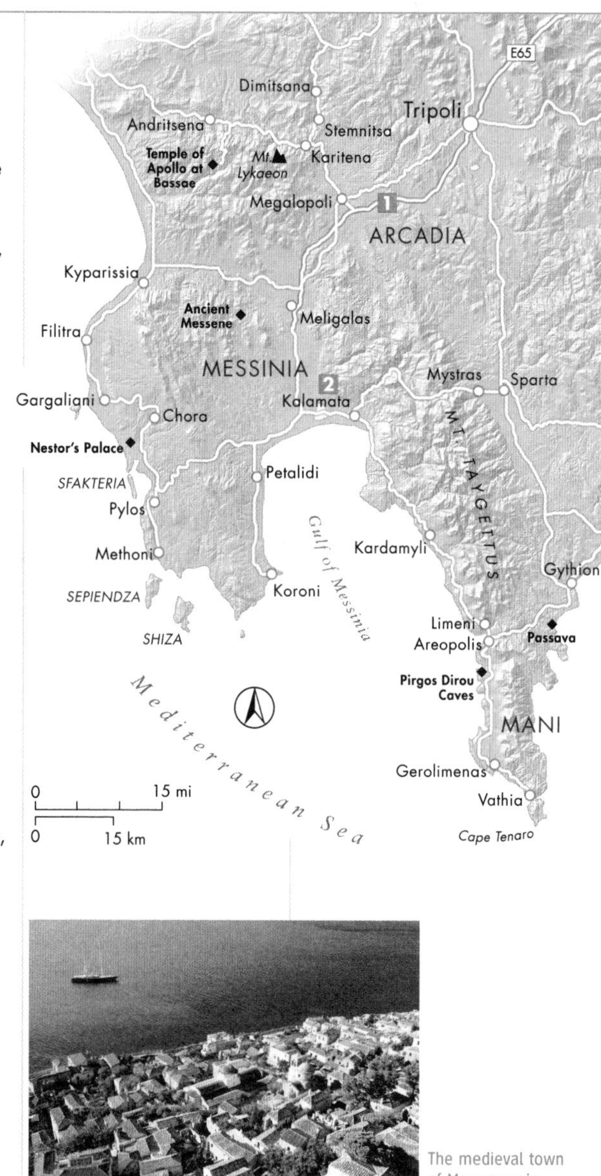

The medieval town of Monenvassia.

Olive grove, Arcadia.

GETTING ORIENTED

Politically, the Southern Peloponnese is divided into regions established by the ancients—Arcadia to the north, Messinia in the southwest, and Laconia in the southeast. These three regions are bisected with rugged mountain ranges. Arcadia is most accessible to Athens; exploring Messinia and Laconia means traveling down the three fingerlike peninsulas that dangle from the southernmost extremes of the Greek mainland. Highway E65 allows travelers to speed from Athens to Tripoli, Sparta, and Gythion in half a day or less.

1 Arcadia. Tripoli is the capital of this mountainous region, which is still somewhat remote and uncrowded, embracing a rural lifestyle. Two of Greece's most beautiful mountain villages, Stemnitsa and Dimitsana, are here, as is one of the most isolated and elegant remnants of the ancient world, the Temple of Apollo at Bassae.

2 Messinia. The fertile plains around Kalamata were home to Nestor of Homeric fame—the ruins of his palace lie west of Kalamata—and to Achilles, who was awarded the seaside village of Methoni by Agamemnon. Pylos, another delightful port, is just to the north. Messinia reaches south into parts of the stark Mani peninsula.

3 Laconia. Surrounded on three sides by mountains and by the sea on the other, Laconia was home to the harsh Spartans and also to the civilized Byzantines, who left splendid cities at Mystras, now in ruin, and Monemvassia, an intact medieval stronghold that clings to a rock above the sea.

Ruins of Methoni stronghold, Messinia,

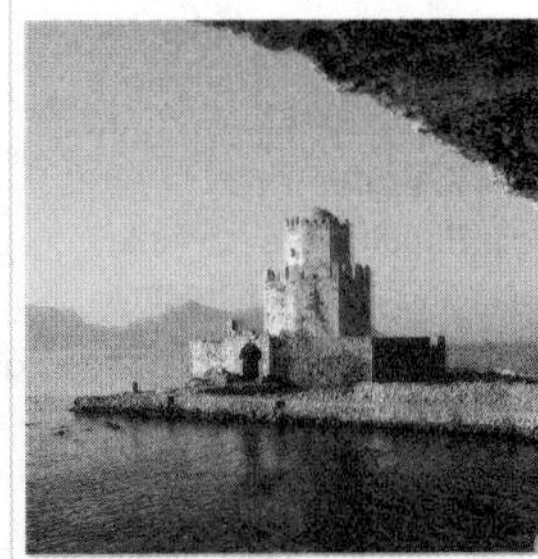

10

SOUTHERN PELOPONNESE PLANNER

Hit the Road

Driving is not only the easiest way to get around the Southern Peloponnese, it's also a real pleasure—a chance to enjoy dramatic scenery and get to out-of-the-way spots. The best driving routes are:

1 **The mountain roads east of Tripoli, to Karitena, Stemnitsa, and Demitsana:** You'll encounter thick forests (though some of it burned in the fires of 2007), stone villages clinging to steep hillsides, and the occasional Frankish castle brooding over a high mountain valley.

2 **The road from Kalamata to Mystras:** A scenic route rises from the plains of Messinia in the west onto the forested flanks of the Taygettus range, where hillsides are heavily forested and scented with pine, then emerges at the ruined city of Mystras before dropping into Sparta.

3 **The road down the Mani peninsula:** Setting out from Gythion (10 mi to the east), the landscape becomes starker the farther south you travel on a highway that is barely more than one-lane in places. It first heads through the so-called outer Mani, around Kardamyli, then south past Areopolis all the way to Cape Tenaro, the mythical entrance to the underworld.

How's the Weather?

May, September, and October are especially comfortable months here, with pleasant temperatures (it's warm enough to swim) and little rain. In summer temperatures can soar to uncomfortable highs in many regions, especially the Mani and on the low-lying plains of Messinia. Mosquitoes are out in force around Methoni and other seaside villages, which are often surrounded by fields and groves, so bring repellant and, more importantly, seek out a hotel room with air-conditioning. Snow renders many of the mountain regions inaccessible in winter.

Where the Crowds Are—and Aren't

Resort life is relatively low-key in the Southern Peloponnese; Methoni and Pylos are busiest in summer yet these towns are rarely too packed. Mountain villages are a delightful getaway in summer and are popular Sunday-afternoon excursions for Greek families, who add a festive air to the otherwise quiet surroundings. Monemvassia is a popular weekend destination for Greeks, and the narrow lanes can seem jammed; the town is much less crowded and more pleasant to visit during the week, when the medieval atmosphere regains a hold. The ancient sites—Nestor's Palace, Ancient Messene, and the Temple of Apollo at Bassae—are far off the tourist path, so you might have the pleasure of having these places to yourself.

Making the Most of Your Time

The Southern Peloponnese is a remarkably diverse region, with landscapes that vary from low coastal plains to stark seascapes to high mountains. Nicely compact, this is a relatively uncrowded area, and you'll appreciate it most if you take time to linger in a village or savor the landscape over a picnic lunch. A short visit forces you to make some difficult choices: any of the three regions covered in this chapter can be explored in a few days, but in that time you may be tempted to explore more than one region.

Great Flavors

The Southern Peloponnese is not as popular as the Northern Peloponnese, so be prepared to find fewer restaurants, and certainly fewer fancy restaurants. On the other hand, one of the great pleasures of traveling in the region is enjoying a meal on a village square or seaside terrace. Villages here were the source of such international favorites as avgolemono soup and lamb fricassee. There are several local specialties to watch for: in the mountain villages near Tripoli, order *stifado* (beef with pearl onions), *arni psito* (lamb on the spit), *kokoretsi* (entrails on the spit), and thick, creamy yogurt. In Sparta, look for *bardouniotiko* (a local dish of chicken stuffed with cheese, olives, and walnuts), and, around Pylos, order fresh ocean fish (priced by the kilo). In the rest of Laconia, try *loukaniko horiatiko* (village sausage), and in the Mani ask for ham.

As for wines, the light white from Mantinea is a favorite, and whenever possible, sample the *hima* (barrel wines), which range from light, dry whites to heavy reds.

A hole-in-the-wall may serve the town's best meals, and what's available is what the butcher, fisherman, and grocer sold that day, despite the printed menu. Vegetables are almost always locally grown and fresh in this region famous for its olives and olive oil as wells as figs, tomatoes, and other produce. Seafood is plentiful, though sometime frozen—menus will usually indicate what's frozen and what's fresh. A fresh catch is usually available at seaside tavernas, and an octopus or two will usually be drying out front. Inland, many tavernas serve grilled pork from local farms, as well as chicken and roosters plucked that morning.

Dining & Lodging Prices in Euros

	¢	$	$$	$$$	$$$$
Restaurants	Under €8	€8–€15	€15–€20	€20–€25	Over €25
Hotels	Under €80	€80–€120	€120–€160	€160–€200	Over €200

Restaurant prices are for one main course at dinner, or for two mezedes (small dishes). Hotel prices are for a standard double room in high season, including taxes. Hotels operate on the European Plan (EP, with no meal provided) unless we note that they use the Continental Plan (CP, with Continental breakfast); Breakfast Plan (BP, with a full breakfast); Modified American Plan (MAP, with breakfast and dinner); or the Full American Plan (FAP, with all meals). Inquire when booking if these meal plans (which can entail higher rates) are mandatory. Guest rooms have air-conditioning, room phones, and TVs unless otherwise noted.

Hiking the Peloponnese

Throughout the Peloponnese there are many small trails, or *kalderimi* (mule paths), to explore, as well as the international E4 European Rambler Trail, which starts in the Pyrenees, winds through Eastern Europe, and traverses Greece to Gythion. The southern half, from Delphi to Gythion, is considered less difficult than the northern section and can be walked most of the year; the best time is mid-May through early October. Pick up the southern section at Menalon Refuge and continue through Vresthena, Sparta, Taygettus Refuge, and Panagia Yiatris monastery to Gythion. More information is available from the **Greek Alpine Club** (✉ *Kapnikereas 2, Athens* ☎ *210/321–2355*) or the **Hellenic Federation of Mountaineering and Climbing** (✉ *Milioni 5, Athens* ☎ *210/363–6617 or 210/364–5904* 🌐 *www.sportsnet.gr*).

10

Finding a Place to Stay

In recent years the region has gained a few distinctive hotels, often in historic structures. You'll find especially atmospheric lodging in Monemvasia and Mystras. Most hotels, though, offer plain, tile-floored rooms, usually with balconies. Newer hotels may have more services and a bit more decorative flair.

Updated by Stephen Brewer

IN THE RELATIVELY REMOTE REACHES of the Southern Peloponnese ungainly yet amiable towns like Tripoli, Sparta, and Kalamata are set amid olive groves, rugged mountains, dizzying gorges, and languorous beaches. Stone towns—Stemnitsa, Dimitsana, and medieval Karitena—and the remote Temple of Apollo in Bassae cling to the rugged hillsides of mountain ranges. Ancient ruins and historic towns and monuments pervade the landscape. The low-key seaside retreat of Methoni is guarded by a seaside Venetian fortress. Ancient Messene, with its mammoth fortifications from the 4th century BC, is on the sandy cape of Messinia. The Mycenaean ruins of Nestor's Palace, almost a millennium older than Ancient Messene, are surrounded by olive groves on a nearby hilltop, and the harbor at Pylos, a whitewashed village that is now a pleasant fishing port and quiet resort, was the scene of a famous 1827 sea battle that paved the way for Greek independence.

Except for the foundations of Artemis's sanctuary and some fragments of Apollo's shrine at Amykles, nothing remains of ancient Sparta—fitting tribute perhaps to what was the first totalitarian state. The Byzantines, however, left the well-preserved town of Mystras, and the still-inhabited medieval city of Monemvassia, a Byzantine gem, is carved into a rock face on the region's southeast coast.

Despite the waves of invaders over the centuries—Franks, Venetians, and Turks—this land is considered the distillation of all that is Greek, with its indulged idiosyncrasy, intractable autonomy, and appreciation of simple pleasures. The Southern Peloponnese is somewhat isolated from the rest of Greece, especially politically, but its people are great respecters of *filoxenia* (hospitality). Though it may be less accessible than other areas of Greece, this part of the Peloponnese has the advantage of a less-hectic pace and fewer crowds. The best moments come when you stray beyond the familiar and take time to have a coffee in the square of a village on Mt. Taygettus, a picnic at the ruins of Bassae, or a sunset swim beneath the brooding towers of a Maniote fishing hamlet.

ARCADIA ΑΡΚΑΔΙΑ

Arcadians are believed to be among the oldest inhabitants of the Peloponnese; this group of tribes first united when they entered the Trojan War. They later founded the powerful Arcadian League, but after Corinth fell to Rome in 146 BC, the region slipped into decline. When the Goths invaded in AD 395, Arcadia was almost entirely deserted. Several centuries later the Franks conquered the area and built many castles; they were succeeded by the Byzantines and then the Turks, who ruled until the War of Independence.

No conqueror ever really dominated the Arcadians. Even when Tripoli was the Turks' administrative center, the mountain villagers lived much as they pleased, maintaining secret schools to preserve the rudiments of Greek language and religion and harassing the Turks in roaming bands. Forested mountainsides and valley farms still lend themselves to a decidedly rural way of life, and the very word "arcadia" has come

Southern Peloponnese
KEY
Ferry lines
0
20 miles
0
30 km
Ionian Sea
Mediterranean Sea
Mirtóön Sea
Gulf of Argolis
Gulf of Messinia
Gulf of Laconia
ARCADIA
ARGOLID
LACONIA
MESSINIA
MANI
MT. PARNON
MT. TAYGETTUS
Mt. Lykaeon
Alphios R.
Nedhas R.
Pamisos R.
Evrotas R.
METHANA
POROS
HYDRA
SPETSES
SFAKTERIA
ELAFONISI
KYTHERA
Cape Tenaro
Dimitsana
Stemnitsa
Karitena
Tripoli
Andritsena
Temple of Apollo at Bassae
Megalopoli
Kyparissia
Kopanaki
Ancient Messene
Meligalas
Mavromati
Filitra
Gargaliani
Chora
Messene
Bouka
Nestor's Palace
Pylos
Methoni
Petalidi
Koroni
Kalamata
Verga
Kardamyli
Stoupa
Itilo
Neo Itilo
Areopolis
Pirgos Dirou Caves
Gerolimenas
Vathia
Mystras
Sparta
Gythion
Passava
Skoutari
Argos
Tiryns
Nauplion
Lerna
Astros
Ayios Petros
Leonidion
Geraki
Kiparissi
Geraka
Gefira
Monemvassia
Viglafia
Neapolis
Ayios Pelagia
Potamos
Kythera Town
Fanari
Galatas
Kranidion
Ermioni
Hydra Town
Porto Heli
Spetses Town
9
76
74
70
E65
E55
1
39
82
86

to suggest the sorts of pastoral pleasures you will encounter here. In recent years many locals have abandoned their pastoral life to look for work in Athens; Arcadia now has no more people than Corinthia, a region half its size.

TRIPOLI ΤΡΙΠΟΛΗ

150 km (93 mi) southwest of Athens, 70 km (43 mi) southwest of Corinth.

Regardless of the direction from which you approach the southern half of the Peloponnese, history, along with the practicalities of the road network in this part of Greece, suggests you're sure to at least pass through the outskirts of Tripoli. In the days of the Ottoman Empire, this crossroads was the capital of the Turkish pasha of the Peloponnese, and during the War of Independence it was the first target of Greek revolutionaries. They captured it in 1821 after a six-month siege, but the town went back and forth between the warring sides until 1827, when Ibrahim Pasha's retreating troops burned it to the ground.

Tripoli is a workaday town with few attractions to keep you here, although if you do hang around, you'll get an eyeful of Greek life. Its most attractive feature is the mountain scenery, with attendant hillside villages, that surrounds it; you will soon understand why this region is nicknamed the Switzerland of Greece. Unless you run out of daylight, you'll probably want to move on from Tripoli to one of these villages.

Catch an authentic Greek experience by visiting one of the *kafeneia* (coffeehouses) on Agiou Vasiliou Square. Here Greek men smoke, play cards, and talk politics; women may feel a little uncomfortable but will be treated with great respect if they enter. You can also grab a quick and juicy (and very inexpensive) souvlaki at E Gonia in a corner of the square (*gonia* means "corner" in Greek).

You can observe Greek life in the squares in the center of town, especially **Areos Square,** one of the largest and most beautiful *platias* (central squares) in Greece—definitely the place to while away the time if marooned in Tripoli.

WHERE TO STAY & EAT

¢ ✕ **Polis.** Tripoli's most popular spot, a trendy indoor-outdoor café on a corner of Areos Square, looks like it might belong in Key West. It is, however, as popular with the old crowd that stops in for a frappé or ice cream as it with Tripoli's young and restless, many of whom are students at the local university. A large assortment of crepes, including one with feta, olives, and toma-

WHAT'S IN A NAME?

Arcadia was named after Arcas, whom Zeus fathered with Callisto. According to one version of the legend, Callisto's father chopped Arcas into bite-size pieces and served him to Zeus for dinner. Zeus managed to give his son new life as a bear, but in a fit of ingratitude, Arcas eventually had his wicked way with his mother. That's when Zeus decided to turn both mother and son into the constellations Ursa Major and Minor, the Big and Little Dipper.

toes, provide the perfect lunch. ✉ *Areos Sq. 5* ☎ *2710/237019* ▭ *No credit cards.*

$$ **Mainalon Hotel.** The fairly luxurious amenities here include a tasteful mix of traditional and contemporary furnishings, silk fabrics in the guest rooms, and commodious marble bathrooms. Ask for a room in the front of the hotel and enjoy a balcony overlooking Areos Square. The hotel's café on the square is one of the town's most popular hangouts. ✉ *Areos Sq., 22100* ☎ *2710/230300* 🖷 *2710/230327* 🌐 *www.mainalonhotel.gr* *42 rooms, 3 suites* *In-room: dial-up. In-hotel: bar* ▭ *AE, MC, V* *BP.*

¢ **Arcadia.** This six-story green cement box is not fancy, but the saving graces are the high ceilings, pleasantly ornate furnishings, terraces, and a roof garden. ✉ *Kolokotronis Sq. 1, 22100* ☎ *2710/225551 through 2710/225553* 🖷 *2710/222464* *45 rooms* *In-hotel: restaurant, bar* ▭ *No credit cards* *CP.*

SPORTS

Mt. Menalon ski center (☎ *2710/232243*), at Oropedio Ostrakina (4,310 feet) northwest of the city, has five downhill runs and three tows; food and overnight accommodations are available. The center is 30 km (19 mi) from Tripoli.

STEMNITSA ΣΤΕΜΝΙΤΣΑ

★ *43 km (27 mi) northwest of Tripoli.*

Also called Ipsous, Stemnitsa is one of the most beautiful towns in southern Greece, wondrously perched 3,444 feet above sea level amid a forest of fir and chestnut trees. For centuries the stone village was one of the Balkans' best-known metalworking centers, and today a minuscule school is still staffed by local artisans. Above the lively square rises the bell tower of the church of Ayios Giorgios, and at the top of a nearby hill is the monument to fighters in the 1821 War of Independence against the Turks. Stemnitsa, in fact, claims to have been the capital of Greece for a few weeks in 1821, when it was the center for rebels who successfully routed the Turks. The views throughout the town are phenomenal, especially at night when the village lies beneath of canopy of bright stars.

From the north side of town, a well-marked path leads through the mountains to the isolated monastery of **Moni Ayiou Ioannitou**, with a little chapel covered in frescoes that is generally open. From the monastery other paths lead through a beautiful, wooded valley to the banks of the River Lousios.

The unusual **Folklore Museum of Stemnitsa** devotes one floor to mock workshops for indigenous crafts such as candle making and bell casting; the other two floors house re-created traditional rooms and a charmingly haphazard collection of costumes, weapons, icons, and plates. ✉ *Off main road* ☎ *27950/81252* 🌐 *www.culture.gr* *Free* ⏲ *Oct.–June, Mon. and Wed.–Fri. 11–1, weekends 11–2; July–Sept., Mon. 11–1, Wed., Thurs., and Sat. 11–1 and 6–8, Fri. 6–8.*

EN ROUTE

The winding road between Stemnitsa and Dimitsana reveals extensive views over the forested rises and valleys of the Arcadian mountains. About halfway between the two villages you'll come to a widening in the road that's a perfect place to stop: A mountain spring supplies cool, refreshing water (make sure you have containers to fill) and a viewpoint overlooks miles of mountain scenery—still beautiful, though badly scarred in the fires of 2007.

DIMITSANA ΔΗΜΗΤΣΑΝΑ

10 km (6 mi) north of Stemnitsa, 50 km (31 mi) northwest of Tripoli.

Dimitsana has stunning views of the Arcadian mountains. Leave your car at the entrance to town, stroll the maze of narrow cobbled lanes, and study the town's ancient churches. Archaeologists found ruins of a cyclopean wall (irregular stones without mortar) and classical buildings near the town; the ruins belonged to the acropolis of Teuthis, an ancient city.

The **Ecclesiastical Museum** houses manuscripts, a 35,000-volume library, and other artifacts from the 19th-century School of Greek Letters, which at one time educated Germanos, a bishop of Patras, and other church leaders. ✉ *Off main square* ☎ *27950/31360* 🎫 *€1.50* ⏲ *Fri.–Tues. 10–1:30 and 5–7.*

On the River Lousios below town is the **Open Air Water Power Museum,** which includes a water mill, tannery, and gunpowder mill. Displays and demonstrations reveal why water power was the force behind the region's economy until the first part of the 20th century. ✉ *Off main road, south of town* ☎ *27950/31217* 🎫 *€1.50* ⏲ *Mid-Apr.–mid-Oct., Wed.–Mon. 10–2 and 5–7; mid-Oct.–mid-Apr., Wed.–Mon. 10–4.*

The **town library** displays manuscripts, rare books, and memorabilia from the Greek revolutionary period, when Dimitsana was a center for revolutionary activity against the Turks. ✉ *Main square* ☎ *27950/31219* 🎫 *Free* ⏲ *Apr.–Oct., weekdays 8–2, Sat. 8–noon.*

WHERE TO STAY

$ **Hotel Dimitsana.** The lounges, restaurant, and many rooms hang right over the deep gorge of the River Lousios, providing stunning views. All rooms have balconies (those over the gorge seem to be suspended in midair), while rooms in front of the hotel overlook the surrounding mountains. In summer the hotel can arrange rafting trips and mountain treks; rates jump in winter when skiers use the hotel as a base for the slopes on Mt. Menalon and other nearby ski centers. ✉ *Main road, south end of town, 22007* ☎ *27950/31518 through 27950/31520* 📠 *27950/31040* 🌐 *www.dimitsanahotel.gr* *20 rooms* *In-hotel: restaurant, public Internet* 💳 *MC, V* 🍴 *BP.*

SPORTS & THE OUTDOORS

The **E2 hiking path,** part of the European trail system, passes through Dimitsana. You can follow the path south along the gorge of the River Lousios or east into the surrounding mountains. The trek south brings

CLOSE UP

A Little Night Music

Dance performances, accompanied by traditional music, are common in the region. In the *tsakonikos,* the dancers wheel tightly around each other and then swing into bizarre spirals; this dance resembles the sacred dance of Delos, first performed by Theseus to mime how he escaped from the Labyrinth. The popular *kalamatianos* is a circular dance from Kalamata. The *tsamikos,* from Roumeli in central Greece, is an exclusively male dance showcasing agility and derring-do. You will see your fill of dancing at local festivals to celebrate a town or village's patron saint, usually in summer. Dancing is also part of a Greek wedding, and it's not entirely unlikely that you might attend one. The guest list usually includes the entire population of a village or section of town, and if you happen to be staying there at the time of a wedding, you may well be invited.

you to several small monasteries tucked into the walls of the gorge and the scanty ruins of the ancient city of Gortys.

KARITENA ΚΑΡΥΤΑΙΝΑ

26 km (16 mi) south of Dimitsana, 54 km (33 mi) west of Tripoli.

Karitena, a medieval village of stone houses topped by a Frankish castle, is inhabited by fewer than 300 people, though the population was 20,000 during the Middle Ages. The buildings reveal the influence of the Franks, Byzantines, and Turks who occupied the area. For a stunning view of the gorge and the town, walk over to the multiarched Frankish bridge that spans the Alpheios gorge.

When the Franks took over from the Byzantines in 1209, they gave the town to Hugo de la Bruyères, who built the hilltop **Frankish castle** (⌧*Off town square*) in 1245 and then bequeathed it to his son Geoffrey, the only well-liked Frankish overlord (he was praised in the *Chronicle of Morea* for his chivalry). The castle was known as the Toledo of Greece because of its strategic position at the mouth of the Alpheios. Later, during the revolution against the Turks, the hero Theodore Kolokotronis again made use of its location, repairing the fortifications and building a house and a church within the walls as his base, out of reach of Ibrahim Pasha. The castle, now partly in ruin, is not open to the public, though you can climb to the walls.

The 11th-century church of **Ayios Nikolaos** (⌧*Below town square*) has vivid and generally well-preserved frescoes, though some of the faces were scratched out during the Ottoman era. Ask in the square for the caretaker, who has the keys.

ANDRITSENA ΑΝΔΡΙΤΣΑΙΝΑ

29 km (18 mi) southwest of Karitena, 83 km (51 mi) west of Tripoli.

Andritsena is a pleasant little collection of stone houses clinging to the sides of a deep valley. The village is the launching point for visits to the Temple of Apollo at Bassae and a good stop for a meal or an overnight.

A small **library** houses 15th-century Venetian and Vatican first editions and documents relating to the War of Independence. ✉ *On main road, 100 yards after square* ☎ *26260/22242* 🎫 *Free* ⏲ *Weekdays 8:30–3.*

WHAT WERE THE FRANKS DOING IN THE PELOPONNESE?

Franks, in the personages of itinerant French noblemen ostensibly on their way to the Fourth Crusade, began settling in the Peloponnese in the early years of the 13th century. One of them, Geoffrey de Villehardouin, made landfall in Methoni during a storm and was enchanted by his surroundings. Meanwhile, his colleagues had sacked Constantinople, making it easy for Villehardouin and other nobles to take control of the Peloponnese, capturing such Byzantine strongholds as Mystras and Monemvassia.

WHERE TO STAY

$ **Theoxenia Hotel.** The only hotel for miles is geared to basic comfort, but the rooms are large and pleasantly furnished and offer vistas of mountains and woods. The hotel serves lunch and dinner in summer, but you're better off at one of the eateries surrounding the main square. ✉ *On main road on edge of village as you enter from Karitena, 27061* ☎ *26260/22219* *35 rooms* *In-hotel: restaurant* *No credit cards* ⏲ *Closed Nov.–Feb.* *CP.*

TEMPLE OF APOLLO AT BASSAE ΝΑΟΣ ΤΟΥ ΑΠΟΛΛΩΝΑ ΣΤΙΣ ΒΑΣΣΕΣ

★ *14 km (9 mi) south of Andritsena, 97 km (60 mi) southwest of Tripoli.*

Isolated amid craggy, uncompromising scenery, the Temple of Apollo Epikourios at Bassae is elegant and untouched by vandalism or commercialism. Despite its setting, the temple has lost some of its impact—it is veiled by a canopy during ongoing long-term restoration to undo weather damage. For many years it was believed that this temple was designed by Iktinos, the Parthenon's architect. Although this theory has recently been disputed, it is one of the best-preserved classical temples in Greece, superseded in its state of preservation only by the Hephaistion in Athens. The residents of nearby Phygalia built it atop an older temple in 420 BC to thank Apollo for delivering them from an epidemic; *epikourious* means "helper." Made of local limestone, the temple has some unusual details: exceptional length compared to its width; a north–south orientation rather than the usual east–west (probably because of the slope of the ground); and Ionic half columns linked to the walls by flying buttresses. Here, too, were the first known Corinthian columns with the characteristic acanthus leaves—only the base remains now—and the earliest example of interior sculptured friezes illustrating the battles between the Greeks and Amazons (now in the British Museum).

Climb to the **summit** northwest of the temple for a view overlooking the Nedhas River, Mt. Lykaeon, and, on a clear day, the Ionian Sea. ✉*Off Rte. 76 and then up a 1-lane road* ☎*26260/22254* 🌐*www.culture.gr* 🎫*€2* ⏲*Daily 8:30–3.*

MESSINIA ΜΕΣΣΗΝΙΑ

Euripides called this region "a land of fair fruitage and watered by innumerable streams ... neither very wintry in the blasts of winter, nor yet made too hot by the chariot of Hellos." Long, relatively cool summers and mild winters may be Messinia's blessing, but nature was no ally in 1986 when a major earthquake razed its capital, Kalamata, which has been rebuilt with an eye to efficiency rather than charm. The region remains deeply rural, and Kalamata has given its name to the olives that grow in mile after mile of groves, punctuated by such ancient sites as Ancient Messene and Nestor's Palace.

KALAMATA ΚΑΛΑΜΑΤΑ

91 km (56 mi) southwest of Tripoli.

Though not Greece's most attractive city, Kalamata does have the animated air of a busy market town. The city is built atop ancient Pharai, described by Homer as subject to the kingdom of Agamemnon. In the 8th century BC, Pharai was annexed as a province of Laconia and, like most towns in the area, was not independent again until the Battle of Leuctra ended Spartan domination, prompting the Theban general Epaminondas to erect the great fortifications of Messene.

The effects of the severe earthquake that nearly leveled the city in 1986 are still evident in the remaining rubble and an ongoing rebuilding boom. Kalamata is a crossroads between such places as Pylos and Ancient Messene to the west, Sparta and Mystras to the east, and the Mani to the south.

10

The small, well-organized **Benakeion Archaeological Museum** exhibits local stone tools, proto-Geometric and Geometric pottery, and a 1st-century AD Roman mosaic floor depicting Dionysus with a panther and a satyr. ✉*Benaki and Papazoglou, near Martiou 25 Sq.* ☎*27210/26209* 🌐*www.culture.gr* 🎫*Free* ⏲*Tues.–Sun. 8:30–3.*

In the early 13th century William de Champlitte divided the Peloponnese into 12 baronies, bestowing Kalamata on Frankish knight Geoffrey de Villehardouin, who built a winter **kastro** (✉*At end of Ipapandis*). Through the centuries the castle was bitterly fought over by Franks, Slavs, and Byzantines, and today it's difficult to tell what of the remains is original. From Martiou 25 Square, walk up Ipapandis past the church, take the first left at the castle gates (which are always open), and climb the small hill; the views of the town, coast, and the Messinian plain are lovely.

The oldest church here is the 13th-century **Ayii Apostoli** (*Holy Apostles* ⊠*Martiou 25 Sq.*), a small Byzantine church dedicated to the Virgin of Kalamata ("of the good eye"), from whom the town may get its name. Restored after the 1986 earthquake, it is one of Greece's double churches, with two naves—one for the Roman Catholics and one for the Orthodox—that resulted from 13th- and 14th-century ecumenical efforts. The Greek War of Independence was formally declared here on March 23, 1821, when Theodoros Kolokotronis captured Kalamata from the Turks. The church is usually open in the late afternoon (5–7).

BEACHES

About 30 km (19 mi) west of Kalamata at **Petalidi** is the beginning of a long chain of sandy beaches that are ideal for children because of the shallow water. **Verga,** about 6 km (4 mi) east of town, and the more crowded **Bouka,** 10 km (6 mi) west of town, both have showers and changing rooms.

WHERE TO STAY & EAT

$–$$ ★ ✕ **Koinakos.** The large, waterfront terrace and handsome dining room are the best places in town to enjoy grilled octopus and fish, mussels steamed in wine, and other seafood dishes, always fresh and deftly prepared. Rather than ordering off the menu, ask to step into the kitchen and see what's fresh that day. ⊠*Navarinou 12* ☎*27210/22016* ▭*MC, V.*

¢–$$ ✕ **Selitsa.** Take in Kalamata and the Gulf of Messinia from the tables at this hillside taverna, set in pine woods next to a stream. It's worth the trip up for the hearty meats such as *katsiki tou fournou* (roasted goat) and roasted lamb. Next door is a small castle, which in summer is a drinks-only bistro. Ask for directions; everyone in Kalamata knows this place well. ⊠*About 3 km (2 mi) northeast of the center; follow Navarinou south toward Verga; signs indicate turn for Selitsa village, Selitsa* ☎*27210/41331* ▭*No credit cards.*

¢–$ ✕ **Kaloutas.** Watch the men laying out their nets to dry at this waterfront restaurant, while you eat copious helpings of tender beef *kokkinisto* (stew) and *arni lemonato* (lamb cooked in a light lemon sauce). Mr. Kaloutas prides himself on his selection, and if he's not too busy, he takes requests. He also prepares large breakfasts with croissants, eggs, orange juice, and drip coffee instead of the drearily ubiquitous *nes* (boiled Nescafé). ⊠*Navarinou 98* ☎*27210/29097* ▭*No credit cards.*

$ **Haikos.** The Haikos brothers run their well-kept seaside hotel meticulously, extend a friendly welcome and readily dispense advice to their guests, and charge very fairly for what they offer. Most of the cool blue bedrooms have balconies and ocean views, and all have showers and comfy chairs and sofas; a pebble-and-sand beach is a few steps away. Breakfast is €7 extra and served in an airy lounge that's a pleasant place to enjoy a coffee or snack any time of the day. ⊠*Navarinou 115,*

24100 ☎27210/82886 or 27210/82888 📠27210/23800 🌐www.haikos.com 65 rooms In-room: dial-up ▭No credit cards 🍽CP.

FESTIVALS

The annual **Independence Day celebration** is held on or around March 25, the national holiday date. Stick around for the festivities—dancing, local bands, and a spirited parade. Contact the Greek National Tourism Organization (GNTO or EOT) for information. In summer Kalamata holds a **theater festival** (☎*27210/29909*).

SHOPPING

Kalamata is most famous for its fleshy black olives and olive oil, but is also known for *pasteli* (sesame-seed-and-honey candy) and figs. You can stock up on these at **Nikniea** (✉*Faron 206* ☎*27210/86724*), which has many tempting local delicacies. Nuns from the convent of the Kalograies (✉*Just below kastro, off square of church of Virgin Ypapanti*) weave beautiful silk scarves and table linens, for sale in a shop just inside the entrance; ask to step into the tranquil cloister while you're there.

ANCIENT MESSENE ΑΡΧΑΙΑ ΜΕΣΣΗΝΗ

★ *31 km (19 mi) north of Kalamata, 75 km (47 mi) southwest of Tripoli.*

The ruins of Ancient Messene, about 20 km (12 mi) north of the modern city of the same name, are set amid olive groves and pine forests on the slopes of majestic Mt. Ithomi (also known as Voulkanos). Epaminondas, the Theban leader, built Ancient Messene, which today incorporates the village of **Mavromati,** in 370–369 BC as a defense against the Spartans, with whom the Messenians had battled during two Messenian Wars, in 743–724 BC and 650–620 BC.

The most striking aspect of the ruins is the city's **circuit wall,** a feat of defensive architecture that rises and dips across the hillsides for an astonishing 9 km (5½ mi). Four gates remain; the best preserved is the north or **Arcadian Gate,** a double set of gates separated by a round courtyard. On the ancient paving stone below the arch, grooves worn by chariot wheels are still visible. The heart of the walled city is now occupied by the village, but excavations have uncovered the most important public buildings, including a **theater,** whose seats have now been restored; the **Synedrion,** a meeting hall for representatives of independent Messene; the **Sebasteion,** dedicated to worship of a Roman emperor; the **sanctuary to the god Asklepios;** and a **temple to Artemis Orthia.** Outside the walls lie a **stadium** and a **cemetery.** The site is a bit confusing, as the ruins are spread over the hillside and approached from different paths; follow the signposts indicating the theater, gates, and other major excavations. Some of the finds are in the village's **small museum.** After exploring the ruins, enjoy a beverage in one of the tavernas that surround the main square of Mavromati. ✉*From modern town of Messene, turn north at intersection of signposted road to Mavromati* ☎*27240/51257* 🌐*www.culture.gr* *Free* ⏲*Daily 8–dusk.*

10

CHORA ΧΩΡΑ

48 km (29¾ mi) west of Kalamata, 64 km (39¾ mi) west of Ancient Messene.

Chora's **Archaeological Museum** (follow the confusing signs from Nestor's Palace; it's at the edge of town) displays golden cups and jewelry from the Mycenaean period; fragments of frescoes from nearby Nestor's Palace, including a warrior in a boar's-tusk helmet described by Homer; and plaster casts of the Linear B tablets—the originals are in the National Archaeological Museum in Athens. ✉*Marinatou* ☎*27630/31358* 🌐*www.culture.gr* 🎫*€2* ⏲*Tues.–Sun. 8:30–3.*

NESTOR'S PALACE ΑΝΑΚΤΟΡΟ ΤΟΥ ΝΕΣΤΟΡΑ

4 km (2½ mi) south of Chora.

Nestor's Palace belonged to the king of Pylos, commander, according to Homer, of the fleet of "ninety black ships" in the Trojan War. Nestor founded the town around 1300 BC—only Mycenae was larger—but the palace was burned a century later. It was here, the *Iliad* recounts, that Telemachus came to ask for news of his father, Odysseus, from Nestor, who welcomed the young man to a feast at the palace. Archaeologists believe the complex, excavated in 1952, was similar to those found in Crete and Mycenae, except that it was unfortified, an indication that surrounding towns had sworn strict allegiance to and depended economically on Pylos. Most of the palace rooms are clearly marked, but it's a good idea to buy the guidebook (available at the site) prepared by the University of Cincinnati, whose archaeologists excavated the site. The illustrations will help you imagine the palace in its original glory, which is indicated by the sheer size of the foundations and wall fragments.

In the **main building,** a simple **entrance gate** is flanked by a **guard chamber** and two **archives,** where 1,250 palm-leaf-shaped tablets were discovered on the first day of excavation. The tablets—records of taxes, armament expenses, and debts in Linear B script—were the first such unearthed on the Greek mainland, thus linking the Mycenaean and Minoan (Crete) civilizations, because the writing (like that in Knossos) was definitely Greek.

The entrance gate opens into a spacious **courtyard** with a balcony where spectators could watch the royal ceremonies. To the left are a **storeroom** that yielded thousands of tall-stemmed vases and a **waiting room** with built-in benches. Beyond the courtyard a **porch of the royal apartments** and a **vestibule** open onto a richly decorated **throne room.** In the middle of the room is a ceremonial **hearth** surrounded by four wooden columns (only the stone bases remain) that probably supported a shaft. Now completely destroyed, the throne once stood in the center of the wall to the right. Each **frescoed wall** depicted a different subject, such as a griffin (possibly the royal emblem) or a minstrel strumming his lyre. Even the columns and the wooden ceiling were painted. Along the southern edge of the throne room were seven **storerooms** for oil, which together with the one on the floor immediately above fueled the fire that destroyed the palace.

Off a corridor to the right of the entrance are a **bathroom,** where the oldest known bathtub stands, along with jars used for collecting bathwater. Next to it are the **queen's apartments.** In the largest room a hearth is adorned with a painted flame, the walls with hunting scenes of lions and panthers. Other rooms in the complex include the **throne room** from an earlier palace, a **shrine, workshops,** and a **conduit** that brought water from a nearby spring. Several **beehive tombs** were also found outside the palace. ✉ *On highway south of Chora* ☎ *27630/31437* 🌐 *www.culture.gr* 🎫 *€3* ⏲ *July–Oct., daily 8–7:30.*

PYLOS ΠΥΛΟΣ

22 km (14 mi) south of Chora, 52 km (32 mi) southwest of Kalamata.

With its bougainvillea-swathed, pristine white houses fanning up Mt. St. Nicholas and the blue waters of its port, Pylos will remind you of an island town. It was built according to a plan drawn by French engineers stationed here from 1828 to 1833 with General Maison's entourage and was the site of a major naval battle in the War of Independence. Ibrahim Pasha chose Sfakteria, the islet that virtually blocks Pylos Bay, from which to launch his attack on the mainland. For two years Greek forces flailed under Turkish firepower until, in 1827, Britain, Russia, and France came in to support the Greek insurgents. They sent a fleet to persuade Turkey to sign a treaty, were accidentally fired upon, and found themselves retaliating. At the end of the battle the allies had sunk 53 of 89 ships of the Turko-Egyptian fleet without a single loss among their 27 war vessels. The sultan was forced to renegotiate, which paved the way for Greek independence. A column rising between a Turkish and a Venetian cannon in the town's main square, Trion Navarchon (Three Admirals) Square, commemorates the leaders of the fleets.

For a closer look of the bay, take an hour-long boat tour to the various monuments on **Sfakteria,** sunken Turkish ships, and the neighboring rock of **Tsichli-Baba,** which has a vast, much-photographed natural arch, nicknamed Tripito, a former pirate hideout with 144 steps. The boats can also take you to the weed-infested 13th-century **Paleokastro,** one of the two fortresses guarding the channels on either side of Sfakteria, and make a stop also at **Nestor's cave.** Boat trips cost about €25; walk along the dock and negotiate with the captains, or ask at the waterside kiosk (staffed only occasionally). The trip is less expensive if you go with a group, but these trips are usually prearranged for the tour buses that drop down to Pylos from Olympia. ✉ *West of Pylos port.*

For views of Pylos, the bay, and the Kamares Roman aqueduct, the **Neokastro,** the newer fortress that dominates the town, is unbeatable. It was built by the Turks in 1573 to control the southern—at that time, the only—entrance to the bay (an artificial embankment had drastically reduced the depth of the northern channel). Neokastro's well-preserved walls enclose the **Church of the Transfiguration,** originally a mosque; cannons; and two anchors from the battle. The highest point of the castle is guarded by a hexagonal fort flanked by towers. A prison in the 18th and 19th centuries, the fort was more secure than most other Greek prisons, because it sometimes housed convicts from the Mani, who continued their blood feuds while behind bars. ✉*Access is by trail from south side of town or off road to Methoni* ☎*27230/22897* 🎫*€2* ⏲*Daily 8–7.*

The small **Antonopouleion Museum,** dedicated to archaeology, has a collection of Hellenistic pottery, Roman bronze statues, engravings, battle memorabilia, gold pots, jewelry, and other objects of the Mycenaean period. ✉*Methonis 8* ☎*27230/22448* 🌐*www.culture.gr* 🎫*€2* ⏲*Tues.–Sun. 8:30–3.*

WHERE TO STAY & EAT

¢–$ ✕**Ta Pente Aderfia.** Grilled meats, popular Greek *magirefta* (precooked dishes served at room temperature), and fresh seafood are served in a plain but attractive room or on the waterfront terrace. Order the special dish called *navomahia* (a seared fillet of beef) served in wine sauce or the *psari macaronada* (an unusual combination of fish and pasta), which has to be ordered a day ahead. All in all, a meal here is a real treat. ✉*Waterfront* ☎*27230/22564* 💳*No credit cards.*

$ 🏨**Karalis Beach.** Set on a piney bluff at the end of town and clinging to rocks above the sea, the bright rooms and their balconies hang directly over the water. The setting—the best thing about the hotel, which could use some renovation—can also be appreciated from a roof terrace that doubles as a breakfast room in good weather. The same management runs the nearby Karalis ($), on a bluff above the bay. ✉*Paralia, 24001* ☎*27230/23021 or 27230/23022* 📠*27230/22970* 🌐*www.karalis.roomstorent.info* 🛏*14 rooms* *In-hotel: bar* 💳*MC, V* ⏲*Closed Nov.–Mar.* 🍽*CP.*

SPORTS & THE OUTDOORS

If you want to putter around the bay on your own, rent a small launch from **Pilos Marine** (✉*Kalamatis 10* ☎*27230/22408* 🌐*www.pilosmarine.com*). Boats seat four to five people, and the cost is €50 for half a day, €60 for a day. A license is not required.

METHONI ΜΕΘΩΝΗ

★ *14 km (9 mi) south of Pylos, 98 km (61 mi) southwest of Kalamata.*

Methoni, a small fishing and farming village and quiet resort on a cape south of Pylos, is so delightful it was one of the seven towns Agamemnon offered Achilles to appease him after his beloved Briseis was carried off. According to Homer, Pedasos, as it was called, was "rich in vines," and tradition says that the town got its modern name because *onoi* (donkeys) carrying the town's wine became *methoun* (intoxicated) from the aroma. The small fishing and farming village is still a delightful place, with long beaches backed by olive groves and vineyards. Modern Methoni is two towns: a low-key settlement huddled on the beach beneath the fortress, and, just above, an animated old town on the crest of a rise—a laid-back, pleasant place to rest travel-weary bones for a few days.

Methoni's principal attraction is its **kastro,** an imposing, well-kept citadel that the Venetians built when they took control of Methoni in 1209. The town already had a long history: After the Second Messenian War in the 7th century BC, the victorious Spartans gave Methoni to the Nafplions, who had been exiled from their homeland for their Spartan alliance. With its natural harbor, the town was an important stop on trade routes between Europe and the East during the Middle Ages. A stone bridge leads over the dry moat to the citadel; various coats of arms mark the walls, including those of Genoa and Venice's Lion of St. Mark. A second bridge joins the kastro with the **Bourtzi,** an octagonal tower built above the crashing surf on a tiny islet during the Turkish occupation (shortly after 1500). ✉ *By coast* ☎ *27310/25363* 🎫 *Free* ⏲ *Nov.–Mar., daily 8:30–3; Apr.–Oct., daily 8:30* AM*–9* PM.

WHERE TO STAY & EAT

$–$$ ✕ **To Akrogiali.** You might want to take off your shoes to reach this seaside fish taverna, tucked against the walls of the fortress right on the beach. The town's small fishing fleet bobs beyond the dining terrace, ensuring that such simple dishes as grilled octopus and mullet are as fresh as you're ever going to find them. ✉ *On beach below fortress* ☎ *27230/31520* ▭ *No credit cards* ⏲ *Closed Nov.–Mar.*

¢–$ ✕ **Alector.** Except in the coldest weather seating here is right in the street—so you get a nice view of village life while enjoying souvlaki and other meats off the wood-fired grill. You can also step into the busy kitchen to choose from the several dishes that are prepared for each meal. ✉ *Main street of town center* ☎ *27230/31830* ▭ *No credit cards.*

¢–$ ✕ **Nikos's.** "The only time this kitchen closes is if I'm sick," says Nikos Vile, who insists on cooking everything from *mamboulas* (a moussaka made with tomatoes) to *maridakia* (lightly fried whitebait) each day. You can sip an aperitif at the bar or hide out in the vine-covered courtyard. ✉ *Miali road near fortress* ☎ *27230/31282* ▭ *No credit cards.*

$ 🏨 **Amalia.** Situated on a hilltop and surrounded by lush gardens, this hotel has a flair that puts it many leagues ahead of other hotels in this category. The basic but pleasant rooms have huge verandas that face the sea and the town, with stunning views of the fortress, about a 15-minute walk away. ✉ *Coastal road to Finikoundas, 24006* ☎ *27230/31129 or 27230/31193* 📠 *27230/31195* 🛏 *36 rooms* 🛎 *In-room: refrigerator. In-hotel: restaurant, bar, no elevator* ▭ *MC, V* ⏲ *Closed Nov.–mid-Mar.* 🍽 *BP.*

¢ ★ 🏨 **Ulysses.** From the shady, well-manicured side garden to the attractive traditional furnishings in the spotless rooms, all aspects of this hotel extend a warm welcome. Balconies have views over the town and sea and each room has an individual heating and cooling unit (important when the mosquitoes are out in force). The breakfast spread is lavish, with fresh orange juice, local yogurt with honey, and freshly baked breads. ✉ *Paralia, 24006* ☎ *27230/31600* 📠 *27230/31646* 🛏 *12 rooms* 🛎 *In-hotel: restaurant, bar, no elevator* ▭ *MC* 🍽 *BP.*

FESTIVAL

On **Kathari Deftera** *("Clean Monday")* , before Lent, Methoni holds a mock village wedding at the town square, a riotous annual performance, in which both the bride and groom are played by men.

LACONIA ΛΑΚΩΝΙΑ

The Laconian plain is surrounded on three sides by mountains and on one side by the sea. Perhaps it was the fear that enemies could descend those mountains at any time that drove the Spartans to make Laconia their training ground, where they developed the finest fighting force in ancient Greece. A mighty power that controlled three-fifths of the Peloponnese, Sparta contributed to the Greek victory in the Second Persian War (5th century BC). Ultimately, Sparta's aggressiveness and jealousy of Athens brought about the Peloponnesian War, which drained the city's resources but left it victorious. The Greek world found Sparta to be an even harsher master than Athens, and this fact may have led to its losses in the Boeotian and Corinthian wars, at the Battle of Leuctra, and, in 222–221 BC, at the hands of the Achaean League, who liberated all areas Sparta had conquered. A second period of prosperity under the Romans ended with the barbarian invasions in the 3rd century AD, and Sparta declined rapidly.

Laconia can also claim two important magnificently medieval sites: Mystras and Monemvassia. The former was an intellectual and political center, the latter a sea fortress meant to ward off invaders from the east.

SPARTA ΣΠΑΡΤΗ

60 km (37 mi) south of Tripoli, 60 km (37 mi) east of Kalamata.

For those who have read about ancient Sparta, the bellicose city-state that once dominated the Greek world, the modern city on the broad Eurotas River might be a disappointment, since ruins are few and far between. Given the area's earthquakes and the Spartans' no-frills approach—living more like an army camp than a city-state—no elaborate ruins remain, a fact that so disconcerted Otto, Greece's first king, that in 1835 he ordered the modern city built on the ancient site. The modern town is not terribly attractive, but it's pleasant enough, with a pedestrian-only city center.

At the **Temple of Artemis Orthia** (✉ *Tripoli road, down path to Eurotas River*), outside town, the young Spartan men underwent *krypteia* (initiations) that entailed severe public floggings. The altar had to be splashed with blood before the goddess was satisfied. Traces of two such altars are among sparse vestiges of the 6th-century BC temple. The larger ruins are the remains of a grandstand built in the 3rd century AD by the Romans, who revived the flogging tradition as a public spectacle.

CLOSE UP

The Spartan Ethic

The Spartans' relentless militarism set them apart from other Greeks in the ancient world. They were expected to emerge victorious from a battle or not at all, and for most of its existence Sparta was without a wall, because according to Lykourgos, who wrote Sparta's constitution sometime around 600 BC, "chests, not walls, make a city." The government was an oligarchy, with two kings who also served as military leaders. Spartan society had three classes: a privileged elite involved with warfare and government; farmers, traders, and craftspeople, who paid taxes; and the numerous Helots, a serf class with few rights.

Selected boys in the reigning warrior class were taken from their parents at the age of seven and submitted to a training regimen without parallel in history for its ruthlessness. Their diet involved mostly herbs, roots, and the famous black broth, which included pork, the blood of the pig, and vinegar. Rich foods were thought to stunt growth. Forbidden to work, boys and young men trained for combat and practiced stealing, an acceptable skill—it was believed to teach caution and cunning—unless one was caught. One legend describes a Spartan youth who let a concealed fox chew out his bowels rather than reveal his theft. Girls also trained rigorously in the belief they would bear healthier offspring; for the same reason, newlyweds were forbidden to make love frequently.

The kingdom's iron coinage was not accepted outside Sparta's borders, creating a contempt for wealth and luxury (and, in turn, rapacious kings and generals). Sparta's warrior caste subjugated the native Achaean inhabitants of the region. Today all that remains of this realm founded on martial superiority is dust.

Ancient Sparta's **acropolis** (⊠*North end of town*) is now part archaeological site, part park. Locals can be seen here strolling, along with many young couples stealing a romantic moment amid the fallen limestone and shady trees. The ruins include a **theater,** a **stadium,** and a **sanctuary to Athena.**

Stop a moment and contemplate the stern **Statue of Leonidas** (⊠*End of Konstantinou*). During the Second Persian War in the 5th century BC, with 30,000 Persians advancing on his army of 8,000, Leonidas, ordered to surrender his weapons, jeered, "Come and get them." For two days he held off the enemy, until a traitor named Efialtes (the word has since come to mean "nightmare" in Greek) showed the Persians a way to attack from the rear. Leonidas ordered all but 300 Spartans and 700 Thespians to withdraw, and when forced to retreat to a wooded knoll, he is said to have commented, "So much the better, we will fight in the shade." His entire troop was slaughtered.

The eclectic collection of the **archaeological museum** reflects Laconia's turbulent history and is worth an hour: Neolithic pottery; jewels and tools excavated from the Alepotripia cave; Mycenaean tomb finds; bright 4th- and 5th-century Roman mosaics; and objects from Sparta. Most characteristic of Spartan art are the bas-reliefs with deities and heroes;

note the one depicting a seated couple bearing gifts and framed by a snake (540 BC). ✉*Ayios Nikonos between Dafnou and Evangelistria* ☎*27310/28575* 🌐*www.culture.gr* 🎫*€2* ⏲*Tues.–Sat. 8:30–3, Sun. 8:30–12:30.*

THE BEST GYRO IN SPARTA

If you find yourself waiting for a bus out of Sparta at dinnertime, cross the street to **Parthenon** (✉*Vrasidou 106* ☎*27310/23767*) for the best gyro you may ever eat. The meat, which has a local reputation for being a cut above the usual, is served in pita with the right amount of chew and generous doses of onion, tomato, and tzatziki sauce.

Olives are thick on the ground in these parts, so it's only fitting that Sparta is home to the **Museum of the Olive and Greek Olive Oil,** a quirky and appealing collection of apparatus and culture related to the staple of Greek economy since ancient times, housed in stunning renovation of the city's first electricity works. Ancient oil lamps and storage jars are especially beautiful, and exhibits tracing the botany and cultivation of the olive are fascinating. ✉*Othonos-Amalias 129* ☎*27310/89315* 🌐*www.piop.gr* 🎫*€2* ⏲*Mar.–Oct. 15, Wed.–Mon. 10–6.*

WHERE TO STAY & EAT

¢–$ ✕**Diethnes.** Locals claim this is one of Sparta's best restaurants, but then again, most head out to village tavernas for a big meal and leave this place to the tour-bus crowd. Classic specialties include a fish dish made with garlic, wine, oil, and rusks; *bardouniotiko* (chicken cooked with cheese and olives); and, occasionally, sheep's heads cooked on a spit. The tree-shaded garden rounds out a perfect meal. ✉*Paleologou 105* ☎*27310/28636* 💳*No credit cards.*

$ ★ ✕🏨**Maniatis Hotel.** The sleek style here begins in the modern marble lobby and extends through the handsome guest rooms, with their contemporary, light-wood furnishings and soft, soothing colors. All rooms have balconies, wall-to-wall carpeting, and sparkling baths. The restaurant serves such specialties as *arni araxobitiko* (lamb with onions, cheese, red sauce, and walnuts) and *bourekakia* (honey-and-nut pastries). ✉*Paleologou 72, 23100* ☎*27310/22665* 📠*27310/29994* 🌐*www.maniatishotel.gr* 🛏*80 rooms* 👍*In-hotel: restaurant, bar* 💳*MC, V* 🍴*BP.*

$$ 🏨**Menelaion Hotel.** The pool sparkling in the courtyard—a welcome sight after a hot day of exploring the ruins of nearby Mystras—is the best thing about this city-center hotel. Guest rooms are nicely if somewhat blandly furnished and well equipped, with modern bathrooms, most with tubs. ✉*Paleologou 91, 23100* ☎*27310/22161 through 27310/22165* 📠*27310/26332* 🌐*www.menelaion.com* 🛏*30 rooms* 👍*In-hotel: restaurant, bar, pool* 💳*AE, MC, V* 🍴*BP.*

MYSTRAS ΜΥΣΤΡΑΣ

4 km (2½ mi) west of Sparta, 64 km (40 mi) southwest of Tripoli.

Fodor'sChoice ★ At Mystras, abandoned gold and stone palaces, churches, and monasteries line serpentine paths; the scent of herbs and wildflowers permeates the air; goat bells tinkle; and silvery olive trees glisten with the slightest breeze. An intellectual and cultural center where philosophers like Chrysoloras, "the sage of Byzantium," held forth on the good and the beautiful, Mystras seems an appropriate place for the last hurrah of the Byzantine emperors in the 14th century. Today the splendid ruins are a UNESCO World Heritage Site and one of the most impressive sights in the Peloponnese. A pleasant modern town adjoins the ruins.

In 1249 William Geoffrey de Villehardouin built the castle in Mystras in an attempt to control Laconia and establish Frankish supremacy over the Peloponnese. He held court here with his Greek wife, Anna Comnena, surrounded by knights of Champagne, Burgundy, and Flanders, but in 1259 he was defeated by the Byzantines. As the Byzantines built a palace and numerous churches (whose frescoes exemplified several periods of painting), the town gradually grew down the slope.

At first the seat of the Byzantine governor, Mystras later became the capital of the Despotate of Morea. It was the despots who made Mystras a cultural phenomenon, and it was the despots—specifically Emperor Constantine's brother Demetrios Palaiologos—who surrendered the city to the Turks in 1460, signaling the beginning of the end. For a while the town survived because of its silk industry, but after repeated pillaging and burning by bands of Albanians, Russians, and Ibrahim Pasha's Egyptian troops, the inhabitants gave up and moved to modern Sparta.

Among the most important buildings in the lower town (Kato Chora) is **Ayios Demetrios,** the *mitropolis* (cathedral) founded in 1291. Set in its floor is a stone with the two-headed Byzantine eagle marking the spot where Constantine XII, the last emperor of Byzantium, was consecrated. The cathedral's brilliant frescoes include a vivid depiction of the Virgin and the infant Jesus on the central apse and a wall painting in the narthex of the Second Coming, its two red-and-turquoise-winged angels sorrowful as they open the records of Good and Evil. One wing of the church houses a **museum** that holds fragments of Byzantine sculptures, later Byzantine icons, decorative metalwork, and coins.

In the Vrontokion monastery are **Ayios Theodoros** (AD 1295), the oldest church in Mystras, and the 14th-century **Church of Panagia Odegetria,** or **Afendiko,** which is decorated with remarkable murals. These include, in the narthex, scenes of the miracles of Christ: *The Healing of the Blind Man, The Samaritan at the Well,* and *The Marriage of Cana.* The fluidity of the brushstrokes, the subtle but complicated coloring, and the resonant expressions suggest the work of extremely skilled hands.

The **Pantanassa monastery** is a visual feast of intricate tiling, rosette-festooned loops, and myriad arches. It is the only inhabited building in Mystras; the hospitable nuns still produce embroidery that you can purchase. Step out onto the east portico for a view of the Eurotas River valley below.

Every inch of the tiny **Perivleptos monastery,** meaning "attracting attention from all sides," is covered with exceptional 14th-century illustrations from the New Testament, including *The Birth of the Virgin*; in a lush palette of reds, yellows, and oranges; *The Dormition of the Virgin* above the entrance (with Christ holding his mother's soul represented as a baby); and, immediately to the left of the entrance, the famous fresco the *Divine Liturgy.*

COVER YOUR HEAD AND WATCH YOUR STEP

In spring Mystras is resplendent with wildflowers and butterflies, but it can be oppressively hot in summer, so get an early start to avoid exploring the site in the midday sun. That said, it's easy to spend half a day here, so bring water, sunscreen, a hat, and sturdy shoes for traction on slippery rocks. And be wary of the occasional snake.

In the upper town (Ano Chora), where most aristocrats lived, stands a rare Byzantine civic building, the **Palace of Despots,** home of the last emperor. The older, northeastern wing contains a guardroom, a kitchen, and the residence. The three-story northwest wing contains an immense reception hall on its top floor, lighted by eight Gothic windows and heated by eight huge chimneys; the throne probably stood in the shallow alcove that's in the center of a wall.

In the palace's **Ayia Sofia chapel,** the Italian wives of emperors Constantine and Theodore Palaiologos are buried. Note the polychromatic marble floor and the frescoes that were preserved for years under whitewash, applied by the Turks when they transformed this into a mosque. Climb to the **castle** and look down into the gullies of Mt. Taygettus, where it's said the Spartans, who hated weakness, hurled their malformed babies. ✉ *Ano Chora* ☎ *27310/83377* 🌐 *www.culture.gr* 🎟 *All Mystras sites €5* ⏲ *Nov.–Apr., daily 8:30–3; May and Oct., daily 8–5; Sept., daily 8–6; June–Aug., daily 8–7.*

WHERE TO STAY & EAT

¢–$ ✕ **Stelakos.** This spot about 2 km (1 mi) east of Mystras, on the road to Sparta, is known for excellent chicken dishes. After enjoying its rustic pleasures, take a stroll outside for an unimpeded view of the Taygettus mountain range. You can sip an after-dinner coffee or ouzo in one of the tavernas in the main square, where waterfalls rush down a cliff face. ✉ *Off village square, Parori* ☎ *27310/83346* ▭ *No credit cards* ⏲ *Closed Sun.*

$$$$ Fodor's Choice ★ 🏨 **Pyrgos of Mystras.** A stone mansion set in a fragrant garden at the edge of the modern town is the setting for a luxurious and stylish hotel where guests feel like pampered visitors in a rather extraordinary home. Rooms are beautifully decorated with rich colors and fabrics; they overlook orange groves and Mt. Taygettus. The stone-walled public rooms (including one with an Arabesque theme) and shady terraces

are a delight as well, as are the friendly welcome and attentive service. ✉*Manousaki 3, 23100 Mystras* ☎*27310/20870* 🌐*www.pyrgosmystra.com* *7 rooms* *In-room: ethernet. In hotel: bar, no elevator* *AE, MC, V* *BP.*

SPORTS & THE OUTDOORS

The Athens travel agency **Trekking Hellas** (✉*Fillelinon 7, 10557 Athens* ☎*210/331–0323* 🌐*www.trekking.gr*) arranges weekend hiking trips to Mystras and a six-day walk through the Taygettus foothills, with visits to the Mani and Mystras.

GYTHION ΓΥΘΕΙΟ

79 km (49 mi) north of Vathia, 46 km (29 mi) south of Sparta.

Gythion, at the foot of the Taygettus range, will seem terribly cosmopolitan once you've been driving through the adjacent stark countryside. Graceful pastel 19th-century houses march up the steep hillside, and along the busy harbor, fruit-laden donkeys sidestep the peanut vendors and gypsies hawking strings of garlic. Laconia's main port, the town is the Laconian gateway to the Mani peninsula. It claims Hercules and Apollo as its founders and survives today by exporting olives, oil, rice, and citrus fruits.

Gythion has a few rather insignificant ruins, including a well-preserved **Roman theater** (✉*Archaio Theatrou*) with stone seats intact.

Some remains of the ancient town (Laryssion) are visible on **Mt. Koumaros** (*2 km [1 mi] north along road to Monemvassia*), a settlement that in Roman times exported the murex shell for dyeing imperial togas purple.

NEED A BREAK?

Take a late-afternoon break for grilled octopus and ouzo; Gythion is the octopus capital of Greece. The best place is Nautilia (✉*Southern end of waterfront, across from pier*); look for the octopuses dangling in the doorway.

On the tiny islet of **Marathonissi** (✉*East of Gythion*), once called Kranae, Paris and Helen (wife of Menelaos) consummated their love affair after escaping Sparta, provoking the Trojan War described in the *Iliad*. A causeway now joins Marathonissi to Gythion.

The **Pyrgos Tzannetaki Tower** on the island houses a museum of the Mani. ✉*Marathonissi* ☎*27330/22676* *€2* *Daily 9:30–5.*

BEACHES

Near Gythion there are beaches on the coast between Mavrovouni and Skoutari and north of town on the road to Monemvassia. About 10 km (6 mi) north of Gythion the Monemvassia road passes a long, sandy beach that, aside from the presence of a rusted freighter that ran aground here, is clean and idyllic.

WHERE TO STAY & EAT

¢–$$ ★ ✕ **Isalos.** Though hardwood floors and tasteful pale walls lend Isalos a sophisticated air, at heart this is a friendly waterfront taverna with seating on the sidewalk and alongside the harbor—and a focus on the freshest fish. The menu lists some pastas and other Italian dishes, alongside traditional Greek fare. All can be accompanied by barrel wine from the family vineyard. ✉ *Vassileos Pavlou 35* ☎ *27330/24024* ▭ *No credit cards.*

¢–$ ✕ **Sinantisi.** The freshest seasonal local produce—artichokes in spring, squash and eggplant in summer, wild greens in winter—enhances the *catserolas* (casserole-style dishes) at this grill. You may also order fresh fish, appetizers such as *tzatziki* (cucumber-yogurt dip) and *taramosalata* (pink fish-roe dip), and homemade sweets such as clove-scented baklava. The restaurant is about 2 km (1 mi) south of Gythion off the main road to Areopolis. ✉ *Town square, Mavrovouni* ☎ *27330/22256* ▭ *MC, V* ⊗ *No lunch.*

$ **Aktaion.** All of the rooms in this neoclassic building face the sea, and all have balconies. The style throughout is traditional, with some modern furnishings and old prints of Maniote life, and the overall ambience is that of a comfortable, well-maintained hotel. ✉ *Vassileos Pavlou 39, 23200* ☎ *27330/23500 or 27330/23501* 🖷 *27330/22294* *22 rooms* ▭ *No credit cards* *CP.*

$ **Gythion Hotel.** A former gentleman's club from 1864 is now a waterfront hotel, entered off a flight of steps from the harbor. Rooms are rather narrow but have high ceilings and face the sea, and many have several beds to accommodate families; two apartments have kitchenettes. A hearty breakfast is served in a vaulted lounge. ✉ *Vassileos Pavlou 33, 23200* ☎ *27330/23452* 🖷 *27330/23523* 🌐 *www.gythionhotel.gr* *5 rooms, 2 apartments* *In-room: kitchen (some), refrigerator* ▭ *No credit cards* *BP.*

MONEMVASSIA ΜΟΝΕΜΒΑΣΙΑ

96 km (60 mi) southeast of Sparta.

Fodor's Choice ★ The Byzantine town of Monemvassia clings to the side of the 1,148-foot rock that was once a headland, but in AD 375 was separated from the mainland by an earthquake. The town was first settled in the 6th century AD, when Laconians sought refuge after Arab and Slav raids. Monemvassia—the name *moni emvasia* (single entrance) refers to the narrow passage to this walled community—once enjoyed enormous prosperity, and for centuries dominated the sea lanes from Western Europe to the Levant. During its golden age in the 1400s, Monemvassia was home to families made wealthy by their inland estates and the export of malmsey wine, a sweet variety of Madeira praised by Shakespeare. When the area fell to the Turks, Monemvassia was controlled first by the pope and then by the Venetians, who built the citadel and most of the fortifications. The newer settlement that has spread out along the water on the mainland is not as romantic as the old town, but it's pleasant and well equipped with shops and services.

Well-to-do Greeks once again live on the rock in houses they have restored as vacation homes. Summer weekends are crowded, but off-season Monemvassia is nearly deserted. Houses are lined up along steep streets only wide enough for two people abreast, among remnants of another age—escutcheons, marble thrones, Byzantine icons. It's a delight to wander through the back lanes and along the old walls, and to find perches high above the town or the sea.

If you walk or drive from the adjoining town of Gefira, the rock looks uninhabited until you suddenly see castellated walls with an opening wide enough for one person. An overnight stay here allows you to enjoy this strange place when the tour groups have departed.

Christos Elkomenos (*Christ in Chains* ✉*Tzamiou Sq. along main street*) is reputedly the largest medieval church in southern Greece. The carved peacocks on its portal are symbolic of the Byzantine era; the detached bell tower—like those of Italian cathedrals—is a sign of Venetian rebuilding in the 17th century.

The 10th-century **Ayios Pavlos** (✉*Across from Tzamiou Sq.*), though converted into a mosque, was allowed to function as a church under the Ottoman occupation, an unusual indulgence.

For solitude and a dizzying view, pass through the upper town's wooden entrance gates, complete with the original iron reinforcement. Up the hill is a rare example of a domed octagonal church, **Ayia Sofia** (✉*At top of mountain*), founded in the 13th century by Emperor Andronicus II and patterned after Dafni monastery in Athens. Follow the path to the highest point on the rock for a breathtaking view of the coast.

OFF THE BEATEN PATH

Island of Elafonisi. Following the Laconic peninsula south from Monemvassia toward Neapolis for 35 km (22 mi) brings you to the village of Viglafia, where car ferries depart about every half hour (€2 for foot passengers, €8 for cars) for the 15-minute crossing to the island of Elafonisi. This is where Greeks retreat for a fish lunch in the delightful little port town and then spend the afternoon on miles-long sandy strands that may well be the best, and least-discovered, beaches in Greece. A number of small hotels on the island may tempt you to linger.

10

BEACHES

Some people swim off the rocks at the base of the old town and along the road leading to the main gate, but safer and more appealing is the pebble beach in the new town. For the most rewarding beach experience, head to the sandy strands at Pori, about 5 km (3 mi) northwest of Monemvassia.

WHERE TO STAY & EAT

¢–$$ ✕**To Kanoni.** After you roll out of bed, wander over to the Kanoni, which serves breakfast on a terrace overlooking the square's *kanoni* (cannon). Choose from omelets, ham and eggs, or thick, creamy yogurt and honey. Among the lunch and dinner offerings are eggplant baked with other fresh vegetables and feta, and *yiouvetsi* (beef baked in a clay pot with orzolike pasta). ✉*Old town* ☎*27320/61387* ▭*No credit cards.*

¢–$ **Marianthi.** You'll feel as if you're dropping into someone's home at dinner here: family photos of stern, mustachioed ancestors hang on the walls along with local memorabilia, and the service, at tables on the street in good weather, is just as homey. Order the wild mountain greens, any of the fish—especially the fresh red mullet—the addictive potato salad (you may have to order two plates), and the marinated octopus sprinkled with oregano. ⊠*Old town* ☎*27320/61371* ▭*No credit cards.*

$$–$$$ ★ **Byzantino.** These comfortable and unusual accommodations are in several stone buildings in the old town. All the rooms are different, embellished with tile work and other distinctive decorations, and some are multilevel. Less-expensive rooms do not have terraces or sea views but are still quite charming. If mobility is a concern, be advised that reaching many of the rooms requires clambering down narrow, unevenly paved lanes and climbing stairs. Breakfast is €6. ⊠*Old town, 23070* ☎*27320/61351 or 27320/61254* ⊕*www.yourgreece.com* *25 rooms* *In-room: kitchen (some), no TV. In-hotel: restaurant, bar* ▭*MC, V.*

$$ ★ **Malvasia.** Three restored buildings in the old town (reached on a trek over sometimes steep and uneven pavement) provide atmospheric lodgings. Rooms are tucked into nooks and crannies under cane-and-wood or vaulted brick ceilings. Each is decorated with bright patchwork rugs, embroidered tapestries, antique marble, and antique wood furniture. Many rooms have terraces and sea views, and some have fireplaces. Reserve well ahead in July and August. ⊠*Old town, 23070* ☎*27320/61323 or 27320/61113* ⎙*27320/61722* *32 rooms* *In-room: kitchen, no TV. In-hotel: bar* ▭*AE, MC, V* *CP.*

¢ **Hotel Pramataris.** When there is no room at the old town's inns, or if you don't like the idea of carting your baggage, this sparkling seaside hotel in the new town is a wonderful alternative and a real bargain. The management is friendly and helpful; the bright, tile-floored rooms have balconies; and the beach is steps away, making this an excellent choice for families. Some units have connecting doors and can be combined. ⊠*New town, on sea, 23070* ☎*27320/61833* ⊕*www.pramatarishotel.gr* *17 rooms, 1 suite* *In-room: refrigerator. In-hotel: beachfront, no elevator* ▭*MC, V* *CP.*

¢ **Ta Kellia.** Built in an old monastery (*kellia* means "cells"), this establishment is now run, albeit a little haphazardly, by the Greek National Tourism Organization. Though the hotel is not glamorous like the competition, the rough-hewn rooms are a good, comfortable alternative. Only a few rooms on the second floor have ocean views, but all face an airy plaza above the sea. ⊠*Old town, on lower square opposite Church of Panagia Chrissafitissa, 23070* ☎*27320/61520* *11 rooms* *In-room: no a/c, no TV* ▭*No credit cards.*

SHOPPING

Ioanna Anghelatou (⊠*Main street, old town* ☎*27320/61163*), established by Ms. Anghelatou in the 1980s, has a loyal clientele for her extraordinary collection of antique and contemporary jewelry, much of it crafted by artisans from throughout Greece.

SOUTHERN PELOPONNESE ESSENTIALS

TRANSPORTATION

BY AIR

Olympic Airlines offers daily one-hour flights from Athens to Kalamata's airport, 10½ km (6½ mi) outside town near Messinia.

Contacts **Kalamata Airport** (*☎ 27210/69442*). **Olympic Airlines** (*☎ 210/926-7555 Athens reservations line ✉ Giatrakou 3, Kalamata ☎ 27210/86410 ⊕ www.olympic-airways.gr*).

BY BIKE & MOPED

A number of agencies in the area rent mopeds. For information on cycling in Greece, contact the Greek Cycling Federation.

Contacts **Greek Cycling Federation** (*✉ Bouboulinas 28, Athens ☎ 210/883-1413*). **Maniatis** (*✉ Iatropoulou 1, Kalamata ☎ 27210/27694 ✉ Faron 202, Kalamata ☎ 27210/26025*).

BY BOAT & FERRY

Anen Lines runs five times weekly in winter and daily in summer between Gythion, Neapolis, and Kythera. There is also weekly service from Kalamata and Gythion to Kissamos (Kastelli) on Crete. In the Peloponnese, call the local port authority for the latest information on boat travel. Unfortunately, Hellas Flying Dolphins, which once connected Athens (Zea Marina in Pireaus) and Monemvassia, no longer operates, though there is talk of restoring service.

Information **Anen Lines** (*☎ 28210/20345 ⊕ www.anen.gr*). **Port Authorities** (*☎ 27330/22262 in Gythion, 27210/22218 in Kalamata, 27320/61113 in Monemvassia, 27210/23100 in Pylos*).

BY BUS

The association of regional bus companies (KTEL) provides frequent service at reasonable prices from Athens to the Southern Peloponnese, with buses several times daily for Gythion, Kalamata, and Tripoli and once a day for Andritsena, Monemvassia, and Pylos. Buses leave from Terminal A on the outskirts of Athens at Kifissou 100 (take Bus 051 at corner of Zinonos and Menandrou streets, near Omonia Square; from the airport, take Bus E93). Pick up a bus schedule from the Athens EOT (*⇨ Visitor Information in Athens Essentials in Chapter 1*) or call the number listed below for departure times or seat reservations.

In the Peloponnese, you may buy tickets at a local bus station. The network of bus routes lets you move easily, even to more remote sites such as the Pirgos Dirou Caves and Nestor's Palace museum in Chora; however, you will be limited by timing, as many remote places are served only by one or two buses a day. Sparta is a major bus hub for the Southern Peloponnese, and from there you can make connections to Monemvassia, Gythion, Areopolis, Andritsena, and other towns and cities, with at least several buses a day. There are fewer buses in winter and on weekends. For short distances, you may buy tickets on board; otherwise purchase them in advance at the station.

Information **KTEL (Greek Coach Services) Station Office** (☎ *210/513–4574 in Andritsena, 210/512–4913 in Gythion, 210/513–4293 in Kalamata, 210/512–4913 in Monemvassia, 210/513–4293 in Pylos, 210/512–4913 in Sparta, 210/513–2834 in Tripoli*). **Local bus stations** (✉ *Main square, Andritsena* ☎ *26260/22239* ✉ *Ebrikleous at north end of harbor, Gythion* ☎ *27330/22228* ✉ *Artemidos 50, Kalamata* ☎ *27210/22851* ✉ *Off main square, Monemvassia* ☎ *27320/61432* ✉ *Trion Navarchon Sq., Pylos* ☎ *27230/22230* ✉ *Vrasidou and Paleologou, Sparta* ☎ *27310/26441* ✉ *Kolokotronis Sq., Tripoli* ☎ *2710/224314*). **Terminal A** (✉ *Kifissou 100, Athens* ☎ *210/512–4910* 🌐 *www.ktel.org*).

BY CAR

Especially off-season, when buses don't run regularly, it's most rewarding to explore this region by car. You can rent a car in Athens or in any of the Peloponnese's bigger towns, such as Kalamata, Tripoli, Gythion, and Sparta.

Even if highways have assigned numbers, no Greek knows them by any other than their informal names, usually linked to their destination. For those traveling on the E92 from Athens to Tripoli, the section of the highway (the Corinth–Tripoli road) now cuts travel time in half, to little more than two hours. From Olympia in the northwest Peloponnese, you may take a smaller local road (74, the Pirgos–Tripoli road). Both approaches have mountainous stretches that occasionally close in winter because of snow, but conditions are otherwise good. Narrow roads cross mountainous terrain throughout the region, providing many a scenic route when not closed due to snow in winter.

You'll need a good map to navigate the back roads of the Southern Peloponnese, as well as a transliteration of the Greek alphabet—many signs on remote roads are in Greek only. Gas stations are few and far between in some places, so top off the tank when you have the chance.

Rental Agencies **Hertz** (✉ *Faron 186, Kalamata* ☎ *27210/88268* 🌐 *www.hertz.com*). **Kottaras Rent-A-Car** (✉ *Menelaon 54, Sparta* ☎ *27310/28966* 🌐 *www.kottaras-car-rentals.com*).

EMERGENCIES The Automobile Touring Club of Greece (ELPA) provides assistance for light repairs around the clock. There are also ELPA main offices in Kalamata and Tripoli.

Contact **Automobile Touring Club of Greece** (*ELPA* ☎ *104 road assistance, 210/606–8800 other information*).

BY TAXI

If you have trouble reaching a site—for example, there is no public transportation to Ancient Messene—take a taxi from a town's main square, which is always near the bus station. In rural areas drivers may not switch on the meter if the destination has a fixed price, but make sure you agree on the cost before getting in—remember that it's the same price whether you're alone or in a company of four. It's the mileage that counts. When leaving town limits, the driver may switch his meter to the higher rate (Tarifa 2). The price also goes up after midnight. If you think you've been had, don't hesitate to protest or threaten to report the driver to the police.

BY TRAIN

Train travel into the area is slower and much more limited than bus travel. Buy tickets before you leave; prices shoot up 50% when purchased on board. If you're traveling during a national holiday, when many Athenians head to the Peloponnese, it's worth paying extra for first class to ensure a seat, especially in no-smoking compartments. Train food is dismal, so stock up for long trips.

Trains run from Athens to Kalamata five times daily with stops in Corinth, Mycenae, and Tripoli, not to be confused with those traveling a second, longer route to Kalamata via Patras. In Athens, the Greek National Railway (OSE) offices are the most convenient if you're staying near Syntagma (Constitution) Square; otherwise purchase your ticket before departure at the Peloponnissos station. You can reach the station by Bus 057, which leaves every 10 minutes from Panepistimiou, or take Line 2 of the metro to the Larissa station, which is adjacent to the Peloponnissos station.

As of this writing, extensive track work is being done on the Peloponnesian line, with a goal of significantly improving service between Athens and Patras. Check for service interruptions and station changes by contacting one of the numbers below.

Information **Greek National Railway (OSE) offices** (✉ *Fillelinon 17, Athens* ☎ *210/323-6747* ✉ *Sina 6, Athens* ☎ *210/362-4402*). **Kalamata station** (✉ *Sidirodromikou Stathmou* ☎ *27210/23904*). **Peloponnissos station** (✉ *Karilou 1, Athens* ☎ *210/522-4302*). **Tripoli station** (✉ *Grigoris Lambraki at Xeniou Dios* ☎ *2710/222402*).

CONTACTS & RESOURCES

EMERGENCIES

Emergency information is listed below by region.

Contacts **Medical assistance** (☎ *27330/51259 first aid in Areopolis, 27330/22315 hospital in Areopolis, 27330/22001 through 27330/22003 clinic in Gythion, 27210/25555 first aid in Kalamata, 27210/23561 hospital in Kalamata, 2731/28671 first aid in Sparta, 2731/28672 hospital in Sparta*). **Police** (☎ *27330/51209 in Areopolis, 27330/22100 in Gythion, 27210/23187 in Kalamata, 27230/31203 in Methoni, 27320/61210 in Monemvassia, 27230/22316 in Pylos, 27310/28701 in Sparta, 2710/222411 in Tripoli*).

TOUR OPTIONS

Unlike in the Northern Peloponnese, the choice of English-language tours in the south is extremely limited. If an agency does venture into the region, it's usually a detour through Tripoli and Sparta for a cursory visit to Mystras, as part of a package to the Northern Peloponnese.

VISITOR INFORMATION

The Southern Peloponnese is underserved by tourist offices, and your best bet will be the tourist police, who usually speak English and can help you find accommodations, restaurants, and sights. You can reach them by dialing 171 or local numbers. Beware of good-intentioned locals if you ask for directions to the tourist office—they may lead you to private travel agents (who can indeed be helpful) or to municipal offices that are not geared to helping the public.

Contacts **Tourist police** (☎ *171, 27210/95555 in Kalamata, 27310/20492 in Sparta, 2710/222411 in Tripoli*).

The Cyclades

TINOS, MYKONOS, DELOS, NAXOS, PAROS, SANTORINI, FOLEGANDROS, SIFNOS & SYROS

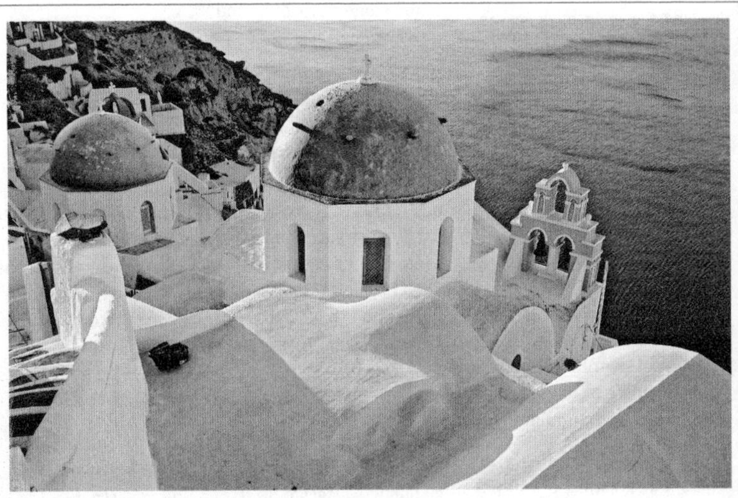

Ia, Santorini

WORD OF MOUTH

"I'd always heard that Naxos has the best beaches in the Cyclades and our visit there last year confirmed it."

—repete

"Yes, I would bring the ring to Santorini . . . suggest a romantic restaurant with a sunset view of the caldera. Catch her at that moment! If she loves you and has a pulse she can't say no."

—worldinabag

www.fodors.com/forums

WELCOME TO THE CYCLADES

Fishing harbors dot the coastof Sifnos

TOP REASONS TO GO

★ **Atlantis Found?:** Volcanic, spectacular Santorini is possibly the last remnant of the "lost continent"—the living here is as high as the towns' cliff-top perches.

★ **Ariadne's Island:** Mythic haunt of the ancient Minoan princess, Naxos is the largest of the Cyclades and is noted for its 16th-century Venetian homes.

★ **Lively, Liberated Mykonos:** The rich arrive by yacht, the middle class by plane, the backpackers by boat—but everyone is out to enjoy the golden sands and Dionysian nightlife.

★ **Cubism, Cycladic Style:** The smiling island of Sifnos is studded with mirage-like, white clusters of houses that tumble down hillsides like so many cubist sculptures.

★ **Tantalizing Antiparos:** Hiding within the shadow of its mother island of Paros, this long-forgotten jewel has been discovered by Hollywood high-rollers like Tom Hanks and Brad Pitt.

1 Tinos. Among the most beautiful of the Cyclades, Tinos's charms remains largely unheralded but include the "Greek Lourdes"—the Panayia Evangelistria church—1,000 traditional stone dovecotes, and idyllic villages like Pirgos.

2 Mykonos. Party Central because of its nonstop nightlife, the chief village of Mykonos, called Mykonos town, is the Cyclades's best preserved—a maze of flatstone streets lined with white houses and flower-filled balconies. A short boat ride away is hallowed Delos, sacred to Apollo.

3 Naxos. Presided over by the historic port of Naxos town, largely the creation of the Venetian dukes of the archipelago, Naxos has a landscape graced with time-stained villages like Sangri, Chalki, and Apeiranthos, many with Venetian-era towers.

4 Paros. West of Naxos and known for its fine beaches and fishing villages, as well as the pretty town of Naousa, Paros often takes the summer overflow crowd from Mykonos. Today, crowds head here for Paros town and its Hundred Doors Church and great ferry harbor.

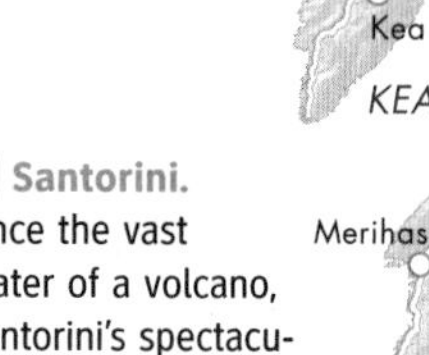

5 Santorini. Once the vast crater of a volcano, Santorini's spectacular bay is ringed by black-and-red cliffs that rise up a thousand feet over the sea. The main towns of Fira and Ia cling inside the rim in dazzling white contrast to the somber cliffs. South lies the "Greek Pompeii" that is ancient Akrotiri.

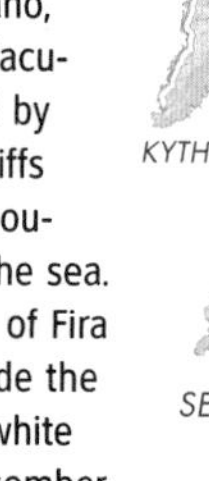

6 Folegandros. Tides of travelers have yet to discover this stark island, which makes it all the more alluring to Cyclades lovers, particularly those who prize its stunning cliff scenery.

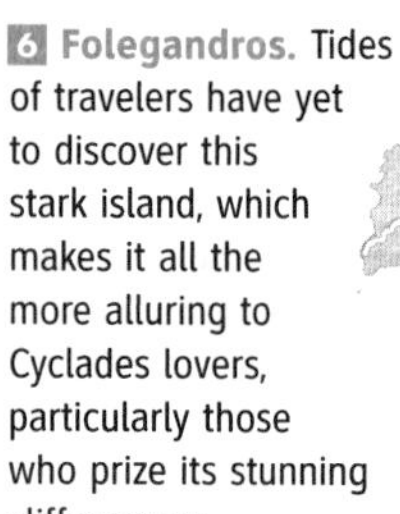

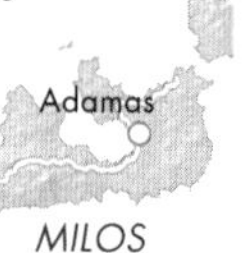

7 Sifnos. In ancient days famed for its silver mines, Sifnos is now noted for its Siphnian cooking, its traditional pottery, and perfect Cycladic houses. The capital of Apollonia extends over three hills, offering jaw-dropping vistas.

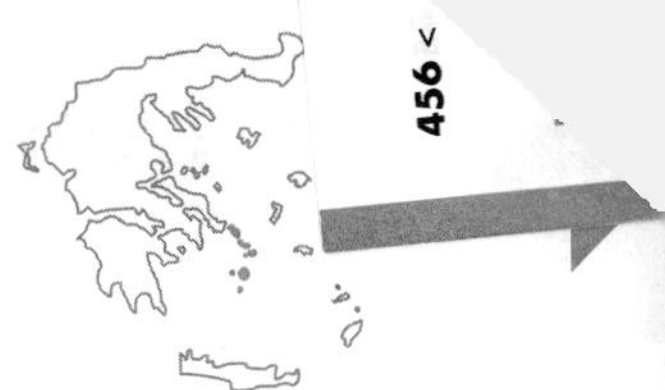

GETTING ORIENTED

Set in the heart of the Grecian Mediterranean, these nearly 2,000 islands and islets are scattered like a ring (Cyclades is the Greek word for "circling ones") around the sacred isle of Delos, birthplace of the god Apollo. All the top spots—Santorini, Naxos, Paros, Mykonos, Tinos, Sifnos, and Folegandros—are beloved for their postcard-perfect olive groves, stark whitewashed cubist houses, and bays of lapis lazuli. Gateways to this Aegean archipelago include the airports on Mykonos and Santorini and the harbors of Paros and Syros.

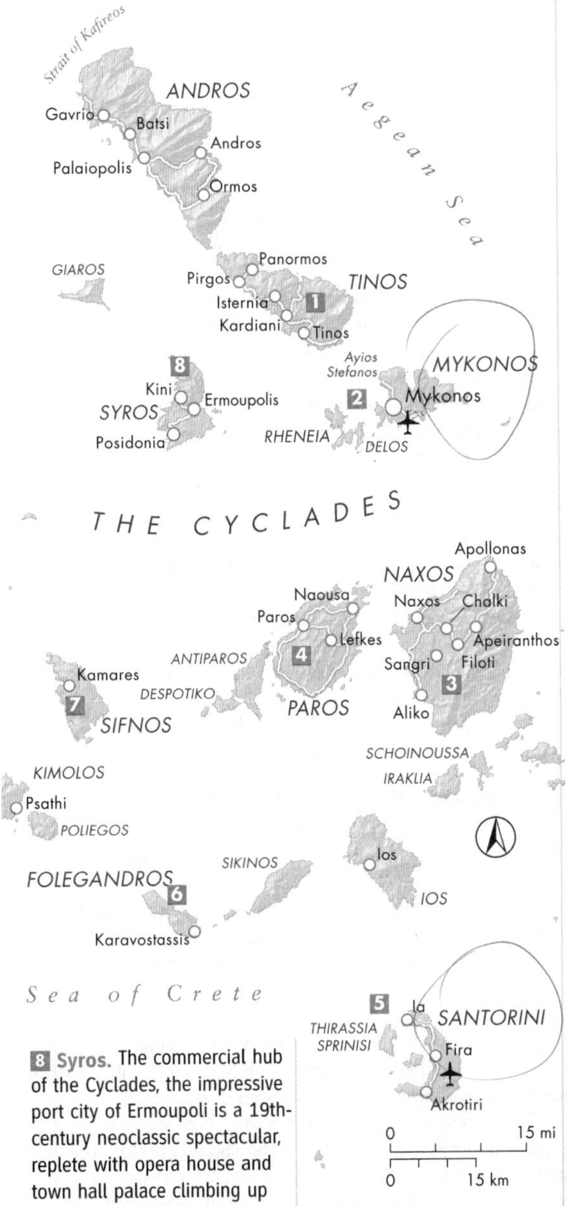

8 Syros. The commercial hub of the Cyclades, the impressive port city of Ermoupoli is a 19th-century neoclassic spectacular, replete with opera house and town hall palace climbing up two mountain peaks.

Man climbing stairs on his donkey, Santorini

THE CYCLADES PLANNER

Water, Water, Everywhere

When it comes to the Cyclades, anyone who invests in a mask, snorkel, and flippers has entry to intense, serene beauty.

But even without this underwater gear, this archipelago is a swimmer's paradise.

Most of the Cycladic islands gleam with beaches, from long blond stretches of sand to tiny pebbly coves.

The best beaches are probably those on the southwest coast of Naxos, though the ones on Mykonos are trendier.

Beaches on Tinos tend to be less crowded than those on other islands in the Cyclades.

The strands on Santorini, though strewn with plenty of bathers, are volcanic; you can bask on sands that are strikingly red and black.

As for water sports, there are many options that entice many sunseekers.

Waterskiing, parasailing, scuba diving, and especially windsurfing have become ever more popular.

Note that many water sports venues change from season to season.

When to Go

The experience of the Cyclades is radically different summer and winter. In summer all services are operating on overload, the beaches are crowded, the clubs noisy, the restaurants packed, and the scene swinging. Walkers, nature lovers, and devotees of classical and Byzantine Greece would do better to come in spring and fall, ideally in late April–June or September–October, when temperatures are lower and tourists are fewer. But off-season travel means less-frequent boat service; in fact, there is sometimes no service at all between November and mid-March, when stormy weather can make the seas too rough for sailing. In winter, many shops, hotels, and restaurants are closed, and the open cafés are full of locals recouperating from summer's intensities. The villages can feel shuttered and the nightlife zilch. Cultural organizations, film clubs, concerts of island music, and religious festivals become more important. The temperature will often seem colder than the thermometer indicates: if it is in the low fifties, cloudy, drizzling, and windy, you will feel chilled and want to stay indoors, and Greece is at her best outdoors.

Making the Most of Your Time

The Cyclades are more for lazing around than for book-nosed tourism. Start with the livelier islands (Mykonos, Santorini), add one or two of the larger islands (Naxos, Paros), and finish up with an untouristy one (Sifnos, Folegandros). While it is true that feverish partying can overwhelm the young in summer, in other seasons the temptations are fewer, gentler, and more profound. If you move fast, you will see little, and the beauty is in the general impression of sea, sky, mountain, and village, and in the details that catch your eye: an ancient column used as a building block, an octopus hung to dry in the sun, a wedding or baptism in a small church you are stopping into (welcome, stranger), a shepherd's mountain hut with a flagstone roof—they are endless. There are important sites such as Delos's ruins but just enjoying the island rhythms often proves as soul-satisfying.

Dining à la Cyclades

Dishes in the Cyclades are often wonderfully redolent of garlic and olive oil. Many of the islands are still more geared to agriculture than to tourism, so you can expect the freshest vegetables. Grilled seafood is a favorite, and you should try grilled octopus with ouzo at least once. Lamb is a staple in the Cyclades and a simply grilled lamb chop can be a memorable meal; lamb on a skewer and keftedes (spicy meatballs) are on many menus. Likewise, a light meal of fresh fried calamari with a salad garnished with locally made feta cheese is the Cyclades equivalent of fast food but is invariably excellent.

Finding a Place to Stay

Overall, the quality of accommodations in the Cyclades is high, whether they be tiny pensions, private houses, or luxury hotels. The best rooms and service (and noticeably higher prices) are on Mykonos and Santorini, where luxury resort hotels are mushrooming. Wherever you stay in the Cyclades, make a room with a view, and a balcony, a priority. Unless you're traveling at the very height of the season (July 15–August 30), you're unlikely to need advance reservations; often the easiest way to find something is to head for a tourist office and describe your needs and price range. Remember few hotels have elevators, and even Santorini's best often have breathlessly picturesque cliffside staircases and no porters.

Dining & Lodging Prices in Euros

	¢	$	$$	$$$	$$$$
Restaurants	Under €8	€8–€11	€11–€15	€15–€20	Over €20
Hotels	Under €60	€60–€90	€90–€120	€120–€160	Over €160

Note that luxury hotel and restaurant prices in Santorini and Mykonos are more comparable to the Athens price chart. Restaurant prices are for one main course at dinner, or for two mezedes (small dishes). Hotel prices are for a standard double room in high season, including taxes. Hotels operate on the European Plan (EP, with no meal provided) unless we note that they use the Continental Plan (CP, with Continental breakfast); Breakfast Plan (BP, with a full breakfast); Modified American Plan (MAP, with breakfast and dinner); or the Full American Plan (FAP, with all meals). Inquire when booking if meal plans (which can entail higher rates) are mandatory. Guest rooms have air-conditioning, room phones, and TVs unless otherwise noted.

Getting There and Around

Transportation to the islands is constantly improving. Five of the Cyclades have airports, and the flight is short. But if you want to understand where you are, you really should travel by boat—after all, these are islands in the fabled Aegean, inhabited even before the days of Homer. But remember that boat schedules depend on Poseidon's weather-whims, and also on the tippling gods of holidays, when they adjust. If you come for Easter, better buy tickets to and from in advance. For details on getting to the Cyclades from mainland Greece and on using island buses, see the Essentials section at the end of this chapter.

Hiking Heaven

The Cyclades are justly famous for their hiking. Ancient goat and donkey trails go everywhere—through fields, over mountains, along untrodden coasts. Since tourists crowd beaches, clubs, and ancient sites, walking is uncrowded even in July and August. Prime walking months, though, are April and May, when temperatures are reasonable, wildflowers seem to cover every surface, and birds migrate. October is also excellent for hiking—plus, olive groves provide their own sort of spectacle when dozens of "gatherers" descend upon them with nets.

Updated by Jeffrey and Elizabeth Carson

THE MAGICAL WORDS "GREEK ISLANDS" conjure up beguiling images. If for you they suggest blazing sun and sea, bare rock and mountains, olive trees and vineyards, white rustic architecture and ancient ruins, fresh fish and fruity oils, the Cyclades are isles of quintessential plenty, the ultimate Mediterranean archipelago. "The islands with their drinkable blue volcanoes," wrote Odysseus Elytis, winner of the Nobel Prize for poetry, musing on Santorini. That Homer—who loved these islands—is buried here is unverifiable but spiritually true.

The major stars in this constellation of islands in the central Aegean Sea—Tinos, Mykonos, Naxos, Paros, Sifnos, and Santorini—are the archetypes of the islands of Greece. Swinging Mykonos and spectacular Santorini remain the most popular of the islands, with relaxing Paros and fertile Naxos right behind them. Delicate Sifnos, the potter's island, is getting more crowded all the time, and for good reason. Tinos is especially beloved by Greeks, while Syros has the Cyclades's only real city, with many notable buildings. Little Folegandros—the smallest of our islands—is for purists. No matter which of these islands you head for it always seems—at least in summer—that Zeus's sky is faultlessly azure, Poseidon's sea warm, and Dionysus's nightlife swinging (especially in Mykonos's clubs). The prevailing wind is the northern *vorias*; called *meltemi* in summer, it cools the always-sunny weather. In a magnificent fusion of sunlight, stone, and sparkling aqua sea, the Cyclades offer both culture and hedonism: ancient sites, Byzantine castles and museums, lively nightlife, shopping, dining, and beaches plain and fancy.

These arid, mountainous islands are the peaks of a deep, submerged plateau; their composition is rocky, with few trees. They are volcanic in origin, and Santorini (also known as Thira), southernmost of the group, actually sits on the rim of an ancient drowned volcano that exploded about 1600 BC. The dead texture of its rock is a great contrast to the living, warm limestone of most Greek islands. Santorini's basic geological colors—black, pink, brown, white, pale green—are not in themselves beautiful; as you arrive by boat, little shows above the cliff tops but a string of white villages—like teeth on the vast lower jaw of some giant monster. Still, the island was called Kállisti, "Loveliest," when it was first settled, and today, appreciative visitors find its mixture of vaulted cliff-side architecture, European elegance, and stunning sunsets all but irresistible.

A more-idyllic rhythm of life can still be found on many of the other Cyclades (and, of course, off-season in Santorini). Tinos has stayed authentically Greek, since its heavy tourism is largely owing to its miracle-working icon, not to its beautiful villages. In the town of Mykonos, the whitewashed houses huddle together against the meltemi winds, and backpackers rub elbows with millionaires in the mazelike white-marble streets. The island's sophistication level is high, the beaches fine, and the shopping varied and upscale. It's also the jumping-off place for a mandatory visit to tiny, deserted Delos. That windswept islet, birthplace of Apollo, still watched over by a row of marble lions, was once the religious and commercial center of the eastern Mediterranean.

Naxos, greenest of the Cyclades, makes cheese and wine, raises livestock, and produces potatoes, olives, and fruit. For centuries a Venetian stronghold, it has a shrinking aristocratic Roman Catholic population, Venetian houses and fortifications, and Cycladic and Mycenaean sites. Paros, a hub of the ferry system, has reasonable prices and is a good base for trips to other islands. It's also good for lazing on long, white-sand beaches and for visiting fishing villages. Of course, throughout the Cyclades, there are countless classical sites, monasteries, churches, and villages to be explored. The best reason to visit them may be the beauty of the walk, the impressiveness of the location, and the hospitality you will likely find off the beaten track.

Despite its depredations, the presence of automobiles has brought life back to Cycladic villages. Many shuttered houses are being authentically restored, and much traditional architecture can still be found in Ia on Santorini, Kardiani on Tinos, and Apeiranthos on Naxos—villages that are part of any deep experience of the islands. In the countryside, many of the sites and buildings are often or permanently closed, though the fencing around sites may have fallen, and monks and nuns may let you in if you are polite and decently dressed—the gods may still be out there.

EXPLORING THE CYCLADES

Each island in the Cyclades differs significantly from its neighbors, so how you approach your exploration of the islands will depend on what sort of experience you are seeking. The busiest and most-popular islands are Santorini, with its fantastic volcanic scenery and dramatic cliff-side towns of Fira and Ia, and Mykonos, a barren island that insinuates a sexy jet-set lifestyle, flaunts some of Greece's most famous beaches, and has a perfectly preserved main town. These two islands have the fanciest accommodations. Naxos has the best mountain scenery and the longest, least-developed beaches, and Andros, too, is rugged and mountainous, covered with forests and laced with waterfalls. Tinos, the least visited and most scenic of the Cyclades, is the place to explore mountain villages, hundreds of churches, and fancifully decorated dovecotes (*peristeriónes*). Sifnos has more than 360 churches, all of which celebrate their name day, and is the most scrupulously whitewashed.

BEEP BEEP

When your feet prove less than bionic, it may be time to rent wheels. Many people opt for scooters, but be careful—island hospitals are frequently filled with people with serious-looking injuries from scooter travels. ATV's are the safest bets, while many places now rent Smart Cars for about 25 to 40 euros a day: these two-seaters are way-cool for getting around.

All these islands are well connected by ferries and faster boats, with the most frequent service being scheduled in summer. Schedules change frequently, and it can be difficult to plan island-hopping excursions in advance. So be flexible and the islands are yours.

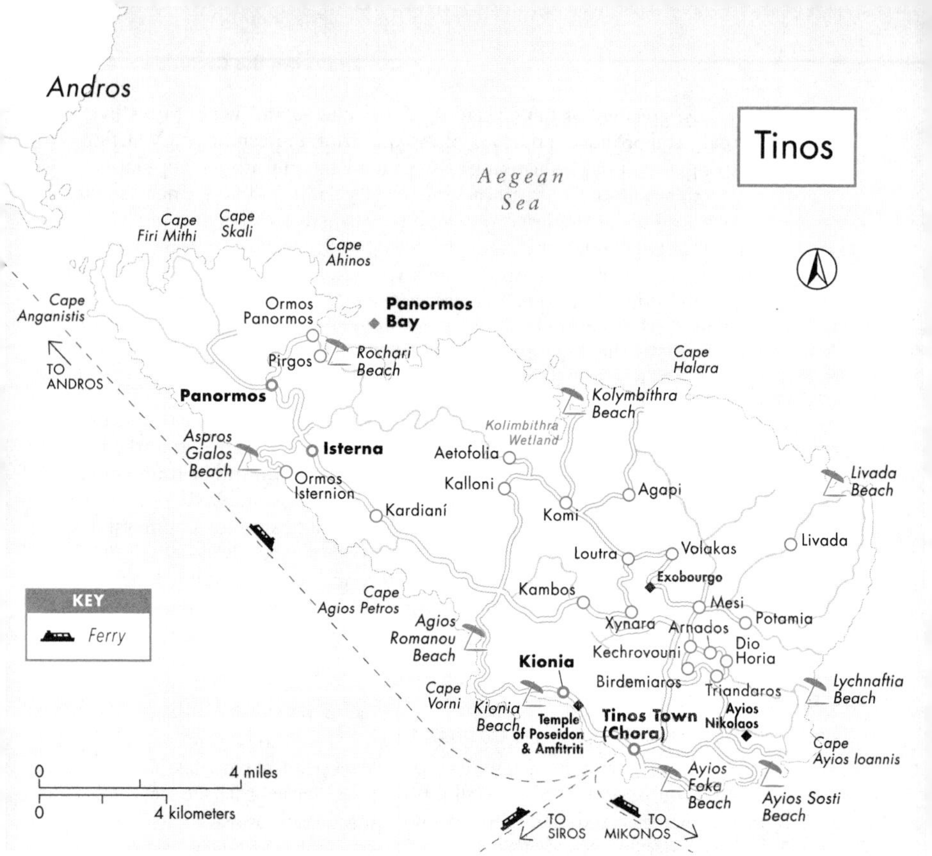

TINOS ΤΗΝΟΣ

Tinos (or, as archaeologists spell it, Tenos) is among the most beautiful and most fascinating of the major Cyclades. The third largest of the island group after Naxos and Andros, with an area of 195 square km (121 square mi), it is inhabited by nearly 10,000 people, many of whom still live the traditional life of farmers or craftsmen. Its long, mountainous spine, rearing amid Andros, Mykonos, and Syros, makes it seem forbidding, and in a way it is. It is not popular among tourists for several reasons: the main village, Tinos town (Chora), lacks charm; the beaches are undeveloped; there is no airport; and the prevailing north winds are the Aegean's fiercest (passing mariners used to sacrifice a calf to Poseidon—ancient Tinos's chief deity—in hopes of avoiding shipwreck). But for Greeks, a visit to Tinos is essential: its great Church of the Evangelistria is the Greek Lourdes, a holy place of pilgrimage and miraculous cures; 799 other churches adorn the countryside. Encroaching development here is to accommodate those in search of their religious elixir and not, as on the other islands, the beach-and-bar crowd.

Tinos is dotted with possibly the loveliest villages in the Cyclades, which, for some welcome reason, are not being abandoned. The dark arcades of Arnados, the vine-shaded sea views of Isternia and Kardiani, the Venetian architecture of Loutra, the gleaming marble squares of Pirgos: these, finally, are what make Tinos unique. A map, available at kiosks or rental agencies, will make touring these villages by car or bike somewhat less confusing, as there are nearly 50 of them. Note that of all the major islands, Tinos is the least developed for sports—the strong winds discourage water sports, and sports outfitters come and go.

LOVEY-DOVEY MCMANSIONS

Tinos is also renowned for its 1,300 dovecotes (*peristeriónes*), which, unlike those on Mykonos or Andros, are mostly well maintained; in fact, new ones are being built. Two stories high, with intricate stonework, carved-dove finials, and thin schist slabs arranged in intricate patterns resembling traditional stitchery, the dovecotes have been much written about—and are much visited by doves.

TINOS TOWN ΤΗΝΟΣ (ΧΩΡΑ)

55 km (34 mi) southeast of Andros's port.

Civilization on Tinos is a millennium older than Tinos town, or Chora, founded in the 5th century BC. On weekends and during festivals, Chora is thronged with Greeks attending church, and restaurants and hotels cater to them. As the well-known story goes, in 1822, a year after the War of Independence began (Tinos was the first of the islands to join in), the Virgin sent the nun Pelagia a dream about a buried icon of the Annunciation. On January 30, 1823, such an icon was unearthed amid the foundations of a Byzantine church, and it started to heal people immediately.

Fodor'sChoice ★ The Tiniots, hardly unaware of the icon's potential, immediately built the splendid **Panayia Evangelistria,** or Church of the Annunciate Virgin, on the site, in 1823. Imposing and beautiful, framed in gleaming yellow and white, it stands atop the town's main hill (*chora*), which is linked to the harbor via Megalochais, a steeply inclined avenue lined with votive shops. Half Venetian, half Cypriot in style, the facade (illuminated at night) has a distinctive two-story arcade and bookend staircases. Lined with the most costly stones from Tinos, Paros, and Delos, the church's **marble courtyards** (note the green-vein Tiniot stone) are paved with pebble mosaics and surrounded by offices, chapels, a health station, and **seven museums.** Inside the **upper three-aisle church** dozens of beeswax candles and precious tin and silver-work votives—don't miss the golden orange tree near the door donated by a blind man who was granted sight—dazzle the eye. You must often wait in line to see the little icon, encrusted with jewels, which was donated as thanks for cures. To beseech the icon's aid, a sick person sends a young female relative or a mother brings her sick infant. As the pilgrim descends from

CLOSE UP

Traditional Festivals

All over Greece, villages, towns, and cities have traditional celebrations that vary from joyous to deeply serious, and the Cyclades are no exception. In Tinos town on Tinos, the healing icon from Panayia Evangelistria church is paraded with much pomp on Annunciation Day, March 25, and especially Dormition Day, August 15. As it is carried on poles over the heads of the faithful, cures are effected, and religious emotion runs high. On July 23, in honor of St. Pelagia, the icon is paraded from Kechrovouni Nunnery, and afterward the festivities continue long into the night, with music and fireworks.

If you're on Santorini on July 20, you can partake in the celebration of St. Elias's name day, when a traditional pea-and-onion soup is served, followed by walnut and honey desserts and folk dancing.

Naxos has its share of festivals to discover and enjoy. Naxos town celebrates the Dionysia festival during the first week of August, with concerts, costumed folk dancers, and free food and wine in the square. During Carnival, preceding Lent, "bell wearers" take to the streets in Apeiranthos and Filoti, running from house to house making as much noise as possible with strings of bells tied around their waists. They're a disconcerting sight in their hooded cloaks, as they escort a man dressed as a woman from house to house to collect eggs. In Apeiranthos, villagers square off in rhyming-verse contests: on the last Sunday of Lent, the *paliomaskari*, their faces blackened, challenge each other in improvising *kotsakia* (satirical couplets). On July 14, Ayios Nikodemos Day is celebrated in Chora with a procession of the patron saint's icon through town, but the Dormition of the Virgin on August 15 is, after Easter and Christmas, the festival most widely celebrated, especially in Sangri, Filoti (where festivities take place on August 4), and Apeiranthos.

On Paros each year on August 23, eight days after the huge festival in Parikia at the Church of a Hundred Doors, Naousa celebrates the heroic naval battle against the Turks, with children dressed in native costume, great feasts, and traditional dancing. The day ends with 100 boats illuminated by torches converging on the harbor. On June 2 there is much feasting in Lefkes for the Holy Trinity.

On Sifnos, which has more than 360 churches, the Ascension (a movable feast in May or June) is celebrated especially fervently at Chrysopigi Monastery. Many people also make the trek on June 26 to Ayios Panteleimon in Cheronisos.

On Syros, you can attend Easter services (except when they coincide) in both the Catholic and Orthodox cathedrals: how different they are!

the boat, she falls to her knees, with traffic indifferently whizzing about her, and crawls painfully up the faded red padded lane on the main street—1 km (½ mi)—to the church. In the church's courtyards, she and her family camp for several days, praying to the magical icon for a cure, which sometimes comes. This procedure is very similar to the ancient one observed in Tinos's temple of Poseidon. The **lower church,** called the Evresis, celebrates the finding of the icon; in one room a baptismal font is filled with silver and gold votives. The chapel to the left commemorates the torpedoing by the Italians, on Dormition Day, 1940, of the Greek ship *Helle*; in the early stages of the war, the roused Greeks amazingly overpowered the Italians. ✉*At end of Megalohari* ☎*22830/22256* 🎫*Free* 🕓*Daily 8:30–3.*

On the main street, near the church, is the small **Archaeological Museum**; its collection includes a sundial by Andronicus of Cyrrhus, who in the 1st century BC also designed Athens's Tower of the Winds. Here, too, are Tinos's famous huge, red storage vases, from the 8th century BC. ✉*Megalohari* ☎*22830/22670* 🎫*€4* 🕓*Tues.–Fri. 8–2.*

Just 1½ km (¾ mi) from Chora you'll see a copse of pines shading a small parking lot, from which a path leads down to Stavros (Holy Cross) chapel; right on the water is the unmarked **Markos Velalopoulos's Ouzeri** (✉*Under church* ☎*22830/23276*), which serves *strophia* (raki), ouzo, and traditional snacks such as fried cheese or figs with sesame. This is Tinos's most romantic spot to watch the sunset. It is also good for swimming. Note that the sunken breakwater along the coastal road in front of the *ouzeri* (casual bar) is ancient.

The **Cultural Center,** in the large and splendid neoclassic building at the south end of the quay, finally opened in 2007 and has a full schedule of traveling exhibitions and a permanent exhibition of the sculptures of Iannoulis Chalepas *(⇨Pirgos, below).* ☎*22830/22742* 🎫*€3* 🕓*Wed.–Mon. 10–2 and 7–9.*

OFF THE BEATEN PATH

Mountain Villages Above Chora. At night the lights of the hill villages surrounding Tinos's highest mountain, Mt. Tsiknias—2,200 feet high and the ancient home of Boreas (the wind god)—glitter over Chora like fireworks. By day they are worth visiting. Take the good road that runs through Dio Horia and Monastiri, which ascends and twists around switchbacks while passing fertile fields and a few of Tinos's most fanciful old dovecotes. After 9 km (5½ mi) you reach **Kechrovouni,** or Monastiri, which is a veritable city of nuns, founded in the 10th century. One cell contains the head of St. Pelagia in a wooden chest; another is a small icon museum. Though a nunnery, Kechrovouni is a lively place, since many of the church's pilgrims come here by bus. Out front, a nun sells huge garlic heads and braids to be used as charms against misfortune; the Greeks call these "California garlic." One kilometer (½ mi) farther on, Tinos's telecommunications towers spike the sky, marking the entrance to **Arnados,** a strange village 1,600 feet up, overlooking Chora. Most of the streets here are vaulted, and thus cool and shady, if a bit claustrophobic; no medieval pirate ever penetrated this warren. In one alley is the **Ecclesiastical Museum,** which displays icons from local churches. Another 1½ km (¾ mi) farther on are the **Dio Horia** (Two Villages), with a marble fountain house, unusual in Tinos. The spreading plane tree in front of it, according to the marble plaque, was planted in 1885. Now the road starts winding down again, to reach **Triandaros,** which has a good restaurant. Many of the pretty houses in this misty place are owned by Germans. Yannis Kyparinis, who made the three-story bell tower in Dio Horia, has his workshop and showroom here.

BEACHES

There is a series of beaches between Chora and Kionia (and beyond, for walkers). **Stavros** is the most romantic of the area beaches. **Ayios Yannis** (✉*Near Porto*) is long, sandy, and peaceful. **Pachia Ammos** (✉*Past Porto, reached by a dirt road*) is undeveloped and sparkling.

> **CALLING ALL FAITHFUL**
>
> Evangelistria, the street parallel to Panagia Evangelistria, the legendary church of Tinos town, is closed to traffic and is a kind of religious flea market, lined with shops hawking immense candles, chunks of incense, tacky souvenirs, tin votives, and sweets. There are several good jewelers' shops on the market street, where, as always on Tinos, the religious note is supreme.

WHERE TO STAY & EAT

$$$ ✕**Metaxi Mas.** On a trellised lane by the harbor, Euripides Tatsionas's restaurant, the best in Tinos, turns out to be no more expensive than a taverna. The name means "between us," and a friendly air prevails. The decor is traditional—pale yellow walls, wooden furniture, high stone arches—and the staff is welcoming. From starters to desserts, the food is homemade, but with an haute-Athenian flair. For a starter, try deep-fried sun-dried tomatoes or hot eggplant slices wrapped around cheese, mint, and green pepper. Among the main dishes, the spicy lamb cooked in paper is especially succulent; the beef fillet with peppers is also exceptional. With a fireplace in winter and an air conditioner for summer, this place stays open year-round. ✉*Kontogiorgi alley* ☎*22830/25945* ▭*AE, MC, V.*

$$ ✕**Symposion.** Yorgos Visdalis's café and restaurant occupies the prettiest and best-kept neoclassic building on Evangelistria street, which is closed to traffic. Its second- and third-floor terraces overlook the Turkish fountain and the passing scene, Tinos's liveliest during shop hours. Marble stairs lead to rooms with elegant furnishings in pastel colors. The second-floor café, open all day, serves snacks and drinks. The third floor is an excellent restaurant. You might start with the ambrosia salad and follow it with burger á la crème (with mushrooms and basmati rice). His mixed plates, combining local meats and vegetables, are perfect to accompany an ouzo on the terrace. The wine list is big and Greek. ✉*Evangelistrias 13* ☎*22830/24368* ▭*AE, MC, V* ⊙*Closed Nov.–Mar.*

$ ✕**Zefki.** It may say Zeyki on the sign out front but no matter the spelling, locals—who always know where to find the freshest food—love this place. Andreas Levantis has converted this old wineshop into an attractive room. The local wines and the raki are carefully chosen. He is a specialist with omelets (local eggs, of course). His main dishes include roasted local goat. The desserts are homemade and change with the season. To find Zefki, walk up Evangelistria street and take your second right. Open all year. ✉*Alex. Lagourou 6* ☎*22930/22231* ▭*AE, MC, V* ⊙*Closed Nov.–Mar.*

$$$ **Porto Tango.** This ambitiously up-to-date resort-hotel strives for the best in decor and service. Greece's late prime minister, Andreas Papandreou, stayed here during his last visit to Tinos. Modular Cycladic architecture lends privacy; the lobby, where an art exhibition is usually on display, has a wooden ceiling, marble floors, and Tiniot furnishings,

both modern and antique. Rooms are simple, white, and private, with basic wood furniture. There are extensive spa facilities, for ultimate relaxation. The price includes transfers. This is an out-of-town resort; you need transportation to go anywhere. ✉ *Follow signed road up hill, 84200Porto (Agios Ioannis)* ☎ *22830/24411 through 22830/24415* 📠 *22830/24416* 🌐 *www.tinosportotangohotel.com* ⇨ *55 rooms, 7 suites* ♨ *In-room: refrigerator. In-hotel: restaurant, bar, pool, gym, spa* ▭ *AE, D, MC, V* ⊙ *Closed Nov.–Mar.* 🍴 *BP.*

$$–$$$ **Favie Suzanne Hotel.** Sleek, posh, and convenient, too: if you are willing to give up a sea view, this is the best place to stay in Tinos town. Set right in the heart of the busy town, it has two wings, with the fancier new section added in 2007. From fanlights to dovecotes, the decoration incorporates many Tiniot details. Guest rooms have massage showers and big plasma TVs. The pool, the first in town, is adjacent to a spa area. Breakfast and transfer are included in the main room rate. ✉ *Antoniou Sochou 22, 84200* ☎ *22830/22693* 📠 *22830/25993* 🌐 *www.faviesuzanne.gr* ⇨ *32 rooms, 2 suites* ♨ *In-room: Ethernet (some). In-hotel: public Internet* ▭ *AE, MC, V* ⊙ *Closed Nov.–Feb.* 🍴 *BP.*

$$ ★ **Alonia Hotel.** Ordinary looking from the road, this is Tinos's most pleasant hotel. Comfortable, family-run, and quietly efficient, it is for you if you dislike snazzy resorts and want to be out of (but still convenient to) hectic Chora. The fairly large rooms all have dazzling views (those overlooking the pool are best) over palms and olive trees to the sea; the bathrooms have bathtubs, a rarity in island hotels. Tinos's largest freshwater pool is surrounded by lawns, trees, and gardens—not baking cement. The price includes transfers. The restaurant (¢) serves home-style meals prepared by the owners, especially son Vangelis. To start, try pita stuffed with meat or vegetables. Entrées include chicken breasts stuffed with bacon, cheese, and herbs, or beef stew with wine and onions—the menu changes, so ask what's available that day. The barrel wine is excellent. Vangelis also has inexpensive (€50) rooms in town by the church. ✉ *2 km (1 mi) from Chora toward Porto (Agios Ioannis), 84200* ☎ *22830/23541 through 22830/23543* 📠 *22830/23544* 🌐 *www.aloniahotel.gr* ⇨ *34 rooms, 4 suites* ♨ *In-hotel: restaurant, bar, pool, no elevator* ▭ *AE, MC, V* 🍴 *BP.*

$ **Akti Aegeou.** The family that runs this little resort is lucky to own such a valuable piece of property. Akti Aegeou, or "Aegean Coast," is right on the uncrowded beach at Porto—a very pretty location (too bad there are so many modern villas being built here). All the airy rooms come with sea-view balconies, marble floors, and traditional rag rugs. The good restaurant specializes in fresh fish. A fishing caïque is set up next to the saltwater pool, which looks out to Delos. ✉ *Beach of Ayios Ioannis, 84200 Porto (Agios Ioannis)* ☎ *22830/24248* 📠 *22830/23523* 🌐 *www.aktiaegeou.gr* ⇨ *5 rooms, 6 apartments* ♨ *In-room: kitchen. In-hotel: restaurant, bar, pool, no elevator* ▭ *AE, MC, V* ⊙ *Closed Nov.–Mar.* 🍴 *BP.*

$ **Anna's Rooms.** The best bet on Tinos for those on a budget, this is a healthful 10-minute walk from town and 5 minutes from Stavros beach. Families like this small pension since each apartment has a full kitchen. The apartments, arranged around a green courtyard, all have balconies with sea views. Except for fresh bread, there is no breakfast. The price includes transfers. ✉*Kiona road, about ½ km (¼ mi) outside town, 84200* ☎*22830/22877* 🌐*www.tinos.nl* *10 rooms* *In-room: kitchen. In-hotel: no elevator, public Internet* *No credit cards.*

NIGHTLIFE

Tinos has fewer bars and discos than the other big islands, but there is plenty of late-night bar action behind the waterfront between the two boat docks. People go back and forth among the popular clubs **Syvilla, Volto,** and **Metropolis,** on the street behind the fish market next to the Archeio Bar.

SHOPPING

FARMERS' & FLEA MARKETS Tinos is a rich farming island, and every day but Sunday, farmers from all the far-flung villages fill the **square** (✉*Between 2 docks*) with vegetables, herbs, and *kritamos* (pickled sea-plant leaves). In a square near town, the local pelican (a rival to Mykonos's Petros) can often be found cadging snacks from the **fish market.**

Tinos produces a lot of milk. A short way up from the harbor, on the right, is the little store of the **Enosis** (*Farmers' Cooperative* ✉*Megalohari, up from harbor* ☎*22830/23289*), which sells milk, butter, and cheeses, including sharp kopanistí, perfect with ouzo; local jams and honeys are for sale, too.

JEWELRY At **Artemis d and b** (✉*Evangelistria 18* ☎*22830/24312*), owned by the Artemis brothers, Christos paints the seascapes; Dimitris, a retired captain, makes ship models; and the classic jewelry is all by Teniots. The selection at **Ostria** (✉*Evangelistria 20* ☎*222830/23893* *22830/24568*) is especially good; in addition to delicate silver jewelry, it sells silver icon covers, silver plate, and 22-karat gold.

WEAVINGS The 100-year-old weaving school, or **Biotechniki Scholi** (✉*Evangelistria, three-quarters of the way up from sea* ☎*22830/22894*), sells traditional weavings—aprons, towels, spreads—made by its students, local girls. The largest of its three high-ceiling, wooden-floor rooms is filled with looms and spindles.

KIONIA KIONIA

2½ km (1¼ mi) northwest of Tinos town.

The reason to come to this small community outside Tinos town is to visit the large, untended **Sanctuary of Poseidon** (✉*Northwest of Tinos town*), also dedicated to the bearded sea god's sea-nymph consort, Amphitrite. The present remains are from the 4th century BC and later, though the sanctuary itself is much older. The sanctuary was a kind of hospital, where the ailing came to camp and solicit the god's help. The marble dolphins in the museum were discovered here. According to the Roman historian Pliny, Tinos was once infested with serpents (goddess symbols) and named Serpenttown (Ophiousa), until supermasculine Poseidon sent storks to clean them out. The sanctuary functioned well into Roman times.

BEACH

The Kiona road ends at a long, sheltered beach, which is unfortunately being worn away by cars heading for the two pretty coves beyond, including the Gastrion cave, whose entrance bears Byzantine inscriptions.

WHERE TO EAT

$ ✕**Tsambia.** Abutting the Sanctuary of Poseidon and facing the sea, this multilevel taverna home makes traditional fare. For starters try the indigenous specialties: *louza* (smoked pork), local Tiniot cheeses rarely sold in stores (especially fried local goat cheese), and homegrown vegetables. Fresh fish is available, depending on the weather. Tried-and-true are pork in red wine with lemon, or goat casserole with oregano. To get here, follow signs for TRADITIONAL TAVERNA before the Sanctuary of Poseidon. ✉*Cement road* ☎*22830/23142* ▭*No credit cards.*

ISTERNIA ΙΣΤΕΡΝΙΑ

24 km (15 mi) northwest of Tinos town.

The village of Isternia (Cisterns) is verdant with lush gardens. Many of the marble plaques hung here over doorways—a specialty of Tinos—indicate the owner's profession, for example, a sailing ship for a fisherman or sea captain. A long, paved road winds down to a little port, **Ayios Nikitas,** with a **beach** and two **fish tavernas**; a small boat ferries people to Chora in good weather.

PIRGOS ΠΥΡΓΟΣ

★ *32 km (20 mi) northwest of Tinos town, 8 km (5 mi) north of Isternia.*

The village of Pirgos, second in importance to Chora, is inland and up from the little harbor of Panormos. Tinos is famous for its marble carving, and Pirgos, a prosperous town, is noted for its sculpture school (the town's highest building) and marble workshops, where craftsmen make fanlights, fountains, tomb monuments, and small objects for tourists; they also take orders. The village's main square is aptly crafted of all marble; the five cafés, noted for *galaktoboureko* (custard pastry), and one taverna are all shaded by an ancient plane tree. The quarries for the green-vein marble are north of here, reachable by car. The cemetery here is, appropriately, a showplace of marble sculpture.

The marble-working tradition of Tinos survives here from the 19th century and is going strong, as seen in the two adjacent museums **Museum Iannoulis Chalepas** and **Museum of Tenos Artists,** which house the work of Pirgos's renowned sculptor, and other works. ✉*1 block from bus stop* ☎*22830/31262* 🎫*€5* ⏲*Daily 10–2 and 6–8.*

BEACHES

The **beaches next to Panormos** are popular in summer.

SHOPPING

A number of marble carvers are, appropriately, found in Pirgos. You may visit the shop of probably the best master carver, **Lambros Diamantopoulos** (⊠*Near main square* ☎*22830/31365*), who accepts commissions for work to be done throughout Greece. He makes and sells traditional designs to other carvers, who may bring a portable slab home to copy, and to visitors.

PANORMOS BAY ΌΡΜΟΣ ΠΑΝΟΡΜΟΥ

35 km (22 mi) northwest of Tinos town, 3 km (2 mi) north of Pirgos.

Panormos bay, an unpretentious port once used for marble export, has ducks and geese, a row of seafood restaurants, and a good beach with a collapsed sea cave. More coves with secluded swimming are beyond, as is the islet of Panormos. There are many rooms to rent.

WHERE TO EAT

$$ ✕ **The Fishbone.** When any Tinos restaurant features fish from Panormos bay, they tell you; happily, the Fishbone always does (that is, when weather permits). This small taverna, decorated with lots of blue and two Tiniot fanlights, is on the quay; boats right out front bring in fresh fish, which owners Belasarius Lais and Nikos Menardos, brothers-in-law, serve with flare. Among the appetizers are small fish pies and mussels in mustard sauce. Fresh fish wrapped in paper to preserve succulence is a specialty; sole with mushrooms is also a top choice. ⊠*Panormos* ☎*22830/31362* ▭*V* ⏲*Closed Nov.–Apr.*

MYKONOS & DELOS ΜΥΚΟΝΟΣ & ΔΗΛΟΣ

From backpackers to the superrich, from day-trippers to yachties, from gays to celebrities (who head here by helicopter), Mykonos has become one of the most popular of the Aegean islands. Today's scene is a weird but attractive cocktail of tradition, beauty, and glitz, but travelers from all over the world have always been drawn to this dry, rugged island—at 16 km (10 mi) by 11 km (7 mi), one of the smallest of the Cyclades—thanks to its many stretches of sandy beach, its thatched windmills, and its picturesque port town. One thing is certain: Mykonos knows how to maintain its attractiveness, how to develop it, and how to sell it. Complain as you will that it is touristy, noisy, and overdeveloped, you'll be back.

Happily, the islanders seem to have been able to fit cosmopolitan New Yorkers, Londoners, and Athenians gracefully into their way of life. You may see, for example, an old island woman leading a donkey laden with vegetables through the town's narrow streets, greeting the suntanned vacationers walking by. The truth is, Mykonians regard a good tourist season the way a fisherman inspects a calm morning's catch; for many, the money earned in July and August will support them for the rest of the year. Not long ago Mykonians had to rely on what they could scratch out of the island's arid land for sustenance,

and some remember suffering from starvation under A
during World War II. In the 1950s a few tourists bega
Mykonos on their way to see the ancient marvels on
of Delos, the sacred isle.

For almost 1,000 years Delos was the religious and political center of the Aegean and host every four years to the Delian games, the region's greatest festival. The population of Delos actually reached 20,000 at the peak of its commercial period, and throughout antiquity Mykonos, eclipsed by its holy neighbor, depended on this proximity for income (it has been memorably described as Delos's "bordello"), as it partly does today. Anyone interested in antiquity should plan to spend at least one morning on Delos, which has some of the most striking sights preserved from antiquity, including the beautiful Avenue of the Lions or the eye-knocking sight of the enormous stone phalli at the entrance to the Sanctuary of Dionysus.

MYKONOS TOWN ΜΥΚΟΝΟΣ (ΧΩΡΑ)

16 km (10 mi) southeast of Tinos town.

Put firmly on the map by Jackie O. in the 1960s, Mykonos town—called Hora by the locals—-remains the Saint-Tropez of the Greek islands. The scenery is memorable, with its whitewashed streets, Little Venice, the Kato Myli ridge of windmills, and Kastro, the town's medieval quarter. Its cubical two- or three-story houses and churches, with their red or blue doors and domes and wooden balconies, have been long celebrated as some of the best examples of classic Cycladic architecture. Luckily, the Greek Archaeological Service decided to preserve the town, even when the Mykonians would have preferred to rebuild, and so the authentic old town has been impressively preserved. Pink oleander, scarlet hibiscus, and trailing green pepper trees form a contrast amid the dazzling whiteness, whose frequent renewal with whitewash is required by law. Any visitor who has the pleasure of getting lost in its narrow streets (made all the narrower by the many outdoor stone staircases, which maximize housing space in the crowded village) will appreciate how its confusing layout was designed to foil pirates—if it was designed at all. After Mykonos fell under Turkish rule in 1537, the Ottomans allowed the islanders to arm their vessels against pirates, which had a contradictory effect: many of them found that raiding other islands was more profitable than tilling arid land. At the height of Aegean piracy, Mykonos was the principal headquarters of the corsair fleets—the place where pirates met their fellows, found willing women, and filled out their crews. Eventually the illicit activity evolved into a legitimate and thriving trade network.

Today, Mykonos makes its living from tourism, though the fishing boats still go out in good weather. The summer crowds have turned one of the poorest islands in Greece into one of the richest. Old Mykonians complain that their young, who have inherited stores where their grandfathers once sold eggs or wine, get so much rent that they have lost ambition, and in summer sit around pool bars at night with their

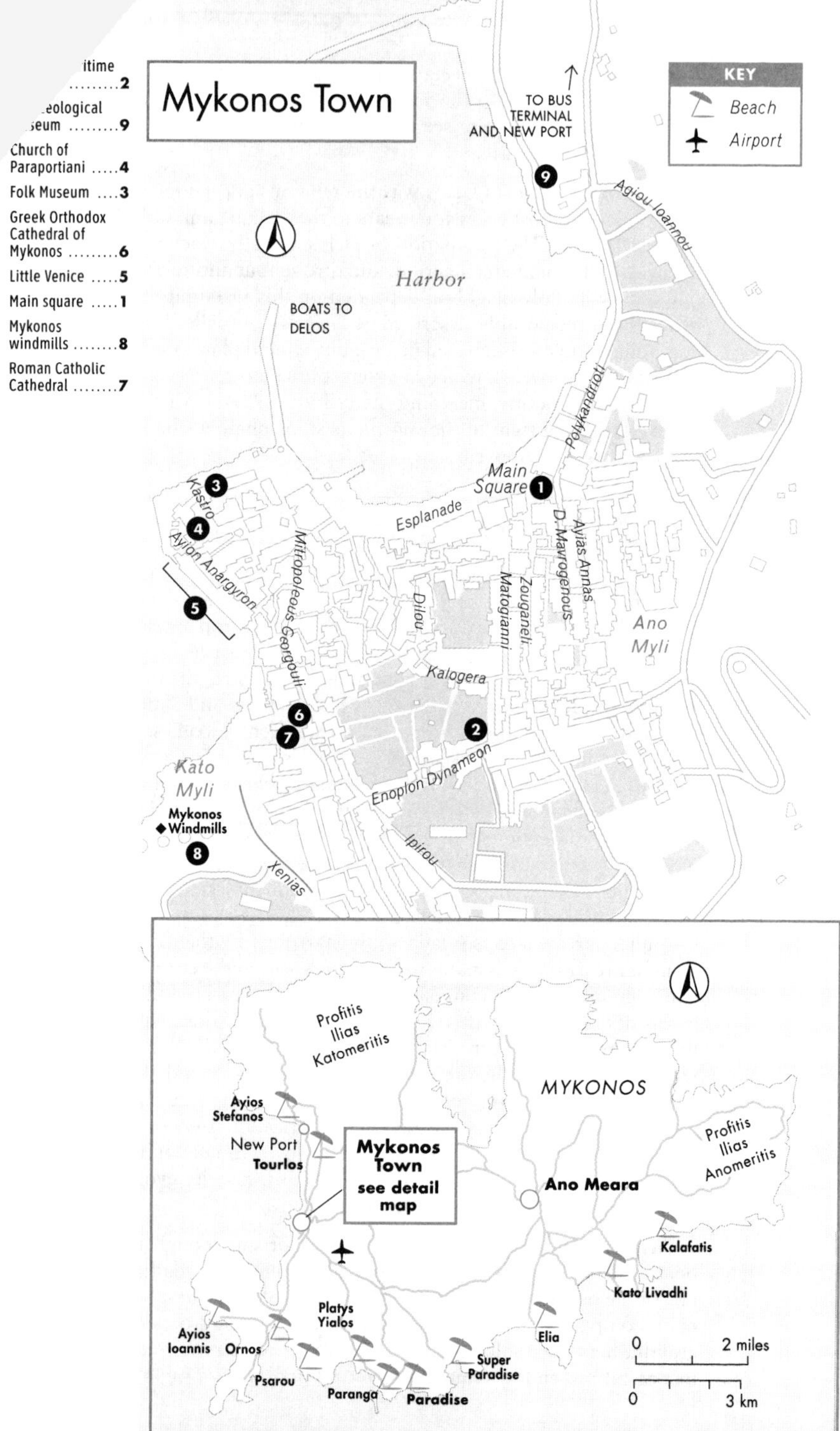

itime 2
eological
seum 9
Church of Paraportiani 4
Folk Museum 3
Greek Orthodox Cathedral of Mykonos 6
Little Venice 5
Main square 1
Mykonos windmills 8
Roman Catholic Cathedral 7
Mykonos Town
TO BUS TERMINAL AND NEW PORT
KEY
Beach
Airport
Agiou Ioannou
Harbor
BOATS TO DELOS
Polykandrioti
Main Square
Esplanade
Kastro
Ayion Anargyron
Mitropoleous Georgouli
Dilou
Matogianni
Zouganeli
D. Mavrogenous
Ayias Annas
Ano Myli
Kalogera
Enoplon Dynameon
Kato Myli
Mykonos Windmills
Ipirou
Xenias
Profitis Ilias Katomeritis
MYKONOS
Ayios Stefanos
New Port
Tourlos
Mykonos Town see detail map
Ano Meara
Profitis Ilias Anomeritis
Kalafatis
Kato Livadhi
Platys Yialos
Ayios Ioannis
Ornos
Psarou
Paranga
Paradise
Super Paradise
Elia
0 2 miles
0 3 km

friends, and hang out in Athens in winter when island life is less scintillating, rather than on Paros, Naxos, Andros, or Tinos.

THE PRANCE OF THE PELICAN

By the time morning's open-air fish market picks up steam in Mykonos town, Petros the Pelican—the town mascot—preens and cadges eats. In the 1950s a group of migrating pelicans passed over Mykonos, leaving behind a single exhausted bird; Vassilis the fisherman nursed it back to health, and locals say that the pelican in the harbor is the original Petros (though there are several).

Morning on the main town quay is busy with deliveries, visitors for the Delos boats, lazy breakfasters, and street cleaners dealing with the previous night's mess. In late morning the cruise-boat people arrive, and the shops are all open. In early afternoon, shaded outdoor tavernas are full of diners eating salads (Mykonos's produce is mostly imported); music is absent or kept low. In mid- and late afternoon, the town feels sleepy, since so many people are at the beach, on excursions, or sleeping in their air-conditioned rooms; even some tourist shops close for siesta. At sunset, people have come back from the beach, having taken their showers and rested. At night, the atmosphere in Mykonos ramps up. The cruise-boat people are mostly gone, coughing three-wheelers make no deliveries in the narrow streets, and everyone is dressed sexy for summer and starting to shimmy with the scene. Many shops stay open past midnight, the restaurants fill up, and the bars and discos make ice cubes as fast as they can.

❶ Start a tour of Mykonos town (Hora) on the main square, **Mando Mavrogenous Square** (sometimes called Taxi Square). Pride of place goes to a bust of Mando Mavrogenous, the island heroine, standing on a pedestal. In the 1821 War of Independence the Mykonians, known for their seafaring skills, volunteered an armada of 24 ships, and in 1822, when the Ottomans landed a force on the island, Mando and her soldiers forced them back to their ships. After independence, a scandalous love affair caused the heroine's exile to Paros, where she died. An aristocratic beauty who becomes a great revolutionary war leader and then dies for love may seem unbelievably Hollywoodish, but it is true.

The main shopping street, **Metoyanni** (⌧*Perpendicular to harbor*), is lined with jewelry stores, clothing boutiques, chic cafés, and candy shops. Owing to the many cruise ships that disgorge thousands of shoppers daily in season, the rents here rival Fifth Avenue's, and the more-interesting shops have skedaddled to less-prominent side streets.

The **Public Art Gallery** (⌧*Metoyanni* ☎*22890/27190*) is also here, with exhibitions changing often.

❷ The charming **Aegean Maritime Museum** contains a collection of model ships, navigational instruments, old maps, prints, coins, and nautical memorabilia. The backyard garden displays some old anchors and ship wheels and a reconstructed 1890 lighthouse, once lighted by oil. ⌧*Enoplon Dynameon* ☎*22890/22700* 💶*€3* ⏲*Daily 10:30–1 and 6:30–9.*

Take a peek into **Lena's House,** an accurate restoration of a middle-class Mykonos house from the 19th century. ⊠*Enoplon Dynameon* ☎*22890/22591* 🎟*Free* ⏲*Apr.–Oct., daily 7* PM–*9* PM.

The **Mykonos Agricultural Museum** displays a 16th-century windmill, traditional outdoor oven, waterwheel, dovecote, and more. ⊠*Petassos, at top of Mykonos town* ☎*22890/22591* 🎟*Free* ⏲*June–Sept., daily 4–6* PM.

3 The **Folk Museum,** housed in an 18th-century house, exhibits a bedroom furnished and decorated in the fashion of that period. On display are looms and lace-making devices, Cycladic costumes, old photographs, and Mykoniot musical instruments that are still played at festivals. ⊠*South of boat dock* ☎*22890/22591 or 22890/22748* 🎟*Free* ⏲*Mon.–Sat. 4–8, Sun. 5:30–8.*

Mykonians claim that exactly 365 churches and chapels dot their land-
4 scape, one for each day of the year. The most famous of these is the
★ **Church of Paraportiani** (*Our Lady of the Postern Gate* ⊠*Ayion Anargyron, near folk museum*). The sloping, whitewashed conglomeration of four chapels, mixing Byzantine and vernacular idioms, looks fantastic, it is solid and ultimately sober, and its position on a promontory facing the sea sets off the unique architecture.

Many of the early ship's captains built distinguished houses directly on the sea here, with wooden balconies overlooking the water. Today
5 this neighborhood, at the southwest end of the port, is called **Little Ven-**
★ **ice** (⊠*Mitropoleos Georgouli*). This area, architecturally unique and one of the most attractive in all the islands, is so called because its handsome houses, which once belonged to shipowners and aristocrats, rise from the edge of the sea, and their elaborate buttressed wooden balconies hang over the water—there are no Venetian marble palazzi reflected in still canals. Many of these fine old houses are now elegant bars specializing in sunset drinks, or cabarets, or shops, and crowds head to the cafés and clubs, many found a block inland from Little Venice. These are usually soundproofed (Mykonians are still sad that a rent fight closed Pierro's, the Mediterranean's most famous gay bar, though maybe residents who lived nearby aren't).

6 The **Greek Orthodox Cathedral of Mykonos** (⊠*On square that meets both Ayion Anargyron and Odos Mitropolis*) has a number of old icons of the post-Byzantine period.

7 Next to the Greek Orthodox Cathedral is the **Roman Catholic Cathedral** (⊠*On square that meets both Ayion Anargyron and Odos Mitropolis*) from the Venetian period. The name and coat of arms of the Ghisi family, which took over Mykonos in 1207, are inscribed in the entrance hall.

Across the water from Little Venice, set on a high hill, are the famous
8 **Mykonos windmills,** echoes of a time when wind power was used to grind the island's grain. The area from Little Venice to the windmills is called **Alefkandra,** which means "whitening": women once hung their laundry here. A little farther toward the windmills the bars chock-

ablock on shoreside decks are barely above sea level, and when the north wind is up (often) surf splashes the tables. Further on, the shore spreads into an unprepossessing beach, and tables are placed on sand or pebbles. After dinner (there are plenty of little tavernas here), the bars turn up their music, and knowing the beat thumps into the night, older tourists seek solace elsewhere.

A SEASIDE MILKY WAY

The best time to visit Mykonos's central harbor is in the cool of the evening, when the islanders promenade along the esplanade to meet friends and visit the numerous cafés. Mykonians, when they see the array of harbor lights from offshore, call it the String of Pearls, though more and more lights are fuzzing the dazzle.

Before setting out on the mandatory boat excursion to the isle of
9 Delos, check out the **Archaeological Museum,** set at the northern edge of town. It affords insight into the intriguing history of its ancient shrines. The museum houses Delian funerary sculptures, many with scenes of mourning; most were moved to Rhenea when the Athenians cleansed Delos in the 6th century, during the sixth year of the Peloponnesian war, and, under instruction from the Delphic Oracle, the entire island was purged of all dead bodies. The most significant work from Mykonos is a 7th-century BC *pithos* (storage jar), showing the Greeks in the Trojan horse and the sack of the city. ✉ *Ayios Stefanos, between boat dock and town* ☎ *22890/22325* 🎫 *€3* ⏲ *Wed.–Mon. 8:30–2:30.*

BEACHES

There is a beach for every taste in Mykonos. Beaches near Mykonos town, within walking distance, are **Tourlos** and **Ayios Ioannis. Ayios Stefanos,** about a 45-minute walk from Mykonos town, has a mini-golf course, water sports, restaurants, and umbrellas and lounge chairs for rent. The south coast's **Psarou,** protected from wind by hills and surrounded by restaurants, offers a wide selection of water sports and is often called the finest beach. Nearby **Platys Yialos,** popular with families, is also lined with restaurants and dotted with umbrellas for rent. **Ornos** is also perfect for families; boats leave from here for more-distant beaches, and there is lively nightlife patronized by locals as well as visitors. **Paranga, Paradise, Super Paradise,** and **Elia** are all on the southern coast of the island, and are famously nude, though getting less so; one corner of Elia is gay. **Super Paradise** is half gay, half straight, and swings at night. The scene at Paradise's bars throbs till dawn. All have tavernas on the beach. At the easternmost end of the south shores is **Kalafatis,** known for package tours, and between Elia and Kalafatis there's a remote beach at **Kato Livadhi,** which can be reached by road.

WHERE TO STAY & EAT

$$$$ ✕ **La Maison de Catherine.** This hidden restaurant's Greek and French
Fodor's Choice ★ cuisine and hospitality—Katerina is still in charge—are worth the search through the Dilou quarter of Mykonos. The splendid air-conditioned interior mixes Cycladic arches and whitewash with a French feeling and a faded 16th-century tapestry from Constantinople. Candles and classical music set the tone for baby squid stuffed with rice and

Greek mountain spices, or soufflé, puffed to perfection and loaded with cheese, mussels, and prawns. For entrées, try leg of lamb with mint sauce or pasta with lobster. The apple tart is divine. ✉ *Ayios Gerasimos, Dilou, 84600* ☎ *22890/22169* 📠 *22890/26946* ✍ *Reservations essential* 💳 *AE, DC, MC, V.*

$$$–$$$$ ✕ **Tagoo.** High Mykonian style can be yours at the eatery of this noted hotel. Haute cuisine is served up in either an all-white room or at outdoor tables, with Mykonos bay on one side and an infinity pool on the other. Start with local louza (smoked pork) with grilled tomatoes and bean mash, seasoned with thyme and marjoram, or with bass carpaccio marinated in olive oil, lemon, and fennel. Other home runs include the sea bream fillet with spinach, rice, and yogurt, or the baby beef fillet with vin santo and coriander. Fish is always fresh and delicately prepared. To top things off, opt for the warm chocolate fondant with ice cream and vanilla sauce. The sommelier helps with the large selection of wines. The restaurant is open April through October. ✉ *Hotel Cavo Tagoo, 84600 (15 mins by foot north of Mykonos town on sea road)* ☎ *22890/23692 through 22890/23694* ✍ *Reservations essential* 💳 *AE, DC, MC, V.*

$$$ ✕ **Chez Maria's.** Dine at this 30-year-old garden restaurant for lively atmosphere—sometimes with live music and dancing—for the zest of Greek living in a lovely candlelit garden. Octopus in wine, great cheese pies, and the fillet of beef with cheese and fresh vegetables will keep you in the mood. So will the apple tart with ice cream and walnuts. ✉ *Kalogera 30, 84600* ☎ *22890/27565* 💳 *AE, MC, V.*

$$$ ★ ✕ **Sea Satin Market–Caprice.** If the wind is up, the waves sing at this magical spot, set on a far tip of land below the famous windmills of Mykonos. The preferred place for Greek shipowners, Sea Satin Market sprawls out onto a seaside terrace and even onto the sand of the beach bordering Little Venice. When it comes to fish, prices vary according to weight. Shellfish is a specialty, and everything is beautifully presented. In summer, live music and dancing add to the liveliness. ✉ *On seaside under windmills* ☎ *22890/24676* 💳 *AE, MC, V.*

$$ ✕ **El Greco.** A fixture for 30 years in Mykonos town's Three Wells district, El Greco has now moved to Tourlos, near the new harbor. Its quiet terrace overlooks the bay (and sunset), although you can go formal in the indoor dark-wood dining room, which has a wine cellar to explore. While wife Barbara provides gracious service, owner Giorgos Rizopoulos cooks "Greek with imagination" and he has a remarkable culinary sensitivity for fresh herbs, which come from the adjacent garden. You might start with *soupies politikes* (cuttlefish, Constantinople style), cooked in their ink and moschato wine; the plate of Mykonos specialties, such as cheeses and cured meats, is the best in town. For a main dish, try rabbit in wine, parsley, and vinegar; or monkfish fricassee (with lettuce and dill). For a fine finale, Giorgos turns his orchard's lemons into an aromatic mousse. Set in the Tourlos suburb, El Greco is located right on the main harbor, about a 20 minute walk from the center of Mykonos town. ✉ *Tourlos* ☎ *22890/22074* 💳 *No credit cards.*

$–$$ ✕ **Kounelas.** This long-established fresh-fish taverna is where many fishermen themselves eat, for solid, no-frills food. The menu depends on the weather—low winds means lots of fish. Note: even in simple places such as Kounelas, fresh fish can be expensive. ✉*Off port near Delos boats* ☎*22890/28220* 💳*No credit cards.*

$–$$ ✕ **Lotus.** For more than 30 years, Giorgos and Elsa Cambanis have lovingly run this tiny restaurant. Elsa is the cook, so compliment her on the fine starter, the mushroom "Lotos" with cream and cheese. The roast leg of lamb with oregano, lemon, and wine is succulent, and the moussaka is almost too good to be traditional. For dessert, have *pralina,* which resembles tiramisu. It's open year-round for dinner only: the porch is covered with bougainvillea in summer, and there's a fireplace in winter. ✉*Metoyanni 47, 84600* ☎*22890/22881* 💳*No credit cards* ⊗*No lunch.*

WORD OF MOUTH

"Tagoo: we absolutely loved it. The owner and her husband were amazing. They helped so much with restaurants, picking us up at the port, rental cars, etc. By the time we left, we felt like family. The pool was wonderful and the bar was fun with lots of interesting people to talk to. They seem to get lots of repeat clients, too. It was a walk into town, though—maybe 10 to 15 minutes. Down hill going and uphill coming back, which was a bit tiring." —Leslie28

¢–$ ✕ **Angolo Bar.** Run by Italians, this place has been serving Mykonos's best espresso for years. In the evening, they also prepare light Italian meals (their full-fledged restaurant is directly across the street). During the day the music is less loud. Set in Mykonos town's busy Lakka area, Angolo can be found 50 yards from the bus stop. ✉*Lakka, 84600* ☎*22890/24207* 💳*No credit cards.*

$$$$ Fodor'sChoice ★ **Belvedere.** You may not have to go to Greece once you view the "movie" presentation on this hotel's Web site—it is almost as relaxing, blue-and-white, and high style as this hotel (but not quite). Favored by the hip, replete with Matsuhisa Mykonos—an outpost of famed sushi chef Nobu—and designed in the best dreamy manner, the Belevedere has a clublike atmosphere, convenient location, and view over Mykonos town and harbor that ensures this hotel's popularity. In the restaurants and bars, you can cut the "cool" attitude with a knife—but when you want to slip off your Tods, repair to the dramatically decorated guest rooms, white-on-white sanctums with sailcloth drapes, rope accents, and a beautifully laid-back touch. Some have magical views, a trade-off for the small dimensions of some of the rooms. For stylishness and class, it's hard to top this one. ✉*School of Fine Arts district, 84600* ☎*22890/25122* 📠*22890/25126* 🌐*www.belvederehotel.com* *42 rooms, 6 suites* *In-room: refrigerator. In-hotel: restaurant, bar, pool, spa, public Internet* 💳*AE, MC, V* ⊗*Closed Nov.–Mar.* 🍽*BP.*

$$$$ ★ **Cavo Tagoo.** Completely redesigned in 2007 in a "barefoot chic" esthetic by the architect-owner, the Cavo Tagoo climbs the hill over the bay in sensuous white curves, with natural projecting rock on the winding path to the guest rooms. The two public pools (one a 38-foot-long eternity) and many private pools make it feel island-aqueous. Drama is on tap in the pool bar where a 43-foot-long aquarium comes stocked with sharks (PETA-lovers, beware). The medley of white cubical suites are furnished in high-drama minimalism, with a

stark white palette enlivened by hot red or cool blue; palm-leaf futons, plasma TVs, and luxurious bathrooms add luxe. Longtime manager Tasos Didimiotis keeps it all gracious. It's a 15-minute walk to town. ✉ *Follow coast road, north of port, 84600* ☎ *22890/23692 through 22890/23695* 🖷 *22890/24923* 🌐 *www.cavotagoo.gr* ⇐ *68 rooms, 5 suites* ♨ *In-room: Ethernet, Wi-Fi. In-hotel: restaurant, bar, pool, no elevator* ▭ *AE, MC, V* ⊙ *Closed Nov.–Mar.* ¶◎| *BP.*

$$$$ ★ **Deliades.** Away from the fray, the Deliades (which translates as "Delian nymphs") is a welcome escape from Mykonos's heat. But these cool Cycladic white cubes offer a lovely retreat made all the more appealing because manager Steve Argiriadis had a hand in their design. The capacious, airy guest rooms (many with beautiful wood beams and 19th-century-style lanterns) all have sea views and terraces, the marble carvings were made especially for this hotel, and the stark white of the architecture is softened with accents in muted sand and sea shades. Eating dinner at the quiet poolside café-restaurant, overlooking the bay, is especially pleasant and it is only a short walk to Ornos beach. The price includes transfers. ✉ *Far end of Ornos beach, follow road up 30 yards, 84600Ornos* ☎ *22890/79430 or 22890/79470* 🖷 *22890/26996* 🌐 *www.hoteldeliadesmykonos.com* ⇐ *30 rooms* ♨ *In-room: refrigerator, dial-up. In-hotel: restaurant, bar, pool, no elevator* ▭ *AE, MC, V* ⊙ *Closed Nov.–Mar.* ¶◎| *BP.*

$$$$ **Hotel Mykonos Adonis.** Set on the edge of town (behind the bus stop) overlooking the sea, this recently renovated option is both convenient and out of the fray. Completely eschewing Mykonos glitz, this place is thoughtfully planned to produce a homelike atmosphere. Result? The clientele, many of them artists and writers, return year after year to let owners Michalis and Roz Apostolou (he's Mykonian, she's American) take care of them. The guest rooms all have balconies, many with views of the sea and the hotel gardens—some of the staffers are passionate gardeners. Breakfast and transfers included. ✉ *Chora, 84600* ☎ *22890/23433* 🖷 *22890/23449* 🌐 *www.mykonosadonis.gr* ⇐ *12 rooms, 12 suites* ♨ *In-room: refrigerator. In-hotel: no elevator* ▭ *AE, D, MC, V* ⊙ *Closed Nov.–Mar.* ¶◎| *BP.*

$$$$ ★ **Kivotos Clubhotel.** Beautifully designed with a vast stonework facade, topped with your usual Cycladic whitewashed house, Spyros Michopoulos's deluxe hotel is architecturally ambitious and designed around an impressive pool. The main floor is all done in a richly decorative island style, with statues in niches and mosaic work, and unexpected little courtyards with bright flowers. The guest rooms, all individually decorated, display local crafts and dazzling objects—ship steering wheels, Fortuny-esque pleated fabrics, fine antiques, and sea views all catch the eye. A hotel minibus runs into town, and to the airport. ✣ *2 km (1 mi) from Mykonos town* ✉ *Ornos bay, 84600* ☎ *22890/25795 or 22890/25796* 🖷 *22890/22844* 🌐 *www.kivotosclubhotel.gr* ⇐ *35 rooms, 5 suites* ♨ *In-room: refrigerator, Ethernet, dial-up. In-hotel: 2 restaurants, bars, pools, no elevator* ▭ *AE, D, MC, V* ⊙ *Closed Nov.–Mar.* ¶◎| *BP.*

$$$$ **Royal Myconian.** You may never leave this light-filled, luxurious hotel, a 20-minute drive from Mykonos town, set high on the bare mountain overlooking quiet Elia beach. A vast fantasia of stone terraces, bou-

gainvillea, Cycladic whitewash, green shutters, spa pools, and sea-view dining, this place may be large enough to boast a vast business convention center but it is also designed with excellent taste. Guest rooms have light teak-wood trim, sheer beige curtains, and Cycladic accents. Their terraces overlook the sea, and suites have private Jacuzzis. The restaurant is elegant inside and out. The price includes transfers. ✉*Elia beach, 84600* ☎*22890/72000* 📠*22890/72027* 🌐*www.royal-myconian.gr* *129 rooms, 20 suites* *In-room: refrigerator. In-hotel: 2 restaurants, pool, spa, public Internet* 💳*AE, D, MC, V* ⏲*Closed Nov.–Mar.* 🍽*BP.*

$$$$ ★ **Semeli.** A carved-marble entrance doorway leads to an old stately home that has been expanded into an elegant hotel in the high Mykoniot style. Named after a Greek nymph, the hotel is now a rambling complex, threaded by stone paths running through sweet gardens. A welcoming lobby allures with coved archways and pretty island handcrafts. Each of the large guest rooms, some with sea views, is differently and traditionally furnished. Though convenient to the town, the pool area, with its terraces and garden view, will tempt you to linger. But the rooms could be larger. ✉*On ring road, 84600* ☎*22890/27466 or 22890/27471* 📠*22890/27467* 🌐*www.semelihotel.gr* *42 rooms, 3 suites* *In-room: refrigerator. In-hotel: restaurant, bar, pool, no elevator, public Internet* 💳*AE, MC, V* 🍽*BP.*

$$$ **Omiros.** Looking for an inexpensive, attractive, convenient, slightly out-of-town accommodation on a hill overlooking the bay? Try this spot, set in the Tagoo area, a 10-minute walk from town (but longer to the center, and the walk back is uphill), on the upper road. The guest rooms are fairly small and simply furnished, some with balconies, and the public terraces lend a convivial atmosphere. Owner Yannis Koukas is efficient, dynamic, and friendly, and a useful expert on Mykonos's less-expensive restaurants; he also edits the local newspaper. Breakfast and transfers are included. ✉*Chora, 84600* ☎*22890/23328* 📠*22890/24369* 🌐*www.hotelomiros.gr* *10 rooms* *In-hotel: no elevator, public Internet.* 💳*AE, D, MC, V* ⏲ 🍽*BP.*

$$$ **Villa Konstantin.** This complex of small apartments, studios, and rooms, located on the ring road, is a 765-yard downhill walk to the town—a theoretically walkable distance, but really not. The owners themselves live here all year, and go to lengths to make it attractive and friendly, as their many returning customers attest. The decor is traditional Mykoniot with built-in furniture, and all rooms have terraces or balconies with sea views. The lovely pool was added in 2006. ✉*Box 1030, 84600* ☎*22890/26204* 📠*22890/26205* 🌐*www.villakonstantin-mykonos.gr* *19 units* *In-room: kitchen, dial-up. In-hotel: no elevator* 💳*MC, V* ⏲*Closed Nov.–Mar.*

$ **Philippi.** Of the inexpensive hotels scattered throughout town, this is the most attractive. The rooms have balconies that overlook the garden—owner Christos Kontizas is a passionate gardener. You can't get there by vehicle, but once there you are in the center of things. If you want to get away from it all, go elsewhere. ✉*Kalogera 25, 84600* ☎*22890/22294* 📠*22890/24680* ✉*chriko@otenet.gr* *13 rooms* *In-room: refrigerator. In hotel: no elevator* 💳*AE, MC, V* ⏲*Closed Nov.–Mar.*

NIGHTLIFE & THE ARTS

Whether it's bouzouki music, break beat, or techno, Mykonos's nightlife beats to an obsessive rhythm until undetermined hours—little wonder Europe's gilded youth comes here *just* to enjoy the night scene. After midnight, they often head to the techno bars along the Paradise and Super Paradise beaches. Some of Little Venice's nightclubs become gay in more than one sense of the word, while in the Kastro, convivial bars welcome all for tequila-*sambukas* at sunset. What is "the" place of the moment? The scene is ever-changing—so you'll need to track the buzz once you arrive.

BARS & DISCOS Little Venice is a good place to begin an evening, and Damianos Griparis's **Galleraki** (☒*Little Venice* ☎*22890/27118*) is one of the best cocktail bars in town; it's so close to the water you may get wet when a boat passes. Upstairs in the old mansion (Delos's first archaeologists lived here), you'll find an art gallery—a handy sanctum for drinks on windy nights. Kostas Karatzas's long-standing **Kastro Bar** (☒*Behind Paraportiani* ☎*22890/23072* 🌐*www.kastrobar.com*), with heavy beamed ceilings and island furnishings, creates an intimate environment for enjoying the evening sunset over the bay; classical music sets the tone. **Montparnasse** (☒*Agion Anargyron 24, Little Venice* ☎*22890/23719* 🌐*www.thepianobar.com*) hangs paintings by local artists; its superb sunset view precedes nights of live cabaret and musicals.

El Pecado–Remezzo (☒*North of waterfront*) is a high-tech, wild dance club.

SPORTS & THE OUTDOORS

DIVING **Mykonos Diving Center** (☒*Psarou* ☎*22890/24808* 🌐*www.dive.gr*) has a variety of scuba courses and excursions at 30 locations.

WATER SPORTS The windy northern beaches on Ornos bay are best for water sports; you can rent surfboards and take lessons. There's windsurfing and waterskiing at Ayios Stefanos, Platys Yialos, and Ornos. **Aphrodite Beach Hotel** (☒*Kalafati beach* ☎*28890/71367* 🖷*22890/71525*) has water sports. The program at **Surfing Club Anna** (☒*Agia Anna* ☎*22890/71205*) is well organized.

SHOPPING

FASHION Yiannis **Galatis** (☒*Mando Mavrogenous Square, opposite Lalaounis* ☎*22890/22255*) has outfitted such famous women as Elizabeth Taylor, Ingrid Bergman, and Jackie Onassis. Yiannis will probably greet you personally and show you some of his coats and costumes, hostess gowns, and long dresses. He also has men's clothes. His memoirs capture the old days on Mykonos, when Jackie O. was a customer. **Jella's** (☒*Nikiou 5* ☎*22890/24153* 🌐*www.mykonos-web.com*), a tiny boutique filled with custom-made silk knits that drape with special elegance, and silk slippers from Turkistan, is next to La Maison de Catherine restaurant; the nearby area is rife with shops. **Loco** (☒*Kalogera 29 N* ☎*22890/23682*) sells cotton and linen summer wear in lovely colors. The Marla knits are from the family factory in Athens. **Parthenis** (☒*Alefkandra Square* ☎*22890/23080* 🌐*www.orsalia-parthenis.gr*) was opened by Dimitris Parthenis in 1978 but now features designs by his daughter Orsalia, all showcased in a large Mykonian-style building on the up side of Alefkandra Square in Little Venice. The collection of cotton and silk garments in white and soft neutral colors are very popular for their soft draping and clinging wrap effect.

FINE & DECORATIVE ART Soula Papadakou's **Venetia** (✉*Ayion Anargyron 16, Little Venice* ☎*22890/24464*) carries authentic copies of traditional handmade embroideries in clothing, tablecloths, curtains, and such, all in white; the women who work for her come from all over Greece, including a nunnery in Ioannina. Mykonos used to be a weaver's island, where 500 looms clacked away. Two shops remain. In **Nikoletta** (✉*Little Venice*), Nikoletta Xidakis sells her skirts, shawls, and bedspreads made of local wool. **Ioanna Zouganelli** (☎*22890/22309*), whose father used to sell the family's weavings from a trunk on his Delos excursion boat, makes mohair shawls and traditional Mykonian weavings in her tiny shop on the square in front of Paraportiani.

JEWELRY **Ilias Lalaounis** (✉*Polykandrioti 14, near taxis* ☎*22890/22444* 🖷*22890/24409* 🌐*www.lalaounismykonos.com*) is known internationally for jewelry based on classic ancient Greek designs, reinterpreted for the modern woman. There are always new variations; the shop is as elegant as a museum. **Precious Tree** (✉*Dilou 2* ☎🖷*2289024685*) is a tiny shop aglitter in gems elegantly set here and in its workshop in Athens; in its creativity, it hardly resembles Mykonos's mainline shops.

ANO MERA ΆΝΩ ΜΕΡΑ

8 km (5 mi) east of Mykonos town.

Monastery buffs should head to Ano Mera, a village in the central part of the island, where the **Monastery of the Panayia Tourliani,** founded in 1580 and dedicated to the protectress of Mykonos, stands in the central square. Its massive baroque iconostasis (altar screen), made in 1775 by Florentine artists, has small icons carefully placed amid the wooden structure's painted green, red, and gold-leaf flowers. At the top are carved figures of the apostles and large icons depicting New Testament scenes. The hanging incense holders with silver molded dragons holding red eggs in their mouths show an Eastern influence. In the hall of the monastery, an interesting **museum** displays embroideries, liturgical vestments, and wood carvings. A good taverna is across the street. The monastery's big festival—hundreds attend—is on August 15. ✉*On central square* ☎*0289/71249* ⏲*By appointment only; call in advance.*

DELOS ΔΗΛΟΣ

Fodor'sChoice ★ *25-min caïque ride southwest from Mykonos.*

Arrive at the mythical, magical, and magnificent site of Delos and you might wonder how this barren islet, which had virtually no natural resources, became the religious and political center of the Aegean. One answer is that Delos provided the safest anchorage for vessels sailing between the mainland and the shores of Asia; another answer is that it had no other utilization. A third is provided if you climb Mt. Kynthos to see that the isle is shielded on three sides by other islands. Indeed, this is how the Cyclades—the word means "circling ones"—got their name: they circle around the sacred island. Delos's amazing saga begins back in the times of myth:

Zeus fell in love with gentle Leto, the Titaness, who became pregnant. When Hera discovered this infidelity, she forbade Mother Earth to give Leto refuge and ordered the Python to pursue her. Finally Poseidon, taking pity on her, anchored the poor floating island of Delos with four diamond columns to give her a place to rest. Leto gave birth first to the virgin huntress Artemis on Rhenea and then, clasping a sacred palm on a slope of Delos's Mt. Kynthos, to Apollo, god of music and light.

By 1000 BC the Ionians, who inhabited the Cyclades, had made Delos their religious capital. Homeric Hymn 3 tells of the cult of Apollo in the 7th century BC. One can imagine the elegant Ionians, whose central festival was here, enjoying the choruses of temple girls—"Delian korai, who serve the Far-Shooter"—singing and dancing their hymn and displaying their graceful tunics and jewelry. But a difficult period began for the Delians when Athens rose to power and assumed Ionian leadership. In 543 BC an oracle at Delphi conveniently decreed that the Athenians purify the island by removing all the graves to Rhenea, a dictate designed to alienate the Delians from their past.

After the defeat of the Persians in 478 BC, the Athenians organized the Delian League, with its treasury and headquarters at Delos (in 454 BC the funds were transferred to the Acropolis in Athens). Delos had its most prosperous period in late Hellenistic and Roman times, when it was declared a free port and quickly became the financial center of the Mediterranean, the focal point of trade, where 10,000 slaves were sold daily. Foreigners from as far as Rome, Syria, and Egypt lived in this cosmopolitan port, in complete tolerance of one another's religious beliefs, and each group built its various shrines. But in 88 BC Mithridates, the king of Pontus, in a revolt against Roman rule, ordered an attack on the unfortified island. The entire population of 20,000 was killed or sold into slavery. Delos never fully recovered, and later Roman attempts to revive the island failed because of pirate raids. After a second attack in 69 BC, Delos was gradually abandoned.

In 1872, the French School of Archaeology began excavating on Delos—a massive project, considering that much of the island's 4 square km (1½ square mi) is covered in ruins. The work continues today. Delos remains dry and shadeless; off-season, the snack bar is often closed; most guards leave on the last boat to Mykonos in the early afternoon. But if on the way to Mykonos you see dolphins leaping (it often happens), you'll know Apollo is about and approves.

1 On the left from the harbor is the **Agora of the Competialists** (circa 150 BC), members of Roman guilds, mostly freedmen and slaves from Sicily who worked for Italian traders. They worshipped the *Lares Competales,* the Roman "crossroads" gods; in Greek they were known as Hermaistai, after the god Hermes, protector of merchants and the

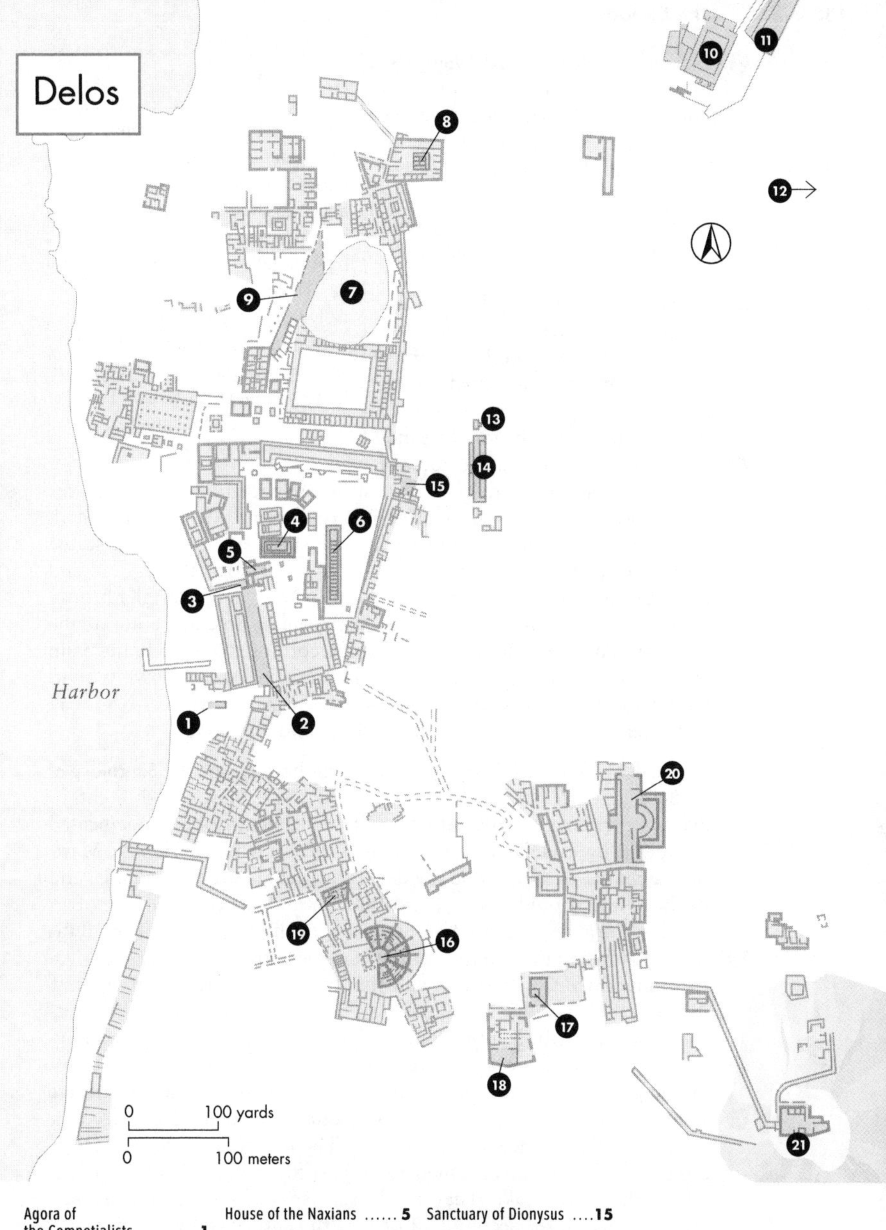

- Agora of the Competialists **1**
- Ancient Theater **16**
- Archaeological Museum ...**14**
- Avenue of the Lions **9**
- Gymnasium **10**
- House of the Dolphins **17**
- House of the Masks **18**
- House of the Naxians **5**
- House of the Trident.......**19**
- Mount Kythos **21**
- Palaestras **8**
- Propylaea **3**
- Sacred Lake **7**
- Sacred Way **2**
- Sanctuary of Apollo **4**
- Sanctuary of Dionysus **15**
- Sanctuary of the Bulls **6**
- Sanctuary of the Syrian Gods **20**
- Stadium **11**
- Synagogue built by Phoenician Jews **12**
- Tourist Pavilion **13**

2 crossroads. The **Sacred Way,** east
of the agora, was the route, during the holy Delian festival, of the
procession to the Sanctuary of
3 Apollo. The **Propylaea,** at the end of
the Sacred Way, were once a monumental white marble gateway with
three portals framed by four Doric
columns. Beyond the Propylaea is
4 the **Sanctuary of Apollo**; though little
remains today, when the Propylaea
were built in the mid-2nd century
BC, the sanctuary was crowded with
altars, statues, and temples—three
of them to Apollo. Inside the sanc-
5 tuary and to the right is the **House of
the Naxians,** a 7th- to 6th-century BC structure with a central colonnade.
Dedications to Apollo were stored in this shrine. Outside the north wall a massive rectangular **pedestal** once supported a colossal statue of Apollo (one of the hands is in Delos's Archaeological Museum, and a piece of a foot is in the British Museum). Near the pedestal a bronze palm tree was erected in 417 BC by the Athenians to commemorate the palm tree under which Leto gave birth. According to Plutarch, the palm tree toppled in a storm and brought the statue of Apollo down with it. Odysseus in The Odyssey compares the Phaeacian princess Nausicaa to the palm he saw on Delos, when the island was wetter.

6 Southeast of the Sanctuary of Apollo are the ruins of the **Sanctuary of
the Bulls,** an extremely long and narrow structure built, it is thought, to
display a trireme, an ancient boat with three banks of oars, dedicated
to Apollo by a Hellenistic leader thankful for a naval victory. Maritime symbols were found in the decorative relief of the main halls, and
the head and shoulders of a pair of bulls were part of the design of an
interior entrance. A short distance north of the Sanctuary of the Bulls
7 is an oval indentation in the earth where the **Sacred Lake** once sparkled.
It is surrounded by a stone wall that reveals the original periphery.
According to islanders, the lake was fed by the River Inopos from its
source high on Mt. Kynthos until 1925, when the water stopped flow-
8 ing and the lake dried up. Along the shores are two ancient **palaestras,**
buildings for physical exercise and debate. One of the most evocative
9 sights of Delos is the 164-foot-long **Avenue of the Lions.** These are replicas; the originals are in the museum. The five Naxian marble beasts
crouch on their haunches, their forelegs stiffly upright, vigilant guard-
ians of the Sacred Lake. They are the survivors of a line of at least nine
lions, erected in the second half of the 7th century BC by the Naxians.
One, removed in the 17th century, now guards the Arsenal of Venice
10 (though with a later head). Northeast of the palaestras is the **gymnasium,** a square courtyard nearly 131 feet long on each side. "Gym"
means naked in Greek, and here men and boys stayed in shape (and,
in those heavily Platonic days, eyed each other). The long, narrow
11 structure farther northeast is the **stadium,** the site of the athletic events

A SITE TO SEE BY SEA

Most travel offices in Mykonos town run guided tours to the ancient isle of Delos that cost about €35, including boat transportation and entry fee. Alternatively, take one of the small passenger boats that visit Delos daily from the port: the round-trip costs about €12, and entry to the site (with no guide) is €6. They leave between 8:30 AM and 1 PM and return noon to 2 PM.

of the Delian Games. East of the stadium site, by the seashore, are the
12 remains of a **synagogue built by Phoenician Jews** in the 2nd century BC.
13 A road south from the gymnasium leads to the **tourist pavilion,** which
14 has a meager restaurant and bar. The **Archaeological Museum** is also on
the road south of the gymnasium; it contains most of the antiquities
found in excavations on the island: monumental statues of young men
and women, stelae, reliefs, masks, and ancient jewelry. Immediately to
15 the right of the museum is a small **Sanctuary of Dionysus,** erected about
300 BC; outside it is one of the more-boggling sights of ancient Greece:
several monuments dedicated to Apollo by the winners of the choral
competitions of the Delian festivals, each decorated with a huge phallus, emblematic of the orgiastic rites that took place during the Dionysian festivals. Around the base of one of them is carved a lighthearted
representation of a bride being carried to her new husband's home. A
marble phallic bird, symbol of the body's immortality, also adorns this
corner of the sanctuary. Beyond the path that leads to the southern part
16 of the island is the **ancient theater,** built in the early 3rd century BC in the
elegant residential quarter inhabited by Roman bankers and Egyptian
and Phoenician merchants. Their one- and two-story **houses** were typically built around a central courtyard, sometimes with columns on all
sides. Floor mosaics of snakes, panthers, birds, dolphins, and Dionysus
channeled rainwater into cisterns below; the best-preserved can be seen
17 18 19 in the **House of the Dolphins,** the **House of the Masks,** and the **House of the
Trident.** A dirt path leads east to the base of Mt. Kynthos, where there
20 are remains from many **Middle Eastern shrines,** including the **Sanctuary of the Syrian Gods,** built in 100 BC. A flight of steps goes up 368 feet
21 to the summit of **Mt. Kynthos** (after which all Cynthias are named), on
whose slope Apollo was born. ✉ *Delos island and historic site, take
a small passenger boat from Mykonos town* ☎ *22890/22259* 🌐 *www.
culture.gr* 🎫 *€5* ⏲ *Apr.–Oct., Tues.–Sun. 8:30–3.*

NAXOS ΝΑΞΟΣ

"Great sweetness and tranquillity" is how Nikos Kazantzakis, premier novelist of Greece, described Naxos, and indeed a tour of the island leaves you with an impression of abundance, prosperity, and serenity. The greenest, largest, and most fertile of the Cyclades, Naxos, with its many potato fields, its livestock and its thriving cheese industry, and its fruit and olive groves framed by the pyramid of Mt. Zas (3,295 feet, the Cyclades's highest), is practically self-sufficient. Inhabited for 6,000 years, the island has memorable landscapes—abrupt ravines, hidden valleys, long and sandy beaches—and towns that vary from a Cretan mountain stronghold to the seaside capital that strongly evokes its Venetian past. It is full of history and monuments—classical temples, medieval monasteries, Byzantine churches, Venetian towers—and its huge interior offers endless magnificent hikes, not much pursued by summer tourists, who cling to the lively capital and the developed western beaches, the best in the Cyclades.

Continued on page 490

MYTH,
BEHAVIN'

GREECE'S GODS AND HEROES

Superheroes, sex, adventure: it's no wonder Greek myths have reverberated throughout Western civilization. Today, as you wander ancient Greece's most sacred sites–such as Delos, island birthplace of the sun god Apollo–these ageless tales will come alive to thrill and perhaps haunt you.

Whether you are looking at 5th century BC pedimental sculptures in Olympia or ancient Red-Figure vase paintings in Athens, whether you are reading the epics of Homer or the tragedies of Euripides, you are in the presence of the Greek mythopoetic mind. Peopled with emblems of hope, fear, yearning, and personifications of melting beauty or of petrifying ugliness, these ancient myths helped early Greeks make sense of a chaotic, primitive universe that yielded no secrets.

Frightened by the murder and mayhem that surrounded them, the Greeks set up gods in whom power, wisdom, and eternal youth could not perish. These gods lived, under the rule of Zeus, on Mount Olympus. Their rivalries and intrigues were a primeval, superhuman version of *Dynasty* and *Dallas*. These astounding collections of stories not only pervaded all ancient Greek society but have influenced the course of Western civilization: How could we imagine our culture—from Homer's *Iliad* to Joyce's *Ulysses*—without them?

IN GODS WE TRUST

To the ancient Greeks, mythology was more than a matter of literature, art, philosophy, and ethics. For them, the whole countryside teemed with spirits and powers. Besides the loftier Olympian gods there were spirits of mountain, sea, trees, and stream—oreads, nereids, dryads, and naiads. The ancients preferred to personify natural phenomena than to depict them realistically.

Nymphs, for example, were primarily personifications of nature—oak trees, pools, sea waves, caves, peaks, isles. Monsters did the same; Scylla, who ate six of Odysseus' men, was the symbolic personification of a shipwrecking cliff in the Straits of Messina. In the darkness of the night (or of the mind), the ancients' ancestral fears and perverse desires became embodied in a world of brutal minotaurs, evil chimeras, mischievous sphinxes, terrifying centaurs, and ferocious Furies. To combat them, people looked to the gods, promoters of peace and justice at home, success in trade and war, and fertility.

YE GODS!

WHO'S WHO IN GREEK MYTHOLOGY

ZEUS

Latin Name: Jupiter

God of: Sky, Supreme God

Attribute: Scepter, Thunder

Roving Eye: Zeus was the ruler of Mount Olympus but often went AWOL pursuing love affairs down on earth with nymphs and beautiful ladies; his children were legion, including Hercules.

DEMETER

Latin Name: Ceres

Goddess of: Earth, Fecundity

Attribute: Sheaf, Sickle

Most Dramatic Moment: After her daughter Persephone was kidnapped by Zeus, Demeter decided to make all plants of the earth wither and die.

ATHENA

Latin Name: Minerva

Goddess of: Wisdom

Attribute: Owl, Olive

Top Billing: The goddess of reason, she gave the olive tree to the Greeks; her uncle was Poseidon, and the Parthenon in Athens was built in her honor.

ARTEMIS

Latin Name: Diana

Goddess of: Chastity, Moon

Attribute: Stag

Early Feminist: Sister of Apollo, she enjoyed living in the forest with her court, frowned on marriage, and, most notoriously, had men torn apart by her hounds if they peeked at her bathing.

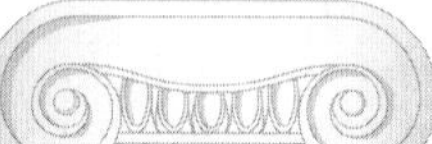

HEPHAESTOS

Latin Name: Vulcan

God of: Fire, Industry

Attribute: Hammer, Anvil

Pumping Iron: The best-preserved Doric style temple in Athens, the Hephaestaion, was erected to this god in the ancient Agora marketplace; today, ironmongers still have shops in the district there.

APOLLO

Latin Name: Phoebus

God of: Sun, Music, and Poetry

Attribute: Bow, Lyre

Confirmed Bachelor: Born at Delos, his main temple was at Delphi; his love affairs included Cassandra, to whom he gave the gift of prophecy; Calliope, with whom he had Orpheus; and Daphne, who, fleeing from his embrace, changed into a tree.

The twelve chief gods formed the elite of Olympus. Each represented one of the forces of nature and also a human characteristic. They also had attributes by which they can often be identified. The Romans, influenced by the arts and letters of Greece, largely identified their own gods with those of Greece, with the result that Greek gods have Latin names as well. Here are the divine I.D.s of the Olympians.

HERA
Latin Name: Juno

Goddess of: Sky, Marriage

Attribute: Peacock

His Cheating Heart: Hera married her brother Zeus, wound up having a 300-year honeymoon with him on Samos, and was repaid for her fidelity to marriage by the many love affairs of her hubby.

HESTIA
Latin Name: Vesta

Goddess of: Hearth, Domestic Values

Attribute: Eternal Fire

Hausfrau: A famous virgin, she was charged with maintaining the eternal flame atop Olympus; the Vestal Virgins of ancient Romans followed in her footsteps.

POSEIDON
Latin Name: Neptune

God of: Sea, Earthquakes

Attribute: Trident

Water Boy: To win the affection of Athenians, Poseidon and Athena were both charged with giving them the most useful gift, with his invention of the bubbling spring losing out to Athena's creation of the olive.

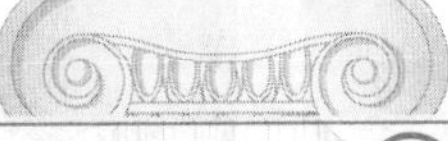

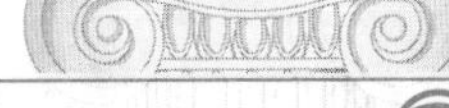

APHRODITE
Latin Name: Venus

Goddess of: Love, Beauty

Attribute: Dove

And the Winner Is: Born out of the foam rising off of Cyprus, she was given the Golden Apple by Paris in the famous beauty contest between her, Athena, and Hera, and bestowed the love of Helen on him as thanks.

HERMES
Latin Name: Mercury

God of: Trade, Eloquence

Attribute: Wings

Messenger Service: Father of Pan, Hermes was known as a luck-bringer, harbinger of dreams, and the messenger of Olympus; he was also worshipped as the god of commerce and music.

ARES
Latin Name: Mars

God of: Tumult, War

Attribute: Spear, Helmet

Antisocial: The most famous male progeny of Zeus and Hera, he was an irritable man; considering his violent temper, few temples were erected in his honor in Greece.

TOGA PARTY

Was all human life doomed to disaster and woe? Zeus, many believed, had two jars—one of good fortune and one of ill—which he dipped into when making his decisions. To most people he distributed portions fairly equally—but Zeus himself often fell prey to pride and envy, and the latter often got this chronic double-dater into trouble. No matter that he had seven wives: He was a very "Your honey or your wife" philanderer and his endless seductions provided innumerable scandals.

One notable case was Leda, queen to King Tyndareus of Sparta. Zeus saw her shapely naked limbs, seduced her by assuming the form of a swan, and she then gave birth to two eggs, one of which hatched with the Dioscuri, Castor and Pollux, the other with Clytemnestra and Helen of Troy, women of serious trouble. Clytemnestra married Agamemnon, king of Mycenae, and Helen married Menelaos, king of Sparta. The Trojan War followed and the rest is history (or something like history). The whole story, embracing fantasy, politics, and cult has been retold endlessly in poems from Homer to Yeats and images from Leonardo to Gustave Moreau's surrealist paintings. The ancient myths turn out to be as modern as today.

GREEK LIGHTNING

Today, historians point to tribal origin-heroes and local cult figures of the ancient Near East as influencing the earliest Greek myths, first professed in the preliterate second millennium BC. Capturing primeval energies from the past that are still in us, these stories provide the back story to great sites like Delos, the legendary birthplace of the god Apollo. The ancients believed that the sun crossed the sky in Apollo's chariot. Other gods were considered the cause of many phenomena. What caused earthquakes? Poseidon with his trident. Who used lighting bolts as weapons? Zeus. Who invented fire? Prometheus brought it down from Olympus. How did pain and sickness come into the world? Through the curiosity of Pandora (that other Eve). Before long, in the non-factual, gravity-free world of the ancient Greek imagination, the deeds of the gods became moralistic parables about man. Is gold the best thing of all? Consider Midas. Would it be a good thing to fly? Icarus did not find it so. Would you like to be married to Helen of Troy, or to Jason, the winner of the Golden Fleece? Consult Menelaus and Medea. How wonderful to be the supremely powerful and popular ruler of a fabulously great city! Not for Oedipus. Without some understanding of the ancient myths, half the meaning of Greece will elude you.

HERCULES THE FIRST ACTION HERO

Greece's most popular mythological personage was probably Heracles, a hero who became a god, and had to work hard to do it. This paragon of masculinity was so admired by the Romans that they vulgarized him as Hercules, and modern entrepreneurs have capitalized on his popularity in silly sandal epics and sillier Saturday morning cartoons. His name means "glory of Hera," though the goddess hated him because he was the son of Zeus and the Theban princess Alcmene. The Incredible Bulk proved his strength and courage while still in the cradle, and his sexual prowess when he impregnated King Thespius' fifty daughters in as many nights. But the twelve labors are his most famous achievement. To expiate the mad murder of his wife and his three children, he was ordered to:

1. Slay the Nemean Lion
2. Kill the Lernaean Hydra
3. Capture the Ceryneian Hind
4. Trap the Erymanthian Boar
5. Flush the Augean stables of manure
6. Kill the obnoxious Stymphalian Birds
7. Capture the Cretan Bull, a Minoan story
8. Steal the man-eating Mares of Diomedes
9. Abscond with the Amazon Hippolyta's girdle
10. Obtain six-armed Geryon's Cattle
11. Fetch the Golden Apples of the Hesperides, which bestowed immortality
12. Capture three-headed Cerberus, watchdog of Hades.

In other words, he had to rid the world of primitive terrors and primeval horrors. Today, some revisionist Hellenistic historians considered him to be a historical king of Argos or Tiryns and his main stomping ground was the Argolid, basically the northern and southern Peloponnese. Travelers can today still trace his journeys through the region, including Lerna (near the modern village of Myli), not far from Nafplion, where the big guy battled the Hydra, now seen by some historians as a symbol for the malarial mosquitoes that once ravaged the area. Herc pops up in the myths of many other heroes, including Jason, who stole the Golden Fleece; Perseus, who killed Medusa; and Theseus, who established Athens' dominance. And his constellation is part of the regularly whirling Zodiac that is the mythological dome over all our actions and today's astrology.

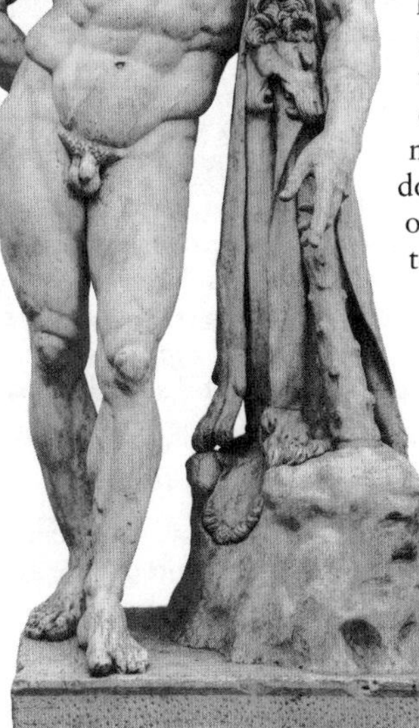

Facing page: left, Disney's *Hercules* (2000); middle, *Apollo*, Olympia Museum; right, Antigone leads Oedipus out of Thebes.
Left: *Hercules Farnese*. National Archaeological Museum, Naples

NAXOS TOWN ΝΑΞΟΣ (ΧΩΡΑ)

LOOK, DON'T TOUCH

If you put on a mask and flippers for a swim in Delos's pellucid water, remember that the site guards will check you, as the offshore waters here are gleaming with shards of Delos past.

7 hrs by ferry from Piraeus; 35 km (22 mi) east of Paros town.

As your ferry chugs into the harbor, you see before you the white houses of Naxos town (Chora) on a hill crowned by the one remaining tower of the Venetian castle, a reminder that Naxos was once the proud capital of the Venetian semi-independent Duchy of the Archipelago.

The tiny church of **Our Lady of Myrtle** (⊠*Perched on sea rock off waterfront*) watches over the local sailors, who built it for divine protection.

While the capital town is primarily beloved for its Venetian elegance and picturesque blind alleys, Naxos's most famous landmark is ancient: ★ the **Portara** (⊠*At harbor's far edge*), a massive doorway that leads to nowhere. The Portara stands on the islet of **Palatia,** which was once a hill (since antiquity the Mediterranean has risen quite a bit) and in the 3rd millennium BC was the acropolis for a nearby Cycladic settlement. The Portara, an entrance to an unfinished Temple of Apollo that faces exactly toward Delos, Apollo's birthplace, was begun about 530 BC by the tyrant Lygdamis, who said he would make Naxos's buildings the highest and most glorious in Greece. He was overthrown in 506 BC, and the temple was never completed; by the 5th and 6th centuries AD it had been converted into a church; and under Venetian and Turkish rule it was slowly dismembered, so the marble could be used to build the castle. The gate, built with four blocks of marble, each 16 feet long and weighing 20 tons, was so large it couldn't be demolished, so it remains today, along with the temple floor. Palatia itself has come to be associated with the tragic myth of Ariadne, princess of Crete.

Ariadne, daughter of Crete's King Minos, helped Theseus thread the labyrinth of Knossos and slay the monstrous Minotaur. In exchange, he promised to marry her. Sailing for Athens, the couple stopped in Naxos, where Theseus abandoned her. Jilted Ariadne's curse made Theseus forget to change the ship's sails from black to white, and so his grieving father Aegeus, believing his son dead, plunged into the Aegean. Seeing Ariadne's tears, smitten Dionysus descended in a leopard-drawn chariot to marry her, and set her bridal wreath, the Corona Borealis, in the sky, an eternal token of his love.

The myth inspired one of Titian's best-known paintings, as well as Strauss's opera *Ariadne auf Naxos*.

North of Palatia, **underwater remains of Cycladic buildings** are strewn along an area called **Grotta.** Here are a series of large worked stones, the remains of the waterfront quayside mole, and a few steps that locals say go to a tunnel leading to the islet of Palatia; these remains are Cycladic (before 2000 BC).

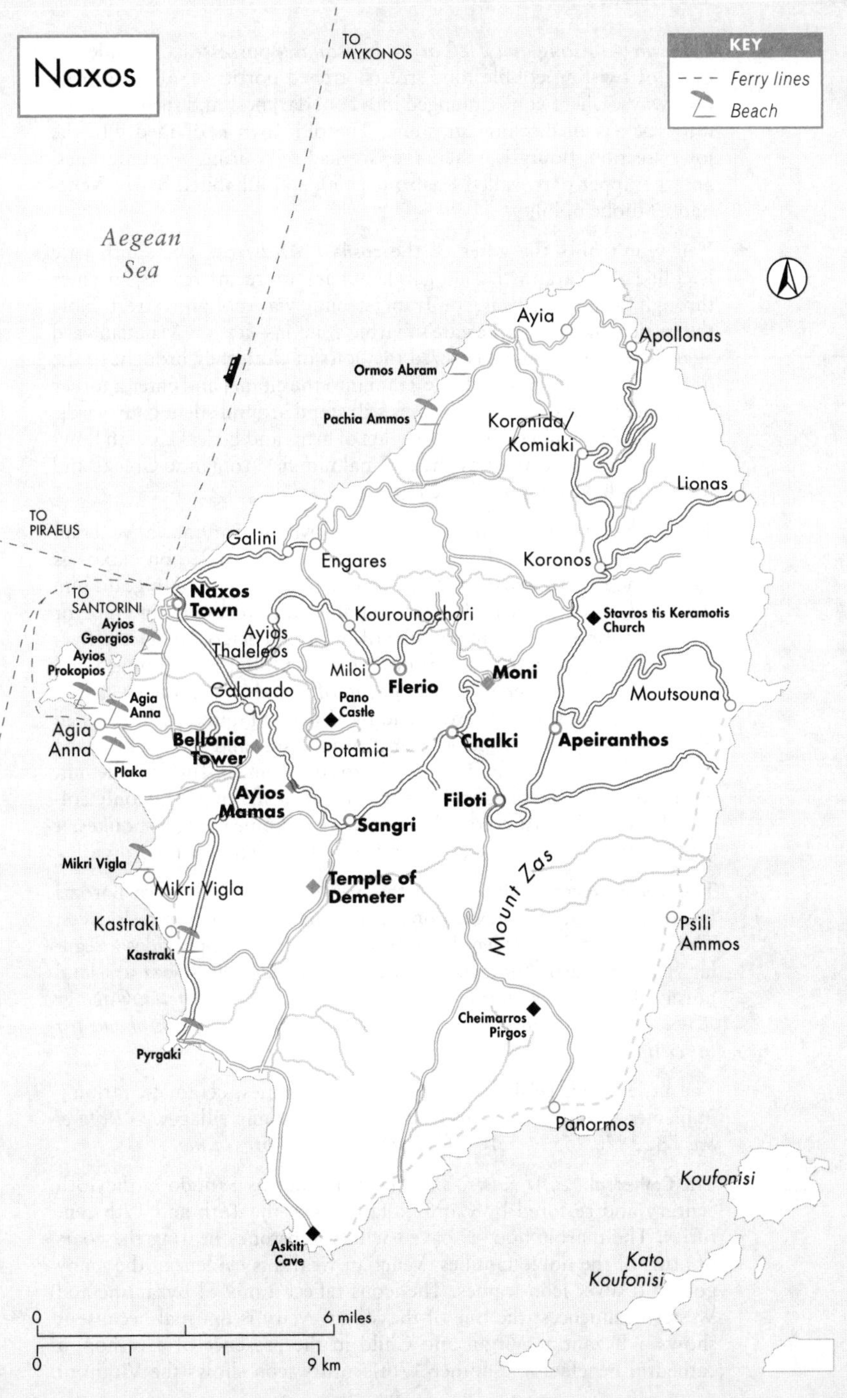

Naxos
KEY
Ferry lines
Beach
TO MYKONOS
Aegean Sea
TO PIRAEUS
TO SANTORINI
Ayia
Apollonas
Ormos Abram
Pachia Ammos
Koronida/ Komiaki
Lionas
Galini
Engares
Koronos
Naxos Town
Kourounochori
Stavros tis Keramotis Church
Ayios Georgios
Ayios Thaleleos
Ayios Prokopios
Miloi
Flerio
Moni
Agia Anna
Galanado
Pano Castle
Moutsouna
Agia Anna
Bellonia Tower
Potamia
Chalki
Apeiranthos
Plaka
Ayios Mamas
Filoti
Sangri
Mikri Vigla
Mikri Vigla
Temple of Demeter
Mount Zas
Kastraki
Kastraki
Psili Ammos
Cheimarros Pirgos
Pyrgaki
Panormos
Koufonisi
Askiti Cave
Kato Koufonisi
0
6 miles
0
9 km

Old town (✉*Along quay, left at 1st big square*) possesses a bewildering maze of twisting cobblestone streets, arched porticoes, and towering doorways, where you're plunged into cool darkness and then suddenly into pockets of dazzling sunshine. The old town is divided into the lower section, **Bourgos,** where the Greeks lived during Venetian times, and the upper part, called **Kastro** (castle), still inhabited by the Venetian Catholic nobility.

★ You won't miss the gates of the **castle** (✉*Kastro*). The south gate is called the **Paraporti** (side gate), but it's more interesting to enter through the northern gate, or **Trani** (strong), via Apollonos street. Note the vertical incision in the gate's marble column—it is the Venetian yard against which drapers measured the bolts of cloth they brought to the noblewomen. Step through the Trani into the citadel and enter another age, where sedate Venetian houses still stand around silent courtyards, their exteriors emblazoned with coats of arms and bedecked with flowers. Half are still owned by the original families; romantic Greeks and foreigners have bought up the rest.

The entire citadel was built in 1207 by Marco Sanudo, a Venetian who, three years after the fall of Constantinople, landed on Naxos as part of the Fourth Crusade. When in 1210 Venice refused to grant him independent status, Sanudo switched allegiance to the Latin emperor in Constantinople, becoming duke of the archipelago. Under the Byzantines, "archipelago" had meant "chief sea," but after Sanudo and his successors, it came to mean "group of islands," i.e., the Cyclades. For three centuries Naxos was held by Venetian families, who resisted pirate attacks, introduced Roman Catholicism, and later rebuilt the castle in its present form. In 1564 Naxos came under Turkish rule but, even then, the Venetians still ran the island, while the Turks only collected taxes. The rust-color Glezos tower was home to the last dukes; it displays the coat of arms: a pen and sword crossed under a crown.

The **Domus Venetian Museum,** in the 800-year-old Dellarocca-Barozzi house, lets you, at last, into one of the historic Venetian residences. The house's idyllic garden, built into the Kastro wall, provides a regular venue in season for a concert series, from classical to jazz to island music. ✉*At Kastro north gate* ☎*22850/22387* ✉*venetian@acn.gr* 🎫*€4, tour €6* ⏲*June–Aug., daily 10–3 and 7–10; check ahead for other times.*

The little **Naxos Folklore Museum** shows costumes, ceramics, farming implements, and other items from Naxos's far-flung villages. ✉*Roubel Sq.* ☎*22850/25531* 🎫*€3* ⏲*Hours not set at press time.*

The **Cathedral** (✉*At Kastro's center*) was built by Sanudo in the 13th century and restored by Catholic families in the 16th and 17th centuries. The marble floor is paved with tombstones bearing the coats of arms of the noble families. Venetian wealth is evident in the many gold and silver icon frames. The icons reflect a mix of Byzantine and Western influences: the one of the Virgin Mary is unusual because it shows a Byzantine Virgin and Child in the presence of a bishop, a cathedral benefactor. Another 17th-century icon shows the Virgin of the Rosary surrounded by members of the Sommaripa family, whose house is nearby.

Today the historic convent and school of the Ursulines houses the **Naxos Archaeological Museum,** best known for its Cycladic and Mycenaean finds. During the early Cycladic period (3200 BC–2000 BC) there were settlements along Naxos's east coast and outside Naxos town at Grotta. The finds are from these settlements and graveyards scattered around the island. Many of the vessels exhibited are from the early Cycladic I period, hand-built of coarse-grain clay, sometimes decorated with a herringbone pattern. Though the museum has too many items in its glass cases to be appreciated in a short visit, you should try not to miss the white marble Cycladic statuettes, which range from the early "violin" shapes to the more-detailed female forms with their tilted flat heads, folded arms, and legs slightly bent at the knees. The male forms are simpler and often appear to be seated. The most common theory is that the female statuettes were both fertility and grave goddesses, and the males servant figures. ✉ *Kastro* ☎ *22850/22725* 🌐 *www.culture.gr* 🎫 *€3* ⏲ *Tues.–Sun. 8:30–3.*

The **Greek Orthodox cathedral** (✉ *Bourgos*) was built in 1789 on the site of a church called Zoodochos Pigis (Life-giving Source). The cathedral was built from the materials of ancient temples: the solid granite pillars are said to be from the ruins of Delos. Amid the gold and the carved wood, there is a vividly colored iconostasis painted by a well-known iconographer of the Cretan school, Dimitrios Valvis, and the Gospel Book is believed to be a gift from Catherine the Great of Russia.

The **Ancient Town of Naxos** was directly on the square in front of the Greek Orthodox cathedral. You'll note that several of the churches set on this square, like the cathedral itself, hint at Naxos's venerable history as they are made of ancient materials. In fact, this square was, in succession, the seat of a flourishing Mycenaean town (1300–1050 BC), a classical agora (when it was a 167-foot by 156-foot square closed on three sides by Doric stoas, so that it looked like the letter "G"; a shorter fourth stoa bordered the east side, leaving room at each end for an entrance), a Roman town, and early Christian church complex. Although much of the site has been refilled, under the square a **museum** (🎫 *Free* ⏲ *Tues.–Sun. 8–2:30*) gives you a well-marked sampling of the foundations. City, cemetery, tumulus, hero shrine: no wonder the early Christians built here. For more of ancient Naxos, explore the nearby precinct of Grotta.

BEACHES

The southwest coast of Naxos, facing Paros and the sunset, offers the Cyclades's longest stretches of beaches. All these have tavernas and rooms. They are listed, in order, heading south. **Ayios Georgios** is now part of town and very developed. **Ayios Prokopios** has a small leeward harbor and lagoons with waterfowl. **Ayia Anna,** very crowded, has a small harbor with connections to Paros. **Plaka,** ringed by sand dunes and bamboo groves, is about 8 km (5 mi) south of town. **Mikri Vigla** is sandy and edged by cedar trees. Seminude **Kastraki** has white marble sand. **Pyrgaki** is the least-developed beach, with idyllic crystalline water.

> **SCHOLARLY IMPRINTS**
>
> The Convent and School of the Ursulines, located a few steps beyond Naxos's cathedral, in the Kastro, was begun in 1739. In a 1713 document, a general of the Jesuits, Francis Tarillon, mentions that the proposed girls' school should be simple; grandeur would expose it to the Turks' covetousness. While it has now been recycled as part of the island's archaeological museum, wealthier Naxian women of a certain age still recall the good education the Ursulines provided.

WHERE TO STAY & EAT

$$ ★ **Old Inn.** Berlin-trained chef Dieter von Ranizewski serves German food informed by Naxos. In a courtyard under a chinaberry tree, with rough whitewashed walls and ancient marbles, two of the old church's interior sides open into the wine cellar and gallery; on the fourth side, with beams and wood paneling, is a fireplace. The menu is extensive. For starters you might try sausages with beer sauce, smoked ham, or liver pâté—all homemade. For entrées, have the signature steak with tomatoes, olives, Roquefort, and bacon-flecked roast potatoes. Barbecue spareribs are also especially good. For dessert the mousse beckons voluptuously. There is a children's menu and small playground. ⊠*Naxos town; take car road off waterfront, turn right into 2nd alley* ☎*22850/26093* ▭*No credit cards.*

$ **Apolafsis.** Rightly named "Enjoyment," Lefteris Keramideas's second-floor restaurant offers a balcony with a great view of the harbor and sunset. You'll enjoy live music (always in summer; often in winter), as well as a large assortment of appetizers (try spinach or zucchini tart), local barrel wine, and fresh fish. The sliced pork in wine sauce is good, too. ⊠*Naxos town waterfront* ☎*22850/22178* ▭*AE, MC, V.*

$ **Gorgona.** Bearded Dimitris and Koula Kapris's beachfront taverna is popular both with sun worshippers on Ayia Anna beach and locals from Chora, who come here winter and summer to get away and sometimes to dance until the late hours, often to live music. The menu is extensive and fresh daily—the fresh fish comes from the caïques that pull up at the dock right in front every morning. Two good appetizers are *kakavia* (fish stew) and shrimp *saganaki* (with cooked cheese), while spaghetti with crab is a fine entrée. The barrel wine is their own (they also bottle it). The small hotel next door is also theirs. ⊠*Ayia Anna near dock* ☎*22850/41007* ▭*No credit cards.*

$ **Labyrinth.** Opened in 2006 in the middle of the old town, Labyrinth was an immediate success with locals. Its more-than-simple food, its cozy flagstone garden, and its good service are all praiseworthy. Good appetizers include a tomato and feta quiche, and crepe rolls with smoked salmon and avocado. Among main dishes are chicken fillet with shrimp, potatoes, and herbs; and roast lamb with tomatoes and mint. And don't miss out on the light and summery lemon mousse. ☎*22850/22253* ▭*No credit cards* ⊙*Closed Oct.–Apr. No lunch.*

$$$ **Galaxy.** All whitewash and marble, this hotel is perfect if you want to be on the beach (and don't mind the crowds at the seaside in summer). Its three buildings have wide stone arches and wooden doors in

shades of green and blue, and balconies with grillwork depicting swans. Archways also span the large rooms, which have beamed ceilings and orange accessories, plus plants, kitchenettes, and dining areas. Most rooms have ocean views (the beach is a minute away). The carefully tended grounds glow with yellow roses and a fountain. Too bad this hotel isn't more convenient to town. ✉ *Ayios Georgios beach, 84300* ☎ *22850/22422 or 22850/22423* 🖷 *22850/22889* 🌐 *www.hotel-galaxy.com* *43 studios, 11 rooms* *In-room: kitchen, Ethernet. In-hotel: pool, no elevator* 💳 *AE, MC, V* ⏲ *Closed Nov.–Mar.* 🍽 *BP.*

$ **Abram Village.** If you love island nature and dislike crowds, this is your place. Set on Naxos's northern coast (the developers only moved in a few years ago when the road was finally paved), Panyiotis Albertis's rooms and villas recline in a green garden on beautiful Abram beach. The scenery is extraordinary and there are many coves with beaches. Most of the accommodations here are rooms, with no TV, air-conditioners (it's cool), or telephones; in addition, there are two villas (which have all these amenities and sleep up to eight; they run about €160); both rooms and villas have balconies with sea views. The inexpensive restaurant, where Panyiotis's mother and wife cook, features traditional food from local products. *Tiliktera* (meatballs with eggplants and spicy sauce) is especially good—and the rosé wine and raki are Panyiotis's own. ✣ *20 km (33 mi) from Chora* ✉ *Abram 84300* ☎ *22850/63244* 🖷 *22850/63223* 🌐 *www.abram.gr* *20 rooms, 2 villas* *In-hotel: no elevator, public Internet* 💳 *MC, V* ⏲ *Closed Oct.–Apr.*

$ ★ **Apollon.** In addition to being comfortable, attractive, and quiet (it's a converted marble workshop), this hotel, set in the Fontana quarter, is convenient to everything in town. Even better, it offers parking facilities, a rarity in town. The lobby blends wood, warm marble, deep greens, and many plants. The rooms are simple and have balconies; bathrooms are small. The outside, of ocher plaster and stone, is adorned with a feast of marble decoration. ✉ *Behind Orthodox cathedral, car entrance on road out of town, 84300Fontana, Chora* ☎ *22850/22468* 🖷 *22850/25200* 🌐 *www.apollonhotel-naxos.gr* *12 rooms, 1 suite* *In hotel: no elevator, parking* 💳 *AE, MC, V.*

$ **Chateau Zevgoli.** If you stay in Chora, try to settle in here. Each room in Despina Kitini's fairy-tale pension, in a comfortable Venetian house, is distinct. The living room is filled with dark antique furniture, gilded mirrors, old family photographs, and locally woven curtains and tablecloths. One of the nicest bedrooms has a private bougainvillea-covered courtyard and pillows handmade by Despina's great-grandmother; the honeymoon suite has a canopy bed, a spacious balcony, and a view of the Portara. Despina also has roomy studios, in Chora's old town, including several on the kastro—stay a day and you'll stay a month. The only downside: The hotel is uphill and you must walk. ✉ *Chora old town (follow signs stenciled on walls), 84300* ☎ *22850/22993 or 22850/26143* 🖷 *22850/25200* 🌐 *www.apollonhotel-naxos.gr* *8 rooms, 1 suite* *In-room: refrigerator. In-hotel: no elevator, public Internet* 💳 *AE, MC, V.*

NIGHTLIFE & THE ARTS

> **A TOP TIME-OUT**
>
> Naxos Café (22850/26343) is one of a number of cafés in Naxos's old town trying for charm and authenticity, and succeeding. It stays open late and there is usually live jazz on Wednesday nights.

BARS Nightlife in Naxos is quieter than it is on Santorini or Mykonos, but there are several popular bars at the south end of Chora. Popularity changes fast, so keep your ears open for the latest places. **Ocean Dance** (☒*Chora* ☎*22850/26766*) opens at 11:30 PM, all year round. Head for **Abyss** (☒*Grotta road, Chora*) for a large, soundproof space with a Portara view; it's active till dawn.

ARTS EVENTS The 17th-century **Bazeos tower** (✥*12 km [18 mi] from Chora toward Chalki,* ☎*22850/31402* ⊕*www.bazeostower.gr*) is one of the island's most beautiful 17th-century Venetian-era monuments and is worth a visit in itself (during high season it is open daily 10–5) but also offers a calendar of exhibitions, concerts, and seminars every summer. The **Catholic Cultural Center** (☒*Kastro, near church* ☎*22850/24729*), among other things, runs art exhibitions; watch for posters. The **Domus Venetian Museum** (☒*At Kastro north gate, Chora* ☎*22850/22387*), in the 800-year-old Dellarocca-Barozzi house, offers a summer concert series in its lovely garden. The **Town Hall Exhibition Space** (☒*Chora's south end* ☎*22850/37100*) offers an ambitious program of art exhibitions, concerts, and other events.

SPORTS & THE OUTDOORS

SAILING & WATER SPORTS For windsurfing rental and lessons near Chora, contact **Naxos-Surf Club** (☒*Ayios Yorgios beach* ☎*22850/29170*). For windsurfing on distant, paradisiacal Plaka beach, contact **Plaka Watersports** (☒*Plaka beach* ☎*22850/41264*).

SHOPPING

ANTIQUES Eleni Dellarocca's shop, **Antico Veneziano** (☒*In Kastro, down from museum* ☎*22850/26206 or 22850/22702*), is in the basement of her Venetian house, built 800 years ago. The columns inside come from Naxos's ancient acropolis. In addition to antiques, she has handmade embroideries, porcelain and glass, mirrors, old chandeliers, and vintage photographs of Naxos. One room is an art gallery.

BOOKS At Eleftherios Primikirios's bookstore **Zoom** (☒*Chora waterfront* ☎*22850/23675 or 22850/23676* ✉*prizoom@otenet.gr*), there's an excellent selection of English-language books about Naxos and much else. No other island bookstore is this well stocked.

CLOTHING Vassilis and Kathy Koutelieris's **Loom** (☒*Dimitriou Kokkou 8, in old market, off main square, 3rd street on right* ☎📠*22850/25531* ✉*loom.naxos@gmail.com*) sells casual clothes made from organically grown Greek cotton (including the Earth Collection in muted natural colors).

JEWELRY At **Midas** (☒*Old town, up main street behind Promponas on Chora waterfront* ☎*22850/24852*), owner Fotis Margaritis creates talismans in different settings. All include a "Naxos eye," which is the operculum, or door, of a seashell with a spiral design that fishermen bring him. The workshop of **Nassos Papakonstantinou** (✉*Ayiou Nikodemou street, on old town's main square* ☎📠*22850/22607*) sells one-of-a-kind pieces both sculptural and delicate. His father was a woodcarver; Nassos has inherited his talent. The shop has no sign—that is Nassos's style.

DAYS FOR WINE & THYME

A large selection of the famous *kitro* (citron liqueur) and preserves, as well as Naxos wines and thyme honey, packed in attractive gift baskets, can be found at Promponas Wines and Liquors, located on the Chora waterfront (22850/22258). It has been around since 1915 and free glasses of kitro are offered.

TRADITIONAL CRAFTS, CARPETS & JEWELS The embroidery and knitted items made by women in the mountain villages are known throughout Greece. They can be bought at **Techni** (✉*Persefonis street, old town* ☎*22850/24767* 🌐*www.techni.gr*). Techni's two shops, almost facing each other, also sell carpets, jewelry in old designs, linens, and more.

BELLONIA TOWER ΠΥΡΓΟΣ ΜΠΕΛΟΝΙΑ

5 km (3 mi) south of Naxos town.

The graceful Bellonia tower (Pirgos Bellonia) belonged to the area's ruling Venetian family, and like other fortified houses, it was built as a refuge from pirates and as part of the island's alarm system. The towers were located strategically throughout the island; if there was an attack, a large fire would be lighted on the nearest tower's roof, setting off a chain reaction from tower to tower and alerting the islanders. Bellonia's thick stone walls, its Lion of St. Mark emblem, and flat roofs with zigzag chimneys are typical of these pirgi. The unusual 13th-century **"double church" of St. John** (✉*In front of Bellonia tower*) exemplifies Venetian tolerance. On the left side is the Catholic chapel, on the right the Orthodox church, separated only by a double arch. A family lives in the tower, and the church is often open. From here, take a moment to gaze across the peaceful fields to Chora and imagine what the islanders must have felt when they saw pirate ships on the horizon.

AYIOS MAMAS ΆΓΙΟΣ ΜΑΜΑΣ

3 km (2 mi) south of Bellonia tower, 8 km (5 mi) south of Naxos town.

A kilometer (½ mi) past a valley with unsurpassed views is one of the island's oldest churches (9th century), Ayios Mamas. St. Mamas is the protector of shepherds and is regarded as a patron saint in Naxos, Cyprus, and Asia Minor. Built in the 8th century, the stone church was the island's cathedral under the Byzantines. Though it was converted into a Catholic church in 1207, it was neglected under the Venetians and is now falling apart. You can also get to it from the Potamia villages.

SANGRI ΣΑΓΚΡΙ

3 km (2 mi) south of Ayios Mamas, 11 km (7 mi) south of Naxos town.

Sangri is the center of an area with so many monuments and ruins spanning the Archaic to the Venetian periods it is sometimes called little Mystras, a reference to the famous abandoned Byzantine city in the Peloponnese.

The name Sangri is a corruption of Sainte Croix, which is what the French called the town's 16th-century monastery of **Timios Stavros** *(Holy Cross)*. The town is actually three small villages spread across a plateau. During the Turkish occupation, the monastery served as an illegal school, where children met secretly to learn the Greek language and culture.

Above the town, you can make out the **ruins of Kastro Apilarou** (⊠ *On Mt. Profitis Ilias*), the castle Sanudo first attacked. It's a hard climb up.

TEMPLE OF DEMETER ΝΑΟΣ ΤΗΣ ΔΗΜΗΤΡΑΣ

★ *5 km (3 mi) south of Sangri.*

Take the asphalt road right before the entrance to Sangri to reach the Temple of Demeter, a marble Archaic temple, circa 530 BC, lovingly restored by German archaeologists during the 1990s. Demeter was a grain goddess, and it's not hard to see what she is doing in this beautiful spot. There is also a small museum here (admission is free).

CHALKI ΧΑΛΚΙ

6 km (4 mi) northeast of Sangri, 17 km (10½ mi) southeast of Naxos town.

You are now entering the heart of the lush Tragaia valley, where in spring the air is heavily scented with honeysuckle, roses, and lemon blossoms and many tiny Byzantine churches hide in the dense olive groves. In Chalki is one of the most important of these Byzantine churches: the white, red-roofed **Panagia Protothrone** *(First Enthroned Virgin Church)*. Restoration work has uncovered frescoes from the 6th through the 13th century, and the church has remained alive and functioning for 14 centuries. The oldest layers, in the apse, depict the Apostles. ⊠ *On main road* ⊙ *Mornings.*

Chalki itself is a pretty town, known for its neoclassic houses in shades of pink, yellow, and gray, which are oddly juxtaposed with the plain but stately 17th-century Venetian **Frangopoulos tower.** ⊠ *Main road, next to Panagia Protothrone* 🎫 *Free* ⊙ *Sometimes open in morning.*

MONI ΜΟΝΗ

6 km (4 mi) north of Chalki, 23 km (14¼ mi) east of Naxos town.

Owing to a good asphalt road, Moni ("monastery"), high in the mountains overlooking Naxos's greenest valley, has become a popular place for a meal or coffee on a hot afternoon. Local women make embroideries for Chora's shops. Just below Moni is one of the Balkans's most important churches, **Panayia Drosiani** (☎*22850/31003*), which has faint, rare Byzantine frescoes from the 7th and 8th centuries. Its name means Our Lady of Refreshment, because once during a severe drought, when all the churches took their icons down to the sea to pray for rain, only the icon of this church got results. The fading frescoes are visible in layers: to the right when you enter are the oldest—one shows St. George the Dragon Slayer astride his horse, along with a small boy, an image one usually sees only in Cyprus and Crete. According to legend, the saint saved the child, who had fallen into a well, and there met and slew the giant dragon that had terrorized the town. Opposite him is St. Dimitrios, shown killing barbarians. The church is made up of three chapels—the middle one has a space for the faithful to worship at the altar rather than in the nave, as became common in later centuries. Next to that is a very small opening that housed a secret school during the revolution. It is open mornings and again after siesta; in deserted winter, ring the bell if it is not open.

FILOTI ΦΙΛΟΤΙ

6½ km (4 mi) south of Moni, 20 km (12½ mi) southeast of Naxos town.

Filoti, a peaceful village on the lower slopes of Mt. Zas, is the interior's largest. A three-day festival celebrating the Dormition starts on August 14. In the center of town are another Venetian tower that belonged to the Barozzi and the Church of Filotissa (Filoti's Virgin Mary) with its marble iconostasis and carved bell tower. There are places to eat and rooms to rent.

SPORTS & THE OUTDOORS

Filoti is the starting place for several walks in the countryside, including the climb up to **Zas cave** (✉*Southeast of town onsmall dirt track*), where obsidian tools and pottery fragments have been found; lots of bats live inside. Mt. Zas, or Zeus, is one of the god's birthplaces; on the path to the summit lies a block of unworked marble that reads *Oros Dios Milosiou*, or "Boundary of the Temple of Zeus Melosios." (Melosios, it is thought, is a word that has to do with sheep.) The islanders say that under the Turks the cave was used as a chapel, and two stalagmites are called the Priest and the Priest's Wife, who are said to have been petrified by God to save them from arrest.

APEIRANTHOS ΑΠΕΙΡΑΝΘΟΣ

★ *12 km (7½ mi) northeast of Filoti, 32 km (20 mi) southeast of Naxos town.*

Apeiranthos is very picturesque, with views and marble-paved streets running between the Venetian Bardani and Zevgoli towers. As you walk through the arcades and alleys, notice the unusual chimneys—no two are alike. The elders sit in their doorsteps chatting, while packs of children shout "Hello, hello" at any passerby who looks foreign.

TOWERING VIEWS

The Cheimarros Pirgos (Tower of the Torrent), a cylindrical Hellenistic tower, can be reached from Filoti by a road that begins from the main road to Apeiranthos, outside town, or by a level, 3½-hour hike with excellent views. The walls, as tall as 45 feet, are intact, with marble blocks perfectly aligned. The tower, which also served as a lookout post for pirates, is often celebrated in the island's poetry: "O, my heart is like a bower/And Cheimarros's lofty tower!"

A very small **Archaeological Museum,** established by a local mathematician, Michael Bardanis, displays Cycladic finds from the east coast. The most important of the artifacts are unique gray marble plaques from the 3rd millennium BC with roughly hammered scenes of daily life: hunters and farmers and sailors going about their business. If it's closed, ask in the square for the guard. ✉ *Off main square* 🎫 *Free* 🕙 *Daily 8:30–3.*

PAROS & ANTIPAROS ΠΑΡΟΣ & ΑΝΤΙΠΑΡΟΣ

In the classical age, the great sculptor Praxiteles prized the incomparably snowy marble that came from the quarries at Paros; his chief rival was the Parian Scopas. Between them they developed the first true female nude and gentle voluptuousness seems a good description of this historic island. Today, Paros is favored by people for its cafés by the sea, golden sandy beaches, and charming fishing villages. It may lack the chic of Mykonos and have fewer top-class hotels, but at the height of the season it often gets Mykonos's overflow. The island is large enough to accommodate the traveler in search of peace and quiet, yet the lovely port towns of Paroikía, the capital, and Naousa also have an active nightlife (overactive in August). Paros is a focal point of the Cyclades ferry network, and many people stay here for a night or two while waiting for a connection. Paros town has a good share of bars and discos, though Naousa has a more-chic island atmosphere. And none of the islands has a richer cultural life, with concerts, exhibitions, and readings, than does Paros. For this, check the English monthly, *Paros Life,* available everywhere (🌐 *www.paroslife.gr,* and also 🌐 *www.parosweb.com*).

Like all the bigger islands, Paros is developing too fast. In the last 15 years 2,000 new homes have been built on the island, which has a population of 14,000. Another thousand are underway—and this equals the total number of homes ever built here. You'll understand why: you're likely to want to build a little house here yourself. The

overflow of visitors is such that it has now washed up on Paros's sister, Antiparos: this island forgetaway still has an off-the-beaten-track vibe, even though the rich and famous—Dolly Goulandris, Brad Pitt, and Tom Hanks, to name three—have discovered it.

PAROIKIA ΠΑΡΟΙΚΙΑ (ΠΑΡΟΣ)

35 km (22 mi) west of Naxos town, 10 km (6 mi) southwest of Naousa.

First impressions of Paroikía (Paros town), pretty as it is, will not necessarily be positive. The port is clogged with too many boats and the traffic problem, now that Athenian families bring two cars and local families own two cars, is insoluble; the new parking area on landfill is one of the Cyclades's disasters. The waterfront is lined with travel agencies, a multitude of car and motorbike rental agencies, and "*fast-food-adika*"—the Greek word means just what you think it does. Then, if you head east on the harbor road, you'll see a lineup of bars, tourist shops, and coffee shops—many, as elsewhere on the more-prosperous islands, rented by Athenians who come to Paros to capitalize on the huge summer influx. Past them are the fishing-boat dock, a partially excavated ancient graveyard, and the post office; then start the beaches (shaded and over-popular), with their hotels and tavernas.

But go the other way straight into town and you'll find it easy to get lost in the maze of narrow, stone-paved lanes that intersect with the streets of the quiet residential areas. The new marble plaza at the town's entrance, finished in 2007, is full of strollers and playing children in the evening (during the day, you can fry eggs on this shadeless space). As you check your laptop (Paroikía is Wi-Fi) along the market street chockablock with tourist shops, you'll begin to traverse the centuries: ahead of you looms the seaside Kastro, the ancient acropolis. In 1207 the Venetians conquered Paros, which joined the Duchy of Naxos, and built their huge marble castle wall out of blocks and columns from three temples. At the crest, next to the church of Saints Constantine and Helen (built in 1689), are the visible foundations of a late-Archaic temple to Athena—the area remains Paros's favorite sunset spot.

PRIDE GOETH BEFORE A FALL

At one point, Justinian the Great (who ruled the Byzantine Empire in 527-65) had the Hundred Doors Church rebuilt. He appointed Isidorus, one of the two architects of Constantinople's famed Hagia Sophia, to design it, but Isidorus sent his apprentice, Ignatius, in his place. On inspection, Isidorus discovered the dome to be so magnificent that, consumed by jealousy, he pushed the apprentice off the roof. Ignatius grasped his master's foot and the two tumbled to their death together. Look for the folk sculpture at the sanctuary's left portal of the two men.

Fodor's Choice ★ The square above the port, to the northwest, was built to celebrate the church's 1,700th anniversary. From there note a white wall with two belfries, the front of the former monastic quarters that surround the magnificent **Panayia Ekatontapyliani** *(Hundred Doors Church)*, the earliest remaining proto-Byzantine church in Greece and one of the oldest unaltered churches in the world. As such, it is of inestimable value to architecture buffs (such as Prince Charles, who has been spotted here).

The story began in 326, when St. Helen—the mother of Emperor Constantine the Great—set out on a ship for the Holy Land to find the True Cross. Stopping on Paros, she had a vision of success and vowed to build a church there. Though she died before it was built, her son built the church in 328 as a wooden-roof basilica. Two centuries later, Justinian the Great (who ruled the Byzantine Empire in 527–65) comissioned the splendid dome.

According to legend, 99 doors have been found in the church and the 100th will be discovered only after Constantinople is Greek again—but the name is actually older than the legend. Inside, the subdued light mixes with the dun, reddish, and green tufa (porous volcanic rock). The columns are classical and their capitals Byzantine. At the corners of the dome are two fading Byzantine frescoes depicting six-winged seraphim. The 4th-century iconostasis (with ornate later additions) is divided into five frames by marble columns. One panel contains the 14th-century icon of the Virgin, with a silver covering from 1777.

The Virgin is carried in procession on the church's crowded feast day, August 15, the Dormition. The adjacent **Baptistery,** nearly unique in Greece, also built from the 4th to the 6th century, has a marble font and bits of mosaic floor. During Easter services, thousands of rose petals are dropped from the dome on the singing celebrants. The church **museum,** at right, contains post-Byzantine icons. ✉ *750 ft east of dock* ☎ *22840/21243* 🎟 *€2* ⏲ *Daily 8 AM–10 PM.*

The **Archaeological Museum** contains a large chunk of the famed Parian chronicle, which recorded cultural events in Greece from about 1500 BC until 260 BC (another chunk is in Oxford's Ashmolean Museum). It interests scholars that the historian inscribed detailed information about artists, poets, and playwrights, completely ignoring wars and shifts in government. Some primitive pieces from the Aegean's oldest settlement, Saliagos (an islet between Paros and Antiparos), are exhibited in the same room, on the left. A small room contains Archaic finds from the ongoing excavation at Despotiko—and they are finding a lot. In the large room to the right rests a marble slab depicting the poet Archilochus in a banquet scene, lying on a couch, his weapons nearby. The ancients ranked Archilochus, who invented iambic meter and wrote the first signed love lyric, second only to Homer. When he died in battle against the Naxians, his conqueror was cursed by the oracle of Apollo for putting to rest one of the faithful servants of the muse. Also there are a monumental Nike and three superb pieces found in the last decade: a waist-down kouros, a gorgon with intact wings, and a dancing-girl relief. ✉ *Behind Hundred Doors Church* ☎ *22840/21231* 🎟 *€3* ⏲ *Tues.–Sun. 8:30–2:30.*

At the **Anthemion Museum**, the Kontogiorgos family has lovingly gathered a large, valuable collection of books, manuscripts, prints, coins, jewels, embroideries, weapons, ceramics, and much more, mostly pertaining to Paros, and lovingly displays it in this house-turned-museum. ✉ *Airport road, before Punta split* ☎📠 *22840/91010* 🎟 *€5* ⏲ *Tues.–Sun. 8:30–2:30.*

The **Scropios Museum** is set next to a garden full of large models of traditional Parian windmills, dovecotes, churches, and other such things, making for an utterly charming setting. It showcases the creations of fisherman Benetos Skiadas, who loves to make detailed models of ships, including his own, and his scrupulous craftsmanship is on view here; you can also order a model of your own design. ✉ *On road to Aliki, just past airport* ☎📠 *22840/91129* 🎟 *€2* ⏲ *May–Sept., changeable hrs.*

BEACHES

From Paros town, boats leave throughout the day for beaches across the bay: to sandy **Krios** and the quieter **Kaminia. Livadia,** a five-minute walk, is very developed but has shade. In the other direction, Delfini has a club with live music, and Parasporos has two music bars.

WHERE TO STAY & EAT

$$ ★ **Levantis.** Owner George Mavridis does his own cooking—always a good sign. Though this spot looks like a garden taverna and, amazingly, is priced like one, the food is sophisticated and eclectic, as George often returns from winter travels with exotic new recipes. Two intriguing starters are roasted eggplant tart with salsa verde, and Greek mussels with a spicy ouzo sauce. Top entrées include handmade ravioli stuffed with gingered beets, goat cheese, and pesto or the caramelized calves' liver with roasted grapes. Then choose, if you can, between banana toffee and cream pie or lemon sorbet with roasted figs and sweet wine. Unusual in Greece, Levantis has a nonsmoking section. ✉ *Central market street* ☎ *22840/23613* ▭ *AE, MC, V* ⊗ *Closed Nov.–Apr.*

$–$$ ★ **Porphyra.** Yannis Gouroyannis knows everything about fish; he fishes, dives, prepares, and greets you with a plate of marinated fish, and his oysters, clams, and urchins couldn't be fresher. The mussels are always superb, and the kakavia (fish soup with a whole fish in each plate) and fresh fish (it changes) in an aromatic white sauce remind you that Paros is seagirt. The interior is simple and authentic, while the outdoor tables border a romantic ancient ruin. All ingredients are local and of the highest quality in Paros's best seafood restaurant. ✉ *Along waterfront toward post office* ☎ *22840/23410* ▭ *AE, MC, V.*

¢ **Gelato Sulla Luna.** Many of the evening strollers on the waterfront of Paroikía cannot pass this authentic gelateria; their willpower melts faster than the gelato. Denise Marinucci's father made ice cream in New Jersey, and Denise continues the tradition, but her recipes come from Venice. She makes everything on the premises. Have another. ✉ *Waterfront* ☎ *22840/22868* 🌐 *www.parosweb.com/sullaluna* ▭ *No credit cards* ⊗ *Closed Dec.–Mar.*

$$$$ ★ **Bicycle House.** The name comes from the bicycle (of the noted late dancer Vasilis Iakoumis) mounted to the front of this house, which contains three lovely units. The complex overlooks the sea and sunset, is surrounded by greenery, and is scrupulously designed in island style with the addition of modern comforts. Owners Len and Marilyn Rooks are warm and helpful and visitors tend to return, if only to hear more about Len's own cycling exploits (guests are often regaled with these stories at his garden barbecues). You should have your own transportation, though there is a bus. Unusually for a place at this price range, no credit cards are taken. It's open all year. ✣ *8 km (12 mi) from Paroikía on airport road* ✉ *84400* ☎📠 *22840/92203* 🌐 *www.paroshome.com/roshome.com* *3 apartments* *In-room: kitchen, Ethernet. In-hotel: no elevator* ▭ *No credit cards.*

$$$ **Pandrossos Hotel.** If you want a good night's sleep away from the pulse of Paros town but you don't want to give up shopping, nightlife, restaurants, and cafés, the Pandrossos—built on a hill with a splendid view overlooking Paros bay—is the best choice. The lobby, restaurant, and terrace form one great expanse of marble, perfect for sunset watching—unless you're watching it from your room's sea-view balcony. Note that some of the rooms are on the small side. To get to this hotel's hill location, take the seaside road from Paros town. ✉ *On hill at southwest edge of Paros town, 84400* ☎ *22840/22903* 📠 *22840/22904*

www.pandrossoshotel.gr 41 rooms, 5 suites In-room: Ethernet. In-hotel: restaurant, bar, pool, no elevator AE, MC, V Closed Nov.–Mar. BP.

$ **Parian Village.** This shady, quiet hotel at the far edge of Livadia beach has small rooms, all with balconies or terraces, most with spectacular views over Paroikía bay. The pool is pretty, but the sea is close. Breakfast is included. *25-min sea walk from center of Paros town, 84400 22840/23187 22840/23880 www.paros-accommodations.gr/parianvillage 28 rooms In-room: refrigerator. In-hotel: pool, no elevator MC, V Closed Nov.–Apr. BP.*

$ ★ **Pension Evangelistria.** Voula Maounis's rooms, all with balconies, are usually full of returnees—archaeologists, painters, and the like—who enjoy its central location near the Hundred Doors Church, olive trees, and gracious welcome. The house is built over a Roman-period ruin; the hotel is open all year. *Near dock, 84400 22840/21481 22840/22464 parosrealmarket@otenet.gr 9 rooms In-room: kitchen. In-hotel: no elevator No credit cards.*

NIGHTLIFE & THE ARTS

MUSIC & BARS Turn right along the waterfront from the port in Paros town to find the town's famous bars; then follow your ears. At the far end of the Paralia is the laser-light-and-disco section of town, which you may want to avoid. In the younger bars, cheap alcohol, as everywhere in tourist Greece, is often added to the more-colorful drinks. For a classier alternative to noisy bars, head for **Pebbles** (*On Kastro hill 22840/22283*), which often has live jazz (Greece's best jazz guitarist, Vasilis Rakopoulos, who summers on Paros, likes to drop by with local bassist Petros Varthakouris) and overlooks the sunset.

THE ARTS The **Aegean Center for the Fine Arts** (*Main cross street to market street 22840/23287 www.aegeancenter.org*), a small American arts college, hosts readings, concerts, lectures, and exhibitions in its splendidly restored neoclassic mansion. Director John Pack, an American photographer, lives on the island with his family. Since 1966 the center has offered courses (two three-month semesters) in writing, painting, photography, and classical voice training.

The **Archilochos Cultural Society** (*Near bus stop 22840/23595 www.archilochos.gr*) runs a film club in winter and offers concerts, exhibitions, and lectures throughout the year.

The **Paros Summer Musical Festival** brings musicians from around the world to perform at the Archilochos Hall. Watch for posters for upcoming events.

Of all the islands Paros has the liveliest art scene (check *Paros Life* for openings and events), with dozens of galleries and public spaces presenting exhibitions. Many artists, Greek and foreign, live on the island or visit regularly—painters Jane Pack and Neva Bergmann, sculptor Britt Spillers, photographers Stavros Niflis and Elizabeth Carson, mosaicist Angelika Vaxevanidou, and ceramist Stelios Ghikas are just a few—and the Aegean Center has proved a strong stimulant. Set on an enchanting alley in the historic Kastro area of Paroikía is the former wine storage space now known as the **Apothiki** (✉*Near bus stop* ☎*22840/28226* 🌐*www.apothiki.com*); artists include sculptor Richard King and painter Ellen Shire, and it's worth a visit just for the beauty of its space.

The **Orange Door Gallery** (✉*Market street* ☎*22840/21590* 🌐*www.orangedoorgallery.com*) is set in a whitewashed town house and has a fine stable of artists, including some great photographers.

SPORTS & THE OUTDOORS

WATER SPORTS Many beaches offer water sports, especially windsurfing. **Aegean Diving College** (✉*Golden beach* ☎📠*22840/43347*) offers scuba lessons and takes you to reefs, shipwrecks, and caves. Director Peter Nikolaides, who discovered the oldest shipwreck known, is a marine biologist involved in many of Greece's ecological projects. Every summer the **F2 Windsurfing Center** (✉*New Golden beach, at Philoxenia Hotel, near Marpissa* ☎*22840/41878*) hosts the International Windsurfing World Cup.

SHOPPING

CERAMICS On Market street, look for the house with the beautifully carved Parian marble facade to find Paros's most elegantly designed shop, **Yria Interiors** (✉*Start of Market street* ☎*22840/24359* 🌐*www.yriaparos.com*). Here Stelios and Monique Ghikas display their pottery from Studio Yria, as well as a carefully chosen range of stylish household items mostly from France.

JEWELRY Vangelis Skaramagas and Yannis Xenos have been making their own delicate, precious jewelry at **Jewelry Workshop** (✉*End of market street* ☎*22840/21008*) for more than 20 years. Local Phaidra Apostolopoulou, who studied jewelry in Athens, now has a tiny shop, **Phaidra** (✉*Near Zoodochos Pyghi church* ☎*22840/23626*), where she shows her silver pieces, many lighthearted for summer.

LOCAL FOODS **Enosis** (*Agricultural Cooperative's shop* ✉*Mando Mavrogenous Sq. at front of Paros town under police station* ☎*22820/22181*) sells homemade pasta, honey, cheeses, and especially Paros's renowned wines. The varietal wine Monemvasia (officially rated "Appellation of High Quality Origin Paros") is made from white monemvasia grapes, indigenous to Paros. You can visit the winery for an evocative slide show, a photography exhibition of Paros's agricultural traditions, and a wine tasting. For an appointment call Alexis Gokas at 22840/22235.

EN ROUTE Halfway from Paros town to Naousa, on the right, the 17th-century **Monastery of Longovarda** (☎*22840/21202*) shines on its mountainside. The monastic community farms the local land and makes honey, wine, and olive oil. Only men, dressed in conservative clothing, are allowed inside, where there are post-Byzantine icons, 17th-century frescoes depicting the Twelve Feasts in the Life of Christ, and a library of rare books; it is usually open mornings.

NAOUSA ΝΑΟΥΣΑ

★ *10 km (6 mi) northeast of Paroikía.*

Naousa, impossibly pretty, long ago discovered the benefits of tourism. Its outskirts are mushrooming with villas and hotels that exploit it further. Along the harbor—which thankfully maintains its beauty and function as a fishing port—red and navy-blue boats knock gently against one another as men repair their nets and foreigners relax in the ouzeri—Barbarossa being the traditional favorite—by the water's edge. From here the pirate Hugue Crevelliers operated in the 1570s, and Byron turned him into the Corsair. Navies of the ancient Persians, flotillas from medieval Venice, and the imperial Russian fleet have anchored in this harbor. The half-submerged ruins of the Venetian fortifications still remain; they are a pretty sight when lighted up at night. Compared to Paroikía, the scene in Naousa is somewhat more chic, with a more-intimate array of shops, bars, and restaurants, but in winter the town shuts down. Unobtrusive Paros's gay scene is here, if it is anywhere.

BEACHES

A boat goes regularly to **Lageri** (⊠*North of Naousa*), a long, sandy beach with dunes. The boat that goes to Lageri also travels to **Santa Maria** (⊠*Northeastern shore of Paros*), the windsurfers' beach. A boat crosses the bay to **Kolimbithres** (⊠*Directly across bay from Naousa*), noted for its anfractuous rock formations, water sports, a choice of tavernas, and two luxury hotels. **Ayios Ioannis** (⊠*Across from Naousa*), served by the boat that goes to Kolimbithres, is a quiet locale, offering a pretty 15-minute walk along a path to a lighthouse.

WHERE TO STAY & EAT

$$$$ ✕ **Poseidon.** Eat here for elegant dining away from the fray, on a spacious terrace with two pools, dozens of palm trees, and the bay of Naousa in front of you. The vegetables are from their own garden, the fish is fresh, and the food has a French accent. To start, try beef (fresh from France) carpaccio in a crush of herbs and spices with arugula and Parmesan, or scallops St-Jacques with parsley butter. Two excellent main courses would be French beef fillet with pepper sauce, sautéed oyster mushrooms, and broccoli; or Dover sole fillet with Mozambique prawns, leeks, and sautéed spinach, and wild rice with a bouillabaisse sauce. If you can still manage dessert (you will want to sit here a long time), try the chocolate pyramid with passion-fruit cream. ⊠*Astir Hotel, Kolimbithres* ☎*22840/51976* 🌐*www.astirofparos.gr* 💳*AE, MC, V* ⏲*Closed Nov.–Apr.*

$$$$ ✕ **Taverna Christos.** For more than 25 years Christos has been Naousa's best restaurant; it still is. Its cool, white, spacious garden—the walls are an art gallery—has an easy elegance; the service is both efficient and gracious. Excellent first courses include fresh sardines rolled in vine leaves with yogurt and saffron, and risotto with fresh cuttlefish in its ink. Among entrées, try the fine veal fillet with fresh tomatoes and basil, and roast lamb with lentils and caramelized onions. Fresh strawberry mousse on chocolate slabs is sinful, to say nothing of the chocolate "Trilogy," with Madagascar vanilla ice cream and caramel sauce. Chris-

Fodor's Choice ★

tos always has local specialties, so ask. ✉ *Up hill from central square, 84401* ☎ *22840/51442* 🌐 *www.christos-restaurant.gr* 💳 *AE, MC, V* ⏲ *Closed Oct.–May.*

WORD OF MOUTH

"The Astir of Paros is a beautiful hotel and situated near the fishing town of Naousa, which has many great tavernas. Paros is greener that the other Cycladic islands and the grounds of the Astir are lovely. There are nice beaches in the area, too. We wish we had stayed there after seeing it." –SuQue

$$$ ★ ✕ **Mario.** Good food is enhanced here by the pretty location, a few feet from the fishing boats on Naousa's harbor. The taverna specializes in fresh fish and also such dishes as eggplant confit, or pastry rolls stuffed with shrimp and soft cheese. For a main dish, have fresh fish wrapped in bacon, or a fillet of beef on potato puree in wine sauce. The fresh strawberry liquor will keep you sitting longer. ✉ *On fishing-boat harbor* ☎ *22840/51047* *tsachoo@hotmail.com* *Reservations essential* 💳 *AE, MC, V.*

$$$$ **Astir of Paros.** Across the bay from Naousa twinkle the lights of this deluxe resort hotel, a graceful and expensive retreat (expensive for Paros, not for Mykonos), with green lawns, tall palm trees, extensive lush gardens, and an art gallery. Guest rooms are elegant and spacious, a vibrant mix of antiques and boldly colored modern paintings, which lose a little compared to the window views of sparkling Naousa bay. The hotel's bars (one set by the sea) are popular and its two restaurants are ambitious. As you stroll through the vast gardens—note the historic Chapel of St. Nicholas (and its Byzantine-era murals) church carefully rebuilt on 12th-century foundations—the bustle of Paros is very far away indeed. ✉ *Take Kolimbithres road from Naousa, 84401* ☎ *22840/51976 or 22840/51984* 📠 *22840/51985* 🌐 *www.astirofparos.gr* *11 rooms, 46 suites* *In-room: refrigerator, Ethernet. In-hotel: 2 restaurants, bars, tennis court, pool, gym, no elevator* 💳 *AE, DC, MC, V* ⏲ *Closed Nov.–Mar.* *BP.*

$ **Svoronos Bungalows.** These bungalow apartments always seem to be fully occupied. The friendly Sovronos family tends the lush garden, and the comfortable apartments and Cycladic whitewashed courtyards are decorated with antiques and objects from the family's extensive travels. Though quiet, the hotel is within easy reach of Naousa's lively shopping and nightlife. There is no air-conditioning, but it is cool. ✉ *Behind big church, 1 block in from Santa Maria road, 84401* ☎ *22849/51211 or 22840/51409* 📠 *22840/52281* 🌐 *www.parosweb.gr/svoronos* *19 apartments* *In-room: no a/c, kitchen, no TV. In-hotel: bar, no elevator* 💳 *MC, V* ⏲ *Closed Nov.–Apr.*

NIGHTLIFE & THE ARTS

BARS **Linardo's** (✉ *At fishing harbor*) is lively and is open into the wee hours. **Agosta** (✉ *At fishing harbor*) is a pretty spot.

DANCE The group **Music–Dance "Naousa Paros"** (☎ *22840/52284* 🌐 *www.users.otenet.gr/~parofolk/index_en.html*), formed in 1988 to preserve the traditional dances and music of Paros, performs all summer long in Naousa in the costumes of the 16th century and has participated in dance competitions and festivals throughout Europe. Keep an eye out for posters.

SPORTS & THE OUTDOORS

If you're traveling with children, **Aqua Paros Waterpark** (✉*Kolimbithres, next to Porto Paros Hotel* ☎*22840/53271*), with its 13 waterslides big and small, will cool a hot afternoon. Admission is €12. **Santa Maria Surf Club** (✉*Santa Maria beach, about 4 km [2½ mi] north of Naousa*) is popular, with windsurfing, jet-skiing, waterskiing, and diving.

SHOPPING

ART & JEWELRY Paros is an art colony and exhibits are everywhere in summer. Petros Metaxas's **Metaxas Gallery** (✉*On 2nd street from harbor toward main church* ☎*22840/52667*) is especially devoted to the jewelry of Aristotelis and Lilly Bessis, who run it, too. There are also exhibits by local artists, and a selection of antiques from Albania.

FASHION Kostas Mouzedakis's **Tango** (✉*On 2nd street from harbor toward main church* ☎*22840/51014*) has been selling classic sportswear for two decades; its most popular line is its own Tangowear.

MARATHI ΜΑΡΑΘΙ

10 km (6 mi) east of Paros town.

During the classical period the island of Paros had an estimated 150,000 residents, many of them slaves who worked the ancient marble quarries in Marathi. The island grew rich from the export of this white, granular marble known among ancient architects and sculptors for its ability to absorb light. They called it *lychnites* ("won by lamplight").

Marked by a sign, **three caverns** (✉*Short walk from main road*) are bored into the hillside, the largest of them 300 feet deep. The most recent quarrying done in these mines was in 1844, when a French company cut marble here for Napoléon's tomb.

SHOPPING

At **Studio Yria** (✣*1½ km [¾ mi] east of Marathi, above road to Kostos village* ☎*22840/29007* 🌐*www.yriaparos.com*) master potters Stelios and Monique Ghikas and other craftspeople can be seen at work. Marble carvers, metalsmiths, painters, and more all make for a true Renaissance workshop. Both the ceramic tableware and the works of art make use of Byzantine and Cycladic motifs in their designs; they have even made ceramic designs for the prince of Wales. Easily accessible by bus, taxi, and rental car, the studio is usually open daily 8–8; call ahead in the off-season.

LEFKES ΛΕΥΚΕΣ

6 km (4 mi) south of Marathi, 10 km (6 mi) southeast of Paros town.

Rampant piracy in the 17th century forced thousands of people to move inland from the coastal regions; thus for many years the scenic village of Lefkes, built on a hillside in the protective mountains, was the island's capital. It remains the largest village in the interior and has maintained a peaceful, island feeling, with narrow streets fragrant of jasmine and honeysuckle. These days, the old houses are being restored, and in summer the town is full of people. Farming is the major source of income, as you can tell from the well-kept stone walls and olive groves. For one of the best walks on Paros, take the ancient Byzantine road from the main lower square to the lower villages.

Two **17th-century churches** of interest are **Ayia Varvara** (St. Barbara) and **Ayios Sotiris** (Holy Savior).

The big 1830 neo-Renaissance **Ayia Triada** *(Holy Trinity)* is the pride of the village.

BEACHES

Piso Livadi (⊠*On road past Lefkes*) was the ancient port for the marble quarries and today is a small resort town convenient to many beaches; the harbor, where boats leave for Naxos and Delos, is being expanded.

WHERE TO STAY & EAT

$ ✕ **Taverna Klarinos.** You go to Nikos and Anna Ragousis's place for the real thing. Nikos grows the vegetables, raises the meat, makes the cheese (even the feta) from his own goats, and makes the wine from his own vineyards; Anna cooks. Traditional dishes such as fried zucchini or beets with garlic sauce are the best you'll taste, and the grilled meats make the gods envious. ⊠*Main entrance street, opposite square, on 2nd fl.* ☎*22840/41608* ▭*No credit cards* ⊙*Closed Oct.–May.*

$$$ ★ **Lefkes Village.** All the rooms in this elegant hotel are white, and the wooden furniture and fabrics are reproductions of traditional styles; all have balconies with magnificent views down the olive-tree valley and over the sea to Naxos. The restaurant is noted for its traditional Greek food; the folk museum here is chockablock with interesting objects. ⊠*East of Lefkes on main road, 84400* ☎*22840/41827* 🖷 *22840/42398* ⊕*www.lefkesvillage.gr* *20 rooms* *In-room: refrigerator. In-hotel: restaurant, bar, pool, no elevator, public Internet* ▭*AE, DC, MC, V* ⊙*Closed Nov.–Mar.* *BP.*

SHOPPING

WEAVINGS On the main street above the lower café square, Nikoletta Haniotis's shop, **Anemi** (☎*22840/41182*), sells handwoven weavings colored with natural dyes and local designs. Also for sale are iron pieces made by her father, Lefkes's blacksmith.

PETALOUDES PARK ΠΕΤΑΛΟΥΔΕΣ

4 km (2½ mi) south of Paros town.

A species of moth returns year after year to mate in Petaloudes (the Valley of the Butterflies), a lush oasis of greenery in the middle of this dry island. In May, June, and perhaps July, you can watch them as they lie dormant during the day, their chocolate-brown wings with yellow stripes still against the ivy leaves. In the evening they flutter upward to the cooler air, flashing the coral-red undersides of their wings as they rise. A notice at the entrance asks visitors not to disturb them by taking photographs or shaking the leaves. ✉*Petaloudes* *€3* *Mid-May–mid-Sept., daily 9–8.*

NEED A BREAK?

Even when the butterflies are not there, it is pleasant to have coffee in the small *kafeneio* (*coffeehouse* ✉*Inside entrance to park*) and enjoy the shade of the cypress, olive, chestnut, mulberry, and lemon trees.

On the summit of a hill beyond the garden reigns a lopped **Venetian tower.** Its founder's name, Iakovos Alisafis, and the date, 1626, are inscribed on it.

WHERE TO EAT

$$$ ★ ✕**Thea.** From the terrace of this fine restaurant you can enjoy the view over the Antiparos strait and the little ferries that ply it. The interior is all of wood and hundreds of bottles of wine shelved from floor to high ceiling. Owner Nikos Kouroumlis is, in fact, a wine fanatic, and Thea has one of the most varied wine lists in all of Greece; his own wine is excellent. In winter, a good bottle of the grape and a warm fire keep Thea popular. Nikos and family hail from northern Greece and Constantinople and so does their food: Caesaria pie, hot and spicy with cheeses, salted meat, and tomatoes; Cappodocian lamb, cooked with dried apricots; Constantinopolitan chicken, with plums, raisins, and rice; or one of their famous T-bone steaks. Save room for one of the traditional Greek sweets, especially the *ekmek* served up with mastic ice cream. Reservations are recommended in summer. ✉ ☎*22840/91220* ▭*MC, V.*

EN ROUTE

A 15-minute walk or 2-minute drive back toward Paros town from the Valley of the Butterflies leads to the convent known as **Christos sto Dasos** *(Christ in the Wood)*, from where there's a marvelous view of the Aegean. The convent contains the tomb of St. Arsenios (1800–77), who was a schoolteacher, an abbot, and a prophet. He was also a rainmaker whose prayers were believed to have ended a long drought, saving Paros from starvation. The nuns are a bit leery of tourists. If you want to go in, be sure to wear long pants or skirt and a shirt that covers your shoulders, or the sisters will turn you away.

ANTIPAROS ΑΝΤΙΠΑΡΟΣ

Fodor's Choice ★ *5 km (2 mi) southwest of Paroikía.*

The smaller, sister isle of Paros, Antiparos is developing all too rapidly, though recent visitors, such as Tom Hanks and Brad Pitt, want to keep this place a secret. Twenty-five years ago you went to the Paros hamlet of Pounta, went to the church, opened its door (as a signal), and waited for a fishing caïque to chug over. Now, 30 car ferries ply the channel all day and a lovely seven-minute ride wafts you from Paros (from Pounta; the ride from Paroikía takes about 20 minutes) to Antiparos. The green, inhabited islet on the way belongs to Dolly Goulandris, benefactress of the Goulandris Cycladic Museum in Athens (and much else). A causeway once crossed the Antiparos strait, which would be swimmable but for the current, and on one of its still emergent islets, Saliagos, habitations and objects have been found dating back almost to 5,000 BC.

Antiparos's one town, also called Antiparos, has a main street and two centers of activity: the quay area and the main square, a block or two in. At both are restaurants and cafés. To the right of the square are houses and the kastro's 15th-century wall. At the other end of the quay from the ferry dock a road goes to an idyllic sandy beach (it is 10 minutes by foot); you can wade across to the islet opposite, Fira, where sheep and goats graze.

BEACHCOMBERS' PARADISE

Pounta is not even a village, just a few houses, three restaurants (one fine one), and a tiny harbor, whence the ferries leave for Antiparos. The road that turns left just before you get there continues on to many beaches. And beyond—it is a beautiful drive—are the peaceful harbor towns of Aliki and Dryos, both with fine beaches and restaurants, especially Faragas. Beyond Dryos toward Naousa are the windsurfers' long beaches, Golden beach and New Golden beach.

In the 19th century the most famous sight in the Aegean was the **Antiparos cave** (9 km [5½ mi] from town), and it still deservedly attracts hundreds of visitors a year. Four hundred steps descend into huge chambers, pass beneath enormous pipe-organ stalactites, and skirt immense stalagmites. In 1673 the French ambassador famously celebrated Christmas Mass here with 500 guests, who feasted for three days. Look for Lord Byron's autograph. Outside is the church of Agios Ioannis Spiliótis, built in 1774.

It is pleasant to go around to the other side of Antiparos on the good road to Ayios Georgios, where there are three excellent taverns, perfect after a swim. On request a boat will take you to the nearby islet of **Despotikon,** uninhabited except for seasonal archaeologists excavating a late-Archaic marble temple complex to Apollo. In autumn the hills are fragrant with purple flowering heather. A great source of information about Antiparos, with a complete listing of hotels can be found at www.antiparos-isl.gr.

WHERE TO EAT

$$ ✕ **Akrogiali.** Far from the madding crowd, you sit and look across the strait to the sacred isle of Despotikon, and, after a swim, eat the fish from right here. The bells you hear belong to the goats of the Pipinos family (yes, they occasionally end up on the table here). Vegetables come from the garden. This is one of three good restaurants by the little dock. *Closed Oct.–Apr. No credit cards.*

SANTORINI (THERA) ΣΑΝΤΟΡΙΝΗ (ΘΗΡΑ)

Undoubtedly the most extraordinary island in the Aegean, crescent-shape Santorini remains a mandatory stop on the Cycladic tourist route—even if it's necessary to enjoy the sensational sunsets from Ia, the fascinating excavations, and the dazzling white towns with a million other travelers. Called Kállisti (the "Loveliest") when first settled, the island has now reverted to its subsequent name of Thera, after the 9th-century BC Dorian colonizer Thiras. The place is better known, however, these days—outside Greece, that is—as Santorini, a name derived from its patroness, St. Irene of Thessaloniki, the Byzantine empress who restored icons to Orthodoxy and died in 802.

You can fly conveniently to Santorini, but don't: the boat trip here provides a spectacular, almost mandatory introduction, a literal rite of passage. After the boat sails between Sikinos and Ios, your deck-side perch approaches two close islands with a passage between them. The bigger one on the left is Santorini, and the smaller on the right is Thirassia. Passing between them, you see the village of Ia adorning Santorini's northernmost cliff like a white geometric beehive. You are in the caldera (volcanic crater), one of the world's truly breathtaking sights: a demilune of cliffs rising 1,100 feet, with the white clusters of the towns of Fira and Ia perched along the top. The bay, once the high center of the island, is 1,300 feet in some places, so deep that when boats dock in Santorini's shabby little port of Athinios, they do not drop anchor. The encircling cliffs are the ancient rim of a still-active volcano, and you are sailing east across its flooded caldera. On your right are the Burnt Isles, the White Isle, and other volcanic remnants, all lined up as if some outsize display in a geology museum. Hephaestus's subterranean fires smolder still—the volcano erupted in 198 BC, about 735, and in 1956.

Indeed, Santorini and its four neighboring islets are the fragmentary remains of a larger landmass that exploded about 1600 BC: the volcano's core blew sky high, and the sea rushed into the abyss to create the great bay, which measures 10 km by 7 km (6 mi by 4½ mi) and is 1,292 feet deep. The other pieces of the rim, which broke off in later eruptions, are Thirassia, where a few hundred people live, and deserted little Aspronissi ("White Isle"). In the center of the bay, black and uninhabited, two cones, the Burnt Isles of Palea Kameni and Nea Kameni, appeared between 1573 and 1925.

There has been too much speculation about the identification of Santorini with the mythical Atlantis, mentioned in Egyptian papyri and by Plato (who says it's in the Atlantic), but myths are hard to pin down. (For the full scoop, *see* our special photo feature, "Santorini: The Lost Atlantis?" in this chapter). This is not true of old arguments about whether or not tidal waves from Santorini's cataclysmic explosion destroyed Minoan civilization on Crete, 113 km (70 mi) away. The latest carbon-dating evidence, which points to a few years before 1600 BC for the eruption, clearly indicates that the Minoans outlasted the eruption by a couple of hundred years, but most probably in a

Continued on page 518

SANTORINI: THE LOST ATLANTIS?

View of Santorini's waters caldera from the town of Ia

Did Atlantis, "the island at the center of the earth," ever really [illegible] if it did, where? Big-budget Hollywood films have placed it in [illegible] of the Atlantic Ocean. Several historians think it was located in the Bay of Naples; others that it was a Sumerian island in the Persian gulf, or a sunken island in the Straits of Gibraltar. Nowadays, more and more experts are making a case for the island of Santorini—and therein lies a tale.

WHOLE LOTTA LAVA

Imagine: A land called Atlantis, with a vast, spectacular city adorned with hanging gardens, gigantic palaces, and marble colossi of Poseidon, ancient god of the sea. One fateful day, more than 3,500 years ago, an enormous earthquake triggers a cataclysmic volcano that destroys the capital. In the space of a few hours, a towering tidal wave washes all traces of this civilization into a fiery cauldron. All, that is, except for a rocky fragment framing a watery caldera. Historical detectives, archaeologists, and volcanologists have long wondered if Greece's fabled isle of Santorini could be that last remnant of Atlantis. But is this theory more fable than fact?

For those who consider Atlantis merely a symbol or metaphor, the question is not important. Surfacing like a rising island in a deep bay, the notion of a Golden Age is ever-present in the human imagination, and the Atlantis story is among our most durable and poignant ideas of it. Reverberating through Western culture and dazzling the mind, the name "Atlantis" glitters with glamour; it titles hotels, Web sites, towns, submarines, book and film companies, even a pop song by Donovan. But historians today remain divided on whether Atlantis was a funtastic shooting-star of history or just a legend with a moral lesson.

PLATO VERSUS THE VOLCANO

Plato (427–347 BC), the most fearless, and the most substantive writer, of all the ancient Greek philosophers, would have supported the latter option. He liked to end his famous Dialogues with a myth, and Atlantis shows up in both his "Timaeus" and his "Critias," as a parable (and history?) of good and bad government. Plato says that the great 6th-century lawgiver-poet of Athens, Solon (630–560 BC), went to Egypt, and there heard

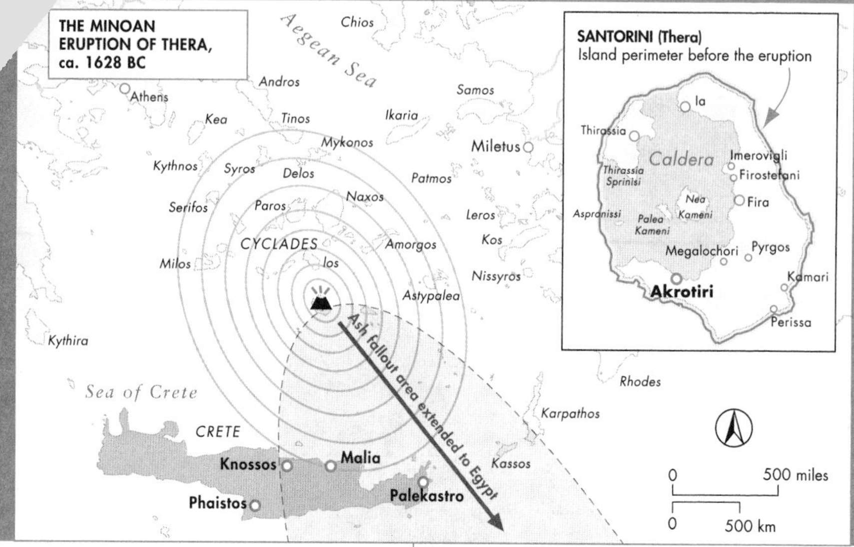

stories of Atlantis. They told him that 9,000 years ago Athens defeated the empire of Atlantis, a huge island in the Atlantic Ocean, in battle.

Then a natural cataclysm destroyed the island in one day, "and Atlantis disappeared in the sea depths." Atlantis was created by and belonged to Poseidon, god of the sea and of earthquakes, and he made it a paradise ruled by his son, King Atlas, with the guidance by wise counselors. When later generations on the island abandoned his prudent ways, catastrophe struck: you mustn't love Power more than you love the Gods. The Bible had Sodom and Gomorrah; Plato had Atlantis.

Some authors claim the story of Atlantis is history, not fantasy. They believe that Solon misread 9,000 years as 900. If so, Atlantis would have flourished at the same time as Santorini, which, as we know and the classical Greeks suspected, was destroyed by earthquakes followed by a cataclysmic volcanic

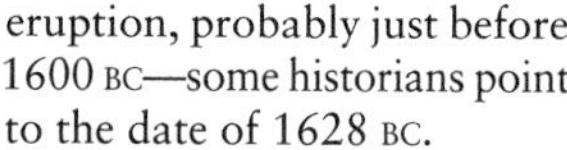

eruption, probably just before 1600 BC—some historians point to the date of 1628 BC.

THE MINOAN CONNECTION

In the late 1960s, when archaeologist Spyridon Marinatos's excavations of Santorini's caldera revealed the ruin of Akrotiri, preserved under 25 feet of volcanic ash, the island's claim to be Atlantis began to outweigh all others. The buried town had been large, comfortable, and attractive, the art beautiful and gentle, and its high Bronze Age civilization resembled Minoan Crete's, 47 miles south. Since a tsunami from the volcano must have devastated the larger island, it is not surprising that Crete, whose dimensions chime better with Plato's, is also called Atlantis.

Crete and its satellite, Santorini (don't call it this to a Santorini scholar, but it's true) were "feminine" civilizations. They worshipped the goddess of fertility; disliked depictions of war and

Imaginary view of Santorini's submerged volcano in eruption in 1866, (below) Akrotiri frescoes.

weapons; kept their towns unwalled; loved magnificent jewelry; and their art eschews the monumental for spontaneous natural forms, such as swallows, octopi, dolphins, and palm trees. They liked pretty people. The women's elaborate costumes exposed their breasts, and the men, nearly naked, wore gold jewelry and fancy hairstyles. They worshipped not in temples, but in caves, springs, and mountaintops. From our sparse evidence, it seems it was indeed a golden age, when "the earth bore freely all the aromatic substances it bears today, roots, herbs, bushes and gums exuded by flowers or fruit." Perfume was as popular here as in Egypt. A mural preserved in Athens from Akrotiri shows blue monkeys opening doors à la Wizard of Oz. Plato, the stern taskmaster, would probably have disapproved.

... ET TU, SANTORINI?

Today, archaeological excavation continues at Akrotiri, situated high—1,300 feet—over the whitecaps of the Aegean Sea. What was Santorini like when the great bay was terra firma, lush with olive trees and abundant harvests? Santorini's own Prehistoric Museum is studying the possibilities, as the writings of historians, poets, and philosophers provide food for thought. The fact remains that the evidence is not all in: there is a possibility that Santorini could, in fact, reawaken from its long slumber and once again erupt, and then subside again. The key to Atlantis's existence may lie in the once and future fury of this fascinating island.

very weakened state. In fact, the island still endures hardships: since antiquity, Santorini has depended on rain collected in cisterns for drinking and irrigating—the well water is often brackish—and the serious shortage is alleviated by the importation of water. However, the volcanic soil also yields riches: small, intense tomatoes with tough skins used for tomato paste (good restaurants here serve them); the famous Santorini fava beans, which have a light, fresh taste; barley; wheat; and white-skin eggplants.

Sadly, unrestrained tourism has taken a heavy toll on Santorini. Fira, and now Ia, could almost be described as "a street with 40 jewelry shops"; many of the natives are completely burned out by the end of the peak season (the best times to come here are shoulder periods); and, increasingly, business and the loud ringing of cash registers have disrupted the normal flow of Greek life here. For example, if a cruise ship comes in during afternoon siesta, all shops immediately open. And you will have a pushy time walking down Fira's main street in August, so crowded is it. Still and all, if you look beneath the layers of gimcrack tourism, you'll find Greek splendor. No wonder Greece's two Nobel poets, Giorgios Seferis and Odysseus Elytis, wrote poems about it. For you, too, will be "watching the rising islands / watching the red islands sink" (Seferis) and consider, "With fire with lava with smoke / You found the great lines of your destiny" (Elytis).

FIRA ΦΗΡΑ

10 km (6 mi) west of the airport, 14 km (8½ mi) southeast of Ia.

Tourism, the island's major industry, adds more than 1 million visitors per year to a population of 7,000. As a result, Fira, the capital, midway along the west coast of the east rim, is no longer only a picturesque village but a major tourist center, overflowing with discos, shops, and restaurants. Many of its employees, East Europeans or young travelers extending their summer vacations, hardly speak Greek. But it soon becomes clear what brings the tourists here: with its white, cubical houses clinging to the cliff hundreds of feet above the caldera, Fira is a beautiful place.

To experience life here as it was until only a couple of decades ago, walk down the much-photographed, winding **staircase** that descends from town to the water's edge—walk or take the cable car back up, avoiding the drivers who will try to plant you on the sagging back of one of their bedraggled-looking donkeys.

The modern Greek Orthodox cathedral of **Panayia Ypapantis** (⊠ *Southern part of town*) is a major landmark; the local priests, with somber faces, long beards, and black robes, look strangely out of place in summertime Fira.

Along **Eikostis Pemptis Martiou** (*25th of March street* ⊠ *East of Panayia Ypapantis*), you'll find inexpensive restaurants and accommodations.

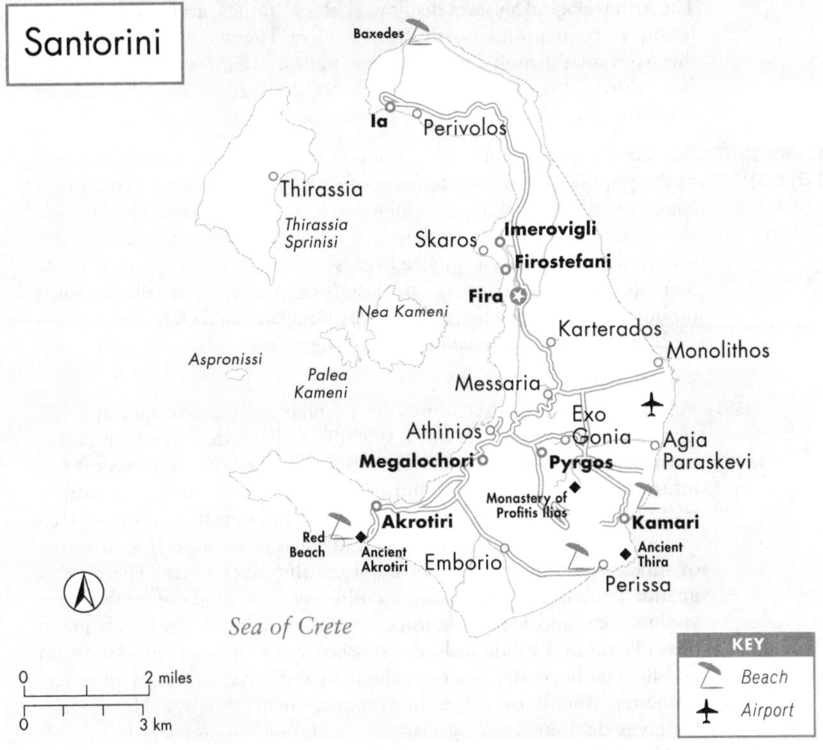

The blocked-off Ypapantis street (west of Panayia Ypapantis) leads to **Kato Fira** *(Lower Fira)*, built into the cliff side overlooking the caldera, where prices are higher and the vista wonderful. For centuries the people of the island have been digging themselves rooms-with-a-view right in the cliff face—many bars and hotel rooms now occupy the caves.

★ The **Museum of Prehistoric Thera** displays pots and frescoes from the famed excavations at Akrotiri. Note the fresco fragments with the painted swallows (who flocked here because they loved the cliffs) and the women in Minoan dresses. The swallows, which still come in spring, remain the island's favorite design motif. The fossilized olive leaves from 60,000 BC prove the olive to be indigenous. ✉ *Mitropoleos, behind big church* ☎ *22860/23217* 🌐 *www.culture.gr* 🎫 *€5 including Archaeological Museum; €8 including Archeological Museum and Akrotiri* ⏲ *Tues.–Sun. 8:30–3.*

WALK ON BY

Tourist touts still like to promote mules as a mode of transport to take you up the zigzag cliff path to the island capital of Fira. But animal rights groups would prefer you didn't. And you should be aware of another reason: the mules on Santorini are piously believed to contain souls of the dead, who are thus doing their purgatory. It is an arduous ascent.

The **Archaeological Museum** displays pottery, statues, and grave artifacts found at excavations mostly from ancient Thera and Akrotiri, from the Minoan through the Byzantine periods. ✉*Stavrou and Nomikos, Mitropoleos, behind big church* ☎*22860/22217* 🎫*€5 including Museum of Prehistoric Thera* ⏲*Tues.–Sun. 8:30–3.*

OFF THE BEATEN PATH

Nea Kameni. To peer into a live, sometimes smoldering volcano, join one of the popular excursions to Nea Kameni, the larger of the two Burnt Isles. After disembarking, you hike 430 feet to the top and walk around the edge of the crater, wondering if the volcano is ready for its fifth eruption during the last hundred years—after all, the last was in 1956. Some tours continue on to Therassia, where there is a village. Tours (about €15) are scheduled regularly by **Nomikos Travel** (☎*22860/23660* 📠*22860/23666* 🌐*www.nomikosvillas.gr*).

WHERE TO STAY & EAT

$$$$ ✕**Selene.** No wonder weddings are popular here: the terrace at Fira's most romantic restaurant has a splendid caldera view, while the time-burnished cliff house is a beaut, with vaulted ceilings, dark-wood furniture, and "Thera-style" banquette benches (the sort you'll find in traditional island homes). The menu is full of interesting starters, such as zucchini with langoustine salad and slices of botargo (roe of tuna), or mixed seafood wrapped in phyllo with fennel sauce. The entrées include lamb chops and roasted lamb—yes, two kinds of lamb—with yogurt, rice, and local tomatoes layered in a mold; beef with green olives is another subtle dish. For dessert try zabaglione with vin santo and flaked chocolate. Georgia, the maître d', oversees all with grace, efficiency, and knowledge. In summer, owner George Hatziyianakis gives daylong cooking classes. ✉*Cliff-side walkway, 310 ft left of Hotel Atlantis* ☎*22860/22249* 🌐*www.selene.gr* ✍*Reservations essential* 💳*AE, DC, MC, V* ⏲*Closed Nov.–Mar.*

$$$$ ✕**Sphinx.** When Fira locals want more than a taverna, they come to this pretty vaulted room, which glows with spotlighted Cycladic sculptures and blush-pink walls. As lush as this is, however, few can resist an outdoor terrace table, thanks to the striking caldera views in one direction and a vista of the giant cathedral in the other. Owner George Psichas is his own chef, and every dish is evidence of his loving care—even the bread and pasta are homemade. Starters include smoked salmon with fresh asparagus and brik caviar with hollandaise sauce, or artichokes with lemon and feta. Fresh fish is usually available—try the fresh grouper steak with grape and grappa sauce. Other high-style delights include the scallops and shrimps with pink peppercorn sauce and the steak fillet with mushrooms, truffle oil, arugula, and Parmesan flakes. Desserts change day by day, but rich chocolate soufflé is always available. The wine list is long and Greek (and the "cave" is very much worth a look). ✉*Cliff-side walkway in front of Panayia Ypapantis* ☎*22860/23823* 🌐*www.sphinx-santorini.com* ✍*Reservations essential in summer* 💳*AE, MC, V.*

$$ ✕**Naoussa.** This family taverna, owned by Kyriakos and Stelios Selios, is easily Fira's most popular among the locals. The food is freshly prepared daily (most tavernas cook in advance, then freeze and

microwave), and so here is the right place to get moussaka, stuffed vegetables, and other Greek specialties; there is always a daily specialty. Winning best bets include the small spinach pies with egg, feta, and spring onions and the walnut-studded eggplant salad. Naoussa can be found on the second-floor terrace on the main shopping street near the Archaeological Museum. ✉*LaGoudera Shopping Center (near cable car)* ☎*22860/22869* 🌐*www.naoussa-restaurant.gr* 💳 ⊗*Closed Dec.–mid-Mar.*

$ ✕**Nicholas.** This is Santorini's oldest taverna, where you'll find the natives camped out in winter. Island dishes are prepared well and served in a simple, attractive room. Try the local yellow lentils and the lamb fricassee with an egg-lemon sauce. ✉*2 streets in from cliff side on Erythrou Stavrou* ☎*No phone* 💳*No credit cards.*

$$$$ **Aigialos.** For a taste of old aristocratic Santorini, venture to Aigialos ("seashore"), a cluster of buildings from the 18th and 19th centuries. The most comfortable and discreetly luxurious—as well as the most poetic and serenely quiet—place to stay in Fira, it comprises an array of one- and two-bedroom villas. Outside, various abodes are built in traditional volcanic stone, lime-washed in heavenly pastels. Inside, you'll find marble floors, magnificently beautiful antique furniture, and walls festooned with 19th-century engravings. Nearly all guest rooms have sublime terraces or balconies overlooking the caldera—no need to venture out at sunset. There's maid service twice daily, impeccable 24-hour service, and fresh flowers. The restaurant serves its Mediterranean cuisine only to residents, and you can eat on your private terrace. Breakfast, included, is served in a deep cave, on the pool terrace, or on your balcony. Note that this complex does have a lot of steps, even for Santorini. ✉*South end of cliff-side walkway, 84700* ☎*22860/25191 through 22860/25195* 📠*22860/22856* 🌐*www.aigialos.gr* *17 villas* *In-room: refrigerator. In-hotel: bar, pool, spa, no elevator, public Internet* 💳*AE, DC, MC, V* ⊗*Closed Nov.–Mar.* *BP.*

Fodor's Choice ★

$$$$ **Hotel Aressana.** Though the Aressana lacks a view of the caldera, its own slant of sea view is effulgent (and helps make you forget the Las Vegas–like hotel sign). The large freshwater pool, spacious lobby with traditional furnishings and wood-panel bar, excellent service, famous breakfast, and location in central Fira make this a popular option. The Aressana specializes in traditional wedding receptions and provides charming bridal suites—so don't be surprised by how many Americans honeymoon here. Renovated in 2007, this is a large full-service hotel, with no steps and an elevator. ✉*South end of cliff-side walkway, 84700* ☎*22860/23900 or 22860/23901* 📠*22860/23902* 🌐*www.aressana.gr* *42 rooms, 8 suites* *In-room: dial-up. In-hotel: bar, pool, no elevator, public Internet, parking* 💳*AE, DC, MC, V* ⊗*Closed Nov.–Mar.* *BP.*

$$$ **Aroma Suites.** For a caldera view, this new (2006) accommodation is an exceptional value. The small white cave-rooms with vaulted ceilings are decorated with warm touches of color and sleek marble fixtures. The common terrace overlooks the caldera, and you will want to sit here mornings and evenings. Transfers and breakfast are extra, and there are stairs, but it is very attractive, small, and friendly. Pool privileges can be

had at the nearby Loizos Apartments. To get to Aroma Suites, head to the southern end of Fira's caldera walkway, then follow the signs down. ✉ *Caldera walkway, 84700* ☎ *22860/24112* 📠 *22860/24116* 🌐 *www.aromasuites.gr* *4 rooms, 4 suites* *In-room: refrigerator. In-hotel: no elevator, public Wi-Fi* 💳 *AE, MC, V.*

$$$ **Dream Island Hotel.** Opened in 2006, well appointed, and family run, this complex of 15 rooms looks like a complete Cycladic village, presiding over a vast (somewhat forlorn) pool terrace and an almost cinematic vista over ancient Thera. Sorry, the view doesn't include the watery caldera (guest rooms take in the view over the sea, in the opposite direction) but that fact helps make this place less expensive than it looks. The rooms (all with plasma satellite TV) and cavernous spacious lobby are decorated in light beige tones with strong color accents. Outside, the pool's terrace is paved with volcanic rock. Breakfast is extra; transfers are included. Owners Roussetos and Georgia Karamelogos are very accommodating. Some other pluses: there are no steps and off-season prices are very low. To get to the hotel, walk north (toward Ia) five minutes from the main (Theotokopoulou) square and turn right at the sign. ✉ *Off Martiou St., 84700* ☎ *22860/24122* 📠 *22860/23922* 🌐 *www.dreamislandhotel.gr* *15 rooms* *In-hotel: no elevator, public Internet, parking* 💳 *MC, V*

$$ ★ **Costa Marina Villas.** Set in a tranquil neighborhood, surrounded by a garden, and vaulted and shimmering-white in archetypal Cycladic fashion, this is a nifty option (built in 2002). Although just a block or so from the main square, the immediate precinct is a quiet, domestic neighborhood. Most guest rooms have a tiny balcony overlooking the garden or with an eastern sea view; "family" rooms (which anyone can book) are most spacious, thanks to their impressive double-height loft ceilings. A bit of luxury: some rooms have a Jacuzzi. Great value for the money, Costa Marina may be a hike from the caldera, but it is romantic all the same. ✉ *Along road leading to camping grounds, 84700* ☎ *22860/28923* 📠 *22860/28926* 🌐 *www.santorini.org/hotels/costamarina-hotel* *21 rooms* *In-room: refrigerator, kitchen (some). In-hotel: no elevator* 💳 *MC, V* *BP.*

$$ **Pelican Hotel.** Just down from the busy main (Theotokopoulou) square on Danezi street, this small hotel is in the center of the commercial part of town. Although not in a picturesque neighborhood, few can complain about the convenient location. Happily, most rooms are sound-insulated, making for an oasis of quiet. The vaulted lobby and white guest rooms are furnished with dark traditional wooden furniture. Some rooms have balconies over a lovely garden. Breakfast is included, but not transfers. There is a self-service laundry room. ✉ *On cobbled road up from main traffic street, near town hall, 84700* ☎ *22860/23133* 📠 *22860/23514* 🌐 *www.pelican.gr* *18 rooms* *In-room: Wi-Fi. In-hotel: pool, no elevator, public Internet* 💳 *AE, D, MC, V.*

$ **Loizos Apartments.** Lefteris Anapliotis's pension, located in a quiet and convenient section of Fira, is the perfect budget choice. The rooms, some with sea views, are spacious and the garden is pretty. The price includes transfers. The excellent breakfast costs €5. Lefteris also runs the even cheaper Loizos Hotel, 3 km (2 mi) outside town. Lefteris makes this place special—he's got lots of handy tips to spread around (just ask him about Santorini wine). ✉ *On cobbled road up from main traffic street, near town hall, 84700* ☎ *22860/24046* 📠 *22860/25118* 🌐 *www.loizos.gr* *23 rooms* *In-room: refrigerator. In-hotel: pool, no elevator, public Internet, public Wi-Fi* 💳 *AE, MC, V.*

A "PRIVATE" BALCONY?

Remember that many of Santorini's hotel cliffside balconies elbow each other out of the way for the best view and, with footpaths often running above and aside them, privacy is often hard to come by.

$ **Pension Delphini I.** Vassilis Rousseas's pension, on the busy main traffic street, is well run, inexpensive, friendly, and open all year. His mother tends the lovely little garden. Although an excellent budget choice, the front rooms are on the noisy car road and a few rooms lack air-conditioning. ✉ *Main traffic street, opposite Piraeus Bank, 84700* ☎ *22860/22780* 📠 *22860/22371* 🌐 *www.delfini-santorini.gr* *10 rooms* *In-room: refrigerator, dial-up. In-hotel: no elevator* 💳 *No credit cards.*

NIGHTLIFE & THE ARTS

DANCING The **Koo Club** (✉ *North end of cliff-side walkway* ☎ *22860/22025*) is Fira's most popular outdoor disco by far. **Santorinia** (✉ *Next to Nomikos Conference Center* ☎ *22860/23777*) is the place for live Greek music and dancing. Nothing happens before midnight. **Casablanca Soul** (✉ *Fira* ☎ *22860/24008*) is in the maze to the north; there is often live music.

FESTIVALS The **Bellonia Cultural Center**, on the main car crossroads, contains a small auditorium, the latest audiovisual equipment, and a large library. In summer, it presents concerts, readings, and theater festivals; in winter, it becomes an educational center. Thank pianist Athena Capodistria for September's **Santorini Music Festival** (✉ *Nomikos Conference Center* ☎ *22860/22220*), which always includes internationally known musicians. In 2007 the **Santorini Jazz Festival** (✉ *Open-air Cinema Kamari* 🌐 *www.jazzserver.nl/festivals/?letter=s*) celebrated its 10th anniversary.

MUSIC The popular **Franco's Bar** (✉ *Below cliff-side walkway* ☎ *22860/24428* 🌐 *www.francos.gr*) plays classical music and serves champagne cocktails. It has a caldera view.

SHOPPING

EMBROIDERY **Costas Dimitrokalis** and Matthew Dimitrokalis sell locally made embroideries of Greek linen and Egyptian cotton, rugs, pillowcases in hand-crocheted wool with local designs, and more. Purchases can be mailed anywhere. ✉ *1 block from cable car* ☎📠 *22860/22957* 💳 *AE, D, MC, V.*

GALLERIES **Art and Glass Gallery.** Aris Carreris's gallery represents seven Greek artists whose crafts range from icons on wood to glass in both sleek modern and traditional designs. He ships everywhere. ✉ *On block that runs* *down from Archaeological Museum to main car street* ☎*22860/25977.* **Phenomenon.** Christoforos Asimis studied painting at Athens University, and has had many exhibitions there and abroad. The nearby cathedral's murals are his. His paintings specialize in the light and landscape of his home island. His wife, Eleni, who also studied in Athens, shows sculptures, ceramics, and jewelry; her jewelry, in elegant designs both classic and modern, is executed with the highest craftsmanship. Few of Fira's proliferating jewelry shops have work to compare with this. ✉*Ypapantis walkway, Palia Fabrika* ☎*22860/23041* 🌐*www.santorini.info/paliafabrika/index.html.*

JEWELRY **Bead Shop.** Marina Tsiagkouri's shop has expanded, but beads are still the main reason to go. Who can resist her unique beads made from Santorini's volcanic rock? ✉*Opposite entrance to Museum of Prehistoric Thera* ☎*22860/25176.* **Kostas Antoniou Jewelry.** Many of Kostas's original pieces were inspired by ancient Thera; some solid gold necklaces are magnificent enough to earn their own names, such as Earth's Engravings, Ritual, and Motionless Yielding. The work is both classic and creative. ✉*In Spiliotica shopping area, near Archaeological Museum* ☎📠*22860/22633* 🌐*www.antoniou-santorini.com* 💳*AE, MC, V.*

SPORTS & THE OUTDOORS

SAILING The **Santorini Sailing Center** (✉*Merovigli* ☎*22860/23058 or 22860/23059*), near Fira, arranges charters and runs weekly two- to three-day sailing trips around the Cyclades for groups of up to 10.

FIROSTEFANI ΦΗΡΟΣΤΕΦΑΝΙ

Firostefani used to be a separate village, but now it is an elegant suburb north of Fira. The 10-minute walk between them, along the caldera, is one of Santorini's highlights. From Firostefani's single white cliff-side street, walkways descend to traditional vaulted cave houses, which are fast becoming pensions. Though close to the action, Firostefani feels calm and quiet.

WHERE TO STAY & EAT

$$$ ★ ✕**Vanilia.** Set in a windmill—built in 1872 and preserved by the government after the 1956 earthquake—Vanilia also encompasses pretty terraces, on which to enjoy the good food. You might start with Santorini fava served with onions, cherry tomatoes, and capers. Homemade pasta, such as ravioli stuffed with Cretan graviera cheese and served with yogurt, is a specialty. An intriguing entrée is grilled pork fillet in thyme-honey sauce. Kazas-tipi (cream custard on cinnamon sugar) will make you want to linger at this friendly place. ✉*Main square* ☎*22860/25631* 💳*AE, D, MC, V* ⊗*Closed Nov.–Apr.*

$$ ★ ✕**Aktaion.** In his tiny taverna, Vangelis Roussos uses mostly his grandfather's recipes. The paintings on the walls are Vangelis's own. Salad Santorini, his mother's recipe, has raw cod flakes, caper leaves, and seasonal ingredients. The moussaka, made with white eggplant, is incomparable. ✉*Main square* ☎*22860/22336* 💳*MC, V.*

WORD OF MOUTH

"Just next to Fira on Santorini is Firostefani, sometimes not designated as a separate village. This is a much shorter walk from Fira than Imerovigli, so if you can get a hotel there you will have the quiet and caldera view without the crowds."

—brotherleelove2004

$$$$ Fodor'sChoice ★ **Tsitouras Hotel.** Architectural Digest–worthy decor and earthy Cycladic charm collide here at this complex of six apartments, and the result is true Santorinian splendor. Little wonder these apartments have been homes-away-from-homes for the likes of Gianni Versace, Joan Kennedy, Harvey Keitel, Nana Mouskouri, and Jean-Paul Gaultier. There's no sign; guests are met (at the airport or harbor) and brought to these sparkling white cubes with volcanic stone trimmings built around an 18th-century mansion. Inside, the decor is a fantasia of Chippendale armchairs, ancient amphorae, Byzantine icons, Corfiot mariner's chests, Picasso ceramics, and gilt-framed engravings; the glowing color schemes were cooked up by legendary British designer David Hicks. Salons are picturesquely dotted with domes, skylights, and interior windows—the showpiece is the "House of the Winds," where the Oscar winner is the grand, double-height, cathedral-roofed living room ashimmer with elegant antiques and robin's-egg-blue walls. The elegant terrace overlooks the caldera, but many choose to enjoy dinner on their own terrace. All this luxe comes at a stiff price, but no doubt many will think their pennies—rates run from €470 to €790—well spent. ✉ *Firostefani cliff face, next to St. Mark's, 84700* ☎ *22860/23747* 🖷 *22860/23918* 🌐 *www.tsitouras.gr* *6 apartments* *In-room: refrigerator. In-hotel: restaurant, no elevator, public Internet* 💳 *AE, D, MC, V* *BP.*

$$–$$$$ ★ **Reverie Traditional Apartments.** Georgios Fytros has converted his family home into an inexpensive and attractive hotel, all cream color with marble insets. Each of the large rooms, white with dark-toned wood furniture, has a winding staircase to a balcony with a metal frame bed. The roof garden has a caldera view. ✉ *Between Firostefani walkway and main traffic road, 84700* ☎ *22860/23322* 🖷 *22860/23044* 🌐 *www.reverie.gr* *13 rooms, 2 suites* *In-room: refrigerator. In-hotel: pool, no elevator, public Internet* 💳 *D, MC, V*

IMEROVIGLI ΗΜΕΡΟΒΙΓΛΙ

Set on the highest point of the caldera's rim, Imerovigli (the name means Watchtower), is what Firostefani was like a decade and a half ago. It is now being developed, and for good reasons: it is quiet, traditional, and less expensive. The 25-minute walk from Fira, with incredible views, should be on everyone's itinerary. The lodgments, some of them traditional cave houses, are mostly down stairways from the cliffside walkway. The big rock backing the village was once crowned by Skaros Castle, whence Venetian overlords reigned after 1207. It collapsed in an earthquake, leaving only the rock. A trail descending from the church of Ayios Georgios crosses the isthmus and encircles Skaros;

it's only 10 minutes to the castle top. After 1 km (½ mi) it reaches the small chapel of Theoskepasti with a memorable caldera view.

WHERE TO STAY & EAT

$$$ ✕**Blue Note.** You can't go wrong with the location: a deck extended over the cliff, a panoramic caldera view, and a sunset as dessert. For a starter try Gruyère flambé. For a main dish, lamb *klephtiko* (stewed in wine and herbs in a ceramic dish) is a good choice, as is shrimp Blue Note (a secret recipe). Blue Note is open for lunch and dinner. ✉*On main walkway near Maltesa.* ☎*22860/23771* ▭*MC, V.*

$$ ✕**Skaros Fish Taverna.** This rustic open-air taverna, one of three restaurants in Imerovigli, has spectacular caldera views. It serves fresh fish and Santorini specialties, such as octopus in onion sauce, and mussels with rice and raisins. ✉*On cliff-side walkway* ☎*22860/23616* ▭*AE, MC, V* ⏲*Closed Nov.–Mar.*

$$$ **Spiliotica Apartments and Suites.** With his lively vibe, Tony Spiliotis (a Greek-American) has created an attractive hideaway that attracts everyone from families to celebrities. Cascading steeply down the cliff side, these cave rooms are individually theme-decorated, with baths built into the deep rock recesses. All rooms have caldera views and little terraces where you can watch the sunset. Breakfast is included; transfers are extra. Beware: there are a lot of steep steps. ✉*On cliff-side walkway, behind church of Panaghia Maltesa, near parking and bus stop, 84700* ☎*22860/22637* 🖷*22860/23590* 🌐*www.spiliotica.com* *4 houses* *In-hotel: pool, no elevator, public Internet* ▭*MC, V* ⏲*Closed Nov.–Mar.* *BP.*

$$ **Annio.** The rooms in this cliff-side lodgment are attractive and simple, with local furnishings both new and old. All have terraces and caldera views, making this a good deal (if you don't care about a pool). Christos Nomikos built it himself on his family property, and his daughter Katerina runs it. They don't provide transfers, but rather lots of beauty, peace, comfort, and quiet. Breakfast costs extra. ✉*Imerovigli, 84700* ☎*22860/24714* 🖷*22860/23550* 🌐*www.annioflats.gr* *11 rooms* *In-room: refrigerator, Ethernet. In-hotel: no elevator* ▭*MC, V* ⏲*Closed Nov.–Apr.*

$$ **Heliades Apartments.** Owner Olympia Sarri knows she has something special. Her father mostly built the apartments, consisting of four cave houses, white with blue-green accents, with verandas and caldera views. The couches and loft beds are traditional, and the arches are outlined in Santorini tufa; the living room areas are especially spacious. Unbelievably, there are just a few steps. Breakfast is extra. ✉*On cliff-side walkway, behind church of Panaghia Maltesa, near parking and bus stop, 84700* ☎*22860/24102* 🖷*22860/25587* 🌐*www.heliades-apts.gr* *4 houses* *In-room: kitchen. In-hotel: no elevator.* ▭*No credit cards* ⏲*Closed Nov.–Mar.*

IA OIA

Fodor'sChoice ★ *14 km (8½ mi) northwest of Fira.*

At the tip of the northern horn of the island sits Ia (or Oia), Santorini's second-largest town and the Aegean's most photographed village. Ia is more tasteful than Fira (for one thing, no establishment here is allowed to play music that can be heard on the street), and the town's cubical white houses (some vaulted against earthquakes) stand out against the green-, brown-, and rust-color layers of rock, earth, and solid volcanic ash that rise from the sea. Every summer evening, travelers from all over the world congregate at the caldera's rim—sitting on whitewashed fences, staircases, beneath the town's windmill, on the old **kastro**—each looking out to sea in anticipation of the performance: the Ia sunset. The three-hour rim-edge walk from Ia to Fira at this hour is unforgettable.

In the middle of the quiet caldera, the volcano smolders away eerily, adding an air of suspense to an already awe-inspiring scene. The 1956 eruption caused tremendous earthquakes (7.8 on the Richter scale) that left 48 people dead (thankfully, most residents were working outdoors at the time), hundreds injured, and 2,000 houses toppled. The island's west side—especially Ia, until then the largest town—was hard hit, and many residents decided to emigrate to Athens, Australia, and America. And although Fira, also damaged, rebuilt rapidly, Ia proceeded slowly, sticking to the traditional architectural style. The perfect example of that style is the restaurant 1800, a renovated ship-captain's villa. In 1900, Ia had nearly 9,000 inhabitants, mostly mariners who owned 164 seafaring vessels and seven shipyards. Now there are about 500 permanent residents, and more than 100 boats. Many of these mariners use the endless flight of stairs from the kastro to descend down to the water and the small port of **Ammoudi,** where the pebble beach is home to some of the island's nicest fish tavernas. Head east to find the fishing port of **Armeni,** home to all those excursion boats that tour the caldera.

Ia is set up like the other three towns—Fira, Firostefani, and Imerovigli—that adorn the caldera's sinuous rim. There is a car road, which is new, and a cliff-side walkway (Nikolaos Nomikou), which is old. Shops and restaurants are all on the walkway, and hotel entrances mostly descend from it—something to check carefully if you cannot negotiate stairs easily. In Ia there is a lower cliff-side walkway writhing with stone steps, and a long stairway to the tiny blue bay with its dock below. Short streets leading from the car road to the walkway have cheaper eateries and shops. There is a parking lot at either end, and the northern one marks the end of the road and the rim. Nothing is very far from anything else.

The main walkway of Ia can be thought of as a straight river, with a delta at the northern end, where the better shops and restaurants are. The most-luxurious cave-house hotels are at the southern end, and a stroll by them is part of the extended evening promenade. Although it is not as crowded as Fira, where the tour boats deposit their thousands of hasty shoppers, relentless publicity about Ia's beauty and tastefulness, accurate enough, are making it impassable in August. The sunset in Ia may not really be much more spectacular than in Fira, and certainly not better than in higher Imerovigli, but there is something tribally satisfying at the sight of so many people gathering in one spot to celebrate pure beauty. Happily, the night scene isn't as frantic as Fira's—most shop owners are content to sit out front and don't cotton to the few revelers' bars in operation. In winter, Ia feels pretty uninhabited.

The **Naval Museum of Thera** is in an old neoclassic mansion, once destroyed in the big earthquake, now risen like a phoenix from the ashes. The collection displays ships' figureheads, seamen's chests, maritime equipment, and models—all revealing the extensive nautical history of the island, Santorini's main trade until tourism took over. ✉ *Near telephone office* ☎ *22860/71156* 🎫 *€4* ⏲ *Tues.–Sun. 8:30–3.*

BEACH

There are no beautiful beaches close to Ia, but you can hike down Ia's cliff side or catch a bus to the small sand beach of **Baxedes** (✉ *Port of Armoudhi*).

WHERE TO STAY & EAT

$$$$ Fodor's Choice ★ ✕ **1800.** Clearly, some of Santorini's old sea captains lived graciously, as you'll note when dining at one of Santorini's most famous restaurants, 1800 (the name refers to the date when the house was built). Owner, architect, and restaurateur John Zagelidis has lovingly restored this magnificent old captain's house with original colors (white, olive green, and gray) and furnishings, including antique sofas, wooden travel chests, and a hand-painted Venetian bed. To top it all off, a superlative roof terrace was constructed, with a vista framed by Ia's most-spectacular church cupolas—a perfect perch on hot nights for taking in the famous Ia sunset. Maître d' Eleni Economou is efficient, knowledgeable, and charming, while the chef, Thanasis Sfougkaris—winner of Greece's prestigious Golden Toque award in 2004—does full honor to the beautiful surroundings. For starters try red mullet baked in vine leaves with tapenade sauce, spring onion coulis, and capers with their leaves; or tomato and mozzarella tart with basil and bell pepper dressing. Entrées include fillet of white grouper with celery mousse, artichokes, capers, and botargo sauce; and baked lamb cutlets with fennel, young peas, and porcini sauce. ✉ *Main street, 84702* ☎ *22860/71485* 📠 *22860/72317* 🌐 *www.oia-1800.com* 💳 *AE, DC, MC, V.*

$$–$$$ ✕ **Red Bicycle.** Once featured on Giada De Laurentis's Food Network show, this sophisticated café, wine bar, and art gallery is located at the north end of Ia's main walkway, just down the steps; its big terrace with sail-like white awnings overlooks the bay. Owner Chara Kourti loves "Chara's Pie" (ground beef, carrots, pistachios, pine nuts baked in phyllo with tahini sauce), and no one will complain about the delicious quiches or large wine list. Desserts are a specialty; try *galaktoboureko* (warm custard pie with dates, raisins, and rosewater syrup). ✉ *Ia* ☎ *22860/71918* 💳 *No credit cards.*

$–$$ ★ **Kastro.** Spyros Dimitroulis's restaurant is primarily patronized for its view of the famous Ia sunset, and at the magical hour it is always filled. Happily, the food makes a fitting accompaniment. A good starter is olives stuffed with cream cheese dipped in beer dough and fried, served on arugula with a balsamic sauce. For a main dish try lamb scallops in wine and rosemary sauce, or pappardelle with asparagus and a sauce of dried tomato and garlic. Lunch is popular. *Near Venetian castle 22860/71045 AE, MC, V.*

$$$$ **Katikies.** Sumptuously appointed, this immaculate white cliff-side complex layered on terraces has sleek modern design, including Andy Warhol wall prints, stunning fabrics, and handsome furniture. Chic as the surroundings are, the barrel-vaulted ceilings and other architectural details lend a traditional air to the place. Suites and villas are small and private; all have private terraces that overlook the caldera and are luxuriously appointed. The restaurant terrace sports a great caldera view, strikingly framed by sleek white columns and chairs slip-covered in the whitest linen. Note: there are a lot of stairs for the weary. *Ia cliff face, edge of main town, 84702 22860/71401 22860/71129 www.katikies.com 7 rooms, 33 suites, 7 villas In-room: kitchen. In-hotel: 3 restaurants, bars, pools, no elevator, public Internet AE, MC, V Closed Nov.–Mar. BP.*

$$$$ **Lampetia Villas.** This EOT Traditional Settlement, 800 feet up the cliff from the sea, offers charm, comfort, and friendliness. The owner, Tom Alafragis, has a charm all his own. Each of the accommodations—all have private balconies with a view—is different in size and furnishings. *Nomikou, Ia cliff face, down from main street 22860/71237 www.lampetia.gr 8 houses In-room: kitchen. In-hotel: pool, no elevator AE, MC, V Closed Nov.–Mar. BP.*

$$$$ ★ **Perivolas.** Immortalized as one of the most famous infinity pools on earth (thanks to nearly a dozen magazine covers), the cliff-hanger here seems to make you feel you could easily swim off the edge into the caldera's blue bay 1,000 feet below. The pool is the jewel in the crown of these 17 houses (all connected by flights of stairs), one of the first hotel complexes built after the big 1956 earthquake. Inside, guest rooms have been converted from old wineries and renovated in archetypal *skafta* (vaulted cave) fashion, with clever nooks for beds, sculpted walls, and full kitchens; all are simply but stunningly furnished with handmade wooden pieces and weavings. Each house has its own terrace. *Nomikou, Ia cliff face, 15 mins by foot from cliff-side street, 84702 22860/71308 22860/71309 www.perivolas.gr 17 houses In-room: kitchen. In-hotel: restaurant, bar, pool, no elevator AE, MC, V Closed Nov.–Mar. BP.*

$ **Delfini Villas.** If you think a comfortable, convenient room in Ia with a caldera view and terrace has to be expensive, think again: Rena Halari's place is affordable and warmly charming. This is a great buy, so don't expect a lot of service. *Lower main traffic street, opposite Piraeus Bank, 84702 22860/71600 22860/71601 www.delfini-villas.com 6 rooms, 4 apartments In-room: kitchen, refrigerator. In hotel: no elevator AE, MC, V Closed Nov.–Mar.*

NIGHTLIFE

There are the usual cafés, bars, and pastry shops along the main street but a peaceful note is struck by the fact that establishments are forbidden to play loud music. The bar at Santorini's most sophisticated restaurant, **1800** (☒*Main street* ☎*22860/71485*), gets lively late, when diners leave. With a balcony overlooking the caldera, **Skiza** (☎*22860/71569*) is well known for the excellence of its pastries. Those in search of a happy-hour beer go to **Zorba's** (☒*On cliff side*).

> **THE REAL DEAL**
>
> Ia mostly abjures the jewelry madness of Fira, and instead offers a variety of handcrafted items. Since the shops are not so dependent on cruise ships, a certain sophistication reigns in the quiet streets. Art galleries, "objets" shops, crafts shops, and icon stores set the tone. More open every year.

SHOPPING

ACCESSORIES You'll know the **Silk Shop** (☒*Main shopping street* ☎*22860/71923*), a tiny outlet near the Red Bicycle restaurant, from the spectacular array of brilliant rainbow colors. Judy Neaves and Theodore Xenos sell woven silk scarves, shawls, and small handmade purses.

ANTIQUES & COLLECTIBLES Manolis and Chara Kourtis's **Loulaki** (☒*Main shopping street* ☎*22860/71856*) sells antiques, odd pieces, jewelry, and art; exploring the shop is a pleasure. Alexandra Solomos's painted plates are a favorite.

ART **Art Gallery** (☒*Main shopping street* ☎📠*22860/71448*) sells large, three-dimensional representations of Santorini architecture by Bella Kokeenatou and Stavros Galanopoulos. Their lifelike depth invites the viewer to walk through a door or up a flight of stairs.

BOOKS **Atlantis Books** (☒*North end of main shopping street* ☎*22869/72346* 🌐*www.atlantisbooks.org*) is a tiny English bookshop that would be at home in New York's Greenwich Village or London's Bloomsbury; its presence here is a miracle. Only good literature makes it onto the shelves. Writers stop by to chat and give readings.

PYRGOS ΠΥΡΓΟΣ

5½ km (3½ mi) south of Fira.

Though today Pyrgos has only 500 inhabitants, until the early 1800s it was the capital of the island. Stop here to see its medieval houses, stacked on top of one another and back to back for protection against pirates. The beautiful neoclassic building on the way up is a luxury hotel. The view from the ruined Venetian castle is panoramic. And reward yourself for the climb up the picturesque streets, which follow the shape of the hill, with a stop at the panoramic terrace of the Café Kastelli, for Greek coffee and homemade sweets. In Pyrgos you are really in old Santorini—hardly anything has changed.

The **Monastery of Profitis Ilias** is at the highest point on Santorini, which spans to 1,856 feet at the summit. From here you can see the surrounding islands and, on a clear day, the mountains of Crete, more than 100 km (66 mi) away. You may also be able to spot ancient Thera on the peak below Profitis Ilias. Unfortunately, radio towers and a NATO radar installation provide an ugly backdrop for the monastery's wonderful bell tower.

Founded in 1711 by two monks from Pyrgos, Profitis Ilias is cherished by islanders because here, in a secret school, the Greek language and culture were taught during the dark centuries of the Turkish occupation. A **museum** in the monastery contains a model of the secret school in a monk's cell, another model of a traditional carpentry and blacksmith shop, and a display of ecclesiastical items. The monastery's future is in doubt because there are so few monks left. ✉ *At highest point on Santorini* 🎫 *Free* ⏲ *No visiting hrs; caretaker is sometimes around.*

VIN BEATS EAU

The locals say that in Santorini there is more wine than water, and it may be true; Santorini produces more wine than any two other Cyclades islands (Paros is second). The volcanic soil, high daytime temperatures, and humidity at night produce 36 varieties of grape, and these unique growing conditions are ideal for the production of distinctive white wine now gaining international recognition. Farmers twist the vines into a basketlike shape, in which the grapes grow, protected from the wind. A highlight of any Santorini trip is a visit to one of its many wineries—log on to www.santorini.org/wineries/ for a helpful intro.

MEGALOCHORI ΜΕΓΑΛΟΧΩΡΙ

4 km (2½ mi) east of Pyrgos, 9 km (5½ mi) southwest of Fira.

Megalochori is a picturesque, half-abandoned town set. Many of the village's buildings were actually *canavas,* wine-making facilities. The tiny main square is still lively in the evening.

On your way south from Megalochori to Akrotiri, stop at **Antoniou Winery** (✉ *Megalochori* ☎ 22860/23557 🌐 *www.antoniou-santorini.com*) and take a tour of the multilevel old facility. It's so beautiful, local couples get married here. An enologist leads a wine tasting with snacks, and a slide show describes local wine production; it costs €5. Many think Antoniou's white wines are Santorini's best—and that's saying a lot.

WHERE TO STAY

$$$$ ★ **Vedema.** Angelina Jolie, Oliver Stone, Susan Sarandon, Danny DeVito ... and now you? Those A-Listers head here because the black-lava environs keep crowds and paparazzi at bay—but you, too, may enjoy the peace of this distant and deluxe outpost. A world unto itself, it was built up around a beautiful 15th-century winery. Trouble is, it kept expanding and expanding, and now tops out at 42 villas, almost like a "planned" gated community in Florida. Inside, the leitmotif is minimalism-meets-Mediterranean: SoHo stone tables below vintage

island-style mirrors, with some guest rooms done in such shocking blues and pinks you may soon be reaching for your Visine. Still, the old vaulted dining room is one of the prettiest on Santorini; the wine cellar, with its many valuable wines, is worth exploration (there are wine tastings nightly). The spacious suites all have marble bathrooms and terraces. Vedema is not cheap, but you'll get what you're paying for, in spades—everyone raves about the food and service. Although the location is relatively isolated, a handy shuttle service ferries you to other parts of the island. ✉*84700Megalochori* ☎*22860/81796 or 22860/81797* 📠*22860/81798* 🌐*www.vedema.gr* *35 rooms, 7 suites* *In-room: kitchen (some). In-hotel: 2 restaurants, pool, no elevator* 💳*AE, D, MC, V* ⏲*Closed Nov.–Mar.* 🍴*BP.*

AKROTIRI ΑΚΡΩΤΗΡΙ

7 km (4½ mi) west of Pyrgos, 13 km (8 mi) south of Fira.

If Santorini is known as the "Greek Pompeii" and is claimant to the
★ title of the lost Atlantis, it is because of the archaeological site of **ancient Akrotiri,** near the tip of the southern horn of the island. At this writing (winter 2007), the site was closed temporarily for structural repairs, so check ahead before you plan your visit.

In the 1860s, in the course of quarrying volcanic ash for use in the Suez Canal, workmen discovered the remains of an ancient town. The town was frozen in time by ash from an eruption 3,600 years ago, long before Pompeii's disaster. In 1967 Spyridon Marinatos of the University of Athens began excavations, which occasionally continue. It is thought that the 40 buildings that have been uncovered are only one-thirtieth of the huge site and that excavating the rest will probably take a century.

Marinatos's team discovered great numbers of extremely well-preserved frescoes depicting many aspects of Akrotiri life, most now displayed in the National Archaeological Museum in Athens; Santorini wants them back. Meanwhile, postcard-size pictures of them are posted outside the houses where they were found. The antelopes, monkeys, and wildcats they portray suggest trade with Egypt.

Culturally an outpost of Minoan Crete, Akrotiri was settled as early as 3000 BC and reached its peak after 2000 BC, when it developed trade and agriculture and settled the present town. The inhabitants cultivated olive trees and grain, and their advanced architecture—three-story frescoed houses faced with masonry (some with balconies) and public buildings of sophisticated construction—is evidence of an elaborate lifestyle. ✉*South of modern Akrotiri, near tip of southern horn* ☎*22860/81366* 🌐*www.culture.gr* *€5* ⏲*Tues.–Sun. 8:30–3.*

BEACH

Red beach (✉*On southwest shore below Akrotiri*) is quiet and has a taverna.

KAMARI ΚΑΜΑΡΙ

6½ km (4¼ mi) east of Akrotiri, 6 km (4 mi) south of Fira.

★ Archaeology buffs will want to visit the site of **ancient Thera.** There are relics of a Dorian city, with 9th-century BC tombs, an engraved phallus, Hellenistic houses, and traces of Byzantine fortifications and churches. At the sanctuary of Apollo, graffiti dating to the 8th century BC record the names of some of the boys who danced naked at the god's festival (Satie's famed musical compositions, *Gymnopedies,* reimagine these). To get here, hike up from Perissa or Kamari or take a taxi up **Mesa Vouna.** On the summit are the scattered ruins, excavated by a German archaeology school around the turn of the 20th century; there's a fine view. ✉ *On a switchback up mountain right before Kamari, 2,110 ft high* ☎ *22860/31366* 🌐 *www.culture.gr* 🎫 *€5* 🕐 *Tues.–Sun. 8:30–3.*

BEACH

The black-sand beach of **Kamari** is a natural treasure of Santorini and crowds head here to rent deck chairs and umbrellas. They also flock to Kamari because tavernas and refreshment stands abound—despite an attractive wooden walkway and lively nightlife, Kamari is the epitome of overdevelopment.

FOLEGANDROS ΦΟΛΕΓΑΝΔΡΟΣ

If Santorini didn't exist, little, bare Folegandros (🌐 *www.folegandros.gr*) would be world famous. Its gorgeous Cycladic main town of Chora, built between the walls of a Venetian fort, sits on the edge of a beetling precipice: this hilltop setting represents, with the exception of Santorini, the finest cliff scenery in the Cyclades. Beyond this, the island does not seem to have much to offer on paper—but in person it certainly does. Beautiful and authentic, it has become the secret island of Cyclades lovers, who want a pure dose of the magic essence of the Aegean every year or so. Only 31 square km (12 square mi) in area and 64 km (40 mi) in circumference, it lacks ruins, villages, green valleys, trees, country houses, and graceful cafés at the edge of the sea. But what it does have—one of the most stunning Chora towns; deliberately downplayed touristic development; several good beaches; quiet evenings; traditional local food; and respectful visitors—make it addictive. There are no discos, no bank, but the sea is shining and, in spring, much of the island is redolent of thyme and oregano.

Visitors to Folegandros—historians are divided on whether the name immortalizes the Cretan explorer Pholegandrus or comes from the Phoenician term for "rock-strewn"—all stay in the main town, and hang around the town's three squares. A walk, a swim at the beach, a visit to the little Folklore Museum at Ano Meria, meeting other people who love the essence of the Greek islands: these require few arrangements. Unless you want to stop on the side of the road to look at views (the island does offer an array of interesting hiking trails), the bus is adequate. There are a number of beaches—Angali and Ayios Nikolaos are especially good. Because Folegandros is so small, it fills up fast in

August, and despite the absence of raucous nightlife, it somewhat loses its special flavor. For travel services and booking boat trips, check out Tours in the Essentials section at the end of this chapter.

CHORA ΧΩΡΑ

42 km (27 mi) northwest of Santorini, 164 km (102 mi) southeast of Athens.

As the boat approaches the little port of Karavostasi, bare, sun-scoured cliffs—with a hint of relieving green in wet winter but only gray glare in summer—let you know where you are. Leaving the port immediately, since there is hardly anything here, visitors climb the road 3 km (2 mi) to Chora on buses (which meet all ferries). On the rugged way up, you'll see the spectacular, whitewashed **church of Koímisis tis Theotókou** (or Dormition of the Mother of God) dominating the town on the high cliff where the ancient settlement first stood. On Easter Sunday the chief icon is carried through the town.

A TASTE OF ITALY

The island's Italian vibe lingers at Flavio Facciolo's Café dei Viaggiatori. Found on the first bus square, Flavio and his wife offer a selection of good Italian wines, serve light Venetian-flavored snacks, and serve the best espresso on the isle.

After a steep ride, cliff-top Chora comes into view. Its sky-kissing perch is well out of sight of the port, an important consideration in the centuries when the seas here were plagued by marauding pirate raiders. Today, Chora—small, white, old, and preserved lovingly by the islanders—is less hidden and is known as the main reason to visit the island. Its main street, starting at the bus stop (past which most streets are pedestrianized) meanders through five little squares—the middle three are the main ones—each with a few restaurants and cafés shaded by bougainvillea and hibiscus. Some of the buildings, including a hotel and café, are set into the walls of the Venetian fort, or kastro, built by the Venetian duke of Naxos in the 13th century. The second street circles the kastro and the precipice on which the town stands and is strikingly lined with two-story cube houses that form a wall atop the towering cliff. The glory days of Venice came to an end in 1715, when the ruling Turks sacked Folegandros and sold the captives as slaves. The old families go back to 1780, when the island was repopulated. As for dining and lodging, the new fancier places at the edge of town miss the meaning of the island. Opt, instead, for the simple tavernas in Chora, all family run. Next to one another and competitive, they are all good.

ANO MERIA ἌΝΩ ΜΕΡΙΑ

The paved road connects the port, the capital, and, after 5 km (3 mi), Ano Meria. On the way there, you can see terraces where barley was coaxed seemingly from stone, though they are hardly farmed now. The tiny town is a smaller version of Chora, and the cafés are perfect places for a drink. Exhibits in the little **Folklore Museum** (*Free* *July–mid-*

Sept., daily 10–6,) reconstruct traditional farming life. The church of Agios Panteleimon celebrates on July 27, and almost everyone goes.

WHERE TO STAY & EAT

¢ ✕**I Piazze.** A middle-square eatery, this popular option has tables set out under trees. Specialties include kalasouna cheese pies and homemade noodles (called *matsata*) with pork or lamb. They also sell their own aromatic thyme honey. ✉*Middle square* ☎*No phone* ▭*No credit cards.*

¢ ✕**O Kritikos.** Set under a tree and abutting a Byzantine church, Kritikos serves exclusively local meats and vegetables. Souroto, a local cheese, makes a fitting appetizer. Kontosouli is usually pork on the spit; here it is a mixture of lamb and pork, and delicious. ✉*Middle square* ☎*22860/41219* ▭*No credit cards.*

$$$ **Anemomilos Apartments.** Much the best place to stay in Folegandros (it is up to the right as you enter the main town), Anemomilos is the friendly domain of Dimitris and Cornelia Patelis. Perched on the cliff overlooking the sea and set amid a series of small garden terraces (perfect for breakfast and drinks), the complex is faced with attractive island-style stonework. The apartments beckon in traditional blue and white; all have terraces, half with sea view. Breakfasts and transfers are extra. ✉*Chora, 84011* ☎*22860/41309* 🖷*22860/41407* 🌐*www.anemomilosapartments.com* *23 rooms* *In-room: refrigerator, Wi-Fi. In-hotel: pool, no elevator* ▭*MC, V* ⏲*Closed mid-Oct.–Easter.*

$ **Meltemi.** If you want a simple, inexpensive, family place to stay, Meltemi does the job. Clean, white, simple, convenient, with good-size rooms, it is open March through October. ✉*Chora, 84011* ☎*22860/41425* 🌐*www.greekhotel.com/cyclades/folegand/chora/meltemi* *11 rooms* *In-hotel: no elevator, public Wi-Fi* ▭*No credit cards* ⏲*Closed Nov.–Feb.*

SHOPPING

JEWELRY Open April through September, **Jewelry Creations** (✉*Middle square* ☎*22860/41524*) features the jewelry of Apostolos and Eleni, who have been creating their striking jewels, often with Greek stones, for 20 years.

SIFNOS ΣΙΦΝΟΣ

Sifnos is a *kore*—one of those elegantly draped young female figures that the Archaic islanders liked to carve out of the finest marble. Her beauty is graceful and modest. Unlike her parched neighbor Seriphos, just 19 km (12 mi) northwest, Sifnos is well watered and fertile, a garden island. But to passing boats she appears formidable, for her sweetness is guarded by steep cliffs, broken suddenly by only a few deep-cut bays with safe anchorage. The main towns of the island, Apollonia and Artemonas, are found along the central ridge, while the popular beaches are in the south; the north, where the ancient silver mines were, is sparsely inhabited. Because Sifnos is small (2,000 people) and relatively undeveloped (though ministers, ambassadors, and artists

have houses here), her 35,000 tourists yearly overwhelm resources in August, when the beaches are clogged and the buses packed.

The history of the island is fabled. Ancient Sifnos enjoyed a brief period of great prosperity when gold was found here; the remains of the Siphnian treasury which was erected at Delphi are impressive. The Siphnians were supposed to give Apollo at Delphi a golden egg annually: once they tried to fob him off with a gilded stone, and in anger, he sent tidal waves to swamp their mines (a drier account simply has them running dry). The island's name, not insignificantly, means "empty."

Buses run regularly all day from Apollonia's clogged central square to the outlying villages and some of the beaches, and this is probably the best way to get around Sifnos. Taxis (22840/33300) start here, too; bikes, quads, and cars are available, but useful only for unusual locations, and if you're heading to some of the beaches, you'll want to access them via small boats from Kamares. Aegean Thesaurus Travel and Tourism (*see* Tours in this chapter's Essentials section) is on the main square; they handle accommodations, tickets, rentals, and are especially good on hiking trips, a chief reason to visit Sifnos. The sights of Sifnos (🌐 *www.sifnos.gr*) can easily be seen in three days; to be seen well, they require years.

KAMARES ΚΑΜΑΡΕΣ

50 km (31 mi) northwest of Folegandros, 105 km (65 mi) northwest of Santorini.

The most protected of Sifnos's anchorages is the port of Kamares, a small white town on a bay on the west coast with high cliffs on either side, a good beach with tamarisk trees, and a narrow green valley whose road takes you to the interior. You'll find some handy travel agencies and rental-car offices here (as well as in the island's main towns). A couple of potters' studios still function, and there is a mining establishment at the north end, in one of whose shafts relics of ancient temples were found. Indeed, the old fishermen who still reside here whisper about Nereids—and they don't mean the scantily clad tourists who lunch at the beachside fish tavernas. Today, however, Kamares is a hectic tourist port, with new Athenian villas, and you'll want to move on quickly to the island interior.

HEAVENLY DATES

Sifnos's main church festivals are Chrysopigi in May or June, a movable feast; Prophet Ilias, July 19; Saint Panteleimonas in Cheronisos, July 16; Saint Simeon, August 31; and Taxiarchis in Vathy, September 5.

The bus ride from Kamares southeast up to Apollonia (5 km [3 mi]) provides a sweet initiation into Sifnos's enchanting landscape. You will see two-story dovecotes, delicate chapels hugging the hillside, ruined windmills, and very narrow terraces with golden wheat, glinting olive trees, or low grape vines buttressed by elegant stone walls that prevent them from washing into the ravines below during winter storms. In spring the hillsides are so yellow with Spanish broom they are hard to look at in bright sunlight. The most notable and numerous accents dotting the landscape are the Hellenistic watchtowers—the *pirgis.* Sifnos has remains of more than 40, testament to the ferocity of Venetian, Maltese, and Turkish pirate raids of centuries gone by.

APOLLONIA ΑΠΟΛΛΩΝΙΑ

4 km (2 ½ mi) southeast of Kamares.

Apollonia, capital of Sifnos since 1836, seems at first glance a gentle, disheveled sprawl on the high undulation of the island's saddle. Once you reach the central crossroads, and take in a jaw-dropping vista of the surrounding countryside, you'll find it is actually a whitewashed constellation of six villages and blue-dome churches. The bus stops at the lively main square, the busy central crossroads for all Sifnos (gridlocked in August). The big building in the central Iroon Square (Heroes' Square) houses the **Folklore Museum,** full of traditional weavings, embroideries, and vestments, a Sifnos specialty. Also on view are examples of ancient Siphnian pottery, which was made at several places on the island, always by the sea, so that it could be shipped with ease. ✉*Iroon Sq.* ☎*22840/33730* 🎟*€2* 🕐*July–mid-Sept., Mon.–Sat., 10–1 and 6–9.*

With their mazelike streets closed to vehicles, the best and only way to explore these villages is on foot. From the main square a main street locals call the Steno winds upward to traverse the prettiest sections of the old town. On the right (east) side of the street, through an archway, gleams the **Panayia Ouranophora,** called the Church of the Heaven-Bearing Virgin. The marble carvings around the door give the date 1767, but the church itself is older; the relief overhead depicts St. George and the Dragon. The marble column by the courtyard well is from the 7th-century BC temple to Apollo, Apollonia's namesake. To fast-forward several millennia: most of Sifnos's nightlife is on the Steno—just follow your aching ears. The street, more officially called Stilianou Proukou, is lined with cafés and shops but debouches, in timeless Greek fashion, at a mammoth cathedral, the Agios Spirídonos (restored 1901) .

Then the road crosses into **Ano Petali,** quiet and pristine, tucked between its larger neighbors, and presided over by the Italianate-style Agios Ioánnis church (not far away is the Panayia Ta Gournía, which has impressive murals and icons). The islanders' scrupulous dedication to whitewash makes the villages of Sifnos seem daintier than those of the other Cyclades. The flagstones here are carefully delineated with very thin white lines reapplied weekly (much more time consuming than the thicker lines preferred elsewhere). It is on Sifnos that the Cycladic cubic type of architecture, seen with small variations in so many islands, is found in its greatest perfection. Here a projecting ledge, over every door or window, adds to the interest of the exteriors (a feature also to be seen on Folegandros, where the houses are also very beautiful).

NEED A BREAK?

At the lower end of the Steno, between it and the car road, is the Gerontopoulos Sweetshop and Café (☎ *22840/32220*); its *bourekia,* a kind of sweetmeats, are to die for.

WHERE TO STAY & EAT

$$ ✕ **Odos Oneiron.** "Dream Street" is one of Sifnos's few restaurants that depart from local cuisine. A good starter is tomato croquettes with grilled haloumi cheese and arugula oil. For a main dish, try stuffed pork fillet with Cyprian white cheese, olive paste, tomato sauce, and mint. The special of the day is always top-notch, as is the dessert of yogurt pie. ✉ *On square behind Taxiarch church on Steno* ☎ *22840/23002* ▭ *No credit cards.*

$$$$ Fodor's Choice ★ **Petali Hotel.** On a hilltop offering spectacular views over several villages, the sea, and Antiparos clear in the distance, the open-all-year Petali is a mini-Cycladic village. Although built recently, it blends in beautifully with its ageless surrounds. Inside, the decor is picture-perfect, with wood-beam ceilings, four-posters, tablecloth drapes, antiques, and a very cozy sense of style; many of the room balconies are exquisitely embowered in ivy. The restaurant is serious, there's a vast and relaxing terrace around a pool, and the amenities are worth the price. Transfers are extra. The Petali is not far from the bustling center of Apollonia, but it's far enough for true peace and quiet: it's located on the pedestrian street leading to Artemonas—there is a sign to it

on the car road, halfway up. ✉*Ano Petali, 84003* ☎*22840/33024* 📠*22840/33391* 🌐*www.hotelpetali.gr* *23 rooms* *In-room: refrigerator, Ethernet. In-hotel: restaurant, pool, no elevator, public Internet* ▭*MC, V* 🍽*BP.*

ARTEMONAS ΑΡΤΕΜΩΝΑΣ

3 km (1 mi) northeast of Apollonia.

The flagstone street from Apollonia's Ano Petali district descends slightly to cross a stone bridge over the seasonal Marinou River. Artemonas, named after Apollo's virginal sister, Artemis, is the most beautiful village on Sifnos. The walls of the **church of the Virgin of the Troughs,** on the rock outcropping to the left, were frescoed in the primitive style by a monk 150 years ago. Inside, note the marble tombstones set into the floor.

Beyond lies the small square built to honor Nicholas Chrysogetos, a local teacher who led a contingent in the 1821 revolution who later became Greece's first minister of education. His marble bust reigns over the tiny town hall and impressive town houses. Soon the same street reaches Artemonas's capacious main square, where the bus turns to go back down to Apollonia. The 18th-century church here, with its ghostly white stairway, is dedicated, like the square, to Saints Constantine and Helen. Right next to the church is an excellent taverna, the Manganas, and the comfortable Hotel Artemon, with a garden restaurant. The main stone-paved street of the town is lined with large neoclassic houses, with gardens in front of them, built by wealthy shipowner families of the late 19th century. The quiet coexistence of elegant edifices and small houses, many with the characteristic Siphnian chimney caps of multi-spouted inverted pots, all united by fresh whitewash, gives Artemonas its graceful appearance. Strolling by the mansions, you'll notice on the main street Katerina Theodorou's Sweet Shop, where she makes her traditional almond sweets and nougat by hand; the shop is in a preserved sitting room of old Sifnos, full of curios.

The main street leads to Artemonas's multi-domed chief church, the **Kochi.** In its courtyard, where Artemis's temple once stood, the Siphnian Cultural Society presents readings and concerts in summer. Just past Kochi, turning left down a narrow lane, you reach, on the right after about 30 yards, a little two-story house marked by a plaque as the place where poet John Gryparis (1871–1942), indifferent to the world's praise (but not, gossip the Siphnians, to his bossy wife's), wrote mournful sonnets. In May, perfumed Easter lilies bloom on every porch in this district—lined with traditional houses and elegant neoclassic mansions—and as you stand here it is easy to see where Gryparis got his inspiration.

WHERE TO STAY & EAT

$ ★ ✕**Lenbessis.** Artemonas's best, Lenbessis is part of chef Stamatis Lenbessis's family hotel (happily, it is open all year). In this quiet garden restaurant, the meat, vegetables, and wine come from Dad's organic farm. Quiche with sun-dried tomatoes starts things off properly, rabbit stew with onions and lamb wrapped in phyllo with cheese and herbs make a hearty main course, and where else can you find crème caramel made from cream fresh from the cow? ✉*Near end of Artemonas's car road* ☎*22830/13103* ▭*No credit cards.*

$ ★ ✕ **Liotrivi.** For 50 years, the famed, beloved outpost of Liotrivi has excelled in traditional Siphnian fare. Caper salad and chickpea croquettes are found everywhere on Sifnos; eat them here. Zucchini stuffed with meat and grilled seafood are specialties. It's open year-round. ✉*In carless entrance square to Artemonas* ☎*22840/31246* ▭*No credit cards.*

$$ **Hotel Artemon.** A true home-away-from-home, this is entirely a family outfit (just note all the memorabilia in the lobby), and many visitors—artists, writers, and hikers among them—come back yearly. Inside the modern, motel-like structure, guest rooms are comfortable and quiet; all come with balconies, with the views particularly nice on the second floor. Be sure to compliment owner-manager Voula Lembessis on her lovely flowering plants. ✉*Near end of car road, 84003* ☎*22840/31303* 📠*22840/32385* 🌐*www.hotel-artemon.com* *26 rooms* *In-room: Wi-Fi (some). In-hotel: public Internet* ▭*MC, V.*

SHOPPING

POTTERY With a grand hilltop vista at its feet, **Kalogirou** (✉*On car road to Ayia Anna, follow sign from Artemonas* ☎*22840/33090* 🌐*www.theworkshops.gr*), also called the Workshops, mostly showcases ceramics made by fifth-generation potter Andonis (whose life has included a 30-year stay in New Jersey, where his creations won prizes in art exhibitions); now returned to his home island, he works with his son, while mother and daughter make traditional weavings and patchwork. **Lembesis** (✉*Between Apollonia and Artemonas, closer to Artemonas* ☎*22840/23010*) shows work made in the family's pottery located on the nearby hill of Ayia Anna, which you can also visit. The designs and glazes are in the old Siphnian tradition. If you want to find the most traditional of Sifnos's potteries, head to the beach of Cheronisos at the northern end of the island; the clay is dug up right there.

KASTRO ΚΑΣΤΡΟ

★ *4 km (2 mi) east of Apollonia.*

An acropolis overlooking a little bay, the hilltop, whitewashed Kastro (Castle) was already a thousand years old when Herodotus knew it. The site of ancient Sifnos, it was wrested by the Da Corogna family from Naxos's control in 1307 and it did not fall to the Turks until 1617. Before 1833 it was the island's capital city, with a population of 2,000. All this history has left much of interest behind, most notably some of the Cyclades's most idiosyncratic architecture; you'll find that one street can pass over the roof of one-story buildings below, then join up by bridges to the upper stories of the opposite houses. Many houses bear Venetian coat of arms and have Italian-style balconies. Today, only 30 families remain all year, but cafés and a restaurant now welcome the many visitors who pass through the five town gates, superb remnants of the former Venetian fortified town. The classical sarcophagi in the main street were brought up from the riverbed below, where they had been used to water cows. Kastro's main **church of the Virgin of Mercy** was last restored in 1635, the date on the marble lintel. The **church of the Dormition of the Virgin,** 1593, is elaborately inlaid in Siphnian style—note the marble holy table, a classical altar adorned with Dionysian bulls' heads and swags. Elsewhere, notably on the promontories near the outskirts of town, are some hyper-picturesque churches with great sea views (and sunrises)—the most famous is the **Eftamartyres** (Seven Martyrs). In the middle of the town, in a Venetian-era building, the **Archaeological Museum** displays locally found objects from pre-Christian times. ☎*22840/31022* ✉*Free* ⏲*Tues.–Sat. 9–2, Sun. 10–2.*

Sifnos has some of the Cyclades's most stunningly beautiful monasteries, including Chrysopigi *(⇨below)*. A healthy hike from Kastro lies

Fodor'sChoice ★ magical **Panagia Pouláti,** a whitewashed sculpture, whose blue dome and soaring bell tower are dazzlingly set off by the dramatic cliffs and rocky bay that surround it—have your Nikon handy. The most famous monastery is the **Profitis Ilias,** an abandoned Byzantine extravaganza that sits atop the island's highest mountain, which you can see after a two-hour hike up from the village of Katavati, just south of Apollonia (a monk can tour you around). Needless to say, the panoramic sea view here stops all conversation. The main feast day honoring the Prophet Elijah falls on either July 19, 20, or 21, and is celebrated with a torch-lighted procession.

EXAMBELA AND VRISI ΕΞΑΜΠΕΛΑ & ΒΡΥΣΗΣ

From Apollonia three paved roads lead to three coastal villages. The road south to Platys Yialos passes through the villages of Katavati and Exambela. Exambela is especially pretty and white, with flowers by every stoop. In Turkish times (from 1617 to 1830) Exambela was considered a hot night spot, renowned for its songs. The ruined neoclassic buildings were schools, and at the edge of the village are the ruins of a Hellenistic watchtower. On the Hill of St. Andrew to the southwest lies an ancient acropolis, but not much is left. Objects from 3,000 to 400 BC keep turning up, but little of Sifnos's ancient splendor has survived to the present day. A bit farther along, whitewash steps climb to the **Vrisi (Fountain) Monastery,** cared for by the Lambrinos family: a deep vaulted gateway opens into the courtyard and church, whose arcaded porch employs classical Doric columns from an earlier temple. Inside is a small museum devoted to religious arts. Vrisi's flowing water is considered the best on Sifnos.

CHRYSOPIGI ΧΡΥΣΟΠΗΓΗ

8 km (5 mi) southeast of Apollonia.

Fodor'sChoice ★ Between the famed beach of Platys Yialos and the harbor of Faros lies Chrysopigi, the spectacular site of the **Golden Wellspring Monastery**

(1650), winner of Sifnos's "Most Picturesque" award. Its dramatic Cape Petálos perch—a rocky peninsula with seagirt views—overlooks the long, sandy beach of Apokofto (home to an excellent taverna). The Siphnians think of the monastery, built in 1650, as paradise, and the simple rooms it rents are booked way in advance. The chief icon here, which fishermen discovered gleaming in the waves, saved Sifnos in 1675 from plague and in 1928 from locusts. The gape in the entranceway, through which the sea whistles and hisses, was cut by another miracle. One dawn some local maidens who came to tend the church found seven pirates asleep. When the brigands awakened and pursued them with impure intentions, the maidens prayed to the Virgin. Aristomenes Provelengios, who often wrote in a cell here, described what took place: "Suddenly a great quake shook the cape and cut it from the shore ... the women fell to their knees and glorified the Virgin for her grace."

WHERE TO EAT

$ ✕ **Chrisopigi.** This taverna, owned by George Lembesis, features top Siphnian specialties, such as caper salad and chickpea croquettes, all freshly made, as well as cooked and grilled dishes. ✉ *Apokofto beach* ☎ *22840/71295* ▭ *No credit cards.*

BEACHES

This region of the island is home to its most beautiful beaches, including **Platys Yialos** (Broad beach), the most developed and popular stretch of sand hereabouts, thanks to its hotels and cafés. Once a potters' beach, it still has potteries, where you can buy what you see being made. The most notable is the shop of the brothers **Apotolides** (☎ *22840/71358*), which offers ceramics based on traditional but modernized designs.

VATHY ΒΑΘΥ

★ *8 km (5 mi) southeast of Apollonia.*

Formerly one of the more-isolated and unblemished districts of Sifnos, Vathy is a green isolated valley leading to a beautiful, crescent-shape bay with a beach looking toward Kimolos. Here, the whitewashed **Taxiarhis Monastery** (16th century) looms into view on its stone mole perch over the water, offering a lovely vision of white domes and cubic blocks. The valley road was laid only in 1997; before that, the village here was accessible only by caïque or donkey, and frequented by potters who worked on the beach (a few remain). Inevitably undergoing development—now including the island's fanciest hotel—it remains one of Sifnos's prettiest and quietest spots to swim, or to lunch on the beach at one of the several tavernas.

WHERE TO STAY

$$$$ Fodor'sChoice ★ **Elies Resort.** Since 2003, little ole Sifnos boasts one of the fanciest hotels in the western Cyclades, a retreat now favored by some big-time Athenian politicians and celebs. Elies (it means "olive trees") climbs a terraced hill with the usual Cycladic village sprawl of white-on-white villas around a pool. In this case, sleekness has nearly steamrolled tra-

ditional Siphnian style, so get ready to vibe with white-on-gray color schemes, spare and elegant furniture, and glittering, cubistic bathrooms. The pool, superfluous so near the sea, is large; the restaurant is Iranian-caviar ambitious; the bar is stocked with Cuban cigars; and all guest rooms have terraces and balconies (and suites have private pools). Although a bit isolated from the island center, the hotel does reach out, offering guests speedboat tours, pottery-making lessons, and photo safaris—bravo! After the time-stained, millennia-old charm of Sifnos, the suave luxury of Elies may be exactly what the doctor ordered. Price includes transfer. ✉ *Vathy bay, 84003* ☎ *22840/34000* 🖷 *22840/34070* 🌐 *www.eliesresorts.com* *20 rooms, 12 suites* *In-room: refrigerator, Ethernet. In-hotel: gym, spa, no elevator, public Internet* ▭ *AE, MC, V* ⊙ *Closed Nov.–Mar.* 🍽 *BP.*

SHOPPING

POTTERY **Andonis and Yannis Atsonios** (☎ *22840/71194*) have a shop right by the main bus stop filled with traditional wares (their work atelier is nearby). The island's **Potter's Union** (15 potteries) has an annual exhibit of local wares, July 15 to August 30, at the Monastery of Phyrogia in Vathy. Foreign painters, photographers, jewelers, and ceramists also participate by invitation.

SYROS ΣΥΡΟΣ

The mercantile bustle of modern Ermoupoli—Syros's port, capital, and the archipelago's business hub since the 18th century—often makes people do a double take. Seen from a far distance out at sea, the city looks like a Cycladic village—one, however, raised to the nth dimension, with thousands of houses climbing their way up twin conical hills. The closer you get, the more impressive things get. As you pull up to the harbor, lined with big mansions and towering churches, you see that Hermesopolis—the city was originally named after Hermes, the god of trade—is a 19th-century neoclassic jewel. A palatial marble town hall, a grand city square that looks airlifted from Paris, an opera house modeled after La Scala; and a British-run gambling casino: these are just a few of the flourishes that announce Ermoupoli as the centuries-old administrative hub of the Cyclades. Partly colonized by one of Greece's largest Catholic populations, Syros is home to more than half the residents of the island chain.

Though it seems arid, Homer praised the island in Book XV of The *Odyssey,* and Markos Vamvakaris, the great Syrian rebetis (performer of rembetika music), wrote a song celebrating the beauty of its women of Venetian and Frankish descent, the "Frankosyriani," perhaps the most popular of all *bouzouki* songs. Herman Melville, writing in 1856–57, gave the men equal time: "Lithe fellows tall with gold-shot eyes, Sunning themselves as leopards may."

Near the center of the Cyclades, due east of Kythnos and west of Mykonos, rocky Syros covers an area of 135 square km (52 square mi). Some might say that Ermoupoli is the only real reason for a stopover on Syros—but it is so architecturally rich that it should not be missed. Also, the island's untouristy urbanity and long, exciting history, much of it visible, make it worthwhile.

ERMOUPOLI ΕΡΜΟΥΠΟΛΗ

35 km (21 mi) west of Mykonos, 135 km (83 mi) northwest of Santorini, 154 km (95 mi) southeast of Athens.

Ermoupoli spills like multicolor lava from the twin colonial hills of Ano Syros and Vrodado, topped respectively by churches Roman Catholic (St. George, on the left-hand peak when viewed from the harbor) and Greek Orthodox (Resurrection, on the right). Capital not only of the island but of the entire Cycladic island group, Ermoupoli was the main port of Greece for half a century after its conception in 1822, during the War of Independence. During the struggle refugees fleeing from the Turkish massacres chose the site of the ancient "town of Hermes," god of travelers and merchants, on which to raise their new city, and crowned it with Vrodado's blue-dome Resurrection church. Following the war, Syros became so important it was seriously considered as a site for the fledgling nation's first capital. Starting at that time, waves of rich immigrants from Smyrna, Chios, Hydra, Psara, and Crete made the island into a cultural and commercial center.

The full splendor of Syros's heyday is on view on Miaoúli Square, located two blocks up Venizelou street from the quay. The square's showpiece is the frescoed Municipal Palace, which today houses the capital's administrative offices and courts. Designed by the noted beaux arts European architect Ernst Ziller in 1876, it also houses two museums, one devoted to historic fire engines, the other Syros's noted **Archaeological Museum.** Located on the left side of the town hall, this contains artifacts from the island's rich ancient history. The collection stretches back to the Neolithic era, with important finds taken from the prehistoric acropolis at Kastri to the north. Particularly illustrious are the Early Cycladic objects from Chalandriani (just south of Kastri), which indicate an advanced culture in the 3rd millennium BC. The museum, while not extensive, is one of the oldest in Greece. ✉*Plateia Miaouli* ☎*22860/86900* 🎫*€3* ⏲*Tues.–Sun. 8:30–2.*

Like the Municipal Palace, the palm-ringed **Miaoúli Square**, or Plateia Miaouli, was the creation of Ernst Ziller (who also is credited with Athens's famous Grande Bretagne hotel). Here a band shell with nine sculpted Muses, and a statue of revolutionary war hero Admiral Andreas Miaoulis, ornament a vast expanse of marble pavement. Families patrician and not still stroll back and forth on their evening *voltes* (strolls), displaying their marriageable members, while skateboarding children skid around them.

Across from the Municipal Palace on Miaoúli Square is another testament to Syros's wealth: the **Apollon Theater** (🌐*www.festivaloftheaegean.com*), 1861, a small-scale version of Milan's La Scala. It is, after decades of restoration, again offering operas and other cultural events in July and August; its third floor displays a collection of cultural memorabilia. Although money poured into Syros since the days of Italian rule after 1207, the high-rollers and opera divas really began to arrive in the 19th century, after the Turkish period, when Ermoupoli became the main port between Europe, the Black Sea, and the Levant. When commerce boomed, Greece's first high school (Eleftherios Venizelos, Greece's greatest modern politician, attended) and first shipyard were established on Syros. Around Miaoúli Square are streets lined with two- and three-story mansions with graceful wrought-iron fanlights washed in pastels; here, too, in the streets to the right of Miaoúli Square (facing the palace), you can find a high-quality concentration of Syros's tavernas.

One of the two towering peaks that rise over town, **Ano Syros** was greatly expanded by Venetians in the 13th century, who erected a walled town over the ancient acropolis, immuring themselves against pirates. From the Roman Catholic bishopric of the church of St. George crowning the hill on down, this lofty retreat maintains its 13th-century integrity. Take a taxi up and walk down, with Omiros street a handy thoroughfare through this picturesque quarter, dotted with castle walls and stone alleyways. High atop the hill is the looming Capuchin Monastery (1633), where visitors on official religious business may enjoy a sojourn in the jasmine-scented garden overlooking all Ermoupoli. Not far away is a belvedere—the town's high point—where a bronze bust of Pherekides commemorates that imaginative 6th-century BC Syrian philosopher, Pythagoras's teacher, who reputedly invented the sundial and was the first to write Greek prose. The bishopric, where bishops have presided since the time of Irenaios (AD 343, is downhill from the monastery. Farther down is the Jesuit Monastery, founded in 1747, and the adjacent church of the Virgin of Carmel. As you can see, the hill of Ano Syros remains mostly Catholic, but just across the townscape is the hill of Vrodado, which reminds us that Syros is now two-thirds Greek Orthodox (happily, relations remain cordial). The Catholic-flavored Venetian influence has given the island's culture and architecture a distinctive flavor: having welcomed so many religious refugees to its shores, Syros came under the protection of Louis XIII in 1640, which accounts for the French-flavored influence.

WHERE TO STAY & EAT

$$$ ★ ✕ **Lilis Taverna.** On a clear day you can flee forever to this spot high above the city on the peak of Ano Syros. You can also see forever—or at least to the shores of Mykonos—if you grab a front-row table on the stone terrace. One of Ermoupoli's top food-with-a-view options, these vistas are yours if you climb the big flight of steps past the Hotel Omiros (or opt for a cab). Grilled meats and fish are the house specialties, but the chef knows his stuff and you can't go wrong no matter what you order. Sometimes *rembetika* musicians play late. ✉ *Ano Syros* ☎ *22810/88087* ▭ *No credit cards* ⊗ *No lunch.*

$$ ✕ **Thalami.** Although this spot, ensconced in a neoclassic mansion, is a top choice for fresh seafood, it is the view that makes Thalami special. Perched on a sea cliff, its two terraces offer vistas as delicious as the

fresher-than-fresh shellfish. Opt for the squid stuffed with feta and green pepper or, if you have a chubby wallet, splurge on the fresh fish of the day. Open March to October; in summer, it's best to make dinner reservations. ✉ *Kalemenopoulo 1 (next to neoclassic Nomarch bldg.)* ☎ *22810/85331* ▭ *AE, MC, V* ⏲ *Closed Nov.–Feb.*

$ ★ ✕ **Kouzina.** Set in a wood-trim taverna setting, with a vast courtyard semi-embowered in pink bougainvillea, Kouzina is a showcase for top Cyprus cuisine, thanks to chef-owner Pavlos Grivas. He pays homage to his homeland with stylish twists, including a wicked beef carpaccio marinated in black truffle oil and lemon garnished with arugula and Parmesan. Top main dishes include the *afelia*, dried pork cooked slowly in red wine and coriander, served with bulgur and minted yogurt. For a different change of pace (and another €10) Pavlos will cook you fresh Argentine beefsteaks. Don't miss out on his exceptional homemade bitter-chocolate ice cream with Talisker whiskey, cardamom, and chili. The wine list is international; ask Pavlos's wife Andrea for some recommendations (although the house wine is excellent). Kouzina is located at the far end of restaurant-lined Stephanou street; walk up Venizelou toward Miaoúli Square and take the third left. ✉ *Androu 5* ☎ *22840/34000* 🌐 *www.kouzinasyros.gr* ▭ *AE, MC, V.*

¢ ✕ **To Kastri.** Located in the central market, To Kastri is run by the Women's Union of Syros. A group comprising 28 women, they cook 10 dishes a day—home cooking so good that local housewives secretly buy food for their midday meals here. Open 9–5 (all year), this cafeteria often sells out by early afternoon. Beef stew, stuffed zucchini, stuffed cuttlefish, and beef in lemon sauce are what you would expect—but better. ✉ *Parou 13 (a small side street off Chiou)* ☎ *22810/83140* ▭ *No credit cards.*

$$ **Nisaki.** Convenient and comfortable, this modern three-story building is set amid neoclassic ones and is nestled next to a little park overlooking the sea. The lobby is comfy-traditional, with modular white furniture and green plants galore. Accessed by elevator, guest rooms all have balconies, half of which have town vistas and half unencumbered and exhilarating sea views. Most customers are Greek, which makes it lively (but they smoke). Breakfast is included. ✉ *E. Padadam 1, 84100* ☎ *22810/88200* 🖷 *22810/82000* 🌐 *www.hotelnisaki.gr* *14 rooms* *In-room: no TV, refrigerator. In-hotel: restaurant, public Internet* ▭ *AE, MC, V* *BP.*

I LOVE THE NIGHTLIFE

Siros is known for its *rembetika* music—the noted songster Markos Vamvakaris was a native. The best places to hear traditional songs are the cafés way up on the Ano Syros hill (reservations needed) but you'll also find fine cafés down by the harbor, including To Rebetadio, a noted restaurant on Eptanisou street (one block up from the waterfront), where, late at night, the music begins to wail. Other nighttime options: the open-air Pallas Cinema (east of Miaoúli Square), concerts at Apollon Theater, or the elegant British-run casino on the quay.

$ ★ **Hotel Omiros.** Perched on a steep hill just above Miaoúli Square and alluringly set in a yellow-stucco neoclassic mansion, Omiros is a friendly place to experience both comfort and old Syros. The lobby's two handsome sitting rooms are much used; the one used in winter looks like a whitewashed farmhouse living room, complete with sculpted Cycladic fireplace and rough stonework walls. Take the spiral staircase up to the guest rooms, many adorned with furniture and marble decorations from the 19th century (some have balconies). Omiros, or Homer, is up the street from the Metamorphosis church. A bar and cafeteria are adjacent; breakfast is extra. ✉ *43 Omirou Metamorfosi, 84100* ☎ *22810/84910* 📠 *22810/89266* 🌐 *www.greekhotel.com/cyclades/syros* *11 rooms, 2 suites* *In-hotel: no elevator, parking* 💳 *AE, MC, V.*

MACHO GREEK FLAVORING

When Athenians want *real* Greek food, they often head to Siros, which has long been known for its culinary brio. Not only was Greece's first cookbook published here in 1828, famed foodie Elizabeth David earned her toques in Mediterranean cooking here. Flavors are strong and accented with cheese, tomato, and fennel. Check out the lemon-and-anise-flavored *loukanika* sausages, the cured-pork louza tenderloin soaked in wine and cloves, the *marathopita*, lemon-herb and fennel bread, and the *kopanisti*, the island's tangy cheese.

BEACHES

Athough its beaches don't equal those of Andros, Mykonos, Paros, and Naxos, Syros has plenty of pleasant stretches of sand. Almost all of these are being developed, and villas, some truly hideous, are going up by the dozen. **Megas Yialos, Poseidon** (or **Dellagrazia**), **Finikas,** and **Galisas** all offer beachfront accommodations and tavernas. No one can deny that eating some fresh squid at a seaside taverna, watching the ducks bob, and having a swim are a pleasant respite from the big-city excitement of Ermoupoli.

CYCLADES ESSENTIALS

TRANSPORTATION

BY AIR

Schedules change seasonally and are often revised; reservations are always a good idea. There are no airports on Tinos, Sifnos, or Folegandros.

CARRIERS Olympic Airways has six flights daily to Mykonos (10 daily during peak tourist season). There are also summer flights between Mykonos and Heraklion (on Crete), and between Mykonos and Rhodes. The Olympic Airways offices in Mykonos are at the port and at the airport. Olympic Airways has two flights daily between Athens and Naxos airport. Olympic also offers five daily flights to the Paros Airport from Athens (up to seven a day in high season) and six daily flights to Santorini Airport from Athens in peak season. Syros has two flights daily. In summer there are flights to Mykonos and Salonica about three times per week.

Aegean Airlines has five daily flights to Mykonos and four to Santorini in summer, but their schedules are often subject to change. Some European countries now have charter flights to Mykonos.

Contacts **Aegean Airlines** (☎ *210/626–1000* 🌐 *www.aegeanair.com*). **Olympic Airways** (✉ *Port, Mykonos town* ☎ *22890/22490 or 22890/22495* 🌐 *www.olympic-air.com* ✉ *Ayia Athanassiou, Santorini, Fira* ☎ *22860/22493 or 22860/22793*).

AIRPORTS Information **Mykonos Airport** (✉ *4 km [2½ mi] southeast of Mykonos town* ☎ *22890/22327*). **Naxos Airport** (✉ *1 km [½ mi] south of Naxos town* ☎ *22850/23969*). **Paros Airport** (✉ *Near Alyki village, 9 km [5½ mi] south of Paros town* ☎ *22840/91257*). **Santorini Airport** (✉ *On east coast, 8 km [5 mi] from Fira, Monolithos* ☎ *22860/31525*). **Syros Airport** (✉ *5 km [3 mi] south of Ermoupoli* ☎ *22810/82634*).

BY BIKE & QUADS

All the major islands have car- and bike-rental agencies at the ports and in the business districts. Motorbikes and scooters start at about €10 a day, including third-party liability coverage. Don't wear shorts or sandals, insist on the helmet (which the law requires), and get a phone number, in case of breakdown. Quads feel safer, but overturn easily.

BY BOAT & FERRY

Most visitors use the island's extensive ferry network, which is constantly being upgraded. Ferries sail from Piraeus (Port Authority) and from Rafina, 35 km (22 mi) northeast of Athens (Port Authority). Leaving from Rafina cuts traveling time by an hour; buses leave for the one-hour trip from Rafina to Athens every 20 minutes 6 AM–10 PM. Traveling time from Piraeus varies with the speed (and price) of the boat.

Economy-class boat tickets cost roughly one-third the airfare, and passengers are restricted to seats in the deck areas and often-crowded indoor seating areas. High-speed boats are more expensive (and there are no scenic outdoor decks). A first-class ticket, which sometimes buys a private cabin and better lounge, costs about half an airplane ticket. For information on interisland connections, contact local travel agents. High season is June through September; boats are less frequent in the off-season. All schedules must be checked soon before departure, as they change with the season, for major holidays, for weather, and for reasons not ascertainable. Many Web sites give official long-range schedules: *holidaytravel.forth-crs.gr/english/npgres.exe?PM=BO* and *www.openseas.gr/OPENSEAS/index_en.vm* are two good examples, as they try to update every five days. Port authorities, who have expertise, generally send you to a travel agent as the best bet for booking the right kind of boat and ticket for you.

On all islands, caïques leave from the main port for popular beaches and interisland trips. For popular routes, captains have posted signs showing their destinations and departure times.

Contacts **Piraeus Port Authority** (*210/451–1311 or 210/415–1321*). **Rafina Port Authority** (*22940/22300*).

Contact **Andros Port Authority** (*22820/22250*).

FOLEGANDROS Two boats a day (not all ferries, as some might be catamarans or steamers) leave from Piraeus. Boats from here also call at Santorini, Paros, Naxos, Ios, and Syros.

Contact **Folegandros Port Authority** (*22860/41530*).

MYKONOS In summer, there are two to three ferries daily to Mykonos from Piraeus and Rafina. There are daily departures to Paros, Syros, Tinos, Naxos, Santorini, and Andros. Destinations are widening monthly. Check which dock they leave from, as there are both new and old docks. For complete information, you must check here with several agencies.

Contact **Mykonos Port Authority** (*Harbor, above National Bank 22940/22218*).

NAXOS In summer, ferries leave Piraeus for Naxos at least three times a day. (The trip takes about four to seven hours.) Boats go daily from Naxos to Mykonos, Ios, Paros, Syros, Tinos, and Santorini; check for other places served.

Contact **Naxos Port Authority** (*22850/22300*).

PAROS About three ferries leave Piraeus for Paros every day in summer. Paros has daily ferry service to Santorini, Mykonos, Tinos, Andros, Syros, and Naxos; there are also weekly boats to Ikaria, Samos, Folegandros, and other islands. Antiparos excursion boats leave from Parikia, car ferries leave from Pounta. Cruise boats leave daily from Paros town and Naousa for excursions to Delos and Mykonos.

Contact **Paros Port Authority** (*22840/21240*).

SANTORINI Santorini is served at least thrice daily from Piraeus; from Santorini, ferries make frequent connections to the other islands—daily to Paros, Naxos, Ios, Anaphi, and Crete. All ferries dock at Athinios port, where taxis and buses meet the boats. Travelers bound for Ia and other towns change at Fira. The port below Fira is used only by cruise ships and small craft. Passengers disembarking here face a half-hour hike, or they can take the cable car (just use the traditional transport donkeys for photo ops).

Contact **Santorini Port Authority** (☎ *22860/22239*).

SIFNOS There are four to five boats daily from Piraeus, mostly ferries and the occasional steamer or catamaran. Sifnos has daily connections with Seriphos and Mylos. There are also boats to Syros and Paros.

Contact **Sifnos Port Authority** (☎ *22840/33617*).

SYROS There are four or five boats, most of them ferries, daily from Piraeus. There are daily connections with Andros, Tinos, and Mykonos, and regular connections with Paros, Naxos, Sifnos, Santorini, and other islands.

Contact **Syros Port Authority** (☎ *22810/82690*).

TINOS Tinos is served in summer by four boats a day from Rafina and Piraeus. There are daily connections with Andros, Syros, Paros, Naxos, and Mykonos and regular boats to Santorini, and sometimes other islands. An excursion boat goes daily to nearby Delos, returning in the afternoon. Only Sea Jets and excursion boats stop at the old dock. For information, you must check with several agencies.

Contact **Tinos Port Authority** (☎ *22830/22348*).

BY BUS

FOLEGANDROS Buses go from the little port to Chora every hour or so throughout the day; buses meet the boats. Buses go almost as often to the southern beaches and to Ano Meria.

MYKONOS In Mykonos town the Ayios Loukas station in the Fabrica quarter at the south end of town has buses to Ornos, Ayios Ioánnis, Platys Yialos, Psarou, Paradise beach, the airport, and Kalamopodi. Another station near the Archaeological Museum is for Ayios Stefanos, Tourlos, Ano Mera, Elia, Kalafatis, and Kalo Livadi. Schedules are posted.

NAXOS On Naxos, the bus system is reliable and fairly extensive. Daily buses go from Chora (near the boat dock) to Engares, Melanes, Sangri, Filoti, Apeiranthos, Koronida, and Apollonas. In summer there is added daily service to the beaches, including Ayia Anna, Pyrgaki, Ayiassos, Pachy Ammos, and Abram. All the many villages have bus service. Schedules are posted.

PAROS From the Paros town bus station, just west of the dock, there is service every hour to Naousa and less-frequent service to Alyki, Pounta, and the beaches at Piso Livadi, Chrysi Akti, and Drios. Schedules are posted.

SANTORINI On Santorini buses leave from the main station in central Fira (Deorgala) for Perissa and Kamari beaches, Ia, Pyrgos, and other villages. Schedules are posted.

SIFNOS Buses meet the boats in Kamares and go to Apollonia, the capital. From Apollonia there are hourly connections to Artemonas, Kastro, and Platys Yialos, and less frequently to Vathy. Schedules are posted.

SYROS From the seaside station between the boat dock and the main street, buses run at least every hour from Ermoupoli to all the other villages. Schedules are posted.

TINOS On Tinos, buses run several times daily from the quay of Chora to nearly all the many villages in Tinos, and in summer buses are added for beaches.

Information **Bus Information** (*☎ 22820/22316 in Andros, 22860/41425 in Folegandros, 22890/23360 in Mykonos, 22850/22440 in Naxos, 22840/21133 in Paros, 22890/25404 in Santorini, 22840/31210 in Sifnos, 22810/82575 in Syros, 22830/22440 in Tinos*).

BY CAR

To take cars on ferries you must make reservations. Though there is bus service on the large and mountainous islands of Andros and Naxos, it is much more convenient to travel by car.

Although islanders tend to acknowledge rules, many roads on the islands are poorly maintained, and tourists sometimes lapse into vacation inattentiveness. Drive with caution, especially at night, when you may well be sharing the roads with motorists returning from an evening of drinking.

All the major islands have car- and bike-rental agencies at the ports and in the business districts. Car rentals cost about €45 per day, with unlimited mileage and third-party liability insurance. Full insurance costs about €6 a day more. Four-wheeled semi-bikes (quads), that look—but are not—safer than bikes, are also available everywhere. Choose a dealer that offers 24-hour service and a change of vehicle in case of a breakdown. Most will take you from and to your plane or boat. Beware: all too many travelers end up in Athenian hospitals owing to poor roads, slipshod maintenance, careless drivers, and excessive partying.

FOLEGANDROS There is not much reason to rent a vehicle in tiny Folegandros; buses will do. The few agencies have offices in the port and in the capital of Apollonia.

Local Agency **Diaplous Travel** (*✉ ☎ 22860/41158 📠 22860/41159 🌐 www.diaploustravel.gr*).

MYKONOS No cars are permitted in town. Many car rentals line the street above the bus terminal, and in the Maouna area near the windmills. Beware of sharp dealing. For friendly, trustworthy service go to Apollon Rent a Car, run by the Andronikos family. They'll meet you at the boat with a car, or bring one to your hotel; they also have offices at Mykonos Airport and at Ornos. Their in-town parking is a boon.

Local Agency **Apollon Rent a Car** (✉ *Maouna, Mykonos* ☎ *22890/24136* 🖷 *22890/23447* 🌐 *www.apolloncars.com*).

NAXOS Car-rental outfits are concentrated in the Chora new town: try Naxos Vision. Or let Despina Kitini, of the Tourist Information Centre *(⇨ Tour Options)*, make arrangements for you.

Local Agency **Naxos Vision** (✉ *Chora, near post office* ☎ *22850/26200* 🖷 *22850/26201* 🌐 *www.naxosvision.com*).

PAROS It is a good idea to rent a vehicle here, because the island is large; there are many beaches to choose from, and taxis are in demand. There are many reputable agencies near the port. Nick Boyatzis's Acropolis is reliable and friendly, and will meet boats and planes.

Major Agency **Sixt** (✉ *Car-rental desk in Polos Travel, by OTE office, Paros town* ☎ *22840/21309* 🌐 *www.polostours.gr/english/rentacar* ✉ *Naousa* ☎ *22840/51544*).

Local Agency **Acropolis Rent a Car** (✉ *On waterfront, 2 blocks east of the port, Parikia* ☎ *22840/21830* 🖷 *22840/24344*).

SANTORINI Europcar has offices in Fira and at Santorini Airport. Ia's Drossos delivers anywhere.

Major Agency **Europcar** (☎ *22860/24610 in Fira, 22860/33290 airport* 🌐 *www.europcar.com.gr*).

Local Agency **Drossos** (☎ *22860/71492, 22860/71668 at port* 🌐 *www.drossos.gr*).

SIFNOS Buses go everywhere, but cars will definitely come in handy if you want to stop at the many little roadside chapels.

Local Agency **Aegean Thesaurus Travel and Tourism** (✉ *Apollonia* ☎ *22840/33151* 🖷 *22840/32190* 🌐 *www.thesaurus.gr*); there is also a branch office in Kamares port ☎ 22840/33527.

SYROS The main sights in Syros are in Ermoupoli, and buses go frequently everywhere else; a car is probably superfluous.

Local Agency **Gaviotis Travel** (✉ *Main quay, Ermoupoli* ☎ *22810/86644* 🖷 *22810/88755* 🌐 *www.syros.com.gr/companies/rentacar/gaviotis/gaviotis_en.htm*).

TINOS Vidalis Rent-a-Car and Dimitris Rental, almost next door to each other, are reliable.

Local Agencies **Dimitris Rental** (✉ *Alavanou, Tinos town* ☎ *22830/23585* 🖷 *22830/22744* 🌐 *www.tinosrentacar.com/index.html*). **Vidalis Rent-a-Car** (✉ *Alavanou 16, Tinos town* ☎ *22830/24300* 🖷 *22830/25995* 🌐 *www.vidalisrentacar.gr*).

BY TAXI

Taxis are privately owned. Taxis on Folegandros meet boats and a stand is at the town entrance. Meters are not used on Mykonos; instead, standard fares for each destination are posted on a notice bulletin board. There is a taxi stand on Naxos near the harbor, and in Paros, there is one across from the windmill on the harbor. Note that in high season taxis are often busy. The main taxi station on Santorini is near Fira's central square (25th of March street). Taxis on Sifnos meet boats, and there is a stand in the main square of Apollonia. On Syros they wait on the quay and on Miaoúli Square. In Tinos, taxis wait near the central boat dock, on the quay.

Contacts **Taxis** (☎ *22820/22171 in Andros, 22890/22400 or 22860/41048 in Folegandros, 22810/31272 in Kythnos, 22890/23700 in Mykonos, 22850/22444 in Naxos, 22840/21500 in Paros, 22860/22555 in Santorini, 22840/31656 or 22840/33570 for 2 of Sifnos's 10 taxis, 22810/86222 in Syros, 22830/22470 in Tinos*).

EMERGENCIES

FOLEGANDROS Contacts **Health Center** (☎ *22860/41222*). **Police** (☎ *22860/41249*).

MYKONOS The hospital in Mykonos has 24-hour emergency service with pathologists, surgeons, pediatricians, dentists, and X-ray technicians.

Contacts **First Aid** (✉ *Ano Mera* ☎ *22890/71395*). **Hospital** (✉ *Mykonos town* ☎ *22890/23998 or 22890/23994*). **Police** (☎ *2289/22235*).

NAXOS The Health Center outside Chora is open 24 hours a day.

Contacts **Health Center** (☎ *22850/23333 or 2285/23676*). **Medical Center of Naxos** (✉ *Quay, Chora* ☎ *22850/23234* 🖷 *22850/23576*). **Police** (☎ *22850/22100 in Chora, 22850/31244 in Filoti*).

PAROS Contacts **Medical Center** (☎ *22840/22500 in Paros town, 22840/51216 in Naousa, 22840/61219 in Antiparos*). **Police** (☎ *22840/23333 in Paros town, 22840/51202 in Naousa*).

SANTORINI Contacts **Medical assistance** (☎ *22860/22237 in Fira, 22860/71227 in Ia*). **Police** (☎ *22860/22649 in Fira*).

SIFNOS Contacts **Medical assistance** (☎ *22840/31315 in Apollonia*). **Police** (☎ *22840/31210 in Fira*).

SYROS Syros has the islands' most fully equipped hospital.

Contacts **Hospital** (✉ *Near Iroon Sq., Ermoupoli* ☎ *22810/86666*). **Police** (☎ *22810/82610 on Miaoúli Sq.*).

TINOS Contacts **Medical assistance** (✉ *East end of town, Chora* ☎ *22830/22210* ✉ *Isternia* ☎ *22830/31206*). **Police** (☎ *22830/22255 in Chora, 22830/31371 in Pirgos*).

TOUR OPTIONS

Contact **Colours Travel** (✉ *Main square, Batsi* ☎ *22820/41252* 🖷 *22820/41608* 🌐 *www.bookandros.com*).

FOLEGANDROS Flavio Facciolo's Sottovento arranges boat trips and general information graciously.

Contact **Maraki Travel and Tours** (✉ *Chora* ☎ *22860/41273* ✉ *maraki@syr.forth.gr*). **Sottovento** (✉ *Main square, Chora* ☎ *22860/41444* 🖷 *22820/41608* 🌐 *www.sottovento.eu*).

MYKONOS Windmills Travel takes a group every morning for a day tour of Delos (€35). The company also has half-day guided tours of the Mykonos beach towns, with a stop in Ano Mera for the Panayia Tourliani Monastery (€20). Windmills also provides excursions to nearby Tinos (€40–€50); arranges private tours of Delos and Mykonos and off-road jeep trips (€50); charters yachts; and, in fact, handles all tourist services. John van Lerberghe's office, the Mykonos Accommodations Center, is small, but he can tailor your trip from soup to nuts.

Contacts **The Mykonos Accommodation Center** (✉ *In picturesque old building, up steep staircase Enoplon Dynameon 10, Mykonos town* ☎ *22890/23160* 🖷 *22890/24137* 🌐 *mykonos-accommodation.com*). **Windmills Travel** (✉ *Fabrica* ☎ *22890/26555 or 22890/23877* 🖷 *22890/22066* 🌐 *www.windmillstravel.com*).

NAXOS The Tourist Information Centre, run by Despina Kitini of the Chateau Zevgoli, offers round-the-island tours (€20). Despina can usually tell exactly what you want after a short discussion and then swiftly arrange it. Zas Travel runs two good one-day tours of the island sights with different itineraries, each costing about €20, and one-day trips to Delos (about €40) and Mykonos (about €35).

Contacts **Tourist Information Centre** (✉ *Waterfront, Chora* ☎ *22850/22993* 🖷 *22850/25200* ✉ *info@naxostownhotels.com*). **Zas Travel** (✉ *Chora* ☎ *22850/23330 or 22850/23331* 🖷 *22850/23419* ✉ *Ayios Prokopios* ☎ *22850/24780* ✉ *zas-travel@nax.forthnet.gr*).

PAROS Trips by land and sea, such as a tour around Antiparos, are arranged by Kostas Akalestos's Paroikia Tours. Erkyna Travel runs many excursions by boat, bus, and foot. For yacht and other VIP services, check out Nikos Santorineos's office.

Contacts **Erkyna Travel** (✉ *On main square, Naousa* ☎ *22840/22654, 22840/22655, or 22840/53180* 🌐 *www.erkynatravel.com/islands/paros.htm*). **Paroikia Tours** (✉ *Market street, Paros town* ☎ *22840/22470 or 22840/22471* 🖷 *22840/22450* ✉ *parikiatours@parosweb.com*). **Santorineos Travel Services** (✉ *Quay, Paros town* ☎ *22840/24245* 🖷 *22840/23922* ✉ *nikos@par.forthnet.gr*).

SANTORINI Pelican Travel runs coach tours, wine tastings, and visits to Ia; it also has daily boat trips to the volcano and Thirassia (half day €12, full day €25) and arranges private tours. Nomikos Travel has tours to the same sights and to the island's wineries and the Monastery of Profitis Ilias. This is the place to sign up for a caldera submarine trip (€60).

Contacts **Nomikos Travel** (✉ *Fira* ☎ *22860/23660* 🖷 *22860/23666* 🌐 *www.nomikosvillas.gr*). **Pelican Travel** (✉ *Fira* ☎ *22860/22220* 🖷 *22860/22570* ✉ *info@pelican.gr* 🌐 *www.pelican.gr*).

SIFNOS Aegean Thesaurus Travel handles private tours, walking tours (€15), cooking classes (€32), and much more.

Contact **Aegean Thesaurus Travel** (✉ *Apollonia* ☎ *22840/33151* 🖷 *22840/32190* ✉ *aegean@thesaurus.gr* 🌐 *www.thesaurus.gr*).

SYROS Konstantinos Gaviotis has a number of tours and excursions.

Contact **Gaviotis Travel** (*Apollonia 22810/86644 22810-88755 gaviotistravel@syr.forthnet.gr www.syros.com.gr/companies/rentacar/gaviotis/gaviotis_en.htm*).

TINOS Sharon Turner at Windmills Travel runs daily guided bus tours of the island for €15, specialty tours by jeep, and unguided Delos–Mykonos trips (€25).

Contact **Windmills Travel** (*Above outer dock, behind playground, Chora 22830/23398 sharon@otenet.gr www.windmillstravel.com*).

VISITOR INFORMATION

Contacts **Colours Travel** (*Batsi main square 22820/41252 22820/41608 www.bookandros.com*). **Police Station** (*Across from ferry dock, Gavrio 22820/71220*).

FOLEGANDROS Flavio Facciolo's Sottovento handles tickets and all other arrangements.

Contact **Sottovento** (*Main square, Chora 22860/41444 22820/41608 www.sottovento.eu*).

MYKONOS Very personal service can be found at John van Lerberghe's Mykonos Accommodations Center, and all services at Windmills Travel.

Contacts **Mykonos Accommodation Center** (*In picturesque old building, up steep staircase Enoplon Dynameon 10, Mykonos town 22890/23160 22890/24137 mykonos-accommodation.com*). **Tourist police** (*Mykonos town harbor, near departure point for Delos 22890/22716*). **Windmills Travel** (*Fabrica 22890/26555 or 22890/23877 22890/22066 www.windmillstravel.com*).

NAXOS Despina Kitini's Tourist Information Centre has free booking service, bus and ferry schedules, international dialing, luggage storage, laundry service, and foreign exchange at bank rates. You can also book airline tickets and rent Kastro houses.

Contact **Tourist Information Centre** (*Waterfront, Chora 22850/24525, 22285/24358, or 22850/22993 222850/25200 info@naxostownhotels.com*).

PAROS For efficient and friendly service—tickets, villa rentals for families, apartments, and quality hotel reservations—try Kostas Akalestos's Paroikia Tours. Kostas, efficient and full of the Greek spirit, has many repeat customers. Polos Tours is big, inclusive, and efficient and will deliver tickets to your Athens hotel. Nikos and Clara Santorineos are very helpful.

Contacts **Paroikia Tours** (*Market street, Paros town 22840/22470 or 22840/22471 22840/22450*). **Polos Tours** (*Next to dockside OTE office, Paros town 22840/22333 222840/21983*). **Santorineos Travel Services** (*Quay, Paros town 22840/24245 22840/23922 nikos@par.forthnet.gr*).

SANTORINI Nomikos Travel, which has offices in Fira and Perissa, can handle most needs.

Contact **Nomikos Travel** (*22860/23660 22860/23666 www.nomikosvillas.gr*).

SIFNOS Aegean Thesaurus Travel is much the best travel office in Sifnos.

Contact **Aegean Thesaurus Travel** (☒ *Apollonia* ☎ *22840/33151* 📠 *22840/32190* ✉ *aegean@thesaurus.gr* 🌐 *www.thesaurus.gr*).

SYROS Konstantinos Gaviotis gives good service for most travel needs.

Contact **Gaviotis Travel** (☒ *Apollonia* ☎ *22810/86644* 📠 *22810/88755* ✉ *gaviotistravel@syr.forthnet.gr* 🌐 *www.syros.com.gr/companies/rentacar/gaviotis/gaviotis_en.htm*).

TINOS For all tourist services (schedules, room bookings, tours, happenings), see friendly Sharon Turner, manager of Windmills Travel; she's a gold mine of information—there's nothing she doesn't know about her adopted island.

Contact **Windmills Travel** (☒ *Above outer dock, behind playground, Chora* ☎📠 *22830/23398* ✉ *sharon@otenet.gr* 🌐 *www.windmillstravel.com*).

Crete

Matala

WORD OF MOUTH

"Under most circumstances, I would consider it a no-brainer to stay in Hania rather than Heraklion. But if all you want to do is visit the [Archaeological] Museum and [the Palace of] Knossos, you should definitely stay in Heraklion . . . you will want to allow yourself a few hours at the museum in Heraklion. It contains all the best artifacts, wall frescoes, etc. that were removed from Knossos for better preservation and safety, including quite a few pieces of world renown."

—Marilyn

www.fodors.com/forums

WELCOME TO CRETE

The fabled ruins of the Palace of Knossos

TOP REASONS TO GO

★ **Minoan Magnificence:** At the Palace of Knossos, get up-close to the mysteries—and the throne room's dazzling murals—of the 3,500-year-old civilization of the Minoans.

★ **Getting Your Sea Major:** From palm-backed Vai to remote Elafonisi, some of the finest beaches in Greece are lapped by Crete's turquoise waters.

★ **Crete's Venice:** Although it has its bright city lights, Rethymnon is most noted for its time-burnished Venetian quarter, threaded with narrow lanes leading to palazzos, fountains, and shady squares.

★ **Walk on the Wild Side:** With its snowcapped peaks and deep gorges, craggy Crete offers lots of escapes for those who want to get away from it all.

★ **Suite Temptation:** New palatial resorts let you live like royalty in a Venetian palace or—at the Elounda Mare—sun-worship the day away in your own private pool.

1 Eastern Crete. Knossos, the most spectacular of the Minoan palaces and Crete's most popular attraction, is here in the east. Just as this sprawling complex was the hub of island civilization 3,500 years ago, nearby Heraklion is Crete's bustling modern capital. Farther east along the coast is the Elounda peninsula, the island's epicenter of luxury, where some of the world's most-sumptuous resort getaways are tucked along a stunning shoreline. The east isn't all hustle, bustle, and glitz, though—the beach at Vai is just one example of the natural beauty that abounds here in the east, and in mountain villages like Kritsa, old traditions continue to thrive.

Traditional red-roofed Cretan church

Life's a beach on Crete

GETTING ORIENTED

Crete is long and slender, approximately 257 km (159 mi) long and only 60 km (37 mi) at its widest. The most development is present on the north shore; for the most part, the southern coast remains blessedly unspoiled. The island's three major cities, Heraklion, Rethymnon, and Hania, are in the north, and are connected by the island's major highway, an east–west route that traverses most of the north coast. All three cities are served by ferry from Piraeus, and Heraklion and Hania have international airports. By car or bus, it's easy to reach other parts of the island from these gateways.

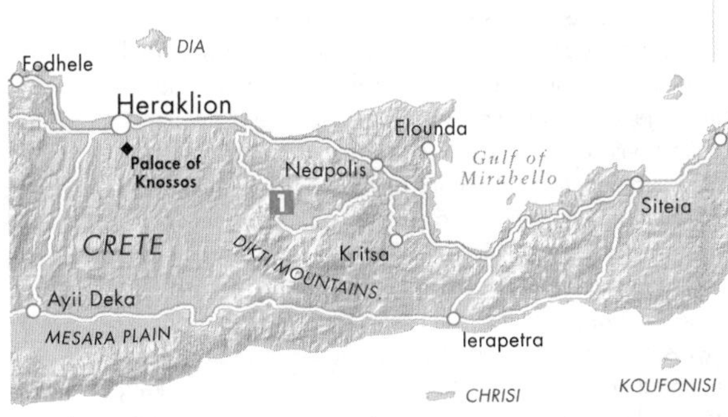

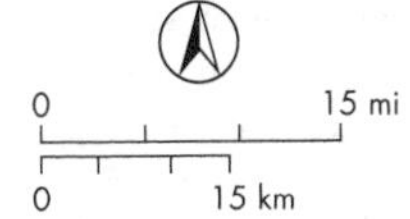

2 Western Crete. The scenery gets more rugged as you head west, where the White mountains pierce the blue sky with snowcapped peaks then plunge into the Libyan Sea along dramatic, rocky shorelines. Mountain scenery and remote seacoast villages—some, like Loutro, accessible only on foot or by boat—attract many visitors to the west. Others come to enjoy the urban pleasures of Rethymnon and Hania, gracious cities that owe their harbors, architectural jewels, and exotic charms to Venetian and Turkish occupiers.

Tread carefully through the Samaria Gorge

CRETE PLANNER

The Serendipitous Shopper

You still occasionally come across the heavy scarlet-embroidered blankets and bedspreads that formed the basis of a traditional dowry chest.

All the villages on the Lasithi plateau have shops selling embroidered linens, made in front of the stove during the cold months.

All over the island, local craftspeople produce attractive copies of Minoan jewelry in gold and silver, as well as some with original modern designs.

A Cretan knife, whether plain steel or with a decorated blade and handle, makes a handy kitchen or camping implement (remember to pack it in your checked luggage when you fly home).

Boot makers in Heraklion and Hania can make you a pair of heavy Cretan leather knee boots to order.

In the village of Thrapsano, potters make terra-cotta vases, candlesticks, and other objects, including pithoi, tall earthenware jars used by the Minoans for storing wine and oil that are popular as flowerpots.

Making the Most of Your Time

Enticing as Crete's beaches are, there is much more to the island than sand and surf. Archaeological sites in Crete open at 8 or 8:30 in summer, so get an early start to wander through the ruins before the sun is blazing. You'll also want to visit some of the folklife museums that pay homage to the island's traditional past. One of the finest collections is in Vori, southwest of Heraklion; there are also excellent folk collections at the Historical and Folk Art Museum in Rethymnon and the Historical Museum of Crete in Heraklion. An evening should begin with a stroll around the shady squares that grace every Cretan town and village, or along a waterfront promenade—those in Hania, Ayios Nikolaos, and Siteia are especially picturesque and jammed with locals. Most evenings are spent over a long meal, almost always eaten outdoors in the warm weather. For entertainment, seek out a *kentron* (a taverna that hosts traditional Cretan music and dancing). The star performer is the *lyra* player, who can extract a surprisingly subtle sound from the small pear-shape instrument, held upright on the thigh and played with a bow. Ask at your hotel where lyra players are performing.

Dining & Lodging Prices in Euros

	¢	$	$$	$$$	$$$$
Restaurants	under €8	€8–€11	€11–€15	€15–€20	over €20
Hotels	under €60	€60–€90	€90–€120	€120–€160	over €160

Note that luxury resort prices on Crete are more comparable to the Athens price chart. Restaurant prices are for one main course at dinner, or for two mezedes (small dishes). Hotel prices are for a standard double room in high season, including taxes. Hotels operate on the European Plan (EP, with no meal provided) unless we note that they use the Continental Plan (CP, with Continental breakfast); Breakfast Plan (BP, with a full breakfast); Modified American Plan (MAP, with breakfast and dinner); or the Full American Plan (FAP, with all meals). Inquire when booking if meal plans (which can entail higher rates) are mandatory. Guest rooms have air-conditioning, room phones, and TVs unless otherwise noted.

12

Dining à la Crete

Cretans tend to take their meals seriously, and like to sit down in a taverna to a full meal. Family-run tavernas take pride in serving Cretan cooking, and a number of the better restaurants in cities now also stress Cretan produce (the fruit is famous) and traditional dishes. One way to dine casually is to sample the mezedes (small plates) served at some bars and tavernas. These often include such Cretan specialties as tyropita (cheese-filled pastry), and a selection of cheeses: Cretan graviera, a hard, smooth cheese, is a blend of pasteurized sheep's and goat's milk that resembles Emmentaler in flavor and texture—not too sharp, but with a strong, distinctive flavor—and Mizythra (a creamy white cheese).

As main courses, Cretans enjoy grilled meat, generally lamb and pork, but there is also plenty of fresh fish. Cretan olive oil is famous throughout Greece; it's heavier and richer than other varieties. The island's wines are special: look for Boutari Kritikos, a crisp white; and Minos Palace, a smooth red. Make sure you try the tsikouthia (also known as raki), the Cretan firewater made from fermented grape skins, which is drunk at any hour, often accompanied by a dish of raisins or walnuts drenched in honey. Many restaurants offer raki free of charge at the end of a meal. Lunch is generally served from 1 to 3 or so. Dinner is an event here, as it is elsewhere in Greece, and is usually served late; in fact, when non-Greeks are finishing up around 10:30 or so, locals usually begin arriving.

Where to Stay

Some of Greece's finest resorts line the shores of Elounda peninsula, offering sumptuous surroundings and exquisite service. Although the atmosphere at these resorts is more international than Greek, you'll find authentic surroundings in the Venetian palaces and old mansions that are being sensitively restored as small hotels, especially in Hania and Rethymnon. For the most authentic experience on Crete, opt for simple, whitewashed, tile-floor rooms with rustic pine furniture in the ubiquitous "room to rent" establishments in mountain and seaside villages. Another common term is "studio," which implies the presence of a kitchen or basic cooking facilities. Standards of cleanliness are high in Crete, and service is almost always friendly.

When to Go

The best times for visiting Crete are April and May, when every outcrop of rock is ablaze with brilliant wildflowers, or September and October, when the sea is still warm and the light golden but piercingly clear.

A spring visit comes with the advantage of long days.

In July and August, the main Minoan sights and towns on the north coast come close to overflowing with tourists.

Take care, special care to avoid such places as Mallia and Limin Hersonissos, hideously developed towns where bars and pizzerias fill up with heavy-drinking northern Europeans on summertime package tours.

Even in the height of summer, though, you can enjoy many parts of the west and the southern coast without feeling too oppressed by crowds.

Crete can also be a pleasure in winter, when you can visit the museums and archaeological sites and enjoy the island's delightful towns and cities without the crush of crowds.

Remember, though, that rainfall can be heavy in January and February.

Remember that some hotels and restaurants close from November through mid-April.

Updated by Stephen Brewer

MOUNTAINS, SPLIT WITH DEEP GORGES and honeycombed with caves, rise in sheer walls from the sea. Snowcapped peaks loom behind sandy shoreline, vineyards, and olive groves. Miles of beaches, some with a wealth of amenities and others isolated and unspoiled, fringe the coast. But spectacular scenery is just the start of Crete's appeal: vestiges of Minoan civilization, which flourished on Crete some 3,000 to 4,000 years ago and is one of the most brilliant and amazing cultures the world has ever known, abound at Knossos, Phaistos, and many other archaeological sites around the island. Other invaders and occupiers—Roman colonists, the Byzantines, Arab invaders, Venetian colonists, and Ottoman pashas—have all left their mark on Heraklion, Hania, Rethymnon, and other towns and villages throughout the island.

Today Crete welcomes outsiders. Openly inviting to guests who want to experience the real Greece, Cretans remain family oriented and rooted in tradition. One of the greatest pleasures on Crete is immersing yourself in the island's lifestyle.

EASTERN CRETE ΑΝΑΤΟΛΙΚΗ ΚΡΗΤΗ

Eastern Crete includes the towns and cities of Heraklion, Ayios Nikolaos, Siteia, and Ierapetra, as well as the archaeological sites of Knossos and Gournia. Natural wonders lie amid these man-made places, including the palm-fringed beach at Vai and the Lasithi plateau, and other inland plains and highlands are studded with villages where life goes on untouched by the hedonism of the coastal resorts. You may well make first landfall in Heraklion, the island's major port. You'll want to spend time here to visit the excellent Archaeological Museum and Knossos, but you're likely to have a more relaxing Cretan experience in Ayios Nikolaos, a charming and animated port town; in the resorts on the stunning Elounda peninsula; or on the beautiful and undeveloped eastern end of the island, around Palaikastro.

HERAKLION ΗΡΑΚΛΕΙΟ

175 km (109 mi) south of Piraeus, 69 km (43 mi) west of Ayios Nikolaos, 78 km (49 mi) east of Rethymnon.

Crete's largest city—the fourth-largest city in Greece—is not immediately appealing: it's a sprawling and untidy collection of apartment blocks and busy roadways. Many travelers looking for Crete's more-rugged pleasures bypass the island's capital altogether, but the city's renowned Archaeological Museum and the nearby Palace of Knossos make Heraklion a mandatory stop for anyone even remotely interested in ancient civilizations. Besides, at closer look, Heraklion is not without its charms. The narrow, crowded alleys of the older city and the thick stone ramparts recall the days when soldiers and merchants clung to the safety of a fortified port. In Minoan times, this was a harbor for Knossos, the largest palace and effective power center of prehistoric Crete. (But the Bronze Age remains were built over long ago, and now

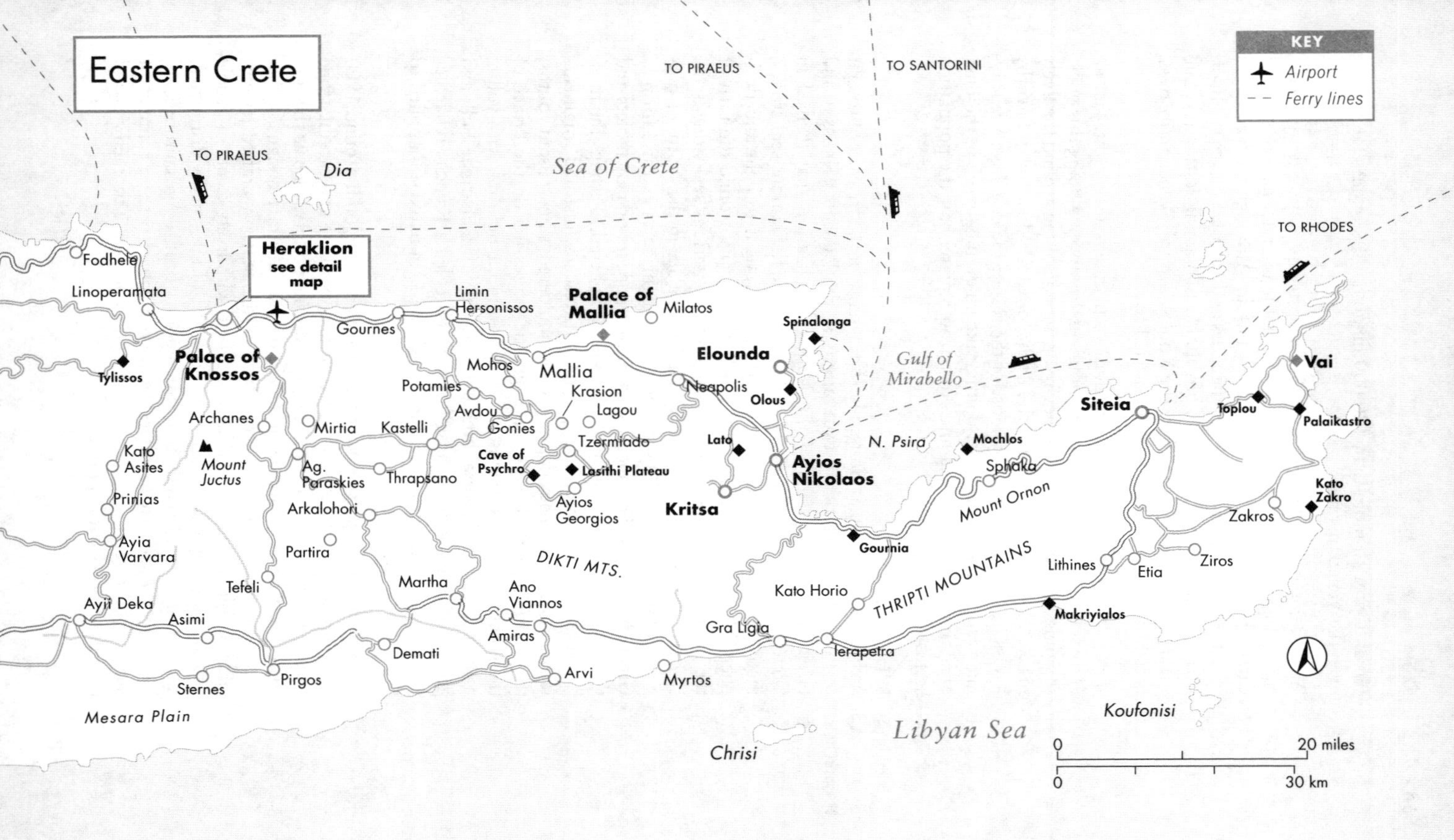
Eastern Crete
KEY
Airport
Ferry lines
TO PIRAEUS
TO PIRAEUS
TO SANTORINI
TO RHODES
Sea of Crete
Dia
Heraklion
see detail
map
Fodhele
Linoperamata
Tylissos
Palace of
Knossos
Gournes
Limin
Hersonissos
Palace of
Mallia
Milatos
Mallia
Mohos
Potamies
Avdou
Gonies
Krasion
Lagou
Tzermiado
Archanes
Mirtia
Kastelli
Kato
Asites
Mount
Juctus
Ag.
Paraskies
Thrapsano
Cave of
Psychro
Lasithi Plateau
Ayios
Georgios
Prinias
Arkalohori
Partira
Ayia
Varvara
DIKTI MTS.
Tefeli
Martha
Ano
Viannos
Ayii Deka
Asimi
Amiras
Demati
Arvi
Sternes
Pirgos
Myrtos
Mesara Plain
Spinalonga
Elounda
Neapolis
Olous
Lato
Ayios
Nikolaos
Kritsa
Gulf of
Mirabello
N. Psira
Mochlos
Sphaka
Mount Ornon
Gournia
Kato Horio
Gra Ligia
Ierapetra
THRIPTI MOUNTAINS
Makriyialos
Lithines
Etia
Ziros
Siteia
Toplou
Vai
Palaikastro
Kato
Zakro
Zakros
Koufonisi
Libyan Sea
Chrisi
0
20 miles
0
30 km

Heraklion, with more than 120,000 inhabitants, stretches far beyond even the Venetian walls.)

A walk down Dedalou and the other pedestrians-only streets provides plenty of amusements, and the city has more than its share of outdoor cafés where you can sit and watch life unfold. Although the waterfront is rather derelict, the seaside promenades and narrow lanes that run off them are slowly coming back to life, thanks to ongoing restoration, and the inner harbor dominated by the Koules, a sturdy Venetian fortress, is richly evocative of the island's storied past.

If you have just a day in Heraklion, your time will be tight. Get an early start and spend a couple of hours in the morning doing this walk, stepping into the churches if they're open and poking around the lively market. Save your energy for the Archaeological Museum and nearby Knossos, which will occupy most of the rest of the day. If you're staying overnight in or near Heraklion, take an evening stroll in the busy area around Ta Leontaria and Kornarou Square; half the population seems to converge here.

WHAT TO SEE

6 **Archaeological Museum.** Housed here are many of the treasures brought to light by the legendary excavations at the Palace of Knossos and other great monuments of the Minoan civilization that thrived in Crete some 3,000 years ago. Holdings include the famous seal stones, many inscribed with Linear B script and brought to light and deciphered by British archaeologist Sir Arthur Evans around the turn of the 20th century. The most stunning and mysterious seal stone is the so-called Phaistos Disk, found at Phaistos Palace in the south, its purpose unknown. (Linear B script is now recognized as an early form of Greek, but the earlier Linear A script that appears on clay tablets and that of the Phaistos Disk have yet to be deciphered.) Perhaps the most arresting treasures are the sophisticated frescoes, restored fragments found in Knossos. They depict broad-shouldered, slim-waisted youths, their large eyes fixed with an enigmatic expression on the Prince of the Lilies; ritual processions and scenes from the bullring, with young men and women somersaulting over the back of a charging bull; and groups of court ladies, whose flounced skirts led a French archaeologist to exclaim in surprise, "*Des Parisiennes!*," a name still applied to this striking fresco.

Fodor's Choice ★

Even before great palaces with frescoes were being built around 1900 BC, the prehistoric Cretans excelled at metalworking and carving stone vases, and they were also skilled at producing pottery, such as the eggshell-thin Kamaresware decorated in delicate abstract designs. Other specialties were miniature work such as the superbly crafted jewelry and the colored seal stones that are carved with lively scenes of people and animals. Though naturalism and an air of informality distinguish much Minoan art from that of contemporary Bronze Age cultures elsewhere in the eastern Mediterranean, you can also see a number of heavy, rococo set pieces, such as the fruit stand with a toothed rim and the punch bowl with appliquéd flowers.

Heraklion

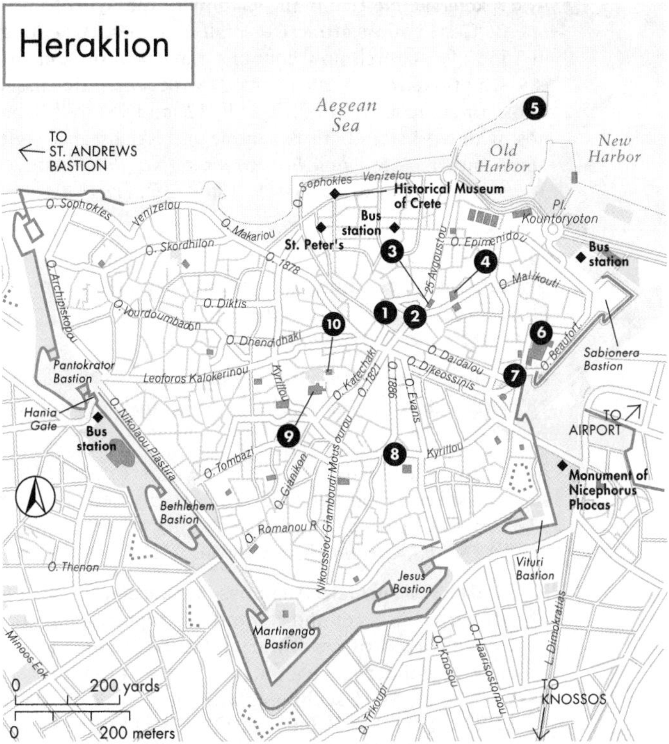

The Minoans' talents at modeling in stone, ivory, and a kind of glass paste known as faience peaked in the later palace period (1700 BC–1450 BC). A famous rhyton, a vase for pouring libations, carved from dark serpentine in the shape of a bull's head, has eyes made of red jasper and clear rock crystal with horns of gilded wood. An ivory acrobat—perhaps a bull-leaper—and two bare-breasted faience goddesses in flounced skirts holding wriggling snakes were among a group of treasures hidden beneath the floor of a storeroom at Knossos. (Bull-leaping, whether a religious rite or a favorite sport, inspired some memorable Minoan art.) Three vases, probably originally covered in gold leaf, from Ayia Triada are carved with scenes of Minoan life thought to be rendered by artists from Knossos: boxing matches, a harvest-home ceremony, and a Minoan official taking delivery of a consignment of hides. The most stunning rhyton of all, from Zakro, is made of rock crystal. It's best to visit the museum first thing in the morning, before the tour buses arrive. Note that, at this writing, the collection is being shown in a one-room annex while the museum undergoes extensive renovation, which is scheduled to be completed in late 2008. ✉ *Eleftherias Sq.* ☎ *2810/224630* 🌐 *www.culture.gr* 🎫 *€4; combined ticket for museum and Palace of Knossos €10* 🕐 *Apr.–mid-Oct., daily 8–7:30; mid-Oct.–Mar., daily 8–5.*

10 **Ayia Aikaterina.** Nestled in the shadow of the Ayios Minas cathedral is one of Crete's most attractive small churches, Ayia Aikaterina, built in 1555. The church now contains a museum of icons by Cretan artists, who traveled to Venice to study with Italian Renaissance painters. Look for six icons (Nos. 2, 5, 8, 9, 12, and 15) by Michael Damaskinos, who worked in both Byzantine and Renaissance styles during the 16th century. ⊠*Kyrillou Loukareos* ☎*No phone* 🎫*€2* ⏲*Mon. and Wed. 9:30–1, Thurs. and Sat. 9–1 and 5–7, Fri. 9–1.*

2 **Ayios Markos.** This 13th-century church (now an exhibition space) is named for Venice's patron saint, but, with its modern portico and narrow interior, it bears little resemblance to its grand namesake in Venice. Hours are irregular; the church is open only for exhibitions. ⊠*Eleftheriou Venizelou Sq.* ☎*No phone.*

9 **Ayios Minas.** This is a huge, lofty, but ultimately unprepossessing 1895 cathedral that can hold up to 8,000 worshippers. ⊠*Kyrillou Loukareos.*

4 **Ayios Titos.** A chapel to the left of the entrance contains St. Tito's skull, set in a silver-and-gilt reliquary. He is credited with converting the islanders to Christianity in the 1st century AD on the instructions of St. Paul. ⊠*Set back from 25 Avgoustou.*

Historical Museum of Crete. An imposing mansion houses a varied collection of early Christian and Byzantine sculptures, Venetian and Ottoman stonework, artifacts of war, and rustic folklife items. The museum provides a wonderful introduction to Cretan culture. Look out for the *Lion of St. Mark* sculpture, with an inscription that says in Latin I PROTECT THE KINGDOM OF CRETE. Left of the entrance is a room stuffed with memorabilia from Crete's bloody revolutionary past: weapons, portraits of mustachioed warrior chieftains, and the flag of the short-lived independent Cretan state set up in 1898. The 19th-century banner in front of the staircase sums up the spirit of Cretan rebellion against the Turks: ELEFTHERIA O THANATOS (Freedom or Death). Upstairs, look in on a room arranged as the study of Crete's most famous writer, Nikos Kazantzakis (1883–1957), the author of *Zorba the Greek* and an epic poem, *The Odyssey, a Modern Sequel*; he was born in Heraklion and is buried here, just inside the section of the walls known as the Martinengo. The top floor contains a stunning collection of Cretan textiles, including the brilliant scarlet weavings typical of the island's traditional handwork, and another room arranged as a domestic interior of the early 1900s. ⊠*Kalokorinou, in a warren of little lanes near the seafront* ☎*2810/283219* 🌐*www.historical-museum.gr* 🎫*€5* ⏲*Apr.–Oct., Mon.–Sat. 9–5; Nov.–Mar., Mon.–Tues. and Thurs.–Sat. 9–3, Wed. 9–3 and 6–9.*

5 **Koules.** Heraklion's inner harbor, where fishing boats land their catch and yachts are moored, is dominated by the Turkish-named fortress. Koules was built by the Venetians in the 16th century and decorated with three stone lions of St. Mark, symbol of Venetian imperialism. On the east side of the fortress are the vaulted arsenal; here Venetian galleys were repaired and refitted, and timber, cheeses, and sweet malmsey

wine were loaded for the three-week voyage to Venice. The view from the battlements takes in the inner as well as the outer harbor, where freighters and passenger ferries drop anchor, and the sprawling labyrinth of concrete apartment blocks that is modern Heraklion. To the south rises Mt. Iuktas and, to the west, the pointed peak of Mt. Stromboli. ✉*North end of 25 Avgoustou* ☎*2810/288484* 🎫*€4* ⏲*Daily 9–1 and 4–7.*

3 **Loggia.** A gathering place for the island's Venetian nobility, this loggia was built in the early 17th century by Francesco Basilicata, an Italian architect. Now restored to its original Palladian elegance, it adjoins the old Venetian Armory, now the City Hall. ✉*25 Avgoustou.*

NEED A BREAK?

Stop in at Kir-Kor, a venerable old *bougatsa* shop (✉ *Eleftheriou Venizelou Sq.*), for an envelope of flaky pastry that's either filled with a sweet, creamy filling and dusted with cinnamon and sugar, or stuffed with soft white cheese. A double portion served warm with Greek coffee is a nice treat. Thick Cretan yogurt and ice cream are other indulgences on offer.

Martinengo Bastion. Six bastions shaped like arrowheads jut out from the well-preserved Venetian walls. Martinengo is the largest, designed by Micheli Sanmicheli in the 16th century to keep out Barbary pirates and Turkish invaders. When the Turks overran Crete in 1648, the garrison at Heraklion held out for another 21 years in one of the longest sieges in European history. General Francesco Morosini finally surrendered the city to the Turkish Grand Vizier in September 1669. He was allowed to sail home to Venice with the city's archives and such precious relics as the skull of Ayios Titos—which was not returned until 1966. Literary pilgrims come to the Martinengo to visit the **burial place of writer Nikos Kazantzakis.** The grave is a plain stone slab marked by a weathered wooden cross. The inscription, from his writings, says: I FEAR NOTHING, I HOPE FOR NOTHING, I AM FREE. ✉*South of Kyrillou Loukareos on N. G. Mousourou.*

7 **Eleftherias Square.** The city's biggest square is paved in marble and dotted with fountains. The Archaeological Museum is off the north end of the square; at the west side is the beginning of Daidalou, the city's main street, which follows the line of an early fortification wall and is now a pedestrian walkway lined with tavernas, boutiques, jewelers, and souvenir shops. ✉*Southeast end of Daidalou.*

8 **Kornarou Square.** This square is graced with a Venetian fountain and an elegant Turkish stone kiosk. Odos 1866, which runs north from the square, houses Heraklion's lively open-air market, where fruit and vegetable stalls and souvenir stands alternate with butchers' displays of whole lambs and pigs' feet. ✉*At Odos 1866, south of Ta Leontaria.*

St. Peter's. Only a shell remains of this medieval church, which was heavily damaged during World War II in the bombing before the German invasion in 1941. ✉*West of harbor along seashore road.*

1 **Ta Leontaria.** "The Lions," a stately marble Renaissance fountain, remains a beloved town landmark. It's the heart of Heraklion's town

center—Eleftheriou Venizelou Square, a triangular pedestrian zone filled with cafés and named after the Cretan statesman who united the island with Greece in 1913. This was the center of the colony founded in the 13th century, when Venice bought Crete, and Heraklion became an important port of call on the trade routes to the Middle East. The city, and often the whole island (known then as Candia), was ruled by the Duke of Crete, a Venetian administrator. ✉ *Eleftheriou Venizelou Sq.*

WHERE TO STAY & EAT

¢–$$ ✕ **Erganos.** One of Heraklion's most traditional restaurants—just outside the old city walls south of Eleftherias Square—takes its name from one of the cities of ancient Crete and serves authentic local fare, including mouthwatering little pies (*pitarakia*) filled with cheese and honey, wild herbs from the mountains, and ground meats. Lunch and dinner both are often accompanied by Cretan music, often provided by a fellow patron. ✉ *Georgiadi 5* ☎ *2810/285629* ▭ *MC, V.*

¢–$ ✕ **Pantheon.** The liveliest restaurant in Heraklion's covered meat market has grilled and spit-roasted meats, as well as deftly prepared versions of moussaka and other traditional dishes. The surroundings are simple, but that doesn't stop locals from pouring in at all hours for a meal, which is nicely accompanied by salads made from the freshest Cretan produce. ✉ *Market off Kornarou Sq.* ☎ *2810/241652* ▭ *No credit cards.*

$$$–$$$$ ★ **Megaron.** A 1930s office building that for decades stood derelict above the harbor now houses an unusually luxurious and restful hotel—the best one in town. Handsome public spaces include a welcoming library/lounge, a rooftop restaurant with stunning views of the city and sea, and a top-floor terrace where a swimming pool is perched dramatically at the edge of the roof. The large and sumptuous guest rooms bring together a tasteful combination of rich fabrics, marble, and woods, and the teak-floored baths are lavish. Special Internet rates are often lower than those at other hotels in this class, making the Megaron a relatively affordable indulgence. ✉ *Doukos Bofor 9, 71202* ☎ *2810/305300* 📠 *2810/305400* 🌐 *www.gdmmegaron.gr* *38 rooms, 8 suites* *In-room: refrigerator, Wi-Fi. In-hotel: 2 restaurants, bar, pool, public Wi-Fi* ▭ *MC, V* 🍽 *CP.*

$$$ **Astoria Capsis.** This sleek hotel opposite the Archaeological Museum in the most animated part of the city is attractive and welcoming, with contemporary rooms decorated in cool shades and furnished with blond wood. All rooms have balconies and all of the modern baths are equipped with bathtubs. Retreat to the rooftop swimming pool from June to August, when bar service is provided, or have coffee at the ground-floor bar, open 24 hours. Rates include a buffet breakfast that is nothing short of lavish. ✉ *Eleftherias Sq., 71201* ☎ *2810/343080* 📠 *2810/229078* 🌐 *www.astoriacapsis.gr* *117 rooms, 14 suites* *In-room: refrigerator, Wi-Fi. In-hotel: restaurant, bar, pool* ▭ *AE, DC, MC, V* 🍽 *BP.*

$ **El Greco.** At this basic-but-comfortable hotel smack dab in the city center, ask for a garden-facing room for a quieter night, or request a street-side balcony to watch the action around Ta Leontaria fountain, just steps away. The carpeted rooms are simply but pleasantly furnished with wood beds and a desk. Rates include a full breakfast, but air-conditioning costs €7 a day extra. Even so, the word is out about what a bargain this is, so it's best to reserve far in advance. ✉ *4 Odos 1821, 71202* ☎ *2810/281071* 📠 *2810/281072* 🌐 *www.elgreco-hotel.gr* *90 rooms* *In-room: no a/c (some)* 💳 *DC, MC, V* 🍽 *BP.*

¢ **Dedalos.** You'd have to look hard to find a more fairly priced accommodation in the city center. On pedestrians-only Daidalou, this place is an easy walk to the Archaeological Museum and other sights. Rooms are modest and not a lot of care goes into the decor, but they're comfortable and all have balconies. Be sure to ask for one that faces the sea and not the street, which is loud with merrymakers into the wee hours. Breakfast is available for €6. ✉ *Daidalou 15, 71202* ☎ *2810/244812* 📠 *2810/244391* *58 rooms* 💳 *MC, V.*

THE MINOANS

They flourished on Crete from around 2700 BC to 1450 BC, and their palaces and cities at Knossos, Phaistos, and Gournia were centers of political power and luxury—they traded in tin, saffron, gold, and spices as far afield as Spain—when the rest of Europe was a place of primitive barbarity. They loved art, farmed bees, and worshipped many goddesses. But what brought about their demise? Some say political upheaval, but others point to an eruption on Thera (Santorini), about 100 km (60 mi) north in the Aegean, which caused tsunamis and earthquakes that brought about the end of this sophisticated civilization.

THE OUTDOORS

Acquaplus Waterpark (✉ *Hersonissos* ☎ *28970/24950* 🌐 *www.acquaplus.gr* *€18* *May–mid-Oct, daily 9 AM–sunset*) is not the place to go if you've come to Crete in search of unspoiled scenery and traditional ways. But this 50-acre water park next to the Crete Golf Club has dozens of slides, pools, and game arcades—a nice reward for little ones who've been letting you drag them through museums and ruins.

PALACE OF KNOSSOS ΑΝΑΚΤΟΡΟ ΚΝΩΣΟΥ

Fodor's Choice ★

5 km (3 mi) south of Heraklion.

This most amazing of archaeological sites once lay hidden beneath a huge mound hemmed in by low hills. Heinrich Schliemann, father of archaeology and discoverer of Troy, knew it was here, but Turkish obstruction prevented him from exploring his last discovery. Cretan independence from the Ottoman Turks made it possible for Sir Arthur Evans, a British archaeologist, to start excavations in 1899. A forgotten and sublime civilization thus came again to light with the uncovering of the great Palace of Knossos.

The site was occupied from Neolithic times, and the population spread to the surrounding land. Around 1900 BC, the hilltop was leveled and the first palace constructed; around 1700 BC, after an earthquake destroyed the original structure, the later palace was built, surrounded by houses and other buildings. Around 1450 BC, another widespread

Central court 3
East bastion 8
Grand staircase 5
North entrance 9
Queen's megaron 6
Royal road 11
South gateway 1
Theatrical area 10
Throne-room complex 4
West wing 2
Workshops 7

Palace of Knossos

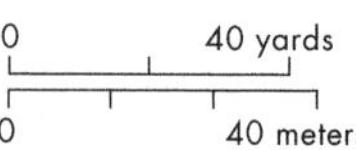

disaster occurred, perhaps an invasion: palaces and country villas were razed by fire and abandoned, but Knossos remained inhabited even though the palace suffered some damage. But around 1380 BC the palace and its outlying buildings were destroyed by fire, and at the end of the Bronze Age the site was abandoned. Still later, Knossos became a Greek city-state.

You enter the palace from the west, passing a bust of Sir Arthur Evans, who excavated at Knossos on and off for more than 20 years. A path leads you around to the monumental **south gateway.** The **west wing** encases lines of long, narrow storerooms where the true wealth of Knossos was kept in tall clay jars: oil, wine, grains, and honey. The **central court** is about 164 feet by 82 feet long. The cool, dark **throne-**

THE REAL THING?

Although excavations at Knossos have revealed houses with mosaic floors, statuary, and a wealth of information about the Minoan civilization, colorful—and controversial—concrete reconstructions form much of the site. Opinions vary, but these restorations and fresco copies do impart a sense of what Knossos must have once looked like. Without the re-creation it would be impossible to experience a full Minoan palace—long, pillared halls; narrow corridors; deep stairways and light wells; and curious reverse-tapering columns.

room complex has a griffin fresco and a tall, wavy-back gypsum throne, the oldest in Europe. The most spectacular piece of palace architecture is the **grand staircase,** on the east side of the court, leading to the domestic apartments. Four flights of shallow gypsum stairs survive, lighted by a deep light well. Here you get a sense of how noble Minoans lived; rooms were divided by sets of double doors, giving privacy and warmth when closed, coolness and communication when open. The **queen's megaron** (apartment or hall) is decorated with a colorful dolphin fresco and furnished with stone benches. Beside it is a bathroom, complete with a clay tub, and next door a toilet, whose drainage system permitted flushing into a channel flowing into the Kairatos stream far below. The east side of the palace also contained **workshops.** Beside the staircase leading down to the **east bastion** is a stone water channel made up of parabolic curves and settling basins: a Minoan storm drain. Northwest of the east bastion is the **north entrance,** guarded by a relief fresco of a charging bull. Beyond is the **theatrical area,** shaded by pines and overlooking a shallow flight of steps, which lead down to the **royal road.** This, perhaps, was the ceremonial entrance to the palace.

For a complete education in Minoan architecture and civilization, consider touring Knossos and, of course, the Archaeological Museum in Heraklion (where many of the treasures from the palace are on view), then traveling south to the Palace of Phaistos, another great Minoan site, which has not been reconstructed. To reach Knossos by bus, take No. 2 (departing every 15 minutes) from Odos Evans, close to the market, in Heraklion. ☎*2810/231940* 🌐*www.culture.gr* 🎫*€6; combined ticket for Knossos and Archaeological Museum in Heraklion €10* ⏲*Apr.–Oct., daily 8–7:30; Nov.–Mar., daily 8–5.*

OFF THE BEATEN PATH

Archanes. If you continue south from Knossos, after about 3 km (2 mi) you'll come to a well-marked road to Archanes, about 5 km (3 mi) beyond the turnoff. After the town received EU funds to do a makeover, streets were repaved with cobblestones, houses were restored and painted in bold shades of ocher and pastels, many fine neoclassic stone structures were spruced up, and new trees and flowers were planted everywhere in town. Archanes now looks a bit like a stage set, but it's lovely, and the handsome squares and surrounding streets are well equipped with places for a snack or a meal—accompany either with a glass of wine from the vineyards that cover the slopes around town.

PALACE OF MALLIA ΑΝΑΚΤΟΡΟ ΜΑΛΙΩΝ

★ *37 km (23 mi) east of Heraklion.*

In its effort to serve mass tourism, the town of Mallia has submerged whatever character it might once have had. The sandy beach, overlooked by the brooding Lasithi mountains, is backed by a solid line of hotels and vacation apartments. The town itself may not be worth a visit, but the Minoan Palace of Mallia on its outskirts definitely is. Like the palaces of Knossos and Phaistos, it was built around 1900 BC; it was less sophisticated both in architecture and decoration, but the layout is similar. The palace appears to have been destroyed by an earthquake around 1700 BC, and rebuilt 50 years later. Across the west court, along one of the paved raised walkways, is a double row of **round granaries** sunk into the ground, which were almost certainly roofed. East of the granaries is the **south doorway,** beyond which is the large, circular limestone table, or *kernos* (on which were placed offerings to a Minoan deity), with a large hollow at its center and 34 smaller ones around the edge. The **central court** has a shallow pit at its center, perhaps the location of an altar. To the west of the central court are the remains of an imposing staircase leading up to a second floor, and a terrace, most likely used for religious ceremonies; behind is a long corridor with **storerooms** to the side. In the north wing is a large **pillared hall,** part of a set of public rooms. The **domestic apartments** appear to have been in the northwest corner of the palace, entered through a narrow dogleg passage. They are connected by a smaller **northern court,** through which you can leave the palace by the **north entrance,** passing two giant old *pithoi* (large earthenware jars for storage of wine or oil). Excavation at the site continues, which is revealing a sizable town surrounding the palace. *3 km (2 mi) northeast of Mallia town ☎28970/31597 www.culture.gr €4 Nov.–June, Tues.–Sun. 8:30–3; July–Oct., Tues.–Sun. 8–7:30.*

MINOS AND THE MINOTAUR

As you tour Knossos, you are stepping into the pages of Greek mythology. It was here, allegedly, that King Minos imprisoned the Minotaur, a monster who was half man and half bull, in a labyrinth designed by Dedalus. As myth has it, Minos coveted the Minoan throne and prayed to Poseidon to send a white bull he would sacrifice in thanksgiving. His wife became smitten and, seducing the animal, gave birth to the Minotaur, for whom Minos ordered the architect Dedalus to build a labyrinthlike prison. The Minotaur was ultimately killed by Theseus.

AYIOS NIKOLAOS ΆΓΙΟΣ ΝΙΚΟΛΑΟΣ

★ *32 km (20 mi) southeast of Mallia, 69 km (43 mi) east of Heraklion.*

Ayios Nikolaos is clustered on a peninsula alongside the Gulf of Mirabello, a dramatic composition of bare mountains, islets, and deep blue sea. Behind the crowded harbor lies a natural curiosity, tiny Lake Voulismeni, linked to the sea by a narrow channel. Hilly, with narrow, steep streets that provide sea views, the town is a welcoming and animated place, far more pleasant than Mallia and the other resort centers in this part of Crete: you can stroll miles of waterside promenades, cafés line the lakeshore, and many streets are open only to pedestrians. Though many visitors bypass Ayios Nikolaos in favor of the nearby Elounda peninsula, the town makes an excellent base for exploring Eastern Crete.

The **Archaeological Museum** at Ayios Nikolaos displays some interesting artifacts, such as the *Goddess of Myrtos,* a statue circa 2500 BC (actually, the entire object is a rhyton, or vessel) of a woman cradling a large jug (the spout) in her spindly arms. There are also examples of late Minoan pottery in the naturalist marine style, with lively octopus and shell designs. ⊠*Odos Palaiologou 74* ☎*28410/24943* *€3* *Tues.–Sun. 8–5.*

The excellent **Folk Museum** showcases exquisite weavings, along with walking sticks, tools, and other artifacts from everyday rural life in Crete. ⊠*Odos Palaiologou 2* ☎*28410/24943* *€3* *Sun.–Fri. 11–3.*

BEACHES

You can dip into the clean waters that surround Ayios Nikolaos from several good beaches right in town. **Kitroplatia** and **Ammos** are both only about a 5- to 10-minute walk from the center. You can rent lounges and umbrellas at both.

WHERE TO STAY & EAT

$$–$$$ ✕ **Migomis.** Dress well (no shorts), try to nab a seat by the windows, and partake of an excellent meal accompanied by stunning views of the town and the sea. At one of the best restaurants in town, the menu embraces both Greece and Italy, with some excellent pastas and Tuscan steaks and the freshest fish and seafood. Reservations are essential in summer. ⊠*Plasira near 28th October* ☎*28410/24353* *AE, MC, V.*

$–$$ ★ ✕ **Pelagos.** An enchanting garden and the high-ceilinged parlors of an elegant mansion are the setting for what many locals consider to be the best seafood tavern in Ayios Nikolaos. Simple is the key word here: fresh catches from the fleet bobbing in the harbor just beyond are grilled and accompanied by local vegetables and Cretan wines. Reservations are recommended. ⊠*Katehaki 10* ☎*28410/25737* *MC, V.*

¢–$ ✕ **Itanos Restaurant.** This old-fashioned taverna is a much better value than most of the seafront establishments and offers a very palatable house wine from a row of barrels in the kitchen. The *tzoutzoukakia* (oven-cooked meatballs) are tender and spicy, and vegetable dishes, such as braised artichokes or green beans with tomato, are full of flavor. ⊠*Iroon Sq.* ☎*28410/25340* *No credit cards.*

¢ ✕ **Sarris.** Irini Sarris shows off her deft culinary skill best in traditional dishes, such as *stifado* (a rich stew made with lamb or sometimes with hare), and in the many *mezedes* (small dishes). The delightful, shady arbor set with tables overlooks an old church. ⊠*Kyprou 15* ☎*28410/28059* *No credit cards* *Closed Nov.–Feb.*

$ ✕ **Hotel Du Lac.** The handsomely appointed dining room with lakeside terrace ($–$$$) is one of the best places in town for a meal. Attentive and polished servers present house specialties such as steaks, other grilled meats, and seafood that's always fresh. The rooms upstairs are airy, spacious, and nicely done with simple, contemporary furnishings; studios, with kitchens and large baths, are enormous and an especially good value. Views from all rooms and their balconies are pleasant, but ask for a room overlooking the lake. ⊠*28th October 17, 72100* ☎*28410/22711* *28410/27211* *www.dulachotel.gr* *18 rooms, 6 studios* *In-room: refrigerator* *AE, MC, V.*

¢ **Hotel Kastro.** At this charming little inn at the end of a quiet street, on top of a hill just above the city center, watch the goings-on at the port from your private balcony. In the pleasant and plain rooms, which cling to the hillside below the main entrance, arches form the doorways and beds are tucked into alcoves. Although rooms have cooking facilities, a homemade breakfast is served in the morning. ✉*Lathenous 23, 72100* ☎*28410/24918* 📠*28410/25827* 🌐*www.meraki.gr* *12 rooms* *In-room: kitchen, no TV. In-hotel: no elevator* 💳*MC, V* 🍽*BP.*

SHOPPING

An appealing array of beads, quartz and silver jewelry, woven tablecloths and scarves, and carved bowls and other handicrafts fills **Chez Sonia** (✉*28th October* ☎*28410/28475*). You can get a very nice taste of the island to take home with you at **Elixir** (✉*Koundourou 15* ☎*28410/82593*) and **Melissa** (✉*Koundourou 18* ☎*28410/24628*), just across the street, both of which are well stocked with Cretan olive oils and wines and locally harvested honey and spices, as well as handmade olive oil soaps.

ELOUNDA ΕΛΟΥΝΤΑ

11 km (7 mi) north of Ayios Nikolaos, 80 km (50 mi) east of Heraklion.

Traversing a steep hillside, a narrow road with spectacular sea views runs north from Ayios Nikolaos around the Gulf of Mirabello to the village of Elounda and the stark peninsula that surrounds it. The beaches tend to be narrow and pebbly, but the water is crystal clear and sheltered from the *meltemi* (the fierce north wind that blows in July and August). Elounda village is becoming a full-scale resort destination: dozens of villas and hotels dot the surrounding hillsides, and the shore of the gulf south of Elounda is crowded with some of the most luxurious hotels in Crete. Don't come here in search of the authentic Greece; expect to meet fellow international travelers.

Olous (*3 km [2 mi] east of Elounda*) is a sunken, ancient city visible beneath the turquoise waters off a causeway that leads to the Spinalonga peninsula (not to be confused with the island of the same name), an undeveloped headland. The combination of warm waters and the promise of seeing the outlines of a Roman settlement on the seabed are alluring to snorkelers and swimmers. A few scant remains, including a mosaic floor, can be seen on dry land (fenced and marked with a sign).

OFF THE BEATEN PATH

Spinalonga. The Venetians built a huge, forbidding fortress on this small, narrow island in the center of the Gulf of Mirabello in the 17th century. In the early 1900s the island became a leper colony, serving this purpose with cruelly primitive conditions for more than 50 years. Travel agents in Ayios Nikolaos and Elounda can arrange boat excursions to the island, some complete with a midday beach barbecue and a swim on a deserted islet; you can also just sign up with any of the many outfitters that leave from the docks in both towns (expect to pay about €10). The real treat is cruising on these azure waters, and as you sail past the islet of Ayioi Pantes, a goat reserve, you're likely to see the *agrimi* (Cretan wild goat), with its impressive curling horns (€2 *Daily 8–7*).

WHERE TO STAY & EAT

$–$$ **Marilena.** In good weather, meals are served in the large rear garden, or you can choose a table on a sidewalk terrace facing the harbor. The kitchen prepares an excellent fresh, grilled fish and a rich fish soup; any meal here should begin with a platter of assorted appetizers. *Harborside, main square 28410/41322 MC, V Closed late Oct.–early Mar.*

¢–$ **Pefko.** Despite the presence of an enormous new resort at the edge of town, Plaka remains a delightful fishing village and Pefko (the Pine Tree) a pleasant place to take in village life and sea views. The menu offers a nice assortment of appetizers, salads, and such basics as moussaka and lamb, to be enjoyed on a shady terrace or in a cozy dining room where music is played some evenings. *Near beach in center of town, Plaka 28410/42510 No credit cards.*

$$$$ **Elounda Beach.** One of Greece's most renowned resort hotels, on 40 acres of gardens next to the Gulf of Mirabello, Elounda Beach has inspired dozens of imitators. The architecture reflects Cretan tradition: whitewashed walls, shady porches, and cool flagstone floors. You can have a room in the central block or a bungalow at the edge of the sea; 25 of the suites have their own swimming pools. Two sandy beaches are the jumping-off point for numerous water sports, including scuba diving. *3 km (2 mi) south of village, 72053 28410/41412 28410/41373 www.eloundabeach.gr 215 rooms, 28 suites In-room: refrigerator, Wi-Fi. In-hotel: 6 restaurants, bars, pool, water sports AE, DC, MC, V Closed Nov.–Mar. BP.*

$$$$ Fodor's Choice ★ **Elounda Mare.** If you plan to stay at one luxurious resort in Crete, make it this extraordinary Relais & Châteaux property on the Gulf of Mirabello, one of the finest hotels in Greece. More than half of the rooms, all bathed in cool marble and stunningly decorated in a soothing blend of traditional and contemporary furnishings, are in villas set in their own gardens with private pools. Verdant gardens line the shore above a sandy beach and terraced waterside lounging areas, a stone's throw from the large pool. *3 km (2 mi) south of village, Elounda, 72053 28410/41102 or 28410/41103 28410/41307 www.eloundamare.gr 38 rooms, 44 bungalows In-room: refrigerator, Wi-Fi. In-hotel: 3 restaurants, pool, water sports AE, DC, MC, V Closed Nov.–mid-Apr. BP.*

$ **Akti Olous.** This friendly, unassuming hotel on the edge of the Gulf of Mirabello outside Elounda and near the sunken city of Olus is a step away from a strip of sandy beach and provides sweeping views of the sea and peninsula. The rooftop pool and terrace are especially pleasant at sunset, and there is a waterside taverna and bar. The bright rooms, decorated in a handsome, modern neoclassic style, all have balconies overlooking the sea. Count on a sea breeze to keep you cool, because use of the air-conditioning costs €6 per day. *Waterfront road, 72053 28410/41270 28410/41425 www.greekhotels.net/aktiolous 70 rooms In-room: refrigerator. In-hotel: restaurant, bar, pool MC, V Closed Nov.–mid-Apr. BP.*

KRITSA ΚΡΙΤΣΑ

20 km (12½ mi) south of Elounda, 80 km (50 mi) southeast of Heraklion.

The mountain village of Kritsa, 9 km (5½ mi) west of Ayios Nikolaos, is renowned for its weaving tradition and surrounds a large, shady town square filled with café tables that afford views down the green valleys to the sea.

The lovely Byzantine church here, the whitewashed **Panayia Kera,** has an unusual shape, with three naves supported by heavy triangular buttresses. Built in the early years of Venetian occupation, it contains some of the liveliest and best-preserved medieval frescoes on the island, painted in the 13th century. ✉ *On main road before town* 🎫 *€1* ⏲ *Sat.–Thurs. 9–3.*

Lato, about 4 km (2½ mi) north of Kritsa, is an ancient city built by the Doric Greeks in a dip between two rocky peaks. Lato was named for the mother of Artemis and Apollo and her image appears on coins found at the site. Make your way over the expanse of ancient masonry to the far end of the site for one of the best views in Crete: on a clear day you can see the island of Santorini, 100 km (60 mi) across the Cretan Sea, as well as inland across a seemingly endless panorama of mountains and valleys. ✉ *Follow marked road from Kritsa* 🎫 *€2* ⏲ *Tues.–Sun. 8:30–3; gate is often open and unattended at other times.*

SITEIA ΣΗΤΕΙΑ

55 km (32 mi) east of Kritsa, 143 km (87 mi) east of Heraklion.

Like Ierapetra, Siteia is an unpretentious town where agriculture is more important than tourism: raisins and, increasingly, bananas are the main crops. Even so, Siteia is a pleasant place to wander, and the whitewashed town with shady lanes behind the harbor seems almost Arabian. Siteia's waterfront, lined with cafés and tavernas, is lively from June through August, and a long, sandy beach that stretches to the east of the waterfront is the town's other principal gathering spot. From Siteia you can fly to Rhodes or take a ferry there via the small islands of Kassos and Karpathos. In July and August, there are usually weekly ferries between Siteia and Piraeus. Siteia is a good choice for an overnight while making the circuit of far eastern Crete.

An old Venetian fort, the **Kazarma,** overlooks Siteia from a height in the west. There's not much to see in the vast enclosed space, used to stage plays and concerts on summer evenings, but the view across the bay is spectacular. ✉ *Follow signs up hill from waterfront.*

Siteia's **Archaeological Museum,** in addition to other artifacts, contains a rare treasure: a Minoan ivory and gold statuette of a young man, found on the east coast at Palaikastro. The figure dates from around 1500 BC and, though incomplete, is a masterpiece of Minoan carving. ✉ *Siteia–Ierapetra road, outskirts of town* ☎ *28430/23917* 🌐 *www.culture.gr* 🎫 *€2* ⏲ *Tues.–Sun. 8:30–3.*

WHERE TO STAY & EAT

$-$$ ★ **The Balcony.** A bit more stylish than you'd expect to find on the backstreets of Siteia, this handsome dining room in an old house focuses on local ingredients and, though a few dishes show an Asian influence, excels at such traditional dishes as lamb cooked in lemon and rabbit stew. An excellent selection of Cretan wines is available. Reservations are recommended. *Fountalido 19 28430/25084 MC, V No lunch Sun.*

$ **Hotel Flisvos.** Small and stylish, this waterfront hotel puts you within steps of the beach and seaside promenades, and is right in the city center. The pleasant rooms all have balconies that overlook the sea or a pretty garden behind the hotel. *Karamanli 4, 72300 28430/27135 21 rooms In room: refrigerator. In hotel: bar MC, V CP.*

¢ **Hotel El Greco.** This friendly establishment on a narrow street several blocks above the waterfront is perfectly comfortable and not without charm. Many of the simple rooms have balconies overlooking the old town and the sea. *G. Arkadiou, 72300 28430/23133 28430/26391 15 rooms In-room: refrigerator. In-hotel: bar MC, V Closed Nov.–Apr. CP.*

EN ROUTE

The fierce north wind that sweeps this region has twisted the few trees on hillsides surrounding the fortified monastery at **Toplou,** 13 km (8 mi) east of Siteia off the road to Vai, into strange shapes. Only a few monks live here now, and the monastery is slowly being renovated. Inside the tall loggia gate, built in the 16th century and from the top of which monks once defended themselves against invading Turks and pirates, the cells are arranged around a cobbled courtyard with a 14th-century church at its center. Each of 61 scenes in its famous icon was inspired by a phrase from the Orthodox liturgy. *Off road to Vai No phone €3 Daily 9–6.*

VAI ΒΑΙ

27 km (17 mi) east of Siteia, 170 km (104 mi) east of Heraklion.

Unique in Europe, the palm grove of the renowned beach at Vai existed in classical Greek times. The sandy stretch with nearby islets in clear turquoise water is one of the most attractive in Crete, but in July and August, it gets very crowded. The appeal of the surrounding, fertile coastal plain was not lost on the ancient Minoans, who left behind some of Crete's most enchanting ruins. Modern towns that surround the old Minoan settlements of Palaikastro, Ano Zakros, and Kato Zakros, are well endowed with tavernas and rooms to rent.

Palaikastro is a sprawling, once densely populated Minoan town, currently being excavated by British and American archaeologists. Although this site, once a working agricultural center, does not have the drama of Knossos or Phaistos, you get a strong sense of everyday life here amid the stony ruins of streets, squares, dwellings, and shops. Follow a narrow track from the site through olive groves to a sandy beach at Hiona. It's rarely crowded, and service is welcoming at the waterside tavernas. *9 km (5½ mi) south of Vai, outside modern vil-*

lage of Palaikastro ⊕www.culture.gr Free ⏲Daily 8:30–3, often later (sight is usually unattended and unlocked).

The ruins of the **Palace of Kato Zakros,** 20 km (12½ mi) south of Palaikastro, are smaller than those of the other Minoan palaces on the island. You can drive down to the site by a circuitous but spectacular route, or stop at Ano Zakro (Upper Zakro) and follow a path that leads down through a deep ravine (known as the Gorge of the Dead) past caves used for early Minoan burials to the Minoan palace. The walk down and back up is steep but not overly arduous, and takes about two hours. The site includes the ruins of a small palace and a surrounding town that from 1650 BC to 1450 BC may have served as a port for trade with Egypt and the Middle East. The ruins, entered from the harbor through a gate and up a ramp, are surrounded by a terraced seaside village, Kato Zakros, which has narrow cobbled streets. On the fine beach is a cluster of tavernas with a few rooms to rent. *✢38 km (25 mi) south of Vai, ascend paved Minoan road from Kato Zakros harbor through gateway to northeast court down stepped ramp ☎28410/22462 €3 ⏲Daily 8–3.*

WHERE TO STAY & EAT

¢ **Hotel Hellas.** Sparkling clean and comfortable, each of the simple rooms here overlooks the town, the surrounding plains, and the sea from a balcony. The ground-floor restaurant (¢) spills into the square and serves excellent traditional Cretan fare, using fresh produce from the fields that run right up to the edge of town. *✉Main square, Palaikastro, 72300 ☎28430/61240 ⊕www.palaikastro.com/hotelhellas 17 rooms In room: refrigerator. In hotel: restaurant No credit cards. CP.*

WESTERN CRETE ΔΥΤΙΚΗ ΚΡΗΤΗ

Much of Western Crete's landscape—soaring mountains, deep gorges, and rolling green lowlands—remains largely untouched by mass tourism; in fact, only the north coast is developed. There is a wealth of interesting byways to be explored. This region is abundant in Minoan sites—including the palace at Phaistos—as well as Byzantine churches and Venetian monasteries. Two of Greece's more-appealing cities are here: Hania and Rethymnon, both crammed with the houses, narrow lanes, and minarets that hark back to Venetian and Turkish occupation. Friendly villages dot the uplands, and there are some outstanding beaches on the ruggedly beautiful and remote west and south coasts. Immediately southwest of Heraklion lies the traditional agricultural heartland of Crete: long, narrow valleys where olive groves alternate with vineyards of sultana grapes for export.

PALACE OF PHAISTOS ΑΝΑΚΤΟΡΟ ΦΑΙΣΤΟΥ

Fodor'sChoice ★ *11 km (7 mi) west of Ayii Deka, 50 km (31 mi) southwest of Heraklion.*

On a steep hill overlooking olive groves and the sea on one side, and high mountain peaks on the other, Phaistos is the site of one of the greatest Minoan palaces. Unlike Knossos, Phaistos has not been reconstructed, though the copious ruins are richly evocative. The palace was built around 1900 BC and rebuilt after a disastrous earthquake around 1650 BC. It was burned and abandoned in the wave of destruction that swept across the island around 1450 BC, though Greeks continued to inhabit the city until the 2nd century BC, when it was eclipsed by Gortyna.

You enter the site by descending a flight of steps leading into the west court, then climb a grand staircase. From here you pass through the **Propylon porch** into a light well and descend a narrow staircase into the **central court.** Much of the southern and eastern sections of the palace have eroded away. But there are large pithoi still in place in the old **storerooms.** On the north side of the court the recesses of an elaborate doorway bear a rare trace: red paint in a diamond pattern on a white ground. A passage from the doorway leads to the **north court** and the **northern domestic apartments,** now roofed and fenced off. The **Phaistos Disk** was found in 1903 in a chest made of mud brick at the northeast edge of the site and is now on display at the Archaeological Museum in Heraklion. East of the central court are the **palace workshops,** with a metalworking furnace fenced off. South of the workshops lie the **southern domestic apartments,** including a clay bath. From there, you have a memorable view across the Messara plain. *⊕Follow signs and ascend hill off Ayii Deka–Mires–Timbaki road ☎28920/42315 ⊕www.culture.gr ✉€4; combined ticket with Ayia Triada €6 ⊙Apr.–Oct., daily 8–7:30; Nov.–Mar., daily 8–5.*

Ayia Triada was destroyed at the same time as Phaistos, which is only a few miles away on the other side of the same hill. It was once thought to have been a summer palace for the rulers of Phaistos but is now believed to have consisted of group of villas for nobility and a warehouse complex. Rooms in the villas were once paneled with gypsum slabs and decorated with frescoes: the two now hanging in the Archaeological Museum in Heraklion show a woman in a garden and a cat hunting a pheasant. Several other lovely pieces, including finely crafted vases, also come from Ayia Triada and are now also on display in Heraklion. Though the complex was at one time just above the sea, the view now looks across the extensive Messara plain to the Lybian Sea in the distance. *⊕Follow signs 3 km (2 mi) west from Phaistos ☎28920/91360 ⊕www.culture.gr ✉€4; combined ticket with Phaistos €6 ⊙May–Sept., daily 10–7:30; Oct.–Apr., daily 8:30–3.*

EN ROUTE

The quickest route from Phaistos, Matala, and other places on the Messara plain to the north coast is the Heraklion road, a small section of which is even four lanes these days. But a very pleasant alternative leads northwest through Ayia Galini (the largest resort on this part of

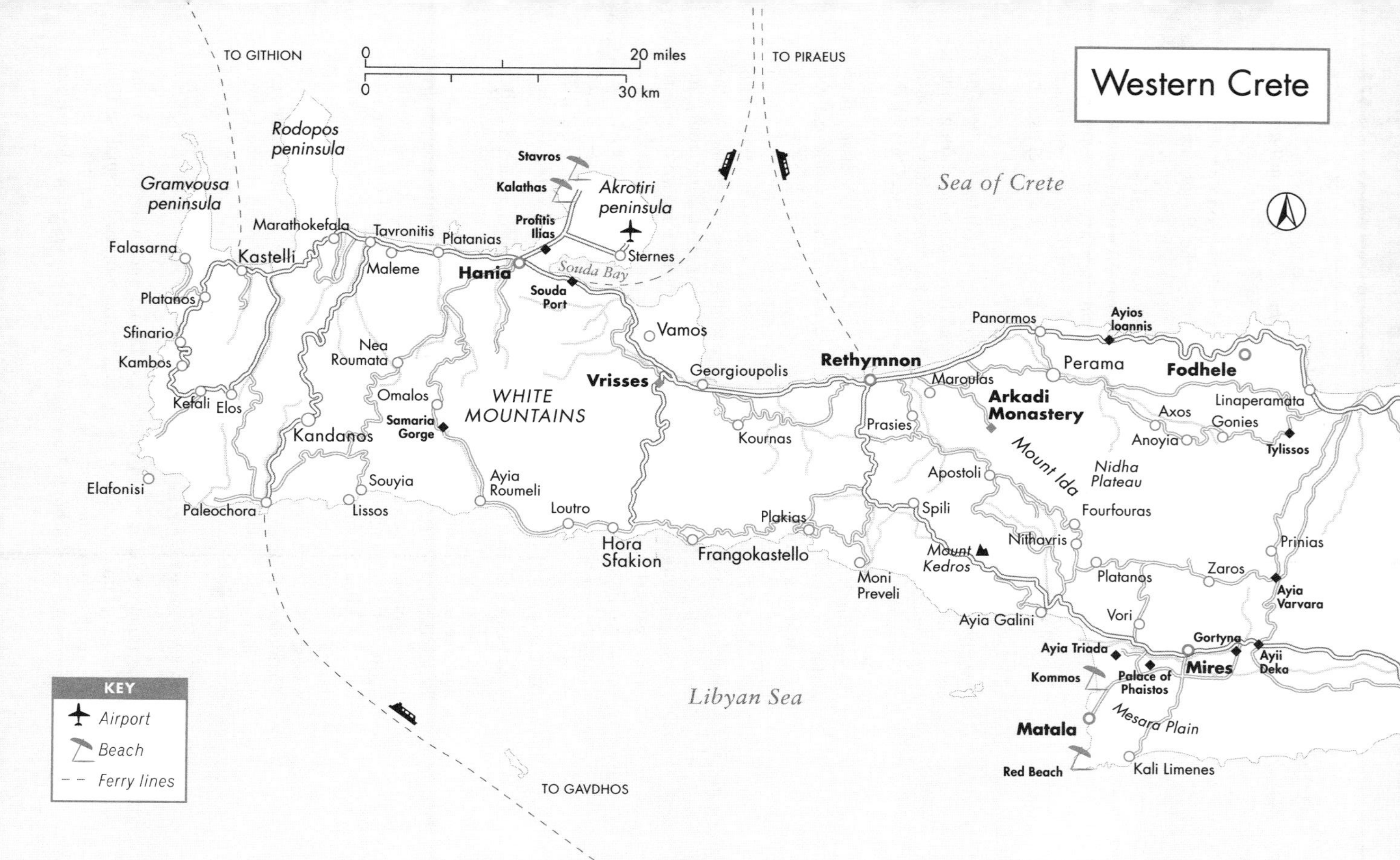

Western Crete
TO GITHION
0
20 miles
0
30 km
TO PIRAEUS
Sea of Crete
Rodopos peninsula
Gramvousa peninsula
Stavros
Kalathas
Akrotiri peninsula
Profitis Ilias
Sternes
Marathokefala
Tavronitis
Platanias
Falasarna
Kastelli
Maleme
Hania
Souda Bay
Souda Port
Platanos
Sfinario
Kambos
Kefali
Elos
Nea Roumata
Omalos
Samaria Gorge
WHITE MOUNTAINS
Vrisses
Vamos
Georgioupolis
Rethymnon
Panormos
Ayios Ioannis
Perama
Fodhele
Maroulas
Arkadi Monastery
Linaperamata
Axos
Gonies
Anoyia
Tylissos
Kandanos
Kournas
Prasies
Mount Ida
Nidha Plateau
Apostoli
Elafonisi
Souyia
Lissos
Paleochora
Ayia Roumeli
Loutro
Hora Sfakion
Frangokastello
Plakias
Spili
Fourfouras
Nithavris
Mount Kedros
Moni Preveli
Prinias
Zaros
Platanos
Ayia Varvara
Vori
Ayia Galini
Gortyna
Ayia Triada
Mires
Ayii Deka
Kommos
Palace of Phaistos
Libyan Sea
Matala
Mesara Plain
Red Beach
Kali Limenes
TO GAVDHOS
KEY
Airport
Beach
Ferry lines

the southern coast) and the mountain town of Spili to Rethymnon. The route shows off the beauty of rural Crete as it traverses deep valleys and gorges and climbs the flanks of the interior mountain ranges. Just beyond Spili, follow signs to Moni Preveli (*€2.50 Daily 8–7*), a stunningly situated monastery perched high above the sea. A monument honors the monks here who sheltered Allied soldiers after the Battle of Crete and helped them escape the Nazi-occupied island via submarine. Below the monastery is lovely Palm Beach, where golden sands are shaded by a palm grove watered by a mountain stream. However, avoid this patch of paradise at midday during high season, when it is packed with day-trippers who arrive by tour boat from Ayia Galini.

FODHELE ΦΟΔΕΛΕ

13 km (8 mi) west of Heraklion, 10 km (6 mi) northwest of Tylissos.

If you are driving west on the north coast from Heraklion toward Rethymnon, a good place to break up the trip is the straggling, sleepy village of Fodhele, said to be the birthplace of Domenico Theotokopoulos, the 16th-century Cretan painter known as El Greco. The claim is disputed by some scholars; nonetheless, a stop in Fodhele allows you to sit in the shady square (where a plaque honors the alleged native son) and enjoy a look at rural Cretan life. Fodhele's **church of the Panayia,** at the edge of town, is a beautiful Byzantine structure with fine 14th-century frescoes. The church is sometimes open for prayer, though it is usually locked, in which case you'll have to look around for a guardian to let you in.

ARKADI MONASTERY ΜΟΝΗ ΑΡΚΑΔΙΟΥ

★ *18 km (11 mi) southwest of Fodhele, 30 km (19 mi) southwest of Heraklion.*

As you approach Arkadi through the rolling lands at the base of Mt. Ida (one of the contenders in the dispute over the alleged Cretan birthplace of Zeus), you'll follow a gorge inland before emerging onto the flat pastureland that is part of the monastery's holdings. Arkadi is a place of pilgrimage for Cretans, a shrine to heroes in the fight against the Turks for independence, and one of the most stunning pieces of Renaissance architecture on the island. The ornate facade, decorated with Corinthian columns and an elegant belfry above, was built in the 16th century of a local, honey-color stone. In 1866 the monastery came under siege during a major rebellion against the Turks, and Abbot Gabriel and several hundred rebels, together with their wives and children, refused to surrender. When the Turkish forces broke through the gate, the defenders set the gunpowder store afire, killing themselves together with hundreds of Turks. The monastery was again a center of resistance when Nazis occupied Crete during World War II. ✉ *South of old Heraklion–Hania road* *€2* *Daily 8–8.*

RETHYMNON ΡΕΘΥΜΝΟ

★ *25 km (15 mi) west of Arkadi Monastery, 78 km (48½ mi) west of Heraklion.*

Rethymnon is Crete's third-largest town, after Heraklion and Hania. The population (about 30,000) steadily increases as the town expands—a new quarter follows the coast to the east of the old town, where the beachfront has been tastelessly developed with large hotels and other resort facilities catering to tourists on package vacations. However, much of Rethymnon's charm perseveres in the old Venetian quarter, which is crowded onto a compact peninsula dominated by the huge, fortified Venetian castle known as the Fortessa. Wandering through the narrow alleyways, you come across handsome carved-stone Renaissance doorways belonging to vanished mansions, fountains, archways, and wooden Turkish houses with latticework screens on the balconies to protect the women of the house from prying eyes.

The most visible sign of the Turkish occupation of Rethymnon is the graceful minaret, one the few to survive in Greece, that rises above the **Neratze,** a mosque–turned–concert hall at the center of town. You can climb its 120 steps for a panoramic view, though access is possible only when a performance takes place. ✉ *Odos Verna and Odos Ethnikis Adistaseos.*

A restored Venetian palazzo almost in the shadow of the minaret houses the delightful **Historical and Folk Art Museum.** Rustic furnishings, tools, and exquisite weavings provide a charming and vivid picture of what life on Crete was like until well into the 20th century. ✉ *Vernadou 28* ☎ *28310/29975* 🎫 *€3* ⏲ *Daily 9:30–2.*

The carefully restored **Venetian loggia** was once the clubhouse of the local nobility. It is now enclosed in glass and houses the Archaeological Museum's shop. ✉ *Arkadiou, near town center.*

Just down the street, at the end of Platanos square, is one of the town's most welcoming sights, the so-called **Rimondi Fountain,** installed by the Venetians and spilling refreshing streams from several lions' heads. You'll come upon several other fountains as you wander through the labyrinth of narrow streets.

Rethymnon's small **Venetian harbor,** with its restored 13th-century lighthouse, comes to life in warm weather, when restaurant tables clutter the quayside. Fishing craft and pleasure boats are crammed chockablock into the minute space, while the outer harbor, protected by a massive breakwater, acts as the port for the ferries that run between Rethymnon and Piraeus. ✉ *Waterfront.*

The west side of the peninsula is taken up almost entirely with the **Fortessa,** strategically surrounded by the sea and thick ramparts. Climbing up to the fortress is a bit of a letdown, because the high, well-preserved walls enclose not much more than a vast empty space occupied by a few scattered buildings—and filled with wildflowers in spring. Forced laborers from the town and surrounding villages built the fortress from 1573 to 1583. It didn't fulfill its purpose of keeping out the Turks: Rethymnon surrendered after a three-week siege in 1646. ✉ *West end of town* 🎫 *€3* ⏲ *Sat.–Thurs. 8:30–7.*

The **Archaeological Museum,** just outside the entrance to the Fortessa will impress you again with just how long Crete has cradled civilizations: a collection of bone tools is from a Neolithic site at Yerani (west of Rethymnon); Minoan pottery is on display; and an unfinished statue of Aphrodite, the goddess of love, is from the Roman occupation (look for the ancient chisel marks). The museum building used to be a Turkish guardhouse and prison. ✉ *West end of town, next to entrance of Fortessa* ☎ *28310/54668* 🎫 *€3* ⏲ *Tues.–Sun. 8:30–3.*

VENETIANS & TURKS

By the 16th century, when the Venetians built the Fortessa in Rethymnon, they had controlled Crete for almost 300 years. Crete was ceded to them by the Crusaders who disbursed the holdings of the Byzantine Empire. Possessing Crete gave Venice control of the very rich trade routes across the southern Mediterranean but Venetians were defeated by Ottoman Turks who overran the island in 1645. They ruled until 1898 when they, in turn, were expelled. Cretan independence fighter Eleftherios Venizelos became premier of Greece in 1910, and under his leadership, Crete became part of the Greek nation in 1913.

12

WHERE TO STAY & EAT

$$–$$$$ ★ ✕ **Avli.** A stone, barrel-vaulted dining room and a multitiered garden are the attractive settings for creative interpretations of Cretan cuisine, made only from grass-fed lamb, fresh-caught fish, garden vegetables, and other organic and natural ingredients. Even a simple *horiatiki* (Greek salad) and grilled lamb chop can be transporting here, as is the excellent selection of the island's finest wines. Reservations are a good idea in summer. ✉ *Paleologou 22* ☎ *28310/26213* 💳 *MC, V.*

$–$$ ✕ **Cavo D'Oro.** This is the most stylish of the handful of fish restaurants around the tiny Venetian harbor. Lobster and fish dishes are always served fresh. The high-ceiling, wood-panel dining room was once a medieval storeroom; diners also sit on the old cobbled waterfront. ✉ *Nearchou 42–43* ☎ *28310/24446* 💳 *DC, MC, V.*

¢–$ ✕ **Kyria Maria.** At this simple, family-run taverna in the center of the old town, good home cooking is served from a small menu of traditional Greek specialties. Neighborhood life buzzes around the tables set beneath an arbor in a narrow lane. This place is open for breakfast daily. ✉ *Moschovitou* ☎ *28310/29078* 💳 *MC, V.*

$$$$ ★ **Palazzino di Corina.** Rethymnon has several hotels occupying old palaces; Corina is the most luxurious and provides stylish surroundings that include a courtyard with wood chaises, topiary planters, and statuary surrounding a small pool. Guest rooms, with exposed-stone walls and wooden beams, are furnished with a mix of antiques and contemporary pieces. ✉ *Damvergi and Diakou, 74100* ☎ *28310/21205* 📠 *28310/21204* 🌐 *www.corina.gr* *21 suites* *In-room: refrigerator, Ethernet. In-hotel: restaurant, pool, no elevator* 💳 *MC, V* 🍽 *BP.*

$$–$$$ Fodor'sChoice ★ **Vetera Suites.** A Venetian-Ottoman house evokes the rich ambience of old Rethymnon, with delightfully atmospheric and comfortable rooms and two-level suites—the most distinctive lodgings in town. All rooms display exposed beams, chimneys, stonework, and other original details, and are furnished with exquisite antiques. Modern comforts abound, too, such as compact stylish bathrooms and kitchenettes that are tucked into alcoves. A delicious breakfast is €10 extra. ✉*Kastrinoyannaki 39, 74100* ☎*28310/23844* 🌐*www.vetera.gr* *2 rooms, 2 suites* *In-room: kitchen* *MC, V* *CP.*

$ **Hotel Fortezza.** Only steps from the fortress, the old town, and the beach, you can enjoy many of the advantages of the larger hotels on Rethymnon's charmless beach strip. The tile-floor rooms, with handsome traditional wood furnishings, are built around a marble atrium and sunny courtyard that has a pool; many rooms have balconies. A buffet breakfast is served. ✉*Melisinou 16, 74100* ☎*28310/55551* *28310/54073* 🌐*www.fortezza.gr* *54 rooms* *In-hotel: restaurant, bars, pool* *AE, DC, MC, V* *BP.*

HIKING CRETE

Crete is excellent hiking terrain, and many trails crisscross the mountains and gorges, especially in the southwest. The Greek National Tourism Organization (GNTO or EOT) is a source of information. **Alpine Travel** (✉*Bonaili 11, Hania* ☎*28210/50939* 🌐*www.alpine.gr*) offers many hiking tours throughout western Crete, while the **Greek Federation of Mountaineering Associations** (☎*28210/44647 in the White Mountains, 2810/289440 on Mt. Ida, 2810/227609 in Heraklion*) operates overnight refuges in the White Mountains and on Mt. Ida.

SPORTS & THE OUTDOORS

★ **Dream Adventure Trips** (✉*Beachfront, Almirida* ☎*6944/357383*) operates highly enjoyable boat excursions off the Vamos peninsula into Almiros Bay (west of Rethymnon), with stops to snorkel, swim, and explore a seaside cave. The two-hour trips cost €20.

The **Happy Walker** (✉*Tombazi 56* ☎*28310/52920* 🌐*www.happywalker.com* *July 1–Sept. 15*) arranges easy hiking tours in the surrounding mountains and gorges, adding a welcome stop for a village lunch to each walk. Each walk costs €30.

SHOPPING

★ The **Archaeological Museum Shop** (✉*Paleologou* ☎*28310/54668*), handsomely housed in a Venetian loggia, has an excellent selection of books, as well as reproductions of artifacts from its collections and from other sites in Crete and throughout Greece. **Avli** (✉*Xanthoudidou 22* ☎*28310/58250*) sells many of the herbs, spices, oils, and other ingredients that flavor the cuisine at the eponymous restaurant around the corner, as well as fine Greek wines. For a souvenir that will be light to carry, stop in at **Kalymnos** (✉*Arampatzouglou 26* ☎*28310/50802*), filled to the rafters with sponges harvested off the eponymous island and in other Greek waters.

EN ROUTE

One of the shortest routes to the remote southwestern coast is the road that climbs mountains and drops through gorges for some 20 km (12 mi) south from Vrisses to Hora Sfakion. Tucked between the sea and the arms of sheltering mountains, Hora has an end-of-the-road atmosphere to it and is a transit hub for the south coast. By car or bus you can make the steep, 12-km (7½-mi) drive up to the charming, unspoiled farming village of Anapoli, on an upland plain near the end of the hiking path through the Aradhena gorge. Or head 14 km (8½ mi) east to Frangokastello, where the romantic-looking shell of a 14th-century castle overlooks a beautiful beach. On foot you can follow the segment of the E4 European hiking path that links Hora with Loutro, a charmingly sleepy seaside village reachable only on foot or by sea. By ferry from Hora you can cruise to Paleochora, Ayia Roumeli, and other ports along the south coast and continue on to Gavdhos Island, 50 km (30 mi) south in the middle of the Lybian Sea.

VRISSES ΒΡΥΣΕΣ

26 km (14 mi) west of Rethymnon, 105 km (65 mi) west of Heraklion.

This appealing old village is famous throughout Crete for its thick, creamy yogurt—best eaten with a large spoonful of honey on top—that is served in the cafés beneath the plane trees at the center of town. Georgioupolis, on the coast about 7 km (4½ mi) due west, is another shady, lovely old town, where the Almiros River flows into the sea. The coast here is being rather unattractively developed, but inland walks—including one through a eucalyptus-scented valley that links Vrisses and Georgioupolis—make it easy to get away from the fray.

HANIA ΧΑΝΙΑ

Fodor'sChoice ★

52 km (33 mi) west of Vrisses, 78 km (48 mi) west of Rethymnon.

Hania surrendered its role of capital of Crete to Heraklion in 1971, but this elegant city of eucalyptus-lined avenues, miles of waterfront promenades, and shady, cobbled alleyways lined with Venetian and Ottoman houses is still close to the heart of all Cretans. It was here that the Greek flag was raised in 1913 to mark Crete's unification with Greece, and the place is simply one of the most beautiful of all Greek cities.

The sizable old town is strung along the harbor (divided by a centuries-old seawall into outer and inner harbors), where tall Venetian houses face a pedestrians-only, taverna-lined waterside walkway, and fishing boats moor beside a long stretch of Venetian arsenals and warehouses. Well-preserved Venetian and Turkish quarters surround the harbors and a covered food and spice market, a remnant of Venetian trade and Turkish bazaars that's set amid a maze of narrow streets.

Kastelli hill, where the Venetians first settled, rises above the east end of the harbor. The hill became the quarter of the local nobility, but it had been occupied much earlier: parts of what may be a Minoan palace have been excavated at its base. ✉ *Above harbor.*

Kastelli hill creates a backdrop to the **Janissaries Mosque,** built at the water's edge when Turks captured the town in 1645 after a two-month siege. You can only enter the building when the town uses it to host temporary art and trade exhibitions, but the presence of the domed structure at the edge of the shimmering sea lends Hania an exotic air. Hours vary from show to show; the place is most often closed. ✉ *East side of inner harbor.*

As you follow the harbor front east from the mosque, you come to a long line of **Venetian Arsenali** from the 16th and 17th centuries, used to store wares and repair craft. The seawalls swing around to enclose the harbor and end at the **old lighthouse** that stands at the east side of the harbor entrance; from here you get a magnificent view of the town, with the imposing White Mountains looming beyond and the animated harbor below.

Just across the narrow channel from the lighthouse and marking the west entrance to the harbor is the **Firka,** the old Turkish prison, which is now the naval museum. Exhibits, more riveting than might be expected, trace the island's seafaring history from the time of the Venetians. Look for the photos and mementos from the World War II Battle of Crete, when Allied forces moved across the island and, with the help of Cretans, ousted the German occupiers. Much of the fighting centered around Hania, and great swaths of the city were destroyed during the war. Almost worth the price of admission alone is the opportunity to walk along the Firka's ramparts for bracing views of the city, sea, and mountains. ✉ *Waterfront at far west end of port* ☎ *28210/91875* *€2.50* *Daily 9–4.*

You'll get some insight into the Venetian occupation *and* the Christian centuries that preceded it at the **Byzantine and Post-Byzantine Collection,** housed in the charming 15th-century church of San Salvadore alongside the city walls just behind the Firka. Mosaics, icons, coins, and other artifacts bring to life Cretan civilization as it was after the Roman Empire colonized the island. ✉ *Theotokopoulou 82* ☎ *28210/96046* *€2; combined ticket with Archaeological Museum €3* *Tues.–Sun. 8:30–3.*

The **Etz Hayyim Synagogue** is tucked away in what was once the Jewish ghetto, a warren of narrow lanes known as Evraki, just off the harbor south of the Firka. The building was formerly the Venetian church of St. Catherine; it became a synagogue in the 17th century. It was stripped of all religious objects by the Nazis; the church was restored in 1999. Hania's once sizable Jewish population was obliterated during World War II; many residents drowned when a British torpedo sunk the ship carrying them toward Auschwitz in 1944. The building contains Venetian Gothic arches, a *mikveh* (ritual bath), and the tombs of three rabbis. ✉ *Parodos Kondylaki* ☎ *28210/86286* *www.etz-hayyim-hania.org* *Free* *May–mid-Oct., weekdays 10–6; mid-Oct.–Apr., weekdays 9:30–2 (hrs may vary).*

Two of the city's museums are at the edge of the old city, amid a busy shopping district in the shadow of the Venetian walls. Artifacts on display at the **Archaeological Museum** come from all over western Crete: the painted Minoan clay coffins and elegant late Minoan pottery indicate that the region was as wealthy as the center of the island in the Bronze Age, though no palace has yet been located. The museum occupies the former Venetian church of St. Francis. ☒*Chalidron* ☎*28210/90334* *€2; combined admission with Byzantine and Post-Byzantine Collection €3* ⏲*Tues.–Sun. 8:30–3.*

A folklife museum, the **Cretan House** is bursting at the seams with farm equipment, tools, household items, wedding garb, and a wealth of other material reflecting the island's traditional heritage. Packed to the rafters as the stuffy house is, the collection is not nearly as extensive or of the same high quality as those in folk and history museums in Heraklion, Vori, and Rethymnon. ☒*Off courtyard at Chalidron 46, near Archaeological Museum* ☎*28210/90816* *€1.50* ⏲*Mon.–Sat. 9–3 and 6–9.*

★ The shop at **Ayia Triada** has some of the island's finest olive oils. Lands at the northeast corner of the Akrotiri peninsula, which extends into the sea from the east side of Hania, are the holdings of several monasteries. The olive groves that surround and finance the monasteries yield excellent oils. ✥*16 km (10 mi) north of Hania, follow road from Chordaki* ☎*No phone* ⏲*Daily 9–3.*

★ From the monastery at **Goubermetou,** on the north end of the Akrotiri peninsula, a path leads down the flanks of a seaside ravine past several caves used as hermitages and churches. A 20-minute walk brings you to the remote monastery of St. John the Hermit; follow the path along a riverbank for another 20 minutes or so to a delightful cove that is the perfect place for a refreshing dip. The return walk requires a steep uphill climb. ✥*19 km (12 mi) north of Hania, follow road north from Chordaki* ☎*No phone* *Free* ⏲*Daily 9–3.*

OFF THE BEATEN PATH

Samaria Gorge. South of Hania a deep, verdant crevice extends 10 km (6 mi) from near the village of Xyloskalo to the Libyan Sea. The landscape—of forest, sheer rock faces, and running streams—is magnificent. The Samaria is the most traveled of the dozens of gorges that cut through Crete's mountains and emerge at the sea, but the walk through it is thrilling nonetheless. Buses depart the central bus station in Hania at 7:30 and 8:30 AM for Xyloskalo. Boats leave in the afternoon from the mouth of the gorge (most people don't hike back up) at Ayia Roumeli for Hora Sfakion, from where buses return to Hania. Travel agents also arrange day trips to the gorge. ☒*25 km (15 mi) south of Hania, Omalos.*

BEACHES

A string of beaches extend west from the city center, and you can easily reach them on foot by following the sea past the old olive-oil factory just west of the walls and the Byzantine Museum. They are not idyllic, but the water is clean. Locals who want to spend a day at the beach often head out to the end of the Akrotiri peninsula, which extends north from the city's eastern suburbs, where **Kalathas** and **Stavros,** both about 15 km (9 mi) north of Hania, have excellent sand beaches. Part of *Zorba the Greek* was filmed at Stavros.

★ **Western Beaches.** Drive west from Hania to the magnificent beaches on the far coast, such as **Falasarna,** near Crete's northwestern tip, and **Elafonisi,** on the southwestern tip of the island. These are rarely crowded even in summer, perhaps because they are a bit off the beaten path. Elafonisi islet has white-sand beaches and black rocks in a turquoise sea (to get there you wade across a narrow channel). You can also head south from Hania across the craggy White Mountains to explore the isolated Libyan Sea villages of Paleochora, the area's main resort, and Souyia.

WHERE TO STAY & EAT

$–$$ ✕ **Apostolis.** What is reputed to be the freshest and best-prepared fish in town is served on a lively terrace toward the east end of the old harbor, near the Venetian arsenals. Choose your fish from the bed of ice and decide how you would like it prepared, or opt for the rich fish soup. ⊠*Akti Enoseos* ☎*28210/41767* ▭*MC, V.*

¢–$ ✕ **Faka.** Much to the delight of the many neighborhood residents who dine here regularly, Faka concentrates on traditional Cretan cooking. House specialties include *boureki,* a delicious casserole of zucchini, potato, and cheese; and *papoutsakia,* a baked dish with ground lamb, eggplant, and béchamel sauce. The generous meze platter is a meal in itself. ⊠*Off Archoleon, behind Venetian arsenals* ☎*28210/42341* ▭*MC, V.*

¢–$ ✕ **Tamam.** An ancient Turkish bath has been converted to one of the most atmospheric restaurants in Hania's old town. Specialties served up in the tiled dining room, and on the narrow lane outside, include peppers with grilled feta cheese and eggplant stuffed with chicken. ⊠*Zambeliou 49* ☎*28210/96080* ▭*No credit cards.*

¢–$ ✕ **Well of the Turk.** It's an adventure just finding this restaurant: ask passersby for help, because everyone in the neighborhood knows the place. Behind the Venetian warehouses on the harbor, it stands in a narrow alley near the minaret in the old Arab quarter. The food ranges from simple Greek fare (a prerequisite is the wonderful, large appetizer platter) to some Continental dishes, such as sautéed chicken in a wine sauce. ⊠*Kalinikou Sarpaki 1–3, Splantiza* ☎*28210/54547* ▭*No credit cards* ⏲*Closed Mon. year-round. Closed Tues. Nov.–Mar.*

$$$$ ★ **Casa Delfino.** In the 1880s this Venetian Renaissance palace was the home of Pedro Delfino, an Italian merchant; today it belongs to two of his descendants. The dramatically decorated guest rooms, four of which are housed in an adjoining building of the same era, are entered through graceful stone archways surrounding a courtyard paved in pebble mosaic. Most have upscale, contemporary wood furniture and rich fabrics, and distinctive architectural details—some occupy two levels, some have enormous marble baths, some have private terraces. ⊠*Theofanous 9, Palio Limani, 73100* ☎*28210/87400* 🖷*28210/96500* 🌐*www.casadelfino.com* *22 suites* *In-room: refrigerator, Ethernet. In-hotel: bar* ▭*AE, DC, MC, V* 🍽*BP.*

12

$$$$ **Villa Andromeda.** The German high command occupied this seaside villa during World War II (Rommel supposedly enjoyed the old swimming pool that is still next to a larger one in the garden). The yellow, neoclassic mansion contains large suites—some on two levels with sleeping areas upstairs—that overlook the garden or face the sea. Ornate painted ceilings, marble floors, and tapestry rugs add to the elegance of the communal spaces. ✉ *Eleftheriou Venizelou Sq. 150, 73100* ☎ *28210/28300 or 28210/28301* 📠 *28210/28303* 🌐 *www.villandromeda.gr* *8 suites* *In-room: refrigerator. In-hotel: bar, pool, no elevator* 💳 *DC, MC, V* *CP.*

$$$ ★ **Doma.** Feel at home for a night in a 19th-century seaside mansion on the eastern edge of town; it stands about a 20-minute walk along the water from the Venetian harbor. The simple guest rooms face either the luxuriant garden or the sea and have elegant, Cretan-style dark-wood furnishings. Carved-wood sofas and local and family photos fill the sitting room, and an exquisite collection of headdresses from around the world is displayed off the wicker-filled garden room. Breakfast, a lavish spread, includes fresh breads, homemade jams, and yogurt with a Turkish topping: a delicious mix of spices, quince preserves, and honey. On request the owners will prepare a traditional Cretan dinner for guests or nonguests and serve it in an airy upstairs dining room. ✉ *Eleftheriou Venizelou Sq. 124, 73100* ☎ *28210/51772 or 28210/51773* 📠 *28210/41578* 🌐 *www.hotel-doma.gr* *22 rooms, 4 suites* *In-room: refrigerator. In-hotel: bar* 💳 *DC, MC, V* *Closed Nov.–Mar.* *BP.*

$$–$$$ **Casa Leone.** A Venetian courtyard with a fountain, and a salon and balcony that hang over the harbor are among the dramatic flourishes at this 600-year-old mansion in the old town. The large and comfortable bedrooms are enhanced with modern baths and such details as curved walls, paneled ceilings, sleeping lofts, and private terraces. ✉ *Theotokopoulou 18, 73100* ☎📠 *28210/76762* 🌐 *www.casa-leone.com* *5 rooms* *In-room: refrigerator. In-hotel: bar, no elevator* 💳 *MC, V* *CP.*

$$ **Porto del Colombo.** This renovated Venetian town house, once the home of Greek prime minister Eleftherios Venizelos, is full of architectural surprises: wood ceilings and floors; small, deep-set windows; and two-story suites with lofts. The wood furnishings throughout are traditional Cretan. Weather permitting, breakfast is served on the narrow, old-town street out front. ✉ *Theofanous and Moshon, 73100* ☎📠 *28210/70945* 🌐 *www.ellada.net/colombo* *8 rooms, 2 suites* *In-room: refrigerator. In-hotel: bar, no elevator* 💳 *MC, V* *CP.*

$–$$ **Hotel Amphora.** Relax on the rooftop terrace and gaze out at views of the harbor, town, and mountains. This comfortable, well-run, and character-filled hotel is in a 14th-century Venetian mansion on a lane above the inner harbor. Rooms are large and many have sea views, as well as such extras as beamed ceilings, fireplaces, private balconies, and kitchenettes. The hotel offers a lavish buffet breakfast for €10, and the dining room, which is on the harbor-front promenade, serves excellent, basic Greek fare and good wines at a discount. ✉ *Parodos Theotokopoulou, 73100* ☎ *28210/93224* 📠 *28210/93226* 🌐 *www.amphora.*

gr 🛏 *20 rooms* 🛁 *In-room: kitchen (some). In-hotel: restaurant, no elevator* 💳 *AE, MC, V.*

SHOPPING

One or two souvenir stores on the waterfront sell English-language books and newspapers. The most exotic shopping experience in town is a stroll through Hania's covered market to see local merchants selling rounds of Cretan cheese, jars of golden honey, lengths of salami, salt fish, lentils, and herbs.

★ The silver jewelry and ceramics at **Carmela** (✉ *Odos Anghelou 7* ☎ *28210/90487*) are striking. The store represents contemporary jewelers and other craftspeople from Crete and throughout Greece, as well as the work of owner Carmela Iatropoulou.

★ **Top Hanas** (✉ *Odos Anghelou 3* ☎ *28210/98571*) sells a good selection of antique blankets and rugs, most of them made for dowries from homespun wool and natural dyes.

CRETE ESSENTIALS

TRANSPORTATION

BY AIR

Olympic Airways connects Athens, and other islands, with Heraklion, Hania, and Siteia. Aegean Airlines flies between Athens and Heraklion and Hania. Airfares have risen substantially in the past few years, and summertime flights from Athens to Crete are expensive—expect to pay at least twice as much (if not much, much more) than you would to make the trip by boat. Fares come down in winter, when special offers are also often available.

Carriers **Aegean Airlines** (☎ *801/112000 reservations within Greece [toll free], 28210/63366 in Hania, 2810/330475 in Heraklion* 🌐 *www.aegeanairlines.gr*). **Olympic Airways** (☎ *801/114444 reservations within Greece [toll free], 2810/244802 in Heraklion, 28210/57702 in Hania, 28430/24666 in Siteia* 🌐 *www.olympicairlines.com*).

AIRPORTS The principal arrival point on Crete is Heraklion Airport, where up to 16 flights daily arrive from Athens, daily flights arrive from Rhodes and Thessaloniki, and two weekly flights arrive from Mykonos. Heraklion is also serviced directly by charter flights from other European cities. There are several daily flights from Athens to Hania Airport, and several a week from Athens to Siteia, which is also connected to Rhodes with a few weekly flights in summer. In summer, Hania is also served by flights to and from other European cities, mostly charters.

Information **Hania Airport** (✉ *15 km [9 mi] northeast of Hania, off road to Sterne, Souda Bay* ☎ *28210/63264*). **Heraklion Airport** (✉ *5 km [3 mi] east of town, off road to Gournes, Heraklion* ☎ *2810/245644*). **Siteia Airport** (✉ *1 km [½mi] northwest of town, off main coast road, Siteia* ☎ *28430/24424*).

AIRPORT TRANSFERS A municipal bus just outside Heraklion Airport can take you to Eleftheriou Square in the Heraklion town center. Tickets are sold from a kiosk next to the bus stop; the fare is €0.80. From Hania Airport, Olympic Airlines buses take you to the airline office in the center for €2. Cabs line up outside all airports to meet flights; the fare into the respective towns is about €5 for Heraklion, €7 for Hania, and €4 for Siteia.

BY BIKE & MOPED

Be cautious: motorbike accidents account for numerous injuries among tourists every year. Reliable rentals can be arranged through Blue Sea Rentals in Heraklion, and you'll find rentals in just about any town on the tourist trail. Expect to pay about €20 a day for a 50cc moped, for which you will need to present only a valid driver's license; law requires a motorcycle license to rent larger bikes. Fees usually cover insurance, but only for repairs to the bike, and usually with a deductible of at least €500. The law, and common sense, mandate that you wear a helmet, but few riders do.

Contact **Blue Sea Rentals** (✉ *Kosmo Zoutou 5–7, Heraklion* ☎ *2810/241097* 🌐 *www.bluesearentals.com*).

BY BOAT & FERRY

Heraklion and Souda Bay (5 km [3 mi] east of Hania) are the island's main ports, and there is regular service as well to Rethymnon, Ayios Nikolaos, and Siteia. The most frequent service is on overnight crossings from these ports to and from Piraeus, though note that Hellenic Seaways runs high-speed, four-hour service between Piraeus and Hania in summer. Ferries also connect Crete with other islands, mostly those in the Cyclades and Dodecanese. Service includes Minoan Lines catamarans between Santorini and Heraklion (cutting travel time to just under two hours) and a ferry linking Siteia with the Dodecanese islands of Kassos, Karpathos, and Rhodes. There is also weekly service from Kalamata and Gythion in the Peloponnese to Kissamos (Kastelli) in the far west of the island. Ships also sail from Heraklion to Limassol, in Cyprus; to Haifa, Israel; and to Venice.

On the overnight runs, you can book either a berth or an airplane-style seat, and there are usually cafeterias, dining rooms, shops, and other services on board. The most economical berth accommodations are in four-berth cabins, which are relatively spacious and comfortable and are equipped with bathrooms. A one-way fare from Piraeus to Heraklion, Rethymnon, or Hania without accommodation costs about €22, and from about €50 with accommodation. A small discount is given for round-trip tickets. Car fares are about €70 each way, depending on vehicle size.

In July and August, a boat service around the Samaria gorge operates along the southwest coast from Hora Sfakion to Loutro, Ayia Roumeli, Souyia, Lissos, and Paleochora, the main resort on the southwest coast. Ferries also sail from Paleochora to Ghavdos, an island south of Crete, and from Ierapetra to Krissi, an island also to the south.

Most travel agencies sell tickets for all ferries and hydrofoils; make reservations several days in advance during the July to August high season.

Contacts **Anek (Piraeus to Heraklion, Rethymnon, and Hania)** (*✉ Karamanlis, Hania ☎ 28210/24163 ⊕ www.anek.gr*). **Anen (Peloponnese to Kissamos)** (*✉ Port, Kissamos ☎ 28210/20345 ⊕ www.anen.gr*). **Hellenic Seaways (Piraeus to Hania via high-speed catamaran)** (*✉ 25 Avgoustou, Heraklion ☎ 2810/346185 ⊕ www.hellenicseaways.gr*). **Lane (Piraeus to Ayios Nikolaos and Siteia)** (*⊕ www.lanesealines.gr*). **Minoan Lines (Piraeus to Heraklion)** (*✉ 25 Avgoustou, Heraklion ☎ 2810/346185 ⊕ www.ferries.gr/minoan*).

BY BUS

You can find schedules and book seats in advance at bus stations, and tourist offices are well equipped with schedules and information about service. As efficient as the bus network is, you might have a hard time getting out of Heraklion, what with its confusing multitude of stations: the bus station for western Crete is opposite the port; the station for the south is outside the Hania Gate to the right of the archaeological museum; and the station for the east is at the traffic circle at the end of Leoforos D. Bofor, close to the old harbor. Ask someone at the tourist information office to tell you exactly where to find your bus and to show you the spot on a map.

Information **KTEL** (*☎ 28410/22234 in Ayios Nikolaos, 28210/93052 in Hania, 2810/245020 in Heraklion, 28310/22785 in Rethymnon ⊕ www.ktel.org*).

BY CAR

Roads on Crete are not too congested, yet the accident rate is high compared to other parts of Europe. Driving in the main towns can be nerve-racking, to say the least. Most road signs are in Greek and English, though signage is often nonexistent or inadequate. Be sure to carry a road map at all times, and to stop and ask directions when the need arises—otherwise, you may drive miles out of your way. Gas stations are not plentiful outside the big towns, and gasoline is more expensive in Crete than it is in the United States—expect to pay about €1 a liter (about €4 a gallon).

Drive defensively wherever you are, as Cretan drivers are aggressive and liable to ignore the rules of the road. Sheep and goats frequently stray onto the roads, with or without their shepherd or sheepdog. In July and August, tourists on motor scooters can be a hazard. Night driving is not advisable.

CAR RENTALS You can arrange beforehand with a major agency in the United States or in Athens to pick up a car on arrival in Crete, or work through one of the many local car-rental agencies that have offices in the airports and in the cities, as well as in some resort villages. For the most part, these local agencies are extremely reliable, provide excellent service, and charge very low rates. Many, such as the excellent Crete Car Rental, will meet your ship or plane and drop you off again at no extra charge. Even without advance reservations, expect to pay about €40 or less a day in high season for a medium-size car with unlimited mileage.

Weekly prices are negotiable, but with unlimited mileage rentals start at about €200 in summer.

Contacts **Avis** (*www.avis.com* *Hania Airport* *28210/63080* *Heraklion Airport* *2810/229402*). **Crete Car Rental** (*28250/32690* *www.crete-car-rental.com*). **Hertz** (*www.hertz.com* *Heraklion Airport* *2810/330452*). **Sixt** (*Akti Konudourou 28, Ayios Nikolaos* *28410/82055* *www.sixt.com* *Hania Airport* *28210/20905* *Heraklion Airport* *2810/280915* *Ikariou 93, Heraklion* *2810/280915*).

12

CONTACTS & RESOURCES

EMERGENCIES

Your hotel can help you call an English-speaking doctor. Pharmacies stay open late by turns, and a list of those open late is displayed in their windows.

Emergency Services **Ambulance** (*166*). **Police (emergency)** (*100*). **Hospitals** (*28410/66000 in Ayios Nikolaos, 28210/22000 in Hania, 2810/368000 in Heraklion, 28310/87100 in Rethymnon*). **Tourist Police** (*171 central operator, 28410/26900 in Ayios Nikolaos, 28210/5332 in Hania, 2810/289614 in Heraklion, 28310/28156 in Rethymnon*).

MEDIA

English-language books, magazines, and newspapers are available in the major towns and resorts, but difficult to find once you get off the well-beaten tourist path. In some of the larger hotels you may find CNN, Star News, or other English-language television broadcasts from the United States and the United Kingdom.

English-Language Bookstores **Astrakianakis** (*Eleftheriou Venizelou Sq., Heraklion* *2810/284248*). **International Press Bookshop** (*Eleftheriou Venizelou Sq. 26, Rethymnon*). **Kouvidis-Manouras** (*Daidalou 6, Heraklion* *2810/220135*).

MAIL & SHIPPING

Post offices are generally open weekdays 7:30–2. You can often buy stamps at magazine kiosks.

Contacts **Post offices** (*Tzanakaki 3, Hania* *Daskaloyianni Sq., Heraklion* *Koundourioti, Rethymnon*).

TOUR OPTIONS

Resort hotels and large agents, such as Canea Travel, organize guided tours in air-conditioned buses to the main Minoan sites; excursions to spectacular beaches such as Vai in the northeast and Elafonisi in the southwest; and trips to Santorini and to closer islands such as Spinalonga, a former leper colony off Ayios Nikolaos. El Greco Tours organizes hikes through the Samaria gorge and other local excursions. The Crete Travel Web site is an excellent one-stop source for tour information, with insights on many of the island's more-worthwhile sights and tours including hiking excursions and visits to out-of-the-way monasteries, as well as car rental and distinctive accommodation information.

A tour of Knossos and the Archaeological Museum in Heraklion costs about €40; a tour of Phaistos and Gortyna plus a swim at Matala costs about €20; a trip to the Samaria gorge costs about €25. Travel agents can also arrange for personal guides, whose fees are negotiable.

Contacts **Canea Travel** (✉ *Bonaili 12–13, Hania* ☎ *28210/52301*). **Crete Travel** (✉ *Monaho, Armenoi Chanion* ☎ *28250/32690* 🌐 *www.cretetravel.com*). **El Greco Tours** (✉ *Theotokopoulou 50, Hania* ☎ *28210/86018* 🌐 *www.elgrecotours.com*).

VISITOR INFORMATION

Tourist offices are more plentiful, and more helpful, on Crete than they are in many other parts of Greece. Offices of the Greek National Tourism Organization (GNTO or EOT), in the major towns, are open daily 8–2 and 3–8:30. The municipalities of Ayios Nikolaos, Siteia, and Ierapetra operate their own tourist offices, and these provide a wealth of information on the towns and surrounding regions, as well as helping with accommodation and local tours; most keep long summer hours, open daily 8:30 AM–9 PM.

Contacts **Ayios Nikolaos** (✉ *Koundourou 21A* ☎ *28410/22357*). **Greek National Tourism Organization** (✉ *Xanthoudidou 1, Heraklion* ☎ *2810/246106* 🌐 *www.gnto.gr* ✉ *Odos Kriari 40, Hania* ☎ *28210/92624* ✉ *Sofokli Venizelou, Rethymnon* ☎ *28310/56350*). **Siteia** (✉ *Port* ☎ *28300/23775*).

Rhodes & the Dodecanese

KOS, SYMI & PATMOS

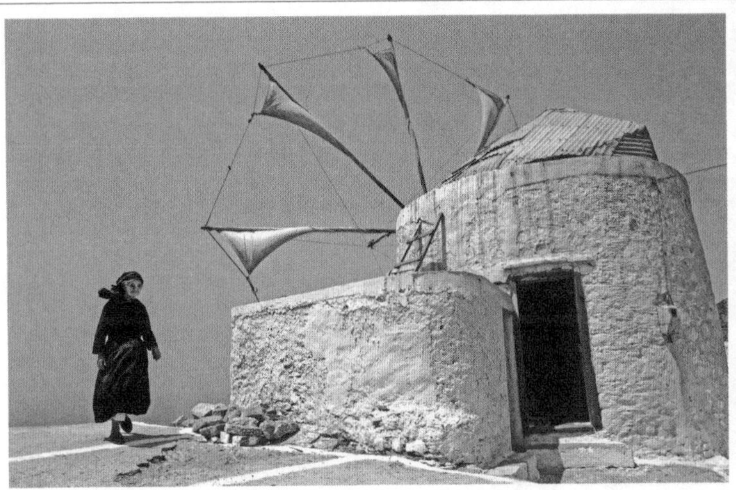

Karpathos

WORD OF MOUTH

"Water parks, discos, nightclubs, crowded resorts? Yes, they exist but we didn't go looking for them. We spent a perfectly pleasant week on Rhodes with plenty to explore, good beaches to relax on, and good food, too—it is still possible to find all the things that attracted people to the island in the first place. Kos town was well worth a visit—for anyone who enjoys wandering around ruins, there were plenty, from 2,000-year-old Greek and Roman remains, to a huge Crusader castle."

—Maria_H

www.fodors.com/forums

WELCOME TO RHODES & THE DODECANESE

TOP REASONS TO GO

★ **Medieval Might:** As much as sun and sand, the monuments the Knights of St. John built some 700 years ago are what draw visitors to Rhodes—no more so than its walled-in Old Town, a remarkably well-preserved and photogenic testimony to the Crusader past.

★ **Healing Hippocrates:** Kos's site of ancient healing, the Asklepieion, was the renowned medical school founded by Hippocrates, father of Western medicine.

★ **Natural Wonders:** The terrain yields butterflies (Rhodes), hot sea springs (Kos), countless coves (Patmos), and mountain paths (Symi).

★ **St. John's Patmos:** Called the "Jerusalem of the Aegean," Patmos is as peaceful as it was when the Apostle John glimpsed the Apocalypse in his cave here—the spiritual mystique of this little island is still strong.

1 Rhodes. Start, like the crusading Knights of St. John did, with the walled city of Rhodes' Old Town with its monuments, shops, and restaurants. Heading south around the island, discover the moth-mecca of the Valley of the Butterflies in Petaloudes, then take the island's mountainous western road to ancient Kameiros city and medieval Monolithos fortress. The eastern road leads to lovely, car-free Lindos and many, many beaches.

Palace of the Grand Masters, Rhodes town

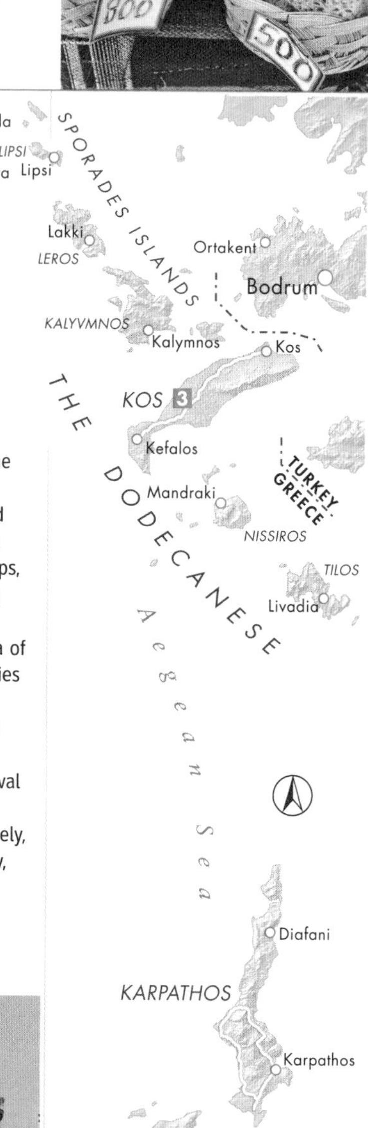

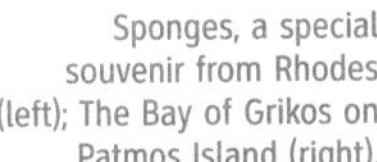

Sponges, a special souvenir from Rhodes (left); The Bay of Grikos on Patmos Island (right).

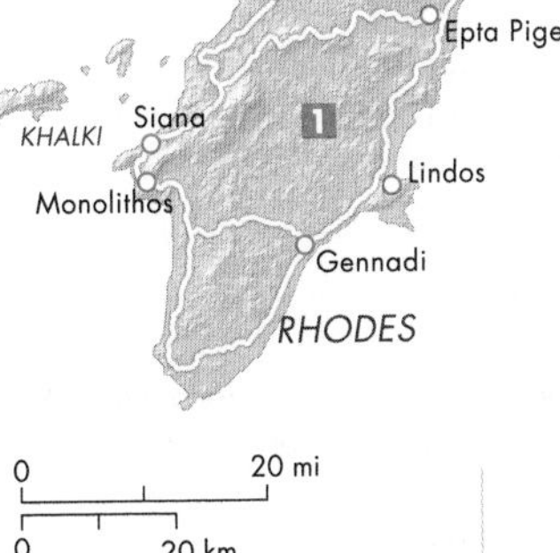

Picturesque" is
ɔr both Yialos
ı its restaurants
and Chorio
t above it. The
d is populated
small churches.
sive Panormitis
is a popular site,
boats.

e port town is
nd of ancient
Northern Euro-
ing teens. A short
f town, Asklepie-
ɔn was once the
greatest heal-
ing site of
the ancient
era. Large
swaths of coast
are perfect for
wimming.

. Make your
to Chora to
e and the sur-
onastery of the
, hallowed by the
f St. John. Tower-
ıora's skyline is
the imposing, fortified Monastery of St. John the Theologian, Skala, a pleasant—if modest—harbor.

GETTING ORIENTED

The Dodecanese (Twelve Islands), wrapped enticingly around the shores of Turkey and Asia Minor, are the easternmost holdings of Greece. Here, classic, Byzantine, and Ottoman architectures deliciously blend and multiculturalism is an old idea. Large, varied Rhodes is the vital linchpin, where Romans, Crusaders, Turks, and Venetians have all left their marks. Heading out, the traveler can discover the cypress-clad hillsides of Patmos, the craggy shoreline of Symi, and the holiday vibe (and lush fields) of Kos.

Agios Stefanos on Kos island

RHODES & THE DODECANESE PLANNER

When to Go

To avoid crowds, just before and after peak seasons (May–June and September) are good seasons to visit.

From October to May, though most archaeological places remain open, most hotels, restaurants, and shops are closed.

On the off-season, resorts go dead and boat travel is limited by the weather's whims. Patmos is packed at Easter.

Getting There

Though you can get to the hubs of Rhodes or Kos in under 10 hours nowadays on the faster boats, if there is limited time, it's best to fly to the airports on these two islands.

Make sure, however, for good rates and an assured spot that you book as far as possible (at least two weeks) in advance.

The big, 15-hours-plus boat rides from the mainland offer both romance and duress.

Remember that deck class passengers claim key spots on the floor, in the lounge areas, and even—in peak season—on the metal deck under the stars.

Pick a Beach, Any Beach

In the Dodecanese it's never hard to find a beautiful beach, or at least a rock from which to swim. Most islands have a beach for every mood. Although many beaches on Rhodes and Kos have been developed to the last grain of sand, on Rhodes the sheltered southeastern coast has long, exquisite, and undeveloped stretches of fine sand. The Gulf of Kefalos on Kos is a haven for those wishing to escape the tourist fray—broad, sandy, scenically magnificent, and for much of its length devoid of development, curving around an enchanting bay. One of the pleasures of being on Patmos is to seek out yet another perfect beach every day: in the morning, caïques make regular runs from Skala to several of the beaches; some can be reached by car or bus, and many delightfully empty strands are the reward for a short trek on foot. The rocky shores of Symi provide many a cove for superb swimming. When you ask your hotel or restaurant for the best beach, include information about what exactly you are seeking—crowds or isolation, shallow water or depths, sand or pebbles. Beach umbrellas and deck chairs are usually rented out (€8–€10), but spread out your towel on the beach instead if you prefer.

Finding a Place to Stay

Except for Athens, Rhodes has more hotels per capita than anywhere else in Greece. Most of them are resort or tourist hotels, with sea views and easy access to beaches. High season can prove extremely crowded and you may have difficulty finding a room in Rhodes if you don't book well in advance. However, there is such a plethora of resort hotels that some remain part-empty, even at the summer's peak. Mass tourist accommodations are also plentiful on Kos but, as in Rhodes, most lodging isn't especially Greek in style. Symi has more small hotels with charm, since the island never encouraged the development of mammoth caravansaries. Similarly, Patmos has attractive, high-quality lodgings that tend to be both more elegant and traditional than its resort-magnet neighbors. It also has a lot of rented rooms—and it is standard practice to check them out before booking.

Proceed with Caution

Unfortunately, because Rhodes and Kos attract so many thousands of tourists, it is easy to sometimes be treated as a number and get ripped off. You can avoid this by avoiding touristy cafés or restaurants, by confirming prices (especially taxis, boats, and sports-equipment rental) in advance, and having the tourist police number handy—and dialing it on the spot if need be.

Dining and Drinking, Dodecanese Style

Throughout the Dodecanese, especially on Rhodes, you can find sophisticated restaurants, as well as simple tavernas serving excellent food. It is sometimes best to wait until after 9 PM to see where the Greeks are eating. Fish, of course, is readily available on all islands. Tiny, tender Symi shrimp, found only in the waters around this island, have such soft shells they can be easily popped in the mouth whole. They are used in dozens of local dishes. Wherever you dine, ask about the specialty of the day, and check the food on display in the kitchen of tavernas. Large fish goes by the kilo, so confirm the exact amount you'd like when ordering. Finally, it is safest to order wine or beer instead of cocktails, as unscrupulous places often serve impure alcohol.

Dining & Lodging Prices in Euros

	¢	$	$$	$$$	$$$$
Restaurants	under €8	€8–€11	€11–€15	€15–€20	over €20
Hotels	under €60	€60–€90	€90–€120	€120–€160	over €160

Restaurant prices are for one main course at dinner, or for two mezedes (small dishes). Hotel prices are for a standard double room in high season, including taxes. Hotels operate on the European Plan (EP, with no meal provided) unless we note that they use the Continental Plan (CP, with Continental breakfast); Breakfast Plan (BP, with a full breakfast); Modified American Plan (MAP, with breakfast and dinner); or the Full American Plan (FAP, with all meals). Inquire when booking if these meal plans (which can entail higher rates) are mandatory. Guest rooms have air-conditioning, room phones, and TVs unless otherwise noted.

Getting Around

Renting a car (for €30–€40 a day) is very useful for exploring Rhodes or Kos, or to hop between Patmos's many beaches. (Make sure it's unlimited mileage, and that the engine has the power for hills!) In Symi, with its one road, a car is of little use and you should opt for the adorable van that serves as the island bus.

The bigger islands and Patmos have regular (if morning-oriented) bus service to sites and beaches. Radio taxis can be slow in coming. It's possible to travel to some spots by boat on Symi and Patmos (be sure to check prices in advance).

If you island-hop through the Dodecanese islands for the day, confirm the return boat schedule, as smaller islands have limited boats.

Feeling Festive?

In Greece, culture shifts to the islands in the summer. On Rhodes, the free international Ecofilms festival of environmental film takes place in late June.

A rich schedule of music and theater is featured at Kos's Ippokratia festival (July–September) and the Symi Festival (June–September).

Patmos's high-profile Festival of Sacred Music brings Byzantine and classical music to the amphitheater outside the Apocalypse Monastery (September).

Updated by Angelike Contis

LYING AT THE EASTERN EDGE of the Aegean Sea, wrapped enticingly around the shores of Turkey and Asia Minor, is the southernmost group of Greek islands, the Dodecanese (Twelve Islands), sometimes known as the Southern Sporades. The archipelago has long shared a common history: Romans, Crusaders, Turks, and Venetians left their mark with temples, castles, and fortresses in exotic towns of shady lanes and tall houses. Of the 12 islands, 4 are highlighted here: strategically located Rhodes has played by far the most important role in history and was for many years one of the most popular vacation spots in the Mediterranean. Kos comes in second in popularity and has vestiges of antiquity; the Sanctuary of Asklepios, a center of healing, drew people from all over the ancient world. Symi is a virtual museum of 19th-century neoclassical architecture almost untouched by modern development, and Patmos, where St. John wrote his *Revelation,* became a renowned monastic center during the Byzantine period and continues as a significant focal point of the Greek Orthodox faith. Symi and Patmos both have a peace and quiet that in large part has been lost on overdeveloped Rhodes and Kos. But despite the invasion of sunseekers, there are still delightful pockets of local color throughout the Dodecanese.

EXPLORING RHODES & THE DODECANESE

Rhodes and Kos unfold in fertile splendor, creased with streams and dotted with large stretches of green; their major towns sit next to the sea on almost flat land, embracing exceptionally large and well-protected harbors facing the mainland of Asia Minor. Both islands are worth visiting for a couple of days each. Patmos and Symi, however, resemble in some ways more the Cycladic islands: rugged hills and mountains are almost devoid of vegetation, with villages and towns clinging in lovely disarray to craggy landscapes. Symi is the closest island to Rhodes, an easy 50-minute hydrofoil ride away.

RHODES ΡΟΔΟΣ

Rhodes (1,400 square km [540 square mi]) is the fourth-largest Greek island and, along with Sicily and Cyprus, one of the great islands of the Mediterranean. It lies almost exactly halfway between Piraeus and Cyprus, 18 km (11 mi) off the coast of Asia Minor, and it was long considered a bridge between Europe and the East. Geologically similar to the Turkish mainland, it was probably once a part of it, separated by one of the frequent volcanic upheavals this volatile region has experienced.

Rhodes saw successive waves of settlement, including the arrival of the Dorian Greeks from Argos and Laconia early in the 1st millennium BC. From the 8th to the 6th century BC Rhodian cities established settlements in Italy, France, Spain, and Egypt and actively traded with mainland Greece, exporting pottery, oil, wine, and figs. Independence and expansion came to a halt when the Persians took over the island at the end of the 6th century BC and forced Rhodians to provide ships

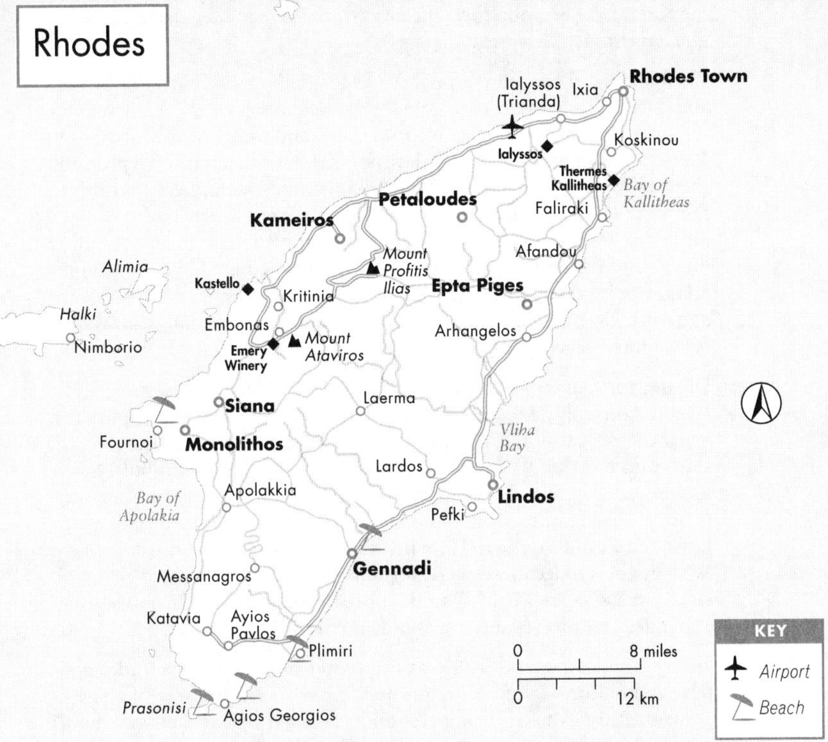

and men for King Xerxes's failed attack on the mainland (480 BC). A league of city-states rose under Athenian leadership. In 408 BC the united city of Rhodes was created on the site of the modern town; much of the populace moved there, and the history of the island and the town became synonymous. As the new city grew and flourished, its political organization became the model for the city of Alexandria in Egypt.

In 42 BC, Rhodes came under the hegemony of Rome, and through the years of the empire it was fabled as a beautiful city where straight roads were lined with porticoes, houses, and gardens. According to Pliny, who described the city in the 1st century AD, the town possessed some 2,000 statues, at least 100 of them of colossal scale. One of the most famous examples of the island's sculptural school is the *Laocöon*—probably executed in the 1st century BC—which showed the priest who warned the Trojans to beware of Greeks bearing gifts (it stands in the Vatican today). The ancient glory of Rhodes has few visible remnants. The city was ravaged by Arab invaders in AD 654 and 807, and only with the expulsion of the Arabs, and the reconquest of Crete by the Byzantine emperors, did the city begin to revive. Rhodes was a crucial stop on the road to the Holy Land during the Crusades. It came briefly under Venetian influence, then Byzantine, then Genoese. In 1309, when the Knights of St. John took the city from its Genoese masters, its most glorious modern era began.

The Knights of St. John, an order of Hospitalers, organized to protect and care for Christian pilgrims. By the beginning of the 12th century the order had become military in nature, and after the fall of Acre in 1291, the Knights fled from Palestine, withdrawing first to Cyprus and then to Rhodes. In 1312 the Knights inherited the immense wealth of the Templars (another religious military order, which had just been outlawed by the pope) and used it to fortify Rhodes. But for all their power and the strength of their walls, moats, and artillery, the Knights could not hold back the Turks. In 1522 the Ottomans, with 300 ships and 100,000 men under Süleyman the Magnificent, began what was to be the final siege, taking the city after six months.

During the Turkish occupation, Rhodes became a possession of the Grand Admiral, who collected taxes but left the Rhodians to pursue a generally peaceful and prosperous existence. They continued to build ships and to trade with Greece, Constantinople (later Istanbul), Syria, and Egypt. The Greek mainland was liberated by the War of Independence in 1821, but Rhodes and the Dodecanese remained part of the Ottoman Empire until 1912, when the Italians took over. After World War II, the Dodecanese were formally united with Greece in 1947. In the years post–World War II, tourism became king, Rhodes town expanded, and the island's farming activities shrank.

Today Rhodes retains its role as the center of Dodecanese trade, politics, and culture. Its diversity ensures it remains a polestar of tourism as well: Rhodes town brings together fascinating artifacts, medieval architecture, and an active nightlife. The island's east coast is blessed with white-sand beaches and dotted with copses of trees, interspersed with fertile valleys full of figs and olives. And though some of the shore is beset by vast resort hotels and holiday villages, there are still some wonderfully unsullied sections of beach to be found all around the island; if you look for it, you'll even find a taste of rural life.

RHODES TOWN ΡΟΔΟΣ (ΠΟΛΗ)

Fodor'sChoice ★

463 km (287 mi) east of Piraeus.

Early travelers described Rhodes as a town of two parts: a castle or high town (Collachium) and a lower city. Today Rhodes town is still a city of two parts: the Old Town, a UNESCO World Heritage site that incorporates the high town and lower city, contains Orthodox and Catholic churches, Turkish structures, and houses, some of which follow the ancient orthogonal plan. Public buildings are all similar in style: staircases are on the outside, either on the facade or in the court; the facades are elegantly constructed of well-cut limestone from Lindos; windows and doors are often outlined with strongly profiled moldings and surmounted by arched casements. Careful reconstruction in recent years has enhanced the harmonious effect. Spreading away from the walls that encircle the Old Town is the modern metropolis, or new town.

In the castle area, a city within a city, the Knights of St. John built most of their monuments. The **Palace of the Grand Masters,** at the highest spot of the medieval city, is the best place to begin a tour of Rhodes; here you can get oriented before wandering through the labyrinthine Old Town. Of great help is the permanent exhibition downstairs, with extensive displays, maps, and plans showing the layout of the city. The palace building withstood unscathed the Turkish siege, but in 1856, an explosion of ammunition stored nearby in the cellars of the Church of St. John devastated it; the present structures are 20th-century Italian reconstructions. Note the Hellenistic and Roman mosaic floors throughout, which came from the Italian excavations in Kos. ✉*Ippoton, Old Town* ☎*22410/25500* 🎫*€6* ⏲*May–Oct., Mon. 12:30–7, Tues.–Sun. 8–7:30; Nov.–Apr., Tues.–Sun. 8–3.*

Before the court of the Palace of the Grand Masters is the **Loggia of St. John,** on the site where the Knights of St. John were buried in an early church. From the loggia, the **Street of the Knights** *(Ippoton)* descends toward the **Commercial Port,** bordered on both sides by the **Inns of the Tongues,** where the Knights supped and held their meetings.

The **Inn of France** was the largest of the Knights' gathering spots and is now the French Consulate. The facade is carved with flowers and heraldic patterns and bears an inscription that dates the building between 1492 and 1509. ✉*About halfway down St. of the Knights from Loggia of St. John.*

The hospital, the largest of the Knights' public buildings, was completed in 1489. The imposing facade opens into a courtyard, where cannonballs remain from the siege of 1522. Today it contains the **Archaeological Museum.** On the main floor there's a collection of ancient pottery and sculpture, including two well-known representations of Aphrodite: the *Aphrodite of Rhodes,* who, while bathing, pushes aside her hair as if she's listening; and a standing figure, known as *Aphrodite Thalassia,* or "of the sea," as she was discovered in the water off the northern city beach. Other important works include a 6th-century BC *kouros* (a statue of an idealized male youth, usually nude) that was found in Kameiros, and the beautiful 5th-century BC funerary stela of Timarista bidding farewell to her mother, Crito. ✉*Mouseou Sq.* ☎*22410/25500* 🎫*€3* ⏲*Tues.–Sun. 8:30–2:40.*

The **Byzantine Museum** collection of icons is displayed within the 11th-century Lady of the Castle church. ✉*Off Mouseou Sq.* ☎*22410/25500* 🎫*€2* ⏲*Tues.–Sun. 8:30–2:40.*

The **Museum of Decorative Arts** exhibits finely made ceramics, crafts, and artifacts from around the Dodecanese. ✉*Argyrokastrou Sq.* ☎*22410/25500* 🎫*€2* ⏲*Tues.–Sun. 8:30–2:40.*

The **Mosque of Süleyman,** (✉*At top of Sokratous* ☎*22410/24918* 🎫*Free*) was built circa 1522 and rebuilt in 1808. At this writing, the restored building was open primarily to groups, by appointment only.

SEE MORE AND SAVE

Plan on hitting all the old-town attractions? Purchase a multi-sight ticket (€10) which gets you admission to the Palace of the Grand Masters, Archaeological Museum, Museum of Decorative Arts, and Byzantine Museum.

The **Turkish Library** dates to the late 18th century. Striking reminders of the Ottoman presence, the library and the mosque are still used by those members of Rhodes's Turkish community who stayed behind after the 1923 population exchange, a mass repatriation of Greek and Turkish migrants after their countries' second war. ✉*Sokratous, opposite Mosque of Süleyman* ☎*22410/74090* 🎫*Free* ⏲*Mon.–Sat. 9:30–4.*

The **walls** of Rhodes in themselves are one of the great medieval monuments in the Mediterranean. Wonderfully restored, they illustrate the engineering capabilities as well as the financial and human resources available to the Knights. (The 20th-century Italian rulers erased much of the Ottoman influence, preferring to emphasize the Knights' past when restoring architecture.) For 200 years the Knights strengthened the walls by thickening them, up to 40 feet in places, and curving them so as to deflect cannonballs. The moat between the inner and outer walls never contained water; it was a device to prevent invaders from constructing siege towers. Part of the road that runs the 4 km (2½ mi) along the top of the walls is usually accessible through municipal **guided tours** (✉*Tours depart from Palace of the Grand Masters entrance in Ippoton, Old Town* ☎*22410/23359*); however, at the time of this writing, the walls were closed temporarily. You can get a sense of the enclosed city's massive scale by walking inside the moat. ✉*Old Town; moat entrances include gate near sound-and-light show* 🎫*Moat free.*

The soaring vaults of the ruins of **Our Lady of the Bourg,** once a magnificent Gothic church, are a startling reminder of Rhodes's Frankish past. ✉*Inside remains of walls, access through Panagias Gate.*

NEED A BREAK?

Partake in an Ottoman-era ritual by visiting Rhodes's Hammam ✉*Arionos Sq.* ☎*22410/27739* 🎫*€1.50* ⏲*Weekdays 10–5, Sat. 8–5*) , built in 1515 and open all year long for steam therapy. Locals visit the traditional Turkish-style public baths (with separate male and female facilities) to soothe arthritis, circulation problems, and muscle aches. Walk-in bathers start in a warm room, then pass into a hotter room, where they "steam" for hours before cooling off with a shower and a massage (€5). A wood-stoked fire heats the stone building, which is very stark apart from the carved stars in the domed shower area. ⚠Check with your doctor before visiting, as the temperatures get very high.

The **commercial harbor,** at the "mouth" of the Old Town, is Rhodes's largest. The port authority and customs offices are here. ✉*Near St. Catherine's Gate.*

The medieval Old Town of Rhodes is now completely surrounded by the **new town.** The city first spread outside town walls during Otto-

Continued on page 608

NECTAR OF THE GODS

The roots of Greek wine run deep: Naughty Dionysus partied his way through mythology as the God of Wine and became a symbol for celebration in Greece. During the ancient festivities called Dionysia, husbands and wives alike let loose and drank themselves to a heady joy. Now that you're in the land of the god, be sure to enjoy some liquid Dionysian delights. Greece's wine is flavorful and original, so much so that some of the wines here you won't find anywhere else.

This is one reason why few can resist taking some bottles home (a bottle of excellent Greek wine will cost at least €15 to €20, but good varieties can be found for around €10). Remember to ask the clerk to pad them with bubble wrap so they won't break in your suitcase on the journey back. Following are some tips about vintners who are leading the new Greek renaissance of wine making, along with a rundown of the grape varietals that Grecian wineries specialize in.

THE GREEK WINES TO LOOK FOR

WHITES

Assyrtiko. One of Greece's finest white wines and found mainly in Santorini, Attica, and Macedonia, it is rich and dry with honeysuckle and citrus aromas and an earthy aftertaste. Pair with grilled fish, poultry, or pork and feta.

Athiri. One of the oldest Greek varieties and found mainly in Santorini, Macedonia, Attica, and Rhodes, it is vibrant and fruity with tropical fruit and honey tones. Pair with poultry or pork, pasta, grilled fish, or white cheeses.

Moschofilero. Originating in the Peloponnese, it is vivid and has rich fruity and floral aromas. Pair with poultry, pasta, and seafood.

Roditis. Popular in Attica, Macedonia, Thessaly, and Peloponnese, it is light and has vibrant scents of pineapple, pear, melon, and jasmine. Pair with poultry, fish, and mild cheeses.

Rombola. Grown in the Ionian island of Cephalonia, it is scented with citrus and peach and has a lemony aftertaste. Pair with fish or poultry.

Savatiano. Cultivated in Attica, it is full-bodied with fruity tones of apple, pear, and peach. Pair with poultry, pork, or fish as well as soft white cheeses.

White Muscat. Cultivated on the Aegean island of Samos and in the northern Peloponnese city of Patras, it is sweet and intense. Pair with desserts and ice cream.

REDS

Aghiorgitiko. The name means St. George and it's mainly found in the Nemea region of the Peloponnese. Richly colored and scented, with scents of sour cherries and pomegranate, it goes well with red meat and yellow soft cheeses.

Kotsifali. Grown mainly in Crete, it is rich and aromatic, with hints of raisins, prunes, and sage. Pair with red meat, light red sauces, and yellow cheeses.

Mantelaria. Mainly cultivated in Rhodes and Crete, it is rich and intense, with hints of pomegranate. Pair with grilled and stewed meats with spicy sauces and mild cheeses.

Mavrodaphne. Found in the Peloponnese regions of Achaia and Ilia and the Ionian Islands, it is a lovely dessert wine. Drink alone or with a light dessert.

Xinomavro. Found in Macedonia, it is rich, acidic, and bursting with aromas such as gooseberry with hints of olives and spices. Pair with grilled meats, casseroles, and yellow spicy cheeses.

WHEN IN RHODES...

Today, Rhodes has become a vibrant wine culture center. While its viticultural history goes back to the ancient Phoenicians, its vintages have become newly popular, thanks to its two delicious grape varieties, the Mandilaria and the aromatic Athiri, and the good showing of the native sweet Muscats. The Cair cooperative produces most of the island's wine, including first-rate Mandilaria and Athiri, as well as reds such as Xinomavro, Cabernet, Grenache, and Syrah. The most prominent winemaking force on the island is the Triantafyllou family, who opened the groundbreaking boutique Emery winery in the village of Embonas (www.emery.gr; see Siana in this chapter). The family has received notice for its Granrose made from Dimitina, a type of Mandelaria. Other top Emery wines include Athiri Vounouplagias, Rodofili, and Zacosta.

PICK OF THE VINE

Wherever you head in Greece, winemakers are perfecting the millennia-old traditions of Greek wine, with high-class estates such as Gaia, Boutari, and Porto Carras leading the way. These wineries can all be visited by appointment. A good introductory Web site is www.allaboutgreekwine.com.

Crete, Nikolaos Douloufakis. He is gaining attention with his Vilana 2000, with its spicy aromas and hints of banana and clementine. He comes from an established winemaking family in Dafnes (www.cretanwines.gr), near the major city of Heraklion in Crete. (His grandfather, Dimitris Douloufakis, used to transport his wine in goatskin when he began in the 1930s.)

Cyclades, Haridimos Hatzidakis. On Santorini, his winery (www.hatzidakiswines.gr) near Pyrgos Kallistis is comprised of a celebrated set of organic vineyards. One of his top organic wines is the Aidani Assyritiko, a dry fruity white.

Macedonia, Yiannis Boutaris. Up north, in Naoussa, Imathia wine lovers make a beeline to Yiannis's Ktima Kir-Yianni winery (www.kiryianni.gr). He split from his family's estate ten years ago to concentrate on producing standout dry reds.

CLOSE UP

The Great Colossus

At the end of the 4th century BC the Rhodians commissioned the sculptor Chares, from Lindos, to create the famous Colossus, a huge bronze statue of the sun god, Helios, and one of the Seven Wonders of the Ancient World. Two bronze deer statues mark the spot where legend says the Colossus once straddled the Mandraki harbor entrance. The 110-foot-high statue only stood for half a century. In 227 BC, when an earthquake razed the city and toppled the Colossus, help poured in from all quarters of the eastern Mediterranean. After the calamity the Delphic oracle advised the Rhodians to let the great Colossus remain where it had fallen. So there it rested for some eight centuries, until AD 654 when it was sold as scrap metal and carted off to Syria allegedly by a caravan of 900 camels. After that, nothing is known of its fate.

man domination. Today, there are many circa 1950s–1970s buildings that resemble those in Athens, though they have fewer stories overall. ✉*North of Old Town walls, bordering Mandraki harbor.*

The city's municipal buildings, an open-air bazaar, and the main shopping areas are along **Mandraki harbor.** The Governor's Palace is constructed in an arcaded Venetian Gothic style.

The town's cathedral, **Evangelismos Church,** which is modeled after the destroyed Church of St. John in the Collachium, dominates the waterfront. ✉*New town* ☎*22410/77916* ⏲*Church daily 7–noon and 5–7:30.*

Mt. Smith rises about 2 km (1 mi) to the west of the town center. Villas and gardens dot its slopes, but many more of them have been torn down to make way for modern apartment buildings. For a dramatic view, walk to the westernmost edge of Mt. Smith, which drops via a sharp and almost inaccessible cliff to the shore below, now lined with enormous hotels.

Atop Mt. Smith are the freely accessible ruins of the **acropolis.** These include a heavily restored **theater,** a **stadium,** the three restored columns of the **Temple of Apollo Pythios,** and the scrappy remains of the **Temple of Athena Polias.** ✉*Mt. Smith* ☎*No phone.*

As you travel south along the east coast, a strange sight meets you: the buildings of the **Thermes Kallitheas** (✉*10 km [6 mi] south of Rhodes town*) look as if they have been transplanted from Morocco. In fact, this mosaic-tile bath complex was built in 1929 by the Italians. As far back as the early 2nd century BC, area mineral springs were prized; the great physician Hippocrates of Kos extolled the springs for alleviating liver, kidney, and rheumatic ailments. Though the baths are no longer in use, you can visit the restored ornate **rotunda** (☎*22410/65691* 🌐*www.kalithea.gr* 🎫*€2.50* ⏲*Apr.–Oct., daily 8–8, Nov.–Mar., daily 8–3*), which houses exhibits. You can also swim on the nearby beach.

BEACHES

The beach at **Elli** (✉ *North of Old Town, near Rhodes Yacht Club*) has fine sand; an easy slope; chairs, umbrellas, and pedal boats for rent; showers; and plenty of sunbathing tourists. All of the coast around Rhodes town is developed, so you can reach some of the best beaches only through the hotels that occupy them.

WHERE TO STAY & EAT

$$$$ ★ ✕ **Ta Kioupia.** In a group of humble farm buildings, Ta Kioupia is anything but modest. The white-stucco rooms with exposed ceiling beams exude rustic elegance: antique farm tools are on display, and linen tablecloths, fine china, and crystal set the tables. In summer you dine in an enclosed garden. Food is presented on large platters and you select what you fancy: pine-nut salad, *tiropita* (four-cheese pie), an eggplant dip that regulars say can't be beat, cheese-and-nut *bourekakia* (stuffed phyllo pastries), *kokorosouvlaki* (rooster kebab) … the list goes on; the food is extraordinary in its variety and quality. ✉ *7 km (4½ mi) west of Rhodes town, Tris* ☎ *22410/91824* ✍ *Reservations essential* ▭ *AE, DC, MC, V* ⊙ *Closed Sun. No lunch.*

$$$–$$$$ ★ ✕ **Dinoris.** The great hall that holds Dinoris was built in AD 310 as a hospital and then converted into a stable for the Knights in 1530. The fish specialties and the spacious, classy setting lure appreciative and demanding clients, from the mayor to hotel owners and visiting VIPs. For appetizers, try the variety platter, which includes *psarokeftedakia* (fish balls made from a secret recipe) as well as mussels, shrimp, and lobster. Other special dishes are sea urchin salad and grilled calamari stuffed with cheese. In warm months, cool sea air drifts through the outdoor garden area enclosed by part of the city's walls. ✉ *Mouseou Sq. 14a* ☎ *22410/25824* ✍ *Reservations essential* ▭ *AE, MC, V* ⊙ *Closed Jan.*

$$–$$$ ★ ✕ **Alexis.** Continuing the tradition begun by his father in 1957, Yiannis Katsimprakis serves the very best seafood and speaks passionately of eating fish as though it's a lost art. Don't bother with the menu; just ask for suggestions and then savor every bite, whether you choose caviar, mussels in wine, smoked eel, or sea urchins. He even cooks up *porphyra*, the mollusk yielding the famous purple dye of the Byzantine emperors. A side dish might be sautéed squash with wild *glistrida* (purslane). If you visit during the off-season, try Katsimprakis's other restaurant, Alexis 4 Seasons (✉ *Aristotelous 33* ☎ *22410/70522 or 22410/70523*), open year-round. ✉ *Sokratous 18* ☎ *22410/29347* ▭ *AE, MC, V* ⊙ *Closed Nov.–Apr. No lunch.*

$$ ✕ **Palia Istoria.** An old house with high ceilings and genteel murals gets a shot of youth with the innovative cooking of Chef Mihalis Boukouris. Tantalizing entrées include shrimp ouzo with orange juice, pork tenderloin in garlic-and-wine sauce, marinated anchovies (which Boukouris calls "Greek sushi"), and spearmint-spice *keftedes* (meatballs). Cleopatra's Salad, with arugula and dried fig, reigns over the extensive salad choices. With 100 Greek wines, a drink may be harder to select. Luckily the flambéed banana dessert wrapped in phyllo and topped with a portlike Komantaria liqueur means you never have to choose between dessert and digestif. Palia Istoria is a bit out of the way, in the

new town—about €3 by taxi from the Old Town. ✉ *Odos Mitropoleos 108, Ayios Dimitrios* ☎ *22410/32421* 💳 *MC, V* ⊙ *Closed Dec.–Apr. No lunch.*

$$$$ **Rodos Park Suites.** Nestled in a green corner of the new town, Rhodes's most luxurious hotel is also one of its quietest retreats, with more staff than guests. The hotel's welcoming common spaces include a warm cigar-cognac lounge, a tranquil landscaped pool area, and a wood-and-stone spa. The guest rooms' large, square headboards are the signature pieces in minimalist rooms with carpet or wood floors and plasma TV screens. Suites have the added luxury of hot tubs. Stunning views sweep the Old Town, which is a few minutes' walk away. ✉ *Odos Riga Fereous 12, 85100* ☎ *22410/89700* 🌐 *www.rodospark.gr* *30 rooms, 30 suites* *In-room: refrigerator. In-hotel: restaurant, bar, pool, spa* 💳 *AE, DC, MC, V* *BP.*

$$$ ★ **Marco Polo Mansion.** Entering this renovated 15th-century Ottoman mansion is like stepping into another world. The trip begins in the maze of the Old Town's colorful Turkish section, which gives a flavor of what's to come inside. Individually styled rooms are painted in deep, warm colors, with Oriental rugs adorning the pitch-pine floors and soft embroidered cushions beckoning from low sofas. Most of the Eastern furnishings are unusual antiques, including the large beds draped with translucent canopies. It's no wonder this truly beautiful hotel has been featured in dozens of glossy magazines. Homemade marmalades and cakes are served at breakfast. ✉ *Aghiou Fanouriou 40–42, 85100* ☎ *22410/25562* 🌐 *www.marcopolomansion.gr* *10 rooms* *In-room: no a/c (some), no phone, no TV, Wi-Fi. In hotel: restaurant, no elevator* 💳 *AE, MC, V* ⊙ *Closed Nov.—Feb.* *CP.*

$$$ ★ **S. Nikolis Hotel.** A charming old-town accommodation occupies a restored house on the site of an ancient agora. The small but tidy rooms are enlivened by arches and other architectural details, and many have balconies overlooking a lovely large garden. Excellent service, including laundry, is provided by Sotiris and Marianne Nikolis with care. Breakfast is served on the roof terrace, which affords a view of a long stretch of the city walls. ✉ *Odos Ippodamou 61, 85100* ☎ *22410/34561* 📠 *22410/32034* 🌐 *www.s-nikolis.gr* *10 rooms, 4 suites* *In-room: kitchen (some), refrigerator. In-hotel: bar, no elevator, public Wi-Fi* 💳 *AE, MC, V* *CP.*

$ **Hotel Andreas.** The owners of this old-town pension, set in a rather ramshackle 15th-century house, say it once belonged to a Turkish vizier and that most of the rooms were bedrooms for his wives. You can guess what the status was of each occupant—some rooms are lovely and have sea views, others are tiny with unconnected (though still private) bathrooms. All are decorated individually with soft washes of color on stucco walls, romantic bed canopies, international folk art, and tapestry bedspreads. Breakfast is €6–€8. You eat on the huge, plant-filled terrace with a magical view of the Old Town. ✉ *Omirou 28D, 85100* ☎ *22410/34156* 📠 *22410/74285* 🌐 *www.hotelandreas.com* *11 rooms* *In-room: no a/c (some), no TV (some). In-hotel: no elevator, airport shuttle* 💳 *AE, MC, V.*

¢ **Pension Sofia.** The Old Town is full of rooms to rent, but budget-priced Sofia's is bright, pleasant, and framed by trailing jasmine; each room has a little bath. ✉ *Aristofanous 27, 85100* ☎ *22410/36181 or 22410/75166* 🌐 *www.sofia-pension.gr* *9 rooms* *In-room: no phone, kitchen (some). In-hotel: no elevator* *No credit cards.*

NIGHTLIFE & THE ARTS

BARS & DISCOS Sophisticated Greeks have created a stylish nightlife using the medieval buildings and flower-filled courtyards of the Old Town. Some bars and cafés here are open all day for drinks, and many—often those with beautiful medieval interiors—stay open most of the year. Nighttime-only spots in the Old Town open up around 10 PM and close around 3 or 4 AM. The action centers around narrow, pebble-paved Miltiadou street, where seats spill out from trendy bars set in stone buildings. Another hot spot is Arionos Square. Those wanting to venture to the new town's throbbing discos should head to Orfanidou street, where bronzed, scantily clad tourists gyrate 'til dawn at massive clubs.

Bar-café **Baduz** (✉ *Arionos Sq.* ☎ *69366/74466*) plays a range of international music and is decorated with old marble basins. *Rembetika* (acoustic music, with blueslike lyrics, played on the bouzouki) fans head to tiny **Cafe Chantant** (✉ *Dimokritou 3* ☎ *22410/32277*) for live music. The biggest area disco is the three-stage complex **Colorado** (✉ *Orfanidou and Akti Miaouli, new town* ☎ *22410/75120*) with live rock, as well as dance hits and R&B.

Hammam (✉ *Aischylou 26* ☎ *22410/33242*), in a 14th-century bath-house, hosts live Greek bands. Mellow **Selini** (✉ *Evripidou 4B* ☎ *No phone*) has frescoes of the moon, art exhibits, cushioned outdoor benches, and jazz. The candlelit **Theatro** (✉ *Miltiadou 2* ☎ *22410/76973*) plays funk and electronic music and even hosts live theater events in the off-season.

ENTERTAINMENT You must show your passport to get into Rhodes's **casino** (✉ *Hotel Grande Albergo Delle Rose, Papanikolaou 4, new town* ☎ *22410/97500* 🌐 *www.casinorodos.gr*). The entry fee is €15 but drinks are free. They're open 24 hours a day, every day, and you have to be at least 23 years old to play.

PERFORMANCES The **Nelly Dimoglou Folk Dance Theatre** (✉ *Andronikou 7, behind Turkish baths, Old Town* ☎ *22410/20157*) has kept alive the tradition of Greek dance since 1971, with strict adherence to authentic detail in costume and performance. From June until October, performances (€12) are held Monday, Wednesday, and Friday at 9:20 PM. The theater also gives dance lessons.

From May through October the **sound-and-light** show (✉ *Grounds of Palace of the Grand Masters in Ippoton, Old Town* ☎ *22410/21922* 🌐 *www.hellenicfestival.gr*) tells the story of the Turkish siege. English-language performances are Monday, Wednesday, and Friday at 9:15 PM; Tuesday, Thursday, and Saturday at 11:15 PM. In September and October, performances start one hour earlier; the cost is €7; free for children up to 10 years old.

SPORTS & THE OUTDOORS

For €50 **Dive Med College** (✉*Lissavonas 33, Rodini* ☎*22410/61115* 🌐*www.divemedcollege.com*) takes you by boat to Thermes Kallitheas and after a 45-minute theory lesson and practice in shallow water, you descend for a 20-minute dive. They also have dives at Ladiko, 15 km (9 mi) south of Rhodes town.

You can rent bicycles, including mountain bikes and racing bikes, as well as ATVs and motor scooters, from **Margaritis Rent a Moto** (✉*Iannou Kazouli 23* ☎*22410/37420*).

SHOPPING

In Rhodes town you can buy good copies of Lindos ware, a delicate pottery decorated with green and red floral motifs. The Old Town's shopping area, on Sokratous, is lined with boutiques selling furs, jewelry, and other high-ticket items. The owner of **Astero Antiques** (✉*Ayiou Fanouriou 4, off Sokratous* ☎*22410/34753*) travels throughout Greece each winter to fill his shop.

EPTA PIGES ΕΠΤΑ ΠΗΓΕΣ

30 km (19 mi) south of Rhodes town.

Seven Springs, or Epta Piges, is a deeply shaded glen watered by mountain springs. In the woods around the springs, imported peacocks flaunt their plumage. The waters are channeled through a 164-yard-long tunnel, which you can walk through, emerging at the edge of a cascading dam and a small man-made lake where you can swim. Here an enterprising local shepherd began serving simple fare in 1945, and his sideline turned into the busy taverna and tourist site of today. Despite its many visitors, Seven Springs' beauty remains unspoiled. To get here, turn right on the inland road near Kolymbia and follow signs.

WHERE TO EAT

$ ✕**Epta Piges.** The family-run taverna spreads out below the plane and pine trees, directly overlooking the springs. There's always charcoal-grill lamb or fish on the menu, and starters include dishes like *pitaroudia* (fried potato balls) or thin fried zucchini and eggplant. ☎*22410/56259* 💳*AE, DC, MC, V* ⊗*Closed Nov.–Mar.*

LINDOS ΛΙΝΔΟΣ

19 km (12 mi) southwest of Epta Piges, 48 km (30 mi) southwest of Rhodes town.

Lindos, cradled between two harbors, had a particular importance in antiquity. Before the existence of Rhodes town, it was the island's principal maritime center. Lindos possessed a revered sanctuary, consecrated to Athena, whose cult probably succeeded that of a pre-Hellenic divinity named Lindia; the sanctuary was dedicated to Athena Lindia. By the 6th century BC, an impressive temple dominated the settlement, and after the foundation of Rhodes, the Lindians set up a *propylaia* (monumental entrance gate) on the model of that in Athens. In the mid-4th century BC, the temple was destroyed by fire and almost immediately rebuilt, with a new wooden statue of the goddess covered by gold leaf, and with arms, head, and legs of marble or ivory. Lindos prospered into Roman times, during the Middle Ages, and under the Knights of St. John. Only at the beginning of the 19th century did the age-old shipping activity cease.

EASY AS 1-2-3

Most of Lindos's mazelike streets don't have conventional names or addresses; instead, buildings are numbered, from 1 through about 500. Lower numbers are on the north side of town, higher numbers on the south.

Lindos is remarkably well preserved, and many 15th-century houses are still in use. Everywhere are examples of the Crusader architecture you saw in Rhodes town: substantial houses of finely cut Lindos limestone, with windows crowned by elaborate arches. Many floors are paved with black-and-white pebble mosaics. Intermixed with these Crusader buildings are whitewashed, Geometric, Cycladic-style houses with square, blue-shuttered windows.

Like Rhodes town, Lindos is enchanting off-season but can get unbearably crowded otherwise, since pilgrims make the trek from Rhodes town daily. The main street is lined with shops selling clothes and trinkets, and since the streets are medieval in their narrowness and twisting course, the passage slows to a snail's pace. Spend a night in Lindos to enjoy its beauties after the day-trippers leave. Only pedestrians and donkeys are allowed in Lindos because the town's narrow alleys are not wide enough for vehicles. If you're arriving by car, park in the lot above town and walk the 10 minutes down (about 1,200 feet) to Lindos.

The **Church of the Panayia** is a graceful building with a beautiful bell tower. The body of the church probably antedates the Knights, although the bell tower bears their arms with the dates 1484–90. The interior has frescoes painted in 1779 by Gregory of Symi. ✉ *Off main square* ☎ *No phone* ⏲ *May–Oct., daily 9–2 and 5–9; Nov.–Mar., call the number posted on the church to have the door unlocked.*

Fodor'sChoice ★ For about €5, you can hire a donkey for the 15-minute climb from the modern town up to the **Acropolis of Lindos.** The winding path leads past a gauntlet of Lindian women who spread out their lace and embroidery like fresh laundry over the rocks. The final approach ascends a steep flight of stairs, past a marvelous 2nd-century BC **relief** of the prow of a Lindian ship, carved into the rock.

The entrance to the Acropolis takes you through the **medieval castle,** with the Byzantine **Chapel of St. John** on the next level above. On the **upper terraces** are the remains of the elaborate **porticoes** and **stoas.** As is the case with Sounion, on the mainland southeast of Athens, the site and temple command an immense sweep of sea, making a powerful statement on behalf of the deity and city to which they belonged; the lofty white columns on the summit must have presented a magnificent picture. The main portico had 42 Doric columns, at the center of which an opening led to the staircase up to the **propylaia.** The temple at the very top is surprisingly modest, given the drama of the approach. As was common in the 4th century BC, both the front and the rear are flanked by four Doric columns. Numerous inscribed statue bases were found all over the summit, attesting in many cases to the work of Lindian sculptors, who were clearly second to none. ✉*Above new town* ☎*22440/31258* 🎫*€6* ⏲*May–Oct., Tues.–Sun. 8:30–7, Mon. 12:30–7; Nov.–Apr., Tues.–Sun. 8:30–2:40.*

Escape the crowds by trekking to the **Tomb of Kleoboulos**, which archaeologists say is incorrectly named after Lindos's early tyrant Kleoboulos; it's actually the final resting place of a wealthy family of the 1st to 2nd century BC. After about 3 km (2 mi), a 30-minute scenic walk, you encounter the small, rounded stone tomb. You can peer inside and see the candle marks, which testify to its later use as the church of St. Emilianos. ✉*Look for sign at parking lot above main square. Follow dirt path along hill on opposite side of bay from Acropolis* ☎*No phone.*

WHERE TO STAY & EAT

In Lindos it's possible through travel agents to rent **rooms** in many of the traditional homes that have mosaic courtyards, gardens, and sea views; an entire house may even be for rent. *Savaidis Travel* ☎*22440/31347* 🌐*www.savaidis-travel.gr.; Lindos Sun Tours* ☎*22440/31333* 🌐*www.lindosuntours.gr.*

$$–$$$ ✕**Mavrikos.** The secret of this longtime favorite is an elegant, perfect simplicity. Seemingly straightforward dishes, such as sea-urchin salad, fried *manouri* cheese with basil and pine nuts, swordfish in caper sauce, and lobster risotto, become transcendent with the magic touch of third-generation chef Dimitris Mavrikos. He combines the freshest ingredients with classical training and an abiding love for the best of Greek village cuisine. ✉*Main square* ☎*22440/31232* ▭*MC, V* ⏲*Closed Nov.–Mar.*

$$$$ ★ ✕🏨**Melenos Hotel.** Michalis Melenos worked for years to make this 12-room stone villa overlooking Lindos bay into a truly special boutique hotel. Each room has a built-in, traditional Lindian village bed with hand-carved woodwork and antique furnishings brought from throughout Greece and Turkey. Colorful Turkish fountains splash throughout the grounds. A tranquil terrace, bathed by lamplight in evening, is the stage for the restaurant's($$$–$$$$) inspired Mediterranean cuisine. Entrées include fish with citrus or herbs, and filet mignon in wine sauce. Parents, take note: a fee of €65 per night applies to children ages 2 to 12 staying in the hotel. If you didn't bring along your computer, laptops are available upon request. ✉*At edge of Lindos, on path to Acropolis, 85107* ☎*22440/32222* 📠*22440/31720* 🌐*www.melenoslindos.com* ⇆*12 suites* ♁*In-room: refrigerator, Ethernet. In-hotel: restaurant, no elevator, public Wi-Fi* ▭*AE, MC, V* 🍽*BP.*

¢ 🏨**Pension Electra.** Linger on the spacious terrace or down in the blossoming garden of this decades-old pension with high ceilings and several levels. Many rooms have sea views, and you can whip up your own breakfasts in one of two large kitchens. ✉*No. 66, 85107*

☎22440/31266 or 69735/15609 7 rooms, 1 with bath in the hall In-room: no phone, refrigerator, no TV. In hotel: no elevator No credit cards.

NIGHTLIFE

Most of Lindos's bars cater to a young, hard-drinking crowd; few are without a television showing soccer. Many are open year-round to serve the locals. The **Captain's House** (*✉Akropoleos 243 ☎22440/31235*), set, naturally, in an old captain's house with a courtyard, plays lounge, ethnic, and Greek music. **Gelo Blu** (*✉Near Theotokou Church ☎22440/31761*), run by the owners of Mavrikos, serves homemade ice cream by day and drinks day and night in its cool, blue-cushioned interior and pebbled courtyard, and on its rooftop terrace. Relaxed **Rainbird** (*✉On road to Pallas beach ☎22440/32169*) is open for coffee and drinks all day and has a romantic sea-view terrace.

13

GENNADI & THE SOUTH COAST ΓΕΝΝΑΔΙ & ΝΟΤΙΑ ΠΑΡΑΛΙΑ

20 km (12½ mi) south of Lindos, 68 km (42 mi) south of Rhodes town.

The area south of Lindos, with fewer beaches and less-fertile soil, is less traveled than the stretch to its north. Though development is increasing, the still-pretty and inexpensive coastal village of Gennadi has pensions, rooms for rent, and a handful of tavernas, nightclubs, and DJ-hosted beach parties.

BEACHES

Lachania beach begins a mile north of Gennadi and stretches uninterrupted for several miles; drive alongside until you come to a secluded spot. Past Lachania is a quiet beach, **Plimiri** (*✉10 km [6 mi] south of Gennadi*), which is reached by following a sign for Taverna Plimiri from the main road. If you're on a quest for the perfect strand and are armed with four-wheel-drive and a good map, aim for the pristine, cedar-lined beach at **Ayios Georgios**—though it will take some doing. (Rental-car companies discourage you from taking regular cars on the poor road.) If you dare, here's how to get there: About 4 km (2½ mi) past Plimiri, you can see the abandoned monastery of Ayios Pavlos. Just before the monastery, turn left down the cypress-lined dirt road. Follow the route about 8 km (5 mi) to a church, where the road forks. Keep going straight to reach Ayios Georgios, one of Rhodes's loveliest secret spots.

MONOLITHOS TO KAMEIROS ΜΟΝΟΛΙΘΟΣ & ΚΑΜΕΙΡΟΣ

28 km (17 mi) northwest of Gennadi, 74 km (46 mi) southwest of Rhodes town.

Rhodes's west coast is more forested, with fewer good beaches than its east coast, but if you're looking to get away from the hordes, it sylvan scenery, august ruins, and vineyards make it worth the trips.

The medieval fortress of **Monolithos**—so named for the jutting, 750-foot monolith on which it is built—rises above a fairy-tale landscape of deep-green forests and sharp cliffs plunging into the sea. Inside the fortress there is a chapel, and the ramparts provide magnificent views of Rhodes's emerald inland and the island of Halki. ✉ *Take western road from middle of Monolithos village; near hairpin turn there's a short path up to fortress* ☎ *No phone* 🎫 *Free.*

Siana (✉ *5 km [3 mi] northeast of Monolithos*) perches above a vast, fertile valley and sits in the shadow of a rock outcropping crowned with the ruin of a castle. The small town is known for souma (which resembles a grape-flavored schnapps); look for roadside stands selling the intoxicant.

For another taste of the town, don't pass through without a stop at **Manos** (✉ *Past town church, on main road* ☎ *22460/61209* ⏲ *Feb.–Nov. 15, 7 AM–10 PM*) or one of several other shops along the street that sell Siana's renowned honey and walnuts.

The **Kastello,** a fortress built by the Knights in the late 15th century, is an impressive ruin, situated high above the sea with good views in every direction. ✉ *13 km (8 mi) northeast of Siana* ☎ *No phone* 🎫 *Free.*

EN ROUTE

Beyond Siana, the road continues on a high ridge through thick pine forests, which carpet the precipitous slopes dropping toward the sea. To the east looms the bare, stony massif of Mt. Ataviros, Rhodes's highest peak, at 3,986 feet. If you follow the road inland rather than continue north along the coast toward Kritinia, you climb the flanks of the mountains to the traditional, arbor-filled village of Embonas, in Rhodes's richest wine country.

The well-respected **Emery Winery** makes many good wines, and occasionally, a few outstanding ones. Tastings are free. ✉ *Embonas* ☎ *22460/41208* 🌐 *www.emery.gr* ⏲ *Weekdays 8–4:30.*

As you continue east you come into the landscape that, in medieval times, earned Rhodes the moniker "emerald of the Mediterranean." The exquisite drive up Mt. Profitis Ilias, overlooking dark-green trees carpeting mountains that plunge into the sea, is one of the loveliest passages of scenery in Greece. Near the 2,200-foot-high summit is the small Church of Profitis Ilias. From the church, you can follow the well-trodden path down to the village of Salakos. It's about a 45-minute walk through the woods.

The site of classical **Kameiros** (23 km [14 mi] northeast of Siana) is one of the three ancient cities of Rhodes. The apparently unfortified ruins, excavated by the Italians in 1929, lie on a slope above the sea. Most of what is visible today dates to the classical period and later, including impressive remains of the early-Hellenistic period. The guards say that the hill hides many more ruins. ✉ *Off main Rhodes road, turn at sign for Ancient Kameiros* ☎ *22410/40037* 🌐 *www.culture.gr* 🎫 *€4* ⏲ *Tues.–Sun. 8:30–2:40.*

PETALOUDES & IALYSSOS ΠΕΤΑΛΟΥΔΕΣ & ΙΑΛΥΣΟΣ

★ *22 km (14 mi) east of Kameiros, 25 km (16 mi) southwest of Rhodes town.*

The Valley of the Butterflies, Petaloudes, lives up to its name, especially in July and August. In summer the *callimorpha quadripunctaria,* actually a moth species, cluster by the thousands around the low bushes of the pungent storax plant, which grows all over the area. Through the years their number has diminished, partly owing to busloads of tourists clapping hands to see them fly up in dense clouds. Don't agitate the butterflies. Access to the valley is through a main road and admission booth and involves a walk up an idyllic trail by a stream in the woods. ⊠*Turn off the coastal road south and follow signs leading to the site with its own parking lot* ☎*22410/81801* *€5* ⏲*Late Apr.–Oct., daily 8–7.*

13

SYMI ΣΥΜΗ

The island of Symi, 45 km (27 mi) north of Rhodes, is an enchanting place, with its star attraction being Chorio, a 19th-century town of neoclassical mansions. The island has few beaches and almost no flat land, so it is not attractive to developers. As a result, quiet Symi provides a peaceful retreat for travelers, who tend to fall in love with the island on their first visit and return year after year.

Nireus, the ancient king of Symi, who sailed with three vessels to assist the Greeks at Troy, is mentioned in Homer. Symi was later part of the Dorian Hexapolis dominated by Rhodes, and it remained under Rhodian dominance throughout the Roman and Byzantine periods. The island has good natural harbors, and the nearby coast of Asia Minor provided plentiful timber for the Symiotes, who were shipbuilders, fearless seafarers and sponge divers, and rich and successful merchants. Under the Ottomans their harbor was proclaimed a free port and attracted the trade of the entire region. Witness to their prosperity are the neoclassical mansions that line the harbor and towns. The Symiotes' continuous travel and trade and their frequent contact with Europe led them to incorporate foreign elements in their furnishings, clothes, and cultural life. At first they lived in Chorio, high on the hillside above the port, and in the second half of the 19th century spread down to the seaside at Yialos. There were some 20,000 inhabitants at this acme, but under the Italian occupation at the end of the Italo-Turkish war in 1912, the island declined; the Symiotes lost their holdings in Asia Minor and were unable to convert their fleets to steam. Many emigrated to work elsewhere, and now there are just a few thousand inhabitants in Chorio and Yialos. Symi is an hour ride by hydrofoil from Rhodes town.

Symi & Kos
Kalimnos
Kalimnos
TO LEROS, PATMOS
Pserimos
Cape Skansdari
Kos Town
Zipari
Marmari
Kos
Asklepieion
Cape Ayios Fokas
Pili
Castle of Antimachia
Mastichari
Andimahia
TO ASTIPALEA
Kardamena
Kefalos
Kamari
Kefalos Bay
Cape Helona
Zini
Cape Krikelos
Giali
Gökova Körfez
Resadiye Yarimadasi
Resadiye
Datca
TURKEY
Kargi
Knidos
Nimos
Simi
Yialos
Chorio
Kasareia
Loryma
Symi
Panormitis
Monastery of Taxiarchis Michael Panormítis
Mandraki
Nisiros
Aegean Sea
KEY
Ferry
TO RHODES
Tilos
Livadia
0
10 miles
0
10 kilometers

YIALOS ΓΙΑΛΟΣ

45 km (27 mi) north of Rhodes.

As the boat from Rhodes to Symi rounds the last of many rocky barren spurs, the port of Yialos, at the back of a deep, narrow harbor, comes into view. The shore is lined with mansions whose ground floors have been converted to cafés with waterside terraces perfect for whiling away lazy hours.

13

The **Church of Ayhios Ioannis** (☒*Near center of Yialos village*), built in 1838, incorporates in its walls fragments of ancient blocks from a temple that apparently stood on this site and is surrounded by a plaza paved in an intricate mosaic, fashioned from inlaid pebbles.

Sponge-diving tools, model ships, 19th-century navigation tools, and anchors fill the teeny **Symi Naval Museum.** It's hard to miss the ornamental blue-and-yellow building. The sea memorabilia within gives a good taste of life in Symi in the 19th and early 20th centuries. ☒*Yialos waterfront* €2 *Tues.–Sun. 10–2.*

WHERE TO STAY & EAT

$$$–$$$$ ★ ✕**Mylopetra.** A delightfully converted old flour mill, Mylopetra is a feast for the eyes: decorations include an ancient tomb embedded in glass beneath the floor. German couple Hans and Eva Sworoski painstakingly oversaw the transition of this extraordinary restaurant and tend to the excellent cooking and gracious service. The menu changes daily, but expect inventive sauces, homemade pasta married with anything from spinach to rabbit to salmon, and abundant seafood and meat (often game) options. ☒*Behind church on the backstreet* ☎*22460/72333* *Reservations essential* *MC, V* *Closed mid-Oct.–Apr.*

¢–$ ✕**Trawlers.** Anna Kanli's home cooking is behind one of Yialos's most-successful, inexpensive tavernas. She prepares traditional meat and fish dishes, not to mention vegetarian moussaka. Weather permitting, you can also dine in a pretty square a few steps from the port. ☒*Economou Sq., harbor front* ☎*22460/71411* *MC, V* *Closed Nov.–Apr.*

$$$ ★ **Aliki Hotel.** A three-story, 1895 mansion on the waterfront houses this attractive hotel. Each of the rooms is different, but all are furnished with a tasteful mix of antiques and newer pieces. The best rooms, of course, are those that face the water. The hotel's lobby has a high, colorful ceiling and its rooftop, an enviable port view. In good weather breakfast is served on a waterside terrace that doubles as a bar in the evening. ☒*Yialos waterfront, 85600* ☎*22460/71665* *22460/71655* *www.hotelaliki.gr* *13 rooms, 2 suites, 2 apartments (in separate building behind hotel)* *In-room: no TV. In-hotel: bar, no elevator* *AE, DC, MC, V* *BP.*

BEACHES

One reason Symi's beaches are so pristine is that almost none are reachable by car. From the main harbor at Yialos, boats leave every half hour between 10:30 AM and 12:30 PM to the beautiful beaches of **Aghia Marina, Aghios Nikolas, Aghios Giorgos,** and **Nanou** bay. Return trips run

4–6 PM. The round-trips cost €5–€10. In summer, there are also small boats for hire from the clock tower.

For a swim near Yialos, you can go to the little strip of beach beyond the **Yialos** harbor—follow the road past the bell tower and the Aliki Hotel and you come to a seaside taverna that rents umbrellas and beach chairs. If you continue walking on the same road for about 3 km (2 mi), you come to the pine-shaded beach at **Niborios** bay, where there is another taverna.

FESTIVAL

The **Symi Festival** brings free dance, music, theater performances, and cinema screenings to the island every year from July through September. Most events take place in the main harbor square in Yialos, but some are scheduled in other places around the island. A schedule of events is posted at the square, and programs can be found at local shops, travel agents, and the town hall.

CHORIO ΧΩΡΙΟ

Fodor's Choice ★ *1 km (½ mi) east of Yialos.*

It's a 10-minute walk from the main harbor of Yialos up to the hilltop town of Chorio, along a staircase of some 400 steps, known as Kali Strata. There is also a road that can be traveled in one of the island's few taxis or by bus, which makes a circuit with stops at the harbor in Yialos, Chorio, and the seaside community of Pedi. The Kali Strata is flanked by elegant neoclassical houses with elaborate stonework, lavish pediments, and intricate wrought-iron balconies. Just before the top of the stairs (and the welcome little Kali Strata bar), a line of windmills crowns the hill of **Noulia.** Most of Chorio's many churches date to the 18th and 19th centuries, and many are ornamented with richly decorated iconostases and ornate bell towers. Donkeys are often used to carry materials through the narrow streets for the town's steady construction and renovation work.

The collection at the **Archaeological Museum** displays Hellenistic and Roman sculptures and inscriptions as well as more-recent carvings, icons, costumes, and handicrafts. ✉*Follow signs from central square to Lieni neighborhood* ☎*22460/71114* 🎫*€2* ⏲*Tues.–Sun. 8–2:30.*

The **kastro** (*castle* ✉*At top of town, in ancient acropolis*) incorporates fragments of Symi's history in its walls. A church and several teeny chapels dominate the area with only a few remnants of the castle walls. The view from here takes in the village of Pedi as well as both Chorio and Yialos.

WHERE TO STAY & EAT

$–$$ ✕ **Georgio and Maria's Taverna.** Meals at this simple Chorio taverna, which is as popular with locals as it is with tourists, are served in a high-ceilinged, whitewashed dining room or on a terrace that is partially shaded by a grape arbor and affords wonderful views over the sea and surrounding hills. Fish is a specialty, and simply prepared *mezedes* (small dishes), such as roasted peppers topped with feta cheese and fried zucchini, can constitute a delicious meal in themselves. If you're lucky, one of the neighbors will stroll in with instrument in hand to provide an impromptu serenade. ✉ *Off main square* ☎ *22460/71984* ▭ *AE, MC, V.*

$ ★ **Hotel Fiona.** This bright, cheerful hotel is perched on the hillside in Chorio, with splendid views. Just about all of the large rooms, with spotless white-tile floors and attractive blue-painted furnishings and pastel fabrics, have a sea-facing balcony. Breakfast, with yogurt and marmalade, is served in the breezy, attractive lobby lounge or on a cozy balcony. ✉ *Near main square* ☎ 📠 *22460/72088* *14 rooms, 3 studios* *In-room: no TV. In-hotel: bar, no elevator* ▭ *No credit cards* *Closed Nov.–Apr.* *CP.*

$ **Village Hotel.** Grand architecture meets quaint surroundings in this traditional neoclassical mansion on a small lane. The hotel has good views in all directions … and requires a steep climb home after a morning coffee in the port. All the rooms open onto a balcony or terrace and surround an attractive garden. ✉ *Off main square* ☎ *22460/71800* 📠 *22460/71802* *17 rooms* *In-room: refrigerator, no TV. In-hotel: bar, no elevator, parking (no fee)* ▭ *MC, V* *Closed Nov.–Apr.* *CP.*

13

MONASTERY OF TAXIARCHIS MICHAEL PANORMITIS
ΜΟΝΗ ΤΑΞΙΑΡΧΗ ΜΙΧΑΗΛ ΠΑΝΟΡΜΙΤΗ

7 km (4½ mi) south of Chorio.

Fodor's Choice ★ The main reason to venture to the atypically green, pine-covered hills surrounding the little gulf of Panormitis is to visit the Monastery of Taxiarchis Michael Panormitis, dedicated to Symi's patron saint, the protector of sailors. The site's entrance is surmounted by an elaborate **bell tower,** of the multilevel wedding-cake variety on display in Yialos and Chorio. In the **courtyard,** which is surrounded by a vaulted stoa, a black-and-white pebble mosaic adorns the floor. The interior of the **church,** entirely frescoed in the 18th century, contains a marvelously ornate wooden iconostasis, flanked by a heroic-size 18th-century representation of Michael, all but his face covered with silver. There are two small **museums** devoted to Byzantine and folk art. The Byzantine includes a collection of votive offerings, including ship models, gifts, and bottles with notes containing wishes and money in them, which, according to local lore, travel to Symi on their own after having been thrown into the sea. A trip to the monastery can be accompanied by a refreshing swim at the designated edges of the deep-blue harbor. There's bus service twice a day from Yialos, which passes through Chorio, and boats from Yialos and Rhodes daily.

If a day trip isn't enough for you, the monastery, which no longer has monks but does have two clergy people, along with a supermarket, bakery, and more, rents 60 spartan rooms (☎ 22460/72414) with kitchens and private baths for about €20. Though the price doesn't include a towel or air-conditioning and there are insects (some rather large), the spiritual aspect makes for an enriching experience. ✉ *Symi's south side, at harbor* ☎ *22460/71581* 🌐 *www.impsymis.gr* 🎫 *Monastery free; museums €1.50* 🕓 *Monastery: daily 7–8; museums: Apr. –Oct. 8:30–1 and 3–4, Nov. –Apr. by appointment.*

KOS ΚΩΣ

The island of Kos, the third largest in the Dodecanese, is certainly one of the most beautiful, with verdant fields and tree-clad mountains, surrounded by miles of sandy beach. Its highest peak, part of a small mountain range in the northeast, is less than 2,800 feet. All this beauty has not gone unnoticed, of course, and Kos undeniably suffers from the effects of mass tourism: its beaches are often crowded, most of its seaside towns have been recklessly overdeveloped, and the main town is noisy and busy between June and September.

In Mycenaean times and during the Archaic period, the island prospered. In the 6th century BC it was conquered by the Persians but later joined the Delian League, supporting Athens against Sparta in the Peloponnesian War. Kos was invaded and destroyed by the Spartan fleet, ruled by Alexander and various of his successors, and has twice been devastated by earthquakes. Nevertheless, the city and the economy flourished, as did the arts and sciences. The painter Apelles, the Michelangelo of his time, came from Kos, as did Hippocrates, father of modern medicine. Under the Roman Empire, the island's Asklepieion and its renowned healing center drew emperors and ordinary citizens alike. The Knights of St. John arrived in 1315 and ruled for the next two centuries, until they were replaced by the Ottomans. In 1912 the Italians took over, and in 1947 the island was united with Greece.

KOS TOWN ΚΩΣ (ΠΟΛΗ)

92 km (57 mi) north of Rhodes.

The modern town lies on a flat plain encircling a spacious harbor called Mandraki and is a pleasant assemblage of low-lying buildings and shady lanes. The fortress, which crowns its west side, where Hippocrates is supposed to have taught in the shade of a large plane tree, is a good place to begin your exploration of Kos town. On one side of little Platanou Square, named after the tree, stands the graceful loggia, actually a mosque, built in 1786.

The **Castle of the Knights,** built mostly in the 15th century and full of ancient blocks from its Greek and Roman predecessors, is a repository of fragments of ancient inscriptions, funerary monuments, and other sculptural material. A walk around the walls affords good views over the town, whose flat skyline is pierced by a few remaining minarets and many palm trees. ✉ *Over bridge from Platanou Sq.* ☎ *22420/27927* 🎫 *€3* 🕓 *Tues.–Sun. 8:30–2:30.*

Excavations by Italian and Greek archaeologists have revealed ancient **agora and harbor ruins** (✉ *Over bridge from Platanou Sq., behind Castle* *of the Knights*) that date from the 4th century BC through Roman times. Remnants include parts of the walls of the old city, of a Hellenistic stoa, and of temples dedicated to Aphrodite and Hercules. The ruins, which are not fenced, blend charmingly into the fabric of the modern city; they are a shortcut for people on their way to work, a place to sit and chat, and an outdoor playroom for children. In spring the site is covered with brightly colored flowers, which nicely frame the ancient gray-and-white marble blocks tumbled in every direction.

13

★ The **Archaeological Museum** contains extremely important examples of Hellenistic and Roman sculpture by Koan artists. Among the treasures are a renowned statue of Hippocrates; a group of sculptures from various Roman phases, all discovered in the House of the Europa Mosaic; and a remarkable series of Hellenistic draped female statues mainly from the Sanctuary of Demeter at Kyparissi and the Odeon. ✉*Eleftherias Sq., west of agora through gate leading to Platanou Sq.* ☎*22420/28326* *€3* *Tues.–Sun. 8–6, Nov.–Mar., and April–late Oct. 8–2:30.*

The **west excavations** (✉*Southwest of agora and harbor ruins*) have uncovered a portion of one of the main Roman streets with many houses, including the **House of the Europa Mosaic.** Part of the **Roman baths** (near main Roman street), it has been converted into a basilica. The **gymnasium,** distinguished by its partly reconstructed colonnade, and the so-called **Nymphaion,** a lavish public latrine that has been restored, are also of interest. These excavations are always open, with free access.

BEACHES

If you must get wet but can't leave Kos town, try the narrow pebble strip of beach immediately south of the main harbor. **Tingaki** (✉*On north coast, 13 km [8 mi] west of Kos town*) has pretty, sandy, but heavily developed resort beaches. At **Mastichari** (✉*On north coast, 32 km [20 mi] west of Kos town*) there's a wide sand beach, tavernas, rooms for rent, and a pier where boats sail on day trips to the uncrowded islet of Pserimos.

WHERE TO STAY & EAT

$$–$$$ ✕**Petrino.** Greek-Canadian brothers Mike and George Gerovasilis have created a calm oasis a few streets in from the hustle and bustle of Kos harbor. A 150-year-old stone house provides cozy dining in cool months, and in summer, tables pepper a garden full of private nooks, fountains, and gentle music. The enormous menu lists Greek recipes, like zucchini pancakes and liver with oregano, side-by-side with European classics like chateaubriand. Servings are generous; the sauces, rich. Actor Tom Hanks has been among the VIP guests. ✉*Ioannou Theologou Sq.* ☎*22420/27251* *AE, DC, MC, V.*

$$–$$$ ✕**To Limanaki.** Buttery Symi shrimp, tender calamari, and lightly fried *atherines* (tiny smelt fish) stand out among the many seafood choices. If fish isn't your thing, the menu also has all the Greek basics. The family-run taverna is even open for bacon and eggs in the morning. On one side of the restaurant is a buzzing street; on the other, silent

ruins and the chapel of St. Ann. ✉ *Odos Megalou Alexandrou 11* ☎ *22420/21153* 💳 *AE, D, DC, MC, V.*

$$$$ ★ **Grecotel Kos Imperial.** On a gentle slope over the Aegean, this spa resort has a private beach as well as seawater and freshwater pools and artificial rivers and lagoons. Indoors, there are glimmering glass-tile hydrotherapy pools, dozens of spa treatments, and many guest rooms with private hot tubs and pools. Grecotel's signature style of simple but beautifully designed luxury is everywhere in evidence, as in the airy rooms with bamboo furniture, sheer white linen, and sweeping blue sea views. ✉ *4 km (2½ mi) east of Kos town, 85300Psalidi* ☎ *22420/58000* 📠 *22420/25192* 🌐 *www.grecotel.com* *177 rooms, 207 bungalows (including 55 suites)* *In-room: refrigerator. In-hotel: 4 restaurants, pools, spa, public Wi-Fi* 💳 *AE, DC, MC, V* *BP.*

¢ **Hotel Afendoulis.** Simple and friendly, the plain, whitewashed rooms with dark-wood furniture are spotless and of far better quality than most in this price range; they're also far enough off the main road, so it stays quiet at night. You can walk to most places in Kos town from here. Enjoy breakfast, which is extra, in the open marble lobby. ✉ *Evripilou 1, 85300* ☎ *22420/25321* 📠 *22420/25797* *20 rooms* *In-hotel: bar, public Wi-Fi* 💳 *MC, V.*

NIGHTLIFE

Things start cooking before 7 PM and in many cases roar on past 7 AM on Akti Koundourioti and in the nearby Exarhia area, which includes rowdy Nafklirou and Plessa streets. Competing bars try to lure in barhoppers with ads for cheap beer and neon-color drinks.

Fashion (✉ *Odos Kanari 2* ☎ *22420/22592*), a massive club off of Delphinia Square, has an outdoor bar, happy hour, and a throbbing indoor dance floor. Guest DJs seek to provide young, international tourists the kind of club music they'd hear back home. The loungey seaside club **H20** (✉ *Aktis Art Hotel, beachfront, Vasileos Georgiou 7* ☎ *22420/47207*) has a small, sleek interior as well as outdoor seating.

FESTIVAL

Every summer from July through mid-September Kos hosts the **Hippocrates Festival** (☎ *22420/28665* ✉ *pkkos@internet.gr*). Music, dance, movie screenings, and theater performances enliven venues such as the Castle of the Knights and the Odeon. The festival also includes exhibits around town and activities for children.

THE OUTDOORS

The island of Kos, particularly the area around the town, is good for bicycle riding. Ride to the Asklepieion for a picnic, or visit the Castle of Antimacheia. Note: be aware of hazards such as cistern openings; very few have security fences around them. You can rent bicycles everywhere—in Kos town and at the more-popular resorts. Try the many shops along Eleftheriou Venizelou street in town. Renting a bike costs about €6 per day.

ASKLEPIEION ΑΣΚΛΗΠΙΕΙΟΝ

4 km (2½ mi) west of Kos town.

One of the great healing centers of antiquity, the Asklepieion is framed by a thick grove of cypress trees and is laid out on several **broad terraces** connected by a monumental staircase. The lower terrace probably held the Asklepieion Festivals. On the middle terrace is an **Ionic temple,** once decorated with paintings by Apelles, including the renowned depiction of Aphrodite often written about in antiquity and eventually removed to Rome by the emperor Augustus. On the uppermost terrace is the **Doric Temple of Asklepios,** once surrounded by colonnaded porticoes. ✉ *Asklepieion* ☎ *22420/28763* 🎫 *€4* ⏲ *Apr.–Oct., Tues.—Sun. 8:30–7; Nov.–Feb., Tues.–Sun. 8:30–2:30.*

OFF THE BEATEN PATH

Mountain villages. Leaving the main road southwest of the Asklepieion (turnoff is at Zipari, 9 km [5½ mi] southwest of Kos town), you can explore an enchanting landscape of cypress and pine trees on a route that climbs to a handful of lovely, whitewashed rural villages that cling to the craggy slopes of the island's central mountains, including Asfendiou, Zia, and Lagoudi. The busiest of them is Zia, with an appealing smattering of churches; crafts shops selling local honey, weavings, and handmade soaps; and open-air tavernas where you can enjoy the views over the surrounding forests and fields toward the sea.

WHERE TO EAT

¢–$ ★ ✕ **Asklipios.** The town is noted for its Muslim minority, and you can have a memorable Turkish-inspired meal at the little restaurant called "Ali." Sit in the shade of an ancient laurel tree and try the selection of exquisite mezedes: *imam bayaldi* (baked eggplant), bourekakia, and home-prepared *dolmadakia* (small stuffed grape leaves). An array of kebabs includes excellent *soutzoukakia* (elongated meatballs); even the boiled cauliflower is perfect. ✉ *3 km (2 mi) west of Kos town, on main square, 85300Platani* ☎ *22420/25264* 💳 *MC, V.*

¢ Fodor'sChoice ★ ✕ **Taverna Ampavris.** The surroundings and the food are both delightful at this charming, rustic taverna, outside Kos town on a lane leading to the village of Platani. Meals are served in the courtyard of an old farmhouse, and the kitchen's emphasis is on local country food—including wonderful stews and grilled meats, accompanied by vegetables from nearby gardens. The owners wait on you, steering you toward meals, like zucchini blossoms stuffed with rice, or offering detailed advice on sightseeing. ✉ *Ampavris, on the way from Rhodes to Platani* ☎ *22420/25696* 💳 *No credit cards.*

CASTLE OF ANTIMACHEIA ΚΑΣΤΡΟ ΑΝΤΙΜΑΧΕΙΑΣ

21 km (13 mi) southwest of Asklepieion, 25 km (15 mi) southwest of Kos town.

The thick, well-preserved walls of this medieval fortress look out over the sweeping Aegean and Kos's green interior. Around the fortress, which has a coat of arms from the Knights of the Order of St. John of Rhodes, are the remains of a ruined settlement. ✉ *On main road from Kos, turn left 3 km (2 mi) before village of Antimacheia, following signs to castle.*

KAMARI ΚΑΜΑΡΙ

10 km (6 mi) south of the Castle of Antimacheia, 35 km (22 mi) southwest of Kos town.

On Kefalos Bay, the little beach community of Kamari is pleasant and less frantic than the island's other seaside resorts. On a summit above is the lovely old town of Kefalos, a pleasant place to wander for its views and quintessential Greekness. Close offshore is a little rock formation holding a chapel to St. Nicholas. Opposite are the ruins of a magnificent 5th-century Christian basilica.

BEACHES

A chunk of the **Ayios Stefanos beach**, just north of Kamari, is now occupied by a Club Med; the rest belongs to beach clubs renting umbrellas and chairs and offering activities that include waterskiing and jet-skiing. Nearby **Paradise beach** (✉ *3 km [2mi] north of Kamari*) has plenty of parking, and thus crowds, but the broad, sandy beach is magnificent and gives its name to a long stretch of sand that curves around the enchanting Gulf of Kefalos and, at its northern end, is undeveloped, almost deserted (and popular with nude bathers).

WHERE TO STAY & EAT

¢–$ ✕ **Faros.** It's not surprising that fish rules the menu at this seaside taverna at the very end of the beach in Kamari. In fact, some patrons arrive by dinghies from their yachts anchored offshore. The friendly staff will take you into the kitchen and show you the fresh catch of the day; then they'll grill or bake it to your liking. ✉ *Beachfront, Kamari* ☎ *22420/71240* ▭ *MC, V.*

¢ **Hotel Kokalakis Beach.** The proprietors of this affordable hotel located on Kamari's beach road say they value quiet, and they're not just paying lip service. Many guests return annually for the peaceful proximity to pebble and sand beaches. The hotel is also walking distance from Kamari's strip of restaurants and cafés. Rooms are whitewashed, with ceramic tile floors, and six include cooking facilities. ✉ *Waterfront, 85301Kamari* ☎ *22420/71496* *32 rooms* *In-room: refrigerator. In-hotel: pool, bar, no elevator, public Internet* ▭ *No credit cards* *Closed May–Oct.*

PATMOS ΠΑΤΜΟΣ

Rocky and barren, the small, 34-square-km (21-square-mi) island of Patmos lies beyond the islands of Kalymnos and Leros, northwest of Kos. Here on a hillside is the Monastery of the Apocalypse, which enshrines the cave where St. John received the Revelation in AD 95. Scattered evidence of Mycenaean presence remains on Patmos, and walls of the classical period indicate the existence of a town near Skala. Most of the island's approximately 2,800 people live in three villages:

Skala, medieval Chora, and the small rural settlement of Kambos. The island is popular among the faithful making pilgrimages to the monastery as well as with vacationing Athenians and a wealthy international set who have bought homes in Chora. Administrators have carefully contained development, and as a result, Patmos retains its charm and natural beauty—even in the busy month of August.

SKALA ΣΚΑΛΑ

161 km (100 mi) north of Kos.

Skala, the island's small but sophisticated main town, is where almost all the hotels and restaurants are located. It's a popular port of call for cruise ships, and in summer the huge liners often loom over the chic shops and restaurants. There's not much to see in the town, but it is lively and very attractive, and, since strict building codes have been enforced, even new buildings have traditional architectural detail. The medieval town of Chora, only 5 km (3 mi) above Skala, and the island's legendary monasteries are nearby.

Take a 20-minute hike up to **Kastelli,** on a hill overlooking Skala, to see the stone remains of the city's 6th- to 4th-century BC town and acropolis.

BEACHES

The small island is endowed with at least 24 beaches. Although most of them, which tend to be coarse shingle, are accessible by land, sun worshippers can sail to a few (as well as to the nearby islet cluster of **Arkoi**) on the caïques that make regular runs from Skala, leaving in the morning. Prices vary with the number of people making the trip (or with the boat); transport to and from a beach for a family for a day may cost around €35. The beach at **Melloi,** a 2-km (1-mi) taxi ride north of Skala or a quick caïque ride, is a sand-and-pebble strip with a taverna nearby. The beach at **Kambos** (✉ *6 km [4 mi] from Skala*) bay is the most popular on the island. It has mostly fine pebbles and sand, nearby tavernas, windsurfing, waterskiing, and pedal boats for rent.

OFF THE BEATEN PATH

Psili Amos, a sand beach located 15 km (9 mi) from Skala, on the south shore, is worth the extra effort to reach; it's arguably the most beautiful of the island. Getting there requires a 45-minute caïque ride (€10) or a 20-minute walk on a footpath from Diakofti, the narrowest point on the island, where visitors can park their cars by the taverna. Nude bathers sometimes line the edges of the beach.

WHERE TO STAY & EAT

$–$$ ★ ✕**Benetos.** A native Patmian, Benetos Matthaiou, and his American wife, Susan, operate this lovely restaurant abutting a seaside garden that supplies the kitchen with fresh herbs and vegetables. Homegrown ingredients, including aromatic cherry tomatoes, find their way into a selection of Mediterranean-style dishes that include phyllo parcels stuffed with spinach and cheese, the island's freshest Greek salad, and a juicy grilled swordfish. Accompany your meal with a selection from the eclectic Greek wine list. Service is gracious and friendly, if a bit slow. ✉ *On harborside road between Skala and Grikos, Sapsila* ☎ *22470/33089* 💳 *MC, V* ⊙ *Closed Mon. and mid-Oct.–May.*

¢–$ ✕ **Ostria.** After a long day of swimming or boating, locals gravitate to this frill-free fish taverna on the harbor. Basic wooden furniture, plastic tablecloths, and bare lightbulbs are the only decor in the tented summer eating area. But this is the perfect place for watching Skala's human traffic pass by while sipping an ouzo and tackling an overflowing fried seafood *pikilia* (appetizer sampler). ✉ *Waterfront* ☎ *69794/38275* 💳 *No credit cards* ⊙ *Closed mid-Oct–May.*

$$$ ★ **Porto Scoutari.** It seems only fitting that Patmos should have a hotel that reflects the architectural beauty of the island while providing luxurious accommodations. Guest rooms are enormous and have sitting and sleeping areas, in addition to large terraces that face the sea and a verdant garden with a swimming pool. Furnishings differ from room to room and include brass beds and reproduction Greek antiques; the lobby and breakfast rooms are also exquisitely decorated with traditional pieces. Owner Elina Scoutari, who lived in Washington, D.C., for many years, is on hand to see to your needs. A short walk takes you to Melloi beach. ✉ *1 km (½ mi) northeast of Skala center, 85500* ☎ *22470/33123* 📠 *22470/33175* 🌐 *www.portoscoutari.com* *30 rooms, 4 suites* *In-room: kitchen, dial-up. In-hotel: bar, pool, no elevator, public Wi-Fi* 💳 *MC, V* ⊙ *Closed Nov.–late Feb.* *BP.*

$ ★ **Captain's House.** One of the very special places to stay in Patmos, largely because the owners are so pleasant, this small pink hotel with green shutters faces the sea at the edge of Skala. Stone arches accent the multilevel lobby, re-creating the feel of old Patmos. The wood-furnished, plain rooms are pleasantly breezy, and all have balconies that face either the harbor or the pool area. The TV in the lounge gets satellite stations. ✉ *Inland, south of main street, 85500* ☎ *22470/31793* 📠 *22470/34077* 🌐 *www.captains-house.gr* *19 rooms* *In-hotel: bar, pool, no elevator* 💳 *MC, V* ⊙ *Closed mid-Oct.–Mar.* *CP.*

SHOPPING

Patmos has some elegant boutiques selling jewelry and crafts, including antiques, mainly from the island. **Katoi** (✉ *Skala–Chora road* ☎ *22470/31487 or 22470/34107*) has a wide selection of ceramics, icons, and silver jewelry of traditional design. **Parousia** (✉ *Past square at beginning of road to Chora* ☎ *22470/32549*) is a good place to purchase Byzantine-style icons, wooden children's toys, and small religious items.

Whether made of ceramic, glass, silver, or wood, each work—by one of 40 different Greek artists—at **Selene** (✉ *Skala harbor* ☎ *22470/31742*) is unique.

CHORA ΧΩΡΑ

5 km (3 mi) south, above Skala.

Atop a hill due south of Skala, the village of Chora, clustered around the walls of the Monastery of St. John the Theologian, has become a preserve of international wealth. Though the short distance from Skala may make walking seem attractive, a steep incline can make this challenging. A taxi ride is not expensive, about €6, and there is frequent bus service (€1) from Skala and other points on the island.

In AD 95, during the emperor Domitian's persecution of Christians, St. John the Theologian was banished to Patmos, where he lived until his reprieve two years later. He writes that it was on Patmos that he "heard ... a great voice, as of a trumpet," commanding him to write a book and "send it unto the seven churches." According to tradition, St. John wrote the text of *Revelation* in the little cave, the Sacred ★ Grotto, now built into the **Monastery of the Apocalypse.** The voice of God spoke through a threefold crack in the rock, and the saint dictated to his follower Prochorus. A slope in the wall is pointed to as the desk where Prochorus wrote, and a silver halo is set on the stone that was the apostle's pillow. The grotto is decorated with wall paintings of the 12th century and icons from the 16th. The monastery, which is accessible via several flights of outdoor stairs, was constructed in the 17th century from architectural fragments of earlier buildings, and further embellished in later years; it also contains chapels to St. Artemios and St. Nicholas. In late August or early September, the monastery hosts the **Festival of Sacred Music of Patmos,** with world-class Byzantine and ecclesiastical music performances in an outdoor performance space. ✉ *2 km (1 mi) south on Skala–Chora road* ☎ *22470/31234 monastery, 22470/29363 festival* *Free* ⏲ *Mon., Wed., Fri., and Sat. 8–1:30; Tues., Thurs., and Sun. 8–1:30 and 4–6.*

MMMMM...

The best goods on the island might be of the baked variety. Be sure to sample specialities like *poogies* (confectioners' sugar–coated cookies stuffed with almond and walnut chunks) and soufflé-like cheese pies. Two places with grin-inducing treats are:

The baker is up long before the roosters at **Fegaros Bakery** (✉ *Dimarxou Ioanni Fegaros, toward central square* ☎ *22470/31394*) nestled in Chora's central whitewashed artery.

Koumanis Bakery (✉ *Off central square* ☎ *22470/32894*) is located near the chic shops.

Fodor's Choice ★ The **Monastery of St. John the Theologian,** on its high perch, is one of the finest extant examples of a fortified medieval monastic complex. Hosios Christodoulos, a man of education, energy, devotion, and vision who built the Theotokos Monastery in Kos, came to Patmos in 1088 to set up the island's now-famous monastery. From its inception, it attracted monks of education and social standing, who made sure that it was ornamented with the best sculpture, carvings, and paintings. It was an intellectual center, with a rich library and a tradition of teaching, and by the end of the 12th century it owned land on Leros, Limnos, Crete, and Asia Minor, as well as ships, which carried on trade exempt from taxes. A broad staircase leads to the entrance, which was fortified by towers and buttresses. The complex consists of buildings from a number of periods: in front of the entrance is the 17th-century **Chapel of the Holy Apostles**; the **main church** dates from the time of Christodoulos (whose skull, along with that of Apostle Thomas, is encased in a silver sarcophagus here); the **Chapel of the Virgin** is 12th century.

The **treasury** contains relics, icons, silver, and vestments, most dating from 1600 to 1800. Many of the objects are votives dedicated by the clerics, nobles, and wealthy individuals; one of the most beautiful is an 11th-century icon of St. Nicholas, executed in the finest mosaic work, in an exquisitely chased silver frame. Another treasure is an El Greco icon. On display, too, are some of the library's oldest codices, dating to the late 5th and the 8th century, such as pages from the Gospel of St. Mark and the Book of Job. The more than 600 vestments are of luxurious fabrics, elaborately embroidered with gold, silver, and multicolor silks. Though not open to the public, the **library** contains extensive treasures: illuminated manuscripts, approximately 1,000 codices, and more than 3,000 printed volumes. The collection was first cataloged in 1200; of the 267 works of that time, the library still has 111. The archives preserve a near-continuous record, down to the present, of the history of the monastery as well as the political and economic history of the region. ✉*3 km (2 mi) south of Monastery of the Apocalypse* ☎*22470/20800* 🌐*www.monipatmou.gr* 🎫*Church and chapels free, treasury €6* ⏲*Daily 8–1:30 (also 4–6 on Sun., Tues., and Thurs.); Dec.–Mar. call to arrange a treasury visit, as hrs are irregular.*

WHERE TO EAT

¢–$ Fodor'sChoice ★ ✕**Vangelis.** At this pleasant taverna, you can choose between a table on the main square (perfect for people-watching) or in the Paradise Garden out back, where a raised terrace has stunning views of the sea. Fresh grilled fish and lemon-and-oregano-flavored goat are the specialties, and simple dishes such as mint-flavored *dolmades* (stuffed grape leaves) and *tzatziki* (yogurt and cucumber dip) are excellent. Want traditional lodging to go with that meal? The management is happy to help find rooms in private homes in Chora. ✉*Main square, 85500* ☎*22470/31967* 💳*No credit cards.*

RHODES & THE DODECANESE ESSENTIALS

TRANSPORTATION

BY AIR

CARRIERS There are more than eight flights per day to Rhodes from Athens on Olympic Airlines or Aegean Airlines, and extra flights are added during high season. The 45-minute flight costs about €115 one way. Olympic flies to Rhodes from Heraklion (1 hour, €100) at least three times per day and several times a week from Thessaloniki (1¼ hours, €117). It is possible to fly directly to Rhodes from a number of European capitals, especially on charters.

To Kos, Olympic Airlines runs three daily flights from Athens, and three flights a week from Rhodes. Schedules are reduced in winter. Neither Patmos nor Symi have airports.

Contacts Aegean Airlines (✉ *Rhodes Airport, Rhodes town* ☎ *22410/98345, 210/626–1000 in Athens* 🌐 *www.aegeanair.gr*). **Olympic Airlines** (✉ *Ierou Lochou 9, Rhodes town, Rhodes* ☎ *22410/24555, 210/966-6666 in Athens* 📠 *210/966-6111* ✉ *Vasileos Pavlou 22, Kos town, Kos* ☎ *22420/28331 or 22420/28332* 🌐 *www.olympicairlines.com*).

AIRPORTS Rhodes Airport is about 20 minutes from Rhodes town, and it's best to take a taxi (about €15). Though private vehicles must have permits to enter the Old Town, a taxi may enter if carrying luggage, no matter what a reluctant driver tells you. Kos airport is located 26 km (16 mi) southwest of Kos town. There is bus and taxi service from there to Kos town.

13

Information Kos Airport (☎ *22420/51229*). **Rhodes Airport** (☎ *22410/88700*).

BY BOAT & FERRY

When traveling from Piraeus to Rhodes by ferry (12–18 hours, €35–€90), you first make several stops, including at Patmos (6–10 hours, €25–€81) and Kos (10–16 hours, €30–€80). Bringing a car aboard can quadruple costs. Of the several ferry lines serving the Dodecanese, Blue Star Ferries and G&A Ferries have the largest boats and the most frequent service, both sailing several times a week out of Piraeus. The Athens–Dodecanese ferry schedule changes seasonally, so contact ferry lines, the Piraeus Port Authority, the Greek National Tourism Organization (GNTO or EOT) in Athens, or a travel agency for details.

BETWEEN THE ISLANDS The easiest way to travel among the Dodecanese islands is by hydrofoil or catamaran. ANES has hydrofoils and catamarans running in the summer between Symi and Rhodes and other islands.

Contacts ANES (✉ *Harbor front, Yialos, Symi* ☎ *22460/71444* 🌐 *www.anes.gr*).

Piraeus Port Authority (☎ *1442*). **Rhodes Port Authority** (☎ *22410/22220*).

BY BUS

There is a decent bus network on all the islands, though there are more-infrequent routes on smaller islands. Buses from Rhodes town leave from two different points on Averoff street for the island's east and west sides. Symi's and Patmos's bus stations are located on the harbor. Kos has a city bus and KTEL island buses; locations of both stations are expected to change by 2009, so call if you can't find the relevant stop.

Information Kos KTEL bus station (✉ *Cleopatras, Kos town, Kos* ☎ *22420/22292*). **Kos town bus station** (✉ *Akti Koundouriotou [main harbor], Kos town, Kos* ☎ *22420/26276*). **Rhodes east-side buses** (✉ *Averoff near end of Rimini Sq., Rhodes town, Rhodes* ☎ *22410/27706*). **Rhodes west-side buses** (✉ *Averoff next to market, Rhodes town, Rhodes* ☎ *22410/26300*).

BY CAR

You may take a car to the Dodecanese on one of the large ferries that sail daily from Piraeus to Rhodes and less frequently to the smaller islands. On Rhodes, the roads are good, there are not many of them, and good maps are available. It is possible to tour the island in one day if you rent a car. Traffic is likely to be heavy only from Rhodes town to Lindos.

In Kos, a car is advisable only if you are interested in seeing points outside Kos town, and even then it's not necessary. In Patmos, a car or motorbike makes it easy to tour the island, though most other sights and outlying restaurants are easily reached by bus or taxi, and a few beaches can be reached by either bus or boat. Symi, which has only one road suitable for cars, is best explored on foot or by boat.

Rental Agencies **Budget Drive Rent-a-Car** (✉ *Km 1 mark on Tsairi–airport road, Rhodes town, Rhodes* ☎ *22410/68243* 🌐 *www.driverentacar.gr* ✉ *Airport, Rhodes* ☎ *22410/81011*). **Holiday Autos** (✉ *Karaiskaki 9, Kos town, Kos* ☎ *22420/22997* 📠 *22420/27608*).

Local Rental Agencies **Autoway** (✉ *Vasileos Georgiou 18, Rhodes, Rhodes* ☎ *22420/25326* 🌐 *www.autowaykos.gr*). **Tassos** (✉ *Skala, Patmos* ☎ *22470/31753* 📠 *22470/32210*).

BY TAXI

Taxis are available throughout the island of Rhodes, including at most resorts. All taxi stands in Rhodes have a sign listing set fares to destinations around the island. Expect a delay when calling radio taxis in high season. ⚠ **Patmos taxi drivers move at breakneck speed on twisty roads. Fortunately, most journeys are short.**

Contacts Taxis (✉ *Agious Apostolous, Rhodes town, Rhodes* ☎ *22410/64712 or 22410/64756*). **Taxis** (✉ *Skala, Patmos* ☎ *22470/31225*).

CONTACTS & RESOURCES

EMERGENCIES

As elsewhere in Greece, pharmacies in the Dodecanese post in their windows a list showing which locations are open 24 hours and on which days.

Information **Hospital** (✉ *Agion Apostolon, Rhodes town, Rhodes* ☎ *22410/80000* ✉ *Ippokratous 34, Kos town, Kos* ☎ *22420/22300* ✉ *Ippokratous 34, Skala, Patmos* ☎ *22470/31211* ✉ *1 mi on the Skala–Chora road, Skala,Patmos* ☎ *22470/31211*). **Medical Clinic** (✉ *Yialos, Symi* ☎ *22460/71290 [Yialos] and 22460/71316 [Chorio]*). **Emergency** (☎ *166 in Rhodes and Kos*). **Police** (✉ *Ethelondon Dodekanissou 45, Rhodes town, Rhodes* ☎ *100 in Rhodes and Kos, 22470/31303 in Patmos, 22460/71111 in Symi*). **Tourist police** (✉ *Odos Karpathou 1, Rhodes town, Rhodes* ☎ *22410/27423* ✉ *Akti Miaouli 2, Kos town, Kos* ☎ *22863, 26666*).

INTERNET, MAIL & SHIPPING

Internet Internet Cafés are not hard to spot in the main port towns. They range from organized operations with scanners and printers, to cafés, bars, or pool halls with one or two computers in the back. Most have high speed connections. **iArena** (✉ *Navarinou 4, Kos town, Kos* ☎ *22420/25333*). **Blue Bay Hotel** (✉ *South edge of Skala Harbor, Patmos* ☎ *22470/31165* 🌐 *www.bluebaypatmos.gr*). **Control Café** (✉ *Alexandrou Diakou 44, Rhodes town, Rhodes* ☎ *22410/24564* 🌐 *www.controlcafe.gr*). **Del Mare** (✉ *Alexander the Great 4a, Kos town, Kos* ☎ *22420/24244* 🌐 *www.cybercafe.gr*). **Kantirimi Café** (✉ *Yialos Central Sq, Yialos, Symi* ☎ *22460/71381*). **Lindianet Internet Café** (✉ *Next to*

Chinese restaurant and Pallas Travel, 85107 Lindos Rhodes ☎22440/32142 🌐www.lindianet.gr).

Mail Post Office (*✉Eleftherias Sq 1, Rhodes town, Rhodes ☎22410/35560 ✉Vas. Pavlou 12, Kos town, Kos ☎22420/22250 ✉Near clock tower and next to police station, Yialos, Symi ☎22460/71315 ✉Harbour, Skala, Patmos ☎22470/31316*).

Shipping Rhodes has a host of international couriers. There are also big courier offices in Kos, and fewer in Patmos. There is courier service on Symi, but ask locals for help in finding local companies doing the shipments as these can change from year to year. **DHL** (*✉Kapodistriou 1, Rhodes town, Rhodes ☎22410/76215 🌐www.dhl.gr ✉Bouboulinas 23, Kos town, Kos ☎22420/21368*). **Speedex** (*✉Ethniki Antistaseos 39, Rhodes town, Rhodes ☎22410/70999 🌐www.speedex.gr ✉Mandilara 56, Kos town, Kos ☎22420/22493 ✉Skala harbour, Skala, Patmos ☎22470/33000*).

MEDIA

The region's only English-language newspaper is found on Symi. The *Symi Visitor*, available at tourist spots, is full of information on events, news, and activities, plus has an overview of the sites, and bus and ferry schedules. The Web site also has weather updates and information on finding accommodations on Symi.

Contact Symi Visitor (*✉Yialos harbor front, near bus station, Yialos, Symi ☎22460/72755 🌐www.symivisitor.com*).

TOUR OPTIONS

From April to October, local island boat tours take you to area sights and may include a picnic on a remote beach or even a visit to the shores of Turkey. For example, Triton Holidays of Rhodes organizes a visit to Lindos by boat; a caïque leaves Mandraki harbor in Rhodes town in the morning, deposits you in Lindos for a day of sightseeing and beachgoing, and returns you in the evening for €20. You can also take their boat trip to Marmaris, Turkey (€35, plus €14 Turkish port tax), which includes a free guided tour of the city. On Symi, Kalodoukas Tours runs boat trips to the Monastery of Panormitis, as well as to secluded beaches and islets, which include swimming and a barbecue lunch. Aeolos Travel in Kos organizes one-day cruises to other islands. A1 Yacht Trade Consortium organizes sailing tours around the Greek islands near the Turkish coast. Many island agencies, such as Symi Tours, on Symi, and Astoria Travel, on Patmos, offer help with yacht-docking paperwork.

If you're not renting a car on Rhodes, it can be worth it to take a bus tour to its southern points and interior. Triton Holidays has, among other trips, a guided bus tour to Thermes Kallitheas, Epta Piges, and Lindos (€30); a bus tour to Kameiros, Filerimos, and Petaloudes (€30); and a full-day trip through several points in the interior and south (€35). Astoria Travel provides day bus trips to Patmos's St. John the Theologian Monastery and the Monastery of the Apocalypse (€20).

On Symi, George Kalodoukas of Kalodoukas Tours leads wonderful guided hiking tours around the island and does an excursion to his

Marathoudas beach–area organic farm. The company sells a short book by Frances Noble (€7) that outlines 25 walks around the island. On Rhodes, you can pick up a book with 18 walks from the Rhodes town EOT office *(⇨ Visitor Information)*.

Contacts **A1 Yacht Trade Consortium** (✉ *Vyronas 1, at Canada, Rhodes town, Rhodes* ☎ *22410/22927* 🌐 *www.a1yachting.com*). **Aeolos Travel** (✉ *Navarinou 55, Kos town, Kos* ☎ *22420/26203* 🌐 *www.tritondmc.gr*). **Astoria Travel** (✉ *Skala harbor, Patmos* ☎ *22470/31205* 🌐 *www.astoriatravel.com*). **Kalodoukas Tours** (✉ *Behind Trawler's taverna, Yialos, Symi* ☎ *22460/71077* 🌐 *www.symi-greece.com*). **Symi Tours** (✉ *Symi harbor, Yialos, Symi* ☎ *22460/71307* 📠 *22460/70011*). **Triton Holidays** (✉ *Plastira 9, Rhodes town, Rhodes* ☎ *22410/21690* 🌐 *www.tritondmc.gr*).

VISITOR INFORMATION

In Rhodes, the Greek National Tourism Organization (GNTO or EOT), close to the medieval walls in the new town, has brochures and schedules for buses and boats. It's open June–September, weekdays 9–9 (8–3 the rest of the year). The central Rhodes Municipal Tourism Office, near the bus station, is open May–October, daily 7:30—11 PM. The city of Rhodes maintains a helpful English Web site.

Contacts **Greek National Tourism Organization (GNTO or EOT)** (✉ *Archbishop Makarios and Papagou, Rhodes town, Rhodes* ☎ *22410/44335 or 22410/44336* 🌐 *www.ando.gr/eot*). **Lindos Tourist Information** (✉ *Central Sq, Lindos, Rhodes* ☎ *22440/31900* 🕒 *Apr.—Oct., 9—9*). **Rhodes official Web site** (🌐 *www.rhodes.gr*). **Rhodes Municipal Tourism Office** (✉ *Averoff 3, Rhodes town, Rhodes* ☎ *22410/35945*).

Kos Municipal Tourism Office (✉ *Vasileos Georgiou 1, Kos town, Kos* ☎ *22420/24460*). **Patmos Municipal Tourism Office** (✉ *Near ferry dock, Skala, Patmos* ☎ *22470/31666*). **Municipality of Southern Rhodes** (✉ *Gennadi* ☎ *22440/43243* 🌐 *www.southrhodes.gr*).

The Northern Aegean Islands

LESBOS, CHIOS & SAMOS

14

St. John the Apostle

WORD OF MOUTH

"If you are looking for someplace a little off the beaten path, and don't care about trendy nightlife, you might want to look at the Northern Aegean islands such as Lesbos and Chios. Both are gorgeous, and very pleasant and relaxing places to spend time. Both have incredibly beautiful beaches. The food in this region of Greece, and particularly the seafood, is wonderful."

—eleni

www.fodors.com/forums

WELCOME TO THE NORTHERN AEGEAN ISLANDS

TOP REASONS TO GO

★ **Samos Block Party:** Pythagoras, Epicurus, and the fabulous Aesop were just a few of this island's brightest stars, and their spirits probably still haunt the ancient Heraion temple.

★ **Mesmerizing Mastic Villages:** Pirgi in Chios is known for the resin it produces, but with its Genoese houses patterned in black and white, it's the Escher-like landscape that's likely to stick with you.

★ **Sappho's Island:** If it's beauty you seek, head to one of Lesbos's oldest towns, Molyvos—a haven for artists and an aesthete's dream.

★ **Sailing to Byzantium:** Colorful Byzantine mosaics make Chios's 11th-century Nea Moni monastery an important piece of history—and a marvel to behold.

★ **Dizzyingly Good Ouzo:** Though you can get this potent potable anywhere in Greece, Lesbos's is reputedly the best—enjoy it with famed salt-baked Kalloni sardines.

Monks at monastery, Lesbos.

1 Lesbos. Birthplace of the erotic songs of poet Sappho (6th century BC), this huge island still reveres women—rarely will you see so many statues of female leaders—and you could easily spend a glorious week exploring its beaches, villages, petrified forests, and rocky mountains. Mytilini has good museums but is in short supply of charm. For that, head to marvelous Molyvos: artists flock here to paint its cobblestone streets and red roofs (mandated by law). Other destinations include Agiassos, the prettiest hill town, and Skala Eressou, birthplace of Sappho.

2 Chios. The island depends on the sea and its mastic production, not tourism, so you'll find the real Greece here. But you'll have to look beyond the chaotic, architecturally unappealing main town to explore the isle's allurements, including black pebble beaches, lush countryside, and quaint village squares. Chios is the "mastic island," producing the highly beneficial resin that is used in cakes, chewing gum, alcoholic drinks, and cosmetic products; the most noted mastic village is Pirgi, famed for the geometric patterns on its house facades. In addition, the 11th century monastery of Nea Moni is celebrated for its Byzantine court art.

3 Samos. Apart from its serene azure-water beaches and verdant landscapes, Samos's cuisine blends the flavors of Asia Minor with those of Greece in a most enticing way. At the top of any sightseer's list are the island's fabled ancient sites, such as the Temple at Heraion—once four times larger than the Parthenon—and the Roman baths and underground aqueduct at Pythagorio. With its close proximity to Turkey, Samos makes for a great stopover in a Greece-Turkey trip.

One of Samos's many churches.

GETTING ORIENTED

About the only thing the islands of Samos, Chios, and Lesbos share is their proximity to Turkey: from their shores, reaching from Macedonia down to the Dodecanese along the coast of Asia Minor, you can see the very fields of Greece's age-old rival. No matter that these three islands may be a long haul from Athens: Few parts of the Aegean have greater variety and beauty of landscape—a stunning blend of pristine shores and craggy (Homer's word) mountains.

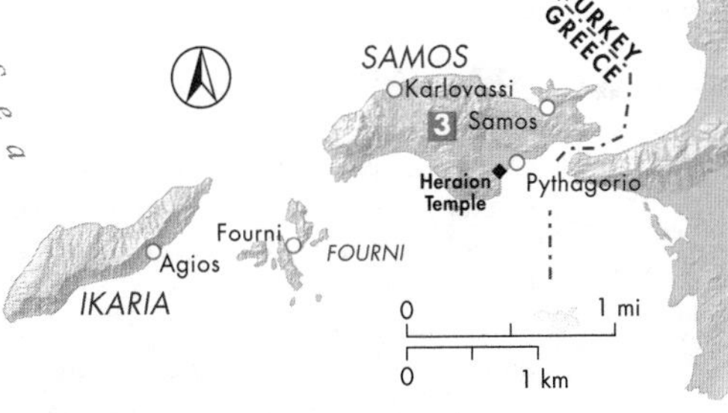

Mytilini's harbor, Lesbos (left).

THE NORTHERN AEGEAN ISLANDS PLANNER

Getting Around

The public (KTEL) bus system on the Northern Aegean islands is reliable, cheap (a few euros one way), and obliging.

Buses run from Chios town to other villages to the north, west, northwest and south, from three to six times per day (usually from 7 AM to 4:30 PM, depending on the part of the island).

Buses depart from Mytilene town chiefly to Petra and Molyvos, and schedules depend largely on the time of year and day of the week, usually leaving at 11 AM and 1:15 PM and taking around two hours each way.

Buses on Samos are, as in Chios, more numbered and regular throughout the summer months, heading to the majority of towns and villages around the island.

Particularly in the case of Lesbos, where bus services leave something to be desired, but also on Chios and Samos, it is worth renting a car or motorbike to really explore the island.

An international driving license is a definite requirement, and fully insured cars will usually cost between 30–50 euros during the high season.

Making the Most of Your Time

If you have time to visit two islands over a 5–14 day period, start by exploring Mytilini, the capital of Lesbos, a bustling center of commerce and learning, with its grand old mansions overlooking the harbour. From there, head to the countryside, to the northern destinations: Molyvos, a medieval town sprawling under the impressive Molyvos castle; Skala Eressou with its fine beach and bars; and the hilltop Agiassos, immersed in verdant forests. For your second stop, take a ferry to Chios, where you can enjoy the nightlife in the main town, and don't miss the old quarter. Travel via Lithi—derived from Alithis limin, meaning "true haven," which is rather apt for this beautiful fishing village—to enjoy a good fish lunch. Next, go to the peaceful and unspoilt Vessa, Pirgi (famous for its unique mosaics), and Mesta, part of the "masticohoria" or mastic villages, world renowned for their cultivation of mastic trees, which preserve a Greece of centuries past. Alternatively, take the ferry from Piraeus directly to Samos, a fine scenario if you can just visit one island. Circle the island, stopping at its lovely beaches and at Pythagorio, the ancient capital, or the temple at Heraion, one of the Wonders of the Ancient World. Consider visiting the traditional fishing village of Kokkari, which has managed to keep its architectural authenticity, then to the beaches Tsamadou and Lemonaki, where the green pine slopes meet the heavenly blue waters of the Mediterranean. If you're drawn to the shores of Turkey, Samos makes a convenient stopover, as there's a daily ferry service.

Top Spots to Stay

On Lesbos, stay on Mytilini if you like a busy, citylike ambiance, on Molyvos for its dramatic medieval beauty or Skala Eressou for its laid-back beach style. On Chios avoid staying in the main town (Chios town) unless you're just stopping over briefly, as it lacks in beauty and style, and opt to stay in the picturesque mastic village of Mesta instead. Vathi (Samos town), the main town, is a good central option in Samos, but even more ideal is the atmospheric and naturally abundant Pythagorio.

Dining à la Lesbos, Chios & Samos

Hospitality and good, fresh food abound on the Northern Islands. Fish is relatively expensive; lobster (crayfish to Americans) is popular and pricey, and sweet fresh shrimp comes from Lesbos's Kalloni gulf. Kakavia, a dish found on many fish tavern menus around the Greek islands, is fisherman's soup made with small fish, seafood, tomatoes, and onions.

Lesbos, especially, is known for its good food: try the keskek (a special meat mixed with wheat, served most often at festivals) and Kalloni bay sardines, the fleshiest in the Mediterranean, which are salted for a few hours and eaten, with a texture reminiscent of succulent sushi. Octopus, simmered in wine or grilled, goes perfectly with the famous island ouzo, of which there are several dozen brands.

Fresh figs, almonds, and raisins are delicious; a Lesbos dessert incorporating one of those native treats is baleze (almond pudding).

Besides being recognized for its mastic products, Chios is known for tangerines. Preserved in syrup, they are served as a gliko koutaliou, or spoon sweet, meaning you spoon them into water or another beverage, or eat them with a spoon. Thyme-scented honey, yiorti (the local version of keskek), and revithokeftedes (chickpea patties), are Samos's edible claims to fame. In Chios you'll find a great variety of mastic-flavor sweets as well as savory foods, while in Samos the cuisine is flavored with interesting Turkish influences.

Dining & Lodging Prices in Euros

	¢	$	$$	$$$	$$$$
Restaurants	under €8	€8–€11	€11–€15	€15–€20	over €20
Hotels	under €60	€60–€90	€90–€120	€120–€160	over €160

Restaurant prices are for one main course at dinner, or for two mezedes (small dishes). Hotel prices are for a standard double room in high season, including taxes. Hotels operate on the European Plan (EP, with no meal provided) unless we note that they use the Continental Plan (CP, with Continental breakfast); Breakfast Plan (BP, with a full breakfast); Modified American Plan (MAP, with breakfast and dinner); or the Full American Plan (FAP, with all meals). Inquire when booking if these meal plans (which can entail higher rates) are mandatory. Guest rooms have air-conditioning, room phones, and TVs unless otherwise noted.

When to Go

Like everywhere else in the world, Greece is affected by the climate change phenomenon, which guarantees unpredictable weather; sometimes periods which are expected to be sizzling hot will be classified by rainfall and wind and vice versa.

However, as changes are not yet completely drastic, one can basically rely on the knowledge that from early May to early June, the weather is sunny and warm and the sea is still a bit chilly for swimming in.

From mid-June until the end of August, the weather goes through quite a sweeping change and can become very hot, although the waters of the Aegean can prove sufficiently refreshing.

In September the weather begins to mellow considerably, and by mid-October is usually at its warmth limit for swimming, although sunshine can continue throughout the year on and off.

Between November and March these islands can make for an enjoyable trip, and although unlike the smaller islands there are enough restaurants, museums, and sites open to visitors, the cold weather can make ferries unreliable.

Updated by Adrian Vrettos

QUIRKY, SEDUCTIVE, FERTILE, SENSUAL, FADED, sunny, worldly, ravishing, long-suffering, hedonistic, luscious, mysterious, legendary—these adjectives only begin to describe the islands of the northeastern Aegean. This startling and rather arbitrary archipelago includes a number of islands, such as Ikaria, Samothraki, and Thassos; in this book we focus on the three largest—Lesbos, Chios, and Samos. Closer to Turkey's coast than to Greece's, and quite separate from one another, these islands are hilly, sometimes mountainous, with dramatic coastlines and uncrowded beaches, brilliant architecture, and unforgettable historic sites. Lesbos, Greece's third-largest island and birthplace of legendary artists and writers, is dense with gnarled olive groves and dappled with mineral springs. Chios, though ravaged by fire, retains an eerie beauty and has fortified villages, old mansions, Byzantine monasteries, and stenciled-wall houses. Samos, the lush, mountainous land of wine and honey, whispers of the classical wonders of antiquity.

Despite the Northern Islands' proximity to Asia Minor, they are the essence of Greece, the result of 4,000 years of Hellenic influence. Lesbos, Chios, and Samos prospered gloriously in the ancient world as important commercial and religious centers, though their significance waned under the Ottoman Empire. They also were cultural hothouses, producing such geniuses as Pythagoras, Sappho, and probably Homer.

These are not strictly sun-and-fun islands with the extent of tourist infrastructure of, say, the Cyclades. Many young backpackers and party seekers seem to bypass the northern Aegean. You can still carve out plenty of beach time by day and wander into lively restaurants and bars at night, but these islands reveal a deeper character, tracing histories that date back to ancient, Byzantine, and post-Byzantine times, and offering landscapes that are both serene and unspoiled. Visitors to the Northern Islands should expect to find history, culture, beauty, and hospitality. These islands offer commodities that are valued ever more highly by travelers—a sense of discovery and the chance to interact with rich, enduring cultures.

EXPLORING THE NORTHERN ISLANDS

The island of Lesbos is carved by two large, sandy bays, the gulfs of Kalloni and Yera. Undulating hills and cultivated valleys, pine-clad mountains, beaches, springs, desert, and even a petrified forest are also part of the Lesbos terrain. Deep green valleys and rolling hills punctuated by mastic villages characterize Chios. Samos, bathed in green, is filled with pine forests, olive groves, citrus trees, and grape vines, as well as soft hills that fall into the breathtaking Aegean Sea.

LESBOS ΛΕΣΒΟΣ

The Turks called Lesbos the "garden of the empire" for its fertility: in the east and center of the island, about 12 million olive trees line the hills in seemingly endless undulating groves. The western landscape is filled with oak trees, sheep pastures, rocky outcrops, and mountains. Wildflowers and grain cover the valleys, and the higher peaks are wreathed in dark green pines. This third-largest island in Greece is filled with beauty, but its real treasures are the creative artists and thinkers it has produced and inspired through the ages.

Lesbos was once a major cultural center, known for its Philosophical Academy, where Epicurus and Aristotle taught. It was also the birthplace of the philosopher Theophrastus, who presided over the Academy in Athens; of the great lyric poet Sappho; of Terpander, the "father of Greek music"; and of Arion, who influenced the later playwrights Sophocles and Alcaeus, inventors of the dithyramb (a short poem with an erratic strain). Even in modernity, artists have emerged from Lesbos: Theophilos, a poor villager who earned his ouzo by painting some of the finest naive modern art Greece has produced; novelists Stratis Myrivilis and Argyris Eftaliotis; and the 1979 Nobel Prize–winning poet Odysseus Elytis.

The island's history stretches back to the 6th century BC, when its two mightiest cities, Mytilini and Mythimna (now Molyvos), settled their squabbles under the tyrant Pittacus, considered one of Greece's Seven Sages. Thus began the creative era, but later times brought forth the same pillaging and conquest that overturned other Greek islands. In 527 BC the Persians conquered Lesbos, and the Athenians, Romans, Byzantines, Venetians, Genoese, and Turks took their turns adding their influences. After the Turkish conquest, from 1462 to 1912, much of the population was sent to Turkey, and traces of past civilizations that weren't already destroyed by earthquakes were wiped out by the conquerors. Greece gained sovereignty over the island in 1923. This led to the breaking of trade ties with Asia Minor, diminishing the island's wealth, and limiting the economy to agriculture.

Lesbos has more inhabitants than either Corfu or Rhodes, with only a fraction of the tourists, so here you can get a good idea of real island life in Greece. Many Byzantine and post-Byzantine sites dot the island's landscape, including castles and archaeological monuments, churches, and monasteries. The traditional architecture of stone and wood, inspired by Asia Minor, adorns the mansions, tower houses, and other homes of the villages. Beach composition varies throughout the island from pebble to sand. Some of the most spectacular sandy beaches and coves are in the southwest.

MYTILINI ΜΥΤΙΛΗΝΗ

350 km (217 mi) northeast of Piraeus. 218 km (135 mi) southeast of Thessaloniki.

Set on the ruins of an ancient city, Mytilini (so important through history that many call Lesbos by the port's name alone) is, like Lesbos, sculpted by two bays, making its coast resemble a jigsaw-puzzle piece. This busy main town and port, with stretches of grand waterfront mansions and a busy old bazaar area, were once the scene of a dramatic

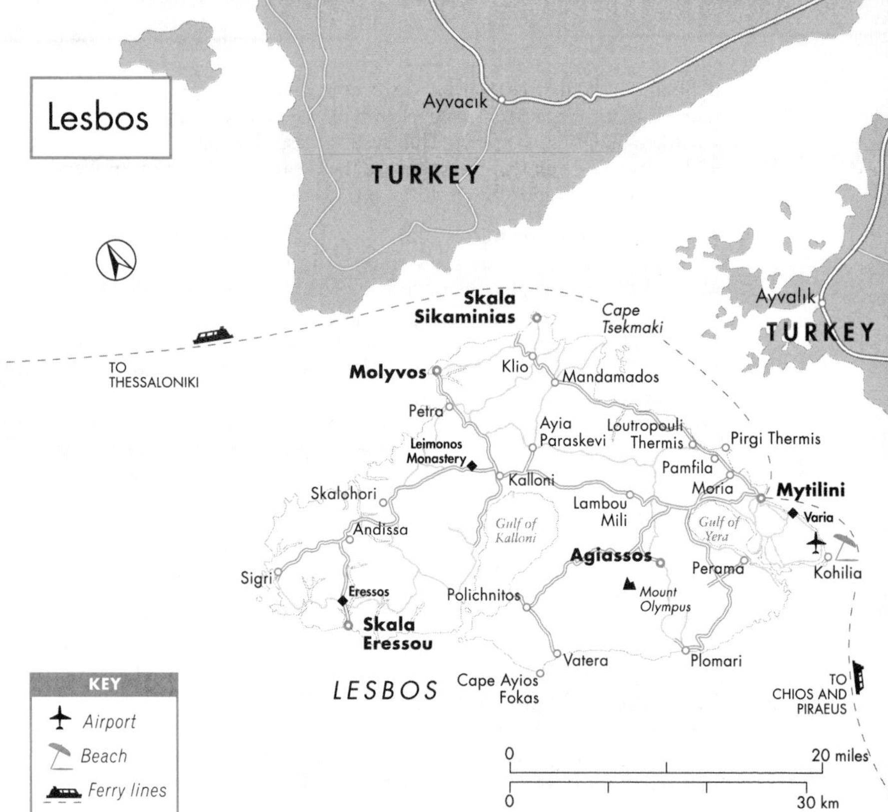

moment in Greek history. Early in the Peloponnesian War, Mytilini revolted against Athens but surrendered in 428 BC. As punishment, the Athens assembly decided to kill all men in Lesbos and enslave all women and children, and a boat was dispatched to carry out the order. The next day a less-vengeful mood prevailed; the assembly repealed its decision and sent a second ship after the first. The second ship pulled into the harbor just as the commander of the first finished reading the death sentence. Just in time, Mytilini was saved. The bustling waterfront just south of the headland between the town's two bays is where most of the town's sights are clustered.

Stroll the main bazaar street, **Ermou,** which goes from port to port. Walk past the fish market on the southern end, where men haul in their sardines, mullet, and octopuses. Narrow lanes are filled with antiques shops and grand old mansions.

The elegant seaside suburb of Varia was home to the modern "naive" artist Theophilos; Tériade, publisher of modern art journals; and poet Odysseus Elytis.

The pine-covered headland between the bays—a nice spot for a picnic—supports a **kastro,** a stone fortress with intact walls that seem to protect the town even today. Built by the Byzantines on a 600 BC temple of Apollo, it was repaired with available material (note the ancient pillars crammed between the stones) by Francesco Gateluzzi of the famous Genoese family. Look above the gates for the two-headed eagle of the Palaiologos emperors, the horseshoe arms of the Gateluzzi family, and inscriptions made by Turks, who enlarged it; today it is a **military bastion.** Inside the castle there's only a crumbling **prison** and a **Roman cistern,** but you should make the visit for the fine view. ✉ *On pine-covered hill* ☎ *22510/27297* 🎫 *€2* 🕙 *Tues.–Sun. 8–2:30.*

The only vestige of ancient Mytilini is the freely accessible ruin of an **ancient theater,** one of the largest in ancient Greece, from the Hellenistic period. Pompey admired it so much that he copied it for his theater in Rome. Though the marbles are gone, the shape, carved out of the mountain, remains beautifully intact. ✉ *In pine forest northeast of town.*

The enormous post-Baroque church of **Ayios Therapon,** built in the 19th century, is reminiscent of some styles in Italy. It has an ornate interior, a frescoed dome, and, in its courtyard, a **Vizantino Mouseio,** or Byzantine Museum, filled with icons. ✉ *Southern waterfront* ☎ *22510/28916* 🎫 *Church and museum €2* 🕙 *Mon.–Sat. 9–1.*

In front of the cathedral of Ayios Athanasios there is a **traditional Lesbos house,** restored and furnished in 19th-century style. Call owner Marika Vlachou to arrange a visit. ✉ *Mitropoleos 6* ☎ *22510/28550* 🎫 *Free* 🕙 *By appointment only.*

The **Archaeological Museum of Mytilene,** in a 1912 neoclassic mansion, displays finds from the Neolithic through the Roman eras, a period of 5,000 years. A garden in the back displays the famous 6th-century Aeolian capitals from the columns of Klopedi's temples. The museum's modern "wing," in a separate building, contains finds from prehistoric Thermi, mosaics from Hellenistic houses, reliefs of comic scenes from the 3rd-century Roman house of Menander, and temporary exhibits. ✉ *Mansion: Argiri Eftaliotis 7, behind ferry dock; modern wing: corner of Noemvriou and Melinas Merkouri* ☎ *22510/28032* 🌐 *www.culture.gr* 🎫 *€3 for both* 🕙 *Mansion Tues.–Sun. 8:30–3, modern wing Tues.–Sun. 8–7:30.*

Crammed to the ceiling in the **Museum of Theophilos** are 86 of the eponymous artist's naive, precise works detailing the everyday life of local folk such as fishermen and farmers, and fantasies of another age. Theophilos lived in poverty but painted airplanes and cities he had never seen. He painted in bakeries for bread, and in cafés for ouzo, and walked around in ancient dress. ✉ *4 km (2½ mi) southeast of Mytilini, Varia* ☎ *22510/41644* 🎫 *€2* 🕙 *Tues.–Sun. 10–4.*

The **Musée–Bibliothèque Tériade** was the home of Stratis Eleftheriadis, better known by his French name, Tériade. His Paris publications *Minotaure* and *Verve* helped promote modern art. Among the works on display are lithographs done for him by Picasso, Matisse, Chagall, Rouault, Giacometti, and Miró. The museum is set among the olive trees of Varia, near the Museum of Theophilos. ✉ *4 km (2½ mi) southeast of Mytilini, Varia* ☎ *22510/23372* 🎫 *€2* 🕙 *Tues.–Sun. 9–2 and 5–8.*

WHERE TO STAY & EAT

> **WORD OF MOUTH**
>
> "There aren't too many sandy beaches [on Mytilini] but what there is is lovely and never crowded because the tourists who frequent Mytilini are usually descendants of those who left there several generations ago. There are no really luxurious hotels . . . You get to live like the natives, who are very artistic . . . and if you take a bus tour beyond the city . . . you will discover lovely surprises, like the remnants of a petrified forest, Turkish ruins, beautiful churches and monasteries, delicious food, ouzo, crafts, etc." —Petruska

$ ✕**Polytechnos.** Locals and visiting Athenians pack the outdoor tables—a solid indication this restaurant has earned its reputation. Some folks choose from the impressive fish selection; others order simple, traditional Greek dishes like souvlaki or succulent pork medallions, and get a small salad of tomatoes and cucumbers to go with it. This casual restaurant lies across from the municipal building on the waterfront, and is the first along the quay. ✉*Fanari quay* ☎*22510/44128* ▭*No credit cards.*

¢–$ ✕**O Stratos.** This no-nonsense, no-decoration restaurant serves the best fish in Mytilini. No surprise, then, that waterfront tables are hard to come by, so plan to come early if you want to sit outside. Ask the genial staff for the catch of the day, or go into the kitchen to take a look at the *sargoi* (sea bream), *tsipoures* (dorado), or *barbounia* (red mullet) before making your pick. If fish is not what you're in the mood for, the barbecue chicken is a worthy substitute. Consider an accompanying wine from the island of Limnos. ✉*Fanari quay* ☎*22510/21739* ▭*MC, V.*

¢ ✕**Hermes.** Founded in 1790 in a building 100 years older, this *ouzeri* (ouzo bar, though the sign calls it a *kafeneion,* or coffeehouse) is where local and visiting artists, poets, and politicians prefer to sip their ouzo on a vine-shaded terrace, with marble-top tables. You might try octopus in wine sauce, long-cooked chickpeas, or homemade sausages. The interior, a popular gathering spot in winter, provides a glimpse of traditional Lesbos design with old wood and mirrors. The long-standing hangout has similarly long hours: from 6 in the morning until the last person leaves at night. ✉*Kornarou 2, near end of Ermou* ☎*22510/26232* ▭*No credit cards.*

$$$$ ★ **Loriet Hotel.** The most-exclusive digs in the area may be in the Loriet's 1880 stone mansion, where high frescoed ceilings, friezes, and antique furniture set the mood—and where visiting dignitaries often stay. Rooms here are called "suites" and start at €550 in high season. These are considerably more enticing than the utilitarian rooms and studios in the hotel's modern section, which is separated from the mansion by a beautiful pool and a grove of tall pines. An on-site restaurant is open July and August. The hotel lies across from the beach and is a five-minute drive from town and the airport. ✉*2 km (1 mi) south of Mytilini, 81100Varia* ☎*22510/43111* 🌐*www.loriet-hotel.com* *35 rooms* *In-room: no a/c (some), kitchen (some), refrigerator. In-hotel: restaurant, bar, pool, no elevator* ▭*AE, MC, V.*

$$–$$$ **Pyrgos of Mytilene.** A restored 1916 mansion in the ornate Second Empire style fuses modern-day amenities and 19th-century nostalgia. The guest rooms are lavish, with period furniture, chandeliers, and stucco moldings, and each has its own style and color scheme, ranging from pistachio green to Venetian red. Particularly charming are the round rooms in the towers. The reception rooms are inviting, elegant, and spacious. On nice mornings, repair to the veranda for the breakfast of local breads, fruits, preserves, and other products. ☒*Eleftherios Venizelou 49, 81100* ☎*22510/27977 or 22510/25069* ⊕*www.pyrgoshotel.gr* *12 rooms* *In-room: refrigerator. In-hotel: bar, no elevator* *MC, AE, V* *CP.*

$ **Porto Lesvos I.** If you want to stay in the center of Mytilini, this old, carefully renovated building a block inland from the harbor is a solid moderately priced choice. You can feel the Papadakis family touch in the furnishings and service. The rooms all have exposed stonework and some have sea views; the breakfast room is nicely done in wood and stone. ☒*Komninaki 21, 81100* ☎*22510/41771* ⊕*www.portolesvos.gr* *12 rooms* *In-room: refrigerator. In-hotel: bar, no elevator* *MC, V* *CP.*

14

NIGHTLIFE

The cafés along the harbor turn into bars after midnight, generally closing at 3 AM. For a relaxed Caribbean-style start to your night, start with a cocktail at **Hacienda** (☒*East end of port* ☎*22510/46850*). You need transportation to reach **Kohilia** (☒*7 km [4½ mi] south of Mytilini, on beach opposite airport* ☎*No phone*), an outdoor beach bar with an upscale, artistic vibe.

SHOPPING

Much of the best shopping is along the Ermou street bazaar. Here you can buy a little of everything, from food (especially olive oil and ouzo) to pottery, wood carvings, and embroidery. Lesbos produces 50 brands of ouzo, and George Spentzas's shop, **Veto** (☒*J. Arisarchi 1* ☎*22510/24660*), right on the main harbor, has made its own varieties on the premises since 1948. It also sells local foods.

SKALA SIKAMINIAS ΣΚΑΛΑ ΣΥΚΑΜΙΝΙΑΣ

★ *35 km (22 mi) northwest of Mytilini.*

At the northernmost point of Lesbos, past Pelopi, is the exceptionally lovely fishing port of Skala Sikaminias, a miniature gem—serene and real, with several good fish tavernas on the edge of the dock. The novelist Stratis Myrivilis used the village as the setting for his *Mermaid Madonna.* Those who have read the book will recognize the tiny chapel at the base of the jetty. The author's birthplace and childhood home are in Sikaminia, the village overlooking Skala Sikaminias—and the Turkish coast—from its perch high above the sea.

WHERE TO EAT

¢–$ ✕ **Skamnia.** Sit at a table of Skala Sikaminias's oldest taverna, under the same spreading mulberry tree where Myrivilis wrote, to sip a glass of ouzo and watch the fishing boats bob. Stuffed zucchini blossoms or cucumbers and tomatoes tossed with local olive oil are food for thought: light, tasty, and ideal for picking at. Other tempting dishes on the creative menu include fresh shrimp with garlic and parsley, and chicken in grape leaves. ✉ *On waterfront* ☎ *22530/55319* ▭ *AE, MC, V.*

> **WORD OF MOUTH**
>
> "I highly recommend Molyvos as a base—stunning town with lots of reasonably priced car, scooter and bicycle rental places. I even managed to rent an automatic car for 35 euros one day!" —murphy89

MOLYVOS ΜΟΛΥΒΟΣ

Fodor's Choice ★ *17 km (10½ mi) southwest of Skala Sikaminias, 61 km (38 mi) west of Mytilini.*

Molyvos, also known by its ancient name, Mythimna, is a place that has attracted people since antiquity. Legend says that Achilles besieged the town until the king's daughter fell for him and opened the gates; then Achilles killed her. Before 1923 the Turks made up about a third of the population, living in many of the best stone houses. Today these balconied buildings with center staircases are weighed down by roses and geraniums; the red-tile roofs and cobblestone streets are required by law. Attracted by the town's charms, many artists live here. Don't miss a walk down to the picture-perfect harbor front.

Come before high season and walk or drive up to the **kastro,** a Byzantine-Genoese fortified castle, for a hypnotic view down the tiers of red-tile roofs to the glittering sea. At dawn the sky begins to light up from behind the mountains of Asia Minor, casting silver streaks through the placid water as weary night fishermen come in. Purple wisteria vines shelter the lanes that descend from the castle and pass numerous Turkish fountains, some still in use. ✉ *Above town* ☎ *22530/71803* 🎫 *€3* ⏲ *Tues.–Sat. 8–2:30.*

★ The stunning 16th-century **Leimonos Monastery** houses 40 chapels and an impressive collection of precious objects. Founded by St. Ignatios Agalianos on the ruins of an older Byzantine monastery, it earned its name from the "flowering meadow of souls" surrounding it. The intimate St. Ignatios church is filled with colorful frescoes and is patrolled by peacocks. A **folk-art museum** with historic and religious works is accompanied by a **treasury** of 450 Byzantine manuscripts. Women are not allowed inside the main church. ✉ *Up a marked road 5 km (3 mi) northwest of Kalloni, 15 km (9 mi) southwest of Molyvos* 🎫 *Museum and treasury €1.50* ⏲ *Daily 9–1 and 5–7:30.*

CLOSE UP

Island Celebrations

Festivals provide a wonderful view into age-old traditions—and lots of fun. Mixing folk traditions with myth and legend, the three-week-long Greek Carnival (Apokreas) is celebrated to varying degrees throughout the islands, including those beyond the northern Aegean. Other festivals, honoring patron saints, history, or the local culture, are unique.

Chios has some notable pre-Lenten events. Greek Carnival, which begins in February and shifts according to the start of Lent, reaches a climax in Thimiana, south of Chios town, where islanders reenact the expulsion of the Berber pirates in the Festival of Mostras. There on the last Friday of Carnival, youths masquerade and wear old men's and women's clothes. Three days later in villages across the island Clean Monday is celebrated with the custom of *Agas,* when an "Aga" is chosen to judge and sentence the people who are present in a humorous, recreational affair. On the evening before Easter the effigy of Judas is burned in Mesta. In Pirgi on August 15 and August 23, villagers perform the local dance, the *pyrgoussikos,* to commemorate the death of the Virgin Mary.

On Lesbos, Clean Monday brings Carnival to a close with lavish costume parades and theater performances at Agiassos.

Molyvos Theater Festival (☎ *22530/71323 tickets*), the best known of the festivals held on these islands, is in July and August. With Molyvos castle as backdrop, artists from Greece and elsewhere in Europe stage entertainments that range from a Dario Fo play to contemporary music concerts.

On August 15 the islanders of Lesbos again flock to Agiassos to celebrate the Feast of the Dormition of the Virgin with dancing, drinking, and eating. Samos has many celebrations: a wine festival in late summer to early fall pleases with Panhellenic dances in Samos town. In high summer, a fisherman's festival centers on the harbor at Pythagorio. Swimming races in Pythagorio commemorate the battle of Cavo Fonias on August 6, a day of celebration for the entire island. On September 14, the Timiou Stavrou monastery celebrates its feast day with a service followed by a *paniyiri* (feast), with music, firecrackers, coconut candy, and *loukoumades* (honey-soaked dumplings).

14

WHERE TO STAY & EAT

$–$$ ★ ✕ **Captain's Table.** At the end of a quay, this wonderful taverna serves seafood caught on its own trawler, moored opposite. The best way to go is to mix and match a series of small dishes, or *mezedes*: maybe try *aujuka* (spicy eggplant slices), smoked mackerel with olives, vegetarian souvlaki, or grilled veggies and rice. Fresh fish may include red snapper, sea bream, lobster, and gilt. Owners Melinda and Theo, who are wonderful resources for visitors, also rent rooms in a house that's a 10-minute walk from the restaurant. Grab a seat at the Table early, as it tends to get busy quickly. ✉ *Molyvos harbor across from Ayios Nikolaos chapel* ☎ *22530/71241* ▭ *MC, V* ⊙ *Closed mid-Oct.–mid-Apr. No lunch.*

$–$$ ✕ **Gatos.** Gaze over the island and harbor from the veranda of this yellow-and-green-dressed charmer, or sit inside and watch the cooks chop and grind in the open kitchen: Gatos is known for its grilled meats. The beef fillet is tender, the lamb chops nicely spiced, and the salads fresh. You might also consider ordering the *kokkinisto* (beef in tomato sauce) with garlic and savory onion. ✉ *Center of old market* ☎ *22530/71661* ▭ *V.*

¢–$ ✕ **Panorama.** High over the town, this terraced restaurant cooks terrific Greek food and, as the name suggests, it has a spectacular view. It's worth coming here just for a sunset drink, to see the sun illumine the red roofs of Molyvos and the sea beyond. Good appetizers include spicy cheese salad, and fried stuffed peppers; among the main courses are meat on the grill and fresh fish. It is also open for breakfast. ✉ *Under kastro* ☎ *22530/71848* ▭ *No credit cards.*

$ **Aeolis.** A little away from the buzz of Molyvos, this cluster of traditional red-roof buildings offers ample chance to relax, with deep-seated sofas in the light, airy lounge, a swimming pool (hard to find in Molyvos proper), and a nearby, if mediocre, beach. The beachside rooms have two or three low-to-the-ground beds, bathrooms with showers or baths, and French doors opening onto a veranda. The view from the veranda takes in the sea and Molyvos castle. A hotel shuttle service runs up to town, as does the local bus. ✉ *On road to Eftalou, 81108* ☎ *22530/71772* 🌐 *www.aeolishotel.gr* *71 rooms* *In-room: kitchen (some), refrigerator. In-hotel: restaurant, bars, pool, no elevator* ▭ *MC, V* ⏲ *Closed Nov.–Mar.* *BP.*

$ ★ **Sea Horse Hotel.** This delightful stone-front hotel on Molyvos harbor overlooks the eateries on the photogenic quay; the lobby even extends into a waterfront café. Twelve of the rooms—simply decorated but perfectly charming with painted wood furniture—have full sea views, an additional three have partial sea views, and one room has a village view. ✉ *Molyvos quay, 81108* ☎ *22530/71320 or 22530/71630* 🌐 *www.seahorse-hotel.com* *16 rooms* *In-room: refrigerator. In-hotel: restaurant, bar, no elevator* ▭ *MC, V* ⏲ *Closed mid-Oct.–mid-Apr.* *CP.*

NIGHTLIFE & THE ARTS

The best-known celebration on the islands is the **Molyvos Theater Festival** (☎ *22530/71323 tickets*) in July and August. With the castle as backdrop, artists from Greece and elsewhere in Europe stage entertainments that range from a Dario Fo play to contemporary music concerts.

Molly's Bar (✉ *On street above harbor* ☎ *22530/71209*) has relaxed music in an environment that's ideal for quiet conversations. **Music Cafe Del Mar** (✉ *Harbor front* ☎ *22530/71588*) hosts live acoustic bouzouki music and has a cocktail terrace with a sea view.

SHOPPING

The **Earth Collection** (✉ *Molyvos quay* ☎ *22530/72094*) sells organic clothes made exclusively of natural products. **Evelyn** (✉ *Kyriakou Sq.* ☎ *22530/72197*) stocks a wide variety of local goods, including ceramics, pastas, olive oil, wines, ouzo, sauces, and marmalades.

SKALA ERESSOU ΣΚΑΛΑ ΕΡΕΣΟΥ

★ *40 km (25 mi) southwest of Molyvos, 89 km (55 mi) west of Mytilini.*

The poet Sappho, according to unreliable late biographies, was born here circa 612 BC. Dubbed the Tenth Muse by Plato because of her skill and sensitivity, she perhaps presided over a finishing school for marriageable young women. She was married herself and had a daughter. Some of her songs erotically praise these girls and celebrate their marriages. Sappho's works, proper and popular in their time, were burned by Christians, so that mostly fragments survive; one is "and I yearn, and I desire." Sapphic meter was in great favor in Roman and medieval times; both Catullus and Gregory the Great used it, and in the 19th century, Tennyson did, too. Today, many gay women come to Skala Eressou to celebrate Sappho (the word "lesbian" derives from Lesbos), although the welcoming town is also filled with heterosexual couples.

On the **acropolis** of ancient Eressos overlooking the coastal area and beach are **remains of pre-Hellenistic walls, castle ruins,** and the AD 5th-century church, **Ayios Andreas.** The church has a mosaic floor and a tiny adjacent **museum** housing local finds from tombs in the ancient cemetery. ✉*1 km (½ mi) north of Skala Eressou* ☎*22530/53332* *Free* ⏲*Tues.–Sun. 7:30–3:30.*

The old village of **Eressos** (✉*11 km [7 mi] inland, north of Skala Eressou*), separated from the coast by a large plain, was developed to protect its inhabitants from pirate raids. Along the mulberry tree–lined road leading from the beach you might encounter a villager wearing a traditional head scarf (*mandila*), plodding by on her donkey. This village of two-story, 19th-century stone and shingle houses is filled with superb architectural details. Note the huge wooden doors decorated with nails and elaborate door knockers, loophole windows in thick stone walls, elegant pediments topping imposing mansions, and fountains spilling under Gothic arches.

BEACH

Some of the island's best beaches are in this area, which has been built up very rapidly—and not always tastefully. Especially popular is the 4-km-long (2½-mi-long) town beach at **Skala Eressou,** where the wide stretch of dark sand is lined with tamarisk trees. A small island is within swimming distance, and northerly winds lure windsurfers as well as swimmers and sunbathers. There are many rooms to rent within walking distance of the beach.

WHERE TO EAT

$–$$ ✕**Soulatso.** The enormous anchor outside is a sign that you're in for some seriously good seafood. On a wooden deck, tables are set just a skipping-stone's throw from the break of the waves. Owner Sarandos Tzinieris serves, and his mother cooks. Fresh grilled squid is mellifluous, and the fish are carefully chosen every morning. ✉*At beach center* ☎*22530/52078* ▭*No credit cards.*

¢–$ ✕**Parasol.** Totem poles, colored coconut lamps, and other knickknacks from exotic travels make this beach bar endearing. The owner and his wife serve omelets, fruits, yogurt, and sweet Greek coffee for breakfast, and simple dishes like pizzas, veggie spring rolls, and cheese platters the rest of the day. But the most obvious reason to come here is to relax after sundown with one of the bar's creative drinks, such as the signature green cocktail, the Wooloomooloo Wonder, made with vodka and fresh melon. The music might be characterized as sophisticated lounge; the owner calls it "intellectual." ✉*Beachfront* ☎*No phone* ▭*No credit cards* ⏲*Closed Nov.–Apr.*

AGIASSOS ΑΓΙΑΣΟΣ

★ *87 km (53 mi) northwest of Skala Eressou, 28 km (17½ mi) southwest of Mytilini.*

Agiassos village, the prettiest hill town on Lesbos, sits in an isolated valley amid thousands of olive trees, near the foot of Mt. Olympus, the highest peak. (In case you're confused, 19 mountains in the Mediterranean are named Olympus, almost all of them peaks sacred to the local sky god, who eventually became associated with Zeus.) Exempted from taxes by the Turks, the town thrived. The age-old charm of Agiassos can be seen in its gray stone houses, cobblestone lanes, medieval castle, and local handicrafts, particularly pottery and woodwork.

The church of **Panayia Vrefokratousa** *(Madonna Holding the Infant)* was founded in the 12th century to house an icon of the Virgin Mary, believed to be the work of St. Luke, and remains a popular place of pilgrimage. Built into its foundation are shops whose revenues support the church, as they have through the ages. The **church museum** has a little Bible from AD 500, with legible, elegant calligraphy. *€0.50* ⏲*Daily 8–1 and 5:30–8:30.*

NEED A BREAK?

Stop at one of several cafés in the winding streets of the old bazaar area past the church of Panayia Vrefokratousa. On weekend afternoons you can listen to a *santoúri* band (hammered dulcimer, accompanied by clarinet, drum, and violin). As the locals dance, rather haphazardly, on the cobblestones, you might be tempted to join in the merriment.

WHERE TO EAT

¢ ✕**Dagielles.** If nothing else, you must stop here for a coffee made by owner Stavritsa and served by her no-nonsense staff. You might also try the *kolokitholouloudia* (stuffed squash blossoms) and the dishes that entice throughout winter: *kritharaki* (orzo pasta) and *varkoules* ("little boats" of eggplant slices with minced meat). For a few short weeks in spring the air is laden with the scent of overhanging wisteria. ✉*Near bus stop* ☎*22520/22241* ▭*No credit cards.*

SHOPPING

For handmade, hand-painted pottery, have a look in **Ceramic Workshop Antonia Gavve** (✉*On main street* ☎*22520/93350*), where you can watch the artist paint.

For woodwork inspired by Byzantine art and Hellenism, stop by the functioning workshop of **D. Kamaros & Son** (✉ *Next to church* ☎ *22213/22520*); the store is opposite the shop. Dimitris Kamaros exports his woodwork throughout the Orthodox world. Although specializing in walnut furniture (the trees are local), the store also sells small pieces such as chessboards, backgammon tables, carved religious pieces, and jewelry boxes.

CHIOS ΧΙΟΣ

"Craggy Chios" is what local boy Homer, its first publicist, so to speak, called this starkly beautiful island, which almost touches Turkey's coast and shares its topography. The island may not appear overly charming when you first see its principal city and capital, Chios town, but consider its misfortunes: the bloody Turkish massacre of 1822 during the fight for Greek independence; major earthquakes, including one in 1881 that killed almost 6,000 Chiotes; severe fires, which in the 1980s burned two-thirds of its pine trees; and, through the ages, the steady stripping of forests to ax-wielding boatbuilders. Yet despite these disadvantages, the island remains a wonderful destination, with friendly inhabitants, and villages so rare and captivating that even having just one of them on this island would make it a gem.

The name Chios comes from the Phoenician word for "mastic," the resin of the *Pistacia lentisca,* evergreen shrubs that with few exceptions thrive only here, in the southern part of the island. Every August, incisions are made in the bark of the shrubs; the sap leaks out, permeating the air with a sweet fragrance, and in September it is harvested. This aromatic resin, which brought huge revenues until the introduction of petroleum products, is still used in cosmetics and chewing gum sold on the island today. Pirgi, Mesta, and other villages where the mastic is grown and processed are quite enchanting. In these towns you can wind your way through narrow, labyrinth-like Byzantine streets protected by medieval gates and peered over by homes that date back half a millennium.

Chios is also home to the elite families that control Greece's private shipping empires: Livanos, Karas, Chandris; even Onassis came here from Smyrna. The island has never seemed to need tourists, nor to draw them. Yet Chios intrigues, with its deep valleys, uncrowded sand and black-pebble beaches, fields of wild tulips, Byzantine monasteries, and haunting villages—all remnants of a poignant history.

CHIOS TOWN ΧΙΟΣ (ΠΟΛΗ)

285 km (177 mi) northeast of Piraeus. 55 km (34 mi) south of Mytilini.

The main port and capital, Chios town, or Chora (which means "town"), is a busy commercial settlement on the east coast, across from Turkey. This is the best base from which to explore the island, and you don't need to venture far from the port to discover the beauti-

Chios & Samos
KEY
Ferry lines
Beaches
Airport
0
15 miles
0
15 km
TURKEY
Bulgurda
Selçuk
Uzunkuyu
Doganbey
Kusadasi
Çesme
TO LESBOS
INOUSSES
TO PSARA
Nagos
Viki
Marmaro
Kardamila
Langada
Pityous
Ayias Galas
Panayia Myrtidiotissa
Vrontados
Volissos
Limnia
Anavatos
Nea Moni
Chios town
Kambos
Avgonima
Vavili
Karfas town
Panayia Krina
Sklavia
CHIOS
Kataraktis
Limani Meston
Komi
Mesta
Pirgi
Emborio
Mavra Volia
TO PIRAEUS
SAMOS
Kalami
Kerveli Bay
Samos town
Kokkari
Ano Vathi
Ayios Konstandinos
Manolates
Vourliotes
Psili Ammos
Mytilini
Karlovassi
Mt. Ambelos
Pondrossos
Chora
Pythagorio
Pirgos
Heraion
Mt. Kerkis
Marathokambos
Ormos Marathokambou
TO PATMOS AND KOS
TO IKARIA, SIROS, MYKONOS AND PIRAEUS
AGATHONISSI
FOURNI

ful mansions of Kambos or the captivating orange groves just south of town. The daytime charm of the port area is limited, in part because no buildings predate the 1881 earthquake, in part because it needs a face-lift. But in the evening when the lights twinkle on the water and the scene is softened by a mingling of blues, the many cafés begin to overflow with ouzo and good cheer, and locals proudly promenade along the bayside.

The capital is crowded with half the island's population, but its fascinating heart is the sprawling **bazaar district.** Merchants hawk everything from local mastic gum and fresh dark bread to kitchen utensils in the morning but typically close in the afternoon. ☒*South and east of Vounakiou Sq. (the main square).*

The **old quarter** is inside the **kastro** (castle) fortifications, built in the 10th century by the Byzantines and enlarged in the 14th century by the Genoese Giustiniani family. Under Turkish rule, the Greeks lived outside the wall; the gate was closed daily at sundown. A deep dry moat remains on the western side. Note the old wood-and-plaster houses on the narrow backstreets, typically decorated with latticework and jutting balconies. An air of mystery pervades this old Muslim and Jewish neighborhood, full of decaying monuments, fountains, baths, and mosques. ☒*In northern highlands.*

The **Giustiniani Museum,** inside a 15th-century building that may have acted as the headquarters of the Genoese, exhibits Byzantine murals and sculptures, post-Byzantine icons, and other small Genoese and Byzantine works of art. ☒*Just inside old quarter* ☎*22710/22819* *€3* *Tues.–Sun. 9–2:30.*

In **Frouriou Square** (☒*At fort, old quarter*), look for the **Turkish cemetery** and the large **marble tomb** (with the fringed hat) of Kara Ali, chief of the Turkish flagship in 1822.

Along the **main street** are the elegant **Ayios Georgios** church (closed most of the time), which has icons from Asia Minor; houses from the Genoese period; and the **remains of Turkish baths** (north corner of fort).

In 1822, in the tiny **prison,** 75 leading Chiotes were jailed as hostages before they were hanged by the Turks, part of the worst massacre committed during the War of Independence. The Turks drove out the Genoese in 1566, and Chios, spurred by Samians who had fled to the island, joined the rest of Greece in rebellion in the early 19th century. The revolt failed, and the sultan retaliated: the Turks killed 30,000 Chiotes and enslaved 45,000, an event written about by Victor Hugo and depicted by Eugène Delacroix in *The Massacre of Chios.* The painting, now in the Louvre, shocked Western Europe and increased support for Greek independence. Copies of *The Massacre of Chios* hang in many places on Chios. ☒*Inside main gate of castle, near Giustiniani Museum.*

The only intact mosque in this part of the Aegean, complete with a slender minaret, houses the **Byzantine Museum,** which at this writing is closed indefinitely for renovation. It holds a *tugra* (the swirling monogram of the sultan that indicated royal possession), rarely seen outside Istanbul; its presence indicated the favor Chios once enjoyed under the sultan. Housed inside are the Jewish, Turkish, and Armenian gravestones leaning with age in the courtyard. ✉ *Vounakiou Sq.* ☎ *22710/26866.*

BEDROCK OF EDUCATION

Daskalopetra *(Teacher's Rock)* where Homer is said to have taught his pupils, stands just above the port of Vrontados, 4 km (2½ mi) north of Chios town. Archaeologists think this rocky outcrop above the sea is part of an ancient altar to Cybele; you can sit on it and muse about how the blind storyteller might have spoken here of the fall of Troy in The *Iliad.*

The **Chios Maritime Museum** celebrates the sea-based heritage of the island with exquisite ship models and portraits of vessels that have belonged to Chios owners over time. One exhibit highlights the Liberty ships and others constructed during World War II that contributed to the beginning of Greece's postwar shipping industry. ✉ *Stefanou Tsouri 20* ☎ *22710/44139* 🌐 *www.nauticalmuseum.com* 🎫 *Free* ⏲ *Mon.–Sat. 10–1.*

The **Chios Archaeological Museum** has a collection that ranges from proto-Helladic pottery dug up in Emborio to a letter, on stone, from Alexander the Great addressed to the Chiotes and dated 332 BC. It also displays beautiful Ionian sculptures crafted by Chiotes. ✉ *Michalon 10, 82100* ☎ *22710/44239* 🎫 *€2* ⏲ *Tues.–Sun. 8:30–1.*

The **Philip Argenti Museum** houses a historic and folkloric collection, and sits on the second floor above the **Korais Library,** Greece's third largest. The museum displays meticulously designed costumes, embroidery, pastoral wood carvings, and furniture of a village home. ✉ *Korais 2, near cathedral* ☎ *22710/28256* 🎫 *€1.50* ⏲ *Weekdays 8–4.*

Mastodon bones were found in the **Kambos district,** a fertile plain of tangerine, lemon, and orange groves just south of Chios town. In medieval times and later, wealthy Genoese and Greek merchants built ornate, earth-color, three-story mansions here. Behind forbidding stone walls adorned with coats of arms, each is a world of its own, with multicolor sandstone patterns, arched doorways, and pebble-mosaic courtyards. Some houses have crumbled and some still stand, reminders of the wealth, power, and eventual downfall of an earlier time. These suburbs of Chios town are exceptional, but the unmarked lanes can be confusing, so leave time to get lost and to peek behind the walls into another world. ✉ *4 km (2½ mi) south of Chios town.*

BEACHES

Karfas beach (✉ *8 km [5 mi] south of Chios town*) fronts a shallow sandy bay. Tavernas are in the area, and in summer there is transportation to town. Farther south, Komi has a fine, sandy beach.

WHERE TO STAY & EAT

> **WORD OF MOUTH**
>
> "When I think of Chios, I think of stepping back in time—as much as you can in the 21st century. It was one of the only places where I could almost feel the past brushing up against the present."
>
> —murphy89

$–$$ ✕ **Bella Vista.** On the coastal road toward the airport, just outside the port, Bella Vista serves the island's best Italian food. Selections include salads with fresh mozzarella, thick crisp pizzas, and numerous pastas, such as spaghetti with fresh, juicy lobster—accompanied by fresh-baked bread. The delicious shrimp "terminator" is a dish of large shrimp smothered with mushrooms, peppers, and cream. The dining room has a mesmerizing tropical aquarium; street noise can disturb the tranquillity of the outdoor veranda. ✉ *South of center, Livanou 2* ☎ *22710/41022* ▭ *MC, V.*

$–$$ ✕ **Pyrgos.** Attentive service, fine food, and pretty surroundings characterize a meal at the poolside garden restaurant of the Grecian Castle hotel. Beef carpaccio and spinach salad are excellent starters, followed by beef *pagiar,* a fillet stuffed with *mastello* (the local goat cheese), sun-dried tomatoes, and pesto-olive sauce. Or try the pork with prunes, mushrooms, and *vin santo* (a sweet wine) sauce. The extensive menu also includes crepes, pastas, and seafood. Mastic ice cream with rose syrup closes a meal on a richly local note. ✉ *Chios harbor* ☎ *22710/44740* ▭ *AE, D, MC, V.*

¢–$ ★ ✕ **Taverna tou Tassou.** Dependably delicious traditional food is why so many locals eat here in a garden courtyard beneath a canopy of trees. Fresh fish and seafood, lamb chops and other meats, stuffed peppers and cooked greens—you can't go wrong. Expect Greek owner Dimitrius Doulos and his son, the chef, to warmly welcome you. The taverna is at the south edge of town toward the airport, and there's a playground nearby for kids. ✉ *Livanou 8, south toward airport* ☎ *22710/27542* ▭ *DC, MC, V* ⊙ *Closed Nov.*

$$$–$$$$ **Chios Chandris.** Only a few minutes' walk from the village center, Chios Chandris has the best location of any hotel in Chios town: it looks out at both the sea and the harbor, and has an inviting pool with panoramic views of both. Balconies have views of the mountains or of the ferries and fishing boats plying the harbor. Although the outside looks a bit worn, comfortable rooms are brightly decorated in shades of Aegean blue and yellow. ✉ *Between port and beach, 82100 Prokymea* ☎ *22710/44401 through 22710/44410* 🌐 *www.chandris.gr* *129 rooms, 10 suites* *In-room: kitchen (some), refrigerator. In-hotel: restaurant, bar, pool, public Wi-Fi* ▭ *AE, MC, V* *BP.*

$$ ★ **Grecian Castle.** With spacious (and a few not-so-spacious) rooms furnished in warm, neutral tones; a pretty pool; and carefully landscaped grounds, this sophisticated hotel sets a high standard for Chios. A stone exterior of the main building, originally a pasta factory, was influenced by Chios's medieval castle; it's complemented by the elegant wood furnishings of the lobby and breakfast room. The hotel is near the sea, toward the airport. ✉ *Leoforos Enosseos, 1 km (½ mi) south toward airport, 82100* ☎ *22710/44740* 🌐 *www.greciancastle.gr* *51 rooms,*

4 suites ⊂*In-room: refrigerator. In-hotel: restaurant, bars, pool* ⊟*AE, D, MC, V.*

$$ **Perleas Mansion.** More than a thousand trees, mostly citrus, grow
Fodor's Choice ★ on the beautiful grounds of this stunning estate. Owners Vangelis and Claire Xydas have painstakingly restored the main stone house, from 1640, and two smaller buildings. Guest rooms, which look out to the orchards, are filled with antique furnishings and the fragrance of jasmine. Common rooms have books and board games, and there are wonderful spots for walking, reading, and relaxing. The service here makes you feel like an aristocrat from a previous era. Should you wish to retain that illusion for dinner, the hostess prepares meals three nights a week upon request: delectable and healthy organic fare fresh from the farm is served on the patio under the stars. ⊠*Vitiadou, Kambos district, 4 km (2½ mi) south of center, 82100* ☎*22710/32217 or 22710/32962* ⊕*www.perleas.gr* *7 rooms* *In-room: no TV, refrigerator. In hotel: no elevator* ⊟*MC, V* *BP.*

$ **Kyma.** Begun in 1917 for a shipping magnate, this neoclassic villa
★ on the waterfront was completed in 1922, when it served as Colonel Plastiras's headquarters after the Greek defeat in Asia Minor (Plastiras went on to become a general and prime minister of Greece). Now the villa is the prettiest hotel in town, run by the friendliest staff, under Theo Spordilis. Many of Kyma's rooms have balconies with sea views, and some are equipped with hot tubs. A large breakfast, including fruits, juices, eggs, jams, yogurt, and honey, is served under frescoed ceilings in the breakfast room. ⊠*Chandris 1, 82100* ☎*22710/44500* *kyma@chi.forthnet.gr* *59 rooms* *In-room: refrigerator* ⊟*No credit cards* *CP.*

NIGHTLIFE

Stylish nightspots along the harbor are more sophisticated than those on most of the other northern Aegean islands, and many of the clubs are filled with well-off young tourists and locals. You can just walk along, listen to the music, and size up the crowd; most clubs are open to the harbor and dramatically lighted. **Cosmo** (⊠*Aigeou 100* ☎*22710/81695*) stands out as an inviting cocktail lounge playing international and Greek music.

SHOPPING

The resinous gum made from the sap of the mastic tree is a best buy in Chios, and makes a fun souvenir and conversation piece; the brand is Elma. You can also find mastic liquor called *mastíha*, and *gliko koutaliou*, sugar-preserved fruit added to water. Stores are typically closed Sunday, and open mornings only on Monday through Wednesday.

At the elegant shop of **Mastic Spa** (⊠*Aigeou 12, on waterfront a block from dock* ☎*22710/40223*), all the beauty and health products contain the local balm. **Moitafiz** (⊠*Venizelou 7* ☎*22710/25330*) sells mastíha, fruit preserves, and other sweets and spirits. **Yiorgos Varias** (⊠*Venizelou 2* ☎*22710/22368*) has a passion for pickles. His tiny store is crammed with 36 varieties, including melon, chestnut, and fig. **Zaharoplasteion Avgoustakis** (⊠*Psychari 4* ☎*22710/44480*) is a traditional candy store where you can buy *masourakia* (crispy rolled pastries dripping in syrup and nuts) and *rodinia* (melt-in-your-mouth cookies stuffed with almond cream).

NEA MONI ΝΕΑ ΜΟΝΗ

Fodor's Choice ★ *17 km (10½ mi) west of Chios town.*

Almost hidden among the olive groves, the island's most important monastery—with one of the finest examples of mosaic art anywhere—is the 11th-century Nea Moni. Emperor Constantine IX Monomachos ("the Dueler") ordered the monastery built where three monks found an icon of the Virgin in a myrtle bush. The octagonal *katholikon* (medieval church) is the only surviving example of 11th-century court art—none survives in Constantinople. The church has been renovated a number of times: the dome was completely rebuilt following an earthquake in 1881, and a great deal of effort has gone into the restoration and preservation of the mosaics over the years. The distinctive three-part vaulted sanctuary has a double narthex, with no buttresses supporting the dome. This design, a single square space covered by a dome, is rarely seen in Greece. Blazing with color, the church's interior gleams with marble slabs and mosaics of Christ's life, austere yet sumptuous, with azure blue, ruby red, velvet green, and skillful applications of gold. The saints' expressiveness comes from their vigorous poses and severe gazes, with heavy shadows under the eyes. On the iconostasis hangs the icon—a small Virgin and Child facing left. Also inside the grounds are an **ancient refectory, a vaulted cistern, a chapel** filled with victims' bones from the massacre at Chios, and a large **clock** still keeping Byzantine time, with the sunrise reckoned as 12 o'clock. ✉ *In mountains west of Chios town* ☎ *22710/79391* 🎫 *Donations accepted* ⊙ *Tues.–Sun. 8–1 and 4–7.*

PIRGI ΠΥΡΓΙ

★ *25 km (15½ mi) south of Nea Moni. 20 km (12½ mi) south of Chios town.*

Beginning in the 14th century, the Genoese founded 20 or so fortified inland villages in southern Chios. These villages shared a defensive design with double-thick walls, a maze of narrow streets, and a square tower, or *pirgos,* in the middle—a last resort to hold the residents in case of pirate attack. The villages prospered on the sales of mastic gum and were spared by the Turks because of the industry. Today they depend on citrus, apricots, olives—and tourists.

Pirgi is the largest of these mastic villages, and in many ways the most wondrous. It could be a graphic designer's model or a set from a mad moviemaker or a town from another planet. Many of the buildings along the tiny arched streets are adorned with *xysta* (like Italian sgraffito); they are coated with a mix of cement and volcanic sand from nearby beaches, then whitewashed and stenciled, often top to bottom, in traditional patterns of animals, flowers, and geometric designs. The effect is both delicate and dazzling. This exuberant village has more than 50 churches (people afraid of attack tend to pray for a continuation of life).

Look for especially lavish xysta on buildings near the main square, including the **Kimisis tis Theotokou church** *(Dormition of the Virgin church)*, built in 1694. ⌧*Off main square* ⏲*Daily 9–1 and 4–8.*

DID A GREEK DISCOVER AMERICA?

About 50 people named Kolomvos live in Pirgi, claiming kinship with Christopher Columbus, known to have been from Genoa, the power that built the town. Some renegade historians claim Columbus, like Homer, was really born on Chios.

Check out the fresco-embellished 12th-century church **Agii Apostoli** *(Holy Apostles)*, a very small replica of the katholikon at the Nea Moni Monastery. The 17th-century frescoes that completely cover the interior, the work of a Cretan artist, have a distinct folk-art leaning. ⌧*Northwest of main square* ⏲*Tues.–Sun. 8:30–3.*

In the small mastic village of **Armolia,** 5 km (3 mi) north of Pirgi, pottery is a specialty. In fact, the Greek word *armolousis* ("man from Armolia") is synonymous with potter.

Earthal Art sells hand-painted pottery and handicrafts, as well as quality, inexpensive oil paintings of the Greek islands. ⌧*Pirgi–Armolia road* ☎*22710/72693.*

BEACH

From Pirgi it's 8 km (5 mi) southeast to the glittering black volcanic beach near Emborio, known by locals as **Mavra Volia** *(Black Pebbles)*. The cove is backed by jutting volcanic cliffs, the calm water's dark-blue color created by the deeply tinted seabed. Here perhaps was an inspiration for the "wine-dark sea" that Homer wrote about.

MESTA ΜΕΣΤΑ

Fodor'sChoice ★ *11 km (7 mi) west of Pirgi, 30 km (18½ mi) southwest of Chios town.*

Pirgi may be the most unusual of the mastic villages, but Mesta is the island's best preserved: a labyrinth of twisting vaulted streets link two-story stone-and-mortar houses that are supported by buttresses against earthquakes. The enchanted village sits inside a system of three-foot-thick walls, and the outer row of houses also doubles as protection. In fact, the village homes were built next to each other to form a castle, reinforced with towers. Most of the narrow streets, free of cars and motorbikes, lead to blind alleys; the rest lead to the six gates. The one in the northeast retains an iron grate.

One of the largest and wealthiest churches in Greece, the 18th-century church of **Megas Taxiarchis** *(Great Archangel)* commands the main square; its vernacular baroque is combined with the late-folk-art style of Chios. The church was built on the ruins of the central refuge tower.

Ask at the main square for Elias, the gentle old man in the village who is the keeper of the keys.

BEACHES

Escape to the string of secluded coves, between Elatas and Trahiliou bays, for good swimming. The **nudist beach** (✉ *2 km [1 mi] north of Lithi*) has fine white pebbles.

WHERE TO STAY & EAT

¢–$ ★ ✕ **Restaurant Café Mesconas.** A traditional Greek kitchen turns out the delicious food served on outdoor tables in the small village square, adjacent to Megas Taxiarchis. You dine surrounded by medieval homes and magical lights at night, but the setting is lovely even for a daytime coffee and relaxed conversation. The best dishes include rabbit *stifado* (stew), made with shallots, tomatoes, and olive oil; and *pastitsio,* a meat pie with macaroni and béchamel sauce. All of the recipes use local ingredients, with herbs and spices gathered from the region. *Souma* is the local equivalent of ouzo but made from figs—it can be blindingly strong, up to 70% alcohol. ✉ *Main square* ☎ *22710/76050* 💳 *MC, V.*

¢ ✕ **Limani Meston.** The fishing boats bobbing in the water only a few feet away supply Limani Meston with a rich daily fish selection. The friendly, gracious owner may well persuade you to munch on some of his smaller catches, such as sardines served with onions and pita, accompanied by calamari and cheese balls. Meats served at the simple taverna include homemade sausage, and lamb or beef on the spit. You can sit outside among the ivy and blossoms, where Mesta's working harbor unfolds before you. On colder days, enjoy the fireplace with the locals. The owner rents studio apartments within walking distance. ✉ *Mesta harbor, 3 km (2 mi) north of Mesta village* ☎ *22710/76389* 💳 *No credit cards.*

¢ ★ 🏨 **Anna Floradi.** The charming Floradi family has remodeled a medieval home into a guesthouse with four studio rooms and a two-bedroom apartment. All have rustic furnishings and cooking facilities—not bad for Byzantine accommodations smack in the center of a mastic village. Ask for one of the rooms upstairs; they open out onto an alfresco den built around an old wood oven, and one has a balcony. Anna Floradi leaves breakfast items (bread, honey, yogurt, or cheese pie) for guests to prepare on their own. ✉ *Village center, 82102* ☎ *22710/28891* 📠 *22710/76455* ✉ *floradis@internet.gr* *4 rooms, 1 apartment* *In-room: kitchen. In hotel: no elevator* 💳 *MC, V* 🍽 *CP.*

NIGHTLIFE

Karnayio (✉ *Leoforos Stenoseos, outside town on road to airport* ☎ *No phone*) is a popular spot for dancing.

SPORTS & THE OUTDOORS

Masticulture leads walking tours to mastic tree groves, where farmers show you how they gather mastic through grooves carved into the trees' bark. There are three daily tours, at 11, 5:30, and 7:30, that include a stop to pick fresh produce from the farm's organic vegetable gardens, to be nibbled during the tour. ✉ *Main square* ☎ *22710/76084* 🌐 *www.masticulture.com* *€15.*

14

SHOPPING

Artists and craftspeople are attracted to this ancient area. **Agnitha** (✉*Delfon 34* ☎*22710/76031*) is a magical shop selling handwoven textiles, silver jewelry, and local art. **Ilias Likourinas** (✉*Workshop: Delfon*) is an icon artist who will paint to order. The shop of **Sergias Patentas** (✉*Mesta–Limenas harbor road, 3 km [2 mi] north of Mesta*) sells sculptural fantasies he creates based on mythology and history.

SAMOS ΣΑΜΟΣ

The southernmost of this group of three north Aegean islands, Samos lies the closest to Turkey of any Greek island, separated by only 3 km (2 mi). It was, in fact, a part of Asia Minor until it split off during the Ice Age. Samos means "high" in Phoenician, and its abrupt volcanic mountains soaring dramatically like huge hunched shoulders from the rock surface of the island are among the tallest in the Aegean, geologically part of the great spur that runs across western Turkey. As you approach from the west, Mt. Kerkis seems to spin out of the sea, and in the distance Mt. Ambelos guards the terraced vineyards that produce the famous Samian wine. The felicitous landscape has surprising twists, with lacy coasts and mountain villages perched on ravines carpeted in pink oleander, red poppy, and purple sage.

When Athens was young, in the 7th century BC, Samos was already a political, economic, and naval power. In the next century, during Polycrates's reign, it was noted for its arts and sciences and was the expanded site of the vast Temple of Hera, one of the Seven Wonders of the Ancient World. The Persian Wars led to the decline of Samos, however, which fell first under Persian rule, and then became subordinate to the expanding power of Athens. Samos was defeated by Pericles in 439 BC and forced to pay tribute to Athens.

Pirates controlled this deserted island after the fall of the Byzantine empire, but in 1562 an Ottoman admiral repopulated Samos with expatriates and Orthodox believers. It languished under the sun for hundreds of years until tobacco and shipping revived the economy in the 19th century.

Small though it may be, Samos has a formidable list of great Samians stretching through the ages. The fabled Aesop, the philosopher Epicurus, and Aristarchos (first in history to place the sun at the center of the solar system) all lived on Samos. The mathematician Pythagoras was born in Samos's ancient capital in 580 BC; in his honor, it was renamed Pythagorio in AD 1955 (it only took a couple of millennia). Plutarch wrote that in Roman times Anthony and Cleopatra took a long holiday on Samos, "giving themselves over to the feasting," and that artists came from afar to entertain them.

In the last decade Samos has become packed with other holiday travelers—European charter tourists—in July and August. Thankfully the curving terrain allows you to escape the crowds easily and feel as if you are still in an undiscovered Eden.

SAMOS TOWN ΣΑΜΟΣ (ΠΟΛΗ)

278 km (174 mi) east of Piraeus. 111 km (69 mi) southeast of Mytilini.

On the northeast coast at the head of a sharply deep bay is the capital, Samos town, also known as Vathi (which actually refers to the old settlement just above the port). Red-tile roofs sweep around the arc of the bay and reach toward the top of red-earth hills. In the morning at the sheltered port, fishermen still grapple with their nets, spreading them to dry in the sun, and in the early afternoon everything shuts down. Slow summer sunsets over the sparkling harbor match the relaxed pace of locals. Tourism has not altered this centuries-old schedule.

14

The stepped streets ascend from the shopping thoroughfare, which ★ meanders from the port to the city park next to the **Archaeological Museum,** the town's most important sight. The newest wing holds the impressive **kouros from Heraion,** a statue of a nude male youth, built as an offering to the goddess Hera and the largest freestanding sculpture surviving from ancient Greece, dating from 580 BC. This colossal statue, the work of a Samian artist, is made of the typical Samian gray-and-white-band marble. Pieces of the kouros were discovered in various peculiar locations: its thigh was being used as part of a Hellenistic house wall, and its left forearm was being used as a step for a Roman cistern. The statue is so large (16½ feet tall) that the wing had to be rebuilt specifically to house it. The museum's older section has a collection of pottery and cast-bronze griffin heads (the symbol of Samos). Samian sculptures from past millennia were considered among the best in Greece, and examples here show why. An exceptional collection of tributary gifts from ancient cities far and wide, including bronzes and ivory miniatures, affirms the importance of the shrine to Hera. ⊠*Dimarhiou Sq.* ☎*22730/27469* *€3* ⏲*Tues.–Sun. 8:30–3.*

In the quaint 17th-century enclave of **Ano Vathi** (⊠*Southern edge of Samos town, beyond museum, to the right*), wood-and-plaster houses with pastel facades and red-tile roofs are jammed together, their balconies protruding into cobbled paths so narrow that the water channel takes up most of the space. From here you have a view of the gulf.

OFF THE BEATEN PATH

Turkey. From Samos town (and Pythagorio), you can easily ferry to Turkey. Once you're there, it's a 13-km (8-mi) drive from the Kuşadası Kud on the Turkish coast, where the boats dock, to Ephesus, one of the great archaeological sites and a major city of the ancient world. (Note that the Temple of Artemis in Ephesus is a copy of the Temple of Hera in Heraion, which is now in ruins.) Many travel agencies have guided round-trip full-day tours to the site (€100), although you can take an unguided ferry trip for €35 with same-day return. You leave your passport with the agency, and it is returned when you come back from Turkey.

BEACHES

One of the island's best beaches is **Psili Ammos** (⊠*Southeast of Samos town, near Mesokambos*), a pristine, sandy beach protected from the wind by cliffs. There are two tavernas here. The beach at **Kerveli bay**

(✉*On the coast east of Samos town*) has an enticing pebbly beach with calm, turquoise waters.

WHERE TO STAY & EAT

$–$$ ✕**The Steps.** Climb the steps and enter a softly lighted, airy terrace draped with ivy and overlooking the harbor. One of the chef's specialties is the mixed plate, which gives you a chance to try the lamb, chicken, beef fillet, and beef steak. He also serves *exohiko*, swordfish grilled with lemon-oil sauce. ✉*Off Samos waterfront, behind Catholic church* ☎*22730/28649* ✍*Reservations essential* ▭*MC, V* ⊙*Closed Nov.–Apr. No lunch.*

WORD OF MOUTH

"The Ino Village Hotel . . . is about five minutes' drive from the hustle of Samos town and is located in a nice treed and peaceful area, high on a hill with lovely sea views. The hotel has a good restaurant located on an outdoor terrace with a view to kill for. There are two to three tavernas within 10 minutes' walk. Staff are friendly. Make sure you ask for an air-conditioned room with a sea view."

—hambo

$ ★ ✕**Karavi.** From the shape of one of Samos town's oldest port-side tavernas it's easy to see that *karavi* in Greek means "boat." To your benefit—and to the frustration of neighboring restaurants—the owner here has arranged for most local fish to be delivered to him. Fish soup, made the local way with vegetables and Aegean fish, tastes like a first-rate bouillabaisse. Other outstanding choices include the fresh grilled calamari, scampi, crawfish spaghetti, and lobster. When you're finished, stop for a cocktail at the stylish adjacent beach bar. ✉*Kefalopoulou 3–5* ☎*22730/24293* ✍*Reservations essential* ▭*AE, DC, MC, V.*

¢–$ ✕**Ostrako.** Greeks come here, amid colored lights, seashell-covered walls, and flowering trees, to devour octopus snacks, steaming hot mussels, shrimp *saganaki* (baked in a tomato sauce with cheese), stuffed calamari, and sea bream. As with other local favorites, Ostrako is a place to order and share mezedes. Meat lovers can choose from among 20 dishes, including lamb chops and grilled tenderloin. Fruit or Samian doughnuts topped with honey and cinnamon end dinner on a sweet note. All the action takes place on the restaurant's back garden patio, which has a small playground next to it. ✉*Them. Soufouli 141, east side of port* ☎*22730/27070* ▭*No credit cards.*

$ **Hotel Samos.** In this value-seeker's paradise, sleek modern rooms come equipped with amenities uncommon in this price range, like soundproof windows, hair dryers, and wireless Internet. There's also a roof garden, rooftop pool, and hot tub. A small marble lobby connects to a chic, street-level café along the town's waterfront, a perfect place for people-watching. ✉*Them. Soufouli 11, 83100* ☎*22730/28377* 🌐*www.samoshotel.gr* *98 rooms, 2 suites* *In-room: refrigerator, Wi-Fi. In-hotel: bar, pool* ▭*AE, DC, MC, V.*

$ **Ino Village Hotel.** North of the port on a sloping hill in residential Kalami, these sand-color stucco buildings draped with fuchsia bougainvillea surround a luminous pool, in a setting of tranquillity you're unlikely to find in Samos town. All rooms have balconies, dark-wood furnishings, and some black-and-white etchings of ancient Samos. Superior rooms include TVs, small refrigerators, and air-conditioning.

Request those in the 800 block for a spectacular view of Samos bay and the mountains beyond. The 15-minute walk to Samos town is downhill (you can call the hotel to arrange for transport back up). ✉ *1 km (½ mi) north of Samos town center, 83100Kalami* ☎ *22730/23241* 🌐 *www.inovillagehotel.com* *65 rooms* *In-room: no a/c (some), refrigerator (some), no TV (some). In-hotel: restaurant, bar, pool, no elevator* 💳 *AE, D, DC, MC, V.*

NIGHTLIFE

Bars generally are open May to September from about 8 or 10 PM to 3 AM. Begin your evening at **Escape** (✉ *Past port police station, on main road out of town, near hospital* ☎ *22730/28095*), a popular gathering place, with a sunset cocktail on the spacious seaside patio (drinks are half price from 8 to 10 PM daily). The music in this hip spot picks up later, and so does the dancing. Friday is theme night (rock, reggae, or funk, for example) and there are full-moon parties.

14

Next to Karavi restaurant, **Selini** (✉ *Kefalopoulou 3–5* ☎ *22730/24293*) is a stylish beachfront cocktail bar designed in Cycladic white. A fashionable Greek and international crowd mixes outside, as blue lights reflect off the sea below. Lounge and dance music is played.

PYTHAGORIO ΠΥΘΑΓΟΡΕΙΟ

14 km (8½ mi) southwest of Samos town.

Samos was a democratic state until 535 BC, when the town now called Pythagorio (formerly Tigani, or "frying pan") fell to the tyrant Polycrates (540–22 BC). Polycrates used his fleet of 100 ships to make profitable raids around the Aegean, until he was caught by the Persians and crucified in 522 BC. His rule produced what Herodotus described as "three of the greatest building and engineering feats in the Greek world." One is the Heraion, west of Pythagorio, the largest temple ever built in Greece and one of the Seven Wonders of the Ancient World. Another is the ancient mole protecting the harbor on the southeast coast, on which the present 1,400-foot jetty rests. The third is the Efpalinio tunnel, built to guarantee that water flowing from mountain streams would be available even to besieged Samians. Pythagorio remains a picturesque little port, with red-tile-roof houses and a curving harbor filled with fishing boats, but it is popular with tourists. There are more trendy restaurants and cafés here than elsewhere on the island.

The underground aqueduct, the **To Efpalinio Hydragogeio,** or Efpalinio tunnel, which Herodotus considered the world's Eighth Wonder, was completed in 524 BC with primitive tools and without measuring instruments. Polycrates, not a man who liked to leave himself vulnerable, ordered the construction of the tunnel to ensure that Samos's water supply could never be cut off during an attack. Efpalinos of Megara, a hydraulics engineer, set perhaps 1,000 slaves into two teams, one digging on each side of Mt. Kastri. Fifteen years later, they met in the middle with just a tiny difference in the elevation between the two halves.

The tunnel is about 3,340 feet long, and it remained in use as an aqueduct for almost 1,000 years. More than a mile of (long-gone) ceramic water pipe once filled the space, which was also used as a hiding place during pirate raids in the 7th century. Today the tunnel is exclusively a tourist site, and though some spaces are tight and slippery, you can walk the first 1,000 feet. ✉ *Just north of town* ☎ *22730/61400* 🎫 *€4* ⏲ *Tues.–Sun. 8:45–2:45.*

Among acres of excavations, little remains from the **archaia polis** (*ancient city* ✉ *Bordering small harbor and hill*) except a few pieces of the **Polycrates wall** and the **ancient theater** a few hundred yards above the tunnel.

Pythagorio's quiet cobblestone streets are lined with mansions and filled with fragrant orange blossoms. At the east corner sits the crumbling ruins of the **kastro** *(castle, or fortress)*, probably built on top of the ruins of the acropolis. Revolutionary hero Lykourgou Logotheti built this 19th-century edifice; his statue is next door, in the **courtyard** of the church built to honor the victory. He held back the Turks on Transfiguration Day, and a sign on the church announces in Greek: CHRIST SAVED SAMOS 6 AUGUST, 1824. On some nights the villagers light votive candles in the church cemetery, a moving sight with the ghostly silhouette of the fortress and the moonlit sea in the background.

The tiny but impressive **Samos Pythagorio Museum** contains local finds, including headless statues, grave markers with epigrams to the dead, human and animal figurines, and beautiful portraits of the Roman emperors Claudius, Caesar, and Augustus. Hours are approximate. ✉ *Pythagora Sq., in municipal bldg.* ☎ *22730/61400* 🎫 *Free* ⏲ *Tues.–Sun. 8:30–3.*

WHERE TO STAY & EAT

¢–$ ✕ **Maritsa.** A regular Pythagorio clientele frequents Maritsa, a simple fish taverna in a garden courtyard on a quiet, tree-lined side street. You might try shrimp souvlaki, red mullet, octopus, or squid garnished with garlicky *skordalia* (a thick lemony sauce with pureed potatoes, vinegar, and parsley). The usual appetizers include a sharp *tzatziki* (tangy garlic-yogurt dip with cucumber) and a large *horiatiki* ("village" or "country" salad) piled high with tomatoes, olives, onion, and feta cheese. Additional recommendations include lamb on the spit, the mixed grill, and stuffed tomatoes. ✉ *Off Lykourgou Logotheti, 1 block from waterfront* ☎ *22730/61957* 💳 *MC, V.*

$$$$ **Doryssa Bay Hotel-Village.** Guests here choose between beachfront accommodations in the plush main hotel building with a view of the sea or in the painstakingly created "village," with its winding cobblestone streets, colorful town-house facades, and rustic main square, complete with shops. Either choice provides elegant contemporary furnishings and gives you access to a well-trained professional staff and a wealth of resort facilities, including an on-site folklore museum. The hotel is popular with Greek and international travelers and receives many tour groups in summer. ✉ *Pythagorio beach, near road to airport 83103* ☎ *22730/88300 or 22730/88400* 🌐 *www.doryssa-bay.gr*

172 rooms, 125 bungalows, 5 suites In-room: refrigerator, Wi-Fi. In-hotel: 2 restaurants, bars, pool, spa, public Internet, some pets allowed AE, DC, MC, V Closed Nov.–Mar.

$$$$ ★ **Proteas Bay.** Standing on the sweeping terrace of the hotel restaurant, or on the balcony of one of the luxurious bungalows that cascade down the steep hillside, is like being on the bridge of a ship: all you see are the blue sea and sky and the mountains of Turkey rising up from the water. The hotel is notably quiet. It's designed in a clean, contemporary style with large, airy spaces, gardens planted with local flowers, an Olympic-size pool, and a beautiful secluded-cove beach. *Samos town, Pythagorio road, 83103 22730/62144 or 22730/62146 www.proteasbay.gr 20 rooms, 72 suites In-room: refrigerator, dial-up. In-hotel: 2 restaurants, bars, pools, spa, public Internet AE, DC, MC, V Closed Oct.–May.*

$ **Fito Bay Bungalows.** A knowledgeable, warm staff makes you feel at home at this relaxed, economical, and family-friendly place just steps from Pythagorio beach. Individual white bungalows with terra-cotta roofs wrap neatly around a sparkling long pool, and paths wind between beds of roses and lavender on the beautifully kept grounds. Rooms are spare (even mini-fridges aren't standard fixtures, though they can be requested), but this is not a place to linger indoors: take breakfast on the vine-covered terrace, relax in a lounge chair on the beach, or have a meal in the excellent taverna. *Pythagorio beach, on road to airport, 83103 22730/61314 www.fitobay.gr 87 rooms, 1 suite In-room: no TV. In-hotel: restaurant, bar, pool, public Internet, no elevator AE, MC, V Closed Oct.–Apr.*

SPORTS & THE OUTDOORS

Sun Yachting (*Poseidonos 21, Kalamaki 210/983–7312 and 210/983–7313 www.sunyachting.gr*) in Athens specializes in charter rentals to Samos; you can pick up the boat in Piraeus or Pythagorio for one- and two-week rentals.

14

HERAION ΗΡΑΙΟΝ

★ *6 km (4 mi) southwest of Pythagorio, 20 km (12½ southwest of Samos town.*

The early Samians worshipped the goddess Hera, believing she was born here beneath a bush near the stream Imbrassos and that there she also lay with Zeus. Several temples were subsequently built on the site in her honor, the earliest dating back to the 8th century BC. Polycrates rebuilt the Iraio, or Temple of Hera, around 540 BC, making it four times larger than the Parthenon and the largest Greek temple ever conceived, with two rows of columns (155 in all). The temple was damaged by fire in 525 BC and never completed, owing to Polycrates's untimely death. In the intervening years, masons recycled the stones to create other buildings, including a basilica (foundations remain at the site) to the Virgin Mary. Today you can only imagine the Iraio's massive glory; of its forest of columns only one remains standing, slightly askew and only half its original height, amid acres of marble remnants in marshy ground thick with poppies.

At the ancient celebrations to honor Hera, the faithful approached from the sea along the **Sacred road,** which is still visible at the site's northeast corner. Nearby are replicas of a 6th-century BC sculpture depicting an aristocratic family; its chiseled signature reads "Genelaos made me." The kouros from Heraion was found here, and now is in the Archaeological Museum in Samos town. Hours may be shortened in winter. ✉*Near Imvisos river* ☎*22730/95277* 🌐*www.culture.gr* 🎫*€3* ⏲*Apr.–Oct., daily 8:30–3.*

KOKKARI ΚΟΚΚΑΡΙ

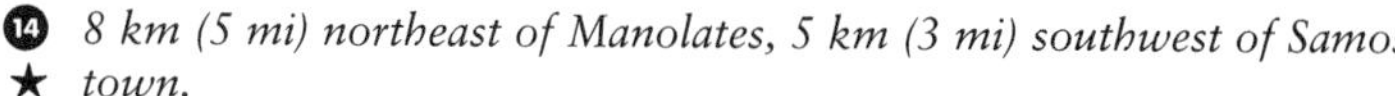

14 ★ *8 km (5 mi) northeast of Manolates, 5 km (3 mi) southwest of Samos town.*

Beyond the popular beaches of Tsabou, Tsamadou, and Lemonakia, the spectacular stretch of coast road lined with olive groves and vineyards ends in the fishing village of Kokkari, one of the most appealing spots on the island. Until 1980, not much was here except for a few dozen houses between two headlands, and tracts of onion fields, which gave the town its name. Though now there are a score of hotels, and many European tourists, you can still traipse along the rocky, windswept beach and spy fishermen mending trawling nets on the paved quay. Cross the spit to the eastern side of the headland and watch the moon rise over the lights of Vathi (Samos town) in the next bay. East of Kokkari you pass by Malagari, the winery where farmers hawk their harvested grapes every September.

BEACHES

Acclaimed coves of the north coast with small pebbly beaches and gorgeous blue-green waters include **Lemonakia, Tsamadou,** and **Tsabou**; all are just a few minutes from one another, and they're to be avoided when the *meltemi* (northern winds) blow, unless you're a professional windsurfer.

WHERE TO STAY & EAT

$ ✕ **Akrogiali Tavern.** Although this small beach shack is not nearly as stylish as some other restaurants up the beach, Akrogiali Tavern serves the town's tastiest fish. Sold by the kilo, the daily selections vary but are always extensive, with red mullet, swordfish, mackerel, salmon, and squid among the possible catches. The menu clearly indicates what's fresh and what's frozen, and Samos olive oil is used in the cooking. For more local flavor, try the native white wine, made from muscat grapes, with your meal. ✉*Kokkari promenade* ☎*22730/92423* 💳*No credit cards* ⏲*Closed Nov.–Mar.*

¢–$ ✕ **Ammos Plaz.** Ammos Plaz serves what many locals consider the best traditional Greek food in Kokkari, and in an ideal location—smack on the beach. Expect the dishes to change daily, but you may find choices like lamb fricassee and rabbit stifado. The owner's father is a fisherman, and he brings his haul to the restaurant daily. Octopus in a sweet white wine sauce and grilled lobster are two favorites, but considerably more expensive than many selections on the menu. ✉ *Kokkari promenade* ☎ *22730/92463* ▭ *AE, MC, V* ⊙ *Closed Nov.–Mar.*

$ **Olympia Beach/Olympia Village.** Flowery Samian ceramics decorate the spare, immaculate rooms with balconies overlooking the sea at the bright-white Olympic Beach hotel. The Olympic Village has apartments with a bedroom, a living room, two baths, and a kitchen. From here you can walk to Tsamadou cove, favored for its shallow water, pine trees, and seclusion. ✉ *Northwest beach road, 83100* ☎ *22730/92324 or 02730/92353* 🌐 *www.olympiabeach.gr* *12 rooms, 22 apartments* *In-room: kitchen (some), refrigerator. In-hotel: restaurant, bar, no elevator* ▭ *MC, V* ⊙ *Closed Nov.–Apr.* *CP.*

¢ **Galini.** Galini means "tranquillity," and this quiet pension deserves the name. Markela Moshous is a wonderfully hospitable host; she serves breakfast in either the garden or the charming breakfast room. Rooms have simple wood furnishings and impressive marble floors, and they come with balconies or terraces facing the town or sea (and access to a refrigerator). ✉ *Panayotis Moshous, 83100* ☎ *22730/92331, 22730/92365, or 22730/28039* *9 rooms* *In-room: no a/c, no TV. In-hotel: bar* ▭ *No credit cards* ⊙ *Closed Nov.–Apr.* *CP.*

14

SPORTS & THE OUTDOORS

In summer **Kokkari Surf and Bike Center** (✉ *On road to Lemonakia* ☎ *22730/92102* 🌐 *www.samoswindsurfing.gr*) rents windsurfing equipment, motorboats, sea kayaks, and mountain bikes. They also provide windsurfing instruction and run treks for hikers and mountain bikers.

NORTHERN ISLANDS ESSENTIALS

TRANSPORTATION

BY AIR

CARRIERS Even if they have the time, many people avoid the 10- to 12-hour ferry ride from Athens and start their island-hopping trip by taking air flights to all three islands; they take less than an hour. Olympic Airlines has at least a dozen flights a week from Athens to Lesbos and Chios in summer; fewer to Samos. Aegean Airlines flies daily from Athens to Chios. There are several Olympic Airlines flights a week from Chios to Lesbos, Limnos, Rhodes, and Thessaloniki; and several a week from Lesbos to Chios, Limnos, and Thessaloniki. From Samos there are several weekly Olympic flights to Limnos, Rhodes, and Thessaloniki; there are few flights (usually only one per week) between Samos and the other Northern Islands.

Be aware that overbooking happens; if you have a reservation, you should be entitled to a free flight if you get bumped.

Contacts **Aegean Airlines** (✉ *Koundouriotou 87, Mytilini, Lesbos* ☎ *22510/37355 and at Odysseas Elitis airport 22510/61120, 22510/61059 and 22510/61889; Chios airport 22710/81051-3; Samos airport 22730/62790* 🌐 *www.aegeanair.gr*).

Olympic Airlines (☎ *80111/44444, 210/626–1000 in Athens* 🌐 *www.olympicairlines.com* ✉ *Egeou, Chios town, Chios* ☎ *22710/44727* ✉ *Kavetsou 44, Mytilini, Lesbos* ☎ *22510/28660* ✉ *Kanari 5, Samos town, Samos* ☎ *22730/27237 or 22730/61219*).

AIRPORTS Lesbos Airport is 7 km (4½ mi) south of Mytilini. Chios Airport is 4½ km (3 mi) south of Chios town. The busiest airport in the region is on Samos, 17 km (10½ mi) southwest of Samos town. More than 40 international charters arrive every week in midsummer.

Contacts **Chios Airport** (☎ *22710/81400*). **Lesbos Airport** (☎ *22510/38700*). **Samos Airport** (☎ *22730/87800*).

BY BOAT & FERRY

Expect ferries between any of the Northern Islands and Piraeus, Athens's port, to take 10 to 12 hours. There are at least four boats per week from Piraeus and three per week from Thessaloniki to Lesbos. Boats arrive daily to Chios from Piraeus. Ferries arrive on Samos at ports in Samos town and Karlovassi (28 km [17 mi] northwest of Samos town) four to nine times per week from Piraeus, stopping at Paros and Naxos; and most of the year two or three ferries weekly serve Pythagorio from Kos and Patmos. Ferries and hydrofoils to Kuşadası, on the Turkish coast, leave from Samos town. Owing to sudden changes, no advance ferry schedule can be trusted. Port authority offices have the most recent ferry schedule information and the Greek Travel Pages Web site is helpful.

BETWEEN THE ISLANDS There is daily service between Lesbos and Chios. The regular ferry takes 3½ hours; the fast ferry 1½ hours. There can be as few as one ferry per week between Lesbos or Chios and Samos (both 3-hour trips). The only other way to reach Samos from Lesbos or Chios is to fly via Athens (an expensive alternative), on Olympic Airlines.

Contacts **Chios Port Authority** (☎ *22710/44433, 22710/44434 in Chios town*). **Greek Travel Pages** (🌐 *www.gtp.gr*). **Lesbos Port Authority** (☎ *22510/47888 in Mytilini*). **Piraeus Port Authority** (☎ *210/422–6000*). **Samos Port Authority** (☎ *22730/27318 in Samos town, 22730/30888 in Karlovassi, 22730/61225 in Pythagorio*).

BY BUS

Lesbos's buses are infrequent, though there are several a day from Mytilini to Molyvos via Kalloni. Buses leave the town of Chios several times per day for Mesta and Pirgi. Samos has excellent bus service, with frequent trips between Pythagorio, Samos town, and Kokkari.

Contacts **Chios Blue and Green Bus System** (✉ *Vlatarias 13, Chios town, Chios* ☎ *22710/23086 or 22710/24257*). **Lesbos Bus Station** (✉ *Konstantinopoleos Sq., Mytilini, Lesbos* ☎ *22510/28873*). **Samos Bus Station** (✉ *Ioannou Lekati and Kanari, Samos town, Samos* ☎ *22730/27262*).

BY CAR

Lesbos and Chios are large, so a car is useful. You might also want to rent a car on Samos, where mountain roads are steep; motorbikes are a popular mode of transport along the coast. Expect to spend about

€35–€50 per day for a compact car with insurance and unlimited mileage. Note that you must have an international driver's license to rent a car on Chios. Though a national license may be sufficient to rent a car at some agencies on other islands, if you are stopped by the police or get into an accident and cannot produce an international or EU license, you may find the rental companies' stance isn't an official one.

Budget, at Lesbos Airport, has newer cars and is cheaper than other agencies. Vassilakis on Chios has reliable, well-priced vehicles. Aramis Rent-a-Car, part of Sixt, has fair rates and reliable service on Samos.

Agencies **Aramis Rent-A-Car** (✉ *Directly across from port, Samos town, Samos* ☎ *22730/23253* 🖷 *22730/23620* ✉ *On main street near National Bank, Pythagorio, Samos* ☎ *22730/62267* ✉ *Town center, opposite Commercial Bank, Kokkari, Samos* ☎ *22730/92385*). **Budget** (✉ *Airport, Mytilini, Lesbos* ☎ *22510/61665* 🌐 *www.budget.com*). **Vassilakis** (✉ *Chandris 3, Chios town, Chios* ☎ *22710/29300* 🖷 *22710/23205* 🌐 *www.rentacar-chios.com*).

BY TAXI

Often there are taxi phones at the port or main bus stops. Due to the small number of cabs, prices are high: expect to shell out around double what you'd pay in Athens, but always check the rates in advance. If you do spring for a ride, it's a good idea to ask for a card with the driver's number in case you need a lift later in your trip.

CONTACTS & RESOURCES

EMERGENCIES

Contacts **Ambulance** (☎ *166*). **Fire** (☎ *199*). **Police** (☎ *100*).

INTERNET, MAIL & SHIPPING

Contacts **Diamonds** (✉ *87 Koundouriotou St., Mytilini, Lesbos* ☎ *22510/43366*). **In Spot Mytilini** (✉ *44 Christougennon St., Mytilini, Lesbos* ☎ *22510/45760*). **In Spot Chios** (✉ *86 Aigaiou Ave., Chios town, Chios* ☎ *22710/23438* ✉ *98 Aigaiou Ave., Chios town, Chios* ☎ *22710/41058*). **Internet Café** (✉ *Themistokli Sofouli St., Samos town, Samos* ☎ *22730/22469*). **Post Office** (✉ *2 Vournazou St., Mytilini, Lesbos* ☎ *22510/28823*). **Post Office** (✉ *Omirou & Rodoukanaki Sts., Chios town, Chios* ☎ *22710/44276*). **Post Office** (✉ *105 Sofouli St., Mytilini, Lesbos* ☎ *22510/45760*).

TOUR OPTIONS

Aeolic Cruises on Lesbos runs several island tours. In Molyvos, Panatella Holidays has two tours that take in villages, monasteries, and other sights. Petra Tours, located in Petra, just south of Molyvos, plans bird-watching, botanical, walking, and scuba-diving excursions. Chios Tours organizes land excursions to the south, central, and northern regions of that island, as well as day trips to Izmir in Turkey. Samina Tours, on Samos, runs an island tour, a one-day boat trip to Patmos island, and a picnic cruise.

Contacts **Aeolic Cruises** (✉ *Prokymea, Mytilini, Lesbos* ☎ *22510/23960 or 22510/23266* 🖷 *22510/43694*). **Chios Tours** (✉ *Aigeou, waterfront, Chios town, Chios* ☎ *22710/29444 or 22710/29555* 🌐 *www.chiostours.gr*). **Panatella Holidays**

(✉ *Possidonion, at town entrance, Molyvos, Lesbos* ☎ *22530/71520, 22530/71643, or 22530/71644* 🌐 *www.panatella-holidays.com*). **Petra Tours** (✉ *Petra, Lesbos* ☎ *22530/41390 or 22530/42011* 🌐 *www.petratours-lesvos.com*). **Samina Tours** (✉ *Them. Sofouli 67, Samos town, Samos* ☎ *22730/22425* 🌐 *www.samina.gr*).

VISITOR INFORMATION

Contacts **Chios Municipal Tourist Office** (✉ *Kanari 18, Chios town, Chios* ☎ *22710/44389 or 22710/44344* 🌐 *www.chios.gr*). **Greek National Tourism Organization** (*GNTO or EOT*) 🌐 *www.gnto.gr*). **Lesbos Municipal Tourist Office** (✉ *Harbor front, Mytilini, Lesbos* ☎ *22510/44165* 🌐 *www.lesvos.gr*). **Mesta's Tourist Information Office** (✉ *Main square, Chios town, Chios* ☎ *22710/76319*). **Samos Municipal Tourist Office** (✉ *Ikosipemptis Martiou 4, Samos town, Samos* ☎ *22730/81031* 🌐 *www.samos.gr*). **Tourist police** (✉ *Harbor front, Mytilini, Lesbos* ☎ *22510/22776* ✉ *Neoriou 37, Chios town, Chios* ☎ *22710/81539* ✉ *Harbor front, Samos town, Samos* ☎ *22730/81000*).

UNDERSTANDING GREECE

GREEK ARCHITECTURE

The Megaron
Showing the development from the "House of the People" to the "House of the God"

A. TROY II

B. TIRYNS

C. OLYMPIA — Temple of Zeus

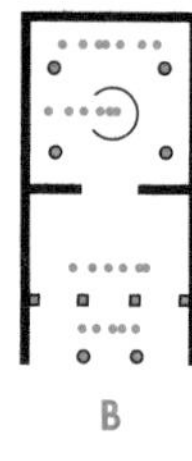

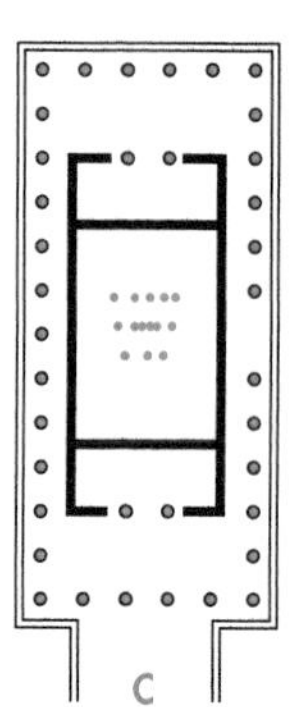

THE ORDERS OF GREEK ARCHITECTURE

DORIC

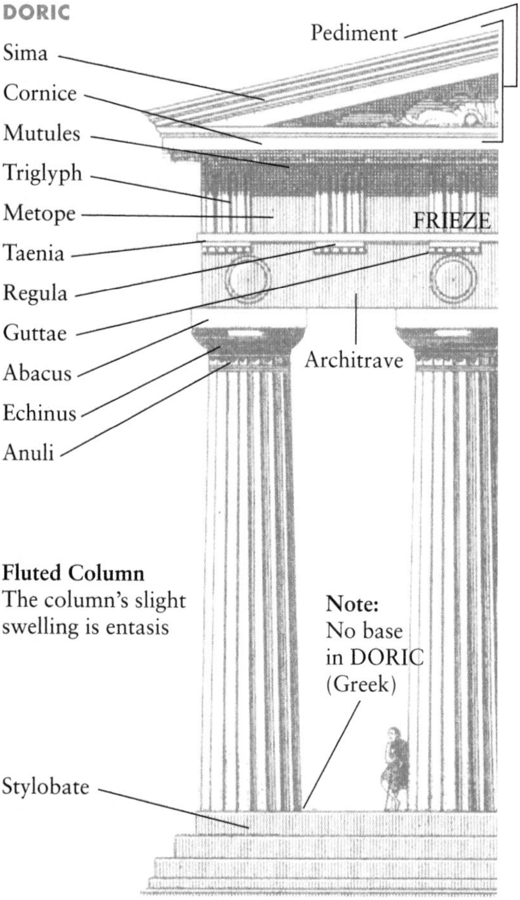

Pediment

Sima

Cornice

Mutules

Triglyph

Metope

FRIEZE

Taenia

Regula

Guttae

Abacus

Architrave

Echinus

Anuli

Fluted Column
The column's slight swelling is entasis

Note:
No base in DORIC (Greek)

Stylobate

Corinthian

Ionic

Composite

BOOKS & MOVIES

BOOKS

A. R. Burn's *The Penguin History of Greece* takes the reader from the Neolithic pioneers to the splendors of Athens to the last dark days when the philosophic schools were closed, capturing the culture of an amazing people. Extremely fluid, it is written for those who are not experts in classical literature. Just as erudite and enthusiastic is the *Oxford History of Greece and the Hellenistic World,* edited by John Boardman, Jasper Griffin, and Oswyn Murray, a comprehensive but never boring view of the ancient Greek world and its achievements. A late convert to classical Greece, Peter France will engage even the laziest reader in his *Greek as a Treat* (Penguin); theme by theme, with a sharp wit, he introduces readers to the greats—Homer, Pythagoras, Aeschylus, Socrates, and Plato—demonstrating how they still can enrich our 20th-century lives.

In Sailing *the Wine-Dark Sea: Why the Greeks Matter* (Nan A. Talese/Doubleday), Thomas Cahill engagingly explores the contributions of the ancient Greeks and examines six key figures (warriors, philosophers, and artists) who exemplify these achievements. Mary Beard's *The Parthenon* (Harvard University Press) is an elegant cultural guide to one of the world's most influential buildings.

C. M. Woodhouse's *Modern Greece: A Short History* (Faber and Faber) succinctly covers the ensuing development of Greece, from the fall of the Byzantine empire to the War of Independence and the monarchy to the ongoing struggle between the socialist PASOK party and the conservative New Democracy party. *The Greeks: The Land and People Since the War* (Penguin; out of print), by James Pettifer, takes readers behind the postcard imagery of lazy beaches and sun-kissed villages to modern Greece's contradictions as the author examines the far-reaching effects of the country's recent troubled past, including civil war and dictatorship. Richard Clogg's *Concise History of Greece* (Cambridge University Press) focuses on the period from the late 1700s to the present. *Eleni* (Ballantine) is journalist Nicholas Gage's account of his mother's struggle for the freedom of her children and her execution in the late 1940s.

John Julius Norwich's three-volume *Byzantium* (Knopf), or his condensed one-volume *A Short History of Byzantium* (Vintage), is a good introduction to the medieval Byzantine empire. Timothy Ware's *The Orthodox Church* (Penguin) provides an introduction to the religion of the Greek people, while Paul Hetherington's *Byzantine and Medieval Greece, Churches, Castles, and Art* (DIANE Publishing) offers a useful introduction to Byzantine and Frankish mainland Greece. *Unearthing Atlantis* (Avon), by Charles Pellegrino, is a fascinating book linking Atlantis to Santorini. The idyllic youth of naturalist Gerald Durrell on the island of Corfu is recalled in many of his books, such as *My Family and Other Animals* (Penguin), which are written with an unpretentious, precise style in a slightly humorous vein and are underrated as works of literature. Lawrence Durrell's 1945 memoir *Prospero's Cell* describes an earlier era on Corfu. Henry Miller's *The Colossus of Maroussi* (New Directions), an enjoyable seize-the-day-as-the-Greeks-do paean that veers from the profound to the superficial—sometimes verging on hysteria—is the product of a trip Miller took to Greece, during which he experienced an epiphany. *Roumeli: Travels in Northern Greece* and *Mani: Travels in Southern Peloponnese,* written by Patrick Leigh Fermor in the mid-20th century, are out of print but worth seeking out for the writer's exquisite evocations of these areas of Greece.

An American poet's account of a year (1992–93) spent in Athens, *Dinner with Persephone* (Vintage), by Patricia Storace, is an unsentimental portrait of modern Greek life and values. *Fodor's Athens: The Collected Traveler,* edited by Barrie Kerper, brings together articles about the city and surrounding areas and extensive bibliographies. *The Most Beautiful Villages of Greece* (Thames & Hudson), by Mark Ottaway and with luscious color photographs by Hugh Palmer, could inspire anyone's travel itinerary.

Greece's premier writer, Nikos Kazantzakis (1883–1957), captured the strengths and weaknesses and the color of traditional Greek culture in his wonderful novel *Zorba the Greek*; he also wrote the classics *Christ Recrucified* and *The Odyssey.* Other modern Greek fiction will immerse readers in the joys and woes of Greece today: Kedros Books has an excellent series, Modern Greek Writers, distributed in the United Kingdom by Forest Books, which includes *Farewell Anatolia,* by Dido Sotiriou, chronicling the traumatic end of Greek life in Asia Minor, and *Fool's Gold,* by Maro Douka, about an aristocratic young woman who becomes enamored of and then disillusioned with the resistance movement to the junta. Noted for his translations of Kazantzakis, the late Kimon Friar demonstrated exquisite taste in his superb translations of modern Greek verse, including works by C. P. Cavafy, and the Nobel Laureates George Seferis and Odysseus Elytis. Friar's *Modern Greek Poetry* is published by the Efstathiadis Group in Athens but is available elsewhere. Readers may have less difficulty finding Edmund Keeley and Philip Sherrard's *Voices of Modern Greek Poetry* (Princeton University Press); both Keeley and Sherrard have written about modern Greek literature.

Some people like to go back to the classics while in Greece. Try either Robert Fitzgerald's or Richmond Lattimore's translations of the *Iliad* and *Odyssey* of Homer, done in verse, unlike the clumsy prose translations you probably read in school. Take the *Iliad* as a pacifist work exposing the uselessness of warfare; read the Odyssey keeping in mind the relationships between men and women as illustrated by Odysseus and Penelope, Circe, and Calypso. Lattimore also translated Greece's early lyric poets, Sappho and her lesser-known contemporaries, in a collection titled *Greek Lyric Poetry.* Aristophanes's play *The Wasps* is one of the funniest pieces of literature ever written; the dramas of Aeschylus, Sophocles, and Euripides are important texts in Western culture. Although it isn't light reading, Thucydides's *Peloponnesian War* details the long struggle of Athens and Sparta, fought openly and through third parties, for and against democracy and autocracy. Pausanias's *Guide to Greece* (Penguin, two volumes) was written to guide Roman travelers to Greece in the 2nd century ad.

MOVIES

A determination to live for the moment coupled with lingering fatalism still pervades Greek society. No film better captures this than Michael Cacoyannis's *Zorba the Greek* (1964; in English), starring the inimitable Anthony Quinn, Alan Bates, and Irene Pappas. Graced with the music of Mikis Theodorakis (the score won an Oscar even though Theodorakis's music was banned at the time in Greece), the film juxtaposes this zest for life with the harsh realities of traditional village society.

In perhaps the second-best-known film about Greece, Hellenic joie de vivre meets American pragmatism in *Never on Sunday* (1960; in English), directed by Jules Dassin. The late Melina Mercouri, a national icon (she also served as the minister of culture in the 1980s), plays a Greek hooker, who in her simple but wise ways takes on the American who has come to reform her and teaches him that life isn't always about getting ahead.

The epic musical drama *Rembetiko* (1983; English subtitles), directed by Costas Ferris and awarded the Silver Bear in 1984, follows 40 years in the life of a rembetika (Greek blues) singer, played by smoldering, throaty-voiced Sotiria Leonardou. The film, notable for its authenticity and the music's raw energy, spans the turbulent political history of Greece and the development of rembetika blues, which flourished from the 1920s until the '40s as 1.5 million Greeks were displaced from Asia Minor. They brought with them their haunting minor-key laments, as well as the Anatolian custom of smoking hashish; today rembetika is enjoying a resurgence with young Greeks.

Mediterraneo (1991; English subtitles) is a nostalgic, humorous depiction of life on a tiny, distant Greek island, occupied by Italian solders during World War II. The soldiers become inextricably involved with the island's vivid personalities—to the point that some refuse to leave when finally informed that the war has long been over. The movie, which won an Oscar for Best Foreign Film, features Vanna Barba, a popular Greek actress whose lusty yet stern gaze captivates the lead role. One of Greece's leading directors, Theodoros Angelopoulos, has made several internationally acclaimed films, including *Journey to Kythera* (1984; English subtitles), which won for Best Screenplay in the 1984 Cannes festival. Considerably shorter than most of his films, it blends the mythical with the contemporary, detailing the life of a Greek civil-war fighter who returns from the Soviet Union to reunite with his son in an adventure that leaves him and his wife on a raft bound for Kythera island. Manos Katrakis, considered one of Greece's finest stage actors, performs superbly (he died soon after), and the music and striking cinematography evoke Cavafy's famous poem "Journey to Ithaki," familiar to all Greeks: "But do not hurry the voyage at all. It is better to let it last for long years; and even to anchor at the isle when you are old, rich with all that you have gained on the way."

A more recent film that portrays life in Greece since tourism hit in the late '60s is *Shirley Valentine* (1989; in English). Set amid marvelous island scenes, the story is a cautionary tale about a bored British housewife who leaves her stultifying life to vacation in Greece. Here, she regains her identity through a liberating romance with the local flirt (Tom Conti, speaking abominable Greek). Although a bit dated, since the "kamaki" (men who prey on foreign women) is no longer in full force given the increased independence of Greek women, the movie is full of humor, sharp dialogue, and dazzling shots of the Aegean.

Captain Corelli's Mandolin (2001; in English) adapted Louis de Bernières's novel of the same name about an Italian captain on the fascist-occupied island of Cephalonia during World War II. Political complexities are simplified into a love story between the captain and a young Greek woman—portrayed by Nicolas Cage and Penelope Cruz—but the Greek scenery is magnificent.

GREEK VOCABULARY

THE GREEK ABC'S

The proper names in this book are transliterated versions of the Greek name, so when you come upon signs written in the Greek alphabet, use this list to decipher them.

Greek	Roman	Greek	Roman
Α, α	a	Ν, ν	n
Β, β	v	Ξ, ξ	x or ks
Γ, γ	g or y	Ο, ο	o
Δ, δ	th, dh, or d	Π, π	p
Ε, ε	e	Ρ, ρ	r
Ζ, ζ	z	Σ, σ, ς	s
Η, η	i	Τ, τ	t
Θ, θ	th	Υ, υ	i
Ι, ι	i	Φ, φ	f
Κ, κ	k	Χ, χ	h or ch
Λ, λ	l	Ψ, ψ	ps
Μ, μ	m	Ω, ω	o

BASICS

The phonetic spelling used in English differs somewhat from the internationalized form of Greek place names. There are no long and short vowels in Greek; the pronunciation never changes. Note, also, that the accent is a stress mark, showing where the stress is placed in pronunciation.

Do you speak English?	Miláte angliká?
Yes, no	Málista or Né, óchi
Impossible	Adínato
Good morning, Good day	Kaliméra
Good evening, Good night	Kalispéra, Kaliníchta
Goodbye	Yá sas
Mister, Madam, Miss	Kírie, kiría, despiní
Please	Parakaló
Excuse me	Me sinchórite or signómi
How are you?	Ti kánete or pós íste
How do you do (Pleased to meet you)	Chéro polí
I don't understand.	Dén katalavéno.
To your health!	Giá sas!
Thank you	Efcharistó

NUMBERS

one	éna
two	dío
three	tría
four	téssera
five	pénde
six	éxi
seven	eptá
eight	októ
nine	enéa
ten	déka
twenty	íkossi
thirty	triánda
forty	saránda
fifty	penínda
sixty	exínda
seventy	evdomínda
eighty	ogdónda
ninety	enenínda
one hundred	ekató
two hundred	diakóssia
three hundred	triakóssia
one thousand	hília
two thousand	dió hiliádes
three thousand	trís hiliádes

DAYS OF THE WEEK

Monday	Deftéra
Tuesday	Tríti
Wednesday	Tetárti
Thursday	Pémpti
Friday	Paraskeví
Saturday	Sávato
Sunday	Kyriakí

MONTHS

January	Ianouários
February	Fevrouários
March	Mártios
April	Aprílios
May	Maíos

June	Ióunios
July	Ióulios
August	Ávgoustos
September	Septémvrios
October	Októvrios
November	Noémvrios
December	Dekémvrios

TRAVELING

I am traveling by car . . .	Taxidévo mé aftokínito . . . me
train . . . plane . . . boat.	tréno . . . me aeropláno . . . me vapóri.
Taxi, to the station . . .	Taxí, stó stathmó . . .
harbor . . . airport	limáni . . . aerodrómio
Porter, take the luggage.	Akthofóre, pare aftá tá prámata.
Where is the filling station?	Pou íne tó vensinádiko?
When does the train leave for . . . ?	Tí óra thá fíyi to tréno ya . . . ?
Which is the train for . . . ?	Pío íne to tréno gía . . . ?
Which is the road to . . . ?	Piós íne o drómos giá . . . ?
A first-class ticket	Éna isitírio prótis táxis
Smoking is forbidden.	Apagorévete to kápnisma.
Where is the toilet?	Póu íne í toaléta?
Ladies, men	Ginekón, andrón
Where? When?	Póu? Póte?
Sleeping car, dining car	Wagonlí, wagonrestorán
Compartment	Vagóni
Entrance, exit	Íssodos, éxodos
Nothing to declare	Den écho típota na dilósso
I am coming for my vacation.	Érchome giá tis diakopés mou.
Nothing	Típota
Personal use	Prossopikí chríssi
How much?	Pósso?
I want to eat, to drink, to sleep.	Thélo na fáo, na pió, na kimithó.
Sunrise, sunset	Anatolí, díssi
Sun, moon	Ílios, fengári
Day, night	Méra, níchta
Morning, afternoon	Proí, mesiméri, or apóyevma
The weather is good, bad.	Ó kerós íne kalós, kakós.

ON THE ROAD

Straight ahead	Kat efthían
To the right, to the left	Dexiá, aristerá
Show me the way to . . .	Díxte mou to drómo . . .
please.	parakaló.
Where is . . . ?	Pou íne . . . ?
Crossroad	Diastávrosi
Danger	Kíndinos

IN TOWN

Will you lead me? take me?	Thélete na me odigíste? Me pérnete mazí sas?
Street, square	Drómos, platía
Where is the bank?	Pou íne i trápeza?
Far	Makriá
Police station	Astinomikó tmíma
Consulate (American, British)	Proxenío (Amerikániko, Anglikó)
Theater, cinema	Théatro, cinemá
At what time does the film start?	Tí óra archízi ee tenía?
Where is the travel office?	Pou íne to touristikó grafío?
Where are the tourist police?	Pou íne i touristikí astinomía?

SHOPPING

I would like to buy	Tha íthela na agorásso
Show me, please.	Díxte mou, parakaló.
May I look around?	Boró na ríxo miá matyá?
How much is it?	Pósso káni? (or kostízi)
It is too expensive.	Íne polí akrivó.
Have you any sandals?	Échete pédila?
Have you foreign newspapers?	Échete xénes efimerídes?
Show me that blouse, please.	Díxte mou aftí tí blouza.
Show me that suitcase.	Díxte mou aftí tí valítza.
Envelopes, writing paper	Fakélous, hartí íli
Roll of film	Film
Map of the city	Hárti tis póleos
Something handmade	Hiropíito
Wrap it up, please.	Tilixteto, parakaló.
Cigarettes, matches, please.	Tsigára, spírta, parakaló.
Ham	Zambón
Sausage, salami	Loukániko, salámi
Sugar, salt, pepper	Záchari, aláti, pipéri

Grapes, cherries	Stafília, kerássia
Apple, pear, orange	Mílo, achládi, portokáli
Bread, butter	Psomí, voútiro
Peach, figs	Rodákino, síka

AT THE HOTEL

A good hotel	Éna kaló xenodochío
Have you a room?	Échete domátio?
Where can I find a furnished room?	Pou boró na vró epiploméno domátio?
A single room, double room	Éna monóklino, éna díklino
With bathroom	Me bánio
How much is it per day?	Pósso kostízi tin iméra?
A room overlooking the sea	Éna domátio prós ti thálassa
For one day, for two days	Giá miá méra, giá dió méres
For a week	Giá miá evdomáda
My name is. . . .	Onomázome. . . .
My passport	Tó diavatirió mou
What is the number of my room?	Piós íne o arithmós tou domatíou mou?
The key, please.	To klidí, parakaló.
Breakfast, lunch, supper	Proinó, messimergianó, vradinó
The bill, please.	To logariasmó, parakaló.
I am leaving tomorrow.	Févgo ávrio.

AT THE RESTAURANT

Waiter	Garsón
Where is the restaurant?	Pou íne to estiatório?
I would like to eat.	Tha íthela na fáo.
The menu, please.	To katálogo, parakaló.
Fixed-price menu	Menú
Soup	Soúpa
Bread	Psomí
Hors d'oeuvre	Mezédes, orektiká
Ham omelet	Omelétta zambón
Chicken	Kotópoulo
Roast pork	Psitó hirinó
Beef	Moschári
Potatoes (fried)	Patátes (tiganités)
Tomato salad	Domatosaláta
Vegetables	Lachaniká
Watermelon, melon	Karpoúzi, pepóni

Desserts, pastry	Gliká or pástes
Fruit, cheese, ice cream	Fróuta, tirí, pagotó
Fish, eggs	Psári, avgá
Serve me on the terrace.	Na mou servírete sti tarátza.
Where can I wash my hands?	Pou boró na plíno ta héria mou?
Red wine, white wine	Kokivó krasí, áspro krasí
Unresinated wine	Krasí aretsínato
Beer, soda water, water, milk	Bíra, sóda, neró, gála
Greek (formerly Turkish) coffee	Ellenikó kafé
Coffee with milk, without sugar, medium, sweet	Kafé gallikó me, gála skéto, métrio, glikó

AT THE BANK, AT THE POST OFFICE

Where is the bank? . . .	Pou íne i trápeza? . . .
post office?	to tachidromío?
I would like to cash a check.	Thélo ná xargiróso mía epitagí.
Stamps	Grammatóssima
By airmail	Aëroporikós
Postcard, letter	Kárta, grámma
Letterbox	Tachidromikó koutí
I would like to telephone.	Thélo na tilephonísso.

AT THE GARAGE

Garage, gas (petrol)	Garáz, venzíni
Oil	Ládi
Change the oil.	Aláksete to ládi.
Look at the tires.	Rixte mia matiá sta lástika.
Wash the car.	Plínete to aftokínito.
Breakdown	Vlávi
Tow the car.	Rimúlkiste tó aftokínito.
Spark plugs	Buzí
Brakes	Fréna
Gearbox	Kivótio tachitíton
Carburetor	Karbiratér
Headlight	Provoléfs
Starter	Míza
Axle	Áksonas
Shock absorber	Amortisér
Spare part	Antalaktikó

Greece Essentials

PLANNING TOOLS, EXPERT INSIGHT, GREAT CONTACTS

There are planners and there are those who, excuse the pun, fly by the seat of their pants. We happily place ourselves among the planners. Our writers and editors try to anticipate all the issues you may face before and during any journey, and then they do their research. This section is the product of their efforts. Use it to get excited about your trip to Greece, to inform your travel planning, or to guide you on the road should the seat of your pants start to feel threadbare.

GETTING STARTED

We're really proud of our Web site: Fodors.com is a great place to begin any journey. Scan Travel Wire for suggested itineraries, travel deals, restaurant and hotel openings, and other up-to-the-minute info. Check out Booking to research prices and book plane tickets, hotel rooms, rental cars, and vacation packages. Head to Talk for on-the-ground pointers from travelers who frequent our message boards. You can also link to loads of other travel-related resources.

RESOURCES

ONLINE TRAVEL TOOLS

While the brunt of the Web sites listed in this book have English translations (look for the American or British flag), there are a few that don't, or that aren't fully translated. If you hit upon a site that's Greek to you, try AltaVista's Babel Fish Translation site (www.babelfish.altavista.com), which converts Greek text and some Web sites to English: just paste in a block of text or the site's URL, select "Greek to English" and hit "Translate." The translations can be amusingly literal but are often sufficient for finding out information like opening hours and prices.

ALL ABOUT GREECE

The U.S. Web site of the Greek National Tourism Organization, 🌐*www.greektourism.com*, is well laid out and packed with information and pictures; it has different content from the GNTO's broader site, 🌐*www.gnto.gr*. You can also check out the official Web site of Athens (🌐*www.cityofathens.gr*); the site of the Hellenic Ministry of Culture (🌐*www.culture.gr*), has basic information about museums, monuments, and archaeological sites. Packed with info about traveling by ferry are 🌐*www.greekferries.gr* and 🌐*www.ferries.gr*, which let you book online. Another source for ferry schedules is 🌐*www.gtp.gr*.

> **WORD OF MOUTH**
>
> After your trip, be sure to rate the places you visited and share your experiences and travel tips with us and other Fodorites in Travel Ratings and Talk on www.fodors.com.

SPECIAL INTEREST

The Hellenic Festival site, 🌐*www.hellenicfestival.gr*, lists summer programs for the Athens Festival and the Festival of Epidauros. The site of the Athens Concert Hall, 🌐*www.megaron.gr*, describes all the activities at this venue. A good resource guide to ancient Greece is 🌐*www.ancientgreece.com*. The Foundation for Environmental Education awards the Blue Flag designation to beaches, including those in Greece, that are clean, safe, and environmentally aware; 🌐*www.blueflag.org* has details.

Currency Conversion **Google** (🌐www.google.com) does currency conversion. Just type in the amount you want to convert and an explanation of how you want it converted (e.g., "14 Swiss francs in dollars"), and then voilà. **Oanda.com** (🌐www.oanda.com) allows you to print out a handy table with the current day's conversion rates. **XE.com** (🌐www.xe.com) is a good currency conversion Web site.

Safety **Transportation Security Administration** (TSA) 🌐www.tsa.gov).

Other Resources **CIA World Factbook** (🌐www.odci.gov/cia/publications/factbook/index.html) has profiles of every country in the world. It's a good source if you need some quick facts and figures.

VISITOR INFORMATION

Tourist police, stationed near the most popular tourist sites, can answer questions in English about transportation, steer you to an open pharmacy or doctor, and locate phone numbers of hotels, rooms, and restaurants. Also helpful are the municipal tourism offices. You can contact the Greek National Tourism Organization (GNTO; EOT in Greece), as well, which has offices throughout the world.

The very complete *Hellenic Traveling Pages,* a monthly publication available at most Greek bookstores, lists travel agencies; yacht brokers; bus, boat, and airplane schedules; and museum hours.

EOT in Greece **EOT** (✉Tsochas 7, Ambelokipi, Athens ☎210/870–7000 🌐www.gnto.gr. ✉Athens International Airport, Spata ☎210/353–0445 or 210/354–5101 ✉Georikis Scholis 46, Thessaloniki ☎2310/471027 ✉Thessaloniki International Airport, Thessaloniki ☎2310/471170 ✉Filopimenos 26, Patras ☎2610/620353).

In the U.S. **Greek National Tourism Organization** (✉Olympic Tower, 645 5th Ave., New York, NY10022 ☎212/421–5777 📠212/826–6940 🌐www.greektourism.com).

Guide Hellenic Traveling Pages (✉Info Publications, Pironos 51, 16341Athens ☎210/994–0109 or 210/993–7551).

THINGS TO CONSIDER

PASSPORTS & VISAS

All citizens (even infants) of the United States, Canada, Australia, and New Zealand, need only a valid passport to enter Greece for stays of up to 90 days. If you leave after 90 days and don't have a visa extension, you will be fined anywhere from €130 to €590 (depending on how long you overstay) by Greek airport officials, who are not flexible on this issue. Worse, you must provide *hartosima* (revenue stamps) for the documents, which you don't want to have to run around and find as your flight is boarding.

PASSPORTS

U.S. passports are valid for 10 years. You must apply in person if you're getting a passport for the first time; if your previous passport was lost, stolen, or damaged; or if your previous passport has expired and was issued more than 15 years ago or when you were under 16. All children under 18 must appear in person to apply for or renew a passport. Both parents must accompany any child under 14 (or send a notarized statement with their permission) and provide proof of their relationship to the child.

TIP→ Before your trip, make two copies of your passport's data page (one for someone at home and another for you to carry separately). Or scan the page and e-mail it to someone at home and/or yourself.

There are 13 regional passport offices, as well as 7,000 passport acceptance facilities in post offices, public libraries, and other governmental offices. If you're renewing a passport, you can do so by mail. Forms are available at passport acceptance facilities and online.

The cost to apply for a new passport is $97 for adults, $82 for children under 16; renewals are $67. Allow six weeks for processing, both for first-time passports and renewals. For an expediting fee of $60 you can reduce this time to about two weeks. If your trip is less than two weeks away, you can get a passport even more rapidly by going to a passport office with the necessary documentation. Private expediters can get things done in as little as 48 hours, but charge hefty fees for their services.

VISAS

A visa is essentially formal permission to enter a country. Visas allow countries to keep track of you and other visitors—and generate revenue (from application fees). You *always* need a visa to enter a foreign country; however, many countries routinely issue tourist visas on arrival, particularly to U.S. citizens. When your passport is stamped or scanned in the immigration line, you're actually being issued a visa. Sometimes you have to stand in a separate line and pay a small fee to get your stamp before going through immigration, but you can still do this at the airport on arrival.

Most visas limit you to a single trip—basically during the actual dates of your planned vacation. Other visas allow you to visit as many times as you wish for a specific period of time. Remember that requirements change, sometimes at the drop of a hat, and the burden is on you to make sure that you have the appropriate visas. Otherwise, you'll be turned away at the airport or, worse, deported after you arrive in the country. No company or travel insurer gives refunds if your travel plans are disrupted because you didn't have the correct visa.

U.S. Passport Information **U.S. Department of State** (☎877/487–2778 🌐travel.state.gov/passport).

U.S. Passport & Visa Expediters

A. Briggs Passport & Visa Expeditors (☎800/806–0581 or 202/338–0111 🌐www.abriggs.com). **American Passport Express** (☎800/455–5166 or 800/841–6778 🌐www.americanpassport.com). **Passport Express** (☎800/362–8196 🌐www.passportexpress.com). **Travel Document Systems** (☎800/874–5100 or 202/638–3800 🌐www.traveldocs.com). **Travel the World Visas** (☎866/886–8472 or 301/495–7700 🌐www.world-visa.com).

BOOKING YOUR TRIP

Unless your cousin is a travel agent, you're probably among the millions of people who make most of their travel arrangements online.

But have you ever wondered just what the differences are between an online travel agent (a Web site through which you make reservations instead of going directly to the airline, hotel, or car-rental company), a discounter (a firm that does a high volume of business with a hotel chain or airline and accordingly gets good prices), a wholesaler (one that makes cheap reservations in bulk and then resells them to people like you), and an aggregator (one that compares all the offerings so you don't have to)?

Is it truly better to book directly on an airline or hotel Web site? And when does a real live travel agent come in handy?

ONLINE

You really have to shop around. A travel wholesaler such as Hotels.com or HotelClub.net can be a source of good rates, as can discounters such as Hotwire or Priceline, particularly if you can bid for your hotel room or airfare. Indeed, such sites sometimes have deals that are unavailable elsewhere. They do, however, tend to work only with hotel chains (which makes them just plain useless for getting hotel reservations outside major cities) or big airlines (so that often leaves out upstarts like jetBlue and some foreign carriers like Air India).

Also, with discounters and wholesalers you must generally prepay, and everything is nonrefundable. Before you fork over the dough, be sure to check the terms and conditions, so you know what a given company will do for you if there's a problem and what you'll have to deal with on your own.

TIP→ To be absolutely sure everything was processed correctly, confirm reservations made through online travel agents, discounters, and wholesalers directly with your hotel before leaving home.

Booking engines like Expedia, Travelocity, and Orbitz are actually travel agents, albeit high-volume, online ones. And airline travel packagers like American Airlines Vacations and Virgin Vacations—well, they're travel agents, too. But they may still not work with all the world's hotels.

An aggregator site, like Kayak, will search many sites and pull the best prices for airfares, hotels, and rental cars from them. Most aggregators compare the major travel-booking sites such as Expedia, Travelocity, and Orbitz; some also look at airline Web sites, though rarely the sites of smaller budget airlines. Some aggregators also compare other travel products, including complex packages—a good thing, as you can sometimes get the best overall deal by booking an air-and-hotel package.

Sometimes you can even bypass the middle man: airlines like Aegean *(⇨ By Air in Transportation, below)* and ferry companies like Hellenic Seaways *(⇨ By Boat in Transportation, below)* offer online booking and discounted fares for booking two or more weeks in advance. Even smaller Greek hotels frequently have Web sites with information about accommodations and rates, and though you can't always book online, you can often e-mail, phone, or fax the hotel directly to do so. When reviewing hotel sites, however, it's advisable to read with a critical eye.

WITH A TRAVEL AGENT

If you use an agent—brick-and-mortar or virtual—you'll pay a fee for the service. And know that the service you get from some online agents isn't comprehensive. For example Expedia and Travelocity don't search for prices on budget airlines like jetBlue, Southwest, or small foreign carriers. That said, some agents (online or not) *do* have access to fares that are difficult to find otherwise, and the savings can more than make up for any surcharge.

A knowledgeable brick-and-mortar travel agent can be a godsend if you're booking a cruise, a package trip that's not available to you directly, an air pass, or a complicated itinerary including several overseas flights. What's more, travel agents that specialize in a destination may have exclusive access to certain deals and insider information on things such as charter flights. Agents who specialize in types of travelers (senior citizens, gays and lesbians, naturists) or types of trips (cruises, luxury travel, safaris) can also be invaluable.

TIP→ **Remember that Expedia, Travelocity, and Orbitz are travel agents, not just booking engines. To resolve any problems with a reservation made through these companies, contact them first.**

A top-notch agent planning your trip will make sure you get the correct visa application and complete it on time; the one booking your cruise may get you a cabin upgrade or arrange to have bottle of champagne chilling in your cabin when you embark. And complain about the surcharges all you like, but when things don't work out the way you'd hoped, it's nice to have an agent to put things right.

For travel in Greece, a good agent is especially useful when you're traveling in high season, and can be invaluable for dealing with oft-frustrating ferry schedules, particularly if boats are canceled due to inclement weather (one phone call to your travel agent can set a seemingly doomed itinerary to rights again). Look for a local agent or one who specializes in Greece.

Agent Resources **American Society of Travel Agents** (☎703/739–2782 🌐www.travelsense.org). **Hellenic Association of Travel & Tourist Agencies** (🌐www.hatta.gr).

Greece Travel Agents **Dolphin Hellas** (☎210/922–7772 through 210/922–7775 🌐www.dolphin-hellas.gr). **Fantasy Travel** (☎210/331–0530 through 210/331–0532, 210/322–8410 🌐www.fantasy.gr). **Horizon** (☎210/947–0700 🌐www.horizon.gr).

ACCOMMODATIONS

Accommodations vary from luxury island resorts to traditional settlements that incorporate local architecture to inexpensive rented rooms peddled at the harbor. Family-run pensions and guesthouses outside Athens and Thessaloniki are often charming and comfortable; they also let you get better acquainted with the locals. Apartments with kitchens are available as well in most resort areas.

Although lodging is less expensive in Greece than in most of the EU and the United States, the quality tends to be lower. However, many hotels in Athens underwent massive renovations before the 2004 Olympics; a number of new hotels were built in the city, and prices have risen dramatically. Often you can reduce the price by eliminating breakfast, by bargaining when it's off-season, or by going through a local travel agency for the larger hotels on major islands and in Athens and Thessaloniki. If you stay longer, the manager or owner will usually give you a better daily rate. An 8% government tax (6% outside the major cities) and 2% municipality tax are added to all hotel bills, though usually the rate quoted includes the tax; be sure to ask. If your room rate covers meals, another 2% tax may be added. Accommodations may be hard to find in smaller resort towns in winter and at the beginning of spring. Remember that the plumbing in rooms and most low-end hotels (and restaurants, shops, and other public places) is delicate enough to require that toilet paper and other detritus be put in the wastebasket and not flushed.

Online Booking Resources

AGGREGATORS		
Kayak	www.kayak.com	also looks at cruises and vacation packages.
Mobissimo	www.mobissimo.com	also looks at car rental rates and activities.
Qixo	www.qixo.com	also compares cruises, vacation packages, and even travel insurance.
Sidestep	www.sidestep.com	also compares vacation packages and lists travel deals.
Travelgrove	www.travelgrove.com	also compares cruises and packages.
BOOKING ENGINES		
Cheap Tickets	www.cheaptickets.com	a discounter.
Expedia	www.expedia.com	a large online agency that charges a booking fee for airline tickets.
Hotwire	www.hotwire.com	a discounter.
lastminute.com	www.lastminute.com	specializes in last-minute travel; the main site is for the U.K., but it has a link to a U.S. site.
Luxury Link	www.luxurylink.com	has auctions (surprisingly good deals) as well as offers on the high-end side of travel.
Onetravel.com	www.onetravel.com	a discounter for hotels, car rentals, airfares, and packages.
Orbitz	www.orbitz.com	charges a booking fee for airline tickets, but gives a clear breakdown of fees and taxes before you book.
Priceline.com	www.priceline.com	a discounter that also allows bidding.
Travel.com	www.travel.com	allows you to compare its rates with those of other booking engines.
Travelocity	www.travelocity.com	charges a booking fee for airline tickets, but promises good problem resolution.
ONLINE ACCOMMODATIONS		
Hotelbook.com	www.hotelbook.com	focuses on independent hotels worldwide.
Hotel Club	www.hotelclub.net	good for major cities worldwide.
Hotels.com	www.hotels.com	a big Expedia-owned wholesaler that offers rooms in hotels all over the world.
Quikbook	www.quikbook.com	offers "pay when you stay" reservations that let you settle your bill at checkout, not when you book.
OTHER RESOURCES		
Bidding For Travel	www.biddingfortravel.com	a good place to figure out what you can get and for how much before you start bidding on, say, Priceline.

The lodgings we list are the cream of the crop in each price category. We always list the facilities that are available—but we don't generally specify whether they cost extra. When pricing accommodations, always ask what's included and what's not. Common items that may add to your basic room rate are breakfast, parking facilities, and, at some places, air-conditioning.

Note that some resort hotels also offer half- and full-board arrangements for part of the year. And all-inclusive resorts are mushrooming. Inquire about your options when booking.

Most hotels and other lodgings require you to give your credit-card details before they will confirm your reservation. If you don't feel comfortable e-mailing this information, ask if you can fax it (some places even prefer faxes). However you book, get confirmation in writing and have a copy of it handy when you check in.

Be sure you understand the hotel's cancellation policy. Some places allow you to cancel without any kind of penalty—even if you prepaid to secure a discounted rate—if you cancel at least 24 hours in advance. Others require you to cancel a week in advance or penalize you the cost of one night. Small inns and B&Bs are most likely to require you to cancel far in advance. Most hotels allow children under a certain age to stay in their parents' room at no extra charge, but others charge for them as extra adults; find out the cutoff age for discounts.

TIP→ Assume that hotels operate on the European Plan (EP, no meals) unless we specify that they use the Breakfast Plan (BP, with full breakfast), Continental Plan (CP, Continental breakfast), Full American Plan (FAP, all meals), Modified American Plan (MAP, breakfast and dinner) or are all-inclusive (AI, all meals and most activities).

HOTELS

The EOT authorizes the construction and classification of hotels throughout Greece. It classifies them into six categories: L (stands for deluxe) and A–E, which govern the rates that can be charged, though don't expect hotels to have the same amenities as their U.S. and northern European counterparts. Ratings are based on considerations such as room size, hotel services, and amenities including the furnishing of the room. Within each category, quality varies greatly, but prices don't. Still, you may come across an A-category hotel that charges less than a B-class, depending on facilities. The classifications can be misleading—a hotel rated C in one town might qualify as a B in another. For the categories L, A, and B, you can expect something along the lines of a chain hotel or motel in the United States, although the room will probably be somewhat smaller. A room in a C hotel can be perfectly acceptable; with a D the bathroom may or may not be shared. Ask to see the room before checking in. You can sometimes find a bargain if a hotel has just renovated but has not yet been reclassified. A great hotel may never move up to a better category just because its lobby isn't the required size.

Official prices are posted in each room, usually on the back of the door or inside the wardrobe. The room charge varies over the course of the year, peaking in the high season when breakfast or half-board (at hotel complexes) may also be obligatory.

A hotel may ask you for a deposit of the first night's stay or up to 25% of the room rate. If you cancel your reservations at least 21 days in advance, you are entitled to a full refund of your deposit.

Unless otherwise noted, in this guide, hotels have air-conditioning (*climatismo*), room TVs, and private bathrooms (*banio*). Bathrooms mostly contain showers, though some older or more luxurious hotels may have tubs.

Beds are usually twins (*diklina*). If you want a double bed, ask for a *diplo krevati*. In upper-end hotels, the mattresses are full- or queen-size. This guide lists amenities that are available but doesn't always specify if there is a surcharge. When pricing accommodations, always ask what costs extra (TV, air-conditioning, private bathroom).

Use the following as a guide to making accommodation inquiries: to reserve a double room, *thelo na kleiso ena diklino*; with a bath, *me banio*; without a bath, *horis banio*; or a room with a view, *domatio me thea*. If you need a quiet room (*isiho domatio*), get one with double-glazed windows and air-conditioning, away from the elevator and public areas, as high up (*psila*) as possible, and off the street.

Information **Hellenic Chamber of Hotels** (✉Stadiou 24, 10564Athens ☎210/331-0022 through 210/331-0026 ⎙210/322-5449); open weekdays 8–2.

RENTAL ROOMS

Most areas have pensions—usually clean, bright, and recently built. On islands in summer, owners wait for tourists at the harbor, and signs in English throughout villages indicate rooms available. The quality of rental rooms has improved enormously in recent years, with many featuring air-conditioning, a small TV set, or a small refrigerator—or all of these. Studios with a small kitchenette and separate living space are good choices for families. Around August 15 (an important religious holiday of the Greek Orthodox Church, commemorating the Assumption of the Virgin Mary), when it seems all Greeks go on vacation, even the most-basic rooms are hard to locate, although you can query the tourist police or the municipal tourist office. On some islands, the local rental room owners' association sets up an information booth. Room touts may show up at the dock when boats arrive; sometimes, they're a good way to find accommodations, but ask to view the rooms before agreeing to a booking. Few rooms are available in winter and early spring. Check the rooms first, for quality and location.

RENTAL CARS

When you reserve a car, ask about cancellation penalties, taxes, drop-off charges (if you're planning to pick up the car in one city and leave it in another), and surcharges (for being under or over a certain age, for additional drivers, or for driving across state or country borders or beyond a specific distance from your point of rental). All these things can add substantially to your costs. Request car seats and extras such as GPS when you book.

Rates are sometimes—but not always—better if you book in advance or reserve through a rental agency's Web site. There are other reasons to book ahead, though: for popular destinations, during busy times of the year, or to ensure that you get certain types of cars (vans, SUVs, exotic sports cars).

TIP→ Make sure that a confirmed reservation guarantees you a car. Agencies sometimes overbook, particularly for busy weekends and holiday periods.

Because driving in Greece can be harrowing, car rental prices are higher than in the United States, and transporting a car by ferry hikes up the fare substantially, think twice before deciding on a car rental. It's much easier to take public transportation or taxis, which are among the cheapest in Europe. The exception is on large islands where the distance between towns is greater and taxi fares are higher; you may want to rent a car or a moped for the day for concentrated bouts of sightseeing.

In summer, renting a small car with standard transmission will cost you about €275 to €400 for a week's rental (including tax, insurance, and unlimited mileage). Four-wheel-drives can cost you anywhere from €80 to €97 a day, depending on availability and the season. Luxury cars are available at some agencies, such as Europcar, but renting a BMW can fetch a hefty price—anywhere from €98 per day in low season to €120 a day in high season. This does not include the 19% V.A.T. (13% on the eastern Aegean islands). Convertibles ("open" cars) and minibuses are also available. Probably the most difficult car to rent, unless you reserve from abroad, is an automatic (which usually goes for €5 more a day). Note that car rental fees really follow laws of supply/demand so there can be huge fluctuations and, in low season, lots of room for bargaining. Off-season, rental agencies are often closed on islands and in less-populated areas.

If you're considering moped or motorcycle rental, which is cheaper than a car, especially for getting around on the islands, try Motorent or Easy Moto Rent, both in Athens. On the islands, independent moped rentals are available through local agents.

You can usually reduce prices by reserving a car through a major rental agency before you leave. Or opt for a midsize Greek agency and bargain for a price; you should discuss when kilometers become free. These agencies provide good service, and prices are at the owner's discretion. It helps if you have shopped around and can mention another agency's offer. If you're visiting several islands or destinations, larger agencies may be able to negotiate a better total package through their local offices or franchises. Some hotels may also have partner agencies that offer discounts to guests.

Official rates in Greece during high season (July–September) are much cheaper if you rent through local agents rather than the large international companies. For example, a small car, such as the Fiat Seicento, will cost you about €290 for a week's rental (including tax, insurance, and unlimited mileage) as opposed to at least €385 if you go through an international chain. Outside high season you can get some good deals with local agents; a car may cost you about €38 per day, all inclusive. Rates are cheaper if you book for three or more days. On the islands, you can often get a lower price by renting for a half day–between the time when a client drops off a car and the next booked rental.

In Greece your own driver's license is not acceptable unless you are a citizen of the European Union. For non-EU citizens an international driver's permit (IDP) is necessary *(⇨ By Car in Transportation, below)*. To rent, you must have had your driver's license for one year and be at least 21 years old if you use a credit card (sometimes you must be 23 if you pay cash); for some car categories, you must be 25. You need the agency's permission to ferry the car or cross the border (Europcar does not allow across-the-border rentals). A valid driver's license is usually acceptable for renting a moped, but you will need a motorcycle driver's license if you want to rent a larger bike.

TRAIN PASSES

Greece is one of 18 countries in which you can use Eurail passes, which provide unlimited first-class rail travel, in all of the participating countries, for the duration of the pass. If you plan to rack up the miles in several countries, get a standard pass. These are available for 15 days ($673), 21 days ($875), one month ($1,086), two months ($1,533), and three months ($1,891).

In addition to standard Eurail passes, ask about special rail-pass plans. Among these are the Eurail Pass Youth (for those under age 26), the Eurail Saverpass (which gives a discount for two or more people traveling together), the Eurail Flexipass (which allows a certain number of travel days within a set period), and the Pass 'n Drive (which combines travel by train and rental car). Among those passes you might want to consider: the Greece Pass allows first-class rail travel throughout Greece; the standard 3 days' unlimited travel in a month costs $131, and the rate rises per day of travel added. The Greece-Italy Pass gives you 4 days' travel time over a span of two months; the cost is $343 for first class, $274 for second. The Balkan Flexipass covers train travel through Greece as well as Bulgaria, Romania, the Former Yugoslav Republic of Macedonia (FYROM), Turkey, and Yugoslavia (including Serbia and Montenegro); there are passes for 5, 10, or 15 travel days in a one-month period for about $248, $433, and $521, respectively (first class). Youths pay about 50% less, senior citizens over 60 20% less.

Whichever pass you choose, remember that you must purchase your pass before you leave for Europe. *For more information about train travel, see By Train in Transportation, below.*

Information & Passes **Rail Europe** (✉500 Mamaroneck Ave., Harrison, NY10528 ☎877/257-2887 or 914/682-5172 📠800/432-1329 ✉2087 Dundas E, Suite 106, Mississauga, Ontario, CanadaL4X 1M2 ☎800/361-7245 📠905/602-4198 🌐www.raileurope.com).

GUIDED TOURS

Guided tours are a good option when you don't want to do it all yourself. You travel along with a group (sometimes large, sometimes small), stay in prebooked hotels, eat with your fellow travelers (the cost of meals sometimes included in the price of your tour, sometimes not), and follow a schedule.

But not all guided tours are an if-it's-Tuesday-this-must-be-Belgium experience. A knowledgeable guide can take you places that you might never discover on your own, and you may be pushed to see more than you would have otherwise. Tours aren't for everyone, but they can be just the thing for trips to places where making travel arrangements is difficult or time-consuming (particularly when you don't speak the language).

Whenever you book a guided tour, find out what's included and what isn't. A "land-only" tour includes all your travel (by bus, in most cases) in the destination, but not necessarily your flights to and from or even within it. Also, in most cases prices in tour brochures don't include fees and taxes. And remember that you'll be expected to tip your guide (in cash) at the end of the tour.

In Greece, True North organizes group and individual tours tailored to travelers' interests, from culinary or hiking tours to wellness retreats, on island and mainland destinations. The company also offers an "alternative" tour of Athens developed to give you an insider's feel for the city—the guide will even follow *your* itinerary. More localized is Culinary Sanctuaries, based in Crete and run by Nikki Rose, who puts together fascinating customized tours with an emphasis on traditional Mediterranean cuisine. In addition, the Skyros Center on the isle of Skyros runs the Atsitsa Retreat, which organizes local island tours as part of a broader program of yoga, writing, and other life-enhancing activities.

Recommended Company **True North** (✉Irodotou 13, Maroussi, 15122Athens ☎210/612-1537 🌐www.truenorthroutes.com). **Crete's Culinary Sanctuaries** (✉info@cookingincrete.com 🌐www.cookingincrete.com). **Skyros Center** (✉Skyros Holidays, 9 Eastcliff Rd., Shanklin, Isle of Wight, England, PO376AA ☎01983/865566 🌐www.skyros.co.uk).

TRANSPORTATION

To make finding your way around as easy as possible, it's wise to learn to recognize letters in the Greek alphabet. Most areas have few road signs in English, and even those that *are* in English don't necessarily follow the official standardized transliteration code, resulting in odd spellings of foreign names. Sometimes there are several spelling variations in English for the same place: Agios, Aghios, or Ayios; Georgios or Yiorgos. Also, the English version may be quite different from the Greek, or even what locals use informally: Corfu is known as Kerkyra; island capitals are often just called Chora (town), no matter what their formal title; and Panepistimiou, a main Athens boulevard, is officially named Eleftheriou Venizelou, but if you ask for that name, no one will know what you're talking about. A long street may change names several times, and a city may have more than one street by the same name, so know the district you're headed for, or a major landmark nearby, especially if you're taking a taxi. In this guide, street numbers appear after the street name. Finally, there are odd- and even-numbered sides of the streets, but No. 124 could be several blocks away from No. 125.

TIP→ Ask the local tourist board about local transportation and hotel packages that include tickets to major museum exhibits or other special events.

BY AIR

Flying time to Athens is 3½ hours from London, 9½ hours from New York, 12 hours from Chicago, 16½ hours from Los Angeles, and 19 hours from Sydney.

Always find out your carrier's check-in policy. Plan to arrive at the airport about 2 hours before your scheduled departure time for flights within the United States and 2½ to 3 hours before international flights from the United States. You may need to arrive earlier if you're flying from one of the busier airports or during peak air-traffic times. Any sharp objects, such as nail files or scissors, may be removed if you take them through airport security. Pack such items in luggage you plan to check.

In Greece, you need to show identification for both domestic and international flights. For domestic flights in Greece, arrive no later than 1 hour before departure time; for flights to the rest of Europe, 1½ hours; and for other international flights, 2 hours. If you get bumped because of overbooking, international carriers try to find an alternative route on another airline, but Olympic Airlines usually puts you on its next available flight, which might not be until the next day. (Under European Union law, you are entitled to receive up to €250 compensation for overbooking on flights of 1,500 km (930 mi) or shorter, €400 on flights between 1,500 km and 3,500 km (2,170 mi), and up to €600 for longer flights. In the past, Olympic Airlines staff and traffic controllers have gone on strike for several hours a day; keep attuned to the local news. Check-in is straightforward and easy at Greece's larger airports, but on small islands, it sometimes gets confusing, since several airlines may use the same check-in counter, indicated by garbled announcements. Watch for movement en masse by the crowd.

If you have been wait-listed on an Olympic flight in Greece, remember that this list does not apply on the day of departure. A new waiting list goes into effect at the airport two hours prior to takeoff for domestic flights and three hours before international flights; you must be there to get a place.

You do not need to reconfirm flights within Greece. Athens International Airport (Eleftherios Venizelos) posts real-time flight information on its Web site (🌐*www.aia.gr*). It also has customer information desks throughout the airport that operate on a 24-hour basis, as well as more than a dozen courtesy phones that put you through to the customer call center. You can contact the Hellenic Civil Aviation Authority or the Quality Management Department, both at the airport, if you have complaints or concerns.

DOMESTIC FLIGHTS

The frequency of flights varies according to the time of year (with an increase between Greek Easter and November), and it is essential to book well in advance for summer or for festivals and holidays, especially on three-day weekends. Domestic flights are a good deal for many destinations. In summer 2007 the one-way economy Athens–Rhodes fare offered by Olympic was €87, excluding taxes; to Corfu, €100; to Santorini, €79; and to Heraklion, €58. Unless the flight is part of an international journey, the baggage allowance is only 33 pounds (15 kilograms) per passenger.

Scheduled (i.e., nonchartered) domestic air travel in Greece is provided predominantly by Olympic Airlines, which operates out of Athens International Airport in Spata. There is service from Athens to Alexandroupolis, Ioannina, Kastoria, Kavala, Kozani, Preveza, and Thessaloniki, all on the mainland; Kalamata in the Peloponnese; the Aegean islands: Astypalaia, Karpathos, Kassos, Kythira, Crete (Hania, Heraklion, and Siteia), Chios, Ikaria, Kos, Lesbos (listed as Mytilini in Greek), Limnos, Leros, Milos, Mykonos, Naxos, Paros, Rhodes, Samos, Skiathos, Syros, Skyros, Kastellorizo (only via Rhodes), and Santorini; Corfu (called Kerkyra in Greek), Kefalonia, and Zakynthos in the Ionian Sea. Flights also depart from Thessaloniki for Chios, Corfu, Hania, Heraklion, Ioannina, Limnos, Lesbos, Mykonos, Rhodes, Samos, and Santorini. You can also fly from Kozani to Kastoria on the mainland. Interisland flights, depending on the season, include the following: from Chios to Lesbos; from Karpathos to Kassos; from Santorini to Rhodes and Heraklion; from Rhodes to Karpathos, Kassos, Kastellorizo, and Mykonos, as well as Kos (summer only); between Kefalonia and Zakynthos (winter); and from Lesbos to Chios, Limnos, and Samos (winter).

For those traveling to Thessaloniki, a good alternative is Aegean Airlines, which has regular scheduled flights and sometimes even cheaper prices than Olympic. It also flies from Athens to Alexandroupolis, Chios, Corfu, Hania, Heraklion, Ioannina, Kavala, Kos, Lesbos, Rhodes, Santorini, and Thessaloniki. Planes depart Thessaloniki for Alexandroupolis, Chios, Corfu, Heraklion, Ioannina, Kavala, Kos, Lesbos, Mykonos, Rhodes, and Santorini. In summer, LTU International Airways operates several flights between points in Greece such as Rhodes and Kos or Athens and Samos.

Airlines & Airports **Airline and Airport Links.com** (🌐www.airlineandairportlinks.com) has links to many of the world's airlines and airports.

Airline Security Issues **Transportation Security Administration** (🌐www.tsa.gov) has answers for almost every question that might come up.

Air Travel Resources in Greece **Hellenic Civil Aviation Authority** (✉Level 3, Room 607, main terminal bldg. ☎210/353–4157 weekdays 9–5, 210/353–4147 at other times). **Quality Management Department** (☎210/353–7240).

AIRPORTS

Athens International Airport at Spata, 33 km (20 mi) southeast of the city center, opened in 2001 as the country's main airport. Officially named Eleftherios Venizelos, after Greece's first prime minister, the airport is user-friendly and high-tech. The main terminal building has two levels: upper for departures, ground level for arrivals. Unless you plan to avoid Athens altogether or to fly via charter directly to the islands, the Athens airport is the most convenient because you can easily switch from international to domestic flights or get to Greece's main harbor, Piraeus, about a 50-minute drive south of the airport. Thessaloniki's airport has modern airport facilities for international travelers, and the airport in Rhodes is being expanded.

Five major airports in Greece, listed below, service international flights. Airports on some smaller islands (Santorini, Syros, Mykonos, and Paros among them) take international charter flights during the busier summer months. Locals will sometimes refer to the airports with their secondary names, so these names—along with the three-letter airport codes—are also given. Information about airports other than Athens is given on the Olympic Airlines Web site (*www.olympic-airlines.com*) and on the Civil Aviation Authority Web site (*www.hcaa.gr*).

Airport Information **Athens International Airport–Eleftherios Venizelos (ATH)** (Spata 210/353–0000 flight information and customer service, 210/353–0445 tourist information, 210/353–0515 lost and found www.aia.gr). **Heraklion International Airport–Nikos Kazantzakis (HER)** (Heraklion, Crete 2810/397129). **Kerkyra (Corfu) Airport–Ioannis Kapodistrias (CFU)** (Corfu town 26610/89600). **Rhodes International Airport (RHO)** (Rhodes town 22410/83200). **Thessaloniki International Airport–Makedonia (SKG)** (Mikras 2310/985000).

GROUND TRANSPORTATION

See Athens Essentials in Chapter 3 for information on transfers between the airport and Athens and Piraeus. In Thessaloniki, municipal Bus 078 (€0.50) picks up travelers about every 40 minutes until 11:15 PM for the 45-minute ride (up to 90 minutes if there is traffic) into town; its final stop is the train station. The EOT office in the airport arrivals terminal has information. At other airports throughout Greece, especially on the islands, public transportation is infrequent or nonexistent; ask your hotel to make arrangements or take a taxi; rates are usually set to fixed destinations.

FLIGHTS

When flying internationally, you must usually choose between a domestic carrier, the national flag carrier of the country you are visiting, and a foreign carrier from a third country. You may, for example, choose to fly Olympic Airlines to Greece. National flag carriers have the greatest number of nonstops. Domestic carriers may have better connections to your home town and serve a greater number of gateway cities. Third-party carriers may have a price advantage.

In Greece, when faced with a boat journey of six hours or more, consider flying. Olympic Airlines has dominated the domestic market, with flights to more than 30 cities and islands. Alternative airlines providing cheaper fares (at times) and better service include Aegean Airlines.

Olympic Airlines, the state-owned Greek carrier, has incurred criticism over the years for its on-time record, indifferent service, and aging aircraft. Three privatization attempts have failed since 2001, and there have been schedule cutbacks. The airline has a fleet of more than 44 aircraft, including A340-300 airbuses. Improved service and fewer cancellations, especially since the opening of Athens International Airport, have left more passengers pleasantly surprised. Olympic is rated among the top three carriers worldwide for safety.

Many European national airlines fly to Athens from the United States and Canada via their home country's major cities. Remember that these are often connecting flights that include at least one stop and may require a change of planes. Air France, British Airways, Delta, KLM, and Lufthansa all now operate code-share flights within Greece; British Airways has some direct flights to Crete.

To & From Greece **Air Canada** (☎800/712-7786 🌐www.aircanada.com). **Air France** (☎800/237-2747 🌐www.airfrance.net). **Alitalia** (☎800/223-5730 🌐www.alitalia.it). **British Airways** (☎800/247-9297 🌐www.britishairways.com). **Continental Airlines** (☎800/523-3273 for U.S. and Mexico reservations, 800/231-0856 for international reservations, 210/353-4312 Athens airport 🌐www.continental.com). **Delta Airlines** (☎800/221-1212 for U.S. reservations, 800/241-4141 for international reservations, 210/353-0116 Athens airport 🌐www.delta.com). **easyJet** (☎0870/600-0000 🌐www.easyjet.com). **Iberia Airlines** (☎800/772-4642, 210/353-7600 in Athens 🌐www.iberia.com). **KLM Royal Dutch Airlines** (☎800/447-4747 🌐www.klm.com). **LOT Polish Airlines** (☎212/869-1074, 210/323-7762 in Athens 🌐www.lot.com). **Lufthansa** (☎800/645-3880 🌐www.lufthansa.com). **Olympic Airlines** (☎800/223-1226 outside New York, 212/735-0200 🌐www.olympicairlines.com). **Swiss International Airlines** (☎800/221-4750, 210/617-5320 in Athens 🌐www.swiss.com).

Within Greece **Aegean Airlines** (✉Viltanioti 3, Kifissia, Athens ☎801/112-0000 🌐www.aegeanair.com). **Air France** (☎801/111-0065). **British Airways** (☎801/115-6000). **KLM Royal Dutch Airlines** (☎210/911-0000). **LTU International Airways** (☎801/113-0320 🌐www.ltu.com). **Lufthansa** (☎210/617-5200). **Olympic Airlines** (Main Athens ticket office and for prepaid tickets, ✉Filellinon 15, near Syntagma Sq. ☎801/114-4444 or 210/966-6666 reservations, 210/356-9111 airport arrival and departure information 🌐www.olympicairlines.com).

BY BOAT

Ferries, catamarans, and hydrofoils make up an essential part of the national transport system of Greece. With so many private companies operating, so many islands to choose from, and complicated timetables with departures changing not just by season but also by day of the week, the most sensible way to arrange island hopping is to select the islands you would like to see, then visit a travel agent to ask how your journey can be put together.

Greece's largest and busiest port is Piraeus, which lies 10 km (6 mi) south of downtown Athens. Every day dozens of vessels depart for the Saronic Gulf islands, the Cyclades, the Dodecanese, and Crete. In fact, the only island groups that are not served by Piraeus are the Ionian islands and the Sporades. Athens's second port is Rafina, with regular daily ferry crossings to Evia (Euboea) and the Cycladic islands Andros, Tinos, and Mykonos. The smaller port of Lavrion, close to Sounion, serves the less-visited Cyclades Kea and Kythnos.

Patras, on the Peloponnese, is the main port for ferries to Italy and the Ionian islands Corfu and Kefalonia. A short distance south of Patras, Killini has ferries to Kefalonia and Zakynthos, also in the Ionian chain. Igoumenitsa, on Greece's northwest coast, has ships to Italy, plus a local ferry to Corfu, which runs several times daily in each direction.

Boats for the Sporades islands depart from Agios Konstantinos and Volos on the central mainland, from Thessaloniki in northern Greece, and from Kimi on the east coast of Evia. The island of Skyros is only served by ferries from Kimi.

In the northeast Aegean, the islands of Limnos, Samothrace (Samothraki), and Thassos are more easily reached from the northern mainland towns of Kavala and Alexandroupolis.

When choosing a ferry, take into account the number of stops and the estimated arrival time. Sometimes a ferry that leaves an hour later gets you there faster. High-speed ferries are more expensive, with airplanelike seating, including fare classes and numbered seats. They'll get you where you're going more quickly but lack the flavor of the older ferries with the open decks. Note that real fast ferries can pitch like crazy (and often don't travel in high seas)—if you're prone to seasickness, chose a boat with an open deck as the breeze keeps queasiness in check.

From Piraeus port, the quickest way to get into Athens, if you are traveling light, is to walk to the metro station and take a 20-minute ride on the electric train to Monastiraki, Omonia, or Syntagma (the latter two involve a train change at Monastiraki). Alternatively, you can take a taxi, though this will undoubtedly take longer because of traffic and will cost around €12, plus baggage and port surcharges. Often, drivers wait until they fill their taxi with debarking passengers headed in roughly the same direction, which leads to a longer, more circuitous route to accommodate everyone's destination. It's faster to walk to the main street and hail a passing cab.

Be aware that Piraeus port is so vast that you may need to walk some distance, or even take a port minibus (gratis) from the port entrance, to your gate (quay) of departure. So be sure to arrive with plenty of time to spare. Confusingly, the gates of departure are occasionally changed at the last moment.

To get to Attica's second port, Rafina, take a KTEL bus, which leaves every half hour 5:30 AM to 9:30 PM from Aigyptou Square near Pedion Areos park in Athens (close to Viktoria metro station). The bus takes about an hour to get to Rafina; the port is slightly downhill from the bus station.

Timetables change in winter and summer, and special sailings are often added around holiday weekends in summer when demand is high. For the Cycladic, Dodecanese, and Ionian islands, small ferry companies operate local routes that are not published nationally; passage can be booked through travel agents on the islands served. Boats may be delayed by weather conditions, especially when the northern wind called *meltemi* hit in August, so stay flexible—one advantage of not buying a ticket in advance. You usually can get on a boat at the last minute. However, it is better to buy your ticket two or three days ahead if you are traveling between July 15 and August 30, when most Greeks vacation, if you need a cabin (good for long trips) or if you are taking a car. If possible, don't travel by boat around August 15, when most ferries are so crowded, the situation becomes comically desperate—although things have improved since strict enforcement of capacity limits. First-class tickets are almost as expensive as flying.

If the boat journey will be more than a couple of hours, it's a good idea to take along water and snacks. Greek fast-food franchises operate on most ferries, and on longer trips boats have both cafeteria-style and full-service restaurants.

If your ship's departure is delayed for any reason (with the exception of force majeure) you have the right to stay on board in the class indicated on your ticket or, in case of prolonged delay, to cancel your ticket for a full refund. If you miss your ship, you forfeit your ticket; if you cancel in advance, you receive a partial or full refund, depending on how far in advance you cancel.

You can buy tickets from a travel agency representing the shipping line you need, from the local shipping agency office, online through travel Web sites (the most reliable is www.greekferries.gr), or direct from ferry companies. Generally you can pay by either credit card or cash, though the latter is often preferred. For schedules, any travel agent can call the port to check information for you, although they may not be as helpful about a shipping line for which they don't sell tickets. On islands the local office of each shipping line posts a board with departure times, or you can contact the port authority (*limenarchio*), where some English is usually spoken. Schedules are also posted online by the Merchant Marine Ministry (www.yen.gr). The English edition of *Kathimerini,* published as an insert to the *International Herald Tribune,* lists daily departures from the capital. Or you can call for a recording, in Greek, of the day's domestic departures from major ports. At 1 PM, a new recording lists boats leaving the following morning.

Information **Agios Konstantinos Port Authority** (☎22350/31759). **Ferry departures** (☎1440). **Igoumenitsa Port Authority** (☎26650/22240 or 26650/22235). **Kimi Port Authority** (☎22220/22606). **KTEL bus to Rafina** (☎210/821-0872 🌐www.ktel.org [in Greek only]). **Lavrion Port Authority** (☎22920/24125). **Patras Port Authority** (☎2610/341002 or 2610/341024). **Piraeus Port Authority** (☎210/412-4585 or 210/459-3000). **Rafina Port Authority** (☎22940/22300). **Thessaloniki Port Authority** (☎2310/531503 or 2310/531504). **Volos Port Authority** (☎24210/28888).

CATAMARANS & HYDROFOILS

Catamarans and hydrofoils, known as *iptamena delphinia* (flying dolphins), carry passengers from Piraeus to the Saronic islands (Aegina, Hydra, Poros, and Spetses) and the eastern Peloponnesian ports of Hermioni and Porto Heli. Separate services run from Piraeus to the Cycladic islands (Amorgos, Folegandros, Ios, Milos, Mykonos, Naxos, Paros, Santorini, Serifos, Sifnos, Syros, and Tinos), and from Rafina to the Cycladic islands (Mykonos, Naxos, Paros, and Tinos). You can also take hydrofoils from Agios Konstantinos or Volos to the Sporades islands Alonissos, Skiathos, and Skopelos). Through summer only, there is a service from Heraklion (on Crete) to the Cycladic islands Ios, Mykonos, Paros, and Santorini.

These boats are somewhat pricey, and the limited number of seats means that you should reserve (especially in summer), but they cut travel time in half. The catamarans are larger, with more space to move around, although on both boats passengers are not allowed outside when the boat is not docked. If the sea is choppy, these boats often cannot travel, and cancellations are common. Tickets can be purchased through authorized agents or one hour before departure. Book your return upon arrival if you are pressed for time.

Information **Hellenic Seaways** (✉Syngrou 98–100, 11745Athens ☎210/419–9000 🌐www.hellenicseaways.gr).

HYDROPLANES

A limited hydroplane service began operating in the Ionian islands in 2005, offering daily flights between Corfu and Paxos. Although the company had initial teething problems, by August 2007 it was operating between Corfu and Paxos, and Corfu and Lefkas. It also began service to the Aegean, with hydroplanes for Mykonos, Santorini, Paros, Ios, Kalymnos, and Kos departing from Lavrion. Prices are lower than regular airfare and higher than boat passage, about €45 one way from Corfu to Paxos.

Information **AirSea Lines** (✉Possidonos 18, 17674 Kallithea, Athens ☎210/940–2880 and 210/940–2012 🌐www.airsealines.com).

INTERNATIONAL FERRIES

You can cross to Turkey from the northeast Aegean islands. The Aegean Shipping Company sails between Rhodes and Marmaris, while Miniotis Lines sails between Chios and Çeşme. In addition, other routes have included Lesbos to Dikeli and from Samos to Kuşadası. Note that British passport holders must have €10 with them to purchase a visa on landing in Turkey, Australian citizens need $20 (American dollars) and U.S. citizens need $100; New Zealanders don't need a visa. Note that rates are due to go up in 2008 or '09. But it is best to purchase the visa beforehand, paying euros, at the Turkish Consulate in Athens (visa hours are weekdays 9 to 1).

There are also frequent sails between Italy and Greece, with stops at Ancona, Bari, Brindisi, and Venice. Note that there are no longer connections from Trieste. The shipping lines covering these routes are Agoudimos/G.A. Ferries (Bari to Igoumenitsa and Patras; Bari to Kefalonia; and Brindisi to Corfu and Igoumenitsa), Anek Lines (Ancona to Igoumenitsa and Patras; and Venice to Igoumenitsa, Corfu, and Patras), Minoan Lines (Venice to Igoumenitsa, Corfu, and Patras; and Ancona to Igoumenitsa and Patras), Ventouris Ferries (Bari to Corfu and Igoumenitsa), and Superfast Ferries (Ancona to Igoumenitsa and Patras; and Bari to Igoumenitsa, Corfu, and Patras).

The most respected (but no longer necessarily the most expensive) company is Superfast Ferries. Its modern, well-maintained vessels are outfitted with bars, a self-service restaurant, a pool, two cinemas, a casino, and shops. The trip from Patras to Ancona takes 19 hours (21 if the ship stops at Igoumenitsa en route), from Patras to Bari 15 hours 30 minutes, and from Igoumenitsa to Bari 9 hours 30 minutes.

Prices range widely, depending on the season and the way you choose to travel (deck, air seat, or cabin). Traveling on Superfast from Patras to Ancona during high season 2007 cost €74 for a one-way ticket on deck; €103 for a one-way ticket with seating; €168 for a one-way ticket with overnight accommodation in an inside cabin with four beds; and €380 for a one-way ticket with overnight accommodation in a deluxe outside cabin with two beds. Taking a car aboard from Patras to Ancona during high season on the same line cost €118. High season runs from late July to early September; prices drop considerably in low season. Some companies offer special family or group discounts, while others charge extra for pets or offer deep discounts on return tickets, so comparing rates does pay off. When booking, also consider when you will be traveling; an overnight trip can be offset against hotel costs, and you will spend more on incidentals like food and drink when traveling during the day.

Contacts **Aegean Shipping Company** (✉Grigoriou Lampraki 46, 85100Rhodes ☎22410/76535 🌐www.seadreams.gr). **Agoudimos/G.A. Ferries** (✉Kapodistriou 2, 18531Piraeus ☎210/414-1300 🌐www.agoudimos-lines.com). **Anek Lines** (✉Amalias 54, Syntagma Sq., 10558Athens ☎210/323-3481 or 210/323-3819, 210/419-7430 international reservations 🌐www.anek.gr). **Miniotis Lines** (✉Neorion 21, Chios, 82100 ☎22710/24670 🌐www.miniotis.gr). **Minoan Lines** (✉Syngrou 100, 11745Athens ☎210/920-0020 🌐www.minoan.gr). **Superfast Ferries** (✉Amalias 30, 10558Athens ☎210/891-9130 🌐www.superfast.com). **Ventouris Ferries** (✉Gr. Lampraki 17, 18533Piraeus ☎210/482-8001 through 210/482-8004 🌐www.ventouris.gr).

Information **Turkish Consulate** (✉Vasilissis Pavlou 22, Paleo Psyhiko, Athens ☎210/671-4828 📠210/677-6430).

BY BUS

Organized bus tours can be booked together with hotel reservations by your travel agent. Many tour operators have offices in and around Syntagma and Omonia squares in Athens. Bus tours often depart from Syntagma or adjacent streets. Most chapters in this guide have information about guided tours.

It is easy to get around Greece on buses, which travel to even the most far-flung villages. The price of public transportation in Greece has risen steeply since the 2004 Olympic year, but it is still cheaper than in other western European cities. Greece has an extensive, inexpensive, and reliable regional bus system (KTEL) made up of local operators. Each city has connections to towns and villages in its vicinity; visit the local KTEL office to check routes or use the fairly comprehensive Web site (🌐*www.ktel.org*, which, as of this writing, was in Greek only) to plan your trip in advance. Buses from Athens, however, travel throughout the country. The buses, which are punctual, span the range from slightly dilapidated and rattly to air-conditioned with upholstered seats. There is just one class of ticket. Board early, because Greeks have a very loose attitude about assigned seating, and ownership is nine-tenths' possession. Taking the bus from Athens to Corinth costs €6.60 and takes about 75 minutes; to Nafplion, €9.70, 2½ hours; to Patras, €13.90, 3 hours 10 minutes; and to Thessaloniki, €30, 7½ hours.

Although smoking is forbidden on KTEL buses, the driver stops every two hours or so at a roadside establishment; smokers can light up then. Drivers are exempt from the no-smoking rule; don't sit near the front seat if smoking bothers you.

In Athens, KTEL's Terminal A is the arrival and departure point for bus lines to northern Greece, including Thessaloniki, and to the Peloponnese destinations of Epidauros, Mycenae, Nafplion, and Corinth. Terminal B serves Evia, most of Thrace, and central Greece, including Delphi. To get into the city center, take Bus 051 from Terminal A (terminus at Zinonos and Menandrou off Omonia Square) or Bus 024 from Terminal B (downtown stop in front of the National Gardens on Amalias). Most KTEL buses to the east Attica coast—including those for Sounion, Marathon, and the ports of Lavrion and Rafina—leave from the downtown KTEL terminal near Pedion Areos park.

In Athens and Thessaloniki avoid riding city buses during rush hour. Buses and trolleys do not automatically stop at every station; you must hold out your hand to summon the vehicle you want. Upon boarding, validate your ticket in the canceling machines at the front and back of buses (this goes for the trolleys and the subway train platforms, too). If you're too far from the machine and the bus is crowded, don't be shy: pass your ticket forward with the appropriate ingratiating gestures, and it will eventually return, properly punched. Keep your ticket until you reach your destination, as inspectors who occasionally board are strict about fining offenders; a fine may cost you up to 40 times the fare. On intracity buses, an inspector also boards to check your ticket, so keep it handy.

The KTEL buses provide a comprehensive network of coverage within the country. That said, the buses are fairly basic in remoter villages and on some of the islands—no toilets or refreshments. However, main intercity lines have preassigned seating and a better standard of vehicle.

See our Athens chapter Planner section for information on the city's convenient multiday transportation passes (good for buses, trolleys, and the metro). In large cities, you can buy individual tickets for urban buses at terminal booths, convenience stores, or at selected *periptera* (street kiosks). KTEL tickets must be purchased at the KTEL station. On islands, in smaller towns, and on the KTEL buses that leave from Aigyptou Square in Athens, you buy tickets from the driver's assistant once seated; try not to pay with anything more than a €5 bill to avoid commotion. Athens bus stops now have signs diagramming each route. It still helps if you can read some Greek, since most stops are only labeled in Greek. The Organization for Urban Public Transportation, north of the National Archaeological Museum, gives Athens route information and distributes maps (weekdays 7:30–3), but the best source for non-Greek speakers is the EOT, which distributes information on Athens and KTEL bus schedules, including prices for each destination and the essential phone numbers for the regional ticket desks.

Throughout Greece, you must pay cash for local and regional bus tickets. For bus tours, a travel agency usually lets you pay by credit card or traveler's checks.

For KTEL, you can make reservations for many destinations free by phone; each destination has a different phone number. Reservations are unnecessary on most routes, especially those with several round-trips a day. Book your seat a few days in advance, however, if you are traveling on holiday weekends, especially if you are headed out of Athens. Because reservations sometimes get jumbled in the holiday exodus, it's best to go to the station and buy your ticket beforehand.

Athens Public Transportation **Organization for Urban Public Transportation** (✉Metsovou 15, Athens ☎185 🌐www.oasa.gr).

Regional Bus Service **Downtown KTEL terminal** (✉Aigyptou Sq., Mavromateon and Leoforos Alexandras, near Pedion Areos park ☎210/823–0179 for Sounion, Rafina, and Lavrion; 210/821–0872 for Marathon 🌐www.ktel.org). **Terminal A** (✉Kifissou 100, Athens ☎210/512–4910 or 210/512–4911). **Terminal B** (✉Liossion 260, Athens ☎210/831–7153).

BY CAR

Road conditions in Greece have improved dramatically in the last decade, yet driving in Greece still presents certain challenges. In Athens, traffic is mind-boggling most of the time and parking is scarce, although the situation has improved somewhat; public transportation or taxis are a much better choice than a rented car. If you are traveling quite a bit by boat, taking along a car increases ticket costs substantially and limits your ease in hopping on any ferry. On islands, you can always rent a taxi or a car for the day if you want to see something distant, and intradestination flights are fairly cheap. The only real reason to drive is if it's your passion, you are a large party with many suitcases and many out-of-the-way places to see, or you need the freedom to change routes and make unexpected stops not permitted on public transportation.

International driving permits (IDPs), required for drivers who are not citizens of an EU country, are available from the American, Australian, Canadian, and New Zealand automobile associations. These international permits, valid only in conjunction with your regular driver's license, are universally recognized; having one may save you a problem with local authorities.

Regular registration papers and insurance contracted in any EU country or a green card are required, in addition to a driver's license (EU or international). EU members can travel freely without paying any additional taxes. *If you are a non-EU member (or are considering bringing your car from the United Kingdom), see Importing Your Car, below.* Cars with foreign plates are exempt from the rule that allows only alternate-day driving in Athens's center depending on whether the license plate is odd or even.

The expansion and upgrading of Greece's two main highways, the Athens–Corinth and Athens–Thessaloniki highways (*ethniki odoi*) and construction of an Athens beltway, the Attiki Odos, has made leaving Athens much easier. These highways (and the new Egnatia Odos, which goes east to west across northern Greece), along with the secondary roads, cover most of the mainland, but on islands, some areas (beaches, for example) are accessible via dirt or gravel paths. With the exception of main highways and a few flat areas like the Thessalian plain, you will average about 60 km (37 mi) an hour: expect some badly paved or disintegrating roads, stray flocks of goats, slowpoke farm vehicles, detours, curves, and near Athens and Thessaloniki, traffic jams. At the Athens city limits, signs in English mark the way to Syntagma and Omonia squares in the center. When you exit Athens, signs are well marked for the National Road, usually naming Lamia for the north and Corinth or Patras for the southwest.

AUTO CLUB

The Automobile Touring Club of Greece, known as ELPA, operates a special phone line for tourist information that works throughout the country; the club also has several branch offices. If you don't belong to an auto club at home, you can join ELPA for €115, which gives you free emergency road service, though you must pay for spare parts. Membership lasts for a year and is good on discounts for emergency calls throughout the EU. Visit your local auto association before you leave for Greece; they can help you plan your trip and provide you with maps. They also can issue you an international driver's permit good for one year. Your local membership may qualify you for cheaper emergency service in Greece and abroad.

In Greece **Automobile Touring Club of Greece** (ELPA ✉Mesogeion 395, Agia Paraskevi, Athens ☎210/606–8800 or 210/606–8838 🌐www.elpa.gr ✉Patroon-Athinon 18, Patras ☎📠2610/426416 or 2610/425411 ✉Papanastasiou 66, Heraklion, Crete ☎📠2810/210581 or 2810/210654 ✉Vas. Olgas 230 and Aegeou, Thessaloniki ☎2310/426319 or 2310/426320 📠2310/412413). **Tourist Information Line** (☎174).

GASOLINE

Gas pumps and service stations are everywhere, and lead-free gas is widely available. However, away from the main towns, especially at night, open gas stations can be very far apart (⇨*Hours of Operation in On the Ground, below*). Don't let your gas supply drop to less than a quarter tank when driving through rural areas. Gas costs about €1.10 a liter for unleaded ("ah-*mo*-leev-dee"), €0.95 a liter for diesel ("*dee*-zel"). Prices may vary by as much as €0.10 per liter from one region to another. You aren't usually allowed to pump your own gas, though you are expected to do everything else yourself. If you ask the attendant to give you extra service (check oil and water or clean the windows), leave a small tip. Want a receipt? The word is *apodiksi*. International chains (BP, Mobil, Shell, and Texaco) usually accept credit cards; Greek-owned stations (Elinoil, EKO, Avin, and Revoil) usually do not unless they are in tourist areas.

Customs Stamps **Directorate for the Supervision and Control of Cars** (DIPEAK) (✉Akti Kondili 32, 1st fl., 18545Piraeus ☎210/462–7325 📠210/462–5182).

INSURANCE

In general, auto insurance is not as expensive as in other countries. You must have third-party car insurance to drive in Greece. If possible, get an insurance "green card" valid for Greece from your insurance company before arriving. You can also buy a policy with local companies; keep the papers in a plastic pocket on the inside right front windshield. To get more information, or to locate a local representative for your insurance company, call the Hellenic Union of Insurance Firms/Motor Insurance Bureau.

Insurance Bureau **Hellenic Union of Insurance Firms/Motor Insurance Bureau** (✉Xenofontos 10, 10557Athens ☎210/323–6733 📠210/333–4149).

PARKING

The scarcity of parking spaces in Athens is one good reason not to drive in the city. Although a number of car parks operate in the city center and near suburban metro stations, these aren't enough to accommodate demand. They can also be quite expensive, with prices of up to €5 an hour. Pedestrians are often frustrated by cars parked on pavements, although police have become stricter about ticketing. "Controlled parking" zones in some downtown districts like Kolonaki have introduced some order to the chaotic system; a one-hour card costs €1, with a maximum of three hours permitted. Buy a parking card from the kiosk or meter and display inside your windshield.

Outside Athens, the situation is slightly better. Many towns and islands have designated free parking areas just outside the center where you can leave your car.

ROAD CONDITIONS

Driving defensively is the key to safety in Greece, one of the most hazardous European countries for motorists. In the cities and on the highways, the streets can be riddled with potholes; motorcyclists seem to come out of nowhere, often passing on the right; and cars may even go the wrong way down a one-way street. In the countryside and on islands, you must watch for livestock crossing the road, as well as for tourists shakily learning to use rented motorcycles.

The many motorcycles and scooters weaving through traffic and the aggressive attitude of fellow motorists can make driving in Greece's large cities unpleasant—and the life of a pedestrian dangerous. Greeks often run red lights or ignore stop signs on side streets, or round corners without stopping. It's a good idea at night at city intersections and at any time on curvy country lanes to beep your horn to warn errant drivers.

In cities, you will find pedestrians have no qualms about standing in the middle of a busy boulevard, waiting to dart between cars. Make eye contact so you can both determine who's going to slow. Rush hour in the cities runs from 7 to 10 AM and 2:30 to 3:30 PM on weekdays, plus 8 to 9 PM on Tuesday, Thursday, and Friday. Saturday mornings bring bumper-to-bumper traffic in shopping districts, and weekend nights guarantee crowding around nightlife hubs. In Athens, the only time you won't find traffic is very early morning and most of Sunday (unless you're foolish enough to stay at a local beach until evening in summer, which means heavy end-of-weekend traffic when you return). Finally, perhaps because they are untrained, drivers seldom pull over for wailing ambulances; the most they'll do is slow down and slightly move over in different directions.

Highways are color-coded: green for the new, toll roads and blue for old, National Roads. Tolls are usually €2. The older routes are slower and somewhat longer, but they follow more scenic routes, so driving is more enjoyable. The National Road can be very slick in places when wet—avoid driving in rain and on the days preceding or following major holidays, when traffic is at its worst as urban dwellers leave for villages.

ROADSIDE EMERGENCIES

You must put out a triangular danger sign if you have a breakdown. Roving repair trucks, manned by skilled ELPA mechanics, patrol the major highways, except the Attiki Odos, which has its own contracted road assistance company. They assist tourists with breakdowns for free if they belong to an auto club such as AAA or ELPA; otherwise, there is a charge. The Greek National Tourism Organization, in cooperation with ELPA, the tourist police, and Greek scouts, provides an emergency telephone line for those who spot a dead or wounded animal on the National Road.

Emergency Services **Automobile Touring Club of Greece** (ELPA ☎10400 for breakdowns, 171 for a dead or hurt animal, 210/606–8800 outside Athens).

RULES OF THE ROAD

International road signs are in use throughout Greece. You drive on the right, pass on the left, and yield right-of-way to all vehicles approaching from the right (except on posted main highways). Cars may not make a right turn on a red light. The speed limits are 120 kph (74 mph) on the National Road, 90 kph (56 mph) outside urban areas, and 50 kph (31 mph) in cities, unless lower limits are posted. The presence of traffic police on the highways has increased, and they are now much more diligent in enforcing speed limits or any other rules. However, limits are often not posted, and signs indicating a lower limit may not always be visible, so if you see Greek drivers slowing down, take the cue to avoid speed traps in rural areas.

In central Athens there is an odd-even rule to avoid traffic congestion. This rule is strictly adhered to and applies weekdays; license plates ending in odd or even numbers can drive into central Athens according to whether the date is odd or even. (The *daktylios,* as this inner ring is called, is marked by signs with a large yellow triangle.) This rule does not apply to rental cars, provided the renter and driver has a foreign passport. If you are renting a car, ask the rental agency about any special parking or circulation regulations in force. Although sidewalk parking is illegal, it is common. And although it's tempting as a visitor to ignore parking tickets, keep in mind that if you've surrendered your ID to the rental agency, you won't get it back until you clear up the matter. You can pay your ticket at the rental agency or local police station. Under a new driving code aimed at cracking down on violations, fines start at €150 (for illegal parking) and can go as high as €300, if your car is towed; fines for running a red light or speeding are now €350, plus you risk having your license revoked for two weeks.

If you are involved in an accident, don't drive away. Accidents must be reported (something Greek motorists often fail to do) before the insurance companies consider claims. Try to get the other driver's details as soon as possible; hit-and-run is all too common in Greece. If the police take you in (they can hold you for 24 hours if there is a fatality, regardless of fault), you have the right to call your local embassy or consulate for help getting a lawyer.

The use of seat belts and motorcycle helmets is compulsory, though Greeks tend to ignore these rules, or comply with them by "wearing" the helmet on their elbows.

BY TAXI

In Greece, as everywhere, unscrupulous taxi drivers sometimes try to take advantage of out-of-towners, using such tricks as rigging meters or tacking on a few zeros to the metered price. All taxis must display the rate card; it's usually on the dashboard, though taxis outside the big cities don't bother. Ask your hotel concierge or owner before engaging a taxi what the fare to your destination ought to be. It should cost between €25 and €40 from the airport (depending on the traffic) to the Athens city center (this includes tolls) and about €15 from Piraeus port to the center. It does not matter how many are in your party (the driver isn't supposed to squeeze in more than four); the metered price remains the same. Taxis must give passengers a receipt (*apodiksi*) if requested.

Make sure that the driver turns on the meter to Tarifa 1 (€0.30), unless it's between midnight and 5 AM, when Tarifa 2 (€0.60) applies. Remember that the meter starts at €1 and the minimum is €2.65. A surcharge applies when taking a taxi to and from the airport (€3) and from (but not to) ports, bus and train stations (€0.80). There is also a surcharge during holiday periods, about €0.30, and a comparable charge for each item of baggage that's over 10 kilograms (22 pounds). If you suspect a driver is overcharging, demand to be taken to the police station; this usually brings them around. Complaints about service or overcharging should be directed to the tourist police; at the Athens airport, contact the Taxi Syndicate information desk. When calling to complain, be sure to report the driver's license number.

Taxi rates are inexpensive compared to fares in most other European countries, mainly because they operate on the jitney system, indicating willingness to pick up others by blinking their headlights or slowing down. Would-be passengers shout their destination as the driver cruises past. Don't be alarmed if your driver picks up other passengers (although he should ask your permission first). Drivers rarely pick up additional passengers if you are a woman traveling alone at night. Each new party pays full fare for the distance he or she has traveled.

A taxi is available when a sign (ELEFTHERO) is up or the light is on at night. Once the driver indicates he is free, he cannot refuse your destination, so get in the taxi before you give an address. He also must wait for you up to 15 minutes, if requested, although most drivers would be unhappy with such a demand. Drivers are familiar with the major hotels, but it's good to know a landmark near your hotel and to have the address and phone number written in Greek. If all else fails, the driver can call the hotel from his mobile phone or a kiosk.

On islands and in the countryside, the meter may often be on Tarifa 2 (outside city limits). Do not assume taxis will be waiting at smaller island airports when your flight lands; often, they have all been booked by arriving locals. If you get stuck, try to join a passenger going in your direction, or call your hotel to arrange transportation.

When you're taking an early-morning flight, it's a good idea to reserve a radio taxi the night before (€2.50 surcharge, €1.50 for immediate response). These taxis are usually quite reliable and punctual; if you're not staying in a hotel, the local tourist police can give you some phone numbers for companies.

Complaints in Athens **Taxi Syndicate** (☎210/353–0575). **Tourist police** (☎171).

BY TRAIN

Fares are reasonable, and trains offer a good, though slow, alternative to long drives, bus rides, or even flights. One of the most impressive stretches is the rack-and-pinion line between Kalavrita and Diakofto, which travels up a pine-crested gorge in the Peloponnese mountains. In fact, the leisurely Peloponnesian train is one of the more-pleasant ways to see southern Greece. In central and northern Greece, the Pelion and Nestos routes cross breathtaking landscapes.

The main line running north from Athens divides into three lines at Thessaloniki, continuing on to Skopje and Belgrade; the Turkish border and Istanbul; and Sofia, Bucharest, and Budapest. The Peloponnese in the south is served by a narrow-gauge line dividing at Corinth into the Tripoli–Kalamata and Patras–Kalamata routes. Two sample fares: Athens–Corinth, €6 and Athens–Volos, €20.70.

The Greek Railway Organization (OSE) has two stations in Athens, side by side, off Diliyianni street west of Omonia Square: Stathmos Larissis and Stathmos Peloponnisou (⇨*Athens Essentials in Chapter 3 for more information*). OSE buses for Albania, Bulgaria, and Turkey also leave from the Peloponnese station. The *Proastiakos* light-rail line (🌐*www.proastiakos.gr*) linking the airport to Stathmos Larissis in Athens has been extended past Corinth to Kiato; fares are €6 from Athens to Corinth and €8 from the airport to Corinth.

InterCity Express service from Athens to Thessaloniki is fast and reliable. The IC costs €45.20 (versus €14.10 for a regular train) but cuts the time by 90 minutes to about 4½ hours. The Athens–Patras IC train (3½ hours) costs €10 (compared to €5.30 and about 4 hours for a regular train). If you order your IC tickets no later than three days in advance, you can have them delivered to you in Athens by courier for a small fee.

If you're planning to make the Athens–Thessaloniki trip several times, buy an Intercity 6+1, which gives you seven trips for the price of six ($203 first class), and a discount on the next card when you return the old one. You can combine this with a Rail 'n Drive package offered by Hertz *(⇨Rental Cars in Booking Your Trip, above)*. They will have a rental car waiting for you at any of the IC stations—Athens, Larissa, Thessaloniki, Volos—at lower prices.

Trains are generally on time. At smaller stations, allow about 10–15 minutes for changing trains; on some routes, connecting routes are coordinated with the main line.

All trains have both first- and second-class seating. On any train, it is best during high season, around holidays, or for long distances to travel first-class, with a reserved seat, as the difference between the first- and second-class coaches can be vast: the cars are cleaner, the seats are wider and plusher, and, most important, the cars are emptier. Without a reservation, in second class you sometimes end up standing among the baggage. The assigned seating of first class (*proti thesi*) is a good idea in July and August, for example, when the Patras–Athens leg is packed with tourists arriving from Italy. First class costs about 20% more than second class (*defteri thesi*).

Many travelers assume that rail passes guarantee them seats on the trains they wish to ride. Not so. You need to book seats ahead even if you are using a rail pass *(for information on Eurail passes, see Train Passes in Booking Your Trip, above)*; seat reservations are required on some European trains, particularly high-speed trains, and are a good idea on trains that may be crowded—particularly in summer on popular routes. You also need a reservation if you purchase sleeping accommodations. On high-speed (IC) trains, you pay a surcharge.

You can pay for all train tickets purchased in Greece with cash (euros) or with credit cards (Visa and MasterCard only). Note that any ticket issued on the train costs 50% more. The best, most efficient contact is OSE's general-information switchboard for timetables and prices. You can get train schedules and fares from EOT and from OSE offices. The Thomas Cook European Timetable is useful, too.

Train Information **Greek Railway Organization** (OSE) (✉Karolou 1, near Omonia Sq., Athens ☎210/529–7006 or 210/529–7007 ✉Sina 6, Athens ☎210/529–8910 🌐www.ose.gr). **InterCity Express** (☎210/529–7313); open Monday–Saturday 8–2:30. **OSE general information switchboard** (☎11100); open daily 7 AM–9 PM.

Train Timetables **Thomas Cook, Timetable Publishing Office** (✉Box 36, Thorpe Wood, Peterborough, CambridgeshirePE3 6SB 🌐www.thomascookpublishing.com).

ON THE GROUND

COMMUNICATIONS

INTERNET

Greece may lag behind other European countries in Internet home penetration, but the country is wired. Major hotels have high-speed Internet connections in rooms and most smaller ones have at least a terminal in the lounge for guests' use. Telecom privatization has helped Greece close the Internet gap with other European countries and, especially on touristed islands, you'll find at least one Internet café with high-speed connections. On the mainland, several villages have created public wireless networks—a trend that seems to be growing.

Although major companies such as Toshiba, Canon, and Hewlett-Packard have representatives in Greece, computer parts, batteries, and adaptors are expensive in Greece and may not be in stock when you need them, so carry spares for your laptop. Your best bets are the national Plaisio and Germanos chains, although some camera shops carry computer equipment, too. Also note that many upscale hotels will rent you a laptop.

If you want to access your e-mail, you can visit one of the Internet cafés that have sprung up throughout Greece. Athens has more than 50, several of which are open 24 hours, and you're sure to find at least one on most islands (⇨ *Essentials at the end of most chapters*). Besides coffee, they offer a range of computer services and charge about €3 per hour; most do not accept credit cards. A few establishments, including Athens Airport and Starbucks, have Wi-Fi service. The City of Athens offers free wireless access in Syntagma Square, and a number of rural towns also have free wireless in public areas. If your cell phone works in Greece and you have a connection kit for your laptop, then you can buy a mobile connect card to get online.

Contacts **Cybercafes** (🌐www.cybercafes.com) lists more than 4,000 Internet cafés worldwide.

PHONES

Greece's phone system has improved markedly. You can direct dial in most better hotels, but there is usually a huge surcharge, so use your calling card or a card telephone in the lobby or on the street. You can make calls from most large establishments, kiosks, card phones (which are everywhere), and from the local office of the Greek telephone company, known as OTE ("oh-*teh*").

Establishments may have several phone numbers rather than a central switchboard. Also, many now use mobile phones, indicated by an area code that begins with 69.

Doing business over the phone in Greece can be frustrating—the lines always seem to be busy, and English-speaking operators and clerks are few. You may also find people too busy to address your problem—the independent-minded Greeks are *not* very service-conscious. It is far better to develop a relationship with someone, for example a travel agent, to get information about train schedules and the like, or to go in person and ask for information face-to-face. Though OTE has updated its phone system in recent years, it may still take you several attempts to get through when calling from an island or the countryside.

The country code for Greece is 30. When dialing Greece from the United States, Canada, or Australia, you would first dial 011, then 30, the country code, before punching in the area code and local number. From continental Europe, the United Kingdom, or New Zealand, start with 0030.

CALLING WITHIN GREECE

For Greek directory information, dial 11888; many operators speak English. In most cases you must give the surname of the shop or restaurant proprietor to be able to get the phone number of the establishment; tourist police are more helpful for tracking down the numbers of such establishments. For operator-assisted calls and international directory information in English, dial the International Exchange at ☎161. In most cases, there is a three-minute minimum charge for operator-assisted station-to-station and person-to-person connections.

Pronunciations for the numbers in Greek are: one ("*eh*-na"); two ("*dhee*-oh"); three ("*tree*-a"); four ("*tess*-ehr-a"); five ("*pen*-de"); six ("*eh*-ksee"); seven ("ef-*ta*"); eight ("och-*toh*"); nine ("eh-*nay*-ah"); ten ("*dheh*-ka").

All telephone numbers in Greece have 10 digits. Area codes now have to be dialed even when you are dialing locally. For cell phones, dial both the cell prefix (a four-digit number beginning with 69) and the telephone number from anywhere in Greece.

You can make local calls from the public OTE phones using phone cards, not coins, or from kiosks, which have metered telephones and allow you to make local or international calls. The dial ring will be familiar to English speakers: two beats, the second much longer than the first.

OTE has card phones virtually everywhere, though some may not be in working order. If you want more privacy—the card phones tend to be on busy street corners and other people waiting to make calls may try to hurry you—use a card phone in a hotel lobby or OTE offices, though these tend to have limited hours. You can also use a kiosk phone. If you don't get a dial tone at first, you should ask the kiosk owner to set the meter to zero. (Bo-*ree*-te na to mee-the-*nee*-ste?)

CALLING OUTSIDE GREECE

To place an international call from Greece, dial 00 to connect to an international network, then dial the country code (for the United States and Canada, it's 1), and then the area code and number. If you need assistance, call 134 to be connected to an international operator. You can use AT&T, Sprint, and MCI services from public phones as well as from hotels.

Long-Distance Carriers **AT&T** (☎800/225-5288). **MCI** (☎800/888-8000 or 800/444-3333). **Sprint** (☎800/877-7746).

Access Codes **AT&T Direct** (☎00/800-1311, 800/435-0812 in the U.S.). **MCI WorldPhone** (☎00/800-1211, 800/444-4141 in the U.S.). **Sprint International Access** (☎00/800-1411, 800/877-4646 in the U.S.).

CALLING CARDS

Phone cards worth €3, €6, €12, or €24 can be purchased at kiosks, convenience stores, or the local OTE office and are the easiest way to make calls from anywhere in Greece. These phone cards can be used for domestic and international calls. Once you insert the phone card, the number of units on the card will appear; as you begin talking, the units will go down. Once all the units have been used, the card does not get recharged—you must purchase another.

MOBILE PHONES

If you have a multiband phone (some countries use different frequencies than what's used in the United States) and your service provider uses the world-standard GSM network (as do T-Mobile, Cingular, and Verizon), you can probably use your phone abroad. Roaming fees can be steep, however: 99¢ a minute is considered reasonable. And overseas you normally pay the toll charges for incoming calls. It's almost always cheaper to send a text message than to make a call, since text messages have a very low set fee (often less than 5¢).

CUSTOMS OF THE COUNTRY

■ Greeks are friendly and openly affectionate. It is not uncommon, for example, to see women strolling arm in arm, or men kissing and hugging each other. Displays of anger are also quite common. You may see a man at a traffic light get out to verbally harangue an offending driver behind him, or a customer berating a civil servant and vice versa, but these encounters rarely become physical. To the person who doesn't understand Greek, the loud, intense conversations may all sound angry—but they're not.

■ But there's a negative side to Greeks' outgoing nature. Eager to engage in conversation over any topic, they won't shy away from launching into political discussions about foreign policy (best politely avoided) or asking personal questions like how much money you earn. The latter isn't considered rude in Greece, but don't feel like you need to respond. Visitors are sometimes taken aback by Greeks' gestures or the ease in which they touch the person they're speaking with—take it all in stride. If a pat on the hand becomes a bit too intimate, just shift politely and the other person will take a hint. On the other hand, kissing someone you've just met good-bye on the cheek is quite acceptable—even between men.

■ A woman who makes long eye contact with a man is interpreted as being interested in romance, but in most cases, Greeks openly stare at anything that interests them, so don't be offended if you are the center of attention wherever you go.

■ In some areas it still doesn't do to over-compliment a baby or a child, thought to provoke others' jealousy and thus bring on the evil eye. You will often see Greeks mock spitting, saying "ftou-ftou-ftou" to ward off harm, as an American might knock on wood after a threatening thought. (At baptisms, the godparent mock-spits three times to discourage Satan.)

■ Respect is shown toward elders; they are seldom addressed by their first name but called "Kiria" (Mrs./Ms.) and "Kirie" (Mr.) So-and-So. In country churches, and at all monasteries and nunneries, shorts are not allowed for either sex, and women may not wear pants. Usually, there is a stack of frumpy skirts that both men and women can don to cover their legs. In very strict places—the Patmos monastery, for example—women cannot reveal bare shoulders or too much cleavage. It's a good idea to carry large scarves for such occasions.

■ Jokes about Greek time abound—and with reason. Although relatively punctual when it comes to professional meetings, many have a more-relaxed attitude about keeping personal appointments, so don't be surprised if someone shows up 20 or 30 minutes late, especially if they know you're waiting at a café or bar or with company. When arranging to meet, pin Greeks down to a specific time, as you may find your definition of morning (before noon) may be quite different from theirs (anytime before 3 PM). If you're invited to someone's home, never turn up early—10 or 15 minutes after the agreed time is acceptable.

■ Globalization has forced Greeks to assimilate new business hours, in offices and shops, and one of the first casualties has been the midday siesta. But some habits are hard to break, and many simply shift their afternoon nap to late evening—especially on weekends, holidays, and during vacations. Still, unless you know someone is at work or doesn't nap, it's considered impolite to phone between 2 and 5 PM.

■ If you make such a mistake, however, it's unlikely Greeks will think you offensive. They're used to foreigners, don't expect you to know all the rules, and will probably chalk up the impropriety to *your* culture's strange dictates.

GREETINGS & GESTURES

■ When you meet someone for the first time, it is customary to shake hands, but with acquaintances the usual is a two-cheek kiss hello and good-bye. One thing that may disconcert foreigners is that when they run into a Greek with another person, he or she usually doesn't introduce the other party, even if there is a long verbal exchange. If you can't stand it anymore, just introduce yourself.

■ Greeks tend to stand closer to people than North Americans and northern Europeans, and they rely more on gestures when communicating. One gesture you should never use is the open palm, fingers slightly spread, shoved toward someone's face. The *moutza* is a serious insult. Another gesture you should remember, especially if trying to catch a taxi, is the Greek "no," which looks like "yes": a slight or exaggerated (depending on the sentiment) tipping back of the head, sometimes with the eyes closed and eyebrows raised. When you wave with your palm toward people, they may interpret it as "come here" instead of "good-bye"; and Greeks often wave good-bye with the palm facing them, which looks like "come here" to English speakers.

GETTING AROUND

■ Greeks can be quite impatient, and queues are nonexistent except in banks and supermarkets. People will push ahead to get on buses, catamarans, and planes—even though the latter have numbered seats.

OUT ON THE TOWN

■ Greeks often eat out of communal serving plates, so it's considered normal in informal settings to spear your tomato out of the salad bowl rather than securing an individual portion. Sometimes in tavernas you don't even get your own plate. Note that it is considered *tsigounia*, stinginess, to run separate tabs, especially because much of the meal is Chinese-style. Greeks either divide the bill equally among the party, no matter who ate what, or one person magnanimously treats. A good host insists that you eat or drink more, and only when you have refused a number of times will you get a reprieve; be charmingly persistent in your "no." Greeks have a loose sense of time. They may be punctual if meeting you to go to a movie, but if they say they'll come round your hotel at 7 PM, they may show up at 8 PM.

LANGUAGE

■ Though it's a byword for incomprehensible ("It was all Greek to me," says Casca in Shakespeare's *Julius Caesar*), much of the difficulty of the Greek language lies in its different alphabet. Not all the 24 Greek letters have precise English equivalents, and there is usually more than one way to spell a Greek word in English. For instance, the letter delta sounds like the English letters "dh," and the sound of the letter gamma may be transliterated as a "g," "gh," or "y." Because of this the Greek for Holy Trinity might appear in English as Agia Triada, Aghia Triada, or Ayia Triada.

■ In most cities and tourist areas, all Greeks know at least one foreign language. It's best to use close-ended queries, however if you ask, "Where is Galissas?" a possible answer will be "Down a ways to the left and then you turn right by the baker's house, his child lives in Chicago, where did you say you went to school?"

■ If you only have 15 minutes to learn Greek, memorize the following: *yiá sou* (hello/good-bye, informal for one person); *yiá sas* (hello/good-bye, formal for one person and used for a group); *miláte angliká?* (do you speak English?); *den katalavéno* (I don't understand); *parakaló* (please/you're welcome); *signómi* (excuse me); *efharistó* (thank you); *ne* (yes); *óhee* (no); *pósso?* (how much?); *pou eéne ...?* (where is...?), ... *ee twaléta?* (... the toilet?), ... *to tahidromío?* (... the post office?), ... *to stathmó?* (... the station?); *kali méra* (good morning), *kali spéra* (good evening); *kali níchta* (good night).

If you just want to make local calls, consider buying a new SIM card (note that your provider may have to unlock your phone for you to use a different SIM card) and a prepaid service plan in the destination. You'll then have a local number and can make local calls at local rates. If your trip is extensive, you could also simply buy a new cell phone in your destination, as the initial cost will be offset over time.

TIP→If you travel internationally frequently, save one of your old mobile phones or buy a cheap one on the Internet; ask your cell phone company to unlock it for you, and take it with you as a travel phone, buying a new SIM card with pay-as-you-go service in each destination.

If you take your cell phone with you, call your provider in advance and ask if it has a connection agreement with a Greek mobile carrier. If so, manually switch your phone to that network's settings as soon as you arrive. To do this, go to the Settings menu, then look for the Network settings and add.

If you're traveling with a companion or group of friends and plan to use your cell phones to communicate with each other, buying a local prepaid connection kit is far cheaper for voice calls or sending text messages than using your regular provider. The most popular local prepaid connection kits are Cosmote's What's Up, Vodafone's A La Carte and CU, or Wind's F2G or For All—these carriers all have branded stores, but you can also buy cell phones and cell phone packages from the Germanos and Plaisio chain stores as well as large supermarkets like Carrefour.

Contacts **Cellular Abroad** (☎800/287-5072 🌐www.cellularabroad.com) rents and sells GMS phones and sells SIM cards that work in many countries. **Mobal** (☎888/888-9162 🌐www.mobalrental.com) rents mobiles and sells GSM phones (starting at $49) that will operate in 140 countries. Per-call rates vary throughout the world. **Planet Fone** (☎888/988-4777 🌐www.planetfone.com) rents cell phones, but the per-minute rates are expensive.

CUSTOMS & DUTIES

You're always allowed to bring goods of a certain value back home without having to pay any duty or import tax. But there's a limit on the amount of tobacco and liquor you can bring back duty-free, and some countries have separate limits for perfumes; for exact figures, check with your customs department. The values of so-called duty-free goods are included in these amounts. When you shop abroad, save all your receipts, as customs inspectors may ask to see them as well as the items you purchased. If the total value of your goods is more than the duty-free limit, you'll have to pay a tax (most often a flat percentage) on the value of everything beyond that limit.

You may bring into Greece duty-free: food and beverages up to 22 pounds (10 kilos); 200 cigarettes, 100 cigarillos, or 50 cigars; 1 liter of alcoholic spirits or 2 liters of wine; and gift articles up to a total of €175. For non-EU citizens, foreign banknotes amounting to more than $2,500 must be declared for re-export, but there are no restrictions on traveler's checks.

Only one per person of such expensive portable items as cameras, camcorders, computers, and the like is permitted into Greece. You should register these with Greek Customs upon arrival to avoid any problems when taking them out of the country again. Sports equipment, such as bicycles and skis, is also limited to one (or one pair) per person.

To bring in a dog or a cat, you need a health certificate issued by a veterinary authority and validated by the Greek Consulate and the appropriate medical authority (in the United States, the Department of Agriculture). It must state that your pet doesn't carry any infectious diseases and that it received a rabies inoculation not more than 12 months prior (for cats, six months) and no fewer than six days before arrival. Dogs must also have a veterinary certificate that indicates they have been wormed against echinococcus. For more information on Greek Customs, check with your local Greek Consulate or the Ministry of Foreign Affairs in Athens, which has more-detailed information on customs and import/export regulations.

Information in Greece **Ministry of Foreign Affairs** (✉Akadimias 3, Stoa Davaki, Athens ☎210/368–2700 Athens 🌐www.mfa.gr).

U.S. Information **U.S. Customs and Border Protection** (🌐www.cbp.gov).

ELECTRICITY

The electrical current in Greece is 220 volts, 50 cycles AC. Wall outlets take Continental-type plugs with two round oversize prongs. If your appliances are dual-voltage, you'll need only an adapter; if not, you'll also need a step-down converter/transformer (United States and Canada).

Consider making a small investment in a universal adapter, which has several types of plugs in one lightweight, compact unit. Most laptops and mobile phone chargers are dual voltage (i.e., they operate equally well on 110 and 220 volts), so require only an adapter. These days the same is true of small appliances such as hair dryers. Always check labels and manufacturer instructions to be sure. Don't use 110-volt outlets marked FOR SHAVERS ONLY for high-wattage appliances such as hair dryers.

Contacts **Steve Kropla's Help for World Travelers** (🌐www.kropla.com) has information on electrical and telephone plugs around the world. **Walkabout Travel Gear** (🌐www.walkabouttravelgear.com) has a good coverage of electricity under "adapters."

EMERGENCIES

Regrettably, vacations are sometimes marred by emergencies, so it's good to know where you should turn for help. In Athens and other cities, hospitals treat emergencies on a rotating basis; an ambulance driver will know where to take you. Or, since waving down a taxi can be faster than waiting for an ambulance, ask a cab driver to take you to the closest "e-phee-me-*re*-von" (duty) hospital. Large islands and rural towns have small medical centers (*iatrikó kéntro*) that can treat minor illnesses or arrange for transport to another facility.

Medications are only sold at pharmacies, which are by law staffed by licensed pharmacists who can treat minor cuts, take blood pressure, and recommend cold medication. Pharmacies are marked with a green-and-white cross and there's one every few city blocks. Outside standard trading hours, there are duty pharmacies offering 24-hour coverage. These are posted in the window of every pharmacy. The *Athens News* and *Kathimerini* (the latter is inserted in the *International Herald Tribune*) have listings for pharmacies that are open late on a particular day. And if you speak Greek, you can call for a recorded message listing the off-hours pharmacies. In cases of emergencies, locals are fairly helpful and will come to your aid. The tourist police throughout Greece (numbers are given in each chapter) can provide general information and help in emergencies and can mediate in disputes.

Foreign Embassy **United States** (✉Vasilissis Sofias 91, Mavili Sq., Athens ☎210/721–2951 through 210/721–2959 🌐www.usembassy.gr).

General Emergency Contacts **Coast Guard** (☎108). **Duty hospitals and pharmacies** (☎1434). **Fire** (☎199). **Forest Service** (☎191 in case of fire). **National Ambulance Service (EKAV)** (☎166). **Off-hours pharmacies** (☎107 in Athens, 102 outside Athens). **Police** (☎100). **Road assistance**

(☎104–ELPA). **S.O.S. Doctors** (☎1016), a 24-hour private medical service. **Tourist police** (✉Dimitrakopoulou 77, Athens ☎171 in Athens, 210/171 from outside Athens).

HEALTH

Greece's strong summer sun and low humidity can lead to sunburn or sunstroke if you're not careful. A hat, long-sleeve shirt, and long pants or a sarong are advised for spending a day at the beach or visiting archaeological sites. Sunglasses, a hat, and sunblock are necessities, and be sure to drink plenty of water. Most beaches present few dangers, but keep a lookout for the occasional jellyfish and, on rocky coves, sea urchins. Should you step on one, don't break off the embedded spines, which may lead to infection, but instead remove them with heated olive oil and a needle. Food is seldom a problem, but the liberal amounts of olive oil used in Greek cooking may be indigestible for some. Tap water in Greece is fine, and bottled spring water is readily available. For minor ailments, go to a local pharmacy first, where the licensed staff can make recommendations for over-the-counter drugs. Most pharmacies are closed in the evenings and on weekends, but each posts the name of the nearest pharmacy open off-hours (⇨*Emergencies, above)*. Most state hospitals and rural clinics won't charge you for tending to minor ailments, even if you're not an EU citizen; at most, you'll pay a minimal fee. Hotels will usually call a doctor for you, though in Athens, you can locate a doctor by calling S.O.S. Doctors (⇨*Emergencies, above)*. For a dentist, check with your hotel, embassy, or the tourist police. Do not fly within 24 hours of scuba diving. In greener, wetter areas, mosquitoes may be a problem. In addition to wearing insect repellent, you can burn coils ("spee-*rahl*") to discourage them or buy plug-in devices that burn medicated tabs ("pah-*steel*-ya"). Hotels usually provide these. The only poisonous snakes in Greece are the adder and the sand viper, which are brown or red, with dark zigzags. The adder has a V or X behind its head, and the sand viper sports a small horn on its nose. When hiking, wear high tops and don't put your feet or hands in crevices without looking first. If bitten, try to slow the spread of the venom until a doctor comes. Lie still with the affected limb lower than the rest of your body. Apply a tourniquet, releasing it every few minutes, and cut the wound a bit in case the venom can bleed out. Do NOT suck on the bite. Whereas snakes like to lie in the sun, the scorpion (rare) likes cool, wet places, in wood piles, and under stones. Apply Benadryl or Phenergan to minor stings, but if you have nausea or fever, see a doctor at once.

HOURS OF OPERATION

A new law passed in 2005 set uniform business hours (weekdays 9–9, Saturday 9–6) for retailers across Greece, although establishments in tourist resorts may remain open longer. For certain categories such as pharmacies, banks, and government offices, hours have always been standardized. Many small businesses and shops close for at least a week around mid-August, and most tourist establishments, including hotels, shut down on the islands and northern Greece from November until mid-spring. Restaurants, especially tavernas, often stay open on holidays; some close in summer or move to cooler locations. Christmas, New Year's, Orthodox Easter, and August 15 are the days everything shuts down, although, for example, bars work full force on Christmas Eve, since it's a very social occasion and not particularly family-oriented. Orthodox Easter changes dates every year, so check your calendar. On Orthodox Good Friday, shops open after church services, around 1 PM.

Banks are normally open Monday–Thursday 8–2, Friday 8–1:30, but select branches of Alpha and Eurobank are open until 8 PM weekdays and on Saturday mornings. Hotels also cash traveler's checks on weekends, and the banks at the Athens airport have longer hours.

Government offices are open weekdays from 8 to 2. For commercial offices, the hours depend on the business: large companies have adopted the 9–5 schedule, but some small businesses stick to the Mediterranean 8–2 workday.

The days and hours for public museums and archaeological sites are set by the Ministry of Culture; they are usually open Tuesday–Sunday 8:30 to 3, and as late as 7:30 in summer. (Summer hours are generally published on the ministry's Web site, www.culture.gr, in April or May.) Throughout the year arrive at least 30 minutes before closing time to ensure a ticket. Archaeological sites and museums close on January 1, March 25, the morning of Orthodox Good Friday, Orthodox Easter, May 1, and December 25–26. Sunday visiting hours apply to museums on Epiphany; Ash Monday, Good Saturday, Easter Monday, and Whitsunday (Orthodox dates, which change every year); August 15; and October 28. Museums close early (around 12:30) on January 2, the last Saturday of Carnival, Orthodox Good Thursday, Christmas Eve, and New Year's Eve. Throughout the guide, the hours of sights and attractions are denoted by the clock icon, ⊙.

All gas stations are open daily 7–7 (some close Sunday), and some pump all night in the major cities and along the National Road and Attica Highway. They do not close for lunch.

Department stores, shops, and supermarkets may stay open until 9 PM on weekdays and 8 PM on Saturday, but some merchants are sticking to the old business hours and continue to close on Monday, Wednesday, and Saturday afternoons. There are no Sunday trading hours, except for the last Sunday of the year and in tourist areas like Plaka in Athens and island or mainland resorts.

Pharmacies are open Monday, Wednesday, and Friday from about 8:30 to 3 and Tuesday, Thursday, and Friday from 8:30 to 2 and 5 until 8 or 8:30 at night. The pharmacy at Athens International Airport operates 24 hours. According to a rotation system, there is always at least one pharmacy open in any area *(⇨ Emergencies, above)*.

If it's late in the evening and you need an aspirin, a soft drink, cigarettes, a newspaper, or a pen, look for the nearest open kiosk, called a *periptero*; these kiosks on street corners everywhere brim with all kinds of necessities. Owners stagger their hours, and many towns have at least one kiosk that stays open late, occasionally through the night. Neighborhood minimarkets also stay open late.

HOLIDAYS

January 1 (New Year's Day); January 6 (Epiphany); Clean Monday (first day of Lent); March 25 (Feast of the Annunciation and Independence Day); Good Friday; Greek Easter Sunday; Greek Easter Monday; May 1 (Labor Day); Pentecost; August 15 (Assumption of the Holy Virgin); October 28 (Ochi Day); December 25–26 (Christmas Day and Boxing Day).

Only on Orthodox Easter and August 15 do you find that just about *everything* shuts down. It's harder getting a room at the last minute on Easter and August 15 (especially the latter), and traveling requires stamina, if you want to survive on the ferries and the highways. On the other hand, the local rituals and rites associated with these two celebrations are interesting and occasionally moving (like the Epitaphios procession on Good Friday).

MAIL

Letters and postcards take about a week to 10 days to reach the United States. That's airmail. It takes even longer in August, when postal staff is reduced; and during Christmas and Easter holidays. If what you're mailing is important, send it registered, which costs about €2.65 in Greece. For about €2.60, depending on the weight, you can send your letter "express"; this earns you a red sticker and faster local delivery. The post office also operates a courier service, EMS Express. Delivery to the continental United States takes about two to three days and costs €26.40. If you're planning on writing several letters, prepaid envelopes are convenient and cost €4.25 for five.

Post offices are open weekdays 7:30–2, although in city centers they may stay open in the evenings and on weekends. The main post offices in Athens and Piraeus are open weekdays 7:30 AM–9 PM, Saturday 7:30–2, and Sunday 9–1:30. The post offices at Athens International Airport and the Acropolis are open weekends, too. Throughout the country, mailboxes are yellow and sometimes divided into domestic and international containers; express boxes are red.

At this writing, airmail letters and postcards to destinations other than Europe and weighing up to 20 grams cost €0.65, and €1.15 for 50 grams (€0.65 and €1, respectively, to other European countries, including the United Kingdom).

Contact American Express (✉ Ermou 7, 10563Athens ☎ 210/322-3380 🌐 www.americanexpress.com).

MEALS & MEALTIMES

Greeks don't really eat breakfast and with the exception of hotel dining rooms, few places serve that meal. You can pick up a cheese pie and rolls at a bakery or a sesame-coated bread ring called a *koulouri* sold by city vendors; order a *tost* ("toast"), a sort of dry grilled sandwich, usually with cheese or paper-thin ham slices, at a café; or dig into a plate of yogurt with honey. Local bakeries may offer fresh doughnuts in the morning. On islands in summer, cafés serve breakfast, from Continental to combinations that might include Spanish omelets and French coffee. Caffeine junkies can get a cup of coffee practically anywhere, but decaf is available only in bigger hotels.

Greeks eat their main meal at either lunch or dinner, so the offerings are the same. For lunch, heavyweight meat-and-potato dishes can be had, but you might prefer a real Greek salad (no lettuce, a slice of feta with a pinch of oregano, and ripe tomatoes) or souvlaki or grilled chicken from a taverna. For a light bite you can also try one of the popular Greek chain eateries such as Everest or Grigori's, found fairly easily throughout the country, for grilled sandwiches or spanakopita and *tiropita* (cheese pie); or Goody's, the local equivalent of McDonald's, where you'll find good-quality burgers.

Coffee and pastries are eaten in the afternoon, usually at a café or *zaharoplastio* (pastry shop). The hour or so before restaurants open for dinner—around 7—is a pleasant time to have an ouzo or glass of wine and try Greek hors d'oeuvres, called *mezedes,* in a bar, ouzeri, or *mezedopoleio* (Greek tapas place). Dinner is often the main meal of the day, and there's plenty of food. Starters include dips such as *taramosalata* (made from fish roe), *melitzanosalata* (made from smoked eggplant, lemon, oil, and garlic), and the well-known yogurt, cucumber, and garlic *tzatziki.* A typical dinner for a couple might be two to three appetizers, an entrée, a salad, and wine. Diners can order as little or as much as they like, except at very expensive establishments. If a Greek eats dessert at all, it will be fruit or a modest wedge of a syrup-drenched cake like *revani* or semolina halvah, often shared between two or three diners. Only in fancier restaurants can diners order a tiramisu with an espresso. One option for those who want a lighter meal is the mezedopoleio.

In most places, the menu is broken down into appetizers (*orektika*) and entrées (*kiria piata*), with additional headings for salads (this includes dips like tzatziki) and vegetable side plates. However, this doesn't mean there is any sense of a first or second "course," as in France. Often the food arrives all at the same time, or as it becomes ready.

Breakfast is available until 10 at hotels and until early afternoon in beach cafés. Lunch is between 1:30 and 3:30 (and on weekends as late as 5), and dinner is served from about 8:30 to midnight, later in the big cities and resort islands. Most Greeks dine very late, around 10 or 11 PM. Unless otherwise noted, the restaurants listed in this guide are open daily for lunch and dinner.

MONEY

Although costs have risen astronomically since Greece switched to the euro currency in 2002, the country will seem reasonably priced to travelers from the United States and Great Britain. Popular tourist resorts (including some of the islands) and the larger cities are markedly more expensive than the countryside. Though the price of eating in a restaurant has increased, you can still get a bargain. Hotels are generally moderately priced outside the major cities, and the extra cost of accommodations in a luxury hotel, compared to in an average hotel, often seems unwarranted.

Other typical costs: authentic Greek sponge: €8; soft drink: (can) €1.50, in a café €2; spinach pie: €1.50; souvlaki: €1.90; local bus: €0.50; foreign newspaper: €2.50–€3.90.

Prices throughout this guide are given for adults. Substantially reduced fees are almost always available for children, students, and senior citizens.

ITEM	AVERAGE COST
Cup of Coffee	€2.60–€5 (in a central-city café; Greek coffee is a bit cheaper)
Glass of Wine	€3–€8
Glass of Beer	€2.80; €2.60–€6.50 in a bar
Sandwich	€2.60
1-mile Taxi Ride in Capital City	€2.50
Archaeological Site Admission	€3–€6; free on Sunday from November to March

TIP→Banks never have every foreign currency on hand, and it may take as long as a week to order. If you're planning to exchange funds before leaving home, don't wait 'til the last minute.

ATMS & BANKS

Your own bank will probably charge a fee for using ATMs abroad; the foreign bank you use may also charge a fee. Nevertheless, you'll usually get a better rate of exchange at an ATM than you will at a currency-exchange office or even when changing money in a bank. And extracting funds as you need them is a safer option than carrying around a large amount of cash.

TIP→PIN numbers with more than four digits are not recognized at ATMs in many countries. If yours has five or more, remember to change it before you leave.

ATMs are widely available throughout the country. Virtually all banks, including the National Bank of Greece (known as Ethniki), have machines that dispense money to Cirrus or Plus cardholders. You may find bank-sponsored ATMs at harbors and in airports as well. Other systems accepted include Visa, MasterCard, American Express, Diners Club, and Eurocard, but exchange and withdrawal rates vary, so shop around and check fees with your bank before leaving home. For use in Greece, your PIN must be four digits long. The word for PIN is pronounced "peen," and ATMs are called *alpha taf mi,* after the letters, or just *to mihanima,* "the machine." Machines usually let you complete the transaction in English, French, or German and seldom create problems, except Sunday night, when they sometimes run out of cash. For most machines, the minimum amount dispensed is €40. Sometimes an ATM may refuse to "read" your card. Don't panic; it's probably the machine. Try another bank.

■ TIP→ **At some ATMs in Greece you may not have a choice of drawing from a specific account. If you have linked savings and checking accounts, make sure there's money in both before you depart.**

CREDIT CARDS

Throughout this guide, the following abbreviations are used: **AE,** American Express; **D,** Discover; **DC,** Diners Club; **MC,** MasterCard; and **V,** Visa.

It's a good idea to inform your credit-card company before you travel, especially if you're going abroad and don't travel internationally very often. Otherwise, the credit-card company might put a hold on your card owing to unusual activity—not a good thing halfway through your trip. Record all your credit-card numbers—as well as the phone numbers to call if your cards are lost or stolen—in a safe place, so you're prepared should something go wrong. Both MasterCard and Visa have general numbers you can call (collect if you're abroad) if your card is lost, but you're better off calling the number of your issuing bank, since MasterCard and Visa usually just transfer you to your bank; your bank's number is usually printed on your card.

If you plan to use your credit card for cash advances, you'll need to apply for a PIN at least two weeks before your trip. Although it's usually cheaper (and safer) to use a credit card abroad for large purchases (so you can cancel payments or be reimbursed if there's a problem), note that some credit-card companies *and* the banks that issue them add substantial percentages to all foreign transactions, whether they're in a foreign currency or not. Check on these fees before leaving home, so there won't be any surprises when you get the bill.

■ TIP→ **Before you charge something, ask the merchant whether or not he or she plans to do a dynamic currency conversion (DCC). In such a transaction the credit-card *processor* (shop, restaurant, or hotel, not Visa or MasterCard) converts the currency and charges you in dollars. In most cases you'll pay the merchant a 3% fee for this service in addition to any credit-card company and issuing-bank foreign-transaction surcharges.**

Dynamic currency conversion programs are becoming increasingly widespread. Merchants who participate in them are supposed to ask whether you want to be charged in dollars or the local currency, but they don't always do so. And even if they do offer you a choice, they may well avoid mentioning the additional surcharges. The good news is that you *do* have a choice. And if this practice really gets your goat, you can avoid it entirely thanks to American Express; with its cards, DCC simply isn't an option.

Should you use a credit card or a debit card when traveling? Both have benefits. A credit card allows you to delay payment and gives you certain rights as a consumer. A debit card, also known as a check card, deducts funds directly from your checking account and helps you stay within your budget. When you want to rent a car, though, you may still need an old-fashioned credit card.

Both types of plastic get you cash advances at ATMs worldwide if your card is properly programmed with your personal identification number (PIN). Both offer excellent, wholesale exchange rates. And both protect you against unauthorized use if the card is lost or stolen. Your liability is limited to $50, as long as you report the card missing. However, shop owners often give you a lower price if you pay with cash rather than credit, because they want to avoid the credit-card bank fees. Note that the Discover card is not widely accepted in Greece. The local Citibank, which issues Diners Club and MasterCard, can't cancel your cards but will pass on the message to the head offices of those cards.

Reporting Lost Cards **American Express** (☎800/528–4800 in the U.S., 336/393–1111 collect from abroad 🌐www.americanexpress.com). **Diners Club** (☎800/234–6377 in the U.S., 303/799–1504 collect from abroad 🌐www.dinersclub.com). **Discover** (☎800/347–2683 in the U.S., 801/902–3100 collect from abroad 🌐www.discovercard.com). **MasterCard** (☎800/627–8372 in the U.S., 636/722–7111 collect from abroad 🌐www.mastercard.com). **Visa** (☎800/847–2911 in the U.S., 410/581–9994 collect from abroad 🌐www.visa.com).

CURRENCY & EXCHANGE

Greece's former national currency, the drachma, was replaced by the currency of the European Union, the euro (€), in 2002. Under the euro system, there are eight coins: 1 and 2 euros, plus 1, 2, 5, 10, 20, and 50 euro cents. Euros are pronounced "evros" in Greek; cents are known as "lepta." All coins have the euro value on one side; the other side has each country's unique national symbol. Greece's range from images of triremes to a depiction of the mythological Europa being abducted by Zeus transformed as a bull. Bills (banknotes) come in seven denominations: 5, 10, 20, 50, 100, 200, and 500 euros. Bills are the same for all EU countries.

Off Syntagma Square in Athens, the National Bank of Greece, Citibank, Alpha Bank, Commercial Bank, Eurobank, and Pireos Bank have automated machines that change your foreign currency into euros. When you shop, remember that it's always easier to bargain on prices when paying in cash instead of by credit card.

If you do use an exchange service, good options are American Express and Eurochange. Watch daily fluctuations and shop around. Daily exchange rates are prominently displayed in banks and listed in the *International Herald Tribune*. In Athens, around Syntagma Square is the best place to look. Those that operate after business hours have lower rates and a higher commission. You can also change money at post offices in even the most remote parts of Greece; commissions are lower than at banks, starting at about €2 for amounts up to €300. To avoid lines at airport exchange booths, get a bit of local currency before you leave home. At this writing the average exchange rate for the euro was €1.47 to the U.S. dollar, €1.47 to the Canadian dollar, €0.71 to the pound sterling, €1.67 to the Australian dollar, and €1.71 to the New Zealand dollar.

■ TIP→ Even if a currency-exchange booth has a sign promising no commission, rest assured that there's some kind of huge, hidden fee. (Oh ... that's right. The sign didn't say no *fee*.) And as for rates, you're almost always better off getting foreign currency at an ATM or exchanging money at a bank.

Athens Exchange Services **American Express Travel Related Services** (✉Ermou 7, Syntagma Sq. ☎210/322–3380 ⏲Weekdays 8:30–4, Sat. 8:30–1:30). **Eurochange** (✉Karageorgi Servias 2, Syntagma Sq. ☎210/331–2462 ⏲Daily 8 AM–11 PM ✉Omonias 10, Omonia Sq. ☎210/523–4816 ⏲Daily 8 AM–10 PM). **National Bank of Greece** (✉Karageorgi Servias 2, Syntagma Sq. ☎210/334–8015 ⏲Mon.–Thurs. 8–2 and 3:15–5:15, Fri. 2:45–5:15, Sat. 9–3, Sun. 9–1); extended foreign exchange.

TRAVELER'S CHECKS

Some consider this the currency of the caveman, and it's true that fewer establishments accept traveler's checks these days. Nevertheless, they're a cheap and secure way to carry extra money, particularly on trips to urban areas. Both Citibank (under the Visa brand) and American Express issue traveler's checks in the United States, but Amex is better known and more widely accepted; you can also avoid hefty surcharges by cashing Amex checks at Amex offices. Whatever you do, keep track of all the serial numbers in case the checks are lost or stolen.

Traveler's checks are a good way to carry your money into Greece, keeping your funds safe until you change them into euros. But it's important to remember that Greece is still a cash society, so plan accordingly. If you're going to rural areas and small towns, go with cash; traveler's checks are best used in cities, though even in Athens most tavernas won't take them. Lost or stolen checks can usually be replaced within 24 hours. To ensure a speedy refund, buy your own traveler's checks—don't let someone else pay for them: irregularities like this can cause delays. The person who bought the checks should make the call to request a refund.

Contact **American Express** (☎888/412-6945 in the U.S., 801/945-9450 collect outside the U.S. to add value or speak to customer service 🌐www.americanexpress.com).

TAXES

Taxes are always included in the stated price, unless otherwise noted. The Greek airport tax (€12 for travel within the EU and €22 outside the EU) is included in your ticket (as are a further €12.15 terminal facility charge and a €5 security charge), and the 8%–12% hotel tax rate is usually included in the quoted price.

Value-added tax, 4.5% for books and about 19% (6%–13% on the Aegean islands) for almost everything else, called FPA (pronounced "fee-pee-ah") by Greeks, is included in the cost of most consumer goods and services, except groceries. If you are a citizen of a non-EU country, you may get a V.A.T. refund on products (except alcohol, cigarettes, or toiletries) worth €117 or more bought in Greece from licensed stores that usually display a Tax-Free Shopping sticker in their window. Ask the shop to complete a refund form called a Tax-Free Check for you, which you show at Greek Customs.

Have the form stamped like any customs form by customs officials when you leave the country or, if you're visiting several European Union countries, when you leave the EU. Be ready to show customs officials what you've bought (pack purchases together, in your carry-on luggage); budget extra time for this. After you're through passport control, take the form to a refund-service counter for an on-the-spot refund, or mail it back in the pre-addressed envelope given to you at the store. You receive the total refund stated on the form, but the processing time can be long, especially if you request a credit-card adjustment.

A refund service can save you some hassle, for a fee. Global Refund is a Europe-wide service with 225,000 affiliated stores and more than 700 refund counters at major airports and border crossings. The service issues refunds in the form of cash, check, or credit-card adjustment, minus a processing fee. If you don't have time to wait at the refund counter, you can mail in the form instead.

V.A.T. Refunds **Global Refund** (☎800/566-9828 🌐www.globalrefund.com).

TIME

Greek time is Greenwich Mean Time (GMT) plus 2 hours. To estimate the time back home, subtract 7 hours from the local time for New York and Washington, 8 hours for Chicago, 9 for Denver, and 10 for Los Angeles. Londoners subtract 2 hours. Those living in Sydney or Melbourne, add 8 hours. Greek Daylight Saving Time starts on the last Sunday in March and ends the last Sunday in October. Stay alert—newspapers barely publicize the change.

TIPPING

How much to tip in Greece, especially at restaurants, is confusing.

On cruises, cabin and dining-room stewards get about €2 a day; guides receive about the same.

TIPPING GUIDELINES FOR GREECE	
Bartender	10% minimum
Bellhop	€1 per bag
Hotel Concierge	€3–€10, if he or she performs a service for you
Hotel Doorman	€1–€2 if he helps you get a cab
Hotel Maid	€1 per night
Hotel Room-Service Waiter	€1 per delivery, even if a service charge has been added
Porter at Airport or Train Station	€1 per bag
Skycap at Airport	€1–€3 per bag checked
Taxi Driver	Round up the fare to the nearest €0.50 or €1; during holidays, drivers legally receive a mandatory "gift"; the amount is posted in the cab during applicable days.
Tour Guide	15%–20%
Waiter	By law a 13% service charge is figured into the price of a meal. However, it is customary to leave an 8%–10% tip if the service was satisfactory. During the Christmas and Greek Easter holiday periods, restaurants tack on an obligatory 18% holiday bonus to your bill for the waiters.
Others	For rest room attendants €0.50 is appropriate. People dispensing programs at cinemas get €0.40.

INDEX

A

N

PHOTO CREDITS

5, *Wayne Linden/Alamy*. **Chapter 1: Experience Greece:** 9, *J.D. Dallet/age fotostock*. 10, *Iraklis Angelos Klampanos/Shutterstock*. 11 (left), *Steve Outram/Alamy*. 11 (right), *Detsis/IML/age fotostock*. 12, *Pierdelune/ Shutterstock*. 13 (left), *IML Image Group Ltd/Alamy*. 13 (right), *Georgios Alexandris/Shutterstock*. 14, *Greek National Tourism Organization*. 15 (left), *Photodisc*. 15 (right), *Jon Arnold Images Ltd/Alamy*. 18, *Dutton Colin/SIME/eStock Photo*. 19 (left), *Fred Goldstein/Shutterstock*. 19 (right), *Patrick Frilet/Hemis.fr/Aurora Photos*. 20 (top left), *Photodisc*. 20 (bottom left), *Giovanni Simeone/SIME/eStock Photo*. 20 (right), *Marc C. Johnson/ Shutterstock*. 21 (left), *Photodisc*. 21 (top right), *Terrance Klassen/age fotostock*. 21 (bottom right), *Pierdelune/ Shutterstock*. 22, *Terry Harris Just Greece Photo Library/Alamy*. 23, *Tommaso di Girolamo/age fotostock*. 24, *Roberto Meazza/IML Image Group/Aurora Photos*. 25 (left), *Danita Delimont/*Alamy. 25 (right), *Deco Images/ Alamy*. 26, *Nils-Johan Norenlind/age fotostock*. 27, *Terry Harris Just Greece Photo Library/Alamy*. 28, *Marco Polo Mansion*. 29, *Pixida/Alamy*. 34, *Loukas Hapsis/IML Image Group/Aurora Photos*. 35, *Vittorio Sciosia/ age fotostock*. 36 (top left), *Elpis Ioannidis/Shutterstock*. 36 (bottom left), *Peter M. Wilson/Alamy*. 36 (right), *Charles Stirling (Travel)/Alamy*. 37 (left), *Walter Bibikow/age fotostock*. 37 (top right), *Inger Anne Hulbaekdal/ Shutterstock*. 37 (bottom right), *Rene Mattes/age fotostock*. 38, *Greece/Alamy*. **Chapter 2: Cruising the Greek Islands:** 39, *J.D. Heaton/age fotostock*. **Chapter 3: Athens:** 73, *Maro Kouri/IML Image Group/Aurora Photos*. 82-83, *SIME s.a.s/eStock Photo*. 84, *Vidler/age fotostock*. 85, *Kord.com/age fotostock*. 86 (top left), *Javier Larrea/age fotostock*. 86 (bottom left) and 86 bottom right), *Visual Arts Library (London)/Alamy*. 87 (top left), *Mary Evans Picture Library/Alamy*. 87 (top right), *Picture History/Newscom*. 87 (bottom), *Popperfoto/Alamy*. 90, *Juha-Pekka Kervinen/Shutterstock*. 92, *Miguel Ángel Muñoz/age fotostock*. 111, *Warner Bros/Everett Collection*. 112 (top right), *Walter Bibikow/age fotostock*. 112 (bottom right), *Eliott Slater/age fotostock*. 113 (left), *Terence Waeland/Alamy*. 113 (top right), *Giulio Andreini/age fotostock*. 113 (bottom right), *Image Asset Management/age fotostock*. 114 (top left), *ACE Stock Limited/Alamy*. 114 (right), *Rene Mattes/age fotostock*. 115 (top left), *Warner Bros/Everett Collection*. 115 (center), *Peter Horree/Alamy*. 115 (bottom), *Keith Binns/ iStockphoto*. 115 (right), *Peter Horree/Alamy*. 116 (top left), *Image Asset Management/age fotostock*. 116 (right), *T. Papageorgiou/age fotostock*. 117 (top left), *Aliki Sapountzi/Aliki Image Library/Alamy*. 117 (bottom left), *Terry Harris/Just Greece Photo Library/Alamy*. 128 (top), *LOOK Die Bildagentur der Fotografen GmbH/ Alamy*. 128 (bottom), *Franco Pizzochero/age fotostock*. 129 (top), *Alvaro Leiva/age fotostock*. 129 (bottom), *Ingolf Pompe/Aurora Photos*. 130 (top), *foodfolio/Alamy*. 130 (2nd from top), *Liv Friis-Larsen/Shutterstock*. 130 (center), *imagebroker/Alamy*. 130 (4th from top), *SIME s.a.s/eStock Photo*. 130 (bottom), *IML Image Group Ltd/Alamy*. 131 (left), *Roberto Meazza/IML Image Group/Aurora Photos*. 131 (top right), *Christopher Leggett/age fotostock*. 131 (center right), *IML Image Group Ltd/Alamy*. 131 (bottom right), *Ingolf Pompe/ Aurora Photos*. **Chapter 4: Attica, The Saronic Gulf & Delfi:** 173, *Stefano Lunardi/age fotostock*. 175 (top), *David Sanger Photography/Alamy*. 175 (bottom), *imagebroker/Alamy*. **Chapter 5: The Sporades:** 235, *SIME s. a.s/eStock Photo*. 236, *Johanna Huber/SIME s.a.s/eStock Photo*. 237 (top), *Roger Cracknell 10/Pagan Festivals/ Alamy*. 237 (bottom), *Terry Harris Just Greece Photo Library/Alamy*. **Chapter 6: Epirus & Thessaly:** 269, *Tolo Balaguer/age fotostock*. 270, *Johanna Huber/SIME s.a.s/eStock Photo*. 271 (top), *Detsis/IML/age fotostock*. 271 (bottom), *Netfalls/Shutterstock*. 292-93, *R. Matina/age fotostock*. 294, *Denis Babenko/Shutterstock*. 295 (top), *Petr Svarc/Alamy*. 295 (bottom), *R. Matina/age fotostock*. 296, *José Fuste Raga/age fotostock*. 297, *R. Matina/age fotostock*. 298, *Walter Zerla/age fotostock*. **Chapter 7: Thessaloniki & Central Macedonia:** 303, *SIME s.a.s/eStock Photo*. 305 (top), *Vito Arcomano/age fotostock*. 305 (bottom), *R. Matina/age fotostock*. **Chapter 8: Corfu:** 345 and 346, *PCL/Alamy*. 347 (top and bottom), *Ljupco Smokovski/Shutterstock*. **Chapter 9: Northern Peloponnese:** 373, *Johanna Huber/SIME s.a.s/eStock Photo*. 375 (top), *Rene Mattes/age fotostock*. 375 (bottom), *T. Papageorgiou/age fotostock*. 410, *SuperStock*. 411, *J.D. Dallet/age fotostock*. 412, *Mary Evans Picture Library/Alamy*. 413 (all), *J.D. Dallet/age fotostock*. 414-15, *ACE Stock Limited/Alamy*. 416, *Wayne Linden/Alamy*. **Chapter 10: Southern Peloponnese:** 421, *Chris Fragassi/Alamy*. 422-23 (all), *T. Papageorgiou/age fotostock*. **Chapter 11: The Cyclades:** 453, *Stefano Brozzi/age fotostock*. 454, *Hemis/Alamy*. 455, *Sylvain Grandadam/age fotostock*. 484, *Anthro/Shutterstock*. 488 (left), *Buena Vista Pictures/Everett Collection*. 488 (center), *INTERFOTO Pressebildagentur/Alamy*. 489, *Ian Fraser/Alamy*. 514-15, *G.V.P./age fotostock*. 516, *Wolfgang Amri/Shutterstock*. 517 (top), *The Print Collector/Alamy*. 517 (bottom), *Wojtek Buss/age fotostock*. **Chapter 12: Crete:** 557, *Alvaro Leiva/age fotostock*. 558 (top), *imagebroker/Alamy*. 558 (bottom), *Irina Korshunova/Shutterstock*. 559 (top), *Paul Cowan/Shutterstock*. 559 (bottom), *LOOK Die Bildagentur de Fotografen GmbH/Alamy*. **Chapter 13: Rhodes & the Dodecanese:** 595, *Giovanni Simeone/SIME s.a.s/eStock Photo*. 596 (top), *Alvaro Leiva/age fotostock*. 596 (bottom), *Werner Otto/age fotostock*. 597 (top), *Franck Guiziou/Hemis.fr/Aurora Photos*. 597 (bottom), *FAN travelstock/Alamy*. 605 (top), *SuperStock*. 605 (bottom), *Walter Bibikow/SuperStock*. 607 (inset), *San Rostro/SuperStock*. 607 (bottles), *blickwinkel/Alamy*. **Chapter 14: The Northern Aegean Islands:** 635, *Walter Bibikow/age fotostock*. 636 (top), *Fausto Giaccone/Marka/age fotostock*. 636 (bottom), *Greek National Tourist Organization*. 637, *Steve Bentley/Alamy*.

ABOUT OUR WRITERS

Alexia Amvrazi spent most of her childhood away from her native Greece but returned there to pursue a full-time career in journalism. She has been working in the English-language newspaper, magazine, Internet, and TV media for 11 years and for the past three has worked at the City of Athens multilingual radio station (where she hosts her own show). For this edition, she helped update our chapters on the Sporades.

Stephen Brewer is a New York–based writer and editor who travels to Crete and other European shores for various national magazines and guidebooks. While he also writes about such northern locales as Ireland, England, and Venice, he especially cherishes his experiences climbing hairpin bends on the roads between Knossos and Phaestos. For this edition, he updated the Crete chapter and wrote our new Experience Greece chapter and photo features on Greek design, history and ancient Olympia.

Jeffrey and Elizabeth Carson, native New Yorkers, have lived on Paros since 1970; they teach at the Aegean Center for the Fine Arts. Jeffrey, a poet, translator, and critic, has published many articles and books. Elizabeth is a photographer who has had numerous solo exhibitions, and has been published widely, including the book *The Church of 100 Doors*. For this edition, they updated and wrote new texts for the Cyclades chapter and also contributed new texts to our photo features on Greek mythology and Atlantis.

Linda Coffman, Fodor's resident Cruise Diva, is a freelance travel writer who has contributed to many publications, including *Consumer's Digest*, the *Chicago Sun-Times*, and *USA Today*. For Fodor's, she has written *The Complete Guide to Caribbean Cruises* and *The Complete Guide to European Cruises*. For this edition, she wrote our new chapter on Greek cruises.

Angelike Contis was raised in Vermont, but took her first baby steps while visiting her grandparents in Arcadia. She has lived in Greece for a decade, writing for publications including the *Athens News* and directing independent documentaries. She is currently writing a book on today's Greek cinema. For this edition, she updated our chapters on the Attica, the Saronic Gulf Islands, and Delphi—along with Natasha Giannousi—and Rhodes and the Dodecanese.

Joanna Kakissis, an Athens-based journalist, was born in Athens, Greece, and grew up in North and South Dakota and Minnesota. She contributes to the *New York Times, USA Today, World Hum,* the *Boston Globe,* the *Washington Post,* and U.S. public radio. She has also taught journalism and essay writing at universities in North Carolina. For this edition, she updated our Athens and Thessaloniki chapters and wrote our special photo features on the Acropolis, Greek dining, and the wines of Greece.

Diane Shugart was lured back to her mother's homeland more than a decade ago by the laid-back lifestyle. A journalist and translator, she makes her home in Athens—a city's whose cultural and history she has explored in the book *Athens by Neighborhood*. Diane updated our Greece Essentials and Corfu chapters for this edition.

Adrian Vrettos first traveled to Greece from London over a decade ago to work as a field archaeologist on prehistoric and classical excavations. All he managed to uncover, however, was the ancient inscription, "The laptop is mightier than the trowel" (loosely translated from Linear B). Thus he set to work decoding modern Greek life instead, and is now a freelance journalist and editor based in Athens. Adrian updated three chapters: Sporades, Epirus and Thessaly, and Northern Aegean Islands.